Southwestern Advantage Integrated Learning System

Software Advantage
- Finest educational software—learning while having fun

Print Advantage
- Curriculum-based study guides
- Easily accessible, easily understood
- Broad range, great depth of material
- Helps students excel, helps parents understand

Advantage Online
- School-subject resources, including thousands of math and science tutorial videos
- Unique language-learning tools
- Parenting skills section
- Life skills coaching
- Rewards for activity, user-community interaction

SOUTHWESTERN
advantage™

www.SWadvantage.com

Sharing the Advantage

Southwestern Advantage has been proven as an effective learning system,
and an important key to a better education and achieving success in life.
Our Mission is to share education and learning skills with
every child and every family, regardless of their circumstances.
So through qualified nonprofit partnerships and local community
involvement with organizations focused on helping young people,
Southwestern will donate one Advantage online membership
for each one sold by student dealers.

Thank you for helping us Share the Advantage!

HONORS: COLLEGE & UNIVERSITY PREP

www.SWadvantage.com

SOUTHWESTERN
advantage™

Printed on Recycled Paper

Reissued 2011 as *Southwestern Advantage Honors: College & University Prep*
Southwestern/Great American, Inc., dba The Southwestern Company
© 2011 The Southwestern Company
Nashville, Tennessee
ISBN 978-0-87197-557-7

Originally published as *Volume Library* (Book 4)
Southwestern/Great American, Inc., dba The Southwestern Company
© 2008 The Southwestern Company
ISBN 978-0-87197-545-4
Reprinted 2009

Henry Bedford
Chief Executive Officer, Southwestern/Great American, Inc.

Dan Moore
President, Southwestern

Dave Kempf
President, FRP, Inc.

Printed in the United States of America by RR Donnelley

5 Steps to a 5: AP U.S. History by Stephen Armstrong
Copyright © 2004 by the McGraw-Hill Companies, Inc. All rights reserved. Reprinted by permission of The McGraw-Hill Companies, Inc.

5 Steps to a 5: AP U.S. Government & Politics by Pamela K. Lamb
Copyright © 2004 by the McGraw-Hill Companies, Inc. All rights reserved. Reprinted by permission of The McGraw-Hill Companies, Inc.

5 Steps to a 5: AP Biology by Mark Anestis
Copyright © 2002 by the McGraw-Hill Companies, Inc. All rights reserved. Reprinted by permission of The McGraw-Hill Companies, Inc.

5 Steps to a 5: AP Calculus by William Ma
Copyright © 2002 by the McGraw-Hill Companies, Inc. All rights reserved. Reprinted by permission of The McGraw-Hill Companies, Inc.

5 Steps to a 5: Writing the AP English Essay by Barbara L. Murphy
Copyright © 2004 by the McGraw-Hill Companies, Inc. All rights reserved. Reprinted by permission of The McGraw-Hill Companies, Inc.

Preface

Welcome to *Southwestern Advantage Honors: College & University Prep*. Athough this book contains review materials originally intended for students taking Advanced Placement tests, it will nonetheless be of great value to any student. You can design a course of study tailored to your unique needs and learning style. The test-taking and study skills and strategies illustrated within these pages can be utilized whether you are in a survey class or college prep class or anywhere in between.

There is a diagnostic test at the beginning of each subject that will enable you to realistically assess your starting point and tell you where your strengths and weaknesses lie. The practice tests on the enclosed CD will afford you the ability to periodically measure your progress. (Practice tests in other subject areas not covered in this book are included on the CD, as well.)

Nothing can substitute for the classroom experience—the give-and-take, the interaction, the growth—but this book will serve as an invaluable supplement to your coursework.

Every effort has been made to ensure that these books are as accurate as possible. If errors or omissions should be discovered, however, we would appreciate hearing from you. Please send comments or suggestions to editor@southwestern.com, or to Editor, The Southwestern Company, P.O. Box 305142, Nashville, Tennessee 37230.

—The Editors

Editorial

Executive Editor and President
Dan Moore

Editorial Director
Mary Cummings

Managing Editor
Judy Jackson

Editors
Georgia L. Brazil
Barbara J. Reed

Research Editors
Trisha McWright
Alison Nash

Copy Editors
Mary Spotswood Box
Julee Hicks
Linda Jones
Cathy Ropp
Debbie Van Mol
Tanis Westbrook

Art

Design Directors
Steve Newman
Starletta Polster

Designers
Bill Kersey
Travis Rader
Jim Scott

Composition
Jessie Anglin
Sara Anglin

Production

Production Manager
Powell Ropp

Production Coordinator
Wanda Sawyer

Sales

Sales Directors
Chris Adams
Dave Causer
Lester Crafton
Grant Greder
Kevin Johnson
Robin Mukherjee
Mark Rau
Tim Ritzer
Chris Samuels
Nate Vogel

About the Authors

Stephen Armstrong (U.S. History) is a social studies teacher and the social studies department chairperson at Manchester High School in Manchester, Connecticut. He is also an adjunct professor of history at Central Connecticut State University in New Britain, Connecticut. He has been a member of the Board of Directors of the National Council for the Social Studies and is presently serving on the NCSS Citizenship Task Force.

Pamela K. Lamb (U.S. Government & Politics) has taught AP U.S. Government and Politics for the past 11 years at Del Rio High School in Del Rio, Texas, and has been a longtime reader of AP tests in History, Government, and Economics.

Mark Anestis (Biology) teaches test preparation courses in AP, SAT I, and SAT II, and other major standardized tests. He has taught AP level biology in Connecticut high schools.

William Ma (Calculus) is the lead Chair of the mathematics department for the Herricks school system in New York. He is responsible for grades 6–12 mathematics curriculum and the supervision of both middle and high school mathematics teachers. He is also the author of online review guides for a number of New York State mathematics exams.

Barbara L. Murphy (English Essay) has taught AP English Language and Composition and other college level courses at Jericho High School for over twenty years. She has been a reader of the AP English Language and Composition exam since 1993 and is a consultant for the College Board's AP English Language and Composition and its Building for Success divisions. She is currently on the faculty of Syracuse University's Project Advance in English.

Estelle Rankin (English Essay) taught AP English Literature at Jericho High School for over 25 years and was honored with the AP Literature Teacher of the Year award by the College Board in 1996. She also received the Long Island Teacher of the Year award in 1990 and the Cornell University Presidential Scholar's award.

CONTENTS

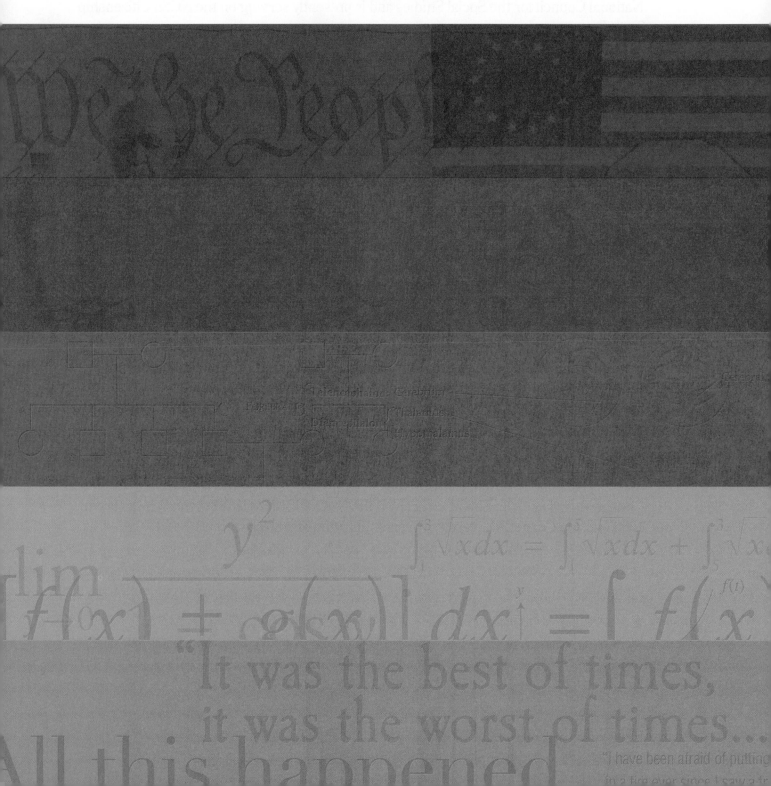

U.S. History / 33

Preface / 34

PART I   HOW TO USE THIS BOOK / 35

Chapter 1   The Five-Step Program / 37
Before We Begin / 37
Introduction to the Five-Step Program / 39
Graphics Used in This Book / 40
Three Approaches to Preparing for the AP U.S. History Exam / 41
Calendars for Preparing for the AP U.S. History Exam / 43
Rapid Review / 47

PART II   WHAT YOU NEED TO KNOW ABOUT
THE AP U.S. HISTORY EXAM / 49

Chapter 2   Introduction to the AP U.S. History Exam / 51
Background Information / 51
The AP U.S. History Examination / 52
Taking the Exam / 57
Getting Started: The Diagnostic/Master Exam / 58
Answers to Diagnostic/Master Exam / 76

PART III   A COMPREHENSIVE REVIEW
OF UNITED STATES HISTORY / 95

Chapter 3   The Settling of the Western Hemisphere and
Colonial America (1450–1650) / 97
Native Americans and European Exploration / 97
A Bringing Together of Three Peoples by the Spanish / 98
The French in Canada / 98
The English in the Americas / 99
Effects of English, French, and British Settlement / 102
Chapter Review / 102

Chapter 4   **The British Empire in America: Growth and Conflict (1650–1750) / 105**
The Impact of Mercantilism / 105
African Slavery in the Americas / 106
Continued Unrest in New England / 107
The Salem Witch Trials / 108
Wars in Europe and Their Impact on the Colonies / 108
The Growth of the Colonial Assemblies / 109
The Era of "Salutary Neglect" / 109
The Great Awakening / 110
Chapter Review / 110

Chapter 5   **Resistance, Rebellion, and Revolution (1750–1775) / 113**
Problems on the Frontier / 113
Additional Conflicts Between the British and
    Their Colonial "Allies" / 114
The Policies of George Grenville / 114
A Sense of Crisis: The Stamp Act / 115
More Protest: The Townshend Acts / 116
Continued Tensions in Massachusetts / 117
The Calm Before the Storm: 1700–1773 / 117
The Boston Tea Party / 117
The Intolerable Acts / 118
The First Continental Congress / 118
Chapter Review / 119

Chapter 6   **The American Revolution and the New Nation (1775–1787) / 122**
The American Revolution / 122
The Second Continental Congress / 123
The Declaration of Independence / 123
The Outbreak of the Revolution: Divisions in the Colonies / 124
Strategies of the American Revolution / 124
Washington as Commander / 125
The War Moves to the South / 126
The Treaty of Paris / 127
The Establishment of Governmental Structures in the New Nation / 127
The Articles of Confederation / 127
The Northwest Ordinances / 128
Shay's Rebellion / 129
Chapter Review / 129

Chapter 7   **The Establishment of New Political Systems (1787–1800) / 132**
Desires for a Stronger Central Government / 132
Government Under the New Constitution / 133

The Issue of Slavery / 133
Ratification of the Constitution / 134
The Presidency of George Washington / 134
The Bill of Rights / 134
Competing Visions: Alexander Hamilton and Thomas Jefferson / 135
The French Revolution / 136
Foreign Policy and Jay's Treaty / 136
Washington's Farewell Address / 137
The Presidency of John Adams / 137
The Alien and Sedition Acts / 138
Chapter Review / 138

Chapter 8   **The Jeffersonian Revolution (1800–1820) / 141**
The Election of 1800 / 141
Reform of the Courts / 142
Westward Expansion / 142
Political Tensions and the Strange Case of Aaron Burr / 144
European Wars Spill Over to America (Again) / 144
The War of 1812 / 145
The American System / 147
The Missouri Compromise / 147
Chapter Review / 147

Chapter 9   **The Rise of Manufacturing and the Age of Jackson (1820–1845) / 150**
The Growth of the Factory / 150
The Monroe Doctrine / 151
Policy Toward Native Americans / 151
The Second Great Awakening / 152
Political Reform: The Jacksonian Era (1829–1841) / 153
The Election of 1824 / 153
The 1828 Presidential Election / 154
Jackson as President / 154
The Nullification Controversy / 155
The Bank Crisis / 155
The Whig Party: A Challenge to the Democratic-Republicans / 156
Chapter Review / 156

Chapter 10   **The Union Expanded and Challenged (1835–1860) / 159**
The Ideology of Manifest Destiny / 159
"Remember the Alamo!" / 160
The Pivotal Election of 1844 / 161
War with Mexico / 161
Political Challenges of the 1850s / 163
Effects of the Compromise of 1850 / 164
The Presidency of Franklin Pierce / 164
The Return of Sectional Conflict / 165

"Bleeding Kansas": Slave or Free? / 165
The Dred Scott Decision / 166
The Lincoln–Douglas Debates / 166
John Brown's Raid / 167
The Presidential Election of 1860 / 167
Chapter Review / 168

Chapter 11   The Union Divided: The Civil War
              (1861–1865) / 171
              Advantages of the North and South in War / 172
              The Attack on Fort Sumter and the Beginning of War / 173
              War Aims and Strategies / 173
              Developments in the South and in the North / 175
              The Emancipation Proclamation / 176
              1863: The War Tips to the North / 177
              War Weariness in the North and South / 177
              The End of the Confederacy / 178
              Chapter Review / 178

Chapter 12   The Era of Reconstruction (1865–1877) / 181
              Lincoln's Plans for Reconstruction / 181
              Andrew Johnson's Plan for Reconstruction / 182
              The Reconstruction of the Radical Republicans / 183
              A Period of Radical Reconstruction / 184
              The Impeachment of Andrew Johnson / 184
              Radical Reconstruction Reinforced / 185
              The End of Reconstruction / 185
              Chapter Review / 186

Chapter 13   Western Expansion and Its Impact on the
              American Character (1860–1895) / 190
              Federal Legislation Encourages Western Settlement / 190
              Farming on the Great Plains / 191
              The Transformation of Agriculture on the Plains / 191
              Women and Minorities on the Plains / 192
              Mining and Lumbering in the West / 193
              Ranching in the West / 193
              The Plight of Native Americans / 194
              The Organization of the American Farmer and Populism / 195
              The Impact of the West on American Society / 197
              Chapter Review / 198

Chapter 14   America Transformed into the Industrial Giant
              of the World (1870–1910) / 201
              The Growth of Industrial America / 201
              The Changing Nature of American Industry / 202
              The Consolidation of Businesses / 203

The Growth of Labor Unions / 205
An Increased Standard of Living? / 206
The Impact of Immigration on American Society / 207
The Transformation of the American City / 208
Politics of the Guilded Age / 209
Cultural Life in the Guilded Age / 212
Chapter Review / 212

Chapter 15   **The Rise of American Imperialism (1890–1913) / 216**
A Period of Foreign Policy Inaction / 216
A Sign of Things to Come: Hawaii / 217
The 1890s: Reasons for American Imperialism / 218
The Spanish-American War / 218
The Role of America: Protector or Oppressor? / 220
The Debate Over the Philippines / 221
Connecting the Pacific and the Atlantic: The Panama
    Canal / 222
The Roosevelt Corollary / 223
Chapter Review / 223

Chapter 16   **The Progressive Era (1895–1914) / 227**
The Origins of Progressivism / 227
The Goals of Progressives / 228
Urban Reforms / 229
The Progressives at the State Level / 229
Women and Progressivism / 230
Reforming the Workplace / 231
The Square Deal of Theodore Roosevelt / 231
Progressivism Under William Howard Taft / 232
The 1912 Presidential Election / 233
The Progressive Legacy of Woodrow Wilson / 234
Did Progressivism Succeed? / 234
Chapter Review / 235

Chapter 17   **The United States and World War I / 238**
The American Response to the Outbreak of War / 238
Increasing American Support for the Allied Powers / 239
America Moves Toward War / 240
America Enters the War / 240
The Impact of the American Expeditionary Force / 241
The Home Front During World War I / 241
Keeping America Patriotic / 242
Woodrow Wilson and the Treaty of Versailles / 243
The Treaty of Versailles and the United States Senate / 244
The Consequences of American Actions After the War / 244
Chapter Review / 245

Chapter 18   **America in the 1920s: The Beginning of Modern America / 248**
A Decade of Prosperity / 248
Republican Leadership in the 1920s / 249
The Presidency of Warren G. Harding / 250
The Scandals of the Harding Administration / 251
The Presidency of Calvin Coolidge / 251
The Election of 1928 / 252
Urban vs. Rural: The Great Divide of the 1920s / 252
Culture in the 1920s / 255
The Jazz Age / 256
The Lost Generation / 257
Chapter Review / 258

Chapter 19   **The Great Depression and the New Deal / 262**
The American Economy of the 1920s: The Roots of the Great
    Depression / 262
The Stock Market Crash / 263
The Social Impact of the Great Depression / 265
The Hoover Administration and the Depression / 266
The 1932 Presidential Election / 266
The First Hundred Days / 267
The Second New Deal / 269
The Presidential Election of 1936 / 270
Opponents of Franklin Roosevelt and the New Deal / 271
The Last Years of the New Deal / 272
The Effects of the New Deal / 273
New Deal Culture / 273
Chapter Review / 274

Chapter 20   **World War II / 278**
American Foreign Policy in the 1930s / 278
The Presidential Election of 1940 and Its Aftermath / 279
The Attack on Pearl Harbor / 280
America Enters the War / 281
The War Against Japan / 283
The Decision to Drop the Atomic Bomb / 284
The Home Front During the War / 284
Discrimination During the War / 286
Chapter Review / 286

Chapter 21   **The Origins of the Cold War (1945–1960) / 290**
The First Cracks in the Alliance: 1945 / 290
The Iron Curtain / 291
The Marshall Plan / 292
Berlin: The First Cold War Crisis / 292
1949: A Pivotal Year in the Cold War / 293

The Cold War at Home / 293
The Heating of the Cold War: Korea / 295
The Rise of McCarthyism / 295
The Cold War Policies of President Eisenhower / 296
A Dangerous Arms Buildup / 298
Chapter Review / 299

Chapter 22   **The 1950s: Prosperity and Anxiety / 302**
Economic Growth and Prosperity / 302
Political Developments of the Postwar Era / 303
Civil Rights Struggles of the Postwar Period / 305
The Conformity of the Suburbs / 306
Chapter Review / 308

Chapter 23   **America in an Era of Turmoil
(1960–1975) / 312**
The 1960 Presidential Election / 312
Domestic Policies Under Kennedy and Johnson / 313
The Struggle of Black Americans: From Nonviolence
    to Black Power / 314
The Rise of Feminism / 316
The Cold War in the 1960s / 317
The Vietnam War and Its Impact on American Society / 318
Chapter Review / 321

Chapter 24   **America from 1968 to 1988:
Decline and Rebirth / 325**
The Presidency of Richard Nixon / 325
The Watergate Affair / 327
The Presidency of Gerald Ford / 330
The Presidency of Jimmy Carter / 331
The Election of 1980 / 332
The Presidency of Ronald Reagan / 333
Chapter Review / 335

Chapter 25   **America from 1988 to 2000: Prosperity
and a New World Order / 339**
The 1988 Election / 339
The Presidency of George Bush / 340
The 1992 Election / 341
The Presidency of Bill Clinton / 342
The 2000 Presidential Election / 344
Chapter Review / 345

PART IV   **"AFTER WORDS" / 348**

Glossary / 349

Preface / 382
Acknowledgments / 383

PART I   **HOW TO USE THIS BOOK / 385**

Chapter 1   **The Five-Step Program / 387**
The Basics / 387
Organization of This Book / 388
Introduction to the Five-Step Program / 388
Graphics Used in This Book / 389
Three Approaches to Preparing for the AP U.S. Government
    and Politics Exam / 390
Calendars for Preparing for the AP U.S. Government and
    Politics Exam / 392

PART II   **WHAT YOU NEED TO KNOW ABOUT THE AP
                  U.S. GOVERNMENT AND POLITICS EXAM / 397**

Chapter 2   **Introduction to the AP U.S. Government
                  and Politics Exam / 399**
Background of the Advanced Placement Program / 399
Reasons for Taking the Advanced Placement Exam / 400
What You Need to Know about the AP U.S. Government
    and Politics Exam / 401
A Look at the Diagnostic/Master Exam / 404
Getting Started: The Diagnostic/Master Exam / 405

Chapter 3   **Section I of the Exam:
                  The Multiple-Choice Questions / 416**
Introduction to the Multiple-Choice Section of the Exam / 416
Types of Multiple-Choice Questions / 417
Strategies for Answering the Multiple-Choice Questions / 417
Scoring the Multiple-Choice Section / 419
Answer Sheet for Diagnostic Multiple-Choice Questions / 421
The Multiple-Choice Section of the Diagnostic/Master Exam / 423
Explanation of the Answers to the Multiple-Choice Questions
    of the Diagnostic/Master Exam / 430

Chapter 4   **Section II of the Exam:**
The Free-Response Essay / 434
Introduction to the Free-Response Essay / 434
Types of Free-Response Prompts / 436
Developing the Free-Response Essay / 436
Rubrics for the Free-Response Essay / 437
Final Comments—Some Helpful Hints / 438
The Free-Response Section of the Diagnostic/Master Exam / 439
Rubrics for Free-Response Essays / 441

PART III   **COMPREHENSIVE REVIEW:**
DEVELOPING THE KNOWLEDGE, SKILLS,
AND STRATEGIES / 443

Chapter 5   **Review: Architecture and Development**
of U.S. Government / 445
Principles of Government / 445
Origins of American Government / 447
The United States Constitution / 452
Review Questions / 457
Answers and Explanations / 458
Rapid Review / 459

Chapter 6   **Review: Federalism / 461**
Federalism / 461
Federalism in Practice / 463
Establishing National Supremacy / 463
Federalism Today / 464
Review Questions / 466
Answers and Explanations / 467
Rapid Review / 468

Chapter 7   **Review: Political Culture / 469**
American Political Environment / 469
Public Opinion / 470
Review Questions / 472
Answers and Explanations / 473
Rapid Review / 473

Chapter 8   **Review: Political Parties / 474**
What Are Political Parties? / 474
Roles of Political Parties / 474
Party Systems / 474
What Do Political Parties Do? / 475
Party Identification and Membership / 476
Two-Party Tradition in America / 476

Third or Minor Parties / 478
Structure and Organization of Political Parties / 479
Future of Political Parties / 480
Review Questions / 481
Answers and Explanations / 482
Rapid Review / 483

Chapter 9   **Review: Voting and Elections / 485**
Participation and Voting / 485
Types of Elections / 488
Campaign Finance / 491
Review Questions / 492
Answers and Explanations / 493
Rapid Review / 494

Chapter 10   **Review: Interest Groups and the Mass Media / 496**
Interest Groups / 496
Mass Media / 499
Biases in the Media / 502
Review Questions / 502
Answers and Explanations / 503
Rapid Review / 504

Chapter 11   **Review: The Legislative Branch / 505**
Congress / 505
Structure of Congress / 505
Organization of Congress / 506
Election to Congress / 506
Leadership of Congress / 507
Committee System / 508
Congressional Staff and Support / 509
Roles of Members of Congress / 509
Powers of Congress / 509
The Lawmaking Process / 510
Legislative Tactics / 511
Influences on Congress / 512
Review Questions / 512
Answers and Explanations / 514
Rapid Review / 514

Chapter 12   **Review: Executive Branch and the Bureaucracy / 516**
Constitutional Origins of Presidency / 516
The Road to the White House / 518
The Vice Presidency / 519
Presidential Powers / 519
Limitations on Presidential Powers / 521
Presidential Character / 521
The Bureaucracy / 522

Executive Office of the President (EOP) / 523
Executive Departments / 524
Review Questions / 525
Answers and Explanations / 526
Rapid Review / 527

Chapter 13   **Review: The National Judiciary / 528**
The Federal Court System / 528
Structure of the Judicial System / 529
Judicial Selection / 530
The Court at Work / 531
Courts as Policymakers / 532
Judicial Philosophy / 533
Review Questions / 534
Answers and Explanations / 535
Rapid Review / 536

Chapter 14   **Review: Civil Liberties and Civil Rights / 537**
Civil Liberties / 537
Freedom of Religion / 538
Freedom of Speech / 539
Freedom of the Press / 541
Freedom of Assembly and Petition / 542
Property Rights / 542
Rights of the Accused / 542
Civil Rights / 543
The Civil Rights Movement / 544
Other Minorities / 545
Affirmative Action / 547
Review Questions / 548
Answers and Explanations / 549
Rapid Review / 549

Chapter 15   **Review: Politics and Public Policymaking / 552**
Policymaking Process / 552
Domestic Policy / 553
Economic Policy / 555
Foreign and Defense Policy / 556
Review Questions / 558
Answers and Explanations / 560
Rapid Review / 560

PART IV   **APPENDIX / 563**

**Websites Related to the Advanced
Placement Exam / 565
Glossary of Terms / 566**

Biology / 573

Preface / 574
Acknowledgments / 575

PART I   HOW TO USE THIS BOOK / 577
The Basics / 579
Organization of the Book / 579
Introduction to the Five-Step Program / 580
Three Approaches to Preparing for the AP Biology Exam / 581
Calendar for Each Plan / 583
Introduction to the Graphics Used in This Book / 586

PART II   WHAT YOU NEED TO KNOW ABOUT
              THE AP BIOLOGY EXAM / 587
Background of the Advanced Placement Program / 589
Who Writes the AP Biology Exam / 589
The AP Grades and Who Receives Them / 589
Reasons for Taking the AP Biology Exam / 589
Questions Frequently Asked about the AP Biology
    Exam / 590
Tips for Taking the AP Biology Exam / 593
Getting Started: The Diagnostic Exam / 595

PART III   COMPREHENSIVE REVIEW / 607

Chapter 1   Chemistry / 609
Introduction / 609
Elements, Compounds, Atoms, and Ions / 609
Lipids, Carbohydrates, and Proteins / 611
Enzymes / 615
pH: Acids and Bases / 616
Reactions / 617
Review Questions / 618
Answers and Explanations / 619
Rapid Review / 620

Chapter 2   Cells / 621
Introduction / 621

Types of Cells / 621
Organelles / 621
Cell Membranes: Fluid Mosaic Model / 623
Types of Cell Transport / 624
Review Questions / 626
Answers and Explanations / 627
Rapid Review / 628

Chapter 3 **Respiration / 630**
Introduction / 630
Aerobic Respiration / 630
Anaerobic Respiration / 636
Review Questions / 638
Answers and Explanations / 638
Rapid Review / 639

Chapter 4 **Photosynthesis / 641**
Introduction / 641
The Players in Photosynthesis / 641
Reactions of Photosynthesis / 643
Types of Photosynthesis / 648
Review Questions / 649
Answers and Explanations / 650
Rapid Review / 651

Chapter 5 **Cell Division / 653**
Introduction / 653
Cell Division in Prokaryotes / 653
The Cell Cycle / 653
Mitosis / 654
Control of Cell Division / 656
Haploid versus Diploid Organisms / 656
Meiosis / 657
Life Cycles / 659
Sources of Cell Variation / 660
Review Questions / 661
Answers and Explanations / 662
Rapid Review / 663

Chapter 6 **Heredity / 665**
Introduction / 665
Terms Important in Studying Heredity / 665
Mendel and His Peas / 666
Intermediate Inheritance / 668
Other Forms of Inheritance / 668
Sex Determination and Sex Linkage / 670
Linkage and Gene Mapping / 671
Heads or Tails? / 672

Pedigrees / 673
Common Disorders / 675
Chromosomal Complications / 675
Review Questions / 676
Answers and Explanations / 678
Rapid Review / 681

Chapter 7   **Molecular Genetics / 683**
Introduction / 683
DNA Structure and Function / 683
RNA Structure and Function / 683
Replication of DNA / 684
Transcription of DNA / 687
RNA Processing / 688
Translation of RNA / 688
Gene Expression / 689
The Genetics of Viruses / 691
The Genetics of Bacteria / 692
Genetic Engineering / 694
Review Questions / 696
Answers and Explanations / 697
Rapid Review / 699

Chapter 8   **Evolution / 701**
Introduction / 701
Definition of Evolution / 701
Natural Selection / 702
Lamarck and Darwin / 703
Adaptations / 704
Types of Selection / 704
Evolution Patterns / 706
Sources of Variation / 706
Speciation / 707
When Evolution Is Not Occurring: Hardy–Weinberg Equilibrium / 708
The Evidence for Evolution / 709
Macroevolution / 710
How Life Probably Emerged / 711
Review Questions / 713
Answers and Explanations / 714
Rapid Review / 715

Chapter 9   **Taxonomy and Classification / 717**
Introduction / 717
Five or Six Kingdoms? / 717
Kingdom Monera / 718
Endosymbiotic Theory / 719
Kingdom Protista / 719
Kingdom Plantae / 721
Kingdom Fungi / 724

Kingdom Animalia / 724
Review Questions / 727
Answers and Explanations / 728
Rapid Review / 728

Chapter 10   **Plants / 731**
Introduction / 731
Anatomy of Plants / 731
Roots / 732
The Shoot System / 733
Plant Hormones / 734
Plant Tropisms / 735
Photoperiodism / 735
Go with the Flow: Osmosis, Capillary Action, Cohesion–Tension
     Theory, and Transpiration / 736
The Changing of the Guard: Regulating Stomata Activity / 737
"Move over, Sugar": Carbohydrate Transport through Phloem / 737
Review Questions / 737
Answers and Explanations / 738
Rapid Review / 739

Chapter 11   **Human Physiology / 741**
Introduction / 741
Circulatory System / 741
Respiratory System / 743
Digestive System / 744
Control of the Internal Environment / 745
Nervous System / 748
Muscular System / 750
Endocrine System / 752
Immune System / 755
Review Questions / 757
Answers and Explanations / 758
Rapid Review / 759

Chapter 12   **Human Reproduction / 762**
Introduction / 762
Sex Differences / 762
Anatomy / 762
Embryonic Development / 766
The Influence of Hormones / 769
Review Questions / 770
Answers and Explanations / 771
Rapid Review / 772

Chapter 13   **Behavioral Ecology and Ethology / 774**
Introduction / 774
Types of Animal Learning / 774

Animal Movement / 775
Animal Communication / 777
Review Questions / 778
Answers and Explanations / 779
Rapid Review / 779

Chapter 14   **Ecology in Further Detail / 782**
Introduction / 782
Population Ecology and Growth / 782
Life History Strategies / 785
Community and Succession / 786
Trophic Levels / 789
Biomes / 790
Biogeochemical Cycles / 792
Review Questions / 793
Answers and Explanations / 794
Rapid Review / 796

Chapter 15   **Laboratory Review / 798**
Introduction / 798
Laboratory Experiment 1: Diffusion and Osmosis / 798
Laboratory Experiment 2: Enzyme Catalysis / 800
Laboratory Experiment 3: Mitosis and Meiosis / 801
Laboratory Experiment 4: Plant Pigments and
    Photosynthesis / 802
Laboratory Experiment 5: Cell Respiration / 804
Laboratory Experiment 6: Molecular Biology / 805
Laboratory Experiment 7: Genetics of Organisms / 807
Laboratory Experiment 8: Population Genetics and
    Evolution / 808
Laboratory Experiment 9: Transpiration / 809
Laboratory Experiment 10: Physiology of the
    Circulatory System / 810
Laboratory Experiment 11: Animal Behavior / 811
Laboratory Experiment 12: Dissolved Oxygen and Aquatic
    Primary Productivity / 811
Review Questions / 812
Answers and Explanations / 813
Rapid Review / 814

PART IV   **APPENDIX / 817**

Bibliography / 819
Websites / 820
Glossary / 821

Calculus / 841

Dedication / 843
Preface / 844
Acknowledgments / 845

PART I   **HOW TO USE THIS BOOK / 847**
How Is This Book Organized? / 849
Introduction to the Five-Step Program / 849
Three Approaches to Preparing for the AP Calculus AB Exam / 850
Overview of the Three Plans / 850
Calendar for Each Plan / 851
Graphics Used in the Book / 855

PART II   **WHAT YOU NEED TO KNOW ABOUT THE AP CALCULUS AB EXAM / 857**
Background on the AP Exam / 859
  What Is Covered in the AP Calculus AB Exam? / 859
  What Is the Format of the AP Calculus AB Exam? / 859
  What Are the Advanced Placement Exam Grades? / 859
  How Is the AP Calculus AB Exam Grade Calculated? / 860
  Which Graphing Calculators Are Allowed for the Exam? / 860
  Calculators and Other Devices Not Allowed for the AP Calculus Exam / 860
  Other Restrictions on Calculators / 861
  How Much Work Do I Need to Show When I Use a Graphing Calculator in Section II, Free-Response Questions? / 861
What Do I Need to Bring to the Exam? / 861
Tips for Taking the Exam / 861
Getting Started! / 863
Diagnostic Test / 865
Answers and Solutions / 873
Scoring and Interpretation / 885

PART III   **COMPREHENSIVE REVIEW / 887**

Chapter 1   **Review of Pre-Calculus / 889**
1.1 Lines / 889
    Slope of a Line / 889

Equations of Lines / 890
Parallel and Perpendicular Lines / 891
1.2 Absolute Values and Inequalities / 893
Absolute Values / 893
Inequalities and the Real Number Line / 894
Solving Absolute Value Inequalities / 895
Solving Polynomial Inequalities / 896
Solving Rational Inequalities / 897
1.3 Functions / 899
Definition of a Function / 899
Operations on Functions / 900
Inverse Functions / 902
Trigonometric and Inverse Trigonometric
    Functions / 904
Exponential and Logarithmic Functions / 907
1.4 Graphs of Functions / 910
Increasing and Decreasing Functions / 910
Intercepts and Zeros / 911
Odd and Even Functions / 913
Shifting, Reflecting, and Stretching Graphs / 914
1.5 Rapid Review / 918
1.6 Practice Problems / 919
1.7 Solutions to Practice Problems / 920

Chapter 2   **Limits and Continuity / 922**
2.1 The Limit of a Function / 922
Definition and Properties of Limits / 922
Evaluating Limits / 923
One-Sided Limits / 924
Squeeze Theorem / 927
2.2 Limits Involving Infinities / 929
Infinite Limits (as $x \to a$) / 929
Limits at Infinity as ($x \to \pm\infty$) / 931
Vertical and Horizontal Asymptotes / 933
2.3 Continuity of a Function / 936
Theorems on Continuity / 936
2.4 Rapid Review / 938
2.5 Practice Problems / 939
2.6 Cumulative Review Problems / 941
2.7 Solutions to Practice Problems / 941
2.8 Solutions to Cumulative Review
    Problems / 943

Chapter 3   **Differentiation / 945**
3.1 Derivatives of Algebraic Functions / 945
Definition of the Derivative of a Function / 945
Power Rule / 948
The Sum, Difference, Product, and Quotient Rules / 949
The Chain Rule / 950

3.2 Derivatives of Trigonometric, Inverse Trigonometric, Exponential, and Logarithmic Functions / 951
  Derivatives of Trigonometric Functions / 951
  Derivatives of Inverse Trigonometric Functions / 953
  Derivatives of Exponential and Logarithmic Functions / 954
3.3 Implicit Differentiation / 956
3.4 Approximating a Derivative / 958
3.5 Derivatives of Inverse Functions / 959
3.6 Higher Order Derivatives / 961
3.7 Rapid Review / 962
3.8 Practice Problems / 963
3.9 Cumulative Review Problems / 964
3.10 Solutions to Practice Problems / 964
3.11 Solutions to Cumulative Review Problems / 967

Chapter 4

Graphs of Functions and Derivatives / 969

4.1 Rolle's Theorem, Mean Value Theorem, and Extreme Value Theorem / 969
  Rolle's Theorem and Mean Value Theorem / 969
  Extreme Value Theorem / 972
4.2 Determining the Behavior of Functions / 973
  Test for Increasing and Decreasing Functions / 973
  First Derivative Test and Second Derivative Test for Relative Extrema / 976
  Test for Concavity and Points of Inflection / 979
4.3 Sketching the Graphs of Functions / 984
  Graphing without Calculators / 984
  Graphing with Calculators / 986
4.4 Graphs of Derivatives / 987
4.5 Rapid Review / 991
4.6 Practice Problems / 994
4.7 Cumulative Review Problems / 996
4.8 Solutions to Practice Problems / 996
4.9 Solutions to Cumulative Review Problems / 1001

Chapter 5

Applications of Derivatives / 1003

5.1 Related Rate / 1003
  General Procedure for Solving Related Rate Problems / 1003
  Common Related Rate Problems / 1003
  Inverted Cone (Water Tank) Problem / 1004
  Shadow Problem / 1006
  Angle of Elevation Problem / 1007
5.2 Applied Maximum and Minimum Problems / 1008
  General Procedure for Solving Applied Maximum and Minimum Problems / 1008
  Distance Problems / 1008
  Area and Volume Problems / 1010
  Business Problems / 1012

5.3 Rapid Review / 1013
5.4 Practice Problems / 1014
5.5 Cumulative Review Problems / 1016
5.6 Solutions to Practice Problems / 1016
5.7 Solutions to Cumulative Review Problems / 1022

Chapter 6   **More Applications of Derivatives / 1024**
6.1 Tangent and Normal Lines / 1024
Tangent Lines / 1024
Normal Lines / 1029
6.2 Linear Approximations / 1032
Tangent Line Approximation / 1032
Estimating the nth Root of a Number / 1034
Estimating the Value of a Trigonometric Function of an
   Angle / 1034
6.3 Motion Along a Line / 1035
Instantaneous Velocity and Acceleration / 1035
Vertical Motion / 1036
Horizontal Motion / 1037
6.4 Rapid Review / 1038
6.5 Practice Problems / 1039
6.6 Cumulative Review Problems / 1040
6.7 Solutions to Practice Problems / 1041
6.8 Solutions to Cumulative Review Problems / 1045

Chapter 7   **Integration / 1046**
7.1 Evaluating Basic Integrals / 1046
Antiderivatives and Integration Formulas / 1046
Evaluating Integrals / 1048
7.2 Integration by U-Substitution / 1051
The U-Substitution Method / 1051
U-Substitution and Algebraic Functions / 1051
U-Substitution and Trigonometric Functions / 1053
U-Substitution and Inverse Trigonometric
   Functions / 1054
U-Substitution and Logarithmic and Exponential
   Functions / 1055
7.3 Rapid Review / 1059
7.4 Practice Problems / 1059
7.5 Cumulative Review Problems / 1060
7.6 Solutions to Practice Problems / 1061
7.7 Solutions to Cumulative Review Problems / 1063

Chapter 8   **Definite Integrals / 1064**
8.1 Riemann Sums and Definite Integrals / 1064
Sigma Notation or Summation Notation / 1064
Definition of a Riemann Sum / 1065
Definition of a Definite Integral / 1066
Properties of Definite Integrals / 1067

8.2 Fundamental Theorems of Calculus / 1068
     First Fundamental Theorem of Calculus / 1068
     Second Fundamental Theorem of Calculus / 1070
8.3 Evaluating Definite Integrals / 1071
     Definite Integrals Involving Algebraic Functions / 1072
     Definite Integrals Involving Absolute Value / 1073
     Definite Integrals Involving Trigonometric, Logarithmic, and
       Exponential Functions / 1074
     Definite Integrals Involving Odd and Even
       Functions / 1075
8.4 Rapid Review / 1076
8.5 Practice Problems / 1077
8.6 Cumulative Review Problems / 1078
8.7 Solutions to Practice Problems / 1078
8.8 Solutions to Cumulative Review Problems / 1081

Chapter 9   **Areas and Volumes / 1083**
9.1 The Function $F(x) = \int_a^x f(t)\,dt$ / 1083
9.2 Approximating the Area under a Curve / 1087
     Rectangular Approximations / 1087
     Trapezoidal Approximations / 1090
9.3 Area and Definite Integrals / 1091
     Area under a Curve / 1091
     Area between Two Curves / 1095
9.4 Volumes and Definite Integrals / 1098
     Solids with Known Cross Sections / 1098
     The Disc Method / 1102
     The Washer Method / 1107
9.5 Rapid Review / 1109
9.6 Practice Problems / 1111
9.7 Cumulative Review Problems / 1112
9.8 Solutions to Practice Problems / 1113
9.9 Solutions to Cumulative Review Problems / 1118

Chapter 10   **More Applications of Definite Integrals / 1121**
10.1 Average Value of a Function / 1121
     Mean Value Theorem of Integrals / 1121
     Average Value of a Function on $[a,b]$ / 1122
10.2 Distance Traveled Problems / 1123
10.3 Definite Integral as Accumulated Change / 1126
     Business Problems / 1126
     Temperature Problems / 1127
     Leakage Problems / 1128
     Growth Problems / 1128
10.4 Differential Equations / 1129
     Exponential Growth/Decay Problems / 1129
     Separable Differential Equations / 1131

10.5 Rapid Review / 1134
10.6 Practice Problems / 1134
10.7 Cumulative Review Problems / 1136
10.8 Solutions to Practice Problems / 1136
10.9 Solutions to Cumulative Review Problems / 1140

APPENDIXES / 1143

Appendix I: Formulas and Theorems / 1145
Appendix II: Special Topic: Slope Fields / 1149
Appendix III: Bibliography / 1154
Appendix IV: Websites / 1155

English Essay / 1157

Preface / 1158
Acknowledgments / 1159

PART I   **INTRODUCTION TO THE TRAINING PROGRAM / 1161**

Chapter 1   **Get with the Program / 1163**
Meet Your Trainers / 1163
Questions About the AP English Essay / 1164
My Personal Writing Profile / 1172
About the Basic Training Program / 1173

PART II   **KNOW THE BASICS: WRITING AEROBICS / 1177**

Chapter 2   **The First Set of Basic Exercises for Your Writing Routine: The Four Modes of Discourse / 1179**
The Basics / 1179

Chapter 3   **"Stretching" and "Aerobic" Exercises for Your Writing Routine: Rhetorical Strategies / 1187**
Rhetorical Strategies / 1187
Exemplification / 1189
Contrast/Comparison / 1194
Cause and Effect / 1199
Classification and Division / 1204
Process / 1207
Definition / 1211
Description / 1215
Narration / 1220
Argument / 1224
A Total Workout / 1231

Chapter 4	"Stretching" and "Aerobic" Exercises for Your Writing Routine: Rhetorical Devices, Techniques, and Writing Style / 1233
	Rhetorical Devices / 1233
	Self-Test / 1251
	Rhetorical Techniques / 1252
	Organization / 1261
	Point of View / 1261
	Style / 1262
	Total Workout / 1266
	• Your Rhetorical Keystone / 1270

PART III	WRITING EXERCISE PROGRAM AND ROUTINE / 1271

Chapter 5	Reading and Working Different Types of AP English Prompts / 1273
	Key Words and Phrases / 1273
	What Constitutes an AP English Prompt or Question? / 1274
	English Language and Composition / 1279
	English Literature and Composition / 1280

Chapter 6	Prewriting and Planning / 1281
	Prewriting / 1281
	Notating the Text / 1282
	• Our Two Sample Texts / 1285

Chapter 7	Introducing the Essay / 1294
	The Professionals Do It / 1296
	• Our Sample Writers / 1301
	• Student Samples / 1303
	Total Workout / 1305

Chapter 8	Writing the Body of the Essay and the Supporting Syntax / 1308
	• Our Body Samples / 1310
	• Student Samples / 1316
	• Supporting Syntax / 1323

Chapter 9	Writing the Conclusion of the Essay and Revising / 1327
	• Our Sample Conclusions / 1328

- Student Samples / 1329
Revision / 1331
- Our Writers' Sample Essays / 1335

PART IV   **TRAINING SUPPLEMENTS / 1339**

Chapter 10   **The College Application Essay / 1341**
- A Sampling of Some Typical College Essay Questions / 1342
- Your Own Personal Interview / 1351
- Working the Material / 1353
- A Few Notes about Writing the College Application Essay / 1354
- Sample Student Essays / 1356

Appendix / 1377
- Bibliography of Recommended Authors and Texts / 1377
- Answers to Questions on Practice Activities / 1383
- Glossary of Terms / 1386
- Websites of Interest to the AP English Student / 1388

5 Steps to a 5
AP U.S. History

Preface

So, you have decided to take AP U.S. History. Prepare to be continually challenged in this course; this is the only way you will attain the grade that you want on the AP exam in May. Prepare to read, to read a lot, and to read critically; almost all students successful in AP U.S. History say this is a necessity. Prepare to analyze countless primary source documents; being able to do this is critical for success on the exam as well. Most importantly, prepare to immerse yourself in the great story that is United States history. As your teacher will undoubtedly point out, it would be impossible to make up some of the people and events you will study in this class. What really happened is much more interesting!

This study guide will assist you along the journey of AP U.S. History. The chapter review guides give you a succinct overview of the major events of U.S. history. At the end of each chapter is a list of the major concepts, a time line, and sample multiple-choice questions for that chapter. In addition, a very extensive glossary is included in the back of this manual. All of the underlined words throughout the book can be found in the glossary (it would also be a good study technique to review the entire glossary before taking the actual AP exam).

The first two chapters of the manual describe the AP test itself and suggest some test-taking strategies. There are also two entire sample tests with answers on the enclosed CD. These allow you to become totally familiar with the format and nature of the questions that will appear on the exam. On the actual testing day you want absolutely no surprises!

In the first chapter you will also find time lines for three approaches to preparing for the exam. It is obviously suggested that your preparation for the examination be a yearlong process; for those students unable to do that, two "alternative calendars" also appear. Many students also find that study groups are very beneficial in studying for the AP test. Students who have been successful on the AP test oftentimes form these groups very early in the school year.

Many students feel frustrated when their AP class doesn't make it all the way to the present day. Don't worry—The number of questions on the test that deal with events after the 1970s will be relatively small.

I hope this manual helps you in achieving the "perfect 5." That score is sitting out there, waiting for you to reach for it.

PART I

HOW TO USE THIS BOOK

Chapter 1

The Five-Step Program

BEFORE WE BEGIN

Reading This Guide

This guide provides you with the specific format of the AP U.S. History test, two sample AP U.S. History tests (on the enclosed CD), and a comprehensive review of U.S. history. After each review chapter you will find a time line and several sample questions that might appear on the AP test.

Reading this guide is a great start to getting the grade you want on the AP U.S. History test, but it is important to read on your own as well. Several groups of students who have all gotten a 5 on the test maintain the key to success is to *read* as much as you can on U.S. history as you possibly can.

Reading this guide will not guarantee you a 5 when you take the U.S. history exam in May. However, by carefully reviewing the format of the exam and the test-taking strategies provided for each section, you will definitely be on your way! The review section that outlines the major developments of U.S. history should augment what you have learned from your regular U.S. history textbook. This book won't "give" you a 5, but it can certainly point you firmly in that direction.

Thinking Historically

Even if you have a photographic memory, there is more to do to get a 5 on the AP U.S. History exam. Unfortunately, knowing all of the dates, names, and important events of U.S. history is not enough. It is important that you develop the ability to analyze these events: to judge their importance, to analyze why they occurred, and to understand what the ramifications of these events were. Historical analysis is somewhat different than the analysis you do in an English or a physics class. There are plenty of examples in this book to help you to develop the skill of historical analysis, or to reinforce the skill if you already have it.

The Importance of Studying U.S. History

Please do not approach U.S. history as a study of old, irrelevant names, places, and dates. U.S. history is *not* an old, dead topic. The events you study in your U.S. history course all, either indirectly or directly, have an influence on the United States today. Also, at the risk of sounding incredibly corny, U.S. history is a *great* story! Allow yourself to become familiar with some of the bizarre and humorous events and people in U.S. history as well. Let the subject come alive! This will put you in the right frame of mind to seriously study the subject matter.

> *"I strongly encourage my students to keep up with current events. It helps to provide some context to the history they are studying."*
>
> —AP Teacher

Why This Particular Guide

The author of this book has taught U.S. history for over 20 years and is very familiar with the AP test and why students succeed (or don't succeed) when taking it. In a sense, my students have taught me a lot of what is in this book; I have seen over the years what works for them, and I have tried to include as much of this as possible in this book. I have also tried to keep this book user-friendly for you. I teach U.S. history to eleventh graders (which I suspect the vast majority of readers of this book are), and I have written the book in the language in which I converse with my students. I sat down and had lengthy conversations with seven groups of AP students (from seven different schools) before beginning this guide; many of their suggestions are included here.

Some of the other specific advantages of this guide are that it will

- Give you a very comprehensive review of the key events and trends of U.S. history
- Anticipate and answer many of the questions you have about the test
- Explain strategies for being successful in each part of the test to you
- Help you to "think historically" (as noted previously)
- Provide you with numerous opportunities to practice the types of questions that will be on the test
- Provide you with a comprehensive glossary of U.S. history terms
- Make you aware of the **Five-Step Program** for mastering the AP U.S. History exam

Organization of This Book

The introductory chapters of this book give you critical information on the AP U.S. History exam in general, and then specific detail on the multiple-choice and the essay sections of the exam. Specific strategies for success are given in each of these sections. Even though the major reason for getting this guide might have been to go through the section that reviews the details of U.S. history, it is strongly advised that you read these sections carefully. Taking the time to do the Diagnostic Exam will give you a good idea of where you stand before you start your preparations.

A 23-chapter review of the major events of U.S. history follows, with sample questions at the end of each chapter. A glossary of key terms used in these chapters is found at the very back of the book.

Two complete sample exams are also included, with all of the correct answers (and why they are correct) also noted.

INTRODUCTION TO THE FIVE-STEP PROGRAM

The **Five-Step Program** is a powerful tool designed to provide you with the best-possible skills, strategies, and practice to help lead you to the perfect 5 on the AP U.S. History examination. Each of these five steps provides you with the opportunity to get closer and closer to the 5, which every AP student strives to achieve.

STEP ONE leads you through a brief process to help determine which type of exam preparation is most comfortable for you:

1. Month-by-month: September through May
2. The calendar year: January through May
3. Basic training: the 4–6 weeks before the exam

STEP TWO helps develop the knowledge you need to do well on the exam:

1. A comprehensive review of the exam
2. A thorough review of the type of questions asked on the exam
3. Explanation of multiple-choice answers
4. A comprehensive review of the two types of essays asked for on the exam
5. A review of the major events and trends of U.S. history
6. A glossary of important terms in U.S. history

STEP THREE helps develop the skills necessary to take the exam and do well:

1. Practice activities in historical thinking
2. Practice activities in multiple choice questions
3. Practice document-based essay questions

STEP FOUR helps you develop strategies for taking the exam:

1. Learning about the test itself
2. Learning to read multiple-choice questions
3. Learning how to answer multiple-choice questions, and the value of guessing
4. Learning what to look for in the essay question
5. Learning how to plan the essay

STEP FIVE helps you develop you confidence in using the skills demanded on the AP U.S. History exam:

1. The opportunity to evaluate yourself with many practice questions
2. Time management techniques and skills
3. Two practice exams that test how well-honed your skills are
4. The opportunity to show you that you know more than you think you do about U.S. history

GRAPHICS USED IN THIS BOOK

To emphasize particular skills, strategies, and practice, we use seven sets of icons throughout this book.

The first icon is an hourglass, which indicates the passage of time during the school year. This hourglass icon will appear in the margin next to an item that may be of interest to one of the three types of students who are using this book (mode A, B, or C students).

For the student who plans to prepare for the AP U.S. History exam during the entire school year, beginning in September through May, I use an hourglass that is full on the top.

For the student who decides to begin preparing for the exam in January of the calendar year, I use an hourglass that is half full on the top and half full on the bottom.

For the student who wishes to prepare during the final 6 weeks before the exam, I use an hourglass that is almost empty on the top and almost full on the bottom.

The second icon is a footprint, which indicates which step in the five-step program is being emphasized in a given analysis, technique, or practice activity.

Plan   Knowledge   Skills   Strategies   Confidence Building

The third icon is a clock, which indicates a timed practice activity or a time management strategy. It will indicate on the face of the dial how much time to allow for a given exercise. The full dial will remind you that this is a strategy which can help you learn to manage your time on the test.

The fourth icon is an exclamation point, which will point to a very important idea, concept, or strategy point that you should not pass over.

The fifth icon is a checkmark, which will alert you to pay close attention. This activity will be most helpful if you go back and check your own work, your calendar, or your progress.

The sixth icon is a lightbulb, which indicates strategies that you may want to try.

The seventh icon is the sun, which indicates a tip that you might find useful.

Boldfaced and <u>underlined</u> words indicate terms that are included in the glossary at the end of the book.

THREE APPROACHES TO PREPARING FOR THE AP U.S. HISTORY EXAM

> *"It really helps to develop a plan for studying for the test; once you have a plan, stick with it."* —AP Student

You are the only person who knows which schedule listed below is right for you. If you were to ask me, I would strongly suggest using approach A, but I know that not everyone can or will. This manual is designed to help you, no matter which of the schedules you decide to adopt.

You're a full-year prep student (Approach A) if

1. You have a definite love of U.S. history.
2. You are certain that history will be your major in college.
3. You are not a procrastinator; you like to get things done.
4. You like detailed planning and everything in its place.
5. You feel you must be thoroughly prepared.
6. You have been successful with this approach in the past.

You are a one-semester prep student (Approach B) if

1. You are pretty interested in U.S. history.
2. You usually plan ahead but sometime skip some of the little details.
3. You feel more comfortable when you know what to expect, but a surprise or two does not floor you.
4. You are always on time for appointments.
5. You have been successful with this approach in the past.

You are a 4- to 6-week prep student (Approach C) if

1. United States history is somewhat interesting to you.
2. You work best under pressure and close deadlines.
3. You think the work you have done in your U.S. history class has prepared you fairly well for the AP test.
4. You decided late in the year to take the exam.
5. You like surprises.
6. You have been successful with this approach in the past.

> *"Do all the reading on U.S. history you possibly can. This WILL help you do better on the test."* —AP Student

CALENDARS FOR PREPARING FOR THE AP U.S. HISTORY EXAM

 ## Calendar for Approach A: Year-Long Preparation for AP U.S. History Exam

Although its primary purpose is to prepare you for the AP U.S. History exam you will take in May, this book can enrich your study of U.S. history.

SEPTEMBER–OCTOBER (Check off the activities as you complete them)

_____ Determine into which student mode you would place yourself.

_____ Carefully read the first three chapters of this manual.

_____ Get on the World Wide Web and see what is said on the College Board AP Web site.

_____ Skim the Comprehensive Review Questions (go to this section all year if you have specific questions).

_____ Buy a highlighter, and use it on this manual and, if possible, your regular textbook (in many schools AP students buy their textbooks ahead of time for this very purpose).

_____ Coordinate the materials in this manual with the curriculum of your AP History class.

_____ Begin to do outside reading on U.S. history topics.

_____ Begin to use this book as a resource.

NOVEMBER (The first 10 weeks have elapsed.)

_____ Do some of the sample questions found throughout the manual.

_____ Look at one of the sample tests to get an idea of what the big picture is.

_____ Intensify your reading of outside sources.

_____ Remind yourself to do historical analysis when you read.

DECEMBER

_____ Review the section on document-based questions, or DBQs. (You will probably have one on your midterm exam in class.)

_____ Carefully review the historical survey sections found in this manual for the areas you have already studied in class. Do the interpretations of events generally match up? If they don't, why might this be so?

JANUARY

_____ Using the eras of U.S. history you have studied in class, create your own document-based question for two of the units, and try to answer it.

_____ Form a study group to prepare for the AP exams. Many successful students on the AP maintain that a good study group was critical to their success.

FEBRUARY–MARCH

_____ Further intensify your outside readings.

_____ Take two U.S. history textbooks and compare and contrast their handling of three events in U.S. history. What do your results tell you?

_____ Carefully analyze the materials in the comprehensive review section of U.S. history for the units you are now studying in your U.S. history class. What events are you studying that directly impact the United States today?

APRIL

_____ Take Practice Exam 1 in the first week of April.

_____ Evaluate your strengths and weaknesses.

_____ Study appropriate chapters to correct weaknesses.

_____ Practice creating and answering multiple-choice questions in your study group.

_____ Develop and review worksheets for and with your study group.

MAY—First Two Weeks (It's Almost Showtime!)

_____ Highlight materials in your textbook (and in this manual) that you are unsure of, and ask your teacher about them.

_____ Write two or three historical essays under timed conditions.

_____ Take Practice Exam 2.

_____ Score and evaluate your performance.

_____ You are well prepared for the test. Go get it!

> "The more sample questions and essays you can go over before the test the better. Definitely take more than one practice exam from start to finish." —AP Student

Calendar for Approach B:
Semester-Long Preparation for the AP U.S. History Exam

Working under the assumption that you've completed one semester of U.S. History, use this calendar and the skills you've learned to prepare for the May exam.

JANUARY–FEBRUARY

_____ Carefully read the introductory three chapters of the book.

_____ Write two or three document-based essay questions and sample multiple choice questions.

_____ "Think historically" about the material you are reading in class.

_____ Read at least one source outside of class on a topic you are studying.

MARCH

_____ Carefully analyze the historical review sections on the material you are now studying in class. Are the interpretations of historical events the same in your textbook and in this manual? If not, why might that be?

_____ Form a study group (these are pivotal to success).

_____ In your study group, practice creating and answering multiple-choice questions.

APRIL

_____ Take Practice Exam 1 in the first week of April.

_____ Evaluate your strengths and weaknesses.

_____ Study appropriate chapters to correct weaknesses.

_____ Practice creating and answering historical essays with your study group.

_____ Develop and review worksheets for and with your study group.

MAY—First Two Weeks (It's Almost Showtime!)

_____ Ask your teacher to clarify things in your textbook or in this manual that you are unclear about.

_____ Carefully review the historical review section for as much of the year as you can.

_____ Take Practice Exam 2.

_____ Score yourself and analyze what you did wrong.

_____ Try to get answers to as many of the nagging details as you can before the test.

_____ It's almost time for the test: Let's do it!

Calendar for Approach C:
4- to 6-Week Preparation for the AP U.S. History Exam

You have been in an AP U.S. History class since September. Undoubtedly, you have read much and learned a lot. The purpose of this guide is not to start from the beginning, but to refine and to further develop all that you have been learning since September.

APRIL

_____ Carefully read the first three chapters about the format of the test.

_____ Read the comprehensive review sections on the events of U.S. history.

_____ Write one sample DBQ question, provided as a sample in this manual.

_____ Complete Practice Exam 1.

_____ Score yourself and analyze your errors.

_____ Go back to chapters on essays or multiple-choice question format if needed.

_____ Develop a weekly study group to prepare for the test (many students say this is crucial).

_____ Skim and highlight the glossary.

MAY

_____ Complete Practice Exam 2.

_____ Score yourself and analyze your errors.

_____ Review entire historical review section to refresh yourself on historical detail.

_____ Be sure to be familiar with the format of the test. Review chapters two and three if needed.

_____ **The test is almost here: Be ready for it!**

> *"Three of my friends and I worked together in a study group last year and it helped us a lot!"* —AP Student

RAPID REVIEW

- Familiarize yourself with the Five-Step Program:

  - Know yourself.

  - Know the plan.

- Develop knowledge:

  - Know the test.

  - Carefully review the section on U.S. history and the glossary.

  - Check out AP Web sites.

- Develop skills:

  - Practice multiple-choice questions.

  - Practice historical essays

  - Practice thinking historically.

- Develop strategies:

  - Explore multiple-choice approaches.

  - Plan the DBQ.

  - Plan the historical essay.

- Develop confidence:

  - Practice time management skills.

  - Find your mode of preparation.

  - Familiarize yourself with the icons used in the text.

  - Choose your calendar.

PART II

WHAT YOU NEED TO KNOW ABOUT THE AP U.S. HISTORY EXAM

PART II

WHAT YOU NEED
TO KNOW ABOUT
THE AP U.S.
HISTORY EXAM

Chapter 2

Introduction to the AP U.S. History Exam

BACKGROUND INFORMATION

What Is the Advanced Placement Program?

 The Advanced Placement program was begun by the College Board in 1955 to construct standard achievement exams that would allow highly motivated high school students the opportunity to be awarded advanced placement as freshmen in colleges and universities in the United States. Today, there are 35 courses and exams with well over a million students taking the annual exams in May

There are numerous AP courses in the social studies besides United States History, including Modern European History, World History, and Government. The majority of students who take AP tests are juniors and seniors; however, some schools do offer AP courses to freshmen and sophomores.

Who Writes the AP U.S. History Exam? Who Corrects Them?

Like all AP exams, the U.S. History exam is written by college and high school instructors of U.S. history. This group is called the AP United States History Development Committee. This group constantly evaluates the test, analyzing the test as a whole and on an item-by-item basis. All questions on the AP U.S. History exam are field-tested before they actually appear on an AP exam.

A much larger group of college and secondary school teachers meet at a central location in early June to correct the exams that were completed by students the previous month. The scoring procedure of each grader during this procedure is carefully analyzed to ensure that exams are being evaluated on a fair and consistent basis.

How Are AP Exams Graded?

Sometime in July the grade you receive on your AP exam is reported. You, your high school, and the colleges you listed on your initial application will receive scores.

There are five possible scores that you may receive on your exams:

- 5 indicates that you are extremely well qualified. This is the highest-possible grade.
- 4 indicates that you are well qualified.
- 3 indicates that you are qualified.
- 2 indicates that you are possibly qualified.
- 1 indicates that you are not qualified to receive college credit.

What Are the Benefits of Taking the AP U.S. History Exam?

There are several very practical reasons for enrolling in an AP U.S. History course and taking the AP U.S. History exam in May. In the first place, during the application process colleges look very favorably upon students who have challenged themselves by taking Advanced Placement courses. Although few would recommend this, it is possible to take any AP exam without taking a preparatory course for that exam.

Most importantly, most colleges will reward you for doing well on your AP exams. Although the goal of this manual is to help you achieve a 5, if you get a 3 or better in your AP U.S. History exam, most colleges will either (a) give you actual college credit for introductory U.S. History or (b) allow you to be exempt from introductory U.S. History courses. You should definitely check beforehand with the colleges you are applying to find out their policy on AP scores and credit. They will vary.

Taking a year of AP U.S. History (or any AP) course will be a very exacting and challenging experience. If you have the capabilities, allow yourself to be challenged! Many students feel a sense of great personal satisfaction after completing an AP course, regardless of the score they eventually receive on the actual AP exam.

THE AP U.S. HISTORY EXAMINATION

The AP U.S. History exam consists of both multiple-choice and essay questions. Each is worth 50 percent of the total exam grade.

Multiple-Choice Questions

!

This section consists of 80 questions. Each question has five possible answers. You will have 55 minutes to complete this section.

The College Board annually publishes material on the breakdown of questions on the multiple-choice test. According to their most recently published information, the multiple-choice is broken down as follows:

HISTORICAL ERAS:

- 1/6 of the questions deal with events from 1600 to 1789.
- 1/2 of the questions deal with events from 1790 to 1914.
- 1/3 of the questions deal with events from 1914 to the present.

TOPICS:

- 37 percent of the questions deal with political institutions and public policy.
- 36 percent of the questions deal with social change.
- 13 percent of the questions deal with diplomacy and international relations.
- 8 percent of the questions deal with economic changes and developments.
- 4 percent of the questions deal with cultural and intellectual developments.

The information provided above is extremely valuable as you prepare for the multiple-choice section of the test. As you study, you should obviously concentrate your efforts on the nineteenth and twentieth centuries. In addition, there are fewer questions on events of the twentieth century than on the nineteenth: The makers of the AP realize how difficult it is to "make it to the present" in the AP U.S. History course. Few questions will be asked on events that occurred after 1970.

It is obviously essential to spend most of your time preparing for questions on political and social changes that have taken place in the United States (again, mostly since 1789). Even though most instructors spend time on cultural and intellectual developments, there will be only a few questions on the AP test on those topics.

Question Format

As stated above, all multiple-choice questions will have five possible answers. In all probability, your teacher will give you plenty of practice on these as the year progresses. A question that might appear on the exam might be as follows:

America during the Great Depression experienced

A. severe drought across the vast majority of the country
B. a vast increase in the number of Americans opposed to the policies of Franklin Roosevelt
C. widespread unemployment in both urban and rural sectors
D. increased employment possibilities for women and blacks
E. an increased sense of militarism

You may also have questions on your exam asking you to interpret a political cartoon or a graph. To answer these, rely on the social studies skills you have developed from all of your social studies courses.

The hardest type of questions that many students encounter on their exam are the "which of the following is not correct" kind. Here is an example:

All of the following are true about America during the Great Depression except:

A. Americans were put to work by programs such as the W.P.A.
B. Americans saw an increase in the power of labor unions through acts such as the Wagner Act.
C. By the end of the decade many Americans favored the policies of Father Coughlin and Charles Townshend.
D. The majority of Americans rejected socialist solutions to the problems of the Great Depression.
E. The majority of Americans favored the programs of the New Deal.

Some Useful Hints on the Multiple-Choice Section

The most commonly asked question about this section is whether or not to guess if you are not completely sure of a question. If you can eliminate at least one of the answers as definitely wrong, the answer is this: Do it! As the College Board notes in its most recent publication on the AP U.S. History exam:

Many candidates wonder whether or not to guess the answers to questions about which they are not certain. In this section of the examination, as a correction for haphazard guessing, one-fourth of the number of questions you answer incorrectly will be subtracted from the number of questions you answer correctly. It is improbable, therefore, that mere guessing will improve your score significantly; it may even lower your score, and it does take time. If, however, you are not sure of the best answer but have some knowledge of the question and are able to eliminate one or more answer choices as wrong, your chance of getting the right answer is improved, and it may be to your advantage to answer such a question.

> *"Go with your gut on multiple-choice questions: you don't have a real lot of time to do much thinking on individual questions."* —*AP Student*

Another suggestion is to make sure you read the question and all of the answers completely before you answer it. Sometimes the question asks you something other than what you think it will be asking. Always use the process of elimination when answering these questions. On the other hand, you have 80 questions to do in 55 minutes, giving you about 40 seconds per question. If you are sure you have the right answer, don't dwell on the question; you can certainly use the time for other questions that you are less certain on.

The Essay Questions

!

There are two types of essays you will be asked to write in your AP U.S. History exam: the document-based question (DBQ) and the "free-response" question. In the DBQ you will be asked to analyze 7 to 10 documents about a certain period in U.S. history to answer a question; the free-response questions are more traditional essay questions (you will be expected to write two of these on the exam). For the DBQ question you will have 15 minutes to read the documents and 45 minutes to construct your essay; for the free-response section you will have 70 minutes to write two essays. The essay section of the exam is also worth 50 percent of your final score.

DBQ Questions

In this section you are asked to analyze a number of documents and to utilize previously acquired knowledge on an era to answer a question. All of the information needed to earn a 5 is not included in the documents: You need to bring what you know to the table as well. In a typical question, you might be presented with several political speeches, the results of public opinion polls, and several political cartoons from the 1960s and be asked to discuss the reasons for political unrest in the decade.

There has been a critical change in the DBQ format beginning with the May 2003 test. Unfortunately, this will not be to your advantage. In prior years, the 50-year period for the DBQ for that year was announced beforehand. This obviously assisted both teachers and students in preparing for the exam. However, the College Board has decided that beginning with the May 2003 exam, the DBQ period will not be released beforehand. It was felt that many historical trends have lasted longer than 50 years and that the 50-year limit was restricting the types of questions that could be asked.

> *"My students hated me during the year for giving them so many DBQs. After the test, they agreed it had been worth it."* —*AP Teacher*

Here are some hints for answering the DBQ questions. Use the standard essay format you have used for all historical essays. Of course, write out an outline before you actually start writing the essay. Students report that it is not always necessary to use every single document to construct your answer; use as many as possible, but make sure that their inclusion in your essay is relevant. In addition, students that have done well on this section note that the *order* of the documents presented to you is crucial. If the documents are presented in chronological order, your answer should also be chronological in nature.

It is not necessary to spend every second of the 45 minutes writing the essay. Answer the question, including what the documents say and what you can say about them, and be done with it. To repeat: *Some of what you already know has to be included in your answer.* As with all historical essays, there must be a logic to your answer. Organization as well as knowledge is important. Please remember that there is no "right answer" to the DBQ question.

Many students ask whether spelling counts. The answer is, generally, no. Scorers know that you are rushed on these essays; in all probability, if you think your writing is bad, they have probably seen worse. Nevertheless, do what you can to make your presentation as readable as possible. I know from personal experience as an instructor that it is hard to give a good grade to a student if you can hardly read what the student is saying.

Free-Response Questions

> "Don't relax after the DBQ; you still have a big chunk of the test to go!" —AP Student

Immediately after taking the DBQ, you will answer two free-response questions. You will receive two questions about the United States before the Civil War, and you will have to answer one of these. You will receive two questions about the United States after the Civil War, and you will have to answer one of these. Most free-response questions ask you to utilize higher-order thinking skills; you will be asked to analyze events and trends of the past. As stated above, you will have 70 minutes to answer these questions.

A typical question might be (again, picking one of the two) this:

I. What were the most important reasons for increased tensions between the American colonies and Great Britain between 1760 and 1776.
II. Analyze the major reasons for the defeat of the Confederacy in the Civil War.

Here are some hints for taking the free-response questions. You probably have had many of these questions in your AP class all year, so use the organizational approaches you have utilized during the year. Always make an outline before you begin to write. *Make sure to answer the question.* Don't just go around in circles with information you know about the topic in question.

Also, this may be obvious, but be sure to pick the questions that you know the most about to answer. I have had students say they chose a question because it "looked easier." Avoid that approach. In addition, *watch your time!* I have had students so intent on constructing the perfect essay for the first free-response question that they didn't realize until it was too late they only had 15 minutes to answer the second question.

One final note: Many teachers spend a great deal of time preparing their students for the DBQ question and stressing the importance of this part of the test to their students. Several students have reported to me that once the DBQ is over, they relaxed a bit. You should keep in mind that immediately after the DBQ is over, you will be beginning the free-response essays. Be ready for them.

TAKING THE EXAM

When you come to the exam, bring the following:

- Several pencils (for the multiple-choice)
- Several black pens (for the essays)
- A watch
- Something to drink—water is best
- A quiet snack, such as Lifesavers
- Tissues
- Your driver's license and some other ID, in case there is a problem with your registration

Other Recommendations

Here are some more tips:

- Don't work the night before. Allow yourself to come to the test refreshed.
- Wear comfortable clothing
- Eat a light breakfast before the test.
- You are well prepared! As you come to the test, remember that.

Final Preparations for the Exam

Some students have reported spending the entire day and night before the test studying, reviewing their notes, and so forth. If you have properly prepared yourself, don't bother; it's not going to improve your score. A quick review of your notes in the early evening of an hour or two might be in order, but by and large, relaxing yourself is the best way to prepare for the test.

> *"Last year a couple of kids in my class crammed for two straight days before the exam. Both ended up getting a "2" on the test."* —AP Student

GETTING STARTED:
THE DIAGNOSTIC/MASTER EXAM
AP U.S. HISTORY

Section I

Time—55 minutes

80 questions

Directions: Each of the questions or incomplete statements below is followed by five suggested answers or completions. Select the one that is best in each case, and write your answer neatly on the answer sheet.

1. The Compromise of 1820 averted sectional conflict by

   A. removing federal troops from the South
   B. preserving the balance of power between free and slave states
   C. implementing a more stringent Fugitive Slave Law
   D. lowering tariff rates
   E. eliminating the constitutional ban on the importation of the slaves

2. All of the following relate to the McCarthy Era *except*

   A. Alger Hiss trial
   B. McCarran Act
   C. Federal Loyalty Program
   D. "Palmer raids"
   E. "Hollywood Ten"

3. Samuel Gompers

   A. used the state militia to break up the Boston police strike
   B. led the American Federation of Labor
   C. directed President Franklin D. Roosevelt's War Labor Board
   D. was a Populist candidate for governor in Kansas
   E. advocated Socialism as head of the Industrial Workers of the World

4. During the Second New Deal, President Franklin D. Roosevelt

   A. sought passage of more long-lasting reform measures
   B. experienced less opposition from conservatives in Congress
   C. attempted to cooperate with business leaders to promote recovery
   D. averted a financial crisis with the Emergency Banking Act
   E. focused primarily on the creation of relief agencies such as the Civilian Conservation Corps

5. The trial of John Peter Zenger in 1735 contributed to the codification of which of the following principles in the Constitution?

   A. Freedom of religion
   B. Freedom of the press
   C. Separation of powers
   D. Checks and balances
   E. Taxation by elected representatives

6. "Vietnamization" of the Vietnam War took place under which of the following presidents?

   A. Harry S. Truman
   B. Dwight D. Eisenhower

C. John F. Kennedy
D. Lyndon B. Johnson
E. Richard M. Nixon

7. The Wilmot Proviso heightened sectional tensions by proposing

   A. to ban the importation of slaves in 1808
   B. to repeal the "three-fifths" compromise
   C. a constitutional amendment to free the slaves
   D. that all Western lands must be purchased with specie rather than paper money
   E. to ban the importation of slaves into land acquired from Mexico

8. Harvard College was founded primarily to

   A. promote the study of science and technology
   B. accommodate new movements in theology
   C. train Puritan ministers
   D. offer women a classical education
   E. give technical training to African-Americans in the South

9. Which of the following statements best summarizes the Rosenberg case?

   A. It represented the height of racial tensions in the 1890s.
   B. It was influenced by the nativism of the 1920s.
   C. It decentralized the power of the federal government in the 1930s.
   D. It exemplified the anticommunist hysteria of the 1950s.
   E. It ensured the rights of those accused of crimes in the 1960s.

10. In response to the disgusting conditions he or she witnessed in the meatpacking houses of Chicago,

which of the following individuals wrote *The Jungle*?

   A. Upton Sinclair
   B. Henry George
   C. John Spargo
   D. Jacob Riis
   E. Ida Tarbell

11. The Civil Rights Act of 1964

   A. completed the desegregation of the armed forces
   B. integrated all colleges and universities
   C. banned segregation in public places
   D. outlawed poll taxes and literacy tests
   E. proposed the Equal Rights Amendment

12. During his administration, President Theodore Roosevelt sought to limit the effects of industrial consolidation. He directed his attorney general to bring suit against specific monopolies under the Sherman Antitrust Act (1890). In *Northern Securities Company* v. *United States* (1904), the Supreme Court ordered the dissolution of a proposed monopoly in which of the following industries?

   A. Steel
   B. Railroad
   C. Oil
   D. Meatpacking
   E. Automotive

13. The following cartoon refers to a scandal that marred the administration of

   A. Ulysses S. Grant
   B. William J. Clinton
   C. Richard M. Nixon
   D. Grover Cleveland
   E. Warren G. Harding

JUGGERNAUT.

The political cartoon, "Juggernaut," April 1924; courtesy of the Library of Congress.

14. The Tea Act (1773) angered American colonists because it

   A. passed a revenue tax on a popular consumer item

   B. pitted eastern merchants against western farmers

   C. followed the closing of Boston Harbor

   D. granted the East India Company a virtual monopoly on the tea trade

   E. ruined colonial trade with the West Indies

15. Federalists opposed the purchase of the Louisiana territory primarily because

   A. it threatened the balance of power between the political parties

   B. they feared a war with Spain

   C. they rejected the idea of the federal government accumulating debt

   D. it would not improve Western commerce

   E. it might jeopardize their goal of purchasing Canada

16. Which of the following Civil War battles resulted in Union control of the Mississippi River?

   A. Vicksburg

   B. Gettysburg

   C. Shiloh

   D. Chancellorsville

   E. New Orleans

17. All of the following were part of President Woodrow Wilson's "New Freedom" legislation *except* the

   A. Federal Trade Commission Act

   B. Pure Food and Drug Act

   C. Underwood Tariff

D. Clayton Antitrust Act

E. Federal Reserve Act

18. In his message to Congress, President Grover Cleveland resisted the annexation of Hawaii mainly because he

A. feared the influx of cheap labor to the West Coast

B. did not want to extend citizenship rights to nonwhites

C. believed that the provisional government had unjustly undermined the existing government

D. had little support for annexation from Republicans in Congress

E. was more concerned with mounting tensions with Spain

19. Cesar Chavez is significant because he

A. led the AIM occupation of Alcatraz Island

B. wrote the *Pentagon Papers*

C. integrated the University of Mississippi in 1962

D. was the first Hispanic mayor of a major U.S. city

E. organized farm workers into a powerful union

20. A "flapper" was

A. a mass-produced automobile

B. a young woman who challenged traditional gender roles in the 1920s

C. a steel ship introduced at the turn of the century

D. an electric record player of the 1930s

E. a jazz instrument

21. The Marshall Plan was

A. an international agreement that outlawed war

B. the blueprint for the Allied invasion at Normandy on June 6, 1944

C. an effort to root out communists from the State Department during the Truman administration

D. an effort to provide economic aid to countries devastated by World War II

E. designed to send military aid to Middle Eastern nations battling communism

22. The "Great Migration," which involved the movement of African-Americans from the South to the industrial cities of the North and West, occurred primarily

A. during the Civil War

B. in the 1880s

C. during and after World War I

D. after World War II

E. during and after the Vietnam War

23. Which of the following statements best expresses the pro-business stance of the Republican administrations of the late nineteenth century?

A. They maintained very high tariff rates to protect American industry.

B. They lowered corporate and income taxes for the wealthy industrialists.

C. They bargained with labor leaders to forestall crippling strikes.

D. They passed legislation limiting investments abroad.

E. They expanded the federal government's role in regulating economic growth.

24. Throughout the 1920s, American farmers suffered from depressed agricultural prices. As a result, President Franklin D. Roosevelt hoped to stabilize the farm economy by attempting to control production and fixing the price of farm goods. The agency in charge of monitoring the agricultural sector of the economy was the

A. Farmer's Holiday Association

B. NRA

C. RFC

D. AAA

E. Farm Board

25. The "supremacy clause" of the Constitution

    A. distributed power among the executive, legislative, and judicial branches of the government
    B. made presidential authority superior to Congress through the chief executive's veto powers
    C. empowered the Chief Justice of the Supreme Court to supervise impeachment proceedings
    D. ensured that all states would be equally represented in the Senate
    E. forced the state legislatures to conform to federal laws

26. During the Spanish-American War, the Teller Amendment stated that

    A. the residents of the Philippines automatically became American citizens with annexation
    B. the United States did not intend to annex Cuba
    C. all of the property of Spanish landholders would be returned after the war
    D. the United States reserved the right to intervene in Cuban affairs after the war
    E. France must abandon its claims to build a canal in Central America

27. "Education, beyond all other devices, is a great equalizer of the conditions of men, the balance wheel of the social machinery. . . . The spread of education, by enlarging the cultivated class or caste, will open a wider area over which the social feelings will expand; and if this education should be universal and complete, it would do more than all things else to obliterate factitious distinctions in society."

    The antebellum reformer who asserted these beliefs was

    A. John Dewey
    B. Lucretia Mott
    C. Horace Mann
    D. Theodore Dwight Weld
    E. Mary Montessori

28. Herbert Hoover oversaw the most successful of President Woodrow Wilson's war boards during World War I. That agency was the

    A. Food Administration
    B. Red Cross
    C. War Industries Board
    D. Committee on Public Information
    E. UNIA

29. In an effort to stabilize the economy, President Kennedy attempted to implement voluntary "wage-price" guidelines for American businesses. Although several industries adopted these standards, one in particular tried to resist the president's initiatives. In response Kennedy threatened to terminate federal contracts and bring suit unless this industry complied. Which industry lowered its prices because of Kennedy's reaction?

    A. Automobile
    B. Oil
    C. Steel
    D. Textiles
    E. Railroad

30. Which of the following contributed to the growth of suburbs before 1900?

    A. Generous federal land grants
    B. Mass production of the automobile
    C. Implementation of the Newlands Act
    D. Developments in mass transit
    E. Corruption of municipal governments

31. All of the following statements about the election of 1860 are true *except*

    A. Abraham Lincoln won the election with a minority of the popular vote

B. the Democratic party was split between two candidates
C. more votes were cast in 1860 than any previous antebellum election
D. Abraham Lincoln's name did not appear on many Southern ballots
E. Southern Unionists did not vote, as no party represented their interests

32. Which of the following represents an attempt to curb the arms race during the Nixon administration?

A. Test Ban Treaty
B. SALT I
C. War Powers Act
D. Strategic Defense Initiative
E. INF Treaty

33. In 1943, Allied leaders met at the Teheran Conference and decided to

A. launch a cross-Channel invasion of France
B. invade Sicily and eliminate Hitler's primary ally
C. outlaw war
D. limit fleet construction as a means to naval disarmament
E. divide German possessions in Africa

34. In the decade preceding the War of 1812, which of the following Indian chiefs attempted to organize a confederation of tribes to halt white expansion?

A. Metacomet (King Philip)
B. Tecumseh
C. Osceola
D. Geronimo
E. Pontiac

35. The Fourteenth Amendment, which ensured the citizenship rights of African-Americans, was ratified

A. when the Southern states seceded from the Union
B. after the Union victory at Antietam

C. as a requirement of "Radical" Reconstruction
D. as part of President Theodore Roosevelt's "Square Deal"
E. as part of the Compromise of 1877

36. Which of the following presidential candidates pursued a "give 'em hell," whistle-stop campaign in which he blasted the "do-nothing" 80th Congress?

A. Thomas Dewey
B. Franklin D. Roosevelt
C. Dwight D. Eisenhower
D. Adlai Stevenson
E. Harry S. Truman

37. The Ballinger-Pinchot Controversy (1909) was

A. a dispute between the Secretary of the Interior and the Chief Forester over the sale of public lands
B. a conflict between a reform governor and a corrupt urban boss
C. an investigation of communist infiltration of the State Department
D. the result of the sinking of an American merchant ship in French waters
E. a reaction to the passage of antitrust legislation

38. "The United States is now involved in a sizeable and 'open-ended' war against communism in the only country in the world which won freedom from colonial rule under communist leadership. . . . My own view is that there is a kind of madness in the facile assumption that we can raise the many billions of dollars necessary to rebuild our schools and cities and public transport and eliminate the pollution of air and water while also spending tens of billions to finance an 'open-ended' war in Asia."

A notable "dove" on the Vietnam War, he wrote an incisive critique of American foreign policy in Southeast Asia (excerpted above) entitled *The Arrogance of Power*. This man was

A. Robert McNamara.
B. Dean Acheson.
C. Dean Rusk.
D. J. William Fulbright.
E. Robert F. Kennedy.

39. The Treaty of Guadalupe Hidalgo

A. formalized the annexation of Texas in 1845
B. ended the Mexican War in 1848
C. ended the war between Mexico and the Texans in 1836
D. applied the Monroe Doctrine to Venezuela in 1824
E. gave Stephen F. Austin the right to sell land titles in Mexico in 1821

40. In 1965, a riot occurred that served as a symbol of African-American frustration to some and rampant lawlessness to others. That riot took place in

A. Oxford, Mississippi
B. Birmingham, Alabama
C. Kent State, Ohio
D. Little Rock, Arkansas
E. Watts, Los Angeles, California

41. The American victory at Yorktown

A. forced the British evacuation of Boston
B. induced Great Britain to negotiate an end to the Revolutionary War
C. ended Pontiac's Rebellion
D. caused French troops to withdraw from British North America
E. led to the removal of General William Howe

42. The United States matched the Soviet Union when the first American (Alan Shepard) was put into space during the administration of

A. Dwight D. Eisenhower
B. John F. Kennedy
C. Lyndon B. Johnson
D. Richard Nixon
E. Jimmy Carter

43. Which of the following statements about immigration to the United States during the period 1890 to 1910 is true?

A. Most immigrants settled in the South to take advantage of agricultural opportunities.
B. Most immigrants tended to be Protestant, skilled workers.
C. Most new immigrants came from Southern and Eastern Europe.
D. All immigrants were accepted into established urban communities.
E. No immigrants went to California or the West Coast during this period.

44. The WCTU promoted

A. prohibition of alcohol in the 1880s
B. isolationism in the 1930s
C. abolitionism in the 1840s
D. suffrage for African-Americans in the 1950s
E. religious fundamentalism in the 1860s

45. In 1830, President Andrew Jackson vetoed the Maysville Road Bill. The bill provided for federal financing, in the amount of $150,000, for construction of a 60-mile road near Maysville, Kentucky. Which of the following statements best summarizes Jackson's reason for vetoing the bill?

A. Westerners opposed the bill because they would have to bear the greatest burden of the taxes demanded by Congress.
B. As a strict constructionist, he never signed internal improvements bills.

C. He wanted to assist his long-time ally, Henry Clay, who opposed the bill.

D. Since the road would run within the borders of one state, he believed that Congress did not have the constitutional authority to finance the road.

E. As a resident of Tennessee, Jackson bore much ill will against Kentuckians.

46. Which of the following individuals presented a direct challenge to President Franklin D. Roosevelt's New Deal with the introduction of his "Share the Wealth" program?

A. Al Smith
B. Alf Landon
C. Thomas E. Dewey
D. Huey Long
E. Francis Townsend

47. Which of the following statements best expresses a tenet of the Puritan faith?

A. The church and state must remain separate entities.
B. Worldly events could be explained through science and reason.
C. Individuals could attain salvation through emotional appeals to God.
D. After creating the universe, God allowed worldly events to operate according to natural law.
E. An omnipotent God predestined some individuals for salvation.

48. During the 1950s, the United States experienced a "baby boom." Doctors and child development specialists spurred the national focus upon the family. The polio vaccine, which prevented the spread of a crippling childhood disease, was developed by

A. Jonas Salk
B. Allen Ginsburg
C. Benjamin Spock
D. John Foster Dulles
E. Albert Einstein

49. Which of the following contributed to the onset of the Great Depression?

A. Overspeculation in Western lands
B. Overproduction of consumer goods
C. Collapse of the Bank of the United States
D. Elimination of the gold standard
E. Significant cuts in federal spending on public works projects

50. In 1896, the *Plessy* v. *Ferguson* decision

A. outlawed monopolies
B. reversed child labor legislation
C. legalized racial segregation
D. empowered the federal government to place Plains Indians on reservations
E. limited free speech through the "clear and present danger" clause

51. In the early nineteenth century, mounting hostilities between France and Great Britain caused a war that threatened American interests abroad. When both nations violated American neutrality, the United States attempted to use economic coercion to force both nations to respect shippers' rights. The Embargo Act, which banned American international commerce, was passed under

A. George Washington
B. John Adams
C. Thomas Jefferson
D. James Madison
E. James Monroe

52. Which of the following best explains the witchcraft phenomenon that swept New England in the late seventeenth century?

A. Conflicts with the Creeks and Seminoles caused widespread panic among Puritan settlers.

B. The Second Great Awakening had undermined many elements of the Puritan faith.

C. New England colonies were more superstitious than other colonies.

D. Polluted water caused physiological disturbances among young women in Massachusetts.

E. Social strains were not being contained within Puritan communities.

53. The immediate cause of the Korean War was

A. an attack upon the USS *Maddux* in the Gulf of Tonkin

B. the assassination of Ngo Dinh Diem

C. U-2 incident

D. North Korean invasion of South Korea

E. creation of the National Security Council

54. Nat Turner's Rebellion (1831) had which of the following results?

A. It shattered the perceptions of those who believed that a bond of mutual affection existed between slaves and their masters.

B. It led to the repeal of the "gag rule" in Congress.

C. It induced Congress to ban the future importation of slaves into the United States.

D. It cemented the bond between North and South on the issue of fugitive slaves.

E. It led to the rapid emancipation of slaves in the Upper South.

55. During World War II, the OPA

A. promoted the purchase of Victory Bonds

B. fixed prices and promoted the rationing of consumer goods

C. led a propaganda campaign that contributed to the persecution of German-Americans

D. attempted to limit the Asian immigration into the United States

E. regulated the purchase of industrial resources and halted nonessential production

56. The Albany Congress (1754) was significant because it

A. was the first effort by American women to win equal rights

B. ended the French and Indian War

C. passed a series of resolutions opposing the passage of the Quebec Act

D. formulated the first bill of rights in the colonies

E. proposed a colonial union for defense against the Indians

57. By 1830, which of the following opened the Great Lakes to Eastern commerce?

A. The National Road

B. The Oregon Trail

C. The Erie Canal

D. The Baltimore and Ohio Railroad

E. The Natchez Trace

58. During Reconstruction, the Freedmen's Bureau achieved a significant measure of success in

A. redistributing the land of former slave masters

B. promoting educational opportunities for African-Americans

C. stripping power from former Confederate leaders

D. eliminating the influence of the Ku Klux Klan

E. revitalizing the devastated Southern economy

59. All of the following attempted to promoted collective security during the Cold War *except*

A. NATO
B. SEATO
C. CENTO
D. Kellogg-Briand Pact
E. the United Nations

60. Which of the following statements is true about Shays's Rebellion, 1787?

A. It was suppressed when President George Washington implemented the powers granted to him under the Constitution.

B. It hurt the Federalist party in the next election.

C. It ended when Daniel Shays was killed by federal troops in a barn in Virginia.

D. It demonstrated the power of the federal government over the states.

E. It alarmed conservatives and landowners in several states.

61. The Lend-Lease Act was designed to

A. help Great Britain in the war against Germany

B. get the nation out of the depths of the Great Depression

C. strengthen Japan against the Soviet Union

D. expand consumer credit

E. improve relations with Middle Eastern nations

62. The following newspaper headline was intended to stir up American hostility toward

A. Germany
B. Spain
C. Great Britain
D. Mexico
E. the USSR

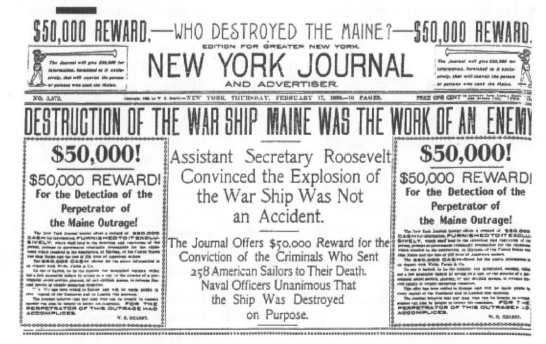

The newspaper article, "Destruction of the Warship Maine," *New York Journal*, February 17, 1898; courtesy of PBS.

63. The concept of "republican motherhood" emerged after which of the following?

    A. The establishment of the Massachusetts Bay colony, 1620
    B. The First Great Awakening, 1734 to 1746
    C. The American Revolution, 1775 to 1783
    D. The end of the Jackson administration, 1837
    E. The election of the first Republican president, 1860

64. Which of the following best represents the results of the election of 1976?

    A. The Republican party regained control of the executive office after 20 years of Democratic administrations.
    B. The Democratic candidate lost support in many Southern states.
    C. The Republicans capitalized upon popular unrest over the Vietnam War.
    D. The Democratic party portrayed his Republican candidate as a war monger.
    E. The Watergate scandal undermined the position of the Republican party.

65. The CIO was founded in order to

    A. organize industrial unions
    B. "pump prime" the economy during the Kennedy administration
    C. achieve diplomatic goals through sabotage and covert operations
    D. monitor the economy during World War I
    E. support passage of the Equal Rights Amendment

66. The phrase "54°40' or fight" was a rallying cry that referred to

    A. the boundary line Confederate soldiers vowed to protect at all costs
    B. a dispute between American and Canadian loggers on the Maine border
    C. a means of tax relief demanded after the Panic of 1819
    D. a border dispute between the United States and Great Britain
    E. the conflict between American farmers and the Mexican government in Texas

67. All of the following were powers that the Articles of Confederation granted to Congress *except* the power to

    A. make treaties
    B. declare war
    C. borrow money
    D. organize a post office
    E. tax

68. In *McCulloch* v. *Maryland*, the Supreme Court

    A. reaffirmed the ability of Congress to regulate interstate commerce
    B. endorsed the constitutionality of the Bank of the United States
    C. attempted to halt the state's efforts to remove Indians from their tribal lands
    D. upheld President Lincoln's suspension of habeas corpus
    E. freed Clement Vallandigham, who had criticized Lincoln's war measures

69. The most significant expansion of American highways began during the administration of

    A. Richard M. Nixon
    B. Franklin D. Roosevelt
    C. Harry S. Truman
    D. Dwight D. Eisenhower
    E. Herbert Hoover

70. In the antebellum period, which of the following contributed to the growth of nativism?

   A. Conflicts with Indian tribes along the frontier
   B. The political beliefs of the Democratic party
   C. The rapid influx of Irish and German immigrants
   D. New congressional restrictions on naturalization
   E. The feeling that Southerners were trying to spread slavery into the territories

71. In response to mounting Anglo-French tensions and French claims that the United States was bound by the Treaty of Alliance of 1778, which of the following presidents issued a proclamation of neutrality that became the cornerstone of American foreign policy?

   A. George Washington
   B. John Adams
   C. Thomas Jefferson
   D. James Madison
   E. James Monroe

72. President Lyndon Johnson was able to enact his "Great Society" programs primarily because the

   A. nation's economy had improved dramatically
   B. Republican party favored reform
   C. Democrats controlled Congress
   D. business community supported the program
   E. Supreme Court favored Republican policies

73. All of the following statements about the election of 1928 are true except that

   A. voters endorsed the pro-business policies of the Republican party
   B. the Democratic candidate received support from urban centers

C. the Republican candidate won some support in southern states
   D. the Republican candidate supported the repeal of Prohibition
   E. it was the first election to feature a Catholic presidential candidate

74. Which of the following statements about life in the colonial South is *not* true?

   A. Life expectancy was lower than in the New England colonies.
   B. Gender ratios were relatively equal in the South.
   C. Disease took more lives than in the New England colonies.
   D. Patriarchal authority exerted far less control than in New England.
   E. The rivers were critically important to the regional economy.

75. Which of the following statements is true about the Battle of the Bulge, 1944?

   A. It was the first battle American soldiers fought upon French soil.
   B. It prevented Japan from invading Australia.
   C. It swept all Nazi forces from Italy.
   D. It enabled American naval vessels to protect Allied merchants ships as they crossed the Atlantic Ocean.
   E. It so weakened the Nazi army that it could no longer stop the Allied advance toward Berlin.

76. Which of the following men was beaten on the floor of the Senate in 1856 because of his "Crime against Kansas" speech in which he scathingly attacked the institution of slavery and insulted fellow senator Andrew Butler?

   A. Charles Sumner
   B. Thaddeus Stevens
   C. Stephen Douglas
   D. John Bell
   E. William Seward

77. During the late nineteenth century, bimetallism received the support of those who wanted to

    A. retire federal bank notes
    B. weaken the Populist party
    C. promote copper mining in the West
    D. inflate the currency and alleviate debts
    E. allow state banks to produce their own currency

78. Although Andrew Jackson is credited for the increasing democratization of the United States in the early ante-bellum period, state governments also expanded democracy by

    A. changing the process for the election of senators
    B. overturning the restrictive Supreme Court decisions of John Marshall
    C. extending manhood suffrage by removing property requirements
    D. granting women the right to vote
    E. passing "slave codes" that gave slaves certain rights in white society

79. All of the following represented social unrest in the 1960s *except*

    A. the SDS
    B. the Black Panthers
    C. the Yippies
    D. Mario Savio and FSM
    E. VISTA

80. "I challenge the warmest advocate of separation to show a single advantage that this continent can reap by being connected with Great Britain. . . . But the injuries and disadvantages we sustain by that connection are without number; and our duty to mankind at large, as well as to ourselves, instruct us to renounce that alliance. . . . Everything that is right or natural pleads for separation. The blood of the slain, the weeping voice of nature cries, 'TIS TIME TO PART.' "

    In an effort to rally popular support for war with Great Britain, which of the following penned these words from *Common Sense*?

    A. Patrick Henry
    B. Thomas Paine
    C. John Adams
    D. Samuel Adams
    E. George Washington

___END OF SECTION I___

Section II

Part A

(Suggested writing time—45 minutes)

Directions: The following question requires you to construct a coherent essay that integrates your interpretation of Documents A to H *and* your knowledge of the period referred to in the question. High scores will be earned only by essays that both cite key pieces of evidence from the documents and draw on outside knowledge of the period.

1. To what extent did the Federalist administrations of George Washington and John Adams promote national unity and advance the authority of the federal government?

Document A
Source: George Washington's First Inaugural Address, April 30, 1789

> *I behold the surest pledges that as on one side no local prejudices or attachments, no separate views or party animosities, will misdirect the comprehensive and equal eye which ought to watch over [Congress] so . . . that the foundation of our national policy will be laid in the pure and immutable principles of private morality, and the preeminence of free government be exemplified by all the attributes which can win the affections of its citizens and command the respect of the world.*

Document B
Source: Virginia Resolutions on the Assumption of State Debts, December 16, 1790

> *The General Assembly of the Commonwealth of Virginia . . . represent [that] . . . in an agricultural country like this . . . to perpetuate a large monied interest, is a measure which . . . must in the course of human events produce . . . the prostration of agriculture at the feet of commerce, or a change in the present form of federal government, fatal to the existence of American liberty.*

Document C

Source: Thomas Jefferson's Opinion on the Constitutionality of the Bank, February 15, 1791

I consider the foundation of the Constitution as laid on this ground—that all powers not delegated to the United States, by the Constitution, nor prohibited by it to the states, are reserved to the states, or to the people. To take a single step beyond the boundaries thus specially drawn around the powers of Congress, is to take possession of a boundless field of power.

Document D

Source: Alexander Hamilton's Opinion on the Constitutionality of the Bank, February 23, 1791

This restrictive interpretation of the word necessary is also contrary to this sound maxim of construction; namely, that the powers contained in a constitution of government, especially those which concern the general administration of the affairs of a country, its finances, trade, defense, etc., ought to be construed liberally in advancement of the public good.

Document E

Source: George Washington's Proclamation on the Whiskey Rebellion, August 7, 1794

Whereas combinations to defeat the execution of the laws laying duties upon spirits distilled within the United States . . . have . . . existed in some of the western parts of Pennsylvania; and whereas the said combinations, proceeding in a manner subversive equally of the just authority of government and the rights of individuals; . . . it is in my judgement necessary under the circumstances to take measures for calling forth the militia in order to suppress the combinations of the combinations aforesaid, and to cause the laws to be duly executed.

Document F

Source: Jay's Treaty, November 19, 1794

His Majesty will withdraw all of his troops and garrisons from all posts and places within the boundary lines assigned by the treaty of peace to the United States. . . . His Majesty consents that the vessels belonging to the United States of America, shall be admitted and hospitably received, in all the seaports of the British territories in the East-Indies.

Document G

Source: The Sedition Act, July 14, 1798

That if any person shall write, print, utter, or publish, any false, scandalous, and malicious writing or writings against the government of the United States . . . with the intent to defame said government, . . . then such person, being convicted before any court of the United States having jurisdiction thereof, shall be punished by a fine not exceeding two thousand dollars, and by imprisonment not exceeding two years.

Document H

Source: Kentucky Resolutions, November 16, 1798

Resolved, that the several States composing the United States of America, are not united on the principle of unlimited submission to their general government; . . . that [the States] retain to themselves the right of judging how far the licentiousness of speech and press may be abridged without lessening their useful freedom . . . therefore [the Sedition Act], which does abridge the freedom of the press, is not law but is altogether void.

Section II

Part B and Part C

(Suggested total planning and writing time: 70 minutes)

Part B

Directions: Choose *one* question from this part. You are advised to spend 5 minutes planning and 30 minutes writing your answer. Cite relevant historical evidence in support of your generalizations and present your arguments clearly and logically.

2. Explain the reaction of the American colonists to *two* of the following acts of Parliament:

Proclamation of 1763

Stamp Act, 1765

Coercive Acts, 1774

3. To what degree were the reform movements of the 1840s liberal or conservative?

Part C

Directions: Choose *one* question from this part. You are advised to spend 5 minutes planning and 30 minutes writing your answer. Cite relevant historical evidence in support of your generalizations and present your arguments clearly and logically.

4. Discuss the impact of third-party candidates in *two* of the following elections:

1912, 1948, 1968

5. In what ways did World War II unleash the movements for racial and gender equality?

END OF SECTION II

ANSWERS TO DIAGNOSTIC/MASTER EXAM

Section I

1. B	21. D	41. B	61. A
2. D	22. C	42. B	62. B
3. C	23. A	43. C	63. C
4. A	24. D	44. A	64. E
5. B	25. E	45. D	65. A
6. E	26. B	46. D	66. D
7. E	27. C	47. E	67. E
8. C	28. A	48. A	68. B
9. D	29. C	49. B	69. D
10. A	30. D	50. C	70. C
11. C	31. E	51. C	71. A
12. B	32. B	52. E	72. C
13. E	33. A	53. D	73. D
14. D	34. B	54. A	74. B
15. A	35. C	55. B	75. E
16. A	36. E	56. E	76. A
17. B	37. A	57. C	77. D
18. C	38. D	58. B	78. C
19. E	39. B	59. D	79. E
20. B	40. E	60. E	80. B

2 Explanations of Answers to the Multiple-Choice Questions

1. **B.** The Compromise of 1820, also known as the Missouri Compromise, admitted Maine as a free state and Missouri as a slave state, and established the 36°30′ line as a demarcation between free and slave territories in the Louisiana Purchase. The Compromise of 1877 removed federal troops from the Southern states. The Compromise of 1850 included the Fugitive Slave Act. The Compromise of 1833 reduced tariff rates to end the Nullification Crisis.

2. **D.** The Palmer Raids attempted to root out subversives in the years following World War I. All other responses pertain to McCarthyism. The House Un-American Activities Committee (HUAC), founded in 1938, raised public concern about subversive activities in the early 1940s. In 1947, the Truman administration warned against the dangers of international communism and began to investigate federal employees. Chaired by J. Parnell Thomas, HUAC began its investigations of the motion picture industry that same year. Alger Hiss, a former member of Franklin D. Roosevelt's State Department, faced perjury charges for denying that he had given top secret government information to the Soviets. In 1950 President Truman signed the

McCarran Internal Security Act requiring all communist organizations to register with the federal government.

3. **C.** Active in unionism through out his career, Gompers served as president of the American Federation of Labor (A.F.L.) from 1886 until his death in 1924. Although some industrial workers were attracted to Populism, Gompers never joined the party. He criticized Socialists and their goals. Gompers opposed Governor Calvin Coolidge's use of the militia to break up the Boston Police Strike. President Roosevelt established the National War Labor Board after Gompers's death.

4. **A.** Roosevelt passed most of his reform legislation (i.e., Social Security Act, Fair Labor Standards Act) during the Second New Deal (1935 to 1939). The First New Deal focused primarily on recovery and relief. He passed the Emergency Banking Act as one of his first measures as president. He also created the Civilian Conservation Corps during his first "hundred days." When business leaders failed to cooperate with his National Recovery Administration, he adopted a more regulatory policy toward industry. Opposition from conservatives in Congress increased throughout the New Deal, as many believed that New Deal measures exceeded constitutional limits on power and approached socialism.

5. **B.** Zenger published articles criticizing New York's unpopular royal governor William Crosby. The governor issued a proclamation condemning the actions of the newspaper. Zenger was arrested for seditious libel in 1734. Noted Philadelphia lawyer Andrew Hamilton defended Zenger. Chief Justice of the New York Supreme Court James Delany, an ally of Crosby, sat on the bench. Hamilton argued the editor's case directly to the jury. The jury acquitted Zenger on the grounds that public statements could not be considered libelous if they could be proven to be true. The Bill of Rights later ensured this freedom of the press.

6. **E.** Vietnamese forces defeated French troops at Dienbienphu in 1954. When France withdraws from North Vietnam, Eisenhower pledges American aid to the noncommunist government of Ngo Dinh Diem in Saigon. Kennedy began sending American military advisors in 1961. By the time of Kennedy's assassination in 1963, the number of advisors in Vietnam rose to 15,000. Congress issued the Tonkin Gulf Resolution in 1964, granting Johnson broad powers to wage war against communism in Southeast Asia. By the time of Nixon's victory in 1968, the number of American ground troops in Vietnam rose to over 500,000. Nixon began withdrawing American troops from Vietnam in 1969, thereby initiating the policy of "Vietnamization".

7. **E.** Congressman David Wilmot (R-PA) feared that the addition of new territory would increase the number of potential slave states. He introduced an amendment to an appropriations bill that would impede the creation of new slave states in any land acquired from the

Mexican War. The Constitution banned the importation of slaves into the United States after 1808. No constitutional amendment abolishing slavery would be introduced until the Civil War. Students should not focus upon the reference to the specie circular, which also pertained to expansion and western lands.

8. **C.** Puritans believed that only trained ministers could propagate the faith. Puritans eschewed the Enlightenment philosophy that science and reason could explain worldly events. They resisted any challenge or alternative teaching of the Puritan orthodoxy. However, seventeenth century women were not admitted. E refers to the Tuskegee Institute, founded in the nineteenth century.

9. **D.** Ethel and Julius Rosenberg were convicted of espionage in 1951 for allegedly organizing a conspiracy to provide the Soviet Union with atomic secrets. They were executed in 1953. Students should avoid the references to *Plessy* v. *Ferguson* (1896), Leopold-Loeb case (1924), and Sacco-Vanzetti case (1920 to 27).

10. **A.** Upton Sinclair wrote *The Jungle* (1906). Henry George identified the great disparity of wealth between the rich and poor in *Progress and Poverty* (1879). The other four authors were "muckrakers." Jacob Riis wrote *How the Other Half Lives,* based on his photographs of urban poverty, in 1890. Ida Tarbell published an exposé of the monopoly practices of Standard Oil Trust in 1904. John Spargo examined the problems of child labor in *The Bitter Cry of Children* (1906).

11. **C.** The Civil Rights Act ordered the desegregation of public accommodations. President Eisenhower completed the integration of the military in 1954. The *Brown* v. *Board of Education* decision required the integration of schools. President Kennedy used military force to integrate public universities before 1964. In the wake of the Selma march, Johnson signed the Voting Rights (Civil Rights) Act of 1965.

12. **B.** Financier J. P. Morgan attempted to orchestrate the merger of the Union Pacific, Burlington, and Northern Pacific railroad lines. This monopoly would virtually eliminate competition among the largest commercial carriers from the Pacific coast to the Midwest. The Supreme Court ordered the dissolution of the Northern Securities Company for "combining to restrain free trade," a violation of the Sherman Antitrust Act. Suits against Swift and Company (1905), and Standard Oil (1911) followed.

13. **E.** Scandal touched the administrations of all five presidents. The "whiskey ring" and Credit Mobilier scandals occurred under Grant. President Clinton faced impeachment charges for lying about his involvement with intern Monica Lewinsky. Nixon resigned after the Watergate scandal surfaced. Cleveland acknowledged that he had an illegitimate child. At the request of his Secretary of the Interior Albert Fall, President Warren G. Harding transferred control of naval oil reserves at Elk Hills, California, and Teapot Dome, Wyoming. Fall

accepted bribes from Harry F. Sinclair and Edward L. Doheny, two wealthy oilmen. He was sentenced to one year in prison.

14. **D.** Parliament passed a revenue tax on tea as part of the Townshend Acts (1767). After colonial boycotts, Lord North repealed most of the duties in 1770, except the tax on tea. The Tea Act enabled the British East India Company to sell its tea directly to its agents in the colonies, thus bypassing the tax on tea. The act bankrupted many colonial merchants who continued to pay the duty. Popular unrest over the Tea Act led to the Boston Tea Party. Parliament closed the port of Boston in the Coercive (Intolerable) Acts (1774) in response to the destruction of the property of the British East India Company.

15. **A.** The election of 1800 marked a transition of power from the Federalists to the Jeffersonian Republicans. Jefferson seemed to favor a limited government and agrarian interests. Many Federalists saw that the acquisition of the vast Louisiana territory portended the creation of several new Republican states, thus further eroding their political power and influence in the federal government.

16. **A.** Vicksburg remained in Confederate hands after New Orleans fell to Admiral David Farragut in 1862. General Grant's victory at Shiloh gave the Union control of much of western Tennessee. His siege at Vicksburg finally gave the Union forces control of the Mississippi River in 1863. Both Gettysburg and Chancellorsville occurred in the eastern theater of war.

17. **B.** During his first administration, Woodrow Wilson intended to address what he called the "triple wall of privilege." To achieve his goals, he lowered tariff rates with the Underwood Tariff. He addressed the problem of trusts by signing the Clayton Act and creating the Federal Trade Commission. He reformed the banking system by passing the Federal Reserve Act, which created the Federal Reserve Board. Theodore Roosevelt previously signed the Pure Food and Drug Act.

18. **C.** In spite of strong Republican support in Congress, President Cleveland opposed the treaty for annexation. He stated before Congress in 1893 that the Americans who had deposed Queen Lilioukalani had committed "an act of war . . . without the authority of Congress" and committed a "substantial wrong [to] our national character as well as the rights of the [Hawaiians]."

19. **E.** Chavez formed the United Farm Workers Union in 1966. He led a boycott that forced grape growers to sign contracts with the UFW. James Meredith integrated the University of Mississippi in 1962. Members of the American Indian Movement occupied Alcatraz Island in 1969. Daniel Ellsberg published the *Pentagon Papers* in 1971. The CIA funded a military junta that overthrew Chilean president Salvador Allende in 1973. The city of San Antonio, Texas elected Henry Cisneros mayor in 1981.

20. **B.** Changing views of women during the 1920s eroded traditional Victorian mores. Some women, especially among the lower-middle and working class, began to smoke, drink, dance, and wear makeup. The "flapper" image emerged during the "Jazz Age" but was not a musical instrument. Mass-produced automobiles of the era were sometimes called "flivvers."

21. **D.** In June 1947, Secretary of State George C. Marshall announced plans to give economic aid to all European nations willing to participate in recovery efforts. The Soviet Union and Eastern bloc nations rejected the plan as "Yankee imperialism." Nevertheless, the United States contributed over $12 billion dollars by 1950 to revive struggling European economies. The Kellogg-Briand Pact (1928) futilely attempted to outlaw war by international agreement. "Operation Overlord" was the code name for the Normandy invasion. The Federal Loyalty Program investigated the loyalty of federal employees. The Eisenhower Doctrine sent military aid to the Middle East.

22. **C.** Although Union forces occupied most of the Confederate states by 1865, former slaves did not leave the South in large numbers. The end of Reconstruction in 1877 did not spark massive migration in the following decade. World War I expanded employment opportunities in the industrial North. Massive migration began in 1915 as thousands of African-Americans sought to escape the poverty, racism, and violence.

23. **A.** During post-Civil War industrial expansion, most Republicans advocated high tariffs to protect American products from foreign competition. Both the McKinley Tariff (1890) and Dingley Tariff (1897) kept rates above 45 percent. Protectionists also succeeded in undermining efforts to lower rates in the Wilson-Gorman Tariff by adding high-tariff revisions to the bill. Republican policy of the era typically avoided significant regulation of the economy and often sided with management during strikes. Republican Secretary of the Treasury Andrew Mellon revised corporate and income taxes during the 1920s.

24. **D.** Headed by Milo Reno, the Farmers' Holiday Association attempted to raise agricultural prices by withholding commodities from the market. Their efforts failed to increase prices. President Hoover's Federal Farm Board failed to control the farm surplus. His Reconstruction Finance Corporation (RFC) also failed to revitalize the industrial economy. President Franklin D. Roosevelt created the National Recovery Administration (NRA) to address industrial recovery and the Agricultural Adjustment Administration (AAA) to regulate the farm economy. Both met with limited success.

25. **E.** Article VI states that the Constitution and federal legislation "shall be the supreme law of the land." All senators, representatives, judges, and members of state legislatures must swear to uphold the Constitution.

26. **B.** Although nationalists readily supported war with Spain, Congress denied any intention of annexing Cuba. American policy seemed to shift after hostilities ceased. In 1901, Congress passed the Platt Amendment and induced Cuba to accept its terms. The Platt Amendment limited Cuba's ability to make treaties, enabled the United States to establish a naval base on the island, and granted the United States the right to intervene in Cuban affairs.

27. **C.** Both John Dewey and Mary Montessori pushed for education reform during the Progressive era. The other three individuals participated in antebellum reform movements. Initially an abolitionist, Lucretia Mott helped organize the Seneca Falls Convention. Weld published abolitionist tracts. Horace Mann served on the Massachusetts Board of Education and revitalized the Massachusetts school system. Other states followed his model.

28. **A.** Herbert Hoover headed the Food Administration, which supervised a highly successful food rationing campaign. The War Industries Board, led by Bernard Baruch, failed to mobilize the American economy fully by the end of the war. George Creel supervised the Committee on Public Information, which produced propaganda.

29. **C.** Kennedy battled a slight recession and above-normal unemployment figures with legislation designed to foster economic expansion. He convinced steelworkers to abandon demands for higher wages temporarily. When U.S. Steel and other companies announced a price increase, Kennedy denounced the industry's actions in a news conference in April 1962. U.S. Steel lowered its prices three days later.

30. **D.** Federal land grants contributed to the construction of railroads in the West. Mass production of automobiles did not occur until the 1920s. Streetcars allowed people to move outside the city limits.

31. **E.** Lincoln won approximately 40 percent of the popular vote. Democrats split their votes between Stephen Douglas and John C. Breckinridge. Some Southern states refused to recognize Lincoln's candidacy. However, many Unionists in the South cast their vote for John C. Bell, the Constitutional Union candidate.

32. **B.** The United States and the Soviet Union signed the Strategic Arms Limitation Talks (SALT I) at the end of Nixon's first term. The War Powers Act set limits on the president's ability to commit troops abroad. The INF Treaty and Strategic Defense Initiative are connected to the Reagan administration. Kennedy negotiated the Test Ban Treaty in 1963.

33. **A.** Roosevelt and Churchill assured Stalin of an impending invasion of France. At Casablanca earlier in 1943, Roosevelt and Churchill had agreed to invade Italy. The Washington Conference (1921 to 1922) attempted naval disarmament; the Kellogg-Briand Pact (1928) sought to eliminate war.

34. **B.** Metacomet fought British colonists in the seventeenth century. Pontiac led his tribe in an uprising in colonial Virginia in the 1760s. Tecumseh forged a loose alliance of tribes in the Northwest that broke down after the defeat at Tippecanoe in 1811 and ended with his death in 1813. Osceola led the Seminoles in war against Americans in the 1830s. Geronimo raided settlements in the Southwest until the mid-1880s.

35. **C.** Congress sent the Fourteenth Amendment to the states in 1866. Tennessee was the only Southern state to ratify it. The next congressional elections increased the power of the "Radical" Republicans. They passed the Reconstruction Act of 1867, which dismantled the existing state governments in the South in favor of military districts. Republicans made ratification of the amendment a requirement for states seeking readmission to the Union.

36. **E.** Many pollsters picked Thomas E. Dewey to win the election of 1948. Truman, who ascended to the presidency upon Roosevelt's death, faced challenges from both the left and right of the Democratic party. He adopted an aggressive campaign style and traveled across the country by train. He delivered over 350 speeches, attacking Republican policy toward organized labor and the agricultural economy. He garnered nearly 50 percent of the popular vote to win an unexpected victory.

37. **A.** President Theodore Roosevelt set aside thousands of acres of public lands for parks. Richard Ballinger, Taft's Secretary of the Interior, attempted to open forests and mineral reserves to private corporations. Chief Forester Gifford Pinchot criticized Ballinger's actions and was eventually dismissed by Taft. Conservationists and progressives generally sided with Pinchot.

38. **D.** McNamara and Rusk favored American involvement in Vietnam. Both Fulbright and Kennedy opposed sending more troops to Vietnam, but Fulbright wrote the book.

39. **B.** Texans defeated General Santa Anna's forces in 1836. Nevertheless, the Mexican government did not recognize Texan independence. President Jackson resisted annexation in spite of the support of Texans for joining the Union. A joint resolution of Congress annexing Texas heightened simmering tensions that subsequently led to war. The Treaty of Guadalupe Hidalgo followed the war, granting the United States the territory from Texas to California.

40. **E.** In 1957 white mobs attempted to prevent black students from entering Little Rock Central High School. Whites rioted over the admission of James Meredith to the University of Mississippi in 1962. Police used fire hoses and police dogs to disrupt nonviolent demonstrations in Birmingham. A week of violence and destruction of property followed an incident of police brutality in Watts in 1965.

Four students died when National Guardsmen fired into a crowd of antiwar protestors on the campus of Kent State University in 1970.

41. **B.** British troops evacuated Boston early in the Revolutionary War, only to return later with reinforcements. William Howe had been removed from his command in 1778. The American victory on the Virginia coast indicated that Britain's former colonies would continue to sustain the war effort. As a result, the possibility of continuing a costly conflict heightened public opposition to the war in Great Britain.

42. **B.** The Soviet Union launched *Sputnik,* an unmanned satellite, into space in 1957. Cosmonaut Yuri Gagarin became the first man in space in April 1961. Alan Shepard followed in May. Neil Armstrong walked on the moon after the inauguration of Richard Nixon.

43. **C.** The agricultural economy had not improved dramatically in the South since the end of the Civil War. Most Southern farmers faced an unending cycle of poverty and debt. Immigrants at the turn of the century differed significantly from their antebellum predecessors. A large percentage of these new Americans were Catholic or Jewish and came from Italy or Russia.

44. **A.** The Women's Christian Temperance Union sprang from the Progressive era. Formed in 1873, this organization led a publicity campaign against the negative effects of alcohol. It reached the pinnacle of its membership before World War I.

45. **D.** Residents of the Western states would benefit from the expansion of the National Road. The proposed route could improve the movement of crops and expand regional commerce. Although Jackson had previously signed some internal improvements bills, he vetoed the Maysville bill. Jackson believed that the federal government had no authority to finance the project, since it did not run between several states and promote interstate commerce.

46. **D.** Landon and Dewey ran against Roosevelt in the presidential elections of 1940 and 1944, respectively. Neither Republican candidate promoted higher taxes as part of their platform. Francis Townsend proposed the creation of a pension program to alleviate the suffering of elderly Americans hit hard by the Depression. Louisiana senator Huey P. Long proposed confiscatory taxes on the wealthy to be redistributed among average Americans.

47. **E.** In Puritan communities, church leaders directed town affairs. Puritans believed in predestination. The Enlightenment, deism, and the First Great Awakening challenged the traditional Puritan view of worldly events and salvation.

48. **A.** Jonas Salk developed the polio vaccine, which the federal government began to distribute in the mid-1950s. Dr. Benjamin Spock promoted a child-centered approach to raising young people in his book *Baby and Child Care.*

49. **B.** Overspeculation in Western land sales and the demise of the Bank of the United States contributed to the Panic of 1837. The United States remained on the gold standard until Franklin Roosevelt took office. The federal government did not begin to spend significant amounts of money on works projects until the New Deal. Overproduction of consumer goods during the 1920s depressed prices by the end of the decade.

50. **C.** During Reconstruction, Congress passed a Civil Rights Act, which outlawed discrimination in public places. Many state legislatures complied until the Supreme Court narrowed the interpretation of the law in the *Civil Rights Cases* (1883). When Homer Plessy challenged segregation laws in New Orleans, the Court ruled in favor of "separate but equal" facilities for blacks and whites. As a result, states applied the principle of segregation to all public accommodations, including restaurants, hotels, and drinking fountains. *Hammer* v. *Dagenhart* (1918) overturned the Keating-Owen Act, which regulated child labor. The Court's decision in *Schenck* v. *U.S.* (1919) limited the interpretation of "free speech."

51. **C.** Washington annunciated the cornerstone of early American foreign policy in his Neutrality Act and Farewell Address. When France and Great Britain began to seize American ships, Jefferson replied with the Embargo Act. He hoped that being cut off from American trade would force the belligerent nations to respect American neutrality. Instead, the act exacerbated economic problems in the United States and revitalized Federalist opposition to Jefferson.

52. **E.** Economic and social tensions increased as Puritan communities grew. Class distinctions emerged and friction followed. Historians differ on explanations of events in Massachusetts. Some point to the economic rivalry between Salem Village and Salem town; others note that the accused transgressed the traditional roles of colonial women. The Second Great Awakening did not occur until the eighteenth century. The Creeks and Seminoles lived primarily in the Southern colonies.

53. **D.** Both the United States and Soviet Union sent troops into Korea during World War II, and agreed to a temporary partition at the 38th parallel. Soviet and American forces withdrew in 1949. The Soviets supported a pro-communist government in the North, while the United States endorsed the pro-Western government of Syngman Rhee in the South. North Korea invaded South Korea in June 1950. Truman mobilized American forces and sought the support of the United Nations. The alleged attack on the *Maddux* led to the Tonkin Gulf Resolution and American involvement in Vietnam.

54. **A.** Antebellum defenders of slavery frequently used paternalistic terminology to describe a purportedly affectionate relationship between masters and slaves. Nat Turner and his followers collected weapons

and attacked families in Southhampton County, Virginia. Nearly 60 whites died; federal and state troops killed over 100 blacks when suppressing the insurrection. Widespread fear of similar slave revolts led to the passage of stricter "slave codes." This fear persisted throughout the antebellum period. Some Southerners believed that Northern abolitionists had inspired the rebellion, which exacerbated sectional tensions. This belief later led to the passage of a "gag rule" in Congress that prevented discussion of abolitionist petitions on the floor of the House.

55. **B.** Franklin Roosevelt created the Office of Price Administration (OPA) in 1942 to combat inflation. As more Americans found employment in the booming war industries, prices increased. The OPA capped prices and wages and promoted rationing with coupon books. Roosevelt's War Production Board (WPB) struggled to convert the economy to wartime production and control military purchases. The Committee on Public Information (CPI) directed the propaganda campaign during World War I.

56. **E.** Tensions with Indians along the frontier brought representatives from several colonies together at Albany. Benjamin Franklin's "Plan of Union" proposed a form of government to administer to colonial affairs. Most colonial assemblies rejected the Albany Plan by the onset of the French and Indian War. The war ended in 1763 with the Treaty of Paris. Parliament did not pass the Quebec Act until 1774. The women's rights convention at Seneca Falls occurred in 1848.

57. **C.** Construction of the Erie Canal began in 1817. Upon its completion in 1825, it linked Lake Erie to the commerce of New York City. The National Road did not extend to Illinois until 1837. Few railroad routes extended as far as the Erie Canal in this period.

58. **B.** Although many former slaves hoped to become landowners, no concerted effort was made to redistribute the property of former slaveholders. The Confiscation Act of 1862 yielded few free homesteads. Some redistribution occurred in the Sea Islands (South Carolina), but the model was not followed throughout the South. The Freedmen's Bureau established schools in several Southern states. Staffed by white and black teachers, these schools enrolled thousands of black students. Military Reconstruction and the election of Republican governments limited the influence of former Confederate leaders to some degree. However, the Ku Klux Klan and similar organizations terrorized white and black Republicans, leading to the reestablishment of Democratic (Conservative) governments.

59. **D.** In the Kellogg-Briand Pact (1928), signatory nations pledged to outlaw war "as an instrument of national policy." Although signed by over 60 nations, the treaty provided no enforcement mechanism. At the end of World War II, delegates from several nations created the United Nations. The Security Council retained the power to

investigate international issues, recommend actions, and use military force when necessary to maintain international peace. The North Atlantic Treaty Organization (NATO) created a defensive alliance among the United States and several European nations in 1949. Similar alliances followed for Southeast Asia (SEATO) and the Middle East (CENTO).

60. **E.** Daniel Shays and followers used armed resistance to prevent collection of taxes and confiscation of property among hard-pressed farmers in western Massachusetts. The Confederation government and state legislature had little money or power to suppress domestic unrest. Perceiving a threat to property, wealthy merchants financed the state militia to end the rebellion. President George Washington used powers granted under the Constitution to call up state militias and suppress the Whiskey Rebellion in 1794.

61. **A.** By 1941, Great Britain faced an uncertain future in their fight against Nazi aggression. Bombing raids and submarine attacks disrupted the British economy. President Franklin Roosevelt favored the lend-lease policy over "cash-and-carry" because it enabled the United States to provide greater assistance to the beleaguered nation. Roosevelt extended lend-lease to the Soviets after Hitler's forces invaded the USSR.

62. **B.** At the end of the nineteenth century, a combination of events drew the United States into war with Spain. In 1898, an explosion on the USS *Maine* killed over 260 sailors in Havana harbor. The "yellow journalism" of newspapers such as William Randolph Hearst's *New York Journal* intensified the war fever in the United States. "Remember the *Maine*" became a popular rallying cry for advocates of war.

63. **C.** One result of the American Revolution was the widespread belief that an effective republic rested upon the active participation of its citizens. Although the Revolution did not significantly alter the social and legal position of women, it placed great emphasis on their influence upon children. Women were expected to instill their children with the virtues of liberty, thus creating the next generation of loyal citizens.

64. **E.** Watergate and his pardon of Richard Nixon cost Gerald Ford a number of votes in 1976. Dwight D. Eisenhower was elected in 1952 after 20 years of Democratic administrations. Dissent over Johnson's Vietnam policy helped the Republican party in 1968. In 1964, Republican candidate Barry Goldwater was cast as imprudent in foreign affairs.

65. **A.** Workers in mass-production industries remained outside the scope of the American Federation of Labor, which organized craft unions. Supporters of industrial unions strove to organize all workers in a particular industry without concern for their particular skill

or function. John L. Lewis, head of the United Mine Workers, attempted to unionize mass-production workers from within the A.F.L. A.F.L. leaders dismissed Lewis and his committee after a series of bitter conflicts. Lewis reestablished the committee as the Congress on Industrial Organization in 1936.

66. **D.** The United States and Great Britain both claimed territory in the Pacific Northwest. President Polk proposed a division of the Oregon Territory at the 49th parallel. When a British ambassador rebuffed Polk's offer, advocates of manifest destiny clamored for action. In spite of nationalistic rhetoric, Polk wanted a peaceful resolution to the issue. The United States and Great Britain avoided armed conflict by settling on the original proposal.

67. **E.** The American states ratified the Articles of Confederation in order to create a loose alliance to fight the Revolutionary War. Individual state legislatures retained a great deal of authority. The states granted the Continental Congress limited powers to wage the war. Each state jealously guarded its authority to tax its citizens.

68. **B.** The state of Maryland attempted to tax the operations of a local branch of the Bank of the United States (B.U.S.). Maryland indicted James McCulloch, cashier for the B.U.S., for refusing to pay the state tax. Chief Justice Marshall ruled that the state tax law violated the supremacy clause of the Constitution and was thus void. Marshall affirmed the "necessary and proper" clause that afforded the creation of the Bank. In *Gibbons* v. *Ogden* (1824), Marshall confirmed congressional authority to regulate interstate commerce in a dispute between steamboat companies. Marshall attempted to counter the Indian removal of the 1830s but was opposed by Andrew Jackson.

69. **D.** Eisenhower signed the Federal Highway Act of 1956, which initiated the construction of tens of thousands of miles of interstates. New Deal public works projects did not complete as many miles of interstate.

70. **C.** Severe economic distress in both Ireland and Germany impelled millions of immigrants to American shores in the antebellum period. The emergence of the American or "Know-Nothing" party reflected the widespread nativism of the era. The Democratic party tended to welcome these new Americans into their ranks. Legislation to restrict naturalization and immigration was not passed until later in the century and in the early twentieth century.

71. **A.** Smoldering friction between Great Britain and France erupted in war in 1793. Washington stated that the United States would "pursue a conduct friendly and impartial towards the belligerent powers." He repeated his position in the Neutrality Act of 1794 and his Farewell Address.

72. C. Johnson enjoyed sizable Democratic majorities in the House and Senate during his first years as president. He promoted a "War on Poverty" with job training programs, aid to education, and urban renewal.

73. D. The election of 1928 pitted Republican Herbert Hoover against Democrat Al Smith. Hoover seemed to represent a continuation of Republican prosperity. He enjoyed the support of rural America and made inroads into the South. As such, he opposed the repeal of Prohibition. Al Smith, the first Catholic presidential candidate, favored the repeal of Prohibition, a policy popular in the Northern cities.

74. B. Many single males moved to the Southern colonies in search of economic opportunities. More family units migrated to the New England colonies. Climate and the prevalence of unfamiliar diseases contributed a lower life expectancy in the colonial South. As a result, frequent deaths undermined patriarchal authority. The river system provided valuable transportation routes for the regional economy.

75. E. After the Normandy invasion in June 1944, Allied forces gained ground in France. The Allies marched into Paris in August. The Nazi army mounted its last major offensive in December 1944 along the Belgian-German border. Allied forces retreated to Bastogne and suffered heavy casualties. However, the Allied line did not break and a successful counteroffensive opened Germany to an invasion from the west.

76. A. Douglas maintained that the residents of a territory should be able to decide the question of slavery. Seward, Stevens, and Sumner opposed the institution of slavery. On May 20, 1856, Sumner launched into a diatribe against the Kansas-Nebraska Act and the expansion of slavery into Kansas. He focused his invective on Senator A. P. Butler of South Carolina. Butler's nephew, Representative Preston Brooks, sought to avenge this insult to his family. Brooks accosted Sumner on the floor of the Senate and beat him with a cane. Brooks and Sumner came to represent opposite sides of the sectional debate brewing in the 1850s.

77. D. Facing rising debts in the late nineteenth century, farmers advocated the free coinage of silver. Adherence to a gold standard contracted the federal money supply; an inflated currency would raise the price of farm goods, providing farmers the income to repay their debts. The Populists endorsed bimetallism in the elections of 1892 and 1896.

78. C. A number of states lifted property or tax-paying qualifications for voting during the first three decades of the nineteenth century. However, the states did not extend voting privileges to women. The states also passed legislation to restrict the freedoms of African slaves. In 1913 the Seventeenth Amendment gave citizens the right to elect senators directly.

79. **E.** Volunteers in the Service of America (VISTA) enlisted idealistic young people to address poverty in urban and rural communities. The Free Speech Movement, led by Mario Savio, and Students for a Democratic Society exemplified the student protest groups of the decade. Both addressed a wide range of issues, from the Vietnam War to university policies. The outlandish Yippies, members of the Youth International Party, clashed with police outside of the 1968 Democratic Convention in Chicago. The militant Black Panther party rejected the nonviolent protests of moderates within the civil rights movement.

80. **B.** A recent immigrant from Great Britain, Paine was an effective propagandist of the rebel cause. Unlike some other colonial writers, Paine focused American hostility on King George III rather than Parliament. To Paine, "common sense" dictated that Americans should declare their independence. Americans bought over 100,000 copies of *Common Sense* within its first few months of publication.

Section II

Part A

Summary Response to Document-Based Question

1. Although the Federalists intended to unify the nation and strengthen the federal government, their political and economic policies split the nation into rival partisan factions. Students might note that debates over ratification of the Constitution set the stage for the emergence of political parties by the end of the 1790s. They could briefly discuss the supporters and opponents of ratification, the Antifederalists, and *The Federalist Papers,* particularly *The Federalist,* no. 10. Students should examine the ideological conflict between loose and strict interpretations of the Constitution, as well as federal versus state authority. They should identify the leading Federalists (Washington, Adams, Hamilton) and Republicans (Jefferson, Madison, Randolph). Document A indicates Washington's desire that Congress may set policy without party division. Students may note, however, that friction stemmed from Hamilton's financial program. They should examine his intention to establish a sound financial foundation for the new nation by creating a national bank, addressing the public debt (Assumption Act, Funding Bill), and raising revenue (excise taxes, tariffs). While Hamilton's program strengthened the federal government, it fostered dissent among the Republicans. Document B reflects Virginia's opposition to the assumption of state debts. Students will note that the conflict over the Bank of the United States in Document C, and D reflects Jefferson's and Hamilton's interpretation of the "necessary and proper clause" of the Constitution. Students may also contrast the Republican view of an agricultural economy in Document B. with Federalist support for the Tariff of 1789 and Hamilton's Report on Manufactures. They may note that opposition to the excise tax led to the Whiskey Rebellion. In Document E, Washington states his intention to enforce federal law and implement powers granted under the Constitution. Washington demonstrated federal authority by calling forth the militias from three states to suppress the rebellion. Some students may refer to Shay's Rebellion. Students may begin a discussion of diplomatic policy with Washington's Neutrality Proclamation (1793) and Neutrality Act (1794). They may explain how the neutrality policy survived the challenge of "Citizen Genet." However, Great Britain challenged the policy by seizing American ships. Students should discuss partisan perceptions of Jay's Treaty (Document F). They may note that it achieved some of its nationalistic goals regarding the Northwest territory and promoting commerce with Great Britain. However, they should also address Republican views of its shortcomings. Some students may address Pinckney's Treaty. Students should discuss Washington's views on parties in his Farewell Address.

They will note how the election of 1796 yielded a Federalist president (Adams) and a Republican vice president (Jefferson). Students will note how the strife in the executive office reflected party differences in the United States. A discussion of the undeclared naval war with France will reveal the pro-British views of Federalists and pro-French sympathies of the Republicans. Students will discuss how opposing perceptions of the war and the XYZ Affair led to the Alien and Sedition Acts of 1798 (Document G). Students will observe how Madison and Jefferson penned the Virginia and Kentucky Resolutions (Document H), which asserted the theory of nullification. They might conclude how the problems of the Adams administration led to the election of Jefferson in 1800.

Part B and Part C

Summary Responses to Standard Free-Response Questions

2. Students may assert that the colonists increasingly believed that Parliament overstepped its legitimate authority. Students should briefly discuss the results of the French and Indian War. They should examine the development of the colonial assemblies and address the differences between virtual and actual representation throughout the essay. Parliament prohibited colonial expansion in the Proclamation of 1763. The policy intended to reduce the costs of governing the empire, prevent war with Indians along the frontier, and advance the British economy over the colonial economy. The colonists ignored the proclamation and expanded west. They grew restive under parliamentary restrictions on land speculation and the fur trade. Students may explain how Parliament passed the Stamp Act to cover the costs of administering an empire. They should note that the tax fell on all paper products, from legal documents to newspapers. Colonists angrily reacted to the imposition of a revenue tax not passed by their assemblies. Students might discuss Patrick Henry, James Otis, the Stamp Act Congress, Thomas Hutchinson, the Sons of Liberty, and/or colonial boycotts. Parliament passed the Coercive (Intolerable) Acts in response to the Boston Tea Party. Some students may address the Tea Act of 1773. Parliament intended to punish Massachusetts, long considered a source of rebellion. Students should address the Boston Port Act, Massachusetts Government Act, new Quartering Act, and/or a provision allowing officials accused of crimes in the colonies to be tried in England. Students will note how the other colonies rallied in support of Massachusetts with legislative resolutions and a new round of boycotts. Some might refer to the formation of the First Continental Congress.

3. A response to this question might begin by examining the results of industrialization, immigration, and the question of slavery. Students will measure the extent to which the reform movements promoted change or

attempted to arrest new developments. They should touch upon the Second Great Awakening. Students may address the education and temperance movements as reactions to the rapid influx of Irish and German immigrants. Discussions of education should refer to Horace Mann and the goals of public schools. However, students might also address the more liberal emphasis on republicanism or the development of female education. In an examination of temperance movement, students might address the various temperance organizations, Lyman Beecher, Neil Dow, and/or state temperance laws. Students might discuss the emergence of utopian communities such as New Harmony, Oneida, and Brook Farm as reactions to industrialization and/or as representations of new social views. They might discuss Dorothea Dix and the movement to improve asylums and hospitals. An examination of efforts to improve women's rights might include the "cult of domesticity," Quakers, Emma Willard, Catherine Beecher, Lucretia Mott, Elizabeth Cady Stanton, and/or the Seneca Falls Convention. A discussion of the antislavery movement could include the American Colonization Society, major abolitionists (including William Lloyd Garrison, Frederick Douglass, Theodore Dwight Weld, Elijah Lovejoy and/or the Grimkes). Students might address the division within the movement over the inclusion of women and/or immediate versus gradual abolitionism.

4. Students might argue that third-party candidates address the interests of groups feeling isolated from the two major parties. These individuals may attract support away from mainstream candidates. In 1912, the Democratic party nominated Woodrow Wilson; incumbent William Howard Taft headed the Republican ticket. However, Taft's candidacy did not satisfy the liberal Republicans. Reformers within the G.O.P. bristled over Taft's apparent support for the policies of the Old Guard Republicans. Students might discuss the passage of the Payne-Aldrich Tariff, the Ballinger-Pinchot Controversy, and the conflict between Speaker of the House Joseph Cannon (R-IL) and progressive Republicans such as George Norris. Students might address Theodore Roosevelt's Osawatomie speech and progressive proposals known as "New Nationalism" (i.e., increased federal regulation of corporations, tariff revision, income tax, etc.). Students might note the final split between Roosevelt and Taft over the U.S. Steel suit in 1911. They would examine how Taft's renomination at the Republican convention in Chicago led to Roosevelt's candidacy for the Progressive ("Bull Moose") party. Roosevelt attracted many progressive Republicans and other liberals to the Progressive banner. Students may note the differences between Roosevelt's New Nationalism and Wilson's New Freedom proposals (regulation versus eradication of monopolies).

Students will observe that the rift in the Republican party ushered in Wilson as the next president. Some students might indicate that Debs' candidacy for the Socialist party, by comparison, did little to take votes away from Wilson. Harry Truman faced third-party candidacies from both the left and right in 1948. Students might review some elements of the Truman administration before the election, including but not limited to the Truman Doctrine, labor issues, postwar inflation, President's Committee on Civil Rights/*To Secure These Rights*, congressional elections of 1946, and/or rejection of "Fair Deal" policies. Students may note that Truman's eroding position spawned the candidacies of Henry Wallace and Strom Thurmond. Students might argue Wallace's candidacy for the Progressive party represented liberals and Democrats alienated by Truman's containment policy, reaction to the UMW strike, and failure to implement effective social reform. Thurmond's States' Rights party opposed Truman primarily because of his stance on civil rights. The "Dixiecrats" advocated the maintenance of segregation. Students should address the candidacy of Republican Thomas E. Dewey and his favorable position before the election. Students may note that some conservatives may have supported Thurmond over Dewey. Others may argue that Truman's aggressive "whistle-stop" campaign enabled him to defeat the third parties as well as his Republican challenger. In 1968 students may begin with Johnson's withdrawal from the race and touch upon the escalation of Vietnam, popular protest, the mixed results of his "Great Society" programs, and/or challenges led by Eugene McCarthy and Robert F. Kennedy. Students may again note the division within the Democratic party and the emergence of Hubert Humphrey. Wallace's American Independent party fed upon the social dislocations of the decade. He won votes from conservatives who opposed Johnson's civil rights legislation and who rejected the disorder fomented Vietnam protestors. Wallace advocated states rights over "big government." Students will want to address Nixon's bid for the votes "Middle America," aspects of his platform (law-and-order, deregulation, Vietnam) and his "Southern strategy." Students may note that Wallace may have attracted votes away from both Humphrey and Nixon, contributing to the slim margin of victory in the popular vote.

5. Student might first examine how the war affected American women. They could discuss employment in war industries ("Rosie the Riveter" versus discrimination in the workplace), increased participation service-sector jobs (clerical, etc.), and enlistment in the military (WAACs, WAVEs). They could explain the impact of this work upon women themselves. Students might discuss the evaporation of wartime advances with the "baby boom" and return of men to the workplace. Students should address the participation of African-Americans in war industries (opportunity versus discrimination) and the armed forces (segregated units). They should examine the effects of increased opportunities or treatment abroad upon African-Americans. They may include a discussion of the second "Great Migration," FEPC (effects/limitations), CORE, and individuals such as A. Philip Randolph, James Farmer, and Bayard Rustin. Some students may also include a discussion of Japanese-Americans (internment, 442nd Combat Team), Native Americans ("code talkers," departure from reservations), and Mexican-Americans (*braceros,* urban migration, "zoot suit riot").

PART III

A COMPREHENSIVE REVIEW OF UNITED STATES HISTORY

Chapter 3

The Settling of the Western Hemisphere and Colonial America (1450–1650)

NATIVE AMERICANS AND EUROPEAN EXPLORATION

Initial Settlement of the Americas

The first settlers in the Western Hemisphere came from Asia beginning about 25,000 B.C. There is some evidence that some of these early Americans arrived by boat, but the vast majority arrived across the Bering Strait and through Alaska when the last Ice Age created a land-bridge across the strait. It is possible that these settlers were not consciously migrating but were simply following animals that they hunted.

By the time that the Spanish arrived in the Americas in the late fifteenth century, there were approximately 4 million Native Americans living in Canada and the United States and over 20 million living in Mexico. Most groups of Native Americans in the Americas were **hunter-gatherers**, although some were farmers.

European Exploration of the Americas

There are several important reasons why Europeans were interested in the Americas in the period 1450 to 1500. Some historians emphasize that only limited economic growth appeared possible in Europe itself. European monarchs and entrepreneurs therefore had to look abroad for future profits. Europeans could now travel faster and further, because of better ship-building techniques and the perfection of the **astrolabe** and the compass. The **Crusades** had whetted the appetites of Europeans for the luxury goods provided by Asia, thus further encouraging exploration abroad. In addition, the growth of nation-states (governed by kings) during this period increased the competition between European powers for both wealth and territory.

A BRINGING TOGETHER OF THREE PEOPLES BY THE SPANISH

It is important to understand that early European exploration and settlement actually brought together people from three societies: European, Native American, and African. It is crucial to understand the complex and sophisticated nature of Native American and African civilization before each came into contact with the Europeans.

The explorations and conquests of Hernando Cortes and Francisco Pizarro should be carefully studied. Both stated a desire to convert as many natives as possible to Catholicism, and economic factors were also careful considerations in their exploits. In 1519 Cortes invaded Mexico and encountered the rich and powerful **Aztecs**, centered at Tenochtitlán (now Mexico City). The Aztecs were defeated two years later by the Spanish, largely because of Spanish technological advantages (they had guns, while the Aztecs did not) and because of the diseases, such as smallpox, that the Europeans gave to the Native Americans. Ten years later Pizarro defeated the **Inca Empire**, located in the Andes Mountains. The effects of these conquests were that shipload after shipload of gold were shipped from the Americans back to Spain; in addition, a large Spanish empire was created in the Americas. In North America both missionaries and economic opportunists from Spain eventually settled in what is now the southwestern United States and in Florida.

The effects of the Spanish conquests were numerous. The number of Native Americans living in the Americas decreased, with disease brought by the Spanish also devastating the Pueblo tribes of the Southwest and other groups in Florida and the Southeast. Territories ruled by the Spanish were harshly maintained; Native Americans were forced to work as near-slaves on Spanish plantations. In addition, horses introduced by the Spanish did much to alter Native American life in both North and South America. Plants, animals, and diseases from the Americas were also introduced for the first time to Europeans.

THE FRENCH IN CANADA

The French didn't have any permanent settlements in Canada until 1608, when Samuel de Champlain founded Quebec. Few colonists ever came to the French territory in Canada: The climate was considered undesirable, and the French government provided few incentives for them to leave France. In addition, the dissident **Huguenots** were legally forbidden from emigrating. It should be noted that over 65 percent of all those who did come to Quebec ended up returning to France.

The French also desired to convert Native Americans to Catholicism but used much less coercive tactics than the Spanish. Samuel de Champlain actually entered into alliances with the Huron and other Native American tribes, largely for protection for his somewhat unstable settlement. The French actually joined with the Huron and the Algonquians in a battle against the Iroquois tribe in 1608.

Those settlers who did stay in Quebec turned from farming to trapping and fur trading. French explorers ventured into the interior of North America to develop the fur-trading industry. **Jesuit** Jacques Marquette and fur trader Louis Joliet reached the Mississippi River, Wisconsin, and Arkansas; Robert La Salle continued to explore along the Mississippi River and named the territory Louisiana (after Louis XIV).

The impact of the French on Native Americans they came into contact with was profound. The diseases they brought wiped out an estimated 30 percent of all tribes they came into contact with. Many Native American tribes desired to dominate the fur trade desired by the French; this created a series of very bloody wars between these tribes. Jesuit priests were effective in converting thousands of Native Americans to Christianity. Jesuits were more successful than the Spanish **Franciscans** were in converting natives, largely because natives were also asked to become forced laborers in Spanish territories. When the French fought the British and British colonists in the French and Indian wars in the late seventeenth and early eighteenth centuries, most Native American tribes sided with the French.

In short, the French territories were successful as a fur-trading enterprise and a place where natives were converted to Christianity; the territories were a failure in the sense that a large number of settlers never took root there.

It should also be noted that during this period the Dutch made their initial entry into the Americas. The Dutch were largely interested in the commercial possibilities that the Americas offered them. In 1609 Henry Hudson discovered and named the Hudson River, and proceeded to establish trading settlements on the island of Manhattan, at Fort Nassau (soon renamed Albany), and in present-day Connecticut, New Jersey, and Pennsylvania. Like the French, the Dutch were unable to attract large numbers of settlers to the Dutch territories. Like the French, the Dutch were successful in fur trading. However, the aggression of the Dutch in expanding their territory brought them into bloody conflict with several Native American tribes, thus limiting the success of Dutch economic endeavors.

THE ENGLISH IN THE AMERICAS

Several factors encouraged English entrepreneurs and settlers to come to America. After 1550 there was huge population growth in England, with high inflation and a decline in wages for many workers. The number of landless laborers increased dramatically; thousands entered London and other English cities. Many observers noted that England appeared to be dangerously overcrowded, and leaders became increasingly convinced that settlement in America could help relieve the population problem.

Many English people became increasingly attracted to the possibility of resettlement in the Americas.

In addition, many English **Puritans** were increasingly disenchanted with the **Church of England**, feeling that the church was too close to Catholicism. Puritans, who followed the Protestant teaching of **John Calvin**, had some measure of religious freedom under Elizabeth I. After her death in 1603, the position of Puritans in England became more difficult, with some Puritan clergymen removed from their pulpits. Thus, by the 1630s many Puritans felt that by moving to the Americas they would be able to practice their religion without interference from either English civil or religious authorities. Another religious group opposed to the Church of England was the Separatists. After several of its leading spokespersons were arrested, this group fled to Holland; from here a percentage of Separatists decided to go to the Americas.

Settlement in Jamestown

The first permanent English settlement in America was the Jamestown colony, founded in 1607 by Captain John Smith. King James I had granted the **London Company** a charter permitting them to establish this colony. The swampy site of the Jamestown colony encouraged disease; in addition, several years of poor harvests created severe food shortages. In addition, early conflict with the **Powhatan Confederacy** of Native Americans placed additional strains on the colony.

Because of a severe shortage of food, John Smith created a trade alliance with the Powhatans; the corn received from the Native Americans kept the colony alive. Pocahontas, the daughter of the Powhatan chief married one of the more influential men in the Jamestown colony, John Rolfe. This marriage helped to temporarily prevent further conflict with Native Americans. Rolfe's main contribution, however, was to begin the cultivation of tobacco in Jamestown. Rolfe's system of cultivation ensured that tobacco would become the main cash crop of Virginia; the demand for tobacco in England helped to ensure the economic success of the colony.

Large numbers of workers were needed in Virginia to harvest the tobacco crop. To meet this demand, **indentured servants** began to arrive in Virginia; many of these men were unemployed, ex-criminals, or both. As an additional measure to meet the demand for labor the first African slaves arrived in Virginia in 1619, the same year that the first white women arrived there. It should be noted that the Virginia colony created the House of Burgesses in 1619; this was the first representative government in any British colony.

Settlement in Massachusetts

Colonization in New England was different. Where economic gain was the major motivation for settlement in Virginia, many religious dissenters settled in New England, thus making religious zeal a primary factor in the colonization of that region.

A group of Separatists received a charter to settle southeast of the Hudson River. The purpose of this journey was to spread the "gospell"; these men saw their journey as a "pilgrimage," and thus became known as Pilgrims. This group, led by William Bradford, encountered a storm as they neared America and landed on Plymouth Rock in Massachusetts. Before landing they produced the Mayflower Compact (1620), a document that promised that their settlement would have a government answerable to the will of the governed. As in the case of Plymouth, the first year of settlement proved to be very difficult, and the settlers were forced to rely on help from the Native Americans. However, after the first year the Pilgrims had some amount of economic success; many of the diseases that ravaged the Virginia colony were absent in colder New England. By 1691 this group joined with the other major settlement in the region, the Massachusetts Bay colony.

The Massachusetts Bay colony was established in 1629 by the Puritans. This colony was established as a location of earth where the will of God could be truly manifested; the colony was established as a commonwealth and was based on the Calvinist view of man's relation to God. By 1640 nearly 25,000 English people had migrated to Massachusetts Bay. Nearly half of these were fleeing bad economic times in England; the remainder were Puritans, who used the Bible as their religious and their legal guide.

In 1629 John Winthrop was elected governor of the Massachusetts Bay colony, a position he held for 20 years. Winthrop envisioned the colony as a "city upon a hill," away from the corrupting influences of England. Here, he felt, residents could freely live according to the precepts of God. Church, community, and political participation were all emphasized.

Massachusetts Bay did not have the devastating first several years experienced by other colonies. The colony came to be governed by a "General Court," which was an assembly elected by Puritan males in good standing. Thus, in both Virginia and in Massachusetts representative government (albeit in a limited form) was established. Additional towns were chartered in the years following the initial arrival of the Puritans near Boston.

It should be noted that there were profound differences between the Virginia and Massachusetts Bay colonies. The slave labor of Virginia never existed in Massachusetts; while many families settled in Massachusetts, Virginia was mostly settled by single men. In Massachusetts religion and political participation went hand in hand, while in Virginia land ownership was a necessity for political participation.

Effects of Religious Dissent: Development in Massachusetts Bay was steady, but leaders continued to emphasize that the main purpose of the colony was to be a place where God would be served. Religious dissent was simply not tolerated, obviously alienating some within the colony. As a result, four new colonies were created. Roger Williams believed that the Puritans in Massachusetts were still too close to the ways of the Church of England, and he preached on the necessity of the total separation of church and state (this was obviously not practiced in Massachusetts Bay).

Williams was finally asked to leave Massachusetts, and he settled in Providence, Rhode Island. Thomas Hooker was another dissenter who was hounded out of the colony; he ended up settling near Hartford, Connecticut. Anne Hutchinson claimed to have received special revelations from God; as a result, she was invited to leave and founded Portsmouth near Narragansett Bay. Finally, John Davenport and other Puritans founded a colony in New Haven. In 1662 Hooker's colony combined with Davenport's to create the colony of Connecticut.

Maryland and the Carolinas

By 1640 the English kings began to create proprietary colonies, which were given to a single individual or groups of individuals and not to a stock company. Maryland was settled in 1632 by George Calvert and was designed as a refuge for English Catholics. North Carolina was very similar to Virginia, while planters in South Carolina used slaves from almost the very beginning. Plantation owners found both Native Americans and indentured servants to be good workers; their search for large numbers of workers inevitably made them turn to slavery as a possible solution.

The importation of slaves will become crucial to the economies of several southern colonies in the seventeenth and eighteenth centuries. It is estimated that over 20 million Africans were brought to the Americas before slavery was outlawed. By the late 1600s laws had been made in several southern colonies regulating the institution of slavery.

EFFECTS OF ENGLISH, FRENCH, AND BRITISH SETTLEMENT

Many effects, intended and otherwise, were created by European settlement in the Americas. Diseases and agricultural products introduced by Europeans dramatically changed the ecosystem of the Americas. Settlement fundamentally altered population patterns in Africa (with the loss of slaves) and in the Americas (with the loss of Native American populations). Settlements in America gradually introduced representative government and freedom of religion when these concepts were not popular in much of Europe.

CHAPTER REVIEW

Rapid Review Guide

To achieve the perfect 5, you should be able to explain that

- Economic difficulties in Europe, the desire to acquire raw materials, and religious tensions all caused Europeans to become interested in the Americas.

- Cortes, Pizarro, and other Spanish conquistadors entered much of Central America, South America, the southeastern section of North America, and the area now known as Florida, conquering the Aztecs, the Incas, and other Native American tribes. Guns, horses, and diseases brought from Europe all aided the Spanish in their efforts to defeat the native tribes.

- French settlers in Canada were less oppressive than the Spanish. Jesuit priests converted thousands of Native Americans to Christianity. French settlers became increasingly interested in fur trading.

- Puritans and other religious dissidents came to the Americas because they felt the Church of England was too close to Catholicism.

- The first English settlement in America was the Jamestown colony, founded in 1607. Tobacco became the main crop in Jamestown, and the first slaves arrived in 1619.

- A group of religious Separatists arrived in Plymouth, Massachusetts, in 1620. The first year of settlement was difficult for these Pilgrims, who had to rely on help from the Native Americans to survive.

- The Massachusetts Bay colony was established in 1629 by the Puritans. This colony was established as a "city upon a hill," where the will of God could be manifested. A limited representative government was established. Religious dissent was not tolerated in this colony: Dissenters were thrown out and founded new colonies in Rhode Island, Connecticut, and Portsmouth.

- The ecosystem of the Americas was tremendously altered by European settlement.

Time Line

10,000 B.C.E.: Migration of Asians to the Americas across the Bering Straight begins

1492: Voyage of Columbus to the Americas

1520–1530: Smallpox epidemic helps wipe out Native American tribes of South and Central America

1519: Cortes enters Mexico

1534–1535: French adventurers explore the St. Lawrence River

1541–1542: Spanish explorers travel through southwestern United States

1607: English settle in Jamestown

1619: Virginia establishes House of Burgesses (first colonial legislature)

1620: Plymouth colony founded

1629: Massachusetts Bay colony founded

1634: Maryland colony founded

1636: Roger Williams expelled from Massachusetts Bay colony and settles in Providence, Rhode Island; Connecticut founded by John Hooker

1642: City of Montreal founded by the French

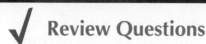

Review Questions

1. By the seventeenth century, Spain had

   A. monopolized New World trade
   B. reached the height of its power and began to decline
   C. failed in its effort to build a New World empire
   D. swept across northern Africa and seized control of the slave trade
   E. pioneered new routes to the East Indies

(Correct Answer: **B.** By this point England was catching up to the Spanish in terms of naval power, and Spanish power in the Americas had reached its highest point.)

2. Which of the following was *not* a religious dissenter in Massachusetts Bay?

   A. William Bradford
   B. Roger Williams
   C. John Davenport
   D. Anne Hutchinson
   E. Thomas Hooker

(Correct Answer: **A.** Bradford was a governor of Massachusetts Bay for twenty years; all of the others left for religious reasons and founded colonies elsewhere.)

3. A colony designated as a refuge for English Catholics was:

   A. North Carolina
   B. Pennsylvania
   C. South Carolina
   D. Maryland
   E. Virginia

(Correct Answer: **D.** George Calvert settled this colony in 1632 for exactly that purpose.)

4. English people came to the New World because of

   A. their dislike for the Church of England
   B. overcrowding in English cities
   C. economic opportunity
   D. A and C
   E. All of the above

(Correct Answer: **E.** The overcrowding of cities was an additional factor in convincing some English people to "try their lot" in the New World)

5. The very first Americans

   A. lived in South America
   B. were nomadic wanderers
   C. lived in permanent sites
   D. were subsistence farmers
   E. predated Spain's arrival in the New World by only two centuries

(Correct Answer: **B.** Almost all early Native American tribes were nomadic in nature.)

Chapter 4

The British Empire in America: Growth and Conflict (1650–1750)

THE IMPACT OF MERCANTILISM

The dominant economic philosophy of the period in Europe was **mercantilism.** This theory proclaimed that it was the duty of the government to strictly regulate a state's economy. Mercantilists believed that it was crucial for a state to import more than it exported, since the world's wealth was limited. The possession of colonies (so a nation wouldn't have to rely on other nations for raw materials), tariffs, and monopolies were other mercantilist tactics of the era. The American colonies were more than adequate from a mercantilist point of view, as they could provide crops such as tobacco and rice from the southern colonies and raw materials such as lumber from the colonies of the north.

Charles II came to the throne in England in 1660 and desired to increase British trade at the expense of its main trading rival, the Dutch. Charles influenced the British Parliament to pass the **Navigation Acts** of 1660 and 1663. These bills had great influence on colonial trade. These stated that certain products from the colonies, such as sugar, tobacco, and indigo, could only be shipped to England; in an effort to help British merchants, the acts required that all goods going from anywhere in Europe to the American colonies must pass through England first.

Resistance to the Navigation Acts came from both the Dutch and the American colonies. Three commercial wars between the Dutch and the British took place in the late 1600s (with one result being the ending of the Dutch monopoly over the West African slave trade). In New England, many wanted to be able to continue to trade with the Dutch, who offered them better prices for their goods. Edmund Randolph, the chief British customs official in Massachusetts Bay, noted that colonial officials welcomed non-British traders, and he called upon the British government to "reduce Massachusetts to obedience." In 1684 a British court ruled that

Massachusetts Bay colony had intentionally violated the Navigation Acts (as well as restricting the Church of England). The charter of the colony was thus declared invalid, and the colony was placed under direct British control. The **Dominion of New England** was created, which revoked the charters of all the colonies from New Jersey to Maine and placed immense powers in the hands of Sir Edmund Andros, the governor.

Similar feelings of resentment against the Navigation Acts developed in Virginia. The price of tobacco dropped sharply after 1663, with many landowners blaming Royal Governor Sir William Berkeley, who was thought to be profiting greatly from his position in Virginia. Some landowners joined in opposition to Berkeley under Nathaniel Bacon. In a dispute over policy toward Native Americans (specifically, how the government could protect farmers against Native American attacks) and how the colony would be governed, Bacon and his followers took control of the colony and burned the city of Jamestown. Some historians view this revolt as a rebellion of poor western farmers against the "eastern elite." The rebellion ended in October 1676 when Bacon and several of his followers died from dysentery. The results of Bacon's Rebellion were a limitation of the power of the royal governor by the Virginia gentry and an increase in the slave trade (some of Bacon's supporters were former indentured servants; the leaders of Virginia believed that African slaves would be much more docile.)

AFRICAN SLAVERY IN THE AMERICAS

For both political and economic reasons, African slavery became widely introduced in the Chesapeake colonies in the 1670s and 1680s. Cultivation of goods such as tobacco required a large number of workers, and by this point fewer and fewer English people were willing to come to Virginia as indentured servants (with increased prosperity, more workers were remaining in England, while others viewed the economic possibilities of the Middle Colonies as more appealing.) The Portuguese and other European powers had engaged in slave trading as early as the 1440s, and African slaves had been imported to the Spanish possessions in the Americas. The first Africans entered Virginia as workers in 1619; few legal differences existed between white and black workers at that time. By 1662 servitude for blacks in Virginia was a legal fact when it was stated that a child born to a mother who was a slave was also a slave.

The trading of slaves was a pivotal part of the **triangular trade system** that tied together the economies of North America, South America, the Caribbean, Africa, and Europe in the late seventeenth century. Under this system, finished products from Europe went to Africa and the Americas, while raw materials from various colonies went to Europe. The shipping of slaves from Africa to America became known as the **middle passage**, as it served as the foundation of the entire trading system.

Until the 1670s the financial risk of owning African slaves was too much for most Virginia plantation owners, who still could be guaranteed a supply of British indentured labor. Yet as that labor force eroded, the desire to own African slaves increased. This desire only expanded when the Dutch monopoly on the slave trade ended in 1682, drastically reducing the prices of slaves in British colonies. Many landowners in the region that could not afford slaves ended up moving westward.

The **middle passage** or journey of African slaves on European slave ships to the Americas is well documented. Disease and death were common on these ships for both the Africans kept chained under the decks and the European crews of the ships. It is estimated that almost 20 percent of all Africans who began the journey on one of these ships perished before reaching the Americas.

Until the 1730s most slaves in the region worked on small farms with two or three other slaves and the plantation owner. Under these conditions it was difficult to create a unique slave culture. However, slave cultures did slowly develop, combining elements of African, European, and local traditions. African religious traditions were sometimes combined with Christianity to create a unique religious culture. Slaves used various methods to demonstrate their hatred of the slave system that had been thrust on them. Many owners reported examples of broken tools, stolen supplies, and imagined illnesses.

Slaves were used in other colonies as well. The most oppressive conditions for slaves existed in South Carolina, where they were used to harvest rice. Overwork and mosquito-borne epidemics caused thousands of slaves to die an early death there.

Slave owners lived in fear of slave revolts, which occasionally did occur. The most famous slave uprising occurred near Charleston, South Carolina, in 1739 and was called the **Stono Rebellion**. Nearly 100 slaves took up arms and killed several plantation owners before they were killed or captured and executed. The effect of the rebellion was that slaves were treated more harshly than they had been before.

CONTINUED UNREST IN NEW ENGLAND

The New England colonies chafed under the harsh and arbitrary rule of Sir John Andros as governor. In 1688 they saw an opportunity to remove him. The **Glorious Revolution** in England removed James II from the throne and replaced him with William of Orange and Mary, who pledged their support to a parliamentary system. Andros was jailed in Massachusetts; colonists there wrote to the new monarchs pledging their loyalty to them and asking what form of government they should adopt. A Protestant revolt also took place in Catholic Maryland, while in New York a revolt put Jacob Leisler, a military officer, in charge.

The colonists soon discovered that William and Mary, like the Stuart monarchs that proceeded them, believed in firm control by Britain over colonial affairs. They sanctioned the rebellion in Maryland because of its religious overtones but ordered Jacob Leisler hung and again established Massachusetts as a royal colony with a governor appointed by the crown.

However, the authoritarian nature of the Dominion of New England ended, as representative political institutions at the local level were restored.

THE SALEM WITCH TRIALS

The Massachusetts colony underwent great economic and social change in the last half of the seventeenth century. Tensions developed between the Puritan ideal of small, tightly knit farming communities and the developing ideal of a colony based on trade and commerce, with less emphasis on strict Puritan beliefs. These tensions were largely responsible for the **Salem Witch Trials** of 1692.

Several women had been killed earlier in the century in Massachusetts for suspicion of witchcraft, but in 1692 a larger group of women were reported to display strange behavior. Observers testified many had strange fits and experienced "great distress." By the end of August over 100 people were jailed for suspicion of witchcraft; 19 people (18 of them women) had already been executed. The new royal governor to Massachusetts arrived and ended the trials, freeing those in prison. As stated previously, the trials demonstrated the social clashes existing in the colony; almost all of the accusers were members of the older farm communities, while the accused all were part of the newer "secular" class.

WARS IN EUROPE AND THEIR IMPACT ON THE COLONIES

Beginning in 1689 and continuing through much of the eighteenth century, England and France fought a series of wars to see which of them would be the dominant power of Western Europe. Various other countries also became involved in these wars in Europe; predictably, English and French colonists would also become involved. Both England and France also used Native American tribes as allies during various campaigns in the American continent.

The War of the League of Augsburg (known in American textbooks as **King William's War**) lasted from 1689 to 1697. During this war, troops from New England fought with allies from the Iroquois tribe against French soldiers, who were allied with the Algonquians. The French destroyed the British settlement in Schenectady, New York, while troops made up largely of residents of Massachusetts captured Port Royal (in present-day Nova Scotia). The Treaty of Ryswick ended this war, reaffirming prewar colonial boundaries and allowing the French to maintain control over half of Santo Domingo (now Haiti).

The War of the Spanish Succession (in American books called **Queen Anne's War**) took place between 1702 and 1713; in this war Spain was also allied with France.

Anticipating an attack by the Spanish from Florida, the British attacked first from South Carolina, burning the settlement at St. Augustine and then arming many Native Americans who had fled the near-slavelike working conditions in the Spanish missions. These Indians attacked the missions, as well as the Spanish settlement at Pensacola. Native Americans allied with the French attacked English settlements in Maine. In 1704 the Iroquois, also allied with the French, attacked Deerfield, Massachusetts, killing 48 settlers there and taking 112 into captivity.

Neither side could conclusively claim victory in several other battles that were to follow, but victories in Europe allowed the British to make sizable gains in the Treaty of Utrecht. In this treaty, France had to give the British Newfoundland, Acadia (Nova Scotia), territory along the Hudson Bay, as well as more access to the Great Lakes region.

THE GROWTH OF THE COLONIAL ASSEMBLIES

After these wars the British attempted to reform their control of the colonies in general but were unable to do that. American colonies existed in a variety of forms. Many were royal colonies, with governors appointed by the Crown; other colonies, such as Connecticut and Rhode Island, elected their own governors and other local officials. Colonies such as the Carolinas, Maryland, and Pennsylvania were **proprietorships**, with residents who owned property-electing assemblies and governors appointed by the proprietors themselves.

One disturbing development during this period for the British was the rise in the independence of **colonial assemblies**. In the 1720s the Massachusetts assembly resisted on three occasions instructions from the Crown to pay the royal governor a permanent salary; similar acts of resistance took place in other assemblies. These developments should not be seen as a move toward democracy in any way; assemblies were made up of members of the landowning elite in every colony. Nevertheless, popular opinion did begin to be expressed during New England town meetings and in political discussions throughout the colonies. Some colonial legislators perceived that the "power of the purse" could be a powerful tool against the British in the future.

THE ERA OF "SALUTARY NEGLECT"

British politics during the reigns of George I (1714–1727) and George II (1727–1760) helped to foster a desire for more self-government in the American colonies. During this period of "**salutary neglect**" British policies were most concerned with defending British territory at home and abroad and strengthening the British economy and trade. Strict control of political affairs in the colonies was not a priority in this era. Many officials appointed to positions in the Americas during this era were appointed because of political connections and not because of political skill. British politics during this era weakened the British political hold in the Americas.

The British did impose policies in this era that increased their economic control over the American colonies. Under the terms of the Navigation

Acts, all "finished products" owned by colonists had to be made in Great Britain. English officials passed additional regulations prohibiting the colonists from producing their own textiles (1699), hats (1732), and iron products (1750). However, the Navigation Acts allowed the colonies to own ships and to transport goods made in the colonies. Colonial ships carried on a lively trade with the French West Indies, importing sugar from there instead of from British colonies producing sugar in the Caribbean. In 1733 Parliament enacted the <u>Molasses Act</u>, which tightened British control over colonial trade. By 1750 Charles Townshend and others on the British Board of Trade were convinced that the colonies had far too much economic freedom, and they were determined to bring the era of salutary neglect to an end.

THE GREAT AWAKENING

A great religious revival, the <u>Great Awakening</u>, swept through the American colonies from the 1720s through the 1740s. Ministers of the movement claimed that local ministers were not devoted enough to God and practiced "cold" preaching. Preachers such as Jonathan Edwards preached of the pitiful condition of man and the terrors of hell that most will confront when they die. Entire congregations were stirred to greater religious devotion; thousands turned up to hear Anglican George Whitefield as he toured the colonies in 1740. Some congregations also split over the message and the tactics of the "Awakeners."

The Great Awakening had several major effects on the colonies. Yale, Harvard, Brown, Dartmouth, Princeton, and Rutgers were all founded to train ministers during this period, yet preachers without college degrees preaching during the Great Awakening claimed to "know God" as well; several historians claim that the movement introduced a sense of social equality to the colonies. By challenging the existing the religious establishment, the Great Awakening introduced a sense of social rebellion to colonial thought that became amplified in the ensuing years. In addition, some historians maintain that the debate and the questioning of religious authority that took place in the Great Awakening reinforced the idea that the questioning of political authority was also acceptable.

CHAPTER REVIEW

Rapid Review Guide

To achieve the perfect 5, you should be able to explain the following:

- The dominant economic theory of the era was mercantilism; British mercantilist measures such as the Navigation Acts created resentment in the American colonies.

- The importation of African slaves became increasingly important for the continued economic growth of several southern colonies.

- The Salem Witch Trials demonstrated the social conflict present in the American colonies.

- Eighteenth-century European wars between the British and the French spilled over to the Americas, with British and French colonists becoming involved.

- In the early eighteenth century, colonial assemblies became increasingly powerful and independent in several colonies, including Massachusetts.

- Even during the era of "salutary neglect," the British attempted to increase their economic control over the colonies.

- The religious revival called the Great Awakening caused some in the colonies to question many of the religious, social, and political foundations on which colonial life was based.

Time Line

1651: First of several Navigation Acts approved by British parliament
1676: Bacon's Rebellion takes place in Virginia
1682: Dutch monopoly on slave trade ends, greatly reducing the price of slaves coming to the Americas
1686: Creation of Dominion of New England
1688: Glorious Revolution in England; James II removed from the throne
1689: Beginning of the War of the League of Augsburg
1692: Witchcraft trials take place in Salem, Massachusetts
1702: Beginning of the War of the Spanish Succession
1733: Enactment of the Molasses Act
1739: Stono slave rebellion in South Carolina
1740: George Whitefield tours the American colonies—the high point of the Great Awakening

✓ Review Questions

1. The creation of the Dominion of New England

   A. increased democracy in the colonies
   B. increased the power of the governor of the area
   C. allowed New England colonies to discuss common grievances
   D. guaranteed direct control of the King over affairs in the New England colonies
   E. was largely a symbolic gesture

   (Correct Answer: **B.** This occurred after resistance in Massachusetts to the Navigation Acts, and it gave increased power to Sir Edmund Andros.)

2. A major effect of the Stono Rebellion was

   A. an increase in the number of slaves brought into the southern colonies
   B. increased fortifications around several southern cities
   C. an attempt by slave owners to lessen the horrors of the "middle passage"
   D. the passage of legislation in southern assemblies calling for mandatory capital punishment for escaped slaves
   E. harsher treatment of slaves in many parts of the south.

(Correct Answer: **E.** Many plantation owners were fearful of additional rebellions and felt that harsh treatment of slaves would prevent rebellious behavior.)

3. The growth of colonial assemblies alarmed the British for all of the following reasons *except:*

   A. At meetings of these assemblies anti-British feelings were expressed.
   B. Assemblies holding the "power of the purse" could ultimately undermine British control.
   C. The assemblies increased democratic tendencies in the colonies.
   D. The assemblies occasionally ignored or resisted instructions from Great Britain.
   E. Governors appointed in Britain had little control over these assemblies in most colonies.

(Correct Answer: **C.** These assemblies were in no way democratic, as in every colony they were dominated by the landowning elite.)

4. For the British, the major economic role of the American colonies was

   A. to produce manufactured goods the English did not want to produce
   B. to produce crops such as tobacco
   C. to provide food and materials for the other British colonies
   D. to produce raw materials such as lumber
   E. B and D above

(Correct Answer: **E.** The role of the colonies under mercantilism was to provide England with crops and raw materials.)

5. What changes in the slave system of the southern colonies began in the 1730s?

   A. The Dutch lost the monopoly on slave trading, thus increasing the number of slaves being brought into the Americas.
   B. Conditions during the "middle passage" began to slightly improve.
   C. Under pressure from religious leaders, slave conditions in South Carolina became less oppressive.
   D. More slaves began to live and work on larger plantations.
   E. A series of slave rebellions created much harsher treatment for slaves.

(Correct Answer: **D.** Before the 1730s, most slaves worked on small farms. The Dutch lost their monopoly on slave trading back in 1682. The Stono Rebellion was the first major slave rebellion and occurred in 1739.)

Chapter 5

Resistance, Rebellion, and Revolution (1750–1775)

PROBLEMS ON THE FRONTIER

An energetic traveler going west of the Appalachian Mountains in 1750 would discover a land inhabited by Native American tribes who had no desire to release their territory to colonial or European settlers. The Iroquois and other tribes of the region had traded and allied with both the English and the French, depending on who offered the best "deal" at the time.

Beginning in the 1740s, English and French interests in this region began to come into conflict. Land speculators from Virginia and other colonies began to acquire land in the Ohio Valley, and they tried to broker further treaties with Native Americans who resided there. French colonial officials viewed this with alarm, as their ultimate aim was to connect Canada and Louisiana with a series of forts and settlements through much of the same region.

In 1754 delegates from seven northern and middle colonies met at the **Albany Congress**, at which the colonies attempted to coordinate their policies concerning further westward settlement and concerning Native Americans. While the representatives couldn't agree on several main points, Governor Robert Dinwiddie of Virginia sent a young militia officer to attempt to stop the French construction of a fort at what is now the city of Pittsburgh. The young officer, George Washington, was defeated in battle there. Several Native American tribes, noting the incompetence of Washington and the colonial army, decided to cast their lot with the French. After hearing of this defeat in early 1756, the British sent a seasoned general, Edward Braddock, to stop French construction of Fort Duquesne. Braddock's army was routed by the French, and he was killed in the battle. When London heard of this, war was officially declared against the French. This was the beginning of the Seven Years War (in American textbooks called the **French and Indian War**).

ADDITIONAL CONFLICTS BETWEEN THE BRITISH AND THEIR COLONIAL "ALLIES"

The war went very badly for the British and the colonial Americans in 1756 and 1757. Much of New York was captured by the French, and even the western New England territories appeared to be in jeopardy. Other than the Iroquois, most Native American tribes sided with the French. The British finally put the war in the hands of William Pitt, who sent nearly 25,000 to the Americas to fight against the French. The British had had little luck in convincing the colonies to supply many men or much material to the war effort. To get the support of the colonies, Pitt agreed to reimburse them for expenses during the war and put the recruiting of troops totally in local hands (Pitt's willingness to incur large debts for Great Britain to finance the war effort should be noted). As a result, a colonial army of nearly 24,000 joined with the British army to battle the French. The French stronghold at Quebec was defeated in 1759, and Montreal was taken one year later.

The Treaty of Paris ending the French and Indian War effectively in 1763 ended French influence in the Americas. Most French territory in the New World was given to the British, who now controlled over half of the continent of North America. France also gave Spain (its ally in the war) the Louisiana territory west of the Mississippi River.

The American colonists and the British both shared a sense of victory in 1763, yet resentments between the two festered. The colonist resented the patronizing attitude that the British had toward them; in addition, many British soldiers had been quartered in the homes of colonists without compensation. Many colonial soldiers viewed with horror the harsh punishments given to British soldiers for trivial infractions. The British felt that the colonists never did their fair share in the war; they also noted that some colonists continued to trade with the French during the first two years of the war.

THE POLICIES OF GEORGE GRENVILLE

George II died in 1660 and was succeeded by his grandson, George III. George III never exhibited even average political skills and was more than willing to give his ministers (who he rapidly replaced) a large amount of political power. In 1763 he selected George Grenville as prime minister.

Grenville faced a difficult financial task. Great Britain had great debt, largely because of the lengthy wars that had taken place both on the continent and in the colonies. British citizens were already very heavily taxed. Grenville felt that one way to relieve the financial burden facing the Crown would be for the American colonists to pay a greater share for colonial administration. Grenville was convinced that Britain should be making more money than it was in the Americas; he was personally disturbed by the illegal trading carried out by colonists during the Seven Years War.

Grenville took measures to "reform" the trading relationship between Britain and the Americas. The **Currency Act** of 1764 made it illegal to print paper money in the colonies. Because of the lack of hard currency in the colonies, the impact of this bill was significant. The **Sugar Act** of the same year conceded that the colonies were importing large amounts of French molasses, but it increased the penalties for colonial smuggling and ensured that colonists would pay the British a duty for all molasses brought into the colonies. In the years after the French and Indian War, colonial economies were already suffering from depression; the Grenville Acts only served to make that depression worse.

Debate over the reforms of Grenville appeared in many colonial newspapers, with many editorials pondering the proper relationship between decisions made in Great Britain and the American colonies.

A SENSE OF CRISIS: THE STAMP ACT

The act proposed by Grenville that created the greatest furor in the colonies was the **Stamp Act**. This act would require a purchased stamp on virtually all printed material purchased in the colonies: Newspapers, wills, dice, official documents, and countless other written documents would require this stamp. This was controversial in the colonies because this was the first time the Parliament would directly tax the colonies; before this, all taxation was self-imposed. Grenville's purpose was two-fold: The Stamp Act would raise needed revenue and would uphold "the Right of Parliament to lay an internal Tax upon the Colonies."

For many colonists the final straw was the **Quartering Act**, which insisted that colonial governments provide food and accommodations for British troops stationed in the colonies.

In several colonies, such as Massachusetts, reaction against the Stamp Act was swift. During July of 1765 the **Sons of Liberty** was created in Boston, led by Samuel Adams. Demonstrations by this group forced the stamp agent in Massachusetts, Andrew Oliver, to resign. Similar outbursts in other colonies forced stamp agents to resign. Some politicians also began to speak in state assemblies against the act. Patrick Henry proclaimed in the Virginia Houses of Burgesses that the act demonstrated the tyranny of George III; several members of the assembly demanded that he be arrested for treason. James Otis from Massachusetts and Benjamin Franklin from Philadelphia both proposed that the colonists be directly represented in the British Parliament. In October of 1765, nine colonies met together at the **Stamp Act Congress**, where representatives reaffirmed the principal that taxation of the colonies be imposed only from within the colonies.

The Repeal of the Stamp Act

The uproar from the colonies may have helped the British Parliament to repeal the Stamp Act. However, the real pressure for repeal came from

British merchants, who feared the act would destroy the profits they made by trading with the colonies. Economic boycotts were threatened in numerous colonies. Lord Rockingham, the new prime minister, urged repeal of the bill not for philosophical but for economic and political reasons. Celebration occurred in many colonies when news of the repeal came from Britain. These celebrations became muted when word arrived that the Parliament had also passed a **Declaratory Act**, which stated that Parliament had the right to tax and pass legislation regarding the colonies "in all cases whatsoever."

MORE PROTEST: THE TOWNSHEND ACTS

In 1766 George III appointed the aging and infirm William Pitt as prime minister. Ill health made him unable to concentrate on his duties concerning the colonies. As a result, Charles Townshend, the **Chancellor of the Exchequer**, had a large hand in creating policy concerning the American colonies. Townshend decided to follow the policies of Grenville and try to extract more income for the government from colonial trade. In 1767 he proposed new duties on glass, paper, and tea. These **Townshend Acts** were different than previous duties on colonial trade; these were for goods produced in Britain. In addition, income from these acts would be used to pay the salaries of certain ranks of British officials in the colonies; colonial assemblies had always authorized these salaries. Townshend also created new courts in the colonies, the Admiralty courts, to try smuggling cases and ordered British soldiers to be stationed in major port cities (to hopefully prevent the protests that had followed the Stamp Act).

The opposition to the Townshend Acts in the colonies was immediate and sustained. Newspaper editorials and pamphlets renounced the acts with vehemence. John Dickinson from Pennsylvania best expressed the colonial position in his **Letters from a Farmer in Pennsylvania** (1767). Dickinson said that Parliament had the right to regulate colonial trade, but not to use that power to raise revenue. By this argument, only duties used to control trade or regulate the affairs of the empire were legal. Benjamin Franklin expressed a different view of the situation. Franklin stated that "Either Parliament has the power to make all laws for us, or Parliament has the power to make no laws for us; and I think the arguments for the latter more numerous and weighty than those of the former."

In early 1768 Samuel Adams in Massachusetts composed a document opposing the Townshend Acts, proclaiming that "taxation without representation is tyranny." The Massachusetts Assembly voted to approve this document and send it along to other colonial assemblies for approval. The royal governor stated that this **Circular Letter** was a form of sedition, and Parliament suggested that and state assembly passing such a resolution be dissolved. Yet similar resolutions were passed in five other colonies. Boycotts of British goods again took place to protest the Townshend Acts. In 1770 a new prime minister came into power in Britain, Lord North. North repealed all of the Townshend Acts except the tax on tea; the tea tax remained to remind the colonists that the British had the right to collect such taxes if they desired to.

CONTINUED TENSIONS IN MASSACHUSETTS

British customs officials and merchants in Massachusetts continued to clash over the smuggling of goods into Boston harbor. In 1768 officials seized a vessel belonging to a well-known smuggler, John Hancock; in the next several days several customs officials were roughed up. As a result, two regiments of regular British soldiers were assigned to the city. Tensions increased notably in the city; many local workers became incensed when, in their off-hours, British soldiers took jobs that had previously been held by Bostonians. Soldiers were taunted on a regular basis. On March 5, 1770, the event that became known as the **Boston Massacre** took place. A confrontation occurred, with laborers throwing snowballs filled with rocks at the soldiers. The soldiers, acting against orders, finally shot into the crowd, killing five men and wounding eight. Sam Adams and others made much of the "massacre," yet members of the **Sons of Liberty** opposed uncontrolled violence. Seven soldiers were later put on trial for the "massacre"; five were acquitted and two were branded on the thumb and then freed.

THE CALM BEFORE THE STORM: 1770–1773

There was an apparent calm in relations between the British and the colonies between 1770 and 1773. Import duties were collected on a regular basis. The tea tax was still in effect; some colonists boycotted British tea, but some drank it openly. Resistance again occurred first in Massachusetts. Samuel Adams established a **Committee of Correspondence** in Boston. Similar groups were created throughout Massachusetts, Virginia, and other colonies as well. These groups were designed to share information on British activities in the Americas, as well as to share details of demonstrations, protests, and so on. Some historians argue that these Committees of Correspondence were the first permanent machinery of protest in the colonies.

THE BOSTON TEA PARTY

The Boston Tea Party occurred because of an effort by the British government to save the near-bankrupt East India Tea Company. American boycotts and smuggled Dutch tea had hurt this company; they asked the government for permission to sell their tea directly to the American colonies without going through English merchants as middlemen. The old tax on tea would remain, but tea would now be cheaper to purchase for the colonists. Lord North and Parliament approved the passage of the **Tea Act** that would legalize these changes.

Colonial leaders were furious. Some pointed out that this measure reaffirmed that Parliament could tax the colonies; others feared a monopoly of the East India Company on all colonial trade. In the fall of 1773, crowds prevented tea from being unloaded in several port cities. Predictably, Boston was the city where resistance was the strongest. On December 16, 1773, in an event called the **Boston Tea Party**, 65 men dressed as Mohawk Indians boarded the tea ships and dumped nearly 350 chests of tea in the harbor.

THE INTOLERABLE ACTS

The British were extremely quick to act in punishing the colonists. The **Intolerable Acts** all took effect by May of 1774. The port of Boston was closed except for military ships and ships specifically permitted by British custom officials. The upper house of the Massachusetts Assembly would now be appointed by the king instead of being elected by the lower house. Town meetings could not be held without the governor's consent, and the Quartering Act was again put into effect. Many concerned citizens in other colonies feared that similar actions could easily occur elsewhere. As a result, several colonial legislatures suggested a meeting of representatives from all the colonies to discuss the situation in Massachusetts. The passage of the Quebec Act by the British further alarmed many colonial leaders. Among other things, this act increased the religious freedom of French Catholics. To many Protestants in the colonies, Catholicism was easily equated with the absolutist French monarchy of the eighteenth century.

THE FIRST CONTINENTAL CONGRESS

Fifty-six delegates from every colony except Georgia attended the Continental Congress in Philadelphia on September 5, 1774. Some of those present, such as Sam Adams, pushed for a total boycott of British goods; others proposed further negotiations with Parliament. John Adams worked out a compromise entitled the **Declaration of Rights and Grievances**, which stated that the colonists would not object to measures designed to regulate their external commerce. The colonies would, however, resist any measures that taxed them without their consent. The mood of the meeting was even clearer when the **Suffolk Resolves** were adopted. This act stated that colonies would continue to boycott English imports and approve the efforts of Massachusetts to operate a colonial government free from British control until the Intolerable Acts were rescinded. Colonies were also urged to raise and train militias of their own.

Before they adjourned, the Continental Congress sent a petition to George III requesting the repeal of all regulatory acts since 1763 and informing him of the continued boycott of British goods. Colonial leaders returned home, wondering what the response of George III to their petition would be.

CHAPTER REVIEW

Rapid Review Guide

To achieve the perfect 5, you should be able to explain the following:

- Tensions between the British and the French intensified in the 1740s when land speculators from the English colonies began to acquire land in the Ohio Valley.
- The Seven Years War (the French and Indian War in American textbooks) was between the English and colonial militias and the French; Native Americans fought on both sides.
- The defeat of the French in this war largely ended their influence in the Americas; after the war, the British attempted to make the colonies pay their fair share for the war effort.
- Parliamentary efforts during this era to produce money for Great Britain by imposing various taxes and duties on the colonies resulted in great unrest in the colonies.
- The impact of the Stamp Act on the colonies was great; as a result, nine colonies met at the 1765 Stamp Act Congress and the Sons of Liberty formed in Boston.
- Boston remained a center of opposition to British policy; the Boston Massacre in 1770 and the Boston Tea Party in 1773 helped to create resistance to the Crown in other colonies as well.
- The 1774 Intolerable Acts, which closed the port of Boston and curtailed freedom of speech in Massachusetts, outraged many in the colonies.
- The 1774 First Continental Congress passed a resolution that firmly stated the colonies would firmly resist measures that taxed them without their consent. At this meeting it was also decided that individual colonies should start to raise and train state militias.

Time Line

1754: Representatives of colonies meet at Albany Congress to coordinate further western settlement
1756: Beginning of Seven Years War
1763: Signing of Treaty of Paris ending Seven Years War
1764: Parliament approves Sugar Act, Currency Act
1765: Stamp Act approved by Parliament; Stamp Act Congress occurs and Sons of Liberty are formed, both in opposition to the Stamp Act
1766: Stamp Act repealed, but in Declaratory Act, Parliament affirms its right to tax the colonies
1767: Passage of the Townshend Acts

1770: Boston Massacre occurs

1773: Boston Tea Party takes place in December in opposition to the Tea Act

1774: Intolerable Acts adopted by Parliament

First Continental Congress held in Philadelphia

✓ Review Questions

1. William Pitt was able to convince the colonies to fight in the Seven Years War by

   A. convincing Native American tribes to attack colonial settlements in the Ohio valley
   B. threatening military reprisals by the British army
   C. threatening to make the colonists fight the French by themselves
   D. putting the recruiting of troops in the colonies totally in the hands of the colonies themselves
   E. paying colonial soldiers generous bonuses to fight against the French

(Correct Answer: **D.** Pitt put the recruiting of colonial troops totally in local hands and agreed to reimburse the colonies for all their expenses during the war.)

2. The Stamp Act created great fury in the colonies because

   A. it imposed massive duties on the colonies
   B. colonial legislatures had expressed opposition to it beforehand
   C. it was the first time Parliament had imposed a duty on the colonies
   D. it took badly needed revenue away from colonial legislatures
   E. this was the first time that Parliament imposed a direct tax on the colonies

(Correct Answer: **E.** All previous taxation of the colonies had been self-imposed.)

3. The statement "taxation without representation is tyranny" was first proclaimed by

   A. Benjamin Franklin
   B. John Hancock
   C. Samuel Adams
   D. John Dickinson
   E. Patrick Henry

(Correct Answer: **C.** This statement was first made by Adams in 1768 in an article he wrote opposing the Townshend Acts.)

4. After the Seven Years War, resentment between the British and the colonists existed for all of the following reasons *except*

   A. the British resented the fact that few colonists had actually helped them in the war against the French
   B. British soldiers had been quartered in colonial homes
   C. the British resented the fact that some colonists continued to trade with the French at the beginning of the war
   D. colonial militiamen felt the British exhibited a patronizing attitude toward them
   E. many colonial militiamen were appalled at the incredibly harsh discipline that British officers imposed on their soldiers

(Correct Answer: **A.** The colonies contributed nearly 24,000 men to the war effort—while the British contributed 25,000.)

5. Most delegates at the First Continental Congress of 1774

A. felt that there should be a total boycott of British goods by the colonies

B. felt that the colonies should firmly resist measures to tax them without their consent

C. felt that it was time to seriously consider military measures against the British

D. wanted the British to totally refrain from regulating trade to the colonies

E. proposed sending Benjamin Franklin and John Dickinson as representatives to the British parliament

(Correct Answer: **B.** Although some, including Sam Adams, wanted a boycott of all British goods, John Adams crafted a compromise that called for the colonies to oppose "taxation without representation.")

Chapter 6

The American Revolution and the New Nation (1775–1787)

THE AMERICAN REVOLUTION

Prelude to Revolution: Lexington and Concord: April, 1775

Events in the colonies had little effect on attitudes in Britain. George III and Lord North both still insisted that the colonies comply with edicts from England. What they failed to realize was that royal authority in the colonies was routinely being ignored. General Thomas Gage was the acting governor of Massachusetts, and in early 1775 he ordered the Massachusetts Assembly not to meet. They met anyway.

Gage also wanted to stop the growth of local militias. On April 19 he sent a group of regular British troops to Concord to seize colonial arms stored there and to arrest any "rebel" leaders that could be found. As you learned in second grade, Paul Revere and other messengers rode out from Boston to warn the countryside of the advance of the British soldiers. At dawn on April 19 several hundred British soldiers ran into 75 colonial militiamen on the town green in **Lexington**. The British ordered the colonists to disperse; in the confusion, shots rang out, with 8 colonists killed and 10 wounded.

The British marched on to **Concord**, where a larger contingent of militiamen awaited them. The British destroyed military stores and food supplies and were ready to return to Boston when the colonists opened fire, with three British soldiers killed and nine wounded. The British were attacked at they retreated to Lexington; they lost 273 men, compared to 95 colonial militiamen killed. At Lexington the British were saved by the arrival of reinforcements.

Several weeks later Ethan Allen and his Green Mountain Boys captured Fort Ticonderoga from the British. Cannons from the fort were dragged to

Boston, where they would be a decisive factor in forcing the British to leave Boston harbor in March 1776.

THE SECOND CONTINENTAL CONGRESS

The purpose of the **Second Continental Congress**, which met in Philadelphia in May of 1775, was clear: to get the American colonies ready for war. It authorized the printing of paper money to buy supplies for the war, established a committee to supervise foreign relations with other countries, and created a Continental Army. George Washington was appointed commander in chief of this new army. Washington was chosen because of his temperament, because of his experiences in the French and Indian Wars, and because he was *not* from Massachusetts, considered by George III the place where the "rabble" were.

The Congress made one final gesture for peace when moderates drafted, and the Congress approved, the sending of the "Olive Branch Petition" to George III. This document, approved on July 5, 1775, asked the king to formulate a "happy and permanent reconciliation." The fact that the king refused to even receive the document strengthened the hand of political radicals throughout the colonies.

The Impact of *Common Sense*

The impact of Thomas Paine's **_Common Sense_** on colonial thought was immense. Paine was a printer and had only been in the colonies for two years when his pamphlet was published in January of 1776. Virtually every educated person in the colonies read this document (within three months 120,000 copies were sold). Paine proclaimed that "monarchy and hereditary succession have laid the world in blood and ashes" and called George III a "royal brute." Paine attacked the entire system of monarchy and empire, expressing confidence that the colonies would flourish once they were removed from British control. Many saw in Paine's document very sensible reasons why the Americas should break from Britain. When discussing the document, one New York **loyalist** bitterly complained that "the unthinking multitude are mad for it . . . ."

THE DECLARATION OF INDEPENDENCE

On June 7, 1776, Henry Lee of Virginia made a motion at the meeting of the Second Continental Congress in Philadelphia. His motion proposed that American colonies should be considered independent states, that foreign relations should begin with other countries, and that a confederate form of government be prepared for future discussion by the colonies. It was decided that the motion would be voted on July 1 (giving delegates time to win the resistant middle colonies over). In the meantime, one committee worked on a potential constitution, while another was appointed to write a declaration of independence. This committee gave the job of writing the first draft to Thomas Jefferson. Jefferson was a perfect choice: He was a student of the thinkers of the **Enlightenment** and other thinkers of the era.

Jefferson's argument maintained that men had certainly "unalienable rights," which included "Life, Liberty, and the pursuit of Happiness." Jefferson stated that when a government "becomes destructive of these ends" those who live under it can revolt against it and create a government that gets its "just powers from the consent of the governed." Jefferson also listed many things the British had done that were oppressive to the colonies. Unlike others who had criticized certain ministers or Parliament, Jefferson personally blamed George III for many of these misdeeds. This document was formally approved on July 2, 1776; this approval was formally announced on July 4.

THE OUTBREAK OF THE REVOLUTION: DIVISIONS IN THE COLONIES

The celebrations surrounding the announcement of the Declaration of Independence took place in every colony, but not every citizen living in the Americas took part. Many loyalists were members of the colonial economic elite and feared the repercussions on their pocketbooks of a break with Great Britain. Other loyalists saw the legitimacy of Britain's control over the colonies; some loyalists were also very practical men, who predicted the easy defeat of the colonies by the seemingly immense British army.

Blacks in America greeted the Declaration of Independence with enthusiasm. Many free blacks saw the a possible revolution as a chance to improve their position; slaves saw the possibilities of freedom from slavery (during the war some slaves managed to escape their masters, and a few even fought on the side of the British). During the fighting, British troops freed slaves in Georgia and South Carolina. In the North, some slaves fought in colonial militias, winning their freedom through military service. The British courted Native American tribes, but their determination to definitively help the British in battle was never strong.

STRATEGIES OF THE AMERICAN REVOLUTION

It is easy to see how the British thought that they would be able to defeat the colonists quickly and decisively. Britain had a strong navy, one of the finest armies of Europe, and considerable support from approximately 150,000 loyalists in the colonies. In addition, in the first years of the war, the Continental Army suffered from poor discipline, frequent desertions, a lack of supplies and money, and a virtually nonexistent navy. However, an obviously long supply line (four to six weeks by ship), divided British policies in London, and a army used to fighting the more "formal" European type of war would end up hindering British efforts. The leadership of George Washington, the willingness to use defensive tactics and only attack when needed, and the fact that they were fighting on home territory all helped aid the colonial military efforts. Washington felt that a lengthy war would assist the colonists, since they were fighting on home ground.

In May of 1775 a bloody battle had taken place at **Bunker Hill** in Boston. The colonists were defeated, but at the expense of nearly 1,000 British dead or wounded.

WASHINGTON AS COMMANDER

The British approach under General William Howe was to slowly move his army through the colonies, using the superior numbers of the British army to wear the colonists down. However, from the beginning things did not go as planned for the British. In March 1776, the British were forced to evacuate Boston. The British then went to New York, which they wanted to turn into one of their major military headquarters (a large number of loyalists lived there). Washington and his troops attempted to dislodge the British from New York in late August of 1776; Washington's army was routed and chased back into Pennsylvania.

During November and December of 1776, Washington's army faced daily desertions and poor morale. On Christmas night Washington boldly led the **Battle of Trenton** against the **Hessian** allies of the British, defeating them. On January 3 Washington defeated a small British regiment at Princeton. These victories bolstered the morale of the colonial army greatly.

Another tremendous advantage for the colonists were the arms shipments from the French that they began receiving in late 1776. French aid for the colonies did not come from any great trust that developed between the two sides; for over a century, France and Britain had been bitter rivals, and the French saw the American Revolution as another situation that they could exploit for their gain against the British. Massive British naval superiority in the Americans was at least partially counterbalanced by the entry of the French navy into the war.

The "British Blunder" of 1777

The British decided on a strategy to strike a decisive blow against the colonists in 1777. Three separate British armies were to converge on Albany, New York, and cut off New England from the rest of the colonies. The British effort is called a blunder because of the poor execution of military plans that might have been effective. An army led by General Howe headed toward Philadelphia; for obvious strategic reasons, it should have been heading toward Albany. Howe was intent on taking on Washington's army in Philadelphia and decisively defeating it. An army under "Gentleman Johnny" Burgoyne carried much heavy equipment that could be carried in preparation for European battles but not through the forests of North America. On October 17, 1777, Burgoyne was forced to surrender at Saratoga. Some military historians claim this defeat was the beginning of the end for the British. The colonial victory convinced the French to send troops to aid the war effort.

Women became increasingly important to the war effort of the colonies. Women were prominent in the boycott of British goods, provided support services for the Continental Army, spied on British troops, and ran numerous households when the "man of the house" was off fighting the British. In a March 1776 letter to her husband John, Abigail Adams reminded him to "Remember the Ladies . . . Do not put such unlimited power in the hands of the Husbands."

THE WAR MOVES TO THE SOUTH

After their defeat at Saratoga, the British abandoned their strategy of fighting in New York and New England and decided to concentrate their efforts in the Southern colonies, where they imagined more loyalists to live. Despite their victory at Saratoga, the winter of 1777–1778 was the low point for the Continental Army. The British camped for the winter in Philadelphia, while Washington's army stayed at **Valley Forge**. Cold weather, malnutrition, and desertion horribly hurt the army. Morale improved when daily drilling began under the leadership of Baron von Steuben, a Prussian who had volunteered to help the colonists. As a result, the Continental Army that emerged in the spring was a much tougher and more disciplined unit.

Nevertheless, at first the British southern strategy was successful. By the summer of 1780, the British captured Georgia and South Carolina. Desertions continued, and General Benedict Arnold went over to the British side.

Things soon turned against the British. A Virginia army under George Rogers Clark defeated a British force and their Native American allies at Vincennes, Indiana, securing the Ohio River region for the colonies. By the summer of 1781, French army forces joined the Continental Army as two regiments marched from New York to Virginia. The British southern campaign, now headed by General Cornwallis, was constantly hampered by attacks by colonial guerrilla bands, led by Francis Marion and other rebel leaders.

Cornwallis decided to abandon the southern strategy and went into Virginia, where he was ordered to take up a defensive position at **Yorktown**. Once the British troops began to dig in, they were cut off by a combination of French and continental forces. Cornwallis hoped to escape by sea, but ships of the French navy occupied Chesapeake Bay. For three weeks Cornwallis tried to break the siege; on October 17, 1781, he finally surrendered. Fighting continued in some areas, but on March 4, 1782, Parliament voted to end the British military efforts in the former colonies.

THE TREATY OF PARIS

British, French, Spanish (also allies with the colonists in the war), and American diplomats gathered in Paris in 1783 to make the treaty ending the war. The British and French diplomats were initially not impressed with the diplomatic efforts of the Americans, but soon the American team of John Jay, Benjamin Franklin, and John Adams demonstrated shrewd diplomatic skills. The Americans negotiated separately with the British, and on September 3, 1783, the **Treaty of Paris** was signed. (Please note that this is a different Treaty of Paris from the one ending the French and Indian War.) By this treaty Great Britain formally recognized American independence. Britain held on to Canada, but all of the territory they had received from France after the French and Indian War (territory between the Appalachian Mountains and the Mississippi River) was given over to the Americans. The American diplomats also negotiated for fishing rights off the coasts of Newfoundland and Nova Scotia. The British insisted on, and received, promises that British merchants would be free to recover prewar debts and that loyalists would be treated as equal citizens and would be able to recover property seized from them during the war. (As might be expected, many loyalists were leaving the Americas during this period.)

THE ESTABLISHMENT OF GOVERNMENTAL STRUCTURES IN THE NEW NATION

The Drafting of State Constitutions

By the end of 1777, 10 new state constitutions had been written. Written into these constitutions were safeguards to prevent the evils that Americans had seen in the colonial governments established by the British. The governor was the most oppressive figure in many colonies; as a result, many new constitutions gave limited power to the governor, who was usually elected by the state assembly. All states except Pennsylvania and Vermont adopted a **bicameral legislature,** with much power usually given to the upper house. Most states also lowered the property qualifications for voting, thus allowing people to vote who had not voted before the Revolutionary War. Many historians comment that writers of these constitutions were making a conscious attempt to broaden the base of American government. Most state constitutions also included some form of a bill of rights.

THE ARTICLES OF CONFEDERATION

In the fall of 1777, the Continental Congress sent a proposed constitution out to the individual states for ratification. This document, called the

Articles of Confederation, intentionally created a very weak national government.

The main organ of government was a **unicameral legislature**, in which each state would have one vote. Executive authority was given to a Committee of Thirteen, with one representative from each state. For both amendment and ratification, the unanimous consent of all 13 state legislatures was required.

The national government was given the power to conduct foreign relations, mediate disputes between states, and borrow money. The weakness of the national government was shown by the fact that it could not levy taxes, regulate commerce, or raise an army. Because of disputes over land claims in the West, all 13 states didn't ratify the Articles of Confederation until 1781.

Economic Distress

Financial problems plagued the new nation in the years immediately after the war. Many merchants had overextended themselves by importing foreign goods after the war. Large numbers of Revolutionary War veterans had never been paid for their service. The national government had large war debts. By the terms of the Articles of Confederation, the national government could not tax, so the national government began to print a large amount of paper money. These bills, called "Continentals," were soon made worthless by inflation. Proposals for the national government to impose import tariffs came three times, and all three times they were defeated. Loans from foreign countries, especially France, propped up the national government during this period.

THE NORTHWEST ORDINANCES

The sale of lands in the West was one way that the national government *could* make money, and westward settlement was encouraged. By 1790 nearly 110,000 settlers were living in Kentucky and Tennessee, despite the threat of Native American attack. The **Northwest Ordinances** of 1784, 1785, and 1787 regulated the sale of lands in the Northwest Territory and established a plan to give these settled territories statehood. The 1784 Ordinance provided governmental structures for the territories and a system by which a territory could become a state. The Ordinance of 1785 spelled out the terms for the orderly sale of land in the Northwest Territory. The Ordinance of 1787 stated that any territory with 60,000 white males could apply for statehood, provided a bill of rights for settlers, and prohibited slavery north of the Ohio River. Controversy over whether slavery should be allowed in these territories was a foreshadowing of the bitter conflicts that would follow on the issue of slavery in newly acquired American territories.

SHAY'S REBELLION

Like farmers in other parts of colonies, farmers in western Massachusetts were in desperate shape in the years after the Revolution. Many owed large amounts to creditors, inflation further weakened their economic position, and in 1786 the Massachusetts Assembly raised taxes. Farmers took up arms, closing government buildings and freeing farmers from debtor's prisons. This rebellion was called Shay's Rebellion, after one of its leaders, war veteran Daniel Shays. The rebellion spread throughout Massachusetts and began to gain supporters in other New England states. The rebellion was put down by an army paid for by citizens of Boston and by a lowering of taxes. To many, Shay's Rebellion demonstrated that stronger state and national governments were needed to maintain order.

CHAPTER REVIEW

Rapid Review Guide

To achieve the perfect 5, you should be able to explain the following:

- The first armed resistance to the British army occurred at Lexington and Concord.
- The Second Continental Congress began to prepare the American colonies for war against the British, but by passing the Olive Branch Petition, they tried to accommodate colonial interests with those of the Crown.
- The impact of the message presented in *Common Sense* by Thomas Paine was widespread throughout the colonies.
- Many loyalists lived in the colonies at the outbreak of the Revolutionary War; many were members of the economic elite.
- Blacks and women played a large role in the war effort of the colonies.
- The defensive tactics of George Washington as leader of the continental forces proved decisive, since a longer war was disadvantageous to the British army.
- French assistance to the continental war effort proved invaluable; the French navy proved to be especially critical as the war progressed.
- The Treaty of Paris ended the Revolutionary War. In this treaty, American independence was recognized by the British and large amounts of territory west of the Appalachian became American territory.
- The Articles of Confederation created a weak national government, partially to avoid replicating the "tyranny" of the Crown in England.
- To many colonial observers, Shay's Rebellion demonstrated that a stronger national government was needed.

Time Line

1775: Battles of Lexington and Concord
Meeting of Second Continental Congress
1776: *Common Sense* published by Thomas Paine
Declaration of Independence approved
Surrender of British forces of General Burgoyne at Saratoga
1777: State constitutions written in 10 former colonies
1777–1778: Continental Army encamped for the winter at
Valley Forge
1778: French begin to assist American war efforts
1781: Cornwallis surrenders at Yorktown
Articles of Confederation ratified
1783: Signing of the Treaty of Paris
1786–1787: Shay's Rebellion in Massachusetts
1787: Northwest Ordinance establishes regulations for settlement of
territories west of the Appalachian Mountains

✓ Review Questions

1. The purpose of the Olive Branch petition was to

   A. rally colonial support for war against Great Britain
   B. petition the king for redress of economic grievances suffered by the colonies
   C. ask the king to craft a solution to end the tensions between Great Britain and the colonies
   D. request formal support of each colony for the formulation of the Second Continental Congress
   E. ask the king to grant independence to the colonies

(Correct Answer: **C.** Although the Second Continental Congress began to prepare the colonies for war against Great Britain, the delegates also voted to send this petition to George III, asking him to create harmony between Great Britain and the colonies.)

2. At the beginning of the Revolutionary War, the British were extremely confident of victory because all of the following reasons *except*

   A. they had outstanding generals that would be commanding British forces in the Americas
   B. there were many loyalists throughout the American colonies
   C. the Continental Army suffered from poor discipline
   D. the British had an outstanding navy
   E. the Continental Army was continually lacking in supplies

(Correct Answer: **A.** Several of the main generals commanding British troops in the Revolutionary War proved early on to be quite ordinary in tactical and leadership skills.)

3. All of the following were contained in the Treaty of Paris of 1783 *except*

   A. Americans got fishing rights off the coast of Newfoundland
   B. territory west of the Appalachian Mountains was ceded to the Americans

C. American independence was recognized by Great Britain
D. Quebec and the area immediately surrounding it was ceded to the Americans
E. former loyalists in the colonies could retrieve property seized from them during the Revolutionary War

(Correct Answer: **D.** None of the British territory in Canada was taken from them as a result of the treaty.)

4. Women were important in the war effort because they

   A. provided much of the financial backing for the colonial cause
   B. provided several delegates to the Second Continental Congress
   C. wrote influential articles in colonial newspapers urging the colonies to resist the British
   D. provided clothing and blankets for the frozen troops at Valley Forge
   E. maintained economic stability in the colonies by managing households across the colonies while men were off fighting the British

(Correct Answer: **E.** Although women assisted the war effort in many ways, they made an important contribution by managing estates and farms while their husbands were serving in the colonial militias or in the Continental Army.)

5. The weakness of the national government created by the Articles of Confederation was demonstrated by the fact that it was *not* given the power to

   A. mediate disputes between states
   B. raise an army
   C. conduct foreign relations
   D. borrow money
   E. print money

(Correct Answer: **B.** The national government was not given the power to issue taxes, regulate commerce, or raise an army.)

Chapter 7

The Establishment of New Political Systems (1787–1800)

DESIRES FOR A STRONGER CENTRAL GOVERNMENT

Many Americans viewed the flaws of the national government established by the Articles of Confederation with dismay. As Alexander Hamilton stated, the American Revolution had taught those living in the former colonies to think "continentally"; yet the government in existence did not foster continental thought or action. To many, a stronger national government was a necessity.

In 1787 delegates from the 13 states went to Philadelphia to amend the Articles of Confederation. Many of the great men of the age were present at this meeting, including Alexander Hamilton, George Washington, James Madison, and Benjamin Franklin (John Adams and Thomas Jefferson were both in Europe during this convention). Debates quickly turned away from reforming the Articles of Confederation to creating a new national government. Most delegates believed that the central government had to be much stronger, with the ability to raise an army, collect taxes, and regulate commerce.

However, some delegates at the convention had doubts about how strong a new central government should actually be. They feared that too much power might fall into the hands of a small group, who would use it to their own advantage. In addition, small states and large states had very different ideas about how representation in a new national legislature should be determined. Smaller states favored the model provided by the Articles of Confederation with one vote per state; larger states proposed that population should determine representation. In addition, Southern and Northern states began to view each other suspiciously. Debates also took place over the future relationship of the national government to the various state governments.

GOVERNMENT UNDER THE NEW CONSTITUTION

Virginia plantation owner Edmund Randolph presented the **Virginia Plan**, which proposed a bicameral legislature with the number of representatives in each house determined by **proportional representation**. The guiding force behind this plan was really James Madison, a 36-year-old scholar and member of the Virginia legislature. Madison also proposed a structure of three branches of government: judicial, legislative, and executive. The importance of the contributions of James Madison in the creation of the Constitution cannot be overemphasized; by proposing branches of government, Madison dispelled the fears held by many critics that in the new government too much power would be placed in the hands of a small number of leaders.

Smaller states, while favoring a strong central government, were opposed to Madison's concept of a national legislature, fearing it would be dominated by the larger states. Smaller states supported the **New Jersey Plan**, which proposed a unicameral legislature where every state would receive one vote. This plan was equally unpopular with the larger states. Delegates from Connecticut finally proposed the plan that was ultimately adopted, the **Great Compromise**. This plan included an upper house, called the Senate, which would have two representatives per state, and a lower house, the House of Representatives, whose members would be elected by proportional representation.

Many representatives remained skeptical of a national government with massive powers. To diminish these fears, it was voted that the chief executive of the national government would be elected by an **Electoral College**, membership to which would be chosen by individual states. In addition, senators would be elected by state legislatures and not by the voters.

THE ISSUE OF SLAVERY

The issue of slavery was discussed several times during the deliberations of the Convention. It was decided that the new national government could not regulate slavery for 20 years. Much debate took place over how slaves should be counted when determining representation for states in the House of Representatives; slave states wanted to count the slaves in their total populations. This issue was resolved by the **Three-Fifths Compromise**, which stated that three-fifths of a state's slave population would be counted when determining representation in the House of Representatives. Southern states applauded the section of the Constitution promising national aid to any state threatened with "domestic violence"; Southern politicians assumed that this meant that federal troops would be utilized to help dispel any future slave revolts.

RATIFICATION OF THE CONSTITUTION

The writers of the new document wanted it to be approved by **ratifying conventions** that would be held in each state. Supporters of the new Constitution began to call themselves **Federalists**, a term used at the time for a supporter of strong *national* government. Federalists had faith that the elites that would come to dominate both federal and state governments would act in the interest of the entire nation. Those opposed to the new, stronger national government were soon called **Antifederalists**. Antifederalists sometimes equated the potential tyranny they saw in the new government with the tyranny that had been practiced by British monarchs. Antifederalists felt that the best protection against the tyranny of a strong central government would be the power of the individual states. In the end, they said that the major problem was that the new government was not based on republican principles and, without a Bill of Rights, was not interested in individual rights. After especially tough fights in New York, Virginia, and Massachusetts, the new Constitution was finally passed by all states (with New York being last) on July 26, 1788.

THE PRESIDENCY OF GEORGE WASHINGTON

Although he did not seek the presidency, the national reputation of George Washington made him the most logical choice to be the first chief executive of the United States of America. For at least the first term of Washington's administration, the future of the United States remained uncertain. Washington felt that it was crucial to establish respect for the office of President of the United States. Washington believed it was his job to administer the laws and not to make them; he almost never made legislative proposals to the Congress.

THE BILL OF RIGHTS

When the Constitution was being written, James Madison opposed including a bill of rights, fearing that such a document might actually limit the rights of citizens. By 1791, he saw the wisdom of such a document, and proposed 12 amendments to the Constitution. Antifederalists unanimously supported the addition of a bill of rights; they felt these would be added protections against the tyranny of the federal government. By the end of year, 10 amendments had been ratified by the individual states. The **Bill of Rights** contains the basic protections that Americans hold dear today; politically it quieted the Antifederalists and their fears of authoritarian government. The Bill of Rights guaranteed the right of free speech, ensured freedom of worship, gave citizens the right to bear arms, forbid the quartering of troops in private homes, and said that warrants were needed before searches took place. In addition, persons could not be forced to testify against themselves, citizens were guaranteed a trial by jury, "due process of law" was guaranteed, and "cruel and unusual punishments" were outlawed. The Ninth Amendment stated that these were not the only rights that Americans had, while the Tenth stated that any powers not specifically given to the federal government belonged to the states. Some historians point out that the basis of the entire American political system can be found in these 10 amendments.

COMPETING VISIONS: ALEXANDER HAMILTON AND THOMAS JEFFERSON

Two of the most brilliant men in the Washington administration were Secretary of State Thomas Jefferson and Secretary of the Treasury Alexander Hamilton. Hamilton was a huge admirer of the British economic system and wanted to turn America, which was still largely agrarian, into a manufacturing society like Britain. Hamilton wanted to institute strong **mercantilist** policies and proposed economic union with Great Britain. Hamilton believed that a strong national government was necessary for economic growth and believed in a broad interpretation of the Constitution. By this interpretation, the federal government had many powers not specifically mentioned in the Constitution and was only denied those powers specifically given to the states.

Jefferson (supported by James Madison) proposed a radically different view of America. He proposed an America that would remain largely agricultural, with industry serving only as "a handmaiden to agriculture." While Hamilton supported the mercantilist policy of high tariffs on foreign goods, Jefferson proposed a system of **free trade** (which would keep prices low). Jefferson came to be influenced by the events of the French Revolution and was fearful of the power of the federal government (emphasizing the importance of state power instead). Jefferson also favored a strict interpretation of the Constitution; by this interpretation the federal government only had the powers it was specifically given in the Constitution.

From these differences emerged the two-party system in the United States. Hamilton and his supporters called themselves **Federalists**; mercantilism would impel them to propose a strong government hand in economic affairs. Jefferson and his followers were called **Republicans**; as stated previously, they favored **laissez-faire economic principles** and the continued vision of America as a largely agricultural nation. The plans of Hamilton were most popular in the commercial cities of the Northeast and the port cities of the South, while the Republican plan was most popular in the Western and Southern sections of the country.

The Plan of Alexander Hamilton

Determined to turn the United States into a manufacturing power, Hamilton began a gigantic economic reform of America. In his **"Report on the Public Credit"** Hamilton proposed that the United States had the obligation to redeem in full all notes that had been issued by the government established by the Articles of Confederation. In addition, he proposed that the federal government take over all of the debts of the individual states. Hamilton also proposed the chartering of a **national bank**, which could provide loans to developing industries. Hamilton proposed that the federal government use subsidies and tax incentives to spur industrial growth. Hamilton proposed that these measures could be paid for largely by high tariffs on foreign imports.

Jefferson and Madison opposed these plans on both practical and philosophical grounds. They maintained that the commercial elite would be the ones to benefit from these programs, largely at the expense of the farmer. Most of Hamilton's programs were adopted, although the plan to increase industrial growth was not. Hamilton's economic vision provided a system of public credit and a steady stream of government revenue through tariffs.

THE FRENCH REVOLUTION

The French Revolution broke out as George Washington was taking over as president in 1789. By 1793 a continent-wide war pitted revolutionary France against most of Europe. Within months Washington issued a Declaration of Neutrality, which allowed American merchants to prosper by trading with both sides. Many Americans sided with the democratic principles that the Revolution appeared to be based on; **Democratic-Republican clubs** in many cities carefully followed events in France. Many of the people supporting the Revolution also supported Jefferson and his republican ideals in America. The entire Revolution and especially the Terror appalled other Americans; many of these men supported federalism in the United States.

Pennsylvania farmers who supported the **Whiskey Rebellion** of 1794 were inspired by the French Revolution (they actually carried signs proclaiming "Liberty, Equality, and Fraternity"). They opposed a tax Alexander Hamilton had placed on distilled alcohol, which reduced the profits on the whiskey that they produced and sold. The tax was necessary because the federal government needed more money; Hamilton's plan of having the federal government assume certain debts of state governments had recently been instituted. Hamilton demonstrated his political skill by taxing whiskey; the grain from which it was made came from Western farmers, most of whom supported Jefferson. Washington raised an army and put the whiskey revolt down; by the time the army was ready to fight, the rebellion had largely ended.

FOREIGN POLICY AND JAY'S TREATY

The war between France and the rest of Europe continued. By 1794 British officials became concerned that the Americans were trading mostly with the French West Indies during their period of "neutrality." The British began to search, and then to seize, American merchants ships, many times imploring that the crews of these ships join the British navy. Washington sent Chief Justice John Jay to negotiate with the British, and the results were mixed at best. Jay was unable to get the British to promise not to undermine American freedom of the seas, and he was forced to comply with the British demand that they had the right to remove French products and materials from American ships. The British did agree to leave some of the forts they still occupied in the Northwest Territory.

Bitter political battles took place in America over **Jay's Treaty**. On the other hand, the treaty negotiated by Thomas Pinckney with Spain was extremely popular; by this treaty the United States gained navigating rights along the Mississippi River. The transport of farm produce from the South and the West got to markets much quicker as a result of this treaty.

WASHINGTON'S FAREWELL ADDRESS

Increased political battles between Federalists and Republicans convinced George Washington not to stand for a third term as president. In his Farewell Address, Washington spoke against party politics, asking political leaders to work together and not against each other. He also warned America not to "interweave our destiny with any part of Europe" and stated that America should not enter into alliances that would cause them to get involved in foreign wars. Political leaders for the next 200 years would invoke the words of Washington when opposing American plans to ally with foreign nations.

THE PRESIDENCY OF JOHN ADAMS

John Adams had been Washington's vice president, was also a Federalist, and served one term as president (1796 to 1800). Adams was opposed in the 1796 election by Thomas Jefferson, running as a Republican. Adams won, but Jefferson came in second in the Electoral College, thus putting candidates of two different parties in as president and vice president.

Despite recent biographies that suggest otherwise, Adams had four largely unsuccessful years in office. Adams spent a great deal of time back home in Quincy, Massachusetts, thus allowing his Cabinet members to make major decisions with little input from the president.

Problems with France

The French were unhappy with a series of American laws and policies that economically favored the British at their expense. For many in France, Jay's Treaty was the last straw. The French impounded several American ships going to England and announced that American sailors doing duty on British ships would be treated as "pirates." A three-member diplomatic delegation went to Paris in 1798 to negotiate with the French. French Minister Talleyrand, through third and fourth parties, informed the Americans that a bribe would have to be paid before negotiations could begin. The American diplomats refused to pay, and word of this caused outrage at home. This affair came to be known as the "XYZ Affair," named for the unnamed "assistants" of Talleyrand who made the bribe offer.

Adams announced the buildup of the American navy in preparation for a potential war against France. Trading with France was temporarily suspended, and American ships were authorized to attack French ships at sea. In 1800 the French and the Americans met again (Napoleon was now in power in France) and tensions decreased. The Convention of 1800 gave the United States compensation for ships that had been seized by the French. In addition, the United States was freed from its diplomatic entanglements with the French.

THE ALIEN AND SEDITION ACTS

During the undeclared war against France, the policies of Adams were attacked by some in the press; several pamphlets written by French emigrants were especially vindictive. As a result, Adams and his administration supported several measures that would threaten the rights of Americans. The **Alien Act** gave the president the right to deport any immigrant who was felt to be "dangerous to the peace and safety of the United States." The **Sedition Act** stated that the administration could prohibit any attacks on the president or Congress that were deemed to be "malicious." Twenty Republican journalists and politicians were arrested under the Sedition Act, with some going to jail. State legislatures in Virginia and Kentucky passed the **Kentucky and Virginia Resolves**, stating that states have the right to not enforce laws that were unconstitutional, such as the Sedition Act. This would later be the philosophy of some Southern states in the years leading up to the Civil War and again in the civil rights struggles of the 1950s and 1960s.

The negative publicity generated by the Sedition Act certainly did not help John Adams as he ran for president against Thomas Jefferson in 1800.

CHAPTER REVIEW

Rapid Review Guide

To achieve the perfect 5, you should be able to explain the following:

- The 1787 meeting on amending the Articles of Confederation turned into a historical session where the Constitution of the United States was drafted.

- The importance of James Madison in the formulation of the Constitution cannot be overemphasized.
- The format of the bicameral legislature, the branches of power established at the federal level, and the division of powers between federal and state governments made the U.S. Constitution a unique document for its time.
- The division between Federalists and Antifederalists demonstrated that very different visions of America and the scope of the federal government existed in the United States at this time.
- The Bill of Rights established the basic freedoms that Americans cherish today.
- During the Washington administration, very different visions of America were expressed by Alexander Hamilton and Thomas Jefferson; the ideas of Hamilton helped spur American economic growth during the Washington administration.
- The United States had a great deal of trouble convincing the British and the French that the United States was a major power during this era.
- Many critics viewed the Alien and Sedition Acts of John Adams as gross overextensions of the power given to the federal government by the Constitution.

Time Line

1787: Constitutional Convention ratifies U.S. Constitution
1788: U.S. Constitution ratified by states
1789: Washington sworn in as first president
1790: Hamilton issues plans proposing to protect infant U.S. industries
1791: Establishment of First National Bank
      Ratification of the Bill of Rights
1793: Democratic-Republican clubs begin to meet
1794: Whiskey Rebellion begins
1795: Jay's Treaty with England/Pinckney's Treaty with Spain
1796: John Adams elected president, Thomas Jefferson vice president
      (each from a different political party)
1798: XYZ affair
      Sedition Act of John Adams issued
      Kentucky and Virginia Resolves
1800: Convention of 1800
      Thomas Jefferson elected president

✓ Review Questions

1. The Connecticut Plan presented to the Constitutional Convention of 1787

   A. proposed a one-house legislature based on population

   B. proposed a two-house legislature based on proportional representation

   C. proposed a one-house legislature based on proportional representation

D. proposed a two-house legislature, with one house based on proportional representation
E. proposed a balance of power between executive, legislative, and judicial branches

(Correct Answer: **D.** The Connecticut plan, also called the Great Compromise, was ratified by the delegates. Under this plan representation in the House of Representatives would be by population, while in the Senate all states would have equal representation.)

2. The Kentucky and Virginia Resolves

A. expressed support for the new U.S. Constitution
B. expressed opposition to the government actions in putting down the Whiskey Rebellion
C. stated that individual states do not have to enforce laws the states consider unconstitutional
D. were written to support John Adams' support of the Sedition Act
E. were written in opposition to the economic policies of Alexander Hamilton

(Correct Answer: **C.** After the passage of the Sedition Act, legislatures in Kentucky and Virginia passed resolutions stating that states do not have to enforce laws they consider to be unconstitutional.)

3. Many in America felt that the English and the French failed to treat the United States as a major power in this era; all of the following are evidence of that *except*

A. the Convention of 1800
B. the treatment of American ships by the French during the 1890s
C. Jay's Treaty
D. the treatment of American ships by the British during the 1890s
E. the XYZ Affair

(Correct Answer: **A.** As a result of the Convention of 1800, the French agreed to compensate the United States for ships seized during the previous decade. Events mentioned in all of the other choices demonstrate that the French and English had little respect for American rights in diplomatic matters and on the high seas during this era.)

4. Thomas Jefferson and Alexander Hamilton had different views on all of the following *except*

A. whether America should be a commercial or agrarian society
B. the amount of power the federal government should have
C. the tariff policy of the United States
D. the importance of a National Bank
E. their belief in the power of the U.S. Constitution

(Correct Answer: **E.** Both believed in the power of the Constitution, although their interpretation of the Constitution was different. Jefferson believed in a strict interpretation of the Constitution, while Hamilton believed in a broad interpretation.)

5. Under the Electoral College system

A. voters directly elect the president of the United States
B. state legislatures elect the president of the United States
C. voters approve electors, who elect the president of the United States
D. it is possible to win the popular vote and lose the election in the Electoral College
E. C and D above

(Correct Answer: **E.** As demonstrated in the presidential election of 2000, it is possible to get the most number of votes nationwide but to lose the presidential election in the Electoral College. This also occurred in the presidential election of 1876.)

Chapter 8

The Jeffersonian Revolution (1800–1820)

THE ELECTION OF 1800

John Adams, despite much criticism over the **Sedition Act**, stood for reelection in 1800. The vice presidential candidate of the Federalists was Charles Pinckney. The candidate for the Republicans was Thomas Jefferson, with Aaron Burr running for vice president. At this point all candidates were eligible for votes in the Electoral College; Jefferson and Burr each received 73 votes (the **Twelfth Amendment** of 1804 would change this, stating that the Electoral College would vote for president and vice president separately). The Constitution in 1800 threw the election to the House of Representatives, where each state received one vote. Federalists supported Burr, and it was only on the thirty-sixth ballot that Jefferson was elected president. Jefferson's victory was only assured when Alexander Hamilton convinced some Federalists to switch their votes to Jefferson, telling them that Burr was "the most unfit man in the United States for the office of president." Some historians term this election the "Revolution of 1800"; as previously stated, Jefferson's vision of America had almost no similarity with the views of the Federalists who had been in power since the beginning of the republic, yet they peacefully gave up power when the balloting was completed in the House of Representatives.

Some historians maintain that Thomas Jefferson was one of the most brilliant men ever to be elected president. Recent movies and exposés on the life of Jefferson have largely ignored his immense political skills and intellect. Jefferson had been a diplomat, was familiar with European affairs, was a skillful politician, and was a distinguished political philosopher. He implemented Republican policies almost as soon as he took office, with the goal of cutting back on the growth of the federal government that had taken place under Adams. The Alien and Sedition Acts of Adams were not renewed, taxes such as the whiskey tax were eliminated, and Jefferson opposed further expansion of the national debt. On the other hand, Jefferson remained a pragmatist. As a member of Washington's Cabinet, he had vigorously opposed the creation of a National Bank, yet as president he supported it (he reasoned that American economic growth was dependent on the existence of the Bank.)

REFORM OF THE COURTS

When Jefferson was inaugurated in 1801, virtually every justice in the court system was a Federalist, since they had all been appointed by either Washington or Adams. Several weeks before Jefferson took office, Congress passed the **Judiciary Act**, creating a large number of new federal courts. In a series of "**midnight appointments**" made just hours before he left office, Adams appointed Federalists to all of these positions.

Jefferson's Republican allies in the Congress repealed the Judiciary Act almost immediately and also impeached two Federalists judges. John Marshall was a Federalist who had been appointed Chief Justice of the Supreme Court by Adams and continued in office during Jefferson's presidency and beyond. Marshall served as Chief Justice from 1801 to 1835 and served to dramatically improve the prestige and the functioning of the federal court system.

Marshall also dramatically increased the power of the Supreme Court itself in the 1803 *Marbury v. Madison* decision. John Adams had appointed John Marbury to be justice of the peace for the District of Columbia in one of his final appointments before leaving office. James Madison, secretary of state under Jefferson, refused to issue the appointment letter signed by Adams. Marbury sued, demanding that the Supreme Court force Madison to release the appointment letter.

Marshall ruled that the Supreme Court did not have the power to force Madison to act. However, the ruling also stated that the Supreme Court did have the right to judge the constitutionality of federal laws and decisions. This began the principal of **judicial review**, making the judiciary an equal branch in every way with the executive and legislative branches.

WESTWARD EXPANSION

As previously mentioned, Thomas Jefferson had a very different view of America than had been held by Alexander Hamilton and many other Federalists. While Hamilton had envisioned America as evolving into a mighty industrial power, Jefferson's view of an ideal America was one made up largely of yeoman farmers, who would possess a spirit of fierce independence and pride. To accomplish this end, Jefferson encouraged further expansion westward (into the area between the Appalachian Mountains and the Mississippi River). Over 1 million settlers lived there in 1800; in 1804 it became even easier to purchase land in this territory, when it became possible to buy 160 acres of land for an initial down payment of $80. New settlers streamed into the area, sometimes settling on land legally owned by Native American tribes.

Jefferson publicly stated that the best approach to Native Americans would be to show them the benefits of farming. He felt that if Native Americans could be turned into farmers that they would not need all of their forest land and they might incorporate themselves as citizens of the U.S. However, Jefferson's desire for western settlement far outweighed his desire for fair treatment for Native Americans. The pattern that began under Jefferson and continued for decades was one where Native Americans were forced to sign treaties in which they gave up more and more of their lands with virtually nothing given in return.

The Louisiana Purchase

In secret treaties between France and Spain signed in 1800 and 1801 France regained the Louisiana territory. Americans did not hear of this until 1802 and were worried that Napoleon's France might attempt to reassert their power in the Americas. Napoleon also expressed his desire to place Haiti back under French control. Concerns increased when in the last two months of their control there the Spanish refused to allow American ships to store products in New Orleans (which had been common practice).

Jefferson feared war with France and sent Virginia governor James Monroe to France to see if France would sell part of the territory to the United States. Napoleon had been unable to recapture Haiti and needed money to finance his army for his European conquests, so he offered to sell the Louisiana Territory to the United States for $15 million. The **Louisiana Purchase** doubled the size of the United States; for Jefferson this was the perfect opportunity to expand the "empire of liberty." Many Northeastern Federalists were opposed to the Louisiana Purchase, fearing it would decrease their economic and political power. Nevertheless, the purchase was overwhelmingly ratified by Congress in late 1803. Jefferson's pragmatism was also displayed when he approved the Louisiana Purchase. The Constitution did not mention that the federal government had the right to acquire new territory; Jefferson had always interpreted the Constitution strictly, and normally stated that the federal government has no powers that were not specifically mentioned in the Constitution. However, in Jefferson's eyes the acquisition of the Louisiana territory was absolutely essential for the continued growth of the United States.

Jefferson and many others in America wanted more accurate information about the geography, the peoples, and the economic possibilities of the rest of the continent. In 1803 the **Lewis and Clark Expedition** began. This expedition of nearly 50 men took two years to complete; despite hardships they crossed the Rockies and eventually made it to the Pacific Ocean. The information they brought back about the possibilities of further expansion in the West intrigued many.

POLITICAL TENSIONS AND THE STRANGE CASE OF AARON BURR

Federalists feared that the country was being debased by virtually every move that Jefferson made. A group of Federalists called the **Essex Junto** existed in Boston and loudly campaigned against the "decline in public virtue" they saw personified in Jefferson. Thomas Pickering, senator from Massachusetts, saw Jefferson as a "Parisian revolutionary monster." A younger group of Federalists tried to improve the image of the party, although the Federalist candidate, Charles C. Pinckney, received only 14 electoral votes in the 1804 election.

Aaron Burr was vice president, but after the fiasco of the 1800 election, he had no meaningful role during Jefferson's first term. Some New England Federalists had spoke of leaving the Union after the Louisiana Purchase and forming a Northern Confederacy. The group tried to get Alexander Hamilton to join them. After he refused, they tried to recruit Aaron Burr, who, seeing no future role in a Washington run by Thomas Jefferson, was trying to become governor of New York. Hamilton accused Burr of attempting to ruin the United States. At this point, Burr challenged Hamilton to a duel (a practice that had been outlawed in the United States). Hamilton died in the duel, and Burr was indicted for murder.

After ending his term as vice president, Burr moved to the West (probably to avoid jail). While in Louisiana, he met up with General James Wilkinson, the military governor there. The two plotted to turn Louisiana into an independent nation, with Burr as its leader. Burr was betrayed by Wilkinson and arrested. Burr was acquitted, but his actions and the actions of other Federalists demonstrate the deep divisions that were developing in the United States. Federalists had plotted secession, President Jefferson wanted a conviction of Burr at all costs, and Federalist John Marshall, who presided over the trial, made several rulings that helped Burr (possibly to discredit the efforts of Jefferson).

EUROPEAN WARS SPILL OVER TO AMERICA (AGAIN)

The Napoleonic Wars of Europe that lasted from 1802 till 1815 had a large impact on the United States. America viewed its role in this war as a neutral, yet came into conflict with both France and Great Britain. By terms of the Continental System, American ships that traded in Britain were sometimes stopped and seized. British ships also seized ships trading with the French West Indies, made merchants pay heavily to get special licenses to send their ships through the British naval blockade of the continent, and practiced **impressment** (forcing deserted British sailors but also American citizens into the British navy). Jefferson banned British warships from American ports, yet impressment and the stopping and seizing of American ships continued.

Many in America wanted war, but Jefferson thought that economic pressure would cause the British and the French to respect the rights of

America as a neutral. He declared the **Embargo of 1807**, by which American ships could not enter the seas until England and France stopped their harassment of American shipping. Predictably, the effect on the American economy was disastrous. Exports dropped dramatically, with Northeastern merchants, Southern plantation owners, and even farmers dramatically affected.

The Embargo of 1807 was by far the most unpopular act championed by Jefferson. In the 1808 presidential election, Congressman James Madison was elected president, even though he was one of the architects of the embargo bill.

Seeing that America had actually fallen into economic depression, Madison in 1808 introduced the **Non-Intercourse Act**, which opened trade with all countries except England and France. An 1810 act again threatened to cut trade with any nation that interfered with American ships, which England and France continued to do.

THE WAR OF 1812

Reasons for War

Frustrated by the continued British policies of impressment and the seizure of ships, Madison formally asked Congress for a Declaration of War against Britain in June of 1812. Many Federalists opposed the war. They regarded Great Britain as a potential trading partner and viewed British citizens as people "like themselves." To many Americans, Madison's argument that the country's political and economic rights as a neutral power had been violated was convincing. A younger group of Republicans, personified by Henry Clay of Kentucky, were especially supportive of war. This group, called the "War Hawks," felt that war would enable the United States to acquire more territory in the West, leading to greater economic growth.

Another stated cause for war revolved around connections between the British and Native Americans. In 1812 two members of the Shawnee Tribe, Tecumseh and his brother Tenskwatawa, decided the time was right to take a stand against further settlement by whites in the region between the Appalachians and the Mississippi River. Tecumseh joined many tribes together, terrifying settlers in the region. James Madison was convinced by Western political leaders that the Native Americans were being encouraged (and being armed) by the British in Canada. The attack on Tecumseh's village by General William Henry Harrison in late 1811 intensified the conflict that would take place with Native Americans in the region.

The Outbreak of War

The United States was totally unprepared for war against Britain when war was first declared. In 1812 the army consisted of 6000 men, and the entire navy was made up of 17 ships. The first military effort was a three-pronged attack against Canada, with the intent of destroying Indian villages, defeating British troops, and taking Montreal. Military efforts were largely unsuccessful, and American troops soon retreated.

The American navy had some initial successes, but American ships were soon driven back and blockaded in their own ports. The naval victories of 1812 at least boosted the morale of the American nation. Native Americans, including Tecumseh and the Shawnee, were fighting on the side of the British. The first big victory for the Americans came in the summer of 1813 when William Henry Harrison and his forces defeated the British and the Native Americans at the Thames River (east of present-day Detroit), killing Tecumseh. In Tennessee a militiaman, Andrew Jackson, lead many victories over Indian forces.

The Attack on Washington

Napoleon was finally defeated in 1814. Many Americans rejoiced at the defeat of the French, but also realized that the United States was now Britain's only enemy. The British began an offensive in New York, but in August 1814, a second British army advanced on Washington. Most Washingtonians (including President Madison) left the city before the British arrived, but the British proceeded to sack the city, including the White House and the Capitol.

Ironically, as the British were burning the Capitol, peace negotiations for ending the war were already in progress in Ghent, Belgium. With the European war over, many of the issues that had driven Britain and America apart, such as blockading and impressment, now appeared to be less important. After sustained battles against Napoleon, public opinion in England did not favor continued military action in the Americas. The strange **Treaty of Ghent**, which ended the war, actually said nothing about impressment or neutral trading rights, but simply restored diplomatic relations between Britain and the United States. Two weeks after peace was declared, Andrew Jackson defeated a large British force at the Battle of New Orleans.

Political Effects of the War

Nine days before the Treaty of Ghent was signed, a group of Federalists met at the **Hartford Convention**. They continued to see the war as disastrous to their interests and viewed with extreme suspicion the growing influence of politicians and military leaders from the West. Proposals regarding **nullification**, and even one concerning **secession**, were debated. When the ending of the war and the victory at New Orleans were announced, the actions of the Federalists appeared foolish. Their influence on political life in America was drawing to an end. With the decline of the Federalists, the United States was united more after the War of 1812 than it had been for years. As a result, the years 1816 to 1823 are called in textbooks the **Era of Good Feelings**, with James Monroe taking over the presidency in 1817.

THE AMERICAN SYSTEM

Henry Clay and other nationalists in Congress proposed the **American System** in the aftermath of the War of 1812. This plan was supported by James Madison and most fully implemented by James Monroe. The purpose of this plan was to make America less economically dependent on Europe by encouraging the production of goods in the United States that had previously been purchased abroad. Important to this economic growth would also be a second national bank, so that credit would be readily available, and a rather large protective tariff, which would encourage production and interstate commerce.

The **Tariff of 1816** raised tariff rates to nearly 22 percent, providing more than adequate protection for American business interests and revenues for improvements in the internal transportation system of the United States. A **Second National Bank** was also chartered in 1816. There was rapid economic growth in the postwar years, as Europeans and others traded for American tobacco, cotton, and grain. Economic growth could not last forever, and a depression gripped America in 1819.

THE MISSOURI COMPROMISE

The issue of slavery was one that increased as more settlers moved westward: Would the territories they were moving into be slave or free? In 1808 the further exporting of slaves was eliminated. Additional states had joined the Union, some slave and some free. By 1819 there were 11 slave states and 11 free states. The issue came to a head that year when Missouri petitioned to join the Union as a slave state. Debate in the Congress and in newspapers around the country was heated; to many Northerners, to have more slave states than free states was unthinkable. Speaker of the House Henry Clay engineered the Missouri Compromise, by which Maine entered the Union as a free state, Missouri entered as a slave state, and in the Louisiana Territory any states north of 36 degrees, 30 minutes had to come in as free states. Many at the time realized that this solution would only be a temporary one.

CHAPTER REVIEW

Rapid Review Guide

To achieve the perfect 5, you should be able to explain the following:

- The election of Thomas Jefferson in 1800 is called the "Revolution of 1800," as the new president had a completely different vision of America than the Federalists whom he replaced.

- Thomas Jefferson was one of the most brilliant men ever to serve as president, and he instituted many "Republican" policies during his eight years in office.
- The role of the federal courts was greatly strengthened during the tenure of John Marshall as Chief Justice of the Supreme Court.
- The Louisiana Purchase more than doubled the size of the United States and allowed the "empire of liberty" to continue to expand.
- The case of Aaron Burr showed the deep political divisions that existed in the United States during this period.
- The Napoleonic wars greatly impacted the relationship between the United States, England, and France.
- American entered the War of 1812 because President Madison convinced the nation that America's rights as a neutral power had been violated and because many in Congress felt that the British were encouraging resistance by Native American tribes.
- The American System of Henry Clay and others was proposed after the War of 1812 and outlined a plan for broad economic growth for the United States.
- The Missouri Compromise temporarily solved the issue of the number of slave versus the number of free states.

Time Line

1800: Thomas Jefferson elected president in "Revolution of 1800"
1801: John Marshall named as Chief Justice of Supreme Court
　　　Alien and Sedition Acts not renewed
1803: Louisiana Purchase
　　　Marbury v. *Madison* case established federal judicial review
1804: Alexander Hamilton killed in duel with Aaron Burr
　　　Thomas Jefferson reelected
　　　Twelfth Amendment ratified (separate voting for president, vice president)
　　　Beginning of Lewis and Clark expedition
1807: Embargo Act greatly harms foreign trade
1808: James Madison elected president
　　　Further importation of slaves into United States made illegal
1812: Beginning of War of 1812
1814: British army sacks Washington
　　　Treaty of Ghent formally ends War of 1812
　　　Indian removal from Southern territories begins in earnest
1814–1815: Hartford Convention (meeting of Federalists)
1815: Victory of Andrew Jackson at Battle of New Orleans (after War of 1812 was officially over)
　　　Henry Clay proposes the "American System"
1816: James Monroe elected president
1816–1823: Era of Good Feelings
1820: Missouri Compromise

✓ Review Questions

1. The *Marbury v. Madison* decision

   A. gave powers to the president that the Republicans of Thomas Jefferson claimed he didn't have
   B. gave broad judicial power to the state courts
   C. declared that the Alien and Sedition Acts were constitutional
   D. established the principle of judicial review
   E. legalized the removal of Native Americans from western lands

(Correct Answer: **D.** The decision stated that the Supreme Court had the right to decide on the constitutionality of federal rulings and laws.)

2. As a result of the election of Thomas Jefferson in 1800,

   A. more assistance was given to the commercial sector
   B. politicians in New York, Boston, and Philadelphia gained power
   C. American foreign policy became more pro-British
   D. the federal debt rose dramatically
   E. federal excise taxes were eliminated

(Correct Answer: **E.** All of the remaining answers would have been true if a Federalist had been elected president. Jefferson favored lessening the power of the federal government, and eliminating federal excise taxes was one way in which he did so.)

3. All of the following are reasons why America entered the War of 1812 *except*

   A. the impressment of American naval crews
   B. the existence of a strong American navy ready to demonstrate its capabilities
   C. the relationship between the British and Native American tribes in the western territories of North America
   D. the violation of America's rights as a neutral power
   E. the desire by American leaders to acquire additional western territories

(Correct Answer: **B.** The United States had an army of 6000 men and 17 ships when war began. All of the other choices are reasons that Americans supported the War of 1812.)

4. The Hartford Convention demonstrated that

   A. the Federalist party had remained a dominant party in American political life
   B. the War of 1812 brought political union to the United States
   C. the concept of nullification was not exclusively a Southern one
   D. the legacy of John Adams was large
   E. the Treaty of Ghent was a controversial treaty

(Correct Answer: **C.** Kentucky and Virginia spoke of nullification after the Sedition Act; New England Federalists saw the War of 1812 as a disaster and at the Hartford Convention also spoke of nullification.)

5. The American System of Henry Clay

   A. favored strong economic growth and a Second National Bank
   B. wanted to make the United States the military equivalent of Great Britain or France
   C. wanted to place a ceiling on the national debt
   D. favored lowering tariffs, so that more goods could be purchased from abroad
   E. advocated the elimination of slavery

(Correct Answer: **A.** The American System favored American economic growth, a national bank, and increased tariffs to protect American businesses and finance new transportation systems within the United States.)

Chapter 9

The Rise of Manufacturing and the Age of Jackson (1820–1845)

THE GROWTH OF THE FACTORY

Economic growth was a key component of Henry Clay's American System, and in the aftermath of the War of 1812, measures were taken to expand American industry. American industries were protected by the Tariff of 1816, which raised import tariffs by 25 percent. At the same time state governments began improving road, river, and canal transportation systems.

Before 1820 almost all products made in America were completed using a system borrowed from Europe called the **putting-out system**. Under this system merchants would buy the raw materials, recruit dozens, or in some case hundreds, of farm families to do the work, and then sell the finished product. Many shoes in New England were made in this manner; women and children would make part of the shoe, which would be finished by experienced shoemakers.

Beginning in the late 1780s the textile industry started to use power-driven machines and interchangeable parts. All power in these early factories came from water, so the early factories all were located along rivers. Most were located in New England or the Middle states. In the 1790s factories like those in Lowell, Massachusetts, began to weave cotton imported from the south. With the introduction of the cotton gin in the same decade, more cotton became available, and production boomed. By 1840 the textile industry employed nearly 75,000 workers, with almost half of them women.

The workforce of many of the early factories was hired using the "<u>Lowell System</u>." Young women from surrounding areas were brought in to work. They worked for a pittance, worked in horrible conditions, and slept in dormitories provided by the factory. The young women saw this as temporary work, as many went home after several years after making some money (and in some cases spending it as well). This constant turnover of workers kept worker demands low, which pleased the factory owners. An economic middle class of manufacturers, bankers, and their families began to grow during this period. Factory towns such as Lowell, Massachusetts, began to grow rapidly in size.

An economic panic hit the United States in 1819, caused by the recovery of European economies after the Napoleonic wars, by money policies of the National Bank, and by the efforts of officials at several branch banks of the National Bank to enrich themselves through speculation. It was not until the 1830s that worker strikes began, along with drives to influence state legislatures to shorten the workday. A real **labor movement** did not develop in the textile industry until the 1840s.

THE MONROE DOCTRINE

The fact that America now was beginning to consider itself a major world power was demonstrated by the **Monroe Doctrine**, announced by President Monroe in 1823. Many Latin American nations had announced their independence in the Napoleonic era, and many in Latin America and in the United States felt that the Spanish and the French might send armies to reassert their control of the region. The Monroe Doctrine stated that countries in the Western Hemisphere were now off-limits to European control (these states "henceforth are not to be considered as subjects for future colonization by any European powers").

POLICY TOWARD NATIVE AMERICANS

In 1824 President James Monroe proposed that all Native Americans be moved west of the Mississippi River. Conflict had continued east of the Mississippi between settlers and various Native American tribes. Even though tribes had signed legal treaties for land, settlement constantly encroached on Native American territories. Monroe claimed that his proposal would benefit the Native Americans, stating that settlers would never bother them as long as they settled west of the Mississippi River Some tribes, such as the Cherokee, adopted systems of government similar to those used in many states, but even that did not stave off the pressure for removal.

The state of Georgia pressured the Cherokee to sell the land they held in that state. The Cherokee felt they held a valid treaty for the land that they lived on and decided to take their case to the federal court system. In a 1831 decision, ***Cherokee Nation v. Georgia***, Chief Justice Marshall stated that Native Americans had no real standing in court, since they were not a state or a foreign country. Nevertheless, Marshall affirmed that the Cherokee had a right to the lands that they possessed.

The Constitution states that it is the job of the executive branch to enforce the laws or decisions of the other two branches. Andrew Jackson was now president, and a large part of his reputation was as a successful Indian fighter. Jackson declined to take action to enforce this decision, stating "John Marshall has made his decision: let him enforce it." In his inaugural speech Jackson affirmed his support for Native American removal. During the War of 1812 Jackson led troops against the Creek tribe. As a result, the Creeks lost over 60 percent of their tribal lands. Congress had already passed and Jackson signed the **Removal Act of 1830**, which authorized the removal of all tribes east of the Mississippi.

Tribes were forced to move beginning in 1831; the horrors of these journeys, sometimes undertaken during winter months, are very well documented. In 1838 the Cherokees were finally marched west at gunpoint in what is now called the **Trail of Tears**; nearly one-third died of disease or exhaustion along the way. Many Native Americans were never able to adjust to the alien environment found west of the Mississippi. Indian resistance continued in Florida until 1841.

THE SECOND GREAT AWAKENING

The rise of industry, the growing commercialization of cities, and westernization all fundamentally altered America in the years 1800 to 1830. Transportation was rapidly changing; a National Road linked the Potomac and the Ohio rivers, and the Erie Canal was completed in 1825. The lives of vast numbers of ordinary people were being altered as a result of these economic and social changes.

In the midst of these transformations, the **Second Great Awakening** reaffirmed the role of religion in the lives of believers. The movement began in the late 1790s and reached its zenith in the 1830s. Where earlier Calvinist preachers had spoke of predestination, preachers of this era such as Timothy Dwight and Charles Finney proclaimed that one's actions on Earth played at least some role in an individual's fate after death. During this period **revival meetings**, some lasting as long as a week, would cause followers to faint, speak in tongues, or writhe uncontrollably. The Second Great Awakening began as a rural phenomenon, but by the 1820s, it spread to the cities as well. Evangelical sects such as the Methodists and the Baptists also grew in popularity.

Women played a significant role in the revivalism of the era. Many women became dedicated Christians and worked as volunteers for Protestant churches. In addition, many of these churches set up "academies" to educate women.

Other Reform Movements

Many individuals involved in the religious fervor of the era wanted to use that enthusiasm to reform society. Many wanted to act to improve the lives of those living in the cities and others with disadvantages. Dorothea Dix campaigned for better treatment of the mentally ill in the 1830s and

1840s. A prison reform movement also developed. In addition, a large **temperance movement** developed in this period, urging the working class to not drink to excess. Individuals such as Horace Mann spoke out for formal education for all children, the expansion of the school year, and the need for rigorous standards of teacher training.

Many Christians, especially in the North, began to speak out forcefully about the treatment of American slaves. In the 1820s and 1830s the **abolitionist movement** gained a large number of supporters. Abolitionists considered slavery to be a sin. The most prominent abolitionist was William Lloyd Garrison, who founded ***The Liberator***, his antislavery newspaper, in 1831. Some were against slavery for other reasons. The **American Colonization Society**, founded in the South in 1817, opposed slavery on the grounds that it encouraged contact between blacks and whites; members of this organization urged slave owners to free their slaves and return them to Africa.

Frederick Douglass, an ex-slave, was another leader of the abolitionist movement, who in 1845 would write the *Narrative of the Life of Frederick Douglass,* a key text for those who opposed slavery. In 1831 Nat Turner, a slave in Virginia, organized a bloody slave revolt that killed 60 whites. As was the case in the Stono Rebellion, the revolt was brutally repressed, and Black Codes and other restrictions on slaves in Southern states became more harsh.

POLITICAL REFORM: THE JACKSONIAN ERA (1829–1841)

Alexis de Tocqueville and other visitors from Europe noticed a different spirit in America than existed in European countries. de Tocqueville viewed with wonder the egalitarian system that he observed in virtually all aspects of American life. Many political changes both before and during the presidency of Andrew Jackson accentuated the sense that the "common man" reigned in this era.

Changes were already taking place in how presidential candidates were chosen. In 1800 only five states chose electors to the Electoral College by popular vote. By 1824, 18 out of 24 states chose electors in this manner. By the 1824 campaign, banners, posters, buttons, and hats were commonplace (the 1828 campaign was the first time when these were mass-produced).

In addition, more and more people could vote. By 1824 the property qualification, long a method to keep the "rabble" away from the political process, had been eliminated in most states. Blacks (even free blacks in the North) and women were still excluded from the political process.

THE ELECTION OF 1824

In this election Secretary of the Treasury William Crawford, Speaker of the House Henry Clay, Secretary of State John Quincy Adams, and

Tennessee's Andrew Jackson all ran for president. All of them considered themselves Republicans (the party was now referred to in many newspapers as **Democratic-Republican**). Jackson won the most popular votes, but only 38 percent of the electoral votes, so the election was turned over to the House of Representatives. Speaker of the House Clay threw his support to Adams, who won in the House and then appointed Clay to the position of Secretary of State.

For the next four years supporters of Jackson did everything they could to sabotage the presidency of John Quincy Adams, constantly reminding themselves of the "corrupt bargain" between Adams and Clay that had decided the 1824 election.

THE 1828 PRESIDENTIAL ELECTION

The 1828 presidential campaign was the model for many political campaigns of the future. Campaign rallies were held by supporters of both Quincy Adams and Jackson. Mudslinging was a daily occurrence during the campaign. Jackson's supporters claimed that Adams stole the 1824 election and gave too many fancy dinners; they also claimed that when he had been envoy to Russia, Adams had helped procure American prostitutes for the Russia tsar. Supporters of Adams said that Jackson was a murderer and an adulterer (the charge was made that his wife was an adulterer as well). Jackson won the election handily; under him the **Democratic party** became the first real political party of the United States.

JACKSON AS PRESIDENT

Andrew Jackson had been born in a log cabin, but when he was elected president in 1828, he was a planter and slaveholder. He was the first president from the West and had first achieved fame by fighting Native Americans. Jackson, however, was not naïve in terms of politics; he had been a congressman and a senator from Tennessee, as well as serving as territorial governor of Florida. Jackson was personally popular, especially with the common people.

Jackson also expressed loyalty to those who supported him politically. He infrequently consulted with his appointed Cabinet, relying instead on his "**Kitchen Cabinet**," the inner circle of his political supporters. Jackson also utilized the **spoils system** to give other political supporters jobs in the government.

Jackson also wanted to return to the Jeffersonian ideal of America as a nation of independent yeoman farmers. He opposed excessive government involvement in economic affairs, fearing that in most cases only wealthy interests benefited from that involvement. In modern terms, Jackson favored "smaller government" and was not afraid to use the power of the presidential veto to stop government programs he thought were excessive. At the end of his presidency Jackson appointed Roger B.

Taney as Chief Justice of the Supreme Court; the Taney court would validate almost all of Jackson's decisions favoring states rights.

To many of his opponents Jackson was a paradox. While he spoke of the need to limit the influence of government in society, he increased the power of the presidency. Opponents often referred to him as "King Andrew I." On the issue of slavery Jackson was no friend of abolitionists; he was a slave owner and was opposed to reform of the slave system.

THE NULLIFICATION CONTROVERSY

Jackson was forced early in his presidency to face the issue of the power of the states in relation to the power of the federal government. In 1828 Congress passed a bill authorizing new tariffs on imported manufacturing cloth and iron. The cost of these goods rose dramatically, and legislators in South Carolina began to revisit the doctrine of **nullification**, whereby individual states could rule on the constitutionality of federal laws. Jackson's own vice president, John C. Calhoun of South Carolina, stated that the practice of nullification was a necessity to protect states from the potential tyranny of the federal government.

In 1830 a debate in the U.S. Senate over western land sales between Robert Hayne of South Carolina and Daniel Webster of Massachusetts evolved into a debate on nullification. In the **Webster-Hayne Debate**, Daniel Webster argued that if nullification were to proceed, the results would be "states dissevered, discordant, belligerent; on a land rent with civil feuds, or drenched . . . in fraternal blood!" President Jackson was a believer in states' rights but firmly opposed the concept of nullification.

New tariffs were imposed on imported goods, and in November of 1832 a specially called convention in South Carolina voted to nullify the law imposing these tariffs. Jackson moved troops and federal marshals to South Carolina to collect the tariff payments there; Congress authorized these decisions when it passed the **Force Act**. John Calhoun resigned as vice president (Jackson suggested privately that he should be hung). A crisis was avoided when the Congress passed a bill, acceptable to South Carolina, that lowered the amount of the tariffs to be collected.

THE BANK CRISIS

The Second Bank of the United States was chartered in 1816 (it was a crucial part of Henry Clay's "American System"). The bank issued national currency, regulated loan rates, and controlled state banks. The bank had been run since 1823 by Nicholas Biddle. As stated previously, Jackson was suspicious of government involvement in the economy. These suspicions extended to the National Bank.

Henry Clay was going to run for president in the 1832 election and wanted to use the bank as a campaign issue. Clay began pushing to have the bank rechartered, even though its original charter did not expire until

1836. Clay was convinced that national support of the bank would swing supporters his way. Jackson vetoed the rechartering proposal, claiming it served special interests and few others. This increased his popularity with the public and helped to ensure his reelection in 1832.

Jackson wanted to destroy the National Bank, and in 1833, he ordered that money be removed from it and placed in state or local banks (Jackson's political enemies called these his "pet banks"). To keep the National Bank going, Biddle increased interest rates and called in loans that had been made to state banks. The results of this **Bank War** would eventually be the **Panic of 1837** and a depression that would last into the 1840s.

THE WHIG PARTY: A CHALLENGE TO THE DEMOCRATIC-REPUBLICANS

In the 1830s the **Whig party** emerged as the major opposition party to the party of Jackson. The Whigs and the Democratic-Republicans battled for elections throughout the 1830s and 1840s. Taking their lead from the legacy of Andrew Jackson, the Democrats generally favored a limited government. They saw urbanization and industrialization as necessary evils; the America they favored was still essentially a Jeffersonian one.

The Whigs favored more governmental involvement in commercial activities and favored the National Bank and industrial growth. They were opposed to rapid and uncontrolled settlement of the West. Consistent with their view of a more activist government, the Whigs also were more likely to sponsor reformist legislation. Predictably, businessmen from the North and Northeast supported the Whigs, as did Southern planters. The Democrats were generally supported by the "common man," which included small farmers, factory workers, and smaller merchants. A Democrat, Martin Van Buren, won the 1836 election, but Whig William Henry Harrison was elected in 1840. Harrison died after one month in office and was seceded by John Tyler. Developments in Texas and American expansionism would become important issues during his presidency.

CHAPTER REVIEW

Rapid Review Guide

To achieve the perfect 5, you should be able to explain the following:

- A new production system developed in textile mills, such as those that existed in Lowell, Massachusetts, in the early nineteenth century.
- The Monroe Doctrine boldly proclaimed that the Western Hemisphere was off-limits to European intrusion.
- Beginning in 1824, it was official American policy to move Native American tribes east of the Mississippi; the horrors of many of these relocations are well documented.

- The Second Great Awakening influenced many to become involved in reform movements, including the abolitionist movement.
- The presidency of Andrew Jackson is celebrated as an era where the "common man" reigned supreme, although Jackson greatly expanded the powers of the presidency.
- The Democratic party of Andrew Jackson was the first real political party in American history.
- Jackson's tariff policy caused a renewal of interest in the policy of nullification in several Southern state legislatures.
- In the 1830s the Whig party emerged as the major party opposing the Democratic party of Jackson.

Time Line

1790s: Beginning of Second Great Awakening
1816: Second Bank of United States chartered
Tariff of 1816 imposes substantial import tariffs
Election of James Monroe
1819: Panic of 1819 (unemployment lasts until 1823)
1820: Missouri Compromise
Reelection of James Monroe
1820s: Growth of New England textile mills
1823: Monroe Doctrine
1824: Proposal by President Monroe to move Native Americans east of the Mississippi River
1825: John Quincy Adams elected president by House of Representatives (no candidate had won a majority in Electoral College)
1828: Andrew Jackson elected president
1830: Passage of Indian Removal Act in Congress
Webster-Hayne debate
1830s: Growth of the Whig Party
1831: Cherokee nation goes to court to defend tribal rights in *Cherokee Nation* v. *Georgia*
First issue of William Lloyd Garrison's *The Liberator* published
1832: Andrew Jackson reelected
Nullification crisis after nullification of tariffs by South Carolina
1834: First strike of women textile workers in Lowell, Massachusetts
1836: Democrat Martin Van Buren elected president
1840: Whig William Henry Harrison elected president

✓ Review Questions

1. President Monroe claimed that westward relocation of Native Americans would be to the advantage of the Native Americans because

A. they would not be bothered west of the Mississippi

B. the American military would protect them during the journey

C. they would be well compensated for the tribal lands that they were leaving

D. they would not have to pay for the lands they were moving to

E. settlers west of the Mississippi were receptive to Native American settlement there

(Correct Answer: **A.** Monroe stated that Native Americans could not avoid being continually harassed if they lived east of the Mississippi, but that this would not happen after they moved.)

2. The concept of nullification became an issue during this period when

A. Georgia opposed congressional legislation concerning slavery

B. South Carolina nullified congressional legislation concerning the removal of Native Americans

C. South Carolina nullified congressional tariff bills

D. Southern representatives to the Electoral College switched their votes in the 1824 election

E. Virginia nullified congressional legislation concerning slavery

(Correct Answer: **C.** Because the tariff bills increased the prices of cloth and iron, the South Carolina legislature first nullified the Tariff of 1828.)

3. Critics of Andrew Jackson would make all of the following claims *except*

A. he was a very common man and not fit to be president

B. he gave too much power to the presidency

C. he gave political offices to his friends

D. his lack of experience in governmental affairs

E. he relied too much on his "Kitchen Cabinet"

(Correct Answer: **D.** All of the other criticisms were often made against Jackson. However, he did have an impressive background: Before becoming president, he had served as a congressman and a senator from Tennessee and as the territorial governor of Florida.)

4. The following are true about the textile mills of New England in the early nineteenth century *except*

A. a large percentage of their workforce was made up of women

B. they depended on water for power

C. they used a system called the putting-out system

D. Almost none still exist today.

E. there was little labor unrest in the mills until the 1830s and 1840s

(Correct Answer: **C.** It was the putting-out system that these mills replaced.)

5. Horace Mann is associated with

A. abolitionism

B. the temperance movement

C. prison reform

D. educational reform

E. reform for conditions of the mentally ill

(Correct Answer: **D.** Horace Mann wrote and spoke about the need to improve schools and to improve teacher training methods.)

Chapter 10

The Union Expanded and Challenged (1835–1860)

THE IDEOLOGY OF MANIFEST DESTINY

The idea of **manifest destiny** fueled the continued American expansion westward. Americans from the time of the Puritans spoke of America as a community with a divine mission. Beginning in the 1830s, some began to express the view that it was "God's plan" that America expand beyond the Mississippi River. Both political leaders and Protestant missionary organizations fervently supported western expansion. In 1845 Democratic newspaperman John O'Sullivan wrote that the most critical need for America was "the fulfillment of our manifest destiny to overspread the continent allotted by Providence for the free development of our yearly multiplying millions."

Americans had begin to settle in Oregon in the 1830s. The six-month, 2000-mile journey along the **Oregon Trail** brought settlers to the Oregon territory; many of them settled in the Willamette Valley. Many settlers in the Ohio Valley began to catch "Oregon Fever" by 1842; stories of a mild climate and the possibility of fur trading fueled the imaginations of many. Missionaries came to "tame" the Native Americans that lived in the region. By 1845 over 5000 had streamed into the Oregon territory. A section of Oregon was controlled by the British and a section by America. "Fifty-four Forty or Fight" became the rallying cry for expansionists who wanted all of Oregon to be under American control. The **Oregon Treaty** of 1846 gave most of Oregon to the Americans. The California territory, controlled by Spain, also attracted the interest of American settlers; American settlers first arrived there in the 1830s. The future of expansion in Oregon and California were key issues in the 1844 presidential campaign.

"REMEMBER THE ALAMO!"

The drive for expansion, which fueled the dreams of many Americans in the first half of the nineteenth century, made eventual conflict with Mexico inevitable. Mexico gained its independence from Spain in 1821 and encouraged the economic development of its northern province of Texas (which consisted of what we now know of as the state of Texas and parts of Kansas, Oklahoma, New Mexico, Wyoming, and Colorado). American economic investment was encouraged in the region: American settlers who would agree to become Mexican citizens, become Catholics, and encourage others Americans to come to Mexico were given large tracts of land for next to nothing. These settlers numbered nearly 30,000 by 1836.

Predictably, many Americans who settled in Texas were not diligent in fulfilling their obligations to the Mexican government, causing the Mexican government to act to reassert control over Texas. In 1836 the American settlers and some Mexicans living in Texas revolted against Mexican control of Texas. On March 2 they declared that Texas was an independent state and established a constitution (in which slavery was legal). Led by Davey Crockett and Jim Bowie, 165 Texans were defeated at the Alamo on March 6 by over 3000 Mexican soldiers, but their cry of "Remember the Alamo!" became the rallying cry for those fighting for the independence of Texas. A declaration of independence was issued in early March of 1836 by a convention of Texans opposed to continued Mexican rule.

Many American adventurers eager for land now poured into Texas and helped the Texans defeat the Mexican army on April 21, 1836. An independent Republic of Texas was proclaimed. General Sam Houston, who had led the army that defeated the Mexicans, became president of the Lone Star Republic. Most people living there (the vast majority being Americans) desired to become part of the United States. Andrew Jackson gave stirring speeches favoring the annexation of Texas and offered diplomatic recognition to the Lone Star Republic just before he left office. However, most Whigs were against annexation, fearing it would cause war with Mexico and domestic dissension. **Abolitionists** in the North were opposed to it, since they feared the entry of another slave state (which Texas would undoubtedly be) into the Union. Jackson feared that the annexation of Texas would hurt the chances of his chosen successor, Martin Van Buren, in the 1836 presidential election. He never acted on the annexation issue, causing the Republic of Texas to turn to Europe for potential allies.

Martin Van Buren also refused to support legislation that would make Texas part of the United States. William Henry Harrison, a Whig, defeated Van Buren in the 1840 presidential election but died after one month in office. Harrison's vice president was John Tyler, a Democrat who had been placed on the ticket to appeal to Southerners. Tyler favored the annexation of Texas and by mid-1844 had completed negotiations with the Texans on a treaty that would bring Texas into the United States. John C. Calhoun, the secretary of state, wrote a note to the British government concerning the situation in Texas; in the note he stated that the continuation of slavery would be good for Texas. This was enough to doom the treaty when it went to the Senate for approval.

THE PIVOTAL ELECTION OF 1844

Democrat James K. Polk was elected president in 1844. Polk was the first American **dark-horse candidate** for president, as he was not one of the announced candidates before the Democratic convention of that year. The campaign of that year showed several trends that would be pivotal to American political life in the 1840s and 1850s. The South and Southern interests increasingly influenced and were reflected in Democratic policies, and the Walker Tariff of 1846 established a very low tariff on imported goods, delighting many in the South and disgusting many Northern industrialists.

Abolitionism officially entered presidential politics in 1844. The Liberty party, with James Birney as its presidential candidate, was an abolitionist party. Although Birney attracted only 62,000 votes, abolitionism, and the sectional divisions it would help to foster, became a permanent part of the political landscape until the Civil War.

The 1844 election also demonstrated that desire for manifest destiny was the most important issue facing America at the time; most historians credit Polk's support of American expansionism as the major reason for his election. Polk was inaugurated in March of 1845. By December Texas had entered the Union. Expansionism and slavery also became increasingly intertwined as a single issue. The status of slavery in each newly acquired territory would have enormous political consequences, as forces in the North and the South were determined that the number of slave and free states remain equal.

WAR WITH MEXICO

The reasons for the Mexican-American War are numerous. Patriots in Mexico were outraged when Texas joined the United States, as they considered Texas still to be part of Mexico. The war served the economic interests of groups both in Mexico and the United States. However, the main reason for war was the determination of President Polk to fulfill what he perceived to be America's mission to occupy the lands all the way to the Pacific Ocean and his willingness to use force to accomplish this aim.

Polk did much to provoke war with the Mexicans. He encouraged settlers in Mexico to occupy territory all the way to the Rio Grande River, which the Mexicans considered to be outside of the territory of Texas (Mexico considered the Nueces River, north of the Rio Grande, as the border between Texas and the rest of Mexico). Polk also wanted to buy territory from Mexico that would allow the United States to expand all the way to California. In October 1845, he offered the Mexican government $5 million for the territory between the Nueces and the Rio Grande rivers, $25 million for California, and $5 million for other Mexican territory in the West. John Slidell, the diplomat sent to Mexico City with Polk's offer, was never even received by the Mexican government. Early in 1846 Polk sent an American force commanded by General Zachary Taylor to defend the territory between the Nueces and the Rio Grande rivers. In early April part of this force was ambushed by the Mexican army. Polk had to do little to convince the American Congress to issue a declaration of war against Mexico on May 13, 1846.

Many Whigs had hoped the conflict with Mexico could be peacefully negotiated; abolitionists feared the conflict with Mexico was little more than a Southern ruse to expand slavery in the American territories. Texas had never achieved real prosperity since its independence from Mexico, and the Mexican government was riddled with corruption. President Polk had predicted that the Mexicans would refuse American efforts to purchase western territories, and he proceeded through officials stationed there to let Americans and Mexicans living in California know that if they rose in opposition to Mexican control of the area, the American army would protect them. Not coincidentally, American naval and infantry forces arrived in California in late 1845 as a show of American force. Shortly after the American declaration of war against Mexico, settlers rose up in revolt, supported by American infantry forces commanded by John C. Fremont. On July 4, 1846, the **Bear Flag Republic** was officially proclaimed in the California territory.

American troops also entered into Mexico itself, easily defeating the Mexican army. Forces under Zachary Taylor were especially successful in winning battles over the Mexicans in late 1846 and early 1847. The Mexican government refused to surrender or negotiate with the Americans. President Polk then sent an American force under General Winfield Scott to Mexico to occupy Mexico City, the capital. Scott landed on Mexican territory at Veracruz on March 8, 1847, and was victorious in several battles against the Mexicans. Mexico still refused to settle for peace, and on September 13, 1847, Scott's army entered Mexico City. Mexican partisans continued guerrilla warfare well into 1848.

Effects of the Mexican War

The **Treaty of Guadalupe Hidalgo** was signed on February 2, 1848, and officially ended the Mexican-American War. Many who had favored war considered the treaty too generous to the defeated Mexicans. For $15 million the United States acquired the Texas territory north of the Rio Grande, New Mexico, and California (the exact territory they had previously offered to buy). The American government also assumed all claims of Americans against the Mexican government.

The territory of the United States increased by one-third as a result of this treaty, yet the controversy over slavery in the new territories was immense. In 1846 David Wilmont, a Democratic Representative from Pennsylvania, introduced an amendment to a bill authorizing funding for the Mexican-American War that stated slavery could not exist in any territory acquired from Mexico. The **Wilmont Proviso** was passed by the House of Representatives four times and rejected by the Senate each time. Nevertheless, each debate concerning the bill stirred up intense sectional differences concerning slavery in the territories. Southerners such as John C. Calhoun strenuously argued that the federal government had no right to outlaw something in an American territory that was legal in a number of American states. President Polk's compromise decision was to continue the line drawn by the **Missouri Compromise** out to the Pacific Ocean, with slavery allowed in territories south of the line and not allowed in territories north of the line.

To avoid being hurt by the controversies surrounding slavery, both the Democrats and the Whigs said little about it in the 1848 presidential election. Zachary Taylor ran as a Whig and was victorious, largely because of his war record in Mexico and because he made no comments whatsoever about the future of slavery in the territories. Some members of the Liberty party and defectors from the Whig and Democratic parties formed the **Free-Soil party**, whose main purpose was to oppose slavery in the newly acquired western territories. The Free-Soilers nominated former president Van Buren, who won 10 percent of the popular vote.

POLITICAL CHALLENGES OF THE 1850s

The controversies of the 1850s largely centered around slavery and its status in the newly acquired American territories. Americans had been able to compromise on such issues in the first half of the nineteenth century. By the 1850s the volatile nature of debate on the issue of slavery made compromise much harder to come by.

The discovery of gold in California in January of 1848 caused a flood of "diggers" to enter the territory. Within a year over 80,000 "forty-niners" entered the state. By the end of 1849 the territory's population swelled to over 100,000. Law enforcement and governmental controls were severely lacking in much of the territory. Zachary Taylor encouraged settlers in California and New Mexico to draft constitutions and to apply for statehood. By the end of 1849 California had adopted a constitution prohibiting slavery; New Mexico did the same six months later.

Taylor's proposal to allow California to enter the Union as a non-slave state infuriated many Southerners. Southern senators railed that much of the California territory was south of the **Missouri Compromise** line: Shouldn't slavery be allowed in that part of California? A convention was called for representatives of Southern states to come together and discuss leaving the Union. John C. Calhoun captured the feeling of many Southerners when he said, "I trust we shall persist in our resistance until restoration or all our rights, or disunion, one or the other, is the consequence."

Henry Clay, the author of the **Missouri Compromise**, spoke forcefully against many of Calhoun's arguments and wrote the parts of the legislation that together would be called the **Compromise of 1850**. Both the North and the South got some of what they wanted in this compromise. Northerners were happy that the legislation allowed California to enter the Union as a free state, that the residents of the New Mexico and Utah territories would decide if these areas would be slave territories, and that slave trading was eliminated in Washington, DC. Southerners were satisfied over several provisions found in the legislation: provisions of the **Fugitive Slave Law** were toughened, Congress stated that it didn't have jurisdiction over interstate slave trade, and slavery was allowed to continue in Washington. Eight months of debate were needed to pass all provisions of the compromise. Senator Stephen A. Douglas of Illinois was the most effective spokesperson for the cause of the compromise. California entering the Union as a free state gave the free states a majority; in the future, that majority would grow, helping to explain the increased tensions between the North and the South between 1850 and 1860.

The presidential election of 1852 was another campaign devoid of much discussion of the slave issue. The Free-Soilers got half the votes they had received in the 1848 election. General Winfield Scott was the candidate of the Whigs. Like Zachary Taylor in 1848, he made few public statements on political issues. Franklin Pierce was another **dark-horse candidate** who won the Democratic nomination and then the presidency.

EFFECTS OF THE COMPROMISE OF 1850

The part of the **Compromise of 1850** that most bothered abolitionists in the North was the strengthening of the **Fugitive Slave Act**. Under the new provisions of the bill, judges in the North determined the fate of blacks accused of being escaped slaves. Accused runaways were denied jury proceedings and often were denied the right to testify in their own trials. Heavy financial penalties were imposed on Northerners who helped slaves escape or who hid slaves. Harriet Beecher Stowe's *Uncle Tom's Cabin* was written as a response to the **Fugitive Slave Act**. Stowe demonstrated the immorality of slavery in her novel, which sold nearly 275,000 copies in its first year of publication.

THE PRESIDENCY OF FRANKLIN PIERCE

Pierce's foreign policy was pro-expansionist. In 1853 he sent a naval force under Commodore Matthew Perry to Japan to open Japan to American trade and diplomatic contact. American diplomats negotiated the **Gadsden Purchase** with Mexico, which gave America an additional southern route for trade (and territory for a proposed transcontinental railroad). Pierce also initiated efforts to purchase Cuba from the Spanish. When this effort proved unsuccessful, many in the Pierce administration favored the seizing of Cuba by force, which infuriated many in the North. Pierce's policies seemed to benefit Southern interests and were viewed with suspicion by many in the North.

The Whig party also died during this period. Many former Whigs became members of the American or **Know-Nothing party** that developed in response to rising immigration from Ireland and Germany, which had begun in the late 1840s. The Know-Nothing party was **nativist** and especially anti-Catholic. The Know-Nothings favored restrictions on further immigration and various schemes that would keep recent immigrants from voting. The fact that it was the second most powerful party in America during the first years of the Pierce administration demonstrates the weakness of the two-party system in this period.

THE RETURN OF SECTIONAL CONFLICT

The desire to organize settlement in Kansas and Nebraska brought tensions between the North and the South back to the forefront. According to the provisions of the Missouri Compromise, slavery would be banned in both of these territories. Stephen A. Douglas, sponsor of the bill that proposed the creation of the Kansas and Nebraska territories, wanted to create a large region free of native Americans so that a transcontinental railroad could be built between Chicago and the West Coast. Douglas was pressured by Southern senators and included a provision in the bill that the existence of slavery in these territories would be decided by a vote of those that lived there. This **Kansas-Nebraska Act** infuriated many in the North. The bill was passed with the support of President Pierce.

The fury over the passage of the Kansas-Nebraska Act caused the creation of the **Republican party**. The party was an exclusively Northern one and was dedicated to the principle that slavery should be prohibited in all territories. Some former Democrats, Whigs, and Free-Soilers made up the base of the Republican party, which would quickly replace the Know-Nothings as the second most important political party in the United States.

"BLEEDING KANSAS": SLAVE OR FREE?

In preparations for elections that would be held in 1855, states and interests supporting and opposing slavery all were active in sending settlers into Kansas that would support their cause. Abolitionists financed the journey to Kansas of many settlers opposed to slavery; at the same time, many Southern states "encouraged" settlers to travel there. Conflicts, often involving bloodshed, erupted between the two sides. Many proslavery settlers flooded into Kansas from Missouri, thus ensuring the election of a pro-slavery legislature in 1855 by casting illegal ballots. The legislature enacted measures designed to protect slavery in the territory (the "Lecompton Constitution" made slavery legal in a constitutional sense). Free-Soilers proceeded to elect their own legislature and adopted equally harsh antislavery legislation. Violence continued in **"Bleeding Kansas"** in 1856: The free-soil settlement at Lawrence was attacked, and in response, abolitionist John Brown and his followers killed five pro-slavery settlers. Fighting between supporters and opponents of slavery continued throughout the year.

Democrat James Buchanan won the presidential election of 1856. The opposition to him was split, with John C. Fremont running as a Republican and ex-president Millard Fillmore running as the Know-Nothing candidate. It should be noted that Fremont and Fillmore together gained nearly 55 percent of the popular vote.

THE DRED SCOTT DECISION

The **Dred Scott case** finally made it to the Supreme Court docket in 1856. Many hoped it would decisively end the controversy over slavery in the territories. Dred Scott was a former slave who was suing for his freedom on the basis that his owner had taken him to stay first in a free state, Illinois, and then into a free territory, Wisconsin.

The final decision of the Supreme Court, in essence, supported the Southern position concerning slavery in the territories. The court ruled that Scott as a slave had no legal right to sue in federal court, that his time in a free state and a free territory did not make him a free man, and that Congress had no right to prohibit slavery in the territories, since the Constitution protected property rights and slaves were still considered property.

Instead of easing tensions between the North and South, the Dred Scott decision only made tensions between the sections worse. Southerners felt their position had been justified and felt little need to compromise with the North; Northerners were more convinced than ever that "slave interests" controlled all the branches of government.

President Buchanan further antagonized Northerners by recommending that Kansas be admitted to the Union as a slave state, even though the legislature in Kansas had been elected by largely illegal means (Kansas was finally admitted to the Union as a free state in 1861).

THE LINCOLN–DOUGLAS DEBATES

Stephen Douglas was opposed by Abraham Lincoln in the 1858 election for senator from Illinois. Lincoln had been a Whig but was now a Republican, having broken from the Whig party over slavery. Lincoln was a practicing attorney, had been in the U.S. Congress during the Mexican War, and narrowly lost an earlier bid for the Senate in 1852. Douglas and Lincoln debated at seven locations throughout Illinois in the months leading up to the election. The issues of slavery and the territories dominated all of these debates. At a debate in Freeport, Lincoln asked Douglas how the residents of a territory could exclude slavery in light of the Dred Scott decision. Douglas responded with the **Freeport Doctrine**, which maintained that a territory could exclude slavery if the laws and regulations written made slavery impossible to enforce. Douglas won the Senate seat, but Lincoln was recognized by many as an up-and-coming force in the Republican party.

JOHN BROWN'S RAID

Radical abolitionist John Brown and 18 followers seized the federal arsenal at Harper's Ferry, Virginia, on the evening of October 16, 1859. Brown hoped to incite a slave uprising by his actions. It would later become known that Brown's actions had been financed by several wealthy Northern abolitionists. Brown was captured, tried for treason, and hung. The response to Brown's death further intensified the tensions between the North and the South. Henry David Thoreau was one of many Northerners to consider Brown as "the bravest and humanest man in all the country," while Southerners were outraged by Northern support of Brown's actions.

THE PRESIDENTIAL ELECTION OF 1860

The election of Abraham Lincoln as president in 1860 virtually ensured that some Southern states would leave the Union. Lincoln campaigned on the need to contain slavery in the territories. The Democratic party split at their nominating convention, with Stephen Douglas receiving the support of Northern Democrats and John Breckinridge getting the backing of Southern Democrats. Douglas stated that the slave issue in the territories should be decided by a vote of those residing in each territory; Breckinridge proposed that slavery should be legally protected in the territories. John Bell also received some ex-Whig support as he ran as a candidate of the Constitutional Union party. Lincoln received nearly 40 percent of the popular vote and easily won the Electoral College vote.

To many Southerners, the election was an insult. A man had been elected president who virtually no one in the South had voted for. Since free states outnumbered slaves states, it was only natural that their representatives would dominate Congress and the Electoral College. Lincoln had repeatedly stated that Republicans had no interest in disturbing slavery in the South, but many Southerners did not believe him.

South Carolina was the first state to leave the Union on December 20, 1860. In the next six weeks, legislatures in Mississippi, Georgia, Florida, Alabama, Texas, and Louisiana all voted to do the same. Representatives of these seven states met in February of 1861 to create the **Confederate States of America**, with former moderate Jefferson Davis elected as president. The only question remaining was when the first shots between the North and the South would actually be fired.

CHAPTER REVIEW

Rapid Review Guide

To achieve the perfect 5, you should be able to explain the following:

- The concept of manifest destiny spurred American expansion into Texas and the far West.

- American settlers much more loyal to the United States than to Mexico entered Texas in large numbers and encouraged Texas to break away from Mexico and eventually become an American state.

- The issue of slavery and slavery in the territories came to dominate American political debate more and more in the 1840s and 1850s.

- California entered the Union as a free state under the Missouri Compromise, upsetting the balance between free and slave states and intensifying the conflict between them.

- The Kansas-Nebraska Act created violence in these territories as they "decided" on whether they would be slave or free; both abolitionists and pro-slavery forces shipped in supporters to help sway the elections in these territories.

- The Dred Scott decision only intensified tensions between the North and the South.

- The election of 1860 was seen as an insult to many in the South, and after its results were announced, the secession of Southern states from the Union was inevitable.

Time Line

1836: Texas territory repels against Mexico; independent republic of Texas created
1841: Beginning of expansion into Oregon territory
1844: James K. Polk elected president
1845: Texas becomes a state of the United States
1846: Oregon Treaty with Britain gives most of Oregon to United States
War with Mexico begins
Wilmont Proviso passed
1848: Gold discovered in California; beginning of California gold rush
Treaty of Guadalupe Hidalgo
Formation of Free-Soil party
Zachary Taylor elected president

1850: Passage of Compromise of 1850
1852: Franklin Pierce elected president
Uncle Tom's Cabin by Harriet Beecher Stowe published
1854: Kansas-Nebraska Act passed
Formation of the Republican party
1856: Democrat James Buchanan elected president
"Bleeding Kansas"
1857: Dred Scott decision announced
1858: Lincoln-Douglas debates
Freeport Doctrine issued by Stephen Douglas
1859: Harper's Ferry rail of John Brown
1860: Abraham Lincoln elected president
South Carolina secedes from the Union (December)

✓ Review Questions

1. Northerners approved all of the provisions of the Compromise of 1850 *except*

    A. the section of the document concerning slavery in California
    B. the section of the document concerning the Fugitive Slave Law
    C. the section of the treaty on slave trading in Washington, DC
    D. the section of the document concerning slavery in New Mexico
    E. the section of the document concerning slavery in Utah

(Correct Answer: **B.** In the Compromise of 1850, provisions of the Fugitive Slave Law were made tougher. California was to enter the Union as a free state, the residents of New Mexico and Utah could decided if they wanted to be slave or free, and slaving trading was outlawed in Washington, DC.)

2. During the presidential election of 1860

    A. the Democratic party had split and ran two candidates
    B. the new president was someone that almost no one in the South had voted for
    C. support for the Constitutional Union party demonstrated that ex-Whigs were not satisfied with either the Democratic or the Republican party
    D. the issue of the future of slavery in the territories was a major issue
    E. All of the above

(Correct Answer: **E.** All of the factors mentioned concerning the 1860 election are true.)

3. According to the concept of manifest destiny

    A. it was primarily economic factors that caused Americans to expand westward
    B. it was primarily political factors that caused Americans to expand westward
    C. the desires of the American military did much to force westward expansion
    D. westward expansion was the fulfillment of America's destiny
    E. overpopulation on the eastern seaboard forced westward expansion

(Correct Answer: **D.** The concept of manifest destiny stated that social, political, and social factors all came together to encourage western expansion, and that western expansion was actually "God's plan" for America.)

4. American settlers first came to Mexico in the early 1830s

   A. to avenge the attack on the Alamo
   B. for religious reasons; most that came were devout Catholics
   C. for political reasons; most that came were disenchanted with American policy toward Native Americans
   D. out of personal loyalty to Davey Crockett or Jim Bowie
   E. because they could receive a large plot of land for next to nothing

(Correct Answer: **E.** Settlers who came and became Mexican citizens and Catholics could receive very large plots of land for almost nothing. The incident at the Alamo did not occur until 1836.)

5. The political party of the era that supported nativist policies was the

   A. Liberty party
   B. Free-Soil party
   C. Democratic party
   D. Know-Nothing party
   E. Whig party

(Correct Answer: **D.** The Know-Nothing party, a popular party in the early 1850s, supported a number of anti-immigrant and anti-Catholic policies.)

Chapter 11

The Union Divided: The Civil War (1861–1865)

The Civil War was the culmination of nearly 40 years of tensions between the North and the South. Northern abolitionists looked forward to the war with great anticipation: Victory over the South would finally allow the dreaded institution of slavery to be eliminated. Northern industrialists saw the war as an opportunity, at long last, to expand their control of American industry. The majority of Southerners rejoiced at the onset of war; they perceived that victory would allow the "Southern way of life" to continue without constant criticism from the North. As in many wars, politicians and generals on both sides predicted a quick victory. Newspapers in both the North and the South declared that the war would be over by Christmas of 1861.

To state that the Civil War was just about slavery is an oversimplification. Certainly, criticism by Northern abolitionists of the "peculiar institution" of slavery, and Southern responses to that criticism, were important factors. However, other tensions between the North and the South also existed. The future of the American economy as seen by Northern industrialists differed drastically from the desires and needs of the leaders of Southern plantation society. Most importantly, the Southern view of "state's rights" differed most dramatically from the view of the Union held in the North. By 1861, many political leaders in the South fervently espoused the views that John C. Calhoun had formulated decades earlier: It was up to the individual state to decided on the validity of any federal law or federal action for that state. This position was intolerable to President Lincoln and most political leaders in the North. If anything, it was debate over the state's rights issue that made the Civil War inevitable.

Other factors increased the animosity between the North and the South. By this point slavery was synonymous with Southern identity; in Southern eyes any attack on slavery was an attack on the South as a whole. The fact that this struggle between the North and the South had gone on for 40 years served to harden positions on both sides. In addition, by this point the population of the North was greater than the population of the South, and the number of free states was greater than the number of slave states. As a result, Southerners knew that Northern antislave interests would control the Congress (and the ability to influence Supreme Court appointments) and the Electoral College for the foreseeable future.

ADVANTAGES OF THE NORTH AND SOUTH IN WAR

Many Southerners were very excited when the Civil War finally began, yet there were some harsh realities facing them as war commenced. Most of the nation's wealth was situated in the North; the industrialization of the North would give Northerners an advantage in producing guns, bullets, and other materials needed for warfare. The Northern railway system was far superior to the existing railways in the South. Most influential banks and financial markets were located in the North. More people (by a nearly 3-to-1 margin) lived in the North. The South could at least say that they were larger than the North; conquering the South would be a formidable task. At the outset of the war, Southerners might also claim that their officer corps, led by men such as Robert E. Lee, was superior to the officer corps of the Union, led by Winfield Scott.

The Aftermath of Secession

As mentioned in the previous chapter, South Carolina, Mississippi, Florida, Louisiana, Texas, Georgia, and Alabama all voted to secede from the Union in late 1860 or early 1861. In February 1861, the **Confederate States of America** was officially created. States in the Upper South (such as Virginia and Kentucky) were not eager to join the secessionist movement (there were fewer slaves in these states). Leaders of Kentucky and Maryland proposed that Congress in Washington enact legislation that would protect slavery in any territory or state where it already existed; the desire of these leaders was the preservation of the Union. President James Buchanan did little to aid the situation. Buchanan stated in December of 1860 that secession from the Union was illegal, but that nowhere in the Constitution was it stated that any state could be forced to remain in the Union.

Politicians in South Carolina and elsewhere in the South interpreted Buchanan's statement as, in essence, stating that he would do nothing to bring back the seceded states and that they were now independent. Leaders in South Carolina demanded the surrender of **Fort Sumter**, a federal fort located in Charleston harbor. To test the will of the leaders of South Carolina, Buchanan sent an unarmed merchant ship to bring supplies to the fort. When the ship was fired on, Buchanan did not send the navy in (which many in South Carolina was sure he would do); "patriots" in South Carolina and elsewhere in the South now felt certain that independence was theirs.

As the crisis continued at Fort Sumter, Senator John Crittenden of Kentucky emerged with a compromise plan. The **Crittenden Plan** proposed that the federal government guarantee the existence of slavery in any state where it existed, and that the line of the Missouri Compromise be extended all the way to the Pacific, with territories to the north of the line being free from slavery and those south of the line having slavery. Republicans in Congress rejected this plan, since it went away from the concept of "free soil" that president-elect Lincoln had just been elected on.

THE ATTACK ON FORT SUMTER AND THE BEGINNING OF WAR

Abraham Lincoln had to walk a political tightrope upon his inauguration in March of 1861. It was necessary to maintain the authority of the federal government, but at the same time to do nothing that would provoke war with the South. Many of Lincoln's advisors thought that negotiations could bring at least some of the states that had seceded back into the Union. In his inauguration speech, however, Lincoln stated that force would be used if necessary to preserve the Union.

The skill of Lincoln as president was immediately called upon. In April of 1861, Lincoln sent another ship to supply **Fort Sumter**. The government of South Carolina was informed that the ship would be arriving and that no troops would land unless the delivery of these supplies was interfered with. Jefferson Davis and the Confederate government saw this as an opportunity to strike against the Union. Confederate guns bombed Fort Sumter for two days, and on April 14 the fort surrendered. Davis was hopeful that early victory would force states in the Upper South to turn to the Confederate cause; Confederates also hoped to obtain British and French assistance. Any thought of compromise between North and South ended with the attack on Fort Sumter.

Three days after the surrender of the fort, Virginia passed a resolution favoring secession. On the same day, Robert E. Lee rejected an offer to command the Union army, resigned from the Union army, and took control of the Confederate army. In the end, Lincoln was able to keep four of the states of the Upper South in the Union (Kentucky, Missouri, Maryland, and Delaware).

WAR AIMS AND STRATEGIES

From the beginning of the war, the Southern defense of the slave system was unrelenting. This position greatly undermined the possibility of the Confederacy receiving aid from the French and the English. Economically, European support of the Confederacy would have made sense; European nations were dependent on cotton cultivated in the American South. However, both France and England firmly opposed slavery and had outlawed it in their countries decades earlier. The South also overestimated the British need for Southern cotton; Britain soon proved that it could get cotton elsewhere.

Both sides began recruiting armies in the spring and early summer of 1861. Lincoln was able to summon support in the Northern states not from speeches on slavery but from the simple claim that the actions of the South was an attack on the very principles of the republican form of government. Both sides predicted early victory. The capital of the Confederacy was moved to Richmond, Virginia, after Virginia joined the Confederacy; cries of "On to Richmond!" filled the Northern newspapers. For political reasons, Lincoln pushed for an early attack against the South (Winfield Scott presented an alternative proposal, stating that the best policy for the North would be to blockade all Southern ports and starve the South into submission). A Union army advanced on Richmond. On July 21, 1861, at the **First Battle of Bull Run**, Union forces retreated in chaos back toward Washington. After this battle Northern political leaders and generals conceded that victory in this war would not be as easy as they initially thought it might be.

The Effects of Bull Run

The Battle of Bull Run showed both sides that new tactics would be necessary for victory. The plan proposed by Winfield Scott, now referred to as the **Anaconda Plan**, was reviewed more carefully by Abraham Lincoln. Lincoln had the United States Navy blockade Southern ports; as the war wore on, this became increasingly important. Industrial goods that the South had imported from the industrial North in earlier years now could not be gotten from Europe either. Also, later in the war Confederate states could not export cotton to Europe for very badly needed currency. Another part of the Anaconda Plan called for Northern naval forces to control the Mississippi River. The Union made major headway with this part of the plan in April of 1862 when a Union naval force captured New Orleans.

The Confederacy also made a major foreign trading mistake in early 1862. Cotton-producing states were convinced not to export cotton to England and France. Confederate leaders thought that textile factory owners in those countries would be so affected by this that they would pressure their governments to help the Confederacy and get their cotton back. Instead, Europeans turned elsewhere for cotton (especially India). As stated previously, when the South wanted to export cotton later in the war, they couldn't because of the naval blockade. It also became obvious that the organization of the South into a confederacy during a period of wartime was a disadvantage; individual state governments had the constitutional right to block critical tax programs and requisitions. The decision of the Confederacy to print paper money with no secure backing also would prove to be detrimental.

The Union Triumphant in the West

The Confederacy won several more battles in 1862, including the **Second Battle of Bull Run**. General George McClellan was named commander of the Union army and began formulating a plan to attack the Confederacy from the west. In February 1862, forces commanded by General Ulysses S. Grant captured Fort Henry and Fort Donelson, in Tennessee. Forces on both sides realized the importance of these victories. Grant continued to conquer Southern territory from this position. On April 6, 1862, the incredibly bloody but inconclusive **Battle of Shiloh** was fought. Up until this point it was the bloodiest battle ever fought in America. McClellan began to develop the reputation as a commander who was afraid to enter his troops into battle, even though the situation warranted it.

The Confederacy attempted to use technology to defeat the Northern naval blockade. In March of 1862 they presented their very first **ironclad** ship, the **Merrimack**. Shortly after the Union displayed the first Union ironclad, the **Monitor**. The two ironclads met once in battle, with neither ship able to do much to damage to the other.

DEVELOPMENTS IN THE SOUTH AND IN THE NORTH

Being a nation founded on the principle of **state's rights** was oftentimes a disadvantage for the Confederacy. Many Confederate soldiers who enlisted for one year in 1861 appeared ready to return home in 1862. General Robert E. Lee insisted that a system of **conscription** had to be introduced to ensure a steady supply of soldiers. In April 1862, the Confederate legislature passed laws requiring three years in the army for all white men from 18 to 35 (after the horrible losses of Antietam, this was extended to 45). Many advocates of state's rights violently objected to these regulations. Three Southern governors tried to block the conscription law in their states, saying that only the individual states had the right to make such laws. In some sections of the South nearly 60 percent of available manpower never served in the army. The Confederacy also adopted a plan to pay plantation owners who released their slaves to serve in the army; this was largely resisted because it was economically harmful to slave owners.

By late 1862 severe shortages of food and other materials began to spread throughout the South. Prices skyrocketed. Many soldiers deserted the army to return home to help their families through these difficult times. Large numbers of deserters and those who had resisted the draft became a problem in some sections of the South. The Confederacy instituted an income tax in order to get needed income for the government. Under existing circumstances, the actual collection of this money was sometimes difficult.

Many similar tensions existed in the North. In 1863 a system of conscription was introduced, requiring service of all men from ages 20 through 45. As in the South, draft dodgers could be found in the North. A provision of the Northern draft law that was very unpopular to many allowed a drafted person to avoid service by hiring a substitute or by paying the government $300; many of the "replacement" soldiers were Irish immigrants. Draft riots took place in New York City in July 1863, with nearly 200 people dying in these protests. Many taking part in the riots were Irish-Americans, and many of those killed were black. Draft offices and other buildings were destroyed; Irish-Americans did not want to take part in a war that would free the slaves, whom they perceived would be their competitors for jobs.

The North also had trouble financing the war. In 1861 a federal income tax was instituted. Still short of money, the government began issuing "**greenbacks**" in 1862; this money, not backed by gold, was considered official legal tender until the end of the war.

In every wartime setting in American history, the power of the executive has expanded. This was certainly true in the Civil War. President Lincoln assumed powers that no previous president had even considered. By executive order parts of Kentucky were placed under **martial law** for much of the war. Some Democrats in the North, nicknamed **Copperheads**, vigorously opposed the war, stating that it would lead to masses of freed slaves coming north and taking jobs. Copperheads were sometimes arrested, and three of them were actually deported from the North. Over 14,000 who opposed the war were imprisoned without trial. In several cases Lincoln ordered the **writ of habeas corpus** suspended.

THE EMANCIPATION PROCLAMATION

When he was elected president, Abraham Lincoln had no thought whatsoever of freeing the slaves; he repeatedly stated that he had no constitutional right to do that. However, on a practical level Lincoln realized that the continued existence of slavery in the South would make Northern victory harder; the existence of slavery allowed Southern landowners to leave their fields and fight in the Confederate army.

The **Emancipation Proclamation** was issued on January 1, 1863. The timing of this was a brilliant political move. Support for the war in the North had been waning; the Emancipation Proclamation gave Northerners a moral justification to continue fighting. This measure was received by different groups in predictable ways. Northern blacks were heartened by it, Southerners condemned it, and in Southern territories controlled by the Union army, slaves were actually freed. Many in England agreed with the proclamation; any last hopes that England might enter the war to aid the Confederacy were dashed at this point. Some whites in the North feared that ex-slaves would end up taking their jobs, and as a result, in the 1862 congressional elections Democrats picked up seats.

Blacks were not accepted into the Union army at the beginning of the war. After the Emancipation Proclamation many ex-slaves from Southern territories and free blacks from the North joined the Union army. By

1865, blacks made up almost 10 percent of the entire Union army. Black soldiers traditionally served in all-black units with white officers (the heroism of the 54th Massachusetts Infantry can be seen in the movie *Glory*).

1863: THE WAR TIPS TO THE NORTH

The darkest days of the war for the Union occurred in late 1862 and early 1863. The Union army suffered major defeats at the **Battle of Fredericksburg** (December 13, 1862) and at the **Battle of Chancellorsville** (May 1 to 3, 1863). Competent leadership of the Union army remained a major problem.

Yet time was an enemy of the Confederate army. As commander, General Robert E. Lee found it increasingly difficult to get men and resources (the Northern naval blockade definitely was affecting Southern military efforts by this point). In June of 1863, Lee decided to move the Confederate army out of Virginia into Pennsylvania. At the **Battle of Gettysburg** (July 1 to 3, 1863). Lee was defeated by the Union army, commanded by General George Meade. This was the bloodiest overall battle of the war, with 24,000 casualties suffered by the North and 28,000 by the South. Lee's army was forced to retreat to Virginia and would never again be able to mount an attack into Northern territory. Some military historians claim that the fate of the Confederate army was sealed by their defeat at Gettysburg.

The tide of the war continued to swing to the North as a result of several victories by armies commanded by Ulysses S. Grant. On July 4, 1863, Grant completed his victory at **Vicksburg**, ending a siege of the city that lasted six weeks. Victory at Vicksburg gave the Union virtual control of the Mississippi River. In November Grant was victorious at the Battle of Chattanooga (November 23 to 25, 1863). Abraham Lincoln's **Gettysburg Address** had been given four days earlier. In January of 1864 Grant was made commander of the Union army. At the same time, some in the Confederate government began speaking of the need for peace negotiations with the North.

Grant and the Army of the Potomac began to advance toward Richmond in the spring of 1864, while an army commanded by William T. Sherman began to advance toward Atlanta.

WAR WEARINESS IN THE NORTH AND SOUTH

In both the North and the South the pressures of a long war were obvious by 1864. To many in the South, it was clear that the Confederacy would be defeated. Severe food and material shortages continued. In the North, the presidential campaign of 1864 produced little excitement. Lincoln's Democratic opponent was General George McClellan. In early September of 1864 Lincoln confided to friends that he thought he would lose the presidency. However, word arrived that General Sherman had taken the key Confederate city of Atlanta. That, along with any real enthusiasm for (and by) McClellan, allowed Lincoln to easily win reelection.

THE END OF THE CONFEDERACY

Sherman employed a scorched earth policy as he marched from Atlanta to Savannah, Georgia, in November and December of 1864. In early April of 1865 General Lee took the Confederate army from Richmond and tried to escape to the south. The Union army caught up to him, and he finally surrendered on April 9, 1865, at the courthouse in **Appomattox**, Virginia. By the first week of June all other Confederate forces also surrendered and began to return home to oftentimes devastated homelands.

Lincoln only had time to begin to plan for what a post-Civil War America would look like. On April 14, 1865, he was assassinated by John Wilkes Booth at Ford's Theater. Booth was a pro-Southerner. He and a group of coconspirators also planned to kill Vice President Andrew Johnson and other members of the Lincoln cabinet. Booth was hunted down several days later and was killed by gunfire; several others conspiring with him were found and, after trials by military tribunals, hung. The incredibly difficult task of reconstruction would have to be handled by the new president, Andrew Johnson, a Tennessee Democrat who Lincoln had chosen to be his vice president.

CHAPTER REVIEW

Rapid Review Guide

To achieve the perfect 5, you should be able to explain the following:

- By 1861 various social, political, economic, and cultural factors made conflict between the North and the South inevitable.

- The North had numerous industrial, transportation, and financial advantages that they utilized throughout the Civil War.

- The Confederate States of America was created in February 1861; the fact that these states were organized as a confederacy had several disadvantages that would become obvious as the war progressed.

- Success for the Confederacy depended on European aid; Southerners overestimated the dependence of Europe on Southern crops.

- Confederate generals proved much more competent than their Union counterparts in several key battles in the first years of the war.

- By late 1862 the war had produced severe effects on the home fronts; food shortages were occurring in the South, and President Lincoln imposed martial law in several locations and suspended the writ of habeas corpus in the cases of some of his political opponents.

- The Emancipation Proclamation provided a moral justification for Northerners to continue the war.

- The war shifted decisively in favor of the North in 1863, with the battles of Gettysburg and Vicksburg proving to be critical victories for the North.

- The surrender of the Confederacy in April 1865 was caused by a severe lack of morale, manpower, and economic stability in the South.

Time Line

1860: Abraham Lincoln elected president
South Carolina secedes from Union
1861: Confederate States of America created
Attack on Fort Sumter
First Battle of Bull Run
Union begins blockade of Southern ports
1862: New Orleans captured by Union navy
Battle of Shiloh
Conscription begins in Confederate states
Emancipation of slaves in Southern states begins
Battle of Antietam
British announce they will not aid the Confederacy in any substantial way
1863: Emancipation Proclamation
Conscription begins in the North; draftees may hire "replacements"
First black soldiers enlist in Union army
Crucial Union victory at Gettysburg
Crucial Union victory at Vicksburg
Draft riots in New York City
1864: Abraham Lincoln reelected
General Sherman carries out his "march to the sea"
Desertion becomes a major problem in the Confederate army
1865: General Lee surrenders at Appomattox
Abraham Lincoln assassinated

✓ Review Questions

1. The North held many advantages at the beginning of the Civil War *except*

   A. most major financial institutions were in the North
   B. the North occupied more territory than the South
   C. the North had more railroad lines
   D. the North had more factories
   E. the North had a larger population

   (Correct Answer: **B.** All of the others were major advantages for the Union war effort.)

2. European states did not aid the Confederacy in the Civil War because

A. Union diplomats made many efforts to convince them not to
B. there were alternative sources of cotton and other crops that they could turn to
C. the Confederacy's position on slavery
D. they did not believe that the Confederacy could win
E. All of the above

(Correct Answer: **E**. All of the reasons given helped convince the Europeans not to assist the Confederacy. The Confederacy's position on slavery proved to be especially troublesome, since slavery had long been outlawed in Europe.)

3. The military draft was unpopular to many in the North because

A. the North already was lacking in men during this period
B. the draft allowed blacks to enter the armed forces
C. the draft allowed Irish-American immigrants to enter the army
D. the draft allowed those drafted to hire "replacements"
E. martial law was needed in many locations to enforce the draft provisions

(Correct Answer: **D**. The fact that replacement soldiers, oftentimes immigrants, could be hired or that a payment of $300 to the government could get a man out of the draft made the system very unpopular to many.)

4. The Battle of Vicksburg was an important victory for the Union because

A. it reversed several Union defeats in the same year
B. it came quickly, with a minimal loss of Union life
C. it gave the Union a pathway to Atlanta
D. it gave the Union virtual control of the Mississippi River
E. it demonstrated that General Lee could, in fact, be beaten

(Correct Answer: **D**. The six-week Battle of Vicksburg occurred in 1863 and helped turn the war in the Union's favor. As a result of Vicksburg, the Mississippi was virtually in the hands of the Union. Lee did not command the Confederate forces at Vicksburg.)

5. Copperheads were

A. Democrats in the North who opposed the war
B. Republicans in the North who suggested that Lincoln be replaced
C. Democrats in the North who switched over to Lincoln
D. Southern Democrats who wanted negotiations with the North as early at 1863
E. Northern Democrats who moved to the South during the war

(Correct Answer: **A**. Copperheads were Democrats in the North who claimed that the war would bring economic ruin to the North, with freed slaves taking jobs that whites now had. Some were arrested and deported.)

Chapter 12

The Era of Reconstruction (1865–1877)

"Some men are born great, some achieve greatness and others lived during the Reconstruction period."

Paul Laurence Dunbar, 1903

LINCOLN'S PLANS FOR RECONSTRUCTION

The preceding quote perfectly expresses the frustrations felt by many Americans during the <u>Reconstruction Era</u>. During this period, political leaders in the North had to decide how the former states of the Confederacy would be assimilated back into the Union. What should be done with former Confederate leaders? What should be done with former slaves? How much punishment (if any) should the former states of the Confederacy be made to endure? There were obviously incredibly complicated questions, and the results *had* to be imperfect in some manner.

Other factors increased the difficulty of the Southern assimilation after the Civil War. It was only when defeated Confederate soldiers returned to their homes that the extent of the devastation of the South during the war became widely known. Virtually the entire Southern railway system and many farms and cities were destroyed by the war. In addition, nearly one-third of all adult males residing in Confederate states died or were wounded during the war. For those plantation owners whose plantations were not destroyed, laborers now had to be hired; many of these owners were now strapped for cash. Many freed blacks wandered the countryside looking for work, while many poorer white men with jobs lived in fear of being replaced by freed black men.

The problems of Reconstruction were compounded by the assassination of Abraham Lincoln at the very end of the Civil War. Lincoln had begun constructing a Reconstruction plan as early as mid-1863. Lincoln devised a plan for former Confederates to rejoin the Union that was entitled the **Ten Percent Plan**. By the provisions of this plan, citizens of former Confederate states would be given the opportunity to swear allegiance to the government in Washington (high-ranking Confederate military and civilian authorities would not be offered this opportunity). When 10 percent of the registered voters in the state signed this pledge, the state was afforded the chance to form its own state government, which obviously had to be loyal to Washington.

Tennessee, Louisiana, and Arkansas all went through the appropriate procedures to form loyal state governments, yet their applications for renewed participation in the Union were not approved by the **Radical Republicans** who dominated the Congress. These men were determined to punish the Southern states in any way possible for their "betrayal" of the Union. This group, led by Thaddeus Stevens, included several who had been ardent abolitionists in the years before the Civil War. They believed that power in the Southern states had to be totally reorganized in order for blacks to achieve equality. The Radical Republicans also saw the creation of Reconstruction policy as a constitutional issue, stating that it was the job of the Congress and not the president to create this policy.

Radical Republicans felt that action was needed to counter the **Black Codes**, which had been passed by all Southern state legislatures in 1866. These sets of regulations limited movement by blacks, prohibited interracial marriage, and insisted that blacks obtain special certificates to hold certain jobs.

The Radical Republicans were insistent on immediate voting rights for blacks in the South; this desire was behind the **Wade-Davis Act**, which was passed by Congress in the summer of 1864. This bill stated that Congress would only authorize a state government in former Confederate states when the majority of voters took an "ironclad" oath, stating that they were not now disloyal to the Union nor had they ever been disloyal. Under these provisions, it would be impossible for any state to reenter the Union without a large number of black voters. President Lincoln killed this bill by a **pocket veto**.

ANDREW JOHNSON'S PLAN FOR RECONSTRUCTION

Much to the disappointment of the Radical Republicans, the Reconstruction plan announced by Andrew Johnson was also a relatively lenient one. Johnson stated that the United States should offer "amnesty and pardon" to any Southerner who would swear allegiance to the Union and the Constitution. Like Lincoln, Johnson felt that ex-Confederate leaders should not be eligible for amnesty; he also opposed amnesty for individuals (almost always plantation owners) whose property was worth over $20,000. Johnson had been a small farmer from Tennessee before he entered politics, and he possessed the typical hatred that small farmers had for plantation owners. Johnson also created a fairly simple plan for Confederate states to reenter the Union.

All of the former Confederate states followed the proscribed procedures and elected members to the Congress of the United States that met in December 1865. However, the "loyalty" of the former Confederate states was still questioned by some in the North. Many former Confederate officials and military officers were elected in local and even congressional elections. In no Southern state legislature were the issues of blacks getting the vote or education for former slaves even considered in the months following the Civil War. The **Radical Republicans** of the North found this totally unacceptable.

THE RECONSTRUCTION OF THE RADICAL REPUBLICANS

The Radical Republicans soon began to implement their own program for Reconstruction in the South. Although they differed on tactics, all agreed that their main goal in the South should be to advance the political, economic, and social position of the **freedmen**, or former slaves. In early 1865 Congress passed legislation creating the Freeman's Bureau, which was designed to help ex-slaves get employment, education, and general assistance as they adjusted to their new lives. By 1866 large numbers of freedmen were back on their original plantations (often against the advice of the Freeman's Bureau), working as **tenant farmers**. Under programs established by the Freeman's Bureau, ex-slaves could receive "40 acres and a mule."

Some Radical Republicans, such as Charles Sumner of Massachusetts, stated that the ex-slave's position would improve the quickest in the South if they were given the vote. Thaddeus Stevens felt that black voters would be strongly influenced by wealthy landowners who oftentimes employed them, and stated that the first goal of the federal government should be to take land from former Confederate leaders and give it to the freedmen. A Joint Committee on Reconstruction first met in January 1866.

The Joint Committee proposed, and the Congress passed, a bill authorizing the continuation of the Freeman's Bureau and a Civil Rights bill early in 1866. Johnson immediately vetoed both, stating they were unconstitutional and emphasizing the need to allow former Confederates to have more of a say in affairs in the South. It is at this point that tensions between the Congress and the president began to increase severely. Johnson gave a Washington's Birthday speech where he claimed the Radical Republicans were traitors and actually wanted to kill him.

Congress eventually overrode the presidential veto of both of these bills. Johnson's actions and demeanor were causing many moderate Republicans to join forces with the radical branch of the party. The **Civil Rights Act of 1866** granted freedmen all the benefits of federal citizenship and promised that federal courts would uphold these rights. In cases where these rights were violated, federal troops would be used for enforcement. The Civil Rights Act also helped to enforce the **Thirteenth Amendment** to the Constitution, which had been ratified in December 1865 and outlawed slavery and other forms of involuntary servitude.

The **Fourteenth Amendment** was passed by the Congress and sent to the states for ratification. The amendment declared that citizenship would be the same in all states, that states that did not give freedmen the vote would have reduced representation in the Congress, and that former Confederate officials could not hold public office. Anti-black riots in New Orleans and Memphis in early 1866 caused the Radical Republicans to push for the passage of the Fourteenth Amendment even more forcefully. President Johnson publicly opposed the ratification of the Fourteenth Amendment. However, Radical Republicans won by large margins in the 1866 congressional elections. After these elections, the Radical Republicans began to dictate the course of Reconstruction in the South.

A PERIOD OF RADICAL RECONSTRUCTION

With many Democrats and even moderate Republicans swept out of office in the 1866 congressional elections, Radical Republicans immediately put their plans for Reconstruction into action. The 1867 **Reconstruction Act** actually placed the Southern states under military rule, with the South being divided into five regions and a military general in control of each region. Former Confederate states were ordered to hold new constitutional conventions to form state constitutions that allowed qualified blacks to vote and provided them equal rights. The legislation barred former supporters of the Confederacy from voting and required that the Fourteenth Amendment be passed in all former Confederate states. To guarantee the assistance of the United States Army in these efforts, Congress also passed the **Army Act**, which reduced the control of the president over the army. To ensure that Secretary of War Edwin Stanton (an ally of the Radical Republicans) would not be dismissed, Congress passed the **Tenure of Office Act**, which stated that the president could not dismiss any Cabinet member without the approval of the Senate.

THE IMPEACHMENT OF ANDREW JOHNSON

In the fall of 1867 President Johnson tried to remove Edwin Stanton as Secretary of War. Radical Republicans loudly proclaimed that Johnson had flouted the United States Constitution by directly violating the Tenure of Office Act, and began **impeachment** proceedings against him. The House of Representatives voted to impeach Johnson on February 24, 1868, making him the first president of the United States to be impeached (Bill Clinton was the second). The trial of Johnson in the Senate began in May. By the Constitution, two-thirds of the Senate have to vote to convict the president for him to be removed; Andrew Johnson escaped conviction by one vote (the deciding vote was a Republican from Kansas by the name of Edmund Ross, who was opposed to Johnson but felt there was insufficient evidence to actually remove him from office).

Johnson served the remainder of his term without incident. In the 1868 presidential election, Ulysses S. Grant, a hero of the Civil War with little political knowledge and few stated political opinions, led the Republican party to victory.

RADICAL RECONSTRUCTION REINFORCED

With the election of Grant, Radical Republicans finally had an ally in the White House. In March of 1870 the final Reconstruction amendment was ratified. The **Fifteenth Amendment** stated that no American could be denied the right to vote "on account of race, color, or previous condition of servitude." Elections in the South in 1870 were regulated by federal troops stationed there. In these elections thousands of Southern blacks voted for the first time; predictably, many Southern whites did not vote in these elections and viewed the entire process with disgust.

In the 1870 elections nearly 630 blacks were elected as representatives in Southern state legislatures. Sixteen blacks were elected to Congress, one to the United States Senate, and a black, P.B.S. Pinchback, was elected governor of Louisiana.

It would be impossible to overstate the resentment with which many Southern whites viewed the entire Reconstruction process. Reconstruction was oftentimes blamed on **carpetbaggers**, who were Northerners who moved to the South during the Reconstruction period, or on **scalawags**, a Southern term for white Southern Republicans.

Groups such as the **Ku Klux Klan** (founded in Tennessee in 1866) fueled white resentment into violence against blacks and their "outside" supporters in the South. The Klan's activities ranged from trying to intimidate blacks at polling places to the burning of crosses to torture and murder. Various federal laws were passed to limit the activities of the Klan, with thousands of members being arrested. The group and its activities persisted, however.

THE END OF RECONSTRUCTION

Grant won reelection in 1872, yet during his second term, federal and Northern interest in the affairs of the South began to wane. The reasons for this were numerous. By this time in history many of the original Radical Republicans had died or no longer were active in government. There were numerous corruption scandals in the second Grant administration (some historians state that this was the most corrupt administration in American history). A recession in 1873 turned the interests of many Northerners to economic and not political and social issues. As a result, Northern troops were gradually removed from the South, allowing whites in Southern states to regain control of Southern governments.

Many Reconstruction-style reforms made by earlier state legislatures were overturned.

The political event that "officially" ended Reconstruction was the **Compromise of 1877**. In the presidential election of 1876, Samuel Tilden, governor of New York, was the Democratic party candidate, running against Republican Rutherford B. Hayes. Tilden won the popular vote and was leading in the electoral vote, but he needed the electoral votes of Florida, Louisiana, and South Carolina, all still occupied by federal troops and under Republican control. Both sides claimed victory in these three states. A special congressional commission was created to resolve this situation. The commission had more Republicans than Democrats on it and was ready to hand the election to Hayes, even though evidence indicated that Tilden had won enough electoral votes to win. When Democrats in Congress stated that they would loudly and publicly protest the Commission's findings, the **Compromise of 1877** was worked out. Hayes was named president; in return, the new president promised to remove all federal troops from the South and to stop the enforcement of much Reconstruction-era legislation concerning the South. As a result, blacks in the South were again reduced to the status of second-class citizens. In addition, Southern hatred of Reconstruction-era Republican policies would make the South solidly Democratic; white Southern support of the Democratic policy would last for nearly 100 years. It should be noted that whites who returned to power in state legislatures in the South in 1878 were called "the redeemers."

CHAPTER REVIEW

Rapid Review Guide

To achieve the perfect 5, you should be able to explain the following:

- Any plan to assimilate the Southern states back into the Union after the Civil War would have major difficulties; a problem was determining the appropriate post-war status of former supporters of the Confederacy.

- The plans for Reconstruction proposed by Abraham Lincoln, the Radical Republicans, and Andrew Johnson all varied dramatically.

- Radical Republicans instituted policies to improve the political and economic status of former slaves; this created great resentment in other segments of Southern society.

- The impeachment of Andrew Johnson went forward because of major disagreements over policy between Johnson and the Radical Republicans in Congress.

- The Thirteenth, Fourteenth, and Fifteenth Amendments outlawed slavery, established the rights of blacks, and established the framework by which Southern states could rejoin the union.

- Profits made by carpetbaggers and scalawags further angered the traditional elements of Southern society; many in the South, including members of the Ku Klux Klan, felt great resentment towards the carpetbaggers and scalawags and towards the political and economic power now held by some Southern blacks.

- The Compromise of 1877 ended Reconstruction in the South; as Union troops left, blacks were again reduced to the status of second-class citizens.

Time Line

1865: Andrew Johnson institutes liberal Reconstruction plan
Whites in Southern legislatures pass Black Codes
Thirteenth Amendment ratified
1866: Civil Rights Act, Freedman's Bureau Act approved by Congress (vetoed by Johnson)
Fourteenth Amendment passes Congress (fails to be ratified in Southern states)
Anti-black riots in New Orleans, Memphis
Republicans who favor Radical Reconstruction win congressional elections, in essence ending Johnson's Reconstruction plan
Ku Klux Klan founded
1867: Tenure of Office Act approved by Congress (Congress had to approve presidential appointments, dismissals)
Reconstruction Act approved by Congress (Southern states placed under military rule)
Constitutional conventions called by former Confederate states
Johnson tries to remove Edwin Stanton as Secretary of War, leading to cries for his impeachment
1868: Impeachment of Andrew Johnson: Johnson impeached in the House of Representatives, not convicted in the Senate
Southern states return to Union under policies established by Radical Republicans
Final ratification of Fourteenth Amendment
Former Civil War general U.S. Grant elected president
1870: Fifteenth Amendment ratified
Many blacks elected in Southern state legislatures
1872: Former Confederates allowed to hold office
U.S. Grant reelected
1876: Disputed presidential election between Tilden, Hayes
1877: Compromise of 1877 awards election to Hayes, ends Reconstruction in the South

✓ Review Questions

1. Radical Republicans favored all of the following *except*

   A. the continuation of the Freedman's Bureau
   B. the governing of the South by military generals
   C. the impeachment of Andrew Johnson
   D. the return of former Confederate leaders to positions of power in the South
   E. the election of newly enfranchised blacks to positions in Southern state legislatures

(Correct Answer: **D.** All of the other choices were favored by Radical Republicans; the Reconstruction Act of 1867 placed the former Confederate states under military rule.)

2. The official reason for impeachment proceedings against Andrew Johnson was

   A. he had violated the Tenure of Office Act
   B. he had violated the Reconstruction Act
   C. his Reconstruction policies were much too lenient to the South
   D. he had failed to enforce the Army Act
   E. he had failed to enforce the Civil Rights Act of 1866

(Correct Answer: **A.** By attempting to remove Edwin Stanton as Secretary of War, many in Congress stated that Johnson had knowingly violated the Tenure of Office Act, thus violating provisions of the United States Constitution.)

3. Black Codes were instituted to

   A. increase black participation in Southern politics during Reconstruction
   B. increase the effectiveness of the Freedman's Bureau
   C. prevent blacks from having certain jobs
   D. maintain slavery in some sections of the Deep South
   E. allow blacks to move more freely in the South

(Correct Answer: **C.** Black Codes were adopted by Southern legislatures in 1866 and limited movement by blacks, prevented them from having certain jobs, and prohibited interracial marriage.)

4. Reconstruction ended as a result of the Compromise of 1877 because

   A. a presidential mandate ordered that Reconstruction end
   B. by the provisions of the compromise, the U.S. Army was removed from Southern states
   C. the new president, Rutherford B. Hayes, was strongly against existing Reconstruction policy
   D. many blacks were now in positions of power in the South, and Reconstruction policies were no longer needed
   E. public opinion in the North no longer favored existing Reconstruction policies

(Correct Answer: **B.** After Hayes was given the presidency by the Compromise of 1877, the U.S. Army left control of the South to the South. Without the army present to enforce Reconstruction policies, these policies ended. Blacks were soon second-class citizens again.)

5. The Fifteenth Amendment
   A. allowed Southern states to reenter the Union
   B. outlawed slavery
   C. stated that a person could not be denied the vote because of his color
   D. said that former Confederate officials could not hold public office
   E. stated that citizenship would be the same in all states

(Correct Answer: C. The Fifteenth Amendment stated that no American could be denied the right to vote "on account of race, color, or previous condition of servitude.")

Chapter 13

Western Expansion and Its Impact on the American Character (1860–1895)

FEDERAL LEGISLATION ENCOURAGES WESTERN SETTLEMENT

Adventurous Americans had settled west of the Mississippi and out to the Pacific in the decades prior to the Civil War. However, several acts passed by the federal government in 1862 set the stage for the massive movement westward that would take place after the Civil War.

The one act that gave land directly to settlers was the **Homestead Act**. This legislation allocated 160 acres to any settler who (1) was an American citizen, or who, in the case of immigrants, had at least filed for American citizenship; (2) was 21 years old and the head of a family; (3) was committed to building a house on the property and living there at least six months of the year; and (4) could pay a $10 registration fee for the land. After actively farming the land for five years, the farmer was given actual ownership of his 160-acre plot. By 1900 nearly 610,000 parcels of land had been given out under the provisions of the Homestead Act, allowing nearly 85 million acres of land to go over to private ownership.

A bill that indirectly gave land to settlers was the 1862 **Morrill Land-Grant Act**. To encourage the building of "land-grant" colleges in Western territories that had already been granted statehood, hundreds of thousands of acres of land were given to state governments. This land could be sold by the states to pay for these colleges. At 50 cents an acre (and sometimes less), settlers and **land speculators** received land from individual states.

The expansion of the railroad was closely tied to western expansion. In acts enacted in 1862 and 1864, the Union Pacific and Central Pacific Railroads received grants of land to extend their rail lines westward. Part of the legislation also gave the railroads 10 square miles on both sides of the track for every mile of track constructed. This land was sometimes sold to settlers as well, sometimes at exorbitant prices.

FARMING ON THE GREAT PLAINS

In the ideology of Thomas Jefferson, the yeoman farmer was the central figure in the development of the American character. The abilities, fortitude, and luck of the yeomen were severely tested as they moved to the Great Plains. Many settlers who went west were immigrants with families (unlike the single male immigrants who lived in New York, Boston, and other Eastern cities).

The harshness of life on the plains was simply too much to bear for many settlers and their families. Temperatures ranged from over 100 degrees in the summer to bitter cold in the winter, and many of the sod houses built by settlers did little to keep out the heat or the cold. Having enough water was a constant problem, with some of the water collected in barrels or buckets carrying "prairie fever" (typhoid fever). In a single year a settler and his land might be attacked by fierce blizzards, howling dust storms, and locusts or grasshoppers. The rosy picture of life on the Great Plains presented in recruitment brochures found in New York or in Currier & Ives prints popular in the East were a harsh contrast with reality. By 1900 two-thirds of the homestead farms failed, causing many ex-farmers to return to the East.

How did the settlers who survived on the Great Plains manage to do so? Survival on the plains largely depended on cooperation with other settlers that lived near you. Groups of men would put up new barns and construct fences; women on the plains would get support from wives of other settlers. In short, successful farmers on the plains were no longer the individual yeomen envisioned by Jefferson.

THE TRANSFORMATION OF AGRICULTURE ON THE PLAINS

More importantly, success on the plains became increasingly dependent on the use of technology and the introduction of business approaches to agriculture. The United States Department of Agriculture was established in 1862 and by late 1863 was distributing information to plains farmers on new farm techniques and developments. New plows and threshers (included some powered by steam) were introduced in the late 1860s and early 1870s.

Slowly, control of agricultural production on the plains was taken from individual farmers as large **bonanza farms** developed. While individual settlers were interested in producing enough for their families to survive, bonanza farms usually produced only one or two crops on them. Produce from these farms was sold to the Eastern United States or abroad. While individual settlers were being driven off of the land because of the hardships of farming on the plains, bonanza farms were run as large businesses and had the technology and professional backing to be successful.

Bonanza farms were plentiful by the late 1870s and demonstrated the transformation that had taken place in agriculture. These farms were truly capitalistic; their success was dependent on the machinery that existed on the farms and on the railroad that would take their crops away for export. Farm production increased dramatically with the advent of bonanza farms. At the same time, the numbers of Americans involved in agriculture decreased (from nearly 60 percent in 1860 to 37 percent in 1900).

The new business techniques practiced by bonanza farms were successful in the short run but created problems for both bonanza farms and individual farmers in the future. Several times in the 1880s and early 1890s there was simply too much grain being produced on these farms, dropping the prices drastically. To remain economically successful, farmers proceeded to do the only logical thing: produce even more, which drove prices down even more. Many plains farmers in this period were unable to pay their mortgages, and farms were foreclosed. Bonanza farms usually had the technology for the production of only one or two crops and could not diversify; they too faced financial distress. Many farmers felt that federal policies had to do more to protect them, and thus started to organize to protect themselves.

WOMEN AND MINORITIES ON THE PLAINS

As stated previously, most settlers came to the plains as families (there were a tiny number of women who filed for land claims on their own). Diaries of many women who lived on the plains spoke of the loneliness of their existence, especially in the non-harvest periods when many men left for other work and women were left on the farms. Perhaps the greatest novel describing prairie life is *O Pioneers!* (1913) by Willa Cather. This book describes both the tremendous challenges and the incredible rewards found in life on the prairie. An equally compelling vision of prairie life is *Giants of the Earth* (1927) by O. E. Rolvaag. In this novel the harshness of prairie life drives the wife of an immigrant settler to madness and to eventual death.

It was in the Western states where the first American women received the vote. In 1887 two towns in Kansas gave women the vote (with one of them electing a woman mayor to a single term in office). The state constitution of Wyoming was the first to give women the vote on a state-wide basis.

Thousands of blacks moved west after the Civil War to escape the uncertainty of life in the Reconstruction South. Many who ended in the plains and elsewhere lacked the finances and farming abilities to be successful, and faced many of the same racial difficulties they had faced in the American South. However, some black farmers did emerge successfully as plains farmers. The most prominent group of Southern blacks who went west was a 1879 group who called themselves the **Exodusters** (modeling their journey after the journey of the Israelites fleeing Egypt to the Promised Land). Less than 20 percent of this group became successful farmers in the plains region.

MINING AND LUMBERING IN THE WEST

The rumors of gold at Pike's Peak, Nevada, silver at Comstock, Nevada, and other minerals at countless other locations drew settlers westward in the quest for instant riches (it should be noted that a large number of Californians traveled eastward for exactly the same reason). Persons of all backgrounds, including women and some Chinese who had left their jobs in railroad construction, all took part in the search for riches. Stories of the wild nature of many early mining towns are generally accurate; stories of the failure of most speculators to find anything to mine are almost always true. Most prospectors who did find something in the ground found it much too difficult to dig for and then to transport; oftentimes they sold their claims to Eastern mining companies, such as the **Anaconda Copper Company**, who did the work for them. For many of these companies, minerals such as tin and copper became just as profitable as gold and silver to mine.

Lumber companies also began moving into the Northwest in the 1870s to start to cut down timber. The lumber industry benefited greatly from the federal **Timber and Stone Act**, passed in 1878. This bill offered land in the Northwest that was unsuitable for farming to "settlers" at very cheap prices. Lumber companies hired seamen from port cities and others who had no interest in "settling" to buy the forest land cheaply and then to transfer the ownership of the land to the companies.

RANCHING IN THE WEST

In Texas the ranching industry was profitable long before either farming or mining was fully developed. Settlers there had learned cattle ranching from the Mexicans. Much of the romantic view many still have of the West comes from of our vision of cowboys driving cattle on the "long drive" from Texas to either Kansas or Missouri (nearly one-third of the cowboys involved were either Mexicans or blacks).

The long drive was economically inefficient, and with the removal of Native Americans and buffalo from the Great Plains in the 1860s and 1870s (to be discussed in the next section), many cattle ranchers moved their herds northward, allowing them to be closer to the cattle markets of Chicago, Kansas City, and St. Louis.

However, conflicts between farmers and ranchers soon developed. Farmers often accused ranchers of allowing herds to trample their farmland. The invention of barbed wire by Joseph Glidden in 1873 was the beginning of the end for the cattle industry; as farmers began to contain their farmlands, the open range began to disappear.

A critical blow to the cattle industry occurred during two very harsh winters of 1885 to 1886 and 1886 to 1887. Many cattle froze to death or starved during these years, with some ranchers losing up to 85 percent of their cattle. Those ranchers that survived turned to the same business techniques that had saved many plains farms; scientific methods of breeding, feeding, and fencing were now utilized by those ranchers that survived. In reality, the independent cowboy present in our myths of the West also died during this transformation.

THE PLIGHT OF NATIVE AMERICANS

The westward stream of settlers in the mid-1800s severely disrupted the lives of Native Americans. The migration patterns of buffalo, which the Native Americans depended on, were disrupted; settlers thought nothing of seizing lands that previous treaties had given to Native Americans. Some tribes tried to cooperate with the onrush of settlers, while others violently resisted. It is unlikely that any Native American approach would have saved Native American territories from the rush of American expansionism. The completion of the transcontinental railroad required that rail lines run through territories previously ceded to Native American tribes. A congressional commission meeting in 1867 stated the official policy of the American government on "Indian affairs": Native Americans would all be removed to Oklahoma and South Dakota, and every effort would be made to transform them from "savages" into "civilized" beings.

The tribe that resisted the onrush of settlement most fiercely were the **Sioux**. In 1865 the government announced their desire to build a road through Sioux territory; the following year tribesmen attacked and killed 88 American soldiers. After negotiations in 1868 the Sioux agreed to move to a reservation in the Black Hills of South Dakota. Yet in late 1874 miners searching for gold began to arrive in the Black Hills. The chief of the tribe, Sitting Bull, and others of the tribe left the Dakota reservation at this point. General George Custer was sent to round up Sitting Bull and the Sioux. He and his force of over 200 men were all killed at the **Battle of the Little Bighorn** in June of 1876. This was the last major Native American victory against the American army. Large numbers of federal troops were brought into the region, returning the Sioux to their reservations.

Conflict with the federal army occurred again in 1890 after the death of Sitting Bull. Some Sioux again attempted to leave their reservation; these tribesmen were quickly apprehended by the federal army. As the male Sioux were handing in their weapons, a shot was fired by someone. The soldiers opened fire on the Native Americans, killing 146 men, women, and children in the **Massacre at Wounded Knee**.

Other tribes such as the **Nez Perce** also initially resisted, only to be eventually driven to reservations. Nez Perce warriors ending up taking part in elaborate **Ghost Dances**, which were supposed to remove the whites from Native American territories, return the buffalo, and bring ancestors killed by the whites back to life. The Ghost Dances terrified white settlers who viewed them and served to bring more federal forces into territories nominally controlled by Native Americans.

The killing off of tribes of buffalo by white settlers for food, hides, and even for pure sport did much to destroy Native American life, since Native Americans depended upon the buffalo for their very existence. A fatal blow to remaining land owned by Native American tribes was the 1887 **Dawes Act**. This act was passed in the spirit of "civilizing" the Native Americans and was designed to give them their own plots of land to farm on. The real intent of the legislation was to attempt to destroy the tribal identities of Native Americans. Many Native Americans had little skill or interest in farming; many eventually sold "their" land to land speculators.

In 1889 there were still 2 million acres of unclaimed land in "Indian territory" in Oklahoma. On April 22 a mad rush took place by white settlers staking out claims on this territory (those who staked claims that day were called "boomers"; settlers who had entered Indian territory a day or more early to stake their claims were called "sooners").

By the end of the century virtually all Native Americans had been placed in reservations. Many young Indians attempted to dress, talk, and act like white men in schools established by white reformers, but their attempts to think like and become whites were much, much more difficult.

THE ORGANIZATION OF THE AMERICAN FARMER AND POPULISM

As stated previously, American farmers from the West were in economic trouble by the mid-1880s. Many farmers from the South shared their plight. Several policies were originating in Washington that farmers felt greatly hurt them economically. Congresses of this era favored high tariffs, which helped Eastern businessmen. Farmers felt they were hurt by the high tariff policy, as it kept foreigners from buying their produce. The issue that farmers were most upset about, however, concerned currency.

The Issue of the Gold Standard

After the Civil War, federal budget officials enacted a "**tight money**" policy and took the paper money used during the Civil War out of circulation. In addition, the dollar during this period was for the first time put on the **gold standard**, meaning that every dollar in circulation had to be backed by a similar amount of gold held by the federal government. This action also served to limit the amount of money in circulation. These financial measures ensured that inflation would not occur, but Western farmers were convinced that depressed farm prices were largely a result of these policies. Several congressional acts to increase the coining and mining of gold and silver met with limited success and were opposed by the presidents of the era.

The Beginning of Organization:
The Grange and the Farmer's Alliances

In 1867 the <u>Grange</u> organization was founded by Western farmers. By 1875 it boasted of over 800,000 members. Through the Grange, farmer cooperatives were formed, allowing farmers to buy in large quantities (and at lower prices). Farmers were also convinced that railroad rates were disadvantageous to them, and legislators in farm states began to receive communications from farmers urging regulation of railroad rates and policies. Some farmers supported the <u>Greenback party</u>, which supported getting more paper money into circulation, in the 1878 election. The Greenbacks managed to elect several congressmen from farm states but got little support elsewhere.

While the Grange organization largely operated on the local level, development of the <u>Farmer's Alliances</u> joined farmers at the statewide and even regional level. By 1889 the Southern Alliance claimed 1 million members, while a separate Colored Farmers' National Alliance also had 1 million members on the books. Membership in the Farmer's Alliances on the Great Plains was nearly 2 million members. The policies endorsed by the Farmer's Alliances included federal regulation of the railroad, putting more money in circulation, the establishment of a state department of agriculture in every state, and readily available farm credits; it was proposed that the federal government have large warehouses where farmers could store their grain and get credit for it if prices were low during harvest season. These measures were spelled out in detail at a national Alliance convention held in 1890 in Ocala, Florida. The <u>Ocala Platform</u> stated the principles that motivated most political activity by farmers for the remainder of the century. Some federal policies did at least partially meet the demands of agricultural interests; the <u>Interstate Commerce Act</u> of 1887 stated that the federal government could regulate interstate railway rates, and the <u>Sherman Antitrust Act</u> of 1890 aimed to control the power of trusts and monopolies.

By 1890 some leaders of the Farmer's Alliances began to plan for political action on the national level. Alliance strength was particularly strong in the South, where four governors owed their election to Alliance support. Forty-seven congressmen in the South were also strongly supported by the Alliance. In the plains states Alliance candidates were successful on the local level. Alliance support extended to women as well; several women held important leadership positions at the top levels of the Farmer's Alliances.

The Populist Campaign of 1892

On July 4, 1892, in a convention held in Omaha, Nebraska, a national convention of Farmer's Alliances created the People's party, whose followers soon became known as Populists. The <u>Populist party</u> was intended to appeal to workers of all parts of the country. Populists desired a much greater role of government in American society. The party platform expressed support for increasing the circulation of money, a progressive income tax (by which wealthy Eastern industrialists would pay the most and farmers would pay the least), government ownership of communication and transportation systems, and more direct methods of democracy (greater use of direct primaries, recall, referendum, etc.). To appeal to urban workers, the platform also supported an eight-hour workday. The Populists nominated James B. Weaver, a Union general from the Civil War, as their candidate.

Despite a spirited campaign by Populist supporters, the party only received 1 million popular votes and 22 electoral votes in the 1892 election. Few voters in the Northeast supported the Populists, and Democratic control of the electoral process in the South remained strong. Only in the western United States did Populism do well.

Populism in the 1890s

The reelection of Grover Cleveland angered the agricultural interests greatly, as he announced his continued support of the gold standard during his inauguration speech. A great depression hit America in 1893, with workers from all parts of the country being laid off (in some cities up to 25 percent of laborers were unemployed). Populist marchers joined with marchers from many groups protesting government financial policy in Washington in 1894.

In the 1896 presidential election, the Republican candidate was William McKinley, who followed Cleveland in his support of the gold standard. The Democratic candidate, endorsed by the Populists, was William Jennings Bryan, campaigned on a policy of free silver and an expanded availability of currency, stating, "You shall not crucify mankind upon a cross of gold!" Many Populist leaders hit the campaign trail for Bryan, yet with little success. Bryan carried the South and the West, but was unable to garner support in the Midwestern or Northeastern states.

As the depression ended at the end of the decade, Populists and others in the agricultural sector began to recognize the massive changes that had taken place in the American economy since the end of the Civil War. The American economy was now a national economy and not a sectional one; the railroad had been largely responsible for this change. In addition, slowly but surely the United States was becoming an industrial nation and not an agricultural one.

THE IMPACT OF THE WEST ON AMERICAN SOCIETY

The myths we now associate with the frontier began to be created as early as the 1870s in dime-store novels by Edward L. Wheeler and others. Wheeler's story of _Deadwood Dick: The Prince of the Road_ portrayed a

Western America filled with gamblers, hard drinkers, and stagecoach robberies. The Wild West shows that began in 1883 and were promoted by Buffalo Bill Cody contributed to the myths begun by Wheeler: Spectators were shown log cabins, spectator rodeos, and mock battles between cavalrymen and seemingly deadly Indians.

A different view of the West was presented by Frederick Jackson Turner, an academic who in 1893 published his "frontier thesis." The **Turner Thesis** states that as Americans moved westward they were forced to adapt and to innovate, and how western expansion had helped to ingrain these characteristics into the fabric of American society. Turner stated that their frontier had created a society of men and women who were committed to self-improvement, who supported democracy, and who were socially mobile. In short, the Turner Thesis maintains that much of the nature of America comes from our experiences in the West.

Each of these views is partially correct. The view of western expansion espoused (and later partially rejected) by Turner ignores the fact that not everyone who settled the West were white Easterners. In addition, the massacre of large numbers of Native Americans violates the basic principles of democracy. There is also some truth to Buffalo Bill's view of western settlement, yet his view ignores the cultural and material progress that did take place in the West as a result of western expansion. In 1893 the Turner Thesis and Buffalo Bill's shows both drew incredible interest. During that year it was clear that the Western frontier was for all practical purpose closed, and Americans were attempting to make sense of what that actually meant for the country. Historians today still revisit this question on a regular basis.

CHAPTER REVIEW

Rapid Review Guide

To achieve the perfect 5, you should be able to explain the following:

- The Homestead Act and the Morrill Land-Grant Act encouraged thousands to go westward to acquire land for farming.

- Farming on the Great Plains proved to be very difficult and was oftentimes accomplished by help from one's neighbor; many farmers were not successful on the Great Plains.

- Bonanza farms were part of a transformation of agriculture that began in the late 1860s.

- Western states were the first states where women received the vote.

- Mining and lumbering also attracted many settlers to the West.

- Native American tribes were gradually forced off of their lands because of American expansion to the west; some resistance to this by

Native Americans did take place, such as at the Battle of the Little Bighorn and through the Ghost Dances.

- The 1887 Dawes Act did much to break up the remaining Native American tribal lands.

- American farmers organized beginning in the late 1860s though the Grange, through the Farmer's Alliances, and eventually through the Populist party.

- Dime-store novels of the era and the Turner Thesis present contrasting views of western settlement and its overall impact on American society.

Time Line

1848: California Gold Rush
1859: Silver Discovered in Comstock, Nevada
1862: Homestead Act, Morrill Land-Grant Act
      Department of Agriculture created by Congress
1867: Founding of the Grange
1869: Transcontinental Railroad completed
1870s: Popularity of *Deadwood Dick,* stories by Bret Harte, and other dime-store novels on the West
1874: Barbed wire invented by Joseph Glidden
1876: Battle of the Little Bighorn
1879: Exoduster movement leaves South for the Great Plains
1880s: Large movement of immigrants westward
1883: "Buffalo Bill's Wild West Show" begins
1886: Beginnings of harsh weather that will help destroy the cattle industry
1887: Dawes Act
1889: Indian territories open for white settlement
1890: Massacre at Wounded Knee
      Wyoming women get the vote
      High point of political influence of the Farmer's Alliances
1893: Beginning of great depression of the 1890s
      Publication of the Turner Thesis
1896: William Jennings Bryan's "Cross of Gold" speech

✓ Review Questions

1. Those farmers who were successful on the Great Plains

   A. came to the West as single men, without families
   B. utilized many farming techniques they had learned in the East
   C. personified the spirit of rugged individualism
   D. relied on the assistance of other settlers around them
   E. personified the image of the yeoman farmer of Thomas Jefferson

(Correct Answer: **D.** Almost every diary of memoir from individuals who lived on the plains noted that rugged individualism was not enough to be successful.)

2. Exodusters were

   A. newly arrived miners in Oregon
   B. Southern blacks who went west to settle
   C. settlers who went to Washington state to be part of the lumbering industry
   D. those who "dusted" or cleaned crops on bonanza farms
   E. immigrants who went west to farm

(Correct Answer: **B.** This group went west to farm in 1879 and modeled their journey after the journey of the Israelites fleeing Egypt to the Promised Land.)

3. The Dawes Act

   A. tried to turn Native Americans into farmers who would farm their own individual plots only
   B. protected Native American land from further encroachment
   C. broke up large Native American reservations into smaller ones
   D. made Ghost Dances illegal
   E. made the further killing of buffalo by Western settlers illegal

(Correct Answer: **A.** The Dawes Act tried to "civilize" Native Americans and destroy their tribal lands.)

4. The organization that expressed the views of farmers to the largest national audience was

   A. the Greenback party
   B. the Populist party
   C. the Grange
   D. the Colored Farmer's National Alliance
   E. the Farmer's Alliances

(Correct Answer: **B.** The Populist party platform was intended to appeal to all workers in society, including those in the city. The policies of the Populist Party were heard nationwide in the 1892 presidential election; however, because of the power of the Democratic party in the South, the Populist presidential candidate received only 1 million votes in the election.)

5. The Turner thesis

   A. agreed with accounts of the West in the dime-store novels of the 1870s concerning the character of western expansion
   B. emphasized the diversity of those who traveled west
   C. takes into account the massacre of Native Americans
   D. notes the impact of western expansion on the American character
   E. emphasized the "hard living" that went on in many western settlements

(Correct Answer: **D.** Turner himself would later revise his thesis based on some of the characteristics of western expansion noted in the other possible answers.)

Chapter 14

America Transformed into the Industrial Giant of the World (1870–1910)

 Immense changes rocked the United States between 1870 and 1910 that transformed the very nature of the American republic. During this period, for the first time in American history, more people lived in urban settings than in rural ones. America began to lose the small town and rural character that had defined the nation since its inception. Many who moved to the cities went to work in factories, helping to turn America into the greatest industrial (and agricultural) producer in the world. It was also during this period that immigrants, many from southern and eastern Europe, began to enter the United States by the millions and further transform the American character. In addition, the presidents during this era were generally weak (with several noticeable exceptions), which put extensive power in the hands of the legislative branch; these presidents were disinclined to exert strong executive action against the trusts and monopolies that were developing at the time.

THE GROWTH OF INDUSTRIAL AMERICA

By 1894 the United States had become the largest manufacturing nation in the world. Compared to industrial growth that had occurred in Europe earlier in the century, the economic growth that took place in America during this period was nearly beyond belief. Massive factories employed very large number of workers. In 1860 nearly one out of every four Americans worked in manufacturing, while by 1900 this number was increased to one out of every two. Radical transformations also took place in the approaches to work taken by former rural dwellers or immigrants who moved to the American city for factory work. Things such as time clocks, scheduled breaks, and the repetition of doing the same tasks over and over made work very different for those who came from rural settings.

The essential characteristics of this **Second Industrial Revolution** developed because of a combination of new developments in both technology and business organization. Initially, this growth was aided by the lack of governmental control over the affairs of business (laissez-faire capitalism was the dominant economic theory of the era).

THE CHANGING NATURE OF AMERICAN INDUSTRY

The massive industrial growth of this period was largely based on the expansion of **heavy industry**. Prior to the Civil War, most American production was based on turning out materials that the American consumer would purchase, such as food products and textiles. These products continued to be produced, but during 1870–1910, rapid industrial growth was fueled by the production of steel, machinery, and petroleum products. Most of these products were designed *not* for the consumer, but for those who produced the goods. Heavy industry produced new machinery that a textile mill might install, or a stronger, more durable steel that a railroad line might use for a new stretch of tracks. Industrial expansion during this era spiraled; new machinery introduced in textile mills, for example, fueled a further expansion of textile manufacturing.

Another key component of the Second Industrial Revolution was the development of new and more efficient sources of power. In 1865 the majority of American industries were still dependent on water power. The discovery of anthracite coal (in Pennsylvania, West Virginia, and elsewhere) caused the price of coal to drastically drop and fueled the transformation in many American industries to steam power. By 1890 nearly 70 percent of American industries used steam. After the turn of the century, the inventiveness of Thomas Edison allowed electricity to replace steam as the cheapest and most efficient source of power in American factories.

Industry expanded in this era into geographic regions where it had scarcely existed before. In the **New South** many former sharecroppers went to work in textile factories, which oftentimes utilized state-of-the-art machinery that had been produced in the North. The American Tobacco Company started to manufacture cigarettes by machine, and the steel mills found in Southern cities such as Birmingham, Alabama, made these cities start to resemble factory cities in the North.

Changes in the Workplace

Production methods changed in virtually every factory in America during this period, as the desire for more efficiently produced goods became paramount. Efficiency experts were utilized by many companies, and most championed the ideas of Frederick W. Taylor, a mechanical engineer who wrote popular treatises on efficiency and scientific management. **Taylorism** emphasized speed and efficiency in the workplace; factories found that paying workers "by the piece" made them produce more. Workers were timed and factories sometimes redesigned to promote efficiency and greater production. One by-product of Taylorism was the elimination of some workers in the factory as other workers did their jobs "more efficiently."

Part of this move toward efficiency was the beginning of assembly line production methods. The application of Taylorism and the introduction of the assembly line best demonstrate the combination of technology and business organization that fueled much of the economic growth of the era. The Ford Motor Company was first established in 1903, and by 1910, it was producing nearly 12,000 cars per year. Henry Ford's factories first used assembly line production methods in 1913; during that year Ford produced nearly 250,000 automobiles. Similar growth occurred in the chemical and electrical industries as new production methods were introduced.

How did the role of workers in the production process change in this era? Critics charged that the individual worker had merely become "one more cog in the machine"; in an automobile assembly line the worker might, for example, put the left door on a whole series of identical automobiles all day long. The need for skilled craftsmen, so important in pre-industrial America, drastically lessened as a result of the assembly line.

Many factory jobs could now be learned in several hours or less. The result of this on the nature of the workforce was immense. Immigrants with no previous training could perform the simple tasks associated with many industrial jobs. In addition, many women left their previous jobs as domestics to go to work in the textile mills (many women took clerical jobs in this era as well). Children could also do some of the more menial tasks associated with factory work and be paid a pittance of what adults were making. By 1900 nearly 20 percent of all children between 10 and 15 were employed, many in textile mills and shoe factories. During this period some states began to pass laws regulating child labor, although these were oftentimes difficult to enforce.

Clear differences were present in this period between the pay offered to men and women in most factories. Skilled women factory workers made $5 a week, while unskilled male workers often made $8 per week. Women still preferred factory work to the very time-consuming and low-paying job of being a domestic worker. Some female workers turned to prostitution; there is some evidence that the number of prostitutes increased in industrial cities at the end of the nineteenth century.

Marriage usually ended a woman's work in the factory; doing all of the chores while the husband was away at work was a back-breaking exercise in this era. Some urban married women also added income to the household by doing knitting or sewing for others at home.

THE CONSOLIDATION OF BUSINESSES

John D. Rockefeller made millions through Standard Oil, as did Andrew Carnegie through U.S. Steel. During this period these businessmen and others attempted to further control the industries in which they were invested. Many of these schemes did allow the rich to get richer, with little or no benefit to those working under them.

Some of these organizational schemes were quickly squashed by governmental intervention. Influential stockholders of companies of the same industry would sometimes agree to limit production, set prices, and even share profits. This type of activity was outlawed in 1887 by the <u>Interstate Commerce Act</u>. This bill was passed with the intent of regulating the railroads, but it generally was not enforced. The commission in charge of enforcement was made of former railroad executives and others who favored the interests of the railroads.

Another popular method of business organization was the creation of <u>trusts</u>, an organizational technique perfected by John D. Rockefeller and Standard Oil. At the time, state laws prohibited one corporation from holding stock in another. However, it was legal to create a trust, by which stockholders in a smaller oil company could be "persuaded" to give control of their shares in that company "in trust" to the board of trustees of Standard Oil. Using this technique, Standard Oil established a <u>horizontal integration</u> of the oil industry in the early 1880s, meaning that the board of trustees of Standard Oil also controlled many other oil-producing companies.

Standard Oil expanded in the late 1880s even further by becoming a <u>holding company</u>. In 1888 New Jersey passed new legislation allowing businesses incorporated there to own stock in other corporations. Standard Oil stockholders began to buy up shares in other companies as well; under the regulations for a holding company, management of various companies could be joint as well. Standard Oil stockholders became the majority holders in other oil companies, allowing Standard Oil management to run these companies also. By the early 1890s Standard Oil had merged 43 oil-producing companies together under their control and produced nearly 90 percent of all oil in America. Standard Oil also achieved <u>vertical integration</u> when the company not only moved to control production but also the marketing and distribution of the finished product. Similar examples of vertical integration were found in many other companies (Gustavus Swift exhibited similar control over the meat-processing industry). Carnegie's steel operation is often cited as the best example of vertical integration in this era.

Those at the very top of the economic pinnacle were able to rationalize their incredible economic successes. American social philosopher William Graham Sumner wrote in this period about <u>Social Darwinism</u>, which proclaimed that God had granted power and wealth to those that most deserved it. Believers in Social Darwinism could thus justify any scheme that could bring more money to the Rockefellers and the Carnegies of America, since God had wanted them to have that economic power. Carnegie spoke and wrote about the "<u>Gospel of Wealth.</u>" According to this theory, the major role of America's industrialists was to act as the "guardians" of the wealth of America (and *not* to give this wealth out in the form of higher wages for the workers). Carnegie stated that is was the duty of the wealthy to return a large portion of their wealth to the community. To the credit of both Rockefeller and Carnegie, foundations they established have contributed over $650 million to various educational and artistic ventures since the time of their deaths. Observers with a less sympathetic view call the giants of business from this era "robber barons."

THE GROWTH OF LABOR UNIONS

Although craft unions existed in the period before the Civil War, the first major strike in American history was the large strike of railroad workers that began in July 1877. Railroad workers protested layoffs and the reduction of their wages. In various parts of the country, railroad property was destroyed and trains were derailed. In Pittsburgh, Pennsylvania, over 30 strikers were killed by militia forces loyal to the railroad companies. President Hayes finally sent in government troops to restore order and break up the strike, although he felt that steps should be taken to "remove the distress which afflicts laborers."

The major union to emerge from the 1870s was the **Knights of Labor**, which was founded in Philadelphia in 1869. Many earlier unions represented single crafts (shoemakers, for example). The Knights of Labor opened their doors to skilled *and* unskilled workers, and welcomed immigrants, blacks, and women as well. Membership in the Knights of Labor peaked around 750,000 in the mid-1880s. Brochures written by the Knights of Labor proposed a new, cooperative society, where laborers would one day work for themselves and not for their industrial bosses. Unfortunately, this rhetoric failed to impress many bosses, and in several large strikes, ownership refused to even negotiate with representatives of the union, causing it to gradually lose members.

On May 1, 1886, a massive labor rally was held in Chicago, with nearly 100,000 workers turning out to support strikers at the nearby McCormick reaper plant. Chicago authorities were aware of the violent tactics practiced by many European socialists at this time and vowed not to let that happen in Chicago. The next evening a large worker's demonstration took place near **Haymarket Square** in downtown Chicago. Police and militia forces arrived to break up the demonstration. At that moment, a bomb went off. Seven people died and nearly 70 were wounded. Eventually, eight anarchists were convicted of setting off the bomb. To many not involved in labor unions, the events at Haymarket Square hurt the labor movement; the press at the time drew little distinction between "hard-working union men" and "foreign" socialists and anarchists. Police forces in cities across the country also increased their supplies of ammunition, guns, and men in preparation for the next outbreak of "anarchism" that might break out. The Knights of Labor suffered a decline in membership as a result of Haymarket Square.

The **American Federation of Labor** (A.F.L.) was the next major national labor organization to achieve national stature. The A.F.L. was organized by crafts and made up almost exclusively of skilled workers. This helped its image, since in the eyes of the public, most anarchists and other radicals were unskilled workers. The union's first leader was Samuel Gompers. Unlike the idealistic philosophy of the Knights of Labor, the A.F.L. bargained for "bread-and-butter issues" like higher wages and shorter hours. By 1917 the A.F.L. had over 2.5 million members. Although the union used strike tactics on many occasions it strenuously avoided the appearance of being controlled by radicals. Major strikes of era included a 1892 strike against the Carnegie Steel Company in Homestead, Pennsylvania, and a 1894 strike by the American Railway Union against the Pullman Palace Car Company. The American Railway Union was founded by Eugene V. Debs, who would later run for president on the Socialist party ticket.

Miners in the West also were engaged in labor activity, and in late 1905 helped to found the **Industrial Workers of the World** (I.W.W.). In spirit this union was close to the old Knights of Labor, as it attracted both skilled and unskilled workers. Union literature spoke of class conflict, violence, and the desirability of socialism. I.W.W. members were called "Wobblies" and included "Mother" Jones, who organized coal miners, and Big Bill Haywood of the Western Federation of Miners. The union was involved in many strikes, many of them bloody, and was destroyed during World War I when many of its leaders were jailed.

Strikes by all of the unions mentioned in the preceding text clearly advanced the condition of the American worker during this era. Their wages had risen, and the hours they worked were less. However, the limitations of unions in this era must also be noted. The Knights of Labor and the Industrial Workers of the World were the only unions that recruited women, blacks, and immigrants. The A.F.L. vigorously rejected the recruitment of these groups, claiming that their acceptance in the workforce would depress the wages of all. Some women did form their own labor unions; the 1909 strike by the International Ladies Garment Workers Union in New York City was one of the largest strikes of the era.

Industrial bosses were able to scare some workers away from joining unions, and many continually suspected that unions were filled by anarchists and other agitators. The government supported industrial owners on several other occasions by sending in the military to end strikes. Pinkerton guards were also used against strikers. Unions had still not achieved widespread acceptance in this era. Even in 1915 only 12 percent of the workforce was unionized.

AN INCREASED STANDARD OF LIVING?

Many history textbooks place great emphasis on the growth of a consumer society in America during this period. These textbooks would note that Americans could now afford things that previously had been luxuries of the upper classes, such as tea and silk stockings. The texts would discuss the fact that average life expectancy increased by over six years between 1900 and 1920, and that things like flush toilets were now present in many houses. The growth of the department store would be emphasized to demonstrate all of the goods that the new consumer could buy.

It should be carefully noted, however, that large segments of American society did not share the newly created wealth found in the pockets and bank accounts of many upper middle-class and upper-class Americans. Many Americans, especially newly arrived immigrants, experienced crushing poverty. Conveniences such as flush toilets were not available in most working-class housing until the late 1920s or 1930s. Wages may have gone up, yet in many parts of the country, increases in living costs were even more profound. Clothing made out of new fabrics and fresh fruits were now available, but with the wages that workers were being paid, actually purchasing any of these goods was absolutely out of the question for the vast majority of workers. For many in the growing middle class, however, families could now not just buy the goods and services that they needed; they could begin to buy merchandise and services that they wanted as well.

THE IMPACT OF IMMIGRATION ON AMERICAN SOCIETY

Immigration patterns shifted dramatically in the late 1880s and 1890s. Before then, most European immigrants coming to the United States came from northern Europe, with large numbers coming from England, Ireland, and Germany. A large segment of these immigrants were English speakers; although assimilation into American society was difficult, the commonality of language made it less so. Starting in the late 1880s, most immigrants arrived from non-English-speaking areas, such as Eastern Europe, Russia, and Italy. Many of these "**new immigrants**" were poorer than those who had arrived in America earlier. This and the language barrier made their assimilation into American society more difficult.

From 1870 to 1920 nearly 28 million immigrants arrived in the United States (peak years for immigration were from 1900 to 1910). Ellis Island opened in 1892, and Europeans desiring to settle in America first had to undergo the physical, psychological, and political testing that was given there. In 1910 Angel Island in San Francisco was completed; this was the West Coast's version of Ellis Island.

Nearly 14,000 Chinese laborers had been recruited to build the transcontinental railroad. Many Chinese avoided racial hostilities by moving to sections of cities like Chinatown in San Francisco. The fear existed that Chinese workers would work for lower wages than "our" workers would, and the Chinese Exclusion Act of 1882 prohibited any new Chinese laborers from entering the country (those who were already here were permitted to stay). After the United States acquired Hawaii in 1898, many Japanese living in Hawaii came to California to work in vegetable and fruit fields there. The Japanese faced many of the same prejudices that the Chinese had faced. In 1906 the Board of Education in San Francisco ruled that separate schools would have to be established for white and Asian students. The 1913 California **Webb Alien Land Law** prohibited Asians who were not citizens from owning land anywhere in the state.

The majority of immigrants on both the West and East Coasts initially settled in coastal cities. Eastern and southern Europeans on the East Coast had come to America to escape oppressive governments, religious persecution, rising taxes, and declining production on their farms. The transformation for many from working in agriculture in Europe to working in a factory in America was massive. To survive, many clung to their old European customs, spoke their native languages at home, lived in neighborhoods dominated by their own ethnic group (thus the development of Chinatown and Little Italy in New York City), became members of mutual benefit associations or other ethnic organizations, or sent their children to religious instead of public schools.

The initial intent of many of these immigrants was to come to America, make money, and then return to their homeland. Some did return, yet those who remained were a crucial component of the economic growth of the era. Eastern and southern Europeans worked in many factories on the East Coast but also provided the manpower for the economic growth of cities such as Milwaukee and Chicago as well. Some immigrants did become involved in agriculture; a small number of Europeans continued on to the mining towns of the West. The one part of the country where few immigrants went was the South; few jobs opened up for them there.

THE TRANSFORMATION OF THE AMERICAN CITY

The construction of new factories and the influx of immigrants from abroad and from the countryside helped to force the radical transformation of many industrial cities in this era. Before the Civil War, cities were relatively small, with most people who lived within the city being able to easily walk to work. Almost all cities had poor sections in them before the Civil War. The rapid influx of poor immigrants turned many of these sections into horribly overcrowded slums.

New methods of transportation aided in the transformation of the industrial city. Elevated trains (first introduced in New York in 1867), cable cars (in San Francisco), electric trolleys, and subways (first found in Boston in 1897) allowed middle- and upper-class citizens to move further and further away from the center of the city. In the early nineteenth century the "best" houses were found in the middle of the city; residents of these houses were now relocating to **suburbia**. Businesses, banks, and offices became located in the business district, usually found in the center of the city. Little housing existed in this part of the city. Located in various sectors surrounding the business district were factories and other centers of manufacturing. Cheap housing for workers usually was located very close to each factory. The upper and lower classes physically lived much further apart in the "modern" cities of the late 1800s than they had earlier in the century.

The conditions of working-class slums are well documented. Many workers lived in "apartments" that were created from residences formerly belonging to middle- and upper-class residents. Room in these buildings were divided and subdivided again so that large numbers of families could live in buildings that formerly housed one family. Tenement buildings were more cheaply constructed and were built to house as many families as possible. Outdoor bathrooms were still the rule in many slum areas. Even those that could receive water inside often emptied waste, human and otherwise, into back alleys (sewage system proved to be woefully inadequate in almost every city). Poverty, disease, and crime were the central elements of life for many living in industrial slums, although in many cities somewhat better conditions were available for workers who were better off. Technology did bring some changes to life even in the slums after the turn of the century, as a few worker residencies started to have gas, electricity, and running water. In the later 1800s cities such as New York also started to develop building codes for all new construction.

Office buildings in many cities became taller during this era. Before the Civil War the tallest buildings in most American cities were four or five stories high. The development of stronger and more durable **Bessemer steel** meant that steel girders could now support taller buildings, and the first elevators began to be installed in buildings in the early 1880s. The first actual "skyscraper" was the building of the Home Insurance Company in Chicago. Finished in 1885 this building was 10 stories high, with four separate elevators taking passengers to the top.

City officials in almost every industrial city realized the necessity of construction and city improvements. After the turn of the century, schools, public buildings, and even sewers began to be built at a rapid rate. However, lack of housing was a major problem that urban planners were unable to solve. Many urban reformers, who will be discussed in a later chapter, had other plans to improve the lives of the urban poor.

POLITICS OF THE GUILDED AGE

Mark Twain coined the term "**The Guilded Age**" to refer to the period between 1875 and 1900. This is not a positive image of the era; it implies a thin layer of gold (symbolizing prosperity) covering all of the problems of the era, including grinding poverty in the time of incredible wealth and political corruption on a wide scale.

The irony of political life in this period was that many Americans were deeply involved in political activity. Large numbers of Americans were involved in party politics; nearly 75 percent of all registered voters voted in the presidential elections of the era, far more than have voted in any recent presidential election. Yet at the same time, much of the political activity at the time was at a superficial level. Few elections of the era had two candidates who differed radically on the issues; most campaigns revolved around different personalities and not around issues. One observer noted that the American politicians of the period were the most "thoroughly ordinary" political leaders in the history of the United States. On top of all this, there was more corruption in the American political system during this period than in any other period of the nineteenth century.

During the 1870s Congress exerted a greater power than the executive branch. This was largely caused by the weak Republican presidents that followed Abraham Lincoln (Andrew Johnson and U.S. Grant). It was during this period that some reformers began to point out the evils of the **spoils system** to the American public. This system, which had been begun by Andrew Jackson, allowed the victorious party in any election to reward their loyal supporters by giving them government jobs.

The lack of controversy or debate on issues during this period was partially because Republicans and Democrats each had roughly the same amount of support. As a result, neither party could risk alienating or turning away anyone from their party ranks. One way to do this was not to talk about real issues. Republican support from bankers, industrialists, and farmers was balanced by Democratic support from immigrants (those who could vote), laborers, and farmers (especially from the West). Democrats of this era (as well as Democrats of today) have always made the claim that their party represents "the people."

President Rutherford B. Hayes, the successor to Grant, did make an attempt to reform the spoils system. After he won the election of 1876, Hayes refused to use the spoils system when he named officials for his new administration, and he removed some individuals from government positions who had been appointed to their position by patronage, including Chester A. Arthur in New York, a future president.

What to do about the spoils system was an important issue in the 1880 election, with Republicans themselves being divided on what to do with it. James Garfield, a congressman from Ohio, suggested that the system be reformed. Garfield was not a strong campaigner but emerged victorious in the presidential election, becoming the fourth consecutive Republican president. Garfield, ironically, was assassinated in July 1881 by a man who was outraged because he was passed over on a job that he thought he should get through the spoils system.

After Garfield's assassination, many major newspapers and some politicians began to call for a thorough reform of the spoils system. Garfield's successor, Chester A. Arthur, urged Congress to pass legislation to that effect. The result was the **Pendleton Civil Service Act**, which went into effect in 1883. This act created a **Civil Service Commission**, which would test applicants and ensure that government jobs were given to those who were qualified to get them. The legislation also stated that government officials couldn't be required to contribute to political campaigns (a practice that had been relatively commonplace). As a result, a **professional bureaucracy** began to be created in both the legislative and executive branches. Aides to cabinet members and congressmen became indispensable to the operations of government. Some at the time suggested that this professional bureaucracy was important because it couldn't be voted out office by the "rabble" who were increasingly being given the vote. As any observer of the American political system knows, however, the reforms of this era did not end corruption as a major influence on the system.

Perhaps the best example of politics focusing on the individual and not the issues was the presidential election of 1884. The regulation of business deserved serious discussion, as did the government's tariff policies (a fiercely debated topic at local political meetings across the nation), yet the campaign largely centered around whether Republican James Blaine had when he was a congressman accepted free railroad stock while voting to support bills favorable to the railroad industry. The second most important issue of the campaign was whether Grover Cleveland had fathered a child before he was married. When all was finished, Cleveland became the first Democrat since 1856 to be elected president.

The issue of tariffs remained a major one throughout the 1880s and into the 1890s, with Eastern business interests leading the charge for higher tariffs. As discussed in the previous chapter, a major depression began in 1893. Millions of Americans lost their jobs. Standard economic and government policy of the time was that it was not the job of the federal government to intervene. A Populist from Ohio named Jacob Coxey led a group of unemployed workers to Washington in 1894 and demanded that the government assist the unemployed of America. **Coxey's Army** did little to affect government policy in Washington, although it did demonstrate the distress felt by unemployed Americans.

The policies of the Populists in the 1890s and William Jennings Bryan and his defeat at the hands of William McKinley were discussed in Chapter 13. McKinley's rout of Bryan in the 1896 election signaled a major shift in American politics. As previously stated, both parties were nearly similar in strength for much of the period discussed in this chapter. The 1896 election ended this. The 1896 election cast the Republicans as a truly national party (Bryan's support was largely sectional). Republicans could claim they were the party of prosperity: Nearly as soon as they were elected, the effects of the depression began to end (a part of this was luck; gold was discovered in parts of Alaska in late 1892, thus increasing the national money supply). Republican domination of politics at the national level filtered down to the state and local levels as well. As a result, many local races were no longer close (in an increasing number Democrats even failed to challenge Republicans in a number of races). One result of this was a striking decrease in political participation and voting by supporters of both major parties. Some historians also argue that William McKinley was the first "modern" president, in that he amassed a large amount of power in the office of the presidency.

Political life in many of the major industrial cities was controlled by **political machines**. These political organizations were designed to keep a certain party, or in many cases a certain individual, in power. Favors, jobs, and in some cases money were promised to voters in return for political support. Many machines used the support of immigrants to remain in power, as newly arrived immigrants were often eager to receive the types of help that political machines could give them. Some machines did make positive reforms in local services and education. The most famous machine existed in New York City, where William Marcy Tweed ("Boss" Tweed) ran New York City through the political club located at **Tammany Hall** beginning in 1870. Tweed and his associates bilked the city treasury out of millions of dollars. The famous political cartoons of

Thomas Nast helped to bring Tweed down and send him to jail, although Tammany Hall ran the politics of New York City for nearly 50 years.

CULTURAL LIFE IN THE GUILDED AGE

There are several literary sources written in the era that expressed strong opinions about the economic changes taking place in society. The Horatio Alger stories published in the era promised that hard work and honesty would oftentimes lead to economic success. Henry George's 1879 book *Progress and Property* was a huge seller; in this book the author advocates a single land tax as a method of greatly improving America by redistributing the wealth.

Several other books present a more critical view of America. *Looking Backward* (1888) by Edward Bellamy was also a very popular book. This book looks ahead to Boston in 2000: In Bellamy's view everyone works hard in efficient factories. A difference, however, was that in Bellamy's view of the future, cooperation between the workers and the bosses has replaced the ruthless capitalism that existed in Bellamy's time.

In 1890 Jacob Riis published *How the Other Half Lives*, a documentary account of slum life in New York City. This book was especially powerful because it also contained photographs he had taken of immigrants and the conditions they lived in. Finally, *The Jungle* (1906) by Upton Sinclair was written as an exposé of the meatpacking industry.

CHAPTER REVIEW

Rapid Review Guide

To achieve the perfect 5, you should be able to explain the following:

- The industrial growth that occurred in the United States during this era made the United States the major industrial producer of the world.

- The industrial growth was largely based on the expansion of heavy industry; the availability of steel was critical to this expansion.

- Taylorism and the assembly line created major changes in the workplace for factory workers.

- Horizontal and vertical integration allowed businesses to expand dramatically during this era; Standard Oil (John D. Rockefeller) and U.S. Steel (Andrew Carnegie) are the best examples of this type of expansion.

- Andrew Carnegie's "Gospel of Wealth" proclaimed it was the duty of the wealthy to return large amounts of their wealth back to the community.

- American workers began to unionize in this era by joining the Knights of Labor, the American Federation of Labor, and the Industrial Workers of the World. Because of intimidation by company bosses and the publicity that came from several unsuccessful strikes, union membership remained low, even into the twentieth century.

- The impact of the "new immigrants" from eastern and southern Europe on American cities and in the workplace was immense.

- The American city became transformed in this era, with new methods of transportation allowing many from the middle and upper class to move to suburbia and still work in the city.

- Political life at the state and city level during this era was dominated by various political machines, although reforms were instituted at the federal level and in some states to create a professional civil service system.

Time Line

1869: Knights of Labor founded in Philadelphia
1870: Beginning of Tammany Hall's control over New York City politics
1879: Publication of *Progress and Prosperity* by Henry George
1881: Assassination of President James Garfield
1882: Chinese Exclusion Act passed by Congress
1883: Pendleton Civil Service Act enacted
1885: Completion of Home Insurance Company Building in Chicago, America's first skyscraper
1886: Haymarket Square demonstration and bombing in Chicago
1887: Interstate Commerce Act enacted
Major strike of railroad workers; President Hayes sends in government troops to break up strike in Pittsburgh
1888: New Jersey passes legislation allowing holding companies
Publication of *Looking Backward* by Edward Bellamy
1890: Publication of *How the Other Half Lives* by Jacob Riis
1892: Ellis Island opens to process immigrants on the East Coast
1893: Beginning of major depression in America
1894: March of Coxey's Army on Washington, DC
United States becomes world's largest manufacturing producer
1896: Decisive victory of Republican William McKinley breaks decades-long deadlock between Democrats and Republicans
America begins to recover from Great Depression of early 1890s
1897: America's first subway begins regular service in Boston
1901: Assassination of President William McKinley
1903: Ford Motor Company established
1905: Industrial Workers of the World formed
1906: Publication of *The Jungle* by Upton Sinclair
1909: Strike of International Ladies Garment Workers Union in New York City

1910: Angel Island opens to process immigrants on West Coast
        Number of American children attending school nears 60 percent
1913: Webb Alien Land Law enacted, prohibiting aliens from owning
        farmland in California
        Ford Motor Company begins to use assembly line techniques;
250,000 automobiles produced

✓ Review Questions

1. The practices championed by Frederick W. Taylor that were championed by many factory owners of the era

    A. made it easier for immigrant workers to assimilate into the American working class
    B. ensured that all workers would receive higher wages and conditions in the factories would improve
    C. emphasized the need for greater efficiency in factory operations
    D. reemphasized the need for extensive training before the worker could do almost any job in the factory
    E. created less profits for factory owners

(Correct Answer: **C**. Taylorism made efficiency in the workplace a science and set the stage for assembly line production techniques.)

2. Many citizens became involved in the political process by actively supporting the Republican and Democratic party for all of the reasons listed *except*

    A. the parades, rallies, and campaigns of the era provided an exciting entry into the American political system
    B. the strength of the two parties was roughly identical in this era, thus creating close and interesting races
    C. the expansion and spread of newspapers in this era made more people aware of political developments
    D. candidates for president for both parties in almost every race of this

era were dynamic and very popular campaigners, thus energizing the forces of both parties
    E. energetic campaign workers were sometimes rewarded with government jobs

(Correct Answer: **D**. Most of the presidential candidates—and presidential winners—of this era were nondescript men, thus allowing much power to go over to the Congress.)

3. An analysis of the march on Washington by "Coxey's Army" in 1894 demonstrates that

    A. large segments of the unemployed in America were willing to become involved politically to protest their situation
    B. all classes in American society were deeply affected by the depression of the early 1890s
    C. the policies of dealing with depression in the 1890s were somewhat similar to policies championed by Herbert Hoover from 1929 to 1932
    D. public opinion had a major effect on government policy in the late 1800s
    E. the march was extremely well covered by the press

(Correct Answer: **C**. The march had little effect on government policy. Coxey's Army was relatively small by the time it got to Washington. Official policy of the time was that it was not the job of the federal government to actively intervene during hard times, a policy similar to that supported by Herbert Hoover in the first years of the Great Depression.)

4. The following statements are true about the new industrial city of the late nineteenth century *except*

   A. the working class lived around the factories, usually somewhat near the center of the city
   B. the factories of the city were almost always found near a source of water, since water power was common
   C. mass transportation allowed workers to travel to various parts of the city, where before they had to walk to work
   D. the central area of the city usually consisted of offices, banks, and insurance buildings
   E. many saloons existed in working-class neighborhoods

(Correct Answer: **B.** By 1890 most American industry had converted to steam power.)

5. Evidence that the standard of living for the working class improved in this era could be found by carefully analyzing all of the following *except*

   A. a comparison of increased wages with increased living costs for factory workers
   B. an analysis of the increased diversity of foods available for purchase by factory workers
   C. a study of former luxuries that were now staples in the homes of some industrial workers
   D. an analysis of the growth of amusement parks, sporting events, and movie theaters in the major cities
   E. a comparison of the wages of most immigrant workers with the wages of workers who remained to work in the "old country"

(Correct Answer: **A.** Many diverse foods were available for purchase by factory workers, but few could afford them. For many workers wages did go up in this period; however, increased living costs oftentimes outstripped higher wages.)

Chapter 15

The Rise of American Imperialism (1890–1913)

 During the 20 years between 1890 and 1910, the United States proved itself to be as powerful as the major European states in every respect. By the turn of the century the United States had already surpassed Germany as the major industrial producer of the world. During this same period the United States was proving that its imperialist aims were as aggressive of those of France, England, and Germany, and that it would vigorously fight to maintain territories that it acquired. There were many constituencies in the United States that opposed American imperialism and many that supported it. American actions in this era, especially in the Philippines, showed that the United States was capable of doing every evil deed abroad that it had criticized various European powers for doing in the previous century.

A PERIOD OF FOREIGN POLICY INACTION

In the years immediately after the Civil War, the United States aggressively sought out new territories to acquire or to economically control. In 1867 the United States purchased Alaska from the Russians. During the same year, the Midway Islands were also annexed, as the United States was also searching for potential bases in the Pacific Ocean.

Beginning in 1871 the Europeans powers began an era of great imperialistic expansion, culminating in the "<u>Scramble for Africa</u>," which left virtually the entire continent colonized by England, France, Germany, or Belgium. The United States did not take part in imperialistic adventures until the 1890s. Several reasons can be cited for this. America was still expanding, but this expansion was still westward; the America frontier did not totally close until the last decade of the century. In addition, rapid industrial growth, urban growth, and a large influx of immigrants kept

America occupied for much of the later nineteenth century. Another factor was that most of the men in power had been veterans of the Civil War or had intimate knowledge of it. These men had little stomach for further warfare, which imperialism was likely to bring.

The results of these factors were obvious. During the 1870s and early 1880s, the American State Department had less than 100 employees. The United States Army and Navy both would have been no match for the military forces of four or five European countries. Virtually no politician spoke of increased imperialistic adventures when campaigning in this era.

A SIGN OF THINGS TO COME: HAWAII

An initial indication that American attitudes toward the use of force abroad was first demonstrated by American actions in Hawaii. American missionaries had first come to Hawaii in the 1820s. The United States was, for obvious reasons, interested in Hawaii's sugar plantations. In 1887 a deal was struck allowing sugar from the islands to be imported into America duty-free. This stimulated the sugar trade in Hawaii. Sugar planters in Hawaii exerted tremendous economic and political power; during that same year they forced King Kalakaua to accept a new constitution that took away some of his political power and put it in their hands.

In 1891 the king died and his sister Queen Liliuokalani replaced him. By this point planters in Hawaii, and some members of the United States Senate, saw the obvious economic advantages of turning Hawaii into a United States protectorate. Queen Liliuokalani vigorously rejected this; her goal was to greatly reduce the influence of foreign countries, especially the United States, in Hawaii. In 1893 pro-American sugar planters, assisted by American marines, overthrew the queen, declared Hawaii to be a republic, and requested Hawaii be annexed by the United States. This takeover was partially a reaction to U.S. tariff policies, which favored domestic producers. If Hawaii was annexed, then planters from Hawaii would be considered domestic producers.

Much debate took place on the floor of the Senate on the proper role of the United States in Hawaii. President Grover Cleveland sent a commission to Hawaii to determine the wishes of the citizens of Hawaii concerning their future. After the commission reported that most people interviewed supported Queen Liliuokalani, Cleveland announced that he was opposed to annexation but recognized the Republic of Hawaii. President McKinley had no such reservations after his election in 1896, stating that it was "**manifest destiny**" that the United States should control Hawaii. The Congress soon approved annexation, largely on the promise that future military bases that could be placed in Hawaii could cement America's strategic position in the Pacific.

It also should be noted that American economic interests desired increased involvement in China during this period as well. The possibility of investment in China would cause Secretary of State John Hay to ask European leaders for an "**Open-Door**" policy in China in 1899, which would allow all foreign nations, including the United States, to establish trading relations with China.

THE 1890s: REASONS FOR AMERICAN IMPERIALISM

By the 1890s many American leaders began to have new attitudes toward imperialistic adventures abroad. The reasons for this were also numerous. At the forefront of those pushing for an aggressive American policy abroad were various industrial leaders, who feared that the United States would soon produce more than it could ever consume. New dependent states could prove to be markets for these goods. Some in business also perceived that in the future, industries would need raw materials that could simply not be found in America (rubber and petroleum products, for example). In the future, America would need dependent states to provide these materials.

Other influential Americans stated that it was important for political reasons that America expand. Bases would be needed in the future in the Pacific, many claimed—thus the need to acquire strategic locations in that region. Many of those interested in reviving the American navy also were very interested in imperialistic adventures; the **Naval Act of 1900** authorized the construction of battleships that would be clearly offensive in nature. A major supporter of naval expansion was Captain Alfred T. Mahan, who in 1890 wrote ***The Influence of Sea Power upon History***, which stated that to be economically successful America must gain new markets abroad; the navy would have to be expanded to accomplish this.

Other factors accounted for increased American interest abroad in the 1890s. The concepts of **Social Darwinism** were used by supporters of imperialism, as were ideas, many imported from Europe, about the racial superiority of the Anglo-Saxon race. *Our Country,* written in 1885 by Josiah Strong, stated that God has appointed the Anglo-Saxons to be their "brother's keepers." Some Americans believed in Kipling's "**White Man's Burden**" and felt it was their duty to go over and civilize the "inferior races" of African and Asia. This was also the period where American missionaries felt the time was right to Christianize the "heathen" of these regions. Others, including Senator Albert J. Beveridge of Indiana, feared that the American spirit would be sapped by the closing of the frontier and suggested that adventures abroad might help to offset this. It should also be remembered that a new generation of Americans, less affected by the horrors of the Civil War, were now in positions of power in Washington, DC.

THE SPANISH-AMERICAN WAR

Those who wanted American adventure abroad finally got their wish with the **Spanish-American War**. In this "splendid little war," America was able to fight against an insignificant European power with little military clout. The steps leading to this war began in 1868, when Cuban colonists revolted against the Spanish who controlled the island. The Spanish made some efforts to control the efficiency of their operations in Cuba, but generally failed in their promises of allowing more self-government on the island. In 1895 an economic depression, caused by falling sugar and tobacco prices, hit the native population especially hard, and another revolt took place.

American investors, plantation owners, and government officials initially did not support the rebellion. The Spanish sent in a huge force of 150,000 troops and instituted a policy of **reconcentration**, which sent civilians, including women and children, who the Spanish thought might be potential allies of the rebels into heavily guarded camps. Conditions in these camps were appalling; it was estimated that in two years up to 225,000 people died in them.

The Cuban exile community in the United States pressured America to intervene on the side of the rebels, yet both President Cleveland and President McKinley resisted these efforts. Pressure on McKinley to intervene increased when Cuban rebels started to destroy American economic interests in Cuba, such as sugar mills.

American public opinion began to swerve toward intervention in Cuba. It is often pointed out that the American press was more responsible for this than were actual events in Cuba. Several American newspapers practiced the most lurid forms of **yellow journalism** when dealing with events in Cuba. Stories of the rape of Cuban girls by Spanish soldiers and brutal torture and execution of innocent Cuban citizens were standard fare in the *New York World* (published by Joseph Pulitzer) and the *New York Morning Journal* (owned by William Randolph Hearst), both of which were competing for circulation in New York. Both papers sent numerous reporters and illustrators to Cuba, and editors in New York demanded sensationalized stories. Newspapers across the country reprinted the accounts published in these papers. As a result of these stories, **jingoism** developed in America; this combined an intense America nationalism with a desire for adventure abroad.

It became harder for McKinley to resist the calls for intervention in Cuba, especially after the sinking of the **USS _Maine_** on February 15, 1898. The *Maine* had been sent to Havana harbor to protect American interests after violent riots broke out in Cuba in January. During the same month a letter stolen from the Spanish ambassador to Washington, in which he called President McKinley "weak," was published in newspapers across the country, further inflaming public opinion. The sinking of the *Maine* was undoubtedly caused by an explosion on board, yet both New York newspapers in banner headlines called for Americans to "Remember the Maine!" An American commission sent to study the sinking of the *Maine* was never able to conclusively determine why or how the ship was sunk.

The Outbreak of War

Theodore Roosevelt was the Assistant Secretary of the Navy at the time, and a vigorous supporter of an increased American role abroad. On February 25 (without the approval of his boss) he cabled all of the commanders in the Pacific to be ready for immediate combat against the Spanish. When the existence of these cables was discovered, President McKinley ordered the content of all of them to be rescinded, except the one to Admiral George Dewey; McKinley reaffirmed that if war broke out in Cuba, Dewey should attack the Spanish fleet quartered in the Philippines.

The pressure on McKinley to go to war was enormous. It should be noted that at this point both American expansionists and those with humanitarian motives supported American intervention in Cuba. McKinley sent the Spanish a list of demands that had to be met to avoid war. The Spanish agreed to the vast majority of them, yet McKinley finally gave in to pressures at home. On April 11, 1898, he finally sent a message to the Congress stating that he favored American intervention in Cuba. The next day Congress authorized the use of force in Spain.

It is still debated whether American disorganization or Spanish disorganization was more pronounced in the Spanish-American War. American efforts to organize an army to go to Cuba were woefully inefficient. Theodore Roosevelt resigned his position in the Naval Department to lead the "**Rough Riders**" up San Juan Hill in the most famous event of the war; his actual role in this battle has been debated. Americans lost 2500 men in this war, the vast majority from malaria or food poisoning. Only 400 died in battle.

It was the American navy earlier championed by Captain (now Admiral) Mahan that proved decisive in the American victory over the Spanish. In seven hours Admiral Dewey destroyed the Spanish fleet in the Pacific; every ship of the Spanish Atlantic force was also destroyed by the American navy. In the Treaty of Paris ending the war, Spain recognized the independence of Cuba and for a payment of $20 million gave the Philippines, Puerto Rico, and Guam over to the United States.

THE ROLE OF AMERICA: PROTECTOR OR OPPRESSOR?

After victory over the Spanish, the United States was placed in a somewhat uncomfortable position. It had criticized Spain for the way it had controlled Cuba, yet many in America did not want Cuba to be totally free either. The dilemma facing Americans after victory was one that would be rethought throughout the twentieth century: how to combine imperialistic intentions with the deep-seated American beliefs in liberty and self-government.

Fearing that America would want to annex Cuba, supporters of Cuban independence in Congress had inserted the **Teller Amendment** in the original congressional bill calling for war against Spain. This amendment stated that America would simply not do that under any circumstances. Nevertheless, President McKinley authorized that the Cubans would be ruled by an American military government (which kept control until 1901). The military government did authorize the Cubans to draft a constitution in 1900 but also insisted that the Cubans agree to all of the provisions of the **Platt Amendment**. This document stated that Cuba could not enter into agreements with other countries without the approval of the United States, that the United States had the right to intervene in Cuban affairs "when necessary," and that America be given two naval bases on the Cuban mainland. The Platt Amendment remained in force in Cuba until the early 1930s.

THE DEBATE OVER THE PHILIPPINES

The debate in America over what to do with the Philippines was a much more intense one. This debate took place on the floor of the Senate and in countless editorial pages across the country. An aggressive policy toward Cuba could be justified, since they were only 90 miles away and seemed important to the United States' position in the Western Hemisphere. Many had second thoughts, however, over controlling the Philippines; the Filipinos seemed a world away, and, after all, were not "like us." In addition, Americans became aware that Filipinos expected that after the Americans helped throw out the Spanish they would then help them achieve independence. What, indeed, should America's role in the Philippines be?

All of the most basic arguments on the merits of imperialism were debated in the aftermath of the Spanish-American War. Didn't the concept of ruling a territory by force violate everything that America stood for? An **Anti-Imperialist League** was formed in 1898 (with Mark Twain and William Jennings Bryan as charter members). The first brochures put out by this organization wondered if America didn't have too many problems at home to be involved abroad, and also expressed the fear that the armies needed for imperialistic adventures abroad might also be used to curb dissent at home.

Others pointed to the huge costs of imperialism and the fear that natives from newly acquired territories might take the jobs (or lower the wages) of American workers. Some pointed out the basic racism involved in American attitudes toward the Filipinos; some Southerners opposed imperialism because they feared it would bring people of the "inferior races" to America in greater numbers.

In the end, those arguing the political, strategic, and economic advantages that control of the Philippines would bring won the national argument. The American frontier *was* closing; wouldn't expansion abroad keep America vital and strong? In addition, religious figures noted that the acquisition of the Philippines would give the Church the opportunity to convert Filipinos to Christianity.

In the end, President McKinley supported American control of the Philippines, stating that if the Americans didn't enter, civil war was likely there. He also proclaimed that the Filipinos were simply "unfit for self-government." The treaty authorizing American control of the Philippines was ratified in February of 1899. It should be noted that American soldiers fought Filipino rebels for the next three years, with nearly 4500 American soldiers killed in this fighting. The American army attacked Filipino rebels with a vengeance; by the end of the insurrection, 200,000 Filipinos had been killed. Many humanitarian groups in America, which had initially enthusiastically supported the Spanish-American War, were appalled. An American commission later criticized the U.S. military for its conduct when dealing with the rebel forces.

CONNECTING THE PACIFIC AND THE ATLANTIC: THE PANAMA CANAL

After the Spanish-American War, most in America and in Europe regarded America as one of the major world powers. Theodore Roosevelt became president after the assassination of President McKinley and, as he had previously demonstrated, favored an aggressive foreign policy. (McKinley was killed during the first year of his second term as president by an anarchist; the next day political boss Mark Hanna lamented "now that damned cowboy is President of the United States".) One of Roosevelt's most cherished goals was the construction of a **Panama Canal,** which would link the Pacific and the Atlantic Oceans. The strategic and economic benefits of such a canal for America at the time were obvious.

A French building company had already acquired the rights to build such a canal in the region of Panama (which was controlled by Colombia). In 1902 the United States bought the rights from the company to construct the land, but this agreement was opposed by the Colombians. A "revolt" was organized in Panama by the French. United States warships sailed off the coast of Panama to help the "rebels." The United States was the first to recognize Panama as an independent country; newly installed Panamanian officials then gave America territory to build a canal. By the terms of the Hay-Bunau-Varilla Treaty of 1904, the United States received permanent rights and sovereignty over a 10-mile-wide area on which they planned to build the canal. In return, Panama was given $10 million. Construction of the canal began shortly afterward.

There was much criticism of American actions in Panama within the United States, but as in the case of the Philippines, the practical benefits of having a canal won out. The canal was finally completed in 1914. American businesses could now ship their goods faster and cheaper, although the acquisition of Panama deepened the suspicion of many in Latin America toward the United States.

THE ROOSEVELT COROLLARY

Theodore Roosevelt's most famous quote was to "speak softly and carry a big stick." In 1904 he also announced the **Roosevelt Corollary** to the Monroe Doctrine to Congress, which stated that the United States had the right to intervene in any country in the Western Hemisphere that did things "harmful to the United States," or if the threat of intervention by countries outside the hemisphere was present. The Roosevelt Corollary strengthened American control over Latin America, justified numerous American interventions in Latin American affairs in the twentieth century, and increased "Yankee go home" sentiment throughout the region. In Santo Domingo (now the Dominican Republic) the government went bankrupt and European countries threatened to intervene to collect their money; under the provisions of the Roosevelt Corollary, Roosevelt organized the American payment of Santo Domingan debt to keep the Europeans out.

In fairness, it should also be noted that Roosevelt won the Nobel Peace Prize for his mediation between the Japanese and the Russians after the Russo-Japanese War of 1904.

William Howard Taft, Roosevelt's successor, was not as aggressive in foreign policy as Roosevelt. He favored "dollars over bullets" and instituted a policy labeled by his critics as "**Dollar Diplomacy**," which stated that American investment abroad would ensure stability and good relations between America and nations abroad. This policy would also be hotly debated throughout the twentieth century.

CHAPTER REVIEW

Rapid Review Guide

To achieve a perfect 5, you should be able to explain the following:

- America became the economic and imperialistic equal of the major European powers by the beginning of the twentieth century.

- The United States acquired territory in the years immediately following the Civil War, but then entered a period where little foreign expansion took place.

- Americans and natives friendly to America increased the economic and political control of Hawaii by the United States, signaling a new trend in foreign policy.

- America desired trade in China; these desires were represented in John Hay's Open-Door policy.

- Economic, political, and strategic motives pushed America to pursue imperialist goals in the 1890s.

- Many in this era also opposed imperialism, often on moral or humanitarian grounds.

- The Spanish-American War allowed American imperialistic impulses to flourish; religious figures also supported imperialism in this era.

- Spanish incompetence and the strength of the American navy were important factors in the American victory in the Spanish-American War.

- America was deeply conflicted but finally decided to annex the Philippines, with three years of fighting between Americans and Filipino rebels to follow.

- The Panama Canal was built by the United States for military, strategic, and economic reasons; its construction began in 1904 and was completed in 1914.

- The Roosevelt Corollary to the Monroe Doctrine increased American control over Latin America.

Time Line

1867: United States purchases Alaska from Russia
United States annexes Midway Islands
1871: Beginning of European "Scramble for Africa"
1875: Trade agreement between United States and Hawaii signed
1885: Publication of *Our Country* by Josiah Strong; book discusses role of Anglo-Saxons in the world
1890: Captain Alfred T. Mahan's *The Influence of Sea Power upon History* published
1893: Pro-American sugar planters overthrow Queen Liliuokalani in Hawaii
1895: Revolt against Spanish in Cuba; harsh Spanish reaction angers many in United States
1898: Explosion of USS *Maine* in Havana harbor; beginning of Spanish-American War
Annexation of Hawaii receives final approval from Congress
Anti-Imperialist League formed
1899: Secretary of State John Hay asks European leaders for an Open-Door policy in China
First fighting between American army forces and Filipino rebels in Manila
1900: Naval Act of 1900 authorizes construction of offensive warships requested by navy
1901: Assassination of President McKinley; Theodore Roosevelt becomes president
1904: Roosevelt Corollary to Monroe Doctrine announced
United States begins construction of Panama Canal
1905: Roosevelt mediates conflict between Japan, Russia in Portsmouth, New Hampshire
1914: Completion of the Panama Canal

√ **Review Questions**

1. The intent of the Roosevelt Corollary to the Monroe Doctrine was

    A. to prevent European powers from becoming directly involved in affairs of the Western Hemisphere
    B. to allow the United States to intervene in Latin American countries causing "trouble" for the United States
    C. to allow the United States to "assist" countries in the area that demonstrated economic or political instability
    D. to allow the United States to remove "unfriendly governments" in the Western Hemisphere
    E. All of the above

(Correct Answer: **E.** The Roosevelt Corollary allowed the United States to intervene in affairs of Latin American countries under several circumstances, but was also intended to keep the European powers out of Latin America.)

2. Many humanitarians in the United States initially supported the Spanish-American War because

    A. they were appalled at the Spanish policy of reconcentration in Cuba
    B. they were able to ignore editorial comments found in most American newspapers
    C. they were following the lead of the Anti-Imperialist League
    D. they desired to assist the Filipino natives
    E. of American economic interests in Cuba

(Correct Answer: **A.** The Spanish policy of placing civilians in camps horrified many Americans. Most American newspapers initially supported the war as well. Concern for the Filipinos only became an issue during the debate over whether or not the United States should annex the Philippines.)

3. The major criticism that some Americans had concerning the construction of the Panama Canal was that

    A. the canal would force America to have a navy in both the Pacific and the Atlantic
    B. the canal would be outlandishly expensive to build
    C. the tactics that the Americans used to get the rights to build the canal were unsavory at best
    D. a French construction team had agreed to build the canal first
    E. American forces would have to be stationed indefinitely in Panama to guard the canal

(Correct Answer: **C.** The United States acquired the rights to territory to build the canal through the encouragement of a "revolt" by Panamanians against Colombia. The American navy wanted the canal. The French construction team had already been bankrupted by the excessive construction costs of the canal project.)

4. The United States was able to annex Hawaii because

    A. Queen Liliuokalani desired increased American investment in Hawaii
    B. pro-American planters engineered a revolt in Hawaii
    C. American marines had forcibly removed the queen from power
    D. public opinion in Hawaii strongly favored annexation
    E. Hawaii felt threatened by other Pacific powers

(Correct Answer: **B.** Queen Liliuokalani desired decreased American involvement in Hawaii. American marines were involved in the removal of the queen from power, but only in a supporting role. Public opinion in Hawaii supported the queen.)

5. American missionary leaders supported imperialism in this era because

   A. they thought their involvement would temper the excess zeal of other imperialists
   B. they admired the "pureness of spirit" found in the Filipinos and other native groups
   C. religious leaders in Europe favored imperialism
   D. they saw imperialism as an opportunity to convert the "heathen" of newly acquired territories
   E. American presidents, especially Theodore Roosevelt, strongly pressured them to take that stance

(Correct Answer: **D.** Missionary leaders worked in conjunction with other imperialists in this era. Little admiration of the natives was demonstrated by missionary leaders; the possibilities of conversions was the major reason for religious support for imperialism.)

Chapter 16

The Progressive Era (1895–1914)

In 1896 and 1897 America emerged from the serious depression that had jolted it in the first part of the decade. It remained obvious to many observers that large social and political problems continued to plague American society. The gap between the poorest and richest members of American society continued to widen. Vast numbers of immigrants continued to pour into eastern cities without any meaningful system to support them. Corrupt political machines continued to dominate many American cities. As a result of these and countless other social problems, a group of largely middle-class men and women attempted to reform American society in many meaningful ways. These individuals, called **progressives**, oftentimes blamed capitalism for many of the problems facing America society. Their goal, however, was not to destroy capitalism in any way; it was to make capitalism and the social structures created by it operate more efficiently and more humanely. This reform impulse was a key influence in American political life until the outbreak of World War I in 1914 and was called **progressivism**. Most progressives were either writers or journalists.

THE ORIGINS OF PROGRESSIVISM

It should be emphasized that progressivism was not a unified movement in any way. There was never a unifying agenda or party; many "progressives" eagerly supported one or two progressive reforms without supporting any others. Thus, progressive reforms could be urban or rural, call for more government or less government, and on occasion could even be perceived as being pro-business.

Progressivism has many sources of origin. Books mentioned in Chapter 14 such as *Progress and Poverty* by Henry George and *Looking*

Backward by Edward Bellamy were read by most early progressives. Taylorism (also discussed in Chapter 14) influenced many progressives; many felt that the efficiency that Taylor proposed for American industry could also be installed in American government, schools, and even in one's everyday life.

Progressive reforms also shared some of the same critiques of society that American socialists were making at the time. Progressives and socialists both were very critical of capitalism and wanted more wealth to get into the hands of the poor working class. However, as stated previously, progressives were interested in reforming the capitalist system, while American socialists wanted to end capitalism (by this point, by the ballot box). It should be noted that many progressive reformers had knowledge of socialism, some attended socialist meetings at some point in their careers, and a few progressives remained socialists throughout their careers. Upton Sinclair, author of *The Jungle,* was both a progressive and a socialist.

Progressivism was also influenced by religious developments of the era. During this era the Social Gospel movement flourished; this movement had its origin in Protestant efforts to aid the urban poor. The Social Gospel movement emphasized the elements of Christianity that emphasized the need to struggle for social justice; followers stated that this fight was much more important than the struggle to lead a "good life" on a personal level. Many progressive leaders (such as Jane Adams) had grown up in very religious homes and found in progressive politics a place where they could put their religious beliefs into action. The Social Gospel movement was strictly a Protestant movement.

Finally, progressives were deeply impacted by the muckrakers. Newspaper editors discovered that articles that exposed corruption increased circulation, and thus exposés of unethical practices in political life and business life became common in most newspapers. The term muckrakers was used in a negative way by Theodore Roosevelt, but writers using that title exposed much corruption in American society. *The Jungle* by Upton Sinclair attacked the excesses of the meatpacking industry. Ida Tarbell wrote of the corruption she found in the Standard Oil Trust company, while Lincoln Steffens exposed political corruption found in several American cities in *The Shame of the Cities.* Jacob Riis exposed life in the slums in *How the Other Half Lives.* Progressives wanted to act on the evils of society uncovered by the muckrakers.

THE GOALS OF PROGRESSIVES

The fact that many in the progressive movement were from the middle class greatly influenced the goals of progressivism. Progressives wanted to improve the life experienced by members of the lower classes; at the same time most desired that the nature and pace of this improvement be dictated by them and not the workers themselves. Progressives greatly feared the potential for revolution found in socialist and anarchist writings of the era; they proposed a series of gradual reforms. *Progressives, as stated previously, wanted to make existing institutions work better.* Factories, they felt, could be changed so that they would be concerned with the quality of life of their workers; governments could be altered so that they would act as protectors of the lower classes.

It should be noted that progressive goals and programs were not universally popular. Progressive programs for the betterment of the poor oftentimes meant that the government would have more control over their lives; many in the lower class were vehemently opposed to this. In addition, progressives wanted to crack down on urban political machines, which in many cases did much to aid the lives and conditions of the lower classes. As a result, the very people that progressive reforms were designed to help were oftentimes resentful of these reforms.

URBAN REFORMS

Many of the early successes of progressivism were actions taken against urban political machines. Yet again, some reforms supported by progressives put more power in the hands of those machines. Certain "reform mayors," such as Tom Johnson in Cleveland and Mark Fagan in Jersey City, were legitimately interested in improving the living and working conditions of the lower classes and improving education. In cities such as Cleveland, municipal utilities were taken over by the city to provide more efficient service. Some reform mayors also pushed citywide relief programs and established shelters for the homeless.

Other progressive reformers wanted to professionalize the administrations of various cities and to enact measures so that mere "political hacks" could not get municipal jobs. It should be noted that some of these reforms appeared to be antidemocratic in nature. By attacking the system of political machines and ward politics, reformers were attacking a system that had given a degree of assistance and influence to the urban working classes. The new "professionals" who reformers envisioned getting municipals jobs would be almost exclusively from the middle class, the same class as the reformers themselves.

THE PROGRESSIVES AT THE STATE LEVEL

It was at the state level that some of the most important political work of the progressives took place. Governors Robert La Follette from Wisconsin and Hiram Johnson from California introduced reforms in their states that would allow citizens to have a more direct role in the political process. These reforms included the following:

1. The adoption of the **Seventeenth Amendment**. Finally adopted in 1913, it allowed voters, instead of the state legislatures, to directly elect United States senators.

2. The adoption of the **initiative process**. This initiative allowed a citizen to propose a new law. If he or she got enough signatures, the proposed law would appear on the next ballot.
3. The adoption of the **referendum process**. Referendum allowed citizens to vote on a law that is being considered for adoption.
4. The adoption of the **recall process**, which allowed the voters to remove an elected official from office before his or her term is up.
5. The adoption of the **direct primary**, which allowed party members to vote for prospective candidates instead of having them hand-chosen by the party boss.

WOMEN AND PROGRESSIVISM

Women played a major role in progressivism from the very beginning. In 1899 Florence Kelley founded the **National Consumers League**, an organization made up largely of women that lobbied at the state and national level for legislation that would protect both women and children at home and in the workplace. Minimum wage laws for women were enacted in various states beginning in 1911; more stringent child labor laws began to be enacted in states one year later.

Women also played a crucial rule in the creation of **settlement houses**. In 1889 Jane Addams and Ellen Gates Starr founded **Hull House** in Chicago, which would become a model for settlement house construction in other cities. Found at Hull House (and at many other centers) were clubs for adults and children, rooms for classes, and a kindergarten. Settlement house workers also gave poor and immigrant women (and their husbands) advice on countless problems that they encountered in the city. Some settlement houses were more successful than others in actually helping lower-class families cope with urban life. Programs at settlement houses were multidimensional, stressing art, music, drama, and dance. Classes in child care, health education, and adult literacy could be found at most settlement houses.

Women differed greatly on how they felt the urban poor could be helped. Some pushed heavily for reforms in the workplace, while others joined organizations such as the **Anti-Saloon League**, whose members felt that alcohol was the major cause for the woes of the lower classes. Still others became deeply involved in the suffrage movement, oftentimes attempting to get lower-class women interested in the vote as well. Women started to get the vote in individual western states beginning with Idaho, Colorado, and Utah in the 1890s. In 1916 Alice Paul founded the radical **National Woman's party**, and Carrie Chapman Catt founded the **National American Woman's Suffrage Association**. Both organizations would be crucial in the final push for women's suffrage after World War I.

In addition, during this era women in public meetings first began to discuss the topic of **feminism**. The word was first used by a group of women meeting in New York City in 1914. Feminists wanted to remove themselves from the restraints that society had placed on them because they were female. A radical feminist of the time was Margaret Sanger, who as a nurse in New York City observed the lack of knowledge that immigrant women had about the reproductive system. Sanger devoted herself to teaching the poor about birth control and opened the first birth control clinic in the United States.

Some laws were passed in the era to protect working women. In *Muller* v. *Oregon,* a case that went all the way to the Supreme Court in 1908, it was ruled constitutional to set limits on the number of hours a woman could work. The rationale given for this, which the Court agreed with, was that too much work would interfere with a woman's prime role as a mother.

REFORMING THE WORKPLACE

Horrible events such as the **Triangle Shirtwaist Fire** convinced many progressives to push for reforms of safety and health conditions in factories. Progressives lobbied hard for the creation of accident insurance programs for workers in New York and elsewhere. From 1910 to 1917, many states adopted legislation that would help to protect families of those killed or injured in workplace and mine accidents.

Progressives and labor unions oftentimes did not see eye to eye. However, one issue that some progressives and unions did agree on was the need to restrict further European immigration, especially from southeastern Europe. Immigrants were not union supporters, and increased immigration would cause a larger supply of labor, thus driving down wages. By not bringing in more immigrants that were "unlike ourselves," supporters stated that city life and morale in the workplace would improve. To some, opposing immigration was a progressive reform. More than anything, this demonstrated that "progressivism" meant very different things to different people.

THE SQUARE DEAL OF THEODORE ROOSEVELT

Theodore Roosevelt's ascendancy to the presidency in 1901 after the assassination of William McKinley brought to office a man unafraid to use the power of the government to address the evils of society. In 1902 Roosevelt helped to mediate a strike between the United Mine Workers and the coal companies. Roosevelt stated that the agreement was a "**Square Deal**" for both sides. This term would be used throughout his time in office to emphasize that government intervention could help the plight of ordinary Americans.

Roosevelt was reelected in 1904, and in 1906 Roosevelt supported legislation that was progressive in nature. He supported the Hepburn Act, which gave teeth to the **Interstate Commerce Commission**, designed to further regulate interstate shippers, and the creation of the **Food and Drug Act** and the **Meat Inspection Act**. The writings of many muckrakers, including Upton Sinclair's *The Jungle,* highlighted many of the problems of the food industry addressed in these bills.

Roosevelt also used the federal government to aggressively investigate and prosecute illegal **trusts** and **holding companies** (both described in Chapter 14). The **Sherman Antitrust Act** had been in place since 1890, yet neither President Cleveland or President McKinley had ordered its enforcement on a regular basis. To many Americans it appeared that a small group of Wall Street bankers controlled the entire American economy (this complaint would be echoed many times in the twentieth century). Roosevelt had the Justice Department sue the Northern Securities Company, a holding company that controlled many American railroads, Standard Oil, and the American Tobacco Company. All were partially broken up as a result of these government actions. By the end of his time in office, Roosevelt had taken on 45 major American corporations. It should be emphasized that Theodore Roosevelt was *not* antibusiness; however, he did strongly believe that corporations who abused their power should be punished.

Roosevelt also enacted other measures applauded by progressives. In 1905 he created the **United States Forest Service**, which soon acted to set aside 200 million acres of land for national forests. The **Sixteenth Amendment**, enacted in 1913, authorized the collection of federal income taxes, which could be collected largely from the wealthy (the income of the federal government had been previously collected from tariffs; progressives argued that to pay for them the prices of goods sold to the working classes were artificially high). In the end the "Square Deal" was based on the idea of creating a level playing field. Roosevelt was not against trusts; he opposed trusts that were harmful to the economy. He supported Standard Oil, for example, because of the benefits he said it brought to America.

PROGRESSIVISM UNDER WILLIAM HOWARD TAFT

Many historians regard Taft as the real trustbuster. More antitrust lawsuits went to court when he was president than during the Roosevelt presidency, although some of them had begun during the Roosevelt administration. In the 1908 presidential election, William Howard Taft, Theodore Roosevelt's hand-picked successor, defeated three-time candidate William Jennings Bryan. In the campaign, Bryan continually came across as supporting more progressive measures than Taft did. Taft did promise to follow Roosevelt's progressive legacy, and to some degree, he followed through on this; during his presidency the Sherman Antitrust Act was used against another 95 corporations.

However, Taft never had the personal magnetism that Roosevelt possessed, and totally unlike Roosevelt, he deferred on important issues to the Congress. Taft was influenced by the conservative wing of the Republican party, which opposed additional progressive reforms. His support of the Payne-Adrich Tariff Act of 1909 further angered progressives, who usually viewed tariffs as hurting the lower classes (since to pay for them the prices of goods were usually higher).

Progressives in the Republican party finally took action against Taft after the **Ballinger-Pinchot Affair**. Richard A. Ballinger was Secretary of the Interior under Taft and allowed private business interests to gain access to several million acres of land in Alaska. A close friend of Roosevelt, Gifford Pinchot, headed the Forest Service. When Pinchot protested against Ballinger's actions in front of a congressional committee, Taft proceeded to fire him. Progressives now labeled Taft as being anti-environment.

Progressive Republicans began to campaign against Taft and the "old guard" of pro-business Republicans. In the 1910 congressional primaries, Taft campaigned against several of these progressives. Theodore Roosevelt, just back from an extended trip to Africa, campaigned for a number of these Republican progressives. His speeches called for more progressive reforms, especially in the workplace. Roosevelt called his program for reform the **New Nationalism**. Roosevelt called again and again for a greatly expanded role of the federal government. As a result of the 1920 congressional elections, progressives dominated the United States Senate.

THE 1912 PRESIDENTIAL ELECTION

By early 1912 Theodore Roosevelt decided that the policies of President Taft were not progressive enough and announced he was running for president. The single event that several biographers say pushed Roosevelt to run was the decision of Taft to go after United States Steel because it had purchased Tennessee Coal and Iron back in 1907. Taft knew that Roosevelt had personally approved this deal. As might be expected, Taft's followers controlled the Republican party machinery, thus allowing Taft to easily win the 1912 Republican nomination.

Roosevelt's followers marched out of the Chicago convention site, proclaimed themselves to be the Progressive party, and nominated Roosevelt for president (with California's progressive governor Hiram Johnson as his running mate). This party soon became known as the **Bull Moose party**. Its platform included many progressive causes, including the elimination of child labor, suffrage for women, and an eight-hour workday. Many women supported the Bull Moose party; in several states where women had the vote, women ran for local offices as members of the party.

The beneficiary of the split in the Republican party was the Democratic candidate Woodrow Wilson, governor of New Jersey. Wilson also campaigned as a progressive, although in his platform, called the

New Freedom policy, he also cautioned against big government. Wilson argued that government was wrong to concentrate on regulating big monopolies; instead, government should be trying to break them up. Wilson won the election, but only received 42 percent of the popular vote. Roosevelt received 27 percent and Taft only 23 percent. It should also be noted that Eugene Debs ran as a candidate of the Socialist party and received 6 percent of the votes. The political will of the times is easily shown in this election: The three candidates openly calling for progressive policies (Wilson, Roosevelt, and Debs) received 75 percent of the popular vote.

THE PROGRESSIVE LEGACY OF WOODROW WILSON

Much legislation was enacted under Woodrow Wilson that pleased reformers. The Underwood Tariff Act of 1913 cut tariffs on imported goods. The Clayton Antitrust Act of 1914 was a continuation of the Sherman Antitrust Act, and outlawed certain specific business practices. A key element of this act also helped the labor movement by making strikes and other labor activities legal. In 1914 the Federal Trade Commission was established; the main job of this organization was to uniformly enforce the antitrust laws. Wilson also signed legislation creating the Federal Reserve system, which established 12 district reserve banks and the creation of Federal Reserve notes. This system was designed to protect the American economy against further panics such as had occurred in the early 1890s.

DID PROGRESSIVISM SUCCEED?

Progressives had done much to improve the condition of American cities, the plight of factory workers, the support available for urban immigrants, and the democratic nature of the American political process. However, progressive reforms did much less for migrant farmers and others outside of the city. Many blacks were disappointed that few alliances ever took place between black leaders and progressives; Theodore Roosevelt met twice with Booker T. Washington but other than that did little to help the conditions of blacks during his presidency. Race riots occurred in Springfield, Illinois, in 1908. The anti-black message of D. W. Griffith's 1915 film *Birth of a Nation* was applauded by many; President Wilson stated that the film presented a "truthful" depiction of the Reconstruction era. In 1909 the National Association for the Advancement of Colored People (NAACP) was founded to further the fight of blacks for political equality in America.

The outbreak of World War I in Europe turned the interests of many away from political reform. Only those reformers concerned with women's suffrage relentlessly pursued their cause during the war years.

CHAPTER REVIEW

Rapid Review Guide

To achieve the perfect 5, you should be able to explain the following:

- Political, economic, and social inequities and problems existed in America in the late 1890s, and the Progressive movement developed to attempt to address some of those problems.

- The Progressive movement did not have a unifying set of goals or leaders.

- Progressives shared some of the critiques of American society as the socialists, but wished to reform and not attack the American system.

- Progressive reformers were closely tied to the Social Gospel movement of the Protestant church; progressivism and religious fervor often marched hand in hand.

- Muckraking magazines and newspapers of the era oftentimes created and published the progressive agenda.

- Many progressives were determined to reform city government and the services provided by city government.

- Progressive political reforms included the initiative process, the referendum, recall, and the direct primary.

- Hull House was an example of a settlement house copied by reformers across the country.

- The presidency of Theodore Roosevelt was a high point of progressivism; Roosevelt's "Square Deal" included many progressive measures.

- Progressive policies were sometimes challenged by Roosevelt's successor, William Howard Taft; the advent of World War I blunted the progressive reform impulse for many.

- Progressivism succeeded in achieving some of its goals but fell short in aiding farmers and minorities in America.

Time Line

1879: Progress and Poverty by Henry George published
1888: Looking Backward by Edward Bellamy published
1889: Formation of National Consumer's league
1890: National American Woman Suffrage Association founded
1901: Theodore Roosevelt becomes president after assassination of William McKinley
  Progressive Robert La Follette elected as governor of Wisconsin
  Progressive Tom Johnson elected as mayor of Cleveland, Ohio

1903: Founding of Women's Trade Union League
1904: The Shame of the Cities by Lincoln Steffens published
1905: IWW (Industrial Workers of the World) established
       Establishment of United States Forest Service
1906: The Jungle by Upton Sinclair published
       Meat Inspection Act enacted
       Pure Food and Drug Act enacted
1908: William Howard Taft elected president
1909: Foundation of the NAACP
1910: Ballinger-Pinchot controversy
1911: Triangle Shirtwaist Company fire
1912: Progressive party ("Bull Moose party") founded
   by Theodore Roosevelt
       Woodrow Wilson elected president
       Establishment of Industrial Relations Committee
1913: Establishment of Federal Reserve System
       Ratification of Sixteenth Amendment, authorizing federal
   income tax
       Ratification of Seventeenth Amendment, authorizing direct elec-
   tion of senators
1914: Clayton Antitrust Act ratified
       Outbreak of World War I in Europe
1915: First showing of D. W. Griffith's film Birth of a Nation

✓ REVIEW QUESTIONS

1. Successful reforms initiated by the progressives included all but which of the following:

   A. Governments became more efficient in American cities such as Cleveland
   B. Health and safety conditions improved in some large factories
   C. The conditions of migrant farmers improved to some degree
   D. Some state governments became more democratic with the introduction of measures such as referendum and recall
   E. The federal government began to collect a national income tax.

(Correct Answer: **C.** Progressives did much less for workers in the agricultural sector than they did for factory workers.)

2. Theodore Roosevelt ran for president in 1912 because

   A. the policies of William Howard Taft's administration were almost exclusively antiprogressive
   B. he desired to split the Republican party and give the election to the Democrats
   C. he was appalled by the results of the Ballinger-Pinchot Affair
   D. of the Taft administration's decision to apply the Sherman Antitrust Act to United States Steel
   E. He felt that Taft was not adequately preparing America for potential war with Europe.

(Correct Answer: **D.** The Taft administration enacted many important progressive measures. Roosevelt considered the actions against United States Steel to be a personal affront to him.)

3. American blacks were discouraged by their lack of racial progress during the

Wilson administration. Which of the following is *not* true.

A. The film *Birth of a Nation* presented a positive view of blacks in Reconstruction states after the Civil War.
B. Black and progressive leaders forged tight political bonds during the Wilson administration and battled for many of the same causes.
C. Springfield, Illinois, was one city that demonstrated positive relations between white citizens and newly arrived blacks.
D. Booker T. Washington and Theodore Roosevelt developed close political ties after their two meetings together.
E. All of the above.

(Correct Answer: **E.** D. W. Griffith's film presented a very negative view of blacks during Reconstruction. Progressives and black leaders never worked closely together. Race riots were held in Springfield, Illinois. Theodore Roosevelt met twice with Booker T. Washington but did little to help the conditions of blacks.)

4. Many progressives agreed with socialists that

A. Capitalism had created massive inequality in America
B. the American factory system had to be fundamentally altered
C. labor unions were inherently evil
D. revolutionary tactics were needed to reform the economic and social systems
E. Factory owners were inherently greedy and could not be trusted

(Correct Answer: **A.** Progressives and socialists were both critical of the effects of capitalism in the United States. Progressives, however, were intent on reforming that system.)

5. Which of the following was least likely to be a progressive in this era?

A. A member of the Industrial Workers of the World
B. A member of the Protestant Social Gospel movement
C. A large stockholder in United States Steel
D. A follower of Eugene Debs
E. A member of the Bull Moose party

(Correct Answer: **C.** Progressives were insistent that corporations like U.S. Steel be made to reform. The IWW shared goals with progressives, as did members of the Social Gospel movement and socialist followers of Debs.)

Chapter 17

The United States and World War I

 Students of world or European history can recall the horrific effects that World War I (or the "Great War," as it was then called) had on France, Germany, and other European nations. Trench warfare, poison gas, and U-boats are known about by virtually everyone who has studied the war. Students of United States history should note that the war had a large effect on America as well. Even though America did not enter the war until 1917, the economic benefits of the war were large; many blacks moved north and found jobs during World War I, and during the war women found that they could be more than stenographers. In addition, during World War I America entered the world stage as a major power. Ironically, America seemed reluctant to accept that role in the immediate postwar years; it was only after World War II that America took on that position with assurance.

THE AMERICAN RESPONSE TO THE OUTBREAK OF WAR

The assassination of the Archduke Franz Ferdinand by Bosnian nationalists on June 28, 1914, set off the series of events that would lead to World War I. Tensions between European powers had been building, with almost all of the major powers undergoing rapid military buildup in the years immediately prior to 1914. These conflicts were caused by increasing nationalism throughout Europe, the competition of imperialism, and the complicated system of alliances that wove together the fates of most European nations. When the war actually began in earnest in August 1914, France, Russia, and Great Britain were the Triple Entente, while Germany, Austria-Hungary, and Italy made up the **Central powers**.

Many Americans felt deeply connected to the events of World War I, as over one-third of the American population was a first- or second-generation immigrant. President Wilson and others personally supported the cause of the Allied powers, especially when reports of the alleged barbarism of the German soldiers in the battles of 1914 appeared in American newspapers.

On August 4, 1914, President Wilson issued an official proclamation of American neutrality in the war. Even though most Americans were sympathetic to the cause of the Allied powers, economic common sense dictated that America remain neutral; America in 1914 desired to continue to trade with both sides. After English ships interfered with American trade with Germany and German submarines interfered with American trade with England, America issued a series of diplomatic protests.

INCREASING AMERICAN SUPPORT FOR THE ALLIED POWERS

American sympathies and practical considerations dictated that American trade with the Allies increase as the war progressed. By 1916 American trade with the Central powers was down to near zero, whereas trade with the Allied powers had increased nearly 400 percent. Many who traded with Great Britain urged Washington to begin to prepare the United States for eventual war against Germany. A private **National Security League** was founded in late 1914 to instill patriotism in Americans and to psychologically prepare Americans for war. By the summer of 1915, Congress was taking the first steps to prepare the American army for actual combat in Europe. It should also be noted that peace movements existed in many major America cities, with women making up a large part of the membership of these organizations.

It was the actions of German U-boats that angered many Americans and caused them to favor entering the war against the "**Hun**." According to existing international law, if one ship were to sink another, it first had to board the ship before sinking it and offer all on board "safe passage." The advantage a U-boat had was that it glided underwater undetected and fired at other ships without warning.

Americans were outraged when a German U-boat sank a British passenger ship, the **Lusitania**, in the Atlantic Ocean on May 7, 1915; 128 Americans on board all perished. President Wilson issued a strong protest, but it should be noted that the ship was carrying weapons on it meant to help the Allied cause (which made it technically legal for the Germans to sink the ship). In addition, Germany had placed advertisements in major American newspapers warning Americans not to travel on the ship that day.

In August the *Arabic,* another passenger liner, was sunk by the Germans. President Wilson again forcefully protested; in response the Germans issued the "Arabic pledge," in which they promised to stop sinking passenger ships without warning as long as the crews of the ships allowed the Germans to search the ships.

Official American concern about the actions of the U-boats continued. On March 24, 1916, a French ship called the *Sussex* was attacked by a U-boat; two Americans on board were badly injured. The United States threatened to entirely cut diplomatic ties with Germany over this incident. In the **Sussex Pledge** the Germans promised to sink no more ships without prior warning. The actions described above all caused public opinion in the United States to increasingly favor military support of the Allied powers.

AMERICA MOVES TOWARD WAR

Woodrow Wilson won the 1916 presidential election over his Republican opponent Charles Evans Hughes, by stating that the Republicans were the party of war. "He kept us out of war" was the popular slogan of Wilson's supporters. This was a promise, however, that Wilson could not keep for long. On January 31, 1917, Germany announced a policy of **unrestricted submarine warfare**, stating that any ship from any country attempting to enter the ports of Allied nations would be sunk. Historians believed that the Germans knew that eventually the United States would enter the war; by beginning this policy at this time, the Germans were gambling that they could win the war before the United States was truly involved. On February 3 Wilson officially broke off American diplomat relations and suggested to Congress that American merchant ships be armed.

American public opinion became increasingly enraged when they heard about the **Zimmermann Telegram**. This was an intercepted message between Arthur Zimmermann, the German foreign ministry, and German officials in Mexico suggesting that when Germany went to war with the United States, the Mexicans should be persuaded to attack the United States. As a reward, the Mexicans would receive Texas, New Mexico, and Arizona after the United States was defeated.

Between March 16 and March 18 three more American ships were sunk by German vessels. On April 2 President Wilson formally asked Congress for a declaration of war; this declaration was enthusiastically passed the following day. Wilson was motivated to declare war by the legitimate danger to American shipping that existed and by his belief that American entry into the war would help to shorten it.

AMERICA ENTERS THE WAR

By the time the Americans entered the war in April of 1917, the English and the French were desperate for American assistance. The Russian army had suffered crushing defeats since 1916, and in March of 1917 the removal of the tsar from power threw into doubt the entire Russian commitment to the war effort. Without Russia in the war, the Germans could place virtually their entire army in the western front.

The initial **American Expeditionary Force** that landed in France in June 1917 under the command of General John J. Pershing consisted of 14,500 men; its main psychological effect was to help boost the morale of the Allies. Volunteers were recruited to serve in the army, but a Selective Service Act was passed in May 1917. Those originally drafted were between 21 and 30; this was later extended to ages 17 and 46.

Both women and blacks were in the armed forces during the war. Some 11,500 women served, primarily as nurses and clerks, and over 400,000 blacks served. Black units were kept segregated and almost always had white officers.

American shipping to Europe became increasingly disrupted by German U-boats after the formal American declaration of war. Starting in May 1917, all American shipping to Europe traveled in a **convoy system**. The navy developed special torpedo boats that were able to destroy submarines. These techniques drastically decreased the damage done by German U-boats and other ships; only two troop transports were sunk from this point onward, and losses suffered by the merchant marine were much less.

THE IMPACT OF THE AMERICAN EXPEDITIONARY FORCE

The size of the American Expeditionary Force (AEF) expanded to over 2 million by November of 1918, and they were definitely needed. Lenin and the Bolsheviks took over in Russia in November of 1917 and pulled the Russians out of the war. With only one front to worry about, by March of 1918 the Germans had almost all of their troops on the western front, and in early June were less than 50 miles from Paris.

American soldiers played a major role in preventing the Germans from taking Paris. The Americans held firm at the **Battle of Chateau-Thierry**, preventing the Germans from crossing the Marne and advancing toward Paris. Americans were also involved in a major offensive against the Germans in July and decisively defeated the Germans at the Battle of St. Mihiel. Over 1 million AEF forces took part in the final **Meuse-Argonne Offensive** of late September 1918, which cut the supply lines of the Germany army and convinced the German general staff that victory was impossible.

The armistice ending the war was signed on November 11, 1918. Nearly 115,000 Americans died in this war, a mere pittance compared to the nearly 8 million European soldiers who died in battle. American military heroes from World War I included American fighter pilot Eddie Rickenbacker and Captain Alvin York, who single-handedly shot 25 German soldiers and captured another 132.

THE HOME FRONT DURING WORLD WAR I

Despite the fact that America was far removed from the physical fighting of World War I, much had to be done to prepare America for the war effort. Americans were encouraged to buy **Liberty Bonds** to support the war; movie stars of the era such as Charlie Chaplin made speeches and short films extolling the virtues of Liberty Bonds.

Poor harvests in 1916 and 1917 made it necessary to regulate food production and consumption during the war years. In August 1917, Congress passed the **Lever Food and Fuel Control Act**; almost immediately the government began to regulate food consumption. The Food Administration was headed by future President Herbert Hoover, who attempted to increase production and decrease consumption. Hoover's approach to problems was centered around voluntary cooperation, as "Wheatless Mondays" and "Meatless Tuesdays" became commonplace. Harvests greatly improved in 1918 and 1919 as well. The introduction of daylight saving time allowed farmers more time in the evenings to work in the fields and also served to save electricity.

Industry was also regulated by the **War Industries Board**, headed by Wall Street financier Bernard Baruch. This board attempted to stimulate production for the war effort by strictly allocating raw materials and by instituting strict production controls. A Fuel Administration also acted to preserve coal and gasoline; "Fuelless Mondays" and "Gasless Sundays" also existed in 1917 and 1918.

Some historians make the point that World War I was actually the high point of **progressivism**. The government regulated the economy in positive ways that could have only been dreamed about in the days of Theodore Roosevelt. Business leaders loudly claimed they were supporting the war effort (many of them were). As a result, the Sherman Antitrust Laws were largely forgotten during World War I.

KEEPING AMERICA PATRIOTIC

Another new agency created in 1917 was the **Committee on Public Information**, headed by George Creel. The job of this agency was to spread anti-German and pro-Allied propaganda through newsreels and lectures, and through the cooperation of the press. Germans were portrayed as beastlike **Huns** wherever possible. Liberty Leagues were established in communities across America; members of these organizations were encouraged to report suspicious actions by anyone (especially foreigners) to their local authorities. George Creel asked newspapers to voluntarily censor themselves and to print only articles that would be helpful to the war effort.

A fine line between patriotism and oppression existed during much of World War I. **The National Security League** convinced Congress to insist on a literacy test for all new immigrants. German language instruction, German music, and even pretzels were banned in some cities. In April 1918 a German-born American citizen was lynched outside of St. Louis; ironically, an investigation found that he had recently attempted to enlist in the American navy.

Most Americans felt they were fighting the war to help the spread of democracy, yet many critics lamented some of the actions taken by the government during the war era. The 1917 **Espionage Act** made it illegal to obstruct the draft process in any way and stated that any material that was sent through the mail that was said to incite treason could be seized. The **Sedition Act** of 1918 stated that it was illegal to criticize the government, the Constitution, the U.S. Army, or the U.S. Navy. Prominent socialist Eugene Debs received a 10-year prison term for speaking against militarism; movie producer Robert Goldstein was even sentenced to 10 years in prison for showing the Americans fighting the British in a Revolutionary War film. Radical labor unions such as the IWW were also harassed during the war years. Over 1000 Americans were found guilty of violations of either the Espionage Act or the Sedition Act.

The war did provide a measure of social mobility for blacks and women. With large numbers of men fighting in Europe and no immigrants entering the country, northern factories needed workers, and encouraged blacks to move north to take factory jobs. This move north was called the **Great Migration**; during the war nearly 600,000 blacks moved north. Many women were able to find jobs on farms or in factories for the very first time during the war. After the war, men would replace them in the labor market and force them to return to the "women's sphere."

WOODROW WILSON AND THE TREATY OF VERSAILLES

The Paris Peace Conference began on January 12, 1919, and had the very difficult task of creating a lasting European peace. The conference was dominated by the "Big Four": the representatives of England, France, Italy (which had switched sides in the middle of the war), and the United States.

Woodrow Wilson was treated as a hero when he arrived in Paris, yet it was obvious in the initial sessions of the peace conference that the leaders of the victorious countries had very different goals. The suffering of England and especially France during the war was horrific; the goals of the French delegation was clearly to punish Germany as much as possible. Woodrow Wilson, on the other hand, came to France supporting his **Fourteen Points**, which called for open peace treaties, freedom of the seas, free trade, arms reduction, a gradual reduction of colonial claims, and some sort of a world organization to ensure peace. Wilson's plan was coolly received in France; the French, as stated previously, were mainly interested in what they could get out of the Germans. It was also coolly received in the United States by those who were opposed to continued American involvement in European affairs.

Wilson's Fourteen Points were largely opposed by the other members of the Big Four. Wilson called for a reduction of colonial claims: England and France had every intention of taking Germany's colonies after the war. When the treaty was finally signed, Wilson got only a fraction of what he initially wanted. Germany was held responsible for the war and was made to pay reparations. The **League of Nations** was created, although initially without Germany and the Bolshevik-led Soviet Union. Wilson believed that this was the most important of the Fourteen Points, so he did not leave Paris totally discouraged.

THE TREATY OF VERSAILLES AND THE UNITED STATES SENATE

Woodrow Wilson had not appointed a Republican member of the Senate to the United States delegation to the Paris Peace Conference. This proved to be a huge political mistake. Wilson returned from Paris, needing Senate confirmation of the Treaty of Versailles. Many Republicans in the Senate had huge reservations about the treaty; all of them centered around American commitment to the League of Nations. A dozen senators were "<u>irreconcilables</u>," opposed to American membership in the League under any circumstances. Another large group, led by Henry Cabot Lodge, were called "<u>reservationists</u>" and wanted restrictions on American membership in the League. Lodge, for example, wanted it stated that the Congress would have to approve any American action on behalf of the League, and that provisions of the Monroe Doctrine remain in place even if the League of Nations opposed them.

To win national support for the Versailles Treaty, Wilson began a national speaking tour on September 3, 1919. On October 2 he suffered a severe stroke and never totally recovered. Lodge stated that he would support passage of the Versailles Treaty with certain reservations; Wilson rejected the reservations, and the treaty never got the two-thirds majority necessary for its passage. Many politicians both at home and abroad urged Wilson to compromise with congressional leaders and to get America into the League of Nations. Wilson was never willing to do this; his chief biographer maintains that his stroke impeded his judgment during this era, and that if he had not had a stroke, a compromise would have been struck. In 1921 the United States formally ended the war with Germany, but the United States never entered the League of Nations.

THE CONSEQUENCES OF AMERICAN ACTIONS AFTER THE WAR

The failure of the United States to join the League of Nations greatly affected European affairs in the succeeding decades. The League of Nations was never the organization it could have been with American involvement. Many European leaders felt that the United States could have been the "honest broker" in the League, and that with U.S. involvement the League could have had more substance. In addition, Europeans expected the United States to be a major player in European and world affairs in the years following the war. Led by the Senate, the United States backed off of the commitment, and entered a period of isolationism that would last through the 1930s. It was only after World War II in 1945 that America finally took the role that many thought it would take in 1920.

CHAPTER REVIEW

Rapid Review Guide

To achieve the perfect 5, you should be able to explain the following:

- World War I greatly impacted the American mind-set and America's role in world affairs; this was the first time that America became directly involved in affairs taking place on the European continent.

- Many Americans expressed support for the Allied powers from the beginning of the war; German U-boat attacks solidified American support for Britain and France.

- The sinking of the *Lusitania* and the Zimmermann Telegram did much to intensify American anger against Germany.

- Germany's decision to utilize unrestricted submarine warfare caused President Wilson to call for war in 1917; Wilson claimed that this policy violated America's rights as a neutral power.

- The American Expeditionary Force did much to aid the Allied war effort, both militarily and psychologically.

- The federal government did much to mobilize the American population at home for the war effort; Liberty bonds were sold, voluntary rationing took place, and propaganda was used to encourage Americans to oppose the "Hun" however possible.

- Many blacks moved to northern cities to work in factories during World War I; this migration would continue through the 1920s.

- Woodrow Wilson's Fourteen Points met opposition from French and English leaders at the Paris Peace Conference; many of them had to be abandoned to secure the creation of the League of Nations.

- The Treaty of Versailles was opposed by U.S. Senators who felt that America should pursue an isolationist policy after the war. As a result, the treaty was never signed by the United States and the United States never joined the League of Nations.

- Many European leaders expected America to be active as a leader in world affairs after World War I. Instead, America adopted neo-isolationist policies that lasted until America entered World War II.

Time Line

1914: Outbreak of World War I in Europe
Woodrow Wilson officially proclaims American neutrality in World War I
National Security League founded to prepare America for war

1915: Sinking of the *Lusitania* by German U-boat

1916: Germany torpedoes *Sussex,* then promises to warn merchant ships if they are to be attacked

Woodrow Wilson reelected with campaign slogan of "He kept us out of war"

1917: Zimmermann Telegram

Germany declares unrestricted submarine warfare

United States enters World War I, stating that U.S. rights as a neutral had been violated

Russian Revolution; Russian-German peace talks

Conscription begins in United States

War Industries Board formed to create a war economy

Espionage Act passed

American Expeditionary Force lands in France

1918: Military success by American Expeditionary Force at Chateau-Thierry

Sedition Act passed; free speech limited (illegal to criticize government or American military forces)

Wilson announces the Fourteen Points

Armistice ends World War I (November 11)

1919: Paris Peace Conference creates Treaty of Versailles

Race riots in Chicago

Wilson suffers stroke during speaking tour promoting Treaty of Versailles

Senate rejects Treaty of Versailles; United States does not join League of Nations

✓ Review Questions

1. All of the following events prepared America for war against Germany *except*

   A. accounts of the conduct of the "Huns" during military operations reported in many American newspapers
   B. the Sussex Pledge
   C. German policy concerning use of U-boats in 1917
   D. the sinking of the *Lusitania*
   E. The Zimmermann telegram

(Correct Answer: **B.** In the Sussex Pledge the Germans actually promised not to sink American merchant ships without warning. All of the other choices deeply angered many in America. It was reported in American newspapers that German soldiers—"Huns"—ate babies in villages they occupied, although there was no evidence that this had ever actually occurred.)

2. The French were opposed to many of Wilson's Fourteen Points because

   A. they were fundamentally opposed to the creation of a world body such as the League of Nations
   B. they felt that the French and the Italians should formulate the major provisions of the treaty
   C. they were angry that Wilson had insisted that the Germans not take part in the creation of the treaty

D. French diplomats had little respect for Wilson and his American counterparts

E. the Fourteen Points disagreed fundamentally with what the French felt should be contained in the Treaty of Versailles

(Correct Answer: **E.** While Wilson saw the treaty as an opportunity to create a democratic world free of old diplomatic entanglements, the French saw the treaty as an opportunity to punish the Germans in as many ways as possible, as much of the fighting of the war had taken place on French territory.)

3. After America declared war in 1917

A. millions of American men showed up at draft boards across the country to volunteer for the war

B. ration cards were issued to all families

C. camps were set up to detain "troublesome" Americans of German background

D. drills took place in American cities to prepare Americans for a possible attack

E. movie stars and other celebrities helped sell Liberty Bonds to the American public

(Correct Answer: **E.** Charlie Chaplin and others appeared at rallies and encouraged Americans to buy Liberty Bonds. A draft was needed to get enough American soldiers for the war; rationing during World War I was voluntary.)

4. Some critics maintained that the United States had no right to be outraged over the sinking of the *Lusitania* because

A. the *Lusitania* was carrying contraband, which meant that it could legally be sunk

B. the Germans had sunk a passenger ship before

C. the Germans had placed advertisements in American newspapers warning Americans not to travel on the *Lusitania*

D. German U-boat policies were well publicized

E. All of the above

(Correct Answer: **E.** Six months earlier the Germans had sunk the *Arabic*, another passenger liner. Many maintain that the advertisements the Germans put in American newspapers were strong enough warnings that the ship was going to be sunk.)

5. Many senators were opposed to American entry into the League of Nations because

A. they feared that the United States would end up financing the organization

B. they feared the U.S. Army would be sent into action on "League of Nations business" without congressional authorization

C. American opinion polls demonstrated that the American public was almost unanimously opposed to American entry into the League

D. they feared that the Germans and the Russians would dominate the League

E. Warren G. Harding, Wilson's vice president, was a staunch isolationist

(Correct Answer: **B.** A major fear of many influential senators was that American entry into the League would cause Congress to lose its right to declare war and approve American military actions. It should be noted that Germany and the Soviet Union were not initially members of the League of Nations.)

Chapter 18

America in the 1920s: The Beginning of Modern America

 During the 1920s tremendous transformations took place in America. Incredible industrial growth created a consumer economy, with washing machines, radios, and automobiles available to every household that was willing to pay for these and other products using the installment plan. The continued migration of America from rural areas to the cities finally created a nation in 1925 where the majority lived in urban settings. A **national culture** was created during the 1920s; this was largely caused by the advent of the radio, the massive increase in advertising, and the incredible increase in popularity of motion pictures.

The nationalization (and urbanization) of American culture was resisted by many in small-town and rural America. Many of the cultural conflicts of the 1920s, including battles over Prohibition, evolution, racism, and immigration, were caused by attempts of the America that was "being left behind" to attempt to keep small-town, rural values prominent in American society.

A DECADE OF PROSPERITY

By the middle of the 1920s many of the dire predictions of the effects of capitalism that had been preached by progressives 15 years earlier seemed like no more than ancient history. Business opportunities were plentiful: The prosecution of trusts, which took up much of the Justice Department's time in World War I, were few in the 1920s. New opportunists with capital could challenge corporations like U.S. Steel and make profits doing it. Nevertheless, certain industries, such as the automobile industry, were virtually impossible to crack; by 1929 Ford, General Motors, and Chrysler controlled nearly 85 percent of all auto sales. Socialist predictions that the plight of the workers were getting worse seemed to be negated by statistics published in 1924 stating that industrial workers were making nearly double what they had made 10 years earlier.

Strikes and union activities were plentiful in the two years immediately following the end of World War I, but diminished greatly after that (many factory owners realized that paying their workers a decent wage would make them less likely to listen to speeches made by union "agitators").

By the mid-1920s products made in American factories were available to Americans and also in many European and other world markets. The assembly line of Henry Ford continued to be perfected to the point that by 1925 a **Model T** was being produced in a Ford plant every 24 seconds. During the decade, the ideas of "scientific management" first proposed by Frederick W. Taylor (see Chapter 14) were utilized in businesses and factories across the country. Production was now being done more efficiently; this ultimately lowered the cost of production and the cost to the consumer.

Many other consumer products, such as vacuum cleaners, refrigerators, and radios, were also churned out by American factories at record rates. Many of the products also were produced by assembly line techniques, and the stream of workers who continued to enter the cities from rural America could get work doing one of the monotonous jobs involved in assembly line production. For the consumer, products that were impossible to even dream about 10 years early could now be purchased with the installment plan. For 36 or 48 "easy" payments, a middle-class family in the 1920s could have an automobile, a refrigerator, *and* a vacuum cleaner. Some economists saw danger in the fact that by 1928 nearly 65 percent of all automobiles were being purchased on credit. Most Americans saw little problem with this, since they could not foresee a time when Americans would be unable to make payments on these goods.

The decade of the 1920s can be certainly seen as the beginning of the **advertising age**. Consumers were warned that if they wanted to live the "good life," they *had* to have the latest model refrigerator or automobile. People living in urban, suburban, and rural areas all saw the same advertisements for products that had been placed in both national and local publications by advertising men. As stated previously, this helped to create a universal national culture: Advertisements showed the farmer in Kansas and the suburbanite in Connecticut that they *had* to have exactly the same product.

REPUBLICAN LEADERSHIP IN THE 1920S

Throughout the 1920s the Republican party was truly dominant at the national level. Both houses of Congress were under Republican control, the three presidents of the decade (Warren G. Harding, Calvin Coolidge, and Herbert Hoover) were all Republicans, and for most of the decade the Supreme Court was dominated by Chief Justice (and ex-president) William Howard Taft. Government policies throughout the decade were almost exclusively pro-business; Republican candidates at all levels during this decade *had* to be acceptable to the business community.

THE PRESIDENCY OF WARREN G. HARDING

Many presidential scholars claim that Warren G. Harding was one of the least qualified men ever nominated for the presidency by a major party in America. Harding, a senator from Ohio, was not even mentioned as a possible candidate before the Republican convention of 1920. Harding finally became the Republican nominee after the party bosses determined that he would be a candidate they could control. He was opposed in the national election by Governor James Cox of Ohio. Harding ran on a platform of low taxes, high tariffs, farmer's assistance, and opposition to the League of Nations.

Where Governor Cox (and his running mate, Assistant Secretary of the Navy Franklin D. Roosevelt) ran a strong and aggressive campaign, Harding was generally content to campaign from own back porch. He ended up winning 61 percent of the national vote. Americans found something they liked in both the message and style of Harding: His message was essentially that it was time to pull back from "schemes" to change the world (the postwar plans of Woodrow Wilson) and "social experiment" (all of the programs of the progressives). Harding's call for a period of "normalcy" struck a chord with Americans and seemed to put the final nail in the coffin of progressivism in American thought.

During the presidency of Harding, efforts were made to prevent America from having any involvement with the League of Nations or any other provision of the Versailles Treaty. One of the outstanding appointments made by Harding was the naming of former Supreme Court Justice Charles Evans Hughes as Secretary of State. Hughes' major accomplishment as Secretary of State took place at the **Washington Conference** of 1921. At this meeting diplomats from the United States, Japan, China, the Netherlands, Belgium, Portugal, France, Great Britain, and Italy met to discuss the possible elimination of further naval development and affairs in China and the rest of Asia. All nine nations agreed to respect the independence of China (and maintaining the Open Door in China), a major goal of American business interests. The United States, Britain, France, Japan, and Italy all agreed to halt the construction of naval vessels (at the time Hughes did not realize that this gave naval superiority in the Pacific to the Japanese).

Another notable appointment by Harding was the naming of Andrew Mellon, the "richest man in America," as Secretary of the Treasury. Mellon firmly believed in the traditional Republican tenant that very low taxes would ultimately encourage business investment and ensure economic prosperity. To do this, Mellon sought to reduce government spending in any way possible, and to reduce taxes, especially for the wealthier business classes. To cut expenses, Harding opposed bonus payments to World War I veterans in 1921; some benefits for veterans were authorized by the Congress. In the Revenue Act of 1921 the administration proposed large reductions in the amounts of taxes that the wealthiest Americans would have to pay (protests from some Republicans from farm states caused these reductions to be less than Mellon desired). In the end, many of Mellon's policies increased the economic pain of the working class while benefiting the rich.

To assist American business interests, Mellon also wanted large tariff increases on imported industrial goods. The **Fordney-McCumber Tariff** of 1922 did increase the tariffs on industrial products. However, to appease Republicans from farm states the largest tariff increases were on imported farm products.

Little was done in the Harding administration to assist organized labor. Many court decisions of the decade took the side of management, including several court decisions that overturned lower-court rulings making child labor illegal. It was clear in the decade that the interests of farmers and the interests of industrial workers were very dissimilar.

THE SCANDALS OF THE HARDING ADMINISTRATION

The Harding administration may have been the most scandal-ridden administration in American political history. No principal whatsoever was involved in these scandals; the participants were only interested in money. There is no knowledge that Harding participated in any way in these scandals; his biggest sin was probably appointing political cronies from his Ohio days to important government positions in his administration and not supervising them.

The scandals of the Harding administration were numerous. Charles Forbes, the director of the Veteran's Bureau, stole or horribly misused nearly $250 million of government money; he was indicted for fraud and bribery concerning government hospital supply contracts. Harding allowed Forbes to go abroad and to resign, although he eventually did go to jail. Attorney General Harry Daugherty had taken bribes from businessmen, bootleggers, and many others. Daugherty failed to go to jail when a hung jury was unable to convict him.

The worst of the scandals was the **Teapot Dome** scandal. Secretary of the Interior Albert Fall maneuvered to have two oil deposits put under the jurisdiction of the Department of the Interior; one of these was a reserve in Wyoming called Teapot Dome. Fall then leased these reserves to private companies and got large sums of money from them for doing it. Fall was convicted and finally went to prison in 1929.

The revelation of these scandals greatly bothered Harding, who died of a stroke on August 2, 1923. He was replaced by his vice president, Calvin Coolidge of Vermont.

THE PRESIDENCY OF CALVIN COOLIDGE

American business leaders could have had no better friend in the White House than Calvin Coolidge. His credo was that "the business of the United States is business." Coolidge did little as president, but this was largely intentional; he was convinced that the major decisions affecting American society should be made by businessmen. Like Harding, Coolidge believed in increased tax cuts for the wealthy and favored policies that would help promote American business.

Several decisions made during Coolidge's presidency demonstrate the administration's thinking. Coolidge proposed that a dam constructed at Muscle Shoals, Alabama, on the Tennessee River by the government during World War I be turned over to private interests; this plan was defeated by the Congress (the dam would become a crucial part of the Tennessee Valley Authority in the 1930s). In the Revenue Act of 1926 large tax cuts were given to the wealthiest members of society. Finally, on the grounds that the government couldn't afford it, Coolidge vetoed payments to World War I veterans (Congress passed the legislation over the president's veto).

THE ELECTION OF 1928

Coolidge announced "I do not choose to run" several months before the 1928 presidential election. The Republicans nominated Secretary of Commerce Herbert Hoover. Hoover was a seemingly perfect candidate for the mood of the era. He was a self-made man, worked his way through Stanford, made his first million in business before he was 40, and had run relief efforts in Belgium and the Commerce Department with tremendous, although unsmiling, efficiency. Hoover's campaign speeches emphasized the achievements of past Republican administrations that had created prosperity and the possibilities for success possible through rugged individualism.

The Democratic candidate was New York Governor Al Smith, an opponent of Prohibition and a Catholic. Many Southern Democrats had obvious suspicions about him; Smith's supporters received their support by promising that the Democratic platform would say nothing about the repeal of Prohibition. The election was a landslide for Hoover, with Smith only winning eight states. Nevertheless, the fact that many people living in the large cities of America voted for Smith showed the divisions that existed in American society in the 1920s.

URBAN VS. RURAL: THE GREAT DIVIDE OF THE 1920S

As stated previously, the 1920s was the decade that the United States, population-wise, became an urban country. Tremendous resentment existed in rural and small-town America against the growing urban mindset that was increasingly permeating America. Many citizens who did not live in America's cities felt that the values associated with urban life needed to be opposed. From these sentiments came many of the great cultural battles that were at the center of American life in the 1920s.

Many in the North and the South shared resentment against black Americans in the years immediately after World War I. A number of blacks had come North during the war to take factory jobs in urban centers; now that the war was over, many Northerners saw them as competitors for prime industrial employment. In 1919 large race riots took place in Washington, DC, and in many other Northern cities; anti-black riots in Chicago lasted nearly two weeks. Press reports of these riots oftentimes noted the participation of white veterans.

During the postwar years violence against blacks intensified in the South as well. Lynchings increased dramatically in the postwar years; over 70 blacks were lynched in 1919 alone. The response by some blacks was to think of leaving the United States altogether; beginning in 1920 sign-ups began for the **Universal Negro Improvement Association**, headed by Marcus Garvey. Garvey called on blacks to come with him to Africa to create a new empire (with him on the throne). By 1925 nearly half a million people had expressed interest in Garvey's scheme. In the end the Garvey program was a failure, since few blacks actually went to Africa, and many of those that did go ended up returning to the United States. Garvey was later arrested and jailed for fraud, but the fact that his plan attracted so many black supporters demonstrated the plight of black Americans.

The **Ku Klux Klan** grew tremendously during the early 1920s; by 1925 the Klan's membership was over 5 million. Unlike the Klan of the Reconstruction era, membership in the Klan was not entirely from the South, although it *was* almost entirely from rural and small-town America (Indiana was a huge hotbed of Klan activity in the 1920s). Blacks continued to be a target of the Klan, as were other groups who appeared to be "enemies" of the rural way of life, such as Catholics and immigrants. The Klan had tremendous political power in several states, although terror tactics such as lynchings and cross burnings remained a dominant part of Klan activity.

The Klan began to lose its popularity in 1925 with revelations of scandals involving Klan members, including the murder conviction of the leader of the Klan in Indiana. Many historians see the popularity of the Klan in the 1920s as a symbol of the intolerance prominent in much of American society; several see it as an American version of totalitarianism, which took control in Germany, the Soviet Union, and Italy during this period.

Many Americans in the years following World War I were also terrified of Bolshevism. America, to no avail, gave military aid and actual manpower to forces attempting to overthrow Lenin and Bolsheviks in the years immediately following the Russian Revolution of 1917. Much about Bolshevism (soon to be called communism) was in opposition to mainstream American thought. Communism taught that capitalism was evil, and that worker's revolutions would soon break out in highly industrialized countries like the United States. As a result, a **Red Scare** developed in America in 1919. Many historians maintain that Americans were not just opposed to the ideas of communism, but that many Americans began to see everything wrong in American society as a creation of the "Reds."

254 • A Comprehensive Review of United States History

Beginning in November of 1919 Attorney General Mitchell Palmer carried out raids on the homes and places of employment of suspected radicals. As a result of the **Palmer Raids**, thousands of Americans were arrested, in many cases for no other crime than the fact that they were not born in the United States. Hundreds of former immigrants were sent back to their countries of origin, even though it was never proven (or even in most cases even charged) that they were political radicals. The Red Scare demonstrated the nativism present in American during the period. This was also one of the worst examples in American history of the trampling of the constitutional rights of American citizens.

Nativism probably also accounts for the results of the case of Sacco and Vanzetti. Both were Italian immigrants, and were charged with the murdering of two employees of a shoe company in Massachusetts in 1920. Although there was little evidence against them, they were convicted and finally executed in 1927.

American nativism also was displayed in immigration legislation that was passed in the early 1920s. Many in small-town America blamed the problems of America on the continued inflow of immigrants to the country; pseudoscientific texts published in the first part of the decade claimed that the white Americans were naturally superior to Southern and Eastern Europeans as well as blacks, but warned that these groups had to be carefully controlled to prevent them from attempting to dominate the country.

The Congress passed the **Emergency Quota Act** of 1921, which limited immigration to 3 percent of the number of persons each country had living in the United States in 1910. This act limited the immigration of Eastern and Southern Europeans, and cut immigration in 1922 to roughly 40 percent of its 1921 totals. A real blow to immigration was the **National Origins Act** of 1924. This legislation took that number of immigrants from each foreign country living in the United States in 1890, and stated that immigration to the United States from these countries could now be no more than 2 percent of that; the bill also stated that no more than 150,000 new immigrants could come from outside the Western Hemisphere. In addition, all immigration from Asia was halted. The intent and the effect of this legislation was obvious. Immigration from countries such as Italy and Poland was virtually halted.

Another area where urban and rural/small-town interests clashed was over the issue of Prohibition. Statistics from 1924 stated that in Kansas 95 percent of citizens were obeying the Prohibition law, while in New York state the number obeying was close to 5 percent. For many small-town observers, alcohol, immigrants, and urban life were viewed together as one giant evil. Many small-town preachers spoke of alcohol as an "instrument of the devil" and were outraged that the law was not enforced in places like New York City.

However, the enforcement of Prohibition in a city like New York would have been virtually impossible. Neither the citizenry nor elected officials favored enforcement (it was reported that Warren Harding had a large collection of bootlegged alcohol that he served to guests). **Speakeasies** were frequented by police officers and city officials in many locations; "bathtub gin," some of it good and some of it absolutely atrocious, was also consumed by thousands eager for some form of alcohol during the Prohibition era. Bootlegging of alcohol allowed many famous gangsters of the 1930s to get their feet wet in the world of organized crime; Al Capone in Chicago became the king of the bootleggers, with judges, newspapers, and elected government officials all eventually under his control.

The final area where urban and rural/small-town mind-sets drastically differed was over religion and evolution. Many in small-town America felt vaguely threatened by the changes that science had brought about, and clung to the literal interpretation of the Bible as a defense. William Jennings Bryan and others led the charge against the teachings of Darwin in the postwar years. In 1925, Bryan assisted a group in Tennessee in drafting a bill that would outlaw the teaching of evolution in the state. The American Civil Liberties Union offered to assist any teacher who would challenge this law, and John Scopes of Dayton, Tennessee, volunteered. For several weeks in 1925, the **Scopes Trial** (or "monkey trial") riveted the nation.

One of America's finest lawyers, Clarence Darrow, assisted Scopes, while Bryan was retained to work with prosecutors who wanted to convict Scopes. Scopes was found guilty and fined (this was later overturned on a technicality), but the real drama of the trial was when Darrow questioned Bryan, who took the stand as an "expert on the Bible." Bryan seriously discredited the entire cause of **creationism** when he admitted on the stand that he personally did not take every fact found in the Bible literally.

CULTURE IN THE 1920S

Vast numbers of Americans were attracted to the culture of business that so permeated American life in the 1920s. It was possible, it was felt, that an individual could start with nothing and become a millionaire (a few buying land in Florida and elsewhere did exactly that). It is no surprise that individual heroes were worshipped in the press, on the radio, and on street corners. Sports heroes such as Babe Ruth were perceived as hardly mortal (members of the press had to cover up the excesses found in the personal lives of Ruth and many other heroes). Newspapers delighted in reporting incidents such as those involving Ruth visiting children's hospitals and promising countless home runs for sick children.

Other heroes of the decade included other athletes, such as boxer Jack Dempsey and movie stars Rudolph Valentino, Charlie Chaplin, Clara Bow, and Mary Pickford. No hero, however, was lionized more than Charles Lindbergh after he became the first person to fly across the Atlantic Ocean by himself in 1927. Incredible numbers of songs and newspaper headlines were devoted to Lindbergh for several years after this historic flight.

THE JAZZ AGE

Many Americans rejected the values of business civilization adopted by many in the decade. These people, both men and women, decided that pleasure and private expression were more important than the virtues of Taylorism. Those associated with the **Jazz Age** adopted more open attitudes toward sex, and adopted jazz music as another symbol of their rejection of traditional society. Rural/small-town America (and some in the cities) saw jazz as "the devil's music," as black music, and as a music that helped to promote lewd dancing and sexual contact. For many who went to jazz clubs in Harlem in the early 1920s, these were probably the very reasons they listened to it.

The typical symbol of the Jazz Age was the **flapper**, a young girl with short hair, a short hemline, a cigarette in her hand, and makeup (all of these things were frowned on in rural/small-town America and in pre-World War I urban America). The number of actual flappers in American cities was always relatively small. Many advertisements of the 1920s portrayed women as sex objects; as a result, in the eyes of many Americans, women lost their respected position as moral leaders of the family.

Statistics do show that both sexual promiscuity and the consumption of alcohol increased among the young during this decade. This revolution was greatly aided by the availability of the automobile, which allowed young people to get away from the prying eyes of parents. Margaret Sanger and others promoted the increased availability and usage of birth control during this period. The behavior of flappers and their male counterparts was looked down on by some urban and by almost all rural observers. It should be noted that this "freer" behavior by young people would be drastically reduced by the massive economic difficulties of the Great Depression and World War II, but would again become pronounced in the 1950s (with critics voicing many of the same criticisms as critics had in the 1920s). By the 1950s rock and roll had replaced jazz as the "devil's music."

After the passage of the Nineteenth Amendment in 1920, which gave women the right to vote, many female leaders thought that women would come to have a pronounced role in American political life. Much to their disappointment, this did not occur in the 1920s. Women did not vote in a block "as women." Yet the overall position of women did increase in the decade. Divorces increased throughout the decade, showing that more women (and men) were leaving unhealthy marriage relationships. The number of women working during the decade also increased, although working women were usually single. Restrictions remained, however. Women seldom received the same pay for doing the same work as a man, and women were almost never put into management positions. Most women still worked in clerical jobs, as teachers, or as nurses.

The Rise of Radio and Motion Pictures

As stated previously, as more and more people read newspapers, listened to the radio, and watched movies, a truly universal mass culture was being created. Movie attendance rose incredibly during the 1920s; in 1922 about 35 million people a week saw movies. By 1929 this figure was up to 90 million people per week. In 1927 *The Jazz Singer*, staring Al Jolson, became the first "talking" motion picture, a trend that would create new movie stars and ruin the careers of others who had been stars in the silent era.

Nothing created a more national mass culture than did the radio. Station KDKA in Pittsburgh was the first station to get a radio station license in 1920. Radio networks began to form (the National Broadcasting Company being the first in 1926) and brought listeners across the country news, variety shows, and (at first) re-created sporting events.

THE LOST GENERATION

Many novels were written during the 1920s that supported the business culture of the decade. The most famous of these was Bruce Barton's 1925 *The Man Nobody Knows,* which portrayed Christ as a businessman. Most famous novelists of the era, however, wrote of deep feelings of alienation from mainstream American culture. These writers, called by Gertrude Stein members of the "**Lost Generation**," turned their backs on the business culture and the Republican political culture of the era. Some of these writers ended up in Paris, while others congregated in Greenwich Village in New York City.

The goal of these writers seemed to be to attack the notion of America that they had either physically or spiritually left behind. In novels such as *Main Street* and *Babbit,* Sinclair Lewis attacked the materialism and narrow thinking of middle-class business-types in small-town America. Sherwood Anderson's *Winesburg, Ohio* was another novel of alienation in small-town America.

F. Scott Fitzgerald was both a celebrant of the Jazz Age and a brilliant commentator on it; his novel *The Great Gatsby* dissects the characters of typical Jazz Age figures. Ernest Hemingway in works such as *A Farewell to Arms* express a deep dissatisfaction with American values, especially concerning war. Perhaps none was more direct in his criticisms of American society than journalist H. L. Mencken, who called the American people an "ignorant mob" and was especially disdainful of the "booboisie," his term for the American middle class.

It should also be remembered that in the 1920s black cultural expression was being celebrated in a cultural movement called the **Harlem Renaissance**. Writers of this movement, including Langston Hughes and Zora Neale Hurston, wrote of the role of blacks in contemporary American society; the theme of blacks "passing" into the white world and the importance of black expression were common themes among writers of the Harlem Renaissance. Many in the Harlem Renaissance studied African folk art and music and anthropology. The goal of many in the movement was reconciling the notions of being black and being American (and also to reconcile the notions of being black and being intellectual). Jazz was the music of the movement, with Louis Armstrong and Duke Ellington playing this "primitive music" in clubs across Harlem.

When Herbert Hoover was inaugurated in early 1929, America looked to the 1930s with eager anticipation. The stock market was at an all-time high, and Hoover had continually promised during the campaign that the Republican goal was to wipe out poverty once and for all. All of this would make the events that would begin to unfold in the fall of 1929 even more cruel and devastating.

CHAPTER REVIEW

Rapid Review Guide

To achieve the perfect 5, you should be able to explain the following:

- A consumer economy was created in the 1920s on a level unprecedented in American history.

- Advertising, newspapers, radio, and motion pictures provided new forms of entertainment in the 1920s and helped to create a uniform national culture.

- The changes of the 1920s were resisted by many in small-town/rural America, creating many of the cultural conflicts of the decade.

- Assembly line techniques and the ideas of scientific management of Frederick W. Taylor helped to make industrial production in the 1920s quicker and more efficient, ultimately creating cheaper goods.

- Installment buying helped to fuel consumer buying in the 1920s.

- The Republican party controlled the White House, the Congress, and the Supreme Court in the 1920s, generally sponsoring government policies friendly to big business.

- The scandals of the Harding administration were among the worst in history.

- Resentment against blacks existed in both the American South and North in the years after World War I, resulting in race riots in the North and lynchings and the rebirth of the Ku Klux Klan in the South.

- The Red Scare of 1919 and 1920 resulted in the suspension of civil liberties and deportation of hundred of immigrants, the vast majority of which had committed no crime.

- Nativist fears also resulted in restrictive quota legislation passed in the early 1920s.

- Cultural conflicts between urban and rural American also developed over the issues of Prohibition and the teaching of evolution in schools (resulting in the Scopes Trial).

- During the Jazz Age many Americans rejected the prominent business values of the decade and turned to jazz, alcohol, and looser sexual mores for personal fulfillment.

- The flapper was the single most prominent image of the Jazz Age.

- Writers of the Lost Generation expressed extreme disillusionment with American society of the era; writers of the Harlem Renaissance expressed the opinions of American blacks concerning American culture.

Time Line

1917: Race riots in East St. Louis, Missouri
1918: Armistice ending World War I
1919: Race riots in Chicago
     Major strikes in Seattle and Boston
     Palmer Raids
1920: Warren Harding elected president
     First broadcast of radio station KDKA in Pittsburgh
     Publication of *Main Street* by Sinclair Lewis
     Arrest of Sacco and Vanzetti
     Prohibition takes effect
1921: Immigration Quota Law passed
     Disarmament conference held
1922: Fordney-McCumber Tariff enacted
     Publication of *Babbitt* by Sinclair Lewis
1923: Teapot Dome scandal
     Death of Harding; Calvin Coolidge becomes president
     Duke Ellington first performs in New York City
1924: Election of Calvin Coolidge
     Immigration Quota Law enacted
     Ku Klux Klan reaches highest membership in history
     Women governors elected in Wyoming and Texas
1925: Publication of *The Man Nobody Knows* by Bruce Barton
     Publication of *The Great Gatsby* by F. Scott Fitzgerald
     Scopes Trial held in Dayton, Tennessee
1926: Publication of *The Sun Also Rises* by Ernest Hemingway
1927: *The Jazz Singer,* first movie with sound, released
     Charles Lindbergh makes New York to Paris flight
     Execution of Sacco and Vanzetti
     15 millionth car produced by Ford Motor Company
     $1.5 billion spent on advertising in United States
     Babe Ruth hits 60 home runs
1928: Election of Herbert Hoover
1929: Nearly 30 million Americans have cars
     Stock market crash

✓ Review Questions

1. Many in rural/small-town America would support legislation that

   A. increased immigration from Eastern Europe
   B. mandated the teaching of creationism in schools
   C. lessened the penalties for those that sold illegal alcohol
   D. made it harder to deport immigrants who might have "Red" ties
   E. None of the above

(Correct Answer: **B.** All of the other "causes"—more immigration, the lessening of Prohibition, and the lessening of methods to deport potential communists—were vehemently opposed by most in small-town America. They would, however, support the elimination of the teaching of evolution, and the continued teaching of creationism in American schools.)

2. The novel that supported the business philosophy of the 1920s most definitively was

   A. *Main Street*
   B. *The Great Gatsby*
   C. *The Man Nobody Knows*
   D. *Babbitt*
   E. None of the above

(Correct Answer: **C.** All of the other novels are unsympathetic to the world of business—both A and D are by Sinclair Lewis. In *The Man Nobody Knows*, Jesus Christ was portrayed as a businessman.)

3. In 1928 in most Eastern cities one could find

   A. a speakeasy
   B. a continual flow of immigrants from Northern, Southern, and Eastern Europe

   C. large numbers of supporters of the Ku Klux Klan
   D. the first bread lines
   E. a large number of political supporters of William Jennings Bryan

(Correct Answer: **A.** The influx of immigrants had been greatly reduced by immigration legislation passed in the first half of the decade. Supporters of the KKK were largely not city dwellers; the KKK had also lessened in importance by 1928. Bread lines were not found until the beginning of the Great Depression. Few supporters of William Jennings Bryan came from eastern urban centers.)

4. Republican leaders of the 1920s believed all of the following *except*

   A. "the business of government is business"
   B. the government should do as little as possible
   C. labor unions should be strengthened through legislation
   D. taxes for the wealthiest should be reduced
   E. All of the above

(Correct Answer: **C.** All of the other answers are solid beliefs of Republican leaders of the 1920s. Republicans did very little for labor unions in the decade.)

5. The election of Herbert Hoover in 1928 demonstrated all of the following *except*

   A. Americans were attracted to self-made businessmen
   B. most Americans believed that Republican policies had been responsible for the prosperity of the 1920s

C. fewer divisions existed between the urban and rural populations than had existed at the beginning of the decade

D. Prohibition was still a "hot-button issue" for many Americans.

E. All of the above

(Correct Answer: **C.** Hoover's overwhelming election demonstrated the appeal of his business background and the fact that many Americans credited the Republicans for prosperity. The fact that Al Smith was stomped in this election demonstrated that his anti-Prohibition statements definitely hurt him. However, many in urban centers voted for him; this demonstrated that the divisions between urban and rural America were still wide at the end of the decade.)

Chapter 19

The Great Depression and the New Deal

 The era of the Great Depression tested the character of the American nation as no previous crisis period in America had (with the obvious exception of the Civil War). The lives of those who struggled through the Great Depression were inexorably changed. The factions that came together to make up the Democratic party in the 1930s continued to control much of American political life for the next 50 years. The New Deal, Franklin Roosevelt's series of experimental programs designed to tackle the monumental problems of the 1930s, greatly changed the role of the federal government in American society. The political, social, and cultural fabric of America was permanently altered by the events of the 1930s.

THE AMERICAN ECONOMY OF THE 1920S: THE ROOTS OF THE GREAT DEPRESSION

The vast majority of Americans in 1929 foresaw a continuation of the dizzying economic growth that had taken place in most of the decade. In his inauguration speech, newly elected president Herbert Hoover reemphasized his campaign promise that it was the goal of the Republican party to permanently wipe out poverty in America. In early September 1929, the average share of stock on the New York Stock Exchange stood near 350, a gain of nearly 200 points in a little over a year.

However, careful observers of the American economy noticed several disturbing trends that only seemed to be increasing. These included the following:

1. *Agricultural problems.* Farm prices were at a record high during World War I, dropped after the war, and never recovered. Many farmers were unable to pay banks back loans they had acquired to purchase land,

tractors, and other equipment; many farms were foreclosed on and in farm states over 6200 banks were forced to close. Legislation to help farmers had been passed by the Congress, but bills to help the farmers were vetoed by President Coolidge on two occasions.

2. *Installment buying.* As stated in the previous chapter, large numbers of Americans purchased automobiles, refrigerators, vacuum cleaners, and similar household products on credit. Many Americans simply did not have anywhere near enough cash to pay for all they had purchased. The money of many families was tied up making installment payments for three or four big-ticket items; this prevented them from purchasing many other items available for sale. In 1928 and 1929 new goods continued to be produced, but many people could simply not afford to buy them. As a result, layoffs began occurring in some industries as early as 1928.

3. *Uneven division of wealth.* America was wealthy in the 1920s, but this wealth did not extend to all segments of society. The gains made by wealthy Americans in the 1920s far outstripped gains made by the working class. By the time of the stock market crash, the upper 0.2 percent of the population controlled over 40 percent of the nation's savings. On the other hand, over three-quarters of American families made less than $3000 a year. Problems that could develop from this situation were obvious. The bottom three-quarters of families were too poor to purchase much to help the economy to continue to flourish. Furthermore, at the early signs of economic trouble, many of the wealthiest Americans, fearing the worst, curtailed their spending.

4. *The stock market.* There were cases in the late 1920s of ordinary citizens becoming very, very rich by purchasing stock. Some of these people were engaged in **speculation**, meaning that they would invest in something (like the previously mentioned Florida lands) that was very risky, but that they could potentially "make a killing" on. Another common practice in the late 1920s was buying shares of stock **on the margin**. A stockbroker might allow a buyer to purchase stock for only a percentage of what it was worth (commonly as low as 20 percent); the rest could be borrowed from the broker. As long as stock prices continued to rise, investors would have no trouble paying brokers back for these loans. After the stock market crash, brokers wanted payment for these loans. Countless numbers of investors had no way to make these payments.

THE STOCK MARKET CRASH

The prices of stock crested in early September of 1929. The price of stock fell very gradually during most of September and early October. Some investors noted that some factories were beginning to lay workers off; whispers were heard around Wall Street that perhaps the price of stock *was* too high, and that it might be good to sell before prices began to fall.

The first signs of panic occurred on Wednesday, October 23, when in the last hour of trading, the value of a share of stock dropped, on the average, 20 points. On October 24 a massive amount of stock was sold, and prices again fell dramatically. Stockbrokers told nervous investors not to worry; Herbert Hoover announced that the stock market and the economy "is on a sound and prosperous basis."

A group of influential bankers and brokers pooled resources to buy stock, but this was unable to stop the downward trend. Prices fell again on Monday, October 28, and on the following day, Black Tuesday, the bottom fell out of the market. Prices fell by 40 points that day; it is estimated that total losses to investors for the day was over $20 million. Stockbrokers and banks frantically attempted to call in their loans; few investors had the money to pay even a fraction of what they owed.

How the Stock Market Crash Caused the Great Depression

In the weeks immediately following the crash, important figures from the banking world and President Hoover all assured the American people that America was still economically sound, and that the crash was no worse than other stock downturns that had had little long-term effect on the economy. In retrospect, it can be seen that through both direct and indirect means, the stock market crash was a fundamental cause of the Great Depression. As a result of the crash:

1. *Bank closings increased.* As stated previously, many banks in rural America had to close when farmers couldn't repay loans. The exact same thing happened to many city banks after 1929 when investors could not repay their loans. In addition, the news of even a single bank closing had a snowball effect; thousands of people went to banks across the country to withdraw their life savings. Banks did not have this kind of money (it had been given out to investors as loans); soon urban banks began to fail as well. It is estimated that by 1932 approximately 5000 banks fell, with the life savings of over 5 million Americans gone forever

2. *Income fell for industrialists.* Many large industrialists invested heavily in the stock market. They had less available cash, and some started to close or reduce the scale of their factory operations. Workers were laid off or made much less money; as a result, they were able to buy fewer products made in other industrial plants, causing layoffs there as well. By 1933 nearly 25 percent of the labor force was out of work.

3. *Effect on the world.* Many European countries, especially Germany, utilized loans from American banks and investment houses in the 1920s and 1930s to remain viable. When American financial institutions were unable to supply these loans, instability occurred in these countries. Some historians make the argument that, perhaps indirectly,

the American stock market crash opened the door for Hitler to come to power in Germany.

THE SOCIAL IMPACT OF THE GREAT DEPRESSION

Many Americans felt a huge sense of uprootedness in the 1930s. By late 1932 virtually all sectors of American society were affected in some way by the Depression. Both professional men and common laborers lost their jobs. It was not uncommon during the Depression for two people to share a job, or for a man who had lost his job to continue to put his suit on every morning and pretend to go to work, somehow averting the shame he felt for being unemployed. Women and minorities were often the first to lose their jobs, although women in certain "female" occupations (such as domestic work) were almost never uprooted by men. "Respectable" white men were willing to take jobs that had been previously seen as fit only for minorities. Many behaviors of the 1920s, such as buying on credit, were forgotten practices by 1932.

Many private agencies established soup kitchens and emergency shelters in the early 1930s, but many more were needed. Many couples postponed marriage and having children. Those with nowhere to live in cities often ended up in <u>Hoovervilles</u>, which were settlements of shacks (made from scrap metal or lumber) usually located on the outskirts of cities. Many unemployed young people, both men and women, took to the road in the 1930s, often traveling in empty railroad cars.

The greatest human suffering of the Depression era might have existed in the <u>Dust Bowl</u>. For most of the decade, massive dust storms plagued the residents of Oklahoma, Kansas, Nebraska, Colorado, and Texas; farm production in this area fell drastically for much of the decade. A severe drought was the major cause of the dust storms, although poor farming practices (stripping the soil of any topsoil) also contributed to them. By decade's end nearly 60 percent of all farms in the Dust Bowl were either ruined or abandoned. Many Dust Bowlers traveled to California to get agricultural jobs there, and discovered that if an entire family picked grapes from sunup to sundown, it might barely scrape by. (John Steinbeck's book *The Grapes of Wrath,* as well as the film version, are highly recommended for further study of Dust Bowlers and their move to California, as are the recordings of Woody Guthrie entitled "Dust Bowl Ballads" and the Depression-era photos taken by Dorothea Lange.)

The behavior and attitudes of many who lived through the Depression changed forever. Many would *never* in their lives buy anything on credit; there are countless stories of Depression-era families who insisted on paying for everything, including automobiles, with cash. Depression-era shortages led many in later life to be almost compulsive "savers" of everything and anything imaginable. Many who lived through the Depression and had children in the 1950s were determined to given their kids all that they had been deprived of in the 1930s.

THE HOOVER ADMINISTRATION AND THE DEPRESSION

To state that Herbert Hoover did nothing to stem the effects of the Great Depression is not entirely accurate. Nevertheless, he did believe that this crisis could be solved through **voluntarism**. Hoover urged Americans to donate all they could to charities, and held several conferences with business leaders where he urged them not to reduce wages or lay off workers. When it became obvious that these measures were not enough, public opinion quickly turned against Hoover.

The Hoover administration did take several specific measures to offset the effects of the Depression. Even before the stock market crash, the **Agricultural Marketing Act** created a Federal Farm Board that had the ability to give loans to the agricultural community and buy crops to keep farm prices up. By 1932 there was not enough money to keep this program afloat. In 1930 Congress enacted the **Hawley-Smoot tariff**, which to this day is the highest import tax in the history of the United States. In response, European countries drastically increased their own tariffs as well; some historians maintain that this legislation did little to improve the economy of the United States, but that its effects did much to ensure that the American Depression would be a worldwide one.

Hoover did authorize more money for public works programs, and in 1932, he authorized the creation of the **Reconstruction Finance Corporation**. This agency gave money to banks, who were then authorized to loan this money to businesses and railroads. Another bill authorized loans to banks to prevent them from failing. To many in America, these bills were merely signs that Hoover was only interested in helping those at the top of society and that he cared little about the common person. Hoover vetoed legislation authorizing a federal relief program, although in 1932 he did sign legislation authorizing federal loans to the states; states could then administer relief programs with this money.

The views of those Americans who felt that Hoover was unconcerned about the plight of the common man had their views seemingly confirmed by federal actions against the **Bonus Army** that appeared in Washington in the summer of 1932. This group of nearly 22,000 unemployed World War I vets came to ask the federal government to give them the bonuses that they were supposed to get in 1945 immediately. At Hoover's urging, the Senate rejected legislation authorizing this. Most of the Bonus Army then went home, but a few thousand stayed, living in shacks along the Anacostia River. Hoover ordered them removed; military forces led by Douglas MacArthur used tear gas and cleared the remaining bonus marchers from their camp and burned down the shacks they had been living in.

THE 1932 PRESIDENTIAL ELECTION

The two candidates in the 1932 presidential election could not have been more different in both content and style. In a joyless convention, the Republicans renominated Herbert Hoover. In newsreels seen by Americans across the country, Hoover came across as unsmiling and utterly lacking in warmth. He insisted that his policies would eventually lead America out of the Depression, stating that history demonstrated that lulls in the American economy are always followed by upturns. Hoover warned against "mindless experimentation" in the creation of government policies. It should be noted that Hoover was echoing standard economic and political theory of the era.

Hoover's opponent in the election was the Governor of New York, Franklin Delano Roosevelt. Roosevelt was a man of wealth. After serving as Assistant Secretary of the Navy under Woodrow Wilson, Roosevelt unsuccessfully tried to get the vice presidential nomination in 1920. During the summer of 1921, he came down with polio, which left him unable to walk for the rest of his life. Several of Roosevelt's biographers maintain that the mental and physical anguish caused by his polio made Roosevelt much more sensitive to the sufferings of others.

Franklin Roosevelt married a distant cousin, Eleanor Roosevelt, in 1905. While Franklin spent much of the 1920s attempting to recover from polio in Warm Springs, Georgia, Eleanor became a tireless worker in New York state politics, pushing for governmental reform and better conditions for working women. The role that Eleanor Roosevelt played during the presidency of Franklin Roosevelt cannot be overestimated. FDR (this shortening of his name was done by a reporter in 1932) oftentimes stated that Eleanor served as his "legs," visiting miners, schools, and countless other groups. Eleanor also discussed policy with Roosevelt and continually urged him to do more to offset the effects of the Depression.

As Governor of New York during the first years of the Great Depression, Roosevelt instituted relief programs that became models for others across the country. During his campaign Roosevelt promised "**The New Deal**" for the American people; unlike Hoover, he also promised to experiment to find solutions to America's problems. Roosevelt's broad smile and personal demeanor contrasted drastically with the public image of Herbert Hoover; Americans were convinced that Roosevelt cared (this would be demonstrated during his presidency by the hundreds of letters that Roosevelt and his wife both received during their presidency, asking for things such as small loans, money to pay doctors, and old clothes; it should also be noted that many Americans had a picture of Franklin Roosevelt on display somewhere in their living quarters during the Depression).

The 1932 presidential election was easily won by Roosevelt, who won by over 7 million votes. Hoover's only strength was in the Northeastern states. In addition, the Democrats won control of both houses of Congress. Some had feared (or hoped) that the Depression would radicalize the American working class, yet the socialist candidate for president, Norman Thomas, received considerably less than 1 million votes.

THE FIRST HUNDRED DAYS

Franklin Roosevelt's inauguration speech in 1933 was one of optimism; the most quoted line of this speech is ". . . so first of all let me assert my firm belief that the only thing we have to fear is fear itself." Within a week of taking office, Roosevelt gave the first of his many **fireside chats**. During these radio addresses, Roosevelt spoke to the listening audience as if they were part of his family; Roosevelt would usually explain the immediate problems facing the country in these speeches and outline the reasons for his decided solution.

Roosevelt surrounded himself with an able Cabinet, as well as a group of unofficial advisors called Roosevelt's "brain trust." In dealing with the problems of the Depression, Roosevelt urged his advisors to experiment. Some programs thus failed, some were continually reformed, and several conflicted with each other. The key, insisted Roosevelt, was to "do something."

During the first **hundred days** of the Roosevelt administration, countless programs were proposed by the administration and passed by the Congress that attempted to stimulate the American economy and provide relief and jobs. A very popular act, for psychological reasons if nothing else, was the repeal of Prohibition, which was actually voted on by the Congress in February 1933.

Roosevelt's economic advisor told him that his first priority should be the banking system. On March 5, 1933, he officially closed all banks for four days and had the federal government oversee the inspection of all banks. By March 15 most banks were reopened; this cooling-off period gave people a renewed confidence in the banks, and slowly people started putting money back into banks instead of taking it out. The Banking Act of 1933 created the **Federal Deposit Insurance Corporation** (FDIC), which insured the bank deposits of individual citizens.

During the hundred days, large amounts of federal money were handed down to local relief agencies, and a Federal Emergency Relief Administration (led by Harry Hopkins) was also established. Efforts were also made to help people find work. Thousands were hired from funds distributed to states by the Public Works Administration; many schools, highways, and hospitals were built under this program.

The **Civilian Conservation Corps** (CCC) was begun during this period and would eventually employ over 2 1/2 million young men. Under this program forest and conservation programs were undertaken. CCC workers were only paid a small amount (this money was actually sent to their families), but in a period where little work was available, many veterans of CCC programs later perceived the program as a godsend.

Roosevelt considered the bolstering of the industrial sector of the American economy to be a top priority. Falling prices had caused layoffs and the failure of many businesses. The **National Industry Recovery Act** (NIRA) was established to try to stop falling prices in industry. Under this act committees of both owners and union leaders in each industry would meet to set commonly agreed on prices, wages, working hours, and working expectations. Unions and collective bargaining were accepted in industry as a result of the NIRA. Wages in many industries rose as a result of this; the thinking in the creation of the NIRA was that as wages rose, workers would then buy more, stimulating the economy and stopping the fall of industrial prices. The goals of this program were largely not met; as wages rose so did prices. As a result, many workers did not buy more, negating any benefit that rising wages were supposed to have.

Another body created by the NIRA was the National Recovery Administration (NRA), which was supposed to enforce the decisions of the NIRA. The entire process of the NIRA was declared unconstitutional in the 1935 Supreme Court case *Schechter* v. *United States*, although the agency had largely lost its effectiveness by then.

Two other important programs developed during the first hundred days. The **Agricultural Adjustment Administration** (AAA) attempted to stop the sharp decline in farm prices by paying farmers *not* to produce certain crops and livestock. It was hoped that this would cause the prices of these goods to rise. The **Tennessee Valley Authority** authorized the construction of a series of dams that would ultimately provide electricity and flood control to those living in the Tennessee River Valley. Thousands who had not had electricity in their homes now did.

The hundred days and the months that followed it provided some relief to those affected by the Depression, but by no means solved the basic economic problems facing the United States. The 1934 midterm congressional elections showed that most Americans favored FDR's policies, yet even in 1935 some 20 percent of all Americans were still out of work.

THE SECOND NEW DEAL

Many wealthy members of American society were appalled by the actions that Roosevelt took during his first year in office; he was called a traitor to his class, a communist, and far worse. Other elements of Roosevelt's brain trust (as well as his wife Eleanor) were advising Roosevelt to do even more to help the unemployed of America. As a result, the **Second New Deal**, beginning in 1935, included another flurry of legislation.

It was obvious that even more dramatic measures were needed to help farmers; many farms were still being foreclosed on because farmers could not make necessary payments on their land. The **Resettlement Administration**, established in May of 1935, offered loans to small farmers who faced foreclosure. In addition, migrant farmers had not been affected by previous New Deal measures dealing with agriculture; funds to help them find work were included under the Resettlement Administration.

One of the outstanding achievements of the Second New Deal was the creation of the **Works Progress Administration** (WPA). The WPA took people that were on relief and employed them for 30 or 35 hours a week. On average, 2 million people per month were employed by the WPA; by 1941 well over 8 million people had worked for the WPA. WPA workers were usually engaged in construction projects, building schools, hospitals, and roads across the country. In addition, unemployed musicians, artists, and actors were all employed by the WPA. WPA artists painted many of the murals found in public buildings, concerts were given for both urban and rural audiences, and plays were performed for audiences who had never seen one before.

Another important piece of legislation from this period was the **Wagner Act**, which reaffirmed the right of workers to organize and to utilize collective bargaining. These rights had been guaranteed by provision 7a of the NIRA guidelines, but when the NIRA was declared to be unconstitutional, additional legislation protecting workers was needed. The Wagner Act also listed unfair labor practices that were outlawed and established the **National Labor Relations Board** (NLRB) to enforce its provisions.

The most important legislation passed during the Second New Deal was the 1935 **Social Security Act**. The critical provision of this act was the creation of a retirement plan for workers over 65 years old. Both workers and employers paid into this retirement fund; the first payments were scheduled to be made in January 1942. It should be noted that the initial social security legislation did not cover agricultural and domestic workers.

Other provisions of this act established a program that provided unemployment insurance for workers who had lost their jobs; this was paid for by a payroll tax that was imposed on all employers with more than eight workers. The federal government also provided financial support to programs at the state level that provided unemployment insurance. The federal government also gave money to the states to provide aid programs for dependent children, for the blind, and for the physically handicapped.

As stated previously, some Americans were exempt from the provisions of the Social Security Act. Nevertheless, this act fundamentally changed the relationship of the federal government to American citizens. At the root of the Social Security Act was the concept that it was the job of the federal government to take care of those who couldn't take care of themselves. This was a fundamentally new role for the federal government to have, and it justified the worst fears of many opponents of the Roosevelt administration.

THE PRESIDENTIAL ELECTION OF 1936

The 1936 election was the first true national referendum on the presidency of Franklin Roosevelt. In his campaign speeches Roosevelt oftentimes railed against the business class; according to Roosevelt they opposed many of his policies only so they could continue to get rich. The Republicans nominated Governor Alfred Landon of Kansas as their presidential candidate. Landon never actually repudiated the programs of the New Deal, but he stated that a balanced budget and less expensive government programs should be top priorities.

The election was one of the most one-sided in American history. Roosevelt won the electoral college 523 to 8; Landon was only able to carry the states of Maine and Vermont. Roosevelt was able to craft a **New Deal Coalition**, which made the Democrats the majority party in America throughout the rest of the 1930s and all the way into the 1980s.

The fact that white urban dwellers supported the Democrats in large numbers was noted during the 1928 defeat of Smith; whites in the Solid South had largely voted Democratic since the nineteenth century. The two groups that joined the Democratic coalition in this era were labor unions and blacks (this was a dramatic shift, as most blacks had voted Republican since the period of Emancipation). Roosevelt enjoyed support in the agricultural community as well.

OPPONENTS OF FRANKLIN ROOSEVELT AND THE NEW DEAL

Despite the overwhelming electoral success of Franklin Roosevelt, many Americans vehemently disagreed with his programs. Some wealthy Americans called him a traitor to his class, while some businessmen called him a socialist or a communist. To others, the programs of Roosevelt were perceived as being designed to benefit the business interests of America and never truly addressed the human suffering of the country. Some of these Americans felt that neither the Democratic nor the Republican parties were really concerned with helping the average American, and perceived socialism as the only viable solution. Many idealistic Americans dabbled with socialism in the 1930s; for some the one or two party meetings they attended became career-threatening during the McCarthy era of the 1950s.

One group that thought the New Deal had gone too far was the **American Liberty League**. This group was led by former presidential candidate Al Smith and several very influential business figures, including prominent members of the du Pont family. The membership of this organization was largely relatively wealthy Republicans; they were particularly incensed by the **Revenue Act of 1935**, which considerably increased the tax rate for those making over $50,000. The American Liberty League equated the New Deal with "Bolshevism" in much of their literature.

The majority of those opposing the New Deal felt that it didn't go far enough. Dr. Francis Townsend of California proposed an **Old Age Revolving Pension Plan**; under this plan a national sales tax would pay for a pension of $200 per month for all retired Americans. Townsend maintained that the benefit would be that more and more money would be put into circulation. In 1934 Upton Sinclair, author of *The Jungle,* ran for governor of California on the Democratic ticket and announced his "End Poverty in California" (EPIC) plan. Under this plan California factories and farms would be under state control. Sinclair was defeated by the Republican candidate and was also sabotaged by members of his own party; the Democratic smear campaign against Sinclair was approved of by Franklin Roosevelt.

The two most vicious opponents of the New Deal were Father Charles Coughlin and Louisiana Senator Huey Long. Millions of people listened to Coughlin on the radio. Originally a supporter of Roosevelt, by the mid-1930s he told his listeners that Roosevelt was a "liar" and "the great betrayer." By the late 1930s Coughlin was praising Mussolini and Hitler on his broadcasts, and making increasing anti-Semitic statements. Per orders of the church, Coughlin was pulled off the air during World War II.

As Governor and later Senator from Louisiana, Huey Long instituted many New Deal-type programs in Louisiana, and also developed the most effective and ruthless political machine in the entire South. By 1934 Long felt that Franklin Roosevelt was not committed to doing enough to end the Depression. Long called for a true redistribution of wealth in his "Share the Wealth" program, which would have allowed no American to make over a million dollars a year (the rest would be taken in taxes). From these taxes Long proposed to give every American family $5000 immediately and an annual income of $2000. Long talked of running against Roosevelt in 1936, but was assassinated by the relative of a Louisiana political enemy in 1935.

THE LAST YEARS OF THE NEW DEAL

Franklin Roosevelt was frustrated that the United States Supreme Court had struck down several New Deal programs. In early 1937 he proposed the **Justice Reorganization Bill**, which would have allowed him to appoint an additional Supreme Court justice for every justice over 70 years old (nothing in the Constitution stated that there had to be only nine Supreme Court justices). Roosevelt would have been able to appoint six new judges under this scheme. Roosevelt claimed that the purpose of this plan was to help the older judges with their workload, but many Republicans and Democrats in Congress believed that Roosevelt was altering the balance of power between branches of government just to get his ideas enacted into law. Newspaper editorial writers and cartoonists compared Roosevelt to the dictators of Europe, Hitler and Mussolini. Many Southern Democrats joined with the Republicans to defeat this bill; the aftereffects seriously damaged Roosevelt's relationship with Congress. Ironically, without the bill several justices retired in the next two years, allowing Roosevelt to appoint justices who would approve his programs anyway.

Any hopes that the New Deal was actually ending the Depression were dashed by a fairly large recession that occurred in mid-1937. Once again, factories began major layoffs. Critics of the New Deal blamed Roosevelt's programs for this recession. Many in the administration were worried that the national debt was too high, and urged Roosevelt to cut programs. The WPA was drastically scaled back, putting some that had worked for it out of work. In addition, a part of every worker's salary was now deducted to be put into the Social Security fund; critics charged that this money would have been better utilized if it was actually being spent on goods and services. By 1940 the administration restored some of the cutbacks made to government programs, slightly improving the economy again.

THE EFFECTS OF THE NEW DEAL

The Wagner Act and other New Deal legislation permanently legitimized labor unions and collective bargaining. Some unions became emboldened by the Wagner Act, and several <u>sit-down strikes</u> occurred in the late 1930s. The most famous occurred at the General Motors plant in Flint, Michigan, in January of 1937. Workers refused to leave the plant; by February management had to give in to the worker's demands. Other strikes of the era turned bloody; at a 1937 strike at Republic Steel in Chicago, 10 strikers were killed. Nevertheless, union membership rose dramatically in the 1930s.

Another development was the creation of the <u>Congress of Industrial Organizations</u> (CIO). The American Federal of Labor, founded in the 1880s, was made up mostly of skilled workers. The first president of the CIO was John L. Lewis; the goal of this union was to organize and represent unskilled factory and textile workers. By 1938 this organization represented over 4 million workers. CIO members were on the front lines of the strikes mentioned in the previous paragraph.

The burden on women and blacks was great during the New Deal. As men lost their jobs, more and more women were forced to take meager jobs to support their families (despite the fact that women workers were oftentimes criticized for "stealing" the jobs of men). It should be noted that Francis Perkins was the Secretary of Labor during the 1930s; Roosevelt employed a number of women in influential roles during his presidency.

Blacks were especially oppressed during the New Deal. Oftentimes they were the first fired from their factory or business; relief programs in Southern states sometimes excluded blacks from receiving benefits. Lynchings continued in the South throughout the 1930s; Roosevelt never supported an antilynching bill for fear of alienating Southern Democrats. The <u>Scottsboro Boys</u> trial received national attention. In 1931 nine black young men were accused of raping two white women on a train. Without any real evidence, eight of the nine were sentenced to die. It is ironic that the American Communist party organized the appeals of the Scottsboro Boys; in the end some of their convictions were overturned.

Nevertheless, blacks did support Franklin Roosevelt, as they felt that he was generally supportive of their cause. Roosevelt did hire blacks for several policy posts in his New Deal administration. Mary McLeod Bethune, founder of the National Council of Negro Women, was appointed in 1936 as Director of the Division of Negro Affairs of the National Youth Administration. Bethune lobbied Roosevelt on the concerns of blacks, and also worked to increase the support of influential black leaders for the New Deal.

NEW DEAL CULTURE

Many authors attempted to capture the human suffering that was so pronounced in the 1930s. Zora Neale Hurston wrote *Their Eyes Were*

Watching God about growing up black in a small Florida town. *Studs Lonigen* by James T. Farrell depicted the lives of the Irish in Chicago. The previously mentioned *The Grapes of Wrath* by John Steinbeck tells the story of Dust Bowlers moving to California for survival, while Erskine Caldwell's *Tobacco Road* describes the suffering of sharecroppers in Georgia. *Gone with the Wind* by Margaret Mitchell offered a romanticized tale of survival from another period of crisis, the Civil War.

Most Americans of the 1930s got their entertainment through radio. Radio in the 1930s offered soap operas, comedies, and dramas. Americans were also offered "high culture" on most radio stations, as symphonic music and operas were standard fare. The response to H. G. Well's dramatization of "War of the Worlds" demonstrated the power of radio in American life.

Going to the movies provided a way for Americans to escape the sufferings of their daily lives; by 1939 nearly 70 percent of all adults went to the movies at least once a week. Lavish sets and dancing in movies such as *The Golddiggers of 1933* allowed people to leave their cares behind, at least for a couple of hours. Shirley Temple charmed millions, and movies such as *Mr. Smith Goes to Washington* showed audiences that in the end, justice would prevail. Promoters attempted to make movie-going itself a special event in the 1930s; theaters were designed to look like palaces, air conditioning was installed, and dishes and other utensils were often given away as theater promotions.

CHAPTER REVIEW

Rapid Review Guide

To achieve the perfect 5, you should be able to explain the following:

- The Great Depression had numerous long-lasting effects on American society.

- Franklin Roosevelt was the first activist president of the twentieth century who used the power of the federal government to help those who could not help themselves.

- The Great Depression's origins lay in economic problems of the late 1920s.

- The 1929 stock market crash was caused by, among others things, speculation on the part of investors and buying stocks "on the margin."

- The stock market crash began to affect the economy almost immediately, and its effects were felt by almost all by 1931.

- Herbert Hoover did act to end the Depression, but believed that voluntary actions by both business and labor would lead America out of its economic difficulties.

- Franklin Roosevelt won the 1932 election by promising "The New Deal" to the American people and by promising to act in a decisive manner.

- Suffering was felt across American society; many in the Dust Bowl were forced to leave their farms.

- During the first hundred days, Roosevelt restored confidence in the banks, established the Civilian Conservation Corps, stabilized farm prices, and attempted to stabilize industry through the National Industrial Recovery Act.

- During the Second New Deal, the WPA was created and the Social Security Act was enacted; this was the most long-lasting piece of legislation from the New Deal.

- Roosevelt was able to craft a political coalition of urban whites, Southerners, union members, and blacks that kept the Democratic party in power through the 1980s.

- The New Deal had opponents from the left who said it didn't do enough to alleviate the effects of the Depression and opponents from the right who said that the New Deal was socialist in nature.

- Roosevelt's 1937 plan to pack the Supreme Court and the recession of 1937 demonstrated that New Deal programs were not entirely successful in ending the Great Depression.

- Many Americans turned to radio and the movies for relief during the Depression.

Time Line

1929: Stock market crash
1930: Hawley-Smoot Tariff enacted
1931: Ford plants in Detroit shut down
      Initial trial of the Scottsboro Boys
1932: Glass-Steagall Banking Act enacted
      Bonus marchers routed from Washington
      Franklin D. Roosevelt elected president
      Huey Long announces "Share Our Wealth" movement
1933: Emergency Banking Relief Act enacted
      Prohibition ends
      Agricultural Adjustment Act enacted
      National Industrial Recovery Act enacted
      Civilian Conservation Corps established
      Tennessee Valley Authority formed
      Public Works Administration established
1934: American unemployment reaches highest point
1935: Beginning of the Second New Deal

Works Progress Administration established
Social Security Act enacted
Wagner Act enacted
Formation of Committee for Industrial Organization (CIO)
1936: Franklin Roosevelt reelected
Sit-down strike against GM begins
1937: Recession of 1937 begins
Roosevelt's plan to expand the Supreme Court defeated
1939: *Gone with the Wind* published
The Grapes of Wrath published

✓ Review Questions

1. Which of the following was *not* a cause of the stock market crash?

   A. Excessive American loans to European countries
   B. Uneven division of wealth
   C. Installment buying
   D. Drop in farm prices
   E. Purchasing of stocks "on the margin"

(Correct Answer: **A.** All of the others were major underlying reasons for the crash. Americans loans to Europe benefited both European countries and American banking houses until the crash.)

2. Wealthy businessmen who objected to the New Deal programs of Franklin Roosevelt claimed that

   A. they unfairly aided the many who did not deserve it
   B. Roosevelt was personally a traitor to his class
   C. New Deal programs smacked of "Bolshevism"
   D. New Deal programs unfairly regulated businesses
   E. All of the above

(Correct Answer: **E.** All of the criticisms listed were heard throughout the 1930s.)

3. The purpose of the Federal Deposit Insurance Corporation (FDIC) was to

   A. ensure that poor Americans had something to fall back on when they retired
   B. inspect the financial transactions of important businesses
   C. insure bank deposits of individual citizens
   D. ensure that businesses were established insurance funds for their workers, as mandated by congressional legislation
   E. increase governmental control over the economy

(Correct Answer: **C.** The FDIC was established after the bank holiday to insure individual accounts in certified banks and to increase confidence in the banking system. Americans began to put money back into banks after its institution.)

4. One group of women who were able to keep their jobs during the Great Depression were

   A. schoolteachers
   B. clerical workers
   C. domestic workers
   D. government employees
   E. professional workers

(Correct Answer: **C.** In the other occupations women were oftentimes fired before men, or had their hours drastically reduced.

Those women who were employed as domestic workers were relatively safe, as this was one occupation that men, as a whole, rejected.)

5. The popularity of Huey Long and Father Coughlin in the mid-1930s demonstrated that

A. most Americans felt that the New Deal had gone too far in under-mining traditional American values
B. more Americans were turning to religion in the 1930s
C. most Americans favored truly radical solutions to America's problems
D. many Americans felt that the government should do more to
end the problems associated with the Depression
E. Franklin Roosevelt was losing the support of large numbers of voters

(Correct Answer: **D.** Many Americans wanted more New Deal-style programs and felt that Roosevelt should have gone even further in his proposed legislation. Many may have listened to Long and Coughlin, but when it came time to vote, cast their ballots for Roosevelt—thus negating answer C. The idea that the New Deal went too far in destroying American capitalism was popular in the business community, but was not widely shared in mainstream America.)

Chapter 20

World War II

World War II altered the American position in the world and ideology at home more than any other event of the twentieth century. For Americans, World War II was the "good war," and Americans at home assisted the war effort in numerous ways. Orders for planes, jeeps, ships, and numerous other war industries had to be quickly filled; this ended the lingering economic effects of the Great Depression.

After World War I, the United States had been reluctant to take on the role of world leader. As a result of World War II, the United States and the Soviet Union emerged as the two major world powers. During the last months of the war, the United States had the awesome responsibility of being the only country to possess the atomic bomb. Decisions made by the United States at the end of World War II helped to usher in the Cold War and the atomic age.

AMERICAN FOREIGN POLICY IN THE 1930S

As Italy, Germany, and Japan all expanded their empires in the 1930s, most Americans favored a continuation of the policy of <u>isolationism</u>. An isolationist group, the <u>America First Committee</u>, attracted nearly 820,000 members by 1940. Isolationists believed that it was in America's best interests to stay out of foreign conflicts that did not directly threaten American interests. A congressional committee led by Senator Gerald Nye investigated the origins of America's entry into World War I and found that bankers and arms manufacturers did much to influence America's entry into the war. On a practical level, Americans were consumed with the problems of the Great Depression and were generally unable to focus on overseas problems.

Congressional legislation passed in the period attempted to keep America out of future wars between other powers. The <u>Neutrality Acts</u>

of 1935 stated that if countries went to war, the United States would not trade arms of weapons with them for six months; in addition, any non-military goods sold to nations at war would have to be paid for up front and would have to be transported in non-American ships (this was called "cash-and-carry").

German expansionism in Europe convinced Franklin Roosevelt that the United States, at some point, would *have* to enter the war on the side of Great Britain (even though public opinion strongly opposed this). On September 1, 1939, Germany invaded Poland, and two days later England and France declared war on Germany. Within three weeks Roosevelt asked Congress to pass the **Neutrality Act of 1939**, which would allow the cash-and-carry sale of arms to countries at war (this legislation was designed to facilitate the sale of American arms to Britain and France). The bill passed on a party-line vote.

News of rapid German advances in Europe began to change American attitudes, with more and more people agreeing with Roosevelt that the best course of action would be to prepare for eventual war. The rapid defeat of France at the hands of the Nazis was stunning to many Americans. In September of 1940 Roosevelt gave Great Britain 50 older American destroyers in return for the rights to build military bases in Bermuda and Newfoundland.

THE PRESIDENTIAL ELECTION OF 1940 AND ITS AFTERMATH

No president in American history had ever served more than two consecutive terms. Just before the Democratic National Convention, Roosevelt quietly stated that if he was nominated, he would accept. Roosevelt was quickly nominated; his Republican opponent was Wendell Wilkie, an ex-Democrat. Roosevelt emerged victorious, but by a smaller margin than in his two previous victories. Most historians say that more Americans voted against Roosevelt was mostly a commentary by the voters on the lingering effects of the Great Depression.

Roosevelt interpreted his victory as a mandate to continue preparations for the eventual U.S. entry into World War II. By early 1941 Roosevelt proposed giving the British aid for the war effort without getting cash in return (it was stated that payment could be made after the war). By the terms of the **Lend-Lease Act**, Congress gave the president the ability to send immediate aid to Britain; Roosevelt immediately authorized nearly $7 billion in aid. As Roosevelt had stated in a 1940 speech, the United States had became an "arsenal of democracy."

In August of 1941 Roosevelt secretly met with British Prime Minister Winston Churchill off the coast of Newfoundland. The two agreed that America would, in all probability, soon be in the war and that the war should be fought for the principles of democracy. Roosevelt and Churchill authorized the publication of their commonly held beliefs in a document called the **Atlantic Charter**. In this document the two leaders proclaimed that they were opposed to territorial expansion for either country, and they were for free trade and self-determination. They also agreed that another world organization would have to be created to replace the League of Nations and that this new world body would have the power to guarantee the "security" of the world. Roosevelt also agreed that the United States would ship lend-lease materials bound for Britain as far as Iceland; this brought the United States one step closer to full support for the Allied cause.

THE ATTACK ON PEARL HARBOR

The Japanese desire to create an Asian empire was the prime motivation behind the Japanese invasion of Manchuria in 1931, Japanese attacks on eastern China in 1937, and the Japanese occupation of much of French Indochina in 1941. As a result of Japanese actions in Southeast Asia, Roosevelt froze all Japanese assets in the United States, cut off the sale of oil to Japan, and closed the Panama Canal to Japanese ships.

From July 1941 until the beginning of December, near-constant negotiations took place between diplomats of Japan and the United States. The Japanese desperately wanted to regain normal trade relations with the United States, but American diplomats insisted that the Japanese leave China first, which the Japanese were unwilling to do. Most Japanese military and civilian leaders were convinced that the Japanese could never achieve their goal of a Pacific empire as long as the United States was active militarily in the region. By December 1 the planning was complete for the Japanese attack on Pearl Harbor.

A few revisionist historians believe that Franklin Roosevelt knew of the impending attack on Pearl Harbor. These historians maintain that Roosevelt was acutely aware that many Americans were still opposed to American entry into war, but that an event such as Pearl Harbor would put the entire country squarely behind the war effort. The vast majority of historians believe that American intelligence knew the Japanese were going to attack somewhere, but didn't know that the attack would be at Pearl Harbor; many in American military intelligence believed the Dutch East Indies would be the next target of the Japanese.

On Sunday morning, December 7, 1941, 190 Japanese warplanes attacked the American Pacific fleet anchored at Pearl Harbor. When the attack was done, 150 American airplanes were destroyed (most on them never left the ground), six battleships were sunk, as were a number of smaller ships, and nearly 2400 Americans were killed. Luckily for the American navy, the aircraft carriers based at Pearl Harbor were out at sea on the morning of the attack.

The next day Roosevelt asked Congress for a declaration of war, stating that December 7 was "a date which will live in infamy." On December 11 Germany and Italy (who had signed a Tripartite Pact with Japan in 1940) declared war on the United States.

AMERICA ENTERS THE WAR

In September of 1940 the President had authorized the creation of a system for the **conscription** of men into the armed forces; in the months immediately after Pearl Harbor, thousands were drafted and countless others volunteered for service. Soldiers in World War II called themselves "**GIs**"; this referred to the "Government Issued" stamp that appeared on the uniforms, tools, weapons, and everything else the government issued to them. A Council for National Defense had also been created in 1940; this body worked rapidly to convert factories over to war production. Additional legislation was also needed to prepare the country for war. In early 1942 the General Maximum Price Regulation Act immediately froze prices and established the rationing system that was in place for most of the war. The **Revenue Act of 1942** greatly expanded the number of Americans who had to pay federal income tax, thus increasing the amount of federal revenue.

America was forced to fight a war in Europe and a war in the Pacific. In the European theater of war, American naval forces first engaged the Germans as they attempted to protect convoys of ships taking critical food and supplies to Great Britain. These convoys were often attacked by German submarines. In this **Battle of the Atlantic** German torpedoes were dreadfully accurate (even though sonar was being used by the Americans). Between January and August of 1942, over 500 ships were sunk by German submarines.

American infantrymen were first involved in actual fighting in North Africa. American and British forces joined to defeat French North Africa in late 1942. American troops also played a role in the battles that eventually forced General Rommel's Africa Korps to surrender in May 1943. American and British soldiers also began a difficult offensive into Sicily and Italy two months later; by June of 1944 Rome had surrendered.

Ever since 1941 the Soviet Union had been the only power to consistently engage the Nazi army (the Soviet Union lost 20 million people in World War II). Stalin had asked on several occasions that a second front be opened in Western Europe; by early 1944 an invasion of France by water was being planned by Dwight D. Eisenhower, commander of all Allied forces (who would become president in 1953).

The D-Day invasion took place on the morning of June 6, 1944. The initial Allied losses on Omaha Beach were staggering, yet the D-Day invasion was the beginning of the end for Nazi Germany. By the end of July over 2 million Allied soldiers were on the ground in France, and the final squeeze of Nazi Germany began. American and British forces liberated French cities and towns as they moved eastward; at the same time Russian troops were rolling westward. By August Paris had been liberated.

The last major German offensive of the war was the **Battle of the Bulge**. Nearly 85,000 American soldiers were killed, wounded, or captured in this battle. The German attack moved the Allied lines back into Belgium, but reinforcement led by General George S. Patton again forced the Germans to retreat. When the German general staff learned that they had not been victorious at the Battle of the Bulge, most admitted that Germany would soon be defeated. American and British bombings did much to destroy several German cities.

Advancing American, British, and German troops were horrified to find concentration camps or the remnants of them. These camps were integral parts of Nazi Germany's **Final Solution** to the "Jewish problem." Between 1941 and 1945 over 6 million Jews were killed in the event now referred to as the **Holocaust**. Historians maintain that if the war continued for another two years, all of European Jewry might have been eliminated. Advancing troops were outraged at what they saw in these camps, and on several occasions shot all of the Nazi guards on the spot. Why the Holocaust occurred, and why it was endorsed by so many Germans, is the subject of hundreds of books and articles in scholarly journals.

Some historians are critical of the diplomatic and military actions of the United States both before and during the Holocaust. During the mid-to late 1930s, the State Department made it very difficult for European Jews to immigrate to the United States; with alarming unemployment figures in the United States because of the Great Depression, American decision makers felt it unwise to admit large numbers of immigrants to the country. Franklin Roosevelt knew of the existence of the concentration camps as early as late 1943, yet chose not to bomb them (which many in the camps say they would have welcomed). Roosevelt maintained that the number one priority of America had to be winning the war.

In March 1945 Allied troops crossed the Rhine River, and met up with advancing Russian troops at the Elbe River on April 25. In fierce fighting the Russians took Berlin. Deep in his bunker, Hitler committed suicide on May 1, and Germany unconditionally surrendered one week later. Celebrations for V-E Day (Victory in Europe Day) were jubilant in London and Paris, but were more restrained in American cities, as the United States still had to deal with the Japanese.

In February of 1945 Roosevelt, Stalin, and Churchill met at the **Yalta Conference**. Franklin Roosevelt had been elected to a fourth term in 1944, but photos reveal him to be very ill at Yalta (he would live only another two months). At Yalta the three leaders made major decisions concerning the structure of postwar Europe. It was agreed that Germany would be split into four zones of occupation (administered by England, France, the United States, and the Soviet Union), and that Berlin, located in the Soviet zone, would also be partitioned. Stalin promised to allow free elections in the Eastern European nations he had freed from Nazi control, and said that the Soviets would join the war against Japan after the surrender of Germany. Many historians consider the decisions made at the Yalta Conference (and the failure of the Soviet Union to totally adhere to them) to be major reasons for the beginning of the Cold War.

Some historians are critical of Franklin Roosevelt for "giving in" to Stalin at Yalta. It should be remembered that at the time of this meeting Roosevelt had only two months to live. In addition, in February 1945 the atomic bomb was not yet a working weapon. American planning for the defeat of Japan was for a full attack on the Japanese mainland; in

Roosevelt's eyes, Soviet participation in this attack was absolutely crucial (in return for this support Roosevelt made concessions to Stalin on Eastern Europe and supported the Soviet acquisition of ports and territories in Korea, Manchuria, and Outer Mongolia). Winston Churchill had strong reservations about the ultimate goals and conduct of Stalin and the Soviet Union at Yalta; these reservations would later intensify, and were articulated by Churchill in his "iron curtain" speech of March 1946.

THE WAR AGAINST JAPAN

In the aftermath of the attack on Pearl Harbor, Japan advanced against British controlled islands and territories in the Pacific. By April of 1942 Hong Kong and Singapore were both in Japanese hands. General Douglas MacArthur controlled a large American and Filipino force in the Philippines. A large Japanese force landed there, and in March MacArthur was forced to abandon his troops and go to Australia. On May 6, 1942, Americans holding out on the Bataan Peninsula were finally forced to surrender. 75,000 American and Filipino prisoners were forced to endure the 60-mile **Bataan Death March,** during which over 10,000 prisoners were executed or died from weakness (it was several years before Washington became aware of this March).

Just two days later the Americans won their first decisive victory at the **Battle of the Coral Sea**. American airplanes launched from aircraft carriers were able to stop the advance of several large Japanese troop transports. Troops on these ships were to be used for an attack on Australia. After this defeat the Japanese could never again mount a planned attack there. American airplanes also played a crucial role in the **Battle of Midway**. This battle took place in early June 1942; in it the Japanese lost 4 aircraft carriers and nearly 300 planes. Many military historians consider the battle to be the turning point of the Pacific War; after this Japan was never able to launch a major offensive. By mid-1942 American industrial might became more and more of a factor; the Americans could simply produce more airplanes than the Japanese could.

The Japanese were again halted at the **Battle of Guadalcanal**, which began in August of 1942 and continued into the following year. American marines engaged in jungle warfare and even hand-to-hand combat. On many occasions Japanese units would fight nearly until the last man. Beginning in 1943 the Allies instituted a policy of **island-hopping**; by this policy key Japanese strongholds would be attacked by air and sea power as American marines would push on around these strongholds. By late 1944 American bombers were able to reach major Japanese cities, and unleashed massive bombing attacks on them.

By 1944 the war had clearly turned against the Japanese. In late October General MacArthur returned to the Philippine island of Leyte (although the city of Manila was not totally liberated until the following March). The Japanese began to use **kamikaze pilots** in a desperate attempt to destroy Allied ships. Several more bloody battles waited ahead for American forces: America suffered 25,000 casualties at the Battle of Iwo Jima, and another 50,000 at the Battle of Okinawa. After these battles, however, nothing was left to stop an Allied invasion of Japan.

THE DECISION TO DROP THE ATOMIC BOMB

The incredibly bloody battles described in the preceding section greatly concerned military officials who were planning for an invasion of Japan. Japanese resistance to such an attack would have been fanatical. Franklin Roosevelt had suddenly died in late 1945; the new president, Harry Truman, was informed in July 1944 about the atomic bomb. The actual planning for this bomb was the purpose of the **Manhattan Project**, begun in August 1942. Construction of this bomb took place in Los Alamos, New Mexico under the direction of J. Robert Oppenheimer. The bomb was successfully tested in the New Mexico desert on July 16, 1945.

Much debate has taken place over the American decision to drop the atomic bomb on Japanese cities. For Harry Truman this was not a difficult decision. Losses in an invasion of Japan would have been large; Truman later admitted that what had happened at Pearl Harbor and on the Bataan Death March also influenced his decision. Some historians also claim that some in both the State Department and the War Department saw the Soviet Union as the next potential enemy of the United States and wanted to use the atomic bomb to "show them what we had." After the atomic bombs were dropped American public opinion was incredibly supportive of Truman's decision. It should be noted that movies, newsreels, and even comic books made the eventual decision to drop the bomb easier by turning the war against the Japanese into a race war. The Japanese were referred to as "Japs," were portrayed with crude racial stereotypes, and were seen as sneaky and certainly not to be trusted (it is interesting to note that the war against Germany was usually portrayed as a war against "Hitler" or against "the Nazis" and almost never as a war against the German people).

On August 6, 1945, the airplane the **Enola Gay** dropped a bomb on the city of Hiroshima. Over 75,000 were killed in the attack. Three days later another bomb was dropped on Nagasaki. Some historians are especially critical of the dropping of the second bomb; there is evidence that the Japanese were pursuing a surrender through diplomatic circles on the day of the attack. Japan surrendered one day later, and V-J celebrations took place in many American cities the following day.

THE HOME FRONT DURING THE WAR

As previously stated, the federal government took actions even before the war began to prepare the American economy for war. Thousands of American businessmen also went to Washington to take on jobs relating to the war effort. These were called "dollar-a-year" men, as almost all still received their regular salary from wherever they worked.

The demand for workers increased dramatically during the war years, thus increasing wages for workers as well. Union membership increased during the war; unions generally honored "no-strike" agreements that were made in the weeks after Pearl Harbor. Beginning in 1943 some strikes did occur, especially in the coal mines.

The government needed money to finance the war effort. As stated previously, more money was raised by expanding greatly the number of Americans who had to pay income taxes. In addition, America followed a policy begun in World War I and sold **war bonds**.

During both wars various celebrities made public appearances to encourage the public to buy these bonds.

Average Americans were asked to sacrifice much during the war. Goods such as gasoline, rubber, meat, sugar, and butter were rationed during the war; American families kept **ration cards** to determine which of these goods they could still buy during any given period. Recycling was commonplace during the war, and many had to simply do without the goods they desired. Women, for example, were desperate for silk stockings; some took to drawing a line up the back of their legs to make it appear that they had stockings on. City dwellers had to take part in "blackouts," where they would have to lower all shades to make any enemy airplane attacks more difficult. Men and boys both took turns at lookout stations, where the skies were constantly scanned for enemy bombers. Many high schools across the country eliminated vacations during the year; by doing this, school could end early and students could go off and do essential work. Many workers stayed for extra shifts at work, called "victory shifts."

Popular culture also reflected the necessities of war. Many movies during the war were light comedies, designed to keep people's minds off the war. Other movies, such as *Casablanca,* emphasized self-sacrifice and helping the war effort. "White Christmas" (sung by Bing Crosby) was a favorite during the war, evoking nostalgia in both soldiers abroad and those on the home front. Professional baseball continued during the war, but rosters were made up of players that had been classified 4-F by local draft boards (unfit for military service). The All-American Girls' Baseball League was founded in 1943 and also provided a wartime diversion for thousands of fans.

Women also entered the American workforce in large numbers during the war. Many women working in "traditional women's jobs" moved to factory jobs vacated when men went off to fight. The figure of **Rosie the Riveter** symbolized American working women during the war. In the 1930s women were discouraged from working (the argument had been that they would be taking jobs from men); during World War II many posters informed women that it was their patriotic duty to work. Problems remained for women in the workplace, however: For many jobs, even in the defense industry, they were paid less than men. It is also ironic that when the war ended women were encouraged that it was now their "patriotic duty" to return home and become housewives.

DISCRIMINATION DURING THE WAR

Many blacks also took important factory jobs and eagerly signed up for military service. However, discrimination against blacks continued during the war. Black military units were strictly segregated and were oftentimes used for menial chores instead of combat. Some American blacks at home began the **Double V campaign**: This pushed for the defeat of Germany and Japan but also the defeat of racial prejudice. CORE (the Congress for Racial Equality) was founded in 1942, and organized the very first sit-ins and boycotts; these actions would become standard tactics of the civil rights movement in the 1950s and 1960s.

Many on the West Coast feared that the Japanese that lived there were sympathizers or even spies for the Japanese cause (even though many had been born and brought up in the United States). On February 19, 1942, Franklin Roosevelt signed Executive Order 9066, which ordered Japanese-Americans to **internment camps**. American public officials told the Japanese that this was being done for their own protection; however, many Japanese noted when they got to their camps that the guns guarding these relocation centers were pointed inward and never outward. Many businesses and homes were lost by Japanese citizens.

Influential Japanese-Americans were outraged by these actions, and a legal challenge was mounted against the internment camps. In a 1944 decision, *Korematsu* v. *United States,* the Supreme Court ruled that the internment camps were legal, since they were based "on military necessity." In 1988 the United States government formally apologized to those who had been placed in camps and gave each survivor $20,000. It should be noted that American units of soldiers of Japanese descent were created during the war, and that they fought with great bravery in the campaign against Hitler.

CHAPTER REVIEW

Rapid Review Guide

To achieve the perfect 5, you should be able to explain the following:

- War production for World War II pulled America out of the Great Depression.

- World War II turned America into one of the two major world powers.

- America continued to pursue a foreign policy of isolationism throughout the 1930s.

- Lend-lease and other measures by Franklin Roosevelt brought America into the war on the side of England one year before America actually entered the war.

- The Pearl Harbor attack was part of an overall Japanese strategy, and it mobilized American public opinion for war.

- Battles fought by American GIs in Africa, Italy, and Western Europe were crucial in creating a "second front" and important in the eventual defeat of Hitler.

- Decision made at the Yalta Conference did much to influence the postwar world.

- Superior American air and sea power ultimately led to the defeat of the Japanese in the Pacific.

- The decision to drop the atomic bomb was based on the calculations of the human cost of an American invasion of Japan and as retaliation for Japanese actions during the war.

- Americans sacrificed greatly during the war and contributed through rationing, extra work, and the purchase of war bonds to the Allied victory.

- American women contributed greatly to the war effort, especially by taking industrial jobs that had been held by departed soldiers.

- Blacks continued to meet discrimination both in and out of the armed services, as did the Japanese. Japanese citizens from the West Coast were forced to move to internment camps. The America government in 1988 issued a formal apology for these actions.

Time Line

1933: Hitler comes to power in Germany
1935: Neutrality Act of 1935
1938: Hitler annexes Austria, Sudetenland
1939: Nazi-Soviet Pact
      Germany invades Poland/beginning of World War II
1940: Roosevelt reelected for third term
      American Selective Service plan instituted
1941: Lend-lease assistance begins for England
      Japanese attack Pearl Harbor/United States officially enters
World War II
      Germany declares war on United States
1942: American troops engage in combat in Africa
      Japanese interment camps opened
      Battle of Coral Sea, Battle of Midway
      Casablanca released
1943: Allied armies invade Sicily
      United Mine Workers strike
1944: D-Day Invasion
      Roosevelt defeats Thomas Dewey, elected for fourth term
      Beginning of Battle of the Bulge

1945: Yalta Conference
       Concentration camps discovered by Allied forces
       FDR dies in Warm Springs, Georgia; Harry Truman becomes president
       Germany surrenders unconditionally
       Atomic bombs dropped on Hiroshima and Nagasaki
       Japan surrenders unconditionally

✓ Review Questions

1. The internment of Japanese-Americans began for all of the reasons listed *except*

   A. large numbers of Japanese lived near Pearl Harbor in Hawaii, and some were suspected of being spies
   B. it was felt that Japanese living in California had divided loyalties when war began
   C. newspapers on the West Coast reported incidents of Japanese-Americans aiding the Japanese military effort
   D. Japanese-Americans needed protection, and the camps would provide it for them
   E. the portrayal of the Japanese in American films and magazines

(Correct Answer: **D.** Although this was the official reason given at the time, the other reasons listed were the actual reasons. California newspapers reported fabricated stories of Japanese-Americans assisting the Japanese war effort.)

2. Which was *not* a reason for the hatred many felt toward the Japanese during the war?

   A. The bombing of Pearl Harbor
   B. The fact that they were physically different in appearance from most Americans
   C. The outrage over the Bataan Death March as soon as Americans first learned of it in late 1941
   D. The portrayal of the Japanese in American films, magazines, and newspapers

(Correct Answer: **C.** The Bataan Death March did not occur until 1942, and most Americans did not know about it until 1945.)

3. Many observers would later be critical of the Yalta Conference for all of the following *except*

   A. at the conference the Soviet Union was given control over more of Germany than the other Allied powers
   B. the Soviet Union did not promise to join the war against Japan immediately
   C. Franklin Roosevelt was near death at the time of the conference
   D. all of the countries liberated by the Soviet Union would remain at least temporarily under Soviet control.

(Correct Answer: **A.** At the conference, the Soviet Union, England, France, and the United States were all to administer parts of Germany; the Soviets did not get more than anyone else. Criticism existed because by the decisions made at Yalta, the Soviet Union joined the war against Japan only days before Japan was defeated. In addition, "temporary" Soviet control over Eastern Europe allowed communist governments to be set up there. Other historians question the decisions Franklin Roosevelt made at Yalta; many wonder if his physical and mental condition were adequate for such a conference.)

4. The United States did little to stop the spread of Hitler and Nazi Germany in the 1930s because

    A. the League of Nations promised to take an active diplomatic and military role beginning in 1935
    B. the United States was much more concerned with diplomatic and political affairs in the Pacific than in Europe in the 1930s
    C. the United States was more interested in solving domestic problems in the 1930s
    D. the findings of the Nye commission did much to sour Americans on future military involvement
    E. C and D above

(Correct Answer: **E.** American policies in the 1930s were largely concerned with solving the problems of the Depression, and the Nye commission reported that arms manufacturers, looking for profits, were largely responsible for pushing America into World War I.)

5. Americans continued to crave diversions during World War II and went in large numbers to see all but which of the following:

    A. Auto racing
    B. Professional baseball
    C. Movies
    D. Big band concerts

(Correct Answer **A.** Because of shortages of gasoline and rubber for tires, auto racing was almost totally eliminated for much of the war.)

Chapter 21

The Origins of the Cold War (1945–1960)

 Winning the **Cold War** was the central goal of the United States from 1945 all the way until the fall of communism in 1990 to 1991. Almost all domestic and foreign policy decisions made in this era related in some way to American efforts to defeat the Soviet Union and their allies. A large part of the success of many sectors of the American economy in the post-World War II era was related to defense and defense-related contracts. Some politicians lost their careers in this era if they were perceived to be "soft on communism."

Exactly whose fault was the Cold War? Initially hundreds of books and articles have been written about that very subject. American historians assigned blame to the Soviet Union for aggressive actions on their part in the period immediately following the end of World War II. "**Revisionist**" American historians have claimed that the Soviets were forced into these actions by the perceived aggressiveness of the United States and its allies. What actually happened in those years immediately following World War II is the subject of this chapter.

THE FIRST CRACKS IN THE ALLIANCE: 1945

The alliance that proved victorious in World War II began to show strains even before the end of the war. In the preceding chapter it was mentioned that tough decisions were made at the **Yalta Conference**, including allowing elections in Eastern European nations. Stalin was especially reluctant to allow free elections in Poland; as Hitler demonstrated, it provided a perfect invasion route into Soviet territory.

The United States would be somewhat handicapped diplomatically by the death of Franklin Roosevelt in April 1945. Roosevelt had excellent personal relations with Winston Churchill and felt that he could at least "understand" Stalin. When Harry Truman took over the presidency, he had little experience in foreign affairs, and Roosevelt had met with him only several times, sharing little about the appropriate way to deal with America's wartime allies.

Truman met Soviet diplomats for the first time at the initial session of the United Nations, which was held in San Francisco two weeks after he took over as president. His first face-to-face meeting with Stalin took place at the **Potsdam Conference**, held at the end of July in 1945. Truman, Stalin, and Clement Atlee (who had just replaced Churchill as Prime Minster) represented the United States, the Soviet Union, and Great Britain at this meeting. Again, the future of Eastern Europe was discussed. It was also decided to hold war-crimes trials for top Nazi leaders (the most famous of these would be known as the Nuremberg Trials). At this meeting Truman announced to Stalin the existence of the atomic bomb (ironically, Stalin had learned of it some two weeks earlier from Soviet spies in the United States).

Great philosophical differences between the two sides were apparent at this meeting. Truman expressed the view that free elections should be held in all Eastern European countries. Stalin, on the other hand, expressed the desire to have Eastern European **satellite countries**, which would act as buffers to potential future invasions of the Soviet Union.

THE IRON CURTAIN

During 1946 and 1947 the Soviet Union tightened its hold on Eastern Europe (Romania, Hungary, Bulgaria, Poland, Czechoslovakia, and East Germany). Promised elections in Europe did not actually take place for two years. In some cases communists backed by Stalin forced noncommunists who had been freely elected out of office.

In March 1946 Winston Churchill made a speech at a college in Fulton, Missouri, where he noted that the Soviet Union had established an **iron curtain** that divided the Soviet Union and its Eastern European satellites from the independent countries of Europe. This speech is often viewed as the symbolic beginning of the Cold War.

Another key document from this era was written by American diplomat and expert in Soviet affairs George F. Kennan. Kennan wrote an anonymous article in *Foreign Affairs* magazine in July 1947 (the author was only identified as "Mr. X"), stating his opinion that Soviet policy makers were deeply committed to the destruction of America and the American way of life. The article maintained that the USSR felt threatened by the United States and felt that it had to expand for self-preservation. Kennan stated that a long-range and long-term **containment policy** to stop communism was needed. According to Kennan, if communism could be contained, it would eventually crumble under its own weight. The policy of containment was central to most American policy toward the Soviet Union for the next 45 years.

If President Truman was looking for an opportunity to apply the containment policy, opportunities soon presented themselves in Turkey and

Greece. The Soviets desperately desired to control the Dardanelles Strait; this Turkish controlled area would allow Soviet ships to go from the Black Sea into the Mediterranean. In addition, communists were threatening the existing government in Greece. In February 1947, the British (still suffering severe economic aftershocks from World War II) stated that they could no longer financially assist the Turkish and Greek governments, and suggested that the United States step in (some historians maintain that this symbolically ended Great Britain's great power status and demonstrated that now the United States was one of the two major players on the world stage). In March 1947, the president announced the **Truman Doctrine**, which stated that it would become the stated duty of the United States to assist all democratic nations of the world who resisted communism. Congress authorized $400 million in aid for Greece and Turkey. The policies outlined in the Truman Doctrine and in George Kennan's article can be found embedded in American foreign policy all the way through the 1980s.

THE MARSHALL PLAN

Most Americans applauded Truman's decision to help countries resisting communism. Others wanted to see a much larger American role in Europe in the postwar era. Several observers stated that Hitler was able to rise to power because of the lack of stability in both the German government and economy in the era following World War I, and that such a situation should never be allowed to develop again.

Many felt that it was the duty of the United States to rebuild the devastated countries of Europe after World War II; it was felt that in the long run this would bring both political and economic benefits to the Western world.

By the terms of the **Marshall Plan** the United States provided nearly $12 billion in economic aid to help rebuild Europe. This assistance was of a strictly nonmilitary nature, and was designed, in large measure, to prevent Western Europe from falling into economic collapse. Seventeen Western European nations received aid under the Marshall Plan; several of them became valuable trading partners of the United States by the early part of the 1950s. The Soviet Union was invited to apply for aid from the Marshall Plan. Stalin refused and ordered the Soviet satellite countries to do so as well.

BERLIN: THE FIRST COLD WAR CRISIS

In 1948 the Americans, French, and British announced that they were to combine their areas of occupation in Germany and create the Federal Republic of Germany. West Berlin (located within the eastern zone of Germany) was supposed to join this Federal Republic. Berlin was already a "problem city" for communist authorities: Many residents of East Berlin (and other residents of Eastern Europe) escaped communism by passing from East Berlin to West Berlin.

In June 1948, Soviet and East German military units blocked off transportation by road into West Berlin. Historians of Soviet foreign policy note that this was the first real test by Stalin of Western Cold War resolve. Truman authorized the institution of the **Berlin Airlift**; for nearly 15 months, American and British pilots flew in enough food and supplies for West Berlin to survive. The Americans and British achieved at least a public relations victory when Stalin ordered the lifting of the blockade in May 1949. Shortly afterward, the French, English, and American zones of occupation were joined together into "West Germany," and the Americans stationed troops there to guard against further Soviet actions.

One month earlier the United States, Canada, and 10 Western European countries announced the formation of **NATO** (North Atlantic Treaty Organization). The main provision of the NATO treaty was that an attack on one signatory nation would be considered an attack on all of them. The NATO treaty placed America squarely in the middle of European affairs for the foreseeable future. NATO would expand in the early 1950s, and in 1955 as a response to NATO, the Soviet Union and its satellite countries created the **Warsaw Pact**.

1949: A PIVOTAL YEAR IN THE COLD WAR

In 1949 two events occurred that rocked American postwar confidence. In September the Soviets announced that they had exploded an atomic bomb. The potential threat of nuclear annihilation was an underlying fear for many Americans throughout the 1950s. Truman quickly gave authorization for American scientists to begin work on the **hydrogen bomb**, a bomb much more powerful than the atomic bombs dropped on Hiroshima and Nagasaki.

An equally horrifying event occurred shortly after the successful Soviet atomic test. Since 1945 the United States had been major financial backers of Nationalist China, led by Chiang Kai-shek. Communist guerrilla forces under Mao Tse-tung was able to capture much of the Chinese countryside. In 1949 Mao's forces captured Peking, the capital city. The People's Republic of China was established by Mao. Nationalist forces were forced to flee to Formosa (now Taiwan). From Formosa Chiang Kai-shek and the Nationalists maintained that they were the "true" government of China, and continued to receive a very sizable aid package from the United States. The question of "who lost China" would be repeatedly asked over the next 10 years in the United States, usually to attack the president, Harry Truman, and the Democratic party, who were in power when Nationalist China fell.

THE COLD WAR AT HOME

During 1949 and 1950 many Americans felt a sense that the tides of the Cold War were somehow shifting over in favor of the Soviet Union. Many felt that the Soviet Union could never do this alone, and that they *had* to have large number of spies within the United States helping them. Thus, under President Truman and later under President Eisenhower, there was a tremendous effort made to rid the United States of a perceived internal "communist menace." As stated in Chapter 19, on the Depression, many idealists had dabbled in communism in the 1930s; this "dabbling" would now come back to haunt them.

The Truman administration began by jailing the leaders of the American Communist party under the provisions of the 1940 Smith Act. This document stated that it was illegal to advocate the overthrow by force of the American government. When some Republicans claimed that the Truman administration was "soft on communism," Truman ordered the creation of a **Loyalty Review Board**, which eventually had the legal jurisdiction to investigate both new and experienced federal workers. Three or four million federal workers were examined by the board; as a result of these investigations, slightly over 100 workers were removed from their jobs. Investigations revealed that some of those investigated were homosexuals, who were oftentimes hounded out of office as well.

While the Truman administration was investigating the executive branch of government, the Congress decided to investigate communists in the government and in the entertainment industry. The congressional committee overseeing these investigations was **HUAC** (the House Un-American Activities Committee). In 1947 HUAC began to investigate the movie industry in earnest. Committee investigators relentlessly pursued actors, directors, and writers who had attended Communist party meetings in the past. Directors of movies made during World War II that cast the Soviet Union in a favorable light (such as *Mission to Moscow* and *North Star*) were brought in for questioning. Dozens of writers, actors, and directors were called in to testify about their political orientation. The Hollywood Ten was an influential group of writers and directors who refused to answer questions posed to them by members of HUAC in an open congressional session. Members of the Hollywood Ten were all sentenced to jail time.

The effects on Hollywood were major. Some Hollywood movies of the late 1940s dealt directly with the problems of society (such as *The Best Years of their Lives*). As a result of pressure from HUAC, Hollywood movies became much more tame. In addition, a **blacklist** was made of actors, directors, and writers who were potentially communist and whom the major studios should *not* hire. Many Hollywood careers were ruined by the blacklist; some writers wrote under false names or had "fronts" turn in their screenplays for them. Some of those blacklisted were unable to get work until the early 1960s.

On the senate side, Senator Pat McCarran sponsored several bills to "stop the spread of communism" in the United States. The **McCarran Internal Security Act** was enacted in 1950; under this bill all communist or communist-front organizations had to register with the government, and members of these organizations could not work in any job related to the national defense. The **McCarran-Walter Act** of 1952 greatly limited immigration from Asia and Eastern Europe; this would hopefully limit the "influx of communism" into the United States. President Truman vetoed both of these bills, but Congress passed both of them over the president's veto.

Were There Spies in America?

The trials of Alger Hiss and the Rosenbergs indicated to many Americans that there just might be communist spies infiltrating America. In 1948 HUAC began an investigation of Hiss, a former official in the State Department and an advisor to Franklin Roosevelt at the Yalta Conference. An editor of Time magazine, Whitaker Chambers had previously been a communist and testified to HUAC that Hiss had been a communist too. After several trials Hiss was finally convicted for perjury and spent four years in jail. To this day, the guilt or innocence of Alger Hiss is still debated.

In 1950 Julius and Ethel Rosenberg were charged with passing atomic secrets to the Soviet Union. The government had much more evidence on Julius than on his wife, but they were both found guilty of espionage in 1952 and executed. Considerable debate has also taken place on the guilt of the Rosenbergs, although materials released from the Soviet archives after the fall of communism strongly implicated Ethel.

THE HEATING OF THE COLD WAR: KOREA

After World War II Korea was divided into a communist North Korea and a noncommunist and pro-American South Korea along the **38th parallel**. In late June of 1950 North Korea invaded the south. The Security Council of the United Nations voted to send in a peacekeeping force (the Soviet Union was protesting the U.N.'s decision not to allow communist China in as a member and failed to attend the Security Council session when this was discussed). Douglas MacArthur was appointed to lead the United Nations forces, and the **Korean War** began.

U.N. forces under MacArthur drove northward into North Korea. In late November forces from communist China forced MacArthur's troops to retreat, yet by March 1951 his troops were on the offensive again. MacArthur was very critical of President Truman's handling of the war, demanding a greatly intensified bombing campaign and suggesting that Truman order the Nationalist Chinese to attack the Chinese mainland. In April 1951 Truman finally fired MacArthur for insubordination. Armistice talks to end the war dragged on for nearly two years; in the end it was decided to divide North and South Korea along the 38th parallel (along virtually the same line that divided them before the war!). More than 57,000 Americans died in this "forgotten war."

THE RISE OF MCCARTHYISM

The seeming American inability to decisively defeat communism both abroad and at home led to the meteoric rise of Senator Joseph McCarthy of Wisconsin. In a speech in Wheeling, West Virginia, on February 9, 1950, McCarthy announced that he had a list of 205 known communists that were working in the State Department. McCarthy's list was sometimes longer and sometimes smaller, and oftentimes also included prominent diplomats, scholars, and Defense Department and military figures. **McCarthyism** was the ruthless searching out for communists in the government that took place in this period, largely without any real evidence.

For four years, McCarthy reigned supreme in Washington, with few in power or in the news media being willing to challenge him. McCarthy offered a simple reason why the United States was not conclusively winning the Cold War: because of communists in the government. The Republican party was a semireluctant supporter of McCarthy in this era; Republicans realized that the issue of communism was getting them votes. McCarthy even accused Harry Truman and former Secretary of State Marshall of being "unconscious" agents of the communist conspiracy.

In March of 1954 McCarthy claimed in a lengthy speech that the United States Army was full of communists as well. It was at this point that McCarthy began to run into major opposition; Republican President Eisenhower (a former general) stated privately that it was definitely time for McCarthy to be stopped. Tensions between the Army and McCarthy increased when it was announced that McCarthy had asked for special privileges for an aide of his that had been drafted.

The **Army-McCarthy Hearings** appeared on network television, and thousands found themselves riveted to them on a daily basis. Over the course of the hearings, it was discovered that McCarthy *had* asked for special favors for his aide, had doctored photographs, and had used bullying tactics on a regular basis. The end was clearly in sight for McCarthy when Joseph Welch, attorney for the Army, received loud applause when he asked McCarthy if he had any "sense of decency" and when reporter Edwin R. Murrow went on CBS News with a negative report about McCarthy and his tactics. In late 1954 McCarthy was formally censured by the Senate. His power gone, McCarthy died only three years later. The McCarthy era is now remembered as one where attack by innuendo was common and where during the investigations to "get at the truth" about communism the civil rights of many were violated.

THE COLD WAR POLICIES OF PRESIDENT EISENHOWER

Foreign policy decisions of the Eisenhower administration were often crafted by the Secretary of State, John Foster Dulles. Dulles felt that the policy of containment was not nearly aggressive enough; instead of merely containment, Dulles often spoke of "**massive retaliation**" against communist advances anywhere in the world. Dulles also spoke of the need to use nuclear weapons if necessary. At one press conference, Dulles stated that instead of containing communism, the goal of the United States should be to "make communism retreat" whenever and wherever possible.

Eisenhower hoped that the death of Stalin in 1953 would allow a "new understanding" between the United States and the Soviet Union. In some ways Nikita Khrushchev was different from Stalin, speaking about the possibilities of "peaceful coexistence" with the United States. However, when Hungary revolted in 1956, Khrushchev ordered this to be brutally stopped by the Soviet army.

The fate of the Hungarian leader Irme Nagy was sealed when the United States failed to assist the anti-Soviet rebellion of his government. Despite the tough talk of John Foster Dulles, who had boldly proclaimed that the United States would come to the aid of any in Eastern Europe who wanted to "liberate" themselves from communism, it was determined that U.S. forces could not be used to help the Hungarian rebels (despite the fact that the CIA operatives in Hungary had promised Nagy this aid), because this might provoke war with the Soviets. Eisenhower was also reluctant to get militarily involved in Southeast Asia, even though he believed in the **domino theory**, which proclaimed that if one country in Southeast Asia fell to the communists, others would follow. In 1954 French forces in Vietnam were being overrun by nationalist forces under the control of Ho Chi Minh. The French desperately asked for aid. Despite segments of the American military who pushed for assisting the French, Eisenhower ultimately refused.

As a result, the French were finally defeated at the **Battle of Dien Bien Phu**. After they left, an international conference took place and the **Geneva Accords** established a North Vietnam under the control of Ho Chi Minh and a South Vietnam under the control of the Emperor, Bao Dai. From the beginning, the United States supplied military aid to South Vietnam. By the terms of the Geneva Accords, a national election was scheduled for 1956 on the potential unification of the entire country. However, a coup in South Vietnam overthrew the emperor and sabotaged the election plans. Nevertheless, the United States continued to support South Vietnam.

Cold War tensions also increased during the Eisenhower administration because of events in the Middle East. After Israel was declared independent in 1948, it was supported by the Americans, while the Arabs opposing Israel were supported by the Soviet Union. In 1953 the Central Intelligence Agency carried out a plan that brought the pro-American Shah of Iran back into power.

The major Middle Eastern crisis during the era was the Suez Canal Crisis. The United States had helped Egyptian leader Colonel Gamal Abdul Nasser build the Aswan Dam. The Egyptians wanted to purchase arms from the United States as well. When the Americans refused, the Egyptians went to the Soviets with the same request. When the United States (and Great Britain), in response, totally cut off all loans to Egypt, Nasser nationalized the British-owned Suez Canal. The British and the French attacked Egypt. In response to Soviet threats that they might join the conflict on the side of the Egyptians, the Americans got the British and French to retreat from Egypt.

Eisenhower and Dulles desperately wanted to prevent the spread of communism in the Middle East. In January 1957, the **Eisenhower Doctrine** was formally unveiled, which stated that American arms would be used in the region to prevent communist aggression. The Americans invoked the Eisenhower Doctrine when they landed troops in Beirut, Lebanon, in mid-1958 to put down a rebellion against the government.

The Americans were equally concerned with the spread of communism in Latin America, where America had numerous economic interests. A defensive alliance of most nations of the Western Hemisphere was signed as the **Rio Pact** in 1947. Critics would argue that the United States was never shy about throwing its weight around in the region. In 1954 the CIA helped orchestrate the overthrow of the president of Guatemala on the grounds that his administration was too friendly with the Soviet Union; during this coup, property that had been seized from American businesses was restored to American hands.

In 1959 Fidel Castro orchestrated the removal of dictator Fulgencio Batista from power. Castro soon seized American businesses located in Cuba and began trade negotiations with the Soviet Union. Thus, beginning in late 1960, the United States cut off trade with Cuba, and eventually cut off diplomatic relations with the island (a situation that still exists today).

A DANGEROUS ARMS BUILDUP

During the Eisenhower administration both the United States and the Soviet Union built up their nuclear arsenals to dangerously high levels. By August of 1953 both countries had exploded hydrogen bombs, which made the bomb used at Hiroshima look primitive in comparison. Both countries carried out nuclear tests, although in 1958 Eisenhower and Khrushchev both agreed to suspend further atomic tests in the atmosphere.

The Soviets concentrated on building up their missile capabilities in this period, causing some Americans to fear that they were falling behind, and that a "missile gap" was developing. The startling fact that the Soviets might be ahead in technology was demonstrated by their 1957 launching of **Sputnik**, the first man-made satellite that could orbit the earth. Americans were shocked as they could look up in the sky and see the satellite whiz by (in the next two years many American high schools and colleges increased the number of math and science courses students had to take so that Americans could "keep up" with the Soviets). Even more troubling was the fact that American tests to create a man-made satellite had all failed.

A final humiliation for the United States came in May of 1960, when the Russians shot down an American **U-2** spy plane. The pilot, Francis Gary Powers, was captured and taken prisoner by Soviet forces. For several days the Americans refused to admit that an American plane had even been shot down; Eisenhower eventually took full responsibility for the incident.

Toward the end of his term in office, Eisenhower warned of the extreme challenge to peace posed by the massive "military-industrial complex" that existed in America in the 1950s. The size of the military-industrial complex would certainly not decline in the 1960s.

CHAPTER REVIEW

Rapid Review Guide

To achieve the perfect 5, you should be able to explain the following:

- Winning the Cold War was the central goal of American policy for 45 years.

- The economic impact of the Cold War on American industry was enormous; many plants continued making military hardware throughout the Cold War era.

- The debate over who "started" the Cold War has occupied the minds of historians since 1945.

- Decisions made at the Yalta and Potsdam Conferences ushered in Cold War tensions between the World War II victors.

- The concept of the "iron curtain" was first articulated by Winston Churchill in 1946.

- The American strategy of containment motivated many foreign policy decisions in the Cold War era.

- The Truman Doctrine, the Marshall Plan, and NATO united America and Western Europe both militarily and economically against the Soviet Union and its satellites.

- America's resolve to oppose communism was tested during the Berlin Crisis and the Korean War.

- 1949 was a critical year in the Cold War, as the Soviet Union got the atomic bomb and mainland China turned communist.

- Some Americans feared that communists had infiltrated the American government and the entertainment industry; investigations by the House Un-American Activities Committee and Senator Joseph McCarthy were dedicated to "rooting out" communists in America.

- Under President Dwight Eisenhower, Secretary of State John Foster Dulles formulated an aggressive foreign policy that would not just contain communism but also attempt to roll communism back whenever possible.

- During the Eisenhower administration, crises in Southeast Asia, the Middle East, and Latin America further tested American resolve.

- Both the Soviet Union and the United States built up their nuclear arsenals to dangerous levels in this era.

Time Line

1945: Yalta Conference
Harry Truman becomes president
Potsdam Conference
1946: Winston Churchill gives "Iron Curtain" speech
Article by George Kennan on containment
1947: HUAC begins probe into movie industry
Introduction of Federal Employee Loyalty program
President Truman articulates Truman Doctrine
1948: Berlin Airlift
Implementation of Marshall Plan
Creation of nation of Israel
Alger Hiss implicated as a communist
1949: NATO established
Soviet Union successfully tests atomic bomb
Mainland China turns communist
1950: Joseph McCarthy gives speech on communists in the
State Department
Alger Hiss convicted of perjury
McCarran Internal Security Act enacted
Beginning of Korean War
1952: Dwight Eisenhower elected president
1953: CIA orchestrates return of Shah of Iran to power
Death of Joseph Stalin
Execution of the Rosenbergs
1954: Army-McCarthy hearings
Government in Guatemala overthrown
French defeated at Dien Bien Phu
Geneva Conference
1955: Creation of the Warsaw Pact
1956: Hungarian Revolt suppressed by Soviet Union
Suez crisis
1957: *Sputnik* launched by Soviet Union
1959: Castro comes to power in Cuba; United States halts trade
with Cuba
1960: U-2 Incident
John Kennedy elected president

✓ Review Questions

1. The Army-McCarthy hearings proved

   A. that a number of communists were serving in the United States Army
   B. that Americans were largely uninterested in the issue of communism
   C. that Eisenhower would support McCarthy at any cost
   D. that McCarthy had little proof for his claims
   E. the massive popularity of Joseph McCarthy

(Correct Answer: **D.** The hearings did much to discredit McCarthy. By this point Eisenhower had broken from McCarthy, and many Americans watched these hearing from beginning to end.)

2. The policy of containment stated that

    A. it would be possible for the United States and the Soviet Union to coexist over a long period of time
    B. America should go out and attempt to dislodge communist leaders where ever possible
    C. America should hold firm against communist encroachment in all parts of the world
    D. America should not hesitate to use atomic weapons against the Soviet Union
    E. the United States should depend on its Western European allies for help against the Soviet Union

(Correct Answer: **C.** Containment emphasized stopping communism whenever it attempted to expand; containment did not emphasize attacking communism where it already existed.)

3. America was especially interested in stopping communist expansion in Latin America because

    A. the United States had many economic interests in the region
    B. both Presidents Truman and Eisenhower were close to many of the Latin American leaders
    C. the Soviet Union expressed a special interest in expanding in this region
    D. the CIA had repeatedly failed in operations in Latin America in the past
    E. political leaders were attempting to gain support from voters of Hispanic origin in the United States

(Correct Answer: **A.** The United States had factories in and active trade relationships with many Latin American countries, and feared that communism would destroy

American economic interests in the region. The CIA had actually been quite successful in their operations in the region in the past—witness their role in Guatemala.)

4. When HUAC began their investigation of the movie industry they looked with suspicion at writers, actors, and directors who

    A. attended Communist party meetings in the 1930s
    B. wrote or appeared in movies that were critical of the "American way of life"
    C. wrote or appeared in World War II-era films that were sympathetic to the Soviet Union
    D. invoked the Fifth Amendment when testifying before HUAC
    E. All of the above

(Correct Answer: **E.** As a result of the HUAC hearings, the American movie industry changed dramatically.)

5. Republicans claimed that the Democrats were "soft on communism" for all of the following reasons *except*

    A. during the Truman administration mainland China had gone communist
    B. Alger Hiss was an advisor to Franklin Roosevelt at Yalta
    C. the Truman administration failed to establish a system to check on the possibility of communists working for the federal government
    D. decisions made by Roosevelt and Truman at the end of World War II made it easier for the Soviet Union to control Eastern Europe
    E. there were perceived communists in the State Department during the Truman administration

(Correct Answer: **C.** All of the other four were used by Republicans to say that the Democrats were indeed "soft on communism." Truman instituted a Loyalty Review Board to verify that nearly 4 million federal workers were "true Americans.")

Chapter 22

The 1950s: Prosperity and Anxiety

 There are two widely contrasting contemporary perspectives of the 1950s. For social critics who deride the political and cultural revolutionary movements of the 1960s, the 1950s serves as a period of stability and "normalcy" before the "evils" of the 1960s ("sex, drugs, and rock and roll") set in. To others, the 1950s was not a period of placid normality, but was a period where the roots of the ferment of the 1960s began to grow. From both perspectives, the 1950s is a critical decade for historical study. Both sides would agree that most people in the 1950s valued stability. After the tremendous unrest of the Great Depression and World War II, many Americans looked forward to a period free from political unrest. The key conflict of the 1950s was the conformity desired by most American versus the stirrings of individualism and rebellion found in the writers of the Beat Generation, singers like Elvis Presley, and other cultural rebels of the decade.

ECONOMIC GROWTH AND PROSPERITY

Some economists feared that the ending of World War II would lead to economic recession. Instead, the American economy enjoyed tremendous growth in the period between 1945 and 1960. In 1945 the American Gross National Product (GNP) stood at just over $200 billion; by 1960 the GNP had grown to over $500 billion dollars.

A significant reason for this growth was the ever-growing spending on defense during the Cold War era. The "military-industrial complex" (a term coined by Dwight D. Eisenhower) was responsible for billions of dollars of new spending during the 1950s (and far beyond). Millions were spent on technological research throughout the era.

Other significant factors were responsible for the economic growth of the era. Consumers had accumulated significant amounts of cash during World War II, but had little to spend it on, as the production of consumer goods was not emphasized in the war era. With the war over, consumers wanted to spend. Credit cards were available to consumers for the first time; Diner's Club cards were issued for the first time in 1950. Two industries that benefited from this were the automobile industry and the housing industry.

Many American households had never owned a new automobile since the 1920s, and in the postwar era, demand for cars was at a record high. If consumers needed assistance in deciding on which automobile to buy, they could receive assistance from the advertisers who were working for the various automobile companies (advertising reached levels in the 1950s equal to the 1920s). As the 1950s wore on, consumers could buy cars with bigger and bigger fins and fancier and fancier interiors. President Eisenhower and Congress encouraged America's reliance on the automobile when they enacted legislation authorizing the massive buildup of the interstate highway system (at the expense of the construction of an effective mass transit system). The highway system was a by-product of national defense plans of the Cold War; planners thought they would be ideal for troop movements and that airplanes could easily land on the straight sections of them.

The other industry that experienced significant growth in the postwar era was the housing construction business. There was a dire shortage of available housing in the immediate postwar era; in many cities two families living in an apartment designed for one was commonplace. Housing was rapidly built in the postwar era, and the demand was insatiable. The **GI Bill** of 1944 authorized low-interest mortgage loans for ex-servicemen (as well as subsidies for education).

William Levitt helped ease the housing crises when he built his initial group of dwellings in Levittown, New York. Several other **Levittowns** were constructed; homes were prefabricated, were built using virtual assembly line practices, and all looked remarkably the same. Nevertheless, William Levitt and developers like him began the move to the suburbs, the most significant population shift of the postwar era.

The economy was also spurred by the mass of appliances desired by consumers for their new homes in the suburbs. Refrigerators, televisions, washing machines, and countless other appliances were found in suburban households; advertising helped to ensure that the same refrigerator and television would be found in homes across the nation. Economist John Kenneth Galbraith noted that during the 1950s America had become an "**affluent society**". It should be noted, however, that even though the economy of the era enjoyed tremendous growth, the wages of many workers lagged behind spiraling prices. For many workers real income declined; this led to labor unrest in the postwar era.

POLITICAL DEVELOPMENTS OF THE POSTWAR ERA

It would have been difficult for anyone to follow Franklin Roosevelt as president, and Harry Truman, in the opinion of many, definitely suffered in comparison. Although Truman stated that "the buck stops here" when decisions were made, many critics felt that he had no consistent set of beliefs to guide him as he decided policy. Truman was considered anti-union by much of organized labor, yet he vetoed a key piece of legislation designed to take power away from labor unions. There were many strikes in 1946 and 1947, and in 1947 the **Taft-Hartley Act** was passed by the Congress over the president's veto (several biographers claim that Truman's veto was primarily symbolic and was done for political reasons). This bill stated that if any strike affected the health and safety of the country, the president could call for a 80-day cooling-off period, during which negotiations could take place and workers would go back to work, that the union contributions of individuals could not be used in federal elections, and that union leaders had to officially declare they were not communists. Unions were furious at these and other restrictions the bill imposed on them.

Truman declared a **Fair Deal policy**, in which he tried to expand the principles of the New Deal. Included in Truman's Fair Deal were plans for national health care and civil rights legislation; Truman also wanted to repeal the Taft-Hartley Act and increase government spending for public housing and education. In early 1948 he sent a civil rights bill to Congress (the first civil rights bill sent to Congress by a president since the Reconstruction). Nevertheless, Truman's popularity in early 1948 was low. Republicans rallied behind second-time candidate Thomas Dewey (who had been defeated by Franklin Roosevelt in 1944) and felt that victory would be theirs. Truman's chances seemed especially dim when Strom Thurmond also ran as a Dixiecrat candidate (in opposition to a civil rights plank in the 1948 Democratic Platform) and Henry Wallace, Truman's Secretary of Commerce, ran as a progressive. The highlight of Truman's political career was his eventual victory over Dewey; Truman's success is attributed to the fact that he campaigned more against the "do-nothing" Republican Congress than he did against Dewey. Truman could never capitalize on his 1948 victory; in the years after this victory, charges of being "soft on communism" plagued the administration.

Truman decided not to seek reelection in 1952, and former general Dwight D. Eisenhower defeated Adlai Stevenson in the general election. As president, Eisenhower saw his role as a crafter of compromise, and not as a creator of new policies. He tried to oversee a scaling back of government programs (some of these cutbacks were later rescinded) and a shift of power to the courts and to the Congress. Eisenhower also shifted much of the power traditionally held by the president to his Cabinet and other advisors. He was similar to the Republican presidents of the 1920s in that he was extremely friendly to business interests; most members of his Cabinet were businessmen. At many levels, Dwight Eisenhower was the perfect president for the 1950s.

Eisenhower's vice president was Richard Nixon, a former member of the House of Representatives and U.S. Senate from California. Nixon had first made a political name for himself in the Alger Hiss case, and his role in the 1952 campaign was largely as an anticommunist hatchet man.

Midway through the campaign it was charged that supporters had set up an illegal campaign fund for his personal use. Candidate Eisenhower gave Nixon the opportunity to give a public speech to try to save himself. During the **Checkers Speech** Nixon declared that he had done nothing wrong, that his wife Pat wore a "very respectable Republican cloth coat," and the only thing given to him had been a dog, Checkers. Nixon remained on the ticket, thus saving a political career that would make him one of the most dominant figures in American politics for the next 25 years.

CIVIL RIGHTS STRUGGLES OF THE POSTWAR PERIOD

Many black veterans who had gone overseas to fight for democracy were appalled to find that conditions for blacks had remained largely unchanged during the war years. After speaking to many leaders from NAACP and CORE in early 1948, Truman outlawed discrimination in the hiring of federal employees and ordered the end to segregation in the armed forces. Change in both the federal government and the armed forces was slow.

Black athletes had often been heroes for large segments of the black population. In the 1930s and early 1940s, it had been Joe Louis; starting in 1947 Jackie Robinson became the first black to play major league baseball, wearing the uniform of the Brooklyn Dodgers. Robinson had to endure threats and racial slurs throughout his first season. Nevertheless, Robinson maintained his dignity and was named National League Rookie of the Year in 1947.

Black leaders had long wanted to strike down the 1896 *Plessy* v. *Feguson* case, which stated that as long as black and white schools or facilities were "equal," it was not unconstitutional that they were separate. In reality, schools in many districts were separate, but they were in no way equal; white schools would get 80 or 85 percent of the financial allocations in some Southern cities and towns. The case that challenged the 1896 law came from Oliver Brown from Topeka, Kansas, who sued the Topeka school district because his daughter had to walk by an all-white school to get to the bus that took her to an all-black school on the other side of town.

The case made it all the way to the Supreme Court and was argued there by NAACP lawyer Thurgood Marshall (later a U.S. Supreme Court justice). The case was heard by a court presided over by Earl Warren, former governor of California and appointed Chief Justice by Eisenhower in 1953. By a unanimous decision, the 1954 ***Brown v. Board of Education*** decision stated that "separate but equal" was unconstitutional, and that local districts should desegregate with "all deliberate speed." Parents, government officials, and students in many districts in the South responded: "2, 4, 6, 8. We don't want to integrate!" Earl Warren was Chief Justice from 1953 to 1969, during which the Court practiced "judicial activism," making important decisions on topics such as the rights of the accused and prayer in schools.

The main battlefield for civil rights in 1955 was in Montgomery, Alabama. Rosa Parks, a secretary for the Montgomery NAACP, refused to give up her seat for a white man to sit in, and was arrested. Civil rights leaders in Montgomery began the **Montgomery bus boycott**, during which blacks in the city refused to ride the city buses; instead, they carpooled or walked. The bus company refused to change its policies; finally the Supreme Court again stepped in and stated that segregation on city buses (like in schools) was unconstitutional. A 27-year-old minister by the name of Martin Luther King, Jr. became the main spokesperson for the blacks of the city.

Another major battle for civil rights took place in Little Rock, Arkansas, in 1957. A small number of black students were set to enroll in Central High School in Little Rock in the fall of 1957. The governor of Arkansas, Orval Faubus, sent the National Guard to Central High School to keep the black students out. President Eisenhower had personally been opposed to the *Brown* v. *Board of Education* decision, but saw this as a direct challenge to a Supreme Court decision and to the authority of the federal government. Eisenhower sent in federal troops and federalized the National Guard; under armed guard, the black students attended Central High School in Little Rock, Arkansas, that year. Decisions by the federal courts outlawing various forms of segregation and federal troops in Southern states enforcing these federal court orders would become an increasingly common sight in the early 1960s.

THE CONFORMITY OF THE SUBURBS

Many young people who had grown up during the Great Depression and had come of age during World War II decided in the postwar era to move to the suburbs and to have families. It was decided by many that **domesticity** would be the avenue to happiness in the postwar world. As a result, the **baby boom** ensued, during which the birthrate soared beyond all expectations. The baby boom lasted from 1945 until 1962; during the peak of the baby boom, 1957, nearly 4 1/2 million babies were born.

The perfect place for large numbers of newly married couples to have these families was, as stated previously, in the suburbs. Many critics of the time noted the conformity of the suburbs: The houses looked much the same, everyone watched the same shows on TV, and because of TV advertising, everyone pretty much used the same appliances and wore the same clothes. Life (especially for women) was centered around their children, as there were endless rounds of PTA meetings, Little League practices, and Boy Scout meetings to get to. Social historians state that young people were using the comfort of the family and home as a buttress against any return to the disruptions they had felt earlier in their lives. William H. Whyte's *The Organizational Man,* written in 1956, analyzed the conformity and conservatism of suburban life.

Many men felt dissatisfaction with their lives in the postwar years. Many who had served in the "good war," World War II, found it difficult to return to civilian life. Many felt civilian jobs to be largely unrewarding; as the book and film *The Man in the Gray Flannel Suit* emphasized, a man who had fought in combat in World War II might find a 9-to-5 job in an office utterly unrewarding. Many men took on hunting and fishing as hobbies; here they could at least symbolically duplicate the war experience. For men the most popular magazines of the 1950s were *Field and Stream* and Hugh Hefner's *Playboy*.

Women felt equal frustration during this era. Many continued to work; yet women's magazines and other publications carried the clear message that now it was the woman's patriotic duty to return to the home and remain a housewife. Doris Day was the star of many films of the decade; she had a "girl-next-door" type of appeal, which was attractive to many women and men of the period. College women saw college as an avenue to meet potential husbands; many dropped out immediately after finding one. Many women *did* find fulfillment as mothers and by doing volunteer work in the community. Yet to others, family life was terribly unsatisfying. Women who felt dissatisfaction with their role in suburban life were routinely told by their doctors that they were neurotics; the sale of tranquilizers to women skyrocketed. Many, many suburban women experienced discontent with their lives in the 1950s and early 1960s. Betty Friedan in *The Feminine Mystique* maintained that the lack of fulfillment experienced by many housewives was the genesis of the feminist revolution of the 1960s. Friedan would found NOW (National Organization for Women) in 1966.

Stereotypically, 1950s teenagers were seen as the "silent generation," interested in only hot rod cars, school mixers, and panty raids. There is a great deal of truth to this characterization. Teenagers in this era were the first teen generation to be targeted by advertisers; many teens wore the same styles and had similar tastes as a result. Adults spent a great deal of time in ensuring that teenagers did nothing in any way rebellious. Educational films in schools taught students to obey authority, to fit in with the group, to control one's emotions, and to not even think about sex. Popular television shows of the era such as *Ozzie and Harriet* showed young people who acted in exactly that manner.

However, there was a youth rebellion in the 1950s. A few brave students would show it in their attitude and attire, using the main character played by James Dean in *Rebel Without a Cause* or Marlon Brando in *The Wild One* as models. Jackson Pollock and other artists were also at the vanguard of another form of cultural rebellion; the significance of their giant "abstract expressionist" painting moved the center of the art world to New York City. Other young people would attempt to copy the writings and attitudes of the **Beat Generation**, a group of writers and artists who rejected an American society obsessed with the atomic bomb and with material culture. In rejecting conventional society, many Beats and their followers enjoyed jazz and drugs, and studied Eastern religious thought. Key works of the Beats include Jack Kerouac's *On the Road*, in which the main characters travel simply for the joy of traveling, and *Howl,* a poem by Allen Ginsberg that outlines in graphic detail the evils of modern society and what that society does to those attempting to live decent lives in it. It should be emphasized that few young people were actual members of the Beat Generation; a larger number went to coffee-houses, dabbled in writing poetry, and sympathized with the plight of Holden Caufield in *Catcher in the Rye.*

The main form of 1950s rebellion for young people was through rock and roll. To many adults, rock and roll was immoral, was the "devil's music," and caused juvenile delinquency; a few even charged that it was sent to America by the communists as part of their plot to conquer the United States. Nevertheless, those who listened and danced to rock and roll were, at some level, rejecting the core values of 1950s America. Young people were told to "control their emotions"; it was very hard to do that when listening to "Good Golly Miss Molly" sung by Little Richard.

The connection in the minds of many adults between rock and roll and blackness accounts for the reaction of many to Elvis Presley. To many, Elvis was very, very dangerous: He covered many black songs, and exuded sex during his live and television performances. For many who feared rock and roll, the best thing that could have possibly happened was when Elvis went into the army in 1958. By the end of the decade, rock had lost much of the ferocity it possessed in 1956 to 1957.

The legacy of the cultural rebels of the 1950s would certainly have tremendous influence in the 1960s. The behavior of members of the Beat Generation would be copied by the hippies. In addition, the rules that were so carefully taught to 1950s teenagers would be very intentionally broken by many teens in the 1960s.

CHAPTER REVIEW

Rapid Review Guide

To achieve the perfect 5, you should be able to explain that

- The 1950s is viewed by some as a decade of complacency and by others as a decade of growing ferment.

- Large-scale economic growth continued throughout the 1950s, spurred by Cold War defense needs, automobile sales, housing sales, and the sale of appliances.

- The advertising industry did much to shape consumer desires in the 1950s.

- The GI Bill gave many veterans low-income mortgages and the possibility of a college education after World War II.

- Many families moved to suburbia in the 1950s; critics maintained that this increased the conformity of American society.

- During the baby boom the birthrate drastically increased; the baby boom lasted from 1945 to 1962.

- Presidents Truman and Eisenhower were both dwarfed by the memory of the personality and the policies of Franklin Roosevelt.

- Jackie Robinson did much to advance the cause of rights in the postwar era.

- *Brown* v. *Board of Education* was a tremendous victory for those pushing for school integration in the 1950s.

- The Montgomery bus boycott and the events at Central High School in Little Rock, Arkansas, demonstrated the techniques that would prove to be successful in defeating segregation.

- Many men and many women felt great frustration with suburban family life of the 1950s.

- 1950s teenagers are often called the "silent generation," although James Dean, the Beat generation of writers, and Elvis Presley all attracted followers among young people who did rebel in the 1950s.

Time Line

1944: GI Bill enacted
1947: Taft-Hartley Act enacted
      Jackie Robinson first plays for Brooklyn Dodgers
1948: Truman elected president in stunning upset
      Truman orders desegregation of armed forces
1950: Diner's Club credit card offered
1951: Publication of *Catcher in the Rye* by J. D. Salinger
1952: Dwight D. Eisenhower elected president
1953: Defense budget at $47 billion dollars
      Allen Freed begins to play rock and roll on the radio in Cleveland, Ohio
1954: *Brown* v. *Board of Education* Supreme Court decision
1955: First McDonald's opens
      Rebel Without a Cause released
      Bus boycott in Montgomery, Alabama
1956: Interstate Highway Act enacted
      Majority of U.S. workers hold white-collar jobs
      Howl by Allen Ginsberg first read
1957: Baby boom peaks
      Publication of *On the Road* by Jack Kerouac
      Resistance to school integration in Little Rock, Arkansas
1960: Three-quarters of all American homes have a TV set

Review Questions

1. Consumer spending increased in the 1950s because of all of the following *except*

   A. many Americans were once again purchasing stock
   B. many Americans were buying appliances for their homes
   C. many families were buying automobiles
   D. many Americans were buying homes
   E. advertising had a major impact on the American consumer

(Correct Answer: **A.** Americans were buying consumer goods in the postwar era. Many had money but not goods to buy in World War II. The purchase of stock would become pronounced only after this post-World War II buying spree ended.)

2. The policies of the presidency of Dwight D. Eisenhower are most similar to the policies of the presidency of

   A. Franklin Roosevelt
   B. William Howard Taft
   C. Calvin Coolidge
   D. Theodore Roosevelt
   E. Woodrow Wilson

(Correct Answer: **C.** Although each was somewhat different in style, Coolidge and Eisenhower were both friends of big business, believed in a balanced budget, and believed in a smaller role for the federal government and the presidency.)

3. How did their experiences in the Great Depression and World War II affect the generation who began to raise families in the postwar era?

   A. They turned inward to family for comfort.
   B. They were likely to want to give their children many of the things they had not been able to have.
   C. Interested in consumer goods, they would be likely to buy many things on credit.
   D. A and B above.
   E. All of the above.

(Correct Answer: **D.** Many of those who lived through the Depression were never comfortable with the idea of buying on credit; some never got credit cards at any point in their lives. Some historians say that this generation of parents spoiled their children, forming the expectations that some of these children would have as young adults in the 1960s.)

4. The most important impact of television on viewers of the early 1950s was that

   A. it provided them with comedies that allowed them to forget the difficult years of the 1950s
   B. it allowed them to receive the latest news of the day
   C. it imposed a sense of conformity on American society
   D. it fostered a growing youth culture
   E. it allowed viewers to view the realities of communism in the Soviet Union

(Correct Answer: **C.** TV viewers could get comedies and news on the radio. There was little on television in the early 1950s that specifically appealed to youth.)

5. Many Americans were especially fearful of rock and roll in the 1950s because

A. many of the musicians who played it were black
B. Elvis Presley and many of the early performers of rock and roll came from a decidedly lower-class background
C. Elvis Presley and many other early rock and roll performers came from the American South
D. the messages found in early rock and roll supported communism
E. young people were buying fewer albums by established stars

(Correct Answer: **A.** Elvis, Carl Perkins, Jerry Lee Lewis, and others were of lower-class backgrounds and were from the South, but the main objection to rock and roll was its connection to black culture—for instance, Fats Domino, Chuck Berry, and Little Richard. No known early rock and roll song supported communism.)

Chapter 23

America in an Era of Turmoil (1960–1975)

 Like the 1950s, the decade of the 1960s is perceived very differently by historians and social critics. Some perceive the changes of the 1960s as a very refreshing antidote to the suffocating conformity of the 1950s. Other observers see the revolts of the 1960s as self-indulgent, harmful to America, and the seed of much that is wrong with the United States today. All would agree that conflicts over civil rights and the Vietnam War greatly influenced virtually every major political figure and many ordinary citizens of the 1960s.

THE 1960 PRESIDENTIAL ELECTION

Many Americans perceived the election of John Kennedy over Richard Nixon in 1960 as the beginning of a new age for America. His statement during his inauguration speech "Ask not what your country can do for you—ask what you can do for your country" is remembered by millions today. At age 43, Kennedy appeared young and vigorous (especially when flanked by his wife, Jacqueline). Kennedy was the son of a former ambassador to Britain and had served as a congressman and senator from Massachusetts. He was also a Roman Catholic.

Some voters considered Richard Nixon to be "too tied to the past"; as previously mentioned, he was the vice president under Dwight D. Eisenhower. Historians note that this was the first election greatly affected by television; in four presidential debates Nixon appeared nervous and tired. Ironically, those who heard the debates on the radio didn't feel that Nixon lost them. Some historians argue that the television image projected by Nixon actually cost him the election. The 1960 popular vote was one of the closest in history; Nixon lost by only 120,000 votes (out of nearly 34 million votes cast).

DOMESTIC POLICIES UNDER KENNEDY AND JOHNSON

Early in his administration John Kennedy stated that America was on the brink of entering into a **New Frontier**. The press from this point on dubbed his domestic policies "New Frontier" policies. Kennedy had plans to stimulate the economy and to seriously attack poverty in America (*The Other America* by Michael Harrington was published in 1962; this book outlined the plight of America's poor and had a great effect on Kennedy and his circle). Kennedy supported several important domestic programs, including a Medicare program (later approved during the administration of Lyndon Johnson) and substantial federal aid to education and to urban renewal.

Very little of Kennedy's domestic agenda was adopted by Congress. His plans to cut taxes and to increase spending on education never even got out of congressional committee. One of Kennedy's domestic successes was to convince Congress to raise the minimum wage from $1.00 per hour to $1.25. Kennedy also established a Peace Corps program, in which young men and women volunteered to help residents in developing countries around the world.

One program that was considered a top priority by both Kennedy and Congress was the space program. Kennedy was barely in office when Soviet cosmonaut Yuri Gagarin became the first human to travel in space. In early May America put its first man in space (Alan Shepard), and in February 1962 John Glenn (later a United States Senator) became the first American astronaut to orbit the earth. During this era Kennedy also made the bold promise that America would land a man on the moon by the end of the 1960s.

The New Frontier programs ended permanently when John Kennedy was assassinated in Dallas, Texas, on November 22, 1963. Kennedy was in Texas to heal wounds in the local Democratic party and to rally support for the 1964 presidential election. Kennedy was riding in a motorcade through downtown Dallas when he was killed. An ex-marine named Lee Harvey Oswald was arrested and charged with Kennedy's death. Oswald never went to trial because he was shot and killed by a Dallas nightclub owner, Jack Ruby, two days later. The **Warren Commission** was formed to investigate the assassination; the report of this committee firmly supported those who said that Oswald acted alone. To this day there are those who maintain that a conspiracy was responsible for Kennedy's death.

Vice President Lyndon Johnson was sworn into office shortly after Kennedy's assassination. In the year after Kennedy's death, Johnson was able to get much of Kennedy's domestic policy plans through Congress. Johnson had been the Senate majority leader before becoming vice president, and in early 1964 was easily able to maneuver the previously rejected Kennedy tax cut through Congress.

Johnson ran for reelection against Senator Barry Goldwater in the 1964 presidential election. Goldwater was a conservative from Arizona who was too far to the right for mainstream America to accept. He spoke of using nuclear weapons in Vietnam and famously stated that "extremism in the defense of liberty is no vice." Lyndon Johnson won nearly 62 percent of the popular vote and was able to institute his own economic plans in 1965; in a speech early in that year, Johnson stated that his goal was to create a **Great Society** in America.

In speech after speech Johnson stated that it would be possible to truly end poverty in America. The Department of Housing and Urban Affairs was created as a Cabinet-level department. In 1964 Johnson had begun the **VISTA** program, which organized volunteers who worked in the poorest communities of the United States. In 1965, Congress passed Johnson's Housing and Urban Development Act, which organized the building of nearly 250,000 new housing units in America's cities and authorized over $3 billion for further urban development. Johnson's major initiatives in education authorized grants to help schools in the poorest sections of America and established **Head Start**, a program to help disadvantaged preschool students. In 1965 Johnson established a **Medicare** system, which provided hospital insurance and medical coverage for America's senior citizens, and Medicaid, which assisted Americans of any age who could not afford health insurance.

The Great Society programs of Lyndon Johnson positively impacted the lives of thousands of Americans, but frustration set in when it appeared that large amounts of poverty remained in America. In addition, the cost of Great Society programs put a strain on American taxpayers (some of whom resented the fact that their taxes were going to help poor people). However, it should be noted that the number of those living in poverty was cut by at least 40 percent by Great Society programs. Many of these programs ended up being reduced or eliminated because of the expenses of America's war in Vietnam.

THE STRUGGLE OF BLACK AMERICANS: FROM NONVIOLENCE TO BLACK POWER

As was noted in the previous chapter, Martin Luther King, Jr. emerged as a key leader of the civil rights movement during the Montgomery, Alabama bus boycott. King and other Southern clergymen founded the Southern Christian Leadership Conference (SCLC), which taught that civil rights could be achieved through nonviolent protest. SCLC leaders taught that violence could never be utilized to achieve their goals, no matter what the circumstance.

Many younger blacks were eager for the fight for civil rights to develop at a quicker pace. In 1960 the Student Nonviolent Coordinating Committee (SNCC) was formed; its leaders were not ministers, and they demanded immediate, not gradual, change. During the first years of its existence, SNCC attracted both black and white members; many of the whites were college students from Northern universities.

An effective technique utilized by the civil rights movement in the early 1960s was the <u>sit-in</u>. Blacks were not allowed to eat at the lunch counters of many Southern stores, even though blacks could buy merchandise at these stores. Black and white civil rights workers would sit down at these lunch counters; when they were denied service, they continued to sit there (preventing other paying customers from taking their spaces). Picketers would oftentimes march outside the store in question. Those participating in sit-ins received tremendous verbal and physical harassment from other whites, yet the tactic of the sit-in helped to integrate dozens of Southern establishments in the first several years of the 1960s.

In May 1961 the Congress for Racial Equality sponsored the <u>Freedom Rides</u>. During the previous year the Supreme Court had ruled that bus stations and waiting rooms in these stations had to be integrated. On the Freedom Rides, both black and white volunteers started in Washington and were determined to ride through the South to see if cities had complied with the Supreme Court legislation. In Anniston, Alabama, a white mob greeted the bus, beating many of the freedom riders and burning the bus. Freedom rides continued throughout the summer; almost all riders experienced some violence or were arrested.

The Freedom Rides introduced an important influence into the civil rights struggle in the South: the public opinion of the rest of the country. Many Americans were horrified at the violence they witnessed; many called their representatives in Congress to urge that the federal government do more to support the freedom riders. By the end of the summer, marshals from the Justice Department were in every city the Freedom Ride buses passed through to ensure a lack of violence.

Under Attorney General Robert Kennedy the federal government became much more involved in enforcing federal civil rights guidelines and court rulings. In September of 1962 President Kennedy nationalized the Alabama National Guard and sent in federal marshals to suppress protesters and allow James Meredith to be the first black to take classes at the University of Mississippi. In Birmingham, Alabama, city officials turned fire hoses and trained dogs on civil rights protesters; the broadcast of these events to the entire nation again created a widespread outrage against those in the South who were opposing court-ordered integration.

President Kennedy went very slowly on civil rights issues, but in the summer of 1963, he presented to Congress a wide-ranging civil rights bill that would have withheld large amounts of federal funding from states that continued to practice segregation. To muster support for this bill, civil rights leaders organized the August 28, 1963 <u>March on Washington</u>. More than 200,000 people showed up to protest for civil rights legislation; it was at this rally that Martin Luther King made his very famous "I have a dream" speech.

In 1964 Lyndon Johnson presented to Congress the most wide-ranging civil rights bill since Reconstruction. The <u>Civil Rights Act of 1964</u> stated that the same standards had to be used to register white and black voters, that racial discrimination could not be used by employers to hire workers, that discrimination was illegal in all public locations, and that an

Equal Employment Opportunity Commission would be created. The Voting Rights Act of 1965 outlawed measures such as literacy tests, which had been used to prevent blacks from voting. Passage of this bill was aided by the public sentiment that followed the revelation that three civil rights workers had been killed the previous summer while attempting to register voters in Mississippi. Television reports of violence against civil rights workers, such as was seen during Martin Luther King's march in Selma, Alabama, in 1965, convinced many Americans that additional civil rights legislation was necessary.

Many blacks who lived in poverty in Northern cities believed that the civil rights movement was doing little or nothing for them. In August 1965 riots broke out in the Watts section of Los Angeles; Chicago, Newark, and Detroit soon experienced similar riots. The **Kerner Commission** was authorized to investigate the cause of these riots, and stated that black poverty and the lack of hope in the black urban communities were the major causes of these disturbances. The Kerner Commission reported that two societies existed in America, one white and rich, and the other poor and black.

One group that preached opposition to integration was the **Nation of Islam**. This organization (also called the Black Muslims) preached that it was to the benefit of white society to keep blacks poor and in ghettoes, and that for blacks to improve their position they would have to do it themselves. Malcolm X would become the most famous representative of this group, preaching **black nationalism**. Eventually Malcolm X rejected the more extreme concepts of the Nation of Islam, and he was killed in February 1965.

The ideas of black nationalism exerted a great deal of influence on many of the younger members of SNCC. One, Stokely Carmichael, began to urge blacks to take up arms to defend themselves against whites; Carmichael also orchestrated the removal of all whites from SNCC. In addition, Carmichael began to urge SNCC members to support **black power**; this concept stated that blacks should have pride in their history and their heritage, and that blacks should create their own society apart from the all-controlling white society.

The most visible group supporting black power were the **Black Panthers**. This San Francisco group, founded by Bobby Seale and Huey Newton, had a militarist image. Several members died after vicious gun battles with police. At the same time, the Black Panthers set up programs that gave food to the poorest members of San Francisco's black population and established schools to teach black history and culture to the children in the community. However, the image of this organization was greatly damaged by its violent reputation.

THE RISE OF FEMINISM

Another group that fought for additional freedoms in the 1960s were women. As discussed in the previous chapter, many women felt extreme frustration with their lives in the 1950s. Some college-aged women were active in the civil rights movement in the early 1960s, but oftentimes felt frustrated when they were always the ones asked to make the coffee or do the typing.

In the mid-1960s even women in suburbia began to notice that the frustrations they had were shared by many of the women living around them. Women's support groups became common on both college campuses and in suburban communities. A pivotal book that helped bolster this growing **feminist** movement was **_The Feminine Mystique_** by Betty Friedan.

In 1966 NOW (**National Organization for Women**) was founded by Friedan. NOW was a decidedly middle-class organization and was dedicated to getting equal pay for women at work and to ending images in the media that objectified women. In 1972 Gloria Steinem founded the feminist magazine **_Ms_**. The key Supreme Court decision of the era concerning women was the 1973 **_Roe v. Wade_** ruling, which, with some restrictions, legalized abortion. Many feminists pushed for the passage of an Equal Rights Amendment, but this amendment was never ratified by enough states to become part of the Constitution.

Other groups protested for equal rights during this period. The **American Indian Movement** (AIM) wanted Native Americans to be knowledgeable about their heritage, and also influenced various tribes to mount legal battles to get back land that had been illegally taken from them. A standoff between AIM members and government authorities took place at Wounded Knee, South Dakota, in 1973; as a result, legislation passed in the 1970s gave Native Americans more autonomy in tribal matters.

Latino groups also began to protest for rights in this era. A large number of Latinos were employed as migrant farm workers in California; Cesar Chavez organized the **United Farm Workers** against farmers (especially grape growers) in California. Environmental groups also became active in this era. _Silent Spring_ by Rachel Carson came out in 1962 and warned about the dangers of DDT. Many also protested throughout the decade against the dangers of nuclear power.

THE COLD WAR IN THE 1960S

Cold War tensions and fears continued to dominate in the early 1960s. The fear of the bomb continued unabated; movies such as _Fail-Safe_ and _Dr. Strangelove_ explored a world where an "accident" with the bomb might occur. Both the United States and the Soviet Union openly tested nuclear weapons during 1961 and 1962.

A plan to liberate Cuba from Castro had actually been formulated during the Eisenhower administration; by this plan the CIA would train Cubans living in America to invade Cuba, and the United States would provide air cover. This operation, called the **Bay of Pigs**, took place in April 1961 and was a complete fiasco, with virtually the entire invasion force killed or captured by Castro's forces. The Bay of Pigs was a major embarrassment for the Kennedy administration in their first months in office.

In Berlin, refugees from the East continued to try to escape to West Berlin on a daily basis; in August of 1961 the East Germans and the Soviets constructed the concrete **Berlin Wall**, dividing the two halves of the city. The issue that almost brought the world to World War III was not in Europe, however; it was in Cuba. In mid-October of 1962 American reconnaissance flights over Cuba indicated Soviet-made missile sights under construction. In the **Cuban Missile Crisis** President Kennedy established a naval blockade of Cuba and told Soviet leader Nikita Khrushchev to remove the missiles from Cuba. Khrushchev backed down and removed the missiles, averting the potential of world war. It is known now that if American forces had landed in Cuba, Soviet authorities were seriously contemplating the use of tactical nuclear weapons against them. Luckily, effective diplomacy prevented the outbreak of a potentially catastrophic crisis. Shortly afterward the United States and the Soviet Union signed a Limited Test Ban Treaty, and a "hot line" was installed, connecting the White House and the Kremlin so that future crises could be dealt with quickly.

THE VIETNAM WAR AND ITS IMPACT ON AMERICAN SOCIETY

Since the 1950s the United States had supported noncommunist South Vietnam against the North, led by communist and nationalist Ho Chi Minh. The South Vietnamese government also had to fight the **Vietcong**, communist guerrillas who lived in South Vietnam but supported the North. During the Kennedy administration the number of American advisors in Vietnam increased. American officials became increasingly suspicious of the effectiveness of South Vietnamese president Diem; in the fall of 1963 these officials supported (or orchestrated, depending on which historian you read) the assassination of Diem.

Shortly after becoming president, Lyndon Johnson decided that to achieve victory, the war in Vietnam had to be intensified. In August 1964, Johnson announced to the nation that light North Vietnamese gunboats had fired on American destroyers in the Gulf of Tonkin, which is in international waters. Some historians are skeptical that these events ever took place. Nevertheless, Congress passed the **Gulf of Tonkin** Resolution, which gave the president the power to "prevent further aggression" in Vietnam; this resolution allowed the president to control the war without the necessity of consulting Congress.

Throughout 1965, 1966, and 1967, America continued to increase its commitment in Vietnam; by early 1968 nearly 540,000 American soldiers were stationed in Vietnam. Beginning in 1965 bombing campaigns against North Vietnam became commonplace. American soldiers in Vietnam became increasingly frustrated by the jungle tactics used by their enemies, by the fact that one's friend by day might be one's enemy by night, and by the seeming lack of effectiveness of the South Vietnamese army.

A key battle of the war was the **Tet Offensive**, which began on January 30, 1968. During the first day of the Vietnamese new year, the Vietcong initiated major offensives in cities across South Vietnam. Saigon, the capital, was even attacked, and for several hours the Vietcong held the American embassy. In the end, the Vietcong and North Vietnamese suffered major losses as a result of the Tet Offensive. Nevertheless, this was the battle that began to conclusively turn American public opinion against the war. The sights on television of American forces trying to recapture their own embassy back certainly made many question the idea that "victory was just around the corner," which is what was being told to the American people by military and civilian officials.

The Vietnam War drove Lyndon Johnson from the White House. Diaries of several in Johnson's inner circle show that he was consumed by the war. In February 1968 Johnson began his reelection bid by taking on Senator Eugene McCarthy of Minnesota, who was running on a peace ticket, in the New Hampshire presidential primary. Johnson won, but got only 48 percent of the total votes to 42 percent for McCarthy. Johnson considered this a humiliation, and one month later pulled out of the presidential race. Johnson endorsed Vice President Hubert Humphrey for president. By this point Robert Kennedy had also announced his candidacy.

Throughout 1968 support for the Vietnam War continued to fade in America. The Republican candidate for president, Richard Nixon, gained support when he proclaimed that he had a "secret plan" to end the war. Reports of the brutality of the war also shocked many Americans. Many were disturbed to find that Americans were using **napalm**, a substance that sticks to the skin and burns, on civilian villages. The story of the 1968 **My Lai Massacre**, where nearly 200 Vietnamese women, children, and elderly men were murdered by American soldiers, horrified many Americans. Some Americans began to wonder what the United States was doing in Vietnam, and what the war was doing to the United States.

The student protest movement also began to furiously campaign against the war. Student activists had previously been active in the civil rights movement. In 1960 the **Students for a Democratic Society** (SDS) organization was formed. The ***Port Huron Statement*** was the founding document of this organization, and called for a less materialistic society that encouraged "participatory democracy." SDS would become one of the major student organizations opposing the war.

The **Free Speech Movement** had grown at the University of California at Berkeley in 1964 when school officials refused to allow political materials to be distributed on campus. Campus buildings were occupied, as students demanded college courses more relevant to their lives. Tactics used by Berkeley students were copied by students at colleges across the country.

The Vietnam War greatly expanded the student protest movement in America. Many students were passionately opposed to the war on moral grounds; to be fair, others were part of the movement because they didn't want to be drafted. Television pictures of young men burning their draft cards were commonplace. Antiwar demonstrations that had attracted a few hundred people in 1964 were now attracting thousands; a 1967 antiwar rally drew 500,000 people to Central Park in New York.

1968 saw the protests grow, both in numbers and in intensity. Events of 1968 convinced many young people that getting involved in mainstream politics (as Eugene McCarthy had tried to get them to do) was fruitless. Martin Luther King and Robert Kennedy were killed in the spring of that year; to many, that left the presidential race between two representatives of the old guard, Richard Nixon and Hubert Humphrey. What, many students asked, was the point of even getting involved in politics if candidates like that were the end result? In the spring of 1968 major protests broke out at Columbia University; in August as protesters chanted "the whole world is watching," Chicago police officers brutally beat students and others who had shown up to protest at the Democratic National Convention. By 1969 disputes over how much violence is acceptable began to tear SDS apart as well.

Another group of revolutionaries in the 1960s rejected political involvement and supported cultural revolution instead. Members of the **counterculture** rejected America and its values as much as antiwar protesters did, but believed that personal revolution was most vital. These "hippies," or countercultural rebels, often had little to do with members of SDS; the revolution of the hippies consisted of growing one's hair long, listening to the "right" music, and partaking of psychedelic drugs. Timothy Leary and other proponents of LSD implored young people to "tune in, turn on, and drop out." Sexual freedom was also commonplace in the counterculture. A birth control pill had been approved by the federal government in 1960; a button worn by many in the 1960s stated "If It Feels Good, Do It!" The Mecca for many of these rebels in 1967 was San Francisco, where the music and lifestyle of groups such as the Grateful Dead personified the counterculture of the 1960s. The **Woodstock Music Festival** of 1969 was the most outward manifestation of the "peace and love" rebels of the 1960s. For members of the counterculture, personal rebellion was a much more valid form of rebellion than political rebellion; it should be remembered that Pete Townshend of "The Who" threw radical political organizer Abbie Hoffman off the stage at Woodstock.

Richard Nixon was elected in November of 1968, and soon announced his policy of **Vietnamization** of the war, which consisted of training the South Vietnamese army and gradually pulling American forces out. By 1972 American forces in Vietnam only numbered 24,000 (as the numbers of soldiers in Vietnam lessened, so did the antiwar protests). In April of 1970, however, Nixon announced that to support the South Vietnamese government, massive bombing of the North was needed and that the war needed to be extended into Cambodia to wipe out communist bases there. Colleges campuses across the country, for one last time, joined together in massive protest. At **Kent State University** four students were killed by National Guardsmen who opened fire on the protesters; two students were killed at Jackson State University in Mississippi. American public opinion at this point was deeply divided on the war; two days after Kent State nearly 100,000 construction workers marched in New York City for the war.

In 1971 the **Pentagon Papers** were leaked by a former Department of Defense employee, Daniel Ellsburg. The Pentagon Papers revealed that the government had deceived the American public and the Congress about Vietnam as early as 1964. By this point, most Americans awaited the end of American involvement in the war.

America was involved in negotiations with the North Vietnamese in Paris. Negotiations intensified in December 1972 when President Nixon ordered the heaviest bombing of the war against North Vietnam. In January 1973 it was announced that American forces would leave Vietnam in 60 days, that all American prisoners would be returned, and that the boundary between North and South Vietnam would be respected. On March 29, 1973, the last American soldiers left Vietnam; 60,000 Americans had died there. On April 30, 1975, the North Vietnamese captured Saigon, the capital of South Vietnam, ending the Vietnam War. The last Americans had left the country one day earlier.

CHAPTER REVIEW

Rapid Review Guide

To achieve the perfect 5, you should be able to explain the following:

- The events that dramatically altered America including protests and cultural rebellion in the 1960s are seen by some in a positive light and others in a negative light.

- John Kennedy projected a new image of presidential leadership, although few of his domestic programs were actually passed by Congress.

- The Cuban Missile Crisis was the critical foreign policy crisis of the Kennedy administration, and may have brought the world close to world war.

- After Kennedy's death Lyndon Johnson was able to get Congress to pass his Great Society domestic programs, which included Head Start and Medicare.

- Nonviolence remained the major tactic of the civil rights movement throughout the 1960s, although some black leaders began to advocate "black power."

- Women strove to achieve equal rights in the 1960s through the National Organization for Women and consciousness-raising groups.

- Lyndon Johnson determined early in his presidency that an escalation in the war in Vietnam would be necessary, and more materials and men went to Vietnam from 1965–1968.

- The military in Vietnam was frustrated by the military tactics of the enemy and by faltering support at home.

- The Tet Offensive did much to turn American public opinion against the war.

- Student protesters held increasingly large demonstrations against the war; SDS was the main organization of student activists.

- Members of the counterculture advocated a personal and not a political rebellion in this era.

- Richard Nixon removed American troops from Vietnam through the policy of Vietnamization; the South Vietnamese government fell two years after American troops departed.

Time Line

1960: John Kennedy elected president
    Sit-ins beginning
    Students for a Democratic Society (SDS) formed
    Student Nonviolent Coordinating Committee (SNCC) formed
1961: Freedom Rides
    Bay of Pigs invasion
    Construction of Berlin Wall
    First American travels in space
1962: James Merideth enters University of Mississippi
    SDS issues *Port Huron Statement*
    Silent Spring by Rachel Carson published
    Cuban Missile Crisis
    The Other America by Michael Harrington published
1963: John Kennedy assassinated; Lyndon Johnson becomes president
    Civil rights march on Washington
    The Feminine Mystique by Betty Friedan published
    President Diem ousted in South Vietnam
1964: Beginning of Johnson's War on Poverty programs
    Civil Rights Act enacted
    Free Speech Movement at Berkeley begins
    Tonkin Gulf Resolution
    Johnson reelected
1965: Elementary and Secondary Education Act passed
    Johnson sends more troops to Vietnam
    Voting Rights Act passed
    Murder of Malcolm X
    Watts riots burn section of Los Angeles
1966: Stokely Carmichael calls for "black power"
    Formation of Black Panther party
    Formation of National Organization for Women (NOW)
1967: Riots in many American cities
    Antiwar demonstrations intensify

1968: Martin Luther King assassinated
Robert Kennedy assassinated
Student protests at Columbia University
Battle between police and protesters at Democratic
National Convention
Richard Nixon elected president
American Indian Movement (AIM) founded
Tet Offensive
My Lai Massacre
1969: Woodstock Music Festival
1970: United States invades Cambodia
Killings at Kent State, Jackson State
1971: *Pentagon Papers* published by the *New York Times*
1972: Nixon reelected
1973: Vietnam cease-fire announced; American troops leave Vietnam
Roe v. *Wade* decision
1975: South Vietnam falls to North Vietnam, ending the Vietnam War

✓ Review Questions

1. The initial fate of the Freedom Riders demonstrated that

   A. Southerners had largely accepted Northern orders to integrate bus stations and other public facilities
   B. state governments were at the forefront in the enforcement of civil rights laws
   C. television news broadcasts had a powerful hold on the American public
   D. by 1961 the federal government was committed to vigorously protecting the civil rights of all citizens
   E. some Southern governors were beginning to moderate their positions

(Correct Answer: **C.** The images of burned buses and beaten freedom riders horrified many Americans. At this point neither the federal or state governments protected the rights of freedom riders.)

2. The Tet Offensive demonstrated that

   A. American forces were fairly close to a decisive victory in Vietnam
   B. military and civilian officials had been less than candid with the American people on the progress of the war
   C. the Vietcong could defeat American soldiers in the battlefield
   D. cooperation between Americans and the South Vietnamese army was improving
   E. despite much criticism, the policies of General Westmoreland were proving to be effective

(Correct Answer: **B.** The Tet Offensive was a military defeat for the Vietcong. However, it did prove that victory was not "around the corner," which is what many military officials were publicly claiming.)

3. The membership rolls of Students for a Democratic Society were at an all-time high when

A. the struggles of the civil rights movement in the South were shown on national television
B. Nixon invaded Cambodia
C. Nixon intensified the bombing to its highest levels of the war in 1972
D. more young men were being sent to Vietnam between 1965 and 1967
E. the organization began to plan violent acts against the government

(Correct Answer: **D.** By the time of the invasion of Cambodia and the massive bombing at the end of the war, SDS had split into factions. The civil rights movement attracted a relatively small number of new members to SDS.)

4. Some Northern blacks were attracted to the call for "black power" for all of the following reasons *except*

A. Martin Luther King and others in the civil rights movement seemed more interested in improving the position of Southern blacks
B. ghetto sections of Northern cities remained poor, and many residents there felt little hope
C. Malcolm X and Stokely Carmichael evoked powerful images of black pride

D. vast numbers of Northern blacks had joined the Nation of Islam
E. economic despair still gripped many blacks living in Northern cities

(Correct Answer: **D.** All of the other reasons caused some Northern blacks to abandon Martin Luther King's call for integration. Only a small proportion of blacks ever joined the Nation of Islam.)

5. Highlights for feminist leaders of this era included all of the following *except*

A. the founding of *Ms.*
B. the formation of NOW
C. the drive for passage of the Equal Rights Amendment
D. the increased awareness of "women's issues" in society
E. the publication of *The Feminine Mystique*

(Correct Answer: **C.** After a long struggle, the drive to get the ERA in the Constitution was finally abandoned when it became obvious that not enough state legislatures would ever pass it.)

Chapter 24

America from 1968 to 1988: Decline and Rebirth

 Some historians claim that the accomplishments of the presidency of Richard Nixon are oftentimes overlooked. Nixon opened diplomatic relations with China, improved relations with the Soviet Union, and began to break the Democratic stranglehold on politics in the South that had existed since the New Deal. Despite these developments, Richard Nixon will always be associated with the Watergate scandal. Watergate began a period where faith in the national government sharply declined; this lasted through the presidencies of Gerald Ford and Jimmy Carter. With the election of Ronald Reagan, many Americans began to "have faith in America again." Just as Nixon began a new relationship with China, under Reagan, America entered into a more positive relationship with its formal rival, the Soviet Union.

THE PRESIDENCY OF RICHARD NIXON

Richard Nixon's election to the presidency in 1968 capped one of the greatest comeback stories in American political history. Nixon's political obituary had been written after successive defeats in 1960 (when he was defeated by John Kennedy for the presidency) and in 1962 (after being defeated by Pat Brown for governor of California; he informed the press on election night that "you won't have Nixon to kick around anymore," as he was resigning from politics).

Nixon was one of the most interesting men to be elected to the presidency in the twentieth century. He was never comfortable with large groups of people, and even in staged photo events sometimes appeared uncomfortable and out of place (such as the time he was pictured walking "informally" along the beach in dress shoes). Nixon was convinced that large numbers of the news media and many members of the Congress were his enemies. He relied on a small group of close-knit advisors, including H. R. Haldeman, his Chief of Staff, and John Ehrlichman, his Advisor for Domestic Affairs.

Nixon's Domestic Policies

As mentioned in the previous chapter, the Vietnam War took up large amounts of Nixon's time and energies. However, other potentially crucial crises also existed. As Nixon entered office in 1969, inflation was growing rapidly, unemployment was rising, the gross national product was experiencing a lack of growth, and the United States had a rather substantial trade deficit. Some of these economic problems can be attributed to the administration of Lyndon Johnson; paying for Great Society programs and the Vietnam War at the same time created serious strains on the federal budget.

At first, Nixon tried to cut government spending and raising taxes; this policy only worsened the economy. The president then imposed a 90-day freeze on prices and wages; after these measures he also established mandatory guidelines for wage and price increases. By 1971 Nixon also directed that a program of **deficit spending** begin. This was somewhat similar to the approach utilized by Franklin Roosevelt in attacking the economic problems of the Great Depression.

The "Southern Strategy" of Richard Nixon

Southern whites had voted firmly Democratic since the Reconstruction era. In the 1968 presidential election cracks in this relationship between the Democratic party and the South began to show. George Wallace, former governor of Alabama, broke from the party and in 1968 ran for president as a candidate of the American Independence Party. He picked up 13.5 percent of the popular vote (a large percentage of these from the South); this aided Richard Nixon in his victory over Hubert Humphrey.

Richard Nixon decided to take decisive measures to appeal to these Southern whites and win them over to the Republican party. Nixon's "**Southern Strategy**" included delaying school desegregation plans (that had been ordered by a federal court) in Mississippi and attempting to block an extension of the Voting Rights Act of 1965. Nixon also attempted to block school integration by busing after the Supreme Court had endorsed busing as a method to achieve integration. Under Nixon the Supreme Court also became much more conservative, especially with Warren Burger as the new Chief Justice (nevertheless, it should be remembered that in **_Roe v. Wade_** this court outlawed state legislation opposing abortion).

Nixon's Foreign Policy

The greatest achievements of the Nixon presidency were undoubtedly in the area of foreign affairs. In formulating foreign policy, Nixon was aided by former Harvard professor Henry Kissinger, his National Security Advisor and beginning in 1973 his Secretary of State. Kissinger had conducted many of the negotiations with the North Vietnamese that allowed American troops to leave Vietnam in 1973. Nixon greatly trusted the judgment of Kissinger on foreign policy affairs.

Nixon's greatest accomplishments included better relationships with both the Soviet Union and China. Nixon had been a fierce anticommunist in the 1950s, but during his first term in office, he instituted a policy of "**détente**" with the Soviet Union. The reduced tensions that this policy created were a welcome relief from the fierce anticommunist rhetoric that had existed through most of the Kennedy and Johnson administrations.

In addition, Nixon realized the foolishness of continued **nuclear proliferation**. He visited the Soviet Union in 1972 and, during discussions with Soviet Premier Leonid Brezhnev, agreed to halt the continued buildup of nuclear weapons. The **SALT I** treaty (Strategic Arms Limitation Talks) was historic, as for the first time the two superpowers agreed not to produce any more nuclear ballistic missiles and to reduce their arsenals of antiballistic missiles to 200 per side.

A journey that Nixon took earlier in 1972 was even more significant. During much of the 1950s and 1960s Nixon spoke about the need to support Nationalist China (who lived on the island of Taiwan) and the need to be vigilant against the expansion of "Red" China (who controlled the Chinese mainland). Henry Kissinger was an admirer of **realpolitik** and convinced Nixon that a new approach to Communist China was necessary. Kissinger maintained that it was foolish to think that the Communist Chinese would ever be overthrown, and that it would be to America's advantage to recognize that fact. In addition, Nixon felt that a friendlier China could be used as a wedge to get future concessions from the Soviet Union.

In February 1972, Nixon and Kissinger made a historic trip to Communist China. Meetings were held with Chinese leader Mao Tse-tung and other officials. At these meetings it was decided that trade talks between the two countries would begin, and that cultural exchanges would start almost immediately. Most importantly, Nixon agreed to support the admission of Communist China to the United Nations (going against what had been traditional U.S. policy for the entire Cold War period).

THE WATERGATE AFFAIR

As a result of his foreign policy successes, Nixon's ratings in public opinion polls were extremely high as the presidential election of 1972 approached. Nixon's opponent was Democrat George McGovern, who campaigned for a faster pullout from Vietnam. Nixon's victory in 1972 was truly staggering; in the Electoral College he won 521 to 17.

The one-sided nature of the 1972 election makes the desires of Richard Nixon and his campaign associates for the events leading up to the **Watergate Affair** difficult to understand. Nixon's paranoid view of the American political system colored the decisions that he and his aids made in the months leading up to the 1972 campaign. In 1971 Nixon created an "enemies list" and suggested various forms of harassment that could be used on everyone on the list (wiretaps, investigating income tax records, etc.). On this list were politicians (Senator Edward Kennedy), newsmen (Daniel Schorr of CBS News), and even sports personalities (New York Jets quarterback Joe Namath).

After the Pentagon Papers were released in the spring of 1971 by Daniel Ellsburg, a former employee of the State Department, a special unit to "plug" leaks was formed by the White House. This unit was known as the **Plumbers**, and included Howard Hunt, a former member of the CIA, and Gordon Liddy, a former agent of the FBI. One of the first actions of the Plumbers was to break into Daniel Ellsburg's psychiatrist's office to try to find incriminating information about Ellsburg. Other aides working for CREEP (the Committee to Reelect the President) performed various "dirty tricks" on political opponents. In the 1972 Democratic primaries, CREEP operatives on two occasions ordered 200 pizzas delivered to an opposing campaign office unannounced, "canceled" political rallies for opponents without the opponents knowing it, and with no basis whatsoever, charged that Democratic Senator Edmund Muskie had made negative remarks about French Canadians living in New Hampshire.

On the night of June 16, 1972, James McCord, an assistant in the office of security of CREEP, led four other men into Democratic National Committee headquarters at the Watergate Hotel in Washington, DC. The goal of this group was to photocopy important files and to install electronic surveillance devices in the Democratic offices. The five were caught and arrested; money they had on their person could be traced back to CREEP. This is the beginning of the chain of events that came to be called **Watergate** or the Watergate scandal.

Five days later Nixon became part of the illegal cover-up of the Watergate break-in. On that day he publicly announced that the White House had absolutely nothing to do with the break-in. More importantly, on the same day Nixon contacted friendly CIA officials and tried to convince them to call the FBI and tell the FBI to cease its investigation of Watergate. This was the first illegal action taken by Nixon in the Watergate Affair.

In the months before the 1972 presidential election, "hush money" was paid to the Watergate burglars and several officials of CREEP committed perjury by denying under oath that Nixon had any knowledge of the break-in.

The Watergate story most assuredly would have died if not for the efforts of reporters Carl Bernstein and Bob Woodward of the *Washington Post*. Despite threats from the White House and other political operatives, the two reporters continued to follow the story. They were aided by a secret source named "Deep Throat," who provided them valuable background information about the case.

James McCord and the other Watergate burglars were found guilty in their January 1973 trial; no mention of White House involvement was made by any of the defendants. It later became known that Nixon personally approved the payment of hush money to one of the defendants during the trial. In February the Senate Select Committee on Presidential Campaign Activities began to investigate the Watergate Affair. During these hearings White House attorney John Dean testified that Nixon was involved in the cover-up and another aide revealed the existence of a taping system in the Oval Office that recorded all conversations held by the President. H. R. Haldeman, John Ehrlichman, and Attorney General Richard Kleindienst all resigned in an attempt to save the presidency of Richard Nixon. Nixon's public approval ratings began to fall.

In an effort to quell the firestorm building around him, Nixon appointed a **special prosecutor** to investigate the Watergate Affair. Almost immediately after being appointed, Archibald Cox demanded that the White House hand over the tapes of all taped conversations.

After losing a court argument that the tapes should be exclusive property of the president, Nixon ordered the new Attorney General to fire Cox. Richardson refused, as did his assistant, William Ruckelhaus, and both resigned. Solicitor General Robert Bork (who would later be an unsuccessful Supreme Court nominee) finally fired Cox. All of these events took place on October 20, 1973, and are referred to as the "**Saturday Night Massacre**."

After these events the president's approval rating dipped dramatically. The Judiciary Committee of the House of Representatives began to discuss the formal procedures for impeaching a president. Nixon turned over heavily edited transcripts of most of the tapes to Leon Jaworski, Cox's replacement; many of the vulgar comments made by Nixon on the tapes shocked both opponents and supporters. Also during this period it was revealed that Spiro Agnew, Nixon's vice president, had taken bribes as an elected official in Maryland before he was vice president. Agnew resigned in October of 1973, and it was two months before his appointed successor, Congressman Gerald Ford of Michigan, was approved as the new vice president.

During the following months the calls for Nixon's resignation increased. In April 1974, Nixon released more, but not all, of the tapes requested by the special prosecutor. In July the House Judiciary Committee formally approved three articles of impeachment, stating that the president had ignored their subpoenas, had misused presidential power, and had obstructed justice. Debate was to begin in the full House on impeachment; Nixon's supporters admitted that Nixon would have been impeached.

Before House hearings could begin, the White House finally complied with a Supreme Court order to release all remaining tapes. One had an 18½-minute gap on it; another was the "smoking gun" that Nixon's opponents had been looking for. Nixon had always denied that he had known about the cover-up, yet a tape made one week after the break-in demonstrated that Nixon was actually participating in the cover-up at that point.

With no support left, Nixon finally resigned on August 9, 1974. Gerald Ford took over as president and announced that "our long national nightmare is over." In retrospect, the Watergate Affair was one of the low points of American political history in the twentieth century, rivaled only by the scandals of the presidency of Warren G. Harding.

THE PRESIDENCY OF GERALD FORD

As described previously, Gerald Ford came to the presidency under the worst of circumstances. To his advantage, he was incredibly well liked in Washington and totally free of any hint of scandal. However, during his time in office, Ford seemed to lack a grand "plan" for what he wanted to accomplish. Several historians note that Ford's presidency was doomed from September 8, 1974, when he pardoned Richard Nixon for any crimes that he might have committed. This soured many Americans on Ford; his later explanation was that up until that point virtually his entire time in office was spent dealing with Watergate-related affairs, and that the only way to move past that was to pardon the former president. The public expressed their opinion in the fall congressional elections, when many Democrats were swept into office.

Ford became the second American president to visit China, and the first to visit Japan. It should be remembered it was during the Ford administration that South Vietnam fell to the North Vietnamese and the Vietcong. The last American troops had left in 1973; by 1975 the North Vietnamese army began to occupy several major South Vietnamese cities. Ford toyed with the idea of sending in troops to aid the South Vietnamese, but ended up asking Congress for a major aid package for South Vietnam. By this point the vast majority of Americans wanted nothing to do with the situation in Southeast Asia, and Congress defeated Ford's request. In late April the North Vietnamese were closing in on Saigon; some of the most gripping photographs of the era were photos of American helicopters evacuating Americans and Vietnamese who had worked for them from the roof of the American embassy in Saigon one day before the city was captured by the North Vietnamese.

The major problem that Ford's presidency faced was the economy. The American economy had always suffered from either unemployment or inflation; during the Ford administration the economy suffered from both. This economic situation was termed **stagflation**. Critics of Ford claimed that his tactics were no different than those of Herbert Hoover, as he tried to restore confidence in the economy by asking people to wear "WIN" buttons ("Whip Inflation Now") and to voluntarily spend less to lessen the effects of inflation. Ford pushed for tax cuts and for less government spending; despite these various approaches, by 1975 unemployment in America stood near 10 percent and inflation remained a problem. On several occasions Ford fell or tripped in public settings, which did not improve the image of the presidency.

In the race for the Republican presidential nomination, in 1976 President Ford was able to fend off the campaign of former Governor of California and actor Ronald Reagan. In the election Ford faced the former Governor of Georgia, Jimmy Carter. During the campaign Carter continually stressed that he would be an outsider in Washington, and not tied to any of the messes that had gone on in Washington since 1968; to many in a post-Watergate America, this message sold perfectly. In addition, Ford did not help himself in the campaign by making several misstatements, such as claiming in one debate that Eastern Europe was not controlled by the Soviet Union. Carter won the presidency by a fairly narrow margin by keeping the New Deal Democratic coalition together. Some Southerners who had voted for Nixon in 1968 and 1972 returned to vote Democrat in 1976 because of Carter's Southern roots.

THE PRESIDENCY OF JIMMY CARTER

Jimmy Carter discovered that coming into the presidency as an outsider has some advantages but also some definite drawbacks. One of the weaknesses of the Carter presidency was his inability to find "insiders" in Congress that he could successfully work with to get legislation passed. Carter hired many women and minorities for his White House staff and did away with some of the pomp and circumstance traditionally associated with the presidency (he sometimes wore sweaters when giving addresses to the nation). To Carter's critics, these were signs that he was not really up to the responsibilities of the presidency.

Domestic problems continued to exist in the Carter presidency. Unemployment and inflation remained as major problems. As Ford had done, Carter asked the American people to voluntarily refrain from spending and excessive energy use to bring down inflation. He then tried to cut government spending to cool the economy, and angered many liberal Democrats by cutting social programs. Another approach tried by the administration was to have the Federal Reserve Board tighten the money supply, hoping this would stop inflation; the resulting high interest rates served to depress the economy. Unfortunately, none of these policies worked, and confidence in Carter's abilities to solve economic problems began to wane; by the end of his term, unemployment still stood near 8 percent, with inflation over 12 percent.

Other domestic measures undertaken by Carter included the granting of amnesty to those who had left America to avoid the draft during the Vietnam era and measures for the federal cleanup of chemical waste dumps. Pressures from **OPEC** drove the price of gasoline higher during the Carter presidency; in 1978 the National Energy Act passed, which taxed cars that were not energy efficient and deregulated the prices of domestic oil and gasoline. During the Carter administration a Cabinet-level Department of Energy was created.

In foreign policy, Carter's early speeches stated that the goal of America should be the spreading of basic human rights around the world. Critics maintained that Carter's idealism blinded him to the real interests of America at the time. Conservatives were very critical of his treaty that gave the Panama Canal back to Panama (this would not actually take place until 1999). Critics also attacked his decision to officially recognize the People's Republic of China as the government of China (thus reducing America's support of Taiwan) and his continued negotiations with the Soviets to limit nuclear weapons (critics stated that America's military might should not be limited). Conservatives were cheered by his response to the 1979 Soviet invasion of Afghanistan. Carter cut aid programs to the Soviet Union and refused to allow the athletes to compete in the 1980 Moscow Summer Olympics.

One of the high points of the Carter presidency was the September 1978 negotiations between Menachem Begin of Israel and Anwar Sadat of Egypt that produced the **Camp David Accords**. These negotiations were mediated by Carter; as a result of these talks, Israel promised to return occupied land to Egypt in return for official recognition of Israel's right to exist by Egypt. Carter was unable to negotiate a solution to the problem of Palestinian refugees (a problem that still exists today).

The nadir of the Carter presidency was the **Iranian Hostage Crisis**. Iran had been governed by the repressive Shah of Iran, who was propped up by arms and economic aid from the United States. In 1978 a revolution of fundamentalist Muslims forced the Shah to leave the country; the Ayatollah Khomeini, a fundamentalist Muslim leader, became leader of Iran. In October 1979, the exiled Shah was suffering from cancer, and Carter allowed him into the United States for treatment. This outraged the Iranians; on November 4 protesters stoned and then seized the American embassy in Tehran, Iran, taking 66 Americans who worked there hostage.

The Americans were kept hostage for 444 days. Some were kept in solitary confinement, while others were not; most were moved around on a regular basis to discourage rescue attempts. Carter tried various attempts to win the release of the hostages, including freezing Iranian assets in America, stopping trade with Iran, and negotiating through third parties. A 1980 attempt to rescue the hostages ended in a military embarrassment when helicopters sent to rescue them either crashed or could not fly because of heavy sand. Carter had been criticized for being ineffectual on domestic programs; as the hostage crisis wore on, he increasingly was seen as ineffectual in the diplomatic sphere as well. The hostages were finally released in January 1981, but only after Carter had left office and Ronald Reagan was sworn in as president.

THE ELECTION OF 1980

Carter was able to win the 1980 Democratic nomination for president over a challenge from Edward Kennedy. Ronald Reagan, portraying himself as the spokesperson for the conservatives of America, won the Republican nomination. Carter was forced to campaign on his record, which was a very difficult thing to do. Reagan promised while campaigning to build up the military; at the same time he promised to cut taxes. He promised strong leadership from Washington and also pledged to take power from Washington and give it to the states. Reagan also pledged support for a renewed emphasis on family and patriotism. Reagan won the election by a decisive margin.

The 1980 election was the first totally successful assault on the New Deal Democratic coalition. Social issues of the era, such as the increasing rights of women, sexual freedom, and **affirmative action**, drew many blue-collar workers away from the Democrats and into the Republican camp. (Conservatives successfully convinced many Americans that the Democrats were the cause of the declining image of America abroad and the reason for the decline in traditional morality at home.) Members of the **religious right** supported the Republicans in large numbers (and would continue this pattern in elections that followed). Many Southerners saw the Republicans and Reagan representing their interests more than Jimmy Carter; others perceived Carter to be "soft on communism." As a result of these factors, the **New Right** had become a major force in American politics; besides electing Reagan, they had also pushed the Republicans to the majority in the Senate in 1980.

THE PRESIDENCY OF RONALD REAGAN

Admirers and detractors of Ronald Reagan both agree that he was a true master of politics (Bill Clinton studied the techniques Reagan used to achieve political success). Reagan used his previously honed skills as an actor to set the right tone and present the right messages at meetings and speeches throughout his presidency. Reagan also used his staff well; on many occasions he would set the general policy and allow staff people to set up the details.

Upon becoming president Reagan instituted traditional conservative economic practices. In 1981 federal taxes were cut by 5 percent, and then cut by another 10 percent in 1982 and 1983. Reagan and his economic staff believed in "**supply-side economics**," which stated that if by cutting taxes you put more money in the hands of wealthy Americans, they would invest it in the economy, thus creating more jobs and additional growth (and eventually additional tax revenue). Capital gains taxes were reduced, also with the intent of encouraging investment.

Political battle lines were drawn early in the Reagan administration. As a result of the tax cuts, the government was taking in less money, causing many domestic programs to be cut, including aid to education, to urban housing programs, and to the arts and the humanities. Liberals were outraged over the fact that at the same time social programs were being cut, Reagan increased the defense budget by nearly $13 billion. Reagan also pushed for funding for a Strategic Defense Initiative (SDI; nicknamed "Star Wars") program. As envisioned, this system could shoot down enemy missiles from outer space. Reagan also pushed to give more power back to the states at the expense of the federal government. Reagan called this plan the **New Federalism**. Under this program, how federal money was spent by states was determined by the states and not by the federal government.

During the Reagan administration the policy of deregulation was intensified; industries such as the energy industry and the transportation industry were freed from "cumbersome" regulations imposed by previous administrations (supporters of these regulations would maintain that they were in the interest of the consumers). In addition, funding for the Environmental Protection Agency was greatly reduced during the Reagan presidency. Many perceived the Reagan administration to be anti-union as well; in 1981 the government actively destroyed the union for the air traffic controllers, and striking controllers were fired.

In response to the perceived foreign policy weakness of America in the Carter years, Reagan worked hard to build up America's image in the world. On a small scale, the American army successfully invaded the island of Grenada in 1983. On a much larger scale, Reagan ended the friendlier relations between the United States and the Soviet Union of the détente era. He put new cruise missiles in Europe and referred to the Soviet Union as the "evil empire." Reagan's harsh rhetoric won him much support in the United States. Reagan's popularity also had gone up after the attempt on his life by John Hinckley in 1981.

Reagan ran for reelection in 1984 against Walter Mondale (Mondale's running mate was Geraldine Ferraro, a congresswoman from New York). Mondale criticized Reagan on economic issues; the supply-side approach had not produced as much growth, and as much income from taxes, as its proponents had said it would. However, Reagan's tough Cold War rhetoric and support of conservative social issues allowed him to continue to break up the Democratic New Deal coalition; Reagan got nearly 60 percent of the popular vote in 1984. Critics who said that the major beneficiaries of Reagan's economic policies were the very rich were still very much in the minority.

Reagan continued to practice conservative policies during his second term. The **Tax Reform Act of 1986** dramatically reduced federal tax rates; the tax the wealthiest Americans had to pay on their income, for example, was reduced from 50 percent to 28 percent. In 1986 and 1987 both unemployment and inflation declined. Under Reagan the Supreme Court also became more conservative, as William Rehnquist became Chief Justice and Antonin Scalia was one of the new justices on the court. Reagan also nominated Sandra Day O'Connor to be the first woman to serve on the Supreme Court. Most women's groups, however, strongly disapproved of the Reagan administration, citing actions such as efforts during Reagan's second term to cut food stamps and the federal school lunch program.

During Reagan's second term, serious economic problems also developed. On October 19, 1987, known as "Black Monday" the average price for a share of stock fell nearly 20 percent. During Reagan's second term, federal government deficits grew drastically; this occurred because less income was coming into the government because of the previously-enacted tax cuts and because of a large increase in defense spending. In addition, for the first time since World War I the United States began to import more than it exported.

Nevertheless, Reagan's foreign policy remained incredibly popular. In April of 1986 the United States bombed Libyan air bases after Muammar al-Qadhafi, the leader of Libya, ordered Libyan gunboats to challenge American ships sailing close to Libya. Reagan and the new leader of the Soviet Union, Mikhail Gorbachev, established a close personal relationship and held meaningful negotiations on the reduction of nuclear weapons. Reagan also supported anticommunist forces fighting in Nicaragua and El Salvador.

Many critics of Reagan had claimed since 1980 that he was unaware of what was being done by others working for him. This view seemed to be validated by the **Iran-Contra Affair** of 1986 and 1987. Apparently without the knowledge of the president, National Security Advisor John Poindexter, Lieutenant Colonel Oliver North, and several others devised a "arms for hostages plan." By this plan the United States sold arms to Iran, hoping that they could use their influence to help free American hostages held in Lebanon. The problem with this plan was that at this point America had an official trade embargo with Iran and had gotten several European countries to support this. The money for this sale was to be used to fund anticommunist fighters in Nicaragua, called the "contras." Again, a problem existed: Congress had passed legislation carefully regulating how much funding could go to the contras. Congressional and legal hearings were held on the Iran-Contra Affair; as a result, nearly a dozen officials of the Reagan administration were forced to resign.

Many Americans felt (and continue to feel) that the political hero of the modern era was Ronald Reagan. Many supporters felt he restored pride to America, stood up to our enemies abroad, restored the economy of America, and reasserted "traditional" American values. Critics of Reagan maintain that the economic policies of the Reagan administration only benefited the wealthiest Americans; they point out that the gap between the richest Americans and the poorest Americans dramatically increased under Reagan, with the real income of middle- and lower-class Americans actually receding. Critics stated that Iran-Contra proved the fact that Reagan was dangerously out of touch on many policy decisions. Nevertheless, Reagan's vice president, George Bush, would certainly have a tough act to follow as he ran for president on his own in 1988.

CHAPTER REVIEW

Rapid Review

To achieve the perfect 5, you should be able to explain the following:

- One of the low points of American political life in the twentieth century was the Watergate Affair.
- Richard Nixon's greatest accomplishments were in the field of foreign policy, as he crafted new relationships with both China and the Soviet Union.

- The Watergate Affair developed from the paranoid view of American politics held by Richard Nixon and several of his top aides.

- Gerald Ford's presidency was tainted from the beginning by his pardoning of Richard Nixon.

- Ford faced huge economic problems as president; during his presidency America suffered from both inflation and unemployment.

- Jimmy Carter and many politicians of the post-Watergate era emerged victorious by campaigning as outsiders.

- President Carter's outsider status hurt him, especially in terms of getting legislation passed in Congress.

- Carter demonstrated his diplomatic skills by forging the Camp David Accords; he was unable to negotiate a release of the American hostages in Iran, and this may have cost him the presidency.

- Ronald Reagan was elected as a conservative and restored the pride of many Americans in America.

- Reagan practiced "supply-side" economics, which benefited the American economy but which also helped to create large deficits.

- Under Reagan the gap between the wealthiest Americans and the poorest Americans increased.

- Reagan reinstituted Cold War rhetoric but later created cordial relations with leaders of the Soviet Union.

- Reagan's lack of direct control over the implementation of presidential policies was demonstrated by the Iran-Contra Affair.

- The legacy of Ronald Reagan is a large one.

Time Line

1968: Richard Nixon elected president
1971: Nixon imposes wage and price controls
Pentagon Papers released
1972: Nixon visits China and Soviet Union
Nixon reelected
SALT I signed
Watergate break-in
1973: Watergate hearings in Congress
Spiro Agnew resigns as vice president
"Saturday Night Massacre"
1974: Inflation peaks at 11 percent
Nixon resigns; Gerald Ford becomes president
Ford pardons Richard Nixon
WIN economic program introduced
1975: South Vietnam falls to North Vietnam, ending Vietnam War
1976: Jimmy Carter elected president

1977: Carter signs Panama Canal treaty
Carter issues Vietnam-era draft amnesty
1978: Camp David Accords
1979: Americans taken hostage in Iran
1980: Ronald Reagan elected president
1981–1982: Major recession
Assassination attempt on Reagan
1981–1983: Major tax cuts instituted
1983: Reagan proposes "Star Wars"
Americans victorious in Grenada
1984: Reagan reelected
1985: Gorbachev assumes power in Soviet Union
1986: Additional tax reform measures passed
Iran-Contra Affair
"Black Monday"
1988: George Bush elected president

 ## Review Questions

1. What tactic was *not* used by supporters of Richard Nixon in the 1972 presidential campaign?

   A. Breaking into private offices
   B. Reviewing income tax records of suspected "enemies"
   C. Falsifying war records of opposing presidential candidates
   D. Attempting to halt official investigations of actions of campaign officials
   E. Planting false stories about opposing candidates in the press

(Answer: **C.** Of all of the "dirty tricks" practiced by the Republicans in 1972, this was not one of them.)

2. According to supply-side economics, when wealthy Americans received tax cuts, they would precede to do all but which of the following:

   A. Invest heavily in the economy
   B. Open new factories
   C. Purchase stocks
   D. Increase their savings dramatically
   E. Buy more consumer goods

(Answer: **D.** The key to supply-side economics is that when tax cuts give individuals large amounts of money, they will turn and reinvest that money in the economy.)

3. Which of the following did *not* help create the deficits of the second term of the Reagan years?

   A. Reduction of federal tax rates
   B. Desperately needed increases in funding for education
   C. Increases in military spending
   D. The SDI program
   E. Changes in the tax code that favored wealthier Americans

(Answer **B.** Even though education advocates were saying that funding had to be drastically increased in many urban school districts, funding for education declined during the Reagan era.)

4. Critics of Ronald Reagan would most emphasize

   A. the relationship between Reagan and Mikhail Gorbachev in 1987 and 1988

B. the effects of the 1981–1983 tax cuts

C. the U.S. response to threats from Libya

D. the effects of Reagan's economic policies on the middle and lower classes

E. his public image and political skills

(Answer: **D.** The 1981 to 1983 tax cuts did help bring down inflation; at this same time employment possibilities increased. Compared to the wealthiest Americans, the middle and lower classes experienced little benefit from Reagan's economic policies, especially from the tax cuts of the second term.)

5. Gerald Ford's WIN program demonstrated to many Americans that Ford

A. had no real grasp of economic issues

B. had the uncanny knack of knowing how to inspire the American public

C. was still under the shadow of Richard Nixon

D. understood sophisticated foreign policy issues

E. was a supporter of supply-side economics

(Correct Answer: **A.** Many Americans saw the WIN program as a public relations gimmick, demonstrating that Ford did not truly understand the economic problems of America; many equated WIN to some of the public pronouncements of Herbert Hoover in 1930 and 1931.)

Chapter 25

America from 1988 to 2000: Prosperity and a New World Order

For much of the post-World War II era, the popularity of a president was largely determined by his success in foreign policy and in handling foreign crises. With the ending of the Cold War at the end of the 1980s, skills in handling domestic issues became equally important for presidents and their staffs. Presidents Bush (I) and Clinton are perfect examples of this: Bush's popularity was sky-high after his Desert Storm victory, yet he ended up being defeated by Bill Clinton largely because of economic problems that developed in the closing years of his term. Despite a mountain of personal and ethical issues that surrounded him, President Clinton was able to keep high approval ratings because of a continuing successful economy.

THE 1988 ELECTION

Republican advertisements in 1988 touted George Bush as "the most qualified man of our times" to be president. Bush has served as a congressman, as the American ambassador to the United Nations, and as the director of the CIA. The **New Right** had never been entirely comfortable with Bush during his eight years as Reagan's vice president; to appease them, he nominated Senator Dan Quayle, a staunch conservative, as his vice presidential nominee.

The Democrats nominated Massachusetts Governor Michael Dukakis as their candidate. Dukakis campaigned on his experience as a governor, touting the "Massachusetts miracle" that had pulled the state out of its economic doldrums. Televisions during the 1988 campaign were glutted with negative advertisements, the most notable being one that linked Dukakis to Willie Horton, a black man who raped a woman while taking advantage of a furlough program established in Massachusetts by the

Governor. Bush won the election rather handily, despite being behind Dukakis in early polls.

THE PRESIDENCY OF GEORGE BUSH

Conservative suspicions of Bush increased during the first months of this presidency. Many considered his stated desires for a "kinder, gentler America" to be efforts to distance himself from the social policies of former-president Reagan. Bush's major domestic problem was an ever-growing federal deficit. To broker a deal with Congress to lower the deficit, Bush broke his campaign promise of "no new taxes" and in 1990 signed a bill authorizing tax increases. Many conservatives never forgave him for his decision. During Bush's term, few substantive domestic programs were instituted; some commentators complained of the **gridlock** created by a Republican president and a Democratic congress.

During the presidency of George Bush, the 45-year-old Cold War ended. In late 1988 Soviet leader Mikhail Gorbachev admitted to Communist party leaders that the incredible amount of the Soviet economy that was devoted to military spending and to "protecting" the satellite countries was preventing economic growth of any type from taking place. In 1989 the Soviets began to withdraw support from the satellite states; many in Moscow naively believed that communist leaders in the satellite states could remain in power without being propped up by the Soviet Union. In Poland, Solidarity, the noncommunist labor party, removed the communist government from power; throughout late 1989 communists were removed from power in all of the satellite nations. Many of the republics of the Soviet Union also desired independence. In December of 1991 Russian President Boris Yeltsin announced the abolition of the Soviet Union and the creation of 11 independent republics.

A large amount of American aid was pumped into Russia and the other Eastern European states. American academics rushed to Moscow and other major centers in the region, explaining to leaders how capitalism could be introduced in the shortest amount of time. This transition proved much more difficult than many would have ever believed; as this volume is being written, this process is still not completed in Russia and Eastern Europe.

American aid was also sent to help several of the former Soviet republics dismantle the nuclear missiles that had been placed there in the Cold War era. The meaning of the Cold War is still being debated by academics; whether the United States won the Cold War or whether the Soviet Union lost it is still a topic of numerous books and historical papers.

The central crisis of the Bush presidency began on August 2, 1990, when the army of Iraq invaded Kuwait. Fears that Saddam Hussein's next target would be Saudi Arabia, the largest importer of oil to the United States, pushed the United States into action. Almost immediately, in Operation **"Desert Shield"** large numbers of American troops were sent to protect Saudi Arabia.

Encouraged by the United States, member states of the United Nations condemned the Iraqi aggression and authorized the creation of a multinational military force to remove Saddam Hussein from Kuwait. The high point of the Bush presidency was the personal diplomacy undertaken by the presidency to get almost all of the states of the Middle East to support military action against Iraq. On February 24, 1991, a ground offensive, termed Operation "<u>Desert Storm</u>," was instituted against Iraq. Iraqi casualties were over 40,000, while the Americans (who made up most of the troops of the UN international force) lost 150 soldiers in battle. Iraqi soldiers surrendered by the hundreds as they retreated from Kuwait. In a decision that would later be questioned, American forces did not move into Iraq and force Saddam Hussein from power. It should be noted that was *not* part of the United Nations mandate, and such an action would have definitely created division in the Middle Eastern coalition so carefully crafted by Bush.

Bush's popularity was at an all time high after Desert Storm. However, problems soon arose that his administration seemed incapable of solving. A recession and continued economic difficulties hit the United States in early 1992. In addition, the end of the Cold War brought new difficulties in several states formerly controlled by the Soviet Union. In the former Yugoslavia, Serbs began to practice "ethnic cleansing" against Bosnian Muslims. Critics of Bush claimed that he lacked any "vision" of what the role of the United States should be in a post-Cold War world.

THE 1992 ELECTION

George Bush and Bill Clinton ran against each other in 1992. The buzzword of politics in 1992 was "change," and both candidates claimed they were prepared to offer it. At the 1992 Republican National Convention speakers of the New Right spoke about the need for "family values" and that a "religious war" against the Democrats was needed.

The former governor of Arkansas, Bill Clinton had the political sense to realize that Americans in the early 1990s were interested in economic rather than social issues, and pledged that as president he would overhaul the health care system and work for the preservation of the Social Security system. Clinton campaigned as a "<u>New Democrat</u>," stating that he was not another typical big-spending advocate of big government. During his presidency Clinton on occasion took Republican concepts and claimed them as his own; right-wing critics such as Rush Limbaugh maintained that he would say or do anything if it meant his position would be improved in the polls.

In the 1990s politicians were under more intense scrutiny than ever. Twenty-four-hour cable news networks needed a continuous input of news; political Web sites and talk radio hosts offered up mountains of political information (with no real need to prove any of it). Bill Clinton was a special target of the conservative press during the 1992 campaign and throughout his presidency; he was the first baby boomer president and had taken part in antiwar demonstrations while he was a graduate student in England. Many also resented his wife, Hillary Rodham Clinton, who maintained that if her husband was elected, she would not sit around the White House and "bake cookies."

A third candidate in the 1992 race was Texas multibillionaire Ross Perot. Perot spent a lot of money on campaign ads, complaining in these ads about how the politicians in Washington were beholden only to special interests, and that if elected he would bring "common sense" back to the White House. However, the charts depicting the American economy that he used on his advertisements were understood by few people.

Clinton won the 1992 election fairly easily. Many from the New Deal Democratic coalition that had deserted the Democrats for Reagan came back to vote for Clinton in 1992. Bush appeared oddly out of touch at several points during the campaign; at one point he was caught looking at his watch in the middle of a presidential debate. Nearly 19 million Americans supported Perot; analysts maintain that the support for Perot hurt Bush more than it did Clinton.

THE PRESIDENCY OF BILL CLINTON

From the beginning Clinton strove to create an administration different than the one that had preceded it. He appointed minorities and women to his Cabinet. During his first term there were several legislative successes, such as the Brady bill, which created a waiting period for handgun purchases and the 1994 Anti-Crime bill, which provided federal funds to hire more policemen. However, several of issues Clinton attempted to tackle during his first term drew the ire of many. His attempt to legislate the proper status of gays in the military caused many in all branches of the military service to distrust him. His attempt to legislate a national health insurance plan was defeated by a combination of effective lobbying by the American Medical Association and intense advertising paid for by the health care industry. In addition, the fact that Hillary Rodham Clinton was actively involved in the formulation of health care policy caused debate over the proper role of a First Lady.

Many also began to question the Clintons concerning their financial dealings. Investments in a failed savings and loan company and in a land development called "**Whitewater**" caused much controversy; in August of 1994 Kenneth Starr became the independent counsel in charge of investigating the Whitewater Affair. Many Clinton supporters felt that Starr moved too vigorously and was out to "get" the Clintons.

The 1994 Congressional elections appeared to be a sweeping rejection of the presidency of Bill Clinton. Republicans, led by new Speaker of the House Newt Gingrich, supported the **Contract with America**, and promised to get rid of many social programs long supported by liberals. Republicans soon learned that the political skills of Bill Clinton were formidable, however. In an attempt to lessen the size of the federal government, there were brief shutdowns of the federal government in 1995 and

1996; on each occasion public opinion polls stated that the American public strongly sided with the president in his argument that all of this was the fault of the Republicans.

Clinton's popularity rose further as the economy improved steadily in 1995 and 1996. The values of stocks rose, economic growth continued at a steady rate, and inflation remained low (many credited Alan Greenspan, chairman of the Federal Reserve, for his ability to skillfully maneuver interest rates to keep inflation low and growth high).

Clinton's role as a "New Democrat" was again demonstrated when he supported passage of the Personal Responsibility and Work Opportunity Reconciliation Act of 1996. This legislation more carefully regulated the welfare system, cut the food stamp program, and gave the power to the states to organize their own "welfare-to-work" programs. This program, which ended "welfare as we know it," was hailed by Clinton supporters as a sign of his pragmatism; many liberals were appalled that he so easily "sold them out."

In foreign policy Clinton faced some of the same criticisms that Bush had: Many claimed that the United States still did not have a post-Cold War foreign policy "focus." Many debated the appropriate role for the U.S. military. A humanitarian mission to Somalia led to the death of 18 American soldiers in 1992. The U.S. military was sent in to restore the government of Jean-Bertrand Aristide in Haiti; Clinton also supported NATO air and military efforts to protect Muslims from the "ethnic cleansing" policies of President Slobodan Milosevic of Serbia. Americans remain as peacekeepers in Bosnia to this day.

President Clinton also favored the continued **globalization** of the economy, which included the lowering of tariffs and the expansion of global markets. Clinton worked with many Republicans to secure the passage of **NAFTA** (North American Free Trade Agreement) in Congress. The goal of NAFTA was to gradually remove all trade barriers between the United States, Canada, and Mexico. As with welfare reform, a segment of the traditional Democratic base was infuriated by one of Clinton's policies: In this case it was the labor unions who felt betrayed.

In 2000 Clinton unsuccessfully attempted to broker a peace between the Palestinians and Israel. He increasingly became aware of the threats of fundamentalist Muslims against the United States. In 1993 bombings took place at the World Trade Center in New York City; American embassies were bombed in Tanzania and Kenya in 1998, and a United States naval ship docked in Yemen was bombed in 2000. Clinton attempted several bombing missions in response to these terrorist attacks, and in one instance came fairly close to killing Osama bin Laden, leader of the Al-Qaeda terrorist network.

Campaigning on the continued strength of the American economy, Clinton became the first Democrat since Franklin Roosevelt to win back-to-back terms when he defeated long-time Senator Robert Dole of Kansas in the 1996 presidential election. Early in Clinton's second term the era of gridlock appeared to be over, as both parties joined in passing legislation to reduce the federal budget. Yet it was the Whitewater Affair that consumed the most political energy in Washington during the last years of Clinton's second term.

As was stated previously, Kenneth Starr and the Whitewater investigation was originally charged with analyzing the financial dealings of the Clintons in Arkansas. However, the investigation soon delved into other areas of the president's life. It was revealed that he had an affair with a White House intern, Monica Lewinsky. Clinton boldly proclaimed on television that he had never had "an affair with that woman." In a lawsuit brought against the president by Paula Jones (for alleged sexual harassment when Clinton was governor of Arkansas), Clinton denied, under oath, having an affair with Lewinsky. Physical evidence obtained from Lewinsky seemed to prove otherwise. Talk show hosts and other opponents stated that the case had long gone beyond merely the matter of the president having an affair; he had actually lied under oath about it.

Clinton's approval ratings remained high throughout his second term; his approval was especially strong in black districts across the country. In the 1996 congressional elections the Republicans lost five seats in the House of Representatives. Congressional calls for impeachment began; others wondered whether the actions of the president were actually the "high crimes and misdemeanors" the Constitution stated were grounds for impeachment. On December 19, 1998, the House of Representatives passed two articles of impeachment (obstruction of justice and perjury), thus preparing the way for a trial in the Senate. Two-thirds of the Senators had to vote for an article of impeachment in order to remove him from office. Senate voting took place on February 12, 1999; neither article of impeachment even got a majority. Many Clinton supporters that spoke during the congressional proceedings noted that despite millions of dollars being spent and years of investigation, the Special Prosecutor was unable to uncover any illegal actions by the president or his wife. After the hearings, several of the president's most vocal adversaries became politically discredited. Popular support for the president remained high, and economic prosperity and expansion continued.

THE 2000 PRESIDENTIAL ELECTION

Excitement for the candidates in the 2000 presidential election was very low. The Democrats nominated Al Gore, Clinton's vice president, who often appeared wooden when giving speeches and stirred little emotion, even among long-time Democrats. George W. Bush, son of the former president, was the Republican nominee; in several early interviews he appeared to lack the knowledge of critical issues that might be expected of a presidential candidate. Ralph Nader ran as a candidate of the Green Party.

When the final results were tabulated, Al Gore actually received some 500,000 votes more than Bush (Nader received less than 3 million votes). However, Gore surprisingly lost his home state of Tennessee, and the winner in the Electoral College would be the winner of the popular vote in Florida. Several recounts were held there, with Bush holding on to a tiny lead. Blacks in several parts of Florida (who voted heavily for Gore) complained that in several parts of the state they had been prevented from voting. Further recounts were planned in contested counties. By a 5-to-4 vote on February 9, 2001, the Supreme Court of the United States temporarily halted all recounts. On February 12 the court ruled, again by a 5-to-4 margin, that recounts in contested counties only was a violation of the Constitution, thus securing the election of George W. Bush. In the first months of his presidency, Bush concentrated much of his effort on domestic affairs; the events of September 11, 2001, would dramatically change the course of his presidency.

CHAPTER REVIEW

Rapid Review

To achieve the perfect 5, you should be able to explain the following:

- The ability to manage domestic issues were critical for a president's political success in the post-Cold War era.

- George Bush alienated many conservatives, especially when he broke his "no new taxes" pledge.

- The end of the Cold War can be attributed to American policy decisions and to weaknesses in the infrastructure of the Soviet Union.

- George Bush skillfully managed the "Desert Storm" operation against Iraq.

- Bill Clinton presented himself as a "New Democrat" and concerned with economic issues in the 1992 presidential campaign; these were important factors in his victory.

- Clinton's failure on national health insurance helped pave the way for large Republican gains in the 1994 congressional elections.

- Clinton and Newt Gingrich were formidable opponents in the budget battles of the mid-1990s.

- The Whitewater Affair and investigations of the personal life of Bill Clinton were the defining political events of the second term of Clinton's presidency.

- George W. Bush's election demonstrated the difficulties of arriving at a "final tally" in any election and was finally secured by the intervention of the United States Supreme Court.

Time Line

1988: George Bush elected president
Solidarity replaces communist government in Poland
1989: Berlin wall opened, communist governments fall in
Eastern Europe
1991: Persian Gulf War
Breakup of the Soviet Union
Beginnings of economic recession
1992: Election of Bill Clinton
American troops killed in Somalia
1993: NAFTA ratified by Senate
Terrorist bombings at World Trade Center
1994: Republicans sweep congressional elections
U.S. military enters Haiti
Kenneth Starr becomes Whitewater independent counsel
1996: Clinton reelected
1998: Federal budget surplus announced
Articles of impeachment passed in House of Representatives
1999: Clinton acquitted in impeachment trial in U.S. Senate
2000: George W. Bush elected president

✓ Review Questions

1. A defining characteristic of the Clinton presidency was his

   A. strict adherence to traditional Democratic values
   B. pragmatic policy making
   C. close alliance with liberals in the Democratic party
   D. unprecedented alliance with labor unions
   E. ability to work closely with fundamentalist religious groups

(Correct Answer: **B.** In claiming to be a "New Democrat," Clinton sometimes adopted traditional Republican ideas as his own. To many critics, the pragmatism of the Clinton White House masked a lack of core values that the president truly believed in.)

2. George Bush alienated many conservative Republicans by

   A. appointing the relatively inexperienced Dan Quayle as vice president
   B. continuing to urge the tearing down of the Berlin Wall
   C. signing the 1990 agreement with the Democrats to reduce the deficit
   D. pursuing policies against Iraq
   E. approving the Willie Horton campaign advertisement in 1988

(Correct Answer: **C.** This was the agreement where Bush broke his "no new taxes" pledge and broke with traditional Republican policy.)

3. Critics accused Bush of lacking "vision" because

   A. he failed to articulate a successful policy to end the economic deficit
   B. he failed to remove Saddam Hussein from power

C. he failed to broker peace between the Palestinians and Egypt

D. he failed to sign an arms treaty with Mikhail Gorbachev

E. he failed to explain his perception of America's role in the post-Cold War world

(Correct Answer: **E.** Several historians state that a weakness of both Bush and Clinton was that they were unable to articulate a coherent post-Cold War foreign policy.)

4. All of the following were reasons for the end of the Cold War *except*

A. the United States military buildup under Ronald Reagan

B. the fact that many producers of military weaponry in the United States did not want to continue to produce this weaponry

C. the weaknesses of the Soviet economy

D. the Cold War rhetoric of both Ronald Reagan and George Bush

E. the tremendous costs to the Soviet Union of continuing to control the satellite countries

(Correct Answer: **B.** Most manufacturers had no desire to stop producing weaponry for the Cold War. When the Cold War finally ended, many of these companies were forced to lay off workers, and some that could not diversify were forced to close.)

5. Bill Clinton was a formidable political opponent for the Republicans for all of the following reasons *except*

A. his ability to eventually win over former Republicans of the New Right

B. his support in the black community

C. his ability to take Republican positions and make them appear to be his own

D. his ability to withstand political scandal

E. his ability to stake out moderate positions, thus gaining support from both Democrats and Republicans

(Correct Answer: **A.** The New Right was the group that came to despise Bill Clinton the most. Members of the New Right interested in social issues were among Clinton's most passionate detractors during the Whitewater Affair.)

PART IV

"AFTER WORDS"

Glossary

abolitionist movement Movement dedicated to the abolition of slavery that existed primarily in the North in years leading up to the Civil War; had both white and black members.

Albany Congress 1754 meeting of representatives of seven colonies to coordinate their efforts against French and Native American threats in the Western frontier regions.

Advertising Age Term first used to describe America's consumer culture of the 1920s, when advertising began to influence the choices of purchasers.

affirmative action Policies that began in the 1970s to make up for past discrimination and give minorities and women advantages in applying for certain jobs and in applying for admission to certain universities.

affluent society Term used by economist John Kenneth Galbraith to describe the American economy in the 1950s, during which time many Americans became enraptured with appliances and homes in the suburbs.

Agricultural Adjustment Administration (AAA) Established by the Agricultural Act of 1932, a New Deal bureau designed to restore economic position of farmers by paying them *not* to farm goods that were being overproduced.

Agricultural Marketing Act 1929 act championed by Herbert Hoover that authorized the lending of federal money to farmer's cooperatives to buy crops to keep them from the oversaturated market; program hampered by lack of adequate federal financial support.

Alien and Sedition Acts Proposed and supported by John Adams, gave the president the power to expel aliens deemed "dangerous to the country's well-being" and outlawed publication and public pronouncement of "false, scandalous, and malicious" statements about the government

Allied Powers Coalition of nations that opposed Germany, Italy, and Japan in World War II; led by England, the Soviet Union, and the United States

America First Committee Isolationist group in America that insisted that America stay out of World War II; held rallies from 1939 to 1941; argued that affairs in Europe should be settled by Europeans and not Americans and stated that the Soviet Union was a greater eventual threat than Nazi Germany.

American Colonization Society Formed in 1817, stated that the best way to end the slavery problem in the United States was for blacks to emigrate to Africa; by 1822 a few American blacks emigrated to Liberia. Organization's views were later rejected by most abolitionists.

American Expeditionary Force Official title of American army sent to Europe to aid England and France after United States entered World War I; army was commanded by General John J. Pershing.

American Federation of Labor (A.F.L.) National labor union founded by Samuel Gompers in 1886; original goal was to organize skilled workers by craft. Merged with Congress of Industrial Organizations (CIO) in 1955.

American Indian Movement (AIM) Native American organization founded in 1968 to protest government policies and injustices suffered by Native Americans; in 1973 organized armed occupation of Wounded Knee, South Dakota.

American Liberty League Formed in 1934 by anti-New Deal politicians and business leaders to oppose policies of Franklin Roosevelt; stated that New Deal policies brought America closer to fascism.

American System Economic plan promoted by Speaker of the House Henry Clay in years following the War of 1812; promoted vigorous growth of the American economy and the use of protective tariffs to encourage Americans to buy more domestic goods.

Anaconda Copper Company Large mining syndicate typical of many companies involved in mining in the western United States in the 1860s and 1870s; used heavy machinery and professional engineers. Many prospectors who found gold, silver, or copper sold their claims to companies such as this.

Anaconda Plan Critical component of initial Union plans to win the Civil War; called for capture of critical Southern ports and eventual control of the Mississippi River, which would create major economic and strategic difficulties for the Confederacy.

Antifederalists Group that opposed the ratification of the proposed Constitution of the United States in 1787; many feared that strong central government would remove the processes of government "from the people" and replicate the excesses of the British monarchy.

Anti-Imperialist League Organization formed in 1898 to oppose American annexation of the Philippines and American imperialism in general; focused the public on the potential financial, military, and especially moral costs of imperialism.

Anti-Saloon League Organization founded in 1893 that increased public awareness of the social effects of alcohol on society; supported politicians who favored prohibition and promoted statewide referendums in Western and Southern states to ban alcohol.

Appomattox In the courthouse of this Virginia city Robert E. Lee surrendered his Confederate army to Ulysses S. Grant on April 9, 1865.

Army-McCarthy hearings 1954 televised hearings on charges that Senator Joseph McCarthy was unfairly tarnishing the United States Army with charges of communist infiltration into the armed forces; hearings were the beginning of the end for McCarthy, whose bullying tactics were repeatedly demonstrated.

Articles of Confederation Ratified in 1781, this document established the first official government of the United States; allowed much power to remain in the states, with the federal government possessing only limited powers. Articles replaced by the Constitution in 1788.

Astrolabe Instrument that enabled navigators to calculate their latitude using the sun and the stars; allowed more accuracy in plotting routes during the Age of Discovery.

Atlantic, Battle of the Began in spring 1941 with the sinking of an American merchant vessel by a German submarine. Armed conflict between warships of America and Germany took place in September of 1941; American merchant vessels were armed by 1942.

Atlantic Charter Fall 1941 agreement between Franklin Roosevelt and Winston Churchill, stating that America and Great Britain would support a postwar world based on self-determination and would endorse a world body to ensure "general security"; U.S. agreement to convoy merchant ships across part of Atlantic inevitably drew America closer to conflict with Germany.

Aztecs Advanced Indian society located in central Mexico; conquered by Spanish conquistador Cortes. The defeat of the Aztecs was hastened by smallpox brought to Mexico by the Spanish.

Baby Boom Large increase in birthrate in United States that began in 1945 and lasted until 1962; new and larger families fueled the move to suburbia that occurred in the 1950s and produced the "youth culture" that would become crucial in the 1960s.

Ballinger-Pinchot Affair Crisis that occurred when William Howard Taft was president, further distancing him from Progressive supporters of Theodore Roosevelt. Richard Ballinger, Taft's Secretary of the Interior, allowed private businessmen to purchase large amounts of public land in Alaska; Forest Service head Gifford Pinchot (a Roosevelt supporter) protested to Congress and was fired by Taft.

Bank War Political battles surrounding the attempt by President Andrew Jackson to greatly reduce the power of the Second Bank of the United States; Jackson claimed the Bank was designed to serve special interests in America and not the common people.

Bataan Death March Forced march of 76,000 American and Filipino soldiers captured by the Japanese from the Bataan Peninsula in early May 1942; over 10,000 soldiers died during this one-week ordeal.

Bay of Pigs Failed 1961 invasion of Cuba by United States-supported anti-Castro refugees designed to topple Castro from power; prestige of the United States, and of the newly elected president, John Kennedy, was damaged by this failed coup attempt.

Bear Flag Republic Declaring independence from Mexican control, this republic was declared in 1846 by American settlers living in California; this political act was part of a larger American political and military strategy to wrest Texas and California from Mexico.

Beat Generation Literary movement of the 1950s that criticized the conformity of American society and the ever-present threat of atomic warfare; *On the Road* by Jack Kerouac, *Howl* by Allen Ginsberg, and *Naked Lunch* by William Burroughs were key works of the Beat Generation.

Berlin Airlift American and British pilots flew in food and fuel to West Berlin during late 1948 and early 1949 because Soviet Union and East Germany blockaded other access to West Berlin (which was located in East Germany); Stalin ended this blockade in May 1949. Airlift demonstrated American commitment to protecting Western allies in Europe during the early Cold War period.

Berlin Wall Concrete structure built in 1961 by Soviets and East Germany physically dividing East and West Berlin; to many in the West, the Wall was symbolic of communist repression in the Cold War era. The wall was finally torn down in 1989.

Bessemer steel First produced in 1856 in converter (furnace) invented by Henry Bessemer; was much more durable and harder than iron. Steel was a critical commodity in the Second Industrial Revolution.

bicameral legislature A legislative structure consisting of two houses, this was adopted by the authors of the U.S. Constitution; membership of the states in one house (the House of Representatives) is determined by population, while in the other house (the Senate) all states have equal representation.

Bill of Rights Added to the Constitution in 1791, the first 10 amendments protected freedom of speech, freedom of the press, the right to bear arms, and other basic rights of American citizens.

Birth of a Nation Epic movie released in 1915 by director D. W. Griffith; portrayed the Reconstruction as a period when Southern blacks threatened basic American values, which the Ku Klux Klan tried to protect; film was lauded by many, including President Woodrow Wilson.

Black Codes Laws adopted by the Southern states in the Reconstruction era that greatly limited the freedom of Southern blacks; in several states blacks could not move, own land, or do anything but farm.

blacklist Prevented persons accused of being communists from getting work in entertainment and other industries during the period of anticommunist fervor of the late 1940s and early 1950s; some entertainers waited until the mid-1960s before working publicly again.

black nationalism Spurred by Malcolm X and other black leaders, a call for black pride and advancement without the help of whites; this appeared to be a repudiation of the calls for peaceful integration urged by Martin Luther King. Race riots in Northern cities in mid-1960s were at least partially fueled by supporters of black nationalism.

Black Panthers Group originally founded in Oakland, California, to protect blacks from police harassment; promoted militant black power; also ran social programs in several California cities. Founded by Bobby Seale and Huey P. Newton.

black power Movement of black Americans in the mid-1960s that emphasized pride in racial heritage and black economic and political self-reliance; term coined by black civil rights leader Stokely Carmichael.

"Bleeding Kansas" As a result of Kansas-Nebraska Act of 1854, residents of Kansas territory could decide if territory would allow slavery or not; as a result, both pro-slavery and antislavery groups flooded settlers into Kansas territory. Much violence followed very disputed elections in 1855.

bonanza farms Large farms that came to dominate agricultural life in much of the West in the late 1800s; instead of plots farmed by yeoman farmers, large amounts of machinery was used, and workers were hired laborers, often performing only specific tasks (similar to work in a factory).

Bonus Army Group of nearly 17,000 veterans who marched on Washington in May 1932 to demand the military bonuses they had been promised; this group was eventually driven from their camp city by the United States Army. This action increased the public perception that the Hoover administration cared little about the poor.

Boston Massacre Conflict between British soldiers and Boston civilians on March 5, 1770; after civilians threw rocks and snowballs at the soldiers, the soldiers opened fire, killing five and wounding six.

Boston Tea Party In response to the Tea Act and additional British taxes on tea, Boston radicals disguised as Native Americans threw nearly 350 chests of tea into Boston harbor on December 16, 1773.

Brown* v. *Board of Education 1954 Supreme Court decision that threw out the 1896 *Plessy* v. *Ferguson* ruling that schools could be "separate but equal"; ruling began the long and painful process of school desegregation in the South and other parts of America.

Bulge, Battle of the December 1944 German attack that was the last major offensive by the Axis powers in World War II; Germans managed to push forward into Belgium but were then driven back. Attack was costly to the Germans in terms of material and manpower.

Bull Moose Party Name given to the Progressive party in the 1912 presidential campaign; Bull Moose candidate ex-president Theodore

Roosevelt ran against incumbent president William Howard Taft and Democrat Woodrow Wilson, with Wilson emerging victorious.

Bull Run, First Battle of July 21, 1861 Confederate victory over Union forces, which ended in Union forces fleeing in disarray toward Washington; this battle convinced Lincoln and others in the North that victory over the Confederates would not be as easy as they initially thought.

Bull Run, Second Battle of Decisive victory by General Robert E. Lee and Confederate forces over the Union army in August 1862.

Bunker Hill, Battle of June 1775 British attack on colonial forces at Breed's Hill outside Boston; despite frightful losses, the British emerged victorious in this battle.

Calvinism Militant Protestant faith that preached salvation "by faith alone" and predestination; desire by Calvinists in England to create a "pure church" in England was only partially successful, thus causing Calvinist Puritans to come to the New World starting in 1620.

Camp David Accords Treaty between Egypt and Israel brokered by President Jimmy Carter and signed in early 1979; Israel agreed to give back territory in the Sinai Peninsula to Egypt, while Egypt agreed to recognize Israel's right to exist as a nation.

carpetbaggers Term used by Southerners to mock Northerners who came to the South to gain either financially or politically during the Reconstruction era.

Central powers The alliance of Germany, Austria-Hungary, the Ottoman Empire, and Bulgaria that opposed England, France, Russia, and later the United States in World War I.

Chancellor of the Exchequer During the era prior to and during the Revolutionary War, this was the head of the department in the British government that issued and collected taxes; many acts issued by the Chancellor of the Exchequer created great resentment in the American colonies.

Chancellorsville, Battle of Brilliant Confederate attack on Union forces led by Stonewall Jackson and Robert E. Lee on May 2 to 3, 1863; Union defeat led to great pessimism in North and convinced many in the South that victory over North was indeed possible.

Chateau-Thierry, Battle of One of the first 1918 World War I battles where soldiers of the American Expeditionary Force fought and suffered severe casualties.

Checkers Speech Speech made by Richard Nixon on national television on September 23, 1952, where he defended himself against charges that rich supporters had set up a special expense account for his use; by the speech Nixon saved his spot on the 1952 Republican ticket (he was running for vice president, with Eisenhower running for president) and saved his political career.

Cherokee Nation v. Georgia 1831 Supreme Court case in which the Cherokee tribe claimed that Georgia had no right to enforce laws in Cherokee territory, since Cherokees were a sovereign nation; ruling by John Marshall stated that Cherokees were a "domestic dependent nation" and had no right to appeal in federal court.

Church of England Also called the Anglican Church, this was the Protestant church established by King Henry VIII; religious radicals desired a "purer" church that was allowed by monarchs of the early seventeenth century, causing some to leave for the Americas.

Circular Letter In reaction to the 1767 Townshend Acts, the Massachusetts assembly circulated a letter to the other colonies, asking that they work together and jointly issue a petition of protest. Strong-willed response of British authorities to the letter influenced the colonial assemblies to work together on a closer basis.

Civilian Conservation Corps (CCC) New Deal program that began in 1933, putting nearly 3 million young men to work; workers were paid little, but worked on conservation projects and maintaining beaches and parks. CCC program for young women began in 1937.

Civil Rights Act of 1866 Act that struck down Black Codes and defined the rights of all citizens; also stated that federal government could act when civil rights were violated at the state level. Passed by Congress over the veto of President Andrew Johnson.

Civil Rights Act of 1964 Key piece of civil rights legislation that made discrimination on the basis of race, sex, religion or national origin illegal; segregation in public restrooms, bus stations, and other public facilities also was declared illegal.

Civil Service Commission Created by the Pendleton Civil Service Act of 1883, this body was in charge of testing applicants and assigning them to appropriate government jobs; filling jobs on the basis of merit replaced the spoils system, in which government jobs were given as rewards for political service.

Clayton Antitrust Act 1914 act designed to strengthen the Sherman Antitrust Act of 1890; certain activities previously committed by big businesses, such as not allowing unions in factories and not allowing strikes, were declared illegal.

Cold War Period between 1945 and 1991 of near-continuous struggle between the United States and its allies and the Soviet Union and its allies; Cold War tensions were made even more intense by the existence of the atomic bomb.

colonial assemblies Existed in all of the British colonies in America; House of Burgesses in Virginia was the first one. Members of colonial assemblies were almost always members of the upper classes of colonial society.

Committees of Correspondence First existed in Massachusetts, and eventually in all of the colonies; leaders of resistance to British rule listed their grievances against the British and circulated them to all of the towns of the colony.

Committee on Public Information Created by Woodrow Wilson during World War I to mobilize public opinion for the war, this was the most intensive use of propaganda until that time by the United States. The image of "Uncle Sam" was created for this propaganda campaign.

Common Sense Very popular 1776 publication in the colonies written by Englishman Thomas Paine, who had come to America in 1774; repudiated the entire concept of government by monarchy. After publication of this document, public sentiment in the colonies turned decisively toward a desire for independence.

Compromise of 1850 Complex agreement that temporarily lessened tensions between Northern and Southern political leaders, and prevented a possible secession crisis; to appease the South, the Fugitive Slave Act was strengthened; to appease the North, California entered the Union as a free state.

Compromise of 1877 Political arrangement that ended the contested presidential election of 1876. Representatives of Southern states agreed not to oppose the official election of Republican Rutherford B. Hayes as president despite massive election irregularities. In return, the Union army stopped enforcing Reconstruction legislation in the South, thus ending Reconstruction.

Concord, Battle of Occurred on April 19, 1775, between British regulars and Massachusetts militiamen. There were 273 British soldiers killed or wounded; as a result, a wider conflict between the colonies and the British became much more probable.

Confederate States of America Eventually made up of 11 former states with Jefferson Davis as its first and only president. Was unable to defeat the North because of lack of railroad lines, lack of industry, and an inability to get European nations to support their cause.

Congress of Industrial Organizations (CIO) Group of unions that broke from the A.F.L. in 1938 and organized effective union drives in automobile and rubber industries; supported sit-down strikes in major rubber plants. Reaffiliated with the A.F.L. in 1955.

conscription Getting recruits for military service using a draft; this method was used by the American government in all of the wars of the twentieth century. Conscription was viewed most negatively during the Vietnam War.

consumer society Many Americans in the 1950s became infatuated with all of the new products produced by technology and went out and purchased more than any prior generation; consumer tastes of the decade were largely dictated by advertising and television.

containment policy Formulated by George Kennan, a policy whereby the United States would forcibly stop communist aggression whenever and wherever it occurred; containment was the dominant American policy of the Cold War era, and forced America to become involved in foreign conflicts such as Vietnam.

Continentals Soldiers in the "American" army commanded by George Washington in the Revolutionary War; victory at the Battle of Trenton on December 16, 1776, did much to raise the morale of the soldiers (and convince many of them to reenlist).

Contract with America 1994 pledge by Republican candidates for House of Representatives; led by Newt Gingrich, candidates promised to support term limits, balancing the budget, and lessening the size of the federal government. In 1994 Congressional elections, Republicans won both houses of Congress for the first time in 40 years.

convoy system System used to protect American ships carrying materials to Great Britain in 1940 and 1941; merchant ships were protected by American warships. Firing took place between these ships and German submarines, with American losses.

Copperheads Democrats in Congress in the first years of the Civil War who opposed Abraham Lincoln and the North's attack on the South, claiming that the war would result in massive numbers of freed slaves entering the North and a total disruption of the Northern economy.

Coral Sea, Battle of the May 1942 American naval victory over the Japanese; prevented Japanese from attacking Australia. First naval battle where losses on both sides came almost exclusively from bombing from airplanes.

counterculture Youth of the 1960s who espoused a lifestyle encompassing drug use, free love, and a rejection of adult authority; actual "hippies" were never more than a small percentage of young people.

Coxey's Army Supporters of Ohio Populist Jacob Coxey who in 1894 marched on Washington, demanded that the government create jobs for the unemployed; although this group had no effect whatsoever on policy, it did demonstrate the social and economic impact of the Panic of 1893.

creationism Belief in the Biblical account of the origin of the universe and the origin of man; believers in creationism and believers in evolution both had their day in court during the 1925 Scopes Trial.

Crittenden Plan 1860 compromise proposal on the slavery issue designed to defuse tension between North and South; would have allowed slavery to continue in the South and would have denied Congress the power to regulate interstate slave trade. On the advice of newly elected President Lincoln, Republicans in Congress voted against it.

Crusades From these attempts to recapture the Holy Land, Europeans acquired an appreciation of the benefits of overseas expansion and an appreciation of the economic benefits of slavery.

Cuban Missile Crisis 1962 conflict between the United States and the Soviet Union over Soviet missiles discovered in Cuba; Soviets eventually removed missiles under American pressure. Crisis was perhaps the closest the world came to armed conflict during the Cold War era.

Currency Act 1764 British act forbidding the American colonies to issue paper money as legal tender; act was repealed in 1773 by the British as an effort to ease tensions between themselves and the colonies.

dark horse candidate A candidate for office with little support before the beginning of the nomination process; James K. Polk was the first dark horse candidate for president in 1844.

Dawes Act 1887 act designed to break up Native American tribes, offered Native American families 160 acres of farmland or 320 acres of land for grazing. Large amounts of tribal lands were not claimed by Native Americans, and thus were purchased by land speculators.

Declaration of Neutrality Issued by President Woodrow Wilson after the outbreak of World War I in Europe in 1914, stating that the United States would maintain normal relations with and continue to trade with both sides in the conflict; factors including submarine warfare made it difficult for America to maintain this policy.

Declaration of Rights and Grievances 1774 measure adopted by the First Continental Congress, stating that Parliament had some rights to regulate colonial trade with Britain, but that Parliament did not have the right to tax the colonies without their consent.

Declaratory Act 1766 British law stating that the Parliament had absolute right to tax the colonies as they saw fit and to make laws that would be enacted in the colonies. Ironically, issued at the same time as the repeal of the Stamp Act.

deficit spending Economic policy where government spends money that it "doesn't have", thus creating a budget deficit. Although "conventional" economic theory disapproves of this, it is commonplace during times of crisis or war (e.g. The New Deal; post-September 11, 2001).

Democratic party Had its birth during the candidacy of Andrew Jackson; originally drew its principles from Thomas Jefferson and advocated limited government. In modern times many Democrats favor domestic programs that a larger, more powerful government allows.

Democratic-Republicans Believed in the ideas of Thomas Jefferson, who wrote of the benefits of a limited government and of a society dominated by the values of the yeoman farmer. Opposed to the Federalists, who wanted a strong national state and a society dominated by commercial interests.

Desert Shield After Iraq invaded Kuwait on August 2, 1990, President Bush sent 230,000 American troops to protect Saudi Arabia.

Desert Storm February 1991 attack on Iraqi forces in Kuwait by United States and other allied forces; although Iraq was driven from Kuwait, Saddam Hussein remained in power in Iraq.

détente The lessening of tensions between nations. A policy of détente between the United States and the Soviet Union and Communist China began during the presidency of Richard Nixon; the architect of policy was National Security Advisor Henry Kissinger.

Dien Bien Phu 1954 victory of Vietnamese forces over the French, causing the French to leave Vietnam and all of Indochina; Geneva Peace Accords that followed established North and South Vietnam.

direct primary Progressive-era reform adopted by some states that allowed candidates for state offices to be nominated by the rank-and-file party members in statewide primaries instead of by the party bosses, who had traditionally dominated the nominating process.

"Dollar Diplomacy" Foreign policy of President William Howard Taft, which favored increased American investment in the world as the major method for increasing American influence and stability abroad; in some parts of the world, such as in Latin America, the increased American influence was resented.

domesticity Social trend of post-World War II America; many Americans turned to family and home life as a source of contentment; emphasis on family as a source of fulfillment forced some women to abandon the workforce and achieve "satisfaction" as homemakers.

Dominion of New England Instituted by King James II in 1686, Sir Edmund Andros governed as a single entity the colonies of Massachusetts, Connecticut, Rhode Island, New York, Plymouth, and New Hampshire without an elective assembly; Andros was finally overthrown by militiamen in Boston in April 1689 (after the Glorious Revolution).

domino theory Major tenet of Cold War containment policy of the United States held that if one country in a region turned communist, other surrounding countries would soon follow; this theory convinced many that to save all of Southeast Asia, it was necessary to resist communist aggression in Vietnam.

Double V campaign World War II "policy" supported by several prominent black newspapers, stating that blacks in America should work for victory over the Axis powers but at the same time work for victory over oppression at home; black leaders remained frustrated during the war by continued segregation of the armed forces.

Dred Scott case Supreme Court case involving a man who was born a slave but had then lived in both a nonslave state and a nonslave territory and was now petitioning for his legal freedom; in 1857 the Court ruled that slaves were not people but were property, that they could not be citizens of the United States, and thus had no legal right to petition the Court for anything. Ruling also stated that Missouri Compromise, which banned slavery in the territories, was unconstitutional.

Dust Bowl Great Plains region that suffered severe drought and experienced severe dust storms during the 1930s; because of extreme conditions many who lived in the Dust Bowl left their farms and went to California to work as migrant farmers.

Eisenhower Doctrine Policy established in 1957 that promised military and economic aid to "friendly" nations in the Middle East; policy was established to prevent communism from gaining a foothold in the region. Policy first utilized later that year when United States gave large amounts of aid to King Hussein of Jordan to put down internal rebellion.

Electoral College Procedure outlined in the Constitution for the election of the president; under this system, votes of electors from each state, and not the popular vote, determine who is elected president. As was demonstrated in 2000 presidential election, this system allows a person to be elected president who does not win the nationwide popular vote.

Emancipation Proclamation Edict by Abraham Lincoln that went into effect on January 1, 1863, abolishing slavery in the Confederate states; proclamation did not affect the four slave states that were still part of the Union (so not to alienate them).

Embargo of 1807 Declaration by President Thomas Jefferson that banned all American trade with Europe. As a result of the war between England and Napoleon's France, America's sea rights as a neutral power were threatened; Jefferson hoped the embargo would force England and France to respect American neutrality.

Emergency Quota Act Also called the Johnson Act, this 1921 bill limited immigration from Southern and Eastern Europe by stating that in a year, total immigration from any country could only equal 3 percent of the number of immigrations from that country living in the United States in 1910.

Enlightenment Eighteenth-century European intellectual movement that attempted to discover the natural laws that governed science and society and taught that progress was inevitable in the Western world. Americans were greatly influenced by the Enlightenment, especially by the ideas of John Locke, who stated that government should exist for the benefit of the people living under it.

Enola Gay The name of the American bomber that on August 6, 1945, dropped the first atomic bomb on the city of Hiroshima, thus initiating the nuclear age.

Era of Good Feelings Term used by a newspaper of the period to describe the years between 1816 and 1823, when after the end of the War of 1812 the United States remained generally free of foreign conflicts and when political strife at home was at a bare minimum (because of the collapse of the Federalist party).

Espionage Act World War I-era regulation passed in 1917 that ordered severe penalties for citizens who criticized the war effort or the government; mandatory prison sentences were also proclaimed for those who interfered with the draft process. Nearly 700 Americans were arrested for violating this act.

Essex Junto Group of Massachusetts Federalists who met to voice their displeasure with the policies of Thomas Jefferson during Jefferson's second term, and proposed that the New England states and New York secede from the Union.

Exodusters Large number of Southern blacks who left the South and moved to Kansas for a "better life" after Reconstruction ended in 1877; many failed to find satisfaction in Kansas because of lack of opportunities and open hostility from Kansas residents.

Fair Deal A series of domestic programs proposed to Congress by President Harry Truman that included a Fair Employment Practices Act, a call for government construction of public housing, an extension of Social Security, and a proposal to ensure employment for all American workers.

Farmer's Alliances After the decline of Grange organizations, these became the major organizations of farmers in the 1880s; many experimented with cooperative buying and selling. Many local alliances became involved in direct political activity with the growth of the Populist Party in the 1890s.

Federalists During the period when the Constitution was being ratified, these were the supporters of the larger national government as outlined in the Constitution; the party of Washington and John Adams, it was supported by commercial interests. Federalists were opposed by Jeffersonians, who favored a smaller federal government and a society dominated by agrarian values. Federalist influence in national politics ended with presidential election of 1816.

Federal Deposit Insurance Corporation (FDIC) Passed during the first Hundred Days of the administration of Franklin Roosevelt, this body insured individual bank deposits up to $2500 and helped to restore confidence in America's banks.

Federal Reserve System Established by Federal Reserve Act of 1913, this system established 12 district reserve banks to be controlled by the banks in each district; in addition, a Federal Reserve Board was established to regulate the entire structure. This act improved public confidence in the banking system.

Federal Trade Commission Authorized after the passage of the Clayton Antitrust Act of 1914, it was established as the major government body in charge of regulating big business. The FTC investigated possible violations of antitrust laws.

Feminine Mystique, The Betty Friedan's 1963 book that was the Bible of the feminist movement of the 1960s and 1970s. Friedan maintained that the post-World War II emphasis on family forced women to think of themselves primarily as housewives and robbed them of much of their creative potential.

feminism The belief that women should have the same rights and benefits in American society that men do. Feminism gained many supporters during the Progressive era, and in the 1960s drew large numbers of supporters. The National

Organization for Women (NOW) was established in 1966 by Betty Friedan and had nearly 200,000 members in 1969.

Fifteenth Amendment Ratified in 1870, this amendment stated that a person could not be denied the right to vote because of the color of their skin or whether or not they had been a slave. This extended the rights of blacks to vote to the North (which the Emancipation Proclamation had not done); some in the women's movement opposed the amendment on the grounds that it did nothing for the rights of women.

Final Solution The plan of Adolf Hitler and Nazi Germany to eliminate Jewish civilization from Europe; by the end of the war in 1945, nearly 6 million Jews had been executed. The full extent of Germany's atrocities was not known in Europe and the United States until near the end of World War II.

fireside chats Broadcasts on the radio by Franklin Roosevelt addressed directly to the American people that made many Americans feel that he personally cared about them; FDR did 16 of these in his first two terms. Many Americans in the 1930s had pictures of Roosevelt in their living rooms; in addition, Roosevelt received more letters from ordinary Americans than any other president in American history.

flapper A "new woman" of the 1920s, who wore short skirts and bobbed hair and rejected many of the social regulations that controlled women of previous generations.

Food and Drug Act 1906 bill that created a federal Food and Drug Administration; example of consumer protection legislation of the progressive era, it was at least partially passed as a result of Upton Sinclair's novel *The Jungle*.

Force Act 1832 legislation that gave President Andrew Jackson the power to invade any state if that action was necessary to enforce federal law; bill was in response to nullification of federal tariff regulation by the legislature of South Carolina.

Fordney-McCumber Tariff 1922 act that sharply increased tariffs on imported goods; most Republican leaders of the 1920s firmly believed in "protectionist" policies that would increase profits for American businesses.

Fort Sumter Federal fort located in Charleston, South Carolina, that was fired on by Confederate artillery on April 12, 1861; these were the first shots actually fired in the Civil War. A public outcry immediately followed across the Northern states, and the mobilization of a federal army began.

Fourteen Points Woodrow Wilson's view of a post-World War I that he hoped the other Allied powers would endorse during the negotiations for the Treaty of Versailles; Wilson's vision included elimination of secret treaties, arms reduction, national self-determination, and the creation of a League of Nations. After negotiations, only the League of Nations remained (which the United States never became part of).

Fourteenth Amendment Ratified in 1868, this amendment stated that "all persons born or naturalized in the United States" were citizens. In addition, all former Confederate supporters were prohibited from holding office in the United States.

Franciscans Missionaries that established settlements in the Southwestern United States in the late 1500s; at their missions Christian conversion was encouraged, but at the same time Native Americans were used as virtual slaves. Rebellions against the missions and the soldiers sent to protect them began in 1598.

Fredericksburg, Battle of Battle on December 13, 1862, where the Union army commanded by General Ambrose Burnside suffered a major defeat at the hands of Confederate forces.

freedmen Term used for free blacks in the South after the Civil War. Freedmen enjoyed some gains in terms of education, the ability to hold office, and economic well-being during the Reconstruction era, although many of these gains were wiped out after the Compromise of 1877.

Freedom Rides Buses of black and white civil rights workers who in 1961 rode on interstate buses to the Deep South to see if Southern states were abiding by the 1960 Supreme Court ruling banning segregation on interstate buses and waiting rooms and restaurants at bus stations. Buses met mob violence in numerous cities; federal marshals were finally called to protect the freedom riders.

Freeport Doctrine Introduced by Stephen Douglas in the Lincoln-Douglas debates, the idea that despite the Dred Scott Supreme Court decision, a territory could still prevent slavery by electing officials who were opposed to it and by creating laws and regulations that would make slavery impossible to enforce.

Free-Soil party Political party that won 10 percent of the vote in the 1848 presidential election; they were opposed to the spread of slavery into any of the recently acquired American territories. Free-Soil supporters were mainly many former members of the Whig party in the North.

Free Speech Movement Protests at the University of California at Berkeley in 1964 and 1965 that opposed the control that the university, and "the establishment" in general, had over the lives of university students. Protesters demanded changes in university regulations and also broader changes in American society.

free trade The philosophy that trade barriers and protective tariffs inhibit long-term economic growth; this philosophy was the basis for the 1994 ratification by the United States of the North American Free Trade Agreement (NAFTA), which removed trade restrictions between the United States, Mexico, and Canada.

French and Indian War Called the Seven Years War in European textbooks, this war between the British and the French was fought for the right to expand their empire in the Americas. Colonists and Native Americans fought on both sides, and the war eventually spilled to Europe and elsewhere. The English emerged victorious, and in the end received all of French Canada.

Fugitive Slave Act Part of the Compromise of 1850, this legislation set up special commissions in Northern states to determine if an accused runaway slave really was one; according to regulations, after the verdict, commissioners were given more money if the black was found to be a runaway than if he or she was found not to be one. Some Northern legislatures passed laws attempting to circumvent the Fugitive Slave Act.

Gadsden Purchase Strip of territory running through Arizona and New Mexico that the United States purchased from Mexico in 1853; President Pierce authorized this purchase to secure that the southern route of the transcontinental railroad (between Texas and California) would be in American territory.

Geneva Accords After the French were defeated in Vietnam, a series of agreements made in 1954 that temporarily divided Vietnam into two parts (along the 17th parallel) and promised nationwide elections within two years. To prevent communists from gaining control, the United States installed a friendly government in South Vietnam and saw that the reunification elections never took place.

Gettysburg Address Speech made by Abraham Lincoln at dedication ceremony for a cemetery for Union soldiers who died at the Battle of Gettysburg; in this November 19, 1863 speech, Lincoln stated that freedom should exist in the United States for *all* men, and that "government of the people, by the people, for the people, shall not perish from the earth."

Gettysburg, Battle of The most important battle of the Civil War, this July 1863 victory by Union forces prevented General Robert E. Lee from invading the North. Defeat at Gettysburg, along with defeat at the Battle of Vicksburg during the same month, turned the tide of war firmly in the direction of Union forces.

Ghent, Treaty of 1814 treaty between the United States and Great Britain ending the War of 1812; treaty restored diplomatic relations between the two countries but did nothing to address the issues that had initially caused war.

Ghost Dances Religion practiced by Lakota tribesmen in response to repeated incursions by American settlers. Ghost dancers thought that Native American messiah would come and banish the whites, return the buffalo, and give all former Native American land back to the Native Americans. Worried territorial officials had Sitting Bull arrested (he was later killed under uncertain circumstances) and killed another 146 Lakota at Wounded Knee Creek.

GI Popular term for American servicemen during World War II; refers to the fact that virtually anything they wore or used was "government issued."

GI Bill Officially called the Serviceman's Readjustment Act of 1944, this legislation gave many benefits to returning World War II veterans, including financial assistance for veterans wanting to go to college or enter other job training programs, special loan programs for veterans wanting to buy homes or businesses, and preferential treatment for veterans who wished to apply for government jobs.

globalization Belief that the United States should work closely with other nations of the world to solve common problems; this was the foreign policy approach of President Clinton. Policies that supported this approach included the ratification of NAFTA, the United States working more closely with the United Nations, and "nation building" abroad. Many policies of globalization were initially rejected by Clinton's successor, George W. Bush.

Glorious Revolution English revolution of 1688 to 1689 where King James II was removed from the throne and his Protestant daughter Mary and her Dutch husband William began to rule. Reaction to this in the American colonies was varied: There was a revolt against appointed Catholic officials in New York and Maryland, and in Massachusetts the governor was sent back to England with the colonial demand that the Dominion of New England be disbanded.

gold standard Economic system that bases all currency on gold, meaning that all paper currency could be exchanged at a bank for gold. Business interests of the late nineteenth century supported this; William Jennings Bryan ran for president three times opposing the gold standard, and supported the free coinage of silver instead.

"Gospel of Wealth" The philosophy of steel magnate Andrew Carnegie, who stated that wealthy industrialists had an obligation to create a "trust fund" from their profits to help their local communities. By the time of his death, Carnegie had given over 90 percent of his wealth to various foundations and philanthropic endeavors.

Grange Initially formed in 1867, the Grange was an association of farmers that provided social activities and information about new farming techniques. Some local Grange organizations became involved in cooperative buying and selling.

Great Awakening A religious revival in the American colonies that lasted from the 1720s through the 1740s; speakers like Jonathan Edwards enraptured speakers with sermons such as "Sinners in the Hands of an Angry God." Religious splits in the colonies became deeper because of this movement.

Great Compromise Plan drafted by Roger Sherman of Connecticut that stated one house of the United States Congress would be based on population (the House of Representatives), while in the other house all states would be represented equally (the Senate). This compromise greatly speeded the ratification of the Constitution.

Great Migration Migration of large numbers of American blacks to Midwestern and Eastern industrial cities that began during World War I and continued throughout the 1920s. Additional workers were needed in the North because of the war and during the 1920s because of immigration restrictions; blacks were willing to leave the South because of continued lynchings there and the fact that their economic situation was not improving.

Great Society Aggressive program announced by President Lyndon Johnson in 1965 to attack the major social problems in America; Great Society programs included the War on Poverty, Medicare and Medicaid programs for elderly Americans, greater protection for and more legislation dealing with civil rights, and greater funding for education. Balancing the Great Society and the war in Vietnam would prove difficult for the Johnson administration.

Greenback party Political party of the 1870s and early 1880s that stated the government should put more money in circulation and supported an eight-hour workday and female suffrage. The party received support from farmers but never built a national base. The Greenback party argued into the 1880s that more greenbacks should be put in circulation to help farmers who were in debt and who saw the prices of their products decreasing annually.

"Greenbacks" Paper money issued by the American government during and immediately after the

Civil War that was not backed up by gold or silver.

gridlock Situation when the president is a member of one political party and the U.S. Congress is controlled by the other party, causing a situation where little legislation is actually passed. This is how some describe the situation with President Clinton and the Republican-controlled Congress after the 1994 congressional elections.

Guadalcanal, Battle of Battle over this Pacific island lasted from August 1942 through February 1943; American victory against fierce Japanese resistance was the first major offensive victory for the Americans in the Pacific War.

Guadeloupe-Hidalgo, Treaty of Treaty ending the war with Mexico that was ratified by the Senate in March 1848 and for $15 million gave the United States Texas territory to the Rio Grande River, New Mexico, and California.

Guilded Age, The Some historians describe the late nineteenth century in this manner, describing it as an era with a surface of great prosperity hiding deep problems of social inequity and shallowness of culture. The term comes from the title of an 1873 Mark Twain novel.

Gulf of Tonkin Resolution 1964 Congressional resolution that gave President Johnson the authority to "take all necessary measures to repel" attacks against American military forces stationed in Vietnam. Later, critics would charge this resolution allowed the president to greatly expand the Vietnam War without congressional oversight.

Harlem Renaissance Black literary and artistic movement centered in Harlem that lasted from the 1920s into the early 1930s that both celebrated and lamented black life in America; Langston Hughes and Zora Neale Hurston were two famous writers of this movement.

Hartford Convention Meeting of New England Federalists in the closing months of the War of 1812 where they threatened that New England would secede from the United States unless trade restrictions imposed by President Madison were lifted. American victory in the war made their protests seem pointless.

Hawley-Smoot Tariff In response to the initial effects of the Great Depression, Congress authorized this tariff in 1930; this established tariff rates on imported goods at the highest level of any point in United States history. Some American companies benefited in the short term, although the effect on world trade was disastrous, as many other countries erected tariff barriers on American imports.

Haymarket Square Location in Chicago of labor rally called by anarchist and other radical labor leaders on May 2, 1886. A bomb was hurled toward police officials, and police opened fired on the demonstrators; numerous policemen and demonstrators were killed and wounded. Response in the nation's press was decidedly anti-union.

Head Start One of Lyndon Johnson's War on Poverty programs that gave substantial funding for a nursery school program to prepare children of poor parents for kindergarten.

Heavy industry The production of steel, iron, and other materials that can be used for building purposes; great increase in heavy industry fueled the massive industrial growth that took place in the last half on the nineteenth century.

Hessians German troops who fought in the Revolutionary War on the side of Great Britain; Hessian troops were almost all paid mercenaries.

Holding company A company that existed to gain monopoly control over an industry by buying large numbers of shares of stock in as many companies as possible in that industry. The best example in American history was John D. Rockefeller's Standard Oil corporation.

Holocaust Historical term used for the extermination of 6 million Jewish victims by Nazi Germany during World War II. Much has been written on the reasons for the Holocaust and why it occurred in Germany.

Homestead Act 1862 enactment by Congress that gave 160 acres of publicly owned land to a farmer who lived on the land and farmed it for five years. The provisions of this bill inspired hundreds of thousands of Americans to move westward in the years after the Civil War.

Hoovervilles Groups of crude houses made of cardboard and spare wood that sprung up on the fringes of many American cities during the first years of the Great Depression. These shacks were occupied by unemployed workers; the name of these communities demonstrated the feeling that President Hoover should have been doing more to help the downtrodden in America.

horizontal integration The strategy of gaining as much control over an entire single industry as possible, usually by creating trusts and holding companies. The most successful example of horizontal integration was John D. Rockefeller and Standard Oil, who had at one point controlled over 92 percent of the oil production in the United States.

HUAC (House Un-American Activities Committee) Committee of the House of Representatives that beginning in 1947 investigated possible communist infiltration of the entertainment industry and, more importantly, of the government. Most famous investigations of the committee were the investigation of the "Hollywood Ten" and the investigation of Alger Hiss, a former high-ranking member of the State Department.

Huguenots Protestants in France, who by the 1630s were believers in Calvinism. Few Huguenots ended up settling in the Americas, as French officials feared they would disrupt the unity of colonial settlements.

Hull House Established by Jane Addams and Ellen Gates Starr in Chicago in 1889, this was the first settlement house in America. Services such as reading groups, social clubs, an employment bureau, and a "day care center" for working mothers could be found at Hull House. The Hull House model was later copied in many other urban centers.

"Hun" Term used in allied propaganda during World War I to depict the German soldier; Germans were portrayed as bloodthirsty beasts. World War I was the first war where propaganda was used on a widespread scale.

Hundred Days The period from March through June of 1933; the first 100 days of the New Deal presidency of Franklin Roosevelt. During this period programs were implemented to assist farmers, the banks, unemployed workers, and businessmen; in addition, prohibition was repealed.

hunter-gatherers Early civilizations that existed not by farming but by moving from region to region and taking what was necessary at the time from the land; some early Native American tribes in northern New England lived as hunter-gatherers.

hydrogen bomb Atomic weapons much more powerful than those used at Hiroshima and Nagasaki, these were developed and repeatedly tested by both the United States and the Soviet Union in the 1950s, increasing dramatically the potential danger of nuclear war.

impeachment The process of removing an elected public official from office; during the Progressive Era several states adopted measures making it easier to do this. Presidents Andrew Johnson and William Jefferson Clinton were both impeached by the House of Representatives, but neither was convicted by the U.S. Senate (the procedure outlined in the Constitution of the United States).

impressment British practice of forcing civilians and ex-sailors back into naval service; during the wars against Napoleon the British seized nearly 7500 sailors from American ships, including some that had actually become American citizens. This practice caused increased tensions between the United States and Great Britain and was one of the causes of the War of 1812.

Inca empire Advanced and wealthy civilization centered in the Andes mountain region; aided by smallpox, Francisco Pizarro conquered the Incas in 1533.

indentured servants Legal arrangement when an individual owed compulsory service (in some cases only 3 years, in others up to 10) for free passage to the American colonies. Many of the early settlers in the Virginia colony came as indentured servants.

Industrial Workers of the World (I.W.W.) Established in 1905, this union attempted to unionize the unskilled workers who were usually not recruited by the American Federation of Labor. The I.W.W. included blacks, poor sharecroppers, and newly arrived immigrants from Eastern Europe. Members of the union were called "Wobblies," and leaders of the union were inspired by Marxist principles.

Influence of Sea Power upon History, The Very influential 1890 book by Admiral Alfred Thayer Mahan, which argued that throughout history the most powerful nations have achieved their influence largely because of powerful navies. Mahan called for a large increase in the size of the American navy, the acquisition of American bases in the Pacific, and the building of the Panama Canal.

initiative process Procedure supported by the Populist party in the 1890s where any proposed law could go on the public ballot as long as a petition with an appropriate number of names is submitted beforehand supporting the proposed law.

internment camps Controversial decision was made after the bombing of Pearl Harbor to place Japanese-Americans living on the West Coast in these camps. President Roosevelt authorized this by Executive Order #9066; this order was validated by the Supreme Court in 1944. In 1988 the U.S. government paid compensation to surviving detainees.

Interstate Commerce Act Passed in 1887, the bill created America's first regulatory commission, the Interstate Commerce Commission. The task of this commission was to regulate the railroad and railroad rates, and to ensure that rates were "reasonable and just."

Intolerable Acts Term used by anti-British speakers across the colonies for the series of bills passed in Great Britain to punish the Massachusetts colony for the Boston Tea Party of December 1773. These included the closing of Boston harbor, prohibiting local meetings, and mandatory quartering of troops in the homes of Massachusetts residents.

Iran-Contra Affair During the second term of the Reagan administration, government officials sold missiles to Iran (hoping that this would help free American hostages held in Lebanon); money from this sale was used to aid anticommunist Contra forces in Nicaragua. Iran was a country that was supposed to be on the American "no trade" list because of their taking of American hostages, and congressional legislation had been enacted making it illegal to give money to the Contras. A major scandal for the Reagan administration.

Iranian Hostage Crisis On November 4, 1979, Islamic fundamentalists seized the American embassy in Tehran, Iran, and took all Americans working there hostage. This was a major humiliation for the United States, as diplomatic and military efforts to free the hostages failed. The hostages were finally freed on January 20, 1981, immediately after the inauguration of Ronald Reagan.

ironclad ship Civil War-era ships that were totally encased in iron, thus making them very difficult to damage; the ironclad of the Confederate army was the *Virginia* (it had been the *Merrimac* when it was captured from the Union), whereas the Union ship was the *Monitor*. The two ships battled each other in March 1862, with both being badly damaged.

Iron Curtain In a March 5, 1946 speech in Fulton, Missouri, Winston Churchill used this term to describe the division that the Soviet Union had created between itself and its Eastern European allies and Western Europe and the United States. Churchill emphasized the need for the United States to stand up to potential Soviet aggression in the future.

"Irreconcilables" After World War I, a group of U.S. senators who were opposed to a continued U.S. presence in Europe in any form. This group was influential in preventing the passage of the Versailles Treaty in the Senate.

island-hopping A successful American military tactic in the Pacific in 1942 and 1943 of taking strategic islands that could be used as staging points for continued military offensives. Increasing American dominance in air power made this tactic possible.

isolationism A policy of disengaging the United States from major world commitments and concentrating on the U.S. domestic issues. This was the dominant foreign policy of the United States for much of the 1920s and the 1930s.

Jay's Treaty 1794 treaty between the United States and Great Britain designed to ease increasing tensions between the two nations; the British did make some concessions to the Americans, including abandoning the forts they occupied in the interior of the continent. However, Britain refused to make concessions to America over the rights of American ships; tensions over this issue would eventually be a cause of the War of 1812.

Jazz Age Term used to describe the image of the liberated, urbanized 1920s, with a flapper as a dominant symbol of that era. Many rural, fundamentalist Americans deeply resented the changes in American culture that occurred in the "Roaring 20s."

Jazz Singer, The 1927 film starring Al Jolson that was the first movie with sound. Story of the film deals with young Jewish man who has to choose between the "modern" and his Jewish past.

Jesuits Missionary group who established settlements in Florida, New Mexico, Paraguay, and in several areas within French territory in North America. Jesuits were organized with military precision and order.

jingoism American foreign policy based on a strident nationalism, a firm belief in American world superiority, and a belief that military solutions were, in almost every case, the best ones. Jingoism was most evident in America during the months leading up to and during the Spanish-American War.

Judiciary Act 1801 bill passed by the Federalist Congress just before the inauguration of President Thomas Jefferson; Federalists in this bill attempted to maintain control of the judiciary by reducing the number of Supreme Court judges (so Jefferson probably wouldn't be able to name a replacement) and by increasing the number of federal judges (who President Adams appointed before he left office). Bill was repealed by new Congress in 1802.

Judicial Review In the 1803 *Marbury* v. *Madison* decision, Chief Justice John C. Marshall stated that the U.S. Supreme Court ultimately had the power to decide on the constitutionality of any law passed by the U.S. Congress or by the legislature of any state. Many had argued that individual states should have the power to do this; the *Marbury* decision increased the power of the federal government.

Justice Reorganization Bill Franklin Roosevelt's 1937 plan to increase the number of Supreme Court justices. He claimed that this was because many of the judges were older and needed help keeping up with the work; in reality he wanted to "pack the court" because the Court had made several rulings outlawing New Deal legislation. Many Democrats and Republicans opposed this plan, so it was finally dropped by Roosevelt.

kamikaze pilots 1945 tactic of Japanese air force where pilots flew at American ships at full speed and crashed into them, in several cases causing ships to sink. This tactic showed the desperate nature of the Japanese military situation at this time; by July 1945, kamikaze attacks were no longer utilized, as Japan was running out of airplanes and pilots.

Kansas-Nebraska Act 1854 compromise legislation crafted by Stephen Douglas that allowed the settlers in the Kansas and Nebraska territories to decide if those territories would be slave or free. Bill caused controversy and bloodshed throughout these territories; in the months before the vote in Kansas, large numbers of "settlers" moved in to influence the vote, and after the vote (won by pro-slavery forces), violence between the two sides intensified.

Kent State University Site of May 1970 antiwar protest where Ohio National Guardsmen fired on protesters, killing four. To many, this event was symbolic of the extreme political tensions that permeated American society in this era.

Kentucky and Virginia Resolves Passed by the legislatures in these two states, these resolutions maintained that the Alien and Sedition Acts championed through Congress by John Adams went beyond the powers that the Constitution stated belonged to the federal government. These resolves predated that later Southern argument that individual states could "nullify" federal laws deemed unconstitutional by the states.

Kerner Commission Established in 1967 to study the reason for urban riots, the commission spoke at length about the impact of poverty and racism on the lives of urban blacks in America, and emphasized that white institutions created and condoned the ghettoes of America.

King William's War Colonial war against the French that lasted from 1689 to 1697; army from New England colonies attacked Quebec, but were forced to retreat because of the lack of strong colonial leadership and an outbreak of smallpox among colonial forces.

Kitchen Cabinet An informal group of advisors, with no official titles, who the president relies on for advice. The most famous Kitchen Cabinet was that of Andrew Jackson, who met with several old political friends and two journalists for advice on many occasions.

Knights of Labor The major labor union of the 1880s; was not a single large union, but a federation of the unions of many industries. The Knights of Labor accepted unskilled workers; publicity against the organization was intense after the Haymarket Square riot of 1886.

Know-Nothing party Political party that developed in the 1850s that claimed that the other political parties and the entire political process was corrupt, that immigrants were destroying the economic base of America by working for low wages, and that Catholics in America were intent on destroying American democracy. Know-Nothings were similar in many ways to other nativist groups that developed at various points in America's history.

Korean War 1950 to 1953 war where American and other United Nations forces fought to stop communist aggression against South Korea. U.S. entry into Korean War was totally consistent with the U.S. Cold War policy of containment. Negotiated settlement divided Korea along the 38th parallel, a division that remains today.

Ku Klux Klan Organization founded in the South during the Reconstruction era by whites that wanted to maintain white supremacy in the region. KKK used terror tactics, including murder. The Klan was revitalized in the 1920s; members of the 1920s Klan also opposed Catholics and Southern and Eastern European immigrants. The KKK exists to this day, with recent efforts to make the Klan appear to be "respectable."

labor movement The drive that began in the second half of the nineteenth century to have workers join labor unions. Divisions existed in nineteenth-century unions on whether unions should focus their energies on political gains for workers or on "bread and butter" issues important to workers. In the twentieth century, unions have broad political powers, as most endorse and financially support candidates in national and statewide elections.

Laissez-faire economic principles Economic theory derived from eighteenth-century economist Adam Smith, who stated that for the economy to run soundly the government should take a hands-off role in economic matters. Those who have favored policies such as high import tariffs do *not* follow laissez-faire policies; a policy like NAFTA has more support amongst the "free market" supporters of Adam Smith.

land speculation The practice of buying up land with the intent of selling it off in the future for a profit. Land speculation existed in the Kentucky territory in the 1780s, throughout the West after the Homestead Act, and in Florida in the 1920s, when hundreds bought Florida swampland hoping to later sell it for a profit.

League of Nations International body of nations that was proposed by Woodrow Wilson and was adopted at the Versailles Peace Conference ending

World War I. The League was never an effective body in reducing international tensions, at least partially because the United States was never a member of it.

Lend-Lease Act Legislation proposed by Franklin Roosevelt and adopted by Congress in 1941, stating that the United States could either sell or lease arms and other equipment to any country whose security was vital to America's interest. After the passage of this bill, military equipment to help the British war effort began to be shipped from the United States.

Letters from a Farmer in Pennsylvania A 1767 pamphlet by Pennsylvania attorney and landowner John Dickinson, in which he eloquently stated the "taxation without representation" argument, and also stated that the only way that the House of Commons could represent the colonies in a meaningful way would be for actual colonists to be members of it.

Lever Food and Fuel Control Act August 1917 measure that gave President Wilson the power to regulate the production and consumption of food and fuels during wartime. Some in his administration argued for price controls and rationing; instead, Wilson instituted voluntary controls.

Levittown After World War II, the first "suburban" neighborhood; located in Hempstead, Long Island, houses in this development were small, looked the same, but were perfect for the postwar family that wanted to escape urban life. Levittown would become a symbol of the post-World War II flight to suburbia taken by millions.

Lewis and Clark Expedition 1803 to 1806 mission sent by Thomas Jefferson to explore and map the newly acquired Louisiana territory and to create good relations with various Native American tribes within the territory. Reports brought back indicated that settlement was possible in much of the region, and that the Louisiana territory was well worth what had been paid for it.

Lexington Massachusetts town where the first skirmish between British troops and colonial militiamen took place; during this April 19, 1775 "battle," eight colonists were killed and another ten were wounded.

Liberator, The The radical abolitionist journal of William Lloyd Garrison that was first published in 1831; Garrison and his journal presented the most extreme abolitionist views during the period leading up to the Civil War.

Liberty Bonds Sold to United States civilians during World War I; a holder who paid $10 for a bond could get $13 back if the holder held onto the bond until it matured. Bonds were important in financing the war effort, and celebrities such as Charlie Chaplin made short films encouraging Americans to buy them.

Little Bighorn, Battle of the 1876 Montana battle where Colonel George Custer and over 200 of his men were killed by a group of Cheyenne and Lakota warriors. This was the last major victory by Native American forces over a U.S. army unit.

London Company In 1603 King James I gave the London Company a charter to settle the Virginia territory. In April 1607, the first settlers from this company settled at Jamestown.

"Lost Generation" Group of American intellectuals who viewed America in the 1920s as bigoted, intellectually shallow, and consumed by the quest for the dollar; many became extremely disillusioned with American life and went to Paris. Ernest Hemingway wrote of this group in *The Sun Also Rises*.

Louisiana Purchase The 1803 purchase of the huge Louisiana territory (from the Mississippi River out to the Rocky Mountains) from Napoleon for $15 million. This purchase made eventual westward movement possible for vast numbers of Americans.

Lowell System Developed in the textile mills of Lowell, Massachusetts, in the 1820s, in these factories as much machinery as possible was used, so that few skilled workers were needed in the process, and the workers were almost all single young farm women, who worked for a few years and then returned home to be housewives. Managers found these young women were the perfect workers for this type of factory life.

Loyalists Individuals who remained loyal to Great Britain during the years up to and during the Revolutionary War. Many who were Loyalists were from the higher strata of colonial society; when war actually broke out and it became apparent that the British were not going to quickly win, almost all went to Canada, the West Indies, or back to Great Britain.

Loyalty Review Boards These were established in 1947 in an effort to control possible communist influence in the American government. These boards were created to investigate the possibility of "security risks" working for the American government, and to determine if those "security risks" should lose their jobs. Some employees were released because of their affiliation with "unacceptable" political organizations or because of their sexual orientation.

Lusitania British passenger liner with 128 Americans on board that was sunk off the coast of Ireland by a German U-boat on May 7, 1915. This sinker caused outrage in the United States and was one of a series of events that drew the United States closer to war with Germany.

Manhattan Project Program begun in 1941 to develop an atomic weapon for the United States; project was aided by German scientists added to the research team who had been working on a similar bomb in Germany. First test of the bomb took place in New Mexico on July 16, 1945.

manifest destiny Term first used in the 1840s, the concept that America's expansion westward was as journalist John O'Sullivan said, "the fulfillment of our manifest destiny to overspread the continent allotted by Providence for the free development of our yearly multiplying millions."

Man in the Gray Flannel Suit, The Early 1950s book and movie that compares the sterility, sameness, and lack of excitement of postwar work and family life with the vitality felt by many World War II veterans during their wartime experiences.

Marbury* v. *Madison 1803 decision of this case written by Chief Justice John Marshall established the principle of judicial review, meaning that the Supreme Court ultimately has the power to decide if any federal or state law is unconstitutional.

March on Washington Over 200,000 came to Washington for this August 1963 event demanding civil rights for blacks. A key moment of the proceedings was Martin Luther King's "I have a dream speech"; the power of the civil rights movement was not lost on Lyndon Johnson, who pushed for civil rights legislation when he became president the following year.

Marshall Plan Plan announced in 1947 whereby the United States would help to economically rebuild Europe after the war; 17 Western European nations became part of the plan. The United States introduced the plan so that communism would not spread across war-torn Europe and bring other European countries into the communist camp.

Massacre at Wounded Knee December 28, 1890 "battle" that was the last military resistance of Native Americans of the Great Plains against American encroachment. Minneconjou Indians were at Wounded Knee creek. American soldiers attempted to take their arms from them; after shooting began, 25 American soldiers died, along with 146 men, women, and children of the Indian tribe.

martial law During a state of emergency, when rule of law may be suspended and government is controlled by military or police authorities. During the Civil War, Kentucky was placed under martial law by President Lincoln.

massive retaliation Foreign policy officials in the Eisenhower administration believed the best way to stop communism was to convince the communists that every time they advanced, there would be massive retaliation against them. This policy explains the desire in this era to increase the nuclear arsenal of the United States.

McCarran Internal Security Act Congressional act enacted in 1950 that stated all members of the Communist party had to register with the office of the Attorney General and that it was a crime to conspire to foster communism in the United States.

McCarran-Walter Act 1952 bill that limited immigration from everywhere except Northern and Western Europe and stated that immigration officials could turn any immigrant away that they thought might threaten the national security of the United States.

McCarthyism Named after Senator Joseph McCarthy of Wisconsin, the title given for the movement that took place during the late 1940s and early 1950s in American politics to root out potential communist influence in the government, the military, and the entertainment industry. Harsh tactics were often used by congressional investigations, with few actual communists ever discovered. This period is seen by many today as an era of intolerance and paranoia.

Meat Inspection Act Inspired by Upton Sinclair's *The Jungle,* this 1906 bill established a government commission that would monitor the quality of all meat sold in America and inspect the meat-packing houses for safety and cleanliness.

Medicare Part of Lyndon Johnson's Great Society program, this program acted as a form of health insurance for retired Americans (and disabled ones as well). Through Medicare, the federal government would pay for services received by elderly patients at doctor's offices and hospitals.

mercantilism Economic policy practiced by most European states in the late seventeenth century that stated the power of any state depended largely on its wealth; thus it was the state's duty to do all that it could to build up wealth. A mercantilist country would not want to import raw materials from other countries; instead, it would be best to have colonies from which these raw materials could be imported.

Merrimack Union ironclad ship captured by Confederates during the Civil War and renamed the *Virginia.*

Meuse-Argonne Offensive American forces played a decisive role in this September 1918 Allied offensive, which was the last major offensive of the war and which convinced the German general staff that victory in World War I was impossible.

Middle Passage The voyage across the Atlantic Ocean taken by slaves on their way to the Americas. Sickness, diseases, and death were rampant as slave ships crossed the Atlantic; on some ships over 20 percent of slaves who began the journey were dead by the time the ship landed.

"midnight appointments" Judicial or other appointments made by an outgoing president or governor in the last hours before he or she leaves office. The most famous were the judicial appointments made by John Adams in the hours before Thomas Jefferson was inaugurated as president.

Midway, Battle of June 4, 1942 naval battle that crippled Japanese offensive capabilities in the Pacific; American airplanes destroyed four aircraft carriers and 245 Japanese planes. After Midway, Japanese military operations were mainly defensive.

Missouri Compromise In a continued effort to maintain a balance between free and slave states, Henry Clay proposed this 1820 compromise, which admitted Maine to the Union as a free state, Missouri to the Union as a slave state, and stated that any part of the Louisiana Territory north of 36 degrees, 30 inches would be nonslave territory.

Model T Automobile produced by Ford Motor Company using assembly line techniques. The first Model Ts were produced in 1907; using the assembly line, Ford produced half of the automobiles made in the world between 1907 and 1926.

Molasses Act In the early 1700s colonists traded for molasses with the French West Indies. British traders wanted to reduce trade between the colonies and the French; in 1733 they pressured Parliament to pass this act, which put prohibitively high duties on imported molasses. Colonists continued to smuggle French molasses in the Americas in spite of British efforts to prevent this.

Monitor Union ironclad ship utilized during the Civil War; fought one battle against the *Virginia*, the South's ironclad ship, and never left port again.

Monroe Doctrine President James Monroe's 1823 statement that an attack by a European state on any nation in the Western Hemisphere would be considered an attack on the United States; Monroe stated that the Western Hemisphere was the hemisphere of the United States and not of Europe. Monroe's statement was scoffed at by certain European political leaders, especially those in Great Britain.

Montgomery bus boycott Yearlong refusal by blacks to ride city buses in Montgomery, Alabama, because of their segregation policies. Boycott began in December 1955; Supreme Court finally ruled that segregation on public buses was unconstitutional. Rosa Parks began the protest when she was arrested for refusing to give up her seat for a white man, and Martin Luther King was a young minister involved in organizing the boycott.

Morrill Land Grant Act 1862 federal act designed to fund state "land-grant" colleges. State governments were given large amounts of land in the western territories; this land was sold to individual settlers, land speculators, and others, and the profits of these land sales could be used to establish the colleges.

Ms. Founded in 1972 by Gloria Steinem, this glossy magazine was aimed at feminist readers.

muckrakers Journalists of the Progressive era who attempted to expose the evils of government and big business. Many muckrakers wrote of the corruption of city and state political machines. Factory conditions and the living and working condition of workers were other topics that some muckrakers wrote about.

My Lai Massacre In 1968 a unit under the command of Lieutenant William Calley killed over 300 men, women, and children in this small Vietnamese village. The antiwar movement took the attack as a symbol of the "immorality" of United States efforts in Vietnam.

NAFTA (North American Free Trade Agreement) Ratified in 1994 by the U.S. Senate, this agreement established a free trade zone between the United States, Mexico, and Canada. Critics of the agreement claim that many jobs have been lost in the United States because of it.

napalm Jellylike substance dropped from American planes during the Vietnam conflict that horribly burned the skin of anyone that came into contact with it. On several occasions, napalm was accidentally dropped on "friendly" villages.

National American Woman's Suffrage Association The major organization for suffrage for women, it was founded in 1890 by Susan B. Anthony and Elizabeth Cady Stanton. Supported the Wilson administration during World War I and split with the more radical National Woman's Party, who in 1917 began to picket the White House because Wilson had not forcefully stated that women should get the vote.

National Association for the Advancement of Colored People (NAACP) Formed in 1909, this organization fought for and continues to fight for the right of blacks in America. The NAACP originally went to court for the plaintiff in the *Brown v. Board of Education* case, and Thurgood Marshall, the NAACP's chief counsel and later a Supreme Court justice, was the main attorney in the case.

National Bank Planned by Alexander Hamilton to be similar to the Bank of England, this bank was funded by government and private sources. Hamilton felt a National Bank would give economic security and confidence to the new nation; Republicans who had originally opposed the bank felt the same way in 1815 when they supported Henry Clay's American System.

National Consumers League Formed in 1899, this organization was concerned with improving the working and living conditions of women in the workplace.

national culture When a general unity of tastes and a commonality of cultural experience exist in a nation; in a general sense, when a country starts to "think the same." This occurred in America for the first time in the 1920s; as many people saw the same movies, read the same magazines, and heard the same things on the radio, a national culture was born.

National Industrial Recovery Act (NIRA) 1933 New Deal legislation that created the Works Progress Administration (WPA) that created jobs to put people back to work right away and the National Recovery Administration (NRA), who worked in conjunction with industry to bolster the industrial sector and create more long-lasting jobs.

National Labor Relations Board (NLRB) Part of the 1935 Wagner Act, which was a huge victory for organized labor. The NLRB ensured that factory owners did not harass union organizers, ensured that collective bargaining was fairly practiced in labor disputes, and supervised union elections. The NLRB was given the legal "teeth" to force employers to comply with all of the above.

National Origins Act Very restrictive immigration legislation passed in 1924, which lowered immigration to 2 percent of each nationality as found in the 1890 census. This lowered immigration dramatically and, quite intentionally, almost eliminated immigration from Eastern and Southern Europe.

National Security League Organization founded in 1914 that preached patriotism and preparation for war; in 1915 they successfully lobbied government officials to set up camps to prepare men for military life and combat. The patriotism of this group became more strident as the war progressed; in 1917 they lobbied Congress to greatly limit immigration into the country.

National Woman's Party Formed by Alice Paul after women got the vote, this group lobbied unsuccessfully in the 1920s to get an Equal Rights Amendment for women added to the Constitution. Desire for this amendment would return among some feminist groups in the 1970s.

Nation of Islam Supporters were called Black Muslims; this group was founded by Elijah Muhammad and preached Islamic principles along with black pride and black separatism. Malcolm X was a member of the Nation of Islam.

NATO (North Atlantic Treaty Organization) Collective alliance of the United States and most of the Western European nations that was founded in 1949; an attack of one member of NATO was to be considered an attack on all. Many United States troops served in Europe during the Cold War era because of the NATO alliance. To counter NATO, the Soviet Union created the Warsaw Pact in 1955.

Naval Act of 1900 Legislation that authorized a large increase in the building of ships to be used for offensive purposes; this measure helped ensure the creation of a world-class American navy.

Navigation Acts 1660 measures passed by Charles II that were designed to increase the dependence of the colonies on England for trade. Charles mandated that certain goods produced in the colonies, such as tobacco, should be sold only to England, that if the colonies wanted to sell anything to other countries it had to come through England first, and that all trade by the colonies to other countries would have to be done in English ships. These measures could have been devastating to the colonies; however, British officials in the colonies did not enforce them carefully.

nativism Nativism states that immigration should be greatly limited or banned altogether, since immigrants hurt the United States economically and also threaten the social well-being of the country. Nativist groups and parties have developed on several occasions in both the nineteenth and the twentieth century; nativist sentiment was especially strong in the 1920s.

Neutrality Act of 1935 To prevent the United States from being drawn into potential European conflicts, this bill said that America would not trade arms with any country at war, and that any American citizen traveling on a ship of a country at war was doing so at his or her own risk.

Neutrality Act of 1939 Franklin Roosevelt got Congress to amend the Neutrality Act of 1935; new legislation stated that England and France could buy arms from the United States as long as there was cash "up front" for these weapons. This was the first military assistance that the United States gave the Allied countries.

New Deal Series of policies instituted by Franklin Roosevelt and his advisors from 1933–1941 that attempted to offset the effects of the Great Depression on American society. Many New Deal policies were clearly experimental; in the end it was the onset of World War II, and not the policies of the New Deal, that pulled the United States out of the Great Depression.

New Deal Coalition The coalition of labor unions and industrial workers, minorities, much of the middle class, and the Solid South that carried Franklin Roosevelt to victories in 1936 and 1940 and that was the basis of Democratic victories on a national level until this coalition started to break up in the late 1960s and early 1970s. A sizable number of this group voted for Ronald Reagan in the presidential elections of 1980 and 1984.

New Democrat Term used to describe Bill Clinton and his congressional supporters during his two terms in office. A New Democrat was pragmatic, and not tied to the old Democratic belief in big government; New Democrats took both Democratic and Republican ideas as they crafted their policies. Some in the Democratic party maintained that Clinton had actually sold out the principles of the party.

New Federalism A series of policies during the administration of Richard Nixon that began to give some power back to the states that had always been held by the federal government. Some tax dollars were returned to state and local governments in the form of "block grants"; the state and local governments could then spend this money as they thought best.

New Freedom policy An approach favored by Southern and Midwestern Democrats, this policy stated that economic and political preparation for World War I should be done in a decentralized manner; this would prevent too much power falling into the hands of the federal government. President Wilson first favored this approach, but then established federal agencies to organize mobilization.

New Frontier The program of President John Kennedy to revitalize America at home and to reenergize America for continued battles against the Soviet Union. Kennedy asked young Americans to volunteer for programs such as the Peace Corps; as he said in his inaugural speech: "Ask not what your country can do for you—ask what you can do for your country."

"new immigrants" Immigrants that came from Southern and Eastern Europe, who made up the majority of immigrants coming into the United States after 1900. Earlier immigrants from Britain, Ireland, and Scandinavia appeared to be "like" the groups that were already settled in the United States; the "new immigrants" were very different. As a result, resentment and nativist sentiment developed against this group, especially in the 1920s.

New Jersey Plan As the U.S. Constitution was being debated and drafted, large states and small states each offered proposals on how the legislature should be structured. The New Jersey Plan stated that the legislature should have a great deal of power to regulate trade, and that it should consist of one legislative house, with each state having one vote.

New Nationalism The series of progressive reforms supported by Theodore Roosevelt as he ran for president on the Progressive or "Bull Moose" ticket in 1912. Roosevelt said that more had to be done to regulate big business and that neither of his opponents were committed to conservation.

New Right The conservative movement that began in the 1960s and triumphed with the election of Ronald Reagan in 1980. The New Right was able to attract many middle-class and Southern voters to the Republican party by emphasizing the themes of patriotism, a smaller government, and a return to "traditional values."

"New South" Concept promoted by Southerners in the late 1800s that the South had changed dramatically and was now interested in industrial growth and becoming a part of the national economy. A large textile industry did develop in the South beginning in the 1880s.

Nez Perce Plains Native American tribe that attempted to resist reservation life by traveling 1500 miles with American military forces in pursuit. After being tracked and suffering cold and hardship, the Nez Perce finally surrendered and were forced onto a reservation in 1877.

Non-Intercourse Act In response to the failure of France and Britain to respect the rights of American ships at sea, President Madison supported this legislation in 1809, which authorized trade with all countries except Britain and France, and stated that trade exist with those countries as soon as they respected America's rights as a neutral power. The British and the French largely ignored this act.

Northwest Ordinances Bills passed in 1784, 1785, and 1787 that authorized the sale of lands in the Northwest Territory to raise money for the federal government; these bills also carefully laid out the procedures for eventual statehood for parts of these territories.

NOW (National Organization for Women) Formed in 1966, with Betty Friedan as its first president. NOW was at first interested in publicizing inequalities for women in the workplace; focus of the organization later turned to social issues and eventually the unsuccessful effort to pass an Equal Rights Amendment for women.

nuclear proliferation The massive buildup of nuclear weapons by the United States and the Soviet Union in the 1950s and into the 1960s; in the United States this was fostered in the belief that the threat of "massive retaliation" was the best way to keep the Soviet Union under control. The psychological effects of the atomic bomb on the populations of the Soviet Union and the United States were also profound.

nullification The belief that an individual state has the right to "nullify" any federal law that the state felt was unjust. Andrew Jackson was able to resolve a Nullification Crisis in 1832, but the concept of nullification was still accepted by many Southerners, and controversy over this was a cause of the Civil War.

Ocala Platform Platform of the Farmer's Alliance, formulated at an 1890 convention held in Ocala, Florida. This farmer's organization favored a graduated income tax, government control of the railroad, the unlimited coinage of silver, and the direct election of United States senators. Candidates supporting the farmers called themselves Populists and ran for public offices in the 1890s.

Old Age Revolving Pension Plan Conceived by California doctor Francis Townsend in 1934, this plan would give every retired American $200 a month, with the stipulation that it would have to be spent by the end of the month; Townsend claimed this would revitalize the economy by putting more money in circulation. A national tax of 2 percent on all business transactions was supposed to finance this plan. A large number of Townsend clubs were formed to support this plan.

"on the margin" The practice in the late 1920s of buying stock and only paying in cash 10 percent of the value of that stock; the buyer could easily borrow the rest from his or her stockbroker or investment banker. This system worked well as long as investors could sell their stocks at a profit and repay their loans; after the 1929 stock market crash, investors had to pay these loans back in cash.

OPEC Acronym for Organization of Petroleum Exporting Countries, this organization sets the price for crude oil and determines how much of it will be produced. The decision of OPEC to raise oil prices in 1973 had a dramatic economic impact in both the United States and the rest of the world.

Open-Door policy The policy that China should be open to trade with all of the major powers, and that all, including the United States, should have equal right to trade there. This was the official American position toward China as announced by Secretary of State John Hay in 1899.

Oregon Trail Trail that took settlers from the Ohio River Valley through the Great Plains and the Rocky Mountains to Oregon. Settlers began moving westward along this trail in 1842; by 1860 over 325,000 Americans had traveled westward along the trail.

Oregon Treaty Both the United States and Great Britain claimed the Oregon Territory; in 1815 they agreed to jointly control the region. In 1843 the settlers of Oregon declared that their territory would become an independent republic.

Palmer Raids Part of the Red Scare, these were measures to hunt out political radicals and immigrants who were potential threats to American security. Organized by Attorney General A. Mitchell Palmer in 1919 and 1920 (and carried out by J. Edgar Hoover), these raids led to the arrest of nearly 5500 people and the deportation of nearly four hundred.

Panama Canal Crucial for American economic growth, the building of this canal was begun by American builders in 1904 and completed in 1914; the United States had to first engineer a Panamanian revolt against Colombia to guarantee a friendly government in Panama that would support the building of the canal. In 1978 the U.S. Senate voted to return the Panama Canal to Panamanian control.

Panic of 1837 The American economy suffered a deep depression when Great Britain reduced the amount of credit it offered to the United States; American merchants and industrialists had to use their available cash to pay off debts, thus causing businesses to cut production and lay off workers.

Paris, Treaty of The treaty ending the Revolutionary War, and signed in 1783; by the terms of this treaty the United States received the land between the Appalachian Mountains and the Mississippi River. The British did keep their Canadian territories.

Pendleton Civil Service Act 1883 act that established a civil service system; there were a number of government jobs that were filled by civil service examinations and not by the president appointing one of his political cronies. Some states also started to develop professional civil service systems in the 1880s.

Pentagon Papers A government study of American involvement in Vietnam that outlined in detail many of the mistakes that America had made there; in 1971 a former analyst for the Defense Department, Daniel Ellsberg released these to the *New York Times*.

Platt Amendment For Cuba to receive its independence from the United States after the Spanish-American war, it had to agree to the Platt

Amendment, which stated that the United States had the right to intervene in Cuban affairs if the Cuban government could not maintain control or if the independence of Cuba was threatened by external or internal forces.

Plumbers A group of intelligence officials who worked for the committee to reelect Richard Nixon in 1972; the job of this group was to stop leaks of information and perform "dirty tricks" on political opponents of the president. The Plumbers broke into the office of Daniel Ellsberg's psychiatrist, looking for damaging information against him and totally discredited the campaign of Democratic hopeful Edmund Muskie.

pocket veto A method a president can use to "kill" congressional legislation at the end of a congressional term. Instead of vetoing the bill, the president may simply not sign it; once the congressional term is over, the bill will then die.

political machine An organization that controls the politics of a city, a state, or even the country, sometimes by illegal or quasi-legal means; a machine employs a large number of people to do its "dirty work," for which they are either given some government job or are allowed to pocket government bribes or kickbacks. The "best" example of a political machine was the Tammany Hall organization that controlled New York City in the late nineteenth century.

Populist party Party that represented the farmers that scored major electoral victories in the 1890s, including the election of several members of the U.S. House of Representatives and the election of one U.S. senator. Populist candidates spoke against monopolies, wanted government to become "more democratic," and wanted more direct government action to help the working classes.

Port Huron Statement The manifesto of Students for a Democratic Society, a radical student group formed in 1962. The Port Huron Statement called for a greater role for university students in the nation's affairs, rejected the traditional role of the university, and rejected the foreign policy goals that America was embracing at the time.

Potsdam Conference July 1945 conference between new president Harry Truman, Stalin, and Clement Atlee, who had replaced Churchill. Truman took a much tougher stance toward Stalin than Franklin Roosevelt had; little substantive agreement took place at this conference. Truman expressed reservations about the future role of the Soviet Union in Eastern Europe at this conference.

Powhatan Confederacy Alliance of Native American tribes living in the region of the initial Virginia settlement. Powhatan, leader of this alliance, tried to live in peace with the English settlers when they arrived in 1607.

professional bureaucracy Government officials that receive their positions after taking competitive civil service tests; they are not appointed in return for political favors. Many government jobs at the state and national level are filled in this manner beginning in the 1880s.

progressivism A movement that desired political and social reform, and was most influential in America from the 1890s up until World War I. Most popular progressive causes included reforming city government, better conditions for urban workers, the education of newly arrived immigrants, and the regulation of big businesses.

proportional representation The belief that representation in a legislature should be based on population; the states with the largest populations should have the most representatives. When the Constitution was being formulated, the larger states wanted this; the smaller states favored "one vote per state." The eventual compromise, termed the Connecticut plan, created a two-house legislature.

proprietorships Settlements in America that were given to individuals, who could govern and regulate the territory in any manner they desire. Charles I, for example, gave the Maryland territory to Lord Baltimore as a proprietorship.

Puritans Group of religious dissidents who came to the New World so they would have a location to establish a "purer" church than the one that existed in England. The Puritans began to settle the Plymouth Colony in 1620 and settled the Massachusetts Bay Colony beginning in 1630. Puritans were heavily influenced by John Calvin and his concept of predestination.

putting-out system The first textile production system in England, where merchants gave wool to families, who in their homes created yarn and then cloth; the merchants would then buy the cloth from the families and sell the finished product. Textile mills made this procedure more efficient.

Quartering Act 1765 British edict stating that to help defend the empire, colonial governments had to provide accommodations and food for British troops. Many colonists considered this act to be the ultimate insult; they perceived that they were paying for the troops that were there to control the colonies.

Queen Anne's War 1702 to 1713 war, called the War of the Spanish Succession in European texts, pitted England against France and Spain. Spanish Florida was attacked by the English in the early part of this war, and Native Americans fought for both sides in the conflict. The British emerged victorious and in the end received Hudson Bay and Nova Scotia from the French.

Radical Republicans Group of Republicans after the Civil War who favored harsh treatment of the defeated South and a dramatic restructuring of the economic and social systems in the South; favored a decisive elevation of the political, social, and economic position of former slaves.

ratifying conventions In late 1787 and in 1788 these were held in all states for the purpose of ratifying the new Constitution of the United States. In many states, approval of the Constitution was only approved by a small margin; in Rhode Island ratification was defeated. The Founding Fathers made an intelligent decision in calling for ratifying conventions to approve the Constitution instead of having state legislatures do it, since under the system proposed by the Constitution, some of the powers state legislatures had at the time would be turned over to the federal government.

ration cards Held by Americans during World War II, these recorded the amount of rationed goods such as automobile tires, gasoline, meat, butter, and other materials an individual had purchased. Where regulation in World War I had been voluntary, consumption in World War II was regulated by government agencies.

realpolitik Pragmatic policy of leadership, in which the leader "does what he or she has to do" in order to be successful. Morality has no place in the mind-set of a leader practicing realpolitik. The late nineteenth-century German chancellor Otto von Bismarck is the best modern example of a leader practicing realpolitik.

Rebel Without a Cause 1955 film starring James Dean exploring the difficulties of family life and the alienation that many teenagers felt in the 1950s. Juvenile delinquency, and the reasons for it, was the subtext of this film, as well as the source of countless other 1950s-era movies aimed at the youth market.

recall One of a number of reforms of the governmental system proposed by progressive-era thinkers; by the process of recall, the citizens of a city or state could remove an unpopular elected official from office in midterm. Recall was adopted in only a small number of communities.

reconcentration 1896 Spanish policy designed to control the Cuban people by forcing them to live in fortified camps; American outrage over this leads some politicians to call for war against Spain.

Reconstruction Act Plan of Radical Republicans to control the former area of the Confederacy and approved by Congress in March 1867; former Confederacy was divided into five military districts, with each controlled by a military commander (Tennessee was exempt from this). Conventions were to be called to create new state governments (former Confederate officials could not hold office in these governments).

Reconstruction era The era following the Civil War where Radical Republicans initiated changes in the South that gave newly freed slaves additional economic, social, and political rights. These changes were greatly resented by many Southerners, causing the creation of organizations such as the Ku Klux Klan. Reconstruction ended with the Compromise of 1877.

Reconstruction Finance Corporation Established in 1932 by Herbert Hoover to offset the effects of the Great Depression; the RFC was authorized to give federal credit to banks so that they could operate efficiently. Banks receiving these loans were expected to extend loans to businesses providing jobs or building low-cost housing.

Red Scare Vigorous repression of radicals, "political subversives," and "undesirable" immigrant groups in the years immediately following World War I. Nearly 6500 "radicals" were arrested and sent to jail; some sat in jail without ever being charged with a crime, while nearly 500 immigrants were deported.

referendum one of a series of progressive-era reforms designed to improve the political system; with the referendum, certain issues would be decided not by elected representatives as voters are called upon to approve or disapprove specific government programs. Consistent with populist and progressive era desire to return government "to the people."

religious right Primarily Protestant movement that greatly grew beginning in the 1970s and pushed to return "morality" to the forefront in American life. The religious right has been especially active in opposing abortion, and since the 1980s has extended its influence in the political sphere by endorsing and campaigning for specific candidates.

Removal Act of 1830 Part of the effort to remove Native Americans from "Western" lands so that American settlement could continue westward, this legislation gave the president the authorization (and the money) to purchase from Native Americans all of their lands east of the Mississippi, and gave him the money to purchase lands west of the Mississippi for Native Americans to move to.

Report on the Public Credit 1790 report by Secretary of the Treasury Alexander Hamilton, in which he proposed that the federal government assume the entire amount of the nation's debt (including state debt), and that the federal government should have an increased role in the nation's economy. Many of America's early leaders vigorously opposed the expansion of federal economic power in the new republic and the expansion of American industry that Hamilton also promoted.

Republican party Formed in 1854 during the death of the Whig party, this party attracted former members of the Free-Soil party and some in the Democratic party who were uncomfortable with the Democratic position on slavery. Abraham Lincoln was the first Republican president. For much of the twentieth century, the party was saddled with the label of being "the party of big business," although Richard Nixon, Ronald Reagan, and others did much to pull middle class and Southern voters into the party.

"Reservationists" This group in the United States Senate was led by Henry Cabot Lodge and was opposed to sections of the Versailles Treaty when it was brought home from Paris by President Woodrow Wilson in 1919. Reservationists were especially concerned that if the United States joined the League of Nations, American troops would be used to conduct League of Nations military operations without the approval of the Congress.

Resettlement Administration In an attempt to address the problems of Dust Bowlers and other poor farmers, this 1935 New Deal program attempted to provide aid to the poorest farmers, resettle some farmers from the Dust Bowl, and establish farm cooperatives. This program never received the funding it needed to be even partially successfully, and in 1937 the Farm Security Administration was created to replace it.

Revenue Act of 1935 Tax legislation championed by Franklin Roosevelt that was called a "soak the rich" plan by his opponents. Under this bill, corporate, inheritance, and gift taxes went up dramatically; income taxes for the upper brackets also rose. By proposing this, Roosevelt may have been attempting to diffuse the popularity of Huey Long and others with more radical plans to redistribute wealth.

Revenue Act of 1942 Designed to raise money for the war, this bill dramatically increased the number of Americans required to pay income tax. Until this point, roughly 4 million Americans paid income tax; as a result of this legislation, nearly 45 million did.

"revisionist" history A historical interpretation not found in "standard" history books or supported by most historians. A revisionist history of the origins of the Cold War, for example, would maintain that the aggressive actions of the United States forced the Soviet Union to seize the territories of Eastern Europe for protection. Historical interpretations that may originally be revisionist may, in time, become standard historical interpretation.

revival meetings Religious meetings consisting of soul-searching, preaching, and prayer that took place during the Second Great Awakening at the beginning of the nineteenth century. Some revival meetings lasted over one week.

Rio Pact 1947 treaty signed by the United States and most Latin American countries, stating that the region would work together on economic and defense matters and creating the Organization of American States to facilitate this cooperation.

Roe v. Wade 1973 Supreme Court decision that made abortion legal (except in the last months of pregnancy). Justices voting in the majority in this 5-to-2 decision stated that a woman's right to privacy gave her the legal freedom to choose to have an abortion. Abortion has remained as one of the most hotly debated social issues in America.

Roosevelt Corollary An extension of the Monroe Doctrine, this policy was announced in 1904 by Theodore Roosevelt; it firmly warned European nations against intervening in the affairs of nations in the Western Hemisphere, and stated that the United States had the right to take action against any nation in Latin America if "chronic wrongdoing" was taking place. The Roosevelt Corollary was used to justify several American "interventions" in Central America in the twentieth century.

Rosie the Riveter Image of a woman factory worker drawn by Norman Rockwell for the *Saturday Evening Post* during World War II. Women were needed to take on factory jobs that had been held by departing soldiers; by 1945 women made up nearly 37 percent of the entire domestic workforce.

"Rough Riders" A special unit of soldiers recruited by Theodore Roosevelt to do battle in the Spanish-American War; this unit was composed of men from many backgrounds, with the commanding officer of the unit being Roosevelt (after he resigned as Assistant Secretary of the Navy). The most publicized event of the war was the charge of the Rough Riders up San Juan Hill on July 1, 1898.

Salem Witch Trials 120 men, women, and children were arrested for witchcraft in Salem, Massachusetts, in 1692; 19 of these were executed. A new governor appointed by the Crown stopped additional trails and executions; several historians note the class nature of the witch trials, as many of those accused were associated with the business and/or commercial interests in Salem, while most of the accusers were members of the farming class.

SALT I (Strategic Arms Limitation Talks) 1972 treaty signed by Richard Nixon and Soviet premier Leonid Brezhnev limiting the development of additional nuclear weapon systems and defense systems to stop them. SALT I was only partially effective in preventing continued development of nuclear weaponry.

salutary neglect British policy announced at the beginning of the eighteenth century stating that as long as the American colonies remained politically loyal and continued their trade with Great Britain, the British government would relax enforcement of various measures restricting colonial activity that were enacted in the 1600s. Tensions between the colonies and Britain continued over British policies concerning colonial trade and the power of colonial legislatures.

satellite countries Eastern European countries that remained under the control of the Soviet Union during the Cold War era. Most were drawn together militarily by the Warsaw Pact; satellite nations that attempted political or cultural rebellion, such as Hungary in 1956 or Czechoslovakia in 1968, faced invasion by Soviet forces.

"Saturday Night Massacre" October 20, 1973 event when Richard Nixon ordered the firing of Archibald Cox, the special investigator in charge of the Watergate investigation. Attorney General Elliot Richardson and several others in the Justice Department refused to carry out this order and resigned. This event greatly damaged Nixon's popularity, both in the eyes of the public and in the Congress.

scalawags Term used by Southerners in the Reconstruction era for fellow Southerners who either supported Republican Reconstruction policies or gained economically as a result of these policies.

Scopes Trial 1925 Tennessee trail where teacher John Scopes was charged with teaching evolution, a violation of state status. The American Civil Liberties Union hired Clarence Darrow to defend Scopes, while the chief attorney for the prosecution was three-time presidential candidate William Jennings Bryan. While Scopes was convicted and ordered to pay a small fine, Darrow was able to poke holes in the theory of creationism as expressed by Bryan.

Scottsboro Boys Nine black young men who were accused of raping two white women in a railway boxcar in Scottsboro, Alabama in 1931. Quick trials, suppressed evidence, and inadequate legal council made them symbols of the discrimination that faced blacks on a daily basis during this era.

Scramble for Africa The competition between the major European powers to gain colonial territories in Africa that took place between the 1870s and the outbreak of World War I. Conflicts created by competing visions of colonial expansion increased tensions between the European powers and were a factor in the animosities that led to World War I.

secession A single state or a group of states leaving the United States of America. New England Federalists threatened to do this during first administration of Thomas Jefferson; Southern states did this in the period prior to the Civil War.

Second Continental Congress Meeting of delegates from the American colonies in May 1775; during the sessions some delegates expressed hope that the differences between the colonies and Britain could be reconciled, although the Congress authorized that the Continental Army be created and that George Washington be named commander of that army.

Second Great Awakening Religious revival movement that began at the beginning of the nineteenth century; revivalist ministers asked thousands of worshippers at revival meetings to save their own souls. This reflected the move away from predestination in Protestant thinking of the era.

Second Industrial Revolution The massive economic growth that took place in American from 1865 until the end of the century that was largely based on the expansion of the railroad, the introduction of electric power, and the production of steel for building. By the 1890s America had replaced Germany as the major industrial producer in the world.

Second National Bank Bank established by Congress in 1816; President Madison had called for the Second Bank in 1815 as a way to spur national economic growth after the War of 1812. After an economic downturn in 1818, the bank shrunk the amount of currency available for loans, an act that helped to create the economic collapse of 1819.

Second New Deal Beginning in 1935 the New Deal did more to help the poor and attack the wealthy; one reason Roosevelt took this path was to turn the American people away from those who said the New Deal wasn't going far enough to help the average person. Two key legislative acts of this era were the Social Security Act of May 1935 and the June 1935 National Labor Relations Act (also called the Wagner Act), which gave all Americans the right to join labor unions. The Wealth Tax Act increased the tax rates for the wealthiest Americans.

settlement houses Centers set up by progressive-era reformers in the poorest sections of American cities; at these centers workers and their children might receive lessons in the English language or citizenship, while for women lessons in sewing and cooking were oftentimes held. The first settlement house was Hull House in Chicago, established by Jane Addams in 1889.

Seventeenth Amendment Ratified in 1913, this amendment allowed voters to directly elect United States senators. Senators had previously been elected by state legislatures; this change perfectly reflected the spirit of progressive-era political reformers who wanted to do all they could to put political power in the hands of the citizenry.

Sherman Antitrust Act 1890 congressional legislation designed to break up industrial trusts such as the one created by John D. Rockefeller and Standard Oil. The bill stated that any combination of businesses that was "in the restraint of trade" was illegal. Because of the vagueness of the legislation and the lack of enforcement tools in the hands of the federal government, few trusts were actually prosecuted as a result of this bill.

Shiloh, Battle of Fierce Civil War battle in Tennessee in April 1862; although the Union emerged victorious, both sides suffered a large number of casualties in this battle. Total casualties in this battle were nearly 25,000. General U.S. Grant commanded the Union forces at Shiloh.

Sioux Plains tribe that tried to resist American westward expansion; after two wars the Sioux were resettled in South Dakota. In 1876 Sioux fighters defeated the forces of General Custer at the Battle of Little Bighorn. In 1890 146 Sioux men, women, and children were killed by federal troops at the Massacre at Wounded Knee.

sit-down strikes A labor tactic where workers refuse to leave their factory until management meets their demands. The most famous sit-down strike occurred at the General Motors plant in Flint, Michigan, beginning December 31, 1936; despite efforts by company guards to end the strike by force, the workers finally saw their demands met after 44 days.

sit-in Tactic used by the civil rights movement in the early 1960s; a group of civil rights workers would typically occupy a lunch counter in a segregated establishment in the South and refuse to leave, thus disrupting normal business (and profits) for the segregated establishment. During sit-ins civil rights workers often suffered physical and emotional abuse. The first sit-in was at the Woolworth's store in Greensboro, North Carolina, on February 1, 1960.

Sixteenth Amendment 1913 amendment that instituted a federal income tax. In debate over this measure in the Congress, most felt that this would be a fairer tax than a national sales tax, which was proposed by some.

Smith-Connally Act 1943 legislation that limited the nature of labor action possible for the rest of the war. Many in America felt that strikes, especially those organized in the coal mines by the United Mine Workers, were detrimental to the war effort.

Social Darwinism Philosophy that evolved from the writings of Charles Darwin on evolution that stated people inevitably compete with each other, as do societies; in the end the "survival of the fittest" would naturally occur. Social Darwinism was used to justify the vast differences between the rich and the poor in the late nineteenth century, as well as the control that the United States and Europe maintained over other parts of the world.

Social Gospel movement Late nineteenth-century Protestant movement preaching that all true Christians should be concerned with the plight of immigrants and other poor residents of American cities and should financially support efforts to improve the lives of these poor urban dwellers. Progressive-era settlement houses were oftentimes financed by funds raised by ministers of the Social Gospel movement.

Social Security Act Considered by many to be the most important act passed during the entire New Deal, this 1935 bill established a system that would give payments to Americans after they reached retirement age; provisions for unemployment and disability insurance were also found in this bill. Political leaders of recent years have wrestled with the problem of keeping the Social Security system solvent.

Sons of Liberty Men who organized opposition to British policies during the late 1760s and 1770s. The Sons of Liberty were founded in and were most active in Boston, where in response to the Stamp Act they burned the local tax collector in effigy and burned a building that he owned. The Sons of Liberty also organized the Boston Tea Party. Samuel Adams was one of the leaders of this group.

"Southern Strategy" Plan begun by Richard Nixon that has made the Republican party dominant in many areas of the South that had previously voted Democratic. Nixon, Ronald Reagan, and countless Republican congressional candidates have emphasized law and order and traditional values in their campaigns, thus winning over numerous voters. Support from the South had been part of the New Deal Democratic coalition crafted by Franklin Roosevelt.

Spanish-American War War that began in 1898 and stemmed from furor in America over treatment of Cubans by Spanish troops that controlled the island. During the war the American navy led by Admiral Dewey destroyed the Spanish fleet in the Pacific, the American ship the *Maine* was sunk in Havana harbor, and Teddy Roosevelt led the Rough Riders up San Juan Hill. A major result of the war was the acquisition by the United States of the Philippines, which made America a major power in the Pacific.

speakeasies Urban clubs that existed in the 1920s where alcohol was illegally sold to patrons. The sheer number of speakeasies in a city such as New York demonstrated the difficulty of enforcing a law such as prohibition.

special prosecutor An official appointed to investigate specific governmental wrongdoing. Archibald Cox was the special prosecutor assigned to investigate Watergate, while Kenneth Starr was the special prosecutor assigned to investigate the connections between President Clinton and Whitewater. President Nixon's order to fire Cox was the beginning of the famous 1973 "Saturday Night Massacre."

speculation The practice of purchasing either land or stocks with the intent of selling them for a higher price later. After the Homestead Act and other acts opened up the western United States for settlement, many speculators purchased land with no intent of ever settling on it; their goal was to later sell the land for profit.

spoils system Also called the patronage system, in which the president, governor, or mayor is allowed to fill government jobs with political allies and former campaign workers. Political reformers of the 1880s and 1890s introduced legislation calling for large numbers of these jobs to be filled by the merit system, in which candidates for jobs had to take competitive examinations. President Andrew Jackson began the spoils system.

Sputnik First man-made satellite sent into space, this 1957 scientific breakthrough by Soviet Union caused great concern in the United States. The thought that the United States was "behind" the Soviet Union in anything worried many, and science and mathematics requirements in universities across the country increased as a result.

Square Deal The philosophy of President Theodore Roosevelt; included in this was the desire to treat both sides fairly in any dispute. In the coal miner's strike of 1902 he treated the United Mine Workers representatives and company bosses as equals; this approach continued during his efforts to reg-

ulate the railroads and other businesses during his second term.

stagflation A unique economic situation faced political leaders in the early 1970s, where inflation and signs of economic recession occurred at the same time. Previously, in times of inflation, the economy was improving, and vice versa. Nixon utilized wage and price controls and increased government spending to end this problem.

Stamp Act To help pay for the British army in North America, Parliament passed the Stamp Act in 1765, under which all legal documents in the colonies had to be issued on officially stamped paper. A tax was imposed on all of these documents, as well as on all colonial newspapers. The resistance to the Stamp Act was severe in the colonies, and it was eventually repealed.

Stamp Act Congress Representatives of nine colonies went to this meeting held in New York in October 1765; the document produced by this congress maintained the loyalty of the colonies to the Crown but strongly condemned the Stamp Act. Within one year the Stamp Act was repealed.

state's rights The concept that the individual states, and not the federal government, have the power to decide whether federal legislation or regulations are to be enforced within the individual states. The mantle of state's rights would be taken up by New England Federalists during the presidency of Thomas Jefferson, by many Southern states in the years leading up to the Civil War, and by some Southern states again in response to federal legislation during the civil rights era of the 1960s.

Stono Rebellion 1739 slave rebellion in South Carolina where over 75 slaves killed white citizens and marched through the countryside with captured guns. After the rebellion was quashed, discipline imposed by many slave owners was much harsher. This was the largest slave rebellion of the 1700s in the colonies.

Students for a Democratic Society (SDS) Founded in 1962, this group was part of the "New Left" movement of the 1960s. SDS believed in a more participatory society, in a society that was less materialistic, and in university reform that would give students more power. By 1966 SDS concentrated much of its efforts on organizing opposition to the war in Vietnam. The *Port Huron Statement* was the original manifesto of SDS and was written by SDS founder Tom Hayden.

suburbia The area outside of the cities where massive number of families flocked to in the 1950s and 1960s. Suburban parents oftentimes still worked in the cities, but the suburban lifestyle shared little with urban life. Critics of 1950s suburbia point to the sameness and lack of vitality noted by some suburban residents and to the fact that suburban women oftentimes had to forget past dreams to accept the role of "housewife."

Sugar Act Another effort to pay for the British army located in North America, this 1764 measure taxed sugar and other imports. The British had previously attempted to halt the flow of sugar from French colonies to the colonies: By the Sugar Act they attempted to make money off this trade. Another provision of the act harshly punished smugglers of sugar who didn't pay the import duty imposed by the British.

Suffolk Resolves These were sent from Suffolk Country, Massachusetts, to the meeting of the First Continental Congress in September 1774 and called for the citizens of all of the colonies to prepare to take up arms against the British. After much debate, the First Continental Congress adopted the Suffolk Resolves.

supply-side economics Economic theory adopted by Ronald Reagan stating that economic growth would be best encouraged by lowering the taxes on wealthy businessmen and investors; this would give them more cash, which they would use to start more businesses, make more investments, and in general stimulate the economy. This theory of "Reaganomics" went against economic theories going back to the New Deal that claimed to efficiently stimulate the economy, more money needed to be held by consumers (who would turn and spend it).

Sussex Pledge A torpedo from a German submarine hit the French passenger liner the *Sussex* in March 1916, killing and injuring many (including two Americans). In a strongly worded statement, President Wilson demanded that the Germans refrain from attacking passenger ships; in the Sussex Pledge the Germans said that they would temporarily stop these attacks, but that they might have to resume them in the future if the British continued their blockade of German ports.

Taft-Hartley Act 1947 congressional legislation that aided the owners in potential labor disputes. In key industries the president could declare an 80-day cooling off period before a strike could actually take place; the bill also allowed owners to sue unions over broken contracts, and forced union leaders to sign anticommunist oaths. The bill was passed over President Truman's veto; Truman only vetoed the bill for political reasons.

Tammany Hall Political machine that ran New York City Democratic and city politics beginning in 1870, and a "model" for the political machines that dominated politics in many American cities well into the twentieth century. William Marcy "Boss" Tweed was the head of Tammany Hall for several years and was the most notorious of all of the political bosses.

Tariff of 1816 An extremely protectionist tariff designed to assist new American industries in the aftermath of the War of 1812; this tariff raised import duties by nearly 25 percent.

Tax Reform Act of 1986 The biggest tax cut in American history, this measure cut taxes by $750 billion over five years and cut personal income taxes by 25 percent. Tax cuts were consistent with President Reagan's belief that more money in the hands of the wealthy would stimulate the economy. Critics of this tax cut would argue that the wealthy were the ones that benefited from it, as little of the money that went to the hands of the rich actually "trickled down" to help the rest of the economy. Critics would also argue that the national deficits of the late 1980s and early 1990s were caused by these tax cuts.

Taylorism Following the management practices of Frederick Winslow Taylor, the belief practiced by many factory owners beginning in 1911 (when Taylor published his first book) that factories should be managed in a scientific manner, with everything done to increase the efficiency of the individual worker and of the factory process as a whole. Taylor describes the movements of workers as if they were machines; workers in many factories resisted being seen in this light.

Tea Act 1773 act by Parliament that would provide the American colonies with cheap tea, but at the same time would force the colonists to admit that Parliament had a right to tax them. The Sons of Liberty acted against this measure in several colonies, with the most dramatic being the Boston Tea Party. Parliament responded with the harsh Coercive Acts.

Teapot Dome Scandal One of many scandals that took place during the presidency of Warren G. Harding. The Secretary of the Interior accepted bribes from oil companies for access to government oil reserves at Teapot Dome, Wyoming; other Cabinet members were later convicted of accepting bribes and using their influence to make millions. The Harding administration was perhaps the most corrupt administration in American political history.

Teller Amendment As Americans were preparing for war with Spain over Cuba in 1898, this Senate measure stated that under no circumstances would the United States annex Cuba. The amendment was passed as many in the muckraking press were suggesting that the Cuban people would be better off "under the protection" of the United States.

temperance movement Movement that developed in America before the Civil War that lamented the effect that alcohol had on American society. After the Civil War members of this movement would become especially concerned about the effect of alcohol on immigrants and other members of the urban poor; out of the temperance movement came the drive for nationwide prohibition.

tenant farmers In the Reconstruction South, a step up from sharecropping; the tenant farmer rented his land from the landowner, freeing him from the harsh supervision that sharecroppers suffered under.

Tennessee Valley Authority Ambitious New Deal program that for the first time provided electricity to residents of the Tennessee Valley; the TVA also promoted agricultural and industrial growth (and prevented flooding) in the region. In all, residents of seven states benefited from the TVA.

Ten Percent Plan Abraham Lincoln's plan for Reconstruction, which would have offered full pardons to persons living in Confederate states who would take an oath of allegiance to the United States (former Confederate military officers and civilian authorities would not be offered this possibility); once 10 percent of the citizens of a state had taken such an oath, the state could take steps to rejoin the Union. Radical Republicans in the U.S. Senate felt that this plan was much too lenient to the South.

Tenure of Office Act 1867 congressional act designed to limit the influence of President Andrew Johnson. The act took away the president's role as commander in chief of American military forces and stated that Congress had to approve the removal of government officials made by the president. In 1868 Johnson attempted to fire Secretary of War Stanton without congressional approval, thus helping set the stage for his impeachment hearings later that year.

Tet Offensive January 1968 attack launched on American and South Vietnamese forces by North Vietnamese and Vietcong soldiers. Although Vietcong troops actually occupied the American embassy in Vietnam for several hours, the end result was a crushing defeat for the anti-American forces. However, the psychological effect of Tet was exactly the reverse: Vietcong forces were convinced they could decisively strike at South Vietnamese and American targets, and many in America ceased to believe that victory was "just around the corner."

Thirteenth Amendment 1865 amendment abolishing slavery in the United States and all of its territories (the Emancipation Proclamation had only ended slavery in the Confederate states). Final approval of this amendment depended on ratification by newly constructed legislatures in eight states that were former members of the Confederacy.

Thirty-Eighth Parallel The dividing line between Soviet-supported North Korea and U.S.-backed South Korea both before and as a result of the Korean War; American forces have been stationed on the southern side of this border continually since the Korean War ended in 1953.

Three-Fifths Compromise As the new Constitution was being debated in 1787, great controversy developed over how slaves should be counted in determining membership in the House of Representatives. To increase their representation, Southern states argued that slaves should be counted as people; Northerners argued that they should not count, since they could not vote or own property. The compromise arrived at was that each slave would could as three-fifths of a free person.

"tight money" Governmental policy utilized to offset the effects of inflation; on numerous occasions the Federal Reserve Board has increased the interest rate on money it loans to member banks; these higher interest rates are passed on to customers of member banks. With higher interest rates, there are fewer loans and other business activity, which "slows the economy down" and lowers inflation.

Timber and Stone Act 1878 bill that allowed private citizens to purchase forest territory in Oregon, Washington, California, and Nevada. Although the intent of the bill was to encourage settlement in these areas, lumber companies purchased large amounts of these land claims from the individuals who had originally purchased them.

Townshend Acts 1767 Parliamentary act that forced colonists to pay duties on most goods coming from England, including tea and paper, and increased the power of custom boards in the colonies to ensure that these duties were paid. These duties were despised and fiercely resisted in many of the colonies; in Boston resistance was so fierce that the British were forced to occupy Boston with troops. The acts were finally repealed in 1770.

Trail of Tears Forced march of 20,000 members of Cherokee tribe to their newly designated "homeland" in Oklahoma. Federal troops forced the Cherokees westward in this 1838 event, with one out of every five Native Americans dying from hunger, disease, or exhaustion along the way.

Trenton, Battle of December 26, 1776 surprise attack by forces commanded by George Washington on Hessian forces outside of Trenton, New Jersey. Nearly 950 Hessians were captured and another 30 were killed by Washington's forces; three Americans were wounded in the attack. The battle was a tremendous psychological boost for the American war effort.

Triangle Shirtwaist Fire March 1911 fire in New York factory that trapped young women workers inside locked exit doors; nearly 50 ended up jumping to their death, while 100 died inside the factory. Many factory reforms, including increasing safety precautions for workers, came from the investigation of this incident.

triangular trade system The complex trading relationship that developed in the late seventeenth century between the Americas, Europe, and Africa. Europeans purchased slaves from Africa to be resold in the Americas, raw materials from the Americas were exported to European states, while manufactured products in Europe were sold throughout the Americas.

Truman Doctrine Created in response to 1947 requests by Greece and Turkey for American assistance to defend themselves against potentially pro-Soviet elements in their countries, this policy stated that the United States would be ready to assist any free nation trying to defend itself against "armed minorities or . . . outside pressures." This would become the major American foreign policy goal throughout the Cold War.

trust Late nineteenth-century legal arrangement that allowed owners of one company to own stock in other companies in the same industry. By this arrangement, John D. Rockefeller and Standard Oil were able to buy enough stock to control other oil companies in existence as well. The Sherman Anti-Trust Act and the Clayton Anti-Trust Act were efforts to "break up" the numerous trusts that were created during this period.

Turner Thesis Published by Frederick Jackson Turner in 1893, "The Significance of the West in American History" stated that western expansion had played a fundamental role in defining the American character, and that the American tendencies toward democracy and individualism were created by the frontier experience.

Twelfth Amendment 1804 amendment that established separate balloting in the Electoral College for president and vice president. This amendment was passed as a result of the electoral deadlock of the 1800 presidential election, when Thomas Jefferson and his "running mate" Aaron Burr ended up with the same number of votes in the Electoral College; the House of Representatives finally decided the election in favor of Jefferson.

U-2 American reconnaissance aircraft shot down over the Soviet Union in May 1960. President Eisenhower initially refused to acknowledge that this was a spy flight; the Soviets finally produced pilot Francis Gary Powers, who admitted the purpose of the flight. This incident created an increase in Cold War tensions at the end of the Eisenhower presidency.

Uncle Tom's Cabin 1852 novel by Harriet Beecher Stowe that depicted all of the horrors of Southern slavery in great detail. The book went through several printings in the 1850s and early 1860s and helped to fuel abolitionist sentiment in the North.

unicameral legislature A governmental structure with a one-house legislature. As written in the Articles of Confederation, the United States would have a unicameral legislature, with all states having equal representation.

United Farm Workers Organized by Cesar Chavez in 1961, this union represented Mexican-Americans engaged in the lowest levels of agricultural work. In 1965 Chavez organized a strike against grape growers that hired Mexican-American workers in California, eventually winning the promise of benefits and minimum wage guarantees for the workers.

United States Forest Service Created during the presidency of Theodore Roosevelt, this body increased and protected the number of national forests and encouraged through numerous progress the efficient use of America's natural resources.

Universal Negro Improvement Association Black organization of the early 1920s founded by Marcus Garvey, who argued that however possible blacks should disassociate themselves from the "evils" of white society. This group organized a "back to Africa" movement, encouraging blacks of African descent to move back there; independent black businesses were encouraged (and sometimes funded) by Garvey's organization.

unrestricted submarine warfare The German policy announced in early 1917 of having their U-boats attack all ships attempting to land at British or French ports, despite their origin or purpose; because of this policy, the rights of the United States as a neutral power were being violated, stated Woodrow Wilson in 1917, and America was forced to declare war on Germany.

USS *Maine* American ship sent to Havana harbor in early 1898 to protect American interests in period of increased tension between Spanish troops and native Cubans; on February 15 an explosion took place on the ship, killing nearly 275 sailors. Later investigations pointed to an internal explosion on board, but all of the muckraking journals of the time in the United States blamed the explosion on the Spanish, which helped to develop intense anti-Spanish sentiment in the United States.

Valley Forge Location where General Washington stationed his troops for the winter of 1777 to 1778. Soldiers suffered hunger, cold, and disease: Nearly 1300 deserted over the course of the winter. Morale of the remaining troops was raised by the drilling and discipline instilled by Baron von Steuben, a former Prussian officer who had volunteered to aid the colonial army.

vertical integration Type of industrial organization practiced in the late nineteenth century and pioneered by Andrew Carnegie and U.S. Steel; under this system all of the various business activities needed to produce and sell a finished product (procuring the raw materials, preparing them, producing them, marketing them, and then selling them) would be done by the same company.

Vicksburg, Battle of After a lengthy siege, this Confederate city along the Mississippi River was finally taken by Union forces in July 1863; this victory gave the Union virtual control of the Mississippi River and was a serious psychological blow to the Confederacy.

Viet Cong During the Vietnam war, forces that existed within South Vietnam that were fighting for the victory of the North Vietnamese. Vietcong forces were pivotal in the initial successes of the Tet Offensive, which did much to make many in America question the American war effort in Vietnam and played a crucial role in the eventual defeat of the South Vietnamese government.

Vietnamization The process begun by Richard Nixon of removing American troops from Vietnam and turning more of the fighting of the Vietnam war over to the South Vietnamese. Nixon continued to use intense bombing to aid the South Vietnamese efforts as more American troops were being pulled out of Vietnam; in 1973 a peace treaty was finally signed with North Vietnam, allowing American troops to leave the country and all American POWs to be released. In March 1975, North Vietnamese and Vietcong forces captured Saigon and emerged victorious in the war.

Virginia Plan A concept of government crafted by James Madison and adopted by delegates to the convention that created the United States Constitution, this plan proposed a stronger central government than had existed under the Articles of Confederation; to prevent too much power being placed in the hands of one person or persons, the plan proposed that the powers of the federal government be divided amongst officials of executive, judicial, and legislative branches.

VISTA (Volunteer in Service to America) Program instituted in 1964 that sent volunteers to help poor Americans living in both urban and rural settings; this program was sometimes described as a domestic peace corps. This was one of many initiatives that were part of Lyndon Johnson's War on Poverty program.

voluntarism The concept that Americans should sacrifice either time or money for the well-being of their country; a sense of voluntarism has permeated America during much of its history, especially during the progressive era and during the administration of John Kennedy ("ask not what your country can do for you—ask what you can do for your country"). President George W. Bush called for a renewed sense of voluntarism in the aftermath of the attacks of September 11, 2001.

Wade-Davis Act Congress passed this bill in 1864 in response to the "10 Percent Plan" of Abraham Lincoln; this legislation set out much more difficult conditions than had been proposed by Lincoln for Southern states to reenter the Union. According to Wade-Davis, all former officers of the Confederacy would be denied citizenship; to vote, a person would have to take an oath that he had never helped the Confederacy in any way, and half of all white males in a state would have to swear loyalty to the Union before statehood could be considered. Lincoln prevented this from becoming law by using the pocket veto.

Wagner Act Also called the National Labor Relations Act, this July 1935 act established major gains for organized labor. It guaranteed collective bargaining, prevented harassment by owners of union activities, and established a National Labor Relations Board to guarantee enforcement of its provisions.

war bonds Also called Liberty Bonds, these were sold by the United States government in both World War I and World War II and used by the government to finance the war effort. A person purchasing a war bond can make money if he or she cashes it in after 5 or 10 years; in the meantime, the government can use the money to help pay its bills. In both wars, movie stars and other celebrities encouraged Americans to purchase war bonds.

War Industries Board Authorized in 1917, the job of this board was to mobilize American industries for the war effort. The board was headed by Wall Street investor Bernard Baruch, who used his influence to get American industries to produce materials useful for the war effort. Baruch was able to increase American production by a staggering 22 percent before the end of the war.

Warren Commission The group that carefully investigated the assassination of John F. Kennedy. After hearing much testimony, the commission concluded that Lee Harvey Oswald acted alone in killing the president. Even today many conspiracy theorists question the findings of the Warren Commission, claiming that Oswald was part of a larger group who wanted to assassinate the president.

Warsaw Pact Defensive military alliance created in 1955 by the Soviet Union and all of the Eastern European satellite nations loyal to the Soviet Union; the Warsaw Pact was formed as a reaction against NATO and NATO's 1955 decision to invite West Germany to join the organization.

Washington Conference 1922 conference where the United States, Japan, and the major European powers agreed to build no more warships for 10 years; in addition, the nations agreed not to attack each other's territories in the Pacific. This treaty came from strong post-World War I sentiment that it was important to avoid conflicts between nations that might lead to war.

Watergate Affair The break-in into Democratic campaign headquarters was one of a series of dirty tricks carried out by individuals associated with the effort to reelect Richard Nixon president in 1972. Extensive efforts were also made to cover up these activities. In the end, numerous government and campaign officials spent time in jail for their role in the Watergate Affair, and President Nixon was forced to resign in disgrace.

Webb Alien Land Law 1913 California law that prohibited Japanese who were not American citizens from owning farmland in California. This law demonstrates the nativist sentiment found in much of American society in the first decades of the twentieth century.

Webster-Hayne Debate 1830 Senate debate between Senator Daniel Webster of Massachusetts and Senator Robert Hayne of South Carolina over the issue of state's rights and whether an individual state has the right to nullify federal legislation. Webster skillfully outlined the dangers to the United States that would be caused by the practice of nullification; this debate perfectly captured many of the political divisions between North and South that would increase in the 1830s through the 1860s.

Whig party Political party that came into being in 1834 in opposition to the presidency of Andrew Jackson. Whigs opposed Jackson's use of the spoils system and the extensive power held by President Jackson; for much of their existence, however, the Whigs favored an activist federal government (while their opponents, the Democrats, favored limited government). William Henry Harrison and Zachary Taylor were the two Whigs elected president. The Whig party dissolved in the 1850s.

Whiskey Rebellion Many settlers in Western frontier territory in the early 1790s questioned the power that the federal power had over them. In 1793 settlers in the Ohio territory refused to pay federal excise taxes on whiskey and attacked tax officials who were supposed to collect these taxes; large numbers of "whiskey rebels" threatened to attack Pittsburgh and other cities. In 1794 President Washington was forced to send in federal troops to put down the rebellion.

"White Man's Burden" From the poem of the same name by Rudyard Kipling, this view justified imperialism by the "white man" around the world, but also emphasized the duty of the Europeans and Americans who were occupying new territories to improve the lives of those living in the newly acquired regions.

Whitewater The name of the scandal that got President Bill Clinton impeached but not convicted. Whitewater was the name of the real-estate deal in Arkansas that Clinton and his wife Hillary Rodham Clinton were both involved in; opponents claimed the actions of the Clintons concerning Whitewater were illegal, unethical, or both. Independent Counsel Kenneth Starr expanded the investigation to include the suicide of Clinton aide Vincent Foster, missing files in the White House, and the relationship of President Clinton with a White House intern, Monica Lewinsky.

Wilmont Proviso In the aftermath of the war with Mexico, in 1846 Representative David Wilmont proposed in an amendment to a military bill that slavery should be prohibited in all territories gained in the treaty ending that war. This never went into law, but in the debate over it in both houses, Southern representatives spoke passionately in defense of slavery; John C. Calhoun even suggested that the federal government had no legal jurisdiction to stop the existence of slavery in any new territory.

Woodstock Music Festival 1969 event that some perceive as the pinnacle of the 1960s counterculture. 400,000 young people came together for a weekend of music and a relative lack of hassles or conflict. The difficulty of mixing the 1960s counterculture with the radical politics of the era was demonstrated when Peter Townshend of the Who kicked Abbie Hoffman off of the Woodstock stage.

Works Progress Administration (WPA) New Deal program established in 1935 whose goal was to give out jobs as quickly as possible, even though the wages paid by the WPA were relatively low. Roads and public buildings were constructed by WPA work crews; at the same time, WPA authors wrote state guidebooks, artists painted murals in newly constructed public buildings, and musicians performed in large cities and small towns across the country.

writ of habeas corpus Allows a person suspected of a crime not to simply sit in jail indefinitely; such a suspect must be brought to court and charged with something, or he or she must be released from jail. Abraham Lincoln suspended the right of habeas corpus during the Civil War so that opponents of his policies could be contained.

Yalta Conference Meeting between Stalin, Churchill, and Roosevelt held two months before the fall of Nazi Germany in February of 1945. At this meeting Stalin agreed to assist the Americans against the Japanese after the Germans were defeated; it was decided that Germany would be divided into zones (each controlled by one of the victors), and Stalin promised to hold free elections in the Eastern European nations the Soviet army had liberated from the Nazis. Critics of the Yalta agreement maintain that Roosevelt was naïve in his dealings with Stalin at this meeting (he was only months from his own death), and that Churchill and Roosevelt essentially handed over control of Eastern Europe to Stalin.

yellow journalism This method uses accounts and illustrations of lurid and sensational events to sell newspapers. Newspapers using this strategy covered the events in Cuba leading up to the Spanish-American War, and did much to shift American opinion toward desiring war with Spain; some critics maintain that many tactics of yellow journalism were used during the press coverage of the Whitewater investigation of Bill Clinton.

Yorktown, Battle of The defeat of the forces of General Cornwallis in this battle in October of 1781 essentially ended the hopes of the British for winning the Revolutionary War. American and French troops hemmed the British in on the peninsula of Yorktown, while the French navy located in Chesapeake Bay made rescue of the British troops by sea impossible.

Zimmermann Telegram January 1917 telegram sent by the German foreign minister to Mexico suggesting that the Mexican army should join forces with the Germans against the United States; when the Germans and Mexicans were victorious, the Mexicans were promised most of the southwestern part of the United States. The British deciphered the code of this telegram and turned it over to the United States; the release of its content caused many in America to feel that war against the Germans was essential.

5 Steps to a 5

AP U.S. Government & Politics

Preface

Welcome to AP U.S. Government and Politics. I am, first and foremost, a teacher who has taught advanced placement to many students who have successfully taken the AP exam. I am also a table leader and reader—one of those crazy teachers who spends a week in the summer reading thousands of student free-response essays. With this guide I hope to share with you what I know, including what I have learned from students and other AP teachers to help you be successful on the exam.

My philosophy is not to teach *only* for the AP exam. Instead, my goal is to help students develop skills and abilities that lead to advanced levels of aptitude in government and politics. These are the same skills that will enable you to do well on the AP U.S. Government and Politics exam. My aim is to remove your nervousness and to improve your comfort level with the test. I believe that you are already motivated to succeed; otherwise, you would not have come this far. And obviously, you would not have purchased this prep book.

Since you have taken or are already taking a government and politics class, this book is going to supplement your course readings, writing, and analysis. I am going to give you the opportunity to practice the skills and techniques that I know from experience *really work*! I am confident that if you apply the techniques and processes presented in this book, you can succeed.

Let's begin.

Acknowledgments

My love and appreciation to Mark H. Lamb for his constant support, encouragement, and belief in my abilities and in me. Without his collaboration, this book would never have been completed. Special thanks to Frances New for her suggestions and encouragement. To Derek James (DJ) New: May this book someday help you in your studies. To my AP Government and Politics colleagues and friends: Thanks for all the ideas you have shared over the years—I'll see you at the reading. To my students, past, present, and future: Thank you for the inspiration you give to all teachers.

PART I

HOW TO USE THIS BOOK

Chapter 1

The Five-Step Program

THE BASICS

The Beginning

It is my belief that if you focus on the beginning, the rest will fall into place. Once you purchase this book and decide to work your way through it, you are beginning your journey to the AP U.S. Government and Politics exam. I will be with you every step of the way.

Why This Book?

"As a student, AP practice materials made me go above and beyond in preparation."
—MT, AP student

I believe that this book has something unique to offer you. I have spoken with many AP government and politics teachers and students, and have been fortunate to learn quite a bit about what they want from a test prep book. The contents of this book reflect genuine student concerns and needs. This is a student-oriented book. I will not try to impress you or overwhelm you with pompous language, mislead you with inaccurate information and tasks, or lull you into a false sense of confidence with easy shortcuts.

Think of this book as a resource and guide to accompany you on your AP U.S. Government and Politics journey throughout the year. This book is designed to serve many purposes. It will:

- Clarify requirements for the AP U.S. Government and Politics exam
- Provide you with test practice
- Help you pace yourself

- Make you aware of the Five Steps to Mastering the AP U.S. Government and Politics exam

ORGANIZATION OF THIS BOOK

I know that your primary concern is to obtain information about the AP U.S. Government and Politics exam. I start by introducing the five-step plan and follow with three different approaches to exam preparation. I then give an overview of the AP exam in general and describe some tips and suggestions on how to approach the various sections of the exam. I next introduce the Diagnostic/Master Exam, which should give you an idea of where you stand before you begin your preparations. I recommend that you spend 45 minutes on this practice exam.

The volume of material covered in AP U.S. Government and Politics is quite intimidating. The next section of this book provides a comprehensive review of all the major sections you may or may not have covered in the classroom. Not every AP U.S. Government and Politics class will get through the same amount of material. This book should help you fill any gaps in your understanding of the coursework.

INTRODUCTION TO THE FIVE-STEP PROGRAM

The Five-Step Program is a powerful program designed to provide you with the best possible skills, strategies, and practice to help lead you to that perfect 5 on the Advanced Placement U.S. Government and Politics exam, administered each May to more than 100,000 high school students. Each of the five steps will provide you an opportunity to get closer to the 5, which is the "Holy Grail" to all AP students.

STEP ONE leads you through a brief process to help determine which type of exam preparation you want:

1. Full-year: September through May
2. One-semester: January through May
3. Basic training: the 6 weeks prior to the exam

STEP TWO helps develop the knowledge you need to succeed on the exam:

1. A comprehensive review of the exam
2. One Diagnostic/Master Exam, which you can go through step by step and question by question to build your confidence level
3. Explanation of multiple-choice answers
4. A glossary of terms related to the AP U.S. Government and Politics exam
5. A list of interesting and related Websites and a Glossary

STEP THREE develops the skills necessary to take the exam and do well:

1. Practice multiple-choice questions
2. Practice free-response questions

STEP FOUR helps you develop strategies for taking the exam:

1. Learning about the test itself
2. Learning to read multiple-choice questions
3. Learning how to answer multiple-choice questions, including whether or not to guess
4. Learning how to plan and write the free-response questions

STEP FIVE will help you develop confidence in using the skills demanded on the AP U.S. Government and Politics exam:

1. The opportunity to take a diagnostic exam
2. Time management techniques and skills
3. Two practice exams that test how well honed your skills are

GRAPHICS USED IN THIS BOOK

To emphasize particular skills, strategies, and practice, we use seven sets of icons throughout this book.

The first icon is an hourglass, which indicates the passage of time during the school year. This hourglass icon will appear in the margin next to an item that may be of interest to one of the three types of students using this book (Approach A, B, or C students).

For the student who plans to prepare for the AP U.S. Government and Politics exam during the entire school year, September through May, we use an hourglass that is full on the top.

For the student who decides to begin preparing for the exam in January, we use an hourglass that is half full on the top and half full on the bottom.

For the student who wishes to prepare during the final 6 weeks before the exam, we use an hourglass that is almost empty on the top and almost full on the bottom.

The second icon is a footprint, which indicates which step in the five-step program is being emphasized in a given analysis, technique, or practice activity.

Plan   Knowledge   Skills   Strategies   Confidence Building

  The third icon is a clock, which indicates a timed practice activity or a time management strategy. The clock's face indicates how much time to allow for a given exercise. The full dial reminds you that this is a strategy to help you manage your time on the test.

 The fourth icon is an exclamation point, which points out a very important idea, concept, or strategy point that you should not pass over.

 The fifth icon is a checkmark, which alerts you to pay close attention. This activity will be most helpful if you go back and check your own work, your calendar, or your progress.

 The sixth icon is a lightbulb, which indicates strategies that you may want to try.

 The seventh icon is the sun, which indicates a tip that you might find useful.

Boldfaced words indicate terms that are included in the glossary at the end of the book.

THREE APPROACHES TO PREPARING FOR THE AP U.S. GOVERNMENT AND POLITICS EXAM

Overview of the Three Plans

No one knows your study habits, likes, and dislikes better than you. So you are the only one who can decide which approach you want or need to prepare for the Advanced Placement U.S. Government and Politics exam. Look at the brief profiles below. These may help you determine a prep mode.

 You're a full-year prep student (Approach A) if

1. You like to plan far in advance
2. You arrive at the airport 3 hours before your flight because "you never know when these planes might leave early"
3. You like detailed planning and everything in its place

4. You feel that you must be thoroughly prepared
5. You hate surprises

You're a one-semester prep student (Approach B) if

1. You get to the airport 1 hour before your flight is scheduled to leave
2. You are willing to plan ahead to feel comfortable in stressful situations, but are okay with skipping some details
3. You feel more comfortable when you know what to expect, but a surprise or two is cool
4. You're always on time for appointments

You're a 6-week prep student (Approach C) if

1. You get to the airport just as your plane's final boarding is announced
2. You work best under pressure and tight deadlines
3. You feel very confident with the skills and background you've learned in your AP U.S. Government and Politics class
4. You decided late in the year to take the exam
5. You like surprises
6. You feel okay if you arrive 10–15 minutes late for an appointment

"AP is tough—organization and planning are essential to success."
—JE, AP teacher

CALENDARS FOR PREPARING FOR THE AP U.S. GOVERNMENT AND POLITICS EXAM

 ## A Calendar for Approach A: Year-Long Preparation for the AP Government and Politics Exam

Although its primary purpose is to prepare you for the AP U.S. Government and Politics exam you will take in May, this book can enrich your study of government and politics, your analytical skills, and your essay writing skills.

SEPTEMBER–OCTOBER (Check off the activities as you complete them.)

_____ Determine the student mode (A, B, or C) that applies to you.

_____ Carefully read Chapters 1 and 2 of this book.

_____ Pay close attention to your walk-through of the Diagnostic/Master exam.

_____ Get on the Web and take a look at the AP Website(s).

_____ Skim the Comprehensive Review section. (Reviewing the topics covered in this section will be part of your year-long preparation.)

_____ Buy a few color highlighters.

_____ Flip through the entire book. Break the book in. Write in it. Highlight it.

_____ Get a clear picture of what your own school's AP Government and Politics curriculum is.

_____ Begin to use the book as a resource to supplement the classroom learning.

NOVEMBER (The first 10 weeks have elapsed.)

_____ Read and study Chapter 5, Architecture and Development of United States Government.

_____ Read and study Chapter 6, Federalism.

DECEMBER

_____ Read and study Chapter 7, Political Culture.

_____ Read and study Chapter 8, Political Parties.

_____ Review Chapters 5–6.

JANUARY (20 weeks have elapsed.)

_____ Read and study Chapter 9, Voting and Elections.

_____ Read and study Chapter 10, Interest Groups and the Mass Media.

_____ Review Chapters 5–8.

FEBRUARY

_____ Read and study Chapter 11, The Legislative Branch.

_____ Read and study Chapter 12, Executive Branch and the Bureaucracy.

_____ Read and study Chapter 13, The National Judiciary.

_____ Review Chapters 5–10.

MARCH (30 weeks have now elapsed.)

_____ Read and study Chapter 14, Civil Liberties and Civil Rights.

_____ Read and study Chapter 15, Politics and Public Policymaking.

_____ Review Chapters 5–13.

APRIL

_____ Take Practice Exam 1 in the first week of April.
_____ Evaluate your strengths and weaknesses.
_____ Study appropriate chapters to correct your weaknesses.
_____ Review Chapters 5–15.

MAY (First 2 weeks) (THIS IS IT!)

_____ Review Chapters 1–15— all the material.
_____ Take Practice Exam 2.
_____ Score yourself.
_____ Get a good night's sleep before the exam. Fall asleep knowing that you are well prepared.

GOOD LUCK ON THE TEST!

"Study groups helped me focus."
—DA, AP student

"My teacher held review sessions right before the exam—they really help!"
—TG, AP student

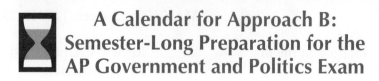

A Calendar for Approach B:
Semester-Long Preparation for the
AP Government and Politics Exam

Working under the assumption that you've completed or are taking one semester of government and politics studies, the following calendar will use the skills you've been practicing to prepare you for the May exam.

JANUARY–FEBRUARY

_____ Carefully read Parts I and II of this book.

_____ Take the Diagnostic/Master exam.

_____ Pay close attention to your walk-through of the Diagnostic/Master exam.

_____ Read and study Chapter 5, Architecture and Development of U.S. Government.

_____ Read and study Chapter 6, Federalism.

_____ Read and study Chapter 7, Political Culture.

_____ Read and study Chapter 8, Political Parties.

_____ Read and study Chapter 9, Voting and Elections.

_____ Read and study Chapter 10, Interest Groups and the Mass Media.

_____ Review Chapters 5–10.

MARCH (10 weeks to go)

_____ Read and study Chapter 11, The Legislative Branch.

_____ Review Chapters 5–6.

_____ Read and study Chapter 12, Executive Branch and the Bureaucracy.

_____ Review Chapters 7–8.

_____ Read and study Chapter 13, The National Judiciary.

_____ Review Chapters 9–10.

_____ Read and study Chapter 14, Civil Liberties and Civil Rights.

_____ Read and study Chapter 15, Politics and Public Policymaking.

APRIL

_____ Take Practice Exam 1 in the first week of April.

_____ Evaluate your strengths and weaknesses.

_____ Study appropriate chapters to correct your weaknesses.

_____ Review Chapters 5–10.

_____ Review Chapters 11–15.

MAY (First 2 weeks) (THIS IS IT!)

_____ Review Chapters 1–15—all the material.

_____ Take Practice Exam 2.

_____ Score yourself.

_____ Get a good night's sleep before the exam. Fall asleep knowing that you are well prepared.

GOOD LUCK ON THE TEST!

A Calendar for Approach C: 6-Week Preparation for the AP Government and Politics Exam

At this point, we assume that you have been building your government and politics knowledge base for more than 6 months. You will, therefore, use this book primarily as a guide to the AP U.S. Government and Politics exam. Given the time constraints, now is not the time to try to expand your AP Government and Politics curriculum. Rather, you should focus on and refine what you already know.

APRIL 1–15

_____ Skim Parts I and II of this book.
_____ Skim Chapters 5–10.
_____ Carefully go over the Rapid Review sections of Chapters 5–10.
_____ Complete Practice Exam 1. Score yourself and analyze your errors.
_____ Skim and highlight the Glossary at the end of the book.

APRIL 16–MAY 1

_____ Skim Chapters 11–15.
_____ Carefully go over the Rapid Review sections of Chapters 11–15.

_____ Carefully go over the Rapid Reviews for Chapters 5–10.
_____ Continue to skim and highlight the Glossary.

MAY (First 2 weeks) (THIS IS IT!)

_____ Skim Chapters 5–15.
_____ Carefully go over the Rapid Review sections of Chapters 5–15.
_____ Complete Practice Exam 2. Score yourself and analyze your errors.
_____ Get a good night's sleep. Fall asleep knowing that you are well prepared.

GOOD LUCK ON THE TEST!

"Relax! Knowing the makeup of the test and how to take the test really helps."
—JB, AP student

WHAT YOU NEED TO KNOW ABOUT THE AP U.S. GOVERNMENT AND POLITICS EXAM

PART II

WHAT YOU NEED
TO KNOW ABOUT
THE AP U.S.
GOVERNMENT AND
POLITICS EXAM

Chapter 2

Introduction to the AP U.S. Government and Politics Exam

BACKGROUND OF THE ADVANCED PLACEMENT PROGRAM

The Advanced Placement program was begun by the College Board in 1955 to construct standard achievement exams that would allow highly motivated high school students the opportunity to be awarded advanced placement as first-year students in colleges and universities in the United States. Today, there are 33 courses and exams with more than 1,000,000 students from every state in the nation, and from foreign countries, taking the annual exams in May.

The AP programs are designed for high school students who wish to take college-level courses. In our case, the AP U.S. Government and Politics course and exam are designed to involve high school students in college-level studies in political science.

Who Writes the AP U.S. Government and Politics Exam?

According to the College Board and several of my AP teacher friends who have worked on the committee, the AP U.S. Government and Politics exam is created by a group of college and high school instructors who serve on the Test Development Committee. The committee's job is to ensure that the annual Government and Politics exam reflects the College Board's course description and what is being taught and studied in college-level government classes in high schools.

This committee writes a large number of multiple-choice questions, which are pre-tested and evaluated for clarity, appropriateness, and range of possible answers. The committee also generates a pool of free-response questions, pre-tests them, and chooses those questions that best represent the full range of the scoring scale, which will allow AP readers to evaluate the responses equitably.

It is important to remember that the AP U.S. Government and Politics exam is thoroughly evaluated after it is administered each year. This way, the College Board can use the results to make course suggestions and to plan future exams.

What Are the Advanced Placement Grades, and Who Receives Them?

Once you have taken the exam and it has been scored, your test will be assigned one of five numbers by the College Board.

- A 5 indicates you are extremely well-qualified.
- A 4 indicates you are well-qualified.
- A 3 indicates you are qualified.
- A 2 indicates you are possibly qualified.
- A 1 indicates that you may not be qualified to receive college credit.

A grade of 5, 4, 3, 2, or 1 will be reported to your designated college or university, your high school, and you. All reporting is usually completed by the middle of July.

REASONS FOR TAKING THE ADVANCED PLACEMENT EXAM

"AP made me a better student in all my classes."
—SH, AP student

At some point during the year, every AP student asks the ultimate question: Why am I taking this exam?

Good question. Why put yourself through a semester or year of intensive study, pressure, stress, and preparation? To be honest, only you can answer that question. Over the years, my students have indicated that there are several reasons they were willing to take the risk and to put forth the effort:

- for personal satisfaction
- to compare themselves with other students across the nation
- because colleges look favorably on the applications of students who elect to enroll in AP courses
- to receive college credit or advanced standing at their colleges or universities
- because they love the subject
- so that their families will really be proud of them

There are plenty of other reasons, but no matter what they might be, the top reason for your enrolling in the AP U.S. Government and Politics course and taking the exam in May is to feel good about yourself and the challenges you have met.

4 WHAT YOU NEED TO KNOW ABOUT THE AP U.S. GOVERNMENT AND POLITICS EXAM

If I Don't Take an AP U.S. Government and Politics Course, Can I Still Take the AP Government and Politics Exam?

Yes. Even though the AP U.S. Government and Politics exam is designed for the student who has had a course in AP U.S. Government and Politics, there are high schools that do not offer this type of course, and the students in these high schools have done well on the exam. However, if your high school does offer an AP U.S. Government and Politics course, by all means take advantage of it and the structured background it will provide you.

How Is the Advanced Placement U.S. Government and Politics Exam Organized?

The exam is divided into two parts and lasts 2 hours and 25 minutes. The first section consists of 60 multiple-choice questions. You will have 45 minutes to complete this part of the exam.

After you complete the multiple-choice section and hand in your test booklet and scan sheet, you will be given a brief break. The length of this break depends on the particular administrator. You will not be able to return to the multiple-choice questions when you return to the examination room.

The second part of the exam is a 100-minute free-response section consisting of four mandatory questions that cover broad topics. Generally, at least one of the free-response questions is a stimulus-based question that uses a table, chart, graph, or other information provided in the question.

Must I Check the Box at the End of the Essay Booklet that Allows the AP People to Use My Essays as Samples for Research?

No. This is simply a way for the College Board to make certain it has your permission if they decide to use one or more of your essays as a model. The readers of your essays pay no attention to whether or not that box is checked. Checking or not checking the box will not affect your score.

How Is My AP U.S. Government and Politics Exam Scored?

Let's look at the basics first. The multiple-choice section counts for 50 percent of your total score, and the free-response section counts for 50 percent. Next, a four-part calculation: the raw scoring of the multiple-choice section, the raw scoring of the free-response section, the calculation of the composite score, and the conversion of the composite score into the AP grade of 5, 4, 3, 2, or 1.

How Is the Multiple-Choice Section Scored?

The scan sheet with your answers is run through a computer that counts the number of wrong answers and subtracts a fraction of that number from the number of correct answers. The AP U.S. Government and Politics questions have five choices; the fraction deducted for a wrong answer is one-fourth (.25) of a point. The formula for the calculation looks like this:

Number right – (number wrong × .25) = raw score rounded up or down to nearest whole number

How Is My Free-Response Section Scored?

Each of your free responses is read by a different, trained AP reader called a *faculty consultant*. The AP/College Board members have developed a highly successful training program for their readers. In addition, many opportunities for checks and double checks of free responses exist to ensure a fair and equitable reading of each free response.

The scoring guidelines are carefully developed by a chief faculty consultant, question leaders, table leaders, and content experts. All faculty consultants are then trained to read and score just one free-response question on the exam. They actually become experts on that one question. No reader knows the identity of any writer. The identification numbers and names are covered, and the exam booklets are randomly distributed to the readers in packets of 25 exams. Table leaders and question leaders review samples of each reader's scores to ensure that quality standards are constant.

Each essay is scored on a scale based on the dynamics of the rubric. Some free-response questions may be scored from 0 to 6, while another may be scored from 0 to 11. Even though the free-response questions receive different scoring, each is weighted equally. Once your free response is graded on this scale, the next set of calculations is completed.

How Is My Composite Score Calculated?

The composite score for the AP U.S. Government and Politics exam is 120. The composite score is determined by adding the score from the multiple-choice section to the score from the essay section and rounding that sum to the nearest whole number.

Over the years there has been an observable trend indicating the number of points required to achieve a specific grade. Data released from previous AP U.S. Government and Politics exams show that the approximate ranges for the five scores are:

mid-80s—120 points = 5
70s—mid-80s points = 4
high 40s—70s points = 3
high 20s—high 40s = 2
0—high 20s = 1

(The ranges change from year to year—use this only as an approximate guideline.)

How Is My Composite Score Turned into the Grade that Is Reported to My College?

Keep in mind that the total composite scores needed to earn a 5, 4, 3, 2, or 1 are different each year. This is determined by a committee of AP/College Board/Educational Testing Service directors, experts, and statisticians. The grading is based on items such as:

- AP distribution over the past three years
- comparability studies
- observations of the chief faculty consultant
- frequency distributions of scores on each section and the free response
- average scores on each exam section and essays

What Should I Bring to the Exam?

You should bring:

- several pencils with erasers
- several black pens (black is easier to read than other colors)
- a watch (no beeping, alarm, or calculator watches)

Is There Anything Else I Should Be Aware of?

"The more you prepare, the more you know."
—OT, AP teacher

You should be aware of the following:

- Allow plenty of time to get to the test site.
- Wear comfortable clothing.
- Eat a light breakfast or lunch.
- Remind yourself that you are well prepared and that the test is an enjoyable challenge and a chance to share your knowledge. Be proud of yourself! You worked hard all semester or all year.

Once test day comes, there is nothing further you can do. It is out of your hands, and your only job is to answer as many questions correctly as you possibly can.

Is There Anything Special I Should Do the Night Before the Exam?

Although I do not advocate last-minute cramming, there may be some value to last-minute review. Spend the night before the exam relaxing with family or friends. Watch a movie, play a game, gab on the phone, then find a quiet spot to study. While you're unwinding, flip through your own textbook, notebook, and review sheets. As you are approaching the exam, you might want to put together a list of topics that have troubled you and review them briefly the night before the exam. Soon you will be ready to drift off. Pleasant dreams.

A LOOK AT THE DIAGNOSTIC/MASTER EXAM

"AP is not just about knowing facts—it's being able to analyze and synthesize the information."
—JE, AP teacher

Over the next several pages you will find a diagnostic exam, which uses the format and style of the AP U.S. Government and Politics Exam. In the next two chapters, I will discuss important aspects of the multiple-choice and free-response sections of the exam. For now, take a look at the exam and familiarize yourself with the format and style. Skim the questions to see what topics are covered. In later chapters, take the diagnostic exam as practice.

GETTING STARTED: THE DIAGNOSTIC/MASTER EXAM

2

U.S. GOVERNMENT AND POLITICS

Section I

Total Time—45 minutes

For the following multiple-choice questions, select the best answer choice and fill in the appropriate blank on the answer sheet.

1. American civil liberties were established by the

   A. Bill of Rights
   B. Articles of Confederation
   C. Declaration of Independence
   D. Judiciary Article of the United States Constitution
   E. Supreme Court decision in *Marbury v. Madison*

2. The only president to resign from office was

   A. Calvin Coolidge
   B. Spiro Agnew
   C. Lyndon Johnson
   D. Richard Nixon
   E. Zachary Taylor

3. Impeachment cases must be tried in the

   I. Senate only
   II. House only
   III. Senate and House
   IV. Senate and House with the Supreme Court presiding

   A. IV
   B. I
   C. I and II
   D. II
   E. III

4. An example of a government corporation would be

   A. the U.S. Treasury Department
   B. the U.S. Postal Service
   C. the U.S. armed forces
   D. the Internal Revenue Service
   E. any independent regulatory agency found within the U.S. government

5. Primary elections are held to

   A. narrow down the field of candidates within a political party
   B. expand the field of candidates within a political party
   C. give the voters more choice
   D. allow state legislatures the opportunity to determine political districts
   E. allow the voter to gain a better understanding of a candidate's views

6. Political parties are

   A. individuals seeking to control government
   B. individuals seeking to control government by influencing public policy
   C. individuals seeking to control government by winning election through peaceful legal actions

D. individuals seeking to elect a candidate to the presidency

E. individuals seeking to organize as a group in order to show support for their group's individual political cause

7. The independent regulatory commission responsible for the supervision of the nation's banking system and regulation of the money supply is the

A. Federal Trade Commission
B. Securities and Exchange Commission
C. Consumer Product Safety Commission
D. Department of Treasury
E. Federal Reserve System

8. How often are senators elected?

A. every 5 years
B. every 2 years
C. every 6 years
D. every 8 years
E. every 4 years

9. The founding fathers' original view of the presidency was to have a president with administrative power be administrator of the Constitution, but not have total control over the government. This view is sometime called the

A. presidential model
B. administrative model
C. congressional model
D. constitutional model
E. executive model

10. Before the Supreme Court hears the oral arguments of a case presented for its review, each side must present written documents supporting that side's legal viewpoint. These written documents are known as

A. legal documents
B. briefs

C. viewpoints of the court
D. a prospectus
E. a writ

11. Which of the following best describes a filibuster?

A. A filibuster is an oratory that can only be used in the Senate.
B. A filibuster is an oratory that can only be used in the House.
C. It is used in both houses to stop or slow down action on legislation.
D. It can easily be avoided or stopped.
E. It is used quite often by the members of Congress and is usually very successful.

12. Interest groups are most associated with

A. matters of economic interest
B. matters of political interest
C. military issues
D. methods of increasing voter participation
E. matters of social interest and value

13. In the United States, the average person's political participation is limited to

A. voting in local elections
B. a basic understanding of government
C. voting in presidential elections
D. ignoring government altogether
E. working for a political party at some level of government

14. How many members comprise the United States House of Representatives?

A. 100
B. 250
C. 438
D. 435
E. 535

15. The electoral college system, when selecting the president, is not a system without defects. Which of the following is a major defect of that system?

    A. The Senate, not the people, decides elections for president.
    B. Electors are not in any way pledged to their candidate.
    C. Electors are directed by the Constitution as to how to cast their ballot.
    D. The candidate winning the popular vote always wins.
    E. Federal law dictates the electoral vote.

16. In *Lemon v. Kurtzman*, the court established the "Lemon test." According to this test, which of the following would apply?

    A. Prayer in public schools is unconstitutional.
    B. Prayer in public schools is constitutional.
    C. Religious freedom is guaranteed by the constitution.
    D. Education laws do not apply to religious freedom.
    E. State aid must be of a secular purpose if it is to be applied to a church school.

17. Which of the following is true about the voting process in America?

    A. The federal government regulates voter registration in all states.
    B. State governments regulate voter registration within their respective state.
    C. All individuals over the age of 18 are required to register to vote.
    D. Anyone may vote regardless of registration status.
    E. Local governments are responsible for voter registration laws.

18. In order to ratify the Constitution of the United States

    A. nine of the 13 states had to approve the document
    B. the people had to approve the Constitution by popular vote
    C. the document had to have unanimous approval by all of the states
    D. a two-thirds vote by both houses of the new government was necessary
    E. a three-fourths vote of all state legislatures had to approve the document

19. Which of the following is not true about the Senate?

    A. The most powerful member is the president of the Senate.
    B. Revenue bills cannot be introduced in the Senate.
    C. The Senate works with the president when treaties are involved.
    D. The Senate's larger number makes it more powerful.
    E. The Senate contains 100 members.

20. The purpose of the 22nd Amendment, passed in 1951, was to

    A. limit presidential terms of office
    B. allow the president to choose a vice presidential running mate
    C. provide more checks and balances on the executive office
    D. allow voters in the District of Columbia to vote
    E. allow for presidential impeachment

21. Which of the following presidents appointed the first woman to the Supreme Court of the United States?

    A. Jimmy Carter
    B. Bill Clinton
    C. Ronald Reagan
    D. Franklin Roosevelt
    E. Gerald Ford

22. Which of the following is a specific power of the House of Representatives?

   I. impeach president
   II. elect president when electoral college fails
   III. initiate revenue bills

    A. I only
    B. II only
    C. III only
    D. I, II, and III
    E. I and II

23. Members of the federal executive bureaucracy tend to represent the interests of

    A. the president
    B. the departments in which they work
    C. the special interests to which they belong
    D. the political party to which they belong
    E. themselves

24. In the United States, the powers of government are divided between a national government, state governments, and several regional and local governments. This system is called

    A. delegated government
    B. federalism
    C. democracy
    D. republican government
    E. democratic government

25. A private organization that attempts to get government officials to respond to its philosophy and way of thinking on particular issues is called a/an

    A. pressure group
    B. political pressure group
    C. interest group
    D. political power group
    E. lobbyist

26. The political belief that the president is the steward of the people and should continually act in the best interests of the people is known as the stewardship theory. Which president most promoted this theory?

    A. Theodore Roosevelt
    B. Thomas Jefferson
    C. George Washington
    D. Franklin Roosevelt
    E. Woodrow Wilson

27. States, which require the winning candidates of each party to have an absolute majority in a primary election, may also require the holding of a/an

    A. open primary
    B. closed primary
    C. runoff primary
    D. nonpartisan primary
    E. presidential primary

28. In the United States, the Congress has created two types of federal courts. These courts are

    A. special and legislative courts
    B. district and constitutional courts
    C. constitutional and appellate courts
    D. constitutional and legislative courts
    E. district and appellate courts

29. What right is protected by the Second Amendment of the United States Constitution?

    A. quarter troops
    B. bear arms and maintain a militia
    C. serve in a militia
    D. petition the federal government
    E. express and exhibit free speech

30. Which of the following is a true statement about political parties in America?

    A. Political parties are detrimental to the American political system.
    B. Membership is voluntary and represents a good cross section of the country's population.

C. Membership is voluntary, but only a small portion of the voting public belongs.

D. Political parties are beginning to die out in the American political scene.

E. Political parties are becoming stronger and more diverse in the American political scene.

31. An incumbent is a

A. first-time office holder
B. candidate running for office
C. current office holder
D. most recently defeated candidate
E. candidate with the most votes

32. In developing the United States Constitution, which of the following plans called for a strong national government with three separate branches?

A. the Virginia Plan
B. the New Jersey Plan
C. the Connecticut Plan
D. the Philadelphia Plan
E. the Hamilton Plan

33. An interest group, a bureaucratic government agency, and a committee of Congress working together would be an example of

A. an iron triangle
B. a government corporation
C. government networks
D. government agencies
E. sub governments

34. The purpose of a poll watcher is to

A. direct the voter to the proper polling station
B. help the election judge count the votes
C. determine exit poll results
D. ensure the election process at the poll is fair and honest
E. ensure that enough ballots are on hand to meet the needs of voter turnout

35. The president's cabinet is designed to

A. advise the president
B. administer a department of the government
C. run the executive branch of the government
D. set the president's agenda before the Congress
E. advise the president and administer a department of government

36. There are many legislative tactics used by members of the Congress. Which of the following terms best describes the legislative tactic of acquiring funds or projects for a Congressman's home district?

A. logrolling
B. pork barrel legislation
C. gerrymandering
D. congressional campaigning
E. bush beating

37. What is the total current membership of the electoral college?

A. 435
B. 535
C. 538
D. 438
E. 270

38. How many courts of appeals are there in the federal court system?

A. one
B. 90
C. six
D. three
E. 12

39. Adding amendments to the United States Constitution is a two-step process that includes

A. proposal by the United States House of Representatives and ratification by the Senate

B. proposal by the United States Senate and ratification by the House of Representatives

C. proposal and ratification by both houses of Congress

D. proposal by the United States Congress and ratification by the states

E. proposal by the executive branch and ratification by the legislative branch

40. Each state in the House of Representatives is allowed a certain number of representatives. That number is determined by:

A. the population of each state
B. constitutional amendment
C. presidential mandate
D. the number of electors each state has in the electoral college
E. a number called for in the Constitution of each state

41. In the case of a tie vote in the electoral college during the selection of the president, who is charged with electing the president?

A. Senate
B. House of Representatives
C. Supreme Court
D. Senate and Supreme Court
E. Supreme Court and House of Representatives

42. Which of the following is an executive power of the Senate?

A. reviewing presidential vetoes
B. trying impeachment cases
C. keeping a check on the House of Representatives
D. proposing constitutional amendments
E. approving appointments and treaties

43. Which of the following Supreme Court cases established the principle of judicial review in the American court system?

A. *McCulloch v. Maryland*
B. *Gibbons v. Ogden*
C. *Marbury v. Madison*
D. *Mapp v. Ohio*
E. *Miranda v. Arizona*

44. Which of the following best describes a public interest group?

A. A public interest group seeks to benefit its self-interest.
B. A public interest group seeks to benefit the nation as a whole rather than its self-interest.
C. A public interest group seeks to destroy government bureaucracy.
D. A public interest group seeks to provide information to certain groups within the Congress.
E. A public interest group seeks to win the support of the president.

45. While the president has the power to make appointments, he or she also has the power to remove some appointed officials from office. Where in the United States Constitution is this power located?

A. Article I
B. Article II
C. Article III
D. Article IV
E. Article V

46. What is the minimum age requirement for a member of the House of Representatives?

A. 25
B. 30
C. 35

D. same age requirement as the president
E. There is no minimum age requirement.

47. Which court was considered to be the most liberal court of the 20th century?

A. Warren Court
B. Burger Court
C. Marshall Court
D. Taney Court
E. Taft Court

48. The civil service system in the United States was created by

A. the Constitution
B. executive order
C. the Pendleton Act
D. the Hatch Act
E. the Civil Service Act of 1850

49. A primary election open only to the known voters of a political party would best be described as a/an

A. open primary
B. indirect primary
C. blanket primary
D. wide-open primary
E. closed primary

50. How many judges serve on the Supreme Court?

A. six
B. nine
C. four
D. ten
E. five

51. Which of the following is not true of the seniority rule?

A. Seniority rule ignores ability.
B. Seniority rule discourages hard work.
C. Seniority rule is not as important today as in the past.

D. Seniority rule is significant in the selection of committee chairpersons.
E. Seniority rule allows the most qualified individual to be selected for the job.

52. Which of the following is not an accurate description of the president's ability to deal with the Congress?

A. In dealing with Congress, the president works under a system of checks and balances.
B. The president must work with the political party influences in Congress.
C. The president is able to enact legislation that he deems necessary.
D. The president may veto acts of Congress.
E. The president must work with Congress on issues important to both branches of the government.

53. If a special session of Congress is necessary after Congress has adjourned, who has the power to call Congress back into session?

A. the speaker of the House and the president pro-tem
B. the president
C. the vice president by virtue of position in the Senate
D. the members of Congress
E. the members of the House and Senate Special Session Committee

54. When a case is appealed to the Supreme Court of the United States on the request of a lower court that is not sure on the point of law, the process is called

A. certificate
B. appeal
C. writ of assistance
D. writ of certiorari
E. brief solicitation

55. Which U.S. president held the most press conferences?

    A. Richard Nixon
    B. George Bush
    C. Jimmy Carter
    D. Franklin Roosevelt
    E. John Kennedy

56. The size of the House of Representatives is determined by

    A. the president
    B. Congress
    C. the Constitution
    D. the population of the states
    E. the Supreme Court

57. The best definition of bicameralism is

    A. a legislative body dominated by two major political parties
    B. a legislative body composed of one house
    C. a legislative body composed of two houses
    D. a legislative body that shares power with a judiciary
    E. a legislative body that shares power with an executive

58. "A President's power originates in his ability to persuade others." This statement can best be attributed to which of the following individuals?

    A. James David Barber
    B. Bill Clinton
    C. Richard Neustadt
    D. Richard Nixon
    E. John Locke

59. The political party system in the United States is based on the principle of a

    A. multi-party system
    B. single-member district system
    C. moderate-liberal system
    D. independent system
    E. two-party system

60. The Supreme Court of the United States has both original and appellate jurisdiction. The court usually hears cases on appeal and decides only a few cases each year. Who decides which cases the court will hear?

    A. chief justice of the Supreme Court
    B. members of the Supreme Court as a group
    C. attorney general of the United States
    D. solicitor general of the United States
    E. chief associate judge of the Supreme Court

END OF SECTION I

Section II

Total Time—100 minutes

1. Legislative strategies are often used to kill or delay the passage of a bill through Congress.

   a. Identify three legislative strategies that can kill or delay the passage of a bill through Congress.

   b. Explain how each of the strategies identified above can kill or delay the passage of a bill through Congress.

Participation in Elections for President and Representatives

Percent of Voting-Age Population: 1972 to 1998

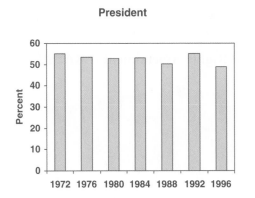

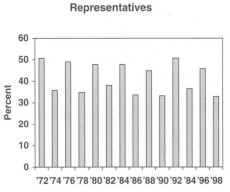

2. The graphs above show participation in elections of the voting-age population for president and members of the House of Representatives. From this information and your knowledge of United States politics, perform the following tasks.

   a. Identify and discuss two patterns displayed in the graphs.

b. Identify two factors that contribute to voter participation in elections. Explain how each affects voter participation.

3. Civil rights may be expanded through the passage of new legislation or constitutional amendment.

   a. Identify and explain two examples of how the expansion of civil rights has been accomplished through the passage of legislation, and two examples of how the expansion of civil rights has been accomplished through constitutional amendment.

   b. Identify and explain one example of a how a restriction has been placed on civil rights through legislation.

   c. Explain how the failure to adopt the Equal Rights Amendment (ERA) affected the civil rights of women.

4. The Constitution creates a Supreme Court for the United States. By hearing disputes, the Supreme Court influences public policy. Several factors may influence the justices in the judicial decision-making process.

   a. Identify and discuss two influences on the judicial decision-making process in the Supreme Court.

b. Discuss and give an example of how the influences you identified have influenced the judicial decision-making process.

<u>END OF SECTION II</u>

So, that's what the Advanced Placement U.S. Government and Politics exam looks like. If you're being honest with yourself, you're probably feeling a bit overwhelmed at this point. Good! This is primarily why I am going to deconstruct this entire Diagnostic/Master exam for you and with you throughout this book. By the time you reach Part IV and Practice Exams 1 and 2, you should be feeling much more confident and comfortable about doing well on the AP U.S. Government and Politics exam.

As you progress through this book you will:

- take each section of the Diagnostic/Master exam;
- read the explanations for the answers to the multiple-choice questions;
- read the rubrics for each of the free-response essays;
- evaluate your own performance in light of this information.

Chapter 3

Section I of the Exam: The Multiple-Choice Questions

 **4** **INTRODUCTION TO THE MULTIPLE-CHOICE SECTION OF THE EXAM**

What Should I Expect in Section I?

For this first section of the U.S. Government and Politics exam, you are allotted 45 minutes to answer 60 objective questions. These are questions that any student in any introductory government and politics class might know. It is not expected that everyone will know the answer to every question; however, you should try to answer as many questions as you can. The AP U.S. Government and Politics questions always have five answer choices. Points are given for every correct answer and partial points (one-fourth) are deducted for every incorrect answer. No points are given or deducted for blank answers.

How Should I Begin to Work with Section I?

Take a quick look at the entire multiple-choice section. This brief skimming of the test will put your mind at ease because you will be more aware of the test and what is expected in Section I. Do not spend too much time skimming. Remember, this is a timed exam.

How Should I Proceed Through This Section of the Exam?

 Timing is important. Always maintain an awareness of the time. Wear a watch. (Some students like to put it directly in from of them on the desk.)

Remember, this will not be your first encounter with the multiple-choice section of the test. You've probably been practicing timed exams in class; in addition, this book provides you with three timed experiences.

Work at a pace that is comfortable. Every question is worth the same number of points, so don't get bogged down on one or two questions. Don't panic if you do not know the answer to a question. Remember, others taking the exam might not know it either. There has to be a bar that determines the 5s and 4s for this exam. Just do your best.

Reading the questions and answer choices carefully is a must. Read the *entire* question. Don't try to guess what the question is asking; read the question. Read *all* the answer choices. Don't jump at the first answer choice. Pay attention to key terms or negative statements, such as, which of the following is NOT; all of the following EXCEPT.

TYPES OF MULTIPLE-CHOICE QUESTIONS

Multiple-choice questions are not written randomly. There are certain general formats you will encounter.

Is the Structure the Same for All of the Multiple-Choice Questions?

No. There are several basic patterns that the AP test makers employ. Some questions may involve general identification, while others may depend on analysis.

1. The straightforward question may involve defining terms or making a generalization.
2. The negative question might include "all of the following except" and requires extra time because it demands that you consider every possibility.
3. The multiple multiple-choice question uses Roman numerals to list several possible correct answers. You must choose which answer or combinations of answers is correct.
4. The stimulus-based question involves interpreting a chart, graph, table, quote, etc. to determine the answer.

STRATEGIES FOR ANSWERING THE MULTIPLE-CHOICE QUESTIONS

You probably have been answering multiple-choice questions most of your academic life, and you've probably figured out ways to deal with them. However, there may be some points you have not considered that will be helpful for this particular exam.

General Guidelines

- Work in order. This is a good approach for several reasons:
  — It's clear.
  — You will not lose your place on the scan sheet.
  — There may be a logic to working sequentially that will help you answer previous questions. But this is your call. If you are more comfortable moving around the exam, do so.
- Write on the exam booklet. Mark it up. Make it yours. Interact with the test.
- Pace yourself and watch your time. Don't spend too much time on one question so that you run out of time and don't complete questions you might know, but which appear later in the exam. Don't rush. There are no bonus points for finishing early.
- Don't be misled by the length or appearance of a question or of answer choices. There is no correlation between length or appearance and the difficulty of the questions.
- Read the questions and answer choices carefully. Make note of key terms such as NOT or EXCEPT.
- Consider all the choices in a given question. This will keep you from jumping to false conclusions. It helps you slow down and really consider all possibilities. You may find that your first choice is not the BEST or most appropriate choice.
- Remember that all parts of an answer must be correct for the answer to be correct.

Specific Techniques

- Process of elimination. This is your primary tool, except for direct knowledge of the answer.

  1. Read the five choices.
  2. If no choice immediately strikes you as correct, you can
     — eliminate those that are obviously wrong
     — eliminate those choices that are too narrow or too broad
     — eliminate illogical choices
     — eliminate answers that are synonymous (identical)
     — eliminate answers that cancel each other out
  3. If two answers are close, do one *or* the other of the following.
     — Find the one that is general enough to cover all aspects of the question.
     — Find the one that is limited enough to be the detail the question is looking for.

- Educated guess. You have a wealth of skills and knowledge. A question or choice may trigger your memory. This may form the basis of your educated guess. Have confidence to use the educated guess as a valid technique. Trust your own resources.

SCORING THE MULTIPLE-CHOICE SECTION

How Does the Scoring of the Multiple-Choice Section Work?

The multiple-choice section of the exam is taken on a scan sheet. The sheet is run through a computer that counts the number of wrong answers and subtracts a fraction of that score from the number of correct answers. The AP U.S. Government and Politics questions have five choices; the fraction deducted for a wrong answer is one-fourth of a point. The formula for the calculation looks like this:

Number right – (number wrong × .25) = raw score rounded up or down to nearest whole number

Let's say you just took the AP U.S. Government and Politics exam. You answered 55 of the 60 questions, leaving five questions blank. After your multiple-choice section was scored, you got 47 questions correct and eight questions incorrect. Your raw score for the multiple-choice section would be determined like this:

47 correct – (8 wrong × .25) = 45 Section I Raw Score

This score would then be added to the free-response score for a composite score on the exam. The composite score would be equated to an AP score of 5, 4, 3, 2, or 1.

If I Don't Know the Answer, Should I Guess?

If you do the math, you will see that a wrong answer is worth one-fourth of a point. Thus, you would have to miss four questions to lose a full point. Therefore, I urge you to try to answer every question, especially if you can eliminate one or more answer choices. You get no points for leaving a question blank, so making educated guesses based on a careful reading of the question and answer choices probably won't seriously hurt you.

The Time Is at Hand

It is now time to try the Diagnostic/Master exam, Section I. Do this entire section in one sitting. Time yourself. Be honest with yourself when scoring your answers.

Note: If the 45 minutes passes before you finish all the questions, stop where you are and score what you have done up to this point. Afterward, answer the remaining questions, but do not count the answers as part of your score. When you have completed all the multiple-choice questions in this Diagnostic/Master exam, carefully read the explanations of the answers. Assess which types of questions give you trouble. Use this book to learn from your mistakes.

ANSWER SHEET FOR
DIAGNOSTIC MULTIPLE-CHOICE QUESTIONS

1. _____	21. _____	41. _____
2. _____	22. _____	42. _____
3. _____	23. _____	43. _____
4. _____	24. _____	44. _____
5. _____	25. _____	45. _____
6. _____	26. _____	46. _____
7. _____	27. _____	47. _____
8. _____	28. _____	48. _____
9. _____	29. _____	49. _____
10. _____	30. _____	50. _____
11. _____	31. _____	51. _____
12. _____	32. _____	52. _____
13. _____	33. _____	53. _____
14. _____	34. _____	54. _____
15. _____	35. _____	55. _____
16. _____	36. _____	56. _____
17. _____	37. _____	57. _____
18. _____	38. _____	58. _____
19. _____	39. _____	59. _____
20. _____	40. _____	60. _____

I _____ did _____ did not finish all the questions in the allotted 45 minutes.

I had _____ correct answers. I had _____ incorrect answers. I left _____ questions blank.

Scoring Formula:

_____ – _____ = _____
number right – (number wrong × .25) = raw score

I have carefully reviewed the explanations of the answers. I need to work on the following types of questions:

2 THE MULTIPLE-CHOICE SECTION OF THE DIAGNOSTIC/MASTER EXAM

✓ The multiple-choice section of the Diagnostic/Master exam follows. You have seen the questions in the "walk-through" in Chapter 2.

U.S. GOVERNMENT AND POLITICS

Section I

Total Time—45 minutes

For the following multiple-choice questions, select the best answer choice and fill in the appropriate blank on the answer sheet.

1. American civil liberties were established by the

   A. Bill of Rights
   B. Articles of Confederation
   C. Declaration of Independence
   D. Judiciary Article of the United States Constitution
   E. Supreme Court decision in *Marbury v. Madison*

2. The only president to resign from office was

   A. Calvin Coolidge
   B. Spiro Agnew
   C. Lyndon Johnson
   D. Richard Nixon
   E. Zachary Taylor

3. Impeachment cases must be tried in the

   I.   Senate only
   II. House only
   III. Senate and House
   IV. Senate and House with the Supreme Court presiding

      A. IV
      B. I
      C. I and II
      D. II
      E. III

4. An example of a government corporation would be

   A. the U.S. Treasury Department
   B. the U.S. Postal Service
   C. the U.S. armed forces
   D. the Internal Revenue Service
   E. any independent regulatory agency found within the U.S. government

5. Primary elections are held to

   A. narrow down the field of candidates within a political party
   B. expand the field of candidates within a political party
   C. give the voters more choice
   D. allow state legislatures the opportunity to determine political districts
   E. allow the voter to gain a better understanding of a candidate's views

6. Political parties are

   A. individuals seeking to control government
   B. individuals seeking to control government by influencing public policy
   C. individuals seeking to control government by winning election through peaceful legal actions

D. individuals seeking to elect a candidate to the presidency
E. individuals seeking to organize as a group in order to show support for their group's individual political cause

7. The independent regulatory commission responsible for the supervision of the nation's banking system and regulation of the money supply is the

A. Federal Trade Commission
B. Securities and Exchange Commission
C. Consumer Product Safety Commission
D. Department of Treasury
E. Federal Reserve System

8. How often are senators elected?

A. every 5 years
B. every 2 years
C. every 6 years
D. every 8 years
E. every 4 years

9. The founding fathers' original view of the presidency was to have a president with administrative power be administrator of the Constitution, but not have total control over the government. This view is sometime called the

A. presidential model
B. administrative model
C. congressional model
D. constitutional model
E. executive model

10. Before the Supreme Court hears the oral arguments of a case presented for its review, each side must present written documents supporting that side's legal viewpoint. These written documents are known as

A. legal documents
B. briefs

C. viewpoints of the court
D. a prospectus
E. a writ

11. Which of the following best describes a filibuster?

A. A filibuster is an oratory that can only be used in the Senate.
B. A filibuster is an oratory that can only be used in the House.
C. It is used in both houses to stop or slow down action on legislation.
D. It can easily be avoided or stopped.
E. It is used quite often by the members of Congress and is usually very successful.

12. Interest groups are most associated with

A. matters of economic interest
B. matters of political interest
C. military issues
D. methods of increasing voter participation
E. matters of social interest and value

13. In the United States, the average person's political participation is limited to

A. voting in local elections
B. a basic understanding of government
C. voting in presidential elections
D. ignoring government altogether
E. working for a political party at some level of government

14. How many members comprise the United States House of Representatives?

A. 100
B. 250
C. 438
D. 435
E. 535

15. The electoral college system, when selecting the president, is not a system without defects. Which of the following is a major defect of that system?

A. The Senate, not the people, decides elections for president.
B. Electors are not legally pledged to their candidate.
C. Electors are directed by the Constitution as to how to cast their ballot.
D. The candidate winning the popular vote always wins.
E. Federal law dictates the electoral vote.

16. In *Lemon v. Kurtzman*, the court established the "Lemon test." According to this test, which of the following would apply?

A. Prayer in public schools is unconstitutional.
B. Prayer in public schools is constitutional.
C. Religious freedom is guaranteed by the constitution.
D. Education laws do not apply to religious freedom.
E. State aid must be of a secular purpose if it is to be applied to a church school.

17. Which of the following is true about the voting process in America?

A. The federal government regulates voter registration in all states.
B. State governments regulate voter registration within their respective state.
C. All individuals over the age of 18 are required to register to vote.
D. Anyone may vote regardless of registration status.
E. Local governments are responsible for voter registration laws.

18. In order to ratify the Constitution of the United States

A. nine of the 13 states had to approve the document
B. the people had to approve the Constitution by popular vote

C. the document had to have unanimous approval by all of the states
D. a two-thirds vote by both houses of the new government was necessary
E. a three-fourths vote of all state legislatures had to approve the document

19. Which of the following is not true about the Senate?

A. The most powerful member is the president of the Senate.
B. Revenue bills cannot be introduced in the Senate.
C. The Senate works with the president when treaties are involved.
D. The Senate's larger number makes it more powerful.
E. The Senate contains 100 members.

20. The purpose of the 22nd Amendment, passed in 1951, was to

A. limit presidential terms of office
B. allow the president to choose a vice presidential running mate
C. provide more checks and balances on the executive office
D. allow voters in the District of Columbia to vote
E. allow for presidential impeachment

21. Which of the following presidents appointed the first woman to the Supreme Court of the United States?

A. Jimmy Carter
B. Bill Clinton
C. Ronald Reagan
D. Franklin Roosevelt
E. Gerald Ford

22. Which of the following is a specific power of the House of Representatives?

I. impeach president
II. elect president when electoral college fails
III. initiate revenue bills

A. I only
B. II only
C. III only
D. I, II, and III
E. I and II

23. Members of the federal executive bureaucracy tend to represent the interests of

A. the president
B. the departments in which they work
C. the special interests to which they belong
D. the political party to which they belong
E. themselves

24. In the United States, the powers of government are divided between a national government, state governments, and several regional and local governments. This system is called

A. delegated government
B. federalism
C. democracy
D. republican government
E. democratic government

25. A private organization that attempts to get government officials to respond to its philosophy and way of thinking on particular issues is called a/an

A. pressure group
B. political pressure group
C. interest group
D. political power group
E. lobbyist

26. The political belief that the president is the steward of the people and should continually act in the best interests of the people is known as the stewardship theory. Which president most promoted this theory?

A. Theodore Roosevelt
B. Thomas Jefferson
C. George Washington
D. Franklin Roosevelt
E. Woodrow Wilson

27. States, which require the winning candidates of each party to have an absolute majority in a primary election, may also require the holding of a/an

A. open primary
B. closed primary
C. runoff primary
D. nonpartisan primary
E. presidential primary

28. In the United States, the Congress has created two types of federal courts. These courts are

A. special and legislative courts
B. district and constitutional courts
C. constitutional and appellate courts
D. constitutional and legislative courts
E. district and appellate courts

29. What right is protected by the Second Amendment of the United States Constitution?

A. quarter troops
B. bear arms and maintain a militia
C. serve in a militia
D. petition the federal government
E. express and exhibit free speech

30. Which of the following is a true statement about political parties in America?

A. Political parties are detrimental to the American political system.
B. Membership is voluntary and represents a good cross section of the country's population.
C. Membership is voluntary, but only a small portion of the voting public belongs.
D. Political parties are beginning to die out in the American political scene.
E. Political parties are becoming stronger and more diverse in the American political scene.

31. An incumbent is a

    A. first-time office holder
    B. candidate running for office
    C. current office holder
    D. most recently defeated candidate
    E. candidate with the most votes

32. In developing the United States Constitution, which of the following plans called for a strong national government with three separate branches?

    A. the Virginia Plan
    B. the New Jersey Plan
    C. the Connecticut Plan
    D. the Philadelphia Plan
    E. the Hamilton Plan

33. An interest group, a bureaucratic government agency, and a committee of Congress working together would be an example of

    A. an iron triangle
    B. a government corporation
    C. government networks
    D. government agencies
    E. sub governments

34. The purpose of a poll watcher is to

    A. direct the voter to the proper polling station
    B. help the election judge count the votes
    C. determine exit poll results
    D. ensure the election process at the poll is fair and honest
    E. ensure that enough ballots are on hand to meet the needs of voter turnout

35. The president's cabinet is designed to

    A. advise the president
    B. administer a department of the government
    C. run the executive branch of the government
    D. set the president's agenda before the Congress
    E. both advise the president and administer a department of government

36. There are many legislative tactics used by members of the Congress. Which of the following terms best describes the legislative tactic of acquiring funds or projects for a Congressman's home district?

    A. logrolling
    B. pork barrel legislation
    C. gerrymandering
    D. congressional campaigning
    E. bush beating

37. What is the total current membership of the electoral college?

    A. 435
    B. 535
    C. 538
    D. 438
    E. 270

38. How many courts of appeals are there in the federal court system?

    A. one
    B. 90
    C. six
    D. three
    E. 12

39. Adding amendments to the United States Constitution is a two-step process that includes

    A. proposal by the United States House of Representatives and ratification by the Senate
    B. proposal by the United States Senate and ratification by the House of Representatives
    C. proposal and ratification by both houses of Congress
    D. proposal by the United States Congress and ratification by the states
    E. proposal by the executive branch and ratification by the legislative branch

40. Each state in the House of Representatives is allowed a certain number of representatives. That number is determined by:

    A. the population of each state
    B. constitutional amendment
    C. presidential mandate
    D. the number of electors each state has in the electoral college
    E. a number called for in the Constitution of each state

41. In the case of a tie vote in the electoral college during the selection of the president, who is charged with electing the president?

    A. Senate
    B. House of Representatives
    C. Supreme Court
    D. Senate and Supreme Court
    E. Supreme Court and House of Representatives

42. Which of the following is an executive power of the Senate?

    A. reviewing presidential vetoes
    B. trying impeachment cases
    C. keeping a check on the House of Representatives
    D. proposing constitutional amendments
    E. approving appointments and treaties

43. Which of the following Supreme Court cases established the principle of judicial review in the American court system?

    A. *McCulloch v. Maryland*
    B. *Gibbons v. Ogden*
    C. *Marbury v. Madison*
    D. *Mapp v. Ohio*
    E. *Miranda v. Arizona*

44. Which of the following best describes a public interest group?

    A. A public interest group seeks to benefit its self-interest.
    B. A public interest group seeks to benefit the nation as a whole rather than its self-interest.
    C. A public interest group seeks to destroy government bureaucracy.
    D. A public interest group seeks to provide information to certain groups within the Congress.
    E. A public interest group seeks to win the support of the president.

45. While the president has the power to make appointments, he or she also has the power to remove some appointed officials from office. Where in the United States Constitution is this power located?

    A. Article I
    B. Article II
    C. Article III
    D. Article IV
    E. Article V

46. What is the minimum age requirement for a member of the House of Representatives?

    A. 25
    B. 30
    C. 35
    D. same age requirement as the president
    E. There is no minimum age requirement.

47. Which court was considered to be the most liberal court of the 20th century?

    A. Warren Court
    B. Burger Court
    C. Marshall Court
    D. Taney Court
    E. Taft Court

48. The civil service system in the United States was created by

A. the Constitution
B. executive order
C. the Pendleton Act
D. the Hatch Act
E. the Civil Service Act of 1850

49. A primary election open only to the known voters of a political party would best be described as a/an

A. open primary
B. indirect primary
C. blanket primary
D. wide-open primary
E. closed primary

50. How many judges serve on the Supreme Court?

A. six
B. nine
C. four
D. ten
E. five

51. Which of the following is not true of the seniority rule?

A. Seniority rule ignores ability.
B. Seniority rule discourages hard work.
C. Seniority rule is not as important today as in the past.
D. Seniority rule is significant in the selection of committee chairpersons.
E. Seniority rule allows the most qualified individual to be selected for the job.

52. Which of the following is not an accurate description of the president's ability to deal with the Congress?

A. In dealing with Congress, the president works under a system of checks and balances.
B. The president must work with the political party influences in Congress.

C. The president is able to enact legislation that he deems necessary.
D. The president may veto acts of Congress.
E. The president must work with Congress on issues important to both branches of the government.

53. If a special session of Congress is necessary after Congress has adjourned, who has the power to call Congress back into session?

A. the speaker of the House and the president pro-tem
B. the president
C. the vice president by virtue of position in the Senate
D. the members of Congress
E. the members of the House and Senate Special Session Committee

54. When a case is appealed to the Supreme Court of the United States on the request of a lower court that is not sure on the point of law, the process is called

A. certificate
B. appeal
C. writ of assistance
D. writ of certiorari
E. brief solicitation

55. Which U.S. president held the most press conferences?

A. Richard Nixon
B. George Bush
C. Jimmy Carter
D. Franklin Roosevelt
E. John Kennedy

56. The size of the House of Representatives is determined by

A. the president
B. Congress
C. the Constitution
D. the population of the states
E. the Supreme Court

57. Bicameralism is
    A. a legislative body dominated by two major political parties
    B. a legislative body composed of one house
    C. a legislative body composed of two houses
    D. a legislative body that shares power with a judiciary
    E. a legislative body that shares power with an executive

58. "A President's power originates in his ability to persuade others." This statement can best be attributed to which of the following individuals?
    A. James David Barber
    B. Bill Clinton
    C. Richard Neustadt
    D. Richard Nixon
    E. John Locke

59. The political party system in the United States is based on the principle of a
    A. multi-party system
    B. single-member district system
    C. moderate-liberal system
    D. independent system
    E. two-party system

60. The Supreme Court of the United States has both original and appellate jurisdiction. The Court usually hears cases on appeal and decides only a few cases each year. Who decides which cases the court will hear?
    A. chief justice of the Supreme Court
    B. members of the Supreme Court as a group
    C. attorney general of the United States
    D. solicitor general of the United States
    E. chief associate judge of the Supreme Court

2 EXPLANATION OF THE ANSWERS TO THE MULTIPLE-CHOICE QUESTIONS OF THE DIAGNOSTIC/MASTER EXAM

1. **A.** Civil liberties were established in America by the Bill of Rights, which guaranteed basic freedoms for citizens.

2. **D.** Richard Nixon resigned from office in 1974, the only president to do so thus far.

3. **B.** According to the Constitution, the House of Representatives brings charges of impeachment and the Senate tries, or sits in judgment of, impeachment cases.

4. **B.** The U.S. Postal Service is a government corporation. The U.S. Treasury is a department, the armed forces are part of the Defense Department, and the IRS is an independent agency.

5. **A.** Primary elections are "first elections," held to nominate candidates from within a political party.

6. **C.** Political parties seek to control government through the winning of elections.

7. **E.** The Federal Reserve System was created in 1913 to supervise the nation's banking system and to regulate the money supply.

8. **C.** According to the Constitution, senators are elected every 6 years.

9. **D.** The constitutional model places restrictions on the powers of the president. Through the system of checks and balances, both Congress and the Supreme Court may limit the powers of the president.

10. **B.** Briefs are written documents given to the court to present each side's views on a case.

11. **A.** A filibuster is a stalling tactic used only in the Senate, where debate is not limited. The House of Representatives limits debate under the Rules Committee. It is difficult to avoid or stop a filibuster, because senators are hesitant to limit each other.

12. **A.** The largest number of interest groups are based on economic issues.

13. **C.** Voting in presidential elections is the method of participation used by the largest number of Americans. Most Americans do not vote in local elections or work for a political party.

14. **D.** The House of Representatives is composed of 435 members.

15. **B.** Electors are not legally pledged to vote for their candidate and may vote for any candidate.

16. **E.** "The Lemon test" created standards for the establishment clause of the first amendment, under which state aid given to a church school must be for a secular purpose.

17. **B.** Voter registration is regulated by state governments.

18. **A.** According to Article VII of the Constitution, ratification would occur with the approval of nine of the 13 states.

19. **D.** The Senate has a smaller number (100) than the House of Representatives (435).

20. **A.** The 22nd Amendment limits the president to two elected terms and not more than 10 years in office. The 23rd Amendment allows voters in the District of Columbia to vote in presidential elections. No amendments address checks and balances, presidential impeachment, or the selection of vice-presidential running mates.

21. **C.** Sandra Day O'Connor, the first woman appointed to the Supreme Court, was appointed by Ronald Reagan in 1981.

22. **D.** The House of Representatives has the power to bring charges of impeachment, elect the president if the electoral college fails, and initiate revenue bills.

23. **B.** Members of the federal bureaucracy tend to represent the departments in which they work.

24. **B.** Federalism in the United States is the division of the powers of government between national, state, and several regional and local governments.

25. **C.** Interest groups are private groups that attempt to get government officials to respond to their issue or philosophy.

26. **A.** Theodore Roosevelt promoted the stewardship theory, which sees the president as the steward of the people, acting in their best interests.

27. **C.** When no candidate receives an absolute majority in a primary, states may require a runoff election between the top candidates.

28. **D.** The United States federal court system is composed of constitutional and legislative courts.

29. **B.** The Second Amendment provides the right to bear arms. Quartering troops is addressed in the Third Amendment. The First Amendment deals with free speech and petitioning the government. No amendment addresses the issue of serving in a militia.

30. **B.** Membership in political parties is voluntary in America. Political parties tend to represent a good cross section of the American public.

31. **C.** Incumbents are current officeholders.

32. **A.** The Virginia Plan provided for a strong central government with three branches.

33. **A.** An iron triangle might consist of an interest group, bureaucratic government agency, and committee of Congress working together.

34. **D.** A poll watcher insures that the election process is fair and honest.

35. **E.** The president's cabinet advises the president, and each secretary administers a department of the government.

36. **B.** Pork barrel legislation is the term for a member of Congress acquiring funds or projects for the home district.

37. **C.** The electoral college is composed of 538 members, each state having the same number of electors as the sum of its representatives and senators. The 23rd Amendment provides that Washington, D.C. shall have the same number of electors as the smallest state—three.

38. **E.** There are 12 courts of appeals in the federal court system.

39. **D.** Adding amendments to the Constitution requires Congress to propose amendments and states to ratify amendments.

40. **A.** A state's representation in the House of Representatives is based on state population.

41. **B.** If the electoral college fails to choose a president, the House of Representatives is charged with choosing a president.

42. **E.** Approving appointments and treaties are executive powers of the Senate, because they are used in conjunction with a power of the president.

43. **C.** *Marbury v. Madison* (1803) established the principle of judicial review.

44. **B.** A public interest group seeks to benefit the nation as a whole rather than its own self-interest.

45. **B.** Article II of the Constitution addresses the powers of the president.

46. **A.** The minimum age for a member of the House of Representatives is 25.

47. **A.** The Supreme Court under Chief Justice Earl Warren is often considered the most liberal court of the 20th century.

48. **C.** The Pendleton Act created the civil service system in the United States.

49. **E.** A primary election would best be described as a closed primary if only the known voters of a political party were able to participate.

50. **B.** There are nine justices on the Supreme Court—a chief justice and eight associate justices.

51. **E.** The seniority rule does not require the selection of the most qualified individual to be chosen as a committee chairperson.

52. **C.** The president is only able to suggest legislation. Congress must pass bills enacting legislation.

53. **B.** Only the president may call special sessions of Congress.

54. **A.** Appealing a case to the Supreme Court because a lower court is not sure on a point of law requires a certificate.

55. **D.** Franklin Roosevelt held the most press conferences, partly due to his long tenure in office and the national emergencies of the times.

56. **B.** Congress determines the size of the House of Representatives through the passage of legislation. The Reapportionment Act of 1929 established the current size at 435 members.

57. **C.** Bicameralism describes a legislative body composed of two houses, such as the United States Congress.

58. **C.** Richard Neustadt stated that the president's power originates in the ability to persuade others.

59. **E.** The United States operates under a two-party system, with only two major parties having a reasonable chance of winning election.

60. **B.** The Supreme Court's members, using the rule of four, decide which cases they will consider.

Chapter 4

Section II of the Exam: The Free-Response Essay

4 INTRODUCTION TO THE FREE-RESPONSE ESSAY

The free-response section of the U.S. Government and Politics exam contains four mandatory free-response or essay questions. This means no choice between questions; you must answer all four. Don't worry though; often a question will allow choice within the question (such as, choose one of the three court cases listed). You will be given 100 minutes for the free-response section; therefore, you should plan on devoting approximately 25 minutes per question. Questions will cover the themes, issues, concepts, and content from all six areas of the course (constitutional underpinnings; political beliefs and behaviors; political parties, interest groups, and the mass media; institutions of national government; public policy; and civil rights and civil liberties).

What Is a Free-Response Essay?

The free-response questions are specific; therefore, your responses must be focused. Responses do not necessarily require a thesis statement, and you must pay close attention to what is being asked. Remember, to gain the highest possible score, answer the question that is asked.

What Is the Purpose of the Free-Response Essay?

The free-response essay assesses your ability to think critically and analyze the topics studied in U.S. Government and Politics. The essays allow students to demonstrate an understanding of the linkages between the various elements of government.

What Are the Pitfalls of the Free-Response Essay?

The free-response question can be a double-edged sword. Students can experience test anxiety (what's "free" in the free-response?) or suffer from overconfidence because of the open nature of this essay. The greatest pitfall is *the failure to plan.* Remember to pace yourself; no one question is more important than another. *Plan your strategy for answering each question, and stick to it.* Don't ramble in vague and unsupported generalities. Rambling may cause you to contradict yourself or make mistakes.

How Do I Prepare for the Free-Response Essay?

You need to begin preparing for the free-response essay as soon as the course begins. Focus on your writing skills, and practice as if you were writing for the AP exam every time you are assigned an essay in your government and politics class. Determine your strengths and weaknesses, and work to correct areas of weakness.

"You must be prepared to read with comprehension and write with consistency."
—JW, AP teacher

- Broaden your knowledge base by reading your textbook and supplemental texts. They will give you basic information to draw from when writing the free-response essay. Do not skim the text—READ—paying attention to details and focusing on people, events, examples, and linkages between different areas of government and politics (for example, interactions between the branches of government or how the media influence lawmakers). Watch the news, and pay attention to current events relating to government and politics.
- Pay attention in class to lectures and discussions. Take notes and study them.

"Pay close attention to examples: You can use them in your essays."
—DC, AP student

- Take advantage of practice writing whenever possible. Watch and correct grammar, spelling, and punctuation in classroom essays. Check out previous year's free-response questions, rubrics, and sample scored student essays on the College Board Website, www.apcentral. collegeboard.com. You will have to register to access the specific course sites, but it is worth your time.

What Criteria Do the AP Readers Use to Score a Free-Response Essay?

The readers look for responses that answer the questions asked. Remember, each free-response is scored by a different AP reader, trained to score that particular question. Care is given to compare each student essay to the standards established in the rubric. The same standards are applied to all essays, and no modifications in the rubrics occur. In general, students should:

- Recognize the subject matter of the question. When you see "Congress," don't just start writing about Congress. Analyze what the question asks about Congress.
- Recognize what task you are being asked to perform in relation to the question, for example, list, explain, describe, identify and explain, or explain and give examples (sometimes you will be asked to perform more than one task).
- NOTE: Remember that there is a general order to the tasks within the question. Organize your essay to answer the question or address the tasks in the order asked.

4 TYPES OF FREE-RESPONSE PROMPTS

Free-response questions are generally straightforward and ask you to perform certain tasks. Understanding what the prompt is asking you to do will help you perform the task correctly.

Prompt Vocabulary

"Pay attention to vocabulary terms."
—AL, AP student

- analyze—examine each part of the whole in a systematic way; evaluate
- define—briefly tell what something is or means
- describe—create a mental picture by using details or examples
- discuss—give details about; illustrate with examples
- explain—make something clear by giving reasons or examples; tell how and why
- argue/defend/justify/support—give evidence to show why an idea or view is right or good
- categorize/classify—sort into groups according to a given set of traits or features
- compare and contrast—point out similarities (compare) and differences (contrast)
- determine cause and effect—decide what leads to an event or circumstance (cause) and what results from an event or circumstance (effect)
- evaluate/judge—determine the worth or wisdom of an opinion, belief, or idea

4 DEVELOPING THE FREE-RESPONSE ESSAY

Strategies for Writing the Free-Response Essay

- Read the question carefully, in its entirety, and determine what you are being asked to write about. Analyze the question and identify the topics, issues, and key terms that define your task (define, discuss, explain). Underline key terms to focus your attention.

"Knowing how to evaluate provided me with confidence in my free-response answers."
—DK, AP student

- Brainstorm ideas.
- Organize ideas and outline your essay before you begin to write. Use the blank space in your test booklet to plan. (Brainstorming and outlining should take about 5–8 minutes per question.)
- Write the essay. Include an introduction that restates the question, the factual information, evidence and examples, and a conclusion. Stick to your outline and keep sentences simple. If time is short, forget the introduction and conclusion and jump into the essay, using bulleted lists with explanations or an outline.
- Reread the question and your essay to determine if you answered the question or questions. NOTE: Many of the free-response questions will have several parts; make sure you answer them all.
- Proofread for grammar, spelling, and punctuation errors. Even though these errors will not count against you, they can make your essay harder to read and your answer less understandable.

"The free-response essays often involve the student choosing between options— look at all options before you begin writing."
—LA, AP teacher

RUBRICS FOR THE FREE-RESPONSE ESSAY

What Is a Rubric?

Rubrics are scoring guidelines used to evaluate your performance on each of the free-response essays. They are based on the sum of points earned by meeting the pre-established criteria.

How Are Rubrics Developed and Applied?

The number of points students may earn for each free-response question is assigned by members of the Test Development Committee. The chief faculty consultant, exam leaders, and question leaders develop preliminary rubrics for each question based on these points. These rubrics are sampled against actual student essays and revised if necessary. Table leaders are then trained using these standards. When the reading begins, table leaders train the AP readers at their table (usually 5–7 readers) in the use of the rubric for that particular question. Once the reading begins, the rubrics are not changed.

Common Characteristics of Rubrics

Since each free-response question is different, each scoring rubric will differ. There are, however, several characteristics common to all U.S. Government and Politics rubrics. Each rubric

- addresses all aspects and tasks of the question. Points are awarded for each task or response requested—one point for a correct identification and two points for the discussion.

- contains evaluative criteria. These distinguish what is acceptable from what is not acceptable in the answer, for example, accept AARP as an interest group but do not accept the Democratic Party.
- has a scoring strategy, a scale of points to be awarded for successfully completing a task. For example, identification of an interest group is worth one point.
- awards points for correct responses; points are not deducted.
- can be applied clearly and consistently by different scorers. If more than one reader were to score a particular essay, it would receive the same score, based on the same standards.

FINAL COMMENTS—SOME HELPFUL HINTS

When writing your free response, consider these do's and don'ts.

"Be sure your free-response essay is brief and gets directly to the point."
—JB, AP student

*"Remember, on free-response questions, AP means answer **all parts** of the question."*
—MN, AP teacher

- **Don't** use words that you are uncomfortable using or not familiar with. Readers are not impressed if you use "big words" but don't understand what they mean or use them incorrectly.
- **Don't** try to "fake out" the reader. They are government professors and teachers.
- **Don't** preach, moralize, editorialize, or use "cute" comments. Remember, you want the reader to think positively about your essay.
- **Don't** "data dump" or create "laundry lists." Do not provide information (names, court cases, laws) without explanation or relevant link.
- **Do** write neatly and legibly. Write or print in blue or black ink (not pencil; it's harder to read) as clearly as you can.
- **Do** use correct grammar, spelling, and punctuation. They make your essay much easier to score.
- **Do** answer all questions and all parts of each question. You may answer the questions in any order. Answer the questions you feel you know best, first. That way, if you run out of time and don't finish, no harm is done. Even though the essays are graded on different scales, they are weighted equally and together count for half your total score. (Each essay is 12.5% of your total score.)
- **Do** support your essay with specific evidence and examples. If the question asks for examples, supply not only the example but also a discussion of how that example illustrates the concept. Provide however many examples the question asks for; hypothetical examples may sometimes be used, if they are backed up with facts.
- **Do** pay attention to dates and terms like "modern." When time frames are used, keep your evidence and examples within that time frame (modern presidency would not include Jefferson, Jackson, Lincoln).
- **Do** stop when you finish your essay. Proofread! If you ramble on after you have answered the question completely, you might contradict yourself, causing the reader to question your answer.
- **Do** your best!

THE FREE-RESPONSE SECTION OF THE DIAGNOSTIC/MASTER EXAM

 The free-response section of the Diagnostic/Master exam follows. You have seen the essays in the "walk-through" in Chapter 2.

U.S. GOVERNMENT AND POLITICS

 ## Section II
Time—100 minutes

1. Legislative strategies are often used to kill or delay the passage of a bill through Congress.

   a. Identify three legislative strategies that can kill or delay the passage of a bill through Congress.

   b. Explain how each of the strategies identified above can kill or delay the passage of a bill through Congress.

Participation in Elections for President and Representatives

Percent of Voting-Age Population: 1972 to 1998

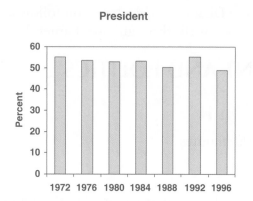

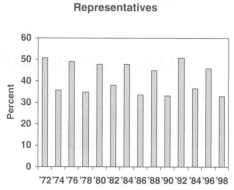

2. The graphs above show participation in elections of the voting-age population for president and members of the House of Representatives. From this information and your knowledge of United States politics, perform the following tasks.

   a. Identify and discuss two patterns displayed in the graphs.

   b. Identify two factors that contribute to voter participation in elections. Explain how each effects voter participation.

3. Civil rights may be expanded through the passage of new legislation or constitutional amendment.

   a. Identify and discuss two examples of how the expansion of civil rights has been accomplished through the passage of legislation

   b. Identify and discuss two examples of how the expansion of civil rights has been accomplished through constitutional amendment.

c. Identify and discuss one example of a how a restriction has been placed on civil rights through legislation.

d. Discuss how the failure to adopt the Equal Rights Amendment (ERA) affected the civil rights of women.

4. The Constitution creates a Supreme Court for the United States. By hearing disputes, the Supreme Court influences public policy. Several factors may influence the justices in the judicial decision-making process.

a. Identify and discuss two influences on the judicial decision-making process in the Supreme Court.

b. Give an example of how the influences you identified have influenced the judicial decision-making process.

RUBRICS FOR FREE-RESPONSE ESSAYS

1. Total Value: 6 points

   Part a: 1 point for each correctly identified legislative strategy = 3 points
   Part b: 1 point for each correct explanation of a legislative strategy = 3 points

2. Total Value: 7 points

   Part a: 1 point for two correctly identified patterns = 1 point
       1 point for each correct discussion of a pattern = 2 points
   Part b: 1 point for each correctly identified factor = 2 points
       1 point for each correct explanation of a factor = 2 points

3. Total Value: 9 points

   Part a: 1 point for two correctly identified examples through legislation = 1 point
       1 point for each correct discussion of an example through legislation = 2 points
   Part b: 1 point for two correctly identified examples through amendment = 1 point
       1 point for each correct discussion for an example through amendment = 2 points

Part c: 1 point for correct identification of example of restriction = 1 point
    1 point for correct discussion of restriction due to legislation = 1 point
Part d: 1 point for correct discussion of ERA = 1 point

4. Total Value: 6 points

Part a: 1 point for each correctly identified influence = 2 points
    1 point for each correct discussion of influence = 2 points
Part b: 1 point for each correct example = 2 points

COMPREHENSIVE REVIEW: DEVELOPING THE KNOWLEDGE, SKILLS, AND STRATEGIES

Chapter 5

Review: Architecture and Development of U.S. Government

 **2 PRINCIPLES OF GOVERNMENT**

What Is Government?

Political scientist Harold Laswell defined government as "who gets what, when, and how." In any nation a **government** is composed of the formal and informal institutions, people, and processes used to create and conduct public policy. **Public policy** is the exercise of government power in doing those things necessary to maintain legitimate authority and control over society.

Purposes of Government

Every nation must decide for itself what goals will be translated into public policy and the methods by which those goals will be translated. The Preamble of the United States Constitution addresses the goals of public policy for the United States:

- forming a more perfect union: creation of a strong union of the states, while also maintaining state sovereignty
- establishing justice: reasonable, fair and impartial law
- insuring domestic tranquility: preservation of public order
- providing for the common defense: protection and maintenance of national defense
- promoting the general welfare: providing public services and economic health of the nation
- securing the blessings of liberty: promoting individual freedoms

Forms of Government

Greek philosopher Aristotle attempted to classify governments based on the number of individuals who participated in making political decisions: rule by one, rule by the few, or rule by the many. His early classification system is still useful in describing governments today:

- anarchy: lack of government
- autocracy: rule by one
  — absolute monarchy: ruler gains power through inheritance; there are no restrictions on the ruler's power
  — constitutional monarchy: ruler gains power through inheritance; formal restrictions limit power, often restricting the monarch to ceremonial status
  — dictatorship: ruler gains power through seizure, keeps power by force and restricts opposition to regime; no restrictions on dictator's power
- oligarchy: rule by a few
  — aristocracy: rule by the elite, usually determined by social status or wealth
  — theocracy: rule by religious leaders
- **democracy:** rule by the people
  — **direct democracy:** citizens meet and make decisions about public policy issues
  — **representative democracy:** citizens choose officials (representatives) who make decisions about public policy

Theories of Democratic Government

Theories of democratic government are theories about who has power and influence over public policy and decision-making at the local, state, and national levels of government.

- **traditional democratic theory:** Government depends on the consent of the governed, which may be given directly or through representatives; may include criteria for the measure of "how democratic."
- **pluralist theory:** Interest groups compete in the political arena, with each promoting its policy preferences through organized efforts. Conflict among groups may result, requiring bargaining and compromise (Robert Dahl).
- **elitist theory:** A small number of powerful elite (corporate leaders, top military officers, government leaders) form an upper class, which rules in its own self-interest (C. Wright Mills).
- **bureaucratic theory:** The hierarchical structure and standardized procedures of modern governments allow bureaucrats, who carry out the day-to-day workings of government, to hold the real power over public policy (Max Weber).

- **hyperpluralism:** Democracy is a system of many groups having so much strength that government is often "pulled" in numerous directions at the same time, causing gridlock and ineffectiveness.

ORIGINS OF AMERICAN GOVERNMENT

Influences on American Government

In 1607 the British established a permanent colony at Jamestown, Virginia. Early colonists brought ideas and traditions that would form the basis of American government as a part of the British colonial empire, and as an independent United States. Two of the early traditions were limited government and representative government.

- *Ancient Greeks and Romans:* Democratic government began with the ancient Greeks and Romans. Their concepts and ideas of direct and representative democracy greatly influenced the American founding fathers.
- *Enlightenment philosophers:* During the Enlightenment Era, philosophers such as John Locke supported the concept of a social contract. Locke viewed the **social contract** as a voluntary agreement between the government and the governed. In *Two Treatises on Civil Government* (1689), Locke argued that people are born with natural rights to life, liberty and property (natural law). Locke also believed that governments are created to support those rights, but that if the government fails to do so, the people may choose to change their government. Thomas Jefferson adopted these ideas in the **Declaration of Independence.**
- *Magna Carta (1215):* The first attempt to limit the power of the British monarch was the Magna Carta, forced upon the monarch by British nobility. The "Great Charter" guaranteed the nobility certain rights such as trial by jury, due process of law, and protections against the arbitrary taking of life, liberty, or property.
- Parliament: Parliament began as an advisory group to the monarch, but as the power of the monarch became more and more limited, Parliament grew to become the lawmaking body of Britain.
- *Petition of Right (1628):* The Petition of Right extended the protections of the Magna Carta to include commoners. The monarch's powers were further limited by restricting the monarch from taxing without the consent of Parliament, declaring martial law or military rule during peacetime, or housing military in private homes without the owner's consent. Guarantees of trial by jury, even for critics of the monarch, were recognized. The Petition of Right was a challenge to the accepted belief in divine-right of the king.
- *English Bill of Rights (1689):* The English Bill of Rights was an agreement between Parliament and King William and Queen Mary, to prevent future monarchs from abusing their powers. The Bill of Rights guaranteed free parliamentary elections; the rights of citizens to a fair

and speedy trial; freedom from excessive bails and cruel and unusual punishment; the right to petition the king; and protections against standing armies during peacetime. Suspension of public laws was prohibited, and taxation without the consent of Parliament was made illegal.

Colonial Experiences

From 1607 to 1776, the American colonies were in a continuous state of political self-development. This was due to several factors, such as the long distance from England, indifference of the colonists to the king's authority, and the disputed political authority in England. As the colonies developed, they made the most of their English heritage but made changes to create a new and unique style of government. This new government was founded on the principles of equality, liberty, and limited government.

- *Colonial charters:* Each colony was founded on the basis of a charter from the king. The charter authorized the colony's existence and established its political authority. Royal, proprietary and charter colonies were founded, each operating with executive, legislative, and judicial roles. The authority of governors, legislatures, and judges depended on the type of colony and its charter.
- *House of Burgesses:* In 1619 Virginia established the first representative legislature in the American colonies. Only adult male property owners could vote for its members.
- *Mayflower Compact:* In 1620 colonists aboard the Mayflower signed an agreement, a social contract, called the Mayflower Compact. This agreement established a government for the colony based on the ideas of consent of the governed and limitations on the authority of government.
- *Difficulties with Britain:* As the colonies grew, so did problems with Britain. Prior to 1750, the British provided defense and manufactured goods for the colonies. The colonies in return provided raw materials and markets for manufactured goods. Britain allowed the colonies to control their own internal affairs. After the French and Indian War (1756–1763), however, the British government expected the colonies to help pay the cost of the war and pay for their own future defense. The British government began enforcing taxes already levied and passed new taxes to replenish the king's treasury. These new taxes included the Sugar Act (1764), the Stamp Act (1765), and the Townshend Acts (1767). As the colonists began protesting, violence and conflict began to break out between the colonies and Britain. After the Boston Massacre (1770) and Boston Tea Party (1772), the British government passed a series of punishing acts collectively known as the Coercive or Intolerable Acts. In response the colonies began to unite in an effort to influence the British government.
- *Continental Congresses:* The First Continental Congress included delegates from 12 colonies (all except Georgia) who met in Philadelphia in 1774. This Continental Congress resolved to send a Declaration of

Rights to the king in protest of Britain's policies. They also agreed to meet again the following year. The Second Continental Congress began meeting in May 1775, more than one month after the battles of Lexington and Concord. The Second Continental Congress became America's first national government. Delegates from all 13 colonies were present, among them John Hancock, George Washington, Ben Franklin, Thomas Jefferson, John Adams, and Patrick Henry. The Second Continental Congress created the Continental Army and appointed George Washington as its Commander-in-Chief; borrowed money from France and the Netherlands; created a monetary system; made treaties with foreign governments; and commissioned the writing of the Declaration of Independence and the Articles of Confederation.

Declaration of Independence

The **Declaration of Independence** is mainly the work of Thomas Jefferson. The principles are based on the works of Enlightenment philosopher John Locke. The Declaration of Independence can be divided into three parts: a theory of government based on social contract and natural rights, a list of grievances against the king and "others" (Parliament), and a statement of colonial unity and separation from Britain.

Articles of Confederation

The **Articles of Confederation** (1781–1789), written by the Second Continental Congress in November of 1777, became the first national constitution for governing the American states. The Articles created a confederation or "league of friendship" among the states. The Confederation would be composed of a relatively weak national government with a unicameral legislature. Congress would have limited powers such as borrowing money, creating a national army and navy, declaring war, creating post offices, and signing treaties with foreign governments. Congress was not given the power to tax, draft soldiers for military service, or regulate commerce. There was no national executive or judicial branch under the Articles of Confederation. Each state was equal, with one vote, regardless of population or size. The votes of nine of the 13 states were required for legislation to pass the Confederation Congress; amending the Articles of Confederation required a unanimous vote.

The weaknesses evident in the Articles of Confederation allowed the states to focus on their own powers. With no central government to control them, the states taxed each other, printed their own money, made treaties with foreign governments, and often refused to uphold the laws of the Confederation government. Even with all these problems, the Confederation Congress was able to approve the signing of the Treaty of Paris, which ended the American Revolution in 1783, and pass the Land Ordinance of 1785 and Northwest Ordinance of 1787. The government under the Articles of Confederation, however, could not deal with the nation's problems. Economic chaos and violence broke out, resulting in conferences at Mt. Vernon and Annapolis. These meetings proved to be unsuccessful, and eventually a rebellion of farmers in Massachusetts (Shays Rebellion) led to the calling of a Constitutional Convention.

Constitutional Convention

The Constitutional Convention was convened in Philadelphia in May of 1787, for the purpose of revising the Articles of Confederation. Delegates representing all the states except Rhode Island attended.

- Very early in the convention, the delegates decided that they would write a new constitution instead of revising the Articles of Confederation.
- The delegates agreed that the new government would be a republic, a **federal system,** and would be composed of three branches (executive, legislative, judicial).
- Several plans were presented to the delegates. (See Figure 5–1.)

Compromises

- Debate over the various plans presented at the Constitutional Convention resulted in the **Connecticut (Great) Compromise.** This compromise settled the disputes between the states over the structure of the legislative branch. Congress would be a bicameral legislature, with representation in the lower house based on the population of the state and equal representation of the states in the upper house.
- A second compromise concerned the counting of slaves for the purpose of determining population for representation in Congress and for tax-

Virginia Plan	New Jersey Plan

Bicameral legislature
  -lower house elected by the people
  -upper house chosen by lower house
    from nominees submitted by state
    legislatures
	Unicameral legislature
	  -representatives chosen by state
	   legislatures
	  -each state receives one vote

Representation in each house based on population and/or monetary contributions to the national government by the state	Representation in house would be equal among the states
Single executive chosen by legislative branch, limited to one term only, could veto legislative acts, removal by Congress	Plural executive chosen by legislative branch, no veto powers, removal by the states
Judges chosen by legislative branch	Judges appointed for life by the executive

Figure 5–1 Comparison of the Virginia and New Jersey Plans.

ation. Southern states wanted slaves to be counted for representation but not taxation. Northern states wanted slaves counted for taxation but not for representation. The **Three-Fifths Compromise** resolved this issue: each state would count three-fifths of its slave population for purposes of determining both representation and taxation.

- The **Commerce and Slave Trade Compromise** resolved other differences between southern and northern states. Congress was prohibited from taxing exports from the states and from banning the slave trade for a period of 20 years.
- Numerous other compromises were made at the Constitutional Convention concerning the executive and judicial branches as well as the electoral process for choosing a chief executive.

"Quiz yourself on the material."
—JS, AP student

Weaknesses of the Articles of Confederation	How the Constitution Remedied Weaknesses
Articles created a "league of friendship" between the states.	Constitution created a federal system of government between the national and state levels.
Congress could not tax; it could only request contributions from the states.	National government was given the power to tax.
Congress could not regulate interstate trade or foreign commerce.	Congress was given the power to regulate commerce between the states and with foreign nations.
No separate executive to enforce the acts of Congress	Article II created a separate executive department whose job is to enforce the laws of Congress.
No national judiciary to handle state disputes	Article III created a national judiciary with a Supreme Court and lower courts as established by Congress.
States and the national government had the authority to coin money.	Only the national government has the authority to coin money.
Each state had one vote, regardless of size or population.	States are represented based on population in the House of Representatives and equality in the Senate.
Nine of 13 states required to pass legislation.	Bills need a simple majority in both houses of Congress.
Unanimous consent required to amend the Articles of Confederation.	Two-thirds of Congress and three-fourths of the states are necessary to amend the Constitution.

Figure 5–2 Weaknesses of Articles of Confederation and Constitutional Remedies.

Ratification of the Constitution

Although the delegates at the convention signed the Constitution on September 17, 1787, it still had to be ratified by nine of the 13 states before it could go into effect. In each state, special ratifying conventions would be held over the next two years. Debate over **ratification** divided citizens into Federalist and Anti-Federalist positions.

- The **Federalists** stressed the weaknesses of the Articles of Confederation and the government it created. They supported a stronger central government with expanded legislative powers. The Federalist cause was helped by James Madison, Alexander Hamilton, and John Jay in a collection of 85 essays published in the New York newspapers under the name "Publius." (Hamilton wrote 51, Madison wrote 26, Jay wrote five, and Hamilton and Madison co-authored three of these essays.) These *Federalist Papers* defended the new government created under the Constitution and even today provide insight into the framers' original intent.
- The **Anti-Federalists** believed that the new Constitution gave too much power to the national government at the expense of the state governments. Another objection was the lack of a **Bill of Rights,** ensuring fundamental liberties.

THE UNITED STATES CONSTITUTION

A **constitution** is a plan of government. The Constitution of the United States is the oldest national constitution in use today. Although the

Federalists	Anti-Federalists
Favored Constitution	Opposed Constitution
Led by Madison, Hamilton, Jay	Led by Henry, Richard Henry Lee, George Mason, Samuel Adams
Stressed weaknesses of Articles; strong government needed to protect nation and solve domestic problems	Wanted strong state governments; feared a strong national government
Checks and balances would protect against abuses.	Created a strong executive similar to monarchy
Protection of property rights	Wanted fewer limits on popular participation
Constitution is a bill of rights with limitations and reserved powers for the states; state constitutions already had protections in bills of rights.	Wanted a bill of rights to protect citizens against government

Figure 5–3 Federalists versus Anti-Federalists.

Constitution is relatively short, it describes the structure and powers of the national government as well as the relationship between the national and state governments.

Basic Principles Within the Constitution

Embodied within the Constitution are the basic principles of:

- *limited government*—belief that government is not all-powerful; government has only those powers given to it
- *popular sovereignty*—the people are the source of government's authority
- *separation of powers*—power is separated among three branches of government; each has its own powers and duties and is independent of and equal to the other branches
- *checks and balances*—each branch is subject to restraints by the other two branches (see Figure 5–4)
- *federalism*—a division of governmental powers between the national government and the states

Checks and Balances

The **Constitution** may be divided into three major parts: the Preamble, articles, and **amendments.**

Preamble

The opening paragraph of the Constitution is called the Preamble. It lists the six goals for American government and explains why the Constitution was written.

Articles

The Constitution is divided into seven articles. Each of the articles covers a specific topic. Article I is the longest, devoted to the legislative branch of government.

- Article I—Legislative Branch
- Article II—Executive Branch
- Article III—Judicial Branch
- Article IV—Intergovernmental Relationships
- Article V—Amendment Process
- Article VI—Supremacy of the Constitution
- Article VII—Ratification Process

Legislative Branch (Passes Laws)

Over Executive:
> May override president's veto by two-thirds vote of both houses
> May impeach and remove president from office
> Senate may refuse to confirm presidential appointments or ratify treaties
> Creates executive agencies and programs
> Appropriates funds

Over Judiciary:
> Creates lower federal courts
> Sets salaries of federal judges
> May refuse to confirm judicial appointments
> May propose constitutional amendments which overrule court decisions
> May impeach and remove federal judges

Executive Branch (Enforces Laws)

Over Legislature:
> President may veto acts of Congress
> President may call special sessions of Congress
> President may recommend legislation

Over Judiciary:
> President appoints federal judges
> President may grant reprieves and pardons to federal offenders
> May refuse to enforce court decisions

Judicial Branch (Interprets Laws)

Over Legislature:
> May rule legislative acts unconstitutional
> Chief justice presides over impeachment of president

Over Executive:
> May rule executive actions unconstitutional

Figure 5–4 Separation of Powers and Checks and Balances.

Formal Amendment Process

One major weakness of the Articles of Confederation was the amendment process, which required unanimous approval for amendments to become effective. The framers of the Constitution anticipated the need to change the Constitution and provided a process to amend the Constitution (Article V) that required both state and national action. Amending the Constitution requires proposal, a national function, and ratification, a state function. Amendments may be proposed in Congress by two methods and ratified by two methods, creating four possible methods for formally amending the Constitution.

- proposed by ⅔ vote of each house of Congress and ratified by ¾ of the state legislatures (used 26 times)
- proposed by ⅔ vote of each house of Congress and ratified by special conventions in at least ¾ of the states (used once, to ratify the Twenty-first Amendment)
- proposed by a national convention called by Congress at the request of ⅔ of the state legislatures and ratified by ¾ of the state legislatures (never used)
- proposed by a national convention called by Congress at the request of ⅔ of the state legislatures and ratified by special conventions in at least ¾ of the states (never used)

Formal Amendments

Formal amendments are written changes to the Constitution. They add to, change the wording of, or delete language from the Constitution. Only 27 formal amendments have been added to the Constitution since its adoption. The first ten amendments, the **Bill of Rights,** were added in 1791.

Informal Amendment Process

Although the United States Constitution has been formally changed only 27 times, there have been many changes in the way in which the American government operates. Most of those changes have come about through the informal amendment process and do not involve actually changing the wording of the Constitution. Informal changes in the Constitution may occur in the following ways:

- *legislative actions:* Congress has passed various acts that have altered or made clear the meaning of the Constitution. For example, under Article III Congress is given the authority to create lower courts, which they did through the Judiciary Act of 1789.
- *executive actions:* The manner in which presidents use their powers can create informal amendments and expand presidential authority. The use of executive agreements rather than treaties allows the president to bypass the Senate.
- *judicial interpretation/judicial review:* The people who serve as judges and the times in which they serve affect how courts interpret laws. The concept of judicial review resulted from *Marbury v. Madison* (1803); it is not mentioned in the Constitution.
- *custom and usage:* Traditions which have been incorporated into the political system and which have lasted over time have changed the meaning of the Constitution. Senatorial courtesy in the Senate and the

Constitutional Amendments

- Amendment 1—guarantees freedom of religion, speech, press, assembly and petition
- Amendment 2—ensures the right to keep and bear arms
- Amendment 3—sets conditions for quartering of troops in private homes
- Amendment 4—regulates search, seizure, and warrants
- Amendment 5—addresses protections against self-incrimination, guarantees of due process, eminent domain, and grand jury indictment for capital crimes
- Amendment 6—guarantees rights to a speedy, public trial, and an impartial jury, to confront witnesses, and to have an attorney
- Amendment 7—preserves right to a jury trial in civil cases
- Amendment 8—ensures no excessive bails or fines, nor cruel and unusual punishment
- Amendment 9—unenumerates rights of the people
- Amendment 10—reserves powers of the states and the people
- Amendment 11—restricts lawsuits against states
- Amendment 12—provides for election of president and vice-president by separate ballot in electoral college
- Amendment 13—abolishes slavery
- Amendment 14—guarantees rights of citizenship, due process, and equal protection
- Amendment 15—guarantees citizens' right to vote regardless of race, color, or previous condition of servitude
- Amendment 16—authorizes income tax
- Amendment 17—establishes direct election of senators by popular vote
- Amendment 18—prohibit intoxicating liquors
- Amendment 19—establishes women's suffrage
- Amendment 20—sets terms and sessions of executive and legislative branches; "lame duck"
- Amendment 21—repeals prohibition (18th amendment)
- Amendment 22—limits presidential terms of office
- Amendment 23—allows for voting rights in District of Columbia in presidential elections
- Amendment 24—abolishes poll taxes
- Amendment 25—addresses presidential succession, disability, and vice-presidential vacancies
- Amendment 26—gives 18-year-olds the right to vote
- Amendment 27—addresses congressional pay

Figure 5–5 Constitutional Amendments.

"no-third-term" tradition in the Presidency (until the 22nd amendment made it part of the Constitution) are examples.

Marbury v. Madison (1803)

In the election of 1800 political parties played an active role. Federalists supported John Adams, and Jeffersonian Republicans supported Thomas Jefferson. At the conclusion of the election, Adams and the Federalists had lost control of the presidency and Congress. In an effort to retain some control in the government, the "lame duck" Federalist Congress created numerous new judicial positions, which outgoing President Adams attempted to fill. Late into the night prior to Jefferson's inauguration, Adams was still signing the commissions of the "midnight appointments" which the Secretary of State was to deliver. Not all the commissions were delivered, and when Jefferson took office, he ordered the commissions withheld, intending to make his own appointments. Marbury expected to receive a commission as a justice of the peace for the District of Columbia. He petitioned the Supreme Court to issue a writ of mandamus (allowed under the Judiciary Act of 1791) ordering Secretary of State James Madison to deliver the commission to Marbury and several others. The Supreme Court under Chief Justice John Marshall ruled that although Marbury was entitled to the commission, the Supreme Court would not order Madison to give it to him because the court did not have authority under the Constitution to decided this type of case, and that the portion of the Judiciary Act of 1791 which allowed the Court to hear these cases was unconstitutional. This case established the principle of **judicial review** and was the first time the court declared an act of Congress unconstitutional.

✓ REVIEW QUESTIONS

1. All of the following are examples of checks and balances EXCEPT

   A. presidential veto
   B. impeachment of the president
   C. appointment of Supreme Court justices
   D. ratification of treaties
   E. declaration of war by Congress

2. Which of the following documents best describes a government based upon unity, natural rights, and the social contract theory?

   A. Articles of Confederation
   B. Declaration of Independence
   C. Mayflower Compact
   D. U.S. Constitution
   E. Petition of Rights

3. The original purpose of the Constitutional Convention was to

   A. write a new constitution
   B. review the problems of the state governments
   C. revise the Articles of Confederation
   D. develop a new plan for the current national government

   E. deal with the unsuccessful economic chaos and violence that resulted from the conferences at Mt. Vernon and Annapolis

4. Compared to government under the Articles of Confederation, the Constitution

   I. can more easily be amended
   II. created a federal republic
   III. called for separation of powers among three branches of government
   IV. created a league of friendship among the states

      A. I only
      B. I and III only
      C. II and IV only
      D. I, II, and III only
      E. I, II, III, and IV

5. Which of the following was not a weakness of government under the Articles of Confederation?

   A. The national judiciary resolved arguments between the states.
   B. Congress lacked the power to tax.
   C. lack of a national judiciary

D. inability to control commercial interests
E. unanimous decisions necessary to amend articles

6. Slavery and taxation were important topics to the founding fathers. Which compromise best describes how the founding fathers resolved both of these issues?

   A. Constitutional Compromise
   B. Commerce and Slave Trade Compromise
   C. Connecticut Compromise
   D. Three-Fifths Compromise
   E. Representation and Taxation Compromise

7. Those who support the pluralist theory of democracy believe that

   A. government depends on the "consent of the governed"
   B. democracy is a hierarchical structure with bureaucrats holding the real power
   C. democracy is based on choosing officials to run the government
   D. a small number of powerful corporate and military leaders rule in their own self interest
   E. interest groups compete to promote their preferences

8. The Supreme Court's decision in *Marbury v. Madison* (1803)

   A. expanded the powers of Congress
   B. established the principle of judicial review
   C. allowed Congress to amend the Constitution
   D. strengthened the powers of the states
   E. supported the concept of national supremacy

9. The Bill of Rights includes

   A. the preamble
   B. the Articles of Confederation
   C. the articles of the Constitution
   D. all the formal amendments
   E. the first ten amendments

10. Amending the Constitution is a multi-step process. Which of the following steps are required to amend the Constitution?

    I.   proposal at the national level
    II. proposal at the state level
    III. presidential signature
    IV. ratification at the state level

    A. II and III only
    B. I and IV only
    C. III and IV only
    D. I, II, and III only
    E. I, II, III, and IV

ANSWERS AND EXPLANATIONS

1. **E.** A declaration of war by Congress is an expressed power of Congress under Article I of the Constitution.

2. **B.** The Declaration of Independence was based on the writings of John Locke. The document unified the colonies to fight for independence by advancing the ideas of natural law, that certain rights cannot be taken away by government, and the social contract between government and the governed.

3. **C.** Because of the problems among the states under the Articles of Confederation, the Constitutional Convention was convened to revise the Articles and strengthen the powers of government.

4. **D.** The Constitution created a federal system of government, allowed for easier amending, and created three separate branches of government—legislative, executive, and judicial.

5. **A.** Under the Articles of Confederation, there was no national judiciary. State courts resolved differences between the states.

6. **B.** Differences between northern and southern interests at the Constitutional Convention led to a compromise concerning the slave trade and the taxation of exports from the states. The Commerce and Slave Trade Compromise prohibited Congress from ending the slave trade for a period of 20 years and prohibited the taxation of exports from the states.

7. **E.** Robert Dahl's pluralist theory is based upon the idea of competing interest groups vying for power.

8. **B.** *Marbury v. Madison* established the principle of judicial review, allowing the courts to determine the constitutionality of acts of Congress.

9. **E.** The Bill of Rights, adopted in 1791, includes the first ten amendments to the Constitution. They were added to ensure the basic rights of all citizens.

10. **B.** Article V of the Constitution outlines the formal amendment process, which includes Congress proposing amendments at the national level and the states ratifying amendments.

RAPID REVIEW

- Political scientist Harold Laswell defined government as "who gets what, when, and how."

- Every nation has defined public policy goals. The United States defines its goals in the Preamble of the Constitution.

- Aristotle's methods of classifying governments are still used today.

- Modern theories about democratic government include traditional democratic theory, pluralist theory, elitist theory, bureaucratic theory, and hyperpluralism.

- The ancient Greeks and Romans, Enlightenment philosophers such as John Locke, British documents, and colonial experiences have influenced American government.

- The Declaration of Independence was a statement of colonial unity and a justification for separation from Britain.

- The Articles of Confederation, the first national constitution, created a "league of friendship" among the states. This weak national government failed to solve the postwar problems of the United States, and its weaknesses led to the writing of the U.S. Constitution.

- The Constitutional Convention, called to revise the Articles of Confederation, realized the need to create a new form of government with broader powers. The resulting Constitution created a federal system of three branches of government, with checks and balances.

- Various plans for the new government resulted in a series of compromises, including the Great (Connecticut) Compromise, Three-Fifths Compromise, and Commerce and Slave Trade Compromise.

- Debates over ratification of the Constitution led to the creation of the Federalists and Anti-Federalists.

- The Constitution is composed of the Preamble, seven articles, and the 27 formal amendments.

- The Constitution is a plan of government based on several basic principles: limited government, popular sovereignty, separation of powers, checks and balances, and federalism.

- Formal amendments are added to the Constitution through the process outlined in Article V. The proposal stage is accomplished at the national level, while ratification takes place within the states.

- The Constitution may be informally amended through legislative actions, executive actions, judicial interpretations, and custom and usage.

- *Marbury v. Madison* established the principle of judicial review.

Chapter 6

Review: Federalism

FEDERALISM

What Is Federalism?

 One of the basic principles embodied in the United States Constitution is federalism. Federalism arose from the framers' desire to create a stronger national government than under the Articles of Confederation but preserve the existing states and state governments. **Federalism** is a political system where the powers of government are divided between a national government and regional (state and local) governments. Each level of government has certain authorities over the same territory and people. A constitution outlines each level of government's authority, powers, and prohibitions.

Constitutional Basis of Federalism

 Although the term federalism is not found in the United States Constitution, it is clearly defined in the delegated, concurrent, and reserved powers of the national and state governments. (See Figure 6–2.)

- **delegated powers:** expressed, or enumerated powers, those specifically given to the national government (Articles I–V)
- **implied powers:** although not expressed, powers that may be reasonably inferred from the Constitution (Article I, Section 8, Clause 18—the **Necessary and Proper** or **Elastic Clause**)
- **inherent powers:** powers that exist for the national government because the government is sovereign

Advantages of Federalism	Disadvantages of Federalism
Ideally suited to large geographic area because it encourages diversity in local government	Inflexibility inherent in a written constitution
Avoids concentration of political power	Complex, with many governments to deal with
Accommodated already existing state governments	Duplication of offices and functions
States serve as training grounds for national leaders.	Conflicts of authority may arise.
Keeps government close to the people	

Figure 6–1 Advantages and Disadvantages of Federalism.

- **concurrent powers:** powers that belong to both the national and state governments
- **reserved powers:** powers belonging specifically to the state because they were neither delegated to the national government nor denied to the states (Article IV; Amendment 10)
- **prohibited powers:** powers that are denied to the national government, state governments, or both (Article I, Sections 9 & 10; Amendments)

National Powers (Expressed, Implied, Inherent)	National and State Powers (Concurrent)	State Powers (Reserved)
Regulate foreign and interstate commerce	Levy taxes	Regulate intrastate commerce
Coin and print money	Borrow money	Establish local governments
Provide an army and navy	Spend for general welfare	Establish public school systems
Declare war	Establish courts	Administer elections
Establish federal courts below the Supreme Court	Enact and enforce laws	Protect the public's health, welfare and morals
Conduct foreign relations	Charter banks	Regulate corporations
Make all laws "necessary and proper"		Establish licensing requirements for certain regulated professions
Acquire and govern U.S. territories and admit new states		
Regulate immigration and naturalization		

Figure 6–2 Powers of Government Under Federalism.

FEDERALISM IN PRACTICE

Interstate Relations

Article IV of the Constitution addresses the issue of relationships between the states. It offers several provisions:

- **full faith and credit clause:** States are required to recognize the laws and legal documents of other states, such as birth certificates, marriage licenses, drivers' licenses, wills.
- **privileges and immunities clause:** States are prohibited from unreasonably discriminating against residents of other states. Nonresidents may travel through other states; buy, sell, and hold property; and enter into contracts (does not extend to political rights such as the right to vote or run for political office, or to the right to practice certain regulated professions such as teaching).
- **extradition:** States may return fugitives to a state from which they have fled to avoid criminal prosecution at the request of the governor of the state.
- **interstate compacts:** States may make agreements, sometimes requiring Congressional approval, to work together to solve regional problems. Some examples are "hot-pursuit agreements," parole and probation agreements, the Port of New York Authority, and regulating the common use of shared natural resources.

Guarantees to the States

Article IV of the Constitution provides national guarantees to the states:

- republican form of government
- protections against foreign invasion
- protections against domestic violence
- respect for the geographic integrity of states

ESTABLISHING NATIONAL SUPREMACY

Article VI of the United States Constitution contains the **Supremacy Clause,** which helps to resolve conflicts between national and state law. Because two levels of government are operating within the same territory and over the same people, conflicts are bound to arise. The Supremacy Clause states that the Constitution, its laws and treaties shall be the "supreme law of the land." The Supreme Court upheld this supremacy in *McCulloch v. Maryland* (1819). The Supreme Court continued to expand the powers of Congress over interstate commerce in *Gibbons v. Ogden* (1824).

McCulloch v. Maryland (1819)

The Supreme Court dealt with the issues of the necessary and proper clause and the supremacy clause when Maryland imposed a tax on the Baltimore branch of the Second National Bank of the United States. Chief cashier James McCulloch refused to pay the tax, Maryland state courts ruled in the state's favor, and the United States government appealed to the Supreme Court. The Marshall court ruled that although no provision of the Constitution grants the national government the expressed power to create a national bank, the authority to do so can be implied by the necessary and proper clause (Article I, Section 8, Clause 18). This ruling established the implied powers of the national government and national supremacy, the basis used to strengthen the power of the national government.

Gibbons v. Ogden (1824)

At issue was the definition of commerce and whether the national government had exclusive power to regulate interstate commerce. The New York legislature gave Robert Livingston and Robert Fulton exclusive rights to operate steamboats in New York waters and Aaron Ogden the right to operate a ferry between New York and New Jersey. Thomas Gibbons had received a national government license to operate boats in interstate waters. Ogden sued Gibbons and won in the New York courts; Gibbons appealed to the Supreme Court. The Marshall court defined commerce as including all business dealings, and the power to regulate interstate commerce belongs exclusively to the national government. Today, the national government uses the commerce clause to justify the regulation of numerous areas of economic activity.

FEDERALISM TODAY

 Since the founding of the United States, society has changed, and federalism has evolved to meet the changes and challenges.

Dual Federalism

The earliest (1789–1932) interpretation of federalism is the concept of **dual federalism,** which views the national and state governments each remaining supreme within their own sphere of influence. This form of federalism is often referred to as "layer cake federalism," because each level of government is seen as separate from the other, with the national government having authority over national matters and state governments having authority over state matters. The early beliefs that states had the sole responsibility for educating their citizens and the national government had the sole responsibility for foreign policy issues, are examples of dual federalism.

Cooperative Federalism

In the 1930's the interpretation of federalism shifted to that of the national and state governments sharing policymaking and cooperating in solving problems. **Cooperative federalism** or "marble cake federalism" as it came to be known, grew from the policies of the New Deal era and the need for the national government to increase government spending and public assistance programs during the Great Depression. The cooperation of the national and state governments to build the national interstate highway system is an example of cooperative federalism. The expansion of cooperative federalism during (President Lyndon B. Johnson's) Great Society required even greater cooperation from the states in return for federal grants.

New Federalism

During the administrations of Richard Nixon, Ronald Reagan, and George H. W. Bush the national government attempted to implement a reversal of cooperative federalism and place more responsibility on the states about how grant money would be spent. The term **devolution**—a transfer of power to political subunits—has been used to describe the goals of new federalism. An example of new federalism is welfare reform legislation, which has returned more authority over welfare programs to the states.

Fiscal Federalism

The national government's patterns of spending, taxation, and providing grants to influence state and local governments is known today as **fiscal federalism**. The national government uses fiscal policy to influence the states through granting or withholding money to pay for programs.

- **grants-in-aid** programs—money and resources provided by the federal government to the state and local governments to be used for specific projects or programs. The earliest grants often covered public works projects such as building canals, roads, and railroads, and land grants for state colleges.
- **categorical grants**—grants that have a specific purpose defined by law, such as sewage treatment facilities or school lunch programs; may even require "matching funds" from the state or local governments; categorical grants may be in the form of project grants (awarded on the basis of a competitive application, such as university research grants) or formula grants (awarded on the basis of an established formula, such as Medicaid)

- **block grants**—general grants which can be used for a variety of purposes within a broad category, such as education, health care, or public services; fewer strings attached so state and local governments have greater freedom in how the money is spent; preferred over categorical grants
- **revenue sharing**—proposed under the Johnson administration and popular under the Nixon administration, a "no strings attached" form of aid to state and local governments; could be used for virtually any project but never exceeded more than two percent of revenues; eliminated during the Reagan administration
- **mandates**—requirements which are imposed by the national government on the state and local governments; for example, the Americans with Disabilities Act (1990) mandates that all public buildings be accessible to persons with disabilities. Mandates often require state or local governments to meet the requirement at their own expense (**unfunded mandates**). After the mid-term elections of 1994, the Republican-controlled Congress passed the Unfunded Mandate Reform Act, which imposed limitations on Congress's ability to pass unfunded mandate legislation.

✓ REVIEW QUESTIONS

1. A major strength of federalism lies in the fact that it promotes both national and state activities in which of the following manners?

   A. provides for complex government activities
   B. avoids concentration of political power
   C. guarantees the inherent inflexibility of a written constitution
   D. allows for the duplication of government offices and functions
   E. allows both the state and the national government to train leaders

2. *McCulloch v. Maryland* (1819) was an important Supreme Court case involving federalism because

   A. it called for a republican form of government
   B. it provided for a national law protecting against domestic violence
   C. following this case, the Supreme Court became the third powerful branch of the national government

   D. the Supremacy Clause of the Constitution was upheld
   E. the Supremacy Clause of the Constitution was established

3. Article IV of the United States Constitution addresses which of the following relationships between the states?

   I. full faith and credit
   II. interstate compacts
   III. respect for geographic integrity

   A. I only
   B. II only
   C. III only
   D. I and II only
   E. II and III only

4. Which of the following is not a concurrent power of national and state governments?

   A. protecting the public's health, welfare and morals
   B. borrowing money
   C. chartering banks

D. establishing courts
E. levying taxes

5. Cooperative federalism can best be described as

A. the national government's ability to help the states through the spending of tax dollars and the providing of project grants
B. placing more responsibility on the states as to how grant money is to be spent
C. "layer cake federalism"
D. an extension of new federalism
E. "marble cake federalism"

6. The president most responsible for the implementation of New Federalism was:

A. George Bush
B. Richard Nixon
C. Ronald Reagan
D. Bill Clinton
E. Gerald Ford

7. Which of the following is an example of fiscal federalism?

I. mandates
II. revenue sharing
III. grants-in-aid
IV. welfare and local grants

    A. I and II only
    B. II and III only
    C. I, II, and III only

D. I, II, and IV only
E. I, II, III, and IV

8. Which of the following has the fewest "strings" attached when it comes to spending government monies?

A. mandates
B. categorical Grants
C. block Grants
D. revenue Sharing
E. grants-in-Aid

9. Federalism as a form of government has many disadvantages. A major disadvantage of federalism is

A. conflicts may arise over authority of government
B. there is no concentration of political power
C. government is not close to the people
D. existing state governments are not accommodated
E. geography is not considered

10. Prohibited powers are powers that are denied to both the national and state governments. These denied powers may be found in

A. Article I, Section 8
B. Article I, Sections 9 & 10
C. Article IV, Section 9
D. Article I, Section 8, Clause 18
E. Article IV, Sections 9 & 10

ANSWERS AND EXPLANATIONS

1. **B.** Power of government is divided between the national and state governments, each operating within the same geographic territory with power over a single population.

2. **D.** *McCulloch v. Maryland* upheld Article VI of the Constitution, which declares the Constitution as the "supreme law of the land."

3. **D.** Geographic integrity of the states is a guarantee of the national government to the states, not the states to each other.

4. **A.** Protecting the public health, welfare, and morals is a reserved power of the states.

5. **E.** Cooperative federalism involves the national government and state governments working together to solve problems, often with a blending (like in a marble cake) of responsibilities.

6. **B.** Richard Nixon began the program of New Federalism to place responsibility on the states for the spending of grant money.

7. **C.** Mandates, revenue sharing, and grants-in-aid are forms of fiscal federalism.

8. **D.** Revenue sharing has a "no strings attached" policy for the states receiving money.

9. **A.** Conflicts between the national and state government may arise under the system of federalism.

10. **B.** Article I, Section 9 denies certain powers to the national government; Article I, Section 10 denies powers to the state governments.

RAPID REVIEW

- Federalism is a system of government in which the powers of government are divided between a national government and regional (state and local) governments.

- There are both advantages and disadvantages to federalism as a form of government.

- Federalism can be found in the delegated, reserved, and concurrent powers of the Constitution.

- Article IV of the Constitution provides for interstate relations, including full faith and credit, privileges and immunities, extradition, interstate compacts.

- Article IV of the Constitution provides national guarantees to the states.

- *McCulloch v. Maryland* and *Gibbons v. Ogden* upheld national supremacy and expanded the powers of Congress under the commerce clause, respectively.

- As practiced in the United States, federalism has evolved through many phases, including dual federalism, cooperative federalism, new federalism, and fiscal federalism.

Chapter 7

Review: Political Culture

AMERICAN POLITICAL ENVIRONMENT

 A **political culture** is a set of basic values and beliefs about a country or government that is shared by most citizens (freedom is precious, for example) and that influences political opinions and behaviors. The U.S. political culture gives citizens a sense of community, creates support for the democratic processes (majority rule, free elections), helps shape attitudes towards public officials, and teaches civic responsibility. The political culture provides a setting for a political system to function.

American Democratic Values

Although America is a diverse society, it is united under a common political culture, or common set of beliefs and attitudes about government and politics. This political culture translates into a consensus of basic concepts that support democracy. Democracy is not guaranteed; therefore the American people must continue to practice these concepts.

- majority rule/minority rights: Although democracy is based upon majority rule, minority rights must be guaranteed.
- equality: equality of every individual before the law and in the political process
- private property: Ownership of property is protected by law and supported by the capitalist system.
- individual freedoms: guarantees of civil liberties and protections of infringements upon them

- compromise: allows for the combining of different interests and opinions to form public policy to best benefit society
- limited government: Powers of government are restricted in a democracy by the will of the people and the law.

Political Socialization

Political socialization is the process by which citizens acquire a sense of political identity. Socialization is a complex process that begins early in childhood and continues throughout a person's life. It allows citizens to become aware of politics, learn political facts, and form political values and opinions. Although the paths to political awareness, knowledge, and values differ, people are exposed to a combination of influences that shape their political identities and opinions:

- Family and home influences often help shape political party identification. It is strongest when both parents identify with the same political party.
- Schools teach patriotism, basic governmental functions and structure, and encourage political participation.
- Group affiliations (interest groups, labor unions, professional organizations) provide common bonds between people which may be expressed through the group or its activities.
- demographic factors (occupation, race, gender, age, religion, region of country, income, education, ethnicity)
- Mass media inform the public about issues and help set the political and public agendas.
- **Opinion leaders,** those individuals held in great respect because of their position, expertise, or personality, may informally and unintentionally exercise influence.
- Events may instill positive or negative attitudes. For example, the Watergate scandal created a mistrust of government.

PUBLIC OPINION

Public opinion is a collection of shared attitudes of many different people in matters relating to politics, public issues, or the making of public policy. It is shaped by people's political culture and political socialization. Public opinion can be analyzed according to distribution (physical shape of responses when graphed), intensity (how strongly the opinions are held), and stability (how much the opinion changes over time). A consensus occurs when there is general agreement on an issue. Public opinion that is strongly divided between two very different views is a divisive opinion.

Measuring Public Opinion

The measurement of public opinion is a complex process often conveying unreliable results. Elections, interest groups, the media, and personal contacts may signal public opinion on certain issues; however, the most reliable measure of public opinion is the public opinion poll. Businesses, governments, political candidates, and interest groups use polls.

Early polling in the United States involved the use of **straw polls,** asking the same question of a large number of people. They were unreliable because they did not necessarily include a cross-section of the general population of the United States. The most famous mishap occurred in 1936 when the *Literary Digest* mailed postcards to more than 10 million people concerning the outcome of the 1936 presidential election. With over 2 million responses, the magazine incorrectly predicted the defeat of Franklin Roosevelt and victory of challenger Alf Landon. The magazine had used automobile registrations and telephone directories to develop its sample, not realizing that during the Depression many people did not have cars or telephones. Many voters who supported Roosevelt had not been polled. The mailings had also been done early, and some voters changed their minds between answering the poll and actually voting.

Modern polling began in the 1930s when George Gallup helped develop the use of a scientific polling process that includes:

- *sampling*—Those chosen to participate in the poll must be representative of the general population and chosen at random.
- *preparing valid questions*—Directions should be clear and questions should be phrased and ordered in a way that does not lead the respondent to a particular answer (clear, fair, and unbiased)
- *controlling how the poll is taken*—Make sure the respondent has some knowledge of the issues addressed in the poll and that the pollster's appearance and tone do not influence the responses. Survey methods may include telephone, mail, and in-person interviews.
- *analyzing and reporting results*—Reporting the results of polls without providing information about how the poll was conducted, **sampling errors,** or when the poll was taken can lead to misinformation and error.

Today, the use of statistical analysis through computers has made polling a major research tool.

Ideology

An **ideology** is a consistent set of beliefs. A **political ideology** is a set of beliefs about politics and public policy that creates the structure for looking at government and public policy. Political ideologies can change over time. Differences in ideology generally occur in the arena of political, economic, and social issues.

Ideology: A Political Spectrum

!

- **radical:** favor rapid, fundamental change in existing social, economic, or political order; may be willing to resort to extreme means, even violence or revolution to accomplish such change (extreme change to create an entirely new social system)
- **liberal:** supports active government in promoting individual welfare and supporting civil rights, and accepts of peaceful political and social change within the existing political system
- **moderate:** political ideology that falls between liberal and conservative and which may include some of both; usually thought of as tolerant of others' political opinions and not likely to hold extreme views on issues
- **conservative:** promotes a limited government role in helping individuals economically, supports traditional values and lifestyles, favors a more active role for government in promoting national security, and approaches change cautiously
- **reactionary:** advocates a return to a previous state of affairs, often a social order or government that existed earlier in history (may be willing to go to extremes to achieve their goals)

✓ REVIEW QUESTIONS

1. Which of the following is not a concept found in the political culture of the American democratic society?

   A. private property
   B. equality
   C. majority rule
   D. minority rule
   E. compromise

2. The process by which citizens acquire a sense of their own political identity would best be defined as

   A. public opinion
   B. political socialization
   C. demographic occupation
   D. political culture
   E. group dynamics

3. Which of the following would be a true statement regarding public opinion?

   A. Public opinion teaches patriotism.
   B. Public opinion allows citizens to become aware of politics, learn facts, and form political values.
   C. Public opinion is shaped by an individual's political culture and political socialization.
   D. A change in public opinion is always a slow process.
   E. Public opinion is usually based on the ideas of small select groups within a given political socialization area.

4. Attempting to measure public opinion by asking the same question to a large number of people is

   A. a straw poll
   B. a sampling poll
   C. a controlling poll
   D. a public opinion poll
   E. a literary poll

5. There are many different ideologies within the political spectrum. An ideology that promotes a limited government role in helping individuals and supports traditional values and lifestyles would best be defined as a

A. liberal ideology
B. reactionary ideology
C. radical ideology
D. moderate ideology
E. conservative ideology

ANSWERS AND EXPLANATIONS

1. **D.** Minority rule is not a part of the American political culture.

2. **B.** Political socialization is the process of acquiring a political identity.

3. **C.** Public opinion is shaped by an individual's political culture and political socialization.

4. **A.** A straw poll is an attempt to measure public opinion by asking the same question to a large number of people.

5. **E.** A conservative ideology promotes a limited government role in helping individuals and supports traditional values and lifestyles.

RAPID REVIEW

- A political culture is a set of basic values and beliefs about a country or government that is shared by most citizens.

- America is a heterogeneous (diverse) society with many political cultures.

- Democracy is not guaranteed. In order to ensure democracy, political concepts must be practiced.

- Political socialization is the process of citizens acquiring a political identity. Several factors influence the process of political socialization.

- Public opinion is a collection of ideas and attitudes about government that are shared by the general public.

- Public opinion is shaped by an individual's political culture and political socialization.

- Public opinion polls are the most reliable measure of public opinion.

- Modern polling began in the 1930s with George Gallup. Today, polling is more scientific and based on statistical analysis.

- An ideology is a consistent set of beliefs. A political ideology is beliefs based on politics and public policy.

- Ideological placement on a political spectrum may include classification as radical, liberal, moderate, conservative, or reactionary.

Chapter 8

Review: Political Parties

WHAT ARE POLITICAL PARTIES?

Political parties are voluntary associations of people who seek to control the government through common principles based upon peaceful and legal actions, such as the winning of elections. Political parties, along with interest groups, the media, and elections serve as a linkage mechanism that brings together the people and the government while holding the government responsible for its actions. Political parties differ from interest groups in that interest groups do not nominate candidates for office.

ROLES OF POLITICAL PARTIES

- party in the electorate—all of the people who associate themselves with one of the political parties
- party in government—all of the appointed and elected officials at the national, state, and local levels who represent the party as members; officeholders
- party in organization—all of the people at the various levels of party organization who work to maintain the strength of the party between elections, help raise money, and organize the conventions and party functions

PARTY SYSTEMS

One-Party System

In a one-party system only one party exists or has a chance of winning election. Generally, membership is not voluntary and those who do belong to the party represent a small portion of the population. Party leaders must approve candidates for political office, and voters have no real choice. The only possible result is dictatorial government.

Two-Party System

In a **two-party system** there may be several political parties but only two major political parties compete for power and dominate elections. Minor parties generally have little effect on most elections, especially at the national level. Systems that operate under the two-party system usually have a general consensus, or agreement, among citizens about the basic principles of government, even though the parties often differ on the means of carrying them out. Voters are given an "either–or" choice, simplifying decisions and the political process. The two-party system tends to enhance governmental stability; since both parties want to appeal to the largest number of voters, they tend to avoid extremes in ideology.

Multi-Party System

Multi-party systems exist when several major parties and a number of minor parties compete in elections, and any of the parties stands a good chance of winning. This type of system can be composed of from five to 20 different parties, based upon a particular region, ideology, or class position, and is usually found in European nations. The idea behind multi-party systems is to give voters meaningful choices. This does not always occur because of two major problems: in many elections, no party has a clear majority of the vote, and not receiving a majority forces the sharing of power by several parties (coalitions). The multi-party system tends to promote instability in government, especially when coalition governments are formed.

WHAT DO POLITICAL PARTIES DO?

- Recruit candidates—find candidates interested in running for public office, especially if no incumbent is running
- Nominate and support candidates for office—help raise money and run candidate campaigns through the party organization
- Educate the electorate—inform the voters about the candidates and encourage voters to participate in the election
- Organize the government—The organization of Congress and state legislatures is based upon political party controls (majority vs. minority party); political appointments are often made based on political party affiliation.

PARTY IDENTIFICATION AND MEMBERSHIP

Membership in American political parties is voluntary. There are no dues to pay; membership is based upon party identification. If you believe you are a member of a particular political party, then you are. Most people choose to belong to a political party that shares their views on issues or the role of government. Several factors may influence party identification:

- ideology
- education
- income
- occupation
- race or ethnicity
- gender
- religion
- family tradition
- region of the country
- marital status

TWO-PARTY TRADITION IN AMERICA

The Constitution did not call for political parties, and the founding fathers had no intention of creating them. James Madison, in Federalist #10, warned of the divisiveness of "factions." George Washington was elected president without party labels and in his farewell address warned against the "baneful effects of the spirit of the party." During the process for ratification of the Constitution, Federalists and Anti-Federalists conflicted over ideals concerning the proper role of government. This conflict resulted in the development of the first political parties: the Federalists and Jeffersonian Republicans, or Democratic-Republicans as they were later called.

Why a Two-Party Tradition?

Although there have been numerous minor parties throughout our history, why has the United States maintained the two-party tradition?

- historical roots—British heritage, Federalist and Anti-Federalist divisions
- electoral system—**single-member districts** mean that only one representative is chosen from each district (one winner per office)
- election laws—vary from state to state which makes it difficult for minor parties to get on the ballot in many states

Rise of Political Parties: Party Development (1789–1800)

The earliest political parties began to develop under the administration of George Washington. Alexander Hamilton, secretary of the treasury, supported a strong national government; his followers became known as Federalists. Secretary of State Thomas Jefferson supported states' rights and a less powerful national government. The clash between these two individuals and their supporters led to the development of political parties. In the election of 1796, Jefferson challenged John Adams, the Federalist candidate, for the presidency but lost. By 1800 Jefferson was able to rally his supporters and win the presidency.

Democratic Domination (1800–1860)

The Jeffersonian Republicans dominated the government from 1800–1824, when they split into factions. The faction led by Andrew Jackson, the Jacksonian Democrats or Democrats, won the presidency in 1828. The major opposition party during this time was the Whig Party. From that election until the election of 1860, Democrats dominated American politics. The Democratic Party became known as the party of the "common man," encouraging popular participation, and helping to bring about an expansion of suffrage to all adult white males.

Republican Domination (1860–1932)

The Republican Party began as a third party, developed from a split in the Whig Party. The Whigs had been the major opposition to the Democrats. By 1860 the Whig party had disappeared and the Republican Party had emerged as the second major party. The Republican Party was composed mostly of former members of other political parties, appealing to commercial and anti-slavery groups. The Republican Party was successful in electing Abraham Lincoln president in 1860, and by the end of the Civil War had become a dominant party. Sometimes called the Grand Ole Party or GOP, the Republican Party often controlled both the presidency and Congress.

Return of Democrats (1932–1968)

With the onset of the Depression, new electoral coalitions were formed and the Republicans lost their domination of government. Franklin Delano Roosevelt was able to unite blacks, city dwellers, blue-collar (labor union) workers, Catholics, Jews, and women to create a voting bloc known as the

New Deal coalition. The election of 1932 brought the Democrats back to power as the dominant party in American politics. Roosevelt was elected to the presidency an unprecedented four times. From 1932–1968 only two Republican presidents (Eisenhower and Nixon) were elected. Not until 1994 did the Republicans gain control of both houses of Congress.

Divided Government (1968–present)

Since 1968 **divided government** has characterized American institutions, a condition in which one political party controls the presidency and the opposing party controls one or both houses of Congress. This division creates a potential **gridlock** when opposing parties and interests often block each other's proposals, creating a political stalemate. In the election of 2000, George W. Bush won the presidency and the Republican party won control of the House of Representatives and Senate (until Jim Jeffords changed affiliation to Independent). In the mid-term election of 2002, the Republicans again gained control of the executive and legislative branches, creating a unified government.

Electoral Dealignment

When significant numbers of voters no longer support a particular political party, **dealignment** has occurred. Often, those voters identify as independents and believe they owe no loyalty to any particular political party.

Electoral Realignment

Historically, as voting patterns have shifted and new coalitions of party supporters have formed, electoral **realignment** has occurred. Several elections can be considered realigning elections, where the dominant party loses power and a new dominant party takes its place. The elections of 1860 and 1932 are examples.

THIRD OR MINOR PARTIES

Although the Republican and Democratic parties have dominated the political scene, there have been minor, or third, parties throughout U.S. history. Minor parties usually have great difficulty in getting candidates elected to office, although they have been more successful at the state and local level. A few minor party candidates have been elected to Congress, but no minor party candidate has ever been elected president. Minor parties have been instrumental in providing important reforms that have been adopted by the major parties. Success rather than failure often brings an end to minor parties, as the major parties often adopt popular reforms or ideas, especially if they appeal to the voters.

Types of Third Parties

Some third parties have been permanent, running candidates in every election; however, many third parties disappear after only a few elections. Several types of minor parties have emerged:

- *ideological*—those based upon a particular set of social, political or economic beliefs (communist, socialist, libertarian)
- *splinter/personality/factional*—those that have split away from one of the major parties; usually formed around a strong personality who does not win the party nomination; may disappear when that leader steps aside (Theodore Roosevelt's "Bull Moose" Progressive, Strom Thurmond's States' Rights, George Wallace's American Independent)
- *single issue*—parties that concentrate on a single public policy matter (Free Soil, Right to Life, Prohibition)
- *protest*—usually rooted in periods of economic discontent; may be sectional in nature (Greenback, Populist)

STRUCTURE AND ORGANIZATION OF POLITICAL PARTIES

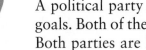

A political party must have an effective organization to accomplish its goals. Both of the major parties are organized in much the same manner. Both parties are highly decentralized, or fragmented. The party of the president is normally more solidly united than the opposition. The president is automatically considered the party leader, while the opposition is often without a single strong leader. Usually one or more members of Congress are seen as the opposition leaders.

National Convention

The national convention serves as the party's national voice. Party delegates meet in the summer of every fourth year to select the party's candidates for president and vice president. They are also responsible for writing and adopting the party's platform.

National Committee

The national committee manages the political party's business between conventions. They are responsible for selecting the convention site, establishing the rules of the convention, publishing and distributing party literature, and helping the party raise campaign contributions.

National Chairperson

The party's national committee, with the consent of the party's presidential nominee, elects the national chairperson. The chairperson is responsible for directing the work of the national committee from their national headquarters in Washington, D.C. The chairperson is involved in fund raising, recruiting new party members, encouraging unity within the party, and helping the party's presidential nominee win election.

Congressional Campaign Committee

Each party has a committee in the House of Representatives and Senate that works to ensure the election or re-election of the party's candidates by raising funds and determining how much money and support each candidate will receive. The committee often works to defeat an opposition party member who appears weak and might be open to defeat.

State and Local Organization

State law largely determines state and local party organization. Differences exist from state to state; however, state and local parties are structured in much the same way as the national party organization. Generally, state parties today are more organized and better funded than in previous years. As a result of **soft money,** money that is distributed from the national political party organization and that does not have to be reported under the Federal Election Campaign Act (1971) or its amendments, state parties have become more dependent upon the national party organization and are subject to their influence.

FUTURE OF POLITICAL PARTIES

The future of political parties in the United States is uncertain. In recent decades, political parties have been in decline. This decline may be attributed to several factors:

- *third-party challenges*—In recent elections third-party challengers have taken votes from the major candidates, lessening their ability to win a majority of the vote.

- *loss of support by party loyalists*—an increase in the number of independent voters
- *increase in split-ticket voting*—Many voters no longer vote a **straight ticket** (only for candidates of one political party) but rather split their vote among candidates from more than one party.
- *lack of perceived differences between the parties*—Voters often believe there are no major differences in the parties or their candidates.
- *party reforms*—Changes within the parties themselves to create greater diversity and openness have allowed for greater conflict within some parties.
- *methods of campaigning*—New technologies have allowed candidates to become more independent of parties and more directly involved with the voters.

✓ REVIEW QUESTIONS

1. Which of the following best describes a multi-party system?

   A. Membership in the party of choice is not generally voluntary.
   B. There is usually a general consensus of agreement as to basic principles of government.
   C. Multi-party systems usually give the voters meaningful choices.
   D. Parties tend to avoid extreme ideologies.
   E. Minor parties have little effect on most elections.

2. Which of the following is not a responsibility of a political party?

   A. create centralized responsibility
   B. politically educate officeholders and candidates for office
   C. serve as a watchdog on party activities
   D. nominate and support candidates for public office
   E. staff the government

3. The Republican and Democratic parties have dominated the political scene throughout American history. Minor parties have often surfaced to fill the void left by the major parties. A splinter minor party can best be characterized by

   A. the single issues supported by the party
   B. the fact that it is usually built around the working class American
   C. the permanence of its presence on the political scene
   D. its presence during times of economic discontent
   E. the fact that it is the result of a revolt within a major party

4. The Republicans dominated party politics during which span of years?

   A. 1860–1932
   B. 1932–1968
   C. 1968–present
   D. 1800–1860
   E. 1789–1800

5. The national convention serves what major purpose for a political party?

   A. to allow the people to direct the work of the national committee through a system of national participation

B. to establish the rules of party campaigning

C. to serve as the party's national voice in the selection of the party's candidate

D. to manage the political party's business by the vote of party constituents

E. to allow the political party to meet as a whole in order to raise funds, recruit new members, and encourage unity within the party

6. Which of the following best describes state party organizations?

A. They are independent of the national party.

B. They are subject to their own jurisdiction according to party doctrines.

C. They are determined and organized by the national party in accordance with national law.

D. They are generally more organized and better funded than they have been in previous years.

E. They have the same organizational structures in all states because they are regulated by state law.

7. Membership in an American political party is voluntary and based on party identification. Which factors influence party identification?

I. education
II. gender
III. public opinion

A. I only
B. II only
C. III only

D. I and II only
E. I and III only

8. Which of the following best describes the structure and organization of a political party?

A. They are close-knit and very organized.

B. They are highly decentralized or fragmented.

C. After election day they are usually less responsible to the people.

D. The president plays no role in party leadership after his election.

E. During the founding of our country, both parties organized in the same manner, along the same lines and with the same political ideas in mind.

9. The shifting of voting patterns and formation of new coalitions of party supporters is known as

A. alignment
B. realignment
C. divided government
D. dealignment
E. party positioning

10. The future of political parties in the United States is uncertain due to

I. decline of third party challenges
II. perceived differences between the parties
III. increase in split-ticket voting
IV. lack of party reform

A. I only
B. III only
C. II and III only
D. I and III only
E. I, II, and IV only

ANSWERS AND EXPLANATIONS

1. **C.** Multi-party systems tend to give voters a greater variety of major and minor party candidate choices.

2. **B.** Political parties educate the electorate about the candidates.

3. **E.** Splinter parties usually develop around a personality within a major party and split from that party when that candidate fails to receive the party nomination.

4. **A.** Republicans often controlled Congress and the executive branch between 1860 and 1932.

5. **C.** Two major functions of the national convention are to write the party platform and nominate the party candidate for president and vice president.

6. **D.** State parties have often received soft money from the national organization, which has allowed them better organization and funding.

7. **D.** Education and gender are two of the several factors which influence party identification.

8. **B.** Political parties tend to be highly decentralized and fragmented, especially at the national level and when no election is immediate.

9. **B.** Realignment creates new voting coalitions, such as the New Deal coalition which elected Franklin Roosevelt in 1932.

10. **B.** The future of political parties is uncertain due to the increase in split-ticket voting, an increase in third party challenges, a lack of perceived differences between the parties, and an increase in party reforms.

RAPID REVIEW

- Political parties are voluntary associations of voters.

- Political parties are different from interest groups.

- Political parties serve the party in the electorate, in government, and in organization.

- One-party, two-party and multi-party systems exist throughout the world.

- Political parties recruit candidates, nominate and support candidates for office, educate the electorate, and organize the government.

- Party identification may be based on several factors.

- The Constitution does not call for political parties. Two parties developed from factions during the ratification process.

- Historically, there have been periods of one-party domination of the government. More recently, divided control of the branches of government has led to potential gridlock.

- Minor parties have existed throughout American history. There are four major types of minor parties: ideological, splinter/personality, single-issue, and protest parties.

- Political parties must have organization to accomplish their goals. American political parties tend to be decentralized and fragmented.

- The future of political parties in America is uncertain.

Chapter 9

Review: Voting and Elections

2 PARTICIPATION AND VOTING

Most people think of political participation in terms of voting, however, there are other forms of political participation, and sometimes they are more effective than voting. Political participation includes all the actions people use in seeking to influence or support government and politics.

Forms of Political Participation

- voting in elections
- discussing politics and attending political meetings
- forming interest groups and PACs
- contacting public officials
- campaigning for a candidate or political party
- contributing money to a candidate or political party
- running for office
- protesting government decisions

Most of these behaviors would be considered conventional or routine, within the acceptable channels of representative government. Less conventional behaviors have been used when groups have felt powerless and ineffective. Although Americans are less approving of unconventional behaviors, those tactics are sometimes effective in influencing government decisions. The often-violent protests against the Vietnam Conflict discouraged Lyndon Johnson from running for reelection in 1968.

The most common form of political participation in the United States is voting. However, Americans are less likely to vote than citizens of other countries.

Participation Through Voting

Democratic government is "government by the people." In the United States, participation through elections is the basis of the democratic process. According to democratic theory, everyone should be allowed to vote. In practice, however, no nation grants universal suffrage; all nations have requirements for voting.

Expansion of Suffrage

Suffrage is the right to vote. It is a political right that belongs to all those who meet certain requirements set by law. The United States was the first nation to provide for general elections of representatives through mass suffrage. The issue of suffrage is left to the states—the only stipulation found in Article I, Section 2 of the Constitution is that individuals who could vote for "the most numerous branch of the state legislature" could also vote for their Congressional representatives.

The composition of the American **electorate** has changed throughout history. Two major trends have marked the development of suffrage: the elimination of a number of restrictive requirements and the transfer of more and more authority from the states to the federal government.

Changes in voting requirements have included:

- elimination of religious qualifications, property ownership, and tax payments after 1800
- elimination of race disqualifications with the passage of the 15th Amendment in 1870
- elimination of gender disqualifications with the passage of the 19th Amendment in 1920
- elimination of grandfather clauses, white primaries, and literacy requirements with the passage of federal civil rights legislation and court decisions (Civil Rights Acts, Voting Rights Act of 1965)
- allowing residents of Washington, D.C., to vote in presidential elections with the passage of the 23rd Amendment in 1961
- elimination of poll taxes in federal elections with the passage of the 24th Amendment in 1964 (all poll taxes were ruled unconstitutional in *Harper v. Virginia State Board of Elections*, 1966)
- lowering the minimum age for voting in federal elections to 18 with the passage of the 26th Amendment in 1971

Issue or Policy Voting

The Progressive Movement of the early twentieth century was a philosophy of political reform that fostered the development of mechanisms for increased direct participation.

- **Direct primary** allows citizens to nominate candidates.
- **Recall** is a special election initiated by petition to allow citizens to remove an official from office before a term expires.
- **Referendum** allows citizens to vote directly on issues called propositions (proposed laws or state constitutional amendments).
- **Initiative** allows voters to petition to propose issues to be decided by qualified voters.

Although the recall, referendum, and initiative do not exist at the national level, several states allow issue voting.

Candidate Voting

Voting for candidates is the most common form of political participation. It allows citizens to choose candidates they think will best serve their interests and makes public officials accountable for their actions. In the United States voters only elect two national officeholders—the president and vice president. All remaining candidates represent state or local constituencies.

Low Voter Turnout

Voting has been studied more closely than any other form of political participation in the United States. Studies have shown that voter turnout in the United States has decreased when compared with other nations and when compared with the U.S. over time. Voter turnout is higher if the election is seen as important; voter turnout is higher in presidential elections than in off-year elections. Several reasons might account for the low voter turnout:

- *expansion of the electorate*—increase in the number of potential voters (26th Amendment)
- *failure of political parties to mobilize voters*—negative campaigning, numerous elections, frequent elections, lack of party identification
- *no perceived differences between the candidates or parties*—both parties and their candidates are seen as virtually the same
- *mistrust of government*—a belief that all candidates are untrustworthy or unresponsive, due in part to the Watergate and Iran-Contra scandals
- *apathy*—a lack of interest in politics; a belief that voting is not important
- *satisfaction with the way things are*—a belief that not voting will keep the status quo
- *lack of **political efficacy***—people do not believe their vote out of millions of votes will make a difference
- *mobility of electorate*—moving around leads to a lack of social belonging

- *registration process*—differences in registration procedures from state to state may create barriers; the National Voter Registration Act of 1995 (**Motor Voter Law**) was designed to make voter registration easier by allowing people to register at drivers' license bureaus and some public offices

Who Votes?

Several factors affect the likelihood of voting:

- *education*—The higher the level of education, the more likely a person is to vote. This is the most important indicator of voting behavior.
- *occupation and income*—These often depend on education level. Those with white-collar jobs and higher levels of income are more likely to vote than those with blue-collar jobs or lower levels of income
- *age*—Older people are more likely to vote than younger people.
- *race*—Minorities such as African-Americans and Hispanics are less likely to vote than whites, unless they have similar socio-economic status.
- *gender*—At one time, gender was not a major predictor, but today women are more likely to vote than men.
- *religion*—Those who are more active within their religion are more likely to vote than those who do not attend religious services, or rarely attend.
- *marital status*—Married people are more likely to vote than those who are not married.
- *union membership*—Unions encourage participation, and union members tend to vote regularly.
- *community membership*—People who are well integrated into community life are more likely to vote than those who have moved recently.
- *party identification*—Those who have a strong sense of party identification are more likely to vote.
- *geography*—Residents of states with inter-party competition and close elections may be more likely to vote than those who live in states with one-party domination.

TYPES OF ELECTIONS

- **Primary elections** are nominating elections in which voters choose the candidates from each party who will run for office in the general election. There are several major types of primaries:
  - **closed primary**—Only voters who are registered in the party may vote to choose the candidate. Separate primaries are held by each political party, and voters must select a primary in advance.
  - **open primary**—Voters may vote to choose the candidates of either party, whether they belong to that party or not. Voters make the decision of which party to support in the voting booth.

> — **blanket primary**—Voters may vote for candidates of either party, choosing a Republican for one office and a Democrat for another; used only in Alaska and Washington.
> — **runoff primary**—When no candidate from a party receives a majority of the votes, the top two candidates face each other in a runoff.

- **General elections** are elections in which the voters choose from among all the candidates nominated by political parties or running as independents.
- Special elections are held whenever an issue must be decided by voters before a primary or general election is held, for example, to fill a vacancy in the Senate.

When Elections Are Held

Local, state, and federal laws determine when elections are held. Congress has established that congressional and presidential elections will be held on the first Tuesday after the first Monday in November. Congressional elections are held every even-numbered year, and presidential elections are held every fourth year.

Congressional Elections

Since congressional elections are held every even-numbered year, **off-year elections** (mid-term elections) occur during the year when no presidential election is held. Voter turnout in off-year elections is generally lower than during presidential election years. During presidential election years, the popularity of a presidential candidate may create a **coattail effect,** allowing lesser-known or weaker candidates from the presidential candidate's party to win by riding the "coattails" of the nominee.

Presidential Elections

The road to the White House and the presidency begins months and even years prior to the election. Some candidates begin the process as soon as the previous election is over. Phases of a candidacy include:

- *exploration*—In deciding whether to run for president, individuals must determine whether they have enough political and financial support to win against other possible candidates. Often a possible nominee will form an exploratory committee to begin lining up support and finances, as well as to attract media coverage and gain widespread recognition.
- *announcement*—Once a candidate has decided to run, an announcement is generally made in a press conference. This announcement is a formal declaration that the candidate is seeking the party's nomination.

- *presidential primaries and caucuses*—In the past, state party officials would meet in a **caucus** to endorse the party candidate prior to presidential primaries. Abuses of the caucus system led to many states abandoning its use. Iowa still uses caucuses to nominate presidential candidates; however, today they are open to all members of the party. Most states today use the **presidential preference primary** to determine whom the state delegates to the national party convention will support. Voters vote in a primary election, and party delegates to the conventions support the winner of the primary election.

- *nominating conventions*—Each political party holds a national nominating convention in the summer prior to the general election. The convention is composed of delegates from each state, with each party determining its method of selecting delegates. The purpose of the nominating convention is to choose the party's presidential and vice presidential nominees, write the party platform, and bring unity to the party in support of their chosen nominees.

- *campaigning and the general election*—After the conventions are over, each candidate begins campaigning for the general election. Generally, candidates travel to states with more electoral votes and often appear more moderate in an effort to win the largest possible number of votes. In recent years the candidates have faced each other in televised debates. The general election is then held to determine which candidate wins the electoral college vote for that state.

- *electoral college*—When voters go to the polls on election day they are casting the popular vote. This vote is actually for electors. Each state has a number of electors equal to its senators and representatives in Congress. Also, Washington, D.C. has three electoral votes. The entire group of 538 electors is known as the electoral college. After the general election, the electors meet in their respective state capitals on the first Monday after the second Wednesday in December. The candidate who wins a majority of popular votes in a state in the general election wins all the state's electoral votes in the electoral college (winner-take-all). Although the electors are not required to vote for their party's candidate, only rarely do they cast a vote for someone else. The votes cast in the electoral college are then sent to Congress, where they are opened and counted before a joint session. The candidate who receives a majority (270) of electoral votes is declared the winner. If no candidate for president receives a majority of electoral votes, the House of Representatives chooses the president from the top three candidates. If no candidate for vice president receives a majority of electoral votes, the Senate chooses the vice president from the top two candidates.

Partisanship in Elections

- **Maintaining elections** occur when the traditional majority power maintains power based on the party loyalty of voters.

- **Deviating elections** occur when the minority party is able to win with the support of majority-party members, independents, and new voters; however, the long-term party preferences of voters do not change.
- **Critical elections** indicate sharp changes in existing patterns of party loyalty due to changing social and economic conditions, for example, elections of 1860, 1896, and 1932.
- **Realigning elections** occur when the minority party wins by building a new coalition of voters that continues over successive elections. This is usually associated with a national crisis such as the Great Depression, when Franklin D. Roosevelt was able to create a new coalition of southerners, African-Americans, the poor, Catholics and Jews, labor union members, and urban dwellers.
- **Dealigning elections** occur when party loyalty becomes less important to voters, as may be seen with the increase in independents and **split-ticket voting.**

CAMPAIGN FINANCE

Campaigning for political office is expensive. For the 2000 elections the Republican and Democratic parties raised more than 1.1 billion dollars.

Campaign Finance Regulations and Reforms

Prior to the 1970s candidates for public office received donations from businesses, labor organizations, and individuals to finance campaigns.

Congress passed the Federal Election Campaign Act (FECA) in 1971, restricting the amount of campaign funds that could be spent on advertising, requiring disclosure of campaign contributions and expenditures, and limiting the amounts candidates and their families could donate to their own campaigns. It also allowed taxpayers to designate a donation on their tax return to the major political party candidates, beginning in the 1976 presidential election.

In 1974, after the **Watergate** scandal, Congress amended the Federal Election Campaign Act to establish a Federal Election Commission (FEC) to enforce the act, and established public financing for presidential candidates in primaries and the general election. The measure also restricted contributions by prohibiting foreign contributions, limiting individual contributions, and restricting the formation of PACs and their contributions. It was further amended in 1976 and 1979.

In 1976 the Supreme Court ruled in *Buckley v. Valeo*, that spending limits established by the FECA Amendments of 1974 were unconstitutional, ruling that those restrictions were in violation of the First Amendment's guarantees of **freedom of expression.**

In 1996 new questions arose over the use of "**soft money,**" donations to political parties that could be used for general purposes. Originally, the money was supposed to be used for voter registration drives, national party conventions, and issue ads. Political parties were allowed to raise unlimited amounts of money because it was not to be used for campaigning. However, soft money has generally been spent in ways that ultimately help individual candidates. By the 2000 election, soft money donations had exceeded $400 million between the two major parties.

Campaign finance reform has been a major issue in Congress. In 2002 Congress passed the Bipartisan Campaign Finance Reform Act (BCRA), banning the use of soft money in federal campaigns and increasing the 1974 limits on individual and group contributions to candidates.

✓ REVIEW QUESTIONS

1. Which of the following would not be a form of political participation?

   A. voting in elections
   B. contacting public officials
   C. paying taxes
   D. forming an interest group
   E. protesting government decisions

2. What is the most common form of political participation in America?

   A. voting
   B. contributing money for candidates
   C. working for a political party
   D. running for office
   E. forming interest groups

3. Which of the following best defines the term recall?

   A. Recall allows voters to petition proposed issues presented before them.
   B. Recall is a form of direct primary.
   C. Recall is a form of indirect primary.
   D. Recall is a special election allowing the voters to remove public officials from office before the end of their term.
   E. Recall allows the voter to vote directly on issues and propositions.

4. Which of the following factors may be attributed to those who are more likely to vote in elections?

   I. age
   II. health status
   III. degree of religious participation
   IV. number of children
   V. gender

      A. I and III only
      B. I, III, and V only
      C. II, III, and IV only
      D. II, IV, and V only
      E. I, II, III, IV, and V

5. Which of the following is not a major type of primary in the United States?

   A. closed primary
   B. blanket primary
   C. general primary
   D. run-off primary
   E. open primary

6. Presidential elections are held on:

   A. the first Tuesday after the first Monday in November
   B. the first Tuesday in November
   C. the first Tuesday after the second Monday in November

D. the first Monday after the first Tuesday in November
E. the first Monday in November

7. Which of the following is a false statement?

A. The first step in running for president of the United States is to explore the possibility of political and financial support.
B. Most candidates running for president of the United States make formal announcements as to the seeking of their party's nomination.
C. After the national convention, candidates begin campaigning for the general election.
D. The purpose of a national nominating convention is to select a party's presidential candidate and write a party platform.
E. Presidential primaries provide little help for the American voter in determining a party's political candidate.

8. The electoral college, along with the popular vote of the people determines the winner of a presidential election. What majority of the electoral vote is needed in order to be declared the winner?

A. 538
B. 435
C. 100
D. 270
E. 271

9. The Federal Election Campaign Act of 1971

A. limits the number of candidates that may run for any one office
B. restricts the amount of campaign funds that may be spent on a single election
C. restricts the amount of campaign donations to $1 per person
D. restricts the amount of campaign contributions to $400 million for the major political parties
E. allows for soft money contributions

10. In 1976, the Supreme Court ruled that spending limits established by the Federal Election Campaign Act were unconstitutional. Which Supreme Court case validated this ruling?

A. *Buckley v. Valentino*
B. *Benjamin v. Buckley*
C. *Buckley v. Valeo*
D. *Buckley v. United States*
E. *United States v. Buckley*

ANSWERS AND EXPLANATIONS

1. **C.** Paying taxes is not a method of political participation.

2. **A.** Voting is the most common form of political participation in the United States.

3. **D.** Recall is an election that allows voters the opportunity to remove a public official from office prior to the end of a term.

4. **B.** Age, degree of religious participation, and gender are characteristics that may determine whether someone is more likely to vote in elections.

5. **C.** A general primary is not a type of primary in the United States.

6. **A.** Presidential elections are held on the first Tuesday after the first Monday in November of every fourth year.

7. **E.** Presidential primaries are often preference primaries where voters may choose which party candidate their party should support at the nominating convention.

8. **D.** Candidates must win at least 270 electoral votes to win election as president or vice president.

9. **B.** The Federal Election Campaign Act of 1971 limits the amount of money that may be spent in federal election campaigns.

10. **C.** In *Buckley v. Valeo* the Supreme Court declared spending limits established by the Federal Election Campaign Act unconstitutional.

RAPID REVIEW

- Political participation includes all the actions people use in seeking to influence or support government and politics.

- Voting is the most common form of political participation in the United States.

- According to democratic theory, everyone should be allowed to vote.

- Suffrage is the right to vote. The expansion of suffrage has allowed a larger number of voters.

- In the early 20th century the Progressive Movement helped bring about an increase in direct participation.

- The president and vice president are the only two nationally elected officeholders.

- Voter turnout in the United States has been decreasing due to numerous reasons.

- Various characteristics have been attributed to those who are more likely to vote.

- Primary elections are intra-party elections held to narrow down the field of candidates.

- General elections are inter-party elections where voters choose the officeholders.

- Federal, state, and local laws determine the holding of elections.

- Congressional elections that take place in years when no presidential election is occurring are called off-year or mid-term elections.

- The presidential election process includes exploration, announcement, primaries, nominating conventions, campaigning, the general election, and the electoral college vote.

- An electoral college elects the president and vice president.

- Partisanship allows for elections to be maintaining, deviating, critical, realigning, or dealigning in scope.

- The Federal Election Campaign Act and its amendments regulate campaign finances. Reforms of campaign financing include the passage of the Bipartisan Campaign Finance Reform Act that bans the use of "soft money" in federal campaigns.

Chapter 10

Review: Interest Groups and the Mass Media

2 INTEREST GROUPS

People form and join groups to take their concerns before public officials at all levels of government. Interest groups are different from a political party in that they have no legal status in the election process. They do not nominate candidates for public office, however, they may actively support candidates who are sympathetic to their cause. While political parties are interested in controlling government, **interest groups** are concerned with influencing the policies of government, usually focusing on issues that directly affect their membership. Membership in interest groups may be restricted or open to all who are interested. Not all interested people belong to interest groups. Many people belong to various interest groups at the same time.

Historical Background of Interest Groups

Interest groups have often been viewed with suspicion. In *Federalist #10*, James Madison warned against the dangers of "factions." Although Madison was opposed to the elimination of factions, he believed that the separation of powers under the Constitution would moderate their effect.

Functions of Interest Groups

Interest groups serve several important functions. They:

- raise awareness and stimulate interest in public affairs by educating their members and the public

- represent membership, serving as a link between members and government
- provide information to government, especially data and testimony useful in making public policy
- provide channels for political participation that enable citizens to work together to achieve a common goal

Types of Interest Groups

Economic Interest Groups

Most interest groups are formed on the basis of economic interests.

- Labor groups promote and protect the interest of organized labor. Examples include the AFL-CIO and the Teamsters Union.
- Business groups promote and protect business interests in general. The Chamber of Commerce of the United States and the National Association of Manufacturers are examples.
- Professional groups maintain standards of the profession, hold professional meetings, and publish journals. Some examples are the National Education Association (NEA), the American Medical Association (AMA), and the American Bar Association (ABA).
- Agricultural groups, such as the National Grange and the National Farmers' Union, promote general agricultural interests.

Groups that Promote Causes

- specific causes
  — American Civil Liberties Union (ACLU)
  — National Rifle Association (NRA)
- welfare of specific groups of individuals
  — American Association of Retired People (AARP)
  — National Association for the Advancement of Colored People (NAACP)
  — Veterans of Foreign Wars (VFW)
- religion-related causes
  — National Council for Churches
  — American Jewish Congress

Public Interest Groups

Public interest groups are concerned with issues such as the environment, consumer protection, crime, and civil rights

- public interests
  — Common Cause
  — League Of Women Voters
  — Mothers Against Drunk Driving (MADD)

Strategies of Interest Groups

- *influencing elections*—encouraging members to vote for candidates who support their views, influencing party platforms and the nomination of candidates, campaigning and contributing money to parties and candidates through **political action committees (PACs)**
- *lobbying*—attempting to influence policymakers, often by supplying data to government officials and their staffs to convince these policymakers that their cases is more deserving than another's
  - *direct lobbying*—uses personal contacts between lobbyists and policymakers
  - *grassroots lobbying*—interest group members and others outside the organization write letters, send telegrams, e-mails and faxes, and make telephone calls to bring influence upon policymakers
  - *coalition lobbying*—several interest groups with common goals join together to bring influence on policymakers
- *litigation*—Groups often take an issue to court if they are unsuccessful in gaining the support of Congress. This strategy was used successfully by the NAACP to argue against segregation during the 1950s.
- *going public*—appealing to the public for support by bringing attention to an issue or using public relations to gain support for the image of the interest group itself

Political Action Committees (PACs)

!

The campaign finance reforms of the 1970s prohibited corporations and labor unions from making direct contributions to candidates running for federal office. Political action committees (PACs) were formed as political arms of interest groups. Federal law regulates PACs; they must register with the federal government, raise money from multiple contributors, donate to several candidates, and follow strict accounting rules.

Regulation of Interest Groups

The first major attempt to regulate lobbying came in 1946 with the passage of the Federal Regulation of Lobbying Act, requiring lobbyists to register with the clerk of the House of Representatives and the secretary of the Senate if their principle purpose was to influence legislation. This law was directed only at those who tried to influence members of Congress. In 1995 Congress passed the Lobbying Disclosure Act, creating much stricter regulations by requiring registration if lobbying was directed at members of Congress, congressional staff, or policymakers within the executive branch. It also required the disclosure of more information concerning the activities and clients of lobbyists.

MASS MEDIA

Mass media refers to all forms of communication that transmit information to the general public. Although the mass media are not the only means of communication between citizens and government (political parties, interest groups, and voting are other means), they are the only linkage mechanism that specializes in communication.

Development of the Modern Media

The development of the mass media in the United States reflects the growth of the country, new inventions and technology, and changing attitudes about the role of government.

Newspapers

The earliest American newspapers, operating during colonial times, were expensive, had small circulations, and were often prepared or financed by political organs or those advocating a particular cause. Improvements in printing, the telegraph, and the rotary press led to the growth of newspapers and newspaper circulations. By the 1890s almost every major city in the United States had one or more daily papers. Circulation wars led to "yellow journalism" and political consequences resulted. Since the 1950s newspaper competition has decreased.

Magazines

Magazines tended to have smaller circulations with less frequent publication. The earliest public affairs magazines were published in the mid-1800s. They often exposed political corruption and business exploitation with the writings of muckrakers such as Ida Tarbell, Lincoln Steffens, and Sinclair Lewis. In the 1920s and 1930s, three weekly news magazines, *Time, Newsweek,* and *U.S. News and World Report* attracted mass readership. Today, they often substitute for daily newspapers.

Radio

The wide use of radio began in the 1920s and made celebrities of news personalities. Franklin Roosevelt successfully used radio to broadcast his "fireside chats" to the American people.

Television

Today, television claims the largest audience of the mass media. After World War II television increased the visibility of broadcast journalists making them celebrities. Television promoted the careers of politicians such as Joe McCarthy, during hearings of the House Unamerican Activities Committee, and John Kennedy, during his campaign debates against Richard Nixon.

Internet as Media

The rapid growth of internet usage has led to media organizations using the internet as a way to convey information. Newspapers, magazines, and radio and television stations have sites on the World Wide Web.

Roles of the Media

The media perform several important functions:

- informing the public
- shaping public opinion
- providing a link between citizens and government
- serving as a watchdog that investigates and examines personalities and government policies, for example, the Trent Lott-Strom Thurmond Controversy
- agenda-setting by influencing what subjects become national political issues. Protests against the Vietnam Conflict are an example.

Media Ownership and Government Regulation

The mass media are privately owned in the United States, giving them more political freedom than in most other countries where they are publicly owned, but also making them more dependent on advertising profits. Government regulation of the media affects the broadcast media (radio and television) more than the print media (newspapers and magazines). Government regulation of the broadcast media falls into three categories:

- *technical regulations*—The Federal Communications Act of 1934 created the Federal Communications Commission (FCC) as an independent regulatory agency to regulate interstate and foreign communication by radio, television, telephone, telegraph, cable, and satellite.
- *structural regulations*—These control the organization and ownership of broadcasting companies; in 1996 the Telecommunications Act broadened competition.
- *content regulations*—although the mass media are protected by the First Amendment, the broadcast media have been subject to regulation of content.

What Is News? Reporting the News

"News" is any important event that has happened within the past 24 hours. The media decide what is news by deciding what to report. News is generally directed through **gatekeepers**—media executives, news editors, and prominent reporters—who decide which events to present and how to present them. Time limitations and the potential impact of the story are major elements in selecting what is news. In political coverage, "horse-race journalism" often focuses on which candidate is winning or losing, rather than the issues of the election.

Media and the President

The major news organizations maintain journalists in major cities and government centers to report political events firsthand. Washington, D.C., has the largest press corps of any city in the United States, with one-third of the press assigned to cover the White House. News events may be staged as **media events.** The White House allows special access to the president, with the press receiving information through the Office of the Press Secretary.

Some ways that journalists receive information are:

- news release—prepared text to be used exactly as written
- news briefing—announcements and daily questioning of the press secretary about news releases
- news conference—questioning of high-level officials, often rehearsed
- leaks—information released by officials who are guaranteed anonymity; may be intentional to interfere with the opposition or to "float" an idea and measure reaction

Reporters are expected to observe "rules" when talking to officials:

- on the record—official may be quoted by name
- off the record—what the official says cannot be printed
- on background—what the official says can be printed but may not be attributed to the official by name
- on deep background—what the official says can be printed, but it cannot be attributed to anybody

Media and Congress

Fewer reporters regularly cover Congress, which does not maintain as tight a control over news stories as the White House. Most of the coverage of Congress concerns the House of Representatives, the Senate, or Congress as an organization, rather than individual members. News about Congress may cover confirmation hearings, oversight investigations, or scandals among members.

C-SPAN (Cable-Satellite Public Affairs Network) was created to increase coverage of Congressional activities. The floor and some committee proceedings of the House of Representatives and Senate are now broadcast on C-SPAN and C-SPAN II. Members of Congress may also record radio and television messages to their constituents.

BIASES IN THE MEDIA

Critics of the media contend the media are biased in reporting. Reporters are said to have a liberal bias, while media owners, publishers, and editors are said to be more conservative. Studies confirm that reporters have a liberal orientation, however the bias tends to be against incumbents and frontrunners. There is also a tendency for "pack journalism," with journalists adopting the viewpoints of other journalists with whom they spend time and exchange information.

✓ REVIEW QUESTIONS

1. How is an interest group different from a political party?

    A. Interest groups often support political candidates for office.
    B. Membership in an interest group is non-restrictive.
    C. Interest groups have no legal status in the election process.
    D. Interest groups control government.
    E. Only interested people belong to interest groups.

2. Which of the following is not a function of an interest group?

    A. provide a system of political "roadblocks" in order to slow down or stop government action
    B. raise awareness and stimulate interest in public affairs
    C. serve as a link between its members and government
    D. provide information to the government
    E. provide a channel for public political participation for the achievement of common goals

3. An example of an interest group that would promote a specific cause is

    A. the National Grange
    B. the Teamsters Union
    C. the American Bar Association
    D. the National Education Association
    E. the National Rifle Association

4. An example of a public interest group is

    A. the League of Women Voters
    B. the American Association of Retired People
    C. the American Bar Association
    D. the National Council for Churches
    E. the American Jewish Congress

5. A method of lobbying by which interest group members and others outside the organization write letters, send telegrams, and make telephone calls to influence policymakers is known as

    A. litigation lobbying
    B. grassroots lobbying
    C. direct lobbying
    D. coalition lobbying
    E. influential lobbying

6. The first major attempt to regulate lobbying in America was in 1946 when Congress passed the

   A. Lobbying Disclosure Act
   B. Congressional Lobbying Act
   C. Federal Lobbying Act
   D. Federal Regulation of Lobbying Act
   E. Federal Lobbying Reform Act

7. "Yellow journalism" is a medium effect that is most associated with

   A. magazines
   B. television broadcast journalism
   C. newspapers
   D. radio journalism
   E. pamphlet journalism

8. In the history of radio as a mode of mass media, which American president was first to make the medium a regular feature of his administration as a method of informing the people?

   A. Ronald Reagan
   B. Franklin Roosevelt
   C. Bill Clinton
   D. George Bush
   E. Harry Truman

9. Which of the following has been an important function in the role of mass media?

   I. directing government
   II. agenda-setting
   III. informing the public
   IV. shaping public opinion

   A. II, III, and IV only
   B. I, II, and III only
   C. I only
   D. II and IV only
   E. II and IV only

10. Those media executives and news editors who decide which events to present and how to present the news are called

   A. content regulators
   B. gatekeepers
   C. technical regulators
   D. telecommunication regulators
   E. media representatives

ANSWERS AND EXPLANATIONS

1. **C.** Interest groups have no political status in the election process while political parties fulfill many role in the election process.

2. **A.** To provide a system of political "roadblocks" in order to slow down or stop government action is not a function of interest groups.

3. **E.** The National Rifle Association promotes the owning of guns as a right of citizens.

4. **A.** The League of Women Voters is a public interest group created to encourage voter participation.

5. **B.** A method of lobbying by which interest group members and others outside the organization write letters, send telegrams, and make telephone calls to influence policymakers is known as grass-roots lobbying.

6. **D.** The Federal Regulation of Lobbying Act was passed in 1946 to regulate lobbying.

7. **C.** Newspapers engaged in "yellow journalism" to create interest and increase circulation.

8. **B.** Franklin Roosevelt used the radio to deliver his "fireside chats" to the American people as a method of informing them about the economy and the war.

9. **A.** Agenda-setting, informing the public, and shaping public opinion are functions of the mass media.

10. **B.** Media executives and news editors who decide which events to present and how to present the news are known as gatekeepers.

RAPID REVIEW

- Interest groups are different from political parties.
- James Madison warned against the dangers of "factions" in *Federalist #10*.
- Interest groups perform many functions: creating awareness among the public, linking the public and government, providing information, and creating avenues for political participation.
- There are three major types of interest groups: economic, cause-related, and public.
- Strategies used by interest groups may include influencing elections, lobbying, litigation, and going public.
- PACs, or political action committees, are political arms of interest groups that raise money for political candidates.
- Federal, state, and local laws regulate interest group activities and fundraising.
- Mass media refers to all the forms of communication that transmit information to the general public. Mass media include newspapers, magazines, radio, television, and the internet.
- One of the major roles of the media is agenda-setting.
- The mass media are privately owned in the United States.
- Government regulation of broadcast media includes technical, structural, and content regulation.
- Gatekeepers are the media executives, news editors, and prominent reporters who decide which events to present and how to present them.
- The Office of the Press Secretary allows the press to have greater access to the president through new releases, briefings, and conferences.
- Media coverage of Congress often centers on the institution rather than individual members.
- Criticism of the media's influence often refers to bias in reporting.

Chapter 11

Review: The Legislative Branch

2 CONGRESS

Article I of the United States Constitution creates a **bicameral,** or two-house, legislature consisting of the House of Representatives and the Senate. The current structure of the Congress was the result of the Connecticut, or Great, Compromise, reached at the Constitutional Convention. The founding fathers based their compromise in part on the belief that each house would serve as a check on the power of the other house. The House of Representatives was to be based on the population in the states, representative of the people, with its members chosen by popular vote. The Senate was to represent the states, with each state having the same number of senators, chosen by the state legislatures.

STRUCTURE OF CONGRESS

	House of Representatives	**Senate**
Membership	435 members (apportioned by population)	100 members (two from each state)
Term of office	2 years; entire House elected every 2 years	6 years; staggered terms with one-third of the Senate elected every 2 years
Qualifications	at least 25 years of age; citizen for 7 years; must live in state where district is located	at least 30 years of age citizen for 9 years must live in state
Constituencies	Smaller, by districts	Larger, entire state
Prestige	Less prestige	More prestige

Figure 11–1 Structure of Congress: A Comparison of the House and Senate.

ORGANIZATION OF CONGRESS

- Two houses meet for terms of two years beginning on January 3 of odd-numbered years; each term is divided into two 1-year sessions
- President may call special sessions in cases of national emergency
- Each house of Congress chooses its own leadership and determines its own rules

ELECTION TO CONGRESS

Getting Elected to the House of Representatives

The Constitution guarantees each state at least one representative. Members are chosen from districts within each state. Some practices related to determining congressional representation are:

- *apportionment*—distribution among the states based on the population of each of the states
- *reapportionment*—the redistribution of Congressional seats after the census determines changes in population distribution among the states
- *congressional districting*—the drawing by state legislatures of congressional districts for those states with more than one representative
- *gerrymandering*—drawing congressional districts to favor one political party or group over another

Getting Elected to the Senate

The Constitution guarantees that "no state, without its consent, shall be deprived of its equal suffrage in the Senate." (Article V)

- Members were originally chosen by the state legislatures in each state.
- Since 1913, the Seventeenth Amendment allows for the direct election of senators by the people of the state.

Incumbency Effect

The **incumbency effect** is the tendency of those already holding office to win reelection. The effect tends to be stronger for members of the House of Representatives and weaker for the Senate. Advantages may include:

- *name recognition*—Voters are more likely to recognize the officeholder than the challenger.
- *credit claiming*—The officeholder may have brought government projects and money into the state or district
- *casework for constituents*—Officeholders may have helped constituents solve problems involving government and the bureaucracy

- *more visible to constituents*—Members can use the "perks" of the office to communicate with constituents. Franking, the privilege of sending official mail using the incumbent's signature as postage, provides communication with constituents.
- *media exposure*—Incumbents are more likely to gain "free" publicity during a campaign through the media.
- *fundraising abilities*—It is generally greater for incumbents
- *experience in campaigning*—Incumbents have already experienced the campaign process.
- *voting record*—Voters can evaluate their performance based on their record.

Term Limits

Although several states have passed legislation establishing term limits for members of Congress, the Supreme Court has ruled that neither the states nor Congress may impose term limits without a constitutional amendment. Therefore, today, there are no limitations on the number of terms a member of Congress may serve.

! LEADERSHIP OF CONGRESS

The majority political party in each house controls the leadership positions of Congress.

House of Representatives

- **Speaker of the House** is the presiding officer and most powerful member of the House. Major duties include assigning bills to committee, controlling floor debate, and appointing party members to committees.
- Majority and Minority **Floor Leaders**
  — The **Majority Floor Leader** serves as the major assistant to the speaker, helps plan party's legislative program and directs floor debate
  — The Minority Floor Leader is the major spokesperson for the minority party and organizes opposition to the majority party.
- Whips help floor leaders by directing party members in voting, informing members of impending voting, keeping track of vote counts, and pressuring members to vote with the party.

Senate

- The U.S. vice president, although not a Senate member, is the presiding officer of the Senate, according to the Constitution. The vice president may not debate and only votes to break a tie.

- The **president pro tempore** is a senior member of the majority party chosen to preside in the absence of the Senate president. It is a mostly ceremonial position lacking real power.
- majority and minority **floor leaders**
  —The majority floor leader is the most influential member of the Senate and often the majority party spokesperson.
  —The minority floor leader performs the same role as the House minority leader.
- Whips serve the same role as whips in the House of Representatives.

COMMITTEE SYSTEM

Most of the work of Congress is accomplished through committees. Committees permit Congress to divide the work among members, thus allowing for the study of legislation by specialists and helping speed up the passage of legislation.

Leadership of Committees

Committee chairpersons are members of the majority party in each house chosen by party caucus. They set agendas, assign members to subcommittees, and decide whether the committee will hold public hearings and which witnesses to call. They manage floor debate of the bill when it is presented to the full House or Senate. Traditionally chairpersons were chosen based on the **seniority system,** with the majority party member having the longest length of committee service chosen as chairperson. Today, reforms allow for the selection of chairpersons who are not the most senior majority-party member on the committee. However most chosen are long-standing members of the committee.

Membership on Committees

The percentage of each committee's membership reflects the overall percentage of Democrats and Republicans in each house. Members try to serve on committees where they can influence public policy relating to their district or state (for example, a Kansas senator on the agriculture committee) or influence national public policy issues (an Iowa representative on the foreign relations committee).

Types of Committees

- A **standing** committee is a permanent committee that deals with specific policy matters (agriculture, energy and natural resources, veterans affairs).

- A **select** committee is a temporary committee appointed for a specific purpose. Most are formed to investigate a particular issue, such as the Senate Watergate Committee.
- A **joint** committee is made up of members of both houses of Congress. It may be a select committee (Iran-Contra Committee) or perform routine duties (Joint Committee on the Library of Congress).
- A **conference** committee is a temporary committee of members from both houses of Congress, created to resolve the differences in House and Senate versions of a bill. It is a compromise committee.

Caucuses

Caucuses are informal groups formed by members of Congress who share a common purpose or set of goals (Congressional Black Caucus, Women's Caucus, Democratic or Republican Caucus).

CONGRESSIONAL STAFF AND SUPPORT

- Personal staff work directly for members of Congress in Washington, D.C., and their district offices in their home states.
- Committee staff work for committees and subcommittees in Congress, researching problems and analyzing information.
- Support agencies provide services to members of Congress (Library of Congress, Government Printing Office).

ROLES OF MEMBERS OF CONGRESS

Members of Congress have several roles.

- policymaker—make public policy through the passage of legislation
- representative—represent constituents
  - delegate—members vote based on the wishes of constituents, regardless of their own opinions
  - **trustee**—after listening to constituents, members vote based on their own opinions
- **constituent servant**—help constituents with problems
- committee member—serve on committees
- politician/party member—work to support their political party platform and get reelected

POWERS OF CONGRESS

Congress has legislative and non-legislative powers.

Legislative powers—power to make laws

- *expressed powers*—powers specifically granted to Congress, mostly found in Article I, Section 8 of the Constitution
- *implied powers*—powers which may be reasonably suggested to carry out the expressed powers; found in Article I, Section 8, Clause 18; "necessary and proper" or elastic clause; allows for the expansion of Congress' powers (expressed power to raise armies and navy implies the power to draft men into the military)
- *limitations on powers*—powers denied Congress by Article I, Section 9 and the Tenth Amendment

Nonlegislative powers—duties other than lawmaking

- *electoral powers*—selection of president by the House of Representatives and/or vice president by the Senate upon the failure of the electoral college to achieve a majority vote
- *amendment powers*—Congress may propose amendments by a two-thirds vote of each house or by calling a national convention to propose amendments if requested by two-thirds of the state legislatures
- *impeachment*—House may bring charges, or impeach, the president, vice president or any civil officer; case is tried in the Senate with the Senate acting as the jury (Andrew Johnson and Bill Clinton were both impeached by the House but not convicted by the Senate)
- *executive powers of Senate*—Senate shares the appointment and treaty-making powers with the executive branch; Senate must approve appointments by majority vote and treaties by two-thirds vote
- *investigative/oversight powers*—investigate matters falling within the range of its legislative authority; often involves the review of policies and programs of the executive branch

! THE LAWMAKING PROCESS

Policymaking: How a Bill Becomes a Law

Bills, or proposed laws, may begin in either house, except revenue bills, which must begin in the House of Representatives.

HOUSE OF REPRESENTATIVES	SENATE
A bill is introduced, numbered, and assigned to a committee.	A bill is introduced, numbered, and assigned to a committee.
The bill may be assigned to a subcommittee for further study.	The bill may be assigned to a subcommittee for further study.
The bill is returned to committee, where it is approved or rejected.	The bill is returned to committee where it is approved or rejected.

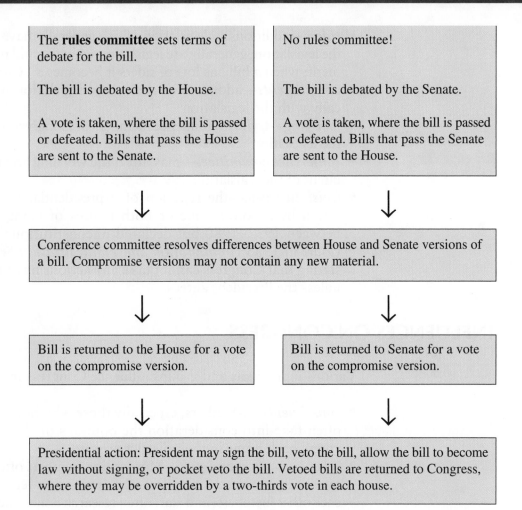

Figure 11–2 How a Bill Becomes a Law.

LEGISLATIVE TACTICS

Legislative tactics are the strategies and devices used by Congress and others in an attempt to block legislation or to get legislation passed.

- *caucuses*—may form voting blocs
- *committee system*—plays a major role in the passage of legislation; bills may die if committees fail to act upon them or reject them
- *filibuster and cloture*—in the Senate only, unlimited debate in an attempt to stall action on a bill; cloture is the method of limiting a filibuster through petition and vote
- *pork barrel legislation*—an attempt to provide funds and projects for a member's home district or state
- *logrolling*—an attempt by members to gain the support of other members in return for their support on the member's legislation; "I'll support your bill, if you will support mine."

- *riders*—additions to legislation which generally have no connection to the legislation; generally are legislation which would not pass on its own merit; when a bill has lots of riders it becomes a "Christmas tree bill"
- *amendments*—additions or changes to legislation which deal specifically with the legislation
- *lobbying*—trying to influence members of Congress to support or reject the legislation
- *conference committees*—may affect the wording and therefore the final intent of the legislation
- *legislative veto*—the rejection of a presidential or executive branch action by a vote of one or both houses of Congress, used mostly between 1932–1980 but declared unconstitutional by the Supreme Court in 1983 (*Immigration and Naturalization Service v. Chadha*) stating that Congress cannot take any actions having the force of law unless the President agrees.

INFLUENCES ON CONGRESS

Various individuals and groups influence Congress members.

- *constituents*—Members, especially those who hope to win reelection, often take into consideration the opinions of their constituents and voters back home in their district or state.
- *other lawmakers and staff*—More senior members often influence newer members; committee members who worked on legislation often influence other members; and staff often research issues and advise members.
- *party influences*—Each party's platform takes a stand on major issues, and loyal members often adhere to the "party line." Members in the House are more likely to support the party position than are Senators.
- *president*—Presidents often lobby members to support legislation through phone calls, invitations to the White House, or even appeals to the public to gain support from voters to bring pressure on members.
- *lobbyists and interest groups*—often provide members with information on topics relating to their group's interest or possible financial support in future campaigns.

✓ REVIEW QUESTIONS

1. After a national census has been taken, changes in population distribution cause the changing of Congressional seats among the states. This effect is commonly called

   A. congressional districting
   B. apportionment
   C. gerrymandering
   D. reapportionment
   E. census apportionment

2. Which of the following is not true of the Congress?

   A. Each house determines its own leadership and rules.
   B. Terms of Congress last for two years.

C. Congress is unicameral in nature.
D. Only the president may call special sessions of Congress.
E. A session of Congress begins on January 3 of odd-numbered years.

3. Which of the following is true about the officers of the House of Representatives?

A. It is the responsibility of the party whip to keep track of vote counts and pressure members to vote with the party.
B. The presiding officer is the majority floor leader.
C. Minority floor leaders direct floor debates.
D. The major duty of the majority floor leader is to assign bills to committee.
E. The whip serves as the major assistant to the speaker in determining the party's legislative program.

4. Temporary committees appointed for the specific purpose of investigating a particular issue are called

A. joint committees
B. select committees
C. standing committees
D. investigating committees
E. compromise committees

5. Members of Congress wear many hats in the performance of their duties. Which of the following does not apply?

A. Members of Congress act as policy-makers and make public policy through the passage of legislation.
B. Members of Congress are constituent servants.
C. Members of Congress work to support their political party platform.
D. After listening to constituents, members vote based on the opinions of those constituents, that is

they become the trustee of the constituent.
E. Members of Congress serve on committees.

6. Congress has both legislative and non-legislative powers. Which of the following best describes a non-legislative power of Congress?

A. power to declare war
B. power to tax
C. impeachment power
D. power to regulate commerce
E. power to make all laws which are necessary and proper

7. Bills are proposed laws that must complete several steps in the houses of Congress in order to become formal laws. Which of the following would not be a step that a proposed bill would encounter on its journey through Congress?

A. The bill is debated.
B. The bill is voted on, at which time it may pass or be defeated.
C. The bill may be assigned to a subcommittee.
D. The bill is numbered.
E. The bill is introduced by a member of the Congress or by a member of the executive department.

8. After receiving a bill the president may

I. sign the bill
II. veto the bill
III. return the bill to Congress for clarification on some point within the bill
IV. allow the Congress to pocket veto the bill, thereby allowing the bill to become law without his signature

A. I only
B. II only
C. I and II only
D. I, II, III only
E. I, II, III, and IV

9. Legislative tactics are used by members of both houses of Congress to get legislation passed that would be favorable to those members and their respective parties. Which legislative tactic is most effectively used only in the Senate?

A. filibustering
B. logrolling
C. caucuses
D. riders
E. pork barrel legislation

10. Which of the following is not considered to be a contributing factor to the incumbency effect?

A. name recognition
B. voting record
C. relationship with the executive
D. experience in campaigning
E. visibility to constituents

ANSWERS AND EXPLANATIONS

1. **D.** Reapportionment is the changing of the number of Congressional seats per state based on state population changes.

2. **C.** Congress is a bicameral legislature, composed of the House of Representatives and the Senate.

3. **A.** The minority and majority whips are responsible for keeping track of vote counts and pressuring members to support the party vote.

4. **B.** Select committees are temporary committees responsible for investigating specific issues.

5. **D.** Members of Congress who vote according to constituent wishes are delegates of the constituents.

6. **C.** The impeachment power of Congress is a non-legislative power, having nothing to do with the passage of legislation.

7. **E.** While bills may be suggested by members of the executive branch, they may only be introduced by members of Congress.

8. **C.** The president does not return bills to Congress for clarification nor does Congress have the power of pocket veto.

9. **A.** Filibustering is a stalling tactic used only in the Senate. Logrolling, caucuses, riders, and pork barrel legislation are used in both houses of Congress.

10. **C.** Name recognition, voting record, experience in campaigning, and visibility to constituents are contributing factors to the incumbency effect. The candidate's relationship with the executive is not a contributing factor.

RAPID REVIEW

- Congress is bicameral in nature.
- Members of the House of Representatives are chosen from districts within a state. The number of representatives per state is based on state population.

- Members of the Senate are elected from the state. States are equally represented, with two Senators from each state.

- Reelection to Congress is often a consequence of the incumbency effect. Several factors may contribute to the incumbency effect.

- There are no term limits in Congress.

- Leaders of the House of Representatives include the speaker of the House, the floor leaders, and the whips. Leaders of the Senate include the president of the Senate (Vice President), the president pro tempore, the floor leaders, and the whips.

- Most of the legislative work of Congress is accomplished through committees. Membership on committees is based on party strength. Types of committees include: standing, joint, select, and conference committees.

- Personal staff, committee staff, and support agencies aid members of Congress and the committees.

- Congressmen serve in many roles.

- Congress has both legislative and nonlegislative powers. Legislative powers include expressed, implied, and denied powers. Nonlegislative powers include electoral powers, amendment powers, impeachment powers, executive powers of the Senate, and **oversight** powers.

- Congress has a specific process for how a bill becomes a law.

- Legislative tactics are used in the process of passing, stopping, or slowing legislation.

- Constituents, other lawmakers, party influences, the president, lobbyists, and interest groups influence members of Congress.

Chapter 12

Review: Executive Branch and the Bureaucracy

 The office of the president is the most important single position in the government of the United States. The president of the United States has many responsibilities and functions originating in Article II of the Constitution. From the time of George Washington to the present, holders of the office of the president have striven to be more than just a ceremonial head of state. The American president is not just a figurehead but also a personality who commands power and respect.

CONSTITUTIONAL ORIGINS OF PRESIDENCY

Delegates to the constitutional convention studied the writings of philosophers Montesquieu and Locke, analyzed the powers of the British monarchs, and studied the role of governors in the American colonial governments. The delegates decided they did not want a king; they wanted power to rest with the people. Debate arose over a single versus a plural executive, and a weak executive appointed by Congress versus a strong executive independent of the legislature. The final compromise created a single executive with powers limited by the checks and balances of the legislative and judicial branches.

Qualifications

Article II of the Constitution establishes the formal qualifications of the president:

- natural-born citizen
- at least 35 years of age
- resident of U.S. 14 years prior to election

Informally, many candidates who have run for the office of the president have also shared several characteristics:

- political or military experience
- political acceptability
- married
- white male
- protestant
- northern European ancestry

Term and Tenure

The concept of a popularly elected president is an American invention. After much debate and compromise, the founding fathers created a single executive, elected indirectly through an electoral college for a four-year term. Until the addition of the 22nd Amendment in 1951, the number of terms of the president was unlimited. After Franklin D. Roosevelt won the office an unprecedented four times, the 22nd Amendment was added, limiting the president to two elected terms.

! Succession and Disability

The Constitution provides that if the president can no longer serve in office, the vice president will carry out the powers and duties of the office. The Constitution does not state that the vice president shall actually become president; that tradition began with the death of W. H. Harrison. After the assassination of John F. Kennedy, the 25th amendment was added to the Constitution, stating that the vice president becomes president if the office of president becomes vacant. That amendment also provides for the new president to nominate a new vice president, with the approval of a majority of both houses of Congress. The first use of the 25th Amendment occurred when Spiro Agnew resigned the vice presidency and was replaced by Gerald Ford in 1973. The following year it was used again when President Richard Nixon resigned; Vice President Gerald Ford became president; and Ford nominated, and Congress confirmed, Nelson Rockefeller as his new vice president.

The 25th Amendment also provides for presidential disability. If the president is unable to perform the duties of his office, the vice president may become "acting president" under one of the following conditions:

- The president informs Congress of the inability to perform the duties of president
- The vice president and a majority of the cabinet inform Congress, in writing, that the president is disabled and unable to perform those duties

The president may resume the duties of office upon informing Congress that no disability exists. If the vice president and a majority of the cabinet disagree, Congress has 21 days to decide the issue of presidential disability by a two-thirds vote of both houses.

! Impeachment and Removal

The Constitution allows for the removal of a president from office through the impeachment process. **Impeachment** involves bringing charges of wrongdoing against a government official. The United States Constitution gives the House of Representatives the authority to impeach the president or vice president for "Treason, Bribery or other High Crimes and Misdemeanors." Once charges of impeachment have been levied against the president or vice president, the Senate then sits in judgment of the charges. The chief justice of the Supreme Court presides over the trial. If found guilty of the charges, the official may be removed from office. Conviction requires a two-thirds vote of the Senate.

THE ROAD TO THE WHITE HOUSE

There are two basic methods of becoming president: succeed to the office or win election to the office. Most presidents have been elected to the office. Many nominees seeking the office have gained political experience through elected or appointed offices—in Congress (mostly the Senate), as state governors, as vice president, or as a cabinet member. Several nominees gained recognition as military leaders.

! Electoral College System

According to the Constitution and the 12th Amendment, an **electoral college** elects the president and vice president. Each state chooses a number of electors equal to its number of members in the House of Representatives and Senate in a method set by the state legislatures. In the general election, voters go to the polls and vote for the candidates of their choice. In December, the electors of the respective candidates meet in each state capital to cast ballots for president and vice president. The electoral college then sends the ballots to the president of the Senate, where they are opened before a joint session of Congress and counted. To win the election, a candidate must receive a majority of electoral votes (270). If no candidate for president receives a majority of electoral votes, the House of Representatives chooses the president from among the top three candidates. If no candidate for vice president receives a majority of electoral votes, the Senate chooses the vice president from the top two candidates.

THE VICE PRESIDENCY

During much of American history, the office of the vice president has been seen as one to be avoided by ambitious politicians. Constitutionally, the vice president has two duties:

- preside over the Senate, casting tie-breaking votes if necessary
- help determine presidential disability under the 25th Amendment and take over the presidency if necessary

Since the vice president may some day become president, the formal qualifications for vice president are the same as those for the president. The vice president serves a four-year term; however, the number of terms a vice president may serve is not limited. The selection of the nominee for vice president occurs at the national convention when the presidential nominee selects a "running mate." Often the choice of nominee is influenced by the party's desire to balance the ticket, that is, to improve a candidate's chances of winning the election by choosing someone from a different faction of the party or from a different geographic section of the country. With the assassination of Kennedy and attempts on the lives of Ford and Reagan, more attention has focused on the vice president. Today, the vice president is often given a larger role in government, taking part in cabinet meetings, serving on the National Security Council, and acting as the president's representative on diplomatic missions. More consideration is also given to the background, health, and other qualifications of vice presidents.

PRESIDENTIAL POWERS

Article II of the Constitution outlines the powers of the president. The checks and balances of the other branches of government limit them. The power of the modern presidency comes from the men who have held the office and have shaped the use of these powers. Historians have often rated presidents as strong or weak. After the 1960s and 1970s, Arthur Schlesinger, Jr., argued that the presidency had become so powerful that an "imperial presidency" existed, applying the term to Richard Nixon and his administration in particular. Richard Neustadt contended that the president's powers lie in the ability to persuade others through negotiation, influence, and compromise.

Presidential powers can be categorized as executive, legislative, diplomatic, military, judicial, and party powers.

Executive Powers

- enforces laws, treaties, and court decisions
- issues executive orders to carry out policies

- appoints officials, removes officials
- assumes emergency powers
- presides over cabinet and executive branch

Legislative Powers

- gives annual State of the Union message (constitutionally required) identifying problems, recommending policies, and submitting specific proposals (president's legislative agenda). Expectations are that the president will propose a comprehensive legislative program to deal with national problems (the Budget and Accounting Act of 1921 requires president to prepare and propose federal budget).
- issues annual budget and economic reports
- signs or vetoes bills
- proposes legislation and uses influence to get it passed
- calls for special sessions of Congress

Diplomatic Powers

- appoints ambassadors and other diplomats
- negotiates treaties and **executive agreements**
- meets with foreign leaders in international conferences
- accords diplomatic recognition to foreign governments
- receives foreign dignitaries

Military Powers

- serves as commander in chief of the armed forces
- has final decision-making authority in matters of national and foreign defense
- provides for domestic order

Judicial Powers

- appoints members of the federal judiciary
- grants reprieves, **pardons,** and amnesty

Party Powers

- Is the recognized leader of the party
- chooses vice presidential nominee
- strengthens the party by helping members get elected (coattails)
- appoints party members to government positions (patronage)
- influences policies and platform of party

LIMITATIONS ON PRESIDENTIAL POWERS

In order to avoid the possibility of abuses by the executive, the founding fathers provided for checks upon the powers of the executive.

- Congressional checks
  - override presidential vetoes—requires a two-thirds vote of both houses of Congress
  - power of the purse Agency budgets must be authorized and appropriated by Congress. In 1974 Congress passed the Congressional Budget and **Impoundment** Control Act, which denied the president the right to refuse to spend money appropriated by Congress and gave Congress a greater role in the budget process.
  - power of impeachment
  - approval powers over appointments
  - legislation that limits the president's powers (for example, the **War Powers Act** limited the president's ability to use military force)
  - **Legislative vetoes** to reject the actions of the president or executive agency by a vote of one or both houses of Congress without the consent of the president; declared unconstitutional by the Supreme Court in 1983
- judicial checks
  - judicial review of executive actions
- political checks
  - public opinion
  - media attention
  - popularity

PRESIDENTIAL CHARACTER

Political scientist James David Barber examined the importance of a president's personality and character, classifying presidents into four distinct types based upon their childhood and other experiences. Barber measured each president's assertiveness in office as active or passive, and how positive or negative his feelings were about the office itself. His classifications were:

- *active-positive*—takes pleasure in the work of the office, easily adjusts to new situations and is confident in himself (FDR, Truman, Kennedy, Ford, Carter, Bush)
- *active-negative*—hard worker but doesn't enjoy the work, insecure in the position, may be obsessive or antagonistic (Wilson, Hoover, LBJ, Nixon)
- *passive-positive*—easygoing, wanting agreement from others with no dissent, may be overly confident (Taft, Harding, Reagan)
- *passive-negative*—dislikes politics and tends to withdraw from close relationships (Coolidge, Eisenhower)

THE BUREAUCRACY

A **bureaucracy** is a systematic way of organizing a complex and large administrative structure. The bureaucracy is responsible for carrying out the day-to-day tasks of the organization. The bureaucracy of the federal government is the single largest in the United States, with 2.8 million employees. Bureaucracies generally follow three basic principles:

- hierarchical authority—similar to a pyramid with those at the top having authority over those below
- job specialization—each worker has defined duties and responsibilities, a division of labor among workers
- formal rules—established regulations and procedures which must be followed

History and Growth

- beginnings—standards for office included qualifications and political acceptability
- spoils system—practice of giving offices and government favors to political supporters and friends
- reform movement—competitive exams were tried but failed due to inadequate funding from Congress
- Pendleton Act—Civil Service Act of 1883, passed after the assassination of Garfield by a disappointed office-seeker; replaced the spoils system with a merit system as the basis for hiring and promotion
- **Hatch Act** of 1939, amended in 1993—prohibits government employees from engaging in political activities while on duty, running for office or seeking political funding while off duty, or if in sensitive positions, may not be involved with political activities on or off duty
- Civil Service Reform Act of 1978—created the office of Personnel Management (replaced the Civil Service Commission) to recruit, train and establish classifications and salaries for federal employees

Organization

The federal bureaucracy is generally divided into four basic types:

- *cabinet departments*—15 executive departments created to advise the president and operate a specific policy area of governmental activity; each department is headed by a secretary, except the Department of Justice, which is headed by the Attorney General (Department of State, Department of Labor, Department of the Interior)
- *independent executive agencies*—similar to departments but without cabinet status (NASA, Small Business Administration)

- *independent regulatory agencies*—independent from the executive; created to regulate or police (Securities and Exchange Commission, Nuclear Regulatory Commission, Federal Reserve Board)
- *government corporations*—created by Congress to carry out business-like activities; generally charge for services (Tennessee Valley Authority, National Railroad Passenger Corporation [AMTRAK], United States Postal Service)

Influences on the Federal Bureaucracy

- *executive influences*—appointing the right people, issuing executive orders, affecting the agency's budget, reorganization of the agency
- *Congressional influences*—influencing appointments, affecting the agency's budget, holding hearings, rewriting legislation or making legislation more detailed
- **iron triangles (sub-governments)**—iron triangles are alliances that develop between bureaucratic agencies, interest groups, and congressional committees or subcommittees. Because of a common goal, these alliances may work to help each other achieve their goals, with Congress and the president often deferring to their influence.
- **issue networks**—individuals in Washington—located within interest groups, Congressional staff, think tanks, universities, and the media—who regularly discuss and advocate public policies. Unlike iron triangles, issue networks continually form and disband according to the policy issues.

EXECUTIVE OFFICE OF THE PRESIDENT (EOP)

The Executive Office of the President includes the closest advisors to the president. Although it was established in 1939, every president has reorganized the EOP according to style of leadership. Within the executive office are several separate agencies.

- White House Office—personal and political staff members who help with the day-to-day management of the executive branch; includes the chief of staff, counsel to the president, press secretary
- National Security Council—established by the National Security Act of 1947; advises the president on matters of domestic and foreign national security
- Office of Management and Budget—helps the president prepare the annual federal budget
- Office of Faith-Based and Community Initiatives—created by George W. Bush to encourage and expand private efforts to deal with social problems
- Office of National Drug Control Policy—advisory and planning agency to combat the nation's drug problems

- Office of Policy Development—gives president domestic policy advice
- Council of Economic Advisors—informs president about economic developments and problems
- Office of U.S. Trade Representative—advises president about foreign trade and helps negotiate foreign trade agreements

EXECUTIVE DEPARTMENTS

- State (1789)—advises President on foreign policy, negotiates treaties, represents U.S. in international organizations
- Treasury (1789)—collects federal revenues, pays federal bills, mints coins and prints paper money, enforces Alcohol, Tobacco and Firearm laws
- Defense (1789)—formed from the Department of War and the Department of the Navy (1789) but changed to the Department of Defense in 1947; manages the armed forces, operates military bases
- Interior (1849)—manages federal lands, refuges, and parks, operates hydroelectric facilities, manages Native American affairs
- Justice (1870)—provides legal advice to the president, enforces federal laws, represents the U.S. in court, operates federal prisons
- Agriculture (1889)—provides agricultural assistance to farmers and ranchers, inspects food, manages national forests
- Commerce (1903)—grants patents and trademarks, conducts the national census, promotes international trade
- Labor (1913)—enforces federal labor laws (child labor, minimum wage, safe working conditions), administers unemployment and job training programs
- Health and Human Services (1953)—administers Social Security and Medicare/Medicaid Programs, promotes health care research, enforces pure food and drug laws
- Housing and Urban Development (1965)—provides home financing and public housing programs, enforces fair housing laws
- Transportation (1967)—promotes mass transit programs and programs for highways, railroads, and air traffic, enforces maritime law
- Energy (1977)—promotes development and conservation of fossil fuels, nuclear energy, research programs
- Education (1979)—administers federal aid programs to schools, engages in educational research
- Veterans Affairs (1989)—promotes the welfare of veterans of the armed forces
- Homeland Security (2002)—prevents terrorist attacks within the United States, reduces America's susceptibility to terrorism, minimizes damage and helps recovery from attacks that do occur; includes Coast Guard, Secret Service, Border Patrol, Immigration and Visa Services, and Federal Emergency Management Agency (FEMA)

✓ REVIEW QUESTIONS

1. The office of the president of the United States can best be described as an office

   A. of great responsibility and function
   B. created as a mere ceremonial head of state
   C. full of conflict and by nature difficult to understand
   D. dominated by the power and experience of the person holding it
   E. dedicated to the service of the government beyond the will of the people

2. Which of the following amendments provides for presidential succession and disability?

   A. 22nd
   B. 20th
   C. 25th
   D. 23rd
   E. 27th

3. When the founding fathers finally decided on the length of the presidential term of office, they established a term

   A. of 8 years
   B. of 4 years
   C. not to exceed 10 years
   D. that could not be renewed after 4 years
   E. that could extend indefinitely if reviewed by Congress

4. Which of the following is a constitutional qualification for being president?

   I.   must be at least 35 years old
   II. must be a natural born citizen
   III. must have lived in the United States for at least 14 years
   IV. must be a naturalized citizen within the first five years of birth

   A. I and II only
   B. II and III only
   C. II, III, and IV only
   D. I, II, III only
   E. I, II, III, IV

5. If the president becomes disabled and cannot perform his duties, how may the vice president take over the office of the president?

   I.   The president may write a letter to the leaders of Congress stating lack of ability to perform the duties of office.
   II. Congress removes the president.
   III. The vice president and a majority of the Cabinet may remove the president.

   A. I only
   B. II only
   C. I and II only
   D. II and III only
   E. I and III only

6. Which of the following is not considered to be a part of the Executive Office of the President?

   A. National Security Office
   B. White House Office
   C. Office of Management and Budget
   D. Office of Emergency Preparedness
   E. Office of Economic Opportunity

7. Members of the president's Cabinet are usually individuals of great ability but little or no political power. Which of the following best describes this statement?

   A. The Senate must approve all appointments made by the president.
   B. Cabinet members must be able to effectively run a department of government and advise the president.

C. Cabinet members serve as long as the president remains in office.

D. Cabinet members serve as an informal advisory body.

E. Only the president may appoint and remove members of the cabinet.

8. Which of the following was not an original cabinet position?

A. secretary of state
B. secretary of war
C. attorney general
D. secretary of interior
E. secretary of treasury

9. Which of the following powers is used by the president for the purpose of enforcing federal law?

A. general administrative power
B. veto power
C. executive agreements
D. patronage
E. judicial power

10. The party power of the president is most recognizable in the fact that the president:

A. is an elected leader
B. checks the power of the party controlling Congress
C. is the head of a political party
D. alone must write the party platform
E. appoints all party members

ANSWERS AND EXPLANATIONS

1. **A.** The presidency is the most important single office in the United States, and the powers of the president extend beyond just ceremonial duties.

2. **C.** The 25th Amendment provides for succession and disability.

3. **B.** The term of office for the president is 4 years.

4. **D.** There are three formal qualifications for president outlined in the Constitution: at least 35 years of age, a natural born citizen, and lived in the U.S. at least 14 years.

5. **E.** Either the president may inform Congress of the inability to perform the duties of office, or the vice president and a majority of the cabinet may inform Congress of the president's inability to perform the duties.

6. **A.** There is no National Security Office in the Executive Office of the President.

7. **B.** Cabinet members must have the ability to run a cabinet level department.

8. **D.** The Secretary of the Interior was not added to the cabinet until 1849.

9. **A.** The president uses administrative powers to enforce federal laws.

10. **C.** The president serves as political party leader.

RAPID REVIEW

- Article II of the Constitution establishes the office of the president and outlines the powers and duties of the office.

- The presidency was a compromise creating a single executive with limited powers.

- There are both formal and informal qualifications for the president.

- The 25th Amendment provides for the succession and disability of the president.

- The House of Representatives impeaches and the Senate tries cases of impeachment of the president. Only two presidents have been impeached, and none has been removed from office.

- To become president one must succeed to the office or win election to the office.

- The electoral college is an indirect method of electing the president.

- The constitutional duties of the vice president include presiding over the Senate and determining presidential disability.

- Presidents have numerous powers: executive, legislative, diplomatic, military, judicial, and party.

- The powers of the president may be limited by Congressional, judicial, and political checks.

- James David Barber described presidential personality and character by classifying president as one of four distinct types: active-positive, passive-positive, active-negative and passive-negative.

- The bureaucracy is a systematic way of organizing government.

- The development of the current bureaucracy has undergone several changes and reforms.

- The organization of the bureaucracy may be divided into four major types: cabinet departments, independent executive agencies, independent regulatory agencies, and government corporations.

- The executive, Congress, iron triangles, and issue networks may influence the federal bureaucracy.

- There are currently 15 executive departments in the executive branch of government.

Chapter 13

Review:
The National Judiciary

2 THE FEDERAL COURT SYSTEM

The United States has a dual system of courts—a federal court system and the court systems of each of the 50 states. Under the Articles of Confederation, there was no national court system. State courts had the sole power to interpret and apply laws. This weakness led to Article III of the Constitution, which states that there shall be one Supreme Court and that Congress may establish a system of inferior courts.

Jurisdiction

Jurisdiction is the authority of the courts to hear certain cases. Under the Constitution, federal courts have jurisdiction in cases involving federal law, treaties, and the interpretation of the Constitution.

- **original jurisdiction**—Lower courts have the authority to hear cases for the first time; in the federal system district courts and the Supreme Court (in a limited number of cases) have original jurisdiction where trials are conducted, evidence is presented, and juries determine the outcome of the case.
- **appellate jurisdiction**—courts that hear reviews or appeals of decisions from the lower courts; Courts of Appeals and the Supreme Court have appellate jurisdiction
- **concurrent jurisdiction**—allows certain types of cases to be tried in either the federal or state courts

STRUCTURE OF THE JUDICIAL SYSTEM

The federal judicial system consists of constitutional courts and legislative courts. **Constitutional courts** are the federal courts created by Congress under Article III of the Constitution and the Supreme Court. Also included are the **district courts, Courts of Appeals,** Court of Appeals for the Federal Circuit, and the U.S. Court of International Trade. Congress has created special or **legislative courts** (Territorial Courts, U.S. Tax Court, U.S. Court of Appeals for the Armed Forces) to hear cases arising from the powers given to Congress under Article I. These legislative courts have a narrower range of authority than the constitutional courts.

District Courts

Congress, under the Judiciary Act of 1789, created the **district courts** to serve as trial courts at the federal level. Every state has at least one district court; larger states may have several, with Washington D.C., and Puerto Rico each having one court. There are currently 94 districts. The district courts have original jurisdiction; they do not hear appeals. District courts decide civil and criminal cases arising under the Constitution and federal laws or treaties. More than 80% of all federal cases are heard in the district courts

Courts of Appeals

Congress created the **Courts of Appeals** in 1891 to help lessen the work load of the Supreme Court. The Courts of Appeals decide appeals from United States district courts and review decisions of federal administrative agencies. There are 13 United States Courts of Appeals. The states are divided into circuits, or geographic judicial districts. There is also a circuit for Washington, D.C., and a Federal Circuit, which hears cases involving federal agencies. The Courts of Appeals have appellate jurisdiction only; they may only review cases already decided by a lower court. A panel of judges decides cases in the Courts of Appeals.

Supreme Court

The only court actually created directly by the Constitution is the Supreme Court. It is the highest court in the federal judicial system. It is the final authority in dealing with all questions arising from the Constitution, federal laws, and treaties. The Supreme Court has both original and appellate jurisdiction. Most of the cases heard in the Supreme Court are on appeal from the district and appellate courts of the federal judicial system, however, cases may come to the Supreme Court from state Supreme Courts, if a federal law or the constitution is involved. The United States

Supreme Court may also hear cases of original jurisdiction if the cases involve representatives of a foreign government, or certain types of cases where a state is a party.

The decisions of the Supreme Court may have a strong impact on social, economic, and political forces in our society. Congress establishes the size of the Supreme Court, having the power to change the number of justices. The current size of the Supreme Court was set in 1869. Today, the Supreme Court consists of nine judges—eight associate justices and one chief justice. They are all nominated by the president and confirmed by the Senate.

JUDICIAL SELECTION

The president appoints federal judges with confirmation by the Senate. Under the Constitution, there are no formal qualifications for federal judges. Federal judges serve "during good behavior," which generally means for life. The notion of the life term was to allow judges to be free from political pressures when deciding cases. Federal judges may be removed from office through impeachment and conviction.

Lower Courts

Because of the large number of appointments made to the lower courts, the Department of Justice and White House staff handle most of these nominations. **Senatorial courtesy,** the practice of allowing individual senators from the president's party who represent the state where the district is located to approve or disapprove potential nominees, has traditionally been used to make appointments to the District Courts. Because the circuits for the **Courts of Appeals** cover several states, individual senators have less influence and senatorial courtesy does not play a role in the nomination process. The Senate tends to scrutinize appeals court judges more closely, since they are more likely to interpret the law and set precedent.

Supreme Court

The higher visibility and importance of the Supreme Court demands that the president give greater attention to the nomination of Supreme Court justices. Presidents only make appointments to the Supreme Court if a vacancy occurs during their term of office. When making appointments, presidents often consider:

- party affiliation—choosing judges from their own political party
- judicial philosophy—appointing judges who share their political ideology
- race, gender, religion, region—considering these criteria may help bring balance to the court or satisfy certain segments of society

- judicial experience—previous judicial experience as judges in district courts, courts of appeals, state courts
- "litmus test"—a test of ideological purity toward a liberal or conservative stand on certain issues such as abortion
- acceptability—noncontroversial and therefore acceptable to members of the Senate Judiciary Committee and the Senate
    — American Bar Association—the largest national organization of attorneys, often consulted by Presidents, rates nominees' qualifications
    — Interest Groups—may support or oppose a nominee based on their position on issues of importance to the interest group; use lobbyists to pressure Senators
    — Justices—endorsements from members of the Supreme Court may help a nominee (O'Connor received strong support from Rehnquist)

Background of Judges

Almost all federal judges have had some form of legal training, have held positions in government, or have served as lawyers for leading law firms, as federal district attorneys or as law school professors. Some federal judges have served as state court judges. Until recently, few African-Americans, Hispanics, or women were appointed as judges to the lower federal courts. Lyndon Johnson appointed the first African-American, Thurgood Marshall, to the Supreme Court; Ronald Reagan appointed the first female, Sandra Day O'Connor.

THE COURT AT WORK

The term of the Supreme Court begins on the first Monday in October and generally lasts until June or July of the following year.

Accepting Cases

Thousands of cases are appealed to the Supreme Court every year; only a few hundred cases are actually heard. Most of the cases are denied because the justices either agree with the lower court decision or believe that the cases does not involve a significant point of law. Cases that are accepted for review must pass the **rule of four**—four of the nine justices must agree to hear the case. Many of the cases accepted may be disposed of in **brief orders**—returned to the lower court for reconsideration because of a related case which was recently decided. Those cases presented to the Supreme Court for possible review may be presented through:

- **writ of certiorari**—an order by the court (when petitioned) directing a lower court to send up the records of a case for review; usually requires the need to interpret law or decide a constitutional question
- **certificate**—a lower court may ask the Supreme Court about a rule of law or procedures in specific cases

Briefs and Oral Arguments

Once a case reaches the Supreme Court, lawyers for each party to the case file a written **brief.** A brief is a detailed statement of the facts of the case supporting a particular position by presenting arguments based on relevant facts and citations from previous cases. Interested parties may also be invited to submit **amicus curiae** ("friends of the court") **briefs,** supporting or rejecting arguments of the case.

Oral arguments allow both sides to present their positions to the justices during a 30 minute period. Justices may interrupt the lawyers during this time, raising questions or challenging points of law.

Research and Conferences

Justices use law clerks to research the information presented in oral arguments and briefs. Throughout the term, the justices meet in private conferences to consider cases heard in oral argument, with the chief justice presiding over the conferences. Each justice may speak about the cases under discussion. An informal poll determines how each justice is leaning in the case.

Writing Opinions

Once the Supreme Court has made a decision in a case, the decision is explained in a written statement called an opinion. If voting with the majority, the chief justice selects who will write the opinion; if voting with the minority, the most senior associate justice of the majority selects who will write the opinion.

- **majority opinion**—a majority of the justices agree on the decision and its reasons
- **concurring opinion**—a justice who agrees with the majority opinion but not with the reasoning behind the decision
- **dissenting opinion**—a justice or justices who disagree with the majority opinion

Opinions of the Supreme Court are as important as the decisions they explain. Majority opinions become **precedents,** standards or guides to be followed in deciding similar cases in the future.

COURTS AS POLICYMAKERS

New Deal Era

Controversy surrounded the Supreme Court during the New Deal era, as Congress passed numerous laws designed to end the Depression and the conservative court ruled these laws unconstitutional. In response, Franklin Roosevelt proposed what opponents termed a "court-packing plan" to increase the number of justices, allowing Roosevelt to appoint justices supportive of New Deal legislation. Although Congress did not pass Roosevelt's plan to expand the court, two justices, Chief Justice Charles Evans Hughes and Associate Justice Owen Roberts, began voting in favor of New Deal legislation (sometimes referred to "the switch in time to save nine.")

Warren Court (1953–1969)

Often termed "the most liberal court ever," the Warren Court under Chief Justice Earl Warren was especially active in the area of civil rights and civil liberties. This court heard *Brown v. Board of Education* (1954), declaring segregation in public schools unconstitutional. The Warren Court also expanded the rights of criminal defendants in *Gideon v. Wainwright* (1963) and *Miranda v. Arizona* (1966).

Burger Court (1969–1986)

Richard Nixon's appointment of Warren Burger as chief justice returned the Supreme Court to a more conservative ideology. The Burger court narrowed defendants' rights, permitted abortions in *Roe v. Wade* (1973), and ruled that Nixon did not have **executive privilege** over information in a criminal proceeding in *U.S. v. Nixon* (1974).

Rehnquist Court (1986–present)

The conservative court under Chief Justice William Rehnquist continues to limit, but not reverse, decisions of the earlier more liberal courts in the areas of defendants' rights, abortion (*Planned Parenthood v. Casey*, 1992), and affirmative action.

JUDICIAL PHILOSOPHY

Judicial philosophy of activism or restraint is not the same as political philosophy such as liberal or conservative. Although some recent justices who supported an activist philosophy (Warren and T. Marshall) were also more liberal, this has not always been the case. The Marshall Court was activist in establishing judicial review but conservative in protecting property rights.

Judicial Activism

The philosophy of **judicial activism,** or judicial intervention, holds that the Court should play an active role in determining national policies. The philosophy advocates applying the Constitution to social and political questions, especially where constitutional rights have been violated or unacceptable conditions exist.

Judicial Restraint

The philosophy of **judicial restraint** holds that the court should avoid taking the initiative on social and political questions, operating strictly within the limits of the Constitution and upholding acts of Congress unless the acts clearly violate specific provisions of the Constitution. Judicial restraint involves only a limited use of judicial powers and advocates the belief that the court should be more passive, allowing the executive and legislative branches to lead the way in policy-making.

✓ REVIEW QUESTIONS

1. Jurisdiction is the authority of the courts to hear certain cases. Under the guidelines of the Constitution, which of the following is not within the jurisdiction of the federal courts?

   A. cases involving federal law
   B. interpretation of state constitutions
   C. interpretation of the federal Constitution
   D. treaties
   E. cases involving territories

2. Federal courts created by Congress under Article III of the Constitution include the Supreme Court, district courts, courts of appeals, Court of Appeals for the Federal Circuit, and the U.S. Court of International Trade. These courts can best be described as

   A. legislative courts
   B. territorial courts
   C. constitutional courts
   D. original courts
   E. inferior courts

3. The Supreme Court is the only court created directly by the Constitution. What type of jurisdiction does this court have?

   I. original
   II. appellate
   III. concurrent

   A. I only
   B. II only
   C. III only
   D. I and II
   E. I, II, and III

4. Which of the following best describes the formal qualifications for a federal judge?

   A. They serve "during good behavior."
   B. The president appoints them with the approval of the House of Representatives.
   C. They serve at the discretion of the president.
   D. They serve at the discretion of the Congress.
   E. They have no formal qualification other than being a loyal follower of the president.

5. Which of the following has no bearing when the president makes an appointment to the Supreme Court?

   A. party affiliation
   B. judicial philosophy
   C. likability

D. "litmus test"
E. judicial experience

6. Until recently, few African-Americans, Hispanics, or women were appointed as judges to the lower courts. Who was the first president to appoint an African-American to the Supreme Court?

A. Richard Nixon
B. Lyndon Johnson
C. Ronald Reagan
D. John Kennedy
E. Jimmy Carter

7. Which of the following terms best describes the Supreme Court's issuance of an order directing a lower court to send up its record for review?

A. certificate
B. rule of four
C. amicus curiae
D. writ of certiorari
E. brief order

8. The majority opinion issued by the Supreme Court as the final decision of a case, becomes the standard or

guide that will be followed in deciding similar cases in the future. This standard or guide is known as a

A. precedent
B. brief
C. argument
D. decision
E. poll of the court

9. Which of the following courts was best known for narrowing the rights of defendants?

A. Warren Court
B. Rehnquist Court
C. Burger Court
D. New Deal Court
E. Nixon Court

10. The judicial philosophy that advocates the courts' active role in policymaking is called

A. **strict constructionist**
B. judicial activism
C. **loose constructionist**
D. judicial restraint
E. liberalism

ANSWERS AND EXPLANATIONS

1. **B.** Federal courts do not hear cases involving state constitutions. They are heard in the state courts.

2. **C.** Constitutional courts include the Supreme Court, district courts, the Courts of Appeals, the Court of Appeals for the Federal Circuit, and the U.S. Court of International Trade.

3. **D.** The Supreme Court has both original and appellate jurisdiction.

4. **A.** There are no Constitutional (formal) qualifications for federal judges. They are appointed by the president with confirmation by the Senate. They serve "during good behavior."

5. **C.** The president may consider party affiliation, judicial philosophy, and experience when appointed justices to the Supreme Court. A "litmus test" may also be a gauge for choosing appointments.

6. **B.** Lyndon Johnson appointed Thurgood Marshall, the first African-American on the Supreme Court, in 1967.

7. **D.** A writ of certiorari is a court order directing a lower court to send up the records of a case for review.

8. **A.** A precedent is a standard used by the courts in deciding similar cases.

9. **C.** The Supreme Court under Chief Justice Warren Burger narrowed the rights of defendants.

10. **B.** The judicial philosophy of judicial activism advocates policy-making by the courts.

RAPID REVIEW

- Article III of the Constitution establishes the Supreme Court and a system of inferior courts.

- Jurisdiction is the authority of the federal courts to hear certain cases. Jurisdiction may be original, appellate, or concurrent.

- The Supreme Court, the Courts of Appeals, and district courts are constitutional courts.

- The Supreme Court was created directly by the Constitution. It is the highest court in the United States, having both original and appellate jurisdiction.

- Federal judges are appointed by the president and confirmed by a majority of the Senate.

- Presidents make appointments to the Supreme Court only when a vacancy occurs during a president's term of office.

- Almost all federal judges have some form of legal training.

- The Supreme Courts only hears a few hundred cases each year from the several thousand cases submitted.

- Cases may be presented to the Supreme Court for possible review by writ of certiorari, certificate, or the submission of an amicus curiae brief.

- Oral arguments allow both sides time to present their arguments to the justices.

- Law clerks research information presented in oral arguments and briefs.

- Supreme Court decisions are explained in written statements known as opinions. Opinions may be majority, concurring, or dissenting.

- Courts are often termed liberal or conservative, depending on the decisions of the court and the guidance of the chief justice.

- Judicial philosophy may follow the lines of judicial activism or judicial restraint.

Chapter 14

Review: Civil Liberties and Civil Rights

2 CIVIL LIBERTIES

In the Declaration of Independence, Thomas Jefferson wrote that all people "are endowed by their creator with certain unalienable rights." **Civil liberties** are those rights that belong to everyone; they are protections against government and are guaranteed by the Constitution, legislation, and judicial decisions.

- Constitution—The original Constitution mentions specific rights considered to be fundamental freedoms by the founding fathers:
  - **writ of habeas corpus**—You must be brought before the court and informed of charges against you.
  - no **bills of attainder**—You cannot be punished without a trial.
  - no **ex post facto** laws—Laws applied to acts committed before the laws' passage are unconstitutional.
  - trial by jury
- Bill of Rights—added in 1791 to the original Constitution to provide specific guarantees by the national government
  - freedom of religion, speech, press, petition and assembly
  - no unreasonable searches and seizure
  - protections against **self-incrimination** and **double jeopardy**
  - protections in criminal procedures
- The Fourteenth Amendment provided for the expansion of individual rights. The Supreme Court in *Gitlow v. New York* (1925) and subsequent cases has interpreted the due process clause of the Fourteenth Amendment to apply the guarantees of the Bill of Rights to state and local governments (**incorporation**). Today, most guarantees of the Bill of Rights have been incorporated to apply to the state and local governments.

- Legislative actions are laws that set limits or boundaries on one person's rights over another's or bring balance between the rights of individuals and the interests of society. For example, false advertising is not protected under the First Amendment guarantee of freedom of speech.
- Court decisions protect rights through the use of judicial review. Flag burning (*Texas v. Johnson*, 1989) is protected, but burning a draft card (*United States v. O'Brien*, 1968) is not protected **symbolic speech.**

FREEDOM OF RELIGION

Two protections for freedom of religion exist: the **establishment clause** and the **free exercise clause.**

Establishment Clause

According to Thomas Jefferson, the Constitution creates a "wall of separation between Church and State." Because the church and government are separate in the United States, Congress cannot establish any religion as the national religion, nor favor one religion over another, nor tax American citizens to support any one religion. Controversy concerning the exact meaning and extent of the establishment clause has led to actions by the Supreme Court in defining the parameters of the clause, including:

- *Everson v. Board of Education* (1947)—The Court upheld a New Jersey policy of reimbursing parents of Catholic school students for the costs of busing their children to school.
- *Engle v. Vitale* (1962)—The Court ruled school-sanctioned prayer in public schools is unconstitutional.
- *Abington School District v. Schempp* (1963)—The Court struck down a Pennsylvania law requiring the reading of a Bible passage at the beginning of each day.
- *Lemon v. Kurtzman* (1971)—The Court struck down a Pennsylvania law reimbursing parochial schools for textbooks and teacher salaries and established the Lemon Test. To pass the test a law must 1) have a primarily secular purpose; 2) its principle effect must neither aid nor inhibit religion; and 3) it must not create excessive entanglement between government and religion.
- *Lynch v. Donnelly* (1984)—The Court upheld the right of governmental entities to celebrate the Christmas holiday with Christmas displays that might include nativity scenes, if secular displays are also sufficiently included.
- *Wallace v. Jaffree* (1985)—The Court overturned a state law setting aside time for "voluntary prayer" in public schools.
- *Edwards v. Aguillard* (1987)—The Court ruled that Louisiana could not force public schools that taught evolution to also teach creationism.

- *Board of Education of Westside Community Schools v. Mergens* (1990)—The Court upheld the Equal Access Act of 1990, which required public secondary schools to provide religious groups the same access to facilities that other extracurricular groups had.
- *Lee v. Weisman* (1992)—The Court ruled against clergy-led prayer at high school graduation ceremonies.
- *Santa Fe Independent School District v. Doe* (2002)—The Court overturned a Texas law allowing high school students to read a prayer at athletic events such as football games.

Free Exercise Clause

The free exercise clause guarantees the right to practice any religion or no religion at all. In its interpretations of the free exercise clause, the Supreme Court has made distinctions between belief and practice. The Court has ruled that religious belief is absolute, while the practice of those beliefs may be restricted, especially if those practices conflict with criminal laws. For example,

- *Reynolds v. United States* (1879)—The Court upheld the federal law that prohibited polygamy even though Reynolds, a Mormon from Utah, claimed it limited his religious freedom.
- *Wisconsin v. Yoder* (1972)—The Court ruled that Wisconsin could not require Amish parents to send their children to public school beyond the eighth grade because it would violate long-held religious beliefs.
- *Employment Division of Oregon v. Smith* (1990)—The Court ruled that Oregon could deny unemployment benefits to workers fired for using drugs (peyote) as part of a religious ceremony.
- *Church of the Lukumi Babalu Aye v. City of Hialeah* (1993)—The Court ruled that laws banning animal sacrifice were unconstitutional because they targeted the Santeria religion.

In 1993 Congress passed the Religious Freedom Restoration Act, giving people the right to practice religious activities unless prohibited by laws that are narrowly tailored and the government can show a "compelling interest." In 1997 the Supreme Court ruled this law unconstitutional in *City of Boerne, Texas v. Flores*.

FREEDOM OF SPEECH

Types of Speech

There are several different classifications of speech:

- **pure speech**—the most common form of speech, verbal speech; given the most protection by the courts

- **symbolic speech**—using actions and symbols to convey an idea rather than words (burning a draft card or flag, wearing an armband in protest); may be subject to government restrictions if it endangers public safety
- **speech plus**—verbal and symbolic speech used together, such as a rally and then picketing; may also be limited

Regulating Speech

Limitations on free speech have generally existed in the area of providing for national security. In 1798 Congress passed the Alien and Sedition Acts, making it illegal to say anything "false, scandalous and malicious against the government or its officials." Although these acts were aimed at John Adams and his Federalist supporters, others were convicted under these laws. The Alien and Sedition Acts were never challenged in court, and they expired in 1801.

After the assassination of President McKinley by an anarchist in 1901 and the entrance of the United States into World War I, Congress again passed sedition laws forbidding verbal attacks on the government, and the states began following suit. These and subsequent laws were challenged in the courts.

- *Schenck v. United States* (1919)—Schenck mailed fliers to draftees during World War I urging them to protest the draft peacefully; he was convicted of violating a federal law against encouraging the disobedience of military orders. Oliver Wendall Holmes wrote in the opinion that such speech was not protected during wartime because it would create a clear and present danger, establishing a standard for measuring what would and would not be protected speech.
- *Gitlow v. New York* (1925)—The Court applied the protections of free speech to the states under the due process clause of the Fourteenth Amendment. This case established the bad tendency test, under which speech could be restricted if it had a tendency to lead to illegal actions.
- *Chaplinsky v. New Hampshire* (1942)—The Court ruled that the first amendment did not protect "fighting words."
- *Tinker v. Des Moines* (1969)—The Court ruled that wearing black armbands in protest of the Vietnam War was "pure speech" or symbolic speech, protected by the First Amendment.
- *Brandenburg v. Ohio* (1969)—The Court made the "clear and present" danger test less restrictive.
- *Miller v. California* (1973)—The Court established the Miller test, which sets standards for measuring obscenity: 1) major theme appeals to indecent sexual desires applying contemporary community standards; 2) shows in clearly offensive way sexual behavior outlawed by state law; and 3) "lacks serious literary, artistic, political, or scientific value."
- *Texas v. Johnson* (1989)—The Court ruled that flag burning is a protected form of symbolic speech.

- *Reno v. ACLU* (1997)—The Court ruled the Communications Decency Act unconstitutional because it was "overly broad and vague" in regulating internet speech.

Since the 1940s the Court has supported the preferred position doctrine: First Amendment freedoms are more fundamental than other freedoms because they provide a basis for other liberties; therefore, they hold a preferred position and laws regulating these freedoms must be shown to be absolutely necessary to be declared constitutional.

FREEDOM OF THE PRESS

Freedom of the press is often protected because it is closely related to freedom of speech; the press is used as a form of expression. Today the press includes newspapers, magazines, radio, television, and the internet.

- *Near v. Minnesota* (1931)—The Court applied the protections of free press to the states under the due process clause of the Fourteenth Amendment and prohibited **prior restraint.**
- *New York Times v. Sullivan* (1964)—The Court protected statements about public officials.
- *New York Times v. United States* (1971)—The Court reaffirmed its position of prior restraint, refusing to stop the publication of the Pentagon Papers.
- *Hazelwood School District v. Kuhlmeier* (1988)—The Court ruled in favor of school district censorship of student newspapers as long as censorship is related to legitimate concerns.

FREEDOM OF ASSEMBLY AND PETITION

The First Amendment guarantees the "right of the people peacefully to assemble, and to petition the Government for a redress of grievances." Freedom of assembly and petition applies to both private and public places, allowing citizens to make their views known to government officials through petitions, letters, picketing, demonstrations, parades, and marches. The courts have protected these rights while allowing the government to set limits to protect the rights and safety of others.

- *Dejonge v. Oregon* (1937)—The Court established that the right of association (assembly) was as important as other First Amendment rights and used the due process clause of the Fourteenth Amendment to apply freedom of assembly to the states.

The courts have generally ruled:

- That to protect public order, government may require groups wanting to parade or demonstrate to first obtain a permit.

- Certain public facilities (schools, airports, jails) not generally open to the public may be restricted from demonstrations.
- Restrictions on assembly must be worded precisely and must apply to all groups equally.
- The right to assemble does not allow groups to use private property for its own uses (creates buffer zones around abortion clinics).
- Police may disperse demonstrations in order to keep the peace or protect the public's safety (if demonstrations become violent or dangerous to public safety).

PROPERTY RIGHTS

The due process clause of the Fifth and Fourteenth Amendments provide for the protection of private property by guaranteeing that the government cannot deprive a person of "life, liberty, or property, without due process of law." Although the Supreme Court has not defined the term due process, it has generally accepted the concept of government acting in a fair manner according to established rules. **Substantive due process** involves the policies of government or the subject matter of the laws, determining whether the law is fair or if it violates constitutional protections. **Procedural due process** is the method of government action or how the law is carried out, according to established rules and procedures. Although the due process clause has often been applied to those accused of crimes (the guarantee of a fair trial would be due process), due process has also been used to protect property rights. The Fifth Amendment states that government cannot take private property for public use without paying a fair price for it. This right of **eminent domain** allows government to take property for public use but also requires that government provide just compensation for that property.

Right to Privacy

The Constitution makes no mention of a "right to privacy," however the Supreme Court has interpreted several rights that might fall under the category of privacy.

- *Griswold v. Connecticut* (1965)—The Court ruled that the Constitution created "zones of privacy" and enhanced the concept of enumerated rights of the Ninth Amendment.
- *Roe v. Wade* (1973)—The outcome was a continuation of the recognition of a constitutional right of privacy for a woman to determine whether to terminate a pregnancy.

RIGHTS OF THE ACCUSED

Several amendments of the Bill of Rights address the rights of those accused of crimes. The Fourteenth Amendment extends those protections to apply to the states.

Fourth Amendment: Search and Seizure

- *Wolf v. Colorado* (1949)—The Court applied protections against unreasonable search and seizure to the states under the due process clause of the Fourteenth Amendment.
- *Mapp v. Ohio* (1961)—The Court ruled that evidence obtained without a search warrant was excluded from trial in state courts.
- *Terry v. Ohio* (1968)—The Court ruled that searches of criminal suspects are constitutional and police may search suspects for safety purposes.
- *Nix v. Williams* (1984)—The Court established the inevitable discovery rule, allowing evidence discovered as the result of an illegal search to be introduced if it can be shown that the evidence would have been found anyway.
- *United States v. Leon* (1984)—The Court established the good faith exception to the exclusionary rule.

Fifth Amendment: Self-Incrimination

- ***Miranda v. Arizona*** (1966)—The Court ruled that suspects in police custody have certain rights and that they must be informed of those rights (right to remain silent, right to attorney).

Sixth Amendment: Right to an Attorney

- *Powell v. Alabama* (1932)—The Court established that the due process clause of the Fourteenth Amendment guarantees defendants in death penalty cases the right to an attorney.
- *Betts v. Brady* (1942)—The Court ruled that poor defendants in non-capital cases are not entitled to an attorney at government expense.

- *Gideon v. Wainwright* (1963)—The Court ruled that in state trials, those who cannot afford an attorney will have one provided by the state, overturning *Betts v. Brady*.

Eighth Amendment: Cruel and Unusual Punishments

- *Furman v. Georgia* (1972)—The Court ruled the death penalty unconstitutional under existing state law because it was imposed arbitrarily.
- *Gregg v. Georgia* (1976)—In this case, the death penalty was constitutional because it was imposed based upon the circumstances of the case.

CIVIL RIGHTS

Civil Rights are the positive acts of government, designed to prevent **discrimination** and provide equality before the law. The Equal Protection

Clause of the Fourteenth Amendment was added to the Constitution after the Civil War to prevent states from discriminating against former slaves and to protect former slaves' rights. The courts recognize that some forms of discrimination may be valid (preventing those under 21 from consuming alcohol) and have therefore devised the rational basis test to determine if the discrimination has a legitimate purpose. The courts have also developed the strict scrutiny test, a much stricter standard. If the discrimination reflects prejudice, the courts automatically classify it as suspect and require the government to prove a compelling reason for the discrimination. For example, if a city had separate schools for different races, the city would have to prove how this serves a compelling public interest.

THE CIVIL RIGHTS MOVEMENT

After the Civil War three amendments were passed to ensure the rights of the former slaves.

- The Thirteenth Amendment abolished slavery.
- The Fourteenth Amendment defined citizenship to include the former slaves, and provided for due process and equal protection, which were used by the Supreme Court to apply the Bill of Rights to the state and local governments.
- The Fifteenth Amendment provided that individuals could not be denied the right to vote based on race or the fact that they were once a slave.

Until the 1950s and 1960s states continued to use discriminatory practices to prevent African-Americans from participating in the political processes.

- Black codes were state laws passed to keep former slaves in a state of political bondage. The laws included literacy tests, poll taxes, registration laws, and white primaries.
- The Civil Rights Act of 1875 outlawed racial discrimination in public places such as hotels, theaters, and railroads but required African-Americans to take their cases to federal court, a time-consuming and costly endeavor. The act was ruled unconstitutional in 1883.
- Jim Crow laws were laws designed to segregate the races in schools, public transportation, and hotels.
- In *Plessy v. Ferguson* (1896) the Supreme Court upheld the Jim Crow laws by allowing separate facilities for the different races if those facilities were equal. This created the separate but equal doctrine.
- With Executive Order 8802 (1941) Franklin Roosevelt banned racial discrimination in the defense industry and government offices.
- With Executive Order 9981 (1948) Harry Truman ordered the desegregation of the armed forces.
- In ***Brown v. Board of Education*** (1954) the Supreme Court overturned the *Plessy* decision, ruling that separate but equal is unconstitutional.

- In *Brown v. Board of Education II* (1955) the Supreme Court ordered the desegregation of schools "with all deliberate speed."
- The Civil Rights Act of 1957 created the Civil Rights Division within the Justice Department and made it a crime to prevent a person from voting in federal elections.
- The Civil Rights Act of 1964 prohibited discrimination in employment and in places of public accommodation, outlawed bias in federally funded programs, and created the Equal Employment Opportunity Commission (EEOC).
- The Twenty-Fourth Amendment (1964) outlawed poll taxes in federal elections.
- The Voting Rights Act of 1965 allowed federal registrars to register voters and outlawed literacy tests and other discriminatory tests in voter registration.
- The Civil Rights Act of 1991 made it easier for job applicants and employees to bring suit against employers with discriminatory hiring practices.

! OTHER MINORITIES

With the successes of the African-American civil rights movement, other minorities have also pressed to end discrimination. Hispanics, American Indians, Asian Americans, women, and people with disabilities have all joined in the quest for protections from discriminatory actions.

Hispanic Americans

Hispanic Americans is a term often used to describe people in the United States who have a Spanish-speaking heritage, including Mexican Americans, Cuban Americans, Puerto Ricans, and Central and South Americans. Today, the Hispanic population is the fastest growing minority in America.

Native Americans

More than two million Native Americans live on reservations in the United States. As a result of discrimination, poverty, unemployment, alcoholism, and drug abuse are common problems. Lack of organization has hampered Native American attempts to gain political power. With the formation of militant organizations (National Indian Youth Council and American Indian Movement) and protests (siege at Wounded Knee), Native Americans have brought attention to their concerns. A 1985 Supreme Court ruling upheld treaty rights of Native American tribes. The Indian Gaming Regulatory Act (1988) allowed Native Americans to have gaming operations (casinos) on their reservations, creating an economic boom in many tribes. In 1990 Congress passed the Native American Languages Act, encouraging the continuation of native languages and culture.

Asian Americans

Discrimination against Asians arriving in the United States began almost immediately as Asian workers began competing for jobs. Beginning in 1882, the Chinese Exclusion Act (and other similar acts) limited the number of Asians permitted to enter the United States. After the bombing of Pearl Harbor, people of Japanese descent were forced into relocation camps. The Supreme Court upheld these actions until 1944, when they declared the internments to be illegal. In 1988 Congress appropriated funds to compensate former camp detainees or their survivors.

The Women's Movement

Throughout much of American history, women have not been given the same rights as men.

- The Nineteenth Amendment (1920) gave women the right to vote.
- The Equal Pay Act (1963) made it illegal to base an employee's pay on race, gender, religion, or national origin. This also affected the African-American civil rights movement.
- The Civil Rights Act of 1964 banned job discrimination on the basis of gender.
- In *Reed v. Reed* (1971) the Supreme Court ruled against a law which discriminated against women.
- The Equal Employment Opportunity Act (1972) prohibited gender discrimination in hiring, firing, promotions, pay, and working conditions.
- The Omnibus Education Act (1972) required schools to give all boys and girls an equal opportunity to participate in sports programs.
- The Equal Credit Opportunity Act (1974) prohibited discrimination against women seeking credit from banks, finance agencies, or the government and made it illegal to ask about a person's gender or marital status on a credit application.
- The Women's Equity in Employment Act (1991) required employers to justify gender discriminations in hiring and job performance.

People with Disabilities

- The Rehabilitation Act (1973) prohibited discrimination against people with disabilities in federal programs.
- The Education for All Handicapped Children Act (1975) guarantees that children with disabilities will receive an "appropriate" education.

- The Americans with Disabilities Act (1990) forbids employers and owners of public accommodations from discriminating against people with disabilities (must make facilities wheel-chair accessible, etc.). The act created the Telecommunications Relay Service, which allows hearing and speech-impaired people access to telephone communications.

Homosexuals

Prior to the 1960s and 1970s few people were willing to discuss their sexual preferences in relation to same-sex relationships. After a riot following a police raid of a gay and lesbian bar in 1969, the gay power movement gained momentum. Organizations such as the Gay Activist Alliance and the Gay Liberation Front began exerting pressure and influence on state legislatures to repeal laws prohibiting homosexual conduct. As a result of the growth of the gay rights movement, the Democratic party has included protection of gay rights as part of its platform, and several states have passed laws prohibiting discrimination against homosexuals in employment, housing, education, and public accommodations. In *Romer v. Evans* (1996) the Supreme Court ruled that a Colorado constitutional amendment invalidating state and local laws that protected homosexuals from discrimination was unconstitutional because it violated the **equal protection clause** of the Fourteenth Amendment.

The Elderly

Discrimination has also been an issue with the elderly. Job discrimination made it difficult for older people to find work. As a result, in 1967 Congress passed the Age Discrimination in Employment Act, prohibiting employers from discriminating against individuals over the age of 40 on the basis of age.

AFFIRMATIVE ACTION

Affirmative action is a policy designed to correct the effects of past discrimination. Most issues of affirmative action are race or gender based. In 1978 the Supreme Court ruled in *Regents of the University of California v. Bakke* that the affirmative action quotas used by the University of California in their admissions policies were constitutional, but that Bakke had been denied equal protection because the university used race as the sole criterion for admissions. In the more recent *Hopwood v. Texas* (1996) the Court struck down the University of Texas Law School's admissions program, stating that race could not be used at all as a factor in admissions. In recent court decisions the court seems to be taking a more conservative view of affirmative action programs and many fear that affirmative action is on the decline.

✓ REVIEW QUESTIONS

1. Which Constitutional amendment provides for the expansion of individual rights found in the Bill of Rights?

   A. Fourteenth Amendment
   B. Fifteenth Amendment
   C. Nineteenth Amendment
   D. Twenty-Second Amendment
   E. Twenty-Fifth Amendment

2. The Constitution creates a "wall of separation between Church and State." Supreme Court interpretations of this barrier have become known as the

   A. elastic clause
   B. establishment clause
   C. exclusionary clause
   D. judiciary clause
   E. expansion clause

3. The Supreme Court case that over-turned a state law setting aside time for "voluntary prayer" in public schools was

   A. *Santa Fe Independent School District v. Doe*
   B. *Lee v. Weisman*
   C. *Edwards v. Aguillard*
   D. *Lemon v. Kurtzman*
   E. *Wallace v. Jaffree*

4. Using actions and symbols to convey an idea rather than words would be an example of

   A. speech plus
   B. pure speech
   C. free speech
   D. symbolic speech
   E. limited speech

5. Which Supreme Court case ruled that flag burning is a protected form of symbolic speech?

   A. *Reno v. ACLU*
   B. *Miller v. California*
   C. *Texas v. Johnson*
   D. *Tinker v. Des Moines*
   E. *Texas v. White*

6. The right of the government to take property for public use as long as the government provides just compensation for the property is called

   A. substantive due process
   B. eminent domain
   C. public domain
   D. procedural due process
   E. emigrant domain

7. The Supreme Court, in *Mapp v. Ohio*, ruled that evidence obtained without a search warrant could be excluded from trial in state courts. This finding upholds the Constitutional guarantee of no unreasonable search and seizure found in the

   A. Fourth Amendment
   B. Fifth Amendment
   C. Fourteenth Amendment
   D. First Amendment
   E. Fifteenth Amendment

8. What government action brought an end to "Jim Crow Laws" and legal segregation in America?

   A. the Civil Rights Act of 1875
   B. Presidential Executive Order 8802
   C. the Supreme Court ruling in *Plessy v. Ferguson*
   D. the Supreme Court ruling in *Brown v. Board of Education*
   E. the Twenty-Fourth Amendment

9. What has been the most recent govern-ment action taken to end discrimination against Native Americans in the United States?

A. the American Indian Movement Act
B. the Native American Tribal Act
C. the Native American Language Act
D. the Indian Gaming Regulatory Act
E. the Native American Reservation Act

10. Throughout American history, women have not been given the same rights as men. Which of the following prohibits gender discrimination in the workplace?

A. Equal Pay Act
B. Equal Unemployment Opportunity Act
C. Women's Civil Rights Act of 1964
D. Nineteenth Amendment
E. Equal Employment Opportunity Act

ANSWERS AND EXPLANATIONS

1. **A.** The Fourteenth Amendment had been used to incorporate the Bill of Rights to apply to the states.

2. **B.** The establishment clause creates a "wall of separation between Church and State."

3. **E.** *Wallace v. Jaffree* overturned a state law setting aside time for voluntary prayer in schools.

4. **D.** Symbolic speech is the use of actions and symbols to convey ideas.

5. **C.** *Texas v. Johnson* was the case in which the Supreme Court ruled that flag burning is a protected form of symbolic speech.

6. **B.** The right of the government to take property for public use as long as the government provides just compensation for the property is called eminent domain.

7. **A.** Constitutional guarantees of protections against unreasonable searches and seizures can be found in the Fourth Amendment.

8. **D.** The Supreme Court ruling in *Brown v. Board of Education* brought an end to "Jim Crow Laws" and legal segregation in America.

9. **C.** The Native American Language Act is the most recent attempt to end discrimination against Native Americans.

10. **E.** The Equal Employment Opportunity Act prohibits gender discrimination in the workplace.

RAPID REVIEW

- Civil liberties are those rights that belong to everyone and are guaranteed by the Constitution, Bill of Rights, Fourteenth Amendment, legislative actions, and court decisions.

- The establishment clause of the First Amendment has been interpreted to mean that there is a separation between church and state, preventing the government from supporting religion or one religion over another.

- The "**Lemon test**" established standards for measuring separation of church and state.

- The free exercise clause guarantees the right to practice any religion or no religion at all.

- There are three classifications of speech: pure speech, symbolic speech, and speech plus.

- The right to free speech is not absolute. Speech may be regulated if national security is at stake; fighting words and obscenity are not protected forms of free speech. The internet has not been regulated.

- Freedom of the press is often protected because it is closely related to free speech. Press includes newspapers, magazines, radio, television, and the internet.

- The First Amendment also guarantees freedom of assembly and petition.

- The due process clauses of the Fifth and Fourteenth Amendments provide for the protection of private property.

- The Constitution makes no mention of the right to privacy, however the Supreme Court ruled that such a right exists under the Constitution.

- Several amendments of the Bill of Rights address the rights of those accused of crimes, including the Fourth, Fifth, Sixth, and Eighth Amendments. The Fourteenth Amendment extends those protections to apply to the states.

- Civil Rights are the positive acts of government designed to prevent discrimination and provide equality before the law.

- The Civil Rights Movement began after the Civil War, with African Americans striving to gain political, social, and economic equality.

- Discriminatory practices were used by the states to prevent political participation by African Americans. These practices included black codes and Jim Crow laws.

- A positive step for African Americans came with the *Brown v. Board of Education* ruling in which the Supreme Court overturned the *Plessy* "separate but equal" ruling.

- The successes of the African American civil rights movement have encouraged other minorities, such as Hispanics, Native Americans, and Asian Americans, to call for an end to discrimination.

- Women have also worked to end discrimination. Their successes include gaining the right to vote and protections against employment discrimination.

- The Americans with Disabilities Act of 1990 forbids discrimination against people with disabilities.

- Affirmative action is a controversial policy designed to correct the effects of past discrimination.

Chapter 15

Review: Politics and Public Policymaking

 Public policy is the method by which government attempts to solve the problems of a nation. Governments are constantly making public policy. Even the decision to keep the status quo is a public policy decision. Public policy is made at all levels of government. Policymaking may be a slow process with only small changes (**incrementalism**) or a major shift from previous policies.

POLICYMAKING PROCESS

The policymaking process involves several steps:

- **agenda-setting**—recognizing an issue as a problem which must be addressed as a part of the political agenda. Problems are often brought to the **political agenda** by citizens, interest groups, the media, or governmental entities.
- **policy formulation**—finding ways to solve the problem; exploring alternative plans of action and developing proposals to solve the problem.
- **policy adoption**—adopting a plan of action to solve the problem; may require the passage of legislation.
- **policy implementation**—executing the plan of action by the appropriate agency or agencies.
- **policy evaluation**—analysis of policy and its impact upon the problem; judging the effectiveness of the policy and making adjustments if necessary.

DOMESTIC POLICY

 Domestic policy often refers to the social policies of the United States in the areas of crime prevention, education, energy, the environment, health care, and social welfare.

Crime Prevention

Although crime prevention has traditionally been a state and local matter, as crime and violence have increased the federal government has become more involved in crime prevention. Lyndon Johnson declared a "war on crime," creating a commission to study the causes of crime and suggest solutions. Today, more crimes are classified as federal crimes, with punishments often more harsh than those for state crimes. Since the shooting of President Ronald Reagan, debate has centered on gun control legislation. President Bill Clinton signed the Brady Bill, requiring a 5-day waiting period and background checks before the purchase of a handgun. Clinton also won congressional support of a ban on the sale of some types of semiautomatic assault weapons and legislation authorizing new federal spending on crime initiatives, including the hiring of new police officers and building new prisons and "boot camps" for juvenile offenders. Clinton's crime bill also listed federal crimes punishable by the death penalty and the "three strikes laws," mandating certain sentences if convicted of a third felony. As the federal government has become more involved in crime prevention, federal agencies have played a larger role.

- The Federal Bureau of Investigation (FBI) collects and reports evidence in matters relating to federal law or the crossing of state borders; provides investigative and lab services to local law enforcement agencies
- Drug Enforcement Administration (DEA) prohibits the flow of illegal narcotics into the United States and patrols U.S. borders
- Bureau of Alcohol, Tobacco, and Firearms (ATF) administers laws dealing with explosives and firearms and regulates the production and distribution of alcohol and tobacco products

Education

Although public education falls under the authority of the state governments, the federal government has played an increasing role in education. Since the 1950s (*Brown v. Board of Education*, 1954, and the Soviet Union's launch of *Sputnik*) the major goal of education policy has been to ensure equal access to educational opportunities. Under Lyndon Johnson's Great Society, Congress passed the Elementary and Secondary Education Act in 1965, providing federal funding to public school districts with low-income populations. In 1979 Congress created the Department of

Education to coordinate education policy. Congress has also provided programs for higher education, including loans and grant programs for college students. Recent proposals in education have concerned the use of school vouchers that would allow parents to choose the schools their children attend at public expense, and the national testing of students.

Energy

Energy policy has traditionally been one of conservation and the study of alternative and renewable sources of fuel. Newer energy policies have addressed issues such as global warming and toxic waste disposal. In 1980 a superfund was established for clean up of toxic waste sites, and current law provides for the tracking of hazardous chemicals and the disposal of toxic waste. Energy policy often involves highly technical issues about which the average citizen may have limited knowledge.

The Environment

In the late eighteenth century, the federal government began setting aside public lands as national parks, monuments, and forests. Not until the 1950s, however, did Congress begin passing legislation aimed at protecting the environment and cleaning up polluted air and water. In the 1970s Congress created the Environmental Protection Agency (EPA) to enforce environmental legislation. The Clean Air Acts of 1970 and 1990 were implemented to reduce air pollution. The Water Pollution Control Act of 1972 was designed to clean up the nation's lakes and rivers. Wilderness areas were established, the Endangered Species Act provided government protection of species listed as endangered, and **environmental impacts statements** required studies and reports of likely environmental impacts be filed with the Environmental Protection Agency.

Healthcare

Unlike Canada or Great Britain, the United States has no national healthcare system, yet the largest percentage of government spending goes to the Medicare and Medicaid programs. Medicare provides hospitalization insurance for the elderly, and Medicaid provides public assistance in healthcare for the poor. The government operates several programs aimed at promoting and protecting public health in the United States. The Public Health Service, Centers for Disease Control (CDC), Veterans Administration (VA), and Food and Drug Administration (FDA) are among the agencies involved in promoting public health. Healthcare was a major campaign issue in the 1992 presidential election, when Bill Clinton campaigned on a plan to address both healthcare's high cost and limited access. Clinton's proposals to reform healthcare in the United States died in Congress.

Social Welfare

Social welfare began during the New Deal era. The Great Depression led citizens to want more government help against economic downturns and poverty. The Social Security Act (1935) was a first step in this fight. Lyndon Johnson's Great Society continued the war on poverty by creating new programs (Medicare, school aid, job training) designed to prevent poverty. Housing programs and urban renewal have been implemented with the goal of providing adequate housing for all citizens. In the 1980s Ronald Reagan reduced benefits and removed people from eligibility in an effort to reform the social welfare system amid claims of increasing government. Bill Clinton continued to bring reform to the social welfare system by limiting how long a person could receive benefits and giving money to the states to run their own programs.

ECONOMIC POLICY

Economic policy can have a profound effect on national elections. The president and Congress are held responsible for the economic "health" of the nation. Economic policy involves improving the overall economic health of the nation through government spending and taxation policies.

Raising Revenue

The government raises revenue through the collection of taxes. The federal government collects individual income taxes, corporate income taxes, social insurance taxes, excise taxes, customs duties, and estate and gift taxes. The government also raises revenue through the sale of government securities by the Federal Reserve and through the collection of fees for services provided, such as patent fees.

Government Spending

Government spending may be discretionary or nondiscretionary (mandatory). **Discretionary spending** is spending about which government planners may make choices, while nondiscretionary spending is required by existing laws for current programs. In recent years the percentage of nondiscretionary spending has grown while the percentage of discretionary spending has decreased. Discretionary spending includes defense spending, education, student loans, scientific research, environmental cleanup, law enforcement, disaster aid, and foreign aid. Nondiscretionary spending includes interest on the **national debt** and social welfare programs such as Social Security, Medicare, Medicaid, veterans' pensions, and unemployment insurance.

The Federal Budget

The **federal budget** indicates the amount of money the federal government expects to receive and authorizes government spending for a fiscal (12-month period) year. The **fiscal year** for the federal government is from October 1 to September 30. The process of preparing the federal budget takes about 18 months and involves several steps:

- *proposals*—Each federal agency submits a detailed estimate of its needs for the coming fiscal year to the Office of Management and Budget (OMB).
- *executive branch*—The OMB holds meetings at which representatives from the various agencies may explain their proposal and try to convince the OMB that their needs are justified. The OMB works with the president's staff to combine all requests into a single budget package, which the president submits to Congress in January or February.
- *Congress*—Congress debates and often modifies the president's proposal. The Congressional Budget Office provides Congress with economic data. Congressional committees hold hearings, analyze the budget proposals, and by September offer budget resolutions to their respective houses (which must be passed by September 15). The Appropriations Committee for each house submits bills to authorize spending.
- *president*—Congress sends **appropriations** bills to the president for approval. If no budget is approved, Congress must pass temporary emergency funding or the government will "shut down."

FOREIGN AND DEFENSE POLICY

Foreign policy involves all the strategies and procedures for dealing with other nations. The purpose of foreign policy is to maintain peaceful relations with other countries through diplomatic, military, or trade relations. The process of carrying out foreign policy is accomplished through foreign relations. Defense policy is the role that the military establishment plays in providing for the defense of the nation.

The President and Foreign Policy

The president is often considered the leader in the development of foreign policy. Presidential authority for foreign policy originates from the constitutional powers, historical precedent, and institutional advantages of the executive. The president is commander-in-chief of the armed forces, negotiates treaties and executive agreements, and appoints foreign ambassadors, ministers, and consuls. Historically, presidents have often issued foreign policy statements (for example, the Monroe Doctrine and the Truman Doctrine) that have not passed through the legislative process but which set the tone for foreign policy. Also, the president can often respond more quickly than Congress when a national crisis requires quick action (for example, the attack on Pearl Harbor or the events of 9-11-2001).

The Department of State

The Department of State is the major organization for carrying out foreign policy. The secretary of state reports directly to the president with advice about foreign policy matters. The secretary of state also supervises the diplomatic corps of ambassadors, ministers, and consuls. The State Department is organized into bureaus, each specializing in a region of the world.

The Department of Defense (DOD)

The Department of Defense provides military information to the president. The Secretary of Defense advises the president on troop movements, military installations, and weapons development. Because the Secretary of Defense is a civilian, the Joint Chiefs of Staff, composed of a chairman and the highest-ranking military officer in the Army, Navy, Air Force and Marines, also provide advice on military matters.

The National Security Council (NSC)

The National Security Council is part of the Executive Office of the President. Membership includes the president, vice-president, the secretaries of state and defense, chairman of the Joint Chiefs of Staff, director of the Central Intelligence Agency, and the president's national security advisor.

The United States Information Agency

The United States Information Agency helps keep the world informed about America, the American way of life, and American views on world problems through information centers around the world. It also sponsors the "Voice of America" radio programs that are broadcast around the world.

Central Intelligence Agency

The Central Intelligence Agency is responsible for gathering secret information essential to national defense. Although the CIA is an independent agency, it operates within the executive branch to gather information, analyze that information, and brief the president and the National Security Council.

Congress and Foreign Policy

Congress also plays a major role in the development of foreign policy. It is the responsibility of the Senate Foreign Relations Committee and the House Committee on Foreign Affairs to make recommendations to Congress and the president on foreign relations. The Senate must approve all treaties between the United States and foreign nations by a two-thirds vote, and all nominations for ambassadors by majority vote. Congress has the power to declare war and must approve spending for national defense.

Current Issues in Foreign Policy

Current foreign policy issues include:

- *nuclear proliferation*—With only a few nations having nuclear capabilities, how do we prevent possible enemies from gaining access to nuclear technology that might someday be used against the United States or our allies?
- *terrorism*—How does the United States defend itself against possible terrorist attacks? What role will the Department of Homeland Security play in intelligence gathering, border security, immigration, and holding, questioning, and prosecuting suspected terrorists?
- *international trade*—Trade can be used as a tool of foreign policy by providing military or economic aid or by reducing or eliminating tariffs through trade agreements such as the **North American Free Trade Agreement** (NAFTA).

✓ REVIEW QUESTIONS

1. During the policymaking process, when a plan of action is executed by an agency or agencies, what important step has taken place?

   A. policy formulation
   B. policy implementation
   C. policy Adoption
   D. agenda-setting
   E. policy evaluation

2. The federal government is playing an ever increasing role in education. What has been the major goal of the government's education policy?

   A. give more power to the states
   B. increase the power of the department of education
   C. provide more money to low-income schools
   D. provide more programs for higher education
   E. ensure equal access to educational opportunity

3. The Environmental Protection Agency was created for the purpose of enforcing environmental legislation. When was the agency created?

   A. 1990s
   B. 1980s
   C. 1960s
   D. 1970s
   E. 1950s

4. In the United States there is no national healthcare system, yet the largest percentage of government spending goes to

A. Medicare and Medicaid programs
B. public health services
C. the Food and Drug Administration
D. Centers for Disease Control
E. the Veterans Administration

5. Social welfare began during the New Deal era. Legislation of this era was designed to give citizens more government economic support. During this era what was the first government act of support?

A. the Great Society Act
B. the Medicare and Medicaid Act
C. the Social Security Act
D. the Welfare Act
E. the Reduction in Poverty Act

6. Which of the following is the best definition of economic policy?

A. The government raises revenue through the collection of taxes.
B. Government spending is both discretionary and non-discretionary.
C. Improvements in the overall economic health of the nation are through government spending and taxation.
D. The government sells government securities to improve the overall spending by the American citizenry.
E. Welfare programs such as Medicaid, Medicare, Social Security, and unemployment insurance help to stabilize the national debt.

7. Which of the following would not be a part of the federal budget process?

A. The Supreme Court would review budget requests that are outside the realm of **constitutional law.**
B. The executive branch (OMB) would hold meetings to review budget proposals.

C. Each federal agency would submit an estimate of needs to the OMB.
D. Congress would debate budget proposals.
E. Congress would send appropriation bills to the president.

8. Which of the following is not a true statement?

A. The purpose of foreign policy is to maintain peaceful relations with foreign nations.
B. Foreign policy is the responsibility of the Congress through the secretary of state.
C. The process of carrying out foreign policy is accomplished through foreign relations.
D. Defense policy is the role that the military establishment plays in providing for the defense of the nation.
E. Foreign policy involves all the strategies and procedures for dealing with other nations.

9. Which of the following departments is most responsible for providing the president with military information that would be useful in dealing with foreign nations?

A. the Department of State
B. the Department of Defense
C. the National Security Council
D. the United States Information Agency
E. the Central Intelligence Agency

10. Current foreign policy issues include all of the following except

A. nuclear proliferation
B. national defense
C. terrorism
D. international Trade
E. national education

ANSWERS AND EXPLANATIONS

1. **B.** Policy implementation is the process of enactment of policy.

2. **E.** The major educational policy goal of the federal government has been to ensure equal access to educational opportunities.

3. **D.** The Environmental Protection Agency was created in the 1970s.

4. **A.** Medicare and Medicaid receive the largest percentage of government spending.

5. **C.** The first act of government to aid citizens during the New Deal era was the Social Security Act.

6. **C. Fiscal policy,** the policies of taxation and spending that comprise the nation's economic policy, are designed to improve the overall economic health of the nation.

7. **A.** The Supreme Court does not participate in the federal budget process.

8. **B.** The president, not Congress, works with the secretary of state to develop foreign policy.

9. **B.** The Department of Defense is responsible for providing military information to the president.

10. **E.** National education is a domestic policy issue.

RAPID REVIEW

- Public policymaking occurs at all levels of government.

- Policymaking is a slow process involving several steps: agenda-setting, policy formulation, policy adoption, policy implementation, and policy evaluation.

- Domestic policies are the social policies of the United States: crime prevention, education, energy, environment, healthcare, and social welfare.

- Crime prevention at the national level is the responsibility of the Federal Bureau of Investigation, the Drug Enforcement Administration, and the Bureau of Alcohol, Tobacco and Firearms.

- Education falls under the authority of state governments, however the federal government has played an increasing role in education.

- The Environmental Protection Agency was created in the 1970s to enforce environmental legislation.

- The government operates several programs aimed at promoting and protecting public health: the Public Health Service, Centers for Disease Control, the Veterans Administration, and the Food and Drug Administration.

- Social welfare programs include Medicare, Medicaid, and Social Security.

- Economic policy can have an impact on national elections.

- Economic policy includes raising revenue, government spending, and formulation of the federal budget.

- The federal budget indicates the amount of money the federal government expects to receive and spend during a fiscal year.

- The Office of Management and Budget (OMB) plays a major role in creating the budget.

- Foreign policy involves all the strategies and procedures for dealing with foreign nations. The president is considered the leader in the development of foreign policy.

- The Department of State, headed by the secretary of state, is responsible for the execution of foreign policy.

- The Department of Defense provides military information to the president.

- Congress plays a role in the development of foreign policy by making recommendations to the president on foreign relations, approving treaties, and approving nominations of ambassadors.

- Current issues in foreign policy include nuclear proliferation, terrorism, and international trade.

PART IV

APPENDIX

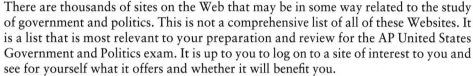

Websites Related to the Advanced Placement Exam

There are thousands of sites on the Web that may be in some way related to the study of government and politics. This is not a comprehensive list of all of these Websites. It is a list that is most relevant to your preparation and review for the AP United States Government and Politics exam. It is up to you to log on to a site of interest to you and see for yourself what it offers and whether it will benefit you.

Since you are preparing for an Advanced Placement exam, go to the source as your first choice.

The College Board—http://www.collegeboard.com/ap/students/index.html
Here you will find:

- Welcome page with student and parent information about AP

- FAQs about AP, with frequently asked questions and answers

- Benefits of AP for students, parents, and schools

- Exam Information, including a calendar of exams, fees, and exam day details

- AP Prep, with College Board resources, study skills, and test-taking tips

- Subjects page, where you can view sample multiple-choice questions for each AP subject, sample free-response questions (with rubrics and student samples) for the past three years, the course description, and links to related sites

    Other Government and Politics sites:

- The White House—http://www.whitehouse.gov

- The House of Representatives—http://www.house.gov

- The Senate—http://www.senate.gov

- The U.S. Supreme Court—http://www.supremecourtus.gov

- Oyez Project—http://oyez.nwu.edu

Each of these Websites will lead you to many others. There are just too many to list here; in fact, there are hundreds of thousands of sites listed on the web.

I suggest you use your favorite search engine (I like www.google.com/) and type in ADVANCED PLACEMENT GOVERNMENT AND POLITICS. From that point you can surf the net for sites that suit your particular needs or interests. You will have to take the time to explore the sites and evaluate their usefulness. Some AP teachers have created great sites with links to other sites that you may find of value.

Glossary of Terms

affirmative action—a policy designed to correct the effects of past discrimination; requirement by law that positive steps be taken to increase the number of minorities in businesses, schools, colleges, and labor

agenda-setting—process of forming the list of matters that policymakers intend to address

amendment—a revision or change to a bill, law, or constitution

amicus curiae brief—friend of the court; interested groups may be invited to file legal briefs supporting or rejecting arguments of the case

Anti-Federalists—opposed the adoption of the U.S. Constitution because it gave too much power to the national government at the expense of the state governments and it lacked a bill of rights

appellate jurisdiction—gives the court authority to hear cases on appeal from the lower courts

apportionment—distribution of representatives among the states based on population of each state

appropriations—money granted by Congress or a state legislature for a specific purpose

Articles of Confederation—the first national constitution of the United States that created a government lasting from 1781–1789; replaced by the current Constitution

at-large—all the voters of a state or county elect their representative

bicameral—a legislature divided into two chambers; Congress has the Senate and the House of Representatives

bill—a law proposed by the legislature

bills of attainder—prohibits a person being found guilty of a crime without a trial

Bill of Rights—The first ten amendments to the Constitution guaranteeing certain rights and liberties to the people

blanket primary—voters may vote for candidates of either party

block grant—money given to states for general programs within a broad category

brief—legal document submitted to the court setting forth the facts of a case and supporting a particular position

brief orders—the returning of a case to a lower court because a similar case was recently decided

Brown v. Board of Education of Topeka, Kansas—overturned Plessy v. Ferguson; ended legal segregation, said school segregation is unconstitutional

bureaucracy—a systematic way of organizing a complex and large administrative structure with responsibility for carrying out the day-to-day tasks of the organization, departments, and agencies of the government

bureaucratic theory—hierarchical structure and standardized procedures of government allow bureaucrats to hold the real power over public policy; proposed by Max Weber

cabinet—government departments headed by presidential appointees to help establish public policy and operate a specific policy area of governmental activity

casework—assistance given to constituents by congressional members, answering questions or doing favors

categorical grant—federal grants for specific purposes defined by law

caucus—locally held meeting in a state to select delegates who, in turn, will nominate candidates to political offices

caucus (congressional)—an association of congressional members who advocate a political ideology, regional ethnic, or economic interest

certificate—lower court asks the Supreme Court about a rule of law or procedure

checks and balances—each branch of government is subject to restraints by the other two branches

civil liberties—constitutional freedoms guaranteed to all citizens

civil rights—positive acts of government designed to prevent discrimination and provide equality before the law

closed primary—only registered party members may vote

cloture rule—prevents filibustering and ends debate in the Senate, by a three-fifths vote of the Senate

coattail effect—weaker or lesser-known candidates from the president's party profit from the president's popularity by winning votes

Commerce and Slave Trade Compromise—resolved differences between northern and southern states; Congress could not tax exports nor ban the slave trade for 20 years

comparable worth—women should be paid salaries equal to men for equivalent job responsibilities and skills

concurrent jurisdiction—authority to hear cases is shared by federal and state courts

concurrent powers—powers shared by the federal and state governments

concurring opinion—justice or justices who agree with the majority's opinion but not with the reason behind the decision

conference committee—a temporary committee to work out a compromise version of a bill that has passed the House of Representatives and Senate in different form

congressional districting—state legislatures draw congressional districts for states with more than one representative

Connecticut Compromise—settled disputes between the states over the structure of the legislative branch

conservative—a person whose political views favor more local, limited government, less government regulations, conformity to social norms and values; tough on criminals

constituency service—casework, assistance to constituents by congressional members

constituent—all residents of the state for Senators, all residents of a district for House members

Constitution—the document setting forth the laws and principles of the government; a plan of government

constitutional courts—federal courts created by Congress under Article III of the Constitution, including the district courts, courts of appeals, and specialized courts such as the U.S. Court of International Trade

constitutional law—laws relating to the interpretation of the Constitution

cooperative federalism—cooperation among federal, state, and local governments; "marble cake" federalism

courts of appeals—federal courts that review decisions of federal district courts, regulatory commissions, and other federal courts

critical election—sharp changes in the existing patterns of party loyalty due to changing social and economic conditions

dealigning elections—party loyalty becomes less important to voters, and they vote for the other party candidate or independents

dealignment—when a significant number of voters choose to no longer support a particular political party

Declaration of Independence—drafted in 1776 by Thomas Jefferson declaring America's separation from Great Britain

deficit—government spending exceeds revenue

delegated powers—powers specifically granted to the national government by the Constitution

democracy—a system whereby the people rule either directly or by elected representation

deviating elections—minority party is able to win the support of majority party members, independents, and new voters

devolution—an effort to shift responsibility of domestic programs (welfare, health care, and job training) to the states in order to decrease the size and activities of the federal government (first-order devolution); some states have attempted to shift responsibilities further to local governments (second-order devolution)

direct democracy—citizens meet and make decisions about public policy issues

direct primary—party members vote to nominate their candidate for the general election

discretionary spending—spending set by the government through appropriations bills, including operating expenses and salaries of government employees

discrimination—unfair treatment of a person based on race or group membership

dissenting opinion—justice or justices who disagree with the majority opinion

district courts—lowest level of federal courts, where federal cases begin and trials are held

divided government—one party controls the executive, and the other party controls one or both houses of Congress

double jeopardy—being tried twice for the same offense

dual federalism—federal and state governments each have defined responsibilities within their own sphere of influence; "layer cake" federalism

elastic clause—the necessary and proper clause, Article I, Section 8, Clause 18 that allows Congress to pass laws to carry out its powers

electoral college—representatives from each state who formally cast ballots for the president and vice president

electorate—people qualified to vote

elitist theory—a small group of people identified by wealth or political power, who rule in their self-interest

eminent domain—allows the government to take property of public use but also requires the government provide just compensation for that property

entitlement program—payments made to people meeting eligibility requirements, such as Social Security

environmental impact statement—required studies and reports of likely environmental impacts, filed with the Environmental Protection Agency prior to the beginning of a project

equal protection clause—constitutional guarantee that everyone be treated equally

establishment clause—prohibits the establishment of a national religion

executive agreement—agreement with another head of state not requiring approval from the Senate

executive order—the president directs an agency to carry out policies or existing laws

executive privilege—the right of the president to withhold information from Congress or refuse to testify; limited by the Supreme Court in *U.S. v. Nixon*

ex post facto law—laws applied to acts committed before the laws' passages are unconstitutional

extradition—states may return a fugitive to a state from which they have fled to avoid criminal prosecution at the request of the state's governor

federal budget—amount of money the federal government expects to receive and authorizes government to spend for a fiscal (12-month period) year

federalism—a division of governmental powers between the national government and the states

Federalist Papers—written by Hamilton, Jay, and Madison to support ratification of the U.S. Constitution

Federalists—supported a strong central government and expanded legislative powers

federal system—power is divided between the states and the federal government

filibuster—a lengthy speech designed to delay the vote on a bill; used only in the Senate

fiscal federalism—national government's use of fiscal policy to influence states through the granting or withholding of appropriations

fiscal policy—the policies of taxation and spending that comprise the nation's economic policy

fiscal year—a 12-month period, October through September, for planning the federal budget

floor leaders—direct party strategy and decisions in the House of Representatives and Senate

free exercise clause—Congress may not make laws restricting or prohibiting a person's religious practices

freedom of expression—freedom of speech or right to petition the government for redress as a First Amendment right

front-loading—choosing an early date to hold the primary election

full faith and credit clause—states are required to recognize the laws and legal documents of other states

gatekeepers—media executives, news editors, and prominent reporters who decide what news to present and how it will be presented

general election—voters choose officeholder from among all the candidates nominated by political parties or running as independents

gerrymandering—drawing of congressional districts to favor one political party or group over another

get-out-the-vote—a campaign near the end of an election to get voters out to the polls

government—the formal and informal institutions, people, and processes used to create and conduct public policy

grants-in-aid—programs, money, and resources provided by the federal government to state and local governments to be used for specific projects and programs

grassroots—average voter at the local level

gridlock—when opposing parties and interests often block each other's proposals, creating a political stalemate or inaction between the executive and legislative branches of government

Hatch Act—prohibits government employees from engaging in political activities while on duty or running for office or seeking political funding while off duty; if in sensitive positions, may not be involved with political activities on or off duty

hyperpluralism—democracy seen as a system of many groups pulling government in many directions at the same time, causing gridlock and ineffectiveness

ideology—a consistent set of beliefs by groups or individuals

impeachment—bringing charges of wrongdoing against a government official by the House of Representatives

implied powers—not expressed, but may be considered through the use of the necessary and proper (elastic) clause

impoundment—refusal of the president to spend money Congress has appropriated

incorporation—application of portions of the Bill of Rights to the states under the 14th Amendment

incorporation doctrine—the Supreme Court ruling that most guarantees in the Bill of Rights are applicable to the states through the 14th Amendment

incrementalism—small changes in policy over long periods of time; usually in reference to budget-making—that the best indicator of this year's budget is last year's budget plus a small increase

incumbency effect—tendency of those already holding office to win reelection due to advantages because they already hold the office

incumbent—the person currently holding office

inherent powers—powers that exist for the national government because the government is sovereign

initiative—allows voters to petition to propose legislation and then submit it for a vote by qualified voters

interest group—a group of private citizens whose goal is to influence and shape public policy

interstate compacts—agreements between states to work together on common issues

iron triangle—alliances that develop between bureaucratic agencies, interest groups, and congressional committees or subcommittees

issue network—individuals in Washington—located within interest groups, congressional staff, think tanks, universities, and the media—who regularly discuss and advocate public policies

joint committee—committee made up of members of both houses of Congress

judicial activism—Court should play an active role in determining national policies

judicial restraint—holds that the Court should avoid taking the initiative on social and political questions, operating strictly within the limits of the Constitution

judicial review—authority given the courts to review constitutionality of acts by the executive, states, or the legislature; established in *Marbury v. Madison*

jurisdiction—the authority of the courts to hear and decide issues in certain cases

legislative courts—courts created by Congress for a specialized purpose with a narrow range of authority

legislative veto—to reject the actions of the president or executive agency by a vote of one or both houses of Congress without the consent of the president; ruled unconstitutional by the Supreme Court in *Immigration and Naturalization Service v. Chadha*

Lemon test—standard set by the Supreme Court in *Lemon v. Kurtzman* to measure the constitutionality of state laws in regard to freedom of religion

liberal—a person whose views favor more government involvement in business, social welfare, minority rights, and increased government spending

line item veto—the president can reject a part of a bill while approving the rest; declared unconstitutional by the Supreme Court

lobbying—attempting to influence policymakers through a variety of methods

lobbyist—uses political persuasion to influence legislation and benefit his or her organization

logrolling—the exchange of political favors for support of a bill

loose constructionist—belief that judges should have freedom in interpreting the Constitution

maintaining elections—traditional majority power maintains power based on voters' party loyalty

majority leader—the elected leader of the party with the most seats in the House of Representatives or Senate

majority–minority districts—drawing district boundaries to give a minority group a majority

majority opinion—the majority of justices agree on the decision and the reasons for the decision

mandates—requirements imposed by the national government on state and local governments to comply with federal rules and regulations

mandatory spending—required government spending by permanent laws

Marbury v. Madison—established the principle of judicial review

markup—rewrite of a bill after hearings have been held on it

mass media—all forms of communication that reach a large portion of the population

McCulloch v. Maryland—Supreme Court decision upholding the supremacy of the national government over the states

media event—a speech or photo opportunity staged to give a politician's view on an issue

Miranda v. Arizona—requires that anyone arrested for a crime be advised of the right to counsel and the right to remain silent

moderate—person whose views are between conservative and liberal and may include some of both ideologies

monetary policy—economic policy in which money is controlled through the Federal Reserve

motor voter law—allows citizens to register to vote at welfare and motor vehicle offices

national chairman—appointed by a committee as head of the party

national debt—amount of money owed by the government

necessary and proper clause—gives Congress the powers to pass all laws necessary to carry out their constitutional duties, found in Article I, Section 8, Clause 18; "elastic clause"

New Deal coalition—alliance of southern conservatives, religious, and ethnic minorities who supported the Democratic Party for 40 years

North American Free Trade Agreement (NAFTA)—created to allow the free movement of goods between Canada, Mexico, and the United States by lessening and eliminating tariffs

off-year election—an election taking place in a year when no presidential elections are occurring; midterm election

open primary—voters may choose the candidates of either party, whether they belong to the party or not

opinion leaders—those individuals held in great respect because of their position, expertise, or personality, who may informally and unintentionally influence others

original jurisdiction—court hears and decides a case for the first time

oversight—Congress monitors policies of the executive branch

pardon—a convicted person is exempt from the penalties of a crime

Plessy v. Ferguson—the Supreme Court case that upheld separate-but-equal segregation in 1896

pluralist theory—interest groups compete in the political arena with each promoting its own policy preferences through organized efforts

policy adoption—the approval of a policy by legislation

policy evaluation—determines if a policy is achieving its goals

policy formulation—the crafting of a policy to resolve public problems

policy implementation—carrying out a policy through government agencies and courts

political action committee—extension of interest group that contributes money to political campaigns

political agenda—issues that merit action, as determined by the public or those in power

political culture—a set of basic values and beliefs about one's country or government that is shared by most citizens and that influences political opinions and behaviors

political efficacy—belief that a person can influence politics and public policymaking

political ideology—a consistent set of beliefs about politics and public policy that sets the framework for evaluating government and public policy

political party—voluntary association of people who seek to control the government through common principles, based on peaceful and legal actions such as the winning of elections

political socialization—complex process by which people get their sense of political identity, beliefs, and values

politics—method of maintaining, managing, and gaining control of government

pork barrel legislation—legislation giving benefits to constituents through sometimes unnecessary or unwise projects within a state or district, to enhance a member's reelection

precedents—standards or guides based on prior decisions that serve as a rule for settling similar disputes

presidential preference primaries—voters select delegates to the presidential nominating convention

president pro tempore—serves as president of the Senate in the absence of the vice president; chosen by the majority party

primary election—nominating election held to choose party candidates who will run in the general election

prior restraint—censorship of information before it is published or broadcast

privileges and immunities—states are prohibited from unreasonably discriminating against residents of other states

procedural due process—method of government action, or how the law is carried out according to established rules and procedures

public opinion—a collection of shared attitudes of citizens about government, politics, and the making of public policy

public policy—the exercise of government power in doing those things necessary to maintain legitimate authority and control over society

pure speech—verbal communication of ideas and opinions

radical—ideological view that favors rapid fundamental change in the existing social, economic, or political order

ratification—method of enacting a constitution or amendment into law

reactionary—ideological view that favors a return to a previous state of affairs

realigning elections—when a minority party wins by building a new coalition of voters that continues over successive elections

realignment—a shift of voting patterns to form new coalitions of party support

reapportionment—redistribution of the congressional seats among the states after the census determines changes in population distribution

recall—special election initiated by petition to allow citizens to remove an official from office before the term expires

referendum—procedure whereby the state submits legislation to its voters for approval, allowing citizens to vote directly on issues

representative democracy—citizens choose officials (representatives) who make decisions about public policy

reserved powers—powers belonging specifically to the states and the people because they were not delegated to the national government nor denied to the states

revenue sharing—giving money back to state and local government with no strings attached

rider—an addition or amendment added to a bill that often has no relation to the bill but that may not pass on its own merits

rule of four—requirement that a case can only be heard by the Supreme Court if four justices vote to hear the case

rules committee—determines the rules of debate for bills in the House of Representatives

runoff primary—when no candidate receives a majority of votes, an election held between the two candidates who received the most votes in the primary

sampling—using a representative cross-section of the general population chosen at random in the polling process

sampling errors—percentage of possible errors in the polling process

select committee—committee selected for a specific purpose

self-incrimination—accusing oneself or giving evidence that may prove oneself guilty

senatorial courtesy—the practice of allowing senators from the president's party who represent the state where a judicial district is located, to approve or disapprove potential nominees for the lower federal courts

seniority system—system in which the chairmanship of a committee is given to the member with the longest continuous service

separation of powers—practice by which power is separated among three branches of government; each branch has its own powers and duties and is independent of and co-equal to the other branches

single-member districts—only one representative is chosen from each district

social contract theory—a voluntary agreement between the government and the governed

social insurance programs—a program to help the elderly, ill, and unemployed if the claimant has paid into it

social welfare policy—government program to enhance quality of life

soft money—money distributed from a national political party organization that was not regulated by law; restricted by the Bipartisan Campaign Finance Reform Act of 2002

sound bite—a brief statement on TV or radio

Speaker of the House—leading officer in the House of Representatives, chosen by the majority party

speech plus—verbal and symbolic speech used together

split ticket voting—voting for candidates from more than one party in the same election

standing committee—permanent committee

stare decisis—let the decision stand; decisions are based on precedents from previous cases

straight ticket voting—voting for candidates all of the same party

straw poll—early form of polling that asks the same question of a large number of people

strict constructionist—view that justices should base decisions on a narrow interpretation of the Constitution

substantive due process—the policies of government or the particular subject matter of the laws determining what the law is about and whether the law is fair or if it violates constitutional protections

suffrage—the right to vote

superdelegates—party officials in the Democratic Party who attend the national convention without having to run in primaries or caucuses

Super Tuesday—day when most southern states hold presidential primaries

supremacy clause—national law supersedes all other laws passed by states; found in Article VI of the Constitution

symbolic speech—using actions and symbols rather than words to convey an idea

Three-Fifths Compromise—agreement that each slave counts as three-fifths of a person in determining representation in the House of Representatives and taxation

traditional democratic theory—government depends upon the consent of the governed

trial balloon—tests the public reaction to policy or appointments by releasing information to the media and gauging public reaction

trustee—after listening to constituents, elected representatives vote based on their own opinions

two-party system—several political parties exist, but only two major political parties compete for power and dominate elections

unfunded mandates—requires states to enforce legislation without the funding necessary

Virginia Plan—Madison's plan for a bicameral legislature, with the executive and judiciary chosen by the legislature

War Powers Act—limits the ability of the president to commit troops to combat

Watergate—break-in at the Democratic National Committee headquarters at the Watergate building in 1972 that resulted in a cover-up and the subsequent resignation of President Nixon

writ of certiorari—order by the court directing a lower court to send up the records of a case for review

writ of habeas corpus—requires a judge to evaluate whether there is sufficient cause to keep a person in jail

5 Steps to a 5

AP Biology

Preface

Hello, and welcome to the AP biology review book that promises to be the most fun you have ever had!!!! Well, ok. . . . It will not be the most fun you have ever had . . . but maybe you will enjoy yourself a little bit. If you let yourself, you may at least learn a lot from this book. It contains the major concepts and ideas to which you were exposed over the past year in your AP biology classroom, written in a manner that, I hope, will be pleasing to your eyes and your brain.

Many books on the market contain the same information that you will find in this book. However, I have approached the material a bit differently. I have tried to make this book as conversational and understandable as possible. I have had to review for countless standardized tests, and I cannot think of anything more annoying than a review book that is a total snoozer. In fact, I had this book "snooze-tested" by over 5000 students, and the average reader could go 84 pages before falling asleep. This is better than the "other" review books whose average snooze time fell within the range of 14–43 pages. Okay, I made up those statistics . . . but I promise that this book will not put you to sleep. ☺

While preparing this book, I spoke to 154,076 students who had taken the AP exam and asked them how they prepared for the test. They indicated which study techniques were most helpful to them and which topics in this book they considered *vital* to success on this test. Throughout the book there are popup windows with these students' comments and tips. Pay heed to these comments because these folks know what they are talking about. They have taken this test and may have advice that will be useful to you.

There is definitely a lot to learn for this AP exam . . . but, of course, you wouldn't get college credit in the subject if there were not. I am not going to mislead you into thinking that you do not need to study to do well on this exam. You will actually need to prepare quite a bit. But this book will walk you through the process in as painless a way as I deem possible. Use the study questions at the end of each chapter to practice applying the material you just read. Use the study tips listed in Part II to help you remember the material you need to know. Take the two practice tests from the enclosed CD as the actual exam approaches to see how well the information is sinking in. Do the practice essays that I have included in the back of the book to prepare yourself for the essays portion. Get used to the format of the essays. They make up 40 percent of the score and should not be ignored.

Well, it's time to stop gabbing, and start studying. Take the diagnostic test that starts in Part 1 of the book and look through the answers and explanations to see where you stand before you dive into the review process. Then look through the hints and strategies in Part 2, which may help you finally digest all the information that comes at you in Part 3. Then, I suggest that you kick back, relax, grab yourself a comfortable seat, and dig in. There is a lot to learn before the exam. Happy reading!

Acknowledgments

This project would not have been completed without the assistance of many dear friends and relatives. To my wife, Stephanie, your countless hours of reading, rereading, and reading once again were of amazing value. Thank you so much for putting in so much time and energy to my cause. You have helped make this book what it is. To my parents and brothers who likewise contributed by reading a few chapters when I needed a second opinion, I thank you. I would like to thank Chris Black, one of my coworkers at College Hill Coaching, for helping me edit and clarify a few of the chapters. I would like to thank Don Reis, whose editing comments have strengthened both the content and the flow of this work. Finally, a big thank you to all the students and teachers who gave me their input and thoughts on what they thought important for this exam. They have made this book that much stronger. Thank you all.

PART I
HOW TO USE THIS BOOK

THE BASICS

The Philosophy of this Book: In the Beginning

If you focus on the beginning, the rest will fall into place. When you purchase this book and decide to work your way through it, you are beginning your journey to the Advanced Placement (AP) Biology exam. I will be with you every step of the way.

Why This Book?

I believe that this book has something unique to offer you. I have spoken with many AP biology teachers and students, and have been fortunate to learn quite a bit from these students about what they want from a test-prep book. Therefore, the contents of this book reflect genuine student concerns and needs. This is a student-oriented book. I did not attempt to impress you with arrogant language, mislead you with inaccurate information and tasks, or lull you into a false sense of confidence through ingenious short-cuts. I have not put information into this book simply because it is included in other review books. I recognize the fact that there is only so much that one individual can learn for an exam. Believe me, I have taken my fair share of these tests—I know how much work they can be. This book is a realistic approach to studying for the AP exam. I have included very little heavy technical detail in this book. (There *is* some . . . I had to . . . but there is not very much.)

Think of this text as a resource and guide to accompany you on your AP Biology journey throughout the year. This book is designed to serve many purposes. It should:

- Clarify requirements for the AP Biology exam
- Provide you with test practice
- Help you pace yourself
- Function as a wonderful paperweight when the exam is completed
- Make you aware of the Five Steps to Mastering the AP Biology Exam

ORGANIZATION OF THE BOOK

I know that your primary concern is to learn about the AP Biology exam. I first start by introducing the five-step plan, and follow it up with three different approaches to exam preparation. I then give an overview of the AP exam in general, and move on to describe some tips and suggestions on how to approach the various sections of the exam. I next introduce our Diagnostic Exam, which should give you an idea of where you stand before you begin your preparations. I recommend that you spend 45 minutes on this practice exam.

The volume of material covered in AP Biology is quite intimidating. Part III of this book provides a comprehensive review of all the major sections you may or may not have covered in the classroom. Not every AP Biology class in the country will get through the same amount of material. This book should help you fill any gaps in your understanding of the coursework.

Part IV of this book is the practice exam section. Here is where you put your skills to the test. The multiple-choice questions provide practice with typical types of questions asked in past AP exams. Keep in mind that they are *not* exact questions taken directly from past exams. Rather, they are designed to focus you in on the key topics that often appear on the actual AP Biology exam. When you answer a question I've written in this book, do not think to yourself, "OK . . . that's a past exam question."

Instead, you should think to yourself "OK, Mark [that would be me] thought that was important, so I should remember this fact. It may show up in some form on the real exam." The essay questions are designed to cover the techniques and terms required by the AP exam. After taking each exam, you can check yourself against the explanations of every multiple-choice question and the grading guidelines for the essays.

The Appendix is also important. It contains a bibliography of sources that may be helpful to you, a list of Websites related to the AP Biology exam, and a glossary of the key terms discussed in this book.

INTRODUCTION TO THE FIVE-STEP PROGRAM

The five-step program is designed to provide you with the skills and strategies vital to the exam and the practice that can help lead you to that perfect score of 5. Each step is designed to provide you with the opportunity to get closer and closer to the "Holy Grail" 5.

STEP ONE leads you through a brief process to help determine which type of exam preparation you want to commit yourself to:

1. Month-by-month: September through May
2. The calendar year: January through May
3. Basic training: the 6 weeks prior to the exam

STEP TWO helps develop the knowledge you need to succeed on the exam:

1. A comprehensive review of the exam
2. One "Diagnostic Exam," which you can go through step by step and question by question to build your confidence level
3. A glossary of terms related to the AP Biology exam
4. A list of interesting and related Websites and a Bibliography

STEP THREE develops the skills necessary to take the exam and do well:

1. Practice multiple-choice questions
2. Practice free-response questions

STEP FOUR helps you develop strategies for taking the exam:

1. Learning about the test itself
2. Learning to read multiple-choice questions
3. Learning how to answer multiple-choice questions, including whether guessing is allowed
4. Learning how to plan and write the free-response questions

STEP FIVE will help you develop your confidence in using the skills demanded on the AP Biology exam:

1. The opportunity to take a diagnostic exam
2. Time management techniques and skills
3. Two practice exams that test how well honed your skills are

THREE APPROACHES TO PREPARING FOR THE AP BIOLOGY EXAM

Overview of the Three Plans

No one knows your study habits, likes, and dislikes better than you do. So you are the only one who can decide which approach you want and/or need to adopt to prepare for the Advanced Placement Biology Exam. Look at the brief profiles below. These may help you determine a prep mode.

You're a full-year prep student (Approach A) if

1. You are the kind of person who likes to plan for everything very far in advance
2. You arrive at the airport 2 hours before your flight because "you never know when these planes might leave early"
3. You like detailed planning and everything in its place
4. You feel that you must be thoroughly prepared
5. You hate surprises

You're a one-semester prep student (Approach B) if

1. You get to the airport 1 hour before your flight is scheduled to leave
2. You are willing to plan ahead to feel comfortable in stressful situations, but are okay with skipping some details
3. You feel more comfortable when you know what to expect, but a surprise or two is cool
4. You're always on time for appointments

You're a 6-week prep student (Approach C) if

1. You get to the airport just as your plane is announcing its final boarding
2. You work best under pressure and tight deadlines
3. You feel very confident with the skills and background you've learned in your AP Biology class
4. You decided late in the year to take the exam
5. You like surprises
6. You feel okay if you arrive 10–15 minutes late for an appointment

Five Steps to a Perfect 5 on the AP Biology Exam: General Outline of Three Different Study Schedules

Month	Year-Long Plan	Calendar Year Plan	6-Week Plan
September–October	Introduction to material	—	—
November	Chapters 1–3	—	—
December	Chapters 4–5	—	—
January	Chapters 6–7	Chapters 1–5	—
February	Chapters 8–9	Chapters 1–5	—
March	Chapters 10–12	Chapters 6–10	—
April	Chapters 13–15; Practice Exam 1	Chapters 11–15; Practice Exam 1	Skim Chapters 1–10; all rapid reviews; Practice Exam 1
May	Review everything; take Practice Exam 2	Review everything; take Practice Exam 2	Skim Chapters 11–15; Practice Exam 2

CALENDAR FOR EACH PLAN

A Calendar for Approach A: Year-Long Preparation for the AP Biology Exam

Although its primary purpose is to prepare you for the AP Biology exam you will take in May, this book can enrich your study of biology, your analytical skills, and your scientific essay writing skills.

SEPTEMBER–OCTOBER (Check off the activities as you complete them.)

_____ Determine the student mode (A, B, or C) that applies to you.
_____ Carefully read Parts I and II of this book.
_____ Pay close attention to your walk through of the Diagnostic/Master exam.
_____ Get on the Web and take a look at the AP Website(s).
_____ Skim the Comprehensive Review section. (Reviewing the topics covered in this section will be part of your year-long preparation.)
_____ Buy a few color highlighters.
_____ Flip through the entire book. Break the book in. Write in it. Toss it around a little bit . . . highlight it.
_____ Get a clear picture of what your own school's AP Biology curriculum is.
_____ Begin to use the book as a resource to supplement the classroom learning.

NOVEMBER (the first 10 weeks have elapsed)

_____ Read and study Chapter 1, Chemistry.
_____ Read and study Chapter 2, Cells.
_____ Read and study Chapter 3, Respiration.

DECEMBER

_____ Read and study Chapter 4, Photosynthesis.
_____ Read and study Chapter 5, Cell Division.
_____ Review Chapters 1–3.

JANUARY (20 weeks have elapsed)

_____ Read and study Chapter 6, Heredity.
_____ Read and study Chapter 7, Molecular Genetics.
_____ Review Chapters 1–5.

FEBRUARY

_____ Read and study Chapter 8, Evolution.
_____ Read and study Chapter 9, Taxonomy and Classification.
_____ Review Chapters 1–7.

MARCH (30 weeks have now elapsed)

_____ Read and study Chapter 10, Plants.
_____ Read and study Chapter 11, Human Physiology.
_____ Read and study Chapter 12, Human Reproduction.
_____ Review Chapters 1–9.

APRIL

_____ Take Practice Exam 1 in the first week of April.
_____ Evaluate your strengths and weaknesses.
_____ Study appropriate chapters to correct your weaknesses.
_____ Read and study Chapter 13, Behavioral Ecology and Ethology.
_____ Read and study Chapter 14, Ecology in Further Detail.
_____ Read and study Chapter 15, Laboratory Review.
_____ Review Chapters 1–12.

MAY (first 2 weeks) (THIS IS IT!)

_____ Review Chapters 1–15—all the material!!!
_____ Take Practice Exam 2.
_____ Score yourself.
_____ Get a good night's sleep before the exam. Fall asleep knowing that you are well prepared.

GOOD LUCK ON THE TEST.

A Calendar for Approach B:
Semester-Long Preparation for the AP Biology Exam

Working under the assumption that you've completed one semester of biology studies,
the following calendar will use those skills you've been practicing to prepare
you for the May exam.

JANUARY–FEBRUARY

_____ Carefully read Parts I and II of this book.
_____ Take the Diagnostic/Master exam.
_____ Pay close attention to your walk through of the Diagnostic/Master exam.
_____ Read and study Chapter 1, Chemistry.
_____ Read and study Chapter 2, Cells.
_____ Read and study Chapter 3, Respiration.
_____ Read and study Chapter 4, Photosynthesis.
_____ Read and study Chapter 5, Cell Division.

MARCH (10 weeks to go)

_____ Read and study Chapter 6, Heredity.
_____ Review Chapters 1–3.
_____ Read and study Chapter 7, Molecular Genetics.
_____ Read and study Chapter 8, Evolution.
_____ Review Chapters 4–6.
_____ Read and study Chapter 9, Taxonomy and Classification.
_____ Read and study Chapter 10, Plants.

APRIL

_____ Take Practice Exam 1 in the first week of April.

_____ Evaluate your strengths and weaknesses.
_____ Study appropriate chapters to correct your weaknesses.
_____ Read and study Chapter 11, Human Physiology.
_____ Review Chapters 1–5.
_____ Read and study Chapter 12, Human Reproduction.
_____ Read and study Chapter 13, Behavioral Ecology and Ethology.
_____ Review Chapters 6–10.
_____ Read and study Chapter 14, Ecology in Further Detail.
_____ Read and study Chapter 15, Laboratory Review.

MAY (first 2 weeks) (THIS IS IT!)

_____ Review Chapters 1–15, all the material!!!
_____ Take Practice Exam 2.
_____ Score yourself.
_____ Get a good night's sleep before the exam. Fall asleep knowing that you are well prepared.

GOOD LUCK ON THE TEST!!

A Calendar for Approach C: 6-Week Preparation for the AP Biology Exam

At this point, we assume that you have been building your biology knowledge base for more than 6 months. You will, therefore, use this book primarily as a specific guide to the AP Biology exam. Given the time constraints, now is not the time to try to expand your AP Biology curriculum. Rather, you should focus on and refine what you already do know.

APRIL 1–15

_____ Skim Parts I and II of this book.
_____ Skim Chapters 1–5.
_____ Carefully go over the Rapid Review sections of Chapters 1–5.
_____ Complete Practice Exam 1.
_____ Score yourself and analyze your errors.
_____ Skim and highlight the Glossary at the end of the book.

APRIL 16–MAY 1

_____ Skim Chapters 6–10.
_____ Carefully go over the Rapid Review sections of Chapters 6–10.

_____ Carefully go over the Rapid Reviews for Chapters 1–5.
_____ Continue to skim and highlight the Glossary.

MAY (first 2 weeks) (THIS IS IT!)

_____ Skim Chapters 11–15.
_____ Carefully go over the Rapid Review sections of Chapters 11–15.
_____ Complete Practice Exam 2.
_____ Score yourself and analyze your errors.
_____ Get a good night's sleep. Fall asleep knowing that you are well prepared.

GOOD LUCK ON THE TEST!

INTRODUCTION TO THE GRAPHICS USED IN THIS BOOK

To emphasize particular skills, strategies, and practice, we use seven sets of icons throughout this book.

The first icon is an hourglass, which indicates the passage of time during the school year. This hourglass icon will appear in the margin next to an item that may be of interest to one of the three types of students who are using this book (mode A, B, or C students).

For the student who plans to prepare for the AP Biology exam during the entire school year, beginning in September through May, I use an hourglass that is full on the top.

For the student who decides to begin preparing for the exam in January of the calendar year, I use an hourglass that is half full on the top and half full on the bottom.

For the student who wishes to prepare during the final 6 weeks before the exam, I use an hourglass that is almost empty on the top and almost full on the bottom.

The second icon is a footprint, which indicates which step in the five-step program is being emphasized in a given analysis, technique, or practice activity.

Plan   Knowledge   Skills   Strategies   Confidence Building

The third icon is a clock, which indicates a timed practice activity or a time management strategy. It will indicate on the face of the dial how much time to allow for a given exercise. The full dial will remind you that this is a strategy which can help you learn to manage your time on the test.

The fourth icon is an exclamation point, which will point to a very important idea, concept, or strategy point that you should not pass over.

The fifth icon is a checkmark, which will alert you to pay close attention. This activity will be most helpful if you go back and check your own work, your calendar, or your progress.

The sixth icon is a lightbulb, which indicates strategies that you may want to try.

The seventh icon is the sun, which indicates a tip that you might find useful.

Boldfaced words indicate terms that are included in the glossary at the end of the book.

Throughout the book you will find marginal notes, boxes, and starred areas. Pay close attention to these areas because they can provide tips, hints, strategies, and further explanations to help you reach your full potential.

PART II

WHAT YOU NEED TO KNOW ABOUT THE AP BIOLOGY EXAM

BACKGROUND OF THE ADVANCED PLACEMENT PROGRAM

The Advanced Placement program was begun by the College Board in 1955 to construct standard achievement exams that would allow highly motivated high school students the opportunity to be awarded advanced placement as first-year students in colleges and universities in the United States. Today, there are 33 courses and exams with more than a million students from every state in the nation, and from foreign countries, taking the annual exams in May.

The AP programs are designed for high school students who wish to take college-level courses. In our case, the AP Biology course and exam are designed to involve high school students in college-level biology studies.

WHO WRITES THE AP BIOLOGY EXAM

After extensive surfing of the College Board Website, here is what I have uncovered. The AP Biology exam is created by a group of college and high school Biology instructors known as the AP Development Committee. The committee's job is to ensure that the annual AP Biology exam reflects what is being taught and studied in college-level biology classes at high schools.

This committee writes a large number of multiple-choice questions, which are pretested and evaluated for clarity, appropriateness, and range of possible answers. The committee also generates a pool of essay questions, pretests them, and chooses those questions that best represent the full range of the scoring scale, which will allow the AP readers to evaluate the essays equitably.

It is important to remember that the AP Biology exam is thoroughly evaluated after it is administered each year. This way, the College Board can use the results to make course suggestions and to plan future tests.

THE AP GRADES AND WHO RECEIVES THEM

Once you have taken the exam and it has been scored, your test will be graded with one of five numbers by the College Board:

- A 5 indicates that you are extremely well qualified.
- A 4 indicates that you are well qualified.
- A 3 indicates that you are adequately qualified.
- A 2 indicates that you are possibly qualified.
- A 1 indicates that you are not qualified to receive college credit.

A grade of 5, 4, 3, 2, or 1 will usually be reported by early July.

REASONS FOR TAKING THE AP BIOLOGY EXAM

Why put yourself through a year of intensive study, pressure, stress, and preparation? Only you can answer that question. Following are some of the reasons that students have indicated to us for taking the AP exam:

- For personal satisfaction
- To compare themselves with other students across the nation
- Because colleges look favorably on the applications of students who elect to enroll in AP courses

- To receive college credit or advanced standing at their colleges or universities
- Because they love the subject
- So that their families will be really proud of them.

There are plenty of other reasons, but no matter what they might be, the primary reason for your enrolling in the AP Biology course and taking the exam in May is to feel good about yourself and the challenges that you have met.

QUESTIONS FREQUENTLY ASKED ABOUT THE AP BIOLOGY EXAM

Here are some common questions student have about the AP Biology exam and some answers to those questions.

If I don't take an AP Biology course, can I still take the AP Biology exam?

Yes. Although the AP Biology exam is designed for the student who has had a year's course in AP Biology, some high schools do not offer this type of course. Many students in these high schools have also done well on the exam although they have not taken the course. However, if your high school does offer an AP Biology course, by all means take advantage of it and the structured background that it will provide you.

How is the Advanced Placement Biology exam organized?

The exam has two parts and is scheduled to last 3 hours. The first section is a set of 120 multiple-choice questions. You will have 90 minutes to complete this part of the test.

After you complete the multiple-choice section, you will hand in your test booklet and scan sheet, and you will be given a brief break. The length of this break depends on the particular administrator. You will not be able to return to the multiple-choice questions when you return to the examination room.

The second section of the exam is a 90-minute essay writing segment consisting of four mandatory, free-response questions that cover broad topics. On average, one essay question covers material relating to molecules and cells, another essay is an examination of heredity and evolution, and two of the questions come from the material relating to organisms and populations. Chapter 15 of the review material is a summary of all the major laboratory experiments performed during the year-long AP Biology course. Pay attention to this chapter, because at least one of the essays will ask you to analyze experimental data and perhaps even design an experiment of your own.

Must I check the box at the end of the essay booklet that allows AP staff to use my essays as samples for research?

No. This is simply a way for the College Board to make certain that it has your permission if they decide to use one or more of your essays as a model. The readers of your essays pay no attention to whether or not that box is checked. Checking the box will not affect your grade.

How is the multiple-choice section scored?

The scan sheet with your answers is run through a computer, which counts the number of wrong answers and subtracts a fraction of that number from the number of correct answers. The AP Biology questions usually have five choices, and the fraction is one fourth. A question left blank receives a zero. The formula for this calculation looks something like this (where N = the number of answers):

$$N_{right} - (N_{wrong} \times 0.25) = \text{raw score rounded up or down to nearest whole number}$$

How are my free-response answers scored?

Each of your essays is read by a different, trained AP reader called a *faculty consultant*. The AP/College Board members have developed a highly successful training program for their readers, together with many opportunities for checks and double checks of essays to ensure a fair and equitable reading of each essay.

The scoring guides are carefully developed by a chief faculty consultant, a question leader, table leaders, and content experts. All faculty consultants are then trained to read and score just *one* essay question on the exam. They actually become experts in that one essay question. No one knows the identity of any writer. The identification numbers and names are covered, and the exam booklets are randomly distributed to the readers in packets of 25 randomly chosen essays. Table leaders and the question leader review samples of each reader's scores to ensure that quality standards are constant.

Each essay is scored on a scale from 1 to 10. Once your essay is graded on this scale the next set of calculations is completed.

How is my composite score calculated?

This is where fuzzy math comes into play. The composite score for the AP Biology exam is 150. The free-response section represents 40 percent of this score, which equals 60 points. The multiple-choice section makes up 60 percent of the composite score, which equals 90 points.

Take your multiple-choice results and plug them into the following formula (keep in mind that this formula was designed for the 1999 AP Biology exam and could be subject to some minor tweaking by the AP Board):

$$N_{correct} - \tfrac{1}{4}\, N_{incorrect} \times 0.7563 = \text{your score for the multiple-choice section}$$

Take your essay results and plug them into this formula:

(Points earned for question 1)(1.50) = score for question 1
(Points earned for question 2)(1.50) = score for question 2
(Points earned for question 3)(1.50) = score for question 3
(Points earned for question 4)(1.50) = score for question 4

Total weighted score for the essay section = sum of scores for questions 1–4

Your total composite score for the exam is determined by adding the score from the multiple-choice section to the score from the essay section and rounding that sum to the nearest whole number.

How is my composite score turned into the grade that is reported to my college?

Keep in mind that the total composite scores needed to earn a 5, 4, 3, 2, or 1 change each year. These cutoffs are determined by a committee of AP, College Board, and Educational Testing Service (ETS) directors, experts, and statisticians. The same exam that is given to the AP Biology high school students is given to college students. The various college professors report how the college students fared on the exam. This provides information for the chief faculty consultant on where to draw the lines for a 5, 4, 3, 2, or 1 score. A score of 5 on this AP exam is set to represent the average score received by the college students who scored an A on the exam. A score of a 3 or a 4 is the equivalent of a college grade B, and so on.

Over the years there has been an observable trend indicating the number of points required to achieve a specific grade. Data released from a particular AP Biology exam shows that the approximate range for the five different scores are (this changes from year to year—just use this as an approximate guideline) as follows:

- Mid 80s–150 points = 5
- Mid 60s–mid 80s points = 4
- High 40s–mid 60s points = 3
- High 20s/low 30s–high 40s points = 2
- 0–high 20s points = 1

What should I bring to the exam?

Here are some suggestions:

- Several pencils and an eraser
- Several black pens (black ink is easier on the eyes)
- A watch
- Something to drink—water is best
- A quiet snack, such as Lifesavers
- Your brain
- Tissues

What should I *avoid* bringing to the exam?

You should not bring:

- A jackhammer
- Loud stereo
- Pop rocks
- Your parents

Is there anything else I should be aware of?

You should

- Allow plenty of time to get to the test site.
- Wear comfortable clothing.
- Eat a light breakfast or lunch.
- Remind yourself that you are well prepared and that the test is an enjoyable challenge and a chance to share your knowledge. Be proud of yourself! You worked hard all year.

Once test day comes, there is nothing further you can do. It is out of your hands, and your only job is to answer as many questions correctly as you possibly can.

What should I do the night before the exam?

Although I do not vigorously support last-minute cramming, there may be some value to some last-minute review. Spending the night before the exam relaxing with family or friends is helpful for many students. Watch a movie, play a game, gab on the phone, then find a quiet spot to study. While you're unwinding, flip through your own notebook and review sheets. As you are approaching the exam, you might want to put together a list of topics that have troubled you and review them briefly the night before the exam. If you are unable to fall asleep, flip through my chapter on taxonomy and classification (Chapter 9). Within moments, you're bound to be ready to drift off. Pleasant dreams.

TIPS FOR TAKING THE AP BIOLOGY EXAM

Following are some suggestions for taking the multiple-choice and free-response parts of the exam:

Multiple-Choice Questions

Here are a few rules of thumb:

1. *Don't outthink the test.* It is indeed possible to be too smart for these tests. Frequently during these standardized tests I have found myself over-analyzing every single problem. If you encounter a question such as, "During what phase of meiosis does crossover (also referred to as *crossing over*) occur?" and you happen to know the answer immediately, this does not mean that the question is too easy. First, give yourself credit for knowing a fact. They asked you something, you knew it, and *wham,* you fill in the bubble. Do not overanalyze the question and assume that your answer is too obvious for that question. Just because you get it doesn't mean that it was too easy.

2. *Don't be afraid to leave questions blank.* This exam penalizes the random guess. It will take off $\frac{1}{4}$ point for *each* wrong answer you give. For this reason, I do not recommend that you wildly guess at questions simply because you don't want to leave anything blank. Think of it this way—let's say that you knew the answer to only 75 out of 120 multiple-choice questions. Imagine that you left the other 45 questions blank—unanswered. If you somehow get all 75 questions right, that gives you a Section 1 raw total of about 57 points. (Look back at the discussion on scoring if I have confused you). Now, to get a 4 on this AP exam, you need to get approximately 50% of the essays correct. But if you randomly guessed on those 45 blank questions, you may need to do better on the essays to get that 4. A random guess is bad; an educated guess is good. If you can eliminate answers that you know for sure are not the right answer, and get it down to two or three choices, go for it! Take a stab! But no random pick guesses, please!

3. *Be on the lookout for trick wording!* Always pay attention to words or phrases such as "least," "most," "not," "incorrectly," and "does not belong." Do not answer the wrong question. There are few things as annoying as getting a $\frac{1}{4}$ point off on this test simply because you didn't read the question carefully enough, especially if you know the right answer.

4. *Use your time carefully.* You have 45 seconds per question on the multiple-choice section of this exam. If you find yourself struggling on a question, try not to waste too much time on it. Circle it in the booklet, and come back to it later if time permits. Remember that to ensure a great score on this exam, you need to correctly answer about 80 multiple-choice questions or more—this test should be an exercise in window

shopping. It does not matter *which* questions you get correct. What is important is that you answer enough questions correctly. Find the subjects that you know the best and answer those questions and save the others for review later on.

5. Be careful about changing answers! If you have answered a question already, come back to it later on, and get the urge to change it . . . make sure that you have a real *reason* to change it. Often an urge to change an answer is the work of exam "elves" in the room who want to trick you into picking a wrong answer. Change your answer only if you can justify your reasons for making the switch.

Free-Response Questions

Here are a few basic guidelines:

1. The makeup of the question. The free-response questions tend to be multipart questions. The test preparers are not unrealistic, and they recognize that nobody knows everything about every topic. Therefore, they show a touch of kindness on the free-response section by often constructing the questions so that the test-taker must answer *two* of three, or *three* of four.

2. Budget your time wisely. You have 90 minutes to answer four free-response questions. This translates into 22.5 minutes per essay. It would be fair to say that you will probably spend 1–3 minutes reading the question to figure out what the exam graders want to know. The next 4–6 minutes should be used to ponder your answer and construct a basic outline of what you want to write for each question. The remaining 14–17 minutes should be spent writing your response. If it is a two-part question, spend approximately half of the time on each section. If it is a three-part section, divide your time up three ways and spend approximately five minutes per section.

3. Spread the wealth! The free-response questions are graded in a way that forces the student to provide information for each section of the question. You can receive only a set maximum number of points for each subquestion. For example, in a question that asks you to answer *three* of the following four choices, most likely the grader's guidelines will say something along the lines of "You can give the student a maximum of only three points for part A, a maximum of three points for part B, and a maximum of four points for part C." This is a very important point for you to realize as a test taker. This means that it is more important for you to attempt to answer every question than to try to stuff every little fact you know about part A into that portion of the essay. You could write the most fantastic essay ever submitted on the subject matter found in part A, and yet receive only a 3 out of 10 on the question if you ignore parts B and C. No matter how great your essay may be, the grader can give you only the maximum points allowed.

Also, be sure to write the various answers to the different parts of the question in separate paragraphs so that the essay reader is definitely able to give you as many points as you deserve.

4. Make an outline. When you have read the question and know what the exam is asking you, it is time to make a quick outline. Don't write the most elaborate outline—just jot down enough notes so that you have an idea of how you are going to construct your essay. While the reader is not grading you according to how well the essay is constructed, it will not hurt your score to attempt to write it in a well-organized and grammatically correct fashion. A quick outline can help you organize your thoughts more clearly, and also help you make sure that you do not leave out any important information.

5. Two wrongs can still make a right. An interesting twist to the free-response section of the AP Biology exam is that wrong information in an essay is simply ignored. You do not lose points for saying things that are incorrect, but you do not *get* points for saying things that are incorrect either. They aren't *that* lenient. So, if you are unsure about something, and *think* it may be right, give it a shot, and include it in your essay. It certainly cannot hurt. This is called "positive scoring."

GETTING STARTED: THE DIAGNOSTIC EXAM

 # DIAGNOSTIC/MASTER EXAM: AP BIOLOGY

Time—45 minutes

For the following multiple-choice questions, select the best answer choice and fill in the appropriate oval on the answer grid.

1. A pH of 10 is how many times more basic than a pH of 7?

   A. 2
   B. 10
   C. 100
   D. 1000
   E. 10,000

2. A reaction that breaks down compounds by the addition of water is known as a

   A. Hydrolysis reaction
   B. Dehydration reaction
   C. Endergonic reaction
   D. Exergonic reaction
   E. Redox reaction

3. Which of the following is not a lipid?

   A. Steroids
   B. Fats
   C. Phospholipids
   D. Glycogen
   E. Cholesterol

4. A compound contains a COOH group. What functional group is that?

   A. Amino group
   B. Carbonyl group
   C. Carboxyl group
   D. Hydroxyl group
   E. Phosphate group

5. The presence of which of the following organelles or structures would most convincingly indicate that a cell is a eukaryote and not a prokaryote?

   A. Plasma membrane
   B. Cell wall
   C. Nucleoid
   D. Lysosome
   E. Ribosome

6. Destruction of microfilaments would most adversely affect which of the following?

   A. Cell division
   B. Cilia
   C. Flagella
   D. Muscular contraction
   E. Chitin

7. Which of the following forms of cell transport requires the input of energy?

   A. Diffusion
   B. Osmosis
   C. Facilitated diffusion
   D. Movement of a solute down its concentration gradient
   E. Active transport

8. Among the following choices, which one would most readily move through a selectively permeable membrane?

   A. Small uncharged polar molecule
   B. Protein hormone
   C. Large uncharged polar molecule
   D. Glucose
   E. Sodium ion

For questions 9–12, please use the following answers:

   A. Glycolysis
   B. Krebs cycle
   C. Oxidative phosphorylation
   D. Chemiosmosis
   E. Fermentation

9. This reaction occurs in the mitochondria and involves the formation of ATP from NADH and $FADH_2$.

10. The coupling of the movement of electrons down the electron transport chain with the formation of ATP using the driving force provided by the proton gradient.

11. This reaction occurs in the cytoplasm and has as its products 2 ATP, 2 NADH, and 2-pyruvate.

12. This reaction is performed by cells in an effort to regenerate the NAD^+ required for glycolysis to continue.

13. Which of the following is a specialized feature of plants that live in hot and dry regions?

    A. Stomata that open and close
    B. Transpiration
    C. Photophosphorylation
    D. C_4 photosynthesis
    E. Carbon fixation

14. The light-dependent reactions of photosynthesis occur in the

    A. Nucleus
    B. Cytoplasm
    C. Mitochondria
    D. Thylakoid membrane
    E. Stroma

15. The oxygen produced during the light reactions of photosynthesis comes directly from

    A. H_2O
    B. H_2O_2
    C. $C_2H_3O_2$
    D. CO_2
    E. CO

16. The cyclic pathway of photosynthesis occurs because

    A. The chloroplasts need to regenerate NAD^+.
    B. The Calvin cycle uses more ATP than NADPH.
    C. It can occur in regions lacking light.
    D. It is a more efficient way to produce oxygen.
    E. It is a more efficient way to produce the NADPH needed for the Calvin cycle.

17. Which of the following statements about mitosis is correct?

    A. Mitosis makes up 30 percent of the cell cycle.
    B. The order of mitosis is prophase, anaphase, metaphase, telophase.
    C. Single-cell eukaryotes undergo mitosis as part of asexual reproduction.
    D. Mitosis is performed by prokaryotic cells.
    E. Cell plates are formed in animal cells during mitosis.

18. An organism that alternates between a haploid and a diploid multicellular stage during its life cycle is most probably a

    A. Shark
    B. Human
    C. Whale
    D. Pine tree
    E. Amoeba

19. Homologous chromosomes are chromosomes that

    A. Are found only in identical twins
    B. Are formed during mitosis
    C. Split apart during meiosis II
    D. Resemble one another in shape, size, and fuction
    E. Determine the sex of an organism

20. Crossover occurs during

    A. Prophase of mitosis
    B. Prophase I of meiosis
    C. Prophase II of meiosis
    D. Prophase I and II of meiosis
    E. All the above

21. Which of the following conditions is an X-linked condition?

    A. Hemophilia
    B. Tay-Sachs disease
    C. Huntington's disease
    D. Cystic fibrosis
    E. Sickle cell anemia

22. In hypercholesterolemia, a genetic condition found in humans, individuals who are HH have normal cholesterol levels, those who are hh have horrifically high cholesterol levels, and those who are Hh have cholesterol levels that are somewhere in between. This is an example of

    A. Dominance
    B. Incomplete dominance
    C. Codominance
    D. Pleiotropy
    E. Epistasis

23. The situation in which a gene at one locus alters the phenotypic expression of a gene at another locus is known as

    A. Dominance
    B. Incomplete dominance
    C. Codominance
    D. Pleiotropy
    E. Epistasis

24. Which of the following is an example of aneuploidy?

A. Cri-du-chat syndrome
B. Chronic myelogenous leukemia
C. Turner's syndrome
D. Achondroplasia
E. Phenylketonuria

25. Which of the following is an incorrect statement about DNA replication?

   A. It occurs in the nucleus.
   B. It occurs in a semiconservative fashion.
   C. Helicase is the enzyme that adds the nucleotides to the growing strand.
   D. DNA polymerase can build only in a 5′-to-3′ direction.
   E. It occurs during the S phase of the cell cycle.

26. A virus that carries the reverse transcriptase enzyme is

   A. A retrovirus
   B. A prion
   C. A viroid
   D. A DNA virus
   E. A plasmid

27. The uptake of foreign DNA from the surrounding environment is known as

   A. Generalized transduction
   B. Specialized transduction
   C. Conjugation
   D. Transformation
   E. Crossover

28. The process by which a huge amount of DNA is created from a small amount of DNA in a very short amount of time is known as

   A. Cloning
   B. Transformation
   C. Polymerase chain reaction
   D. Gel electrophoresis
   E. Generalized transduction

29. In a large pond that consists of long-finned fish and short-finned fish, a tornado wreaks havoc on the pond, killing 50 percent of the fish population. By chance, most of the fish killed were short-finned varieties, and in the subsequent generation there were fewer fish with short fins. This is an example of

   A. Gene flow
   B. Natural selection
   C. Bottleneck
   D. Balanced polymorphism
   E. Allopatric speciation

30. Imagine that for a particular species of moth, females are primed to respond to two types of male mating calls. Males who produce an in-between version will not succeed at obtaining a mate and will therefore have low reproductive success. This is an example of

   A. Directional selection
   B. Stabilizing selection
   C. Artificial selection
   D. Honest indicators
   E. Disruptive selection

31. Traits that are similar between organisms that arose from a common ancestor are known as

   A. Convergent characters
   B. Homologous characters
   C. Vestigial characters
   D. Stabilizing characters
   E. Divergent characters

32. Imagine that 9 percent of a population of anteaters have a short snout (recessive), while 91 percent have a long snout (dominant). If this population is in Hardy–Weinberg equilibrium, what is the expected frequency (in percent) of the heterozygous condition?

   A. 26.0
   B. 30.0
   C. 34.0
   D. 38.0
   E. 42.0

33. Which of the following is the *least* specific taxonomic classification category?

   A. Class
   B. Division
   C. Order
   D. Family
   E. Genus

34. Which of the following is not a characteristic of bryophytes?

   A. They are the first land plants.
   B. They contain a waxy cuticle to protect against water loss.
   C. They package their gametes into gametangia.
   D. They do not contain xylem.
   E. The dominant generation is the sporophyte.

35. Halophiles would be classified into which major kingdom?

   A. Monera
   B. Protista

C. Plantae
D. Fungi
E. Animalia

36. Plants that produce a single spore type that gives rise to bisexual gametophytes are called

A. Heterosporous
B. Tracheophytes
C. Gymnosperms
D. Homosporous
E. Angiosperms

37. A vine that wraps around the trunk of a tree is displaying the concept known as

A. Photoperiodism
B. Thigmotropism
C. Gravitropism
D. Phototropism
E. Transpiration

38. These cells control the opening and closing of a plant's stomata:

A. Guard cells
B. Collenchyma cells
C. Parenchyma cells
D. Mesophyll cells
E. Sclerenchyma cells

39. You have just come back from visiting the Red Wood Forests in California and were amazed at how *wide* those trees were. What process is responsible for the increase in width of these trees?

A. Growth of guard cells
B. Growth of collenchyma cells
C. Growth of apical meristem cells
D. Growth of lateral meristem cells
E. Growth of trachied cells

40. This hormone is known for assisting in the closing of the stomata, and inhibition of cell growth

A. Abscisic acid
B. Auxin
C. Cytokinin
D. Ethylene
E. Gibberellin

41. In which of the following structures would one most likely find smooth muscle?

A. Biceps muscle
B. Heart

C. Digestive tract
D. Quadriceps muscle
E. Gluteus maximus muscle

42. Which of the following hormones is *not* released by the anterior pituitary gland?

A. Follicle-stimulating hormone (FSH)
B. Anti-diuretic hormone (ADH)
C. Growth hormone (GH or STH)
D. Adrenocorticotropic hormone (ACTH)
E. Luteinizing hormone (LH)

43. Most of the digestion of food occurs in the

A. Mouth
B. Esophagus
C. Stomach
D. Small intestine
E. Large intestine

44. Antigen invader → B-cell meets antigen → B-cell differentiates into plasma cells and memory cells → plasma cells produce antibodies → antibodies eliminate antigen. The preceding sequence of events is a description of

A. Cell-mediated immunity
B. Humoral immunity
C. Nonspecific immunity
D. Phagocytosis
E. Cytotoxic T-cell maturation

45. In humans, spermatogenesis, the process of male gamete formation, occurs in the

A. Interstitial cells
B. Seminiferous tubules
C. Epididymis
D. Vas deferens
E. Seminal vesicles

46. The trophoblast formed during the early stages of human embryology eventually develops into the

A. Placenta
B. Embryo
C. Epiblast
D. Hypoblast
E. Morula

47. Which of the following structures would not have developed from the mesoderm?

A. Muscle
B. Heart

C. Kidneys
D. Bones
E. Liver

48. In humans, the developing embryo tends to attach to this structure

    A. Fallopian tube
    B. Oviduct
    C. Endometrium
    D. Cervix
    E. Ovary

For questions 49–52 please use the following answer choices:

    A. Associative learning
    B. Insight learning
    C. Optimal foraging
    D. Imprinting
    E. Altruistic behavior

49. The ability to reason through a problem the first time through with no prior experience.

50. Action in which an organism helps another, even if it comes at its own expense.

51. Process by which an animal substitutes one stimulus for another to get the same response.

52. Innate behavior learned during critical period early in life.

53. Warning coloration adopted by animals that possess a chemical defense mechanism is known as

    A. Cryptic coloration
    B. Deceptive markings
    C. Aposemetric coloration
    D. Batesian mimicry
    E. Müllerian mimicry

54. Ants live on acacia trees and are able to feast on the sugar produced by the tree. The tree is protected by the ants' attack on any foreign insects that may harm the tree. This is an example of

    A. Parasitism
    B. Commensualism
    C. Mutualism
    D. Symbiosis
    E. Competition

55. This biome is known for having the greatest diversity of species

    A. Taiga
    B. Temperate grasslands
    C. Tropical forest
    D. Savanna
    E. Deciduous forest

56. Which of the following is a characteristic of an R-selected strategist?

    A. Low reproductive rate
    B. Extensive postnatal care
    C. Relatively constant population size
    D. J-shaped growth curve
    E. Members include humans

For questions 57–60, please use the information from the following laboratory experiment:

You are working as a summer intern at the local university laboratory, and a lab technician comes into your room, throws a few graphs and tables at you, and mutters, "Interpret this data for me . . . I need to go play golf. I'll be back this afternoon for your report." Analyze the data this technician so kindly gave to you, and use it to answer questions 57–60. The reaction rates reported in the tables are relative to the original rate of the reaction in the absence of the enzymes. The three enzymes used are all being added to the same reactants to determine which should be used in the future.

Room Temperature (25°C), pH 7

Enzyme	Reaction Rate
1	1.24
2	1.51
3	1.33

Varying Temperature, Constant (pH 7)

Enzyme	0°C	5°C	10°C	15°C	20°C	25°C	30°C	35°C	40°C
1	1.00	1.02	1.04	1.19	1.20	1.24	1.29	1.27	1.22
2	1.01	1.12	1.35	1.39	1.65	1.51	1.40	1.12	1.01
3	1.06	1.21	1.55	1.44	1.35	1.33	1.15	1.10	1.06

Varying pH, Constant Temperature = 25°C

Enzyme	4	5	6	7	8	9	10
1	1.54	1.51	1.33	1.24	1.20	1.08	1.05
2	1.75	1.71	1.62	1.51	1.32	1.10	1.01
3	1.52	1.45	1.40	1.33	1.20	1.09	1.04

57. If you had also been given a graph that plotted the moles of product produced versus time, what would have been the best way to calculate the rate for the reaction?

   A. Calculate the average of the slope of the curve for the first and last minute of reaction.
   B. Calculate the slope of the curve for the portion of the curve that is constant.
   C. Calculate the slope of the curve for the portion where the slope begins to flatten out.
   D. Add up the total number of moles produced during each time interval and divide by the total number of time intervals measured.
   E. The rate of reaction cannot be determined from the graph.

58. Over the interval measured, at what temperature does enzyme 2 appear to have its optimal efficiency?

   A. 10°C
   B. 15°C
   C. 20°C
   D. 25°C
   E. 30°C

59. Which of the following statements about enzyme 3 is incorrect?

   A. At pH 6 and a temperature of 25°C, it is more efficient than enzyme 2, but less efficient than enzyme 1.
   B. It functions more efficiently in the acid pH range than the basic pH range.
   C. At 30°C and pH 7, it is less efficient than both enzymes 1 and 2.
   D. Over the interval given, its optimal temperature at pH 7 is 10°C.
   E. Over the interval given, its optimal pH at a temperature of 25°C is 4.

60. Which of the following statements can be made from review of these data?

   A. Enzyme 1 functions most efficiently in a basic environment and at a lower temperature.
   B. All three enzymes function most efficiently above 20°C when the pH is held constant at 7.
   C. Enzyme 1 functions more efficiently than enzyme 2 at 10°C and pH 7.
   D. The pH does not affect the efficiency of enzyme 3.
   E. All three enzymes function more efficiently in an acidic environment than a basic environment.

Answers and Explanations

 This test was designed to include four questions from each of the 15 review chapters. They are in chronological order for simplicity.

Questions from Chapter 1

1. **D**—This question deals with the concept of pH: acids and bases. The pH scale is a logarithmic scale that measures how much acidity or basicity a solution contains. A pH of 4 is 10 times more acidic than a pH of 5. A pH of 6 is 10^2 or 100 times more basic than a pH of 4, and so on. Therefore a pH of 10 is 10^3 or 1000 times more basic than a pH of 7.

2. **A**—This question deals with the five types of reactions you should be familiar with for the AP Biology exam. A hydrolysis reaction is one in which water is added, causing the formation of a compound.

3. **D**—Glycogen is a carbohydrate. The three major types of lipids you should know are fats, phospholipids, and steroids. Cholesterol is a type of steroid.

4. **C**—Functional groups are a pain in the neck. But you need to be able to recognize them on the exam. Most often, the test asks students to identify functional groups by structure.

Questions from Chapter 2

5. **D**—Prokaryotes are known for their simplicity. The do not contain a nucleus, nor do they contain membrane-bound organelles. They do have a few structures to remember: cell wall, plasma membrane, ribosomes, and a nucleoid. Lysosomes are found in eukaryotes, not prokaryotes.

6. **D**—This question deals with the cytoskeleton of cells. Cell division, cilia, and flagella would be compromised if the microtubules were damaged. Microfilaments, made from actin, are important to muscular contraction. Chitin is a polysaccharide found in fungi.

7. **E**—Active transport requires energy. The major types of cell transport you need to know for the exam are diffusion, osmosis, facilitated diffusion, endocytosis, exocytosis, and active transport.

8. **A**—The selectively permeable membrane is a lipid bilayer composed of phospholipids, proteins, and other macromolecules. Small uncharged polar molecules and lipids are able to pass through these membranes without difficulty.

Questions from Chapter 3

9. **C**—Each NADH is able to produce up to 3 ATP. Each $FADH_2$ can produce up to 2 ATP.

10. **D**—You have to know the concept of chemiosmosis for the AP exam. Make sure you study it well in Chapter 3.

11. **A**—Glycolysis is the conversion of glucose into pyruvate that occurs in the cytoplasm and is the first step of both aerobic and anaerobic respiration.

12. **E**—Fermentation is anaerobic respiration, and it is the process that begins with glycolysis and ends with the regeneration of NAD^+.

Questions from Chapter 4

13. **D**—C_4 photosynthesis is an adaptive photosynthetic process that attempts to counter the problems that hot and dry weather causes for plants. Be sure that you read about and understand the various forms of photosynthesis for the exam.

14. **D**—The light-dependent reactions occur in the thylakoid membrane. The dark reactions, known as the *Calvin cycle*, occur in the stroma.

15. **A**—The inputs to the light reactions include light and water. During these reactions, photolysis occurs, which is the splitting of H_2O into hydrogen ions and oxygen atoms. These oxygen atoms from the water pair together immediately to form the oxygen we breathe.

16. **B**—The Calvin cycle uses a disproportionate amount of ATP relative to NADPH. The cyclic light reactions exist to make up for this disparity. The cyclic reactions do not produce NADPH, nor do they produce oxygen.

Questions from Chapter 5

17. **C**—Mitosis makes up 10 percent of the cell cycle; the correct order of the stages is prophase, metaphase, anaphase, telophase; mitosis is not performed by prokaryotic cells; and cell plates are formed in plant cells.

18. **D**—This life cycle is the one known as "alternation of generations." It is the plant life cycle. Pine trees are the only ones among the choices that would show such a cycle.

19. **D**—Homologous chromosomes resemble one another in shape, size, and function. They pair up during meiosis and separate from each other during meiosis I.

20. **B**—You have to know this fact. I don't want them to get you on this one if they even ask it. ☺

Questions from Chapter 6

21. **A**—Tay-Sachs disease, cystic fibrosis, and sickle cell anemia are all autosomal recessive conditions. Huntington's disease is an autosomal dominant condition. It will serve you well to learn the most common autosomal recessive conditions, X-linked conditions, and autosomal dominant conditions.

22. **B**—Incomplete dominance is the situation in which the heterozygous genotype produces an "intermediate" phenotype rather than the dominant phenotype; neither allele dominates the other.

23. **E**—Epistasis exists when a gene at one locus affects a gene at another locus.

24. **C**—Turner's syndrome (XO) is an example of aneuploidy—conditions in which individuals have an abnormal number of chromosomes. These conditions can be

monosomies, as is the case with Turner's, or they can be trisomies, as is the case with Down's, Klinefelter's, and other syndromes.

Questions from Chapter 7

25. **C**—DNA polymerase is the superstar enzyme of the replication process, which occurs during the S phase of the cell cycle in the nucleus of a cell. The process does occur in semiconservative fashion. You should learn the basic concepts behind replication as they are explained in Chapter 7.

26. **A**—Retroviruses are RNA viruses that carry with them the reverse transcriptase enzyme. When they take over a host cell, they first use the enzyme to convert themselves into DNA. They next incorporate into the DNA of the host, and begin the process of viral replication. The HIV virus of AIDS is a well-known retrovirus.

27. **D**—It will serve you well to be reasonably familiar with the biotechnology laboratory techniques for this exam. Lab procedures show up often on free-response questions and the later multiple-choice sections of the exam.

28. **C**—Polymerase chain reaction is the high-speed cloning machine of molecular genetics. It occurs at a much faster rate than does cloning.

Questions from Chapter 8

29. **C**—A bottleneck is a specific example of genetic drift: the sudden change in allele frequencies due to random events.

30. **E**—This is a prime example of disruptive selection. Take a look at the material from Chapter 8 on the various types of selection. The illustrations there are worth reviewing.

31. **B**—Traits are said to be homologous if they are similar because their host organisms arose from a common ancestor. For example, the bone structure in bird wings is homologous in all bird species.

32. **E**—If 9 percent of the population is recessive (ss), then $q^2 = 0.09$. Taking the square root of 0.09 gives us $q = 0.30$. Knowing like we do that $p + q = 1$, $p + 0.30 = 1$, and $p = 0.70$. The frequency of the heterozygous condition = $2pq = 2(0.30)(0.70) = 42\%$.

Questions from Chapter 9

33. **B**—The stupid phrase I use to remember this classification hierarchy is "Karaoke players can order free grape soda"—kingdom, phylum, class, order, family, genus, and species. This question is sneaky because it requires you to know that a division is the plant kingdom's version of the phylum. The kingdom is the least specific subdivision, and the species the most specific. Therefore B is the correct answer.

34. **E**—The dominant generation for bryophytes is the gametophyte (n) generation. They are the only plants for which this is true.

35. **A**—Halophiles are a member of the archaebacteria subgroup of the monerans.

36. **D**—Homosporous plants, such as ferns, give rise to bisexual gametophytes.

Questions from Chapter 10

37. **B**—Thigmotropism, phototropism, and gravitropism are the major tropisms you need to know for plants. Thigmotropism, the growth response of a plant to touch, is the least understood of the bunch.

38. **A**—Guard cells are the cells responsible for controlling the opening and closing of the stomata of a plant.

39. **D**—This is known as *cambium*.

40. **A**—There are five plant hormones you should know for the exam. Auxin seems to come up the most, but it would serve you well to know the basic functions of all five of them.

Questions from Chapter 11

41. **C**—Smooth muscle is found in the digestive tract, bladder, and arteries, to name only a few. Answer choices A, B, and E are skeletal muscles.

42. **B**—This hormone, which is involved in controlling the function of the kidney, is released from the posterior pituitary.

43. **D**—The small intestine hosts the most digestion of the digestive tract.

44. **B**—Humoral immunity is antibody-related specific immunity. Cell-mediated immunity involves T cells, viruses, and direct cellular destruction of invaders.

Questions from Chapter 12

45. **B**—You should learn the general processes of spermatogenesis and oogenesis in humans for the AP Biology exam.

46. **A**—The inner cell mass gives rise to the embryo which eventually gives rise to the epiblast and hypoblast. The morula is an early stage of development.

47. **E**—You should learn the list of structures derived from endoderm, mesoderm, and ectoderm. (This could be an easy multiple-choice question for you if you do.)

48. **C**—Fertilization tends to occur in the oviduct, also known as the *fallopian tube*. The ovum is produced in the ovary, and the cervix is the passageway from the uterus to the vagina.

Questions from Chapter 13

49. **B**—Chapter 13 is fairly short and concise. I left it to the bare bones for you to learn. I would learn this chapter well because it could be worth a good 5–7 points for you on the exam if you are lucky. ☺

50. E

51. A

52. D

Questions from Chapter 14

53. **C**—Learn the defense mechanisms well from predator–prey relationships in Chapter 14. They will be represented on the exam.

54. **C**—Mutualism is the interaction in which both parties involved benefit.

55. **C**—Biomes are annoying and tough to memorize. Learn as much as you can about them without taking up too much time. . . . More often than not there will be two to three multiple-choice questions about them. But you want to make sure you learn enough to work your way through a free-response question if you were to be so unfortunate as to have one on your test.

56. **D**—A J-shaped growth curve is characteristic of exponentially growing populations. That is a characteristic of R-selected strategists.

Questions from Chapter 15

57. **B**—The rate of reaction for an enzyme-aided reaction is best estimated by taking the slope of the constant portion of the moles–time plot.

58. **C**—They will test your ability to interpret data on this exam. You should make sure that you are able to look at a chart and interpret information given to you. This enzyme does indeed function most efficiently at 20°C. Above and below that temperature, the reaction rate is lower.

59. **A**—At a pH of 6 and a temperature of 25°C, enzyme 3 is actually more efficient than enzyme 2, and less efficient than enzyme 1.

60. **E**—This question requires you to know that a pH below 7 (pH < 7) is acidic and a pH above 7 (pH > 7) is basic. It is true that all three enzymes increase the rate of reaction more when in acidic environments than basic environments.

Scoring and Interpretation

Now that you have finished the diagnostic exam and scored yourself, it is time to try to figure out what it all means. First, see if there are any particular areas that you personally struggled in. By this I mean, were there any questions during which you were thinking to yourself something like, "I learned this . . . *when*?!?!" or "What the heck is *this*?!?!" If so, put a little star next to the chapter that contains the material for which this occurred. You may want to spend a bit more time on that chapter during your review for this exam. It is quite possible that you *never* learned some of the material in this book. Not every class is able to cover all the same information.

To get your baseline score for this practice exam, use the following formula (where N represents the number of answers):

$$(N_{correct} - {}^1\!/_4\, N_{incorrect}) = \text{raw score for the multiple-choice section}$$

There are no free-response questions in the diagnostic since I did not want to put you through the torture of that procedure yet, as you are just beginning your journey. As a result, we will guesstimate your score on the basis of multiple-choice questions alone. I will spare you my convoluted calculations and just show you what range I came up with in my analysis. Remember, these are just rough estimates on questions that are not actual AP exam questions . . . do not read too much into them.

Raw Score	Approximate AP Score
35–60	5
26–34	4
19–25	3
11–18	2
0–10	1

If this test went amazingly well for you . . . rock and roll . . . but as I just said earlier, your journey is just beginning and that means that you have time to supplement your knowledge even more before the big day! Use your time well.

If this test went poorly for you, don't worry; as has been said twice now, your journey is just beginning and you have plenty of time to learn what you need to know for this exam. Just use this as an exercise in focus that has shown you what you need to concentrate on between now and mid-May. Good luck!

PART III

COMPREHENSIVE REVIEW

Chapter 1

Chemistry

INTRODUCTION

What is the name of the test you are studying for? The AP Biology exam. Then why in tarnation am I starting your review with a chapter entitled *Chemistry*?!?!? Because it is important that you have an understanding of a few chemical principles before we dive into the deeper biological material. I will keep it short, don't worry. ☺

ELEMENTS, COMPOUNDS, ATOMS, AND IONS

By definition, **matter** is anything that has mass and takes up space; an **element** is defined as matter in its simplest form; an **atom** is the smallest form of an element that still displays its particular properties (terms boldfaced in text are listed in Glossary at the end of the book). For example, sodium (Na) is an element mentioned often in this book, especially in Chapter 11, Human Physiology. The element sodium can exist as an atom of sodium, in which it is a neutral particle containing an equal number of protons and electrons. It can also exist as an **ion,** which is an atom that has a positive or negative charge. Ions such as sodium that take on a positive charge are called **cations,** and are composed of more protons than electrons. Ions with a negative charge are called **anions,** and are composed of more electrons than protons.

Elements can be combined to form **compounds.** The two major types of compounds you need to be familiar with are **organic** and **inorganic** compounds. Organic compounds contain carbon and usually hydrogen; inorganic compounds do not. Some of you are probably skeptical, at this point, as to whether any of what I have said thus far matters for this exam. Bear with me because it does. You will deal with many important organic compounds later on in this book, including **carbohydrates, proteins, lipids,** and **nucleic acids** (Chapter 7).

John: 11th grade "My teacher wanted me to know these structures . . . she was right!"

Before moving onto the next section, where we discuss these particular organic compounds in more detail, I would like to cover a topic that many find confusing and therefore ignore in preparing for this exam. This is the subject of **functional groups.** These poorly understood groups are the chaps responsible for the chemical properties of organic compounds. They should not intimidate you, nor should you spend a million hours trying to memorize them in full detail. You should remember one or two examples of each group and be able to identify the functional groups on sight, as you are often asked to do so on the AP exam.

The following is a list of the functional groups you should study for this exam:

1. *Amino group.* An amino group has the following formula:

$$R - N \begin{array}{c} H \\ H \end{array}$$

The symbol R stands for "rest of the compound" to which this NH_2 group is attached. One example of a compound containing an amino group is an **amino acid.** Compounds containing amino groups are generally referred to as **amines.** Amino groups act as bases and can pick up protons from acids.

2. *Carbonyl group.* This group contains two structures:

$$\begin{array}{c} R \\ | \\ C = O \\ | \\ R \end{array} \qquad R - C \begin{array}{c} O \\ \\ H \end{array}$$

ketone   **aldehyde**

If the C=O is at the end of a chain, it is an **aldehyde.** Otherwise, it is a **ketone.** (*Note:* In aldehydes there is an H at the end; there is no H in the word *ketone.*) A carbonyl group makes a compound **hydrophilic** and **polar.** *Hydrophilic* means water-loving, reacting well with water. A *polar* molecule is one that has an unequal distribution of charge, which creates a positive side and a negative side to the molecule.

3. *Carboxyl group.* This group has the following formula:

$$R \begin{array}{c} O \\ \\ C \\ \\ OH \end{array}$$

A *carboxyl group* is a carbonyl group that has a hydroxide in one of the R spots and a carbon chain in the other. This functional group shows up along with amino groups in amino acids. Carboxyl groups act as acids because they are able to donate protons to basic compounds. Compounds containing carboxyl groups are known as *carboxylic acids.*

4. *Hydroxyl group.* This group has the simplest formula of the bunch:

$$R - OH$$

A hydroxyl group is present in compounds known as **alcohols.** Like carbonyl groups, hydroxyl groups are polar and hydrophillic.

5. *Phosphate group.* This group has the following formula:

$$\begin{array}{c} O \\ || \\ R - O - P = O \\ | \\ O^- \end{array}$$

Phosphate groups are vital components of molecules that serve as cellular energy sources: ATP, ADP, and GTP. Like carboxyl groups, phosphate groups are acidic molecules.

6. *Sulfhydryl group.* This group also has a simple formula:

$$R - SH$$

This functional group does not show up much on the exam, but you should recognize it when it does. This group is present in the amino acids methionine and cysteine and assists in structure stabilization in many proteins.

LIPIDS, CARBOHYDRATES, AND PROTEINS

Lipids

Lipids are organic compounds used by cells as long-term energy stores or building blocks. Lipids are hydrophobic and insoluble in water because they contain a hydrocarbon tail of CH_2s that is nonpolar and repellant to water. The most important lipids are **fats, oils, steroids,** and **phospholipids.**

Fats, which are lipids made by combining **glycerol** and three **fatty acids,** (see Figure 1.1) are used as long-term energy stores in cells. They are not as easily metabolized as carbohydrates, yet they are a more effective means of storage; for instance, one gram of fat provides two times the energy of one gram of carbohydrate. Fats can be **saturated** or **unsaturated.** Saturated fat molecules contain no double bonds. Unsaturated fats contain one (mono-) or more (poly-) double bonds, which means that they contain fewer hydrogen molecules per carbon than do saturated fats. Saturated fats are the bad guys and are associated with heart disease and atherosclerosis. Most of the fat found in animals is saturated, whereas plants tend to contain unsaturated fats. Fat is formed when three fatty acid molecules connect to the OH groups of the glycerol molecule. These connecting bonds are formed by dehydration synthesis reaction (see Figure 1.2).

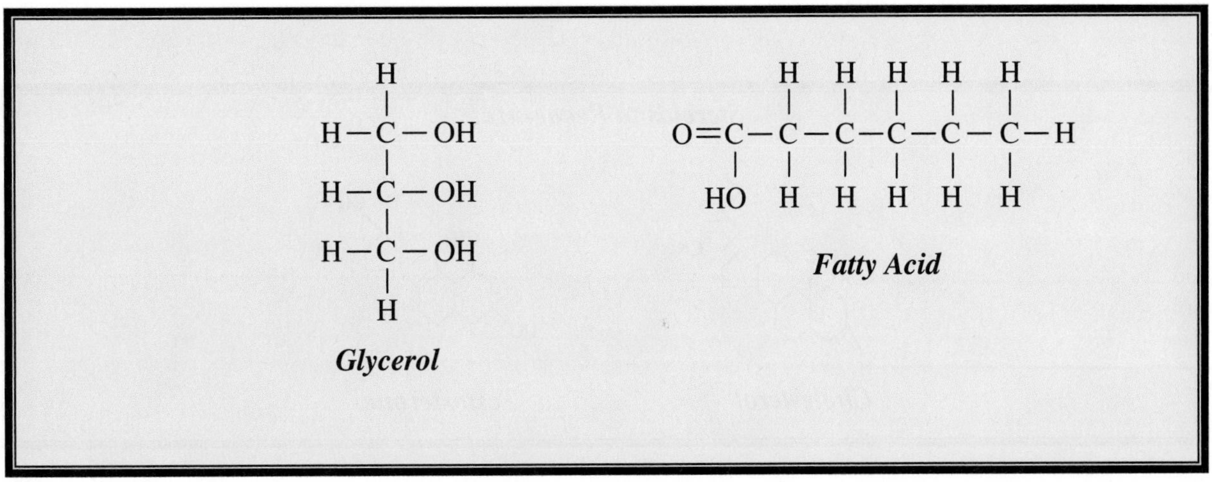

Figure 1.1
Structure of glycerol and fatty acids.

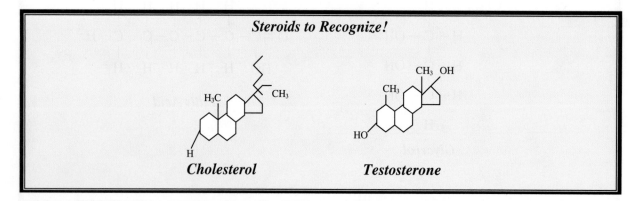

Figure 1.2
Fat (glycerol plus three fatty acids).

Steroids are lipids composed of four carbon rings that look like chicken-wire fencing in pictorial representations. One example of a steroid is cholesterol, an important structural component of cell membranes that serves as a precursor molecule for another important class of steroids: the sex hormones (testosterone, progesterone, and estrogen). You should be able to recognize the structures shown in Figure 1.3 for the AP exam.

A **phospholipid** is a lipid formed by combining a glycerol molecule with two fatty acids and a phosphate group (Figure 1.4). Phospholipids are bilayered structures; they have both a hydrophobic tail (a hydrocarbon chain) and a hydrophilic head (the phosphate group) (see Figure 1.5). They are the major component of cell membranes; the hydrophilic phosphate group forms the outside portion and the hydrophobic tail forms the interior of the wall.

Steroids to Recognize!

Cholesterol   Testosterone

Figure 1.3
Steroid structures.

```
                              H   H   H   H   H
                              |   |   |   |   |
           H      O=C—C—C—C—C—C—H
                              |   |   |   |   |
       H—C————O   H   H   H   H   H
                              H   H   H   H   H
                              |   |   |   |   |
                  O=C—C—C—C—C—C—H
                              |   |   |   |   |
       H—C————O   H   H   H   H   H


                              O
                              ||
       H—C—O—P=O
           |          |
           H          O⁻
```

Figure 1.4
Structure of phospholipid.

Carbohydrates

Carbohydrates can be simple sugars or complex molecules containing multiple sugars. Carbohydrates are used by the cells of the body in energy-producing reactions and as structural materials. Carbohydrates have the elements C, H, and O. Hydrogen and oxygen are present in a 2 : 1 ratio. The three main types of carbohydrates you need to know are monosaccharides, disaccharides, and polysaccharides:

A **monosaccharide**, or simple sugar, is the simplest form of a carbohydrate. The most important monosaccharide is glucose ($C_6H_{12}O_6$), which is used in cellular respiration to provide energy for cells. Monosaccharides with five carbons ($C_5H_{10}O_5$) are used in compounds such as genetic molecules (RNA) and high-energy molecules (ATP). The structural formula for glucose is shown in Figure 1.6.

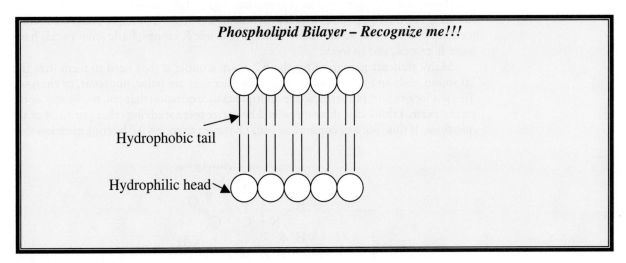

Figure 1.5
Bilayered structure of phospholipids.

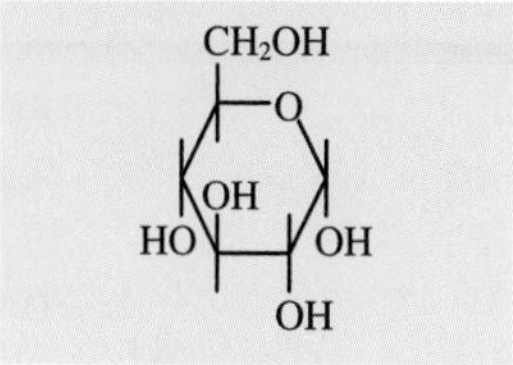

Figure 1.6
Glucose structures.

A **disaccharide** is a sugar consisting of two monosaccharides bound together. Common disaccharides include sucrose, maltose, and lactose. Sucrose, a major energy carbohydrate in plants, is a combination of fructose and glucose; maltose, a carbohydrate used in the creation of beer, is a combination of two glucose molecules; and lactose, found in dairy products, is a combination of galactose and glucose.

A **polysaccharide** is a carbohydrate containing three or more monosaccharide molecules. Polysaccharides, usually composed of hundreds or thousands of monosaccharides, act as a storage form of energy, and as structural material in and around cells. The most important carbohydrates for storing energy are **starch** and **glycogen.** Starch, made solely of glucose molecules linked together, is the storage form of choice for plants. Animals store much of their energy in the form of glycogen, which is most often found in liver and muscle cells. Glycogen is formed by linking many glucose molecules together.

Two important structural polysaccharides are **cellulose** and **chitin.** Cellulose, a compound composed of many glucose molecules, is used by plants in the formation of their cell wall. Chitin is an important part of the exoskeletons of arthropods such as insects, spiders, and shellfish (see Chapter 9, Taxonomy and Classification).

Julie: 11th grade
"Remembering these 4 came in handy on the test!"

Proteins

A **protein** is a compound composed of chains of amino acids. Proteins have many functions in the body—they serve as structural components, transport aids, enzymes, and cell signals, to name only a few. You should be able to identify a protein or an amino acid by sight if asked to do so on the test.

An amino acid consists of a carbon center surrounded by an amino group, a carboxyl group, a hydrogen, and an R group (see Figure 1.7). Remember that the R stands for "rest" of the compound, which provides an amino acid's unique personal characteristics. For instance, acidic amino acids have acidic R groups, basic amino acids have basic R groups, and so forth.

Many students preparing for the AP exam wonder if they need to memorize the 20 amino acids and their structures, and whether they are polar, nonpolar, or charged. This is a lot of effort for perhaps one multiple-choice question that you might encounter on the exam. I think that this time would be better spent studying other potential exam questions. If this is of any comfort to you, I have yet to see an AP biology question that

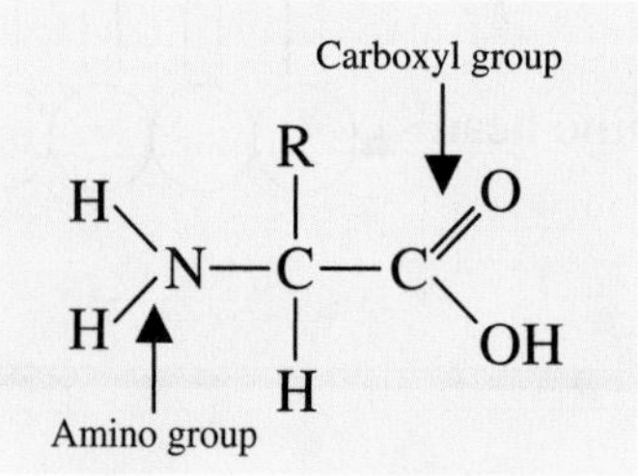

Figure 1.7
Structure of an amino acid.

asks something to the effect of "which of these 5 amino acids is nonpolar?" (*Disclaimer:* This does not mean that it will never happen ☺.) It is more important for you to identify the general structure of an amino acid and know the process of protein synthesis, which we discuss in Chapter 7.

A protein consists of amino acids linked together as shown in Figure 1.8. They are most often much larger than that depicted here. Figure 1.8 is included to enable you to identify a peptide linkage on the exam. Most proteins have many more amino acids in the chain.

The AP exam may expect you to know about the structure of proteins:

Primary structure. The order of the amino acids that make up the protein.

Secondary structure. Three-dimensional arrangement of a protein caused by hydrogen bonding at regular intervals along the polypeptide backbone.

Tertiary structure. Three-dimensional arrangement of a protein caused by interaction among the various R groups of the amino acids involved.

Quaternary structure. The arrangement of separate polypeptide "subunits" into a single protein. Not all proteins have quaternary structure; many consist of a single polypeptide chain.

Proteins with only primary and secondary structure are called *fibrous* proteins. Proteins with only primary, secondary, and tertiary structures are called *globular* proteins. Either fibrous or globular proteins may contain quaternary structure if there is more than one polypeptide chain.

! ENZYMES

Teacher: CT
The topic of enzymes is full of essay material. Know it well.

Enzymes are proteins that act as organic catalysts and will be encountered often in your review for this exam. **Catalysts** speed up reactions by lowering the energy (activation energy) needed for the reaction to take place but are not used up in the reaction. The substances that enzymes act on are known as **substrates.**

Enzymes are selective; they interact only with particular substrates. It is the shape of the enzyme that provides the specificity. The part of the enzyme that interacts with the substrate is called the **active site.** The **induced-fit model** of enzyme-substrate interaction describes the active site of an enzyme as specific for a particular substrate that fits its shape. When the enzyme and substrate bind together, the enzyme is *induced* to alter its shape for a tighter active site–substrate attachment. This tight fit places the substrate in a favorable position to react, speeding up (accelerating) the rate of reaction. After an enzyme interacts with a substrate, converting it into a product, it is free to find and react with another substrate; thus, a small concentration of enzyme can have a major effect on a reaction.

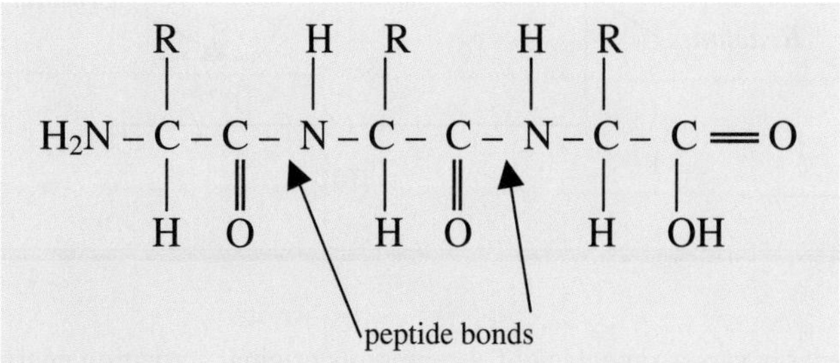

Figure 1.8
Amino acid structure exhibiting peptide linkage.

Every enzyme functions best at an optimal temperature and pH. If the pH or temperature strays from those optimal values, the effectiveness of the enzyme will suffer. The effectiveness of an enzyme can be affected by four things:

1. The temperature
2. The pH
3. The concentration of the substrate involved
4. The concentration of the enzyme involved

You should be able to identify the basic components of an activation energy diagram if you encounter one on the AP exam. The important parts are identified in Figure 1.9.

The last enzyme topic to cover is the difference between competitive and noncompetitive inhibition. In **competitive inhibition** (see Figure 1.10) an inhibitor molecule resembling the substrate binds to the active site and physically blocks the substrate from attaching. Competitive inhibition can sometimes be overcome by adding a high concentration of substrate to outcompete the inhibitor. In **noncompetitive inhibition** (Figure 1.11) an inhibitor molecule binds to a different part of the enzyme, causing a change in the shape of the active site so that it can no longer interact with the substrate.

pH: ACIDS AND BASES

The pH scale is used to indicate how acidic or basic a solution is. It ranges from 0 to 14; 7 is neutral. Anything less than 7 is acidic; anything greater than 7 is basic. The pH scale is a logarithmic scale and as a result, a pH of 5 is 10 times more acidic than a pH of 6. Following the same logic, a pH of 4 is 100 times more acidic than a pH of 6. Remember that as the pH of a solution *decreases,* the concentration of hydrogen ions in the solution *increases,* and vice versa. For the most part, chemical reactions in humans function at a neutral pH. The exceptions to this rule are the chemical reactions involving the enzymes of the digestive system (see Chapter 11, Human Physiology).

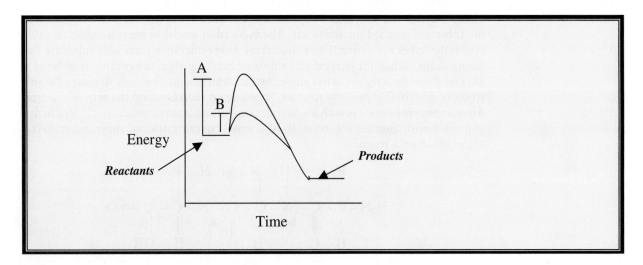

Figure 1.9

Plot showing energy versus time. Height *A* represents original activation energy; height *B* represents the lowered activation energy due to the addition of enzyme.

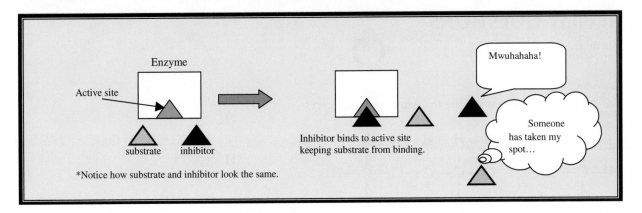

Figure 1.10
Competitive inhibition.

REACTIONS

There are five types of reactions you should know for this exam:

1. Hydrolysis reaction. A reaction that breaks down compounds by the addition of H_2O.
2. Dehydration synthesis reaction. A reaction in which two compounds are brought together with H_2O released as a product.
3. Endergonic reaction. A reaction that requires input of energy to occur.

$$A + B + energy \rightarrow C$$

4. Exergonic reaction. A reaction that gives off energy as a product.

$$A + B \rightarrow energy + C$$

5. Redox reaction. A reaction involving the transfer of electrons. Such reactions occur along the electron transport chain of the mitochondria during respiration (Chapter 3).

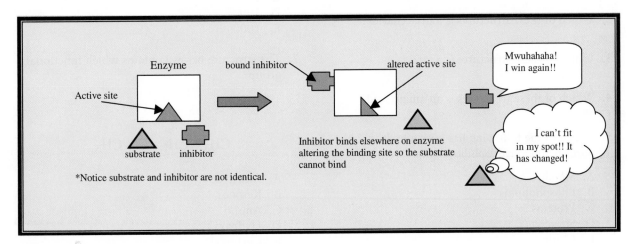

Figure 1.11
Noncompetitive inhibition.

REVIEW QUESTIONS

For questions 1–4 please use the following answer choices:

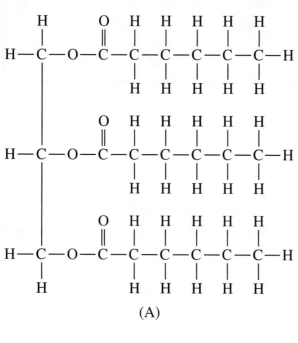

(A)

(B)

(C)

(D)

1. Which of the structures shown above is a polypeptide?

2. Which of these structures is a disaccharide?

3. Which of these structures is a fat?

4. Which of these structures is an amino acid?

5. Which of the following has both a hydrophobic portion and a hydrophilic portion?

   A. Starch
   B. Phospholipids
   C. Proteins
   D. Steroids
   E. Chitin

6. A substance that has a pH of 2 is how many times more acidic than one with a pH of 5?

   A. 2
   B. 5
   C. 10
   D. 100
   E. 1000

7. The structure below contains which functional group?

$$CH_3 - CH_2 - \overset{\overset{\textstyle O}{\|}}{C} - CH_3$$

   A. Aldehyde
   B. Ketone
   C. Amino
   D. Hydroxyl
   E. Carboxyl

8. Which of the following will least affect the effectiveness of an enzyme?

A. Temperature
B. pH
C. Concentration of substrate
D. Concentration of enzyme
E. Original activation energy of system

9. Which of the following is similar to the process of competitive inhibition?

A. When you arrive at work in the morning, you are unable to park your car in your (assigned) parking spot because the car of the person who parks next to you has taken up just enough space that you cannot fit your own car in.

B. When you arrive at work in the morning, you are unable to park your car in your parking spot because someone with a car exactly like yours has already taken your spot, leaving you nowhere to park your car.

C. As you are about to park your car in your spot at work, a giant bulldozer comes along and smashes your car away from the spot,

preventing you from parking your car in your spot.

D. When you arrive at work in the morning, you are unable to park your car in your parking spot because someone has placed a giant cement block in front of your spot.

10. All the following are carbohydrates except

A. Starch
B. Glycogen
C. Chitin
D. Glycerol
E. Cellulose

11. An amino acid contains which of the following functional groups?

A. Carboxyl group and amino group
B. Carbonyl group and amino group
C. Hydroxyl group and amino group
D. Carboxyl group and hydroxyl group
E. Carbonyl group and carboxyl group

ANSWERS AND EXPLANATIONS

1. **D**

2. **C**

3. **A**

4. **B**

5. **B**—A phospholipid has both a hydrophobic portion and a hydrophilic portion. The hydrocarbon portion, or tail of the phospholipid, dislikes water, and the phosphate portion, the head, is hydrophilic.

6. **E**—Because the pH scale is logarithmic, 2 is 1000 times more acidic than 5.

7. **B**—This functional group is a carbonyl group. The two main types of carbonyl groups are ketones and aldehydes. In this case, it is a ketone because there are carbon chains on either side of the carbon double bonded to the oxygen.

8. **E**—The four main factors that affect enzyme efficiency are pH, temperature, enzyme concentration, and substrate concentration.

9. **B**—Competitive inhibition is the inhibition of an enzyme–substrate reaction in which the inhibitor resembles the substrate and physically blocks the substrate from attaching to the active site. This parking spot represents the active site, your car is the substrate, and the other car already in the spot is the competitive inhibitor. Examples A and D more closely resemble noncompetitive inhibition.

10. **D**—Glycerol is not a carbohydrate. It is an alcohol. Starch is a carbohydrate stored in plant cells. Glycogen is a carbohydrate stored in animal cells. Chitin is a carbohydrate used by arthropods to construct their exoskeletons. Cellulose is a carbohydrate used by plants to construct their cell walls.

11. A

$$\text{H}_2\text{N} - \overset{\overset{\displaystyle R}{|}}{\underset{\underset{\displaystyle H}{|}}{C}} - \overset{\overset{\displaystyle O}{\parallel}}{C} - \text{OH}$$

carboxyl group

amino group

RAPID REVIEW

Try to rapidly review the following material:

Organic compounds: contain carbon; examples include lipids, proteins, and carbs (carbohydrates).

Functional groups: amino (NH_2), carbonyl (RCOR), carboxyl (COOH), hydroxyl (OH), phosphate (PO_4), sulfhydryl (SH).

Fat: glycerol + 3 fatty acids.

Saturated fat: bad for you; animals have it; solidifies at room temperature.

Unsaturated fat: better for you, plants have it; liquifies at room temperature.

Steroids: lipids whose structures resemble chicken-wire fence. Includes cholesterol and sex hormones.

Phospholipids: glycerol + 2 fatty acids + phosphate. Phospholipids make up membrane bilayers of cells. They have hydrophobic interior, hydrophilic exteriors.

Carbohydrates: Energy and structural. Monosaccharides (glucose), disaccharides (sucrose, maltose, lactose), storage polysaccharides [starch (plants), glycogen (animals)], structural polysaccharides [chitin (fungi), cellulose (arthropods)].

Proteins: made in ribosomes out of amino acids; serve many functions (e.g., transport, enzymes, cell signals, receptor molecules, structural components, and channels).

Enzymes: catalytic proteins that react in an induced-fit fashion with substrates to speed up the rate of reactions by lowering the activation energy. Enzyme effectiveness is affected by changes in pH, temperature, and substrate and enzyme concentrations.

Competitive inhibition: inhibitor resembles substrate and binds to active site.

Noncompetitive inhibition: inhibitor binds elsewhere on enzyme; alters active site so that substrate cannot bind.

pH: logarithmic scale 0–7 acidic, 7 neutral, 7–14 basic (alkaline); pH 4 is 10 times more acidic than pH 5.

Reaction types

   Hydrolysis reaction: break down compounds by adding water

   Dehydration reaction: two components brought together, producing H_2O

   Endergonic reaction: reaction that requires input of energy

   Exergonic reaction: reaction that gives off energy

   Redox reaction: electron transfer reactions

Chapter 2

Cells

INTRODUCTION

A cell is defined as a small room, sometimes a prison room, usually designed for only one person (but usually housing two or more inmates, except for solitary-confinement cells). It is a place for rehabilitation—whoops! I'm looking at the wrong notes here. Sorry, let's start again. A cell is the basic unit of life (that's more like it), discovered in the seventeenth century by Robert Hooke. There are two major divisions of cells: prokaryotic and eukaryotic. This chapter starts with a discussion of these two cell types, followed by an examination of the organelles found in cells. We conclude with a look at the fluid mosaic model of the cell membrane and a discussion of the different types of cell transport: diffusion, facilitated diffusion, osmosis, active transport, endocytosis, and exocytosis.

TYPES OF CELLS

The **prokaryotic** cell is a *simple* cell. It has no nucleus, and no membrane-bound organelles. The genetic material of a prokaryotic cell is found in a region of the cell known as the **nucleoid.** Bacteria are a fine example of prokaryotic cells and divide by a process known as *binary fission*; they duplicate their genetic material, divide in half, and produce two identical daughter cells. Prokaryotic cells are found only in the kingdom Monera (bacteria group).

Steve: 12th grade "5 questions on my test dealt with organelle function, know them."

The **eukaryotic** cell is much more complex. It contains a nucleus, which functions as the control center of the cell, directing DNA replication, transcription, and cell growth. Eukaryotic organisms may be unicellular or multicellular. One of the key features of eukaryotic cells is the presence of membrane-bound organelles, each with its own duties. Two prominent members of the "Eukaryote Club" are animal and plant cells; the differences between these types of cells are discussed in the next section.

ORGANELLES

You should familiarize yourselves with approximately a dozen organelles and cell structures before taking the AP biology exam:

Prokaryotic Organelles

You should be familiar with the following structures:

Plasma membrane. This is a selective barrier around a cell composed of a double layer of phospholipids. Part of this selectivity is due to the many proteins that either rest on the exterior of the membrane or are embedded in the membrane of the cell. Each membrane has a different combination of lipids, proteins, and carbohydrates that provide it with its unique characteristics.

Cell wall. This is a wall or barrier that functions to shape and protect cells. This is present in all prokaryotes.

Ribosomes. These function as the host organelle for protein synthesis in the cell. Found in the cytoplasm of cells and composed of a large unit and a small subunit.

Eukaryotic Organelles

You should be familiar with the following structures:

Ribosomes. As in prokaryotes, eukaryotic ribosomes serve as the host organelle for protein synthesis. Eukaryotes have *bound* ribosomes, which are attached to endoplasmic reticula and form proteins that tend to be exported from the cell or sent to the membrane. There are also *free* ribosomes, which exist freely in the cytoplasm and produce proteins that remain in the cytoplasm of the cell. Eukaryotic ribosomes are built in a structure called the **nucleolus.**

Smooth endoplasmic reticulum. This is a membrane-bound organelle involved in lipid synthesis, detoxification, and carbohydrate metabolism. Liver cells contain a lot of **smooth endoplasmic reticulum** (SER) because they host a lot of carbohydrate metabolism (glycolysis). It is given the name "smooth" endoplasmic reticulum because there are no ribosomes on its cytoplasmic surface. The liver contains much SER for another reason—it is the site of alcohol detoxification.

Rough endoplasmic reticulum. This membrane-bound organelle is termed "rough" because of the presence of ribosomes on the cytoplasmic surface of the cell. The proteins produced by this organelle are often secreted by the cell and carried by vesicles to the **Golgi apparatus** for further modification.

Golgi apparatus. Proteins, lipids, and other macromolecules are sent to the Golgi to be modified by the addition of sugars and other molecules to form **glycoproteins.** The products are then sent in vesicles (escape pods that bud off the edge of the Golgi) to other parts of the cell, directed by the particular changes made by the Golgi. I think of the Golgi apparatus as the post office of the cell—packages are dropped off by customers, and the Golgi adds the appropriate postage and zip code to make sure that the package reaches the proper destination in the cell.

Mitochondria. These are double-membraned organelles that specialize in the production of ATP. The innermost portion of the mitochondrion is called the *matrix,* and the folds created by the inner of the two membranes are called *cristae.* The mitochondria are the host organelle for the Krebs cycle (matrix) and oxidative phosphorylation (cristae) of respiration, which we discuss in Chapter 3. I think of the mitochondria as the power plants of the cell.

Lysosome. This is a membrane-bound organelle that specializes in digestion. It contains enzymes that break down (hydrolyze) proteins, lipids, nucleic acids, and carbohydrates. This organelle is the stomach of the cell. Absence of a particular lysosomal hydrolytic enzyme can lead to a variety of diseases known as **storage diseases.** An example of this is **Tay-Sachs disease** (discussed in Chapter 6), in which an enzyme used to digest lipids is absent, leading to excessive accumulation of lipids in the brain. Lysosomes are often referred to as "suicide sacs" of the cell. Cells that are no longer needed are often destroyed in these sacs. An example of this process involves the cells of the tail of a tadpole, which are digested as a tadpole changes into a frog.

Nucleus. This is the control center of the cell. In eukaryotic cells, this is the storage site of genetic material (DNA). It is the site of replication, transcription, and posttranscriptional modification of RNA. It also contains the nucleolus, the site of ribosome synthesis.

Vacuole. This is a storage organelle that acts as a vault. Vacuoles are quite large in plant cells but small in animal cells.

Peroxisomes. These are organelles containing enzymes that produce hydrogen peroxide as a by-product while performing various functions, such as breakdown of fatty acids and detoxification of alcohol in the liver. Peroxisomes also contain an enzyme that converts the toxic hydrogen peroxide by-product of these reactions into cell-friendly water.

Chloroplast. The site of photosynthesis and energy production in plant cells. Chloroplasts contain many pigments, which provide leaves with their color. Chloroplasts are divided into an inner portion and outer portion. The inner fluid portion is called the **stroma,** which is surrounded by two outer membranes. Winding through the stroma is an inner membrane called the **thylakoid membrane system,** where the light-dependent reactions of photosynthesis occur. The light-independent (dark) reactions occur in the stroma.

Cytoskeleton. The skeleton of cells consists of three types of fibers that provide support, shape, and mobility to cells: microtubules, microfilaments, and intermediate filaments. **Microtubules** are constructed from tubulin and have a lead role in the separation of cells during cell division. Microtubules are also important components of cilia and flagella, which are structures that aid the movement of particles (Chapter 11). **Microfilaments,** constructed from actin, play a big part in muscular contraction. **Intermediate filaments** are constructed from a class of proteins called *keratins* and are thought to function as reinforcement for the shape and position of organelles in the cell.

> **Remember me!!!!**
> Of the structures listed above, animal cells contain *all except* cell walls and chloroplasts, and their vacuoles are small. Plant cells contain *all* the structures listed above and their vacuoles are large. Animal cells have centrioles (cell division structure); plant cells *do not!*

CELL MEMBRANES: FLUID MOSAIC MODEL

As discussed above and in Chapter 1, a cell membrane is a selective barrier surrounding a cell that has a phospholipid bilayer as its major structural component. Remember that the outer portion of the bilayer contains the hydrophilic (water-loving) tail of the phospholipid, while the inner portion is composed of the hydrophobic (water-fearing) head of the phospholipid (Figure 2.1).

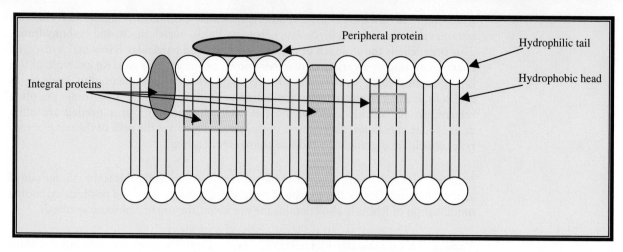

Figure 2.1
Cross section of a cell membrane showing phospholipid bilayer.

The **fluid mosaic model** is the most accepted model for the arrangement of membranes. It states that the membrane consists of a phospholipid bilayer with proteins of various lengths and sizes interspersed with cholesterol among the phospholipids. These proteins perform various functions depending on their location within the membrane.

The fluid mosaic model consists of **integral proteins,** which are implanted within the bilayer and can extend partway or all the way across the membrane, and **peripheral proteins,** such as receptor proteins, which are not implanted in the bilayer, and are often attached to integral proteins of the membrane. These proteins have various functions in cells. A protein that stretches across the membrane can function as a channel to assist the passage of desired molecules into the cell. Proteins on the exterior of a membrane with binding sites can act as receptors that allow the cell to respond to external signals such as hormones. Proteins embedded in the membrane can also function as enzymes, increasing the rate of cellular reactions.

The cell membrane is "selectively" permeable, meaning that it allows some molecules and other substances through, while others are not permitted to pass. The membrane is like a bouncer at a popular nightclub. What determines the selectivity of the membrane? One factor is size and charge of molecules. The bouncer lets small, uncharged polar molecules and hydrophobic molecules such as lipids through the membrane, whereas larger uncharged polar molecules (such as glucose) and charged ions (such as sodium) cannot pass through. The other factor determining what is allowed to pass through the membrane is the particular arrangement of proteins in the lipid bilayer. Different proteins in different arrangements allow different molecules to pass through.

! TYPES OF CELL TRANSPORT

There are six basic types of cell transport:

1. **Diffusion,** which is the movement of molecules down their concentration gradient without the use of energy. It is a *passive* process during which molecules move from a region of higher concentration to a region of lower concentration. The rate of diffusion of substances will vary from membrane to membrane because of different selective permeabilities.

2. **Osmosis,** which is the *passive* diffusion of water down its concentration gradient across selectively permeable membranes. Water moves from a region of *high* water concentration to a region of *low* water concentration. Thinking about osmosis another way, water will flow from a region with a *lower* solute concentration

(hypotonic) to a region with a *higher* solute concentration (hypertonic). This process does not require the input of energy. For example, visualize two regions—one with 10 particles of sodium per liter of water; the other, with 15. Osmosis would drive water from the region with 10 particles of sodium toward the region with 15 particles of sodium.

3. **Facilitated diffusion,** that is, the diffusion of particles across a selectively permeable membrane with the assistance of the membrane's transport proteins. These proteins will not bring any old molecule looking for a free pass into the cell; they are specific in what they will carry and have a binding site designed for molecules of interest. Like diffusion and osmosis, this process does not require the input of energy.

4. **Active transport,** which is the movement of a particle across a selectively permeable membrane *against* its concentration gradient (from low concentration to high). This movement requires the input of energy, which is why it is termed "active" transport. As is often the case in cells, adenosine triphosphate (ATP) is called on to provide the energy for this reactive process. These active-transport systems are vital to the ability of cells to maintain particular concentrations of substances despite environmental concentrations. For example, cells have a very high concentration of potassium and a very low concentration of sodium. Diffusion would like to move sodium in and potassium out to equalize the concentrations. The all-important **sodium–potassium pump** actively moves potassium *into* the cell and sodium *out of* the cell against their respective concentration gradients to maintain appropriate levels inside the cell. This is the major pump in animal cells.

5. **Endocytosis,** a process in which substances are brought into cells by the enclosure of the substance into a membrane-created vesicle that surrounds the substance and escorts it into the cell (Figure 2.2). This process is used by immune cells called **phagocytes** to engulf and eliminate foreign invaders.

6. **Exocytosis,** a process in which substances are exported out of the cell (the reverse of endocytosis). A vesicle again escorts the substance to the plasma membrane, causes it to fuse with the membrane, and ejects the contents of the substance outside the cell (Figure 2.2). In exocytosis, the vesicle functions like the trash chute of the cell.

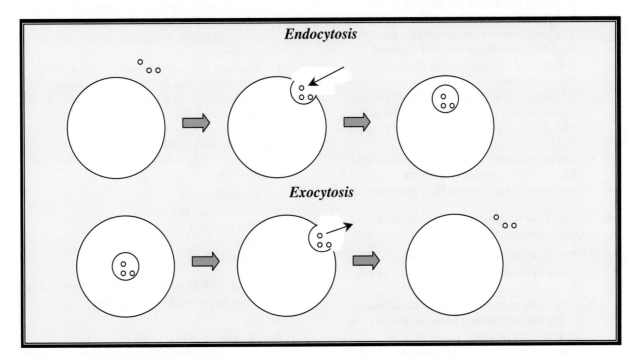

Figure 2.2
Endocytosis and exocytosis.

REVIEW QUESTIONS

For questions 1–4, please use the following answer choices:

    A. Cell wall
    B. Mitochondrion
    C. Ribosome
    D. Lysosome
    E. Golgi apparatus

1. This organelle is present in plant cells, but not animal cells.

2. Absence of enzymes from this organelle can lead to storage diseases such as Tay-Sachs disease.

3. This organelle is the host for the Krebs cycle and oxidative phosphorylation of respiration.

4. This organelle is synthesized in the nucleolus of the cell.

5. Which of the following best describes the fluid mosaic model of membranes?

    A. The membrane consists of a phospholipid bilayer with proteins of various lengths and sizes located on the exterior portions of the membrane.
    B. The membrane consists of a phospholipid bilayer with proteins of various lengths and sizes located in the interior of the membrane.
    C. The membrane is composed of a phospholipid bilayer with proteins of uniform lengths and sizes located in the interior of the membrane.
    D. The membrane contains a phospholipid bilayer with proteins of various lengths and sizes interspersed among the phospholipids.
    E. The membrane consists of a phospholipid bilayer with proteins of uniform length and size interspersed among the phospholipids.

6. Which of the following types of cell transport requires energy?

    A. The movement of a particle across a selectively permeable membrane down its concentration gradient
    B. The movement of a particle across a selectively permeable membrane against its concentration gradient
    C. The movement of water down its concentration gradient across selectively permeable membranes

    D. The movement of a sodium ion from an area of higher concentration to an area of lower concentration
    E. The movement of a particle across a selectively permeable membrane with the assistance of the membrane's transport proteins

7. Which of the following structures is present in prokaryotic cells?

    A. Nucleus
    B. Mitochondria
    C. Cell wall
    D. Golgi apparatus
    E. Lysosome

8. Which of the following represents an *incorrect* description of an organelle's function?

    A. *Chloroplast:* the site of photosynthesis and energy production in plant cells
    B. *Peroxisome:* organelle that produces hydrogen peroxide as a by-product of reactions involved in the breakdown of fatty acids, and detoxification of alcohol in the liver
    C. *Golgi apparatus:* structure to which proteins, lipids, and other macromolecules are sent to be modified by the addition of sugars and other molecules to form glycoproteins
    D. *Rough endoplasmic reticulum:* membrane-bound organelle lacking ribosomes on its cytoplasmic surface, involved in lipid synthesis, detoxification, and carbohydrate metabolism
    E. *Nucleus:* the control center in eukaryotic cells, which acts as the site for replication, transcription, and posttranscriptional modification of RNA

9. The destruction of which of the following would most cripple a cell's ability to undergo cell division?

    A. Microfilaments
    B. Intermediate filaments
    C. Microtubules
    D. Actin fibers
    E. Keratin fibers

10. Which of the following can easily diffuse across a selectively permeable membrane?

    A. Na^+
    B. Glucose
    C. Large uncharged polar molecules
    D. Charged ions
    E. Lipids

ANSWERS AND EXPLANATIONS

1. **A**—Cell walls exist in plant cells and prokaryotic cells, but not animal cells. They function to shape and protect cells.

2. **D**—The lysosome acts like the stomach of the cell. It contains enzymes that break down proteins, lipids, nucleic acids, and carbohydrates. Absence of these enzymes can lead to storage disorders such as Tay-Sachs disease.

3. **B**—The mitochondrion is the power plant of the cell. This organelle specializes in the production of ATP and hosts the Krebs cycle and oxidative phosphorylation.

4. **C**—The ribosome is an organelle made in the nucleolus that serves as the host for protein synthesis in the cell. It is found in both prokaryotes and eukaryotes.

5. **D**—The fluid mosaic model says that proteins can extend all the way through the phospholipid bilayer of the membrane, and that these proteins are of various sizes and lengths.

6. **B**—Answer choice B is the definition of active transport, which requires the input of energy. Facilitated diffusion (answer choice E), simple diffusion (answer choices A and D), and osmosis (answer choice C) are all passive processes that do not require energy input.

7. **C**—Prokaryotes do not contain many organelles, but they do contain cell walls.

8. **D**—This is the description of the *smooth* endoplasmic reticulum. I know that this is a tricky question, but I wanted you to review the distinction between the two types of endoplasmic reticulum.

9. **C**—Microtubules play an enormous role in cell division. They make up the spindle apparatus that works to pull apart the cells during mitosis (Chapter 5). A loss of microtubules would cripple the cell division process. Actin fibers (answer choice D) are the building blocks of microfilaments (answer choice A), which are involved in muscular contraction. Keratin fibers (answer choice E) are the building blocks of intermediate filaments (answer choice B), which function as reinforcement for the shape and position of organelles in the cell.

10. **E**—Lipids are the only substances listed above that are able to freely diffuse across selectively permeable membranes.

RAPID REVIEW

Try to rapidly review the materials presented in the following table and list:

Organelle	Prokaryotes	Animal Cells Eukaryotes	Plant Cells Eukaryotes	Function
Cell wall	+	–	+	Protects and shapes the cell
Plasma membrane	+	+	+	Selective barrier consisting of phospholipids, proteins, and carbohydrates
Ribosome	+	+	+	Host for protein synthesis; formed in nucleolus
Smooth ER*	–	+	+	Lipid synthesis, detoxification, carbohydrate metabolism; no ribosomes on cytoplasmic surface
Rough ER	–	+	+	Synthesizes proteins to secrete or send to plasma membrane. Contains ribosomes on cytoplasmic surface.
Golgi	–	+	+	Modifies lipids, proteins, etc. and sends them to other sites in the cell
Mitochondria	–	+	+	Power plant of cell; hosts major energy-producing steps of respiration.
Lysosome	–	+	+	Contains enzymes that digest organic compounds; serves as cell's stomach
Nucleus	–	+	+	Control center of cell. Host for transcription, replication, and DNA
Peroxisome	–	+	+	Breakdown of fatty acids, detoxification of alcohol
Chloroplast	–	–	+	Site of photosynthesis in plants
Cytoskeleton	–	+	+	Skeleton of cell; consists of microtubules (cell division, cilia, flagella), microfilaments (muscles), and intermediate filaments (reinforcing position of organelles)
Vacuole	–	+, small	+, large	Storage vault of cells
Centrioles	–	+	–	Part of microtubule separation apparatus that assists cell division in animal cells

*Endoplasmic reticulum.

Fluid mosaic model: plasma membrane is selectively permeable phospholipid bilayer with proteins of various lengths and sizes interspersed with cholesterol amongst the phospholipids.

Integral proteins: proteins implanted within lipid bilayer of plasma membrane.

Peripheral proteins: proteins attached to exterior of membrane.

Diffusion: passive movement of molecules down their concentration gradient (from high to low concentrations).

Osmosis: passive movement of water from low solute to high solute (hypotonic to hypertonic).

Facilitated diffusion: assisted transport of particles across membrane (no energy input needed).

Active transport: movement of molecules against concentration gradient (low to high concentrations; requires energy input).

Endocytosis: phagocytosis of particles into a cell through the use of vesicles.

Exocytosis: process by which particles are ejected from the cell, similar to movement in a trash chute.

Chapter 3

Respiration

INTRODUCTION

In this chapter we explore how cells obtain energy. It is important that you do not get lost or buried in the details. You should finish this chapter with an understanding of the basic process. The AP Biology exam will not ask you to identify by name the enzyme that catalyzes the third step of glycolysis, nor will it require you to name the fourth molecule in the Krebs cycle. But it *will* ask you questions that require an understanding of the respiration process.

There are two major categories of respiration: **aerobic** and **anaerobic.** Aerobic respiration occurs in the presence of oxygen, while anaerobic respiration occurs in situations where oxygen is not available. Aerobic respiration involves three stages: glycolysis, the Krebs cycle, and oxidative phosphorylation. Anaerobic respiration, sometimes referred to as *fermentation,* also begins with glycolysis, and concludes with the formation of NAD^+.

AEROBIC RESPIRATION

Glycolysis

Glycolysis occurs in the cytoplasm of cells and is the beginning pathway for both aerobic and anaerobic respiration. During glycolysis, a glucose molecule is broken down through a series of reactions into two molecules of pyruvate. It is important to remember that oxygen plays no role in glycolysis. This reaction can occur in oxygen-rich and oxygen-poor environments. However, when in an environment lacking oxygen, glycolysis slows because the cells run out (become depleted) of NAD^+. For reasons we will discuss later, a lack of oxygen prevents oxidative phosphorylation from occurring, causing a buildup of NADH in the cells. This buildup causes a shortage of NAD^+. This is bad for glycolysis because it requires NAD^+ to function. Fermentation is the solution to this problem—it takes the excess NADH that builds up and converts it back to NAD^+ so that glycolysis can continue. More to come on fermentation later . . . be patient. ☺

To reiterate, the AP Biology exam will not require you to memorize the various steps of respiration. Your time is better spent studying the broad explanation of the process of respiration, to understand the basic process, and become comfortable with respiration as a whole. Major concepts are the key. I will explain the specific steps of glycolysis because they will help you understand the big picture—but do not memorize them all. Save the space for other facts you have to know from other chapters of this book.

Examine Figure 3.1, which illustrates the general layout of glycolysis. The beginning steps of glycolysis require energy input. The first step adds a phosphate to a molecule of glucose with the assistance of an ATP molecule to produce *glucose-6-phosphate* (G6P). The newly formed G6P rearranges to form a molecule named *fructose-6-phosphate* (F6P). Another molecule of ATP is required for the next step, which adds another phosphate group to produce fructose 1,6-biphosphate. Already, glycolysis has used two of the ATP molecules that it is trying to produce—seems stupid . . . but be patient . . . the genius is yet to show its face. F6P splits into two 3-carbon-long fragments known as **PGAL** (glyceraldehyde phosphate). With the formation of PGAL, the energy-producing portion of glycolysis begins. Each PGAL molecule takes on an inorganic phosphate from the cytoplasm to produce 1,3-diphosphoglycerate. During this reaction, each PGAL gives up two electrons and a hydrogen to molecules of NAD$^+$ to form the all-important NADH molecules. The next step is a big one, as it leads to the production of the first ATP molecule in the process of respiration—the 1,3-diphosphoglycerate molecules donate one of their two phosphates to molecules of ADP to produce ATP and 3-phosphoglycerate (3PG). You'll notice that there are *two* ATP molecules formed here because before this step, the single molecule of glucose divided into *two* 3-carbon fragments. After 3PG rearranges to form 2-phosphoglycerate, phosphoenolpyruvate (PEP) is formed, which donates a phosphate group to molecules of ADP to form another pair of ATP molecules and pyruvate. This is the final step of glycolysis. In total, two molecules each of ATP, NADH, and pyruvate are formed during this process. Glycolysis produces the same result under anaerobic conditions as it does under aerobic conditions: two ATP molecules. If oxygen is present, more ATP is later made by oxidative phosphorylation.

> *!*
>
> If you are going to memorize one fact about glycolysis, remember that one glucose molecule produces two pyruvate, two NADH, and two ATP molecules.
>
> One glucose → 2 pyruvate, 2 ATP, 2 NADH

The Krebs Cycle

The pyruvate formed during glycolysis next enters the **Krebs cycle,** which is also known as the *citric acid cycle.* The Krebs cycle occurs in the matrix of the **mitochondria.** The pyruvate enters the mitochondria of the cell and is converted into acetyl coenzyme A (CoA) in a step that produces an NADH. This compound is now ready to enter the eight-step Krebs cycle, in which pyruvate is broken down completely to H_2O and CO_2. You do not need to memorize the eight steps.

As shown in Figure 3.2, a representation of the Krebs cycle, the 3-carbon pyruvate per se does not enter the Krebs cycle. It is converted, with the assistance of CoA and NAD$^+$, into 2-carbon acetyl CoA and NADH. The acetyl CoA dives into the Krebs cycle and reacts with oxaloacetate to form a 6-carbon molecule called *citrate.* The citrate is converted to a molecule named isocitrate, which then donates electrons and a hydrogen to NAD$^+$ to form 5-carbon α-ketoglutarate, carbon dioxide, and a molecule of NADH. The α-ketoglutarate undergoes a reaction very similar to the one leading to its formation and produces 4-carbon succinyl CoA and another molecule each of NADH and CO_2. The succinyl CoA is converted into succinate in a reaction that produces a molecule of ATP. The succinate then transfers electrons and a hydrogen atom

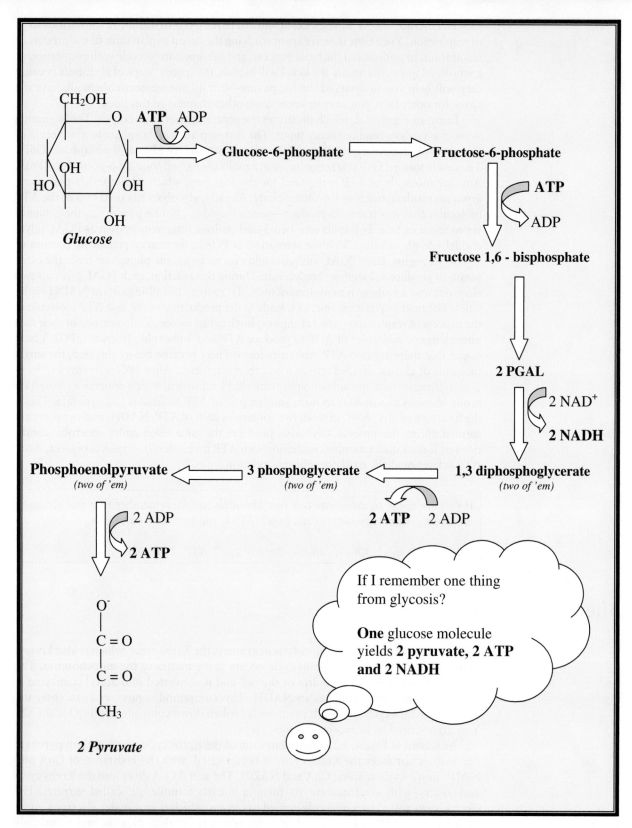

Figure 3.1
Glycolysis.

(C = Carbon)

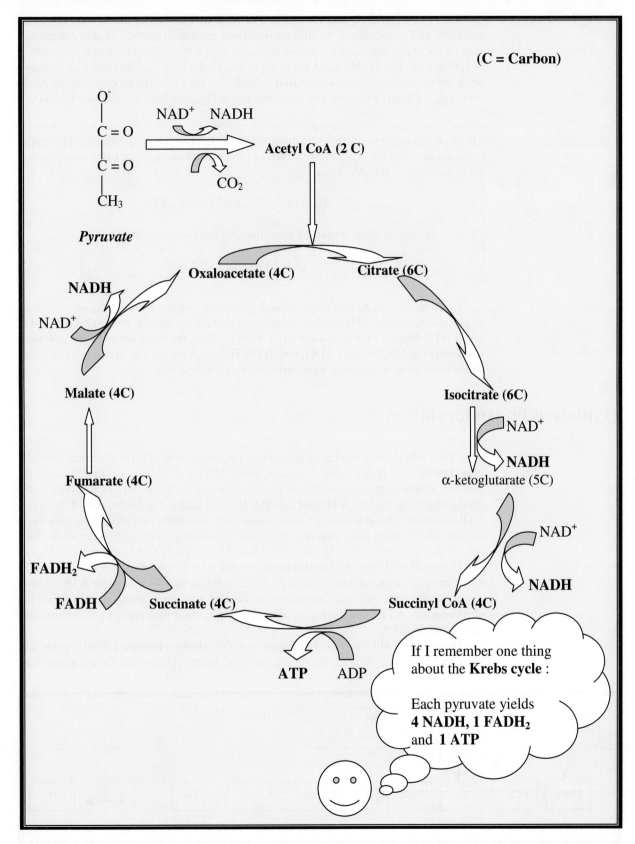

Figure 3.2
The Krebs cycle.

to FAD to form $FADH_2$ and fumarate. The next-to-last step in the Krebs cycle takes fumarate and rearranges it to another 4-carbon molecule: malate. Finally, in the last step of the cycle, the malate donates electrons and a hydrogen atom to a molecule of NAD^+ to form the final NADH molecule of the Krebs cycle, at the same time regenerating the molecule of oxaloacetate that helped kick the cycle off. One turn of the Krebs cycle takes a single pyruvate and produces one ATP, four NADH, and one $FADH_2$.

> If you are going to memorize one thing about the Krebs cycle, remember that for each glucose dropped into glycolysis, the Krebs cycle occurs twice. Each pyruvate dropped into the Krebs cycle produces
>
> 4 NADH, 1 $FADH_2$, 1 ATP, and 2 CO_2
>
> Therefore, the *pyruvate* obtained from the original glucose molecule produces:
>
> 8 NADH, 2 $FADH_2$, and 2 ATP

Up to this point, having gone through glycolysis and the Krebs cycle, one molecule of glucose has produced the following energy-related compounds: 10 NADH, 2 $FADH_2$, and 4 ATP. Not bad for an honest day's work . . . But, the body wants more and needs to convert the NADH and $FADH_2$ into ATP. This is where the electron transport chain, chemiosmosis, and oxidative phosphorylation come into play.

Oxidative Phosphorylation

After the Krebs cycle comes the largest energy-producing step of them all: **oxidative phosphorylation.** During this aerobic process, the NADH and $FADH_2$ produced during the first two stages of respiration will be used to create ATP. Each NADH will lead to the production of up to three ATP, and each $FADH_2$ will lead to the production of up to two ATP molecules. This is an inexact measurement—those numbers represent the maximum output possible from those two energy components if all goes smoothly. For each molecule of glucose, up to 30 ATP can be produced from the NADH molecules and up to 4 ATP from the $FADH_2$. Add to this the four total ATP formed during glycolysis and the Krebs cycle for a grand total of 38 ATP from *each glucose.* Two of these ATP are used during aerobic respiration to help move the NADH produced during glycolysis into the mitochondria. All totaled during aerobic respiration, each molecule of glucose can produce up to *36* **ATP.**

Do not panic when you see the illustration for the **electron transport chain** (Figure 3.3). Once again, the big picture is the most important thing to remember. Do not waste your

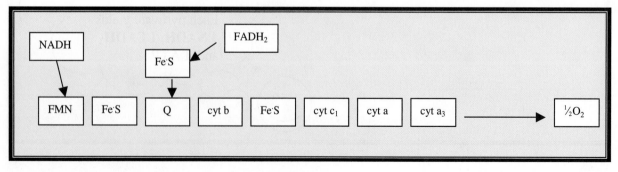

Figure 3.3
Electron transport chain (ETC).

time memorizing the various cytochrome molecules involved in the steps of the chain. Remember that the $\frac{1}{2}$ O_2 is the final acceptor in the chain, and that without the O_2 (anaerobic conditions) the production of ATP from NADH and $FADH_2$ will be compromised. Remember that each NADH that goes through the chain can produce three molecules of ATP, and each $FADH_2$ can produce two.

The *electron transport chain* (ETC) is the chain of molecules, located in the mitochondria, that passes electrons along during the process of chemiosmosis to regenerate NAD^+ to form ATP. Each time an electron passes to another member of the chain, the energy level of the system drops. Do not worry about the individual members of this chain—they are unimportant for this exam. When thinking of the ETC, I am reminded of the passing of a bucket of water from person to person until it arrives at and is tossed onto a fire. In the ETC, the various molecules in the chain are the people passing the buckets; the drop in the energy level with each pass is akin to the water sloshed out as the bucket is hurriedly passed along, and the $\frac{1}{2}$ O_2 represents the fire onto which the water is dumped at the end of the chain. As the $\frac{1}{2}$ O_2 accepts the electrons, it actually picks up a pair of hydrogen ions to *produce* water.

Chemiosmosis is a very important term to understand. It is defined as the coupling of the movement of electrons down the electron transport chain with the formation of ATP using the driving force provided by a proton gradient. So, what does that mean in English? Well, let's start by first defining what a coupled reaction is. It is a reaction that uses the product of *one* reaction as part of *another* reaction. Thinking back to my baseball card collecting days helps me better understand this coupling concept. I needed money to buy baseball cards. I would baby-sit or do yardwork for my neighbors and use that money to buy cards. I coupled the money-making reaction of hard labor to the money-spending reaction of buying baseball cards.

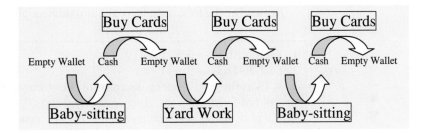

Let's look more closely at the reactions that are coupled in chemiosmosis. If you look at Figure 3.4a, a crude representation of a mitochondrion, you will find the ETC embedded within the inner mitochondrial membrane. As some of the molecules in the chain accept and then pass on electrons, they pump hydrogen ions into the space between the inner and outer membranes of the mitochondria (Figure 3.4b). This creates a proton gradient that drives the production of ATP. The difference in hydrogen concentration on the two sides of the membrane causes the protons to flow back into the matrix of the mitochondria through ATP synthase channels (Figure 3.4c). **ATP synthase** is an enzyme that uses the flow of hydrogens to drive the phosphorylation of an ADP molecule to produce ATP. This reaction completes the process of oxidative phosphorylation and chemiosmosis. The proton gradient created by the movement of electrons from molecule to molecule has been used to form the ATP that this process is designed to produce. In other words, the formation of ATP has been coupled to the movement of electrons and protons.

Chemiosmosis is not oxidative phosphorylation per se; rather, it is a major *part* of oxidative phosphorylation. An important fact I want you to take out of this chapter is that chemiosmosis is not unique to the mitochondria. It is the same process that occurs in the chloroplasts during the ATP-creating steps of photosynthesis (see Chapter 4). The difference is that light is driving the electrons along the ETC in plants. Remember that chemiosmosis occurs in both mitochondria and chloroplasts.

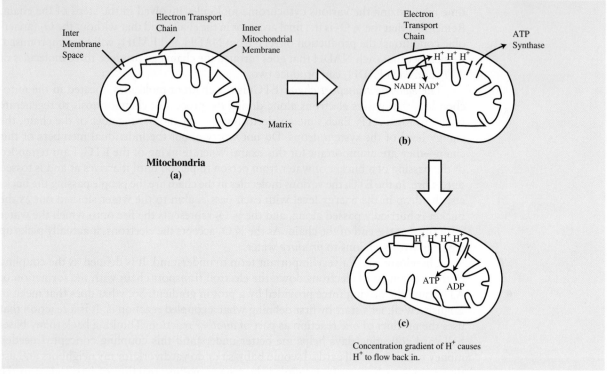

Figure 3.4
Chemiosmosis.

Remember the following facts about oxidative phosphorylation (Ox-phos):

1. Each NADH → 3 ATP.
2. Each FADH$_2$ → 2 ATP.
3. ½ O$_2$ is the final electron acceptor of the electron transport chain and the chain will not function in the absence of oxygen.
4. Ox-phos serves the important function of regenerating NAD$^+$ so that glycolysis can continue.
5. Chemiosmosis occurs in photosynthesis as well as respiration.

ANAEROBIC RESPIRATION

Anaerobic respiration, or *fermentation*, occurs when oxygen is unavailable or cannot be used by the organism. As in aerobic respiration, glycolysis occurs and pyruvate is produced. The pyruvate enters the Krebs cycle, producing NADH, FADH$_2$, and some ATP. The problem arises in the electron transport chain—because there is no oxygen available, the electrons do not pass down the chain to the final electron acceptor, causing a buildup of NADH in the system. This buildup of NADH means that the NAD$^+$ normally regenerated during oxidative phosphorylation is not produced, and this creates an NAD$^+$ shortage. This is a problem because in order for glycolysis to proceed to the pyruvate stage, it needs NAD$^+$ to help perform the necessary reactions. **Fermentation** is the process that begins with glycolysis and ends when NAD$^+$ is regenerated. A glucose molecule that enters the fermentation pathway produces two net ATP per molecule of glucose, representing a tremendous decline in ATP efficiency.

Under aerobic conditions, NAD$^+$ is recycled from NADH by the movement of electrons down the electron transport chain. Under anaerobic conditions, NAD$^+$ is recycled from NADH by the movement of electrons to pyruvate, namely, fermentation. The two main types of fermentation are **alcohol fermentation** and **lactic acid fermentation**. Refer to Figures 3.5 and 3.6 for the representations of the different forms of fermentation.

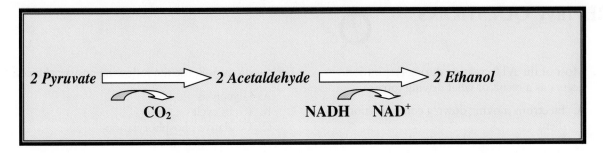

Figure 3.5
Alcohol fermentation.

Alcohol fermentation (Figure 3.5) occurs in fungi, yeast, and some bacteria. The first step involves the conversion of pyruvate into two 2-carbon acetaldehyde molecules. Then, in the all-important step of alcohol fermentation, the acetaldehyde molecules are converted to ethanol, regenerating two NAD^+ molecules in the process.

Lactic acid fermentation (Figure 3.6) occurs in human muscle cells when oxygen is not available. This is a simpler process than alcoholic fermentation—the pyruvate is directly reduced to lactate by NADH to regenerate the NAD^+ needed for the resumption of glycolysis. Have you ever had a cramp during exercise? The pain you felt was the result of lactic acid fermentation. Your muscle was deprived of the necessary amount of oxygen to continue glycolysis, and it switched over to fermentation. The pain from the cramp came from the acidity in the muscle.

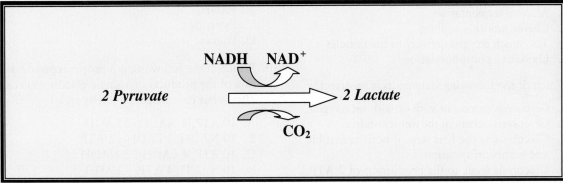

Figure 3.6
Lactic acid fermentation.

If I remember one thing about fermentation...

Yeast, fungi, and bacteria produce ethanol.

Humans produce lactic acid. (Only during O_2 deficit)

REVIEW QUESTIONS

1. Most of the ATP creation during respiration occurs as a result of what driving force?

   A. Electrons moving down a concentration gradient
   B. Electrons moving down the electron transport chain
   C. Protons moving down a concentration gradient
   D. Sodium ions moving down a concentration gradient
   E. Movement of pyruvate from the cytoplasm into the mitochondria

2. Which of the following processes occurs in both respiration and photosynthesis?

   A. Calvin cycle
   B. Chemiosmosis
   C. Citric acid cycle
   D. Krebs cycle
   E. Glycolysis

3. What is the cause of the cramps you feel in your muscles during strenuous exercise?

   A. Lactic acid fermentation
   B. Alcohol fermentation
   C. Chemiosmotic coupling
   D. Too much oxygen delivery to the muscles
   E. Oxidative phosphorylation

4. Which of the following statements is *incorrect*?

   A. Glycolysis can occur with or without oxygen.
   B. Glycolysis occurs in the mitochondria.
   C. Glycolysis is the first step of both anaerobic and aerobic respiration.
   D. Glycolysis leads to the production of 2 ATP, 2 NADH, and 2 pyruvate.

For questions 5–8, use the following answer choices:

   A. Glycolysis
   B. Krebs cycle
   C. Oxidative phosphorylation
   D. Lactic acid fermentation
   E. Chemiosmosis

5. This reaction occurs in the matrix of the mitochondria and includes $FADH_2$ among its products.

6. This reaction is performed to recycle NAD^+ needed for efficient respiration.

7. This process uses the proton gradient created by the movement of electrons to form ATP.

8. This process includes the reactions that use NADH and $FADH_2$ to produce ATP.

9. Which of the following molecules can give rise to the most ATP?

   A. NADH
   B. $FADH_2$
   C. Pyruvate
   D. Glucose

10. Which of the following is a proper representation of the products of a single glucose molecule after it has completed the Krebs cycle?

   A. 10 ATP, 4 NADH, 2 $FADH_2$
   B. 10 NADH, 4 $FADH_2$, 2 ATP
   C. 10 ATP, 4 $FADH_2$, 2 NADH
   D. 10 NADH, 4 ATP, 2 $FADH_2$
   E. 10 NADH, 4 $FADH_2$, 2 ATP

ANSWERS AND EXPLANATIONS

1. **C**—This is the concept of chemiosmosis: the coupling of the movement of electrons down the electron transport chain and the formation of ATP via the creation of a proton gradient. The protons are pushed out of the matrix during the passage of electrons down the chain. They soon build up on the other side of the membrane, and are driven back inside because of the difference in concentration. ATP synthase uses the movement of protons to produce ATP.

2. **B**—This is an important concept to understand. The AP examiners love this topic!

3. **A**—Lactic acid fermentation occurs in human muscle cells when oxygen is not available. Answer choice B would be incorrect because alcohol fermentation occurs in

yeast, fungi and some bacteria. During exercise, if your muscle becomes starved for oxygen, it will switch over to fermentation. The pain from the cramp is due to the acidity in the muscle caused by the increased concentration of lactate.

4. **B**—Glycolysis occurs in the cytoplasm. All the other statements are correct.

5. **B.**

6. **D.**

7. **E.**

8. **C.**

9. **D**—Glucose can net 36 ATP, NADH can net 3, FADH₂ can net 2, and pyruvate can net 15.

10. **D**—During glycolysis, a glucose molecule produces 2 ATP, 2 NADH, and 2 pyruvate. The 2 pyruvate then go on to produce 8 NADH, 2 FADH₂, and 2 ATP during the Krebs cycle to give the total listed in answer choice D.

RAPID REVIEW

There are two main categories of respiration: aerobic and anaerobic.

Aerobic respiration: glycolysis → Krebs cycle → oxidative phosphorylation → 36 ATP

Anaerobic respiration (fermentation): glycolysis → regenerate NAD^+ → much less ATP

Glycolysis: conversion of glucose into 2 pyruvate, 2 ATP, and 2 NADH; occurs in the cytoplasm, and in both aerobic *and* anaerobic respiration; *must* have NAD^+ to proceed.

Total energy production to this point → 2 ATP + 2NADH

Krebs cycle: conversion of pyruvate into 4 NADH, 1 FADH₂, 1 ATP, H_2O, and CO_2; occurs *twice* for each glucose to yield 8 NADH, 2 FADH₂, and 2 ATP; occurs in mitochondria.

Total energy production to this point → 4 ATP + 10 NADH + 2 FADH₂

Oxidative phosphorylation: production of large amounts of ATP from NADH and FADH₂

- Occurs in the mitochondria; *requires presence of oxygen to proceed.*

- NADH and FADH₂ pass their electrons down the electron transport chain to produce ATP.

- Each NADH can produce up to 3 ATP; Each FADH₂ up to 2 ATP.

- ½ O_2 is the final acceptor in the electron transport chain.

- Movement of electrons down the chain leads to movement of H^+ out of matrix.

- Ox-phos *regenerates NAD^+* so that glycolysis can continue!

Chemiosmosis: coupling of the movement of electrons down the ETC with the formation of ATP using the driving force provided by the proton gradient; occurs in *both* cell respiration *and* photosynthesis to produce ATP.

ATP synthase: enzyme responsible for using protons to actually produce ATP from ADP.

Total energy production to this point → 38 ATP (use 2 in process) → 36 ATP total

Fermentation (general): process that regenerates NAD^+ so glycolysis can begin again

- Occurs in the absence of oxygen.

- Begins with glycolysis: 2 ATP, 2 pyruvate, and 2 NADH are produced.

- Because there is no oxygen to accept the electron energy on the chain, there is a shortage of NAD^+, which prevents glycolysis from continuing.

Fermentation (alcohol): occurs in fungi, yeast, and bacteria; causes conversion of pyruvate to ethanol.

Fermentation (lactic acid): occurs in human muscle cells; causes conversion of pyruvate → lactate; causes cramp sensation when oxygen runs low in muscle cells.

Chapter 4

Photosynthesis

INTRODUCTION

In Chapter 3 we discussed how human and animal cells generate the energy needed to survive and perform on a day-to-day basis. Now we are going to look at how plants generate their energy from light—the process of **photosynthesis.** I stress again in this chapter what I said about respiration—do not get caught up in the memorization of every fact. Make sure that you understand the basic, overall concepts and the major ideas. Remember that most of plant photosynthesis occurs in the plant's leaves. The majority of the chloroplasts of a plant are found in mesophyll cells. Remember that there are two stages to photosynthesis: the light-dependent reactions and the light-independent reactions, commonly called the "dark reactions." The simplified equation of photosynthesis is

$$H_2O + CO_2 + light \rightarrow O_2 + glucose + H_2O$$

THE PLAYERS IN PHOTOSYNTHESIS

The host organelle for photosynthesis is the **chloroplast,** which is divided into an inner and outer portion. The inner fluid portion is called the **stroma,** which is surrounded by two outer membranes. In Figure 4.1, you can see that winding through the stroma is an inner membrane called the **thylakoid membrane system.** This is where the first stage of photosynthesis occurs. This membrane consists of flattened channels and disks arranged in stacks called **grana.** I always remember the thylakoid system as resembling stacks of poker chips, where each chip is a single thylakoid. It is within these poker chips that the light-dependent reactions of photosynthesis occur.

Before we examine the process of photosynthesis, here are some definitions that will make things a bit easier as you read this chapter.

Autotroph: an organism that is self-nourishing. It obtains carbon and energy without ingesting other organisms. Plants and algae are good examples of autotrophic organisms—

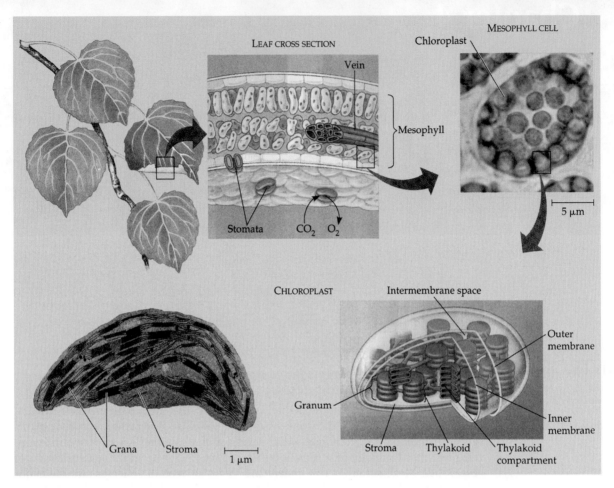

Figure 4.1
An overall view of photosynthesis. (*From Biology, 4th ed., by Neil A. Campbell©1987, 1990, 1993, 1996 by the Bejamin/Cummings Publishing Company, Inc. Reprinted by permission of Addison Wesley Longman Publishers, Inc.*)

they obtain their energy from carbon dioxide, water, and light. They are the producers of the world.

Bundle sheath cells: cells that are tightly wrapped around the veins of a leaf. They are the site for the **Calvin cycle** in C_4 plants.

C_4 plant: plant that has adapted its photosynthetic process to more efficiently handle hot and dry conditions.

Heterotroph: organisms that must consume other organisms to obtain nourishment. They are the consumers of the world.

Mesophyll: interior tissue of a leaf.

Mesophyll cells: cells that contain many chloroplasts and host the majority of photosynthesis.

Photolysis: process by which water is broken up by an enzyme into hydrogen ions and oxygen atoms; occurs during the light-dependent reactions of photosynthesis.

Photophosphorylation: process by which ATP is produced during the light-dependent reactions of photosynthesis. It is the chloroplast equivalent of oxidative phosphorylation.

Photorespiration: process by which oxygen competes with carbon dioxide and attaches to RuBP. Plants that experience photorespiration have a lowered capacity for growth.

Photosystem: a cluster of light-trapping pigments involved in the process of photosynthesis. Photosystems vary tremendously in their organization and can possess hundreds of pigments. The two most important are photosystems I and II of the light reactions.

Pigment: a molecule that absorbs light of a particular wavelength. Pigments are vital to the process of photosynthesis and include **chlorophyll, carotenoids,** and **phycobilins.**

Rubisco: an enzyme that catalyzes the first step of the Calvin cycle in C_3 plants.

Stomata: structure through which CO_2 enters a plant and water vapor and O_2 leave.

Transpiration: natural process by which plants lose H_2O via evaporation through their leaves.

THE REACTIONS OF PHOTOSYNTHESIS

The process of photosynthesis can be neatly divided into two sets of reactions: the light-dependent reactions and the light-independent reactions. The light-dependent reactions occur first and require an input of water and light. They produce three things: the oxygen we breathe, NADPH, and ATP. These last two products of the light reactions are then consumed during the second stage of photosynthesis: the dark reactions. These reactions, which need CO_2, NADPH, and ATP as inputs, produce sugar and recycle the $NADP^+$ and ADP to be used by the next set of light-dependent reactions. Now, I would be too kind if I left the discussion there. Let's look at the reactions in more detail. Stop groaning . . . you know I have to go there.

Light-Dependent Reactions

Light-dependent reactions occur in the thylakoid membrane system. The thylakoid system is composed of the various stacks of poker-chip look alikes located within the stroma of the chloroplast. Within the thylakoid membrane is a photosynthetic participant termed **chlorophyll.** There are two main types of chlorophyll that you should remember: chlorophyll a and chlorophyll b. Chlorophyll a is the major pigment of photosynthesis, while chlorophyll b is considered to be an accessory pigment. The pigments are very similar structurally, but the minor differences are what account for the variance in their absorption of light. Chlorophyll absorbs light of a particular wavelength, and when it does, one of its electrons is elevated to a higher energy level (it is "excited"). Almost immediately, the excited electron drops back down to the ground state, giving off heat in the process. This energy is passed along until it finds chlorophyll a, which, when excited, passes its electron to the primary electron acceptor; then, the light-dependent reactions are under way.

The pigments of the thylakoid space organize themselves into groups called *photosystems.* These photosystems consist of varying combinations of chlorophylls a, b, and others; pigments called **phycobilins;** and another type of pigment called **carotenoids.** The accessory pigments help pick up light when chlorophyll a cannot do it as effectively. An example is red algae on the ocean bottom. When light is picked up by the accessory pigments, it is fluoresced and altered so that chlorophyll a can use it.

Imagine that the plant represented in Figure 4.2 is struck by light from the sun. This light excites the **photosystem** of the thylakoid space, which absorbs the photon and transmits the energy from one pigment molecule to another. As this energy is passed along, it loses a bit of energy with each step and eventually reaches chlorophyll a, which proceeds to kick off the process of photosynthesis. It initiates the first step of photosynthesis by passing the electron to the primary electron acceptor.

Before we continue, there are two major photosystems I want to tell you about—you might want to get out a pen or pencil here to jot this down, because the names for these

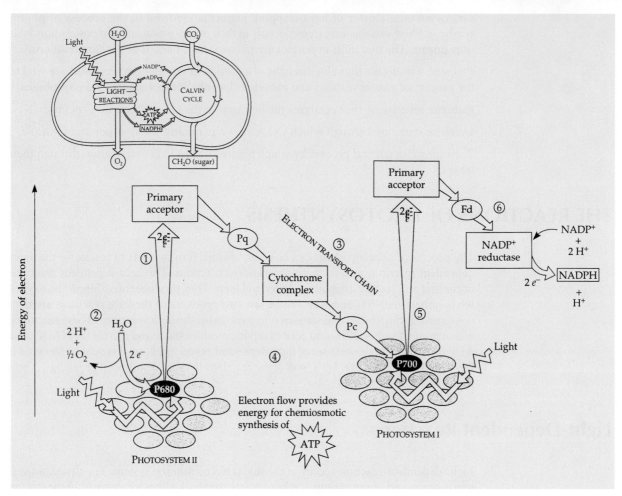

Figure 4.2
Light dependent reactions. (*From Biology, 4th ed., by Neil A. Campbell©1987, 1990, 1993, 1996 by Benjamin/Cumming Publishing Company, Inc. Reprinted by permission of Addison Wesley Longman Publishers, Inc.*)

photosystems may seem confusing. They are photosystems I and photosystem II. The only difference between these two **reaction centers** is that the main chlorophyll of photosystem I absorbs light with a wavelength of 700 nm while the main chlorophyll of photosystem II absorbs light with a wavelength of 680 nm. By interacting with different thylakoid membrane proteins, they are able to absorb light of slightly different wavelengths.

Now let's get back to the reactions. Let's go through the rest of Figure 4.2 and talk about the light-dependent reactions. For the sole purpose of confusing you, plants start photosynthesis by using photosystem II before photosystem I. As light strikes photosystem II, the energy is absorbed and passed along until it reaches the P680 chlorophyll. When this chlorophyll is excited, it passes its electrons to the primary electron acceptor. This is where the water molecule comes into play. **Photolysis** in the thylakoid space takes electrons from H_2O and passes them to P680 to replace the electrons given to the primary acceptor. With this reaction, a lone oxygen atom and a pair of hydrogen ions are formed from the water. The oxygen atom quickly finds another oxygen atom buddy, pairs up with it, and generates the O_2 that the plants so graciously put out for us every day. This is the first product of the light reactions.

The light reactions do not stop here, however. We need to consider what happens to the electron that has been passed to the primary electron acceptor. The electron is passed to photosystem I, P700, in a manner reminiscent of the electron transport chain. As the electrons are passed from P680 to P700, the lost energy is used to produce ATP (remember chemiosmosis). This ATP is the second product of the light reactions and is produced in a manner mechanistically similar to the way ATP is produced during oxidative phosphorylation of respiration. In plants, this process of ATP formation is called **photophosphorylation.**

After the photosystem I electrons are excited, photosystem I passes the energy to its own primary electron acceptor. These electrons are sent down another chain to **ferredoxin,** which then donates the electrons to $NADP^+$ to produce NADPH, the third and final product of the light reactions. (Notice how in photosynthesis there is NADPH, instead of NADH. The symbol P stands for photosynthesis.☺)

Remember the following about the light reactions:

---

1. The light reactions occur in the thylakoid membrane.
2. The inputs to the light reactions are water and light.
3. The light reactions produce three products: ATP, NADPH, and O_2.
4. The oxygen produced in the light reactions comes from H_2O, not CO_2.

Two separate light-dependent pathways occur in plants. What we have just discussed is the **noncyclic light reaction** pathway. Considering the name of the first one, it is not shocking to discover that there is also a **cyclic light reaction** pathway (see Figure 4.3). One key difference between the two is that in the noncyclic pathway, the electrons taken from chlorophyll a are not recycled back down to the ground state. This means that the electrons do not make their way back to the chlorophyll molecule when the reaction is complete. The electrons end up on NADPH. Another key difference between the two is that the cyclic pathway uses only photosystem I; photosystem II is not involved. In the cyclic pathway, sunlight hits P700, thus exciting the electrons and passing them from P700 to its primary electron acceptor. It is called the cyclic pathway because these electrons pass down the electron chain and eventually back to P700 to complete the cycle. The energy given off during the passage down the chain is harnessed to produce ATP—the only product of this pathway. Neither oxygen nor NADPH are produced from these reactions.

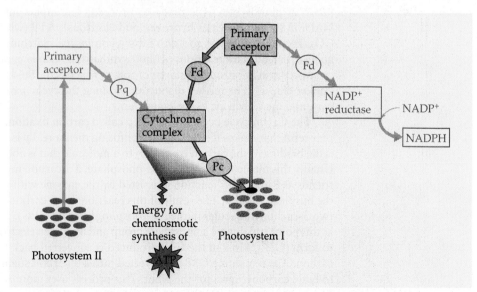

Figure 4.3
Cyclic phosphorylation. (*From Biology, 4th ed., by Neil A. Campbell©1987, 1990, 1993, 1996 by the Benjamin/Cummings Publishing Company, Inc. Reprinted by permission of Addision Wesley Longman Publishers, Inc.*)

!

A question that might be forming as you read this is "Why does this pathway continue to exist?" or perhaps you are wondering "Why does he insist on torturing me by writing about all of this photosynthesis stuff?" I will answer the first question and ignore the second one. The cyclic pathway exists because the Calvin cycle, which we discuss next, uses more ATP than it does NADPH. This eventually causes a problem because the light reactions produce equal amounts of ATP and NADPH. The plant compensates for this disparity by dropping into the cyclic phase when needed to produce the ATP necessary to keep the light-independent reactions from grinding to a halt.

Before moving on to the dark reactions, it is important to understand how ATP is formed. I know, I know. . . . You thought I was finished . . . but I want you to be an expert in the field of photosynthesis. You never know when these facts might come in handy. For example, just the other day I was offered $10,000 by a random person on the street to recount the similarities between photosynthesis and respiration. So, this stuff *is* useful in everyday life. As the electrons are passing from the primary electron acceptor to the next photosystem, hydrogen ions are picked up from outside the membrane and brought back into the thylakoid compartment, creating a H^+ gradient similar to what we saw in oxidative phosphorylation. During the light-dependent reactions, when hydrogen ions are taken from water during photolysis, the proton gradient grows larger, causing some protons to leave, leading to the formation of ATP.

You'll notice that this process in plants is a bit different from oxidative phosphorylation of the mitochondria, where the proton gradient is created by pumping protons from the matrix *out* to the intermembrane space. In the mitochondria, the ATP is produced when the protons move back *in*. But in plants, photophosphorylation creates the gradient by pumping protons in from the stroma to the thylakoid compartment, and the ATP is produced as the protons move back *out*. The opposing reactions produce the same happy result—more ATP for the cells.

Light-Independent Reactions (Dark Reactions)

After the light reactions have produced the necessary ATP and NADPH, the synthesis phase of photosynthesis is ready to proceed. The inputs into the dark reactions are NADPH (which provides hydrogen and electrons), ATP (which provides energy), and CO_2. From here on, just so I don't drive you *insane* switching from term to term, I am going to call the dark reactions of photosynthesis the *Calvin cycle* (Figure 4.4). The Calvin cycle occurs in the stroma of the chloroplast, which is the fluid surrounding the thylakoid "poker chips." (For further distinctions among the cyclic pathway, the noncyclic pathway, and the Calvin cycle, see Figure 4.5.)

The Calvin cycle begins with a step called **carbon fixation.** This is a tricky and complex term that makes it sound more confusing then it really is. Basically, carbon fixation is the binding of the carbon from CO_2 to a molecule that is able to enter the Calvin cycle. Usually this molecule is ribulose bis-phosphate, a 5-carbon molecule known to its closer friends as RuBP. This reaction is assisted by the enzyme with one of the cooler names in the business: **rubisco.** The result of this reaction is a 6-carbon molecule that breaks into two 3-carbon molecules named *3-phosphoglycerate* (3PG). ATP and NADPH step up at this point and donate a phosphate group and hydrogen electrons, respectively, to (3PG) to form (G3P). Most of the G3P produced is converted back to RuBP so as to fix more carbon. The remaining G3P is converted into a 6-carbon sugar molecule, which is used to build carbohydrates for the plant. This process uses more ATP than it does NADPH. This is the disparity that makes cyclic photophosphorylation necessary in the light-dependent reactions.

I know that for some of you the preceding discussion contains many difficult scientific names, strangely spelled words, and esoteric acronyms. So, here's the bottom line—you should remember the following about the Calvin cycle:

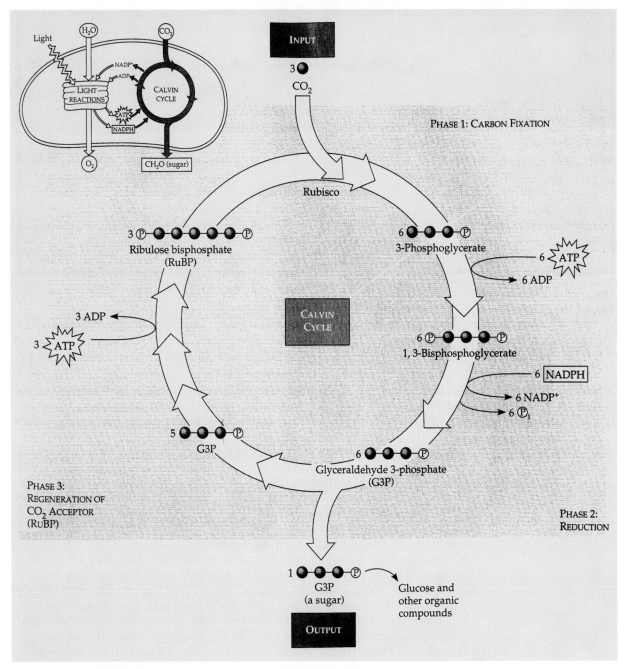

Figure 4.4
The Calvin cycle. (*From Biology 4th ed., by Neil A. Campbell©1987, 1990, 1993, 1996 by the Benjamin/Cummings Publishing Company, Inc. Reprinted by permission of Addison Wesley Longman Publishers, Inc.*)

1. The Calvin cycle occurs in the stroma of the chloroplast.
2. The inputs into the Calvin cycle are NADPH, ATP, and CO_2.
3. The products of the Calvin cycle are $NADP^+$, ADP, and a sugar.
4. More ATP is used than NADPH, creating the need for cyclic photophosphorylation to create enough ATP for the reactions.
5. The carbon of the sugar produced in photosynthesis comes from the CO_2 of the Calvin cycle.

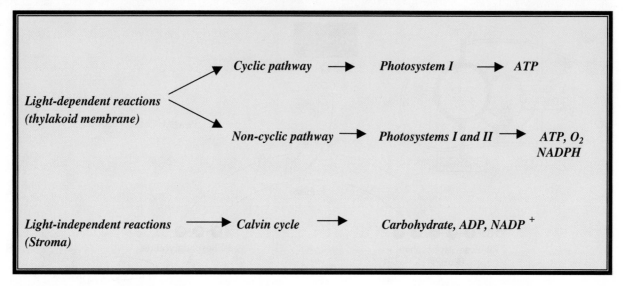

Figure 4.5
Summary of photosynthesis.

TYPES OF PHOTOSYNTHESIS

Plants do not always live under ideal photosynthetic conditions. Some plants must make changes to the system in order to successfully use light and produce energy. Plants contain a structure called a **stomata,** which consists of pores through which oxygen exits and carbon dioxide enters the leaf to be used in photosynthesis. **Transpiration** is the natural process by which plants lose water by evaporation from their leaves. When the temperature is very high, plants have to worry about excess transpiration. This is a potential problem for plants because they need the water to continue the process of photosynthesis. To combat this evaporation problem, plants must close their stomata to conserve water. But this solution leads to two different problems: (1) how will they bring in the CO_2 required for photosynthesis and (2) what will the plants do with the excess O_2 that builds up when the stomata are closed.

When plants close their stomata to protect against water loss, they experience a shortage of CO_2, and the oxygen produced from the light reactions is unable to leave the plant. This excess oxygen competes with the carbon dioxide and attaches to RuBP in a reaction called **photorespiration.** This results in the formation of one molecule of PGA and one molecule of phosphoglycolate. This is not an ideal reaction because the sugar formed in photosynthesis comes from the PGA, not phosphoglycolate. As a result, plants that experience photorespiration have lowered capacity for growth. Photorespiration tends to occur on hot, dry days when the stomata of the plant are closed.

A group of plants called C_4 **plants** combat photorespiration by altering the first step of their Calvin cycle. Normally, carbon fixation produces two 3-carbon molecules. In C_4 plants, the carbon fixation step produces a 4-carbon molecule called **oxaloacetate.** This molecule is converted into malate and sent from the mesophyll cells to the bundle sheath cells, where the CO_2 is used to build sugar. The **mesophyll** is the tissue of the interior of the leaf, and **mesophyll cells** are cells that contain bunches of chloroplasts. **Bundle sheath cells** are cells that are tightly wrapped around the veins of a leaf. They are the site for the Calvin cycle in C_4 plants.

What is the difference between C_3 plants and C_4 plants? One difference is that C_4 plants have two different types of photosynthetic cells: (1) tightly packed bundle sheath cells, which surround the vein of the leaf, and (2) mesophyll cells. Another difference involves the first product of carbon fixation. For C_3 plants, it is PGA, whereas for C_4 plants it is oxaloacetate. C_4 plants are able to successfully perform photosynthesis in these hot areas because of the presence of an enzyme called PEP *(phosphoenolpyruvate) carboxylase.* This enzyme really wants to bind to CO_2 and is not tricked by the devious oxygen into using it instead of the necessary CO_2. PEP carboxylase prefers to pair up with CO_2 rather than O_2, and this cuts down on photorespiration for C_4 plants. The conversion of PEP to oxaloacetate occurs in the mesophyll cells; then, after being converted into malate, PEP is shipped to the bundle sheath cells. These cells contain the enzymes of photosynthesis, including our good pal rubisco. The malate releases the CO_2, which is then used by rubisco to perform the reactions of photosynthesis. This process counters the problem of photorespiration because the shuttling of CO_2 from the mesophyll cells to the bundle sheath cells keeps the CO_2 concentration high enough so that it is not beat out by oxygen for rubisco's love and attention.

One last variation of photosynthesis that we should look at is the function performed by **CAM** (Crassulacean acid metabolizing) **plants**—water-storing plants, such as cacti, which close their stomata by day and open them by night to avoid transpiration during the hot days, without depleting the plant's CO_2 reserves. The carbon dioxide taken in during the night is stored as organic acids in the vacuoles of mesophyll cells until daybreak when the stomata close. The Calvin cycle is able to proceed during the day because the stored CO_2 is released, as needed, from the organic acids to be incorporated into the sugar product of the Calvin cycle.

To sum up these two variations of photosynthesis:

C_4 *photosynthesis:* Photosynthetic process that first converts CO_2 into a 4-carbon molecule in the mesophyll cells, converts that product to malate, and then shuttles the malate into the bundle sheath cells. There, malate releases CO_2, which reacts with rubisco to produce the carbohydrate product of photosynthesis.

CAM photosynthesis: plants close their stomata during the day, collect CO_2 at night, and store the CO_2 in the form of acids until it is needed during the day for photosynthesis.

REVIEW QUESTIONS

Questions 1–4 refer to the following answer choices—use each answer only once:

A. Transpiration
B. Calvin cycle
C. CAM photosynthesis
D. Cyclic photophosphorylation
E. Noncyclic photophosphorylation

1. Plants use this process so that they can open their stomata at night and close their stomata during the day to avoid water loss during the hot days, without depleting the plant's CO_2 reserves.

2. Uses NADPH, ATP, and CO_2 as the inputs to its reactions.

3. Photosynthetic process that has ATP as its sole product. There is no oxygen and no NADPH produced from these reactions.

4. The process by which plants lose water via evaporation through their leaves.

5. The photosynthetic process performed by some plants in an effort to survive the hot and dry conditions of climates such as the desert.

A. Carbon fixation
B. C_3 photosynthesis
C. C_4 photosynthesis
D. Cyclic photophosphorylation
E. Noncyclic photophosphorylation

6. Which of the following is the photosynthetic stage that produces oxygen?

A. The light-dependent reactions
B. Chemiosmosis
C. The Calvin cycle
D. Carbon fixation
E. Photorespiration

7. Which of the following reactions occur in both cellular respiration and photosynthesis?

A. Carbon fixation
B. Fermentation
C. Reduction of NADP+
D. Chemiosmosis
E. Formation of NADH

8. Which of the following is *not* a product of the light-dependent reactions of photosynthesis?

A. O_2
B. ATP
C. NADPH
D. Sugar

9. Which of the following is an advantage held by a C_4 plant?

A. More efficient light absorption
B. More efficient photolysis
C. More efficient carbon fixation
D. More efficient uptake of carbon dioxide into the stomata
E. More efficient ATP synthesis during chemiosmosis

10. Carbon dioxide enters the plant through the

A. Stomata
B. Stroma
C. Thylakoid membrane
D. Bundle sheath cell

11. Which of the following is the source of the oxygen released during photosynthesis?

A. CO_2
B. H_2O
C. Rubisco
D. PEP carboxylase
E. Pyruvate

12. Which of the following is an *incorrect* statement about the dark reactions of photosynthesis?

A. The main inputs to the reactions are NADPH, ATP, and CO_2.
B. The main outputs of the reactions are $NADP^+$, ADP, and sugar.
C. More NADPH is used than ATP during the dark reactions.
D. Carbon fixation is the first step of the process.
E. The reactions occur in the stroma of the chloroplast.

13. Which of the following is the source of the carbon in sugar produced during photosynthesis?

A. CO_2
B. H_2O
C. Rubisco
D. PEP carboxylase
E. Pyruvate

14. The light-dependent reactions of photosynthesis occur in the

A. Stroma
B. Mitochondrial matrix
C. Thylakoid membrane
D. Cytoplasm
E. Nucleus

ANSWERS AND EXPLANATIONS

1. **C**—CAM plants open their stomata at night and close their stomata during the day to avoid water loss due to heat. The carbon dioxide taken in during the night is incorporated into organic acids and stored in vacuoles until the next day when the stomata close and CO_2 is needed for the Calvin cycle.

2. **B**—The Calvin cycle uses ATP, NADPH, and CO_2 to produce the desired sugar output of photosynthesis.

3. **D**—Cyclic photophosphorylation occurs because the Calvin cycle uses more ATP than it does NADPH. This is a problem because the light reactions produce an equal amount of ATP and NADPH. The plant compensates for this disparity by dropping into the cyclic phase when needed to produce the ATP necessary to keep the light-independent reactions from grinding to a halt.

4. **A**—Transpiration is the process by which plants lose water through their leaves. Not much else to be said about that. ☺

5. **C**—One of the major problems encountered by plants in hot and dry conditions is that of photorespiration. In hot conditions, plants close their stomata to avoid losing water to transpiration. The problem with this is that the plants run low on CO_2 and fill with O_2. The oxygen competes with the carbon dioxide and attaches to RuBP, leaving the plant with a lowered capacity for growth. C_4 plants cycle CO_2 from mesophyll cells to bundle sheath cells, creating a higher concentration of CO_2 in that region, thus allowing rubisco to carry out the Calvin cycle without being distracted by the O_2 competitor.

6. **A**—The light-dependent reactions are the source of the oxygen given off by plants.

7. **D**—Chemiosmosis occurs in both photosynthesis and cellular respiration. This is the process by which the formation of ATP is driven by electrochemical gradients in the cell. Hydrogen ions accumulate on one side of a membrane, creating a proton gradient that causes them to move through channels to the other side of that membrane, thus leading, with the assistance of ATP synthase, to the production of ATP.

8. **D**—Sugar is a product not of the light-dependent reactions of photosynthesis but of the Calvin cycle (the dark reactions). The outputs of the light-dependent reactions are ATP, NADPH, and O_2.

9. **C**—C_4 plants fix carbon more efficiently than do C_3 plants. Please see the explanation for question 5 for a more detailed explanation of this answer.

10. **A**—The stomata is the structure through which the CO_2 enters a plant and the oxygen produced in the light-dependent reactions leaves the plant.

11. **B**—The source of the oxygen produced during photosynthesis is the water that is split by the process of photolysis during the light-dependent reactions of photosynthesis. In this reaction, two hydrogen ions and an oxygen atom are formed from the water. The oxygen atom immediately finds and pairs up with another oxygen atom to form the oxygen product of the light-dependent reactions.

12. **C**—This is a trick question. I reversed the two compounds (NADPH and ATP) in this one. More ATP than NADPH is used in the Calvin cycle. It is for this reason that cyclic photophosphorylation exists—to produce ATP to make up for this disparity.

13. **A**—The carbon of CO_2 is used to produce the sugar created during the Calvin cycle.

14. **C**—The light-dependent reactions occur in the thylakoid membrane of the chloroplast. Remember, the thylakoid system resembles the various stacks of poker chips located within the stroma of the chloroplast. The light-independent reactions occur in the stroma of the chloroplast.

RAPID REVIEW

The following terms should be thoroughly familiar to you:

Photosynthesis: process by which plants use the energy from light to generate sugar

- Occurs in chloroplast
- Light reactions (thylakoid)
- Calvin cycle (stroma)

Autotroph: self-nourishing organism that is also known as a *producer* (plants).

Heterotroph: organisms that must consume other organisms to obtain energy—*consumers* (humans).

Transpiration: loss of water via evaporation through the stomata (natural process).

Photophosphorylation: process by which ATP is made during the light reactions.

Photolysis: process by which water is split into hydrogen ions and oxygen atoms (light reactions).

Stomata: structure through which CO_2 enters a plant, and water vapor and oxygen leave a plant.

Pigment: molecule that absorbs light of a particular wavelength (chlorophyll, carotenoid, phycobilins).

There are three types of photosynthesis reactions:

(Noncyclic) light-dependent reactions

- Occur in thylakoid membrane of chloroplast.

- Inputs are light and water.

- Light strikes photosystem II (P680).

- Electrons pass along until they reach primary electron acceptor.

- Photolysis occurs—H_2O is split to H^+ and O_2.

- Electrons pass down an ETC to P700 (photosystem I), forming ATP by chemiosmosis.

- Electrons of P700 pass down another ETC to produce NADPH.

- Three products of light reactions are NADPH, ATP, and O_2.

- Oxygen produced comes from H_2O.

(Cyclic) light-dependent reactions

- Occur in thylakoid membrane

- Only involves photosystem I; no photosystem II.

- ATP is the only product of these reactions.

- No NADPH or oxygen are produced.

- These reactions exist because the Calvin cycle uses more ATP than NADPH; this is how the difference is made up

Light-independent reactions (Calvin cycle)

- Occurs in stroma of chloroplast.

- Inputs are NADPH, ATP, and CO_2.

- First step is carbon fixation, which is catalyzed by an enzyme named rubisco.

- A series of reactions lead to the production of $NADP^+$, ADP, and sugar.

- More ATP is used than NADPH, which creates the need for the cyclic light reactions.

- The carbon of the sugar product comes from CO_2.

Also:

C_4 *plants*—plants that have adopted their photosynthetic process to more efficiently handle hot and dry conditions;

C_4 *photosynthesis*—process that first converts CO_2 into a 4-carbon molecule in the mesophyll cells, converts *that* product to malate and shuttles it to the bundle sheath cells, where the malate releases CO_2 and rubisco picks it up as if all were normal;

CAM plants—plants close their stomata during the day, collect CO_2 at night and store the CO_2 in the form of acids until it is needed during the day for photosynthesis.

Chapter 5

Cell Division

INTRODUCTION

Cell division, the process by which cells produce more of their kind, can occur in several ways. In this chapter we discuss cell division in prokaryotes (binary fission), the cell cycle, and cell division in eukaryotes (mitosis and meiosis). After comparing mitosis and meiosis, we will touch on the life cycles of various organisms.

CELL DIVISION IN PROKARYOTES

Prokaryotes are simple single-celled organisms without a nucleus. Their genetic material is arranged in a single circular chromosome of DNA, which is anchored to the cell membrane. As in eukaryotes, the genetic material of prokaryotes is duplicated before division. However, instead of entering into a complex cycle for cell division, prokaryotes simply elongate until they are double their original size. At this point, the cell pinches in and separates into two identical daughter cells in a process known as **binary fission** (Figure 5.1).

THE CELL CYCLE

Eukaryotic cell reproduction is a bit more complicated. The cell cycle functions as the daily planner of growth and development for the eukaryotic cell. It tells the cell when and in what order it is going to do things, and consists of all the necessary steps required for the reproduction of a cell. It begins after the creation of the cell and concludes with the formation of two daughter cells through cell division. It then begins again for the two daughter cells that have just been formed. There are four main stages to the cell cycle and they occur in the following sequence: **phases G_1, S, G_2, and M** (Figure 5.2). Segments G_1 and G_2 are growth stages, S is the part of the cell cycle during which the DNA is duplicated, and the M phase stands for mitosis: the cell division phase.

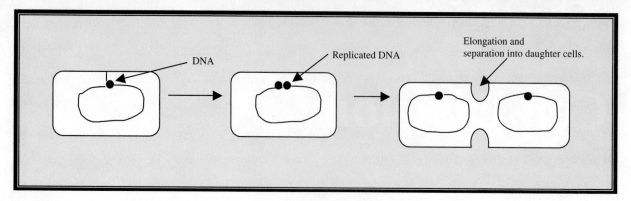

Figure 5.1
Binary fission.

Stages of the Cell Cycle

G₁ phase. the first growth phase of the cell cycle. The cell prepares itself for the synthesis stage of the cycle, making sure that it has all the necessary raw materials for DNA synthesis.

S phase. The DNA is copied so that each daughter cell has a complete set of chromosomes at the conclusion of the cell cycle.

G₂ phase. second growth phase of the cycle. The cell prepares itself for mitosis and/or meiosis, making sure that it has the raw materials necessary for the physical separation and formation of daughter cells.

M phase. mitosis. This is the stage during which the cell separates into two new cells.

The first three stages of the cycle (G_1, S, and G_2) make up the portion of the cell cycle known as **interphase.** A cell spends approximately 90 percent of its cycle in this phase. The other 10 percent is spent in the final stage, mitosis.

The amount of time that a cell requires to complete a cycle varies by cell type. Some cells complete a full cycle in hours, while others can take days to finish. The rapidity with which cells replicate also varies. Skin cells are continually zipping along through the cell cycle, whereas nerve cells do not replicate—once they are damaged, they are lost for good. This is one reason why the death of nerve cells is such a problem—these cells cannot be repaired or regenerated through mitotic replication.

MITOSIS

During mitosis, the fourth stage of the cell cycle, the cell actually takes the second copy of DNA made during the S phase and divides it equally between two cells. Single-cell

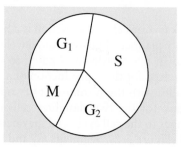

Figure 5.2
Pie chart showing the four main stages of the cell cycle.

eukaryotes undergo mitosis for the purpose of asexual reproduction. More complex multicellular eukaryotes use mitosis for other processes as well, such as growth and repair.

Mitosis consists of four major stages: prophase, metaphase, anaphase, and telophase. These stages are immediately followed by **cytokinesis**—the physical separation of the newly formed daughter cells. During interphase, chromosomes are invisible. The **chromatin**—the raw material that gives rise to the chromosomes—is long and thin during this phase. When the chromatin condenses to the point where the chromosome becomes visible by microscope, the cell is said to have begun mitosis. The AP Biology exam is not going to ask you detailed questions about the different stages of mitosis; just have a *general* understanding of what happens during each step.

Mitosis

Prophase. Nucleus and nucleolus disappear; chromosomes appear as two identical, connected sister chromatids; mitotic spindle (made of microtubules) begins to form; centrioles move to opposite poles of the cell (plant cells do not have centrioles).

Metaphase. For metaphase, think middle. The sister chromatids line up along the middle of the cell, ready to split apart.

Anaphase. For anaphase, think apart. The split sister chromatids move via the microtubules to the opposing poles of the cell. The chromosomes are pulled to opposite poles by the spindle apparatus. After anaphase, each pole of the cell has a complete set of chromosomes.

Telophase. The nuclei for the newly split cells form; the nucleoli reappear, and the chromatin uncoils.

Cytokinesis. Newly formed daughter cells split apart. Animal cells are split by the formation of a cleavage furrow, plant cells by the formation of a cell plate.

Figure 5.3 is a pictorial representation of the stages of mitosis.

Here are the definitions for words you may need to know:

Cell plate: plant cell structure, constructed in the Golgi apparatus, composed of vesicles that fuse together along the middle of the cell, completing the separation process.

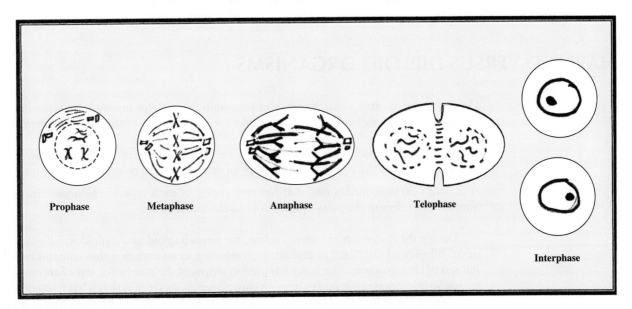

Prophase   Metaphase   Anaphase   Telophase   Interphase

Figure 5.3
The stages of mitosis.

Cleavage furrow: groove formed (in animal cells) between the two daughter cells that pinches together to complete the separation of the two cells after mitosis.

Cytokinesis: the actual splitting of the newly formed daughter cells that completes each trip around the cell cycle—some consider it part of mitosis; others regard it as the step immediately following mitosis.

Mitotic spindle: apparatus constructed from microtubules that assists the cell in the physical separation of the chromosomes during mitosis.

CONTROL OF CELL DIVISION

Sam: 12th grader "Control mechanisms are an important theme for this test. Be able to write about them."

Control of the cell cycle is important to normal cell growth. There are various ways in which the cell controls the process of cell division:

1. *Checkpoints.* There are checkpoints throughout the cell cycle where the cell verifies that there are enough nutrients and raw materials to progress to the next stage of the cycle. The G_1 checkpoint, for example, makes sure that the cell has enough raw materials to progress to and successfully complete the S phase.
2. *Density-dependent inhibition.* When a certain density of cells is reached, growth of the cells will slow or stop because there are not enough raw materials for the growth and survival of more cells. Cells that are halted by this inhibition enter a quiescent phase of the cell cycle known as G_0. Cancer cells can lose this inhibition and grow out of control.
3. *Growth factors.* Some cells will not divide if certain factors are absent. Growth factors, as their name indicates, assist in the growth of structures.
4. *Cyclins and protein kinases.* **Cyclin** is a protein that accumulates during G_1, S, and G_2 of the cell cycle. A **protein kinase** is a protein that controls other proteins through the addition of phosphate groups. Cyclin-dependent kinase (CDK) is present at all times throughout the cell cycle and binds with cyclin to form a complex known as MPF (maturation or mitosis promoting factor). Early in the cell cycle, because the cyclin concentration is low, the concentration of MPF is also low. As the concentration of cyclin reaches a certain threshold level, enough MPF is formed to push the cell into mitosis. As mitosis proceeds, the level of cyclin declines, decreasing the amount of MPF present and pulling the cell out of mitosis.

HAPLOID VERSUS DIPLOID ORGANISMS

One thing that is often a major source of confusion for some of my students is the distinction between being haploid and being diploid. Let's start with a definition of the terms:

A *haploid* (*n*) organism is one that has only one copy of each type of chromosome. In humans, this refers to a cell that has one copy of each type of homologous chromosome.

A *diploid* (*2n*) organism is one that has two copies of each type of chromosome. In humans this refers to the pairs of homologous chromosomes.

During the discussion of meiosis below, the terms haploid and diploid will be used often. Whenever I say "*2n*," or diploid, I am referring to an organism that contains two full *sets* of chromosomes. The letter *n* is used to represent the number of sets of chromosomes. So if an organism is said to have *4n* chromosomes, this means that it has four complete sets of chromosomes. Humans are diploid, and consist of *2n* chromosomes at all times except as gametes, when they are *n*. Humans have 23 *different* chromosomes, and two full *sets* of these 23 chromosomes, one from each parent, for a total of 46 chromosomes. Human sex cells have 23 chromosomes each.

MEIOSIS

Now that I have armed you with the knowledge of the distinction between haploid and diploid, it is time to dive into the topic of meiosis, which occurs during the process of sexual reproduction. A cell destined to undergo meiosis goes through the cell cycle, synthesizing a second copy of DNA just like mitotic cells. But after G_2, the cell instead enters meiosis, which consists of *two* cell divisions, not one. The second cell division exists because the gametes to be formed from meiosis must be haploid. This is because they are going to join with another haploid gamete at conception to produce the diploid zygote. Meiosis is like a two-part made-for-TV miniseries. It has two acts: meiosis I and meiosis II. Each of these two acts is divided into four steps, reminiscent of mitosis: prophase, metaphase, anaphase, and telophase.

Homologous chromosomes resemble one another in shape, size, function, and the genetic information they contain. In humans, the 46 chromosomes are divided into 23 homologous pairs. One member of each pair comes from an individual's mother, and the other member comes from the father. Meiosis I is the separation of the homologous pairs into two separate cells. Meiosis II is the separation of the duplicated sister chromatids into chromosomes. As a result, a single meiotic cycle produces *four* cells from a single cell. The cells produced during meiosis in the human life cycle are called **gametes**.

Again, the AP Biology exam is not going to test your mastery of the minute details of the meiotic process. However, a general understanding of the various steps is important:

Meiosis I

Prophase I. Each chromosome pairs with its homolog. Crossover (synapsis) occurs in this phase. The nuclear envelope breaks apart and spindle apparatus begins to form.

Metaphase I. Chromosomes align along the metaphase plate matched with their homologous partner. This stage ends with the separation of the homologous pairs.

Anaphase I. Separated homologous pairs move to opposite poles of the cell.

Telophase I. Nuclear membrane reforms; process of division begins.

Cytokinesis. After the daughter cells split, the two newly formed cells are haploid (*n*).

As discussed earlier, meiosis consists of a single synthesis period during which the DNA is replicated, followed by two acts of cell division. With the completion of the first cell division, meiosis I, the cells are haploid because they no longer consist of two full *sets* of chromosomes. Each cell has one of the duplicated chromatid pairs from each homologous pair. The cell then enters meiosis II.

Meiosis II

Prophase II. Nuclear envelope breaks apart and spindle apparatus begins to form.

Metaphase II. Sister chromatids line up along the equator of the cell.

Anaphase II. Sister chromatids split apart and are called *chromosomes* as they are pulled to the poles.

Telophase II. The nuclei and the nucleoli for the newly split cells return.

Cytokinesis. Newly formed daughter cells physically divide.

In humans the process of gamete formation is different in women and men. In men, **spermatogenesis** leads to the production of four haploid sperm during each meiotic cycle. In women the process is called **oogenesis.** It is a trickier process than spermatogenesis, and each complete meiotic cycle leads to the production of a single ovum, or egg. After meio-

Figure 5.4 is a pictorial representation of the stages of meiosis I and II.

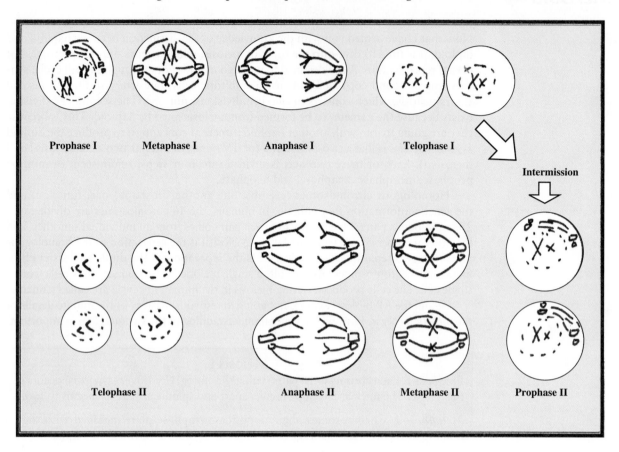

Figure 5.4
The stages of meiosis.

sis I in females, one cell receives half the genetic information and the majority of the cytoplasm of the parent cell. The other cell, the **polar body,** simply receives half of the genetic information and is cast away. During meiosis II, the remaining cell divides a second time, and forms a polar body that is cast away, and a single haploid ovum that contains half the genetic information and nearly all the cytoplasm of the original parent cell. The excess cytoplasm is required for proper growth of the embryo after fertilization. Thus the process of oogenesis produces two polar bodies and a single haploid ovum.

To review, why is it important to produce haploid gametes during meiosis? During fertilization, a sperm (n) will meet up with an egg (n), to produce a diploid zygote ($2n$). If either the sperm or the egg were diploid, then the offspring produced during sexual reproduction would contain more chromosomes than the parent organism. Meiosis circumvents this problem by producing gametes that are haploid and consist of one copy of each type of chromosome. During fertilization between two gametes, each copy will match up with another copy of each type of chromosome to form the diploid zygote.

Before moving on, there are a few important distinctions between meiosis and mitosis that should be emphasized.

	Mitosis	Meiosis
Resulting daughter cells	Two diploid ($2n$) daughter cells	Four haploid (n) daughter cells
Crossover?	No	Yes—prophase I
Types of cells in which it occurs for humans	All cells of the body other than the cells of the gonads	Cells of gonads to produce gametes

In meiosis during prophase I, the homologous pairs join together. This matching of chromosomes into homologous pairs does not occur in mitosis. In mitosis, the 46 chromosomes simply align along the metaphase plate alone.

An event of major importance that occurs during meiosis that does not occur during mitosis is known as **crossover** (also known *crossing over*) (Figure 5.5). When the homologous pairs match up during prophase I of meiosis, complementary pieces from the two homologous chromosomes wrap around each other and are exchanged between the chromosomes. Imagine that chromosome A is the homologous partner for chromosome B. When they pair up during prophase I, a piece of chromosome A containing a certain stretch of genes can be exchanged for the piece of chromosome B containing the same genetic information. This is one of the mechanisms that allows offspring to differ from their parents. Remember that crossing over occurs between the homologous chromosome pairs, *not* the sister chromatids.

LIFE CYCLES

The AP Biology exam characteristically will ask a question or two about the various types of life cycles for plants, animals, and fungi. A **life cycle** is the sequence of events that make up the reproductive cycle of an organism. Let's take a quick look at the three main life cycles.

The most complicated life cycle of the three is that of plants, also called the **alternation of generations** (Figure 5.6). It is referred to by this term because during the life cycle, plants sometimes exist as a diploid organism and at other times as a haploid organism. It alternates between the two forms. Similar to the other life cycles, two haploid gametes combine to form a diploid zygote, which divides *mitotically* to produce the diploid multicellular stage: the **sporophyte.** The sporophyte undergoes *meiosis* to produce a haploid spore. *Mitotic division* leads to the production of haploid multicellular organisms called **gametophytes.** The gametophyte undergoes *mitosis* to produce haploid gametes, which combine to form diploid zygotes . . . and around and around they go.

The human life cycle is (Figure 5.7) pretty straightforward. The only haploid cells present in this life cycle are the gametes formed during meiosis. The two haploid gametes combine during fertilization to produce a diploid zygote. Mitotic division then leads to formation of the diploid multicellular organism. Meiotic division later produces haploid gametes, which continue the cycle.

The life cycle for fungi (Figure 5.8) is different from that of humans. Fungi are haploid organisms, with the zygote being the only diploid form. Like humans, the gametes for fungi are haploid (*n*), and fertilization yields a diploid zygote. But in this life cycle, instead of dividing by mitosis, the zygote divides by meiosis to form a haploid organism. Another difference in this life cycle is that the gametes are formed by *mitosis*, not meiosis—the organism is *already* haploid, before forming the gametes.

Here is some trivia about life cycles that might come in handy on the exam. The only diploid stage for a fungus is the zygote. The only haploid stage for a human is the gamete. Of the plant life cycles, the moss (bryophyte) is an exception in that its prominent gener-

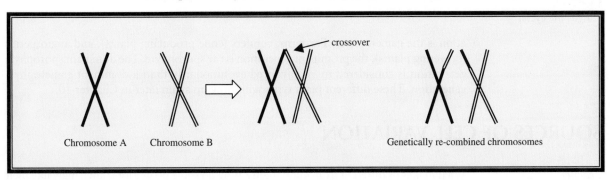

Figure 5.5
Crossover.

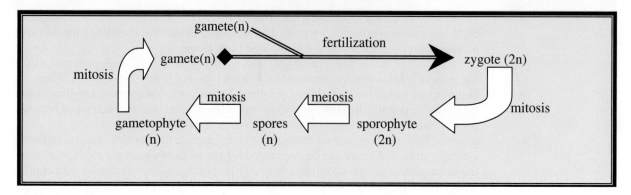

Figure 5.6
Plant life: alternation of generations.

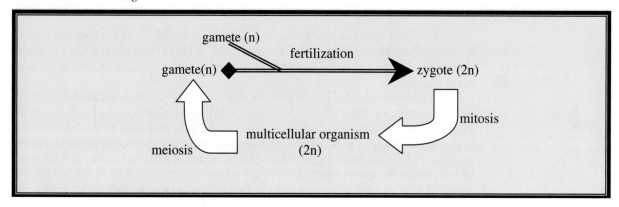

Figure 5.7
Human life cycle.

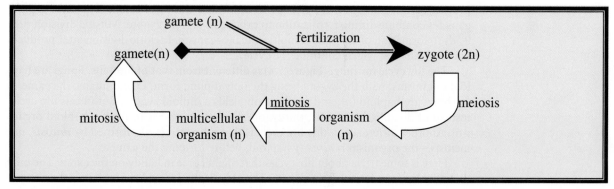

Figure 5.8
Fungus life cycle.

ation is the gametophyte. For ferns, conifers (cone producing plants), and angiosperms (flowering plants), the prominent generation is the sporophyte. The dominant sporophyte generation is considered more advanced evolutionarily than a dominant gametophyte generation. These different plant types will show up again later in Chapter 10.

SOURCES OF CELL VARIATION

Teacher: NYC
"Knowing the sources of variation is important."

What makes us different from our parents? Why do some people look amazingly like their parents while others do not? The process of cell division provides ample opportunity for variation. Remember that during meiosis, homologous chromosome pairs align together along the metaphase plate. This alignment is a completely random process, and there is a

50 percent chance that the chromosome in the pair from the individual's mother will go to one side, and a 50 percent chance that the chromosome in the pair from the individual's father will go to that side. This is true for all the homologous pairs in an organism. This means that $2n$ possible gametes that can form from any given set of n chromosomes. For example, in a 3 chromosome organism, there are $2^3 = 8$ possible gametes. In humans, there are 23 homologous pairs. This comes out to 2^{23} (8,388,608) different ways the gametes can separate during gametogenesis.

Another source of variation during sexual reproduction is the random determination of which sperm meets up with which ovum. In humans, the sperm represents one of 2^{23} possibilities from the male gamete factory; the ovum, one of 2^{23} possibilities from the female gamete factory. All these factors combine to explain why siblings may look nothing like each other.

A third major source of variation during gamete formation is the **crossover** (or *crossing over*) that occurs during prophase I of meiosis. It is very important for you to remember that this process happens *only* during that stage of cell division. It does not occur in mitosis.

REVIEW QUESTIONS

1. Which of the following plant types has the gametophyte as its prominent generation?

   A. Angiosperms
   B. Bryophytes
   C. Conifers
   D. Gymnosperms
   E. Ferns

2. During which phase of the cell cycle does crossing over occur?

   A. Metaphase of mitosis
   B. Metaphase I of meiosis
   C. Prophase I of meiosis
   D. Prophase of mitosis
   E. Anaphase I of meiosis

For questions 3–6 please use the following answer choices:

   A. Prophase
   B. Metaphase
   C. Anaphase
   D. Telophase
   E. Cytokinesis

3. During this phase the split sister chromatids, now considered to be chromosomes, are moved to the opposite poles of the cell.

4. During this phase the nucleus deteriorates and the mitotic spindle begins to form.

5. During this phase the two daughter cells are actually split apart.

6. During this phase the sister chromatids line up along the equator of the cell, preparing to split.

7. Which of the following organisms is diploid ($2n$) only as a zygote and is haploid for every other part of its life cycle?

   A. Humans
   B. Bryophytes
   C. Fungi
   D. Bacteria
   E. Angiosperms

8. Which of the following statements is true about a human meiotic cell after it has completed meiosis I?

   A. It is diploid ($2n$).
   B. It is haploid (n).
   C. It has divided into four daughter cells.
   D. It proceeds directly to meiosis II without an intervening intermission.

9. Which of the following is *not* true about cyclin-dependent kinase (CDK)?

   A. It is present only during the M phase of the cell cycle.
   B. When enough of it is combined with cyclin, the MPF (mitosis promoting factor) formed initiates mitosis.

C. It is a protein that controls other proteins using phosphate groups.

D. It is present at all times during the cell cycle.

10. Which of the following statements about meiosis and/or mitosis is incorrect?

A. Mitosis results in two diploid daughter cells.

B. Meiosis in humans occurs only in gonad cells.

C. Homologous chromosomes line up along the metaphase plate during mitosis.

D. Crossover occurs during prophase I of meiosis.

E. Meiosis consists of one replication phase followed by two division phases.

ANSWERS AND EXPLANATIONS

1. **B**—Bryophytes, or mosses, are the plant type that has the gametophyte (haploid) as its dominant generation. The others in this question have the sporophyte (diploid) as their dominant generation.

2. **C**—Crossover occurs in humans only in prophase I. Propase I is a major source of variation in the production of offspring.

3. **C**

4. **A**

5. **E**

6. **B**

7. **C**—The life cycle for fungi is different from that of humans. Fungi exist as haploid organisms and the only time they exist in diploid form is as a zygote. Like humans, the gametes for fungi are haploid (n) and combine to form a diploid zygote. Unlike humans, the fungus zygote divides by meiosis to form a haploid organism.

8. **B**—Human cells start with 46 chromosomes arranged in 23 pairs of homologous chromosomes. At this time they are $2n$ because they have two copies of each chromosome. After the S phase of the cell cycle, the DNA has been doubled in preparation for cell division. The first stage of meiosis pulls apart the homologous pairs of chromosomes. This means that after meiosis I, the cells are n, or haploid—they no longer consist of *two* full sets of chromosomes.

9. **A**—CDK is present at all times during the cell cycle. It combines with a protein called *cyclin*, which accumulates during interphase of the cell cycle, to form MPF. When enough MPF is formed, the cell is pushed to begin mitosis. As mitosis continues, cyclin is degraded, and when the concentration of MPF drops below a level sufficient to maintain mitotic division, mitosis grinds to a halt until the threshold is reached again next time around the cycle.

10. **C**—Answer choices A, B, D, and E are all correct. C is incorrect because homologous pairs of chromosomes pair together only during meiosis. During mitosis, the sister chromatid pairs align along the metaphase plate, separate from the homologous counterpart.

RAPID REVIEW

You should be familiar with the following terms:

Binary fission: prokaryotic cell division; double the DNA, double the size, then split apart

Cell cycle: $G_1 \rightarrow S \rightarrow G_2 \rightarrow M \rightarrow growth_1 \rightarrow synthesis \rightarrow growth_2 \rightarrow mitosis \rightarrow$ etc.

Interphase: $G_1 + S + G_2 = 90$ percent of the cell cycle

Stage	Mitosis	Meiosis
Prophase	Nucleus, nucleolus disappear; mitotic spindle forms	—
Metaphase	Sister chromatids line up at middle	—
Anaphase	Sister chromatids are split apart	—
Telophase	Nuclei of new cells reform; chromatin uncoils	—
Prophase I	—	Each chromosome pairs with its homolog; this is *crossover*
Metaphase I	—	Chromosome pairs align along middle of cell, ready to split apart
Anaphase I	—	Homologous chromosomes split apart
Telophase I	—	Nuclear membrane reforms; daughter cells are haploid now (n)
Prophase II	—	Nucleus disappears, spindle apparatus forms
Metaphase II	—	Sister chromatids line up at middle
Anaphase II	—	Sister chromatids are split apart
Telophase II	—	Nuclei of new cells reform; chromatin uncoils

Cytokinesis: physical separation of newly formed daughter cells of cell division.

Cell division control mechanisms:

1. *Growth factors:* factors that when present, promote growth and when absent, impede growth.
2. *Checkpoints:* a cell stops to make sure it has the nutrients and raw materials to proceed.
3. *Density-dependent inhibition:* cell stops growing when certain density is reached—runs out of food!!!
4. *Cyclins and protein kinases:* cyclin combines with cyclin-dependent kinase to form a structure known as MPF that pushes cell into mitosis when enough is present.

Haploid (n): one copy of each chromosome

Diploid (2n): two copies of each chromosome

Homologous chromosomes: chromosomes that are similar in shape, size, and function

Spermatogenesis: male gamete formation (four sperm from one cell)

Oogenesis: female gamete formation (one ovum from each cell)

Life cycles: Sequence of events that make up the reproductive cycle of an organism

- *Human:* zygote ($2n$) → multicellular organism ($2n$) → gametes (n) → zygote ($2n$)

- *Fungi:* zygote ($2n$) → multicellular organism (n) → gametes (n) → zygote ($2n$)

- *Plants:* zygote ($2n$) → sporophyte ($2n$) → spores (n) → gametophyte (n) → gametes (n) → zygote ($2n$)

Sources of variation: crossover, $2n$ possible gametes that can be formed, random pairing of gametes

Chapter 6

Heredity

INTRODUCTION

How many times have you heard someone say as they look at a baby, "awwww, he looks like his daddy" or "she has her mother's eyes"? What exactly is it that causes an infant to look like his or her parents? This question is the basis of the study of heredity—the study of the passing of traits from generation to generation. Its basic premise is that offspring are more like their parents than less closely related individuals.

In this chapter, we begin by discussing some terms that will prove important to your study of heredity. This is followed by an examination of Mendel's *law of segregation* and The *law of independent assortment,* including how they were discovered and how they can be applied. We will examine the *law of dominance,* which arose from Mendel's work, and we will also discuss some exceptions to Mendel's fundamental laws such as intermediate inheritance (incomplete dominance and codominance), multiple alleles, polygenic traits, epistasis, and pleiotropy.

In the next section we will examine Thomas Morgan's work on fruit flies, which paved the way for the discovery of linked genes, genetic recombination, and sex-linked inheritance. This discussion concludes with a look at gene linkage and linkage maps.

Finally, since chromosomes carry the vital genes necessary for proper development and passage of hereditary material from one generation to the next, it is important to discuss the types of chromosomal errors that can occur during reproduction. This includes the various forms of nondisjunction, or the improper separation of chromosomes during meiosis (which leads to an abnormal number of chromosomes in offspring). The chapter concludes with an examination of the other major types of chromosomal errors: deletions, duplications, translocations, and inversions.

TERMS IMPORTANT IN STUDYING HEREDITY

The following is a list of terms that will help in your understanding of heredity:

Allele: a variant of a gene for a particular character. For example, the two alleles for eye color discussed later in the chapter are B (dominant) and b (recessive).

F_1: the first generation of offspring, or the first "filial" generation in a genetic cross.

F_2: the second generation of offspring, or the second "filial" generation in a genetic cross.

Genotype: an organism's genetic makeup for a given trait. A simple example of this could involve eye color where B represents the allele for brown and b represents the allele for blue. The possible genotypes include homozygous brown (BB), heterozygous brown (Bb), and homozygous blue (bb).

Heterozygous (hybrid): an individual is heterozygous (or a hybrid) for a gene if the two alleles are different (Bb).

Homozygous (pure): an individual is homozygous for a gene if both of the given alleles are the same (BB or bb).

Karyotype: a chart that organizes chromosomes in relation to number, size, and type.

Nondisjunction: the improper separation of chromosomes during meiosis, which leads to an abnormal number of chromosomes in offspring. A few classic examples of non-disjunction-related syndromes are Down's syndrome, Turner's syndrome, and Klinefelter's syndrome.

P_1: the parent generation in a genetic cross.

Phenotype: the physical expression of the trait associated with a particular genotype. Some examples of the phenotypes for Mendel's peas were round or wrinkled, green or yellow, purple flower or white flower.

MENDEL AND HIS PEAS

The person whose name is most often associated with heredity is Gregor Mendel. Mendel spent many years working with peas. It was a very strange hobby, indeed, but it proved quite useful to the world of science. He mated peas to produce offspring and recorded the phenotype results in order to determine how certain characters are inherited. A **character** is a genetically inherited characteristic that differs from person to person.

Before he began his work in the 1850s, the accepted theory of inheritance was the **"blending" hypothesis,** which stated that the genes contributed by two parents mixed as do colors. For example, a blue flower mixed with a yellow flower would produce a green flower. The exact genetic makeup of each parent could never be recovered; the genes would be as inseparable as the blended colors. Mendel used plant experiments to test this hypothesis and developed his two fundamental theories: the law of segregation and the law of independent assortment.

When Mendel was observing a single character during a mating, he was doing something called a **monohybrid cross**—a cross that involves a single character in which both parents are heterozygous (Bb × Bb). A monohybrid cross between heterozygous gametes gives a 3 : 1 phenotype ratio in the offspring (Figure 6.1). As you can see in Figure 6.1, an offspring is three times more likely to express the dominant B trait than the recessive b trait.

	B	b
B	BB	Bb
b	Bb	bb

Figure 6.1
Monohybrid cross.

Mendel also experimented with multiple characters simultaneously. The crossing of two different hybrid characters is termed a **dihybrid cross** (BbRr × BbRr.) A dihybrid cross between heterozygous gametes gives a 9:3:3:1 phenotype ratio in the offspring (Figure 6.2).

	BR	**Br**	**bR**	**br**
BR	BBRR	BBRr	BbRR	BbRr
Br	BBRr	BBrr	BbRr	Bbrr
bR	BbRR	BbRr	bbRR	bbRr
br	BbRr	Bbrr	bbRr	bbrr

Figure 6.2
Dihybrid cross.

From his experiments, Mendel developed two major hereditary laws: the law of segregation and the law of independent assortment.

The law of segregation. Every organism carries pairs of factors, called *alleles,* for each trait, and the members of the pair segregate (separate) during the formation of gametes. For example, if an individual is Bb for eye color, during gamete formation one gamete would receive a B, and the other made from that cell would receive a b.

The law of independent assortment. Members of each pair of factors are distributed independently when the gametes are formed. Quite simply, inheritance of one trait or characteristic does not interfere with inheritance of another trait. For example, if an individual is BbRr for two genes, gametes formed during meiosis could contain BR, Br, bR, or br. The B and b alleles assort *independently* of the R and r alleles.

The law of dominance. Also based on Mendel's work, this states that when two opposite pure-breeding varieties (homozygous dominant vs. homozygous recessive) of an organism are crossed, all the offspring resemble one parent. This is referred to as the *dominant* trait. The variety that is hidden is referred to as the *recessive* trait.

It is time for you to answer a question for me (of course, I have no way of knowing whether or how you will answer this question): Can the phenotype of an organism be determined from simple observation? Yes—just look at the organism and determine whether it is tall or short, has blue eyes or brown eyes, and so on. However, the genotype of an organism *cannot* always be determined from simple observation. In the case of a recessive trait, the genotype is known. If a person has blue eyes (recessive to brown), the genotype is bb. But if that person has brown eyes, you cannot be sure if the genotype is Bb or BB—the individual can be either homozygous dominant or heterozygous dominant. To determine the exact genotype, you must run an experiment called a **test cross.** Geneticists breed the organism whose genotype is unknown with an organism that is homozygous recessive for the trait. This results in offspring with observable phenotypes. If the unknown genotype is heterozygous, probability indicates one-half of the offspring *should* express the recessive phenotype. If the unknown genotype is homozygous dominant, *all* the organism's offspring *should* express the dominant trait. Of course, such experiments are not done on humans.

Remember me!!!

Mendel discovered many statistical laws of heredity. He learned that a monohybrid cross such as Yy × Yy will result in a phenotype ratio of 3:1 in favor of the dominant trait. He learned that a dihybrid cross, such as YyRr × YyRr, will result in a phenotype ratio of 9:3:3:1 (9 RY, 3 rY, 3 Ry, 1 ry). These two ratios, when they appear in genetic analysis problems, imply mono- and dihybrid crosses.

INTERMEDIATE INHERITANCE

The inheritance of traits is not always as simple as Mendel's pea experiments seem to indicate. Traits are not always dominant or recessive, and phenotype ratios are not always 9:3:3:1 or 3:1. Mendel's experiments did not account for something called **intermediate inheritance,** in which an individual heterozygous for a trait (Yy) shows characteristics not exactly like *either* parent. The phenotype is a "mixture" of both of the parents' genetic input. There are two major types of intermediate inheritance:

Marcy: College freshman "Understanding this concept is worth 2 points on the exam."

1. Incomplete dominance or "blending inheritance"
2. Codominance

Incomplete Dominance ("Blending Inheritance")

In **incomplete dominance** ("blending inheritance") the heterozygous genotype produces an "intermediate" phenotype rather than the dominant phenotype; neither allele dominates the other. A classic example of incomplete dominance is flower color in snapdragons—crossing a snapdragon plant that has red flowers with one that has white flowers yields offspring with pink flowers.

One genetic condition in humans that exhibits incomplete dominance is **hypercholesterolemia**—a recessive disorder (hh) that causes cholesterol levels to be many times higher than normal and can lead to heart attacks in children as young as 2 years old. Those who are HH tend to have normal cholesterol levels, and those who are Hh have cholesterol levels somewhere in between the two extremes. As with many conditions, the environment plays a major role in how genetic conditions express themselves. Thus, people who are HH do not necessarily have normal cholesterol levels if, for example, they have poor diet or exercise habits.

One important side note—try not to confuse the terms blending "hypothesis" and blending "inheritance." The latter is another name for incomplete dominance, whereas the former was the theory on heredity before Mendel worked his magic. The blending "hypothesis" says that the HH and hh extremes can never be retrieved. In reality, and according to blending inheritance, if you were to cross two Hh individuals, the offspring could still be HH or hh, which the blending "hypothesis" says cannot happen once the blending has occurred.

Codominance

Codominance is the situation in which both alleles express themselves fully in a heterozygous organism. A good example of codominance involves the human blood groups: M, N, and MN. Individuals with group M blood have M molecule on the surface of the blood cell, individuals with group N blood have N molecules on the blood cell, and those with group MN blood have *both*. This is not incomplete dominance because both alleles are fully expressed in the phenotype—they are codominant.

OTHER FORMS OF INHERITANCE

Polygenic Traits

Another interesting form of inheritance involves **polygenic traits,** or traits that are affected by more than one gene. Eye color is an example of a polygenic trait. The *tone* (color), *amount* (blue eyes have less than brown eyes), and *position* (how evenly distributed the pigment is) of pigment *all* play a role in determining eye color. Each of these characteristics is determined by separate genes. Another example of this phenomenon is skin color, which is determined by at least three different genes working together to produce a wide range of possible skin tones.

Multiple Alleles

Many monogenic traits (traits expressed via a single gene) correspond to two alleles; one dominant and one recessive. Other traits, however, involve more than two alleles. A classic example of such a trait is the human blood type. On the most simplistic level, there are four major blood types: A, B, AB, and O. They are named based on the presence or absence of certain carbohydrates on the surface of the red blood cells. The gene for blood type has three possible alleles (multiple alleles): I^A, which causes carbohydrate A to be produced on the surface of the red blood cell; I^B, which causes carbohydrate B to be produced; and i, which causes *no* carbohydrate to be produced. The following are the possible genotypes for human blood type: I^Ai (type A), $I^A I^A$ (type A), I^Bi (type B), $I^B I^B$ (type B), $I^A I^B$ (type AB), ii (type O). Type AB blood displays the *codominance* of blood type. As we saw in MN blood groups, both the A and the B alleles succeed in their mission—their carbohydrate appears on the surface of the red blood cell (see Figure 6.3). Analyzing blood type can be really complex because human blood types involve not only multiple alleles (I^A, I^B, and i) and codominance (type AB blood), but classic dominance of I^A and I^B over i as well.

If you have ever watched an episode of *ER* (Emergency Room) on television, you have heard one of the doctors frantically scream, "We need to type her and bring some O blood down here *stat*!" Why is it important for the physician to determine what type of blood the patient has, and why is it okay to give the patient O blood in the meantime? People with type A blood produce anti-B antibodies, because the B carbohydrate that is present on type B and type AB blood is a foreign molecule to someone with type A blood. This is simply the body's defense mechanism doing its job. Following the same logic, those with type B blood make anti-A antibodies, and those with type O blood make anti-A *and* anti-B antibodies. People who are type AB make none, and are therefore the universal acceptor of blood. It is important to find out what kind of blood a person has because if you give type B blood to a person with type A blood, the recipient will have an immune response to the transfused blood. Why is O blood given while they wait to see what blood type the patient is? This is because type O blood has neither carbohydrate on the surface of red blood cells. People with type O blood are universal donors because few people will have an adverse reaction to type O blood. Immune reactions are discussed in further detail in Chapter 11, Human Physiology.

Blood Type	Carbohydrates on surface of RBC	Antibodies produced by the body	Can be transfused with which types of blood?	Can be donated to individuals of which type?
A	Carb A	Anti B	Type A, O	Type A, AB
B	Carb B	Anti A	Type B, O	Type B, AB
AB	Carb A & B	None	All types	Type AB
O	No Carbs	Anti A and Anti B	Only O	All Types

Figure 6.3
Several human blood type characteristics.

Epistasis

In **epistasis** the expression of one gene affects the expression of another gene. A classic example of epistasis involves the coat color of mice. Black is dominant over brown; brown fur has the genotype bb. There is also another gene locus independent of the coat color gene that controls the deposition of pigment in the fur. If a mouse has a dominant allele of this pigment gene (Cc or CC), it leads to pigment deposition and the coloring of the fur according to the coat color gene's instructions. If a mouse is double recessive for this trait (cc), it will have white fur no matter what the coat-color gene wants because it will not put any pigment into the fur. It is almost as if the pigment gene were overruling the coat color gene. If you mate two black mice that are BbCc, the ratio of phenotypes in the offspring would not be the 9:3:3:1 ratio that Mendel predicts, but rather 9:4:3 black: white: brown because the epistatic gene alters the phenotype.

Pleiotropy

In **pleiotropy** a single gene has multiple effects on an organism. A good example of pleiotropy is the mutation that causes sickle cell anemia. This single gene mutation "sickles" the blood cells, leading to systemic symptoms such as heart, lung, and kidney damage; muscle pain; weakness; and generalized fatigue. The problems do not stop there, as these symptoms can lead to disastrous side effects such as kidney failure. The mutation of a single gene is wreaking havoc on the system as a whole.

SEX DETERMINATION AND SEX LINKAGE

Mendel was not the only one to make progress in the field of heredity. In the early 1900s, Thomas Morgan made key discoveries regarding sex linkage and linked genes.

In human cells, all chromosomes occur in structurally identical pairs except for two very important ones: the sex chromosomes, X and Y. Women have two structurally identical X chromosomes. Men have one X, and one Y.

Sex-Linked Traits

Morgan experimented with a quick-breeding fruitfly species. The fruit flies had 4 pairs of chromosomes: three autosomal pairs and one sex chromosome pair. An **autosomal chromosome** is one that is not directly involved in determining gender. In fruit flies, the more common phenotype for a trait is called the **wild type phenotype** (e.g., red eyes). Traits that are different from the normal are called **mutant phenotypes** (e.g., white eyes). Morgan crossed a white-eyed male with a red-eyed female, and all the F$_1$ offspring had red eyes. When he bred the F$_1$ together, he obtained Mendel's 3:1 ratio. But, there was a slight difference from what Mendel's theories would predict—the white trait was restricted to the males. Morgan's conclusion was that the gene for eye color is on the X chromosome. This means that the poor male flies get only a single copy and if it is abnormal, they are abnormal. But, the lucky ladies have two copies and are normal even if one copy is not.

It is this male–female sex chromosomes difference that allows for sex-linked conditions. If a gene for a recessive disease is present on the X chromosome, then a female must have two defective versions of the gene to show the disease while a male needs only one. This is so because males have no corresponding gene on the Y chromosome to help counter the negative effect of a recessive allele on the X chromosome. Thus, more males than females show recessive X-linked phenotypes. In a pedigree (see Figure 6.6, later in this chapter), a pattern of sex-linked disease will show the sons of carrier mothers with the disease.

The father plays no part in the passage of an X-linked gene to the male children of a couple. Fathers pass X-linked alleles to their daughters, but not to their sons. Do you understand why this is so? The father does not give an X chromosome to the male off-spring because he is the one that provides the Y chromosome that makes his son a male. A mother can pass a sex-linked allele to both her daughters *and* sons because she can pass only X chromosomes to her offspring.

Three common sex-linked disorders are Duchenne's muscular dystrophy, hemo-philia, and red-green colorblindness. **Duchenne's muscular dystrophy** is a sex-linked disorder that is caused by the absence of an essential muscle protein. Its symptoms include a progressive loss of muscle strength and coordination. **Hemophilia** is caused by the absence of a protein vital to the clotting process. Individuals with this condition have difficulty clotting blood after even the smallest of wounds. Those most severely affected by the disease can bleed to death after the tiniest of injuries. Females with this condition rarely survive.

People afflicted with **red-green colorblindness** are unable to distinguish between red and green colors. This condition is found primarily in males.

Emily: 12th grader "Be able to categorize diseases for this exam!"

X Inactivation

Here is an important question for you to ponder while preparing for this exam: "Are all the cells in a female identical?"

The answer to this question is "No." Females undergo a process called **X inactiva-tion.** During the development of the female embryo, one of the two X chromosomes in each cell remains coiled as a **Barr body** whose genes are not expressed. A cell expresses the alleles only of the active X chromosome. X inactivation occurs separately in each cell and involves random inactivation of one of a female's X chromosomes. But not all cells inactivate the same X. As a result, different cells will have different active X chromosomes.

Why don't females always express X-linked diseases when this X inactivation occurs? Sometimes they do, but usually they will have enough cells with a "good" copy of the allele to compensate for the presence of the recessive allele.

One last sex-related inheritance pattern that needs to be mentioned is **holandric traits,** which are traits inherited via the Y chromosome. An example of a holandric trait in humans is ear hair distribution.

LINKAGE AND GENE MAPPING

Each chromosome has hundreds of genes that tend to be inherited together because the chromosome is passed along as a unit. These are called **linked genes.** Linked genes lie on the same chromosome and do not follow Mendel's law of independent assortment.

Morgan performed an experiment in which he looked at body color and wing size on his beloved fruitflies. The dominant alleles were G (gray) and V (normal wings); while the recessive alleles were g (black) and v (vestigial wings). GgVv females were crossed with ggvv males. Mendel's law of independent assortment predicts offspring of four dif-ferent phenotypes in a 1:1:1:1 ratio. But that is not what Morgan found. Because the genes are linked, the gray/normal flies produce only (GV) or (gv) gametes. Thus, Morgan expected the ratio of offspring to be 1:1, half GgVv and half ggvv. Morgan found that there were more wild-type and double-mutant flies than independent assortment would predict, but, surprisingly, some (Gv) and (gV) were also produced.

How did those other combinations result from the cross if the genes are linked? **Cross over** (also known as *crossing over*), a form of genetic recombination that occurs during prophase I of meiosis, led to their production. The less often this recombination occurs, the closer the genes must be on the chromosome. The further apart two genes are on a chromosome, the more often crossover will occur. Recombination frequency can be used to determine how close two genes are on a chromosome through the creation of linkage maps, which we will look at next.

Linkage Maps

A **linkage map** is a genetic map put together using crossover frequencies. Another unit of measurement, the **map unit** (also known as *centigram*), is used to geographically relate the genes on the basis of these frequencies. One map unit is equal to a 1 percent crossover frequency. A linkage map does not provide the *exact* location of genes; it gives only the relative location. Imagine that you want to determine the relative locations of four genes: A, B, C, and D. You know that A crosses over with C 20 percent of the time, B crosses over with C 15 percent of the time, A crosses over with D 10 percent of the time, and D crosses over with B 5 percent of the time. From this information you can determine the sequence (Figure 6.4). Gene A must be 20 units from gene C. Gene B must be 15 units from C, but B could be 5 or 35 units from A. But, because you also know that A is 10 units from D and that D is 5 units from B, you can determine that B must be 5 units from A as well if A is also to be 10 units from D. This gives you the sequence of genes as ABDC.

HEADS OR TAILS?

Probability is a concept important to a full understanding of heredity and inheritance. What is the probability that a flipped coin will come up heads? You can answer that easily: ½. What is the probability that two coins flipped simultaneously will *both* be heads? This is a little harder—it is ½ × ½ = ¼. Take a look at Figure 6.5. The first time you toss the coin, there is a probability of ½ that it will land heads and ½ that it will land tails. When you toss it again, it again has a probability of ½ that it will land heads, and ½ that it will land tails. So in the figure, just concentrate on the ½ of the tosses that land heads. Of those, ½ of them will land heads the second time—or ½ of ½. Multiplied together, this results in the ¼ chance of getting heads twice with two coin tosses. This example illustrates the **law of multiplication** with probabilities. This law states that to determine the probability that two random events will occur in succession, you simply multiply the probability of the first event by the probability of the second event.

This is the same thought process that we follow to understand Mendel's law of segregation. If you are Aa for a trait, what is your chance or passing the A on? That's right—½. If you are AaBb, what is the chance you pass both A and B on? Clever you are—you multiply ½ × ½ to get ¼.

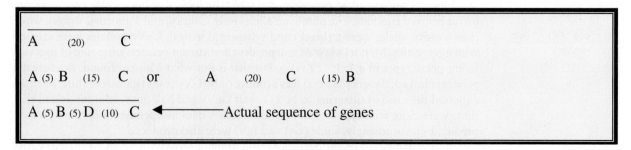

Figure 6.4
A genetic linkage map.

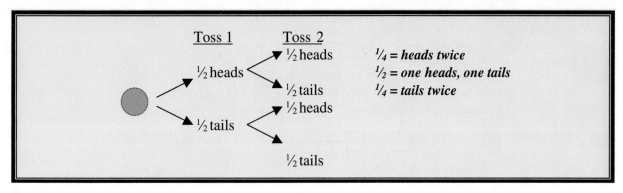

Figure 6.5
Probability in the law of multiplication.

PEDIGREES

Pedigrees are family trees used to describe the genetic relationships within a family. Comprehension of the probability concept is important for a full understanding of pedigree analysis. Squares represent males, and circles are used for females. A horizontal line from male to female represents mates that have produced offspring. The offspring are listed below their parents from oldest to youngest. A fully shaded individual possesses the trait being studied. If the condition being studied is a monogenic recessive condition (rr), then those shaded gray have the genotype rr. If the condition being studied is a dominant condition (Rr or RR), then those that are *un*shaded have the genotype rr. A line through a symbol indicates that the person is deceased. A sample pedigree is shown in (Figure 6.6).

Pedigrees can be used in many ways. One use is to determine the risk of parents passing certain conditions to their offspring. Imagine that two people want to have a child and they both have a family history of a certain autosomal recessive condition (dd). Neither has the particular condition, but the man has a brother who died of the disease and the woman's mother died of the disease at an older age. They want to know the probability of having a child with the condition. You must first determine the probability that each parent is a carrier, and then determine the probability of the parents having a child with the disease, *given* that they are carriers. See the pedigree in Figure 6.7.

!

Teacher: CT
"Test almost always has 2–3 questions about this topic."

First, we can determine the father's (second generation) probability of being a carrier. We know that both of his parents must be carriers with a genotype of Dd. Why is this the case? Although neither parent has the condition, they must both be carriers in order for his brother to have received two recessive alleles and thus contract the disease.

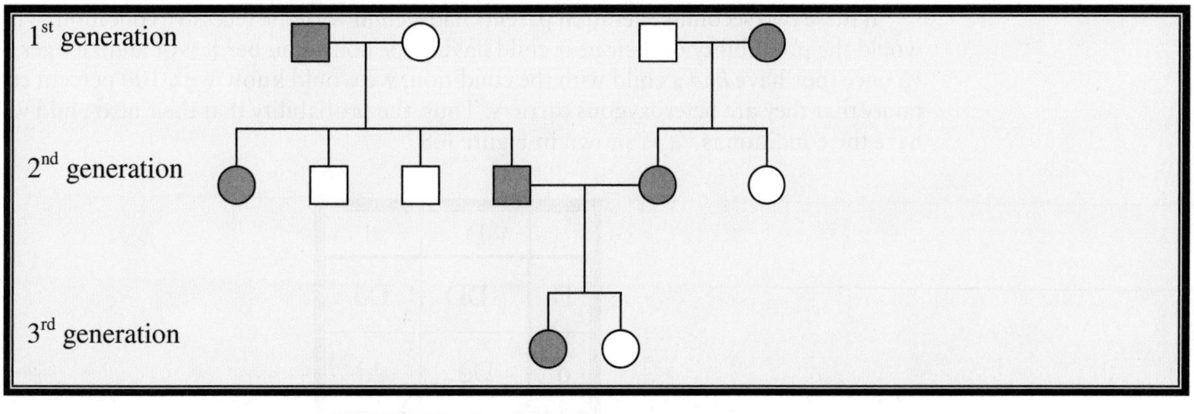

Figure 6.6
Schematic of a pedigree.

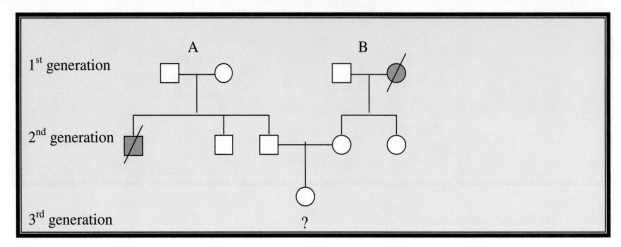

Figure 6.7
Three-generation pedigree indicating probability of inheriting a particular disease.

How can we calculate the potential probability of the father being a carrier? We construct a Punnett square for a monohybrid cross of the father's parents (first generation) (Figure 6.8).

We know with certainty that he is not dd, otherwise he would have the condition. This leaves three equally likely possible genotypes for the father, two of which are "carrier" genotypes (Dd). Thus the probability of his being a carrier is $\frac{2}{3}$.

What is the probability that the mother (second generation) is a carrier? We don't even need a Punnett square to determine this one. Her mother (first generation) died of the condition, which means that she must have been dd, and thus must have passed along a d to each of her children. The mother in question does not have the condition, so she must have a D as well. Therefore her genotype *must* be Dd.

To determine the probability that *both* parents are carriers, apply the law of multiplication with probabilities (similar to tossing a coin), we can use the following formula:

$$P_F \times P_M = \frac{2}{3} \times 1 = \frac{2}{3}$$

(where P_F, P_M = probabilities of father, mother being carriers)

Now that we have determined the probability that they are both carriers, we need to determine the probability that one of their offspring will have the condition. Their Punnett square would be the same as that shown in Figure 6.8, and we can see that the probability of having a child with the recessive condition is $\frac{1}{4}$. Again, we use the law of multiplication and see that the probability of this couple having a child with the condition is $\frac{2}{3} \times \frac{1}{4} = \frac{1}{6}$.

If these two second-generation parents had a child with the recessive condition, what would the probability of their next child having the condition be? It would no longer be $\frac{1}{6}$; once they have *had* a child with the condition, we would know with 100 percent certainty that they are heterozygous carriers. Thus, the probability that their next child will have the condition is $\frac{1}{4}$, as shown in Figure 6.8.

	D	d
D	DD	Dd
d	Dd	dd

Figure 6.8
A Punnett square.

❗ COMMON DISORDERS

There are many simple recessive disorders in which a person must be homozygous recessive for the gene in question to have the disease. Some of the most common examples are Tay-Sachs disease, cystic fibrosis, sickle cell anemia, phenylketonuria, and albinism. These diseases are commonly used as examples on the AP Biology exam and could also aid you in constructing a well-supported essay answer to a question about heredity and inherited disorders.

Tay-Sachs disease is a fatal genetic disorder that renders the body unable to break down a particular type of lipid that accumulates in the brain and eventually causes blindness and brain damage. Individuals with this disease typically do not survive more than a few years. Carriers of this disease do not show any of the effects of the disease, and thus the allele is preserved in the population because carriers usually live to reproduce and potentially pass on the recessive copy of the allele. This disease is found in a higher than normal percentage of people of eastern European Jewish descent.

Cystic fibrosis (CF), a recessive disorder, is the most common fatal genetic disease in this country. The gene for this disease is located on chromosome 7. The normal allele for this gene is involved in cellular chloride ion transport. A defective version of this gene results in the excessive secretion of a thick mucus, which accumulates in the lungs and digestive tract. Left untreated, children with CF die at a very young age. Statistically, 1 in 25 Caucasians is a carrier for this disease.

Sickle cell anemia is a common recessive disease that occurs as a result of an improper amino acid substitution during translation of an important red blood cell protein called *hemoglobin*. It results in the formation of a hemoglobin protein that is less efficient at carrying oxygen. It also causes hemoglobin to deform to a sickle shape when the oxygen content of the blood is low, causing pain, muscle weakness, and fatigue.

Sickle cell anemia is the most common inherited disease among African-Americans. It affects 1 out of every 400 African-Americans, and 1 out of 10 African-Americans are carriers of the disease. The recessive trait is so prevalent because carriers (who are said to have sickle cell "trait") have increased resistance to malaria. In tropical regions, where malaria occurs, the sickle trait actually increases an individual's probability of survival, and thus the trait's presence in the population increases (heterozygote advantage).

Phenylketonuria (PKU) is another autosomal recessive disease caused by a single gene defect. Children with PKU are unable to successfully digest phenylalanine (an amino acid). This leads to the accumulation of a by-product in the blood that can cause mental retardation. If the disease is caught early, retardation can be prevented by avoiding phenylalanine in the diet.

Dominant disorders are less common in humans. One example of a dominant disorder is **Huntington's disease,** a fatal disease that causes the breakdown of the nervous system. It does not show itself until a person is in their 30s or 40s and individuals afflicted with this condition have a 50 percent chance of passing it to their offspring.

Why are lethal dominant alleles less common than lethal recessive alleles? Think about how recessive alleles often are passed on from generation to generation. An individual can be a carrier of a recessive condition and pass it along without even knowing it. On the other hand, it is impossible to be an unaffected carrier of a dominant condition, and many lethal conditions have unfortunately killed the individual before reproductive maturity has been achieved. This makes it more difficult for the dominant gene to be passed along. To remain prevalent in the population, a dominant disorder must not kill the individual until reproduction has occurred.

CHROMOSOMAL COMPLICATIONS

We have spent a lot of time discussing how genes are inherited and passed from generation to generation. It is also important to discuss the situations in which something goes wrong with the chromosomes themselves that affects the inheritance of genes by the off-spring. **Nondisjunction** is an error in homologous chromosome separation. It can occur during meiosis I or II. The result is that one gamete receives too many of one kind of chromosome, and another gamete receives none of a particular chromosome. The fusing of an abnormal gamete with a normal one can lead to the production of offspring with an abnormal number of chromosomes (**aneuploidy**).

Down's syndrome is a classic aneuploid example, affecting 1 out of every 700 children born in this country. It most often involves a trisomy of chromosome 21, and leads to mental retardation, heart defects, short stature, and characteristic facial features. Most with trisomy 21 are sterile.

Trisomy 21 is not the only form of nondisjunction caused by error in the chromosome separation process. Trisomy 13, also known as the **Patau syndrome,** causes serious brain and circulatory defects. Trisomy 18, also known as the **Edwards syndrome,** can affect all organs. It is rare for a baby to survive for more than a year with either of these two conditions. There are also syndromes involving aneuploidy of the sex chromosomes. Males can receive an extra Y chromosome (XYY). Although this nondisjunction does not seem to produce a major syndrome, XYY males tend to be taller than average, and some geneticists believe they display a higher degree of aggressive behavior. A male can receive an extra X chromosome, as in the **Klinefelter syndrome** (XXY). These infertile individuals have male sex organs but show several feminine body characteristics. Nondisjunction occurs in females as well. Females who are XXX have no real syndrome. Females who are missing an X chromosome (XO) have a condition called **Turner's syndrome.** XO individuals are sterile females that possess sex organs that fail to mature at puberty.

Trisomies are not the only kind of chromosomal abnormalities that lead to inherited diseases. A **deletion** occurs when a piece of the chromosome is lost in the developmental process. Deletions, such as **cri-du-chat syndrome,** can lead to problems. This syndrome occurs with a deletion in chromosome 5 that leads to mental retardation, abnormal facial features and a small head. Most die very young.

Chromosomal translocations, in which a piece of one chromosome is attached to another, nonhomologous chromosome, can cause major problems. **Chronic myelogenous leukemia** is a cancer affecting white blood cell precursor cells. In this disease, a portion of chromosome 22 has been swapped with a piece of chromosome 9.

A **chromosome inversion** occurs when a portion of a chromosome separates and reattaches in the opposite direction. This can have no effect at all, or it can render a gene nonfunctional if it occurs in the middle of a sequence. A **chromosome duplication** results in the repetition of a genetic segment. A chromosome **duplication** results in the repetition of a segment . . . whoops . . . sorry. . . . Duplications often have serious effects on an organism.

These are the major concepts of heredity with which the AP Biology exam writers would like you to be familiar. Try the practice problems that follow and be sure that you are able to construct, read, and analyze both Punnett squares and pedigrees, keeping in mind the laws of probability.

REVIEW QUESTIONS

1. The following crossover frequencies were noted via experimentation for a set of five genes on a single chromosome:

   A and B → 35%
   B and C → 15%

   A and C → 20%
   A and D → 10%
   D and B → 25%
   A and E → 5%
   B and E → 40%

Pick the answer that most likely represents the relative positions of the five genes.

A. |------|------------|------------|------------------|
     e   a   d   c   b

B. |------|------------|------------|------------------|
     a   e   c   d   b

C. |------|------------|------------|------------------|
     e   a   c   d   b

D. |------------|------------|------|------|
     b   c   d   e   a

E. |------|------|------------|------------------|
     a   e   d   c   b

2. Imagine that in squirrels gray color (G) is dominant over black color (g). A black squirrel has the genotype gg. Crossing a gray squirrel with which of the following would let you know with the most certainty the genotype of the gray squirrel?

   A. GG
   B. Gg
   C. gg
   D. Cannot be determined from the information given

3. From a cross of AABbCC with AaBbCc, what is the probability that the offspring will display a genotype of AaBbCc?

   A. ½
   B. ⅓
   C. ¼
   D. ⅛
   E. ¹⁄₁₆

Use the following pedigree of an autosomal recessive condition for questions 4–6.

4. What is the genotype of person A?

   A. Bb
   B. BB
   C. bb
   D. Cannot be determined from the given information.

5. What is the most likely genotype of person B?

   A. Bb
   B. BB
   C. bb
   D. Cannot be determined from the information given.

6. What is the probability that persons C and D would have a child with the condition?

   A. ½
   B. ¼
   C. ⅙
   D. ⅛
   E. ¹⁄₁₀

7. Which of the following disorders is X-linked?

   A. Tay-Sachs disease
   B. Cystic fibrosis
   C. Hemophilia
   D. Albinism
   E. Huntington's disease

8. A court case is trying to determine the father of a particular baby. The mother has type O blood, and the baby has type B blood. Which of the following blood types would mean that the man was definitely *not* the father of the baby?

   A. B and A
   B. AB and A
   C. O and B
   D. O and A
   E. None can prove conclusively

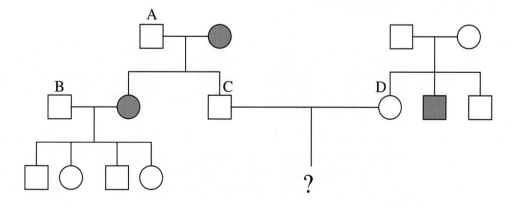

9. Assume that gray squirrel color results from a dominant allele G. The father squirrel is black, the mother squirrel is gray, and their first baby is black. What is the probability that their second baby is also black?

A. 1.00
B. 0.75
C. 0.50
D. 0.25
E. 0.00

10. Imagine that tulips are either yellow or white. You start growing tulips and find out that if you want to get yellow tulips, then at least one of the parents must be yellow. Which color is dominant?

A. White
B. Yellow
C. Neither; it is some form of intermediate inheritance
D. Cannot be determined from the given information

11. Suppose that 200 red snapdragons were mated with 200 white snapdragons and they produced only pink snapdragons. The mating of two pink snapdragons would most likely result in offspring that are

A. 50 percent pink, 25 percent red, 25 percent white
B. 100 percent pink
C. 25 percent pink, 50 percent red, 25 percent white
D. 75 percent red, 25 percent white
E. 100 percent red

12. Which of the following represents the number of possible gametes produced from a genotype of RrBBCcDDEe?

A. 2
B. 4
C. 8
D. 16
E. 32

13. Which of the following diseases is *not* caused by trisomy nondisjunction?

A. Down's syndrome
B. Klinefelter's syndrome
C. Turner's syndrome
D. Patau's syndrome
E. Edward syndrome

14. The pedigree below is most likely a pedigree of a condition of which type of inheritance?

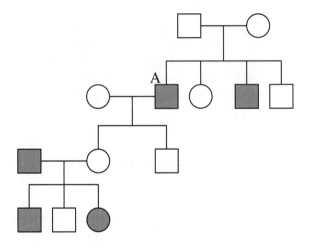

A. Autosomal dominant
B. Autosomal recessive
C. Sex-linked dominant
D. Sex-linked recessive
E. A gene present only on the Y chromosome (holandric)

ANSWERS AND EXPLANATIONS

1. **A**—The crossover frequencies are an indication of the distance between the different genes on a chromosome. The farther apart they are, the greater chance there is that they will cross over during prophase I of meiosis. You are first told that A and B cross over with a frequency of 35 percent, so imagine that they are 35 units apart on a chromosome map.

<u>A   (35)   B</u>   <u>B   (15)   C</u>   <u>A   (20)   C</u>

I then tell you that B and C have a frequency of 15 percent. They are 15 units apart on the map, but you cannot yet be sure what side of gene A that C is on. Gene A and C cross with 20 percent frequency. This means that gene C must be in between A and B.

$$\underline{A \quad (20) \quad C \quad (15) \quad B} \qquad \underline{A \quad (10) \quad D} \qquad \underline{D \quad (25) \quad B}$$

Gene A crosses over with D 10 percent of the time and D crosses with B 25 percent of the time; therefore, D must also be in between A and B. It is closer to A than it is to B. You can use this knowledge to eliminate answer choices B and C.

$$\underline{A \quad (10) \quad D \quad (10) \quad C \quad (15) \quad B}$$

Gene A crosses over with E with a frequency of 5 percent. You do not know which side of A gene E is on until you know its crossover frequency with B. Since the question tells you that it has a 40 percent frequency with B, you know that it must be on the *left* of A. This completes your map, leaving A as the correct answer.

2. **C**—This is a test cross. To determine the genotype of an individual showing the dominant phenotype, you cross that individual with a homozygous recessive individual for the same trait. If they have no offspring with the recessive phenotype, then the individual displaying the dominant phenotype is most likely FF. If approximately one-half of the offspring have the recessive phenotype, you know the individual has the genotype Ff.

3. **D**—The Punnett square shown below shows all the possible gamete combinations from this cross. Two-sixteenths or one-eighth of the possible gametes will be AaBbCc. A quick way to determine the number of possible gametes that an individual can produce given a certain genotype is to use the formula 2^n. For example, an individual who is AABbCc can have $2^2 = 4$ possible gametes because Bb and Cc are heterozygous.

	ABC	**AbC**	**ABc**	**Abc**	**aBC**	**abC**	**aBc**	**abc**
ABC	AABBCC	AABbCC	AABBCc	AABbCc	AaBBCC	AaBbCC	AaBBCc	AaBbCc
AbC	AABbCC	AAbbCC	AABbCc	AAbbCc	AaBbCC	AabbCC	AaBbCc	AabbCc

4. **A**—Person A must have genotype Bb because he has some children that have the recessive condition and some that do not. Since his wife is pure recessive, she can contribute only a b. The father must therefore be the one who contributes the B to the child who does not have the condition, and the second b to the one with the condition.

5. **B**—Person B most likely has a genotype of BB. Because he does not have the condition, we know that his genotype is either BB or Bb. If it were Bb, then when crossed with his wife who has a genotype of bb, 50 percent of his children would be expected to have the recessive condition. None of the children have the condition, which leads you to believe that he is most likely BB. (This test is, of course, not 100 percent accurate. Answer choice B is not certain, but is the most probable conclusion.)

6. **C**—We know that neither parent in question has the recessive condition. We therefore need to calculate the probability that each of them is Bb. The probability that person C is Bb is 1. Because his mother has the condition, she *must* pass a b to him during gamete formation. So the only possible genotypes he can have are Bb and bb. Since he does not have the condition, he must be Bb with a probability of 1. The probability that person D is Bb is 0.67. Neither of her parents has the condition, but she has a brother who is bb. This means that each of her parents *must* be a carrier for the condition (Bb). You know that this woman is not rr, because she does not have the condition. As a result, there are only *three* possible genotypes from the cross remaining. Two of these three are Bb, giving her a probability of ⅔, or 0.67, of being Bb. The probability that *both* person C and person D are Bb is (1) × (0.67) = (0.67). Now it is necessary to calculate the probability that two Bb parents will produce a kid who is bb. The Punnett square says that there is a 0.25 chance of this result. To

calculate the probability that they will have a child with the recessive condition, you multiply the probability that they are both Bb (0.67) times the probability that two individuals Bb will produce a bb child (0.25). Thus, the probability of an affected child being produced from these two parents is ⅙.

7. **C**—Hemophilia is an X-linked condition. An XY male with hemophilia gets his Y chromosome from his father, and his X chromosome from his mother. All that is needed for the hemophilia condition to occur is a copy of the defective recessive allele from his mother.

8. **D**—Types O and A would prove that he was not the father of this particular child. If the mother has type O blood, this means that her genotype is ii and she *must* pass along an i allele to her child. The baby has type B blood, and her genotype could be I^Bi or I^BI^B. Since the mother must give an i, then the baby's genotype must be I^Bi. It follows that the father must provide the I^B allele to the baby to complete the known genotype. If he is type O, he won't have an I^B to pass along since his genotype would be ii. This would also be the case if he were type A, because his genotype would be either I^AI^A or I^Ai. Therefore, those two blood types would prove that he is *not* the father of this child.

9. **C**—To figure out this problem, you need to know the genotype of the mother. The father is black, meaning that his genotype is gg. The two of them produced a squirrel that is also black, which means that the gray mother gave a g to the baby. The mother's genotype is Gg. A cross of Gg × gg produces a phenotype ratio of 1:1 gray:black. They have a 0.5 chance of producing another black baby.

10. **B**—According to this scenario, yellow and white are the only colors possible. If white were dominant, and both parents were Ww, you *could* produce a yellow offspring if the two recessive w's combined. If it were intermediate inheritance, you probably would not produce a straight yellow tulip in the offspring because they would either meet halfway (incomplete dominance), or both express fully (codominance). If yellow were dominant, then you could produce a yellow offspring only if there were a Y allele in one of the parents. A cross of yy × yy would produce only white tulips if white were recessive.

11. **A**—This problem involves incomplete dominance. The genotype of the pink offspring from the first generation is RW. When the two RW snapdragons are mated together, they produce the following results:

	R	**W**
R	RR	RW
W	RW	WW

The offspring will be 25 percent red (RR), 50 percent pink (RW), and 25 percent white (WW).

12. **C**—In a problem like this, you will save time by thinking about the laws of probability. The genotype is RrBBCcDDEe. How many possible combinations of the R-gene are there? There are two: R and r. How many for B? Only one: B. Following the same logic, C has two, D has one, and E has two as well. Now you multiply the possibilities: $(2 \times 1 \times 2 \times 1 \times 2) = 8$. There are 8 possible gametes from this genotype. Another way to arrive at this answer is by use of the expression 2^n, where *n* is the number of hybrid traits being examined. In this case it would be 2^3 or 8 possible gametes.

13. **C**—Down's syndrome is most often due to a trisomy of chromosome 21. Klinefelter's syndrome is a trisomy of the sex-chromosomes (XXY). Patau's syndrome is a trisomy of chromosome 15. Edward syndrome is a trisomy of chromosome 18. Turner's syndrome, the only nontrisomy listed in this problem, is a *monosomy* of the sex chromosomes (XO).

14. **D**—This is most likely a sex-linked recessive disease. The father in the first generation does not have the condition, so his genotype would be $X^N Y$. The original couple has four children, two boys with the condition, and one girl and one boy without the condition. The genotype of the boys with the condition would be $X^n Y$. This means that the original mother's genotype would be $X^N X^n$—Thus she is a carrier. One of the children who inherited the condition has children with a woman from a different family and neither of their two children display the condition. However, the daughter of son A has three children with a man who is $X^n Y$, and she has a daughter and a son who show the recessive condition and one normal son. This means that the daughter of son A is most likely $X^N X^n$—another carrier of the condition. This disease is a condition that is, according to the pedigree, more often seen in men, and passed along to men by the X chromosome from the mother. However, it is important to note that if a father who has the X-linked condition has a child with a female carrier for the condition, that couple can indeed produce a female with the condition.

RAPID REVIEW

You should be familiar with the following terms:

Character: heritable feature, such as flower color.

Monohybrid cross: cross involving one character (Bb × Bb) → (3 : 1 phenotype ratio).

Dihybrid cross: cross involving two different characters (BbRr × BbRr) → (9 : 3 : 3 : 1 phenotype ratio).

Law of segregation: the two alleles for a trait separate during the formation of gametes— one to each gamete.

Law of independent assortment: inheritance of one trait does not interfere with the inheritance of another trait.

Law of dominance: if two opposite pure-breeding varieties (BB × bb) are crossed, all offspring resemble BB parent.

Intermediate inheritance: heterozygous (Yy) individual shows characteristics unlike *either* parent.

- *Incomplete dominance:* Yy produces an intermediate phenotype between YY and yy (snapdragons).

- *Codominance:* both alleles express themselves fully in a Yy individual—(MN blood groups).

Polygenic traits: traits that are affected by more than one gene (eye color, skin color).

Multiple alleles: traits that correspond to more than two alleles (ABO blood type: I^A, I^B, i).

Epistasis: a gene at one locus alters the phenotypic expression of a gene at another locus (coat color in mice).

Pleiotropy: a single gene has multiple effects on an organism (sickle cell anemia).

Sex determination: males are XY, females are XX.

Autosomal chromosome: not involved in gender.

Fruitflies: wild-type traits are the normal phenotype; mutant traits are those that are different from normal.

Sex-linked traits: passed along the X chromosome; more common in males than females (males have only one X) [e.g., hemophilia (can't clot blood), Duchenne's muscular dystrophy (muscle weakness), colorblindness].

X inactivation: one of two X chromosomes is randomly inactivated and remains coiled as a **Barr body.**

Holandric trait: one that is inherited via the Y chromosome.

Linked genes: genes that lie along the same chromosome and do not follow the law of independent assortment.

- *Crossover:* a form of genetic recombination that occurs during prophase I of meiosis.

- The further apart two genes are along a chromosome, the more often they will cross over.

Linkage map: genetic map put together using crossover frequencies.

- Can determine the relative location of a set of genes according to how often they cross over.

- If two genes cross over in 20 percent of the crosses, they are 20 map units apart, etc.

Law of multiplication: To determine the probability that two random events will occur in succession, multiply the probability of the first event by the probability of the second event. (Useful in pedigree analysis!)

Pedigree: family tree used to describe genetic relationships (use pedigree diagram in review question 14 for clearer understanding). To calculate the risk a couple faces of having a child that has a recessive (bb) condition, first determine the probability that *both* parents are Bb (if neither have the condition), or the probability that one is Bb (if one *has* the condition). Once determined, multiply this probability times the probability that a Bb × Bb cross will produce a bb ($\frac{1}{4}$) or that a bb × Bb will produce a bb ($\frac{1}{2}$).

Autosomal Recessive Disorders

Tay Sachs: fatal, storage disease, lipid builds up in brain, mental retardation, increased incidence in eastern European Jews.

Cystic fibrosis: increased mucus buildup in lungs; untreated children die at young age; 1 in 25 Caucasians are carriers.

Sickle cell anemia: caused by error of single amino acid; hemoglobin is less able to carry O_2, and sickles when O_2 content of blood is low; 1 in 10 African Americans is a carrier. Heterozygous condition protects against malaria.

Phenylketonuria: inability to digest phenylalanine, which can cause mental retardation if not avoided in diet.

Autosomal dominant disorders: Huntington's disease (nervous system disease) and achondroplasia (dwarfism)

Nondisjunction: error in which homologous chromosomes do not separate properly

- *Monosomy:* (one copy): Turner's syndrome.

- *Trisomy:* (three copies): Down's syndrome (21), Patau's syndrome (13), Edward's syndrome (18).

Klinefelter syndrome: XXY; *XYY males, XXX females.*

Chromosome disorders: deletion (cri-du-chat), inversions, duplications, and translocations (leukemia).

Chapter 7

Molecular Genetics

INTRODUCTION

Genetics has implications for all of biology. We begin our study of this subject with an introduction to DNA and RNA, followed by a description of the various processes in cells that take DNA from gene to protein: replication, transcription, posttranscriptional modification, translation, and the regulation of all these processes. The genetics of viruses and bacteria follows, and the chapter concludes with a discussion of genetic engineering.

DNA STRUCTURE AND FUNCTION

Deoxyribonucleic acid, known to her peers as DNA, is composed of four **nitrogenous bases:** adenine, guanine, cytosine, and thymine. Adenine and guanine are a type of nitrogenous base called a **purine,** and contain a double-ring structure. Thymine and cytosine are a type of nitrogenous base called a **pyrimidine,** and contain a single-ring structure. Two scientists, James D. Watson and Francis H. C. Crick, spent a good amount of time devoted to determining the structure of DNA. Their efforts paid off, as they were the ones given credit for realizing that DNA was arranged in what they termed a **double helix** composed of two strands of nucleotides held together by hydrogen bonds. They noted that adenine always pairs with thymine (A=T) held together by two hydrogen bonds and that guanine always pairs with cytosine (C≡G) held together by three hydrogen bonds. Each strand of DNA consists of a sugar-phosphate backbone that keeps the nucleotides connected with the strand. The sugar is deoxyribose. (See Figure 7.1 for a rough sketch of what purine-pyrimidine bonds look like.)

One last structural note about DNA that can be confusing is that DNA has something called a 5′ end and a 3′ end (Figure 7.2). The two strands of a DNA molecule run antiparallel to each other; the 5′ end of one molecule is paired with the 3′ end of the other molecule, and vice versa.

RNA STRUCTURE AND FUNCTION

Ribonucleic acid is known to the world as RNA. There are some similarities between DNA and RNA. They both have a sugar-phosphate backbone. They both have four

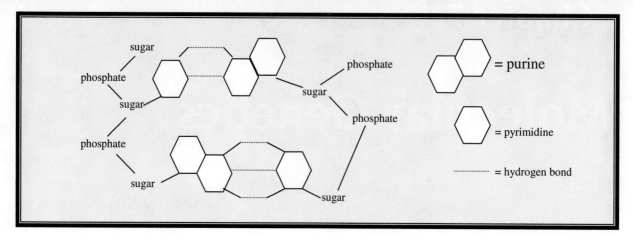

Figure 7.1
Purine-pyrimidine bonds.

different nucleotides that make up the structure of the molecule. They both have three letters in their nickname—don't worry if you don't see that last similarity right away, . . . remember that I have been studying these things for years. These two molecules also have their share of differences. RNA's nitrogenous bases are adenine, guanine, cytosine, and **uracil.** There is no thymine in RNA–uracil beat out thymine for the job (probably had a better interview during the hiring process). Another difference between DNA and RNA is that the sugar for RNA is ribose instead of deoxyribose. While DNA exists as a double strand, RNA has a bit more of an independent personality and tends to roam the cells as a single-stranded entity.

There are three main types of RNA that you should know about, all of which are formed from DNA templates in the nucleus of eukaryotic cells: (1) messenger RNA (mRNA), (2) transfer RNA (tRNA), and (3) ribosomal RNA (rRNA).

REPLICATION OF DNA

Human cells do not have copy machines to do the dirty work for them. Instead, they use a system called **DNA replication** to copy DNA molecules from cell to cell. As we

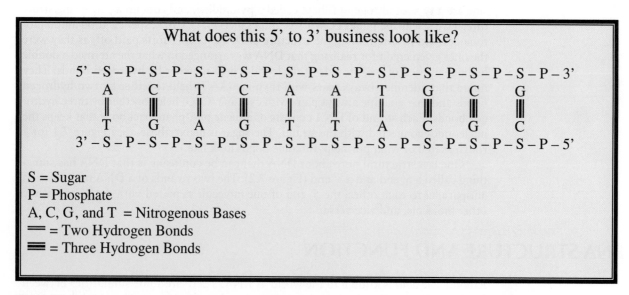

Figure 7.2
The 5' and 3' ends in DNA structure.

discussed in Chapter 5, this process occurs during the S phase of the cell cycle to ensure that every cell produced during mitosis or meiosis receives the proper amount of DNA.

The mechanism for DNA replication was the source of much debate in the mid-1900s. Some argued that it occurred in what was called a "conservative" (**conservative DNA replication**) fashion. In this model, the original double helix of DNA does not change at all; it is as if the DNA is placed on a copy machine and an exact duplicate is made. DNA from the parent appears in only one of the two daughter cells. A different model called the **semiconservative DNA replication** model agrees that the original DNA molecule serves as the template, but proposes that before it is copied, the DNA unzips, with each single strand serving as a template for the creation of a new double strand. One strand of DNA from the parent goes to one daughter cell, the second parent strand to the second daughter cell. A third model, the **dispersive DNA replication model**, suggested that every daughter strand contains *some* parental DNA, but it is dispersed among pieces of DNA not of parental origin. Figure 7.3 is a simplistic sketch showing these three main theories. Watson and Crick would not be pleased to see that I did not draw the DNA as a double helix . . . but as long as you realize this is not how the DNA truly looks, the figure serves its purpose.

An experiment performed in the 1950s by Meselson and Stahl helped select a winner in the debate about replication mechanisms. The experimenters grew bacteria in a medium containing ^{15}N (a heavier-than-normal form of nitrogen) to create DNA that was denser than normal. The DNA was denser because the bacteria picked up the ^{15}N and incorporated it into their DNA. The bacteria were then transferred to a medium containing normal ^{14}N nitrogen. The DNA was allowed to replicate and produced DNA that was half ^{15}N and half ^{14}N. When the first generation of offspring replicated to form the second generation of offspring, the new DNA produced was of two types—one type that had half ^{15}N and half ^{14}N, and another type that was completely ^{14}N DNA. This gave a hands-down victory to the semiconservative theory of DNA replication. Let's take a look at the mechanism of semi-conservative DNA replication.

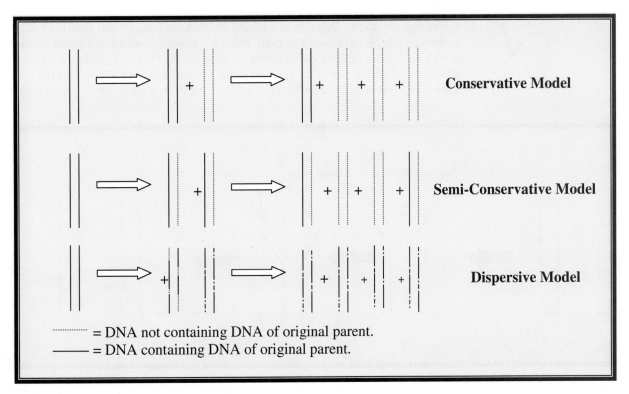

Figure 7.3
Three DNA replication models.

During the S phase of the cell cycle, the double-stranded DNA unzips and prepares to replicate. An enzyme called **helicase** unzips the DNA just like a jacket, breaking the hydrogen bonds between the nucleotides and producing the **replication fork.** Each strand then functions as a template for production of a new double-stranded DNA molecule. Specific regions along each DNA strand serve as **primer sites** that signal where replication should originate. Primase binds to the primer, and **DNA polymerase,** the superstar enzyme of this process, attaches to the primer region and adds nucleotides to the growing DNA chain in a 5′-to-3′ direction. DNA polymerase is restricted in that it can only add nucleotides to the 3′ end of a parent strand. This creates a problem because, as you can see in Figure 7.4, this means that only one of the strands can be produced in a continuous fashion. This continuous strand is known as the **leading strand.** The other strand is affectionately known as the **lagging strand.** You will notice that in the third step of the process in Figure 7.4 the lagging strand consists of tiny pieces called **Okazaki fragments,** which are later connected by an enzyme called DNA ligase to produce the completed double-stranded daughter DNA molecule. This is the semiconservative model of DNA replication.

Unliek my worck, DNA replication is not a perfect process—mistakes are made. A series of proofreading enzymes function to make sure that the DNA is properly replicated each time. During the first runthrough, it is estimated that a nucleotide mismatch is made during replication in one out of every 10,000 basepairs. The proofreaders must do a pretty good job since there is a mismatch error in replication in only one out of every *billion* nucleotides replicated. DNA polymerase proofreads the newly added base right after it is added on to make sure that it is the correct match. Repair is easy—the polymerase simply removes the incorrect nucleotide, and adds the proper one in its place. This process is known as **mismatch repair.** Another repair mechanism is **excision repair,** in which a *section* of DNA containing an error is cut out and the gap is filled in by DNA polymerase. There are other proteins that assist in the repair process, but their identities are not of major importance. Just be aware that DNA repair exists and is a very efficient process.

Here is a short list of mutation types that you should know:

1. *Frameshift mutations.* Deletion or addition of DNA nucleotides that does not add or remove a multiple of three nucleotides. mRNA is produced on a DNA template, and is read in bunches of three called **codons,** which tell the protein synthesis machinery which amino acid to add to the growing protein chain. If the mRNA reads: THE FAT CAT ATE HER HAT, and the F is removed because of an error somewhere, the frame

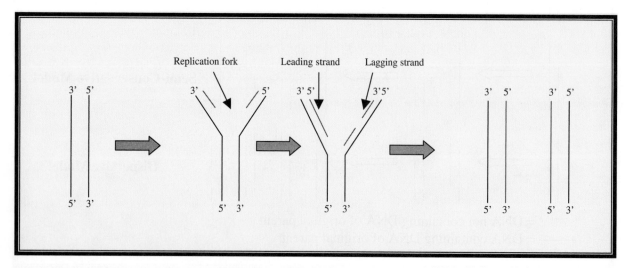

Figure 7.4
Semiconservative DNA replication.

has now *shifted* to read THE ATC ATA THE ERH AT . . . (gibberish). This kind of mutation usually produces a nonfunctional protein unless it occurs late in protein production.

2. *Missense mutation.* Substitution of the wrong nucleotides into the DNA sequence. These substitutions still result in the addition of amino acids to the growing protein chain during translation, but they can sometimes lead to the addition of *incorrect* amino acids to the chain. It could cause no problem at all, or it could cause a big problem as in sickle cell anemia, where a single amino acid error caused by a substitution mutation leads to a disease that wreaks havoc on the body as a whole.

3. *Nonsense mutation.* Substitution of the wrong nucleotides into the DNA sequence. These substitutions lead to premature stoppage of protein synthesis by the early placement of a **stop codon,** which tells the protein synthesis machinery to grind to a halt. The stop codons are UAA, UAG, or UGA. This type of mutation usually leads to a nonfunctional protein.

4. *Thymine dimers.* Result of too much exposure to UV (ultraviolet) light. Thymine nucleotides located adjacent to one another on the DNA strand bind together when this exposure occurs. This can negatively affect replication of DNA and help cause further mutations.

TRANSCRIPTION OF DNA

Teacher: NY
"Know the basic principles. They'll ask you about this process."

Up until this point, we have just been discussing DNA *replication,* which is simply the production of more DNA. In the rest of the chapter, we discuss transcription, translation, and other processes involving DNA. While DNA is the hereditary material responsible for the passage of traits from generation to generation, the DNA does not directly produce the proteins that it encodes. The DNA must first be transcribed into an intermediary: mRNA. This process is called *transcription* (Figure 7.5) because both DNA and RNA are built from nucleotides—they speak a similar language. The DNA acts as a template for the mRNA, which then conveys to the ribosomes the blueprints for producing the protein of interest. Transcription occurs in the nucleus.

Transcription consists of three steps: initiation, elongation, and termination. The process begins when **RNA polymerase** attaches to the promoter region of a DNA strand (initiation). A **promoter region** is simply a recognition site that shows the polymerase where transcription should begin. The promoter region contains a group of nucleotides known as the **TATA box,** which is important to the binding of RNA polymerase. As in DNA replication, the polymerase of transcription needs the assistance of helper proteins to find and attach to the promoter region. These helpers are called **transcription factors.** Once bound, the RNA polymerase works its magic by adding the appropriate RNA nucleotide to the 3′ end of the growing strand (elongation). Like DNA polymerase of replication, RNA polymerase adds nucleotides 5′ to 3′. The growing mRNA strand

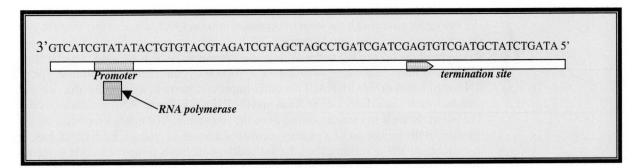

Figure 7.5

separates from the DNA as it grows longer. A region called the **termination site** tells the polymerase when transcription should conclude (termination). After reaching this site, the mRNA is released and set free.

RNA PROCESSING

In bacteria, mRNA is ready to rock immediately after it is released from the DNA. In eukaryotes, this is not the case. The mRNA produced after transcription must be modified before it can leave the nucleus and lead the formation of proteins on the ribosomes. The 5′ and the 3′ ends of the newly produced mRNA molecule are touched up. The 5′ end is given a guanine cap, which serves to protect the RNA and also helps in attachment to the ribosome later on. The 3′ end is given something called a *polyadenine tail*, which may help ease the movement from the nucleus to the cytoplasm. Along with these changes, the **introns** (noncoding regions produced during transcription) are cut out of the mRNA, and the remaining **exons** (coding regions) are glued back together to produce the mRNA that is translated into a protein. This is called **RNA splicing.** I admit that it does seem strange and inefficient that the DNA would contain so many regions that are not used in the production of the gene, but perhaps there is method to the madness. It is hypothesized that introns exist to provide flexibility to the genome. They could allow an organism to make different proteins from the same gene; the only difference is which introns get spliced out from one to the other. It is also possible that this whole splicing process plays a role in allowing the movement of mRNA from the nucleus to the cytoplasm.

TRANSLATION OF RNA

Now that the mRNA has escaped from the nucleus, it is ready to help direct the construction of proteins. This process occurs in the cytoplasm, and the site of protein synthesis is the ribosome. As mentioned in Chapter 1, proteins are made of amino acids. Each protein has a distinct and particular amino acid order. Therefore, there must be some system used by the cell to convert the sequences of nucleotides that make up a mRNA molecule into the sequence of amino acids that make up a particular protein. The cell carries out this conversion from nucleotides to amino acids through the use of the **genetic code.** A mRNA molecule is divided into a series of codons that make up the code. Each **codon** is a triplet of nucleotides that codes for a particular amino acid. There are 20 different amino acids, and there are 64 different combinations of codons. This means that some amino acids are coded for by more than one codon. For example, the codons GCU, GCC, GCA, and GCG all call for the addition of the amino acid alanine during protein creation. Of these 64 possibilities, one is a **start codon**, AUG, which establishes the reading frame for protein formation. Also among these 64 codons are three **stop codons:** UGA, UAA, and UAG. When the protein formation machinery hits these codons, the production of a protein stops.

Before we go through the steps of protein synthesis, I would like to introduce to you the other players involved in the process. We have already spoken about mRNA, but we should meet the host of the entire shindig, the **ribosomes,** which are made up of a large and a small subunit. A huge percentage of a ribosome is built out of the second type of RNA mentioned earlier, rRNA. Two other important parts of a ribosome that we will discuss in more detail later are the **A site** and the **P site,** which are tRNA attachment sites. The job of tRNA is to carry amino acids to the ribosomes. The mRNA molecule that is involved in the formation of a protein consists of a series of codons. Each tRNA has, at its attachment site, a region called the **anticodon,** which is a three-nucleotide sequence that is perfectly complementary to a particular codon. For example, a codon that is AUU has an **anticodon** that reads UAA in the same direction. Each tRNA molecule carries an amino acid that is coded for by the codon that its **anticodon** matches up with. Once the tRNA's amino acid has been incorporated into the growing protein, the tRNA leaves the site to pick up another amino acid just in case its services are needed again at the ribosome. An enzyme known as **aminoacyl tRNA synthetase** makes sure that each tRNA molecule picks up the appropriate amino acid for its anticodon.

Uh-oh . . . there is a potential problem here. There are fewer than fifty different types of tRNA molecules. But there are more codons than that. Oh, dear . . . but wait! This is not a problem, because there are some tRNA that are able to match with more than one codon. How can this be? This works thanks to a phenomenon known as **wobble,** where a uracil in the third position of an anticodon can pair with A or G instead of just A. There are some tRNA molecules that have an altered form of adenine, called inosine (I), in the third position of the anticodon. This nitrogenous base is able to bind with U, C, or A. Wobble allows the 45 tRNA molecules to service all the different types of codons seen in mRNA molecules.

We have met all the important players in the translation process (see also Figure 7.6), which begins when a mRNA attaches to a small ribosomal subunit. The first codon for this process is always AUG. This attracts a tRNA molecule carrying methionine to attach to the AUG codon. When this occurs, the large subunit of the ribosome, containing the A site and the P site, binds to the complex. The elongation of the protein is ready to begin. The P site is the host for the tRNA carrying the growing protein, while the A site is where the tRNA carrying the next amino acid sits. Think of the A site as the on-deck circle of a baseball field, and think of the P site as the batter's box. So, AUG is the first codon bound, and in the P site is the tRNA carrying the methionine. The next codon in the sequence determines which tRNA binds next, and that tRNA molecule sits in the A site of the ribosome. An enzyme helps a peptide bond form between the amino acid on the A site tRNA and the amino acid on the P site tRNA. After this happens, the amino acid from the P site moves to the A site, setting the stage for the tRNA in the P site to leave the ribosome. Now a step called **translocation** occurs. During this step, the ribosome moves along the mRNA in such a way that the A site becomes the P site and the next tRNA comes into the new A site carrying the next amino acid. This process continues until the stop codon is reached, causing the completed protein to leave the ribosome.

GENE EXPRESSION

Let's cover some vocabulary before diving into this section:

Promoter region: a base sequence that signals the start site for gene transcription; this is where RNA polymerase binds to begin the process.

Operator: a short sequence near the promoter that assists in transcription by interacting with regulatory proteins (transcription factors).

Operon: a promoter/operator pair that services multiple genes; the **lac operon** is a well-known example (see also Figure 7.7).

Repressor: Protein that prevents the binding of RNA polymerase to the promoter site.

Enhancer: DNA region, also known as a "regulator," that is located thousands of bases away from the promoter; it influences transcription by interacting with specific transcription factors.

Inducer: a molecule that binds to and inactivates a repressor (e.g., lactose for the lac operon).

*Teacher: CT
"Be able to write
about operons."*

The control of gene expression is vital to the proper and efficient functioning of an organism. In bacteria, operons are a major method of gene expression control. The lactose operon services a series of three genes involved in the process of lactose metabolism. This contains the genes that help the bacteria digest lactose. It makes sense for

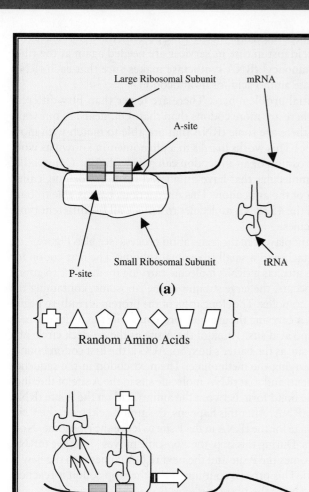

Large Ribosomal Subunit

mRNA

A-site

tRNA

P-site

Small Ribosomal Subunit

(a)

{ Random Amino Acids }

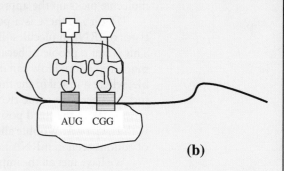

AUG CGG

(b)

♦To start, the P-site lies over the AUG codon of the mRNA and the tRNA carrying the appropriate amino acids binds to the site.

The tRNA carrying the next amino acid arrives at the A-site.

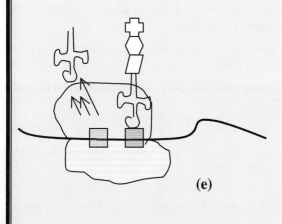

(c)

♦A peptide bond forms between the two amino acids. The amino acid from the P-site hops onto the A-site amino acid freeing the tRNA in the P-site to leave and find another amino acid to carry.

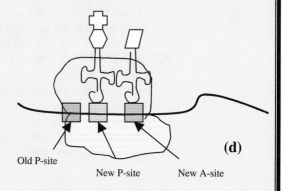

Old P-site

New P-site

New A-site

(d)

Translocation: The ribosome slides along the mRNA in such a way that the A-site becomes the new P-site, and the next tRNA comes into the new A-site carrying the next amino acid.

(e)

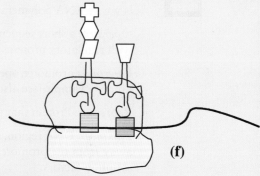

(f)

♦ This process continues until the stop codon is reached and the protein is complete.

Figure 7.6
A pictorial representation of translation.

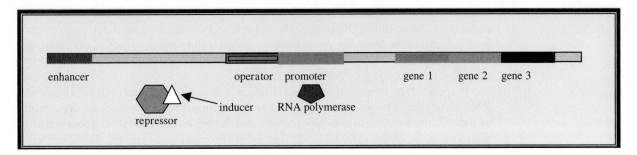

Figure 7.7
General layout of an operon.

bacteria to produce these genes only if lactose is present. Otherwise, why waste the energy on unneeded enzymes? This is where operons come into play—in the absence of lactose, a repressor binds to the promoter region and prevents transcription from occurring. When lactose is present, there is a binding site on the repressor where lactose attaches, causing the repressor to let go of the promoter region. RNA polymerase is then free to bind to that site and initiate transcription of the genes. When the lactose is gone, the repressor again becomes free to bind to the promoter, halting the process.

Because gene expression in eukaryotes involves more steps, there are more places where gene control can occur. Here are a few examples of eukaryotic gene expression control:

Transcription: controlled by the presence or absence of particular transcription factors, which bind to the DNA and affect the rate of transcription.

Translation: controlled by factors that tend to prevent protein synthesis from starting. This can occur if proteins bind to mRNA and prevent the ribosomes from attaching, or if the initiation factors vital to protein synthesis are inactivated.

DNA methylation: The addition of CH_3 groups to the bases of DNA. Methylation renders DNA inactive. **Barr bodies,** discussed in Chapter 6, are highly methylated.

These are only a few of the examples of gene expression control that occur in eukaryotes. Do not get lost in the specifics.

THE GENETICS OF VIRUSES

A **virus** is a parasitic infectious agent that is unable to survive outside of a host organism. Viruses do not contain enzymes for metabolism, and they do not contain ribosomes for protein synthesis. They are completely dependent on their host. Once a virus infects a cell, it takes over the cell's machinery and uses it to produce whatever it needs to survive and reproduce. How a virus acts once it enters a cell depends on what type of virus it is. Classification of viruses is based on many factors:

Genetic material: DNA, RNA, protein, etc.?

Capsid: type of capsid?

Viral envelope: present or absent?

Host range: what type of cells does it affect?

All viruses have a genome (DNA or RNA), and a protein coat (capsid). A **capsid** is a protein shell that surrounds the genetic material. Some viruses are surrounded by a structure called a **viral envelope,** which not only protects the virus but also helps the virus attach to the cells that it prefers to infect. The viral envelope is produced in the endoplasmic reticulum (ER) of the infected cell and contains some elements from the host cell and some from the virus. Each virus has a **host range,** which is the range of cells that the virus is able to infect. For example, the HIV virus infects the T cells of our body and bacteriophages infect only bacteria.

A special type of virus that merits discussion is one called a **retrovirus.** This is an *RNA* virus that carries an enzyme called **reverse transcriptase.** Once in the cytoplasm of the cell, the RNA virus uses this enzyme and "reverse-transcribes" its genetic information from RNA into DNA, which then enters the nucleus of the cell. In the nucleus the newly transcribed DNA incorporates into the host DNA and is transcribed into RNA when the host cell undergoes normal transcription. The mRNA produced from this process gives rise to new retrovirus offspring, which can then leave the cell in a lytic pathway. A well-known example of a retrovirus is the HIV virus of AIDS.

Once inside the cell, a DNA virus can take one of two pathways—a lytic or a lysogenic pathway. In a **lytic cycle** the cell actually produces many viral offspring, which are released from the cell—killing the host cell in the process. In a **lysogenic cycle** the virus falls dormant and incorporates its DNA into the host DNA as an entity called a **provirus.** The viral DNA is quietly reproduced by the cell every time the cell reproduces itself, and this allows the virus to stay alive from generation to generation without killing the host cell. Viruses in the lysogenic cycle can sometimes separate out from the host DNA and enter the lytic cycle. (Like a bear awaking from hibernation.)

Viruses come in many shapes and sizes. Although many viruses are large, **viroids** are plant viruses that are only a few hundred nucleotides in length, showing that size is not the only factor in viral success. Another type of virus you should be familiar with is a **prion**—an incorrectly folded form of a brain cell protein that works its magic by converting other normal host proteins into misshapen proteins. An example of a prion disease that has been getting plenty of press coverage is "mad cow" disease. Prion diseases are degenerative diseases that tend to cause brain dysfunction—dementia, muscular control problems, and loss of balance.

THE GENETICS OF BACTERIA

Bacteria are prokaryotic cells that consist of one double-stranded circular DNA molecule. Present in the cells of many bacteria are extra circles of DNA called **plasmids,** which contain just a few genes and have been useful in genetic engineering. Plasmids replicate independently of the main chromosome. Bacterial cells reproduce in an asexual fashion, undergoing **binary fission.** Quite simply, the cell replicates its DNA, and then physically pinches in half, producing a daughter cell that is identical to the parent cell. From this description of binary fission, it seems unlikely that there could be variation among bacterial cells. This is not the case, thanks to mutation and genetic recombination. As in humans, DNA mutation in bacteria occurs very rarely, but some bacteria replicate so quickly that these mutations can have a pronounced effect on their variability.

Transformation

An experiment performed by Griffith in 1928 provides a fantastic example of **transformation**—the uptake of foreign DNA from the surrounding environment. Transformation occurs through the use of proteins on the surface of cells that snag pieces of DNA from around the cell that are from closely related species. This particular experiment involved a bacteria known as *Streptococcus pneumoniae,* which existed as either a rough strain (R), which is nonvirulent, or as a smooth strain (S), which is virulent. A virulent strain is one that can lead to contraction of an illness. The experimenters exposed mice to different forms of the bacteria. Mice given live S bacteria died. Mice given live R bacteria survived. Mice given heat-killed S bacteria survived. Mice given heat-killed S bacteria combined with live R bacteria died. This was the kicker . . . all the other results to this point were expected. Those exposed to heat-killed S combined with live R bacteria contracted the disease because the live R bacteria underwent transformation. Some of the R bacteria picked up the portion of the heat-killed S bacteria's DNA, which contained the instructions on how to make the vital component necessary for successful disease transmission. These R bacteria became virulent.

Transduction

To understand transduction, you first need to be introduced to something called a **phage** (Figure 7.8)—a virus that infects bacteria. The mechanism by which a phage virus infects a cell reminds me of a syringe. A phage contains within its capsid the DNA that it is attempting to deliver. A phage latches onto the surface of a cell and like a syringe, fires its DNA through the membrane and into the cell. **Transduction** is the movement of genes from one cell to another by phages. The two main forms of transduction you should be familiar with are generalized and specialized transduction.

Generalized Transduction

Imagine that a phage virus infects and takes over a bacterial cell that contains a functional gene for resistance to penicillin. Occasionally during the creation of new phage viruses, pieces of host DNA instead of viral DNA are accidentally put into a phage. When the cell breaks, expelling the newly formed viral particles, the phage containing the host DNA may latch onto another cell, injecting the host DNA from one cell into another bacterial cell. If the phage attaches to a cell that contains a nonfunctional gene for resistance to penicillin, the effects of this transduction process can be observed. After injecting the host DNA containing the functional penicillin resistance gene, crossover could occur between the comparable gene regions, switching the nonfunctional gene with the functional gene. This would create a new cell that is resistant to penicillin.

Specialized Transduction

This type of transduction involves a virus that is in the lysogenic cycle, resting quietly along with the other DNA of the host cell. Occasionally when a lysogenic virus switches cycles and becomes lytic, it may bring with it a piece of the host DNA as it pulls out of the host chromosome. Imagine that the host DNA it brought with it contains a functional gene for resistance to penicillin. This virus, now in the lytic cycle, will produce numerous copies of new viral offspring that contain this resistance gene from the host cell. If the new phage offspring attaches to a cell that is not penicillin-resistant and injects its DNA and crossover occurs, specialized transduction will have occurred.

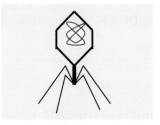

Figure 7.8
A phage.

Conjugation

This is the raciest of the genetic recombinations that we will cover . . . the bacterial version of sex. It is the transfer of DNA between two bacterial cells connected by appendages called **sex pili.** Movement of DNA between two cells occurs across a cytoplasmic connection between the two cells and requires the presence of an **F plasmid,** which contains the genes necessary for the production of a sex pilus.

GENETIC ENGINEERING

DNA technology is advancing at a rapid rate, and you need to have a basic understanding of the most common laboratory techniques for the AP Biology exam.

Restriction enzymes are enzymes that cut DNA at specific nucleotide sequences. When added to a solution containing DNA, the enzymes cut the DNA wherever the enzyme's particular sequence appears. This creates DNA fragments with single-stranded ends called "**sticky-ends,**" which find and reconnect with other DNA fragments containing the same ends (with the assistance of DNA ligase). Sticky ends allow DNA pieces from different sources to be connected, creating **recombinant DNA.** Another concept important to genetic engineering is the **vector,** which moves DNA from one source to another. Plasmids can be removed from bacterial cells and used as vectors by cutting the DNA of interest and the DNA of the plasmid with the same restriction enzyme to create DNA with similar sticky ends. The DNA can be attached to the plasmid, creating a vector that can be used to transport DNA.

✓ Gel Electrophoresis

Steve: 12th grade
"Know this COLD. *It was all over my exam!"*

This technique is used to separate and examine DNA fragments. The DNA is cut with our new friends, the restriction enzymes, and then separated by electrophoresis. The pieces of DNA are separated on the basis of size with the help of an electric charge. DNA is added to the wells at the negative end of the gel. When the electric current is turned on, the migration begins. Smaller pieces travel further along the gel, and larger pieces do not travel as far. The bigger you are, the harder it is to move. This technique can be used to sequence DNA and determine the order in which the nucleotides appear. It can be used in a procedure known as **Southern** (after Edwin M. Southern, a British biologist) **blotting** to determine if a particular sequence of nucleotides is present in a sample of DNA. Electrophoresis is used in forensics to match DNA found at the crime scene with DNA of suspects. This requires the use of pieces of DNA called *restriction fragment length polymorphisms* (RFLPs). DNA is specific to each individual, and when it is mixed with restriction enzymes, different combinations of RFLPs will be obtained from person to person. Electrophoresis separates DNA samples from the suspect, and whatever sample is found at the scene of the crime. The two are compared, and if the RFLPs match, there is a high degree of certainty that the DNA sample came from the suspect. In Figure 7.9, if well A is the DNA from the crime scene, then well C is the DNA of the guilty party.

Cloning

Sometimes it is desirable to obtain large quantities of a gene of interest, such as insulin for the treatment of diabetes. The process of cloning involves many of the steps we just

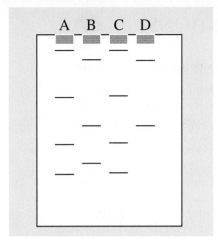

Figure 7.9
A sample gel electrophoresis.

mentioned. Plasmids used for cloning often contain two important genes—one that provides resistance to an antibiotic, and one that gives the bacteria the ability to metabolize some sugar. In this case we will use a galactose hydrolyzing gene and a gene for ampicillin resistance. The plasmid and DNA of interest are both cut with the same restriction enzyme. The restriction site for this enzyme is right in the middle of the galactose gene of the plasmid. When the sticky ends are created, the DNA of interest and the plasmid molecules are mixed and join together. Not every combination made here is what the scientist is looking for. The recombinant plasmids produced are transformed into bacterial cells. This is where the two specific genes for the plasmid come into play. The transformed cells are allowed to reproduce and are placed on a medium containing ampicillin. Cells that have taken in the ampicillin resistance gene will survive, while those that have not will perish. The medium also contains a special sugar that is broken down by the galactose enzyme present in the vector to form a colored product. The cells containing the gene of interest will remain white since the galactose gene has been interrupted and rendered nonfunctional. This allows the experimenter to isolate cells that contain the desired product. Now, it is time for us to quit cloning around and move onto the other genetic engineering techniques.

Polymerase Chain Reaction

Think of this technique as a high-speed copy machine. It is used to produce large quantities of a particular sequence of DNA in a very short amount of time. If the cloning reaction is the 747 of copying DNA, then polymerase chain reaction (PCR) is the Concorde. This process begins with double-stranded DNA containing the gene of interest. DNA polymerase, the superstar enzyme of DNA replication, is added to the mixture along with a huge number of nucleotides and primers specific for the sequence of interest, which help initiate the synthesis of DNA. PCR begins by heating the DNA to split the strands, followed by the cooling of the strands to allow the primers to bind to the sequence of interest. DNA polymerase then steps up to the plate and produces the rest of the DNA molecule by adding the nucleotides to the growing DNA strand. Each cycle concludes having doubled the amount of DNA present at the beginning of the cycle. The cycle is repeated over and over, every few minutes, until a huge amount of DNA has been created. PCR is used in many ways, such as to detect the presence of viruses such as HIV in cells, diagnose genetic disorders, and to amplify trace amounts of DNA found at crime scenes.

REVIEW QUESTIONS

1. Which of the following statements is *incorrect*?

   A. Messenger RNA must be processed before it can leave the nucleus of a eukaryotic cell.
   B. A virus in the lysogenic cycle does not kill its host cell, whereas a virus in the lytic cycle destroys its host cell.
   C. DNA polymerase is restricted in that it can add nucleotides only in a 5′-to-3′ direction.
   D. During translation, the A site holds the tRNA carrying the growing protein, while the P site holds the tRNA carrying the next amino acid.
   E. Viroids are plant viruses that are only a few hundred nucleotides in length.

2. The process of transcription results in the formation of

   A. DNA
   B. Proteins
   C. Lipids
   D. RNA
   E. Carbohydrates

3. Which of the following codons signals the beginning of the translation process?

   A. AGU
   B. UGA
   C. AUG
   D. AGG
   E. UAG

4. Which of the following is an improper pairing of DNA or RNA nucleotides?

   A. Thymine-adenine
   B. Guanine-thymine
   C. Uracil-adenine
   D. Guanine-cytosine
   E. Pyrimidine-purine

5. Which of the following is responsible for the type of diseases that includes "mad cow" disease?

   A. Viroids
   B. Plasmids
   C. Prions
   D. Provirus
   E. Retrovirus

6. Which of the following is the correct sequence of events that must occur in order for translation to begin?

   A. Transfer RNA binds to the small ribosomal subunit, which leads to the attachment of the large ribosomal subunit. This signals to the mRNA molecule that it should now bind, with its first codon in the correct site, to the protein synthesis machinery, and translation begins.
   B. Messenger RNA attaches to the small ribosomal subunit, with its first codon in the correct site, thus attracting a tRNA molecule to attach to the codon. This signals to the large subunit that it should now bind to the protein synthesis machinery, and translation can begin.
   C. Messenger RNA attaches to the large ribosomal subunit with its first codon in the correct site, attracting a tRNA molecule to attach to the codon. This signals to the small subunit that it should now bind to the protein synthesis machinery, and translation can begin.
   D. Transfer RNA binds to the large ribosomal subunit, which leads to the attachment of the small ribsomal subunit. This signals to the mRNA molecule that it should now bind with its first codon in the correct site to the protein synthesis machinery, and translation begins.
   E. Transfer RNA attaches to the large ribosomal subunit, which attracts the mRNA molecule to attach with its first codon in the correct site to the large ribosomal subunit. This signals to the small subunit that it should now bind to the protein synthesis machinery, and translation can begin.

7. All the following are players involved in the control of gene expression *except*

   A. Episomes
   B. Repressors
   C. Operons
   D. Methylation
   E. Hormones

8. Which of the following does *not* occur during RNA processing in the nucleus of eukaryotes?

   A. The removal of introns from the RNA molecule
   B. The addition of a string of adenine nucleotides to the 3′ end of the RNA molecule
   C. The addition of a guanine cap to the 5′ end of the RNA molecule
   D. The ligation of exons of the RNA molecule
   E. The addition of methyl groups to certain nucleotides of the RNA molecules

9. Which of the following statements is *not* true of a tRNA molecule?

   A. The job of transfer RNA is to carry amino acids to the ribosomes.
   B. At the attachment site of each tRNA there is a region called the *anticodon,* which is a three-nucleotide sequence that is perfectly complementary to a particular codon.
   C. Each tRNA molecule has a short lifespan and is used only once during translation.
   D. The enzyme responsible for ensuring that a tRNA molecule is carrying the appropriate amino acid is aminoacyl tRNA synthase.
   E. Transfer RNA is transcribed from DNA templates within the nucleus of eukaryotic cells.

For questions 10 and 11, please use the following gel:

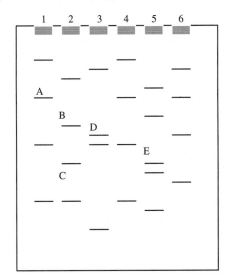

10. Which of the DNA pieces in the gel is smallest in size?

    A. A
    B. B
    C. C
    D. D
    E. E

11. If well 1 is DNA from a crime scene, which individual should contact a lawyer?

    A. Person 2
    B. Person 3
    C. Person 4
    D. Person 5
    E. Person 6

ANSWERS AND EXPLANATIONS

1. **D**—During translation, the **P site** holds the tRNA carrying the growing protein, while the **A site** holds the tRNA carrying the next amino acid. When translation begins, the first codon bound is the AUG codon, and in the P site is the tRNA with the methionine. The next codon in the sequence determines which tRNA binds next, and the appropriate tRNA molecule sits in the A site of the ribosome. A peptide bond forms between the amino acid on the A site tRNA and the amino acid on the P site tRNA. The amino acid from the P site then moves to the A site, allowing the tRNA in the P site to leave the ribosome. Next the ribosome moves along the mRNA in such a way that the A site is now the P site and the next tRNA comes into the A site carrying the next amino acid. Answer choices A, B, C, and E are all true.

2. **D**—The process of transcription leads to the production of RNA. The RNA is not immediately ready to leave the nucleus after it is produced. It must first be processed, during which a 3′ poly-A tail and a 5′ cap are added and the introns are spliced from the RNA molecule. After this process, the RNA is free to leave the nucleus and lead the production of proteins.

3. **C**—AGG codes for the amino acid arginine. AGU codes for the amino acid serine. UGA and UAG are stop codons, which signal the end of the translation process. AUG is the start codon, which also codes for methionine.

4. **B**—Guanine does not pair with thymine in DNA or RNA. Watson and Crick discovered that adenine pairs with thymine (A=T) held together by two hydrogen bonds and guanine pairs with cytosine (C≡G) held together by three hydrogen bonds. One way that RNA differs from DNA is that it contains uracil instead of thymine. But in RNA, guanine still pairs with cytosine and adenine instead pairs with uracil. Watson and Crick also discovered that in order for the structure of DNA they discovered to be true, a purine must always be paired with a pyrimidine. Adenine and guanine are the purines, and thymine and cytosine are the pyrimidines.

5. **C**—Prions are the culprit for mad cow disease. Viroids are tiny viruses that infect plants. *Plasmids* are small circles of DNA in bacteria that are separate from the main chromosome. They are self-replicating and are vital to the process of genetic engineering. A *provirus* is that which is formed during the lysogenic cycle of a virus when it falls dormant and incorporates its DNA into the host DNA. A *retrovirus* is an RNA virus that carries an enzyme called reverse transcriptase. A classic example of a retrovirus is HIV.

6. **B**—Translation begins when the mRNA attaches to the small ribosomal subunit. The first codon for this process is always AUG. This attracts a tRNA molecule carrying methionine to attach to the AUG codon. When this occurs, the large subunit of the ribosome, containing the A site and the P site, binds to the complex. The elongation of the protein is ready to begin after the complex has been properly constructed. Answers A, C, D, and E are all in the incorrect order.

7. **A**—Episomes are not involved in gene expression regulation. **Episomes** are plasmids that can be incorporated into a bacterial chromosome. *Repressors* are regulatory proteins involved in gene regulation. They work by preventing transcription by binding to the promoter region. *Operons* are a promoter-operator pair that controls a group of genes, such as the lac operon. Methylation is involved in gene regulation. Barr bodies, discussed in Chapter 6, are found to contain a very high level of methylated DNA. Methyl groups have been associated with inactive DNA that does not undergo transcription. Hormones can affect transcription by acting directly on the transcription machinery in the nucleus of cells.

8. **E**—The mRNA produced after transcription must be modified before it can leave the nucleus and lead the translation of proteins in the ribosomes. Introns are cut out of the mRNA, and the remaining exons are ligated back together to produce the mRNA ready to be translated into a protein. Also, the 5′ end is given a guanine cap, which serves to protect the RNA and also helps the mRNA attach to the ribosome. The 3′ end is given the poly-A tail, which may help ease the movement from the nucleus to the cytoplasm. Methylation does not occur during posttranscriptional modification—it is a means of gene expression control.

9. **C**—tRNA does not have a short lifespan. Each tRNA molecule is released and recycled to bring more amino acids to the ribosomes to aid in translation. It is like a taxicab constantly picking up new passengers to deliver from place to place. Answer choices A, B, D, and E are all true.

10. **C**—Gel electrophoresis separates DNA fragments on the basis of size—the smaller you are, the farther you go. Because C went the farthest in this gel, this must be the smallest of the five selected DNA pieces. Of the five labeled, piece A must be the largest, since it moved the least.

11. **C**—Person 4 should contact a lawyer. The DNA from the crime scene seems to match the DNA fingerprint from person 4. Electrophoresis is a very useful tool in forensics and can very accurately match DNA found at crime scenes with potential suspects.

RAPID REVIEW

Briefly review the following terms:

DNA: contains A, G (purines), C, T (pyrimidines), arranged in a double helix of two strands held together by hydrogen bonds (A with T, and C with G).

RNA: contains A, G (purines), C, U (pyrimidines), single stranded. There are three types: mRNA (blueprints for proteins), tRNA (bring a. acids to ribosomes), and rRNA (make up ribosomes).

DNA replication: occurs during S phase, semiconservative, built in 5′ to 3′ direction. Helicase unzips the double strand, DNA polymerase comes in and adds on the nucleotides. Proofreading enzymes minimize errors of process.

Frameshift mutation: deletion or addition of nucleotides (not a multiple of 3); shifts reading frame.

Missense mutation: substitution of wrong nucleotide into DNA (e.g., sickle cell anemia); still produces a protein.

Nonsense mutation: substitution of wrong nucleotide into DNA that produces an early stop codon.

Transcription: process by which mRNA is synthesized on a DNA template.

RNA processing: introns (noncoding) are spliced out, exons (coding) glued together: 3′ poly-A tail, 5′ G cap.

Translation: process by which the mRNA specified sequence of amino acids are lined up on a ribosome for protein synthesis.

Codon: triplet of nucleotides that codes for a particular amino acid: **start codon** = AUG; **stop codon** = UGA, UAA, UAG. (For specifics on translation, please flip to text for a good description.)

Promoter: base sequence that signals start site for transcription.

Repressor: protein that prevents the binding of RNA polymerase to promoter site.

Inducer: molecule that binds to and inactivates a repressor.

Operator: short sequence near the promoter that assists in transcription by interacting with transcription factors.

Operon: on/off switch for transcription. Allows for production of genes only when needed. Remember the lac operon—lactose is the inducer, when present, transcription on; when absent, it is off.

Viruses: Parasitic infectious agent unable to survive outside the host; can contain DNA or RNA, or have a viral envelope (protective coat).

- *Lytic cycle:* one in which the virus is actively reproducing and kills the host cell
- *Lysogenic cycle: one in which the virus lies dormant within the DNA of the host cell*

Retrovirus: RNA virus that carries with it reverse transcriptase (HIV).

Prion: virus that converts host brain proteins into misshapen proteins (mad cow disease).

Viroids: tiny plant viruses.

Phage: virus that infects bacteria.

Bacteria: prokaryotic cells; consist of one double-stranded circular DNA molecule; reproduce by binary fission (e.g., **plasmid**—extra circle of DNA present in bacteria that replicate independently of main chromosome).

Genetic Recombination

Transformation: uptake of foreign DNA from the surrounding environment (smooth vs rough pneumococcus).

Transduction: movement of genes from one cell to another by phages, which are incorporated by crossover.

- *Generalized:* lytic cycle accidently places host DNA into a phage, which is brought to another cell
- *Specialized:* virus leaving lysogenic cycle brings host DNA with it into phage

Conjugation: transfer of DNA between two bacterial cells connected by sex pili.

Genetic Engineering

Restriction enzymes: enzymes that cut DNA at particular sequences, creating sticky ends.

Vector: mover of DNA from one source to another (plasmids are good vectors).

Cloning: somewhat slow process by which a desired sequence of DNA is copied numerous times.

Gel electrophoresis: technique used to separate DNA according to size (small = faster). DNA moves from: − to +.

Polymerase chain reaction (PCR): produces large quantities of sequence in short amount of time.

Chapter 8

Evolution

INTRODUCTION

This chapter begins with an introduction to the concept of evolution and the four major modes in which it occurs. From there we focus more closely on natural selection and the work of Lamarck and Darwin. We then briefly touch on adaptations before looking at the various types of selection: directional, stabilizing, disruptive, sexual, and artificial selection. This is followed by a quick look at the sources of variation within populations followed by a look at the two main types of speciation: allopatric and sympatric. Next will come the yucky math portion of the chapter: the Hardy–Weinberg equation, and the conditions necessary for its existence. The chapter concludes with a look at the existing evidence in support of the theory of evolution and a discussion of how life on this planet emerged so many years ago.

DEFINITION OF EVOLUTION

How often have you heard executives report that "the idea evolved into a successful project" or popular science show narrators describe how a star "has been evolving for millions of years"? *Evolution* is no longer strictly a biological term since every academic field and nonacademic industry uses it. Such uses of the verb "evolve" reveal its meaning in its simplest form—to evolve means to change. For the AP Biology exam, however, you should remember the biological definition of evolution: *descent with modification*. Don't let the general uses of the word mislead you; a key part of this definition is *descent,* which can happen only when one group of organisms gives rise to another. When you see the word evolution, think of something that happens in populations, not in individuals.

More specifically, evolution describes change in allele frequencies in populations over time. When one generation of organisms (whether algae or giraffes or ferns) reproduces and creates the next, the frequencies of the alleles for the various genes represented in the population may be different from what they were in the parent generation. Frequencies can change so much that certain alleles are lost or others become fixed—all individuals have the same allele for that character. Over many generations, the species can change so much that it becomes quite different from the ancestral species, or a part of the population can branch off and become a new species (**speciation**). Why do we see this change in allele frequencies with time?

Allele frequencies may change because of random factors or by natural selection. Let's consider chance events first. Imagine a population of fish in a large pond that exhibits two alleles for fin length (short and long) and is isolated from other populations of the same species. One day a tornado kills 50 percent of the fish population. Completely by chance, most of the fish killed possess the long-fin allele and very few of these individuals are left in the population. In the next generation, there are many fewer fish with long fins because fewer long finned fish were left to reproduce; that allele is much more poorly represented in the pond than it was in the original parent generation before the catastrophe. This is an example of **genetic drift**: a change in allele frequencies that is due to chance events. When drift dramatically reduces population size, we call it a **bottleneck**.

Now imagine that the same pond becomes connected to another pond by a small stream. The two populations mix, and by chance, all the long-finned fish migrate to the other pond, and no long-finned fish migrate in. Again, which individuals migrated was random in this example; thus, there will be a change in the allele frequencies in the next generation. This is an example of **gene flow,** or the change in alleles frequencies as genes from one population are incorporated into another.

Gene flow (also more loosely known as *migration* when the individuals are actively relocating) is random with respect to which organisms succeed, but keep in mind that we could think of situations in which migration is not random. For example, if only the short-finned fish could fit in the stream connecting the two ponds, the alleles represented in the subsequent generation would *not* be random with respect to that allele. We also have not stated that the short-finned fish have an advantage by swimming to the other pond—if they did, this would be an example of natural selection, which we'll discuss below.

Finally, let's consider **mutation**, the third random event that can cause changes in allele frequencies. Mutation is *always* random with respect to which genes are affected, although the changes in allele frequencies that occur as a result of the mutation may not be. Let's say that a mutation occurs in the offspring of a fish in our hypothetical pond. The mutation creates a new allele. As a result, the allele frequencies in the offspring generation has changed, simply because we have added a new allele (remember that allele frequencies for a given gene always add up to one). As you can imagine, one mutation on its own does not have the potential to dramatically alter the allele frequencies in a population, unless this is a *really* small pond! But mutation is extremely important because it is the basis of the variation we see in the first place and it is a very strong force when it is paired with natural selection:

!

The four major modes of evolution are

1. Genetic drift
2. Gene flow (also called *migration*)
3. Mutation
4. Natural selection

Remember that the first three factors act randomly with respect to the alleles in the population—which alleles increase and which decrease in frequency is determined by chance events, not because some alleles are inherently better than others are. We'll now turn to the fourth mode or process of evolution, natural selection, where the modification that occurs with descent is *non*random.

NATURAL SELECTION

Probably the biggest mistake people make when thinking about natural selection is thinking that it is synonymous with evolution. **Natural selection** is only one process by which evolution occurs (the others are discussed in the previous section). However, it is an important process because it has been instrumental in shaping the natural world. Because of the theory of natural selection we can explain why organisms look and behave the way they do.

Natural selection is based on three conditions:

1. *Variation:* for natural selection to occur, a population must exhibit phenotypic variance—in other words, differences must exist between individuals, even if they are slight.
2. *Heritability:* parents must be able to pass on the traits that are under natural selection. If a trait cannot be inherited, it cannot be selected for or against.
3. *Differential reproductive success:* this sounds complicated but it's a simple concept. **Reproductive success** measures how many offspring you produce that survive relative to how many the other individuals in your population produce. The condition simply states that there must be variation between parents in how many offspring they produce as a result of the different traits that the parents have.

It is easiest to illustrate natural selection with an example. Let's revisit our pond before the tornado came, where short- and long-finned fish inhabit murky waters. A new predator invades the pond. Fin length determines swimming speed (longer fins allow a fish to swim faster), and only the fastest fish can escape the predator. How would you expect the allele frequencies to change under these conditions? Fish with what length fin would be eaten the most? Because the short-finned fish would be the slowest, they would be featured on the menu. But the long-finned fish, able to escape this new predator, would survive, reproduce, and the frequency of the long-fin allele would increase relative to the short fin allele. We have created a situation in which allele frequencies change as a result of a nonrandom event; the predator's presence results in a predictable decrease in the short-fin allele and a consequent increase in the long-fin allele. Remember that allele frequencies always add up to 100 percent, so the long-finned fish don't have to do particularly well for the long-fin allele to increase—they only have to do well *relative* to the short-finned fish. The actual numbers of fish could decrease for both variants of this fish species.

Why aren't organisms perfectly adapted to their environments? Since natural selection increases the frequencies of advantageous alleles, why don't we get to a point where all individuals have all the best alleles? For one, different alleles confer different advantages in different environments. Furthermore, remember that the environment—which includes everything from habitat, to climate, to competitors, to predators, to food resources—is constantly changing. Species are therefore also constantly changing as the traits that give them an advantage also change. In cases where a trait becomes unconditionally advantageous, we do in fact see fixed alleles; for example, all spiders have eight legs because the alternatives just aren't as good under any circumstances. But where there are heritable characters that both vary and confer fitness advantages (or disadvantages) on their host organisms, natural selection can occur.

LAMARCK AND DARWIN

The two key figures whose research you should know for the evolution section of the AP Biology exam are Jean-Baptiste Lamarck and Charles Darwin. Lamarck proposed the idea that evolution occurs by the inheritance of acquired characters. The classic example is giraffe necks: Lamarck proposed that giraffes evolved long necks because individuals were constantly reaching for the leaves at the tops of trees. A giraffe's neck lengthened during its lifetime, and then that giraffe's offspring had a long neck because of all that straining its parents did. The key here is that change happened within organisms during their lifetimes and then the change in the trait was passed on.

What's wrong with Lamarck's theory? Try explaining to yourself how the changed character could be passed on to the offspring. The answer is that it couldn't—the instructions in the sex chromosomes that direct the production of offspring cannot be changed after they are created at the birth of an organism. Lamarck confused genetic and environmental (postconceptive) change, which is not surprising since no one had discovered genes yet.

Darwin had another idea, one that ended up being entirely consistent with mendelian genetics (although Mendel had already written his thesis during Darwin's time, it is rumored that his book sat on Darwin's shelf, with the pages still uncut, until Darwin's death). Darwin suggested the idea of natural selection described above, and coined the term "survival of the fittest." Although he didn't call them *genes,* he proposed a hypothetical unit of heredity that passed from parent to offspring. Incidentally, a man named Wallace also came up with the idea of natural selection during the same time, but Darwin got the publication out first and has become famous as a result.

ADAPTATIONS

An **adaptation** is a trait that if altered, affects the fitness of the organism. Adaptations are the result of natural selection, and can include not only physical traits such as eyes, fingernails, and livers but also the intangible traits of organisms. For example, lifespan length is an adaptation, albeit a variable one. Mating behavior is also an adaptation—it has been selected by natural selection because it is an effective strategy. An individual with a different form of mating behavior may do better or worse than the average, but a change is likely to have some effect on reproductive success. For example, individuals whose mating strategy is to attempt to court women by running at them, arms flailing while screaming wildly, and salivating heavily, do worse than the average male.

Let's take a look at how such a behavioral adaptation can evolve. Reproductive maturity is a good example. Female chimpanzees become reproductively mature at around the age of 13. Females that mature at age 12 spend less time growing and may therefore be more susceptible to problems with pregnancy. Females that mature at 14 have lost valuable time—their earlier-maturing peers have gained a year on them. You can imagine that from generation to generation, females that matured at age 13 became better represented in the population compared to faster and slower maturers. Although there will always be individuals that differ from the mode, we can view age at reproductive maturation as an adaptation.

! TYPES OF SELECTION

Mike: Freshman in college
"Learn these selection types . . . they make good multiple-choice questions."

Natural selection can change the frequencies of alleles in populations through various processes. The most commonly described are the following three:

1. *Directional selection.* This occurs when members of a population at one end of a spectrum are selected against, while those at the other end are selected for. For example, imagine a population of elephants with various sized trunks. In this particular environment, much more food is available in the very tall trees than in the shorter trees. Elephants with what length trunk will survive and reproduce the most successfully? Those with the longest trunks. Those with shorter trunks will be strongly selected against (and those in the middle will also be in the middle in terms of success). Over time we expect to see an increasing percentage of elephants with long trunks (how quickly this change occurs depends on the strength of selection—if all the short-trunked elephants die, we can imagine that the allele frequencies will change very quickly) (see Figure 8.1).

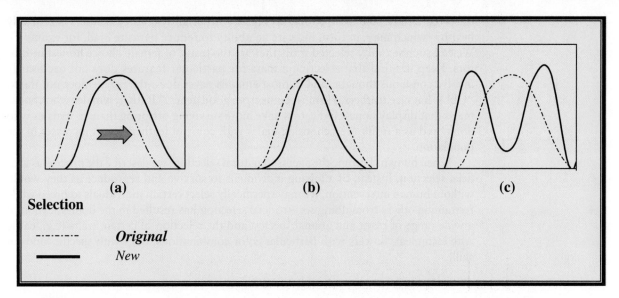

Figure 8.1
Three types of selection: (a) directional; (b) stabilizing; (c) disruptive

2. *Stabilizing selection.* This describes selection for the mean of a population for a given allele. A real example of this is human infant birth weight—it is a disadvantage to be really small *or* really big, and it is best to be somewhere in between. Stabilizing selection has the effect of reducing variation in a population (see Figure 8.1).

3. *Disruptive selection.* Also known as *diversifying selection,* this process can be regarded as being the opposite of stabilizing selection. We say that selection is disruptive when individuals at the two extremes of a spectrum of variation do better than the more common forms in the middle. Snail shell color is an example of disruptive selection. Imagine an environment in which snails with very dark shells and those with very light shells are best able to hide from predators. Those with an in-between shell color are gulped up like escargot at a cocktail party, creating the double-hump curve seen in Figure 8.1.

These three processes describe the way in which allele frequencies can change as a result of the forces of natural selection. It is also important to remember two other types of selection that complement natural selection: sexual selection and artificial selection.

Sexual selection occurs because individuals differ in mating success. In other words, since not all individuals will have the maximum number of possible offspring, there must be some reason why some individuals have greater reproductive success than others. Think about how this is different from natural selection, which includes both reproduction and survival. Sexual selection is purely about access to mating opportunities.

Sexual selection occurs by two primary processes: **within-sex competition** and **choice.** In mammals and many nonmammalian species, females are limited in the number of offspring they can produce in their lifetimes (because of internal gestation), while males are not (because sperm are cheap to produce and few males participate in offspring care). Which sex do you think will compete, and which sex will be choosier? In mammals, males compete and females choose. It makes sense that males have to compete because females are a limiting resource, and it makes sense that females are choosy because they invest a lot in each reproductive effort. This leads to the evolution of characters that are designed for two main functions: (1) as weaponry or other tools for male competition (e.g., large testes for sperm competition) and (2) as traits that increase mating opportunities because females prefer to mate with males who have them (e.g., colorful feathers in many birds).

On what do females base their choices? While you need not become an expert on this matter, it is important to remember that female mate choice for certain characters is not random. One hypothesis for why females choose males with colorful feathers, for example, is that colorful feathers indicate good genes, which is important for a female's offspring. Bright colors are costly, so a male with brightly colored feathers is probably healthy (which may, in turn, indicate an ability to reduce parasite load, for example). We call such sexually selected traits that are the result of female choice **honest indicators.** Keep in mind that selecting a mate for particular features does not necessarily involve conscious thought, and in most animals never does; the female does not think, "Oh! What nice feathers. He must come from good genes." Rather, females who choose males that display honest indicators have more surviving offspring than do females who don't, and as a result the "choosing males with colorful feathers" trait increases in the population.

When humans become the agents of natural selection, we describe the process as **artificial selection.** Instead of allowing individuals to survive and reproduce as they would without human intervention, we may specifically select certain individuals to breed while restraining others from doing so. Artificial selection has resulted in the domestication of a wide range of plant and animal species, and the selection of certain traits (e.g., cattle with lean meat, flowers with particular color combinations, dogs with specific kinds of skill).

EVOLUTION PATTERNS

There are four basic patterns of evolution:

Coevolution. The mutual evolution between two species, which is exemplified by predator–prey relationships. The prey evolves in such a way that those remaining are able to escape predator attack. Eventually some of the predators survive that can overcome this evolutionary adapation in the prey population. This goes back and forth, over and over.

Convergent evolution. Two unrelated species evolve in a way that makes them *more* similar (think of them as converging on a single point). They are both responding in the same way to some environmental challenge, and this brings them closer together. We call two *characters* **convergent characters** if they are similar in two species, even though the species do *not* share a common ancestor. For example, birds and insects both have wings in order to fly, despite the fact that insects are not directly related to birds.

Divergent evolution. Two related species evolve in a way that makes them *less* similar. Divergent evolution can lead to speciation (allopatric or sympatric).

Parallel evolution. Similar evolutionary changes occurring in two species that can be related or unrelated. They are simply responding in a similar manner to a similar environmental condition.

! SOURCES OF VARIATION

Remember that one of the conditions for natural selection is variation. Where does this variation within populations come from?

1. *Mutation.* We already discussed mutations as a mechanism by which evolution occurs. Random changes in the DNA of an individual can introduce new alleles into a population.
2. *Sexual reproduction.* Refer to Chapter 12, Human Reproduction, and the discussion of why offspring are not identical to their parents (cross over, independent assortment of homologous pairs, and the fact that all sperm and ova are unique and thus create a unique individual when joined).

3. *Balanced polymorphism.* Some characters are fixed, meaning that all individuals in a species or population have them: for example, all tulips develop from bulbs. However, other characters are polymorphic, meaning that there are two or more phenotypic variants. For example, tulips come in a variety of colors. If one phenotypic variant leads to increased reproductive success, we expect directional selection to eventually eliminate all other varieties. However, we can find many examples in the natural world where variation is prominent and one allele is not uniformly better than the others. The various ways in which balanced polymorphism is maintained are presented in Figure 8.2.

SPECIATION

A **species** is a group of interbreeding (or potentially interbreeding) organisms. **Speciation,** the process by which new species evolve, can take one of several forms. You should be familiar with the two main forms of speciation:

1. *Allopatric speciation.* Interbreeding ceases because some sort of barrier separates a single population into two (an area with no food, a mountain, etc.). The two populations evolve independently (by any of the four processes discussed earlier), and if they change enough, then even if the barrier is removed, they cannot interbreed.
2. *Sympatric speciation.* Interbreeding ceases even though no physical barrier prevents it. This may take several forms:

   Two other important terms are **polyploidy** and **balanced polymorphism:**

Polyploidy. A condition in which an individual has more than the normal number of sets of chromosomes. Although the individual may be healthy, it cannot reproduce with nonpolyploidic members of its species. This is unusual, but in some plants it has resulted in new species because polyploidic individuals are only able to mate with each other.

Mechanism	Description	Example
Heterozygote advantage	The heterozygous condition has an advantage over either homozygote, so both alleles are maintained (AA is worse off than Aa)	Sickle cell trait, a heterozygous condition, gives people in malarial environments an advantage because they are resistant to this disease
Hybrid vigor and outbreeding	Two unrelated individuals are less likely to have the same recessive, deleterious allele than are relatives; therefore their offspring are less likely to be homozygous for that allele; in addition, outbreeding increases the number of heterozygous alleles, increasing heterozygote advantage	Artificially selected plants are carefully outbred in order to increase hybrid vigor; mating two inbred strains of potato will increase the number of heterozygous loci and increase the species' resistance to disease
Frequency-dependent selection	The least common phenotype is selected for, while common phenotypes have a disadvantage	In some fruitflies, females choose to mate with males that have the rarer phenotype, resulting in selection against the more common variants

Figure 8.2
How balanced polymorphism is maintained.

Balanced polymorphism. This condition (described above) can also lead to speciation if two variants diverge enough to no longer be able to interbreed (if, e.g., potential mates no longer recognize each other as possible partners).

One more term to mention before moving on is **adaptive radiation,** which is a rapid series of speciation events that occur when one or more ancestral species invades a new environment. This process was exemplified by Darwin's finches. If there are many ecological niches (see Chapter 14, Ecology in Further Detail), several species will evolve because each can fill a different niche.

WHEN EVOLUTION IS NOT OCCURRING: HARDY–WEINBERG EQUILIBRIUM

Evolutionary change is constantly happening in humans and other species; this seems sensible since evolution is the change in allele frequencies over time. It makes sense that these frequencies are highly variable and subject to change as the environment changes. However, biologists use a theoretical concept called the **Hardy–Weinberg equilibrium** to describe those special cases where a population is in stasis, or not evolving.

Only if the following conditions are met can a population be in Hardy–Weinberg equilibrium:

Hardy–Weinberg Conditions

1. No mutations
2. No gene flow
3. No genetic drift (and for this, the population must be large)
4. No natural selection (so that the traits are neutral; none give an advantage or disadvantage)
5. Random mating

Notice items 1–4 in this list are the four modes of evolution, which makes sense—if we are trying to establish the conditions under which evolution does *not* occur, we must keep these processes of evolution from occurring! The fifth condition, random mating, is included because if individuals mated nonrandomly (e.g., if individuals mated with others that looked like them), the allele frequencies could change in a certain direction and we would no longer be in equilibrium.

Determining Whether a Population Is in Hardy–Weinberg Equilibrium

Unfortunately for you, there is an equation associated with the Hardy–Weinberg equilibrium that the test writers love to put on the exam. Don't let it scare you!

$$p + q = 1$$

This equation is used to determine if a population is in Hardy–Weinberg equilibrium. The symbol p is the frequency of allele 1 (often the *dominant allele*) and q is the frequency of allele 2 (often the recessive allele). Remember that the frequency of two alleles always adds up to 1 *if the population is in Hardy–Weinberg equilibrium.* For example, if 60 percent of the alleles for a given trait are dominant (p), then $p = 0.6$, and q (the recessive allele) $= 1 - 0.6$, or 0.4 (40 percent).

There is a second equation that goes along with this theory: $p^2 + 2pq + q^2 = 1$, where p^2 and q^2 represent the frequency of the two homozygous conditions (AA and

---

Teacher: CT
"Knowing how to do Hardy-Weinberg problems is worth 2 points to you . . . easy points"

continued

aa). The frequency of the heterozygotes is pq plus qp or $2pq$ (Aa and aA). Since p represents the dominant allele, it makes sense that p^2 represents the homozygous dominant condition. By the same logic, q^2 represents the homozygous recessive condition.

Let's say that you are told that a population of acacia trees is 16 percent short (which is a, recessive) and 84 percent tall (which is A, dominant). What are the frequencies of the two alleles? Remember that it is not 0.16 and 0.84 because there are also the heterozygotes to consider!

In a problem like this, it is important to determine the value of q first because we know that all individuals with the recessive phenotype must be aa (q^2). You cannot begin by calculating the value of p, because it is *not* true that all the individuals with the dominant phenotype can be lumped into p^2. Some folks displaying the dominant phenotype are heterozygous Aa (pq).

We know that $q^2 = 0.16$, so we find q by calculating $\sqrt{0.16} \rightarrow q = 0.400$. Now remember that they do not let you use a calculator. So these problems will give numbers that are fairly easy to work with. Do not despair.

What about p? Since $p + q$ is 1, and we know $q = 0.40$, then p must equal $1 - 0.40$ or 0.600.

You may also be asked to go a step further and give the percentages of the homozygous dominant and heterozygous conditions (remember, we know that the recessive condition is 16 percent—all these individuals must be aa in order to express the recessive trait). This is simple—just plug in what you know about p and q:

$$2pq = (2)(0.6)(0.4) = 0.48 \text{ or } 48\%$$

$$p^2 = (0.6)(0.6) = 0.36 \text{ or } 36\%$$

Now, check your math: do the frequencies add up to 100 percent?

$$16 + 48 + 36 = 100$$

Why do we ever use the Hardy–Weinberg equation if it rarely applies to real populations? This can be an excellent tool to determine whether a population is evolving or not; if we find that the allele frequencies do not add up to one, then we need to look for the reasons for this (perhaps the population is too small and genetic drift is a factor, or perhaps one of the alleles is advantageous and is therefore being selected for and increasing in the population). Therefore, although the Hardy–Weinberg equilibrium is largely theoretical, it does have some important uses in evolutionary biology.

THE EVIDENCE FOR EVOLUTION

Support for the theory of evolution can be found in varied kinds of evidence:

1. *Homologous characters.* Traits are said to be homologous if they are similar because their host organisms arose from a common ancestor (which implies that they have evolved). For example, the bone structure in bird wings is homologous in all bird species.

2. *Embryology.* The study of embryos reveals remarkable similarities between organisms at the earliest stages of life, although as adults (or even at birth) the species look completely different. Human embryos, for example, actually have gills for a short time during early development, hinting at our aquatic ancestry. I kept my gills. I'm a good swimmer. Darwin used embryology as an important piece of evidence for the process of evolution. In 1866, the scientist Ernst Haeckel uttered the phrase, "Ontogeny recapitulates phylogeny." **Ontogeny** is an *individual's* development; **phylogeny** is a **species'** evolutionary history. What Haeckel meant was that during an organism's embryonic development, it will at some point resemble the adult form of all its ancestors before it. For example, human embyros at some point look a lot like fish embryos. The important conclusion from this is that Haeckel and others thought that embryologic similarity between developing individuals could be used to deduce phylogenetic relationships. By the end of the nineteenth century it was clear this law rarely holds. The real development of organisms differs in several important ways from Haeckal's schemes.

3. *Vestigial characters.* Most organisms carry characters that are no longer useful, although they once were. This should remind you of our short discussion about why organisms are not perfectly adapted to their environments (because the environment is constantly changing). Sometimes an environment changes so much that a trait is no longer needed, but is not deleterious enough to actually be selected against and eliminated. Darwin used vestigial characters as evidence in his original formulation of the process of evolution, listing the human appendix as an example.

Keep in mind that the kinds of evidence described above are often found in the **fossil record**–the physical manifestation of species that have gone extinct (including things like bones as well as imprints). The most important thing to remember is that adaptations are the result of natural selection.

MACROEVOLUTION

Biologists distinguish between microevolution and macroevolution. **Microevolution** includes all of what we have been discussing so far in this chapter—evolution at the level of species and populations. Think of **macroevolution** as the big picture, which includes the study of evolution of groups of species over very long periods of time.

There are disagreements in the field as to the typical pattern of macroevolution. Those who believe in **gradualism** assert that evolutionary change is a steady, slow process, while those who think that evolution is best described by the **punctuated equilibria model** believe that change occurs in rapid bursts separated by large periods of stasis (no change) (see comparison in Figure 8.3). Because the fossil record is incomplete,

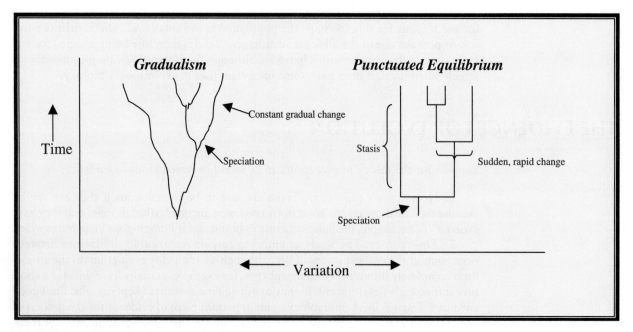

Figure 8.3
Gradualism versus punctuated equilibrium.

it is very hard to test the two theories—if we find no fossils for a species over a contested period, how can we determine whether change was occurring? The debate therefore continues.

HOW LIFE PROBABLY EMERGED

The AP Biology exam often includes questions on how life originated. It is therefore wise to learn the steps of the **heterotroph theory** (see Figure 8.4), so named because it posits that the first organisms were **heterotrophs,** organisms that cannot make their own food:

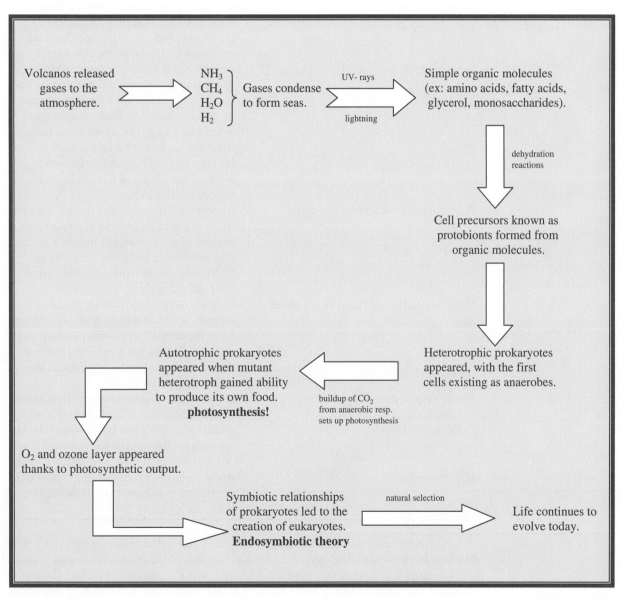

Figure 8.4
Flowchart representation of heterotroph theory.

Step	Description
The earth's atmosphere formed	Emerging from volcanoes, gases such as NH_3, CH_4, $H_2O(g)$, and H_2 (but not oxygen) invaded the atmosphere
The seas formed	The gases condensed to form the seas as the earth cooled
Simple organic molecules appeared	Energy (from UV light, lightning, heat, radioactivity) transformed inorganic molecules to organic ones, including amino acids
Polymers and self-replicating molecules appeared	These may have been formed through dehydration, or the removal of water molecules; e.g., proteinoids can be produced from polypeptides by dehydrating amino acids with heat
Protobionts appeared	These are cell precursors, formed from organic molecules; they are unable to reproduce, but can carry out chemical reactions and have permeable membranes
Heterotrophic prokaryotes appeared	Heterotrophs consume organic substances to survive (an example is pathogenic bacteria); since there was a limited amount of organic material, heterotrophs competed and natural selection occurred—these first cells were anaerobic; thus, the buildup of CO_2 from fermentation allowed for plenty of CO_2 to be available for photosynthesis
Autotrophic prokaryotes appeared	A heterotroph mutated and gained the ability to produce its own food using light energy, making it an autotroph (e.g., photosynthetic bacteria); this was a highly successful strategy compared to the heterotroph's
Oxygen and the ozone layer appeared	As you know, photosynthesis produces oxygen, which interacts with UV light to form the ozone layer—this production of oxygen allowed for aerobic respiration; the ozone layer blocks UV light from reaching the earth's surface
Eukaryotes appeared (specifically mitochondria types and chloroplast types)	**Endosymbiotic theory** proposes that groups of prokaryotes associated in symbiotic relationships to form eukaryotes (the various organelles in cells today invaded a cell and eventually became one organism)
Life evolved	Natural selection produced the variety of organisms that have existed throughout the earth's history

Why is it important that there was no oxygen to start? Alexander Oparin and J. B. S. Haldane hypothesized that oxygen would have prevented the formation of simple molecules because it is too reactive, and would have taken the place of any other element in chemical reactions. Stanley Harold Miller and Urey tested this hypothesis by simulating a primordial environment, and found that in the absence of oxygen they were able to form organic molecules (including amino acids).

REVIEW QUESTIONS

1. Which of the following is an evolutionary process *not* based on random factors?

   A. Genetic drift
   B. Natural selection
   C. Mutation
   D. Gene flow
   E. Bottlenecks

2. Which of the following is not a sexually selected trait?

   A. Fruitfly wings
   B. A male baboon's canine teeth
   C. Peacock tail feathers
   D. Male/female dimorphism in body size in many species
   E. A frog's throat sac

3. An adaptation

   A. Can be shaped by genetic drift
   B. Cannot be altered
   C. Evolves because it specifically improves an individual's mating success
   D. Affects the fitness of an organism if it is altered
   E. Can be deleterious to an organism

4. Which of the following is *not* a requirement for natural selection to occur?

   A. Variation between individuals
   B. Heritability of the trait being selected
   C. Sexual reproduction
   D. Differences in reproductive success among individuals
   E. Survival of the fittest

5. Why can Hardy–Weinberg equilibrium occur only in large populations?

   A. Large populations are likely to have more variable environments.
   B. More individuals means less chance for natural selection to occur.
   C. Genetic drift is a much stronger force in small versus large populations.
   D. Large populations make random mating virtually impossible.
   E. Large populations tend to last longer than small ones.

6. A population of frogs consists of 9 percent with speckles (the recessive condition) and 91 percent without speckles. What are the frequencies of the p and q alleles if this population is in Hardy–Weinberg equilibrium?

   A. $p = 0.49$, $q = 0.51$
   B. $p = 0.60$, $q = 0.40$
   C. $p = 0.70$, $q = 0.30$
   D. $p = 0.49$, $q = 0.30$
   E. $p = 0.49$, $q = 0.09$

7. Frequency-dependent selection is

   A. Particularly important during speciation
   B. One way in which multiple alleles are preserved in a population
   C. Possible only when there are two alleles
   D. Most common in bacteria
   E. The same as heterozygote advantage

8. All the following provide evidence for evolution *except*

   A. Vestigial characters
   B. Darwin's finches
   C. Homologous characters
   D. Embryology
   E. Mutations

9. Why do we assume that oxygen was not present in the original atmosphere?

   A. The presence of O_2 would have resulted in the evolution of too many species too fast.
   B. Oxygen would have slowed down the rate of evolution.
   C. We know the ozone layer, which is formed by oxygen, has not been around that long.
   D. Inorganic molecules could not have formed in the presence of oxygen.
   E. All the oxygen was held in the volcanoes.

10. All these are examples of random evolutionary processes *except*

   A. An earthquake divides a single elk species into two populations, forcing them to no longer interbreed.
   B. A mutation in a flower plant results in a new variety.
   C. An especially long winter causes a group of migrating birds to shift their home range.
   D. A mutation results in a population of trees that spread their seeds more widely than their peers, causing their population to grow.
   E. A spider species declines in an area because individuals are consistently moving out of an old range and into a new range.

ANSWERS AND EXPLANATIONS

1. B—Natural selection is the selective increase in certain alleles because they confer an advantage to their host organism. All other factors are random with respect to the alleles (a "bottleneck" is a type of genetic drift where a population is drastically reduced in size).

2. A—All fruitflies need to fly not only to find mates but also to survive. All the other characters listed are sexually selected, meaning that they have evolved because they confer specific advantages in mating (and not survival).

3. D—Adaptations are defined as traits that affect fitness if they are altered. Although adaptations may have evolved to increase mating success (answer C), they are not always intended for that function (e.g., they may have remained because they increase survival).

4. C—Natural selection can occur in asexually reproducing organisms, as long as the other three necessary conditions are met. "Survival of the fittest" (answer E) is another way of saying that certain organisms have higher reproductive success than others.

5. C—Genetic drift is change in allele frequencies as a result of random factors (e.g., natural disasters or environmental change). In small populations, genetic drift is a much more powerful force because each individual represents a greater percentage of the population's total genes than that person would in a much larger population. Think of it this way—if you have a population of 10 cheetahs, and 3 die, you have lost 30 percent of the genes in that pool. If you have a population of 100 cheetahs, and 3 die, you have lost only 3 percent. Since Hardy–Weinberg equilibrium depends on no genetic drift, it is much more likely to occur in very large populations.

6. C—Remember that p and q must add up to 1 for a population to be in Hardy–Weinberg equilibrium (this eliminates answers d and e). Calculate q first by taking the square root of 0.09, which is 0.30. Then simply subtract 0.30 from 1, to get $p = 0.70$.

7. B—Frequency-dependent selection is one process by which multiple alleles are preserved in a population. For traits that are selected for or against on the basis of frequency, an allele becomes more advantageous when it is rare, and therefore increases. In this way, it is impossible for the allele to become extinct (because as soon as it gets that low, it increases again). When it gets too high, the other allele is low, and that one then increases. Frequency-dependent selection often exhibits itself in this kind of seesaw effect.

8. E—Mutations in themselves are not evidence for evolution, although they are necessary if evolution is going to occur.

9. D—Inorganic molecules could not have formed in the presence of oxygen because oxygen would have taken the place of other elements in every chemical reaction (because it is such a highly reactive element).

10. D—This is the only answer that shows evidence of natural selection, which is the *non*random process by which evolution occurs. The two elk species splitting

(answer A) is an example of allopatric speciation caused by a random factor (a geologic event). A mutation is also a random event (answer B); for example, if I had said that the new variety became the dominant allele in a population because it had an advantage over other variants, then that *would* be natural selection. A home range shift (answer C) is not evolution, but rather a behavioral change within an organism's lifetime. Finally, a spider species declining in an area because individuals are slowing changing territory is an example of gene flow, which we know to be a random process of evolution.

RAPID REVIEW

There are four modes of *evolution*:

1. *Genetic drift*: change in allele frequencies because of chance events (In small populations)
2. *Gene flow*: change in allele frequencies as genes move from one population to another
3. *Mutation*: change in allele frequencies due to a *random genetic change* in an allele
4. *Natural selection*: process by which characters or traits are maintained or eliminated in a population, based on their contribution to the differential survival and reproductive success of their "host" organisms

There are three requirements for *natural selection* to occur:

1. *Variation*: differences must exist between individuals.
2. *Heritability*: the traits to be selected for must be able to be passed along to offspring. Traits that are not inherited, cannot be selected against.
3. *Differential reproductive success*: there must be variation among parents in how many offspring they produce as a result of the different traits that the parents have.

Adaptation is a trait that, if altered, affects the fitness of an organism. Includes physical or intangible traits.

Selection types are as follows:

1. *Directional*: members at one end of a spectrum are selected against and population shifts toward that end.
2. *Stabilizing*: selection for the mean of a population; reduces variation in a population.
3. *Disruptive (diversifying)*: selects for the two *extremes* of a population; selects against the middle.
4. *Sexual*: certain characters are selected for because they aid in mate acquisition.
5. *Artificial*: human intervention in the form of selective breeding (cattle).

Sources of *variation within populations* are

1. *Mutation*: random changes in DNA can introduce new alleles into a population.
2. *Sexual reproduction*: cross over, independent assortment, random gamete combination.
3. *Balanced polymorphism*: the maintenance of two or more phenotypic variants.

Speciation is the process by which new species evolve:

1. *Allopatric speciation*: interbreeding stops because some physical barrier splits the population into two. If two populations evolve separately and change so they cannot interbreed, speciation has occurred.

2. *Sympatric speciation:* interbreeding stops even though no physical barrier prevents it.
   - *Polyploidy:* condition in which individual has higher than normal number of chromosome sets. Polyploidic individuals cannot reproduce with nonpolyploidics . . . a barrier.
   - *Balanced polymorphism:* two phenotypic variants become so different that the two groups stop interbreeding.

Other terms to remember are

Adaptive radiation: rapid series of speciation events that occur when one or more ancestral species invades a new environment.

Hardy–Weinberg equilibrium: $p + q = 1$, $p^2 + 2pq + q^2 = 1$. Evolution is *not* occurring. The *rules* for this are no mutations, no gene flow, no genetic drift, no natural selection, and random mating.

Homologous character: traits similar between organisms that arose from a common ancestor.

Vestigial character: character contained by organism that is no longer functionally useful (appendix).

Gradualism: evolutionary change is a slow and steady process.

Punctuated equilibria: evolutionary change occurs in rapid bursts separated by large periods of no change.

Heterotroph theory: theory that describes how life evolved from original heterotrophs.

Convergent character: traits similar to two or more organisms that do *not* share common ancestor; parallel evolution.

Convergent evolution: two unrelated species evolve in a way that makes them *more* similar.

Divergent evolution: two related species evolve in a way that makes them *less* similar.

Chapter 9

Taxonomy and Classification

INTRODUCTION

Taxonomy is the brainchild of Linnaeus, who came up with a **binomial system of classification** in which each species was given a two-word name. The first word describes the **genus**—the group to which the species belongs. The second word is the name of the particular *species*. For example, *Homo sapiens* is the binomial system name for humans.

Taxonomy is the field of biology that classifies organisms according to the presence or absence of shared characteristics in an effort to discover evolutionary relationships among species. A *taxon* is a category that organisms are placed into and can be any of the levels of the hierarchy. There are seven common categories of classification; listed from broadest to most specific, they are kingdom, phylum, class, order, family, genus, species. A way to remember this sequence is through the use of a silly sentence such as this:

"*Karaoke players can order free grape soda*" or

"*King Phillip came over for good spaghetti.*"

Kingdom–phylum–class–order–family–genus–species.

A **kingdom** consists of organisms that share characteristics such as cell structure, level of cell specialization, and mechanisms to obtain nutrients. Kingdoms are split into *phyla,* which are split into classes, which are further divided into *orders*. Orders are split into *families,* which are made up of the different *genera*. The final and most specific division is the *species*. This is the only naturally occurring taxon. These seven categories apply to many but not *all* organisms. The plant kingdom has **divisions** instead of phyla. Bacterial species tend to be placed into groups called **strains.**

! FIVE OR SIX KINGDOMS?

The current system of classification is a five-kingdom system that divides all the organisms of the planet into one of five kingdoms: Monera, Protista, Plantae, Fungi, and Animalia. Do not be confused and/or alarmed if you hear mention of a six-kingdom system. The difference in the six-kingdom system is that the kingdom Monera is split into Eubacteria and Archaebacteria. Other than that, the kingdom delineations are similar. Let's begin the tour of the various kingdoms with the kingdom Monera.

KINGDOM MONERA

The members of this kingdom are prokaryotes: single-celled organisms that have no nucleus or membrane-bound organelles. Since this chapter is an exercise in painful amounts of classification, and subclassification and further classification, based on the previous classification of classifications, and so on, I thought I would point out a few of the many different ways that the kingdom Monera can be subdivided. The Monera kingdom can be further classified by nutritional class, reactivity with oxygen, and whether they are eubacteria or archaebacteria.

Nutritional Class

Moneran organisms can be classified as either autotrophs or heterotrophs. **Autotrophs** are the producers of the world:

1. *Photoautotrophs:* photosynthetic autotrophs (used to be called blue-green algae) that produce energy from light.
2. *Chemoautotrophs:* produce energy from inorganic substances (e.g., S bacteria).

Heterotrophs are the consumers of the world. Examples of prokaryotic heterotrophs, including parasitic bacteria that feed off hosts, and **saprobes,** such as bacteria of decay, which feed off dead organisms.

Reactivity with Oxygen

A second way to classify moneran organisms is by their ability to react with oxygen: whether they *must* react with oxygen to survive, whether they must be *without* oxygen to survive, or if they can survive with or without oxygen. There are three classes of oxygen reactivity: obligate aerobes and obligate anaerobes at the two extremes of the spectrum, and facultative anaerobes somewhere in between. **Obligate aerobes** require oxygen for respiration—they must have oxygen to grow; **obligate anaerobes** must avoid oxygen like the plague—oxygen is a poison to them; and **facultative anaerobes,** which are happy to use O_2 when available, but can survive without it.

Archaebacteria versus Eubacteria

There are two major branches of prokaryotic evolution: eubacteria and archaebacteria. **Archaebacteria** tend to live in extreme environments and are thought to resemble the first cells of the earth. The major examples you should be familiar with include (1) **extreme halophiles**—these are the "salt lovers" and live in environments with high salt concentrations, (2) **methanogens**—bacteria that produce methane as a by-product, and (3) **thermoacidophiles**—bacteria that love hot, acidic environments.
   Eubacteria are categorized according to their mode of acquiring nutrients, their mechanism of movement, and their shape, among other things. The following is a list of the names of a few groups of bacteria that you should be familiar with for the AP exam:

1. Proteobacteria
2. Gram-positive bacteria
3. Cyanobacteria
4. Spirochetes
5. Chlamydias
6. Chemosynthetic bacteria
7. Nitrogen-fixing bacteria

The three basic shapes of bacteria you might want to be familiar with include

1. *Rod-shaped bacteria:* also known as *bacilli* (e.g., *Bacillus anthracis,* the bug that causes anthrax)
2. *Spiral-shaped bacteria:* also known as *spirilla* (e.g., *Treponema pallidum,* the bug that causes syphilis)
3. *Sphere-shaped bacteria:* also known as *cocci* (e.g., *Streptococcus,* the fine bug that gives us strep throat)

To summarize, the kingdom Monera can be subdivided according to the following characteristics:

Nutrition type?	Autotroph versus heterotroph
Oxygen preference?	Obligate aerobes versus anaerobes versus facultative anaerobes
Evolutionary branch?	Archaebacteria versus Eubacteria

ENDOSYMBIOTIC THEORY

Bill, 11th grade
"Important concept to know."

Endosymbiotic theory states that eukaryotic cells originated from a symbiotic partnership of prokaryotic cells. This theory focuses on the origin of mitochondria and chloroplasts from aerobic heterotrophic and photosynthetic prokaryotes, respectively.

I can see why scientists examining these two organelles would think that they may have originated from prokaryotes. They share many characteristics: (1) they are the same size as eubacteria, (2) they also reproduce in the same way as prokaryotes (binary fission), and (3), if their ribosomes are sliced open and studied, they are found to more closely resemble those of a prokaryote than those of a eukaryote. They are prokaryotic groupies living in a eukaryotic world.

The eukaryotic organism that scientists believe most closely resembles prokaryotes is the **archezoa,** which does not have mitochondria. One phylum grouped with the archezoa is the **diplomonads.** A good example of a diplomonad you should remember is *Giardia*—an infectious agent you would do well to avoid. Giardia is a parasitic organism that takes hold in your intestines and essentially denies your body the ability to absorb any fat. This infection makes for very uncomfortable and unpleasant GI (gastrointestinal) issues and usually results from the ingestion of contaminated water.

KINGDOM PROTISTA

The evolution of protists from prokaryotes gave rise to the characteristics that make eukaryotes different from their prokaryotic predecessors. Protists were around a long time before fungi, plants, or animals graced our planet with their presence. Most protists use aerobic metabolism. Since this is a chapter on classification, it would be silly, if not too kind of me, to not mention how these different protists are organized. They are usually grouped into three major categories:

1. *Plantlike protists:* photosynthetic protists, also called *algae*
2. *Animal-like protists:* heterotrophic protists, also called *protozoa*
3. *Funguslike protists:* protists that resemble fungi; also called *absorptive protists*

Protists are usually unicellular or colonial. This is why they are *not* considered plants, animals, or fungi. All protists are capable of asexual reproduction. Some reproduce only asexually, and others can reproduce sexually as well. This variability in the life cycles found among various members of the protist kingdom is just one reason why they are considered to be one of the most diverse kingdoms in existence.

Animal-like Protists (Protozoa)

This division includes protists that *ingest* foods—as do animals. As with the rest of this chapter, you do not need to become an expert on protozoans and know everything about every member. But the following is a list that contains basic information about some names that may help you on the multiple-choice section of the test. I will italicize the most important things to remember about each of them.

1. *Rhizopoda.* These *unicellular* and *asexual* organisms are also known as *amoebas.* They get from place to place through the use of **pseudopods,** which are extensions from their cells. Every living creature has to eat, and they do so through *phagocytosis.*
2. *Foraminifera.* These *marine* protists live attached to structures such as rocks and algae. Their name is derived from the word *foramen* because of the presence of calcium carbonate ($CaCO_3$) shells full of holes. Some of these protists obtain nutrients through *photosynthesis* performed by symbiotic algae living in their shells.
3. *Actinopoda.* These organisms move by *pseudopodia* and make up part of plankton, the organisms that drift near the surface of bodies of water. The two divisions of actinopoda include heliozoans and radiozoans. Just recognize the names, do not worry about anything more than that.
4. *Apicomplexa.* These *parasites* are the protists formerly known as sporozoans. They spread from place to place in a small infectious form known as a **sporozoite.** They have both *sexual* and *asexual* stages, and their life cycle requires two different host species for completion. An example of an apicomplexa is **plasmodium,** the causative agent of malaria (two hosts—mosquitoes, then humans).
5. *Zooflagellates.* These *heterotrophic* protists are known for their *flagella,* which they use to move around. Like rhizopoda, they eat by *phagocytosis,* and can range from being *parasitic* to their hosts to living *mutualistically* with them. A member of this group is *trypanosoma,* which is known to cause African sleeping sickness.
6. *Ciliophora.* Their name is fitting because these protists use *cilia* to travel from place to place. They live in *water,* and contain *two types of nuclei:* a **macronucleus** (which controls everyday activities) and many **micronuclei** (a function in **conjugation**). A ciliaphora you may recognize is paramecium.

Funguslike Protists (Slime Molds and Water Molds)

This division includes protists that resemble fungi. Once again, I am going to provide a list that contains basic information about some names that may help you on multiple choice questions. The most important things to remember are boldfaced or italicized.

1. *Myxomycota.* These *heterotrophic* brightly colored protists include the **plasmodial slime molds,** and are not photosynthetic. Unlike the acrasiomycota, they do not like to eat alone—they eat and grow as a single clumped *unicellular* mass known as a **plasmodium** (same name as the causative agent of malaria). This mass ingests food

by *phagocytosis*. When Mother Hubbard's cupboard is bare and there is no more food, the plasmodium stops growing and instead produces spores that allow the protist to reproduce.

2. *Acrasiomycota.* Known to their closer friends as **cellular slime molds,** these protists have a bit of a strange eating strategy. When there is plenty of food around, these organisms eat alone as solitary beings, but when food becomes scarce, they clump together in a manner similar to slime molds and work together as a unit.

3. *Oomycota.* These *water-mold* protists can be *parasites* or *saprobes*. They are able to munch on their surrounding environment owing to the presence of *filaments* known as *hyphae,* which release digestive enzymes. They are often multicellular, or *coenocytic.* One difference between these organisms and actual fungi is that their cell wall is made of *cellulose,* and not *chitin* as seen in fungi.

Plantlike Protists

This division includes protists that are mostly photosynthetic. All of these organisms contain chlorophyll a. Focus your attention on the italicized points.

1. *Dinoflagellata.* Protists known for having *two flagella* that rest perpendicular to each other that allow them to swim with a funky spinning motion that makes them the envy of all other protist observers (or at least makes them really dizzy). Most dinoflagellates are *unicellular*. These protists are very important producers in many aquatic food chains.

2. *Golden algae.* Known as the *chrysophyta,* these protists move through the use of *flagella* and can also be found swimming among plankton.

3. *Diatoms.* These yellow and brown protists are also known as bacillariophyta, and are a major component of plankton. They mostly reproduce in an *asexual* fashion, although they do rarely enter a *sexual* life cycle. They have ornate *walls* made of *silica* to protect them.

4. *Green algae.* Known as *chlorophyta,* they have chlorophyll a and b. Most of these protists live in freshwater and can be found among the algae that are part of the mutualistic *lichen* conglomerate. Most have both *asexual* and *sexual* reproductive stages. These organisms are considered to be the ancestors of plants.

5. *Brown algae.* Known as *phaeophyta,* most of these protists are *multicellular* and live in *marine* environments. Two members to know are *kelp* and *seaweed*.

6. *Red algae.* Known as rhodophyta, they get their color from a pigment called *phycobilin.* Most of these *multicellular* protists live in the ocean and produce gametes that do not have flagella. Many live in deep waters and absorb non-visible light via accessory pigments.

KINGDOM PLANTAE

Classification of plants is very similar to classification of the animal kingdom, except that plants are divided into divisions instead of phyla. So, instead of "Karaoke players can order free grape soda," remember "Karaoke *dancers* can order free grape soda."

Reality again, folks . . . you do not need to become experts in the evolutionary history of plants, but you should be able to understand a phylogenetic representation of how the various plant types evolved.

Chlorophytes→bryophytes→seedless vascular plants→gymnosperms→angiosperms

Chlorophytes are green algae. Scientists have found enough evidence to conclude that they are the common ancestors of land plants. Plants are said to have experienced four major evolutionary periods since the dawn of time, described in the following sections.

Bryophytes

Teacher: CT "Know plant evolution very well. There are a lot of potential questions here. Including essays"

Bryophytes were the first land plants to evolve from the chlorophytes. They include mosses, liverworts, and hornworts. Prior to bryophytes, there was no reason for these organisms to worry about water loss because they lived in water and had unlimited access to the treasured resource. But in order to survive on land, where water was no longer unlimited, two evolutionary adaptations in particular helped them survive:

1. A waxy **cuticle** cover to protect against water loss.
2. The packaging of gametes in structures known as **gametangia.**

Bryophyte sperm is produced by the male gametangia, the **antheridia.** Bryophyte eggs are produced by the female gametangia: the **archegonium.** The gametangia provide a safe haven because the fertilization and development of the zygote occur within the protected structure.

Because they lack xylem and phloem, bryophytes are also known as *nonvascular plants.* This lack of vascular tissue combined with the existence of flagellated sperm results in a dependence on water. For this reason, bryophytes must live in damp areas so that they do not dry out. There are three nonvascular plants you should know about: mosses, liverworts, and hornworts. Mosses are special in that, unlike all other plants, the dominant generation in their life cycle is the haploid gametophyte. The moss sporophyte is tiny, short-lived, and reliant on the gametophyte for nutritional support. One interesting fact about liverworts is that in addition to the alternation of generations life cycle, they are able to reproduce asexually.

Seedless Vascular Plants

The transition for plants from water to land was a tricky one. They needed to find a way to use the nutritional resources of the minerals and water found in soil, while not denying themselves access to the light needed for photosynthesis. Another problem facing these early land plants was the need to find a way to distribute water and nutrients throughout the plant—not as much of an issue when the plant was submerged in water. The solution to this issue was the development of the xylem and phloem, which you will read about in Chapter 10, Plants. The **xylem** is the water superhighway for the plant, transporting water throughout the plant. The **phloem** is the sugar food highway for the plant, transporting sugar and nutrients to the various plant structures.

The first vascular plants (also referred to as **tracheophytes**) to evolve did not have seeds. Two major evolutionary changes occurred that allowed the transition from bryophytes to seedless vascular plants:

1. The switch from the gametophyte to the sporophyte as the dominant generation of the life cycle
2. The development of branched sporophytes, increasing the number of spores produced

The major seedless vascular plants you should know are **ferns**, which are **homosporous plants** that produce a single spore type that gives rise to bisexual gametophytes. The spores tend to exist on the underside of the fern leaves. A **heterosporous plant** produces two types of spores, some of which yield male gametophytes (**microspores**), and others produce female gametophytes (**megaspores**). The dominant generation for ferns is the sporophyte.

Seed Plants

Gymnosperm

The third major plant category to branch off the phylogenetic tree is the seed plant. Three major evolutionary changes occurred between the seedless vascular plants and the birth of seed plants:

1. Further decline in the prominence of the gametophyte generation of the life cycle
2. The birth of pollination
3. The evolution of the seed

A seed is a package containing an embryo and the food to feed the developing embryo that is surrounded by a nice protective shell. The first major seed plants to surface were the **gymnosperm**. These plants are heterosporous and usually transport their sperm through the use of **pollen**—the sperm-bearing male gametophyte. Not all gymnosperms have pollen; some have motile sperm. The major gymnosperms you should remember are the **conifers**, plants whose reproductive structure is a cone. Members of this division include pine trees, firs, cedars, and redwoods. These plants survive well in dry conditions and keep their leaves year-round. They are evergreens and usually have needles for leaves.

Angiosperm

The final major plant evolutionary category to branch off the phylogenetic tree is the flowering plant. Today there are more **angiosperm** around than any other kind of plant. There are two major classes of angiosperms to know: monocots (**monocotyledons**) and dicots (**dicotyledons**). A **cotyledon** is a structure that provides nourishment for a developing plant. One distinction between monocots and dicots is that monocots have a single cotyledon, while dicots have two.

One interesting evolutionary change from the gymnosperm to the angiosperm is the adaptation of the xylem. In gymnosperms, the xylem cells in charge of water transport are the **tracheid cells**, whereas in angiosperms the xylem cells are the more efficient **vessel elements.** Don't worry too much about this distinction, but store away in the back of your mind that vessel elements are seen in angiosperm, while tracheid cells are seen in gymnosperm.

What is a flower, really? Are they just another visually pleasing structure? No . . . they are so much more. Flowers are the main tools for angiosperm reproduction. Do not waste too much time learning every little part of a flower. Here are the most important parts to remember:

Stamen: male structure composed of an **anther,** which produces pollen.

Carpel: female structure that consists of an *ovary,* a **style,** and a **stigma.** The stigma functions as the receiver of the pollen, and the style is the pathway leading to the ovary.

Petals: structures that serve to attract pollinators to help increase the plant's reproductive success.

Below is a quick display that lists many of the major evolutionary trends observed during the phylogenetic development of plants:

KINGDOM FUNGI

Nearly all fungi are multicellular and are built from filamentous structures called **hyphae.** These hyphae form meshes of branching filaments known as a **mycelium,** which function as mouthlike structures for the fungus, absorbing food. Many fungi contain **septae,** which divide the hyphae filaments into different compartments. The septa have pores, which allow organelles and other structures to flow from compartment to compartment. Fungi that do not contain septae are called **coenocytic fungi.** Fungus walls are built using the polysaccharide **chitin.** As was discussed in Chapter 5, Cell Division, the fungus life cycle is predominately haploid. The only time they are diploid is as the 2*n* zygote.

The following is a list of fungus-related organisms that you should know:

1. *Zygomycota.* These *coenocytic* and *land-dwelling* fungi have very few septa and reproduce sexually. A classic example of a zygomycete is bread mold.
2. *Basiodiomycota.* These club-shaped fungi are known for their haploid basidiospores and love of decomposing wood. They like piña coladas and getting caught in the rain. Famous members include mushrooms and rusts.
3. *Ascomycota.* Many members of this group of saprobic fungi live as part of the symbiotic relationship called **lichen.** These fungi produce sexual **ascospores,** which are contained in sacs. Famous ascomycetes you may have heard of are yeasts and mildews. These are discussed again in Chapter 15, Laboratory Review.
4. *Lichens.* These are formed by a *symbiotic association* of photosynthetic organisms grouped together with fungal hyphae (*usually an ascomycete*). The algae member of this group tends to be *cyanobacteria or chlorophyta* and provides the food (sugar from photosynthesis). The fungus provides protection and drink (water).
5. *Molds.* These are *asexual, quick-growing* fungus known as *deuteromycota* or the "imperfect fungi." If you check any college refrigerator, you can find many fine samples of this organism.
6. *Yeasts.* These are *unicellular* fungi that can be asexual *or* sexual. One member of this group, *Candida,* is known to cause yeast infections in humans.

KINGDOM ANIMALIA

Animals are the final kingdom to be discussed in this chapter. There are some characteristics that separate animals from other organisms:

Adaptation	Description
Cell wall	Animals lack cell walls
Mode of reproduction	Sexual reproduction is the norm
Dominant life cycle stage	The diploid stage is usually the dominant generation in the life cycle
Motile	Most animals are mobile

continued

Continued

Adaptation	Description
Nutritional class	Animals are multicellular heterotrophs
Storage of energy	Animals store carbohydrates as glycogen, not starch as is seen in plants
Special embryological events	Most animals undergo a process in which specialized tissue layers (endoderm, mesoderm, ectoderm) form during a process known as **gastrulation**
Nervous and muscle tissue	Animals have specialized nervous and muscle tissue
Cellular junctions	Animal cells contain tight junctions and gap junctions

As is the case with all of the other kingdoms in this chapter, you do not need to become the master of animal phylogeny and taxonomy. But it is definitely useful to know the general evolutionary history of the animal kingdom and how it diversified so quickly over time (see Figure 9.1).

Many people believe that the original common ancestor that started the whole process of animal evolution was most likely the **choanoflagellate.** During the evolutionary progression from choanoflagellate to present date, there are *four* major branchpoints on which you should focus. Let's take a look at all the important changes that have allowed such diversity of life.

The first major branchpoint occurred after the development of multicellularity from choanoflagellates. Off of this branch of the tree emerged two divisions:

1. *Parazoa:* sponges; these organisms have no true tissues.
2. *Eumetazoa:* all the other animals with true tissue.

After this split into parazoa and eumetazoa, the second major branchpoint in animal evolutionary history occurred: the subdivision of eumetazoa into two further branches on the basis of body symmetry. The eumetezoans were subdivided into

1. *Radiata:* those that have radial symmetry, which means that they have a single orientation. This can be a top and a bottom, or a front and back. This branch included jellyfish, corals, and hydras.
2. *Bilateria:* those that have bilateral symmetry, which means that they have a top and a bottom (dorsal/ventral) as well as a head and a tail (anterior/posterior).

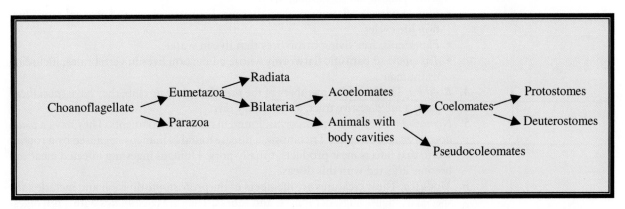

Figure 9.1
The animal phylogenetic tree.

The next major split in the phylogenetic tree for animal development involved the split of bilateral organisms into two further branches—one of which subdivides into two smaller branches:

1. *Acoeleomates:* animals with no blood vascular system and lacking a cavity between the gut and outer body wall. An example of a member of this group is the flatworm.
2. Animals *with* a vascular system and a body cavity.
   - *Pseudocoelomates:* animals that have a fluid-filled body cavity that is *not* enclosed by mesoderm. Roundworms are a member of this branch.
   - *Coelomates:* a **coelom** is a fluid-filled body cavity found between the body wall and gut that has a lining. It comes from the mesoderm.

The final major branchpoint comes off from the coelomates. It branches into two more divisions:

1. *Protostomes:* a bilateral animal whose first embryonic indentation eventually develops into a *mouth.* Prominent members of this society include *annelids, arthropods,* and *mullusks.*
2. *Deuterostomes:* a branch that includes *chordates* and *echinoderms.* The first indentation for their embryos eventually develops into the *anus.*

These two divisions differ in their embryonic developmental stages. As already mentioned, the protostomes' first embryonic indent develops into the mouth, whereas for the dueterostome it becomes the anus. Another difference is the *angle* of the cleavages that occur during the early cleavage division of the embryo. A third difference is the tissue from which the coelom divides.

That concludes the evolutionary development portion of this chapter. Now let's take a quick look at a few members of the various branches we mentioned above.

1. *Porifera (sponges).* These are simple creatures, which, for the most part, are able to perform both male and female sexual functions. They have no "true tissue," which means that they do *not* have organs, and their cells do not seem to be specialized in function.
2. *Cnidaria.* These organisms are of *radial symmetry* and include jellyfish and coral animals, and *lack* a *mesoderm.* A cnidarian's body is a digestive sac that can be one of two types: a polyp or a medusa. A **polyp** (asexual) is *cylinder-shaped* and lives *attached* to some surface (sea anemones). A **medusa** (sexual) is *flat* and roams the waters looking for food (jellyfish). Cnidarians use tentacles to capture and eat prey.
3. *Platyhelminthes.* These are *flatworms,* members of the *acoelomate* club. They have *bilateral symmetry* and a touch of *cephalization.* There are three main types of flatworms, you should be familiar with:
   - *Flukes:* parasitic flatworms that alternate between sexual and asexual reproduction life cycles.
   - *Planarians:* free-living carnivores that live in water.
   - *Tapeworms:* parasitic flatworms whose adult form lives in vertebrates, including us (humans)
4. *Rotifera.* These are also members of the *pseudocoelomate* club; they have *specialized organs,* a full digestive tract, and are very tiny.
5. *Nematoda.* These are *roundworms,* found in moist environments. They have a *psuedocoelomate* body plan. Trichinosis, a disease found in humans, is caused by a roundworm that infects meat products, usually pork. Humans ingesting infected meat can become afflicted with this disease.
6. *Mollusca.* These creatures are members of the *protostome* division and include such species as snails, slugs, octopuses, and squids. They are *coelomates* with a full digestive system. **Bivalves,** such as clams and oysters, are mollusks that have hinged shells that are divided into two parts.

7. *Annelida*. These are segmented worms such as earthworms and leeches.

8. *Arthropoda*. This is the most heavily represented group on the planet. These creatures are *segmented, contain a hard exoskeleton* constructed out of *chitin*, and have *specialized appendages*. Some well known members include spiders, crustaceans, and insects. One interesting tidbit about arthropods is that, like humans, some members of this group, when born, are miniature versions of their adult selves that grow in size to resemble adults. Others look completely different from adults and exist in a larva form in their youth. At some point, the larvae undergo a metamorphosis and change to the expected adult form.

9. *Echinodermata*. These are *sea stars*. These coelomates are of the deuterostrome body plan. One neat characteristic of echinoderms is the presence of a **water vascular system,** which is a series of tubes and canals within the organism that play a role in ingestion of food, movement of the organism, and gas exchange.

10. *Chordata*. This group includes **invertebrates** (animals lacking backbones), and **vertebrates** (animals with backbones). Just in case you are asked to identify some vertebrates on a multiple-choice question, here are some members—fish, amphibians, reptiles, birds, and mammals. There are four features common to chordates you should know:

   • *Dorsal hollow nerve cord:* forms the nervous system and becomes the brain and spinal cord in some
   • *Notochord:* long support rod that is replaced by bone in most (mesodermal in origin)
   • *Pharyngeal gill slits:* slit-containing structure, which functions in respiration and/or feeding
   • *Tail:* extension past the anus that is lost by birth in many species

REVIEW QUESTIONS

1. Which of the following is thought to be the common ancestor to plants?

   A. Chemoautotrophs
   B. Choanoflagellates
   C. Chordata
   D. Chlorophytes
   E. Cnidaria

2. Which of the following pairs of organisms is most closely interrelated?

   A. Sponge and halophile
   B. Jellyfish and coral
   C. Oyster and conifer
   D. Lichen and roundworm
   E. Bryophyte and mold

3. Which of the following was an evolutionary adaptation vital to the survival of the bryophytes?

   A. The switch from the gametophyte to the sporophyte as the dominant generation of the life cycle
   B. The development of branched sporophytes
   C. The birth of pollination

   D. The packaging of gametes into gametangia
   E. Evolution of the seed

4. Which of the following is the most specific category of classification?

   A. Class
   B. Family
   C. Order
   D. Division
   E. Phylum

5. Which of the following is *not* associated with flowers?

   A. Carpel
   B. Stigma
   C. Style
   D. Hypha
   E. Anther

6. Which of the following was the latest to branch off the animal phylogenetic tree?

   A. Radiata
   B. Acoelomates
   C. Eumetazoa

D. Pseudocoelomates
E. Deuterostomes

For questions 7–10, please use the following answer choices:

A. Kingdom Animalia
B. Kingdom Fungi
C. Kingdom Plantae
D. Kingdom Protista
E. Kingdom Monera

7. Thermoacidophiles are grouped into this kingdom that consists of single-celled organisms lacking nuclei and membrane-bound organelles.

8. Arthropods are grouped into this kingdom whose members are multicellular heterotrophs that have the diploid stage as their dominant generation in the life cycle.

9. This kingdom is divided into plantlike, animal-like, and funguslike divisions.

10. Molds, or deuteromycota, are grouped into this kingdom that consists of mostly multicellular organisms that are constructed out of hypha.

ANSWERS AND EXPLANATIONS

1. **D**—Chlorophytes are green algae that are the common ancestors of land plants. Chemoautotrophs are monerans that produce energy from inorganic substances. Choanoflagellates are the organisms thought to be the starting point for the animal kingdom's phylogenetic tree. Chordata includes the invertebrates and vertebrates, and cnidarians are radially symmetric organisms such as jellyfish.

2. **B**—Jellyfish and coral are both cnidarians of the animal kingdom.

3. **D**—Since the bryophytes were the first plants to brave the land, they were still somewhat dependent on water and also needed protection for their gametes. The gametangia provided a safe haven for the gametes where fertilization and zygote development could occur. Answer choices A and B were adaptations made by seedless vascular plants. Answer choices C and E were adaptations made by the gymnosperms.

4. **B**—*Karaoke players can order free grape soda or King Phillip came over for good spaghetti* (enough said).

5. **D**—Hyphae are associated with fungi. The other parts are all associated with flowers.

6. **E**—Take a look at Figure 9.1 for this one; the dueterostomes are indeed the last to branch off.

7. **E.**

8. **A.**

9. **D.**

10. **B.**

RAPID REVIEW

Quickly review the following terms:

Taxonomy—Classification of organisms based upon the presence or absence of shared characteristics: kingdom → phylum (division) → class → order → family → genus → species

Five-kingdom system: Monera → Protista → Plantae → Fungi → Animalia

Six-kingdom system: Archaebacteria → Eubacteria → Protista → Plantae → Fungi → Animalia

---

Kingdom Monera

Autotrophs (producers) versus *heterotrophs* (consumers)

Obligate aerobes (require O_2), versus *obligate anaerobes* (*no* O_2), versus *facultative anaerobes* (either/or)

Archaebacteria: halophiles (salt), methanogens (methane-producers), thermoacidophiles (hot and acidic)

Eubacteria: bacteria classified according to movement, shape, nutritional methods

---

Endosymbiotic theory: eukaryotes originated from a symbiotic partnership of prokaryotic cells

---

Kingdom Protista

Plantlike protists: photosynthetic algae; all contain chlorophyll a

Animal-like protists: heterotrophic protists (protozoa)

Funguslike protists: absorptive protists that resemble fungi

Kingdom Plantae

Chlorophytes: green algae that are the common ancestor of land plants

Bryophytes: first land plants; two important adaptations—waxy cuticle (stop water loss), gametangia:

- *Gametangia:* protective structures to aid survival of gametes on land.

- *Mosses:* important bryophyte, dominant life cycle generation is a **haploid gametophyte**

Seedless vascular plants: came after bryophytes, and had two further changes:

- Switch from haploid gametophyte to diploid sporophyte as dominant generation

- Development of branched sporophytes

- *Ferns:* important member, **homosporous** (bisexual gametophytes).

Gymnosperm: came after seedless vascular plants and had three evolutionary adaptations:

- Further increase in dominance of sporophyte generation

- Birth of pollination

- Evolution of the seed

Conifers: plants whose reproductive structure is a cone

Angiosperm: flowering plants that came after gymnosperms divided into **monocots** and **dicots**

Kingdom Fungi

Multicellular, built from hyphae, which can be separated by septae. Fungus walls are constructed from **chitin**.

Life cycle is predominately **haploid**

Kingdom Animalia

Important characteristics: no cell walls, $2n$ is dominant, mobile, multicellular, heterotrophic, gastrulation.

Four major branchpoints (see Figure 9.1).

Common ancestor: **choanoflagellate.**

Important members (in order of split from phylogenetic tree): sponges (parazoa), jellyfish (Radiata), flatworms (Acoelomates), roundworms (Pseudocoeloomate nematodes), arthropods (protostomes), humans (Chordates).

Skim the information by each subdivision of this kingdom a couple pages back for more information.

Chapter 10

Plants

INTRODUCTION

This chapter begins with a quick tour of the anatomy of plants, starting with the roots and moving to the shoots. During these two sections, the mechanisms of root and shoot growth will be examined, and the important players identified. From there we will turn our focus to plant hormones and tropisms. A discussion on photoperiodism follows, and the chapter concludes with a look at the mechanism by which water and nutrients travel through plants from roots to shoots and back.

ANATOMY OF PLANTS

The anatomy of a plant in its most simplistic form can be divided into the roots and the shoots. **Roots** are the portions of the plant that are below the ground, while **shoots** are the portions of the plant that are above the ground. The roots wind their way through the terrain, working as an anchor to keep the plants in place, and also working as gatherers, absorbing the water and nutrients vital to a plant's survival.

Tissue Systems

There are *three* plant tissue systems to know: ground, vascular, and dermal.

Ground Tissue

The ground tissue makes up most of the body of the plant, is found between the dermal and vascular systems, and is subdivided into three cell types: **collenchyma cells,** live cells that provide flexible and mechanical support—often found in stems and leaves; **parenchyma cells,** the most prominent of the three types, with many functions— parenchyma cells found in leaves are called *mesophyll cells,* and allow CO_2 and O_2 to diffuse through intercellular spaces (owing to the presence of large vacuoles, these cells play a role in storage and secretion for plants); and **sclerenchyma cells,** which protect seeds and support the plant.

Vascular Tissue

Plant vascular tissue comes up often on the AP Biology exam. The two characters you need to be familiar with are the xylem and the phloem.

Xylem. This structure has multiple functions. It is a support structure that strengthens the plant, and also functions as a passageway for the transport of water and minerals from the soil. One interesting (and sad) note about xylem cells is that most of them are dead and are simply there as cell walls that contain the minerals and water being passed along the plant. Xylem cells can be divided into two categories: **vessel elements** and **tracheid cells.** They both function in the passage of water, but vessel elements move water more efficiently because of structural differences that are not pertinent to this exam ☺ .

Phloem. This structure also functions as a "highway" for plants, assisting in the movement of sugars from one place to another. Unlike the xylem, the functionally mature cells of a phloem, *sieve-tube elements,* are alive and well.

Dermal Tissue

Dermal tissue provides the protective outer coating for plants. It is the skin, or **epidermis.** This coating attempts to keep the bad guys (infectious agents) out, and the good guys (water and nutrients) in. Within the epidermis are cells called **guard cells,** which control the opening and closing of gaps called *stomata* that are vital to the process of photosynthesis as was discussed back in Chapter 4, Photosynthesis.

ROOTS

Root Systems

How do plants get their nutrients? Through the hard work of roots, whose tips absorb nourishment for the plant (minerals and water) via root hairs. Most of the water and minerals are absorbed by plants at the root tips, which have **root hairs** extending from their surface. These hairs create a larger surface area for absorption in much the same way as the **brush border** does in the human intestines—improving the efficiency of nutrient and water acquisition.

A root is not just a root, for not all root structures are the same. In Chapter 9, Taxonomy and Classification, two types of angiosperm plants were mentioned: dicots and monocots. Dicots are known for having a taproot system, while monocots are associated with fibrous roots. The **taproot** (e.g., carrot) **system** branches in a way similar to the human lungs; the roots start as one thick root on entrance into the ground, and then divide into smaller and smaller branches called **lateral roots** underneath the surface, which serve to hold the plant in place. **Fibrous roots** provide plants with a very strong anchor in the ground without going very deep into the soil. The root system can be summarized as follows:

Dicots → taproot → thick entry root → division into smaller branches

Monocots → fibrous root → shallow entry into ground → strong anchor effect

Root Structure

Let's take a look at the structure of a root moving from outside to inside. The root is lined by the **epidermis,** whose cells give rise to the root hairs that plants must thank for their ability to absorb water and nutrients. Moving further in, we come to the cortex, the majority of the root that functions as a starch storage receptacle. The innermost layer of the cortex is composed of a cylinder of cells known as the **endodermis.** These cells are important to the plant because the walls between these cells create an obstacle known as the **casparian strip,** which blocks water from passing. This is one of the mechanisms by which plants control the flow of water. Moving in through the endodermis we come to the **vascular cylinder,** which is composed of a collection of cells known as the *pericycle.* The lateral roots of the plant are made from the pericycle, and hold the vascular tissue of the root—our friends from earlier, the xylem and phloem.

Root Growth

Plants grow as long as they are alive as a result of to the presence of **meristemic cells.** Early on in the life of a plant, after a seed matures, it sits and waits until the time is right for germination. At this point, water is absorbed by the embryo, which begins to grow again. When large enough, it busts through the seed coat, beginning its journey to planthood. At the start of this journey, the growth is concentrated in the actively dividing cells of the **apical meristem.** Growth in this region leads to an increase in the length of a plant: **primary plant growth.** Later on growth occurs in cells known as the **lateral meristems,** which extend all the way through the plant. This growth that leads to an increase in the width of a plant and is known as **secondary plant growth.**

Regions of Growth

Root cap: protective structure that keeps roots from being damaged during push through soil

Zone of cell division: section of root where cells are actively dividing

Zone of elongation: next section up along the root, where cells absorb H_2O and increase in length to make the plant taller

Zone of maturation: section of root past the zone of elongation where the cells differentiate to their finalized form (phloem, xylem, parenchyma, epidermal, etc)

THE SHOOT SYSTEM

Now that we have discussed roots—the part of the plant that is *in* the ground—let's take a look at shoots (leaves and stems), the parts of the plant that are *out of* the ground.

Structure of a Leaf

Leaves are protected by the waxy **cuticle** of the epidermis, which functions to decrease the transpiration rate. Inside the epidermis lies the ground tissue of the leaf, the mesophyll, which is involved in the ever-so-important process of photosynthesis. There are two important layers to the mesophyll: the **palisade mesophyll** and the **spongy mesophyll.** Most of the photosynthesis of the leaf occurs in the palisade mesophyll, where there are *many* chloroplasts. Inside a bit further is the spongy mesophyll whose cells provide CO_2 to the cells performing photosynthesis. Important structures to successful photosynthesis are **stomata,** which are controlled by the guard cells that line the walls of the epidermis. Extending a bit further inside the leaf, we find the *xylem,* the supplier of water to photosynthesizing cells; and the *phloem,* which carries *away* the products of photosynthesis. In C_4 plants, a second type of cell called a *bundle sheath cell* surrounds the vascular tissue to make the use of CO_2 more efficient and allow the stomata to remain closed during the hot daytime hours. These cells prevent excessive transpiration.

Structure of Stems

Again, let's travel from the outside in and discuss the basic structure. The epidermis for the stem provides protection and is covered by **cutin,** a waxy protective coat. The cortex of a stem contains the parenchyma, collenchyma, and schlerenchyma cells mentioned earlier in this chapter. You'll notice that there is no endodermis in the stem because this portion of the plant is not involved in the *absorption* of water. As a result, the next structure we see as we move inward is the vascular cylinder and our friends the xylem and phloem.

A term to know is the **vascular cambium,** which extends along the entire length of the plant and gives rise to secondary xylem and phloem. Over time, the stem of a plant will increase in width because of the secondary xylem produced each year.

Another term to know is the **cork cambium,** which produces a thick cover for stems and roots. This covering replaces the epidermis when it dries up and falls off the stem during secondary growth, forming a protective barrier against infection and physical damage.

The growth of plants is not a continuous process in seasonal environments. There are periods of dormancy in between phases of growth. Have you ever seen the rings of a tree after it has been cut down? These rings produced each year, are a window into the past, and give insight into the amount of rain a tree has encountered in a given year. The wider the ring, the more water it saw.

PLANT HORMONES

Hormones perform the same general function for plants that they do for humans—they are signals that can travel long distances to affect the actions of another cell. There are five main plant hormones you should study for this exam.

1. *Abscisic acid.* This is the "baby-sitter" hormone. It makes sure that seeds do not germinate too early, inhibits cell growth, and stimulates the closing of the stomata to make sure the plant maintains enough water.
2. *Auxin.* This is a popular AP Biology exam plant hormone selection. Auxin is a hormone that performs several functions—it leads to the elongation of stems, and plays a role in phototropism and gravitropism, which we will discuss a bit later.
3. *Cytokinins.* Hormones that promote cell division and leaf enlargement. They also seem to have an element of the "fountain of youth" in them, as they seem to slow down the aging of leaves. Supermarkets use synthetic cytokinins to keep their veggies fresh.
4. *Ethylene.* This hormone initiates fruit ripening and causes flowers and leaves to drop from trees (associated with aging).
5. *Gibberellins.* Another hormone group that assists in stem elongation. When you think gibberellins, think "grow." It is thought to induce the growth of dormant seeds, buds, and flowers.

PLANT TROPISMS

A **tropism** is growth that occurs in response to an environmental stimulus such as sunlight or gravity. The three tropisms you should familiarize yourself with include gravitropism, phototropism, and thigmotropism.

1. *Gravitropism.* This is a plant's growth response to gravitational force. Two of the hormones mentioned earlier play a role in this movement: **auxin** and **gibberellins.** A plant placed on its side will show gravitropic growth in which the cells on the upward-facing side will not grow as much as those on the downward side. It is believed that the relative concentrations of these hormones in the various areas of the plant are responsible for this imbalanced growth of the plant.
2. *Phototropism.* This is a plant's growth response to light. Auxin is the hormone in charge here. Auxin works its magic in the zone of elongation. While the mechanics of the phototropism process may not be vital to this exam, it is still quite interesting to know. When a plant receives light on all sides, auxin is distributed equally around the zone of elongation and growth is even. When one half of a plant is in the sun, and the other is in the shade, auxin (almost as if it feels bad for the shady portion), focuses on the darker side. This leads to unequal growth of the stem with the side receiving less light growing faster—causing the movement of the plant *toward* the light source.
3. *Thigmotropism.* This is a plant's growth response to contact. One example involves vines, which wind around objects with which they make contact as they grow.

How in the world did we figure out that auxin played such a large role in phototropism? A series of experiments performed by two scientists proved vital to the understanding of this process. Grass seedlings are surrounded by a protective structure known as the **coleoptile.** Peter Boysen-Jensen performed an experiment in which a gelatin block permeable to chemical signals was placed in between this coleoptile structure and the body of a grass seedling. When the piece of grass was exposed to light on one side, it grew toward the light. When a barrier impermeable to chemical signals was placed in between the two structures instead, this growth toward light did not occur. Another scientist, F. W. Went, came onto the scene and took Jensen's experiment a step further. Went wanted to show that it was indeed a chemical and not the coleoptile tip itself that was responsible for the phototropic response. He cut off the tip and exposed it to light while the tip was resting on an agar block that would collect any chemicals that diffused out. The block was then placed on the body of a tipless grass seedling sitting in a dark room. Even in the absence of light, a block placed more toward the right side of a seedling, caused the seedling to bend to the left. A block placed more toward the left side of a seedling caused the seedling to bend to the right. Because there was no further light stimulation causing the growth, the agar block must indeed have contained a chemical that induced a phototropic response. This chemical was given the name *auxin.*

PHOTOPERIODISM

Like all of us, plants have a biological clock that maintains a **circadian rhythm**—a physiologic cycle that occurs in time increments that are roughly equivalent to the length of a day. The month of June has the longest days of the year—the most sunlight. The month of December has the shortest days of the year—the least sunlight. How is it that plants, that are so dependent on light, are able to survive through these varying conditions? This is thanks to **photoperiodism,** the response by a plant to the change in the length of days. One commonly discussed example of photoperiodism involves flowering plants (angiosperms). A hormone known as **florigen** is thought to assist in the blooming of flowers. An important pigment to the process of flowering is **phytochrome,** which is involved in the production of florigen. Because plants differ in the conditions required for flowering to occur, different amounts of florigen are needed to initiate this process from plant to plant.

One interesting application of photoperiodism involves the distinction between **short-day plants** and **long-day plants,** which flower only if certain requirements are met:

Plant type	Example	Flowering Requirements	Flowers during
Short-day plants	Poinsettias	Exposure to a night *longer* than a certain number of hours (e.g., 10 hours)	End of summer to end of winter
Long-day plants	Spinach	Exposure to a night *shorter* than a certain number of hours (e.g., 8 hours)	Late spring to early summer

GO WITH THE FLOW: OSMOSIS, CAPILLARY ACTION, COHESION–TENSION THEORY, AND TRANSPIRATION

Osmosis drives the absorption of water and minerals from the soil by the root tips. Water then moves deeper into the root until it reaches the endodermis. Once there, because of the casparian strip, it can only travel through the selective endodermal cells that choose which nutrients and minerals they let through to the vascular cylinder beyond. The casparian strip essentially lets only those with a backstage pass through. Potassium has a backstage pass, and can go into the vascular cylinder . . . sodium does not and gets denied. Once the water gets to the xylem, it has reached the H_2O superhighway and is ready to go all over the plant.

There are a few driving forces responsible for the movement of a plant's water supply. The three main forces we will cover here are osmosis, capillary action, and cohesion–tension theory. Of those three, the cohesion–tension theory pulls the most weight.

Osmosis

Osmosis is the driving force that moves water from the soil into xylem cells. How in the world does the plant keep the concentration gradient such that it promotes the movement of water in the appropriate direction? There are two contributing factors: (1) the water is constantly moving away from the root tips creating the space for more water to enter, and (2) osmosis is defined as the passive diffusion of water down its concentration gradient across selectively permeable membranes. It will flow from a region with a high water concentration to a region with a low water concentration. There is a higher mineral concentration inside the vascular cylinder, which drives water into the xylem contained in this cylinder by a force known as **root pressure.**

Capillary Action

Capillary action is the force of adhesion between water and a passageway that pulls water up along the sides. Along with osmosis, this mechanism is a minor contributor to the movement of water up the xylem, due to the counteracting force of gravity.

Cohesion–Tension Theory and Transpiration

This process is the major mover of water in the xylem. Transpiration creates a negative pressure in the leaves and xylem tissue due to the evaporative loss of water. Water molecules display molecular attraction (cohesion) for other water molecules, in effect creating a single united water molecule that runs the length of the plant. Imagine that you tie a bunch of soda cans to a rope. If you are standing in a tree, and pull up on the cans at the top of the rope, the cans at the bottom will follow. Not really because they are loyal to the other cans, but because they are connected to them—they are bonded. This is similar to the movement of water through the xylem. When water evaporates off the surface of the leaf, the water is pulled up through the xylem toward the leaves—transpiration is the force pulling water through the plant.

THE CHANGING OF THE GUARD: REGULATING STOMATA ACTIVITY

The stomata are structures vital to the daily workings of a plant. When closed, photosynthesis is halted because water and carbon dioxide are inaccessible. When open, mesophyll cells have access to water and carbon dioxide. But with every reward there is always a risk. When the stomata are open, the plant could dry out as a result of excessive transpiration. This process of opening and closing the stomata must therefore be very carefully controlled. Guard cells are the ones for the job. They surround and tightly regulate the actions of the stomata. When water flows into neighboring guard cells (leading to an increase in turgor pressure), a structural change occurs that causes the opening of the stomata. When the water flows out of the guard cells (a decrease in turgor pressure), the stomata will close. It is by this mechanism that guard cells control the opening and closing of the stomata.

"MOVE OVER, SUGAR": CARBOHYDRATE TRANSPORT THROUGH PHLOEM

The transport of carbohydrates through the phloem is called **translocation (plants)**. After their production, carbohydrates, the all-important product of photosynthesis, are dumped into the phloem (the sugar superhighway) near the site of their creation, to be distributed throughout the plant. The movement of the sugar into the phloem creates a driving force because it establishes a concentration gradient. This gradient leads to the passive diffusion of water into the phloem, causing an increase in the pressure of these cells. This pressure drives the movement of sugars and water through the phloem. As the sugars arrive at various destination sites, the sugar is consumed by plant cells, causing a reversal in the driving force for water that pushes water out of the phloem. As water exits the phloem, the increased pressure disappears and all is good once again.

REVIEW QUESTIONS 5

1. Which of the following is *not* a time when most stomata tend to be open?

   A. When CO_2 concentrations are low inside the leaf

   B. When temperatures are low

   C. When the concentration of water inside the plant is low

   D. During the day

   E. On a cold rainy day

For questions 2–5, please use the following answer choices:

    A. Abscisic acid
    B. Auxin
    C. Cytokinins
    D. Ethylene
    E. Gibberellins

2. This hormone is used by supermarkets for its "fountain of youth" effect.

3. This hormone initiates fruit ripening and works hard during the autumn months.

4. This hormone prevents seeds from germinating prematurely.

5. This hormone is known to induce growth in dormant seeds, buds, and flowers.

6. A vine is observed to wrap around a tree as it grows in the forest. This is an example of

    A. Gravitropism
    B. Phototropism
    C. Thigmotropism
    D. Photoperiodism
    E. Phototaxis

7. This portion of the root of a plant is responsible for the visual perception of growth:

    A. Zone of cell division
    B. Vascular cylinder
    C. Zone of elongation
    D. Endodermis
    E. Zone of maturation

For questions 8–10, please use the following answers:

    A. Sieve-tube elements
    B. Vessel elements
    C. Tracheids
    D. Guard cells
    E. Collenchyma cells

8. These cells are responsible for controlling the opening and closing of the stomata.

9. These cells are the more efficient of the two types of xylem cells.

10. These cells are live cells that function as structural support for a plant.

11. The unequal growth of the stem of a plant in which the side in the shade grows faster than the side in the sun is an example of

    A. Gravitropism
    B. Phototropism
    C. Thigmotropism
    D. Photoperiodism
    E. Phototaxis

ANSWERS AND EXPLANATIONS

1. C—When the concentration of water inside the plant is low, the stomata close in an effort to minimize transpiration.

2. C.

3. D.

4. A.

5. E.

6. C—Thigmotropism is a plant's growth in response to touch. Phototropism is growth in response to light, and gravitropism is growth in response to gravitational force. Photoperiodism is the response by a plant to the change in the length of days, and phototaxis is the sad phenomenon where moths fly kamikazi-style into burning hot lights at night.

7. C.

8. D.

9. **B.**

10. **E.**

11. **B**—Phototropism, a plant's growth response to light, is controlled by auxin. This hormone is produced in the apical meristem, and sent to the zone of elongation to initiate growth toward the sun.

RAPID REVIEW

The following terms and topics are important in this chapter:

Anatomy of plants: tissue systems are divided into *ground, vascular,* and *dermal.*

Ground tissue: the body of the plant is divided into three cell types:

- *Collenchyma cells:* provide flexible and mechanical support; found in stems and leaves

- *Parenchyma cells:* play a role in storage, secretion, and photosynthesis in cells

- *Sclerenchyma cells:* protect seeds and support the plant

Vascular tissue: xylem (transports water and minerals) and *phloem* (transports sugar)

Dermal tissue: protective outer coating for plants: *epidermis*

Roots

Types: **taproot system** (dicots)—system that divides into lateral roots which anchor the plant; **fibrous root system** (monocots)—anchoring system that does not go deep down into soil

Structure: epidermis → endodermis (casparian strip) → vascular cylinder → xylem/phloem

Growth: occurs for lifetime of the plant thanks to **meristem** cells:

- *Primary growth:* increased *length* of a plant (occurs in region of apical meristems)

- *Secondary growth:* increased *width* of a plant (occurs in region of lateral meristems, limited in monocots)

- Three main growth regions: zone of *cell division* (cells divide), zone of *elongation* (cells elongate), zone of *maturation* (cells mature to specialized form)

Stems (Shoots)

Structure: epidermis (cutin) → cortex (ground tissue) → vascular cylinder → xylem/phloem

Vascular cambium: gives rise to secondary xylem/phloem; runs entire length of plant

Cork cambium: produces protective covering that replaces epidermis during secondary growth

> ## Leaves (Shoots)
>
> *Structure:* epidermis (cuticle) → mesophyll (photosynthesis) → vascular bundles → xylem/phloem
>
> *C$_4$ plants:* leaves contain another cell type, **bundle sheath cells,** which assist in respiration in hot and dry regions
>
> *Stomata:* structure, controlled by **guard cells,** that when open allows CO_2 in, and H_2O and O_2 out

Plant hormones: **abscisic acid** (inhibits cell growth, helps close stomata), **auxin** (stem elongation, gravitropism, phototropism), **cytokinins** (promote cell division, leaf enlargement, slows aging of leaves), **ethylene** (ripens fruit and causes leaves to fall), **gibberellins** (stem elongation, induce growth in dormant seeds, buds, flowers).

Plant tropisms: **gravitropism** (a plant's growth in response to gravity—auxin, gibberellins), **phototropism** (plant's growth in response to light—auxin), **thigmotropism** (plant's growth in response to touch).

Photoperiodism: response of a plant to the change in length of days; remember **florigen** and **phytochrome.**

Driving force for H$_2$O movement in plants: transpiration is the major driving force that draws H_2O up the xylem because of the cohesive nature of water molecules that stick together. Osmosis and capillary action are minor contributors.

Driving force for sugar movement in plants: sugar, when created, is dumped into the phloem, creating a concentration gradient that draws water in, increasing the pressure that drives the sugar through the phloem.

Chapter 11

Human Physiology

INTRODUCTION

Welcome to the tour of the human body. During this tour, we will discuss how our bodies work. We will be making eight stops, lunch will not be served, and I don't want to hear any requests for bathroom breaks (although we will be learning about things of that nature). Buckle up—here we go.

CIRCULATORY SYSTEM

Heart

Welcome to the heart. The human heart is a four-chambered organ whose function is to circulate blood by rhythmic contraction. The heart pumps oxygenated blood from the left ventricle out to the aorta (see Figure 11.1). From there it travels through **arteries** to feed the organs, muscles, and other tissues of the body. The blood returns to the heart via the **veins**. The **vena cava system** of veins returns deoxygenated blood from the body to the lungs to pick up more oxygen. The blood reenters the heart into the right atrium, passes through to the right ventricle, and from there flows to the lungs to pick up more oxygen. At this point, the blood has made a complete cycle through the body. The blood is at its most oxygenated stage just after leaving the lungs as it enters the left side of the heart and travels into the aorta. The blood is in its least oxygenated stage as it reenters the right atrium of the heart.

Structure–function relationships come up often on the AP Biology exam, and the circulatory system provides a good example you could add to an essay on the topic. The left ventricle of the heart is the thickest and most muscular part of the heart and the most pressure is exerted on it. Why does this make sense functionally? Because the left ventricle is the portion of the heart that needs to pump the blood into the aorta and to the rest of the body. The left ventricle is structurally designed to fit its function. The right ventricle is smaller and less muscular because it only pumps blood a short distance to the lungs for reoxygenation.

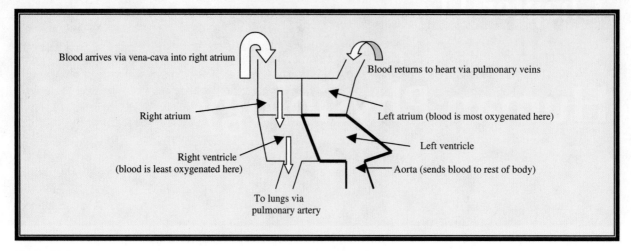

Figure 11.1
Oversimplified diagram of the heart and bloodflow.

Blood

If you look off to your right, you will see some of the blood and its components passing us now. If you look closely, you will see little *red blood cells* traveling in the bloodstream, which carry oxygen. Thanks to a molecule termed **hemoglobin,** the red blood cells are able to carry and deliver oxygen throughout the body to hardworking organs and tissues. Iron is a major component of hemoglobin. If you do not have enough iron in your diet, your ability to deliver oxygen via the blood can be compromised, and you may suffer from **anemia.**

Blood is able to flow so efficiently because it contains primarily water. The liquid portion of the blood, the **plasma,** contains minerals, hormones, antibodies, and nutritional materials. Another common cell seen in the bloodstream is the **platelet,** which is involved in the clotting of blood. You might ask "What are the white cells flowing around?" The white blood cells are the protection system for our body. We will be seeing those up close when we talk about the immune system.

The **lymphatic system** is worth a brief mention here because it is an important part of the circulatory system. When blood flows through the capillaries of the body, proteins and fluid leak out during the exchange. The lymphatic system functions as the route by which these poor lost souls find their way back into the bloodstream. The lymphatic system also functions as a protector for our body because of the presence of structures known as **lymph nodes,** which are full of white blood cells that live to fight infection. If your neck sometimes swells when you are *sick* with the flu, for instance, it is probably the multiplication of white blood cells in the lymph node.

Diseases of the Cardiovascular System

Two diseases that you should be familiar with for the exam are *hypertension* and *arteriosclerosis*. *Hypertension* is high blood pressure and is a major cause of strokes and heart attacks. *Arteriosclerosis* is a big word that means hardening of the arteries. These hardened arteries become narrower and are a prime risk factor for death by embolism—the breaking off of a piece of tissue that lodges in an artery, blocking the flow of blood to vital tissues.

RESPIRATORY SYSTEM

We are going to head down to the lungs now. Please stay close, because it will get a little loud in these windy tunnels. Air comes into the body through the mouth and the nose. We are currently in the nasal passages, and along with the air that came into the nose, we are being warmed and moistened in the *nasal cavity* before we head down toward the **pharynx** region, where the air and food passages cross. We will come back to this area again later on in the tour when we take the road that food uses to get from the mouth to the stomach. During inhalation, the air goes through a structure called the *glottis* into the **larynx** (human voicebox). From there the air moves into the **trachea,** which contains rings of cartilage that help it maintain its shape. The trachea is the tunnel that leads the air into the *thoracic cavity*. If you look outside your windows, you will notice some tiny arms waving at us as we go by. They are the **cilia,** which beat in rhythmical waves to carry foreign particles (like our tour bus) and mucus away from the lungs.

We are now at a fork in the road. Here the trachea divides into two separate tunnels: the two **bronchi,** which are also held open by cartilage rings, one going to the left lung, and one going to the right lung. The bronchus divides into smaller branches, which divide into even smaller branches, which divide into tunnels called **bronchioles.** These bronchioles branch repeatedly until they conclude as tiny air pockets containing **alveoli.**

In Figure 11.2, notice how thin the walls of the alveoli are. They are usually a single cell in thickness, are covered by a thin film of water, and are surrounded by a dense bed of capillaries. You might have questioned earlier exactly where the exchange of O_2

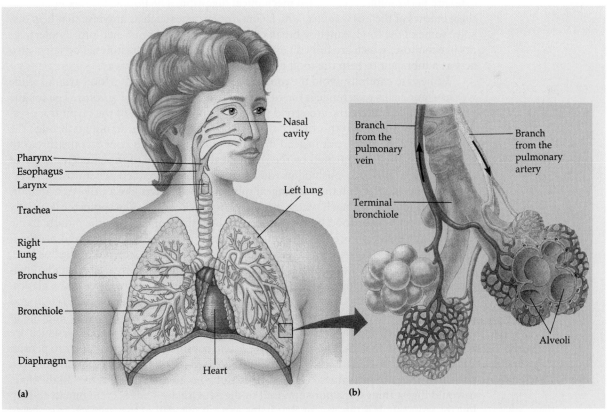

Figure 11.2
The human lungs, with closeup view of alveoli, bronchi, and bronchioles. (*From Biology, 4th ed., by Neil A. Campbell ©1987, 1990, 1993, 1996 by the Benjamin/Cummings Publishing Company, Inc. Reprinted by permission of Addison Wesley Longman Publishers, Inc.*)

and CO_2 actually occurs—this is the place. The alveoli are considered to be the primary functional unit of the lung. Oxygen enters the alveolus the same way we just did—it dissolves in the water lining of the wall and diffuses across the cells into the bloodstream. At the same time, the CO_2, which is carried by the blood, primarily in the form of bicarbonate (HCO_3^-), passes out of the blood in a similar manner. The O_2 moves easily into the bloodstream because it is moving down its concentration gradient. Once there, it travels with the blood to the rest of the body.

Before we move on to the digestive system, we should discuss the mechanism by which breathing actually occurs. The rib cage and the diaphragm play important roles in the breathing process. Inhalation causes the volume of the thoracic cavity to increase. As a result, the air pressure in the chest falls below that of the atmosphere, and air flows into the body. This is accompanied by a contraction of the ribcage muscles and the diaphragm, allowing for the increase in thoracic volume. After the air exchange occurs, the muscles relax, causing the diaphragm to move up against the lungs, reducing the thoracic volume. This causes the pressure in the lungs to exceed that of the atmosphere—driving the air containing CO_2 out of the body.

DIGESTIVE SYSTEM

Okay, folks, it is time to take the tour of the digestive system. Hang on tight—we are going to take a shortcut to the mouth as we are exhaled back through the system. Here we go: bronchioles, bronchi, trachea, larynx, pharynx, and mouth!

Here we sit in the oral cavity. This is where the digestion of food begins. Food is, of course, tasted and smelled in the oral cavity, and the teeth that help us chew (masticate) are performing a task called **mechanical digestion.** The liquid sloshing up against the windows of the bus is *saliva,* which contains enzymes such as **amylase** that help dissolve some of the food. Amylase breaks down the starches in our diet into simpler sugars like maltose, which are fully digested further down in the intestines. The saliva also acts as a lubricant to help the food move along the digestive pathway.

We need to carefully avoid the **tongue,** which functions to move food around while we chew and helps to arrange it into a ball that we swallow called a *bolus.* The tongue pushes the food toward the crossroad we visited during the tour of the respiratory system. You may notice that this time, as the swallowing occurs, we do not go through the glottis toward the lungs, but instead into the **esophagus,** which connects the throat to the stomach. The force created by the rhythmical contraction of the smooth muscle of the esophagus (currently pushing us toward the stomach) is called **peristalsis.**

After passing through the **esophageal sphincter,** which acts like a valve or trapdoor, food enters into the stomach where more digestion will occur. The sphincter is usually closed in order to keep food from returning back up the esophagus to the mouth. In the stomach, the digestion occurs by a churning action that mixes the food and breaks it into smaller pieces. Folks, I would recommend that you do not step out of the bus here, because the pH is way down in the 1.5–2.5 range, which provides *quite* an acidic environment. If you look closely along the edges of the stomach, you will see many glands. Some of these glands secrete gastric juice, composed of hydrochloric acid (HCl) and digestive enzymes, which helps in digestion and lowers the pH. The major enzyme of the stomach is **pepsin,** which breaks proteins down into smaller polypeptides, which are handled by the intestines. The glands here secrete **pepsinogen**—the precursor to pepsin. Pepsinogen is activated into pepsin by HCl. Pepsin is picky and will function only in a particular range of pH values. This is a good thing because if it were active all the time, it would digest things it is not supposed to digest. Other glands secrete mucus to help line the stomach. It is this mucus that helps prevent the wall of the stomach from being digested along with the food.

Now we move on to the *small intestine.* To get to the small intestine, we need to pass through the Panama Canal of the body: the **pyloric sphincter.** For those of you interested in useful AP exam trivia, the small intestine is where most of the digestion and absorption occur. The terrain is a bit different in this organ. The walls are arranged into folds and ridges, which have more waving structures, this time called *villi*, similar to what we saw in the respiratory tract. The walls in the small intestine contain something called a **brush border,** which is composed of a large amount of microvilli that increases the surface area of the small intestine to improve absorption efficiency. Digested nutrients absorbed in the small intestine are dumped into various veins that merge to form the hepatic portal vessel, which leads to the liver. The liver then gets first crack at the newly absorbed nutrients before they are sent to the rest of the body. As the food moves into the small intestine, it brings with it an acidity that promotes the secretion of numerous enzymes from the *pancreas* and the local glands. (*Important note to remember*: Hormones are vital to the turning on and off of the digestive glands.)

Those of you on the left side of the bus have a good view of the pancreatic duct as it expels **lipase, amylase, trypsin,** and **chymotrypsin.** Lipase is the major fat-digesting enzyme of the body. It receives some help in the handling of the fat from a product made in the liver called **bile.** Bile contains bile salts, phospholipids, cholesterol, and bile pigments such as bilirubin. The bile is stored in the *gallbladder* and is dumped into the small intestine upon the arrival of food. The bile salts help digest the fat by *emulsifying* it into small droplets contained in water. (Emulsification is a physical change—bile does not contain any enzymes.) Amylase continues the breakdown of carbohydrates into simpler sugars. *Maltase, lactase,* and *sucrase* break maltose, lactose, and sucrose, respectively, into monosaccharides. Trypsin and chymotrypsin work together to handle the digestion of the peptides in our diet. Trypsin cuts peptide bonds next to arginine and lysine; chymotrypsin cuts bonds by phenylalanine, tryptophan, and tyrosine. Like pepsin, these two proteolytic enzymes are secreted as inactive forms: trypsinogen and chymotrypsinogen. Trypsinogen is activated first to become trypsin, which, in turn, activates chymotrypsin. Some of you might ask "If the proteolytic enzymes only cut at certain sites, how do we finish digesting the proteins?" Trypsin and chymotrypsin are examples of *enteropeptidases*. It is the **exopeptidases** that complete the digestion of proteins by hydrolyzing all the amino acids of the remaining fragments.

After the small intestine comes the large intestine (colon). The two meet up in the lower right corner of the abdomen. The colon has three main parts: the *ascending, transverse,* and *descending colon.* There are two major functions for this part of the system–the first is to reabsorb water used in the digestive process. A failure to reabsorb enough water in this process will lead to diarrhea. A second function of the colon is the excretion of salts when their concentration in the blood is too high. The food enters the large intestine, travels up the ascending colon, across the transverse colon, down the descending colon into the rectum, where it is stored until it gets eliminated . . . but we don't need to go there. We've seen enough for now.

CONTROL OF THE INTERNAL ENVIRONMENT

The next stop on our tour is the kidney (see Figure 11.3 for an overview of the human excretory system). The kidneys lie on the posterior wall of the abdomen. The renal artery and vein bring blood to and from the kidney, respectively. Kidneys are divided into two major regions: an outer region called the **cortex,** and an inner region called the **medulla.** These two regions are full of **nephrons,** the functional units of the kidney. The medulla is divided into structures called *renal pyramids,* which dump urine into the *major and minor calyces.* From here, the urine is sent toward the *bladder* via the *ureter.* When contracted to urinate, the bladder sends the urine through the *urethra* to the outside world.

We've pulled the bus right up to one of over a million nephrons in each kidney. The nephron is composed of a *renal corpuscle, proximal tubule, loop of Henle, distal tubule,*

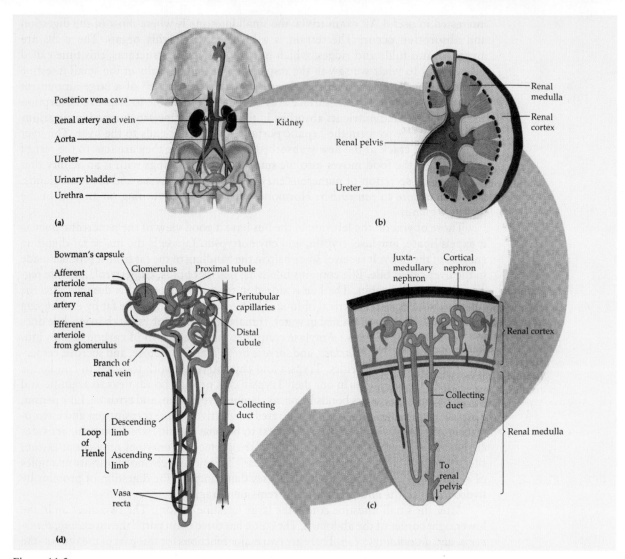

Figure 11.3
The human excretory system on four size scales. (a) The kidneys produce urine and regulate the composition of the blood. Urine is conveyed to the urinary bladder via the ureter and to the outside via the urethra. Branches of the aorta, the renal arteries convey blood to the kidneys; renal veins drain blood from the kidneys into the posterior vena cava. (b) Urine is formed in two distinct regions of the kidney: the outer renal cortex and inner renal medulla. It then drains into a central chamber, the renal pelvis, and into the ureters. (c) Excretory tubules (nephrons and collecting ducts) and associated blood vessels pack the cortex and medulla. The human kidney has about a million nephrons, representing about 80 km of tubules. Cortical nephrons are restricted mainly to the renal cortex. Juxtamedullary nephrons have a long, hairpinlike portion that extends into the renal medulla. Several nephrons empty into each collecting duct, which drains into the renal pelvis. (d) Each nephron consists of a glomerulus, or capillary cluster, surrounded by Bowman's capsule; a proximal tubule; a loop of Henle; and a distal tubule. Blood enters the glomerulus via an afferent arteriole and leaves via an efferent arteriole, which conveys it to peritubular capillaries surrounding the proximal and distal tubules, and to the vasa recta, capillaries surrounding the loop of Henle. The nephrons, collecting duct, and associated blood vessels produce urine from a filtrate (water and small solutes) forced into Bowman's capsule to the collecting duct; its chemical makeup is changed as substances pass via the interstitial fluid between the nephron and the surrounding capillaries. Filtrate processing continues in the collecting duct. The flow of blood in the vasa recta is opposite that of the filtrate in the loop of Henle (arrows). (*From Biology, 4th ed., by Neil A. Campbell ©1987, 1990, 1993, 1996 by the Benjamin/Cummings Publishing Company, Inc. Reprinted by permission of Addison Wesley Longman Publishers, Inc.*)

and *collecting duct system.* If you look closely, you will see that the renal corpuscle is made up of **glomerular capillaries** surrounded by *Bowman's capsule.*

Osmoregulation and Excretion

The blood that enters via the renal artery is sent to the various nephrons by the branching of the renal artery into smaller and smaller vessels that culminate in the capillaries of the glomerulus. The *blood pressure* is the force that leads to the movement of solutes such as water, urea, and salts into the lumen of Bowman's capsule from the glomerular capillaries. From here, the fluids pass down the proximal tubule, through the loop of Henle, and into the distal tubule, which dumps into the collecting duct. The various collecting ducts of the kidney collectively merge into the renal pelvis, which leads via the ureter to the bladder.

As I mentioned moments ago, fluid moves from the capillaries into the lumen of the nephron as a result of the force of blood pressure. During this process of **filtration,** the capillaries are able to let small particles through the pores of their endothelial linings, but large molecules such as proteins, platelets, and blood cells tend to remain in the vessel. As the filtrate progresses along the tubule, plasma solutes such as urea are added by the process of *secretion,* a selective process that helps to create a solute gradient. It is important to realize that much of what is dumped into the tubule originally is reabsorbed—nearly all the sugars, water, and organic nutrients. The combination of reabsorption and secretion help the nephron to control what gets released in the urine. The following chart outlines in detail what happens in the various parts of the nephron:

Proximal tubule	Reabsorbs 75 percent of NaCl and water of filtrate. Nutrients such as glucose and amino acids are reabsorbed unless their concentration is higher than the absorptive capacity. Glucose in urine is an indicator of diabetes, for this reason.
Descending loop of Henle	Freely permeable to H_2O but not NaCl. Assists in control of water and salt concentrations.
Ascending loop of Henle	Freely permeable to NaCl but not water. Assists in control of salt concentration.
Distal tubule	Regulates concentration of K^+ and NaCl. Helps control pH by reabsorbing HCO_3^- and secreting H^+.
Collecting duct	Determines how much salt is actually lost in urine. The osmotic gradient created in the earlier regions of the nephron allows the kidney control in the final concentration of the urine.

The body controls the concentration of the urine according to the needs of the system. When dehydrated, the body can excrete a small volume of hypertonic concentrated urine (little water in the urine; it is dark yellow). But, in times of excessive fluid, the body will excrete a large volume of hypotonic dilute urine to conserve the necessary salts (lots of water in the urine; it is clear). This is controlled by hormones and is discussed in more detail in a later section, but briefly: **ADH** (antidiuretic hormone) is released by the pituitary gland; it increases permeability of the collecting duct to water, leading to more concentrated urine. **Aldosterone,** released from the adrenal gland, acts on the distal tubules to cause the reabsorption of more Na^+ and water to increase blood volume and pressure.

Thermoregulation

A fairly constant body temperature is important for many living organisms. The process by which this temperature is maintained is known as **thermoregulation.** A major organ involved in thermoregulation is the skin, which also plays a role in excretion through sweating. Four major thermoregulatory processes are conduction, convection, evaporation, and radiation. **Conduction** is the process by which heat moves from a place of higher temperature to a place of lower temperature. For example, let's say that two people are sleeping in the same bed, and that person A is cold all the time. Person A would not make it through the night if it were not for this process. Since person B tends to be warmer than person A, person A takes advantage of conduction by pulling the heat from person B's body to hers. **Convection** is heat transfer caused by airflow. Thinking about my baseline warmth (similar to that of person B), if it were not for my air conditioner in the summer, I would probably not be here today to write this book. But we curse convection in the winter as the cold wind removes heat from our bodies, making it feel that much colder outside. **Evaporation** is the process by which water leaves our bodies in the form of water vapor: sweat. Why do humid days feel so much warmer than nonhumid days? Because humidity increases the amount of water in the air, decreasing the driving force for water to leave our bodies. **Radiation** is the loss of heat through ejection of electromagnetic waves.

Before moving on to the nervous system, I must mention two more terms: endotherm and ectotherm. An **endotherm** is an organism whose body temperature is not dramatically affected by the surrounding temperature. We humans are endothermic creatures. Sure, a cold day can feel really cold, but at least it does not dramatically lower the human body temperature. **Ectothermic animals** are organisms whose body temperatures *are* affected by the surrounding temperature. Fish, reptiles, and amphibians are good examples of ectothermic organisms.

NERVOUS SYSTEM

The nervous system is divided into two systems: the **central nervous system** (CNS) and the **peripheral nervous system** (PNS). The CNS contains the brain and the spinal cord. The PNS can be broken down into a sensory and a motor division. The sensory division carries information *to* the CNS while the motor division carries information *away* from the CNS. Another subdivision of the PNS is the **autonomic nervous system** (ANS). The CNS controls skeletal muscles and voluntary movement, while the ANS controls the involuntary activities of the body: smooth muscle, cardiac muscle, and glands. The ANS is divided into the **sympathetic** and **parasympathetic** divisions.

Before delving into the various divisions of the nervous system, it is important to look at the mechanics of nerve cell transmissions (see Figure 11.4). The functional unit of the nervous system is the *neuron.* Outside to the left of the bus is a nerve cell from the

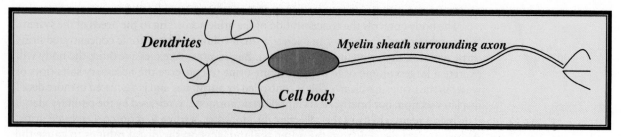

Figure 11.4
The components of nerve cell transmission. A neuron.

CNS. There are three main parts to a nerve cell: the cell body, the dendrite, and the axon. The **cell body** is the main body of the neuron. The **dendrite** is one of many short, branched processes of a neuron that help bring the nerve impulses toward the cell body. The **axons** are longer extensions that leave from a neuron and carry the impulse away from the cell body toward target cells. CNS nerve cells are **myelinated neurons,** which means that they have a layer of insulation around the axon, allowing for faster transmission. It is the cable Internet of the body.

The nerve cells can be divided into three main classes: sensory neurons, motor neurons, and interneurons. **Sensory neurons** receive and communicate information from the sensory environment. **Interneurons** function to make synaptic connections with other neurons. Located in the CNS, they tie together sensory input and motor output and are the intermediaries of the operation. **Motor neurons** take the commands of the CNS and put them into action as motor outputs. This relationship is the basis for the *reflex arc,* which is the basic unit of response in the CNS. A sensory neuron sends an impulse to the spinal cord, which is transmitted via a series of interneurons to a motor neuron whose impulse causes a muscular contraction such as a knee-jerk reaction.

Whoa! Did you see that spark zip past just now? That was a perfect example of a nerve impulse. The membranes of these neurons all around us are full of pumps and special gated ion channels that allow the cell to change its membrane potential in response to certain stimuli. The opening of sodium channels causes the potential to become less negative and the cell is **depolarized.** If the threshold potential is reached (electrical potential that, when reached, initiates an action potential), an action potential is triggered, which is the nerve impulse that we just saw zip by. Action potentials are quick changes in cell potential due to well-controlled opening and closing of ion channels. The cell also contains potassium channels that open slowly in response to depolarization. After a short period of time, the sodium gate closes, and potassium rushes out of the cell causing **repolarization** of the cell and lowering the potential back down to its initial level, stopping the transmission. Let's move further down this axon to see where this impulse is going.

Here we are at the end of the axon, sometimes called the **synaptic knob.** This is where calcium gates are opened in response to the changing potential, which causes vesicles to release substances called **neurotransmitters** into the synaptic gap between the axon and the target cell. These neurotransmitters diffuse across the gap, causing a new impulse in the target cell. Two of the most common neurotransmitters used in the body are acetylcholine and epinephrine. Substances called cholinesterases function to clear the neurotransmitters from the synaptic gap after an action potential by binding to the neurotransmitters and recycling them back to the neuron.

The ANS regulates involuntary activities in the body. As mentioned earlier, it is subdivided into the parasympathetic and sympathetic divisions. For the most part, the parasympathetic response is one that promotes energy conservation: slower heart rate, decreased blood pressure, and bronchial muscle and urinary bladder constriction. The sympathetic response is one that prepares us for "fight or flight"—increased heart rate, dilated bronchial muscles, increased blood pressure, and digestive slowdown.

The CNS consists of the brain and spinal cord. The brain is divided into various sections that control the different regions of our bodies (see Figure 11.5). The **cerebellum** is in charge of coordination and balance. The **medulla oblongata** is the control center for involuntary activities such as breathing. The **hypothalamus** is the thermostat and hunger-meter of the body, regulating temperature, hunger, and thirst. The **amygdala** is the portion of our brain that controls impulsive emotions and anger. The **cerebrum** is split into two "hemispheres" that connect to each other in the middle via the **corpus callosum.** Each half is divided into four different lobes, each specializing in various functions:

Lobes of the Brain and Their Functions

Frontal lobe	Speech, motor cortex
Parietal lobe	Speech, taste, reading, somatosensory
Occipital lobe	Vision
Temporal lobe	Hearing and smell

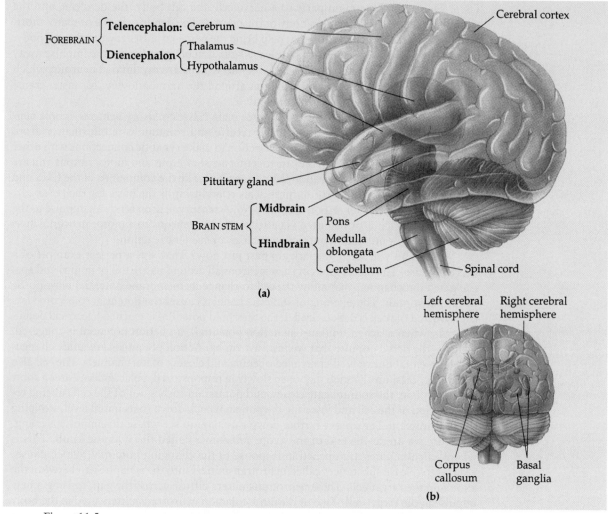

Figure 11.5

Major structures of the human brain. (a) Of the brain's three ancestral regions, the forebrain is massively developed and contains the most sophisticated integrating centers. One of its subdivisions, the telencephalon, consists mainly of the cerebrum (cerebral hemispheres), which extends over and around most other brain centers. The diencephalon contains the thalamus and hypothalamus. The other two ancestral regions, the midbrain and hindbrain, make up the brian stem. (b) This rear view shows the bilateral nature of the brain components. The cerebral hemispheres, corpus callosum (large fiber tracts connecting the hemispheres), and basal ganglia are parts of the telencephalon. (*From Biology, 4th ed., by Neil A. Campbell ©1987, 1990, 1993, 1996 by the Benjamin/Cummings Publishing Company, Inc. Reprinted by permission of Addison Wesley Longman Publishers, Inc.*)

MUSCULAR SYSTEM

Our tour of the muscle types of the body will include a look at the types of muscles and a quick demonstration of muscle contraction. There are three main types of muscle: **skeletal**, **smooth**, and **cardiac**:

1. Skeletal muscle. Muscle type that works when you do pushups, lift a book, and other voluntary activities. Skeletal muscle cells contain multiple nuclei. This muscle type has a *striated* appearance.

2. Smooth muscle. Involuntary muscle that contracts slowly and is controlled by the ANS. Smooth muscle cells contain a single nucleus. Found in arteries, walls of digestive tract, bladder, and elsewhere. Smooth muscle is not striated in appearance.

3. Cardiac muscle. Involuntary muscle of the heart. Cardiac muscle cells contain multiple nuclei. Cardiac muscle cells are striated in appearance.

Muscle cells are activated by the mechanism described earlier involving the action potentials and ion channels. When an action potential reaches a muscle cell, acetylcholine is released at the **neuromuscular junction**—the space between the motor neuron and the muscle cell. This neurotransmitter depolarizes the muscle cell and through a series of intracellular reactions causes the release of large amounts of stored calcium inside the cell, leading to muscle contraction. Muscle contraction stops when the calcium is taken back up by the sarcoplasmic reticulum of the cell.

Folks, we are going to be treated to a demonstration of skeletal muscle contraction. Skeletal muscle consists of fiber bundles, which are composed of myofibrils. What are myofibrils? Good question. They are structures that are made up of a combination of *myofilaments* called *thin filaments* (actin) and *thick filaments* (myosin).

Teacher: CT
"Know the functional units of the various systems discussed in this chapter. How the structure of these functional units relates to their function could be a nice essay."

The Actin-Myosin "Tango"

It takes two to tango, and myosin and actin are up to the task. Myosin is the lead partner of this dynamic duo and powers muscle contraction. Myosin, the heart of the thick fibers, has a "head" and a "tail." The tails of the numerous myosin molecules unite to form the "thick filament" seen in Figure 11.6. The heads of the myosin molecules stick out from the thick filament and serve as the contact point with the actin. The head can exist in two forms: low and high energy. A relaxed muscle begins with the myosin heads

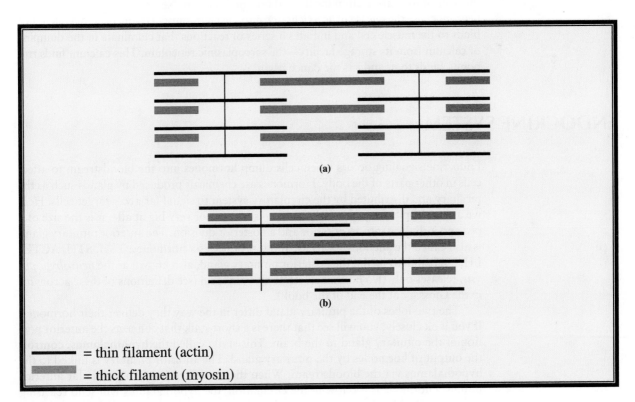

—— = thin filament (actin)

▭ = thick filament (myosin)

Figure 11.6
Actin–myosin interaction: (a) relaxed muscle; (b) contracted muscle.

in the low-energy form, attached to ATP. If the ATP is converted into ADP and phosphate, the myosin changes to the higher-energy form and is ready to dance. Myosin smoothly approaches its beloved partner, actin. When ready, the myosin and actin attach to each other, forming the "cross-bridge." As they get ready to slide, myosin loses its ADP and phosphate, releasing its energy, and causing it to elegantly tilt its head to one side . . . sliding the beautiful actin toward the center of the sarcomere (Figure 11.6b). The two part ways when myosin again binds to ATP, bringing us back to where we started (Figure 11.6a).

:::Applause:::

Control mechanisms are often mentioned on the AP Biology exam and make good essay material. It would be really annoying and awkward if our muscles were contracting all the time. So, it makes sense that there must be some way to control the contraction. Myosin is only able to dance with actin if a regulatory protein, known as **tropomyosin,** is not blocking the attachment site on actin. The key to the removal of tropomyosin is the presence of calcium ions. Tropomyosin is also bound to *another* regulatory protein known as troponin. Calcium causes these two to do their own little dance and shuffle away from the actin-myosin binding site. This allows the actin–myosin dance to occur, and muscle contraction to follow. When the calcium is gone, the dance is complete and the filaments separate from each other.

What causes this calcium release seen in muscle contraction? This brings us back to the neuromuscular junction mentioned not too long ago. Nervous impulses from motor neurons cause the release of acetylcholine into the neuromuscular junction. Acetylcholine binds to the muscle cell and initiates a series of reactions that culminate in the dumping of calcium from its storage facility—the sarcoplasmic reticulum. This calcium finds troponin, binds to it, and lets the dance begin.

ENDOCRINE SYSTEM

Endocrine signaling occurs when cells dump **hormones** into the bloodstream to affect cells in other parts of the body. Hormones are chemicals produced by glands such as the pituitary and distributed by the circulatory system to signal far away target cells. Here we are at the pituitary gland. As you can see, it is not very big at all—it is the size of a pea and is divided into an anterior and a posterior division. The anterior pituitary gland is also called the adenohypophysis, and it produces six hormones: **TSH, STH, ACTH, LH, FSH,** and **prolactin;** the posterior pituitary gland, also known as the *neurohypophysis,* releases only two hormones: **ADH** and **oxytocin** (see definitions of these acronyms in the Glossary at the end of the book).

The two lobes of the pituitary gland differ in the way they deliver their hormones. If you look closely, you will see that there is a short stalk that connects the anterior portion of the pituitary gland to the brain. This stalk, called the **hypothalamus,** controls the output of hormones by the pituitary gland. The anterior pituitary is linked to the hypothalamus via the bloodstream. When the concentration of a particular anterior pituitary hormone is too low in the circulation, the hypothalamus will send releasing factors via the bloodstream that stimulate the production of the needed hormone. The posterior lobe of the pituitary gland is different—it is derived from neural tissue. Because of this, its connection to the hypothalamus is neural. ADH and oxytocin are produced by the nerve cell bodies that are located in the hypothalamus, where they are packaged into secretory granules and sent down the axons to be stored in the posterior pituitary. The posterior pituitary gland releases the hormones when appropriately stimulated by a nervous impulse from the hypothalamus. The following is a breakdown of the hormones you should be familiar with for the exam:

Hormones of the *anterior pituitary* are

Teacher: CT
"Have a good general understanding of these hormones and their functions."

FSH	Follicle-stimulating hormone. A gonadotropin—stimulates activities of the testes and ovaries. In females, it induces the development of the ovarian follicle, which leads to the production and secretion of estrogen.
LH	Luteinizing hormone. A gonadotropin—stimulates ovulation and formation of corpus luteum. Stimulates synthesis of estrogen and progesterone.
TSH	Thyroid-stimulating hormone. Works to stimulate the synthesis and secretion of thyroid hormones, which in turn regulate the rate of metabolism in the body.
STH (or HGH)	Somatotropic hormone (or human growth hormone). Stimulates protein synthesis and general growth in the body.
ACTH	Stimulates the secretion of adrenal cortical hormones, which work to maintain electrolytic homeostasis in the body.
Prolactin	Controls lactogenesis—production of milk by the breasts. Decreases the synthesis and release of GnRH (gonadotropin-releasing hormone), inhibiting ovulation.

Hormones of the *posterior pituitary* are

ADH	Stimulates reabsorption of water by the collecting ducts of the nephron.
Oxytocin	Stimulates uterine contraction and milk ejection for breastfeeding.

Hormones of the *adrenal gland* are

Cortisol	Stress hormone released in response to physiological challenges.
Aldosterone	Regulates sodium concentration of body.
Epinephrine	Raises blood glucose level, increases metabolic activity—"fight or flight" hormone. Also known as *adrenaline*.

Pancreatic hormones are

Insulin	Secreted in response to high blood glucose levels to promote glycogen formation. Lowers blood sugar.
Glucagon	Stimulates conversion of glycogen into glucose. Raises blood sugar.

The *parathyroid* hormone (PTH): Increases serum concentration of Ca^{2+}, assisting in process of bone maintenance.

Sex hormones are

Progesterone	Regulates menstrual cycle and pregnancy.
Estrogen	Stimulates development of sex characteristics in women. Secreted in ovaries. Induces the release of LH, including the LH surge of the menstrual cycle. With progesterone, helps maintain the endometrium during pregnancy.

| Testosterone | Stimulates sex characteristics in men. Secreted in testes. |

Thyroid hormones are

| *Calcitonin* | Lowers blood calcium. Works antagonistically to PTH. |
| *Thyroxine* | Stimulates metabolic activities. |

The thymus hormone is *thymosin,* a hormone involved in the development of the T cells of the immune system.

The pineal gland hormone is *melatonin,* a hormone that is known to be involved in our biological rhythms (circadian). It is released at night.

How is the hormone secretion process of the body regulated? The two main types of regulation with which you should be familiar are negative feedback and positive feedback. **Negative feedback** occurs when a hormone acts to directly or indirectly inhibit further secretion of the hormone of interest. A good example of negative feedback involves insulin, which is secreted by the pancreas. When the blood glucose gets too high, the pancreas is stimulated to produce insulin, which causes cells to use more glucose. As a result of this activity, the blood glucose level declines, halting the production of insulin by the pancreas. **Positive feedback** occurs when a hormone acts to directly or indirectly cause increased secretion of the hormone. An example of this feedback mechanism is the LH surge that occurs prior to ovulation in females. Estrogen is released as a result of the action of FSH, and travels to the anterior pituitary to stimulate the release of LH, which acts on the ovaries to stimulate further secretion of estrogen.

Homeostasis

!

Teacher: NYC
"This could make a nice subquestion to an essay. Understand these relationships."

Homeostasis is the maintenance of balance. Hormones can work antagonistically to maintain homeostasis in the body. Two examples we will talk about are insulin-glucagon and calcitonin/PTH:

1. *Insulin/glucagon.* Both are hormones of the pancreas and have opposing effects on blood glucose. Let's say that you eat a nice sugary snack that pushes the blood glucose above its desired level. This results in the release of insulin from the pancreas to stimulate the uptake of glucose from the blood to the liver to be stored as glycogen. It also causes other cells of the body to take up glucose to be used for energy. Sometimes if you go a long time between meals, your blood glucose can dip *below* the desired level. This sets glucagon into action and causes its release from the pancreas. Glucagon acts on the liver to stimulate the removal of glycogen from storage to produce glucose to pump into the bloodstream. When the glucose level gets back to the appropriate level, glucagon release ceases. This back-and-forth dance works to keep the glucose concentration in our bodies relatively stable over time.

2. *Calcitonin/PTH.* Like glucose, the body has a desired calcium (Ca^{2+}) level it tries to maintain. If it drops below this level, PTH is released by the parathyroid gland and works to increase the amount of Ca^{2+} in circulation in three major ways: (a) release of Ca^{2+} from bones, (b) increased absorption of Ca^{2+} by the intestines, and (c) increased absorption of Ca^{2+} by the kidneys. If the blood Ca^{2+} level gets too high, the thyroid gland releases calcitonin, which pretty much performs the three *opposite* responses to PTH's work: (a) puts Ca^{2+} *into* bone, (b) decreased absorption of Ca^{2+} by the intestines, and (c) decreased absorption of Ca^{2+} by the kidneys

One last distinction I want to make before we move on is to touch on the difference between protein hormones and steroid hormones.

Protein hormones are too large to move into cells, and thus bind to receptors on the surface of cells. In response to the binding of a protein hormone, a change occurs in the receptor that leads to the activation of molecules inside the cell, called **second messengers,** which serve as intermediaries, activating other proteins and enzymes that carry out the mission. The second messenger to know for this exam is cyclic adenosine monophasphate (cAMP), involved in *numerous* signal cascade pathways. Protein hormones activate cAMP through a multi-step process that begins with protein–hormone activation of relay proteins such as **G proteins.** These proteins are able to directly activate a compound known as *adenyl cyclase,* which in turn produces cAMP.

Since we discussed regulatory mechanisms earlier, it is important to point out that there are G proteins that function to *inhibit* cAMP and work antagonistically to hormones that activate cAMP.

Steroid hormones are lipid-soluble molecules that pass through the cell membrane and combine with cytoplasmic proteins. These complexes pass through to the nucleus to interact with chromosomal proteins and directly affect transcription in the nucleus of cells.

IMMUNE SYSTEM

Teacher: CT
"Concentrate on the various cell types and the difference between specific and nonspecific defense."

What we are about to witness is an absolute treat. We just got word from the central office that the body we are touring has just received a **vaccination.** A vaccine is given to a patient in an effort to prime the immune system for a fight against a specific invader. This truly is a rare opportunity for us to see the immune system in action.

We have reentered the general bloodstream circulation of the body in an attempt to find some activity. While we are in transit, I will explain some basic immune system terms to you.

The immune system is a two-tiered defense mechanism. It consists of **nonspecific immunity** and **specific immunity.** Nonspecific immunity is exactly how it sounds—it is the nonspecific prevention of the entrance of invaders into the body. Saliva contains an enzyme called **lysozyme** that can kill germs before they have a chance to take hold. Lysozyme is also present in our tears, providing a nonspecific defense mechanism for our eyes. The skin covering the entire body is a nonspecific defense mechanism—it acts as a physical barrier to infection. The mucous lining of our trachea and lungs prevent bacteria from entering cells and actually assists in the expulsion of bacteria by ushering the bacteria up and out with a cough. Finally, remember how I told you that you did not want to get out of the bus in the stomach? That is also the case for bacteria—it is a dangerous place for them as well. The acidity of the stomach can wipe out a lot of potential invaders.

A nonspecific cellular defense mechanism is headed up by cells called **phagocytes.** These cells, *macrophages* and *neutrophils,* roam the body in search of bacteria and dead cells to engulf and clear away. Some assistance is offered to their cause by a protein molecule called **complement.** This protein makes sure that molecules to be cleared have some sort of identification displaying the need for phagocyte assistance. Complement coats these cells, stimulating phagocytes to ingest them. Cells involved in mechanisms that need cleanup assistance, such as platelets, have the ability to secrete chemicals that attract macrophages and neutrophils to places such as infection sites to help in the elimination of the foreign bacteria. They are nonspecific because they are not seeking out particular garbage . . . they are just looking for something to eat.

A prime example of a nonspecific cellular response is inflammation. Let's say that you pick up a tiny splinter as you grab a piece of wood. Within our tissues lie cells known as mast cells. These cells contain the signal **histamine** that calls in the cavalry and initiates the inflammation response. Entrance of the splinter damages these mast cells, causing them to release histamine, which migrates through the tissue toward the bloodstream. Histamine causes increased permeability and bloodflow to the injured tissue. The splinter also causes the release of signals that call in our nonspecific phagocytic cell friends, which come to the site of the injury to clear away any debris or pathogens within the tissue. The redness and warmth associated with inflammation occur because of the increase in bloodflow to the area that occurs in this process.

The immune system also contains defense mechanisms, which are quite specific. One such defense mechanism involves white blood cells, also called **lymphocytes.** There are two main flavors of lymphocytes: B cells and T cells. These cells are made in the bone marrow of the body and come from cells called **stem cells.** B cells mature in the bone marrow, and T cells mature in the thymus. The two main types of B cells are plasma cells and memory

B cells, and the two main types of T cells are helper T cells and cytotoxic T cells. Cytotoxic T cells are the main players involved in cell-mediated immunity. **Helper T cells,** which assist in the activation of B cells, recognize foreign antigens on the surface of phagocytic cells and bind to these cells. After binding, they multiply to produce a bunch of T cells that pump out chemical signals, which bring in the B cells to respond.

We have arrived at the vaccination site in the left arm, and things are definitely heating up here. An **antigen** is a molecule that is foreign to our bodies and causes our immune system to respond. What is occurring right now is the process called the **primary immune response.** Every B cell has a specific (randomly generated) antigen recognition site on its surface. B cells patrol the body looking for a particular invader. When a B cell meets and attaches to the appropriate antigen, it becomes activated and the B cell undergoes mitosis and differentiation into the two types of cells mentioned earlier: **plasma cells** and **memory cells.** The plasma cells are the factories that produce antibodies that function in the elimination of any cell containing on its surface the antigen that it has been summoned to kill. These antibodies, when released, bind to the antigens, immobilizing them and marking them for the macrophages to engulf and eliminate. This type of immune response falls under the category of **humoral immunity**—immunity involving antibodies.

Someone had a question? How do antibodies recognize the antigen they are designed for? Excellent question. Antibodies are protein molecules with two functional regions. One end is called the *fragment antigen binding region* or F_{ab}—this is what allows an antibody to recognize a specific antigen. It is designed by the plasma cell to have an F_{ab} that binds to the antigen of interest. The other end, which binds to effector cells, is called the F_c region. There are five types of F_c regions, one for each of the five types of antibodies: IgA, IgD, IgE, IgM, IgG. Each antibody type serves a slightly different function and is present in different areas of the body. When the antibodies bind to an antigen, complement gets involved, and this combination of antibodies and complement leads to the elimination of the invader.

I see a hand raised in the back. Yes, you are correct that I neglected to mention the memory cells. Very good. Memory cells contain the basis for the body's **secondary immune response** to invaders. Memory cells are stored instructions on how to handle a particular invader. When an invader returns to our body, the memory cells recognize it, produce antibodies in rapid succession, and eliminate the invader very quickly. The secondary immune response is much more efficient than the primary response. This is why few people are infected by sicknesses such as chickenpox after they have had them once already—their memory cells protect them. One important fact that does come up on the exam is that the secondary immune response produces a *much* larger concentration of antibodies than does the primary response.

Well, this is too good to be true . . . we just got word that this body was just recently infected by a virus. This will allow us to look at the other side of the immune response: **cell-mediated immunity.** This type of immunity involves *direct* cellular response to invasion as opposed to antibody-based defense. The virus that infected this poor sap made it past the humoral immunity system because it entered into the host's cells. This brings the cytotoxic T cells into play. The cells infected by the virus are forced to produce viral antigens, some of which show up on the surface of the cell. The cytotoxic T cells recognize these cells and wipe them out.

You might wonder how these T-cells avoid killing *all* cells. All the cells of the body, except for red blood cells, have on their surface antigens called **class I histocompatability antigens** [major histocompatibility complex (MHC)]. The MHC I antigens for each person are slightly different and the immune system accepts as friendly any cell that has the identical match for this antigen. Anything with a different MHC is foreign. This is the reason that organ donation often fails—the donor and the recipient have incompatible MHCs. There are also **class II histocompatibility antigens,** which are found on the surface of the immune cells of the body. These antigens play a role in the interaction between the cells of the immune system.

Well, I'd like to thank you for joining us on our tour of the body. We've seen a lot of things today and—whoa! We've been hit by something—and hit hard! Oh, dear. . . .

Folks, I don't want you to be alarmed, but it appears that our rival tour company has played a bit of a practical joke on us. Apparently as we were observing the B cell's inter-action with the vaccine, they attached a series of antigens and complement proteins to the surface of our bus. That loud noise you just heard was the sound of a macrophage taking us in . . . oh, dear, this is bad. Oh, no . . . folks, brace yourselves! The macrophage is about to ———— (transmission ended).

REVIEW QUESTIONS

1. In what form is most of the carbon dioxide of the body transported in the bloodstream?

    A. Complexed with hemoglobin
    B. As CO_2
    C. As HCO_3^-
    D. As CO
    E. As ferredoxin

For questions 2–5, use the following answer choices:

    A. LH
    B. FSH
    C. Estrogen
    D. Aldosterone
    E. TSH

2. This hormone is involved in the regulation of the body's metabolic rate.

3. This gonadotropin induces ovulation in females.

4. This hormone is involved in the regulation of the body's sodium concentration.

5. This hormone is vital to the maintenance of the endometrium during pregnancy.

6. The major emulsifier of fats in the digestive system is

    A. Lipase
    B. Amylase
    C. Trypsin
    D. Chymotrypsin
    E. Bile salts

7. Which cell type keeps humans from being infected by the same organism twice?

    A. Plasma cell
    B. Memory cell
    C. Macrophage
    D. Neutrophil
    E. Phagocyte

8. Which of the following muscle sites does not contain smooth muscle?

    A. Aorta
    B. Bladder
    C. Esophagus
    D. Quadriceps
    E. Renal artery

9. Which of the following is the functional unit of the respiratory system?

    A. Bronchus
    B. Bronchioles
    C. Alveolus
    D. Larynx
    E. Trachea

10. Which of the following regions of the brain controls breathing?

    A. Cerebellum
    B. Medulla
    C. Cerebrum
    D. Hypothalamus
    E. Amygdala

11. Which of the following is the major digestive enzyme of the stomach?

    A. Trypsin
    B. Chymotrypsin
    C. Pepsin
    D. Amylase
    E. Sucrase

12. Which of the following is *not* an example of nonspecific immunity?

    A. Lysosyme of saliva
    B. Skin
    C. Mucous lining of the lungs and trachea
    D. Lower pH of the stomach
    E. Plasma cells

13. Which of the following is true about the filtrate of the glomerulus.

    A. It contains little or no glucose.
    B. It contains little or no protein.
    C. It contains little or no sodium.
    D. It contains little or no urea.
    E. It contains little or no potassium.

14. Which of the following is not a hormone secreted by the anterior pituitary?

    A. TSH
    B. FSH
    C. ADH
    D. LH
    E. STH

15. Which of the following scenarios would be *least* likely to initiate a response from the sympathetic nervous system of the body?

    A. Getting called on in class by the teacher when you do not know the answer
    B. Seeing a cop while you are driving too fast on the highway
    C. Walking through the woods and seeing a bear in the near distance
    D. Waking from a midafternoon nap as sunlight strikes your face
    E. Hearing a dish break on the kitchen floor right behind you

ANSWERS AND EXPLANATIONS

1. **C**—Most of the carbon dioxide traveling through the bloodstream of the body is in the form of the bicarbonate ion—HCO_3. Oxygen is the one that likes to complex with hemoglobin. You should try to avoid answer choice D when possible; carbon monoxide is poisonous. Ferredoxin has nothing to do with the transport of CO_2—it is involved in photosynthesis.

2. **E**—The thyroid gland is important to the maintenance of the body's metabolic rate. An increase in TSH leads to an increase in thyroxin (thyroid hormone), which leads to an increase in the metabolic rate of the body.

3. **A**—The LH surge brought about by the combined effect of FSH and LH during the menstrual cycle leads to ovulation in females. This is essentially the release of an egg from its holding pattern in the ovary that allows it to move toward the uterus.

4. **D**—Aldosterone is released by the adrenal gland in an effort to maintain appropriate levels of sodium in the body. Its main site of action is the kidney.

5. **C**—Estrogen and progesterone work together to maintain the endometrium, which is the site of attachment for the growing fetus during pregnancy. Without these two hormones, the endometrium sloughs off and is lost.

6. **E**—Lipase is the major fat *digesting* enzyme of our body. Bile salts help digest the fat by *emulsifying* it into small droplets contained in water. Amylase digests carbohydrates. Trypsin and chymotrypsin break down polypeptides.

7. **B**—Memory cells are produced after the body first reacts to a foreign invader. The next time the body is exposed to that invader, it can respond a much more quickly and efficiently. Plasma cells produce the antibodies designed to wipe out the antigens. Macrophages and neutrophils are both types of phagocytes, which generally roam around looking for nonspecific garbage to pick up and destroy.

8. **D**—The quadriceps is the only muscle type on this list that is not a smooth muscle. It is a skeletal muscle involved in voluntary movements.

9. **C**—The alveolus is the functional unit of the lung. It is the true site of gas exchange during the respiratory process. The trachea, larynx, bronchus, and bronchioles are all tubes that the air passes through on its way to this exchange center.

10. **B**—The medulla oblongata controls the involuntary actions of the body, including respiration. The cerebellum controls balance, the cerebrum is in charge of higher thinking, the hypothalamus monitors the concentration of many substances throughout the body and determines when certain hormones of the pituitary should be released or cut down on. The amygdala controls our emotions and is associated with rage and anger.

11. **C.**

12. **E**—Plasma cells are designed to produce antibodies that combat a particular antigen. They are a great example of *specific* immunity. All the other answer choices are examples of nonspecific immunity.

13. **B**—The filtrate in the glomerulus contains almost everything that is in the blood plasma except for large proteins, which are unable to fit through the pores. Glucose does pass into the filtrate but is usually reabsorbed if present in normal concentrations in the blood. Sodium and potassium are always present in the filtrate. Urea is one of the major waste products that the excretory system is attempting to eliminate, so it is definitely present in the filtrate.

14. **C**—ADH is secreted by the posterior pituitary.

15. **D**—A sympathetic response is one that comes in a time of fight or flight. It is designed to get you ready for action. All the other choices are things that rev you up, whereas waking from a nap as sunlight strikes your face is a rather passive and tranquil experience that doesn't usually make you want to flee the scene or fight a great battle.

RAPID REVIEW

The following terms are important in this chapter:

Circulatory system: bloodflow—left side of heart → aorta → via arteries to organs, muscles → into the venous system of the body (vena cava) → right side of heart → lungs (pick up O_2) → left side of heart.

Respiratory pathway: nose/mouth → pharynx → larynx → trachea → thoracic cavity → bronchi → bronchioles → alveoli (functional unit of the lungs; this is where gas exchange occurs).

Digestive system: digestion begins in mouth, continues in the stomach, and completes in the intestines.

- *Amylase:* enzyme that breaks down starches in the diet (mouth and small intestine).
- *Pepsin:* main digestive enzyme of the stomach that breaks down proteins.
- *Lipase:* major fat digesting enzyme of the body (small intestine).
- *Trypsin* and *chymotrypsin:* major protein digesting endopeptidases of the small intestine.
- *Bile:* contains phospholipids, cholesterol, and **bile salts** (major emulsifier of fat).
- *Maltase, lactase,* and *sucrase:* carbohydrate digesting enzymes of the small intestines.
- Most of the digestion of food occurs in the small intestine.
- Function of the large intestine is to reabsorb water and to excrete salts.

Excretory system: kidneys lie on the posterior wall of the abdomen. Kidney is divided into the cortex and the **medulla.** The functional unit of the kidney is the **nephron.** The medulla is divided into renal pyramids, which dump the urine produced into the calyces

→ bladder via the ureter → out of the body via the urethra.

- Most of what is dumped into the glomerular system is reabsorbed—nearly all the sugar, vitamins, water, and nutrients. If sugar appears in urine it is because there is too much in the system (diabetes).

- Two important hormones of the excretory system are **ADH** (controls water absorption) and **aldosterone** (controls sodium reabsorption).

Muscular System

Muscle type	Striated?	Nuclei?	Control?	Where is it found?
Skeletal	Yes	Multiple	Voluntary	Biceps, triceps, etc.
Smooth	No	Single	Involuntary	Digestive tract, bladder, arteries.
Cardiac	Yes	Multiple	Involuntary	Heart.

Endocrine System

Anterior pituitary hormones

- *FSH:* stimulates ovaries and testes
- *LH:* stimulates ovulation, increased estrogen/progesterone release
- *TSH:* increased release of thyroid hormone
- *STH:* increased growth
- *ACTH:* increased secretion of adrenal hormones
- *Prolactin:* controls lactogenesis, decreased GnRH

Pancreatic hormones

- *Insulin:* increased glycogen formation
- *Glucagon:* increased glycogen breakdown

Parathyroid hormone (PTH): increased Ca^{2+} involved in bone maintenance

Posterior pituitary hormones

- ADH: stimulates H_2O reabsorption
- *Oxytocin:* stimulates uterine contraction and milk ejection

Adrenal gland hormones

- *Aldosterone:* regulates sodium concentration of body
- *Cortisol:* stress hormone

Sex hormones

- *Progesterone:* involved in menstrual cycle and pregnancy
- *Estrogen:* made in ovaries; increased release of LH (LH surge)
- *Testosterone:* (testes): develops male sex characteristics

Negative feedback: hormone acts to directly, or indirectly, inhibit further release of the hormone of interest.

Positive feedback: hormone acts to directly, or indirectly, cause increased secretion of the hormone.

Nervous system: divided into two parts: **central nervous system** (CNS) and **peripheral nervous system** (PNS).

- *CNS:* controls skeletal muscles and voluntary actions.

- *ANS:* controls involuntary activities of body.

- *ANS: sympathetic* (prepare for fight): increased heart rate, increased blood pressure, digestive slowdown, dilate bronchial muscles; *parasympathetic* (conserve energy): decreased heart rate, decreased blood pressure, bladder constriction.

- Brain: cerebellum (coordination/balance): **medulla** (involuntary actions such as breathing), **hypothalamus** (regulates hunger, thirst, temperature), **amygdala** (emotion control center).

Immune system

- *Nonspecific immunity:* nonspecific prevention of entrance of invaders into the body (skin, mucus).

- *Specific immunity:* Multilayered defense mechanism: (1) first line of defense—phagocytes, macrophage, neutrophils, complement; (2) second line of defense: B cells (plasma/memory), T cells (helper/cytotoxic).

- *Primary immune response:* antigen invader → B cell meets antigen → B cell differentiates into plasma cells and memory cells → plasma cells produce antibodies → antibodies eliminate antigen (**humoral immunity**).

- *Secondary immune response:* antigen invader → memory cells recognize antigen and pump out antibodies much quicker than primary response → antibodies eliminate antigen.

- *Cell-mediated immunity:* involves T cells and direct cellular response to invasion. Defense against **viruses.**

Chapter 12

Human Reproduction

INTRODUCTION

Finally, the racy chapter you have all been waiting for: human reproduction! The topic was introduced in Chapter 5 in our discussion of cell division—meiosis and mitosis. This chapter begins by examining the differences between the sexes. A discussion of reproductive anatomy and the wild ride that a sperm must take to fertilize the female egg will follow. Then we will review the formation of gametes and the development of the embryo. Embryology is excessively detailed and not something you should get hung up on. You will want to know some details about development, but like glycolysis, the big picture is key. The AP Biology exam is not an embryology exam. Finally, the chapter concludes with a discussion of hormones and their effects on the reproductive system.

SEX DIFFERENCES

What are the biologic differences between a man and a woman? For the purposes of *this* exam, you should keep in mind that one of the first distinctions is that boys have a Y chromosome in the nuclei of their cells, and girls do not. Another major difference lies in the sex characteristics. **Primary sex characteristics** are the internal structures that assist in the vital process of procreation. Among these are the testes, ovaries, and uterus. **Secondary sex characteristics** are the noticeable physical characteristics that differ between males and females such as facial hair, deepness of voice, breasts, and muscle distribution. These characteristics come into play as indicators of reproductive maturity to those of the opposite sex.

ANATOMY

Since we males tend to be a bit impatient, I will cover male anatomy first. The male sexual anatomy is designed for the delivery of sperm to the female reproductive system. Let's follow the journey of a sperm from the beginning to the end.

Sperm's "Wild Ride"

Here we stand in the **testis.** The male has two testes, located in a sac called the scrotum. This is the sperm factory—a portion of the testis called the **seminiferous tubules** is where the sperm are actually made. We return later to look at how these sperm are created. Notice in the other corner of the testis a structure called the **interstitial cells.** These are the structures that produce the hormones involved in the male reproductive system. Remember that the testis is the site of sperm and hormone production in the male reproductive system.

We are going to move along the production line to the **epididymis**—the coiled region that extends from the testes. The epididymis is where the sperm completes its maturation and waits until it is called on to do its duty. From here, when called into action, the sperm moves through a tunnel called the **vas deferens.** Each epididymis connects to the **urethra** via this tunnel. The urethra is the passageway through which the sperm exits during ejaculation. Yes . . . that is indeed the same tunnel that the urine uses to get out . . . good observation in back.

We're not done yet—let's look at some other important players in this process (see also Figure 12.1). I am sure you have all heard about the **prostate gland,** and how prostate cancer is currently one of the major cancers among men. But do you know what the prostate gland does? Here we are standing by this fine structure whose function in the male reproductive system is to add a basic (pH > 7) liquid to the mix to help neutralize any urine that may remain in the common urethral passage. It also helps to combat the acidity of the vaginal region of the female toward which the sperm is heading.

Follow me, everyone, more to see, more to see. . . . Here on either side of us are the structures called the **seminal vesicles.** These characters play an important role in the success of the sperm on its way to the female ovum. When the male ejaculates, the seminal vesicles dump fluids into the vas deferens to send along with the sperm. Think of the seminal vesicle as a convenience store. It provides three important goods to the sperm: energy by adding fructose; power to progress through the female reproductive system by adding *prostaglandins* (which stimulates uterine contraction); and mucus, which helps the sperm swim more effectively.

The sperm is ready to enter the female reproductive system at this point, but before we observe the sperm as it does so, I want to take a quick tour of the female reproductive structures.

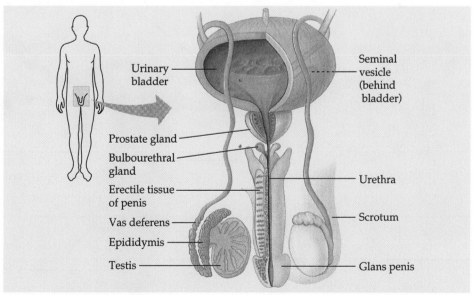

Figure 12.1
The human male urinary system. (*From Biology, 4th ed., by Neil A. Campbell ©1987, 1990, 1993, 1996 by the Benjamin/Cummings Publishing Company, Inc. Reprinted by permission of Addison Wesley Longman Publishers, Inc.*)

We begin in the **ovary**, the site of egg production. Females have two ovaries—one on either side of the body. The egg leaves the ovary before it has fully matured and enters a structure called the **oviduct**. The oviduct is also known as the **fallopian tube**—you may be more familiar with that term. Eggs travel through here from the ovary to the **uterus**. When fertilized by an incoming sperm in the fallopian tube, after several days' transit from the tube to the uterus, the egg usually attaches itself to the inner wall of the uterus, which is known as the **endometrium**. The uterus connects to the vaginal opening via a narrowed portion called the **cervix**. As we pass through the cervical area, we now find ourselves in the vagina, and it is here that the sperm enters the female reproductive system.

As the sperm enters, it must survive the different environment that the female body presents (see Figure 12.2). Its task is to find its way to the fallopian tube, where it must meet the egg and penetrate its outer surface to achieve successful fertilization. The sperm works its way through the vaginal region, up through the cervix, through the uterus, and into the fallopian tube. Here, if the timing is appropriate, there will be a willing and waiting egg that is hoping to meet with a sperm to produce a new diploid zygote. After successful fertilization, the new happy couple moves down to the uterus and builds a nice house along the endometrium where it will develop into an embryo and remain until it is ready to be born.

The Formation of Gametes

In Chapter 5, we discussed cell division and mentioned the process by which gametes are formed. Remember that the mechanics of gamete formation are different in women and men.

Oogenesis

In women, the process of gamete formation is called **oogenesis** (Figure 12.3), which begins quite early—as the embryo develops. Mitotic division turns fetal cells into cells known as

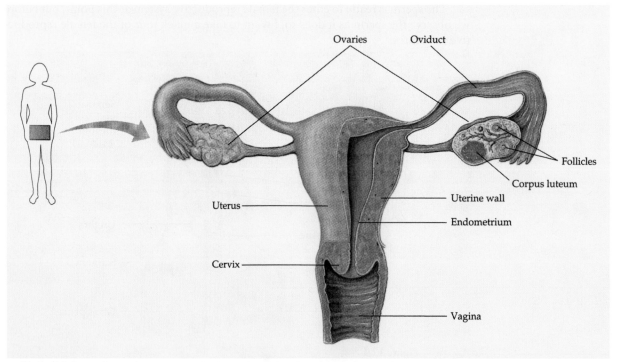

Figure 12.2
The human female reproductive system. (*From Biology, 4th ed., by Neil A. Campbell ©1987, 1990, 1993, 1996 by the Benjamin/Cummings Publishing Company, Inc. Reprinted by permission of Addison Wesley Longman Publishers, Inc.*)

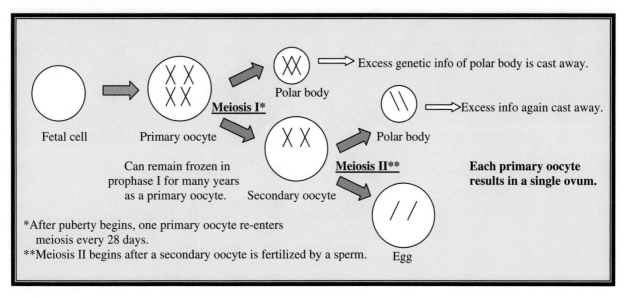

Figure 12.3
Oogenesis.

primary oocytes, which begin the process of meiosis and progress until prophase I; then the wait begins. The primary oocyte sits halted in prophase I until the host female enters puberty a number of years later. Most oocytes pass this time by watching movies, reading magazines, and exercising until they are called back into action. This is where the menstrual cycle begins. Each month, one of the primary oocytes frozen in the first act of meiosis returns to action and completes meiosis I. As we saw earlier, this phase produces a polar body, which has almost no cytoplasm and half of the genetic information of the parent cell, and a secondary oocyte, which has half the genetic information of the parent cell, but the majority of its cytoplasm. This asymmetrical meiosis occurs because the developing embryo will need enough food, organelles, mitochondria, and other such structures for proper development.

As the menstrual cycle continues, ovulation frees the secondary oocyte to travel into the fallopian tube to make its way down to the uterus. Fertilization usually occurs in the oviduct. If a successful fertilization occurs, the secondary oocyte enters meiosis II, again producing a polar body, as well as an egg that combines with the sperm to form an embryo.

What is important to remember about this oogenesis business?
1. It doesn't all happen at once for the ova. A primary oocyte could sit in the ovary for 40 years before completing the first stage of meiosis.
2. The beginning of each menstrual cycle causes a primary oocyte to resume meiosis I.
3. Oocytes undergo meiosis II only after fertilization with the sperm.

Spermatogenesis

For men, the process is less time-intensive. Let's face it, guys . . . we are lazy. Less effort is better. Less time makes sense and leaves us more time and energy to watch sports and play videogames. Males produce gametes through a process called spermatogenesis (Figure 12.4). Unlike females, males do not begin forming gametes until puberty. Spermatogenesis occurs in our old friends, the seminiferous tubules. Here, primary spermatocytes are produced by mitotic division. These primary spermatocytes undergo meiosis I to pro-

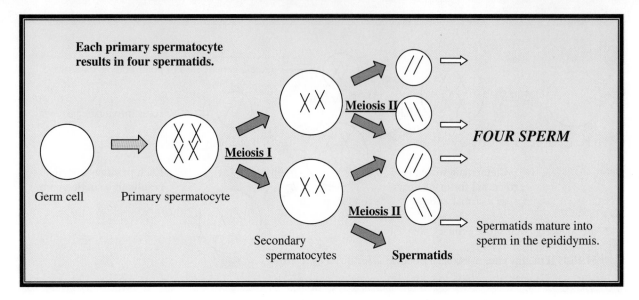

Each primary spermatocyte results in four spermatids.

Germ cell → Primary spermatocyte → **Meiosis I** → Secondary spermatocytes → **Meiosis II** → **Spermatids** → **FOUR SPERM**

Spermatids mature into sperm in the epididymis.

Figure 12.4
Spermatogenesis.

duce two **secondary spermatocytes,** which undergo meiosis II to produce four **spermatids,** which are immature sperm. After production, they enter the epididymis, where their waiting game begins and the maturation completes.

EMBRYONIC DEVELOPMENT

Embryology, the study of embyronic development, is a detailed and complex field. Fortunately, you are not taking an AP exam in embryology. Stick to the basics here, and do not let the complex details bog you down. Follow along with the pretty pictures, and the review questions at the end of this chapter will give you a good indication of the level of detail required for success on the embryology questions of the AP Biology exam.

Cleavage

Embryonic development begins as soon as the egg is fertilized to produce a diploid zygote ($2n$). This zygote then divides mitotically many times without increasing the embryo's overall size. During these **"cleavage"** divisions (Figure 12.5), cytoplasm is distributed unevenly to the daughter cells but genetic information is distributed equally. This disparity exists because different cells will later produce different final products and the uneven distribution of cytoplasm plays a role in that process.

These cleavage divisions take a while in humans. The first three divisions take 3 days to complete. After the fourth division, the one cell has become 16 cells and is now called a **morula.** As it undergoes its next round of cell divisions, fluid fills the center of the morula to create the hollow-looking structure known to embryologists as the **blastula.** The fluid-filled cavity in the blastula is known as the blastocoel. Up to this point, much of the dividing has occurred as the embryo moves toward the uterus through the fallopian tube. By the time the blastula has formed, it has reached the uterus and has implanted on the wall. The blastula contains two parts: an **inner cell mass,** which later becomes the embryo, and a **trophoblast,** which becomes the placenta for the developing fetus and aids in attachment to the endometrium. The trophoblast also produces *human chorionic gonadotropin* (HCG), which maintains the endometrium by ensuring the continued production of progesterone. The trophoblast later gives rise to the chorion, which we will discuss later.

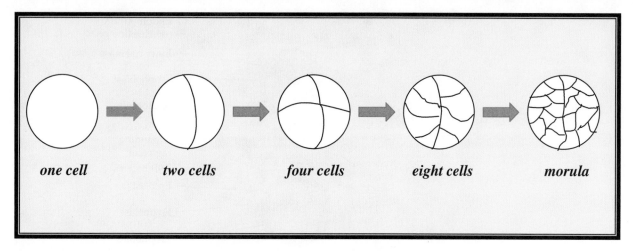

one cell   *two cells*   *four cells*   *eight cells*   *morula*

Figure 12.5
Embryonic cleavage divisons.

Gastrulation

Okay, here's where the discussion of embryology gets a little bit tricky. The next major stage of embryonic development after cleavage is **gastrulation** (also called *morphogenesis*). During gastrulation, cells separate into three primary layers called *germ layers*, which eventually give rise to the different tissues of an adult.

Let's look at this process in a bit more detail (see also Figure 12.6). After the embryo attaches to the uterine wall, the inner cell mass divides into two major cell masses: the **epiblast** and the **hypoblast**. The hypoblast gives rise to the yolk sac, which produces the embryo's first blood cells. In birds and reptiles, the yolk sac provides nutrients to the embryo. In humans, the **placenta** fills this role.

The epiblast develops into the three germ layers of the embryo: the **endoderm**, the **mesoderm**, and the **ectoderm**.

Lindsay: 12th grade "Take the time to learn these. Know which layer produces what. It's worth a point on the exam."

> *Endoderm:* inner germ layer; gives rise to the inner lining of the gut and the digestive system, liver, thyroid, lungs, and bladder
>
> *Mesoderm:* intermediate germ layer; gives rise to muscle, the circulatory system, reproductive system, excretory organs, bones, and connective tissues of the gut and exterior of the body
>
> *Ectoderm:* outer germ layer; gives rise to nervous system and skin, hair, and nails

The separation of cells into the three primary germ layers sets the stage for cellular differentiation by which different cells develop into different structures with different functions. As far as this specific structural and functional differentiation is concerned, keep your focus to the basic development of the nervous system.

The human nervous system derives primarily from the ectoderm, but the mesoderm contributes a structure known as the **notochord**, which serves to support the body. In vertebrates, this is present only in the embryo. The cells of the ectoderm that lie above the notochord form the **neural plate**, which becomes the **neural groove**, which eventually becomes the **neural tube**. This neural tube later gives rise to the central nervous system. One other term you should be familiar with in the development of the mammalian embryo is the **somite**, which gives rise to the muscles and vertebrae in mammals.

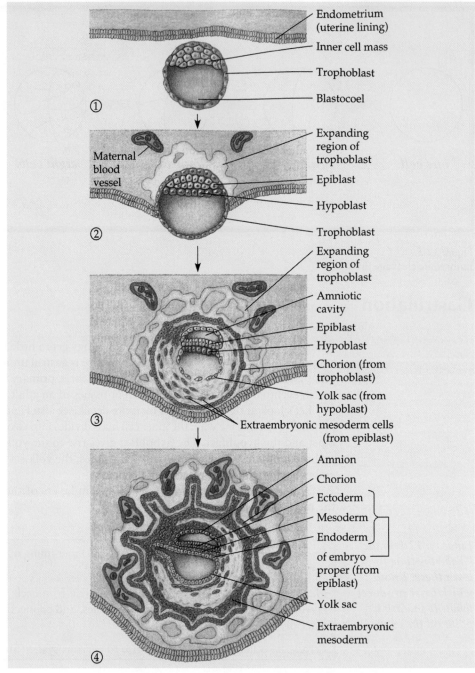

Figure 12.6
Components in the gastrulation process. (*From Biology, 4th ed., by Neil A. Campbell ©1987, 1990, 1993, 1996 by the Benjamin/Cummings Publishing Company, Inc. Reprinted by permission of Addison Wesley Longman Publishers, Inc.*)

There are four extraembryonic structures necessary to the healthy development of the embryo:

1. *Yolk sac:* derived from the hypoblast; site of early blood cell creation in humans. Source of nutrients for bird and reptile embryos.
2. *Chorion:* formed from the trophoblast; the outer membrane of the embryo. Site of implantation onto the endometrium. Contributes to formation of the **placenta** in mammals.

3. *Allantois:* mammalian waste transporter. Later it becomes the **umbilical cord,** which carries oxygen, food, and waste (CO_2) back and forth from placenta to embryo.
4. *Amnion:* formed from epiblast. Surrounds fluid-filled cushion that protects the developing embryo. Present in birds, lizards, and humans, to name only a few.

How Do Cells Know What to Do?

How do the various cells of the developing embryo differentiate into cells with different functions if they come from the same parent cell? As mentioned earlier, not every cell receives the same amount of cytoplasm during the cleavage divisions. It is thought that this asymmetric distribution of cytoplasm plays a role in the differentiation of the daughter cells. Cells containing different organelles or other cytoplasmic components are able to perform different functions. Two other factors, induction and homeotic genes, contribute to cellular differentiation.

Induction is the influence of one group of cells on the development of another, through physical contact or chemical signaling. Just in case you are asked to write an essay on induction, it is good to know a bit about the experiments of the German embryologist Hans Spemann. His experiments revealed that the notochord induces cells of the dorsal ectoderm to develop into the neural plate. When cells from the notochord of an embryo are transplanted to a different place near the ectoderm, the neural plate will develop in the new location. The cells from the notochord region act as "project directors," telling the ectoderm where to produce the neural tube and central nervous system.

Homeotic genes regulate or "direct" the body plan of organisms. For example, a fly's homeotic genes help determine how its segments will develop and which appendages should grow from each segment. Scientists interfering with the development of these poor creatures have found that mutations in these genes can lead to the production of too many wings, legs in the wrong place, and other unfortunate abnormalities. The DNA sequence of a homeotic gene that tells the cell where to put things is called the **homeobox.** It is similar from organism to organism and has been found to exist in a variety of organisms—birds, humans, fish, and frogs.

Factors in Cellular Differentiation	
Cytoplasmic distribution	Asymmetry contributes to differentiation since different areas have different amounts of cytoplasm, and thus perhaps different organelles and cytoplasmic structures.
Induction	One group of cells influences another group of cells through physical contact or chemical signaling.
Homeotic genes	Regulatory genes that determine how segments of an organism will develop.

THE INFLUENCE OF HORMONES

In Chapter 11 we discussed the hormones that will be included in the AP exam. A few of those play a critical role in human sexual development and reproduction. The hormones involved include LH, FSH, estrogen, progesterone, and testosterone. You do not need to know every detail, just the big picture. As proper etiquette requires, ladies first. Let's talk about the hormones involved in the female reproductive system.

Estrogen and progesterone continually circulate in the female bloodstream, and the hypothalamus monitors these levels to determine when to release certain hormones. For example, when the concentrations of estrogen and progesterone are low, the hypothalamus secretes GnRH, which travels to the anterior pituitary gland to induce the release of FSH and LH. (Just to remind you, FSH is follicle-stimulating hormone, LH is luteinizing hormone, and GnRH is gonadotropin-releasing hormone.) FSH induces the development of the follicle that surrounds the primary oocyte during its development. It also causes the follicle to release estrogen, which triggers the hypothalamus to dump more GnRH into the system. This GnRH acts on the anterior pituitary to produce the **LH surge** that initiates **ovulation**—the release of a secondary oocyte from the ovary.

This LH surge causes further release of estrogen and progesterone from the follicle, which has now become a structure called the corpus luteum, The corpus luteum induces the thickening of the endometrium, the site of future fertilized egg attachment. At this point in the cycle, the levels of estrogen and progesterone elevate enough to make the folks in charge in the hypothalamus cut off production of GnRH so that the LH and FSH levels drop back down. (This decrease in production, due to high levels in circulation, is called **negative feedback**.) Here lies a fork in the road for the female reproductive system. If fertilization has occurred in the fallopian tube, and if the embryo attaches successfully to the uterine wall, HCG will be secreted, which works to keep the corpus luteum alive. As a result, the levels of estrogen and progesterone remain high and keep the endometrium intact. If an embryo does not implant, production of estrogen or progesterone from the corpus luteum will cease, causing the destruction of the endometrium.

This cycle of hormonal activity is known as the *menstrual cycle*. A woman repeats this cycle, on average, every 28 days. This cycle is disrupted when a sperm fertilizes the egg, and successful implantation occurs. During pregnancy, hormone levels in the body change as a result of the presence of the corpus luteum, which maintains constant levels of estrogen and progesterone. This halts ovulation for the remainder of the pregnancy. If a sperm does not fertilize the egg, however, negative feedback reduces the levels of LH and FSH and leads to the deterioration of the endometrium, which then sloughs off during the menstrual cycle. When the levels of hormones circulating in the blood drop low enough, the cycle will begin again with the release of LH and FSH, culminating in the next menstrual cycle.

In males, as in females, GnRH causes the pituitary to release LH and FSH. The LH causes the continual production of testosterone in men. FSH and testosterone work together to assist the maturation of sperm produced during spermatogenesis. The baseline levels of testosterone are vital to the development of secondary sex characteristics in men.

REVIEW QUESTIONS

For questions 1–4, please use the following answer selections:

A. Blastula
B. Morula
C. Somite
D. Trophoblast
E. Hypoblast

1. After the fourth cleavage division, the one cell has become 16 cells and is now given this name.

2. Gives rise to the yolk sac of the developing embryo.

3. Forms the placenta for the developing fetus.

4. Gives rise to the muscles and vertebrae in mammals.

5. Which of the following is not a structure involved in the ejaculation of sperm?

A. Epididymis
B. Seminal vesicles
C. Cervix
D. Vas deferens
E. Interstitial cells

6. Which of the following hormones feeds back to cause the LH surge of the menstrual cycle?

A. Estrogen
B. Progesterone
C. FSH
D. LH
E. GnRH

7. Which of the following structures is *not* derived from the endoderm of a developing embryo?

    A. Liver
    B. Thyroid
    C. Heart
    D. Bladder
    E. Lungs

For questions 8–10, please use the following answer selections:

    A. FSH
    B. LH
    C. Testosterone
    D. Estrogen
    E. HCG

8. This hormone ultimately triggers ovulation in females.

9. This hormone is produced in the interstitial cells.

10. This hormone is responsible for maintenance of the corpus luteum during early pregnancy.

11. This hormone works with testosterone to assist in maturation of the sperm produced during spermatogenesis.

12. This structure is usually the site of fertilization in humans:

    A. Cervix
    B. Uterus
    C. Oviduct
    D. Ovary
    E. Endometrium

13. Which of the following explains the mechanism by which the neural plate develops in human embryos?

    A. Induced fit
    B. Homeotic gene determination
    C. Induction
    D. Negative feedback
    E. Gastrulation

ANSWERS AND EXPLANATIONS

1. B.

2. E.

3. D.

4. C.

5. C—The cervix is the only structure listed here that is a part of the female reproductive anatomy. The epididymis is the site of sperm storage and maturation while it awaits ejaculation. The seminal vesicles are the convenience store, providing the sperm with the necessary materials to survive its journey from ejaculation to fertilization. The vas deferens is the tunnel connecting the epididymis to the urethra. The interstitial cells are the cells that produce the hormones, such as testosterone, vital to male sexual function.

6. A—At the beginning of each menstrual cycle, GnRH is released from the hypothalamus and travels to the anterior pituitary gland to induce the release of FSH and LH. FSH induces the development of the follicle and causes the follicle to release estrogen, which triggers the hypothalamus to dump more GnRH into the system. This GnRH acts on the anterior pituitary to produce the LH surge, which triggers ovulation. The estrogen feeds back to the hypothalamus to induce the release of large amounts of LH that ultimately lead to increased production of even more estrogen.

7. C—The heart is part of the circulatory system and is derived from the mesoderm.

8. B.

9. C.

10. **E.**

11. **A.**

12. **C**—The oviduct, or the fallopian tube, is where fertilization normally occurs in humans. The uterus is where implantation and development of the embryo normally occur. The embryo usually implants on the wall of the uterus—the endometrium. The cervix is the narrow pathway from the uterus to the vaginal opening. The ovary is the site of egg production.

13. **C**—Remember induction. It is a concept loved by the AP Biology exam. *Induction* is the ability of cells to influence the development of other cells by either physical contact or chemical signals. *Homeotic genes* are genes that determine how segments of an organism will develop. *Induced fit* is how enzymes and substrates interact. *Gastrulation* is the separation of the cells of the developing embryo into the three primary germ layers. *Negative feedback* is the reduction in production of a substance due to high levels already present in circulation.

RAPID REVIEW

Quickly review the following terms:

Primary sex characteristics: internal structures that assist in reproduction

Secondary sex characteristics: physical characteristics that differ between men and women.

Male anatomy:

- Two **testes** enclosed in the *scrotum*—site of sperm production, which occurs in the **seminiferous tubules**
- **Interstitial cells,** which produce hormones involved in male reproduction
- **Epididymis,** a coiled region where sperm completes maturation
- **Vas deferens,** a tunnel that connects epididymis to urethra, where sperm and urine are ejected
- **Prostate gland,** a gland that adds basic liquid to neutralize urine acidity so that sperm don't die on the way out
- **Seminal vesicles,** which dump fluid into vas deferens to send with sperm, which helps sperm in various ways (adds energy, power, help with swimming)

Female anatomy:

- *Ovary:* site of egg production; eggs move from here through the *fallopian tube* (**oviduct**) to the **uterus,** which is where a fertilized egg attaches (called an **endometrium**)
- *Cervix:* narrowed opening that connects the uterus and vagina

Formation of gametes:

- *Oogenesis:* formation of eggs; starts in embryonic development and doesn't finish for each egg until that egg matures during a menstrual cycle (hence, an egg could wait 40 years to finish maturation).

- *Meiosis II:* oocytes undergo this process only after fertilization by a sperm in the oviduct.
- *Spermatogenesis:* one primary spermatocyte produces 4 spermatids, which mature in epididymis.

Embryology (the study of embryonic development):

- *Cleavage divisions:* mitotic divisions that occur as soon as zygote is formed; these divisions don't increase the overall size of the embryo; cytoplasm distributed unevenly, genetic information distributed evenly.
- *Morula:* what we call the embryo when it has become 16 cells.
- *Blastula:* what we call the embryo when it has become 32 cells—by this time it is implanted in endometrial wall.
- *Gastrulation:* cells separate into three germ layers, which give rise to different adult tissues.

    Endoderm: inner layer; lining of gut and digestive system, liver, lungs

    Mesoderm: intermediate layer; muscle, circulation, bones, reproductive system

    Ectoderm: outer layer; nervous system, skin, hair, nails.

Factors in cellular differentiation:

1. *Cytoplasmic distribution:* different amounts of cytoplasm signal different structures
2. *Induction:* ability of one group of cells to influence another
3. *Homeotic genes:* regulate or direct the body plan of organisms

Hormones play a major role in directing reproductive development and reproduction:

- *FSH:* creates follicle that surrounds the primary oocyte during development.
- *LH:* surge in this hormone triggers ovulation (release of secondary oocyte from ovary).
- *GnRH:* causes pituitary to release LH and FSH.
- *Progesterone and estrogen:* female sex hormones involved in reproduction.
- *Testosterone:* male sex hormone involved in reproduction.

Chapter 13

Behavioral Ecology and Ethology

INTRODUCTION

Teacher: CT
"This chapter has a lot of multiple choice-type questions in it. Learn the general concepts . . ."

Behavioral ecology and ethology both involve the study of animal behavior. **Behavioral ecology** focuses on the interaction between animals and their environments, and usually includes an evolutionary perspective. For example, a behavioral ecologist might ask "Why do two bird species that live in the same environment eat two different types of seeds?" **Ethology** is a narrower field, focused particularly on animal behavior and less on ecological analysis. Historically, ethology has involved a lot of experimental work, which has given us insight into the nature of animal minds.

This chapter introduces you to some of the basic terms and concepts used in behavioral ecology and ethology.

TYPES OF ANIMAL LEARNING

Associative learning is the process by which animals take one stimulus and associate it with another. Ivan Pavlov demonstrated **classical conditioning,** a type of associative learning, with dogs. As will come to be a pattern in this chapter, some poor animals were tampered with to help us understand an important biological principle. Pavlov taught dogs to anticipate the arrival of food with the sound of a bell. He hooked these dogs up to machines that measured salivation. He began the experiments by ringing a bell just moments before giving food to the dogs. Soon after this experiment began, the dogs were salivating at the sound of the bell before food was even brought into the room. They were conditioned to associate the noise of the bell with the impending arrival of food; one stimulus was substituted for another to evoke the same response.

A **fixed-action pattern** (FAP) is an innate, preprogrammed response to a stimulus. Once this action has begun, it will not stop until it has run its course. For example, male stickleback fish are programmed to attack any red-bellied fish that come into their territory. Males do not attack fish lacking this red coloration; it is specifically the color that stimulates aggressiveness. If fake fish with red bottoms are placed in water containing these stickleback fish, there's bound to be a fight! But if fake fish lacking a red bottom are dropped in, all is peaceful.

Habituation is the loss of responsiveness to unimportant stimuli. For example, as I started working on this book, I had just purchased a new fish tank for my office and was struck by how audible the sound of the tank's filter was. As I sit here typing tonight about 2 months later, I do not even hear the filter unless I *think* about it; I have become habituated to the noise. There are many examples of habituation in ethology. One classic example involves little ducklings that run for cover whenever birdlike objects fly overhead. If one were to torture these poor baby ducks and throw bird-shaped objects over their heads, in the beginning they would head for cover each time one flew past them, but over time as they learned that the fake birds did not represent any real danger, they would habituate to the mean trick and eventually not react at all. One side note is that ethologists who study wild animals usually have to habituate their study subjects to their presence before recording any behavioral data.

Imprinting is an innate behavior that is learned during a critical period early in life. For example, when geese are born, they imprint on motion that moves away from them, and they follow it around accepting it as their mother. This motion can be the baby's actual mother goose, it can be a human, or it can be an object. Once this imprint is made, it is irreversible. To this day, I believe that I was fed macaroni and cheese just moments after birth, which explains why I just can't get enough of the stuff . . . it's the only reason I can come up with. I was imprinted to this dish. If given an essay about behavioral ecology, and imprinting in particular, the work of Konrad Lorenz would be a nice addition to your response. He was a scientist who became the "mother" to a group of young geese. He made sure that he was around the baby geese as they hatched and spent the critical period with them creating that mother–baby goose bond. These geese proceeded to follow him around everywhere and didn't recognize their real mother as their own.

Insight learning is the ability to do something right the first time with no prior experience. It requires reasoning ability—the skill to look at a problem and come up with an appropriate solution.

Observational learning is the ability of an organism to learn how to do something by watching another individual do it first, even if they have never attempted it themselves. An example of this involves young chimpanzees in the Ivory Coast, who watch their mothers crack nuts with rock tools before learning the technique themselves.

Operant conditioning is a type of associative learning that is based on trial and error. This is different from classical conditioning because in operant conditioning the association is made between the animal's *own* behavior and a response. This is the type of conditioning that is important to the aposometrically colored organisms that we discuss in Chapter 14, on ecology. For example, a brightly colored lizard with a chemical defense mechanism (it can spray predators in an attempt to escape) relies on this type of conditioning for survival. The coloration pattern is there in the hope that the predator will, in a trial-and-error fashion, associate the coloration pattern with an uncomfortable chemical spraying experience that it had in the past. This association might make the predator think twice before attacking in the future and provide the prey with enough time to escape.

ANIMAL MOVEMENT

There are three major types of animal movement that you should familiarize yourself with for the AP exam: kinesis, migration, and taxis.

Kinesis. This is a seemingly random change in the *speed* of a movement in response to a stimulus. When an organism is in a place that it enjoys, it slows down, and when in a bad environment, it speeds up. Overall this leads to an organism spending more time in favorable environments. In Chapter 15, Laboratory Review, an example of kinesis involving pill bugs is discussed. These bugs prefer damp environments to dry ones, and when placed into a contraption that gives them the choice of being on the dry or damp side, they move quickly toward the damp side (where the speed of their movement slows).

Migration. This is a cyclic movement of animals over long distances according to the time of year. Birds are known to migrate south, where it is warmer, for the winter. It is amazing that these animals know where to go . . . I have a hard enough time getting to the post office without getting lost.

Taxis. These are cars taken by people who need transportation. Hmm . . . Actually, *taxis,* the biological term, is a reflex movement toward or away from a stimulus. I always think about summer evenings, sitting on the porch with the bug light near by, watching the poor little moths fly *right* into the darn thing because of the taxis response. They are drawn to the light at night (**phototaxis**).

Behave Yourselves, You Animals!

There are several typical behavior patterns that you should familiarize yourself with before the exam.

1. *Agonistic behavior.* Behavior that results from conflicts over resources. It often involves intimidation and submission. The battle is often a matter of who can put on the most threatening display to scare the other one into giving up, although the displays can also be quite subtle. Agonistic behaviors can involve food, mates, and territory, to name only a few. Participants in these displays do not tend to come away injured since most of these interactions are just that: displays.
2. *Altruistic behavior.* An *altruistic* action is one in which an organism does something to help another, even if it comes at its own expense. An example of this behavior involves bees. Worker bees are sterile, produce no offspring, and play the role of hive defenders, sacrificing their lives by stinging intruders that pose a threat to the queen bee. (Sounds to me that they need a better agent.) Another example involves vampire bats that vomit food for group mates that did not manage to find food.
3. *Coefficient of relatedness.* This statistic represents the average proportion of genes that two individuals have in common. Siblings have a coefficient of relatedness (COR) of 0.5 since they share 50 percent of their genes. This coefficient is an interesting statistic because it can be expected that an animal that has a high COR with another animal will be more likely to act in an altruistic manner toward that animal.
4. *Dominance hierarchies.* A dominance hierarchy among a group of individuals is a ranking of power amongst the members. The member with the most power is the "alpha" member. The second-in-command, the "beta" member, dominates everyone in the group except for the alpha. It pretty much rocks to be at the top of the dominance hierarchy because you have first dibs (choice) on *every*thing (food, mates, etc.). The dominance hierarchy is not necessarily permanent—there can always be some shuffling around. For example, in chimpanzees an alpha male can lose his alpha status and become subordinate to another chimp if power relationships change. One positive thing about these hierarchies is that since there is an order, known by all involved, it reduces the energy wasted and the risk from physical fighting for resources. Animals that know that they would be attacked if they took food before a higher-ranking individual wait until it is their turn to eat so as to avoid conflict. Keep in mind that dominance hierarchies are a characteristic of group-living animals.
5. *Foraging.* A word that describes the feeding behavior of an individual. This behavior is not as random as it may seem as animals tend to have something called a **search image** that directs them toward their potential meal. When searching for food, few fish look for a particular food; rather, they are looking for objects of a particular size that

seem to match the size of what they usually eat. This is a search image. In an aquarium at mealtime, if you watch the fish closely, you will see them zoom around taking food into their mouths as they swim. Unfortunately, sometimes the "food" they ingest is the bathroom output of another fish that happens to be the same size as the food and is floating nearby. Simply because the fish dropping is the appropriate size and fits the search image, the fish may take it into its mouth for a second before emphatically spitting it out.

6. *Inclusive fitness.* This term represents the overall ability of individuals to pass their genes on to the next generation. This includes their ability to pass their *own* genes through reproduction as well as the ability of their relatives to do the same. Reproduction by relatives is included because related individuals share many of the same genes. Therefore, helping relatives to increase the success of passage of their genes to the next generation increases the inclusive fitness of the helper. The concept of inclusive fitness can explain many cases of altruism in nature.

7. *Optimal foraging.* Natural selection favors animals that choose foraging strategies that take into account costs and benefits. For example, food that is rich in nutrients but far away may cost too much energy to be worth the extra trip. There are many potential costs to traveling a long distance for some food—the animal itself could be eaten on the way *to* the food, and the animal could expend more energy than it would gain *from* the food. You *know* that you have displayed optimal foraging behavior before. "Hey, do you want to go to Wendy's?" "Uhh . . . not really, it's a really long drive . . . let's go to Bill's Burgers down the road instead."

8. *Reciprocal altruism.* Why should individuals behave altruistically? One reason may be the hope that in the future, the companion will return the favor. A baboon may defend an unrelated companion in a fight, or perhaps a wolf will offer food to another wolf that shares no relation. Animals rarely display this behavior since it is limited to species with stable social groups that allow for exchanges of this nature. The bats described above represent a good example of reciprocal altruism.

9. *Territoriality.* Territorial individuals defend a physical geographic area against other individuals. This area is defended because of the benefits derived from it, which may include available mates, food resources, and high-quality breeding sites. An individual may defend a territory using scent marking, vocalizations that warn other individuals to stay away, or actual physical force against intruders. Animal species vary in their degree of territoriality (in fact, some species are *not* territorial), and both males and females may exhibit territorial behavior.

ANIMAL COMMUNICATION

Animals communicate in many ways. Communication need not always be vocal, and we will discuss the various communication mechanisms in this next section: visual, auditory, chemical, tactile, and electrical signals.

Chemical communication. Mammals and insects use chemical signals called **pheromones,** which in many species play a pivotal role in the mating game. Pheromones can be powerful enough to attract mates from miles away.

Visual communication. We mentioned a few visual communication examples earlier, such as agonistic displays. Another example of a visual display is a male peacock's feather splay, which announces his willingness to mate.

Auditory communication. This mode of communication involves the use of sound in the conveying of a message. In many parts of the United States, if one sits on one's porch on a summer night, one hears the song of night frogs and crickets. These noises are often made in an effort to attract mates.

Tactile communication. This mode of communication involves touch in the conveying of a message, and is often used as a greeting (handshake in humans). A major form of primate tactile communication involves grooming behavior.

Bees provide an example of communication that involves chemical, tactile, and auditory components. The beehive is a dark and crowded place, and when a worker bee returns after having found a good food source, how in the world is it going to get the attention of all of the co-workers? Unfortunately, intercom systems in hives are yet to be developed. What these bees do instead is a little dance; a dance in a tight circle accompanied by a certain wag signifies to the co-workers "hey guys . . . food source is *right* down the street." But if the food is farther away, the bee changes the dance to one that provides directional clues as well. The bee will instead perform a different combination of funky moves. Along with amusement, and a reason to point and laugh at the bee, this dance provides distance and directional information to the other workers and helps them find the far-away source. The ever so pleasant chemical component to this process is the regurgitation of the food source to show the other bees what kind of food they are chasing. Imagine if humans did that . . . "Dude, I just found the greatest burger place like 2 miles from here . . . (burp) here . . . try this burger . . . it's delightful!"

REVIEW QUESTIONS

1. When horses hear an unusual noise, they turn their ears toward the sound. This is an example of

   A. A fixed-action pattern
   B. Habituation
   C. Associative learning
   D. Imprinting
   E. Kinesis

2. Why do animal behaviorists have to account for a habituation period when undertaking an observational study?

   A. They have to make sure that the study animals do not imprint on them.
   B. They have to wait until their presence no longer affects the behavior of the animals.
   C. The animals need a period of time to learn to associate the observer with data collection.
   D. Before insight learning can be observed, the animals must practice.
   E. The animals must remain cautious of the observer at all times.

3. Which of the following is an example of an agonistic behavior?

   A. A subordinate chimpanzee grooms a dominant chimpanzee.
   B. Two lionesses share a fresh kill.
   C. A female wolf regurgitates food for her nieces and nephews.
   D. A blackbird approaches and takes the feeding position of another blackbird, causing it to fly away.

   E. Two fish in a stream pass each other without changing course.

4. In which of the following dyads do we expect *not* to see any altruistic behavior?

   A. Two sisters who are allies
   B. Two half-brothers
   C. Two individuals migrating in opposite directions
   D. Two group members who have frequent conflicts and reconciliations
   E. Two adolescents who are likely to eventually transfer into the same group

5. Which of the following is not a requirement for reciprocal altruism to occur?

   A. Ability to recognize the other individual
   B. Long lifespan
   C. Opportunity for multiple interactions
   D. Good long-term memory
   E. High coefficient of relatedness

6. A female tamarin monkey licks her wrists, rubs them together, and then rubs them against a nearby tree. What kind of communication is the probably an example of?

   A. Chemical
   B. Visual
   C. Auditory
   D. Territorial
   E. Tactile

For questions 7–10, please use the following answers:

A. Fixed-action pattern
B. Habituation
C. Imprinting
D. Associative learning
E. Operant conditioning

7. This type of learning is the lack of responsiveness to unimportant stimuli that do not provide appropriate feedback.

8. Trial-and-error learning important to animals displaying aposometric coloration.

9. Process by which animals associate one stimulus with another.

10. Innate behavior that is learned during a critical period in life.

ANSWERS AND EXPLANATIONS

1. **A**—This is a fixed-action pattern—an innate behavior that is a programmed response to a stimulus that appears to be carried out without any thought by the organisms involved.

2. **B**—If the scientist does not allow for a period of habituation, the behavioral observations will be inaccurate since the behavior of the animal will be altered by the presence of the scientist.

3. **D**—An agonistic behavior is a contest of intimidation and submission where the prize is a desired resource. In this case, the resource is the feeding position.

4. **C**—Altruistic behavior cannot be expected from two migrating individuals for a couple of reasons: (a) there is no reason for either of them to believe that they will see the other in the future, taking the "If I help them now, perhaps they will help me sometime in the future" element out of play; and (2) if they are migrating in different directions, it is reasonably likely that they are probably not related, which takes the "I'll help because it'll increase the chance more of my genes get passed along" element out of play.

5. **E**—Reciprocal altruism need not occur between related individuals.

6. **A.**

7. **B.**

8. **E.**

9. **D.**

10. **C.**

RAPID REVIEW

Quickly review the following terms:

Behavioral ecology: study of interaction between animals and their environments

Ethology: study of animal behavior

Types of Animal Learning

- *Fixed-action pattern:* preprogrammed response to a stimulus (stickleback fish)

- *Habituation:* loss of responsiveness to unimportant stimuli or stimuli that provide no feedback

- *Imprinting:* innate behavior learned during critical period early in life (baby ducks imprint to mama ducks)

- *Associative learning:* one stimulus is associated with another (classical conditioning—Pavlov)

- *Operant conditioning:* trial-and-error learning (aposometric predator training)

- *Insight learning:* ability to reason through a problem the first time through with no prior experience

- *Observational learning:* learning by watching someone else do it first

Types of Animal Movement

- *Kinesis:* change in the speed of movement in response to a stimulus. Organisms will move faster in bad environments and slower in good environments.

- *Migration:* cyclic movement of animals over long distances according to the time of year.

- *Taxis:* reflex movement toward or away from a stimulus.

Animal Behaviors

- *Agonistic behavior:* conflict behavior over access to a resource. Often a matter of which animal can mount the most threatening display and scare the other into submission.

- *Dominance hierarchies:* ranking of power amongst the members of a group; subject to change. Since members of the group know the order, less energy is wasted in conflicts over food and resources.

- *Territoriality:* defense of territory to keep others out.

- *Altruistic behavior:* action in which an organism helps another at its own expense.

- *Reciprocal altruism:* animals behave altruistically toward others who are *not* relatives, hoping that the favor will be returned sometime in the future.

- *Foraging:* feeding behavior of an individual. Animals have a search image that directs them to food.

- *Optimal foraging:* natural selection favors those who choose foraging strategies that maximize the differential between costs and benefits. If the effort involved in obtaining food outweighs the nutritive value of the food, forget about it.

- *Inclusive fitness:* the ability of individuals to pass their genes not only through the production of their own offspring, but also by providing aid to enable closely related individuals to produce offspring.

- *Coefficient of relatedness:* statistic that represents the average proportion of genes two individuals have in common. The higher the value, the more likely they would be to altruistically aid one another.

Communication

- *Chemical:* communication through the use of chemical signals, such as pheromones
- *Visual:* communication through the use of visual cues, such as the tail feather displays of peacocks
- *Auditory:* communication through the use of sound, such as the chirping of frogs in the summer
- *Tactile:* communication through the use of touch, such as a handshake in humans

Chapter 14

Ecology in Further Detail

INTRODUCTION

Ecology is the study of the interaction of organisms and their environments. This chapter covers the main concepts of ecology, including population growth, biotic potential, life-history "strategies," and predator–prey relationships. The chapter will also look at within-community and between-community (intra- and intercommunity) interactions. Finally we will talk about succession, trophic levels, energy pyramids, biomass pyramids, biomes, and biogeochemical cycles.

POPULATION ECOLOGY AND GROWTH

Like many fields of biology, the study of ecology contains hierarchies of classification. A **population** is a collection of individuals of the same species living in the same geographic area. A collection of populations of species in a geographic area is known as a **community.** An **ecosystem** consists of the individuals of the community and the environment in which it exists. Ecosystems can be subdivided into abiotic and biotic components: **biotic components** are the living organisms of the ecosystem, while **abiotic components** are the *non*living players in an ecosystem, such as weather and nutrients. Finally, the **biosphere** is the entire life-containing area of a planet—all communities and ecosystems.

Three more terms for you: (1) the **niche** of an organism, which consists of all the biotic and abiotic resources used by the organism; (2) **population density,** which describes how many individuals are in a certain area; and (3) **distribution,** which describes how populations are dispersed over that area. There are three main types of dispersion patterns that you should know (see also Figure 14.1):

1. *Clumped:* the individuals live in packs that are spaced out from each other, as in schools of fish or herds of cattle.
2. *Uniform:* the individuals are evenly spaced out across a geographic area, such as birds on a wire sitting above the highway—notice how evenly spaced out they are

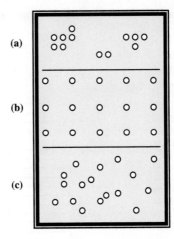

Figure 14.1
Distribution patterns: (a) clumped; (b) uniform; (c) random.

3. *Random:* the species are randomly distributed across a geographic area, such as a tree distribution in a forest.

Population ecology is the study of the size, distribution, and density of populations and how these populations change with time. It takes into account all the variables we have mentioned already and many more. The size of the population, symbolized N, indicates how many individuals of that species are in a given area. **Demographers** study the theory and statistics behind population growth and decline. The following is a list of demographic statistics you should be familiar with for the AP Biology exam:

Birth rate	Offspring produced per time period. Highest among those in the middle of the age spectrum.
Death rate	Number of deaths per time period. Highest among those at two extremes of the age spectrum.
Sex ratio	Proportion of males and females in a population.
Generation time	Time needed for individuals to reach reproductive maturity.
Age structure	Statistic that compares the relative number of individuals in the population from each age group (Figure 14.2).
Immigration rate	Rate at which individuals relocate into a given population.
Emigration rate	Rate at which individuals relocate out of a given population.

All these statistics together determine the size and growth rate of a given population. Obviously, a higher birth rate and a lower death rate will give a faster rate of population growth. A high female sex ratio could lead to an increase in the number of births in a population (more females to produce offspring). A short generation time allows offspring to be produced at a faster rate. An age structure that consists of more individuals in the middle of their reproductive years will grow at a faster rate than one weighted toward older people.

Population Growth and Size

Biotic potential is the maximum growth rate of a population given unlimited resources, unlimited space, and lack of competition or predators. This rate varies from species to

!

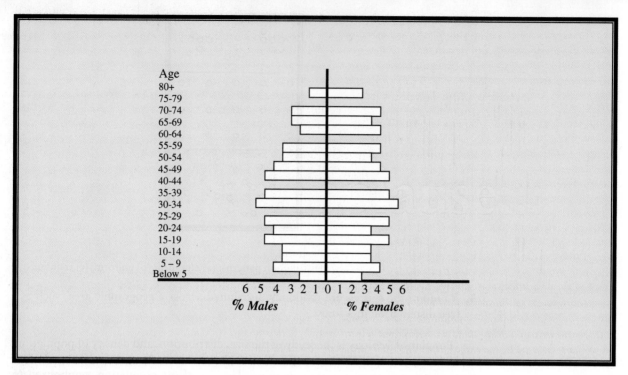

Figure 14.2
A typical age structure chart.

Liz (college freshman): "Know how to read these charts"

species. The **carrying capacity** is defined as the maximum number of individuals that a population can sustain in a given environment.

If biotic potential exists, then why isn't every inch of this planet covered with life? Because of the environment in which we live, numerous **limiting factors** exist that help control population sizes. A few examples of limiting factors include predators, diseases, food supplies, and waste produced by organisms. There are two broad categories of limiting factors:

Density-dependent factors. These limiting factors rear their ugly heads as the population approaches and/or passes the carrying capacity. Examples of density-dependent limiting factors include food supplies, which run low; waste products, which build up; and population-crowding-related diseases such as the bubonic plague, which just stink.

Density-independent factors. These limiting factors have nothing to do with the population size. Examples of density-independent limiting factors include floods, droughts, earthquakes, and other natural disasters and weather conditions.

There are two main types of population growth:

1. *Exponential growth.* the population grows at a rate that creates a J-shaped curve. The population grows as if there are no limitations as to how large it can get (biotic potential).
2. *Logistic growth.* the population grows at a rate that creates an S-shaped curve similar to the initial portion of Figure 14.3. Limiting factors are the culprits responsible for the S shape of the curve, putting a cap on the size to which the population can grow.

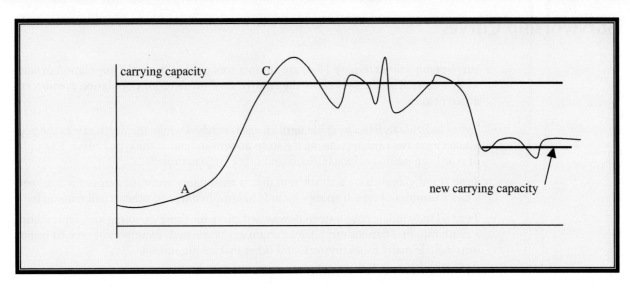

Figure 14.3
Carrying capacity.

Take a look at Figure 14.3. As the population size increases exponentially from point A to point C, there seem to be enough natural resources available to allow the growth rate to be quite high. At some point, however, natural resources, such as food, will start to run out. This will lead to competition between the members of the population for the scarce food. Whenever there is competition, there are winners and losers. Those who win survive, those who lose do not. Notice that the population rises above the carrying capacity. How can this be? This is short-lived, as the complications of being over-populated (lack of food, disease from increased population density, buildup of waste) will lead to a rise in the death rate that pushes the population back down to the carrying capacity or below. When it drops below the carrying capacity, resources replenish, allowing for an increase in the birth rate and decline in the death rate. What you are looking at in Figure 14.3 is the phenomenon known as a **population cycle.** Often, as seen in the figure, when the population size dips below the carrying capacity, it will later come back to the capacity and even surpass it. However, another possibility shown in this figure is that when a population dips below the carrying capacity due to some major change in the environment, when all is said and done, it may equilibrate at a new, lower carrying capacity.

LIFE HISTORY STRATEGIES

You should be familiar with two primary life history "strategies," which represent two extremes of the spectrum:

K-selected populations. Populations of a roughly constant size whose members have low reproductive rates. The offspring produced by these *K*-selected organisms require extensive postnatal care until they have sufficiently matured. Humans are a fine example of a *K*-selected population.

R-selected populations. Populations that experience rapid growth of the J-curve variety. The offspring produced by *R*-selected organisms are numerous, mature quite rapidly, and require very little postnatal care. These populations are also known as **opportunistic populations** and tend to show up when space in the region opens up as a result of some environmental change. The opportunistic population grows fast, reproduces quickly, and dies quickly as well. Bacteria are a good example of an *R*-selected population.

Survivorship Curves

Survivorship curves (Figure 14.4) are another tool used to study the population dynamics of species. These curves show the relative survival rates for population members of different ages.

Type I individuals live a long life until an age is reached where the death rate in the population increases rapidly, causing the steep downward end to the type I curve. Examples of type I organisms include humans and other large mammals.

Type II individuals have a death rate that is reasonably constant across the age spectrum. Examples of type II species include lizards, hydra, and other small mammals.

Type III individuals have a steep downward curve for those of young age, representing a death rate that flattens out once a certain age is reached. Examples of type III organisms include many fishes, oysters, and other marine organisms.

COMMUNITY AND SUCCESSION

Community

Most species exist within a community. Because they share a geographic home, they are bound to interact. These interactions range from positive to neutral to negative.

Forms of Species Interaction

1. *Symbiosis.* A symbiotic relationship is one between two different species that can be classified as one of three main types: commensalism, mutualism, or parasitism.

Del: 12th grade "Know for the multiple-choice questions. I should have...."

    A. *Commensalism.* One organism benefits while the other is unaffected. Commensalistic relationships are rare and examples are hard to find. Cattle egrets feast on insects that are aroused into flight by cattle grazing in the insects' habitat. The birds benefit because they get food, but the cattle do not appear to benefit at all.

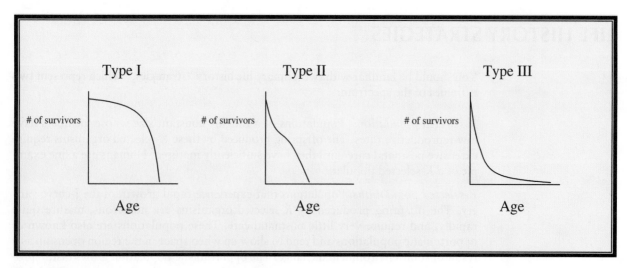

Figure 14.4
Survivorship curves.

B. *Mutualism.* Both organisms reap benefits from the interaction. One popular example of a mutualistic relationship is that between acacia trees and ants. The ants are able to feast on the yummy sugar produced by the trees, while the trees are protected by the ants' attack on any potentially harmful foreign insects. Another example involves a lichen, which is a collection of photosynthetic organisms (fungus and algae) living as one. The fungus component pulls its weight by helping to create an environment suitable for the lichen's survival, while the alga component supplies the food for the fungus. Without each other's contribution, they are doomed.

C. *Parasitism.* One organism benefits at the other's expense. A popular example of a parasitic relationship involves tapeworms, which live in the digestive tract of their hosts. They reap the benefits of the meals that their host consumes by stealing the nutrients and depriving the host of nutrition. Another less well-known example of parasitism involves myself and my younger brother's Playstation 2 console.

2. *Competition.* Both species are harmed by this kind of interaction. The two major forms of competition are intraspecific and interspecific competition. **Intraspecific competition** is *within*-species competition. This kind of competition occurs because members of the same species rely on the same valuable resources for survival. When resources become scarce, the most fit of the species will get more of the resource and survive. **Interspecific competition** is competition between different species.

3. *Predation.* This is one of the "negative" interactions seen in communities (well, for one half of those involved it is negative ☺.) One species, the predator, hunts another species, the prey. Not all prey give in to this without a fight, and the hunted may develop mechanisms to defend against predatory attack. The next section describes the various kinds of defense mechanisms developed by prey in an effort to survive.

Defense Mechanisms

Aposematic coloration is a very impressive-sounding name for this defense mechanism. Stated simply, it is warning coloration adopted by animals that possess a chemical defense mechanism. Predators have grown cautious of animals with bright color patterns due to past encounters in which prey of a certain coloration have sprayed the predator with a chemical defense. It is kind of like the blinking red light seen in cars with elaborate alarm systems. Burglars notice the red light and may think twice about attempting to steal that car because of the potential for encountering an alarm system.

In **batesian mimicry,** an animal that is harmless copies the appearance of an animal that is dangerous to trick predators. An example of this is a beetle whose colors closely resemble those of bees. Predators may fear that the beetle is a bee and avoid confrontation.

In **cryptic coloration,** those being hunted adopt a coloring scheme that allows them to blend in to the colors of the environment. It is like camouflage worn by army soldiers moving through the jungle. The more you look like the terrain, the harder you are to see.

Some animals have patterns called **deceptive markings,** which can cause a predator to think twice before attacking. For example, some insects may have colored designs on their wings that resemble large eyes, causing individuals to look more imposing than they truly are.

In **müllerian mimicry,** two species that are aposematically colored as an indicator of their chemical defense mechanisms mimic each other's color scheme in an effort to increase the speed with which their predators learn to avoid them. The more often predators see dangerous prey with this coloration, the faster the negative association is made.

Looking at Figure 14.5, we can see how the predator–prey dance plays out. When the prey population starts to decrease because of predation, there is a reactionary reduction in the predator population. Why does this happen? Because the predators run low on a valuable resource necessary to their survival—their prey. Notice in the figure that as the predator population declines, an increase in the population of the prey begins to

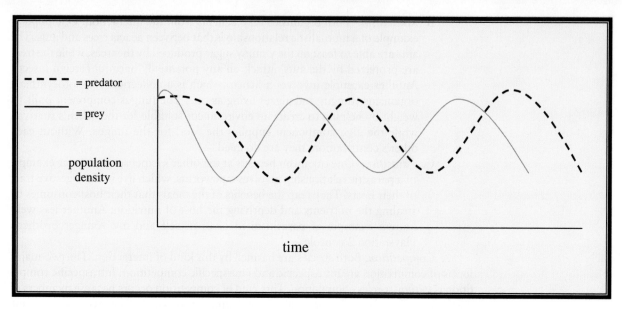

Figure 14.5
Predator–prey population curves.

appear, because more of those prey animals are able to survive and reproduce. As the prey population density rises, the predators again have enough food available to sustain a higher population, and their population density returns to a higher level again. Unless disturbed by a dramatic environmental change, this cyclical pattern continues.

Coevolution is mutual evolution between two species and is often seen in predator–prey relationships. For example, imagine that the hunted prey adapts a new character trait that allows it to better elude the predator. In order to survive, the predator must evolve so that it can catch its victim and eat.

Succession

When something happens to a community that causes a shift in the resources available to the local organisms, it sets the stage for the process of **succession**—the shift in the local composition of species in response to changes that occur over time. As time passes, the community goes through various stages until it arrives at a final stable stage called the **climax community.** Two major forms of succession you should know about are primary and secondary succession.

Primary succession occurs in an area that is devoid of life and contains no soil. A **pioneer species** (usually a small plant) able to survive in resource-poor conditions takes hold of a barren area such as a new volcanic island. The pioneer species does the grunt work, adding nutrients and other improvements to the once uninhabited volcanic rock until future species take over. As the plant species come and go, adding nutrients to the environment, animal species are drawn in by the presence of new plant life. These animals contribute to the development of the area with the addition of further organic matter (waste). This constant changing of the guard continues until the **climax community** is reached and a steady-state equilibrium is achieved. **Bare-rock succession** involves the attachment of lichen to rocks, followed by the step-by-step arrival of replacement species up to the climax community. **Pond succession** is kicked off when a shallow, water-filled hole is created. As time passes, animals arrive on the scene as the pioneer species deposit debris, encouraging the growth of vegetation on the pond floor. Over time, plants develop whose roots are underwater and whose leaves are above the water. As these plants begin to cover the entire area of the pond, the debris continues to build up, transforming the once-empty pond into a marsh. When enough trees fill into the area, the marsh becomes a swamp. If the conditions are appropriate, the swamp can eventually become a forest or grassland, completing the succession process. One trivia fact to take out of primary succession is that usually the pioneer species is an *R*-selected species, while the later species tend to be *K*-selected species.

Secondary succession occurs in an area that once had stable life, but has since been disturbed by some major force such as a forest fire. This type of succession is different from primary succession because there is already soil present on the terrain when the process begins.

TROPHIC LEVELS

As we discussed earlier, an ecosystem consists of the individuals of the community and the environment in which they exist. Organisms are classified as either producers or consumers. The producers of the world are the autotrophs mentioned in Chapter 4, Photosynthesis. The autotrophs you should recognize can be one of two types: photosynthetic or chemosynthetic autotrophs. **Photoautotrophs** (photosynthetic autotrophs) start the earth's food chain by converting the energy of light into the energy of life. **Chemoautotrophs** (chemosynthetic autotrophs) release energy through the movement of electrons in oxidation reactions.

The consumers of the world are the heterotrophs. They are able to obtain their energy only through consumption of other living things. One type of consumer is a **herbivore**, which feeds on plants for nourishment. Another consumer, the **carnivore**, obtains energy and nutrients through the consumption of other animals. A third consumer, the **decomposer**, or **detritivore**, obtains its energy through the consumption of dead animals and plants. Fungi, bacteria, earthworms, and vultures are prime examples of detritivores.

Here comes another hierarchy for you to remember. The distribution of energy on the planet can be subdivided into a hierarchy of energy levels called **trophic levels.** Take a look at the energy pyramid in Figure 14.6. The primary producers make up the first trophic level. The next trophic level consists of the organisms that consume the primary producers: the herbivores. These organisms are known as **primary consumers.** The primary consumers are consumed by the **secondary consumers,** or primary carnivores, that are the next trophic level. These primary carnivores are consumed by the secondary car-

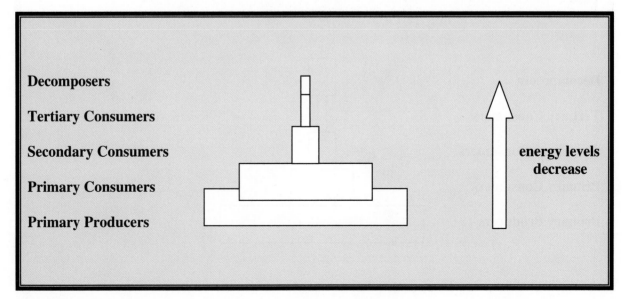

Figure 14.6
Energy pyramid, indicating increase in energy level.

nivores to create the next trophic level. This is an oversimplified yet important basic explanation of how trophic levels work. Usually there are only four or five trophic levels to a food chain because energy is lost from each level as it progresses higher.

The energy pyramid is not the only type of ecological pyramid that you might encounter on the AP Biology exam. Be familiar with a type of pyramid known as a *biomass pyramid* (Figure 14.7), which represents the cumulative weight of all of the members at a given trophic level. These pyramids tend to vary from one ecosystem to another. Like energy pyramids, the base of the biomass pyramid represents the primary producers, and tends to be the largest.

There is also the **pyramid of numbers,** which is based on the *number* of individuals at each level of the biomass chain. Each box in this pyramid represents the number of members of that level. The highest consumers in the chain tend to be quite large, resulting in a smaller number of those individuals spread out over an area.

Two more terms to cover before moving onto the biomes are **food chains** and **food webs.** A *food chain* is a hierarchical list of who snacks on who. For example, bugs are eaten by spiders, who are eaten by birds, who are eaten by cats. A *food web* provides more information than a food chain—it is not so cut and dry. Food webs recognize that, for example, bugs are eaten by more than only spiders. Food webs can be regarded as overlapping food chains that show all the various dietary relationships.

BIOMES

The various geographic regions of the earth that serve as hosts for ecosystems are known as **biomes.** Read through the following list so that you will be able to sprinkle some biome knowledge into an essay on ecological principles.

1. *Deserts.* The driest land biome of the group, **deserts** experience a wide range of temperature from day to night and exist on nearly every continent. Deserts that do not receive adequate rainfall will not have any vegetative life. However, plants such as cacti seem to have adjusted to desert life and have done quite nicely in this biome, given enough water. Much of the wildlife found in deserts is nocturnal, and con-

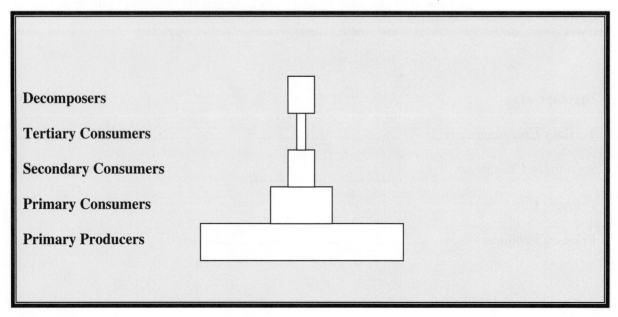

Figure 14.7
Biomass pyramid.

serves energy and water during the heat of the day. This biome shows the greatest daily fluctuation in temperature due to the fact that water moderates temperature.

2. *Savanna.* **Savanna** grasslands, which contain a spattering of trees, are found throughout South America, Australia, and Africa. Savanna soil tends to be low in nutrients, while temperatures tend to run high. Many of the grazing species of this planet (herbivores) make savannas their home.

3. *Taiga.* This biome, characterized by lengthy cold and wet winters, is found in Canada and has gymnosperms as its prominent plant life. **Taigas** contain coniferous forests (pine and other needle-bearing trees).

4. *Temperate deciduous forests.* A biome that is found in regions that experience cold winters where plant life is dormant, alternating with warm summers that provide enough moisture to keep large trees alive. **Temperate deciduous forests** can be seen in the northeastern United States, much of Europe, and eastern Asia.

5. *Temperate grasslands.* **Temperate grasslands** are found in regions with cold winters. The soil of this biome is considered to be among the most fertile of all. This biome receives less water than tropical savannas.

6. *Tropical forests.* Found all over the planet in South America, Africa, Australia, and Asia, **tropical forests** come in many shapes and sizes. Near the equator, they can be rainforests, whereas in lowland areas that have dry seasons, they tend to be dry forests. Rainforests consist primarily of tall trees that form a thick cover, which blocks the light from reaching the floor of the forest (where there is little growth). Tropical rainforests are known for their rapid recycling of nutrients and contain the greatest diversity of species.

7. *Tundras.* The **tundra** biome experiences extremely cold winters during which the ground freezes completely. The upper layer of the ground is able to thaw during the summer months, but the land directly underneath, called the **permafrost,** remains frozen throughout the year. This keeps plants from forming deep roots in this soil and dictates what type of plant life can survive. The plant life that tends to predominate is short shrubs or grasses that are able to withstand difficult conditions.

8. *Water biomes.* Both freshwater and marine **water biomes** occupy the majority of the surface of the earth.

The general distribution of biomes on the earth's surface is shown in Figure 14.8.

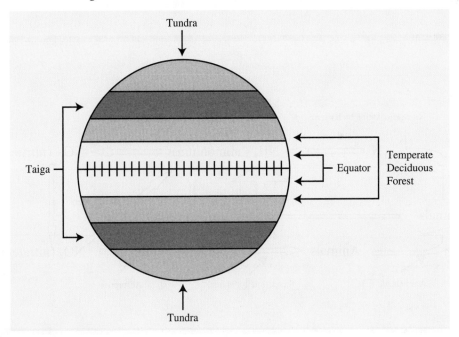

Figure 14.8
General distribution of biomes on the earth's surface. (The other land biomes such as grassland and desert are interspersed in temperate and tropical regions with water as the limiting factor.)

BIOGEOCHEMICAL CYCLES

One last topic to briefly cover before we wave good bye to ecology is that of **biogeochemical cycles**. These cycles represent the movement of elements, such as nitrogen and carbon, from organisms to the environment and back in a continuous cycle. Do not attempt to become a master of these cycles, but you should understand the basics.

Carbon cycle. Carbon is the building block of organic life. The **carbon cycle** begins when carbon is released to the atmosphere from volcanoes, aerobic respiration (CO_2), and the burning of fossil fuels (coal). Most of the carbon in the atmosphere is present in the form of CO_2. Plants contribute to the carbon cycle by taking in carbon and using it to perform photosynthetic reactions, and then incorporating it into their sugars. The carbon is ingested by animals, who send the carbon back to the atmosphere when they die.

Nitrogen cycle. Nitrogen is an element vital to plant growth. In the **nitrogen cycle** (Figure 14.9), plants have nitrogen to consume thanks to the existence of organisms that perform the thankless task of **nitrogen fixation**—the conversion of N_2 to NH_3 (ammonia). The only source of nitrogen for animals is the plants they consume. When these organisms die, their remains become a source of nitrogen for the remaining members of the environment. Bacteria and fungi (decomposers) chomp at these organisms and break down any nitrogen remains. The NH_3 in the environment is converted by bacteria into NO_3 (nitrate), and this NO_3 is taken up by plants and then eventually by animals to complete the nitrogen cycle. **Denitrification** is the process by which bacteria themselves use nitrates and release N_2 as a product.

Water cycle. The earth is covered in water. A considerable amount of this water evaporates each day and returns to the clouds. Eventually, this water is returned to the earth in the form of precipitation. This process is termed the **water cycle**.

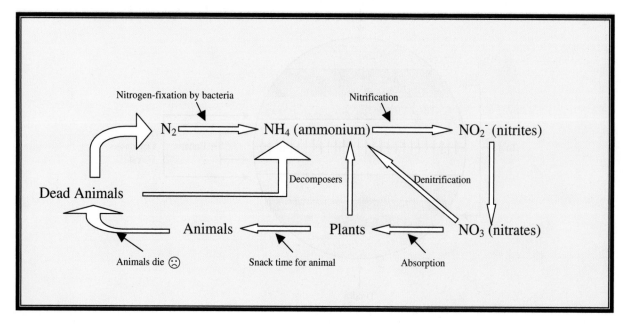

Figure 14.9
The nitrogen cycle.

REVIEW QUESTIONS

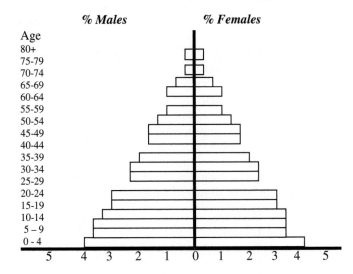

1. How would you describe the population depicted in the age structure graph shown here?

   A. Growing rapidly
   B. Growing slowly
   C. Not growing at all
   D. Experiencing slow negative growth
   E. Experiencing rapid negative growth

2. Carbon is most commonly present in the atmosphere in what form?

   A. CCl_4
   B. CO
   C. CO_2
   D. CH_2
   E. $C_6H_{12}O_6$

3. Which of the following is a density-dependent limiting factor?

   A. Flood
   B. Drought
   C. Earthquake
   D. Famine
   E. Tornado

4. The process by which bacteria themselves use the nitrate of the environment, releasing N_2 as a product, is called:

   A. Nitrogen fixation
   B. Abiotic fixation
   C. Denitrification
   D. Chemosynthetic autotrophism
   E. Nitrogen turnover

For question 5, please use the following curve:

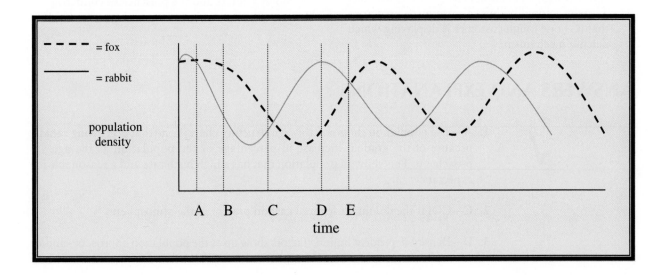

5. At what point on the graph does the decline in rabbit population act as a limiting factor to the survival of the foxes, leading to a decline in their population size?

   A. A
   B. B
   C. C
   D. D
   E. E

6. A collection of all the individuals of an area combined with the environment in which they exist is called a

   A. Population
   B. Community
   C. Ecosystem
   D. Biosphere
   E. Niche

For questions 7–10, please use the following answer choices:

   A. Aposometric coloration
   B. Batesian mimicry
   C. Müllerian mimicry
   D. Cryptic coloration
   E. Deceptive markings

7. A beetle that has the coloration of a yellow jacket is displaying which defense mechanism?

8. A moth whose body color matches that of the trees in which it lives is displaying which defense mechanism?

9. Two different lizard species, each possessing a particular chemical defense mechanism and share a similar body coloration is displaying which defense mechanism?

10. A lizard with a chemical defense mechanism has a bright-colored body as a warning to predators that it is one tough customer is displaying which defense mechanism?

11. Which of the following is *not* a characteristic of a K-selected population?

    A. Populations tend to be of a relatively constant size.
    B. Offspring produced tend to require extensive postnatal care.
    C. Primates are classified as *K*-selected organisms.
    D. Offspring are produced in large quantities.
    E. Offspring produced tend to be relatively large in size compared to *R*-selected offspring.

12. Which of the following would have the survivorship curve shown in the following diagram?

    A. Humans
    B. Lizards
    C. Oysters
    D. Fish
    E. Whales

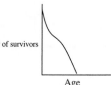

For questions 13–16, please use the following answer choices:

    A. Desert
    B. Taiga
    C. Tundra
    D. Tropical rain forest
    E. Deciduous forest

13. This biome is known for having the most diverse variety of species.

14. This biome is the driest of the land biomes.

15. The predominate plant life of this biome is short shrubs or grasses.

16. This biome is known for its cold, lengthy, and snowy winters and the presence of coniferous forests.

ANSWERS AND EXPLANATIONS

1. **A**—The population shown in this age structure chart is one that is growing rapidly because of the gradual increase in percentage of the population as the age approaches 0. This shows a population that has a high birth rate and a reasonable life expectancy.

2. **C**—CO_2 is the dominant form of carbon present in the atmosphere.

3. **D**—Density-dependent limiting factors show up as the population approaches and/or passes the carrying capacity. Examples of density-dependent limiting factors include

availability of food resources, waste buildup, and density-induced diseases. The other four choices are examples of density-independent factors, which affect population size regardless of how large or small it may be.

4. **C**—*Denitrification* is defined as the process by which bacteria themselves use nitrates and release nitrogen gas as a product. Bacteria also perform the necessary task of nitrogen fixation, which takes atmospheric nitrogen and converts it to NH_3. They later take this NH_3 and convert it to nitrate, which plants require for photosynthetic success. (*Abiotic fixation* and *nitrogen turnover* are terms that I made up because they sounded cool.) Chemiosynthetic autotrophs are the producers of the planet that produce energy through the movement of electrons in oxidation reactions.

5. **B**—At this point, the population of rabbits has declined to the point where the foxes are starting to feel the reduction in their food supply. The fox survival curve soon begins its decline that leads to the revival of the rabbits.

6. **C**—An *ecosystem* consists of all the individuals in the community and the environment in which they exist. A *population* is a collection of individuals of the same species living in the same area. A *community* is a collection of all the different populations of the various species in a geographic area. A *biosphere* is the collection of all the life-containing areas of the planet. A *niche* is a representation of all the biotic and abiotic resources a given organism requires.

7. **B**—An animal that is harmless copies the appearance of an animal that *is* dangerous as a defense mechanism to make predators think twice about attacking.

8. **D**—Cryptic coloration is the animal kingdom's version of army clothes. Their coloration matches that of their environment so they can blend in and hide from their predators.

9. **C**—Two species that are aposematically colored as an indicator of their chemical defense mechanism mimic each other's color scheme in an effort to increase the speed with which their predators learn to avoid them. This, of course, requires a predator that can learn based on experience.

10. **A**—This defense mechanism is warning coloration adopted by animals that possess a chemical defense mechanism. Ideally, predators will learn to avoid the species, helping the prey survive longer.

11. **D**—*K*-selected populations tend to be populations of a roughly constant size, with low reproductive rates and whose offspring require extensive postnatal care until they have sufficiently matured. *R*-selected populations tend to produce many offspring per birth.

12. **B**—Lizards follow a type II survivorship curve as illustrated in the diagram in review question 12. Humans (answer A) and whales (answer E) follow a type I curve, while oysters and fish (answers C and D) follow a type III survivorship curve.

13. **D.**

14. **A.**

15. **C.**

16. **B.**

RAPID REVIEW

The following terms are important in this chapter:

Population: collection of individuals of the same species living in the same geographic area

Community: collection of populations of species in a geographic area

Ecosystem: community + environment

Biosphere: communities + ecosystems of planet

Biotic components: living organisms of ecosystem

Abiotic components: nonliving players in ecosystem

Dispersion patterns: **clumped dispersion** (animals live in packs spaced from each other—cattle), **uniform distribution** (animals are evenly spaced out across an area, e.g., birds on a wire), **random distribution** (animals are randomly distributed across an area, e.g., trees in a forest).

Biotic potential: maximum growth rate for a population.

Carrying capacity: maximum number of individuals that a population can sustain in a given environment.

Limiting factors: factors that keep population size in check: **density-dependent** (food, waste, disease), **density-independent** (weather, natural disasters).

Population growth: **exponential growth** (J-shaped curve, unlimited growth), **logistic growth** (S-shaped curve, limited growth)

Life-history strategies: ***K*-selected populations** (constant size, low reproductive rate, extensive postnatal care—humans); ***R*-selected populations** (rapid growth, J-curve style, little postnatal care, reproduce quickly, die quickly—bacteria)

Survivorship curves: show survival rates for different aged members of a population:

- *Type I:* live long life, until age is reached where death rate increases rapidly—humans, large mammals

- *Type II:* constant death rate across the age spectrum—lizards, hydra, small mammals

- *Type III:* steep downward death rate for young individuals that flattens out at certain age—fish, oysters

---

Forms of Species Interaction

- *Parasitism:* one organism benefits at another's expense (tapeworms and humans).

- *Commensalism:* one organism benefits while the other is unaffected (cattle egrets and cattle).

- *Mutualism:* both organisms reap benefits from the interaction (acacia trees and ants, lichen)

- *Competition:* both species are harmed by the interaction (**intraspecific vs. interspecific**).

- *Predation:* one species, the predator, hunts the other, the prey.

Defense Mechanisms

- *Cryptic coloration:* coloring scheme that allows organism to blend into colors of environment.

- *Deceptive markings:* patterns that cause an animal to appear larger or more dangerous than it really is.

- *Aposematic coloration:* warning coloration adopted by animals that possess a chemical defense mechanism.

- *Batesian mimicry:* animal that is harmless copies the appearance of an animal that is dangerous.

- *Müllerian mimicry:* Two aposemetrically colored species have a similar coloration pattern.

Primary succession: occurs in area devoid of life that contains no soil. **Pioneer species** come in, add nutrients, and are replaced by future species, which attract animals to the area, thus adding more nutrients. Constant changing of guards until the **climax community** is reached and a steady-state equilibrium is achieved.

Secondary succession: occurs in area that once had stable life but was disturbed by major force (fire).

Biomes: The Special Facts

I recommend that you read the biome material in the chapter for more detail.

- *Desert:* driest land biome

- *Taiga:* lengthy cold, wet winters; lots of conifers

- *Temperate grasslands:* most fertile soil of all

- *Tundra:* permafrost, cold winters, short shrubs

- *Savanna:* grasslands, home to herbivores

- *Deciduous forest:* cold winters/warm summers

- *Tropical forest:* greatest diversity of species

- *Water biomes:* freshwater and marine biomes of earth

Trophic levels: hierarchy of energy levels on a planet. Energy level decreases from bottom to top (Figure 14.7). Primary producers (bottom) → primary consumers (herbivores) → secondary consumers → tertiary consumers → decomposers.

Chapter 15

Laboratory Review

INTRODUCTION

Teacher: CT
"This chapter will show up in the free answer section. Understand the experiments and how to set them up. Study the rapid review well."

In this chapter we take a look at each of the 12 lab experiments that are included in the AP Biology curriculum. We summarize the major objectives from each experiment and the major skills and conclusions that you should remember. This chapter is important, so do not just brush it aside if lab experiments are not your cup of tea. Of the four essay questions found on the AP exam each year, on average, one of the four deals with these very labs. They will, of course, not be an exact duplication of the experiment, but they will test your understanding of the objectives and main ideas that are discussed in this chapter. So, only a dozen experiments separate us and the end of the review material for this exam. Let's finish this thing because I'm tired!

LABORATORY EXPERIMENT 1: DIFFUSION AND OSMOSIS

This lab draws on information covered in Chapter 2, Cells. If you feel uncomfortable with this material, take a few moments to flip back to Chapter 2 and scan the information about diffusion, osmosis, and cell transport.

This experiment is designed to examine the diffusion rate of small particles through selectively permeable membranes—dialysis tubing is the membrane of choice for the experiment.

Basic Setup for Part 1 of the Experiment

In the first part of this experiment, the student places a solution of glucose and starch into a bag of dialysis tubing. This dialysis bag is then placed into a beaker of distilled water. Every experimenter's favorite step follows: the 30-minute wait. After this time, both the bag and the beaker are examined to determine if starch and/or glucose are present.

Results Obtained from Part 1

The bottom line is that glucose leaves the bag, the starch sits still, and water enters the bag. Why do they move in a particular direction? Because of the concentration gradients present at the beginning of the experiment. These two substances move *down* their concentration gradient from a place of higher concentration to a place of lower concentration. The starch does not move anywhere during all this activity. Why not? Because the starch molecules are too large for the pores of the dialysis bag. The water and glucose molecules are able to move through the bag because of their small size. The rate of diffusion is found to be inversely proportional to size. The smaller you are, the higher the rate of diffusion.

Basic Setup for Part 2 of the Experiment

The second part of the experiment deals with *osmosis,* the diffusion of water down its concentration gradient. It is important that you know the following three terms. **Isotonic** solutions have identical solute concentrations. A **hypertonic** solution has a solute concentration higher than that of a neighboring solution. A **hypotonic** solution is one that has a lower solute concentration than a neighboring solution.

The bottom line here is that osmosis moves water from hypotonic to hypertonic. In this part of the experiment, six dialysis bags are filled with various concentrations of solute, weighed, and then dropped into a beaker full of distilled water. Once again, good things come to those who wait, and after 30 minutes of waiting, the bags are removed and examined.

Results Obtained from Part 2

The higher the original concentration in the dialysis bag, the more water that moves into the bag during the 30 minutes. The water is driven from a region of lower solute concentration to a region with higher solute concentration (or from high water concentration to low water concentration). If a dialysis bag with a solute concentration of 0.2 M were placed into a beaker having a solute concentration of 0.4 M, the water would flow *out* of the dialysis bag and into the beaker.

Other Important Concepts from Experiment 1

Another concept covered in this experiment is **water potential** (ψ)—the force that drives water to move in a given direction. It is important to recognize that solute concentration is only one part of this potential force. Another factor is the pressure potential of the solution. Increased pressure potential translates into increased water movement. Water moves from a region of higher water potential to a region of lower water potential. Water will continue to pass from one region to another until the net water potential difference between the two regions has equilibrated at zero.

In this part of the experiment, each student takes four cut pieces of potato, weighs them, places them into a 250-mL beaker filled with water, and lets them sit overnight. The next day, the potatoes are removed and weighed to determine what changes have occurred. Potatoes placed in distilled water *absorbed* water. As the solute concentration of the solution in which the potatoes rested overnight is increased, the amount of water that flows *out* of the potatoes increases as well:

$$\psi = \psi_{solute} + \psi_{pressure}$$

The last main concept covered in this experiment is **plasmolysis**—the shriveling of the cytoplasm of a cell in response to loss of water to hypertonic surroundings. This causes the plasma membrane to separate from the cell wall. When a cell is placed into a hypertonic environment, diffusion of water from the cell to that environment will cause this plasmolytic response. Just remember that it can happen when a cell is hypotonic to its surroundings.

LABORATORY EXPERIMENT 2: ENZYME CATALYSIS

This experiment draws on information from Chapter 1, Chemistry. The experiment is designed to practice the calculation of the rate of enzyme-catalyzed reactions through the measurement of the products produced. In this particular experiment, the enzyme **catalase** is used to convert hydrogen peroxide to water and oxygen, and the products are measured to assist in the determination of the rate of reaction. If you do not feel comfortable with your knowledge of enzyme–substrate interactions, refer to Chapter 1 before continuing this section.

The Nitty Gritty about Experiment 2

The reaction of interest in this experiment is:

$$2H_2O_2 \rightarrow 2H_2O + O_2$$

This reaction does indeed occur without the assistance of catalase, but it occurs at a slow rate. When our friend catalase is added to the mix, the reaction occurs at a much faster clip. Take a look at the enzymatic activity curve in Figure 15.1. Notice the constant rate of reaction in the first 6 minutes of the experiment.

However, after the sixth minute, the rate slows, as if the enzyme has become tired. This is because as the reaction proceeds, the number of substrate molecules remaining declines, and this means that fewer enzyme–substrate interactions can occur.

When calculating the **rate of reaction**, it is the constant linear portion of the curve that matters. That is the accepted rate value for the enzyme. Do not attempt to factor in the slowing portion of the curve.

In this particular experiment, catalase is added to a beaker that holds H_2O_2 and is allowed to react for a certain period of time. After the reaction stops, the amount of H_2O_2 remaining in the beaker is measured. The information is then plotted on a curve similar to that in Figure 15.1 to determine the rate of reaction (the slope of the straight portion of the graph).

At one point during the experiment, acid is added to the beaker to stop the reaction. Why does this halt the reaction? Because it alters the pH, which has negative effects on the active sites of many enzymes, adversely affecting their ability to interact with substrates. Likewise, temperature has a negative effect on the rate of enzymatic activity

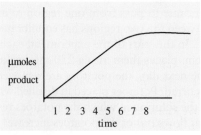

Figure 15.1
Enzyme–activity curve.

because if the temperature is too low, the kinetic energy of the system will be such that very few collisions between enzymes and substrates may occur. If the temperature is too high, the enzyme itself might actually be denatured and break apart.

Things to Take Away from Experiment 2

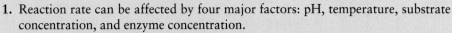

There are a few points to be gleaned from this experiment that reinforce concepts mentioned both in this chapter and in Chapter 1:

1. Reaction rate can be affected by four major factors: pH, temperature, substrate concentration, and enzyme concentration.
2. The "rate of reaction" can be found by measuring either the appearance of product or the disappearance of reactant. Either measure can provide insight into the effectiveness of an enzyme's presence.
3. When calculating the rate of reaction, if you are examining a graph, remember that the rate is actually the portion of the graph with a constant slope.
4. To design an experiment to test the rate of reaction of an enzyme compared to the speed of the normal reaction, first run the reaction *without* the enzyme, then run the reaction *with* the enzyme and compare the two rates of reaction.
5. To determine the ideal temperature (or pH) at which an enzyme functions, run the enzyme reaction at a series of different temperatures (or pH values) and measure the various reaction rates to compare the effects of temperature (or pH) on a particular enzyme. (*Remember:* Do not change both pH and temperature at the same time! Change them separately.)

LABORATORY EXPERIMENT 3: MITOSIS AND MEIOSIS

Part 1: Mitotic Cells of an Onion Root

This experiment draws on information found in Chapter 5, Cell Division. The first part focuses on mitosis and involves the examination of slides containing pictures of cells frozen at various stages of the cell cycle. The experimenter's task is to examine a collection of cells and determine the relative amount of time spent in each stage.

In Chapter 10, Plants, we briefly discuss the regions of plant growth that the mitotic slides of this experiment are reviewing: the apical meristem, the zone of elongation, and the zone of maturation. Take a quick look back there for a refresher if necessary. The onion root slide used in this experiment contains a nice fat apical meristem area that the student is able to scan to discover the various stages of the cell cycle.

So, how the heck are you supposed to estimate how much time a cell that is sitting dead on a slide in front of you spends in the relative stages of the cell cycle? That is a fair question. Your task is to measure how many cells in the slide are in each of the following stages: prophase, metaphase, anaphase, telophase, and interphase.

Say, for example, that you record your findings and get the following breakdown. Of 300 cells examined, 268 are in interphase, 15 are in prophase, 8 are in metaphase, 6 are in anaphase, and 3 were in telophase. This would mean that the cell spent 89.3 percent of its time in interphase. Don't look at me funny . . . here's how I got that number. I took the number of cells in interphase, 268, and divided that by the number of cells examined, 300. This provided a number of 0.893. I moved the decimal over two places to get the percentage, 89.3 percent. By the same logic, these data also show that 5 percent are in prophase, 2.7 percent in metaphase, 2 percent in anaphase, and 1 percent in telophase.

Part 2: Meiosis

The second part of the experiment takes a closer look at meiosis. Here, students take strands of beads of various colors, which represent chromosomes. In an attempt to visualize crossing over, the beads are arranged in a manner similar to the homologous chromosomes pictured in Figure 5.5–Crossover. Chromosome beads of the same color are considered to be sister chromatids. Chromosome beads of different colors are considered to be homologous chromosomes. Crossover, which occurs during prophase I of meiosis, is represented by switching some of the beads of one color to the chromosome with beads of another color, and vice versa. This part of the experiment is essentially playtime . . . you get to play with beads, move them around on the table, and see how the different stages of meiosis play out. Refer to Chapter 5 for an explanation of meiosis if you don't remember the various meiotic stages.

This experiment points out a couple of mechanical distinctions between meiosis and mitosis: (1) during prophase I of meiosis, crossover occurs and genetic recombination is seen—this does not happen during prophase of mitosis; and (2) during metaphase I of meiosis, the chromosome *pairs* line up at the metaphase plate, as opposed to line up of *individual* chromosomes seen in mitosis.

Part 3: Crossover in Sordaria

The title to this section makes *Sordaria* sound like some posh vacation spot in Europe. In reality it is a haploid ascomycete fungus. Anyway, the final portion of this experiment looks at the crossover that occurs during meiosis of this fungus and briefly discusses how recombination maps can be created using such data. Meiosis in *Sordaria* results in the formation of eight haploid **ascospores,** each of which can develop into a new haploid fungus.

Crossover in *Sordaria* can be observed by making hybrids between wild-type and mutant strains. Wild-type *Sordaria* have black ascospores, and mutants have different colored ascospores (e.g., tan). When mycelia of these two different strains come together and undergo meiosis, and if no crossover occurs, the asci that develop will contain four black and four tan ascospores in a 4:4 pattern. If crossover occurs, the ratio will change to either 2:2:2:2 or 2:4:2.

Chapter 6, Heredity, discusses gene maps constructed from crossover frequencies. You would construct the map here by first determining the percentage of asci that showed crossover. Referring to Figure 15.2, count the number of 2:2:2:2 and 2:4:2 asci, and divide that sum into the total number of offspring. This result multiplied by 100 will give the crossover percentage. This number can then be used to determine how far away the gene is from the centromere. The crossover percentage is divided by 2 to determine this distance because a crossover involves only half the spores in each ascus.

LABORATORY EXPERIMENT 4: PLANT PIGMENTS AND PHOTOSYNTHESIS

This experiment draws on material from Chapter 4, Photosynthesis. The general objective here is to use chromatography to separate plant pigments and to measure the rate of photosynthesis in chloroplasts.

Part 1: Separation by Chromatography

Before diving into this experiment, let's briefly review how paper chromatography works in relation to this lab. An extract from the leaves is dabbed onto a piece of paper, which

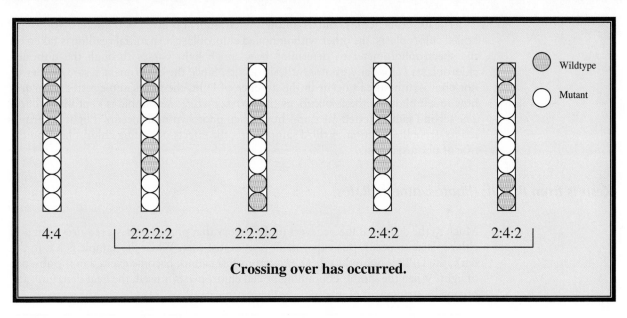

4:4 2:2:2:2 2:2:2:2 2:4:2 2:4:2

Crossing over has occurred.

Wildtype

Mutant

Figure 15.2
Crossover patterns in *Sordaria*.

is hung in such a way that its bottom tip is touching the chromatography solvent. As time passes, this solvent, by way of capillary action, runs up the paper and like a public bus, carries any dissolved substances along for the ride. The rate with which a pigment migrates up the paper depends on two variables: how well it dissolves into the chromatography solvent and how well it can form bonds with the cellulose in the paper. Faster pigments dissolve more and bond less to the paper. Slower pigments dissolve less and bond more to the paper.

Of the plant pigments studied in this lab, the order of migration rate is as follows:

Beta carotene > xanthophyll > chlorophyll a > chlorophyll b

The last concept to take from part 1 of this experiment is R_f—a number that relates the relative rate at which one molecule migrates compared to the solvent of a paper chromatography. The faster a substance migrates, the larger its R_f will be. Beta carotene has the largest R_f of the four pigments listed above. R_f values change depending on the solvent used for the chromatography, because different substances have different solubilities in different solvents.

Part 2: Photosynthetic Rate

The second portion of this experiment examines photosynthetic rates and tests the theory that photosynthesis requires light and chloroplasts to occur. If you are feeling shaky about your grasp of photosynthesis, it might be wise to review Chapter 4 before looking at the rest of this experiment.

The three products of the light reactions of photosynthesis are ATP, NADPH, and oxygen. NADPH is formed by the reduction of $NADP^+$. In this experiment, the $NADP^+$ is replaced by a compound, DPIP (2, 6-dichloroindopheno), which changes from a beautiful blue color to colorless when reduced. Thus, when the light reactions have occurred, one can tell by the color of the solution. A machine called a **spectrophotometer** is used to determine how much light can pass through the sample. This is useful because it will help us know exactly how much of the DPIP has changed from blue to colorless—and thus determine how much photosynthesis has occurred.

The experiment plays out as follows. Each student is given two beakers—one with boiled chloroplasts, the other with unboiled chloroplasts. An initial reading is taken on the spectrophotometer to determine how much light passes through the unboiled chloroplasts *before* any photosynthesis occurs. Since the experiment tests whether or not photosynthesis can occur in the absence of light, the first sample tested measures how much photosynthesis occurs as time passes while the sample is kept in the dark. The second sample tested measures how much photosynthesis occurs if light is permitted to strike the solution. A third sample tests the effects of boiling chloroplasts on the rate of photosynthesis.

Results from Part II: (Photosynthetic Rates)

Much to the delight of the believers of the theory that photosynthesis requires light and chloroplasts to occur, this experiment proves just that. When the sample is left in the dark, the DPIP is not reduced. The electrons just cannot become excited in the absence of light. When the sample containing boiled chloroplasts is used, the heat denatures the organelle, stripping it of its photosynthetic capacity.

!

Bottom-Line Result of This Experiment	
Light + unboiled chloroplasts	Photosynthesis occurs
Light + boiled chloroplasts	Photosynthesis is compromised
Dark + unboiled chloroplasts	Photosynthesis does not occur

LABORATORY EXPERIMENT 5: CELL RESPIRATION

This experiment focuses on cellular respiration, which can be found in Chapter 3. A brief review of the major concepts of Chapter 3 might help you understand this experiment, which attempts to examine the rate at which respiration occurs.

This experiment points out three ways to measure respiration:

1. *Oxygen consumption:* how much O_2 is actually consumed
2. *Carbon dioxide production:* how much CO_2 is actually produced
3. *Energy released during respiration:* how much energy is released

This particular experiment examines germinating peas by measuring the volume of gas that surrounds the peas at certain intervals in an effort to determine the rate of respiration. Two gases contribute to the volume around the pea: O_2 and CO_2. How can we use the amount of oxygen consumed during respiration as our measuring point if there is CO_2 present as well? Something needs to be done with the CO_2 released during respiration. Otherwise we would not get a true representation of how much the volume is changing as a result of oxygen consumption. The CO_2 would skew the numbers by making it appear as if less O_2 were being consumed.

The CO_2 problem can be handled by adding potassium hydroxide, which reacts with CO_2 to produce K_2CO_3. This reaction allows us to limit the number of variables that could be affecting the volume around our beloved peas to

1. Change in the volume of oxygen
2. Change in the temperature $(PV = nRT)$
3. Change in pressure of the surrounding atmosphere

Aerobic respiration requires and uses oxygen. So, one would expect the volume around the pea to decline as respiration occurs. The reactions of interest for this experiment occur in a tubelike device known as a **respirometer.** To calculate the change in volume that occurs with these peas, one first has to measure the initial volume around the peas. A control group must then be set up that consists of peas that are not currently germinating and will have a rate of respiration lower than that of germinating seeds. This will give the experimenter a baseline with which to compare the respiration rate of the germinating seeds. Since temperature and pressure are also able to affect the volume around the peas, it is important to set up another control group that can calculate the change in volume that is due to temperature and pressure as opposed to respiration. Any changes in this control group should be subtracted from the changes found in the germinating seeds to determine how much of the volume change is actually due to oxygen consumption and respiration.

Just a side thought—can you imagine how awkward it could have been if one of Mendel's lab partners had decided to run this experiment way back then? I can see it now: Mendel walks into the lab and asks "Has anyone seen my peas? After 7 long years . . . I've nearly completed my research. Just need to tally up that last generation of peas. . . . Very exciting. . . . Hmm. . . . I thought my peas were sitting here on this desk by my respirometer."

Anyway, the significant points from this experiment are

1. Germinating seeds consume *more* oxygen than do nongerminating seeds. This makes sense, since they have more reactions going on.
2. Seeds germinating at a lower temperature consume *less* oxygen than do seeds germinating at a higher temperature.
3. You can determine how much oxygen is consumed by watching how much water is drawn into the pipettes as the experiment proceeds. (Refer to your classroom lab manual if you are confused by the pipette portion of this lab.) This water is drawn in as a result of the drop in pressure caused by the consumption of oxygen during respiration.

LABORATORY EXPERIMENT 6: MOLECULAR BIOLOGY

This experiment deals with material from Chapter 7, Molecular Genetics. This is the kind of a experiment that can make you feel like a biotech junkie. Here, you use plasmids to move DNA from one cell to another cell—**transformation.** You get to play with restriction enzymes, e-coli (*Escherichia coli*—eww), and gel electrophoresis.

Full understanding of this experiment requires a basic knowledge of:

1. What vectors are and how they are made
2. What gel electrophoresis is and how it works
3. What a restriction enzyme is and why it is so important to the field of biotechnology

You will find all this information waiting for you in Chapter 7. I am not going to cave in and explain to you now what those things are. That is something you should do on your own.

Okay, I'll tell you now . . . e-coli (usually abbreviated *E. coli* in the scientific literature) is a bacteria that is present in everyone's intestinal tract. It grows in the laboratory as well and contains extrachromosmal DNA circles called **plasmids.** This experiment deals with the process of *transformation*: the uptake of foreign DNA from the surrounding environment. This is made possible by the presence of proteins on the surface of cells that snag pieces of DNA from around the cell; these DNA pieces are from closely related species.

The goal of this experiment is to take a bacterial strain that has ampicillin resistance, and transform the gene for this resistance to a strain that dies when exposed to ampicillin. After attempting to successfully transform the bacteria, the experimenter can check to see if it was successful by growing the potentially transformed bacteria on a plate containing ampicillin. If it grows as if all is well, the transformation has succeeded. If nothing grows, something has gone wrong . . .

Part I: Attempting the Transformation

The first part of this experiment is the attempted transformation. The student adds a colony of *E. coli* to each of two test tubes. In one tube she adds a solution that contains a plasmid that carries the ampicillin-resistance gene; the other tube receives no such plasmid. The waiting game follows, and after 15 minutes on ice, the two tubes are quickly heated in an effort to shock the cells into taking in the foreign DNA from the plasmid. The tubes are returned to ice and the colonies spread out on an agar plate. They are sent to the incubator to sleep for the night and grow on the plate.

Results from Part 1 (Attempted Transformation)

Four plates are created: two with ampicillin and two without. The bacteria from both test tubes should happily grow on the plates lacking ampicillin. The ampicillin-coated plate that is spread with bacteria from the nontransformed tube is bare—there is, indeed, no growth. The ampicillin-coated plate that is spread with bacteria from the attempted-transformation tube shows growth . . . it may not be the greatest growth ever seen, but it is growth. This means that some of the *E. coli* originally susceptible to ampicillin has picked up the resistance gene from the surrounding plasmid and is transformed.

Important point to take from this part of the experiment; "How in the world does transformation work?" Restriction enzymes are added, which cut the DNA at a particular sequence and open the DNA so that it can be inserted into another such region in the main *E. coli* chromosome, which is treated with the *same* restriction enzyme. If the opened DNA from the plasmid happens to find and attach to DNA of the *E. coli* that is added to the tube, hallelujah, transformation occurs. In order for this transformation to succeed, the *E. coli* bacteria must be **competent,** which means ready to accept the foreign DNA from the environment. This competence is ensured by treating the cells with calcium or magnesium. Don't worry too much about how this competence business really works. Just know that bacteria must be competent for transformation to occur.

Part II: Fun with Electrophoresis

For this exam, it is very important that you understand how gel electrophoresis works. *Gel electrophoresis* is a lab technique used to separate DNA on the basis of size. When there is an electric current running from one end of the gel to the other, the fragments of DNA dumped into the wells at the head of the gel will migrate to the other side, with the smaller pieces moving the fastest. The more voltage there is running through the gel, the *faster* the DNA will migrate. The longer the voltage is run through the gel, the *farther* the DNA will migrate. The more DNA cut by the same restriction enzymes you put into each well, the *thicker* the bands will be on the gel. If you reverse the flow of the current on the gel, the DNA will migrate in the opposite direction. The DNA just wants to go towards the positive charge . . . optimists, I suppose.

> **Important Facts about Electrophoresis**
> 1. DNA migrates from negative to positive charges.
> 2. Smaller DNA travels faster.
> 3. The DNA migrates only when the current is running.
> 4. The more voltage that runs through the gel, the faster the DNA migrates.
> 5. The more time the current runs through the gel, the farther the DNA goes.

LABORATORY EXPERIMENT 7: GENETICS OF ORGANISMS

This experiment deals with material from Chapter 6, Heredity. This is your chance to be Mendel or Morgan for a few weeks. You will be breeding fruitflies to apply the principles of genetics and heredity you learned during the course of the year. The basic goal of this experiment is to teach you how to determine what kind of inheritance patterns certain genes are displaying.

The life cycle of a fruitfly (*Drosophila*) is in the ball park of about 12–14 days in length. The basic life plan is as follows:

Eggs	→	Larva	→	Pupae	→	Adults

Egg stage: hatch to become larva after about 24 hours

Larva stage: 4–7 days in duration, major growth period for the fruitfly

Pupal stage: lasts about 4 days; wings, legs, and eyes become visible

Adult stage: live for about 30 days.

Here is an interesting fruitfly fact you can pull out at a party to impress everyone around you (or at least use to grind the party conversation to a halt as everyone stares at you wondering what planet you are from). Once female fruitflies have mated, they store sperm that they can use for fertilization for quite a long time. This means that if you are going to run a Morgan-like experiment, you must use virgins because otherwise you cannot be sure who the daddy is.

In this experiment different students study different inheritance modes—monohybrid, dihybrid, and sex-linked. Essentially, each group of students takes a vial of experimental flies, which will be the parental generations. That vial contains eggs and larva that represent the F_1 generation. During the first portion of the experiment, the phenotypes for the characteristics that you are attempting to study are recorded—which flies had which phenotypes. Next the phenotypes of the F_1 flies are noted and recorded. When the F_2 generation has reached adulthood, their phenotypes are recorded as well. As is often the case, the more the merrier, since experimental results tend to pull more weight when the sample size is larger.

Results from Fruitfly Matings

After several weeks pass and all the phenotypic data have been collected, it is now time to analyze the data. In Chapter 6, Heredity, some genetic ratios were mentioned; I will rewrite them here for you:

3:1	Monohybrid cross
9:3:3:1	Dihybrid cross
9:4:3	Epistasis
1:1	Linked genes
4:4:1:1	Linked genes, with some crossover

In this experiment, you were taught how to do chi-square (χ^2) analysis to evaluate the results of your genetic crosses. It is unlikely that you will be asked to perform this type of analysis on the AP Biology exam. It is more realistic that you simply know what a chi-square test is used for: to determine if your results conform to the expected Mendelian frequencies. For example, if you get 96:31:45:2 in your F_2 generation, a chi-square test will help you decide if your experiment was a dihybrid cross. If your observed frequencies do not match your expected frequencies, perhaps some nonrandom mating or even crossover, is occurring.

LABORATORY EXPERIMENT 8:
POPULATION GENETICS AND EVOLUTION

This experiment reviews material from Chapter 8, Evolution. After completing this experiment you want to be sure you know how to use the Hardy–Weinberg equation and how microevolution throws the whole concept of Hardy–Weinberg equilibrium out the window. There is a good example of how to use the equation in Chapter 8. I will not go into the gruesome detail again here. ☺ This lab also discusses the effects that natural selection can have on a population.

The equations to know for this experiment are $p + q = 1$ and $p^2 + 2pq + q^2 = 1$.

Back in Chapter 8, I listed five conditions required for the existence of Hardy–Weinberg equilibrium:

1. Large population size (no genetic drift)
2. Random mating
3. No mutation
4. No gene flow
5. No natural selection

If any one of these five conditions does not hold true, then the population will experience microevolution and the frequencies of the alleles will be subject to change.

The first part of this experiment examines how to experimentally measure the frequencies of certain alleles. The second part studies a population in Hardy–Weinberg equilibrium, and the final part examines **heterozygote advantage**—situations, (e.g., sickle cell anemia in malarial regions) in which being heterozygous for a condition provides some benefit.

There is not really too much to this experiment. The class gets to be the heterozygous breeding population, and each student has the initial genotype of Aa. Each student is given four cards: two A cards and two a cards. These represent the four outcomes from meiosis. The experiment attempts to imitate a Hardy–Weinberg scenario by having students randomly find another person to exchange cards with to produce two offspring. After producing these offspring, both parents now pretend that they are the newly produced offspring, to mimic the creation of another generation. This process is to be repeated many times until enough data are collected. The point is to see if the allele frequency changes in the classroom as a whole by the end of the last generation as compared to the initial frequency of 50 percent A and 50 percent a. The results *should* be the same, but the size of the classroom might be in violation of the "large population" requirement for Hardy–Weinberg equilibrium, leading to a shift in the frequencies.

You can design an experiment to measure the effect of selection, heterozygote advantage, and genetic drift using a similar experiment structure:

Selection. Imagine that an individual homozygous recessive for the condition that the cards represent does not survive to reproduce. Each time two students exchange cards and produce an aa child, they simply exchange cards again until a different pairing is obtained. This is because the aa would not survive to reproduce, anyway. This will cause a shift in allele frequencies to include more A children and fewer a children.

Heterozygote advantage. Run the experiment with the same cards, but this time, if two students produce an AA child, flip a coin, and if it comes up tails, then the AA child dies and they must produce another match. The a allele will still decrease, but not as fast as in the selection lab.

Genetic drift. Have the class produce the F_1 generation of offspring, and then randomly select 60 percent of the students to be symbolically killed in some horrific environmental disaster. This leaves the other 40 percent to continue breeding and exchanging cards. The random nature in which the students are eliminated can lead to a shift in the allele frequency and the p and q will probably to change depending on the geneotype of those who are left behind.

There are a few questions to ponder as you finish this experiment:

1. *Why is it so difficult to eliminate a recessive allele?* It is difficult because the allele remains in the population, hidden as part of the heterozygous condition, safe from selection, which can act only against genes that are expressed. So, although the q for a population may decline, it will not disappear completely because of the pq individuals.
2. *Why does heterozygote advantage protect recessive genes from being eliminated?* Those who are heterozygous for the condition are receiving some benefit. For example, those who have sickle trait are protected against malaria. This positive benefit for heterozygous individuals helps keep the recessive condition alive in the population.

LABORATORY EXPERIMENT 9: TRANSPIRATION

This experiment takes the principles of water transport covered in experiment 1 and in Chapter 2 of the text, and applies them to the material in Chapter 10, Plants. You might want to review the material on plant anatomy and vascular tissue.

Just a quick reminder of how water moves from the soil to the leaves and branches of a plant. Three minor players in the transport of water are capillary action, osmosis, and root pressure. Water is drawn into the xylem (the water superhighway for the plant) by osmosis. The osmotic driving force is created by the absorption of minerals from the soil, increasing the solute concentration within the xylem. Once in the xylem, root pressure aids in pushing the water a small way up the superhighway. The main driving force for the movement of water in a plant from root to shoot is transpiration. When water evaporates from the plant, it causes an upward tug on the remaining water in the xylem, pulling it toward the shoots. The cohesive nature of water molecules contributes to this transpiration-induced driving force of water through the xylem of the plants. Water molecules like to stick together, and when one of their kind is pulled in a certain direction, the rest seem to follow.

The first part of the experiment examines various environmental factors that affect the rate of transpiration: air movement, humidity, light intensity, and temperature. The rate of transpiration increases with increased air movement, decreased humidity, increased light intensity, and increased temperature. It is not hard to remember that increased temperature leads to increased transpiration—think about how much more you sweat when it is hot. It also makes sense that decreased humidity would lead to an increase in the rate of transpiration. When it is less humid, there is less moisture in the air, and thus there is more of a driving force for water to leave the plant. Imagine that you are standing with a 40-watt (W) bulb shining on your neck, and then a 100-W bulb shining on your neck. The higher-wattage bulb will probably cause you to sweat more. The same thing with plants—the higher the intensity of the light, the more transpiration that occurs. Air movement is less obvious. If there is good airflow, then evaporated water on leaves is removed more quickly, increasing the driving force for more water to transpire from the plant.

 To design an experiment to test the effects of various environmental factors on the rate of transpiration, measure the amount of water that evaporates from the surface of plants over a certain amount of time under normal conditions. You can do this using a piece of equipment known as a **potometer,** a device that aids in the measurement of water loss by plants. Then compare the normal rate to the rates obtained when the temperature, humidity, airflow, or light intensity are altered. (Remember: Change only one variable at a time!) If you run a lab of this nature, it is important to measure the surface area of the leaves involved because larger surface areas can transpire more water more quickly.

The rest of this experiment examines the structure of various cells found in plants. For a review of this material, return to Chapter 10, Plants, and take a gander at the various cell types and their characteristics.

LABORATORY EXPERIMENT 10: PHYSIOLOGY OF THE CIRCULATORY SYSTEM

This experiment discusses material from Chapter 11, Human Physiology. The first part focuses on how blood pressure (BP) is measured and how various environmental changes can affect an individual's BP. The second part of the lab examines the Q_{10} **value** of a water flea—*Daphnia*. This statistic is a number that shows how an increase in temperature affects the metabolic activity of an organism:

$$Q_{10} = \frac{\text{heart rate at higher temperature}}{\text{heart rate at lower temperature}}$$

Part 1: Blood Pressure

Blood pressure (BP) is the force that allows the circulatory system to deliver its precious cargo, oxygen and nutrients, to the tissues of the body. This experiment uses students as the test subjects and measures their blood pressures in various situations.

Measurement 1. Take blood pressure after the student has been lying down for 5–10 minutes. This measurement serves as a baseline to compare the effects of physical challenges on the blood pressure of an individual.

Measurement 2. Take blood pressure right after standing up. The expected change is that the BP will increase in an effort to overcome the force of gravity that makes the movement of blood through the circulatory system more difficult.

Measurement 3. Now the pulse rate is taken after standing for a few minutes. This is to provide a baseline to compare the effects of physical challenges on an individual's pulse.

Measurement 4. The pulse rate is taken after lying down for 5–10 minutes. The expected change here is that the pulse rate will decline when lying down just as blood pressure does because the force of gravity has been reduced and thus less effort is required to move blood through the system.

Measurement 5. The pulse rate is taken right after standing up. As with blood pressure, the expected change is that the pulse rate will increase on standing up, owing to gravity.

Measurement 6. The subject performs some form of exercise, and then immediately measures his or her heart rate. The subject then measures his or her pulse every 30 seconds after the completion of the exercise, until the pulse has returned to the original level determined in measurement 2. The increase in exercise is expected to increase both the pulse rate and the BP of an individual because of increased oxygen demand from the tissues.

The point of the repeated pulse readings in measurement 6 is to determine the "physical fitness" of an individual. The quicker an individual's heart rate and BP return to normal, the more "fit" that individual is. Following that same logic, it takes longer for people who are in better shape to reach their maximum heart rate because their hearts are "trained" to pump out more volume per beat.

Part 2: Ectothermic Cardiovascular Physiology

An **ectothermic animal** is one whose basic metabolic rate increases in response to increases in temperature. In this experiment, water fleas, *Daphnia,* are used to measure the effect of temperature changes on ectothermic animals. An experiment to measure this effect would require the measurement of a baseline heart rate for the animal. After this, the temperature should be raised in 5-degree increments, and the heart rate recorded every 5 degrees. The expected result from an experiment such as this is that ectothermic creatures will experience an increase in heart rate as the surrounding temperature rises because their temperature rises as a result. (In contrast—an **endothermic animal** such as a bird, whose body temperature is relatively unaffected by external temperature, would not experience the same rise in heart rate.) From this portion of the experiment, remember that the metabolic rate of an ectotherm responds to changes in environmental temperature, whereas that of an endotherm does not change much, if at all. Also remember how you would perform an experiment to show whether an organism is responding like an ectotherm or an endotherm.

LABORATORY EXPERIMENT 11: ANIMAL BEHAVIOR

This experiment draws on information found in Chapter 13, Behavioral Ecology and Ethology. This experiment is basically an exercise in messing with pillbugs' heads. Each student takes about a dozen of these fine bugs and place them into a container. In the first portion of the experiment the student simply observes the behavior of the bugs for approximately 10 minutes. This is done to get a general idea of what kind of behaviors these bugs will undertake when in a somewhat normal situation (although you have to imagine that they will spend a good portion of that time wondering what the heck just happened to them and how they ended up getting dumped into this container).

This experiment is designed to study kineses—the change in the *speed* of a movement in response to a stimulus. When an organism is in a place that it enjoys, it slows down, and when in an unfavorable environment, it speeds up. The student is to create something called a **choice chamber.** In this experiment, the chamber consists of two Petri dishes taped together with a passageway that allows the bugs to move from one to the other. One of the dishes is dry, the other wet, and a dozen or so bugs are placed into the choice chamber, half on each side. Then the choice begins; every 30 seconds the student records the number of bugs on each side of the chamber.

It is not important that you take away from this experiment the fact that pillbugs spend more time in the wet chamber than the dry chamber. What is important is that you recognize how to set up an experiment such as this one involving the choice chamber to measure kinesis in animals. Other variables measured include temperature, humidity, and light. The cooler and darker it is, the better as far as pillbugs are concerned.

LABORATORY EXPERIMENT 12: DISSOLVED OXYGEN AND AQUATIC PRIMARY PRODUCTIVITY

This experiment deals with material from Chapter 14, Ecology in Further Detail. The experiment is an examination of the various environmental factors that can affect the amount of oxygen dissolved (DO) in water. The variables measured include salinity, pH, and temperature. **Primary productivity** is the rate at which carbon-containing compounds are stored.

The technique used in this experiment is the light/dark-bottle method. One can measure the amount of O_2 consumed in respiration by measuring the concentration of dissolved oxygen in a sample of water before exposing the sample to either light or darkness. After this exposure, the new concentration of dissolved oxygen is taken and compared to the original. The difference between the original and dark bottles is an indication of the amount of oxygen that is being consumed in respiration by organisms in the bottle. The dark bottle involves only respiration because there is no light for photosynthesis to occur. In the bottle given light, both photosynthesis and respiration occur, which means that the difference between the concentration of dissolved oxygen for the initial and light bottle represents a quantity known as the **net productivity**. The difference over time between the DO concentrations of the light and dark bottles is the total oxygen production and therefore an estimate of the **gross productivity**.

Take from this confusing experiment the following points:

1. Dissolved-oxygen levels can be measured by titration. Stated in an oversimplified way, you can determine how much oxygen is present in a sample of water by measuring how much of a particular solvent you must add (titrate) to the water to achieve a desired reaction that tells you whether all the oxygen has reacted.
2. If you want to run an experiment to measure primary productivity, you can do so by observing the rate of CO_2 uptake, oxygen production, or biomass production.
3. As water temperature rises, the amount of oxygen dissolved decreases; it is an inverse relationship.
4. Photosynthesis increases the amount of DO found in water while respiration usually decreases the DO of water.
5. There is more oxygen in air than in water.
6. The amount of oxygen in a body of water can depend on the time of day. For example, there is more DO in a lake at 3 P.M. than at 6 A.M. because when it is dark, photosynthesis halts and there is no oxygen being produced by the plants to make up for the oxygen being consumed during respiration. By 3 P.M., the photosynthesis helps to make up for this loss of oxygen and increases the DO of the water.
7. *Net primary productivity* is the difference between the rate at which producers acquire chemical energy and the rate at which they consume energy through respiration.
8. *Respiratory rate* is the rate at which energy is consumed through respiration.

REVIEW QUESTIONS

1. If a dialysis bag with a solute concentration of 0.6 M is placed into a beaker with a solute concentration of 0.4 M, in which direction will water flow?

   A. Water will flow from the dialysis bag to the beaker.
   B. Water will flow from the beaker into the dialysis bag.
   C. Water will first flow out of the bag, and then back into the bag.
   D. The solution is already in equilibrium, and water will not move at all.
   E. It cannot be determined from the given information.

2. What is the rate of reaction for the enzyme–substrate interaction shown in the graph below?

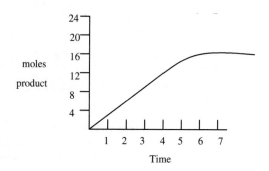

A. 6 μmol/minute (micromoles per minute)
B. 5 μmol/minute
C. 4 μmol/minute
D. 3 μmol/minute
E. 2 μmol/minute

3. In an experiment involving *Sordaria*, an ascomycete fungus, it was found that of 450 offspring produced, 58 yielded a 2:2:2:2 ratio; and 32, a 2:4:2 ratio. Approximately how far apart is the gene from the centromere?

A. 10.0 map units
B. 15.0 map units
C. 20.0 map units
D. 25.0 map units
E. 30.0 map units

4. A plant would show the highest rate of transpiration under which of the following conditions?

A. High humidity
B. Low temperature
C. High light intensity
D. Low air movement
E. A cold rainy day

5. Which of the following will result in a quicker rate of DNA migration on an electrophoresis gel?

A. Increase in temperature of the gel
B. Increase in amount of DNA added to the well
C. Reversal of charge of gel, switching positive and negative sides
D. Increase in current flowing through the gel
E. Increase in length of time that the current is run through the gel

6. A lab experiment is set up in which the participants represent heterozygous individuals (Aa)

and each carry four notecards: two A cards and two a cards. Each member of the class produces the F_1 generation by exchanging cards with another participant. Then 40 percent of the participants are randomly removed from the experiment and the remaining 60 percent are left to continue breeding and exchange cards. This experiment would be used to show what phenomenon?

A. Natural selection
B. Genetic drift
C. Gene flow
D. Mutation
E. Transformation

7. Which of the following would have the highest Q_{10} value?

A. Individual with a heart rate of 60 at 30°C and a heart rate of 80 at 40°C
B. Individual with a heart rate of 80 at 30°C and a heart rate of 60 at 40°C
C. Individual with a heart rate of 60 at 30°C and a heart rate of 70 at 40°C
D. Individual with a heart rate of 70 at 30°C and a heart rate of 60 at 40°C
E. Individual with a heart rate of 60 at 30°C and a heart rate of 60 at 40°C

8. An experiment shows the respiration rate of a sample to be 200 mg C/m² per day and gross primary productivity to be 500 mg C/m² per day. What would you expect the *net* primary productivity to be?

A. 100 mg C/m² per day
B. 200 mg C/m² per day
C. 300 mg C/m² per day
D. 400 mg C/m² per day
E. 500 mg C/m² per day

ANSWERS AND EXPLANATIONS

1. **B**—The water will flow into the dialysis bag because the solute concentration in the bag is higher than that of the beaker. This creates an osmotic driving force that moves water into the bag in an effort to equalize the discrepancy in solute concentrations.

2. **D**—The rate of reaction can be approximated by calculating the slope of the straight portion of the graph. In this case it is 15 μmol of product produced in 5 minutes for an approximate rate of 3 μmoles/minute.

3. **A**—The distance between the gene and the centromere in *Sordaria* is determined by adding up the number of crossovers that occur, and dividing that by the number of offspring produced. This quotient should be multiplied by 100, and that product represents the percent of the offspring that experienced crossover. This percentage

should be divided by 2 to obtain the distance from the centromere to the gene of interest.

$$\frac{\left(32 \text{ offspring} - 4:2:4\right) + \left(58 \text{ offspring} - 2:2:2:2\right)}{450 \text{ total offspring}}$$

$0.200 \times 100 = 20.0\%$ crossover frequency

$\dfrac{20.0}{2} = 10.0$ map units apart

4. **C**—The factors that increase the rate of transpiration are high light intensity, high temperature, low humidity, and high airflow.

5. **D**—The more current you put through the gel, the faster the DNA will migrate. Adding more DNA will result in thicker bands. Reversing the positive and negative ends will swap the direction in which the DNA migrates. Running the gel for a longer amount of time will increase the distance that the DNA fragments travel, and increasing the temperature really won't have too much of an effect.

6. **B**—This is an example of genetic drift, in which a random chunk of the population is eliminated resulting in a potential change in the frequencies of the alleles being studied.

7. **A**—Q_{10} = (heart rate at higher temperature) ÷ (heart rate at lower temperature). The Q_{10} for answer A is 1.33; answer B, 0.75; answer C, 1.16; answer D, 0.86; answer E, 1.00.

8. **C**—Gross primary productivity (GPP) = net primary productivity (NPP) + respiration rate (RESP). Since this question asks the value of the net primary productivity, GPP − RESP = NPP. 500 − 200 = 300.

RAPID REVIEW

Experiments 1–12 are summarized.

Experiment 1: diffusion and osmosis
- Water flows from **hypotonic** (low solute) to **hypertonic** (high solute).
- To measure diffusion and osmosis, take dialysis bags containing solutes of varying concentrations, place them into beakers containing solutions of various concentrations, and record the direction of flow during each experiment.

Experiment 2: enzyme catalysis
- Enzyme reaction rate is affected by pH, temperature, substrate concentration, and enzyme concentration.
- To test the rate of reactivity of an enzyme and the difference it makes compared to the speed of the normal reaction, run the reaction without an enzyme, then run it with your enzyme and compare.
- To determine the ideal pH (or temperature) for an enzyme, run the reaction at varying pH values (or temperatures) and compare.

Experiment 3: mitosis and meiosis
- To determine experimentally the percentage of cells in a particular stage of the cell cycle, examine an onion root slide and count the number of cells per stage. Divide the number in each stage by the total number of cells to determine the relative percentages.

- To determine how far a gene for an ascomycete fungus is from its centromere, cross a wild-type strain with a mutant and examine the patterns among the ascospores. Ratios $4:4$ (no crossover), $2:2:2:2$, or $2:4:2$ (crossover). Total number of crossover divided by total number of offspring = percent crossover. Divide this by 2 to get distance from the centromere.

Experiment 4: plant pigments and photosynthesis

- To experimentally determine the photosynthetic rate of various plants in various environments, replace $NADP^+$ with DPIP (a compound that changes to a clear color when reduced), and measure the rate of photosynthesis with a spectrophotometer, which determines how much light can pass through a sample. Expose different plants to different environmental conditions, and measure how much photosynthesis occurs, and then compare.

Experiment 5: cell respiration

- To experimentally determine the rate of respiration in peas, use a respirometer to calculate the change in volume that occurs around the peas. Set up (1) a control group of nongerminating peas that will have a lower baseline respiration rate, (2) a control group that measures the change in oxygen due to pressure and temperature changes, and (3) an experimental group that contains the group whose respiration rate you want to measure.

Experiment 6: molecular biology

- To run a transformation, add ampicillin-sensitive bacteria to two tubes, and to only one of the two, add a plasmid containing both the gene you would like to transform and the gene for ampicillin resistance. The other is the control. Ice the two tubes for 15 minutes, then quickly heat-shock the cells into picking up foreign DNA. Ice the tubes again, spread the bacteria out on ampicillin-coated plates, and incubate overnight. If transformation occurs, your bacteria will grow on the ampicillin plate and a successful transformation will have occurred.
- Gel electrophoresis can be used in court to determine if an individual committed a crime, or if an individual is the parent of a particular child. Each person has a particular DNA fingerprint. When that individual's DNA is cut with restriction enzymes, and run on an electrophoresis gel, it will show a unique pattern that only that person has. By matching their DNA fingerprint with that of the child of interest, or the evidence from the crime scene, proper identifications can be made.

Experiment 7: genetics of organisms

- To experimentally determine how particular traits in a fruitfly are passed from generation to generation, simply put together a P generation consisting of males and virgin females. Observe and record their phenotypes for the traits of interest. Allow these individuals to mate and produce an F_1 generation. Observe and record the phenotypes for the F_1 generation, and allow them to mate to produce an F_2 generation, and so on. After many generations, pool the data, and determine the inheritance pattern on the basis of your knowledge of heredity.

Experiment 8: population genetics and evolution

- To design an experiment to study the effect of selection, heterozygote advantage, and genetic drift on a population, create a population of individuals all Aa for some trait. Each individual will have four notecards: two A cards and two a cards. Offspring are produced in this experiment by individuals randomly matching up a card with another individual to produce a pair. To measure selection, assume that individuals that are aa for the trait will not survive to reproduce. Each time a couple produces an aa child, they must shuffle and try again. This will mimic the effect of natural selection, eliminating aa individuals and lowering the frequency of the a allele.
- To design an experiment to study heterozygote advantage, decide that if two students produce an AA child, they flip a coin and if it comes up heads, the child dies and they must produce another match. This will mimic the force of nature that prevents the a allele from disappearing as quickly as it might otherwise.

- To experimentally study the effects of genetic drift, have the participants produce an F_1 generation and then randomly eliminate 50 percent of the population and have the remaining 50 percent of the F_1 generation continue to produce offspring. Then measure the allele frequencies and see if they have shifted.

Experiment 9: transpiration

- To design an experiment to test the effects of various environmental factors on the rate of transpiration, measure the amount of water that evaporates from the surface of plants over a certain amount of time under normal conditions. You can do this using a piece of equipment known as a *potometer,* a device that measures water loss by plants. Compare the normal rate to the rates obtained when the temperature, humidity, airflow, or light intensity is altered. If you run an experiment of this nature, it is important to measure the surface area of the leaves involved because larger surface areas can transpire more water more quickly.

Experiment 10: physiology of the circulatory system

- To experimentally determine whether an organism is an endotherm or an ectotherm, run an experiment in which you first take a baseline pulse rate for the organism. Next, increase the temperature in 5-degree increments, stopping to measure the pulse rate each time. Whether the pulse rate is affected by the changes indicates whether it is an ectotherm or an endotherm.

Experiment 11: animal behavior

- To study kinesis of an insect such as a pillbug, create a contraption known as a *choice chamber,* which is designed to study which of two environments an organism prefers. For example, one-half of the choice chamber can be wet; the other, dry. Place the organism of interest into the choice chamber, and record how many of that organism are on each side of the chamber every 30 seconds. This procedure can be performed for a choice chamber that has differing temperatures, humidities, light intensities, and salinities and other varying parameters.

Experiment 12: dissolved oxygen and aquatic primary productivity

- If you want to run an experiment to measure primary productivity, you can do so by observing the rate of CO_2 uptake, oxygen production, or biomass production.
- The amount of oxygen dissolved in a sample can be measured experimentally by titration.
- One can measure the amount of oxygen consumed in respiration by measuring the concentration of dissolved oxygen in a sample of water before exposing it to either light or darkness. After this exposure, the new concentration of dissolved oxygen is compared to that of the original.
- To measure **net productivity,** find the difference between the concentration of dissolved oxygen for the initial bottle and that for the light bottle.
- To measure **gross productivity,** find the difference between the dissolved oxygen concentration for the light bottle and that for the dark bottle.

PART IV

APPENDIX

Bibliography

Campbell, Neil A., *Biology*, 4th ed., The Benjamin/Cummings Publishing Company, Inc., Menlo Park, CA, 1996.

Futuyma, Douglas J., *Evolutionary Biology*, 3d ed., Sinauer Associates, Inc., Sunderland, MA, 1998.

Kotz, John C. and Keith F. Purcell, *Chemistry and Chemical Reactivity*, 2d ed., Saunders College Publishing, Fort Worth, TX, 1991.

Starr, Cecie, *Biology: Concepts and Applications*, 2d ed., Wadsworth Publishing Company, Belmont, CA, 1994.

Strauss, Eric, and Marylin Lisowski, *Biology: The Web of Life* (teacher's edition), Addison-Wesley Longman, Inc., Menlo Park, CA, 1998.

Wilbraham, Antony C., Dennis D. Staley, and Michael S. Matta, *Chemistry*, 4th ed., Addison-Wesley Publishing Company, Menlo Park, CA, 1997.

Websites

Here is a list of Websites that contain information and links that you might find useful to your preparation for the AP Biology exam:

http://apbio.biosci.uga.edu

http://step.sdsc.edu/personal/vanderschaegen/home/links.html

http://www.collegeboard.com

http://www.prs.k12.nj.us/Schools/PHS/Science_Dept/APBio/

http://maxpages.com/aptest/AP_Biology

http://www.asms.net/~bmcph/apbio.html

http://www.guilford.k12.ct.us/~faitschb/links.html

Glossary

abiotic components The *non*living players in an ecosystem, such as climate and nutrients.

abscisic acid Plant hormone that inhibits cell growth, prevents premature germination, and stimulates closing of the stomata.

achondroplasia Autosomal dominant form of dwarfism seen in one out of 10,000 people.

ACTH See **adrenocorticotropic hormone.**

active site Part of the enzyme that interacts with the substrate in an enzyme–substrate complex.

active transport The movement of a particle across a selectively permeable membrane *against* its concentration gradient. This movement requires the input of energy, which is why it is termed "active" transport.

adaptation A trait that, if altered, affects the fitness of the organism. Adaptations are the result of natural selection, and can include not only physical traits such as eyes and fingernails but also the intangible traits of organisms, such as lifespan.

adaptive radiation A rapid series of speciation events that occur when one or more ancestral species invades a new environment.

ADH See **antidiuretic hormone.**

adrenocorticotropic hormone (ACTH) A hormone that stimulates the secretion of adrenal cortical hormones, which work to maintain electrolytic homeostasis in the body.

aerobic respiration Energy-producing reactions in animals that involve three stages: glycolysis, the Krebs cycle, and oxidative phosphorylation. Requires oxygen.

age structure Statistic that compares the relative number of individuals in the population from each age group.

agonistic behavior Behavior that results from a conflict of interest between individuals; often involves intimidation and submission.

alcohol Organic compound that contains a hydroxyl (—OH) functional group.

alcohol fermentation Occurs in fungi, yeast, and bacteria. Pyruvate is converted in two steps to ethanol, regenerating two molecules of NAD^+.

aldehyde Carbonyl group in which one R is a hydrogen and the other is a carbon chain. Hydrophilic and polar.

aldosterone Released from the adrenal gland, this hormone acts on the distal tubules to cause the reabsorption of more Na^+ and water. This increases blood volume and pressure.

allantois Transports waste products in mammals to the placenta. Later it is incorporated into the umbilical cord.

allele A variant of a gene for a particular character.

allopatric speciation Interbreeding ceases because some sort of barrier separates a single population into two (an area with no food, a mountain, etc.). The two populations evolve independently, and if they change enough, then, even if the barrier is removed, they cannot interbreed.

alternation of generations Plant life cycle, so named because during the cycle, plants sometimes exist as a diploid organism and at other times as a haploid organism.

altruistic behavior Behavior pattern that reduces the overall fitness of one organism while increasing the fitness of another.

alveoli Functional unit of the lung where gas exchange occurs.

amines Compounds containing amino groups.

amino acid A compound with a carbon center surrounded by an amino group, a carboxyl group, a hydrogen, and an R group that provides an amino acid's unique chemical characteristics.

aminoacyl tRNA synthetase Enzyme that makes sure that each tRNA molecule picks up the appropriate amino acid for its anticodon.

amino group A functional group that contains —NH_2 and that acts as a base; an example is an amino acid.

amnion Structure formed from epiblast that encloses the fluid-filled cavity that helps cushion the developing embryo.

amygdala The portion of the human brain that controls impulsive emotions and anger.

amylase Enzyme that breaks down the starches in the human diet to simpler sugars such as maltose, which are fully digested further down in the intestines.

anaerobic respiration Energy-producing reactions, known as *fermentation,* that do not involve oxygen. It begins with glycolysis and concludes with the formation of NAD⁺.

anemia Illness in which a lack of iron causes red blood cells to have a diminished capacity for delivering oxygen.

aneuploidy The condition of having an abnormal number of chromosomes.

angiosperm Flowering plant divided into monocots and dicots (monocotyledons and dicotyledons).

anion Ion with a negative charge that contains more electrons than protons.

anterior pituitary gland Structure that produces six hormones: TSH, STH (or HGH), ACTH, LH, FSH, and prolactin.

anther Pollen-producing portion of a plant.

antheridia Male gametangia in bryophytes and ferms designed to produce flagellated sperm that swim to meet up with the eggs produced by the female gametangia.

anticodon Region present at a tRNA attachment site; a three-nucleotide sequence that is perfectly complementary to a particular codon.

antidiuretic hormone (ADH) A hormone produced in the brain and stored in the pituitary gland; it increases the permeability of the collecting duct to water, leading to more concentrated urine content.

antigen A molecule that is foreign to our bodies and causes our immune systems to respond.

apical meristem Region at the tips of roots and shoots where plant growth is concentrated and many actively dividing cells can be found.

apoplast pathway Movement of water and nutrients through the nonliving portion of cells.

aposematic coloration Warning coloration adopted by animals that possess a chemical defense mechanism.

archaebacteria One of two major prokaryotic evolutionary branches. These organisms tend to live in extreme environments and include halophiles, methanogens, and thermoacidophiles.

archegonium Female gametangia in bryophytes, ferns, and gymnosperms.

archezoa Eukaryotic organism that allegedly most closely resembles prokaryotes.

arteries Structures that carry blood away from the heart.

artificial selection When humans become the agents of natural selection (breeding of dogs).

ascospores Haploid meiotic products produced by certain fungi.

A site Region on protein synthesis machinery that holds the tRNA carrying the next amino acid.

associative learning Process by which animals take one stimulus and associate it with another.

atom The smallest form of an element that still displays its unique properties.

ATP synthase Enzyme that uses the flow of hydrogens to drive the phosphorylation of an adenosine diphosphate molecule to produce adenosine triphosphate.

auditory communication Communication that involves the use of sound in the conveying of a message.

autonomic nervous system (ANS) A subdivision of the peripheral nervous system (PNS) that controls the involuntary activities of the body: smooth muscle, cardiac muscle, and glands. The ANS is divided into the sympathetic and parasympathetic divisions.

autosomal chromosome One that is not directly involved in determining gender.

autotroph An organism that is self-nourishing. It obtains carbon and energy without ingesting other organisms.

auxin Plant hormone that leads to elongation of stems and plays a role in phototropism and gravitropism.

axon A longer extension that leaves a neuron and carries the impulse away from the cell body toward target cells.

balanced polymorphism When there are two or more phenotypic variants maintained in a population.

bare-rock succession The attachment of lichen to rocks, followed by the step-by-step arrival of replacement species.

Barr bodies Inactivated genes on X chromosomes.

batesian mimicry An animal that is harmless copies the appearance of an animal that *is* dangerous as a defense mechanism to make predators think twice about attacking.

behavioral ecology Science that studies the interaction between animals and their environments from an evolutionary perspective.

bile Contains bile salts, phospholipids, cholesterol, and bile pigments such as bilirubin, is stored in the gallbladder, and is dumped into the small intestine on the arrival of the food.

bile salts Help to mechanically digest fat by emulsifying it into small droplets contained in water.

binary fission Mechanism by which prokaryotic cells divide. The cell elongates and pinches into two new daughter cells.

binomial system of classification System created by Linnaeus in which each species is given a two-word name: Genus + species (e.g., *Homo sapiens*).

biogeochemical cycles Cycles that represent the movement of elements, such as nitrogen and carbon, from organisms to the environment and back in a continuous cycle.

biomass pyramid *Biomass* represents the cumulative weight of all of the members at a given trophic level.

biome The various geographic regions of the earth that serve as hosts for ecosystems.

biosphere The entire life-containing area of a planet—all ecosystems and communities.

biotic components Living organisms of an ecosystem.

biotic potential The maximum growth rate for a population given unlimited resources, unlimited space, and lack of competition or predators.

birth rate Offspring produced per a specific time period.

bivalves Mollusks with hinged shells such as oysters and clams.

blastula As a morula undergoes its next round of cell divisions, fluid fills its center to create this hollow-looking structure.

"blending" hypothesis Theory that the genes contributed by two parents mix as if they are paint colors and the exact genetic makeup of each parent can never be recovered: the genes are as inseparable as blended paint.

bottleneck A dramatic reduction in population size that increases the likelihood of genetic drift.

bronchi Tunnels that branch off the trachea that lead into the individual lungs and divide into smaller branches called bronchioles.

bronchioles Tiny lung tunnels that branch repeatedly until they conclude as tiny air pockets containing alveoli.

brush border Large numbers of microvilli that increase the surface area of the small intestine to improve absorption efficiency.

bryophytes The first land plants to evolve from the chlorophytes. Members of this group include mosses, liverworts, and hornworts.

bundle sheath cells Cells that are tightly wrapped around the veins of a leaf. They are the site for the Calvin cycle in C_4 plants.

C_4 photosynthesis Photosynthetic process that alters the way in which carbon is fixed to better deal with the lack of CO_2 that comes from the closing of the stomata in hot, dry regions.

C_4 plant Plant that has adapted its photosynthetic process to more efficiently handle hot and dry conditions.

Calvin cycle A name for the light-independent (dark) reactions of photosynthesis.

CAM (crassulacean acid metabolism) photosynthesis Plants close their stomata during the day, collect CO_2 at night, and store the CO_2 in the form of acids until it is needed during the day for photosynthesis.

capsid A protein shell that surrounds genetic material.

carbohydrate Organic compound used by the cells of the human body in energy-producing reactions and as structural material. The three main types of carbohydrates are monosaccharides, disaccharides, and polysaccharides.

carbon cycle The movement of carbon from the atmosphere to living organisms and back to the environment in a continuous cycle.

carbon fixation The attachment of the carbon from CO_2 to a molecule that is able to enter the Calvin cycle, assisted by rubisco.

carbonyl group A functional group that is hydrophilic and polar. It has a central carbon connected to R groups on either side. If both Rs are carbon chains, it is a ketone. If one R is a hydrogen, and the other a carbon chain, it is an aldehyde.

carboxyl group An acidic functional group (COOH). This functional group shows up along with amino groups in amino acids.

cardiac muscle Involuntary muscle of the heart that is striated in appearance and contains multiple nuclei.

carnivore A consumer that obtains energy and nutrients through consumption of other animals.

carotenoid A photosynthetic pigment.

carrying capacity The maximum number of individuals a population can sustain in a given environment.

casparian strip Obstacle that blocks the passage of water through the endodermis of plants.

catalase Enzyme that assists in the conversion of hydrogen peroxide to water and oxygen. Found in peroxisomes.

catalysts Molecules that speed up reactions by lowering the activation energy of a reaction.

cation Ion with a positive charge that contains more protons than electrons.

cell body The main body of the neuron.

cell cycle A cycle that consists of four stages: G_1, S, G_2, and M. G_1 and G_2 are growth stages, S is the part of the cell cycle in which the DNA is duplicated, and the M phase stands for mitosis—the cell division phase.

cell-mediated immunity This type of immunity involves *direct* cellular response to invasion as opposed to antibody-based defense.

cell plate Plant cell structure constructed in the Golgi apparatus composed of vesicles that fuse together along the middle of the cell, completing the separation process.

cellular slime molds Protists with a unique eating strategy. When plenty of food is available, they eat alone. When food is scare, they clump together and form a unit.

cellulose Polysaccharide composed of glucose used by plants to form cell walls.

cell wall Wall that functions to shape and protect cells. Present in plant but not animal cells.

central nervous system (CNS) The CNS is made up of the brain and the spinal cord. The CNS controls skeletal muscles and voluntary movement.

cephalization The concentration of sensory machinery in the anterior end of a bilateral organism.

cerebellum Portion of brain in charge of coordination and balance.

cerebrum Portion of the brain that controls functions such as speech, hearing, sight, and motor control. Divided into two hemispheres and four lobes per hemisphere.

cervix The uterus connects to the vaginal opening via this narrowed region.

CF See **cystic fibrosis.**

character A heritable feature, such as flower color, that varies among individuals.

checkpoints Stop points throughout the cell cycle where the cell verifies that there are enough nutrients and raw materials to progress to the next stage of the cycle.

chemical communication Mammals and insects communicate through the use of chemical signals called *pheromones.*

chemiosmosis The coupling of the movement of electrons down the electron transport chain with the formation of ATP using the driving force provided by a proton gradient. Seen in both photosynthesis and respiration.

chemoautotrophs Autotrophs that produce energy through oxidation of inorganic substances.

chitin Polysaccharide that is an important part of the exoskeletons of arthropods such as insects, spiders, and shellfish.

chlorophyll A photosynthetic pigment.

chlorophytes Green algae that are probably the common ancestors of land plants.

chloroplast The site of photosynthesis and energy production in plant cells and algae.

choanoflagellate Accepted to be the common ancestor of the animal kingdom.

choice Refers to the selection of mates by one sex (in mammals, it is usually females who exercise choice over males).

choice chamber Chamber used in scientific experiments to study kinesis.

cholesterol Steroid that is as an important structural component of cell membranes and serves as a precursor molecule for steroid sex hormones.

chorion Formed from the trophoblast, it is the outer membrane of the embryo and the site of implantation onto the endometrium. It contributes to formation of the placenta in mammals.

chromatin The raw material that gives rise to the chromosomes (genetic material is uncoiled).

chromosomal translocations Condition in which a piece of one chromosome is attached to another, non-homologous chromosome.

chromosome duplication Error in chromosomal replication that results in the repetition of a genetic segment.

chromosome inversion Condition in which a piece of a chromosome separates and reattaches in the opposite direction.

chronic myelogenous leukemia A cancer affecting white blood cell precursor cells. In this disease, a portion of chromosome 22 has been swapped with a piece of chromosome 9.

chymotrypsin Enzyme that cuts protein bonds in the small intestine.

cilia Structures that beat in rhythmical waves to carry foreign particles and mucus away from the lungs.

circadian rhythm A physiologic cycle that occurs in time increments that are roughly equivalent to the length of a day.

class I histocompatability antigens The surface of all the cells of the human body, except for red blood cells, have these antigens, which are slightly different for each individual. The immune system accepts any cell that has the identical match for this antigen as friendly. Anything with a different major histocompatibility complex is foreign.

class II histocompatibility antigens Antigens found on the surface of the immune cells of the body. These antigens play a role in the interaction between the cells of the immune system.

classical conditioning Type of associative learning that Ivan Pavlov demonstrated with his experiments involving salivation in dogs.

cleavage divisions Developing embryo divides; cytoplasm is distributed unevenly to the daughter cells while the genetic information is distributed equally.

cleavage furrow Groove formed, in animal cells, between the two daughter cells; this groove pinches together to complete the separation of the two cells after mitosis.

climax community Final stable stage at the completion of a succession cycle.

clumped dispersion Scenario in which individuals live in packs that are spaced out from each other.

codominance Both alleles express themselves fully in a heterozygous organism.

codon A triplet of nucleotides that codes for a particular amino acid.

coefficient of relatedness Statistic that represents the average proportion of genes that two individuals have in common.

coelom Fluid-filled body cavity found between the body wall and the gut that has a lining and is derived from the mesoderm.

coelomates Animals that contain a true coelum.

coencytic fungi Fungi that do not contain septae.

coevolution The mutual evolution between two species, which is exemplified by predator–prey relationships.

coleoptile Protective structure found around a grass seedling.

collenchyma cells Live plant cells that provide flexible and mechanical support.

commensalism One organism benefits from the relationship while the other is unaffected.

community A collection of populations of species in a given geographic area.

competent Describes a cell that is ready to accept foreign DNA from the environment.

competition Both involved are harmed by this kind of interaction. The two major forms of competition are intraspecific and interspecific competition.

competitive inhibition Condition in which an inhibitor molecule resembling the substrate binds to the active site and physically blocks the substrate from attaching.

complement A protein that coats cells that need to be cleared, stimulating phagocytes to ingest them.

compounds Elements are combined to form entities called compounds.

conduction Process by which heat moves from a place of higher temperature to a place of lower temperature.

conifers Gymnosperm plants whose reproductive structure is a cone.

conjugation The transfer of DNA between two bacterial cells connected by appendages called *sex pili.*

conservative DNA replication The original double helix of DNA does not change at all; it is as if the DNA is placed on a copy machine and an exact duplicate is made. DNA from the parent appears in only one of the two daughter cells.

convection Heat transfer caused by airflow.

convergent characters Characters are convergent if they look the same in two species, even though the species do *not* share a common ancestor.

convergent evolution Two unrelated species evolve in a way that makes them *more* similar. They both respond the same way to some environmental challenge, bringing them closer together.

cork cambium Area that produces a thick cover for stems and roots. It produces tissue that replaces dried-up epidermis lost during secondary growth.

cork cells Cells produced by the cork cambium that die and form a protective barrier against infection and physical damage.

corpus callosum Bridge that connects the two hemispheres of the brain.

cortex Outer region of the kidney or adrenal gland.

cortisol Stress hormone released in response to physiological challenges.

cotyledon Structure that provides nutrients for a developing angiosperm plant.

cri-du-chat syndrome This syndrome occurs with a deletion in chromosome 5 that leads to mental retardation, unusual facial features, and a small head. Most die in infancy or early childhood.

crossover Also referred to as "crossing over." When the homologous pairs match up during prophase I of meiosis, complementary pieces from the two homologous chromosomes wrap around each other and are exchanged between the chromosomes. This is one of the mechanisms that allows offspring to differ from their parents.

cryptic coloration Those being hunted adopt a coloring scheme that allows them to blend in to the colors of the environment.

cuticle Waxy covering that protects terrestrial plants against water loss.

cutin Waxy coat that protects plants.

cyclic light reactions Pathway that produces only ATP and uses only photosystem I.

cyclin Protein that accumulates during interphase; vital to cell cycle control.

cystic fibrosis (CF) A recessive disorder that is the most common lethal genetic disease in the United States. A defective version of a gene on chromosome 7 results in the excessive secretion of a thick mucus, which accumulates in the lungs and digestive tract. Left untreated, children with CF die at a very young age.

cytokinesis The physical separation of the newly formed daughter cells during meiosis and mitosis. Occurs immediately after telophase.

cytokinin Plant hormone that promotes cell division and leaf enlargement, and slows down the aging of leaves.

cytoskeleton Provides support, shape, and mobility to cells.

death rate Number of deaths per time period.

deceptive markings Patterns that can cause a predator to think twice before attacking. For example, some insects may have colored designs on their wings that resemble large eyes, making individuals look more imposing than they are.

decomposer (See *detritivore*)

dehydration reaction A reaction in which two compounds merge, releasing H_2O as a product.

deletion A piece of the chromosome is lost in the developmental process.

demographers Scientists who study the theory and statistics behind population growth and decline.

dendrite One of many short, branched processes of a neuron that help send the nerve impulses toward the cell body.

denitrification The process by which bacteria use nitrates and release N_2 as a product.

density-dependent inhibition When a certain density of cells is reached, cell growth will slow or stop. This is because there are not enough raw materials for the growth and survival of more cells.

density-dependent limiting factors Factors related to population size that come into play as population size approaches and/or passes the carrying capacity. Examples of density-dependent limiting factors include food, waste, and disease.

density-independent limiting factors Factors that limit population growth that have nothing to do with the population size, such as natural disasters and weather.

depolarization The electric potential becomes less negative inside the cell, allowing an action potential to occur.

desert The driest land biome on earth, which experiences a wide range of temperatures from day to night and exists on nearly every continent.

detritivore Also known as *decomposer*. A consumer that obtains its energy through the consumption of dead animals and plants.

dicot (Dicotyledon) An angiosperm plant that has two cotyledons.

diffusion The movement of molecules down their concentration gradient without the use of energy. It is a passive process during which molecules move from a region of higher concentration to a region of lower concentration.

dihybrid cross The crossing of two different characters (BbRr × BbRr). A dihybrid cross between heterozygous gametes gives a 9:3:3:1 phenotype ratio in the offspring.

diploid (*2n*) An organism that has two copies of each type of chromosome. In humans this refers to the pairs of homologous chromosomes.

diplomonads A phylum that is associated with the archezoan eukaryotes.

directional selection Occurs when members of a population at one end of a spectrum are selected against and/or those at the other end are selected for.

disaccharide A sugar consisting of two monosaccharides bound together. Common disaccharides include sucrose, maltose, and lactose.

dispersive DNA replication A theory that suggests that every daughter strand contains *some* parental DNA, but it is dispersed among pieces of DNA not of parental origin.

disruptive selection Selection is disruptive when individuals at the two extremes of a spectrum of variation do better than the more common forms in the middle.

distribution Describes the way populations are dispersed over a geographic area.

divergent evolution Two related species evolve in a way that makes them less similar, sometimes causing speciation.

division The classification category that replaces the phylum in plant classification.

DNA methylation The addition of CH_3 groups to the bases of DNA, rendering DNA inactive.

DNA polymerase The main enzyme in DNA replication that attaches to primer proteins and adds nucleotides to the growing DNA chain in a 5′-to-3′ direction.

DNA replication The process by which DNA is copied. This process occurs during the S phase of the cell cycle to ensure that every cell produced during mitosis or meiosis receives the proper amount of DNA.

dominance hierarchy A ranking of power among the members of a group of individuals.

double helix The shape of DNA—two strands held together by hydrogen bonds.

Down's syndrome A classic aneuploid syndrome affecting one out of every 700 children born in the United States. It most often involves a trisomy of chromosome 21, and leads to mental retardation, heart defects, short stature, and characteristic facial features.

Duchenne's muscular dystrophy Sex-linked disorder caused by the absence of an essential muscle protein that leads to progressive weakening of the muscles combined with a loss of muscle coordination.

ecosystem All the individuals of a community and the environment in which it exists.

ectoderm Outer germ layer that gives rise to the nervous system, skin, hair, and nails.

ectothermic animal Animal whose basic metabolic rates increase in response to increases in temperature.

Edwards' syndrome The presence of trisomy 18, which occurs in one out of every 10,000 live births and affects almost every organ of the body.

electron transport chain (ETC) The chain of molecules, located in the mitochondria, that passes electrons along during the process of chemiosmosis to regenerate NAD^+ to form ATP. Each time an electron passes to another member of the chain, the energy level of the system drops.

element The simplest form of matter.

embryology The study of embryonic development.

emigration rate Rate at which individuals relocate *out of* a given population.

endergonic reaction A reaction that requires *input* of energy to occur. A + B + energy → C.

endocytosis Process by which substances are brought into cells by enclosure into a membrane-created vesicle that surrounds the substance and escorts it into the cell.

endoderm Inner germ layer that gives rise to the inner lining of the gut, digestive system, liver, thyroid, lungs, and bladder.

endodermis Cells that line the innermost layer of the cortex in plants that give rise to the casparian strip.

endometrium Inner wall of the uterus to which the embryo attaches.

endopeptidases Enzymes that initiate the digestion of proteins by hydrolyzing all the polypeptides into small amino acid groups.

endosymbiotic theory Proposes that groups of prokaryotes associated in symbiotic relationships to form eukaryotes (mitochondria and chloroplasts).

endothermic animal Animal whose body temperature is relatively unaffected by external temperature.

enhancer DNA region, also known as a "regulator," that is located thousands of bases away from the promoter that influences transcription by interacting with specific transcription factors.

enzymes Catalytic proteins that are picky, interacting only with particular substrates. However, the enzymes can be reused and react with more than one copy of their substrate of choice and have a major effect on a reaction.

epiblast Develops into the three germ layers of the embryo: the endoderm, the mesoderm, and the ectoderm.

epidermis (plants) The protective outer coating for plants.

epididymis The coiled region that extends from the testes. This is where the sperm completes its maturation and waits until it is called on to do its duty.

episomes Plasmids that can be incorporated into a bacterial chromosome.

epistasis A gene at one locus alters the phenotypic expression of a gene at another locus. A dihybrid cross involving epistatic genes produces a 9:4:3 phenotype ratio.

esophageal sphincter Valvelike trapdoor between the esophagus and the stomach.

esophagus Structure that connects the throat to the stomach.

estrogen Hormone made (secreted) in ovaries that stimulates development of sex characteristics in women and induces the release of luteinizing hormone (LH) before the LH surge.

ETC See **electron transport chain.**

ethology The study of animal behavior.

ethylene Plant hormone that initiates the ripening of fruit and the dropping of leaves and flowers from trees.

eubacteria One of two major prokaryotic evolutionary branches. Categorized according to their mode of nutritional acquisition, mechanism of movement, shape, and other characteristics.

eukaryotic cell Complex cell that contains a nucleus, which functions as the control center of the cell, directing DNA replication, transcription, and cell growth. Organisms can be unicellular or multicellular and contain many different membrane-bound organelles.

evaporation Process by which a liquid changes into a vapor form. Functions in thermoregulation for humans when water leaves our bodies in the form of water vapor—sweat.

evolution Descent with modification. Evolution happens to populations, not individuals, and describes change in allele frequencies in populations with time.

excision repair Repair mechanism for DNA replication in which a section of DNA containing an error is cut out and the gap is filled by DNA polymerase.

exergonic reaction A reaction that *gives off* energy as a product. A + B → energy + C.

exocytosis Process by which substances are exported out of the cell. A vesicle escorts the substance to the plasma membrane, fuses with the membrane, and ejects its contents out of the cell.

exons Coding regions produced during transcription that are glued back together to produce the mRNA that is translated into a protein.

exopeptidases Enzymes that complete the digestion of proteins by hydrolyzing all the amino acids of the fragments remaining.

exponential growth A population grows at a rate that creates a J-shaped curve.

extreme halophiles Archaebacteria that live in environments with high salt concentrations.

F_1 The first generation of offspring, or the first "filial" generation in a genetic cross.

F_2 The second generation of offspring, or the second "filial" generation in a genetic cross.

facilitated diffusion The diffusion of particles across a selectively permeable membrane with the assistance of transport proteins that are specific in what they will carry and have a binding site designed for molecules of interest. This process requires no energy.

facultative anaerobe Organisms that can survive in oxygen-rich or oxygen-free environments.

fallopian tube (see *oviduct*)

fats Lipids, made by combining glycerol and fatty acids, used as long-term energy stores in cells. They can be saturated or unsaturated.

fatty acid Long carbon chain that contains a carboxyl group on one end that combines with glycerol molecules to form lipids.

fermentation Anaerobic respiration pathway that occurs in absense of oxygen. Produces less ATP than aerobic respiration.

ferredoxin Molecule that donates the electrons to NADP$^+$ to produce NADPH during the light reactions of photosynthesis.

fibrous root system Root system found in monocots that provides the plant with a very strong anchor without going very deep into the soil.

filtration Capillaries allow small particles through the pores of their endothelial linings, but large molecules such as proteins, platelets, and blood cells tend to remain in the vessel.

fixed-action pattern An innate behavior that seems to be a programmed response to some stimulus.

florigen Hormone thought to assist in the blooming of flowers.

fluid mosaic model Model that states that the membrane is made of a phospholipid bilayer with proteins of various length and size, interspersed with cholesterol.

fluke Parasitic flatworm that alternates between sexual and asexual reproductive cycles.

follicle-stimulating hormone (FSH) A gonadotropin that stimulates activities of the testes and ovaries. In females, it induces the development of the ovarian follicle, leading to the production and secretion of estrogen.

food chain A hierarchical list of who snacks on who. For example, bugs are eaten by spiders, who are eaten by birds, who are eaten by cats.

food web Can be regarded as overlapping food chains that show all the various dietary relationships in an environment.

foraging The behavior of actively searching and eating a particular food resource.

fossil record The physical manifestation of species that have gone extinct (e.g., bones and imprints).

F-plasmid Plasmid that contains the genes necessary for the production of a sex pillus.

frameshift mutations Deletion or addition of DNA nucleotides that does not add or remove a multiple of three nucleotides. Usually produces a nonfunctional protein unless it occurs late in protein production.

frequency-dependent selection Alleles are selected for or against depending on their relative frequency in a population.

FSH See **follicle-stimulating hormone.**

functional groups The groups responsible for the chemical properties of organic compounds.

G$_1$ phase The first growth phase of the cell cycle that produces all the necessary raw materials for DNA synthesis.

G$_2$ phase Second growth phase of the cycle that produces all the necessary raw materials for mitosis.

gametangia Protective covering that provides a safe haven for the fertilization of the gametes and the development of the zygote in bryophytes, ferns, and some gymnosperms.

gametes Sex cells produced during meiosis in the human life cycle.

gametophyte A haploid multicellular organism.

gastrulation Cells separate into three primary layers called *germ layers,* which eventually give rise to the different tissues of an adult.

gene flow The change in frequencies of alleles as genes from one population are incorporated into another.

generalized transduction Transduction caused by the accidental placement of host DNA into a phage instead of viral DNA during viral reproduction. This host DNA may find its way into another cell where crossover could occur.

generation time Time needed for individuals to reach reproductive maturity.

genetic code Code that translates codons found on mRNA strands into amino acids

genetic drift A change in allele frequencies that is due to chance events.

genotype An organism's genetic makeup for a given trait. A simple example of this could involve eye color, where B represents the allele for brown and b represents the allele for blue. The possible genotypes include homozygous brown (BB), heterozygous brown (Bb), and homozygous blue (bb).

genus Taxonomic group to which a species belongs.

gibberellin Plant hormone that assists in stem elongation and induces growth in dormant seeds, buds, and flowers.

glomerular capillaries The early portion of the nephron where the filtration process begins.

glucagon Hormone that stimulates conversion of glycogen into glucose.

glycerol Three-carbon molecule that combines with fatty acids to produce a variety of lipids.

glycogen Storage polysaccharide made of glucose molecules used by animals.

glycolysis Occurs in the cytoplasm of cells and is the beginning pathway for both aerobic and anaerobic respiration. During glycolysis, a glucose molecule is broken down through a series of reactions into two molecules of ATP, NADH, and pyruvate.

glycoprotein Protein that has been modified by the addition of a sugar.

Golgi apparatus Organelle that modifies proteins, lipids, and other macromolecules by the addition of sugars and other molecules to form glycoproteins. The products are then sent to other parts of the cell.

G-proteins Proteins vital to signal cascade pathways. Directly activate molecules such as adenyl cyclase to assist in a reaction.

gradualism The theory that evolutionary change is a steady, slow process.

grana Flattened channels and disks arranged in stacks found in the thylakoid membrane.

gravitropism A plant's growth response to gravitational force. Auxin and gibberellins are involved in this response.

gross productivity The difference over time between the dissolved oxygen concentrations of the light and dark bottles calculated in primary productivity experiments.

growth factors Assist in the growth of structures.

guard cells Cells within the epidermis of plants that control the opening and closing of the stomata.

gymnosperm First major seed plant to evolve. Heterosporous plant that *usually* transports its sperm through the use of pollen. Conifers are the major gymnosperm to know.

habituation Loss of responsiveness to unimportant stimuli that do not provide appropriate feedback.

haploid (*n*) An organism that has only one copy of each type of chromosome.

Hardy–Weinberg equilibrium A special case where a population is in stasis, or not evolving.

helicase Enzyme that unzips DNA, breaking the hydrogen bonds between the nucleotides and producing the replication fork for replication.

helper T cell Immune cells that assist in activation of B cells.

hemoglobin Molecule that allows red blood cells to carry and deliver oxygen throughout the body to hard-working organs and tissues.

hemophilia Sex-linked disorder caused by the absence of a protein vital to the clotting process. Individuals with this condition have difficulty clotting blood after even the smallest of wounds.

herbivore Consumer that obtains energy and nutrients through consumption of plants.

heterosporous plant Plant that produces two types of spores, male and female.

heterotroph An organism that must consume other organisms to obtain nourishment. They are the consumers of the world.

heterotroph theory Theory that posits that the first organisms were heterotrophs (organisms that cannot produce their own food).

heterozygote advantage The situation, such as sickle cell anemia in malarial regions, in which being heterozygous for a condition provides some benefit.

heterozygous (hybrid) An individual is heterozygous (or a hybrid) for a gene if the two alleles are different (Bb).

histamine Chemical signal responsible for initiation of the inflammation response of the immune system.

holandric trait A trait inherited via the Y chromosome.

homeobox DNA sequence of a homeotic gene that tells the cell where to put body structures.

homeotic genes Genes that regulate or "direct" the body plan of organisms.

homologous characters Traits are said to be homologous if they are similar because their host organisms arose from a common ancestor.

homologous chromosomes Chromosomes that resemble one another in shape, size, function, and the genetic information they contain. They are not identical.

homosporous plant Plants that produce a single spore type that gives rise to bisexual gametophytes.

homozygous (pure) An individual is homozygous for a gene if both of the given alleles are the same (BB or bb).

honest indicators Sexually selected traits that are the result of female choice and signal genetic quality.

hormones Chemicals produced by glands such as the pituitary and used by the endocrine system to signal distant target cells.

host range The range of cells that a virus is able to infect. For example, the HIV virus infects the T-cells of our body.

humoral immunity Immunity involving antibodies and circulating fluids.

Huntington's disease An autosomal dominant degenerative disease of the nervous system that shows itself when a person is in their 30's or 40's and is both irreversible and fatal.

hybrid vigor Refers to the fact that hybrids may have increased reproductive success compared to inbred strains. This is due to the fact that inbreeding increases the likelihood that two deleterious, recessive alleles will end up in the same offspring.

hydrolysis reaction A reaction that breaks down compounds by the addition of H_2O.

hydrophilic Water-loving.

hydroxyl group A hydrophillic and polar functional group (—OH) that is present in compounds known as *alcohols*.

hypercholesterolemia Recessive disorder (hh) that causes cholesterol levels to be many times higher than normal and can lead to heart attacks in children as young as two years old.

hypertonic Characterizes a solution that has a higher solute concentration than does a neighboring solution.

hypha Filament found in fungi made of chitin that separates fungi into multicellular compartments.

hypoblast Forms the yolk sac, which produces the embryo's first blood cells.

hypothalamus The thermostat and "hunger meter" of the body, regulating temperature, hunger, and thirst.

hypotonic Characterizes a solution that has a lower solute concentration than a neighboring solution.

immigration rate Rate at which individuals relocate *into* a given population.

imprinting Innate behavior that is learned during a critical period early in life.

inclusive fitness An individual's fitness gain that is a direct result of his or her contribution to the reproductive effort of closely related kin. This results from the fact that close kin share copies of identical genes.

incomplete dominance Blending inheritance. The heterozygous genotype produces an intermediate phenotype rather than the dominant phenotype; neither allele dominates the other.

induced-fit model Theory that suggests that when an enzyme and a substrate bind together, the enzyme is *induced* to alter its shape for a tighter active-site/substrate attachment, which places the substrate in a favorable position to react more quickly.

inducer Molecule that binds to and inactivates a repressor.

induction The ability of one group of cells to influence the development of another. This influence can be through physical contact or chemical signaling.

inner cell mass Portion of the blastula that develops into the embryo.

inorganic compounds For the most part, compounds containing no carbon. There are some exceptions such as carbon dioxide, carbon monoxide, and others.

insight learning The ability to do something correctly the first time even with no prior experience.

insulin Hormone secreted in response to high blood glucose levels to promote glycogen formation.

integral proteins Proteins that are implanted within the bilayer and can extend part way or all the way across the membrane.

intermediate filaments Substances constructed from a class of proteins called keratins; function as reinforcement for the shape and position of organelles in a cell.

intermediate inheritance An individual heterozygous for a trait (Yy) shows characteristics not exactly like those of *either* parent. The phenotype is a "mixture" of both of the parents' genetic input.

interneurons Function to make synaptic connections with other neurons. They work to integrate sensory input and motor output.

interphase The first three stages of the cycle, G_1, S, and G_2. Accounts for approximately 90 percent of the cell cycle.

interspecific competition Competition between different species that rely on the same resources for survival.

interstitial cells The structures that produce the hormones involved in the male reproductive system.

intraspecific competition *Within*-species competition that occurs because members of the same species rely on the same valuable resources for survival.

introns Noncoding regions produced during transcription that are cut out of the mRNA.

invertebrate Animal without a backbone.

ion An atom with a positive or negative charge.

isotonic solution Solution that has the same solute concentration as surrounding solutions.

karyotype A chart that organizes chromosomes in relation to number, size, and type.

ketone Carbonyl group in which both Rs are carbon chains; hydrophillic and polar.

kinesis A random change in the speed of movement in response to a stimulus. Organisms speed up in places they don't like and slow down in places they do like.

kingdom The broadest of the classification groups.

Klinefelter syndrome (XXY) These individuals have male sex organs but are sterile and display several feminine body characteristics.

Krebs cycle Energy-producing reaction that occurs in the matrix of the mitochondria, in which pyruvate is broken down completely to H_2O and CO_2 to produce 3 NADH, 1 $FADH_2$, and 1 ATP.

***K*-selected populations** Populations of a roughly constant size whose members have low reproductive rates. The offspring produced by *K*-selected organisms require extensive post-natal care.

lac operon Operon that aids in control of transcription of lactose metabolising genes.

lactic acid fermentation Occurs in human muscle cells when oxygen is unavailable. Pyruvate is directly reduced to lactate by NADH to regenerate the NAD^+ needed for the resumption of glycolysis.

lagging strand The discontinuous strand produced during DNA replication.

larynx Passageway from the pharynx to the trachea. Commonly called the "voicebox."

lateral meristems Cells that extend all the way through the plant from roots to shoots that provide the secondary growth that increases the girth of a plant.

lateral roots Roots that serve to hold a plant in place in the soil.

law of dominance When two opposite pure-breeding varieties (homozygous dominant vs. homozygous recessive) of an organism are crossed, all the offspring resemble one parent. This is referred to as the "dominant" trait. The variety that is hidden is referred to as the "recessive" trait.

law of independent assortment Members of each pair of factors are distributed independently when the gametes are formed. In other words, inheritance of one particular trait or characteristic does not interfere with inheritance of another trait (in unlinked genes). For example, if an individual is BbRr for two genes, gametes formed during meiosis could contain BR, Br, bR, or br. The B and b alleles assort *independently* of the R and r alleles.

law of multiplication Law that states that to determine the probability that two random events will occur in succession, you simply multiply the probability of the first event by the probability of the second event.

law of segregation Every organism carries pairs of factors, called *alleles,* for each trait, and the members of the pair segregate out (separate) during the formation of gametes. For example, if an individual is Bb for eye color, during gamete formation one gamete would receive a B and the other made from that cell would receive a b.

leading strand The continuous strand produced during DNA replication.

LH See **luteinizing hormone.**

LH surge Giant release of LH that triggers ovulation—the release of a secondary oocyte from the ovary.

lichen A symbiotic collection of organisms (fungus and algae) living as one.

life cycle Sequence of events that make up the reproductive cycle of an organism.

limiting factors Environmental factors that keep population sizes in check (predators, diseases, food supplies, and waste).

linkage map A genetic map put together using crossover frequencies.

linked genes Genes along the same chromosome that tend to be inherited together because the chromosome is passed along as a unit.

lipase The major fat-digesting enzyme of the human body.

lipids Hydrophobic organic compounds used by cells as energy stores or building blocks. Three important lipids are fats, steroids, and phospholipids.

logistic growth A population grows at a rate that creates an S-shaped curve.

long day plants Plants, such as spinach, which flower if exposed to a night that is shorter than a critical period.

luteinizing hormone (LH) A gonadotropin that stimulates ovulation and formation of a corpus luteum, as well as the synthesis of estrogen and progesterone.

lymphatic system Important part of the circulatory system that functions as the route by which these proteins and fluids that have leaked out of the bloodstream can return to circulation. The lymphatic system also functions as a protector for the body because of the presence of lymph nodes.

lymph nodes Structures found in the lymphatic system that are full of white blood cells that live to fight infection. These nodes will often swell up during infection as a sign of the body's fight against the infectious agent.

lymphocyte White blood cell. There are two main types of lymphocyte: B cells and T cells. These cells are formed in the bone marrow of the body and arise from stem cells.

lysogenic cycle The virus falls dormant and incorporates its DNA into the host DNA as an entity called a *provirus.* The viral DNA is quietly reproduced by the cell every time the cell reproduces itself, and this allows the virus to stay alive from generation to generation without killing the host cell.

lysosome Membrane-bound organelle that specializes in digestion and contains enzymes that break down proteins, lipids, nucleic acids, and carbohydrates.

lysosyme An enzyme, present in saliva and tears, that can kill germs before they have a chance to take hold.

lytic cycle The cell actually produces many viral offspring, which are released from the cell, killing the host cell in the process.

macroevolution The big picture of evolution, which includes the study of evolution of groups of species over very long periods of time.

macronucleus A nucleus present in some protists (Ciliophora) and controls the everyday activities of organisms.

macrospores Female gametophytes produced by heterosporous plants.

map unit Also termed *centigram.* Unit used to geographically relate the genes on the basis of crossover frequencies. One map unit is equal to a 1 percent recombination frequency.

matter Anything that has mass and takes up space.

mechanical digestion The physical breakdown of food that comes from chewing.

medulla Inner region of the kidney.

medulla oblongata The control center for involuntary activities such as breathing.

medusa A cnidarian that is flat and roams the waters looking for food (e.g., jellyfish).

melatonin Hormone that is known to be involved in our biological rhythms (circadian).

memory cells Stored instructions on how to handle a particular invader. When an invader returns to the body, the memory cells recognize it, produce antibodies in rapid fashion, and eliminate the invader very quickly.

meristemic cells Cells that allow plants to grow indeterminately.

mesoderm Intermediate germ layer that gives rise to muscle, the circulatory system, the reproductive system, excretory organs, bones, and connective tissues of the gut and exterior of the body.

mesophyll Interior tissue of a leaf.

mesophyll cells Cells that contain many chloroplasts and host the majority of photosynthesis.

methanogens Archaebacteria that produce methane as a by-product.

microevolution Evolution at the level of species and populations.

microfilaments Substances built from actin that play a major role in muscle contraction.

micronucleus Present in some protists (Ciliophora) and functions in conjugation.

microspores Male gametophytes produced by heterosporous plants.

microtubules Substances constructed from tubulin; play a lead role in the separation of cells during cell division; also are important components of cilia and flagella.

migration This is a cyclic movement of animals over long distances according to the time of year.

mismatch repair Process during DNA replication by which DNA polymerase replaces an incorrectly placed nucleotide with proper nucleotide.

missense mutation Substitution of the wrong nucleotides into the DNA sequence. These substitutions still result in the addition of amino acids to the growing protein chain during translation, but they can sometimes lead to the addition of *incorrect* amino acids to the chain.

mitochondrion Double-membraned organelle that specializes in the production of ATP; host organelle for the Krebs cycle (matrix) and oxidative phosphorylation (cristae).

mitotic spindle Apparatus constructed from microtubules that assists in the physical separation of the chromosomes during mitosis.

monocot (Monocotyledon) angiosperm with a single cotyledon.

monohybrid cross A cross that involves a single character in which both parents are heterozygous (Bb × Bb). A monohybrid cross between heterozygous gametes gives a 3:1 phenotype ratio in the offspring.

monosaccharide The simplest form of a carbohydrate. The most important monosaccharide is glucose, which is used in cellular respiration to provide energy for cells.

morula A structure formed during the cleavage divisions of the embryo.

motor neurons Nerve cells that take the commands from the central nervous system (CNS) and put them into action as motor outputs.

M phase mitosis This is the stage during which the cell separates into two new cells.

müllerian mimicry Two species that are aposematically colored as an indicator of their chemical defense mechanism; they mimic each other's color scheme in an effort to increase the speed with which predators learn to avoid them.

mutant phenotypes Characters that are not the wild-type strain in fruitflies and other organisms.

mutation A random event that can cause changes in allele frequencies. It is *always* random with respect to which genes are affected, although the change in allele frequencies that occur as a result of the mutation may not be.

mutualism Scenario in which two organisms benefit from an interaction or relationship.

mycelium Meshes of branching filaments formed from hyphae that function as mouthlike structures for fungi.

myelinated neurons Neurons with a layer of insulation around the axon, allowing for faster transmission. They form the cable Internet of the body.

natural selection The process by which characters or traits are maintained or eliminated in a population, based on their contribution to the differential survival and reproductive success of their "host" organisms.

negative feedback Occurs when a hormone acts to directly or indirectly inhibit further secretion of the hormone of interest.

nephron The functional unit of the kidney.

net productivity Difference between the concentration of dissolved oxygen for the initial and light bottle in a primary productivity experiment.

neural plate Structure that becomes the neural groove, which eventually becomes the neural tube. This neural tube later gives rise to the central nervous system.

neural tube Embryonic structure that gives rise to the central nervous system.

neuromuscular junction The space between the motor neuron and the muscle cell.

neurotransmitter Chemical released by neurons that functions as a messenger, causing a nearby cell to react and continue the nervous impulse.

niche Term used to describe all the biotic and abiotic resources used by the organism.

nitrogen cycle The shuttling of nitrogen from the atmosphere, to living organisms, and back to the atmosphere in a continuous cycle.

nitrogen fixation The conversion of N_2 to NH_3 (ammonia).

nitrogenous bases Monomers such as adenine, guanine, cytosine, thymine, and uracil out of which DNA and RNA are constructed.

noncompetitive inhibition Condition in which an inhibitor molecule binds to an enzyme away from the active site, causing a change in the shape of the active site so that it can no longer interact with the substrate.

noncyclic light reactions Pathway that produces ATP, NADPH, and O_2. Uses both photosystem I and II.

nondisjunction The improper separation of chromosomes during meiosis, which leads to an abnormal number of chromosomes in offspring. Examples include Down's syndrome, Turner's syndrome, and Klinefelter's syndrome.

nonsense mutation Substitution of the wrong nucleotides into the DNA sequence. These substitutions lead to premature stoppage of protein synthesis by the early placement of a stop codon. This type of mutation usually leads to a nonfunctional protein.

nonspecific immunity The nonspecific prevention of the entrance of invaders into the body.

notochord Structure that serves to support the body. Found in the embryos of chordates.

nucleic acid Macromolecule composed of nucleotides, sugars, and phosphates that serves as genetic material of living organisms (DNA and RNA).

nucleoid Region of a prokaryotic cell that contains the genetic material.

nucleolus Eukaryotic structure in which ribosomes are constructed.

nucleus The control center of eukaryotic cells that is the storage site of the genetic material (DNA). It is the site of replication, transcription, and post-transcriptional modification of RNA.

obligate aerobe Organism that requires oxygen for respiration.

obligate anaerobe Organism that only survives in oxygen-free environments.

observational learning The ability of an organism to learn how to do something by watching another individual do it first.

oil Type of lipid.

Okazaki fragments The lagging DNA strand consists of these tiny pieces that are later connected by an enzyme, DNA ligase, to produce the completed double-stranded daughter DNA molecule.

ontogeny The development of an individual.

oogenesis Process by which female gametes are formed. Each meiotic cycle leads to the production of a single ovum, or egg.

operant conditioning Type of associative learning that is based on trial and error.

operator A short sequence near the promoter that assists in transcription by interacting with regulatory proteins (transcription factors).

operon A promoter/operator pair that services multiple genes.

opportunistic populations *R*-selected organisms that tend to appear when space in the region opens up due to some environmental change. They grow fast, reproduce quickly, and die quickly as well.

optimal foraging Theory that predicts that natural selection will favor animals that choose foraging strategies that maximize the differential between benefits and costs.

organic compounds Carbon-containing compounds. Important examples include carbohydrates, proteins, lipids, and nucleic acids.

osmosis The passive diffusion of water down its concentration gradient across selectively permeable membranes. It will flow from a region with a lower solute concentration (hypotonic) to a region with a higher solute concentration (hypertonic).

outbreeding Mating between unrelated individuals of the same species.

ovary The site of egg production. In animals, females often have two, one on either side of the body. Plants *usually* only have one ovary.

oviduct Known also as the *fallopian tube,* this is the site of fertilization and connects the ovary to the uterus. Eggs move through here from the ovary to the uterus (in animals only).

ovulation Stage of menstrual cycle in which the secondary oocyte is released from the ovary.

oxaloacetate Compound that plays an important role in C_4 photosynthesis of plants and the Krebs cycle in animals.

oxidative phosphorylation Aerobic process in which NADH and $FADH_2$ pass their electrons down the electron transport chain to produce ATP.

oxytocin Hormone that stimulates uterine contraction and milk ejection for breastfeeding.

P_1 The parent generation in a genetic cross.

palisade mesophyll Host to many chloroplasts and much of the photosynthesis of a leaf.

parallel evolution Similar evolutionary changes occurring in two either related or unrelated species that respond in a similar manner to a similar environment.

parasitism Scenario in which one organism benefits at the other's expense.

parathyroid hormone (PTH) Hormone that increases serum concentration of Ca^{2+}, assisting in the process of bone maintenance.

parenchyma cells Plant cells that play a role in photosynthesis (mesophyll cells), storage, and secretion.

parasympathetic nervous system Branch of automic nervous system that shuts body down to coserve energy.

Patau syndrome Presence of trisomy 13, which occurs in 1 out of every 5000 live births and causes serious brain and circulatory defects.

pedigrees Family trees used to describe the genetic relationships within a family. One use of a pedigree is to determine whether parents will pass certain conditions to their offspring.

pepsin The major enzyme of the stomach, which breaks proteins down into smaller polypeptides to be handled by the intestines.

pepsinogen The precursor to pepsin that is activated by active pepsin (a small amount of which normally exists in the stomach).

peripheral nervous system (PNS) The PNS can be broken down into a sensory and a motor division. The sensory division carries information *to* the CNS while the motor division carries information *away* from the CNS.

peripheral proteins Proteins, such as receptor proteins, not implanted in the bilayer, which are often attached to integral proteins of the membrane.

peristalsis The force created by the rhythmical contraction of the smooth muscle of the esophagus and intestines.

permafrost Frozen layer of soil just underneath the upper soil layer, found in the tundra biome.

peroxisome Organelle that functions to break-down fatty acids, and detoxify.

petals Structures that serve to attract pollinators.

PGAL (Glyceraldehydephosphate) Molecule important to energy producing reactions photosynthesis and respiration.

phage A virus that infects bacteria

phagocytes Immune cells (macrophages and neutrophils) that use endocytosis to engulf and eliminate foreign invaders.

pharynx Tube through which both food and air pass after leaving the mouth.

phenotype The physical expression of the trait associated with a particular genotype. Some examples of the phenotypes for Mendel's peas were round or wrinkled, green or yellow, purple flower or white flower.

phenylketonuria (PKU) An autosomal recessive disease caused by a single gene defect that leaves a person unable to break down phenylalanine, which results in a by-product that can accumulate to toxic levels in the blood and cause mental retardation.

pheromones Chemical signals important to communication.

phloem Important part of plant vascular tissue that functions to transport sugar from their production site to the rest of the plant.

phosphate group An acidic functional group that is a vital component of molecules that serve as cellular energy sources: ATP, ADP, and GTP.

phospholipid Lipid with both a hydrophobic tail *and* a hydrophillic head; the major component of cell membranes with the hydrophilic phosphate group forming the outside portion, and the hydrophobic tail forming the interior of the wall.

photoautotrophs Photosynthetic autotrophs that produce energy from light.

photolysis Process by which water is broken up by an enzyme into hydrogen ions and oxygen atoms. Occurs during the light reactions of photosynthesis.

photoperiodism The response by a plant to the change in the length of days.

photophosphorylation Process by which ATP is made during the light-dependent reactions of photosynthesis. It is the chloroplast equivalent of oxidative phosphorylation.

photorespiration Process by which oxygen competes with carbon dioxide and attaches to RuBP. Plants that experience photorespiration have a lowered capacity for growth.

photosynthesis The process by which plants generate energy from light and inorganic raw materials. This occurs in the chloroplasts and involves two stages: the light-dependent reactions and the light-independent reactions.

photosystem Cluster of light-trapping pigments involved in the process of photosynthesis.

phototaxis Reflex movement toward light at night.

phototropism A plant's growth in response to light. Auxin is the hormone involved with this process.

phycobilin Photosynthetic pigment.

phylogeny The evolutionary history of a species.

phytochrome Important pigment in the process of flowering. Leads to the production of florigen.

pigment A molecule that absorbs light of a particular wavelength.

pioneer species A species that is able to survive in resource-poor conditions and takes hold of a barren area such as a volcanic island. Pioneer species do the grunt work, adding nutrients and other improvements to the once-uninhabited volcanic rock until future species take over.

PKU See **phenylketonuria.**

placenta In humans, this structure provides the nutrients for the developing embryo.

planarians Free-living platyhelminthe carnivore that lives in the water.

plasma The liquid portion of the blood that contains minerals, hormones, antibodies, and nutritional materials.

plasma cells The factories that will produce antibodies that eliminate any cell containing on its surface the antigen that the plasma cell has been summoned to kill.

plasma membrane Selective barrier around a cell composed of a double layer of phospholipids that controls what is able to enter and exit a cell.

plasmids Extra circles of DNA in bacteria that contain just a few genes and have been useful in genetic engineering. Plasmids replicate independently of the main chromosome.

plasmodial slime molds Nonphotosynthetic heterotrophic funguslike protists. Eat and grow as a unified clumped unicellular mass known as a *plasmodium.*

plasmodium This word has two meanings in this book. It can be the causative agent of malaria, or it can be the clumped unicellular mass that fungi form under certain feeding conditions.

plasmolysis The shriveling of the cytoplasm of a cell in response to loss of water in hypertonic surroundings.

platelet Blood cell involved in the clotting of blood.

pleiotropy A single gene has multiple effects on an organism.

PNS See **peripheral nervous system.**

polar A molecule that has an unequal distribution of charge, which creates a positive and a negative side to the molecule.

polar body Castaway cell produced during female gamete formation that contains only genetic information.

pollen Sperm-bearing male gametophyte of gymnosperms and angiosperms.

polygenic traits Traits that are affected by more than one gene (e.g., eye color).

polymerase chain reaction Techinque used to create large amounts of a DNA sequence in a short amount of time.

polyp Cylinder-shaped cnidarian that lives attached to a surface (e.g., sea anemone).

polyploidy A condition in which an individual has more than the normal number of sets of chromosomes.

polysaccharide A carbohydrate usually composed of hundreds or thousands of monosaccharides, which acts as a storage form of energy, and as structural material in and around cells. Starch and glycogen are storage polysaccharides; cellulose and chitin are structural polysaccharides.

pond succession Process by which a hole filled with water passes through the various succession stages until it has become a swamp, forest, or grassland.

population A collection of individuals of the same species living in the same geographic area.

population cycle When a population size dips below the carrying capacity, it will later come back to the capacity and even surpass it. However, the population could dip below the carrying capacity as a result of some major change in the environment, and equilibrate at a new, lower carrying capacity.

population density The number of individuals per unit area in a given population.

population ecology The study of the size, distribution, and density of populations and how they change with time.

positive feedback Occurs when a hormone acts to directly or indirectly cause increased secretion of a hormone.

posterior pituitary gland Structure that produces only two hormones: ADH and oxytocin.

potometer Lab apparatus used to measure transpiration rates in plants.

predation Scenario in which one species, the predator, hunts another species, the prey.

primary consumers The consumers that obtain energy through consumption of the producers of the planet. Known as *herbivores.*

primary immune response When a B cell meets and attaches to the appropriate antigen, it becomes activated and undergoes mitosis and differentiation into plasma cells and memory cells.

primary oocytes Cells that begin the process of meiosis and progress until prophase I, where they sit halted until the host female enters puberty.

primary plant growth Increase in the length of a plant.

primary productivity Rate at which carbon-containing compounds are stored.

primary sex characteristics The internal structures that assist in the vital process of procreation; includes the testes, ovaries, and uterus.

primary spermatocytes Produced by mitotic division, these cells immediately undergo meiosis I to produce two secondary spermatocytes, which undergo meiosis II to produce four spermatids.

primary structure The sequence of the amino acids that make up the protein.

primary succession Succession that occurs in an area that is devoid of life and contains no soil.

primer sites DNA segments that signal where replication should originate.

prion Incorrectly folded form of a brain cell protein that works by converting other normal host proteins into misshapen proteins. Prion diseases tend to cause dementia, muscular control problems, and loss of balance.

progesterone Hormone involved in menstrual cycle and pregnancy.

prokaryotic cell A *simple* cell with no nucleus, or membrane-bound organelles; divides by binary fission and includes bacteria, both heterotrophic and autotrophic types.

prolactin Hormone that controls the production of milk and leads to a decrease in the synthesis and release of GnRH, thus inhibiting ovulation.

promoter region A recognition site that shows the polymerase where transcription should begin.

prostate gland Structure whose function in the male reproductive system is to add a basic (pH > 7) liquid to the mix to help neutralize the acidity of the urine that may remain in the common urethral passage.

protein Organic compound composed of chains of amino acids that function as structural components, transport aids, enzymes, and cell signals, among other things.

protein hormones Hormones too large to move inside a cell that bind to receptors on the surface of the cell instead.

protein kinase Protein that controls the activities of other proteins through the addition of phosphate groups.

provirus Viral DNA that sits dormant in a host all controlled by a virus in a lysogenic cycle.

pseudocoelomate Animal that has a fluid-filled body cavity that is not enclosed by mesoderm.

pseudopods Extensions from protists (organisms of the kingdom Protist) that assist in collection of nutrients.

P site Region in protein synthesis machinery that holds the tRNA carrying the growing protein.

PTH See **parathyroid hormone.**

punctuated equilibria model Theorizes that evolutionary change occurs in rapid bursts separated by large periods of stasis (no change).

purine A nitrogenous base that contains a double ring structure (adenine, guanine).

pyloric sphincter The connection point between the stomach and the small intestine.

pyramid of numbers Pyramid based on the *number* of individuals at each level of the biomass chain. Each box in this pyramid represents the number of members of that level. The highest consumers in the chain tend to be quite large, resulting in a smaller number of those individuals spread out over a given area.

pyrimidine A nitrogenous base that contains a single ring structure (cytosine, thymine).

Q_{10} value Statistic that shows how an increase in temperature affects the metabolic activity of an organism.

quaternary structure The arrangement of separate polypeptide "subunits" into a single protein. Seen only in proteins with more than one polypeptide chain.

radiation The loss of heat through ejection of electromagnetic waves.

random distribution Random distribution of species in a given geographic area.

rate of reaction Rate at which a chemical reaction occurs.

reaction centers Control centers made up of pigments.

reciprocal altruism Altruistic behavior performed with the expectation that the favor will be returned.

recombinant DNA DNA that contains DNA pieces from multiple sources.

red blood cells Cells in body that contain hemoglobin and serve as the oxygen delivery system in the body.

red-green colorblindness Sex-linked condition that leaves those afflicted unable to distinguish between red and green colors.

redox reaction A reduction–oxidation reaction involving the transfer of electrons.

replication fork Fork opened in DNA strand that allows DNA replication to occur.

repolarization The lowering of the potential back down to its initial level, stopping the transmission of neural signals at that point.

repressor Protein that prevents the binding of RNA polymerase to the promoter site.

reproductive success A measure of how many surviving offspring one produces relative to how many the other individuals in one's population produce.

RER See **rough endoplasmic reticulum.**

respirometer Machine that can be used to calculate the respiration rate of a reaction.

restriction enzymes Enzymes that cut DNA at specific nucleotide sequences. This results in DNA fragments with single stranded ends called "sticky ends," which find and reconnect with other DNA fragments containing the same ends (with the assistance of DNA ligase).

retrovirus An RNA virus that carries an enzyme called *reverse transcriptase* that reverse-transcribes the genetic information from RNA into DNA. In the nucleus of the host, the newly transcribed DNA incorporates into the host DNA and is transcribed into RNA when the host cell undergoes normal transcription.

R_f Variable that indicates the relative rate at which one molecule migrates compared to the solvent of a paper chromatograph.

ribosomes Host organelle for protein synthesis composed of a large subunit and a small subunit. Ribosomes are built in a structure called the *nucleolus.*

reverse transcriptase Enzyme carried by retroviruses that function to convert RNA to DNA.

RNA polymerase Enzyme that runs transcription and adds the appropriate nucleotides to the 3′ end of the growing strand.

RNA splicing Process that removes introns from newly produced mRNA and then glues exons back together to produce the final product.

root Portion of the plant that is below the ground.

root cap Protective structure found around the apical meristem of a root that keeps it together as it pushes through the soil.

root hairs Hairs extending off the surface of root tips that increase the surface area for absorption of water and nutrients from the soil.

root pressure Driving force that contributes to the movement of water through the xylem of a plant.

rough endoplasmic reticulum (RER) Membrane-bound organelle with ribosomes on the cytoplasmic surface of the cell. Proteins produced by RER are often secreted and carried by vesicles to the Golgi apparatus for further modification.

rRNA Ribosomal RNA, which makes up a huge portion of ribosomes.

***R*-selected populations** Populations that experience rapid growth of the J-curve variety. The offspring produced by *R*-selected organisms are numerous, mature quite rapidly, and require very little postnatal care.

rubisco Enzyme that catalyzes the first step of the Calvin cycle in C_3 plants.

saprobe Organism that feeds off dead organisms.

saturated fat Fat that contains no double bonds. It is associated with heart disease and atherosclerosis.

savanna Grassland that contains a spattering of trees found all over South America, Australia, and Africa. Savanna soil tends to be low in nutrients, while temperatures tend to run high.

sclerenchyma cells Plant cells that function as protection and mechanical support.

search image Mental image that assists animals during foraging. It directs them to food of interest.

secondary consumers Consumers that obtain energy through consumption of the primary consumers.

secondary immune response Memory cells are the basis for this efficient response to invaders.

secondary oocyte An oocyte that has half the genetic information of the parent cell, but the majority of its cytoplasm.

secondary plant growth Growth that leads to an increase in plant girth.

secondary sex characteristics The noticeable physical characteristics that differ between males and females such as facial hair, deepness of voice, breasts, and muscle distribution.

secondary spermatocyte Cells formed during spermatogenesis that give rise to spermatids and eventually sperm.

secondary structure The three-dimensional arrangement of a protein caused by hydrogen bonding.

secondary succession Succession in an area that previously had stable plant and/or animal life but has since been disturbed by some major force such as a forest fire.

second messenger molecule which serves as an intermediary, activating other proteins and enzymes in a chemical reaction.

semiconservative DNA replication Before the parent strand is copied, the DNA unzips, with each single strand serving as a template for the creation of a new double strand. One strand of DNA from the parent goes to one daughter cell; the second parent strand, to the second daughter cell.

seminal vesicles Structures that dump fluids into the vas deferens to send along with the sperm, providing three important advantages to the sperm: energy by adding fructose; power to progress through the female reproductive system by adding prostaglandin (which stimulates uterine contraction); and mucus, which helps the sperm swim more effectively.

seminiferous tubules Actual site of sperm production.

sensory neurons Nerve cells that receive and communicate information from the sensory environment.

septae Structures that divide the hypha filaments of fungi into different compartments.

SER See **smooth endoplasmic reticulum.**

sex pili bacterial appendage vital to process of conjugation.

sex ratio Proportion of males and females in a given population.

sexual selection The process by which certain characters are selected for because they aid in mate acquisition.

shoots Parts of a plant that are above the ground.

short-day plants Plants, such as poinsettias, which flower if exposed to nighttime conditions longer than a critical period of length.

sickle cell anemia A recessive disease caused by the substitution of a single amino acid in the hemoglobin protein of red blood cells, leaving hemoglobin less able to carry oxygen and also causing the hemoglobin to deform to a sickle shape when the oxygen content of the blood is low. The sickling causes pain, muscle weakness, and fatigue.

sieve-tube elements Functionally mature cells of the phloem that are alive.

sink Site of carbohydrate consumption in plants.

skeletal muscle Striated muscle that controls voluntary activities and contains multiple nuclei.

smooth endoplasmic reticulum (SER) Membrane-bound organelle involved in lipid synthesis, detoxification, and carbohydrate metabolism; has no ribosomes on its cytoplasmic surface.

smooth muscle Involuntary muscle that contracts slowly and is controlled by the autonomic nervous system (ANS).

sodium–potassium pump A mechanism that actively moves potassium *into* the cell and sodium *out of* the cell against their respective concentration gradients to maintain appropriate levels inside the cell.

solute A substance dissolved in a solution.

somatotropic hormone (STH) A hormone that stimulates protein synthesis and growth in the body.

somite Structure that gives rise to the muscles and vertebrae in mammals.

source Site of carbohydrate creation in plants.

southern blotting Procedure used to determine if a particular sequence of nucleotides is present in a sample of DNA.

specialized transduction Transduction involving a virus in the lysogenic cycle that shifts to the lytic cycle. If it accidentally brings with it a piece of the host DNA as it pulls out of the host chromosome, this DNA could find its way into another cell.

speciation The process by which new species evolve.

species A group of interbreeding (or potentially interbreeding) organisms.

specific immunity Complicated multilayered defense mechanism that protects a host against foreign invasion.

spectrophotometer Machine used to determine how much light can pass through a sample.

spermatids Immature sperm that enter the epididymis, where their waiting game begins and maturation is completed.

spermatogenesis Process by which the male gametes are formed. Four haploid sperm are produced during each meiotic cycle. This does not begin until puberty, and it occurs in the seminiferous tubules.

S phase The DNA is copied so that each daughter cell has a complete set of chromosomes at the conclusion of the cell cycle.

spongy mesophyll Region of a plant where the cells are more loosely arranged, aiding in the passage of CO_2 to cells performing photosynthesis.

sporophyte The diploid multicellular stage of the plant life cycle.

sporozoite Small infectious form that apicomplexa protists take to spread from place to place.

stabilizing selection This describes selection for the mean of a population for a given allele; has the effect of reducing variation in a given population.

stamen Male structure of a flower that contains the pollen-producing anther.

starch Storage polysaccharide made of glucose molecules; seen in plants.

start codon (AUG) Codon that establishes the reading frame for protein formation.

stem cells Cells that give rise to the immune cells of the human body.

steroid hormones Lipid-soluble molecules that pass through the cell membrane and combine with cytoplasmic proteins. These complexes pass through to the nucleus to interact with chromosomal proteins and directly affect transcription in the nucleus.

steroids Lipids composed of four carbon rings. Examples include cholesterol, estrogen, progesterone, and testosterone.

STH See **somatotropic hormone.**

sticky ends Single stranded DNA fragments formed when DNA is treated with restriction enzymes. These fragments find and reconnect with other fragments with the same ends.

stigma Flower structure that functions as the receiver of pollen.

stomata Structure through which CO_2 enters a plant, and water vapor and O_2 leave.

stop codons (UGA, UAA, UAG) Codons that stop the production of a protein.

storage diseases Diseases such as Tay-Sachs that are caused by the absence of a particular lysosome hydrolytic enzyme.

strain Bacterial species are placed in these groups.

stroma The inner fluid portion of the chloroplast that plays host to the light-independent reactions of photosynthesis.

style Pathway in flower that leads to the ovary.

substrates Substances that enzymes act upon.

succession Shift in the local composition of species in response to changes that occur over time.

sulfhydryl group A functional group that helps stabilize the structure of many proteins.

survivorship curves A tool used to study the population dynamics of species.

symbiosis A relationship between two different species that can be classified as one of three main types: commensalism, mutualism, and parasitism.

sympathetic nervous system Branch of the autonomic nervous system that gets the body ready to move.

sympatric speciation Interbreeding ceases even though no physical barrier prevents it. Can occur as a result of polyploidy and balanced polymorphism.

symplast pathway Movement of water and nutrients through the living portion of plant cells.

synaptic knob The end of the axon. This is where calcium gates are opened in response to the changing potential, which causes vesicles to release substances called *neurotransmitters* (NTs) into the synaptic gap between the axon and the target cell. These NTs diffuse across the gap, causing a new impulse in the target cell.

tactile communication Communication that involves the use of touch in the conveying of a message.

taiga Biome characterized by lengthy, cold, and wet winters. This biome is found in Canada and has gymnosperms as its prominent plant life. This biome contains coniferous forests (pine and other needle-bearing trees).

tapeworm Parasitic flatworm whose adult form lives in vertebrates.

taproot system System of roots found in many dicots that starts as one thick root and divides into many smaller lateral roots, which serve as an anchor for the plant.

tata box Group of nucleotides found in the promoter region that assists in binding of RNA polymerase to the DNA strand for transcription.

taxis The reflex movement toward or away from a stimulus.

taxonomy The field of biology that classifies organisms according to the presence or absence of shared characteristics in an effort to discover evolutionary relationships between species.

Tay-Sachs disease A fatal genetic storage disease that renders the body unable to break down a particular type of lipid.

temperate deciduous forests A biome that is found in regions that experience cold winters where plant life is dormant, alternating with warm summers that provide enough moisture to keep large trees alive.

temperate grasslands Found in regions with cold winter temperatures. The soil of this biome is considered to be among the most fertile of all.

termination site Region of DNA that tells the polymerase when transcription should conclude.

territoriality Scenario in which territorial individuals defend their territory against other individuals.

tertiary structure The 3D (three-dimensional) arrangement of a protein caused by interaction among the various R groups of the amino acids involved.

test cross Crossing of an organism of unknown dominant genotype with an organism that is homozygous recessive for the trait, resulting in offspring with observable phenotypes. Test crosses are used to determine the unknown genotype.

testis The site of sperm production in animals; males have two testes, located in the scrotum.

testosterone Sex hormone produced in testes that stimulates the growth of male sex characteristics.

thermoacidophiles Archaebacteria that live in hot, acidic environments.

thermoregulation The process by which temperature is maintained.

thigmotropism A plant's growth in response to touch.

thylakoid membrane system Inner membrane that winds through the stroma of a chloroplast. Site of the light-dependent reactions of photosynthesis.

thymine dimers Thymine nucleotides located adjacent to one another on the DNA strand bind together when excess exposure to UV light occurs. This can negatively affect replication of DNA and assist in the creation of further mutations.

thymosin Hormone involved in the development of the T cells of the immune system.

thyroid-stimulating hormone (TSH) A hormone that stimulates the synthesis and secretion of thyroid hormones, which regulate the rate of metabolism in the body.

thyroxin Hormone released by the thyroid gland that functions in the control of metabolic activities in the body.

tongue Structure that functions to move food around while we chew and helps to arrange the food into a swallowable bolus.

trachea The tunnel that leads air into the thoracic cavity.

tracheid cells Xylem cells in charge of water transport in gymnosperm.

tracheophytes Vascular plants.

transcription factors Helper proteins that assist RNA polymerase in finding and attaching to the promoter region.

transduction The movement of genes from one cell to another by phages.

transformation The transfer of genetic material from one cell to another, resulting in a genetic change in the receiving cell.

translocation Movement of the ribosome along the mRNA in such a way that the A site becomes the P site and the next tRNA comes into the new A site carrying the next amino acid.

translocation (plants) Movement of carbohydrates through the phloem.

transpiration Process by which plants lose water through evaporation through their leaves.

trichinosis Disease found in humans caused by a roundworm that infects meat products.

trophic levels Hierarchy of energy levels that describe the energy distribution of a planet.

trophoblast Forms the placenta for the developing fetus, and aids in attachment to the endometrium. This structure also produces human chorionic gonadotropin (HCG), which maintains the endometrium by ensuring the continued production of progesterone.

tropical forests These forests consist primarily of tall trees that form a thick cover, which blocks the light from reaching the floor of the forest (where there is little growth). Tropical rain forests are known for their rapid recycling of nutrients and contain the greatest diversity of species.

tropism Plant growth that occurs in response to an environmental stimulus such as sunlight or gravity.

tropomyosin Regulatory protein known to block the actin–myosin binding site and prevent muscular contraction in the absence of calcium.

trypsin Enzyme that cuts protein bonds in the small instestine.

TSH See **thyroid-stimulating hormone.**

tundra This biome experiences extremely cold winters during which the ground freezes completely. Short shrubs or grasses that are able to withstand the difficult conditions dominate.

Turner's syndrome Affects females who are missing an X chromosome.

umbilical cord Structure that transports oxygen, food, and waste (CO_2) between the embryo and the placenta.

uniform distribution Scenario in which individuals are evenly spaced out across a given geographic area.

unsaturated fat Fat that contains one or more double bonds; found in plants.

uracil The nucleotide that replaces thymine in RNA.

urethra Exit point for both urine and sperm from males and urine for females.

uterus Site of embryo attachment and development in mammals.

vaccination Inoculation of medicine into a patient in an effort to prime the immune system to be prepared to fight a specific sickness if confronted in the future.

vacuole A storage organelle that is large in plant cells but small in animal cells.

vascular cambium A cylinder of tissue that extends the length of the stem and root and gives rise to the secondary xylem and phloem.

vascular cylinder Structure in plants that is composed of cells that produce the lateral roots of the plant.

vas deferens Tunnel that connects the epididymis to the urethra.

vector Agent that moves DNA from one source to another.

veins Structures that return blood to the heart.

vena cava system System of veins that returns deoxygenated blood from the body to the heart to be reoxygenated in the lungs.

vertebrate Animal with a backbone.

vessel elements Xylem cells in charge of water transport in angiosperms. More efficient than tracheid cells.

vestigial characters Characters that are no longer useful, although they once were.

viral envelope Protective barrier that surrounds some viruses but also helps them attach to cells.

viroids Plant viruses that are only a few hundred nucleotides in length.

virus A parasitic infectious agent that is unable to survive outside a host organism. Viruses do not contain enzymes for metabolism or ribosomes for protein synthesis.

visual communication Communication through the use of the visual senses.

water biomes Both freshwater and marine biomes, which occupy the majority of the surface of the earth.

water cycle The earth is covered in water. A lot of this water evaporates each day and returns to the clouds. This water is returned to the earth in the form of precipitation.

water potential The force that drives water to move in a given direction. Combination of solute potential and pressure potential.

water vascular system Series of tubes and canals within echinoderms that play a role in ingestion of food, movement, and gas exchange.

wild-type phenotype The normal phenotype for a character in fruitflies and other organisms.

within-sex competition Competition for mates between members of the same sex.

wobble Nucleotides in the third position of an anticodon are able to pair with many nucleotides instead of just their normal partner.

X-inactivation During the development of the female embryo, one of the two X chromosomes in each cell remains coiled as a Barr body whose genes are not expressed. A cell expresses the alleles of the active X chromosome only.

xylem The "superhighway," or important part of the vascular tissue in plants, through which water and nutrients travel throughout the plant. Also functions as a support structure that strengthens the plant.

yolk sac Derived from the hypoblast, this is the site of early blood cell formation in humans and the source of nutrients for bird and reptile embryos.

zone of cell division Region at the tip of a root formed by the actively dividing cells of the apical meristem.

zone of elongation Cells of this region elongate tremendously during plant growth.

zone of maturation Region in the plant where cells differentiate into their final form.

5 Steps to a 5

AP Calculus AB

Dedication

To my mother, *Lai-ping*, who borrowed money

to hire a tutor for me when I was in 7th grade.

Preface

Congratulations! You are an AP Calculus student. Not too shabby! As you know, AP Calculus is one of the most challenging subjects in high school. You study mathematical ideas that helped change the world. Not that long ago, calculus was taught in graduate schools. Today, smart young people like yourself study calculus in high school. Most colleges will give you credit if you score a 3 or more on the AP Calculus Exam.

So how do you do well on the AP Exam? How do you get a 5? Well, you've already taken the first step. You're reading this book. The next thing you need to do is to make sure that you understand the materials and do the practice problems. In recent years, the AP Calculus exams have gone through many changes. For example, today the questions no longer stress long and tedious algebraic manipulations. Instead, you are expected to be able to solve a broad range of problems including problems presented to you in the form of a graph, a chart, or a word problem. For many of the questions, you are also expected to use your calculator to find the solutions.

After having taught AP Calculus for many years and having spoken to students and other calculus teachers, I understand some of the difficulties that students might encounter with the AP Calculus exams. For example, some students have complained about not being able to visualize what the question was asking and others students said that even when the solution was given, they could not follow the steps. Under these circumstances, who wouldn't be frustrated? In this book, I have addressed these issues. Whenever possible, problems are accompanied by diagrams and solutions are presented in a step-by-step manner. The graphing calculator is used extensively whenever it is permitted. The book also begins with a big chapter on review of precalculus. The purpose is to make the book self-contained so that if a student needs to look up a formula, a definition, or a concept in precalculus, it is right there in the book. You might skip this chapter and begin with Chapter 2.

So how do you get a 5 on the AP Calculus AB exam?

Step 1: Pick one of the study plans from the book.
Step 2: Study the chapters and do the practice problems as scheduled.
Step 3: Take the Diagnostic Test and Practice Tests.
(The practice tests are on the enclosed CD.)
Step 4: Get a good night's sleep the day before the exam.

As an old martial artist once said, "First you must understand. Then you must practice." Have fun and good luck!

Acknowledgments

I could not have written this book without the help of the following people:

My high school calculus teacher, *Michael Cantor*, who taught me calculus.

Professor *Leslie Beebe* who taught me how to write.

David Pickman who fixed my computer and taught me Equation Editor.

Jennifer Tobin, who was a senior at Herricks High School and is now attending The College of New Jersey, who tirelessly edited many parts of the manuscript and with whom I look forward to co-author a math book in the future.

Robert Teseo and his calculus students who field-tested many of the problems.

All the students in my BC Calculus class at Herricks for their comments and support.

Mark Reynolds who proofread part of the manuscript.

Robert Main who meticulously edited the entire manuscript.

Maxine Lifshitz who offered many helpful comments and suggestions.

Don Reis whose patience and encouragement kept me writing.

Barbara Gilson, the sponsoring editor, *Grace Freedson,* the project editor, *Maureen Walker,* the editing supervisor, and *Betsy Winship,* the production manager, for all their assistance.

Sam Lee and *Derek Ma* who were on 24-hour call for technical support.

My older daughter *Janet* for not killing me for missing one of her concerts.

My younger daughter *Karen* who helped me with many of the computer graphics.

My wife *Mary* who gave me many ideas for the book and who often has more confidence in me than I have in myself.

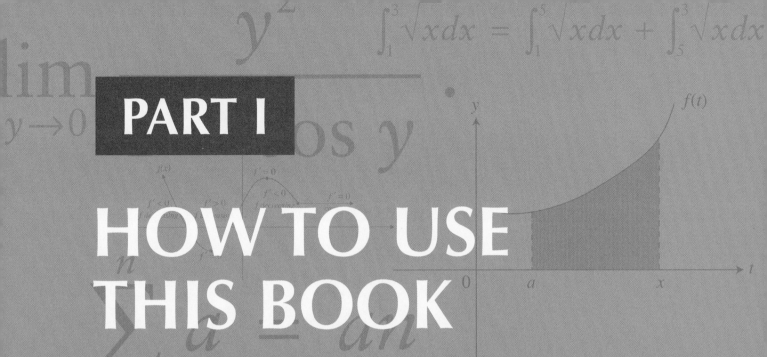

PART I

HOW TO USE THIS BOOK

HOW IS THIS BOOK ORGANIZED?

Part I contains an introduction to the Five-Step Program and three study plans for preparing for the AP Calculus AB exam.

Part II contains a full-length diagnostic test. The diagnostic test contains the same number of multiple-choice and free-response questions as an AP Calculus AB exam.

Part III (Comprehensive Review) contains 10 chapters. Chapter 1 is a review of pre-calculus. It is included in the book so that you do not have to look for a pre-calculus book in the event you need to refer to a previous concept. You may skip this chapter if you wish and begin with Chapter 2. At the end of each chapter you will find a set of 20 practice problems and, beginning with Chapter 2, a set of 5 cumulative review problems. These problems have been created to allow you to practice your skills. They have also been designed to avoid unnecessary duplications. At the end of each chapter, a Rapid Review gives you some of the highlights of the chapter.

The enclosed CD contains two full-length practice tests as well as the answers, explanations, and worksheets to compute your scores.

Note: The exercises in this book are done with the TI-89 graphing calculator.

INTRODUCTION TO THE FIVE-STEP PROGRAM

The Five-Step Program is designed to provide you with the skills and strategies vital to the exam and the practice that can help lead you to that perfect 5. Each of the five steps will provide you with the opportunity to get closer and closer to the "Holy Grail" 5.

Step One leads you through a brief process to help determine which type of exam preparation you want to commit yourself to.

1. Month-by-month: September through May.
2. The calendar year: January through May.
3. Basic training: Six weeks prior to the exam.

Step Two helps develop the knowledge you need to succeed on the exam.

1. A comprehensive review of the exam.
2. One "Diagnostic Test" which you can go through step-by-step and question-by-question to build your confidence level.
3. A summary of formulas related to the AP Calculus AB exam.
4. A list of interesting and related websites and a bibliography.

Step Three develops the skills necessary to take the exam and do well.

1. Practice multiple-choice questions.
2. Practice free-response questions.

Step Four helps you develop strategies for taking the exam.

1. Learning about the test itself.
2. Learning to read multiple choice questions.
3. Learning how to answer multiple choice questions, including whether or not to guess.
4. Learning how to plan and write the free-response questions.

Step Five will help you develop your confidence in using the skills demanded on the AP Calculus AB exam.

1. The opportunity to take a diagnostic exam.
2. Time management techniques/skills.
3. Two practice exams that test how well-honed your skills are.

THREE APPROACHES TO PREPARING FOR THE AP CALCULUS AB EXAM

Overview of the Three Plans

No one knows your study habits, likes and dislikes better than you. So, you are the only one who can decide which approach you want and/or need to adopt to prepare for the Advanced Placement Calculus AB exam. Look at the brief profiles below. These may help you to place yourself in a particular prep mode.

You are a full-year prep student (Approach A) if:

1. You are the kind of person who likes to plan for everything far in advance . . . and I mean far . . . ;
2. You arrive at the airport 2 hours before your flight because, "you never know when these planes might leave early . . .";
3. You like detailed planning and everything in its place;
4. You feel you must be thoroughly prepared;
5. You hate surprises.

You are a one-semester prep student (Approach B) if:

1. You get to the airport 1 hour before your flight is scheduled to leave;
2. You are willing to plan ahead to feel comfortable in stressful situations, but are okay with skipping some details;
3. You feel more comfortable when you know what to expect, but a surprise or two is cool;
4. You're always on time for appointments.

You are a 6-week prep student (Approach C) if:

1. You get to the airport just as your plane is announcing its final boarding;
2. You work best under pressure and tight deadlines;
3. You feel very confident with the skills and background you've learned in your AP Calculus AB class;
4. You decided late in the year to take the exam;
5. You like surprises;
6. You feel okay if you arrive 10–15 minutes late for an appointment.

CALENDAR FOR EACH PLAN

A Calendar for Approach A:
A Year-Long Preparation for the AP Calculus AB Exam

Although its primary purpose is to prepare you for the AP Calculus AB Exam you will take in May, this book can enrich your study of calculus, your analytical skills and your problem solving techniques.

SEPTEMBER–OCTOBER (Check off the activities as you complete them.)

_____ Determine into which student mode you would place yourself.
_____ Carefully read Parts I and II.
_____ Get on the web and take a look at the AP website(s).
_____ Skim the Comprehensive Review section. (These areas will be part of your year-long preparation.)
_____ Buy a few highlighters.
_____ Flip through the entire book. Break the book in. Write in it. Toss it around a little bit . . . Highlight it.
_____ Get a clear picture of what your own school's AP Calculus AB curriculum is.
_____ Begin to use the book as a resource to supplement the classroom learning.
_____ Read and study Chapter 1—Review of Pre-Calculus.
_____ Read and study Chapter 2—Limits and Continuity.
_____ Read and study Chapter 3—Differentiation.

NOVEMBER (The first 10 weeks have elapsed.)

_____ Read and study Chapter 4—Graphs of Functions and Derivatives.
_____ Read and study Chapter 5—Applications of Derivatives.

DECEMBER

_____ Read and study Chapter 6—More Applications of Derivatives.
_____ Review Chapters 1–3.

JANUARY (20 weeks have now elapsed.)

_____ Read and study Chapter 7—Integration.
_____ Review Chapters 4–6.

FEBRUARY

_____ Read and study Chapter 8—Definite Integrals.
_____ Read and study Chapter 9—Areas and Volumes.
_____ Take the Diagnostic Test.
_____ Evaluate your strengths and weaknesses.
_____ Study appropriate chapters to correct weaknesses.

MARCH (30 weeks have now elapsed.)

_____ Read and study Chapter 10—More Applications of Definite Integrals.
_____ Review Chapters 7–9.

APRIL

_____ Take Practice Exam 1 in first week of April.
_____ Evaluate your strengths and weaknesses.
_____ Study appropriate chapters to correct weaknesses.
_____ Review Chapters 1–10.

MAY—First Two Weeks (THIS IS IT!)

_____ Take Practice Exam 2.
_____ Score yourself.
_____ Study appropriate chapters to correct weaknesses.
_____ Get a good night's sleep the night before the exam. Fall asleep knowing you are well prepared.

GOOD LUCK ON THE TEST!

A Calendar for Approach B:
A Semester-Long Preparation for the AP Calculus AB Exam

Working under the assumption that you've completed one semester of calculus studies, the following calendar will use those skills you've been practicing to prepare you for the May exam.

JANUARY

_____ Carefully read Parts I and II.
_____ Read and study Chapter 1—Review of Pre-Calculus.
_____ Read and study Chapter 2—Limits and Continuity.
_____ Read and study Chapter 3—Differentiation.
_____ Read and study Chapter 4—Graphs of Functions and Derivatives.

FEBRUARY

_____ Read and study Chapter 5—Applications of Derivatives.
_____ Read and study Chapter 6—More Applications of Derivatives.
_____ Read and study Chapter 7—Integration.
_____ Take the Diagnostic Test.
_____ Evaluate your strengths and weaknesses.
_____ Study appropriate chapters to correct weaknesses.
_____ Review Chapters 1–4.

MARCH (10 weeks to go.)

_____ Read and study Chapter 8—Definite Integrals.

_____ Read and study Chapter 9—Areas and Volumes.
_____ Read and study Chapter 10—More Applications of Definite Integrals.
_____ Review Chapters 5–7.

APRIL

_____ Take Practice Exam 1 in first week of April.
_____ Evaluate your strengths and weaknesses.
_____ Study appropriate chapters to correct weaknesses.
_____ Review Chapters 1–10.

MAY—First Two Weeks (THIS IS IT!)

_____ Take Practice Exam 2.
_____ Score yourself.
_____ Study appropriate chapters to correct weaknesses.
_____ Get a good night's sleep the night before the exam. Fall asleep knowing you are well prepared.

GOOD LUCK ON THE TEST!

A Calendar for Approach C:
A Six-Week Preparation for the AP Calculus AB Exam

At this point, we are going to assume that you have been building your calculus knowledge base for more than six months. You will, therefore, use this book primarily as a specific guide to the AP Calculus AB Exam. Given the time constraints, now is not the time to try to expand your AP Calculus AB curriculum. Rather, it is the time to limit and refine what you already do know.

APRIL 1st–15th

_____ Skim Parts I and II.
_____ Skim Chapters 1–5.
_____ Carefully go over the "Rapid Review" sections of Chapters 1–5.
_____ Take the Diagnostic Test.
_____ Evaluate your strengths and weaknesses.
_____ Study appropriate chapters to correct weaknesses.

APRIL 16th–May 1st

_____ Skim Chapters 6–10.
_____ Carefully go over the "Rapid Review" sections of Chapters 6–10.

_____ Complete Practice Exam 1.
_____ Score yourself and analyze your errors.
_____ Study appropriate chapters to correct weaknesses.

MAY—First Two Weeks (THIS IS IT!)

_____ Complete Practice Exam 2.
_____ Score yourself and analyze your errors.
_____ Study appropriate chapters to correct weaknesses.
_____ Get a good night's sleep. Fall asleep knowing you are well prepared.

GOOD LUCK ON THE TEST!

Summary of the Three Study Plans

Month	Approach A: September Plan	Approach B: January Plan	Approach C: 6-Week Plan
September–October	Chapters 1, 2 & 3		
November	4 & 5		
December	6 Review 1–3		
January	7 Review 4–6	Chapters 1, 2, 3 & 4	
February	8 & 9 Diagnostic Test	5, 6 & 7 Diagnostic Test Review 1–4	
March	10 Review 7–9	8, 9 & 10 Review 5–7	
April	Practice Exam 1 Review 1–10	Practice Exam 1 Review 1–10	Diagnostic Test Review 1–5 Practice Exam 1 Review 6–10
May	Practice Exam 2	Practice Exam 2	Practice Exam 2

GRAPHICS USED IN THE BOOK

To emphasize particular skills, strategies, and practice, we use four sets of icons throughout this book. You will see these icons in the margins of Parts I, II, and III.

The first icon is an hourglass. We've chosen this to indicate the passage of time during the school year. This hourglass icon will be in the margin next to an item which may be of interest to one of the three types of students who are using this book.

For the student who plans to prepare for the AP Calculus exam during the entire school year, beginning in September through May, we use an hourglass which is full on the top.

For the student who decides to begin preparing for the exam in January of the calendar year, we use an hourglass which is half full on the top and half full on the bottom.

For the student who chooses to prepare during the final 6 weeks before the exam, we use an hourglass which is empty on the top and full on the bottom.

The second icon is a clock that indicates a timed practice activity or a time management strategy. It indicates on the face of the dial how much time to allow for a given exercise. The full dial will remind you that this is a strategy that can help you learn to manage your time on the test.

The third icon is an exclamation point that points to a very important idea, concept, or strategy point you should not pass over.

The fourth icon, a sun, indicates a tip that you might find useful.

PART II

WHAT YOU NEED TO KNOW ABOUT THE AP CALCULUS AB EXAM

BACKGROUND ON THE AP EXAM

What Is Covered in the AP Calculus AB Exam?

The AP Calculus AB exam covers the following topics:

- Functions, Limits and Graphs of Functions, Continuity
- Definition and Computation of Derivatives, Second Derivatives, Relationship between the Graphs of Functions and their Derivatives, Applications of Derivatives
- Finding Antiderivatives, Definite Integrals, Applications of Integrals, Fundamental Theorem of Calculus, Numerical Approximations of Definite Integrals, and Separable Differential Equations.

Students are expected to be able solve problems that are expressed graphically, numerically, analytically, and verbally. For a more detailed description of the topics covered in the AP Calculus AB exam, visit the College Board website at: *www.collegeboard.org/ ap/calculus.*

What Is the Format of the AP Calculus AB Exam?

The AP Calculus AB exam has 2 sections:

Section I contains 45 multiple-choice questions with 105 minutes.

Section II contains 6 free-response questions with 90 minutes.

The time allotted for both sections is 3 hours and 15 minutes. Below is a summary of the different parts of each section.

Section I Multiple-Choice	Part A	28 questions	No Calculator	55 Minutes
	Part B	17 questions	Calculator	50 Minutes
Section II Free-Response	Part A	3 questions	Calculator	45 Minutes
	Part B	3 questions	No Calculator	45 Minutes

During the time allotted for Part B of Section II, students may continue to work on questions from Part A of Section II. However, they may not use a calculator at that time. Please note that you are not expected to be able to answer all the questions in order to receive a grade of 5. If you wish to see the specific instructions for each part of the test, visit the College Board website at: *www.collegeboard.org/ap/calculus.*

What Are the Advanced Placement Exam Grades?

Advanced Placement Exam grades are given in a 5-point scale with 5 being the highest grade. The grades are described below:

5	Extremely Well Qualified
4	Well Qualified
3	Qualified
2	Possibly Qualified
1	No Recommendation

How Is the AP Calculus AB Exam Grade Calculated?

- The exam has a total raw score of 108 points: 54 points for the multiple-choice questions in Section I and 54 points for the free-response questions for Section II.
- Each correct answer in Section I is worth 1.2 points, an incorrect answer is worth $(\frac{1}{4})(-1.2)$ points, and no points for unanswered questions. For example, suppose your result in Section I is as follows:

Correct	Incorrect	Unanswered
36	4	5

Your score for Section I would be:

$$36 \times 1.2 - 4 \times (\tfrac{1}{4})(1.2) = 43.2 - 1.2 = 42.\text{ Not a bad score!}$$

- Each complete and correct solution for Section II is worth 9 points.
- The total raw score for both Section I and II is converted to a 5-point scale. The cut-off points for each grade (1–5) vary from year to year. Visit the College Board website at: *www.collegeboard.com/ap* for more information. Below is a rough estimate of the conversion scale:

Total Raw Score	Approximate AP Grade
75–108	5
60–74	4
45–59	3
31–44	2
0–30	1

Remember, these are approximate cut-off points.

Which Graphing Calculators Are Allowed for the Exam?

The following calculators are allowed:

Texas Instruments	Hewlett-Packard	Casio	Sharp
TI-82	HP-28 series	FX-9700 series	EL-9200 series
TI-83/TI-83 Plus	HP-38G	FX-9750 series	EL-9300 series
TI-85	HP-39G	CFX-9800 series	EL-9600 series
TI-86	HP-40G	CFX-9850 series	
TI-89	HP-48 series	CFX-9950 series	
	HP-49 series	CFX-9970 series	
		Algebra FX 2.0 series	

For a more complete list, visit the College Board website at: *www.collegeboard.com/ap*. If you wish to use a graphing calculator that is not on the approved list, your teacher must obtain written permission from the ETS before April 1st of the testing year.

Calculators and Other Devices Not Allowed for the AP Calculus Exam

- TI-92, HP-95 and devices with QWERTY keyboards
- Non-graphing scientific calculators
- Laptop computers
- Pocket organizers, electronic writing pads or pen-input devices

Other Restrictions on Calculators

- You may bring up to 2 (but no more than 2) approved graphing calculators to the exam.
- You may not share calculators with another student.
- You may store programs in your calculator.
- You are not required to clear the memories in your calculator for the exam.
- You may not use the memories of your calculator to store secured questions and take them out of the testing room.

How Much Work Do I Need to Show When I Use a Graphing Calculator in Section II, Free-Response Questions?

- When using a graphing calculator in solving a problem, you are required to write the setup that leads to the answer. For example, if you are finding the volume of a solid, you must write the definite integral and then use the calculator to compute the numerical value, e.g., Volume $= \pi \int_0^3 (5x)^2 \, dx = 225\pi$. Simply indicating the answer without writing the integral would only get you one point for the answer but no other credit for the work.
- You may *not* use calculator syntax to substitute for calculus notations. For example, you may *not* write "Volume $= \int (\pi)(5 * x)^2, x, 0, 3 = 225\pi$" instead of "Volume $= \pi \int_0^3 (5x)^2 \, dx = 225\pi$."
- You are permitted to use the following 4 built-in capabilities of your calculator to obtain an answer: plotting the graph of a function, finding the zeros of a function, finding the numerical derivative of a function, and evaluating a definite integral. All other capabilities of your calculator can only be used to *check* your answer. For example, you may *not* use the built-in Inflection function of your calculator to find points of inflection. You must use calculus using derivatives and showing change of concavity.

What Do I Need to Bring to the Exam?

- Several Number 2 pencils
- A good eraser and a pencil sharpener
- Two black or blue pens
- One or two approved graphing calculators with fresh batteries. (Be careful when you change batteries so that you don't lose your programs.)
- A watch
- An admissions card or a photo I.D. card if your school or the test site requires it.
- Your Social Security number
- Your school code number if the test site is not at your school
- A simple snack *if the test site permits it.* (Don't try anything you haven't eaten before. You might have an allergic reaction.)
- A light jacket if you know that the test site has strong air conditioning
- Do *not* bring Wite Out or scrap paper.

TIPS FOR TAKING THE EXAM

General Tips

- Write legibly.
- Label all diagrams.

- Organize your solution so that the reader can follow you line of reasoning.
- Use complete sentences whenever possible. Always indicate what the final answer is.

More Tips

- Do easy questions first.
- Write out formulas and indicate all major steps.
- Guess if you can eliminate some of the choices in a multiple-choice question.
- Leave a multiple-choice question blank if you have no clue what the answer is.
- Be careful to bubble in the right grid, especially if you skip a question.
- Move on. Don't linger on a problem too long.
- Go with your first instinct if you are unsure.

Still More Tips

- Indicate units of measure.
- Simplify numeric or algebraic expressions only if the question asks you to do so.
- Carry all decimal places and round only at the end.
- Round to 3 decimal places unless the question indicates otherwise.

- Watch out for different units of measure, e.g., the radius, r, is 2 feet, find $\dfrac{dr}{dt}$ in inches per second.
- Use calculus notations and not calculator syntax, e.g., write $\int x^2 dx$ and not $\int (x^2, x)$.
- Use only the four specified capabilities of your calculator to get your answer: plotting graph, finding zeros, calculating numerical derivatives, and evaluating definite integrals. All other built-in capabilities can only be used to *check* your solution.
- Answer all parts of a question from Section II even if you think your answer to an earlier part of the question might not be correct.

Enough Already . . . Just 3 More Tips

- Be familiar with the instructions for the different parts of the exam before the day of the exam. Visit the College Board website at: *www.collegeboard.com/ap* for more information.
- Get a good night sleep the night before.
- Have a light breakfast before the exam.

GETTING STARTED!

Answer Sheet for Diagnostic Test—Section I

PART A

1. _____

2. _____

3. _____

4. _____

5. _____

6. _____

7. _____

8. _____

9. _____

10. _____

11. _____

12. _____

13. _____

14. _____

15. _____

16. _____

17. _____

18. _____

19. _____

20. _____

21. _____

22. _____

23. _____

24. _____

25. _____

26. _____

27. _____

28. _____

PART B

76. _____

77. _____

78. _____

79. _____

80. _____

81. _____

82. _____

83. _____

84. _____

85. _____

86. _____

87. _____

88. _____

89. _____

90. _____

91. _____

92. _____

DIAGNOSTIC TEST

Section I—Part A

Number of Questions	Time	Use of Calculator
28	55 Minutes	No

Directions:

Use the answer sheet provided in the previous page. All questions are given equal weight. There is no penalty for unanswered questions. However, ¼ of the number of the incorrect answers will be subtracted from the number of correct answers. Unless otherwise indicated, the domain of a function f is the set of all real numbers. The use of a calculator is not permitted in this part of the test.

1. Evaluate $\int_1^4 \frac{1}{\sqrt{x}}\, dx$.

2. If $f(x) = -2\csc(5x)$, find $f'\left(\frac{\pi}{6}\right)$.

3. Evaluate $\lim_{x \to -\infty} \frac{\sqrt{x^2 - 4}}{2x}$.

4. Given the equation $y = \sqrt{x - 1}$, what is an equation of the normal line to the graph at $x = 5$?

5. The graph of f is shown in Figure D-1. Draw a possible graph of f' on (a, b).

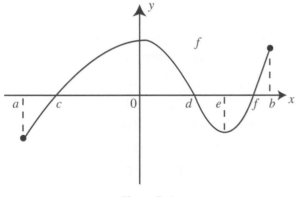

Figure D-1

6. If $f(x) = \left|2xe^x\right|$, what is the value of $\lim_{x \to 0^+} f'(x)$?

7. Evaluate $\int \frac{1 - x^2}{x^2}\, dx$.

8. If $\int_{-1}^{k} (2x - 3)\, dx = 6$, find k.

9. The graph of the velocity function of a moving particle is shown in Figure D-2. What is the total distance traveled by the particle during $0 \le t \le 6$?

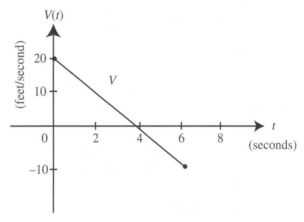

Figure D-2

10. If $h(x) = \int_{\pi/2}^{x} \sqrt{\sin t}\, dt$, find $h'(\pi)$.

11. What is the average value of the function $y = e^{-4x}$ on $[-\ln 2, \ln 2]$?

12. The graph of f consists of four line segments, for $-1 \le x \le 5$ as shown in Figure D-3. What is the value of $\int_{-1}^{5} f(x)\, dx$?

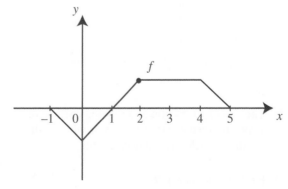

Figure D-3

13. Given the equation $y = (x + 1)(x - 3)^2$, what is the instantaneous rate of change of y at $x = -1$?

14. If $h(x) = \begin{cases} \sqrt{x} & \text{if } x > 4 \\ x^2 - 12 & \text{if } x \le 4 \end{cases}$, find the $\lim\limits_{x \to 4} h(x)$.

15. What is the slope of the tangent to the curve $y = \cos(xy)$ at $x = 0$?

16. If $f'(x) = g(x)$ and g is a continuous function for all real values of x, then $\int_0^2 g(3x)dx$ is

    (A) $\dfrac{1}{3}f(6) - \dfrac{1}{3}f(0)$

    (B) $f(2) - f(0)$

    (C) $f(6) - f(0)$

    (D) $\dfrac{1}{3}f(0) - \dfrac{1}{3}f(6)$

    (E) $3f(6) - 3f(0)$

17. What is $\lim\limits_{\Delta x \to 0} \dfrac{\tan\left(\dfrac{\pi}{4} + \Delta x\right) - \tan\left(\dfrac{\pi}{4}\right)}{\Delta x}$?

18. The graph of the function g is shown in Figure D-4. Which of the following is true for g on (a, b)?

    I. g is monotonic on (a, b).
    II. g' is continuous on (a, b).
    III. $g'' > 0$ on (a, b).

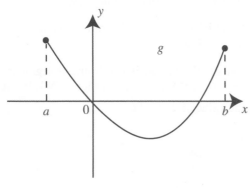

Figure D-4

19. The velocity function of a moving particle on the x-axis is given as $v(t) = t^2 - t$. For which values of t is the particle's speed decreasing?

20. Evaluate $\int_\pi^x \sin(2t)\, dt$.

21. A function f is continuous on $[-2, 0]$ and some of the values of f are shown below.

x	-2	-1	0
f	4	b	4

    If $f(x) = 2$ has no solution on $[-2, 0]$, then b could be

    (A) 3
    (B) 2
    (C) 1
    (D) 0
    (E) -2

22. Find the area of the region enclosed by the graph of $y = x^2 - x$ and the x-axis.

23. If $\int_{-k}^{k} f(x)dx = 0$ for all real values of k, then which of the graphs in Figure D-5 (see page 21) could be the graph of f?

24. If $f(x)$ is an antiderivative of $\dfrac{e^x}{e^x + 1}$ and $f(0) = \ln 2$, find $f(\ln 2)$.

25. If $\dfrac{dy}{dx} = 2 \sin x$ and at $x = \pi$, $y = 2$, find a solution to the differential equation.

26. When the area of a square is increasing four times as fast as the diagonals, what is the length of a side of the square?

27. The graph of f is shown in Figure D-6 on page 21 and f is twice differentiable, which of the following statements is true?

    (A) $f(10) < f'(10) < f''(10)$

    (B) $f''(10) < f'(10) < f(10)$

    (C) $f'(10) < f(10) < f''(10)$

    (D) $f'(10) < f''(10) < f(10)$

    (E) $f''(10) < f(10) < f'(10)$

28. If a function f is continuous for all values of x, which of the following statements is always true?

    I. $\int_a^c f(x)dx = \int_a^b f(x)dx + \int_b^c f(x)dx$

    II. $\int_a^b f(x)dx = \int_a^c f(x)dx - \int_b^c f(x)dx$

    III. $\int_b^c f(x)dx = \int_b^a f(x)dx - \int_c^a f(x)dx$

(A)

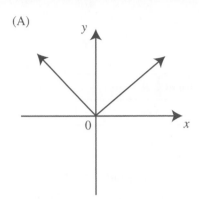

(B)

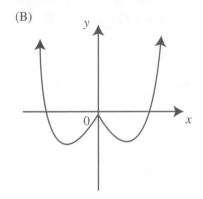

(C)

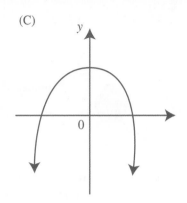

(D)

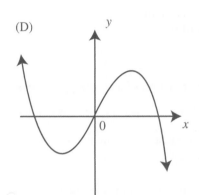

(E)

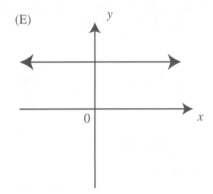

Figure D-5

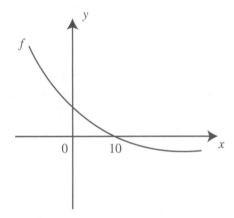

Figure D-6

Section I—Part B

Number of Questions	Time	Use of Calculator
17	50 Minutes	Yes

Directions:

Use the same answer sheet as for Part A. *Please note that the questions begin with number 76. This is not an error. It is done to be consistent with the numbering system of the actual AP Calculus AB Exam.* All questions are given equal weight. There is no penalty for unanswered questions. However, ¼ of the number of incorrect answers will be subtracted from the number of correct answers. Unless otherwise indicated, the domain of a function *f* is the set of all real numbers. The use of a calculator is *permitted* in this part of the test.

76. The area under the curve $y = \sqrt{x}$ from $x = 1$ to $x = k$ is 8. Find the value of k.

77. If $g(x) = \int_{\pi/2}^{x} 2 \sin t \, dt$ on $\left[\dfrac{\pi}{2}, \dfrac{5\pi}{2} \right]$, find the value(s) of x where g has a local minimum.

78. If $g(x) = \left| x^2 - 4x - 12 \right|$, which of the following statements about g are true?

    I. g has a relative maximum at $x = 2$.
    II. g is differentiable at $x = 6$.
    III. g has a point of inflection at $x = -2$.

79. The graph of f', the derivative of f is shown in Figure D-7. At which value(s) of x is graph of f concave up?

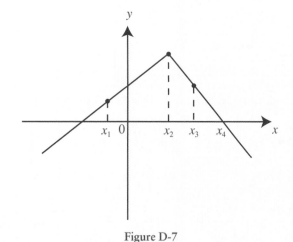

Figure D-7

80. How many points of inflection does the graph of $y = \sin(x^2)$ have on the interval $[-\pi, \pi]$?

81. The velocity function of a moving particle is
$$v(t) = \frac{t^3}{3} - 2t^2 + 5 \text{ for } 0 \le t \le 6.$$
What is the maximum acceleration of the particle on the interval $0 \le t \le 6$?

82. Water is leaking from a tank at the rate of $f(t) = 10 \ln(t + 1)$ *gallons per hour* for $0 \le t \le 10$, where t is measured in hours. How many gallons of water have leaked from the tank at exactly after *5 hours*?

83. Write an equation of the normal line to the graph of $y = x^3$ for $x \ge 0$ at the point where $f'(x) = 12$.

84. If $g(x) = \int_{a}^{x} f(t) dt$ and the graph of f is shown in Figure D-8, which of the graphs in Figure D-9 on page 23 is a possible graph of g?

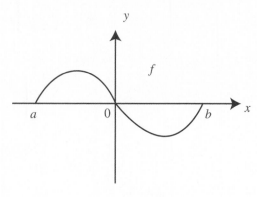

Figure D-8

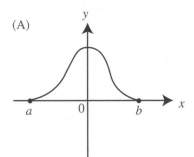

(A)

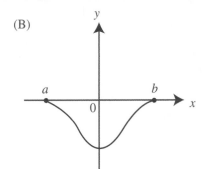

(B)

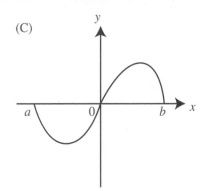

(C)

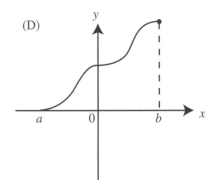

(D)

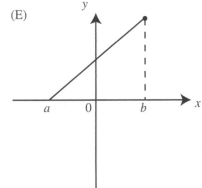

(E)

Figure D-9

85. For $0 \le x \le 3\pi$, find the area of the region bounded by the graphs of $y = \sin x$ and $y = \cos x$.

86. Carbon-14 has a half-life of *5730 years*. If y is the amount of carbon-14 present and y decays according to the equation $\dfrac{dy}{dt} = ky$, where k is a constant and t is measured in years, find the value of k.

87. Given a differentiable function f with $f\left(\dfrac{\pi}{2}\right) = 3$ and $f'\left(\dfrac{\pi}{2}\right) = -1$. Using a tangent line to the graph of $x = \dfrac{\pi}{2}$, what is an approximate value of $f\left(\dfrac{\pi}{2} + \dfrac{\pi}{180}\right)$?

88. Find the volume of the solid generated by revolving about the x-axis the region bounded by the graph of $y = \sin 2x$ for $0 \le x \le \pi$ and the line $y = \dfrac{1}{2}$.

89. The graphs of f', g', p' and q' are shown in Figure D-10 on page 24. Which of the functions f, g, p or q have a point of inflection on (a, b)?

90. At what value(s) of x do the graphs of $f(x) = \dfrac{\ln x}{x}$ and $y = -x^2$ have perpendicular tangent lines?

91. Let f be a continuous function on $[0, 6]$ and has selected values as shown below:

x	0	1	2	3	4	5	6
$f(x)$	1	2	5	10	17	26	37

Using three midpoint rectangles of equal lengths, what is the approximate value of $\int_0^6 f(x)\,dx$?

92. What is the volume of the solid whose base is the region enclosed by the graphs of $y = x^2$ and $y = x + 2$ and whose cross sections perpendicular to the x-axis are squares?

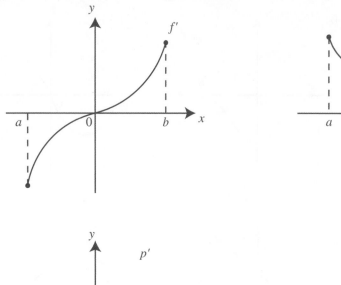

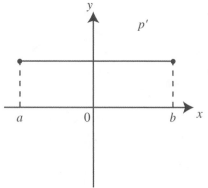

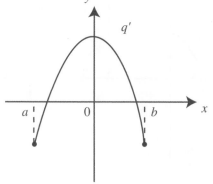

Figure D-10

Section II—Part A

Number of Questions	Time	Use of Calculator
3	45 Minutes	Yes

Directions:

Show all work. You may *not* receive any credit for correct answers without supporting work. You may use an approved calculator to help solve a problem. However, you must clearly indicate the setup of your solution using mathematical notations and *not* calculator syntax. Calculators may be used to find the derivative of a function at a point, compute the numerical value of a definite integral, or solve an equation. Unless otherwise indicated, you may assume the following: (a) the numeric or algebraic answers need not be simplified, (b) your answer, if expressed in approximation, should be correct to 3 places after the decimal point, and (c) the domain of a function f is the set of all real numbers.

1. The slope of a function f at any point (x, y) is $\dfrac{4x + 1}{2y}$. The point $(2, 4)$ is on the graph of f.

   (a) Write an equation of the line tangent to the graph of f at $x = 2$.
   (b) Use the tangent line in part (a) to approximate $f(2.1)$.
   (c) Solve the differential equation $\dfrac{dy}{dx} = \dfrac{4x + 1}{2y}$ with the initial condition $f(2) = 4$.
   (d) Use the solution in part (c) and find $f(2.1)$.

2. A drum containing *100 gallons* of oil is punctured by a nail and begins to leak at the rate of

   $10 \sin\left(\dfrac{\pi t}{12}\right)$ *gallons/minute* where t is measured

   in minutes and $0 \le t \le 10$.

   (a) How much oil to the nearest gallon leaked out after $t = 6$ minutes?
   (b) What is the average amount of oil leaked out per minute from $t = 0$ to $t = 6$ to the nearest gallon?

   (c) Write an expression for $f(t)$ to represent the total amount of oil in the drum at time t, where $0 \le t \le 10$.
   (d) At what value of t to the nearest minute will there be 40 gallons of oil remaining in the drum?

3. Given the function $f(x) = xe^{2x}$.

   (a) At what value(s) of x, if any, is $f'(x) = 0$?
   (b) At what value(s) of x, if any, is $f''(x) = 0$?
   (c) Find $\lim\limits_{x \to \infty} f(x)$ and $\lim\limits_{x \to -\infty} f(x)$.
   (d) Find the absolute extrema of f and justify your answer.
   (e) Show that if $f(x) = xe^{ax}$ where $a > 0$, the absolute minimum value of f is $\dfrac{-1}{ae}$.

Section II—Part B

Number of Questions	Time	Use of Calculator
3	45 Minutes	No

Directions:

The use of a calculator is *not* permitted in this part of the test. When you have finished this part of the test, you may return to the problems in Part A of Section II and continue to work on them. However, you may not use a calculator. You should *show all work*. You may *not* receive any credit for correct answers without supporting work. Unless otherwise indicated, the numeric or algebraic answers need not be simplified, and the domain of a function *f* is the set of all real numbers.

4. The graph of f', the derivative of the function f, for $-4 \le x \le 6$ is shown in Figure D-11.

   (a) At what value(s) of x does f have a relative maximum value? Justify your answer.

   (b) At what value(s) of x does f have a relative minimum value? Justify your answer.

   (c) At what value(s) of x does $f''(x) > 0$? Justify your answer.

   (d) At what value(s) of x, if any, does the graph of f have a point of inflection? Justify you answer.

   (e) Draw a possible sketch of $f(x)$, if $f(-2) = 3$.

5. Let R be the region enclosed by the graph of $y = x^3$, the x-axis and the line $x = 2$.

   (a) Find the area of region R.

   (b) Find the volume of the solid obtained by revolving region R about the x-axis.

   (c) The line $x = a$ divides region R into two regions such that when the regions are revolved about the x-axis, the resulting solids have equal volume. Find a.

   (d) If region R is the base of a solid whose cross sections perpendicular to the x-axis are squares, find the volume of the solid.

6. Given the equation $x^2 y^2 = 4$,

   (a) Find $\dfrac{dy}{dx}$.

   (b) Write an equation of the line tangent to the graph of the equation at the point $(1, -2)$.

   (c) Write an equation of the line normal to the curve at point $(1, -2)$.

   (d) The line $y = \dfrac{1}{2}x + 2$ is tangent to the curve at the point P. Find the coordinates of point P.

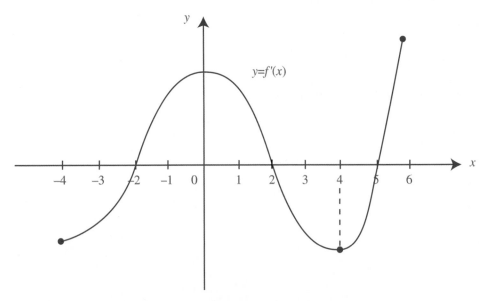

Figure D-11

ANSWERS AND SOLUTIONS

Answers to Diagnostic Test—Section I

Part A

1. 2

2. $-20\sqrt{3}$

3. $-1/2$

4. $y = -4x + 22$

5. See solution.

6. 2

7. $\dfrac{-1}{x} - x + c$

8. $\{-2, 5\}$

9. 50 feet

10. 0

11. $\dfrac{255}{128 \ln 2}$

12. 2

13. 16

14. Does not exist.

15. 0

16. A

17. 2

18. II & III

19. $\left(\dfrac{1}{2}, 1\right)$

20. $\dfrac{-1}{2}\cos(2x) + \dfrac{1}{2}$

21. A

22. $\dfrac{1}{6}$

23. D

24. $\ln 3$

25. $y = -2\cos x$

26. 4

27. C

28. I & III

Part B

76. $13^{2/3}$

77. 2π

78. I

79. $x < x_2$

80. 8

81. 12

82. 57.506

83. $y = \dfrac{-1}{12x} + \dfrac{49}{6}$

84. A

85. 5.657

86. $\dfrac{-\ln 2}{5730}$

87. 2.983

88. 1.503

89. q

90. 1.370

91. 76

92. $\dfrac{81}{10}$

Answers to Diagnostic Test—Section II

Part A

1. (a) $y = \dfrac{9}{8}(x - 2) + 4$ (3 pts.)
   (b) 4.113   (1 pt.)
   (c) $y = \sqrt{2x^2 + x + 6}$ (4 pts.)
   (d) 4.113   (1 pt.)

2. (a) 38 gallons   (3 pts.)
   (b) 6 gallons   (2 pts.)
   (c) $f(t) = 100 - \int_0^t 10\sin\left(\pi x / 12\right)dx$ (1 pt.)
   (d) 8 minutes   (3 pts.)

3. (a) -0.5 (1 pt.)
   (b) -1 (1 pt.)
   (c) $\lim\limits_{x\to\infty} f(x) = \infty$ & $\lim\limits_{x\to-\infty} f(x) = 0$ (2 pts.)
   (d) $-\dfrac{1}{2e}$ (3 pts.)
   (e) See solution.   (2 pts.)

Part B

4. (a) $x = 2$ (2 pts.)
   (b) $x = 5$ (2 pts.)
   (c) $(-4, 0)$ and $(4, 6)$ (1 pt.)
   (d) $x = 0$ and $x = 4$ (2 pts.)
   (e) See solution.   (2 pts.)

5. (a) 4   (2 pts.)
   (b) $\dfrac{128\pi}{7}$ (2 pts.)
   (c) $2^{5/7}$ (3 pts.)
   (d) $\dfrac{128}{7}$ (2 pts.)

6. (a) $\dfrac{dy}{dx} = \dfrac{-y}{x}$ (3 pts.)
   (b) $y = 2x - 4$ (2 pts.)
   (c) $y = -\dfrac{1}{2}x - \dfrac{3}{2}$ (2 pts.)
   (d) $(2, -1)$ and $(-2, 1)$ (2 pts.)

Solutions to Diagnostic Test—Section I

Part A—No calculators.

1. From Chapter 8

$$\int_1^4 \frac{1}{\sqrt{x}}\, dx = \int_1^4 x^{-\frac{1}{2}}\, dx = \left. \frac{x^{\frac{1}{2}}}{\frac{1}{2}} \right]_1^4 = 2x^{\frac{1}{2}} \bigg]_1^4$$

$$= 2(4)^{\frac{1}{2}} - 2(1)^{\frac{1}{2}} = 4 - 2 = 2$$

2. From Chapter 3

$$f(x) = -2\csc(5x)$$
$$f'(x) = -2(-\csc 5x)[\cot(5x)](5)$$
$$= 10\csc(5x)\cot(5x)$$
$$f'\left(\frac{\pi}{6}\right) = 10\csc\left(\frac{5\pi}{6}\right)\cot\left(\frac{5\pi}{6}\right)$$
$$= 10(2)(-\sqrt{3}) = -20\sqrt{3}$$

3. From Chapter 2

$$\lim_{x\to-\infty} \frac{\sqrt{x^2-4}}{2x} = \lim_{x\to-\infty} \frac{\dfrac{\sqrt{x^2-4}}{-\sqrt{x^2}}}{\dfrac{2x}{x}}$$

$$\left(\text{note: as } x \to -\infty, \ x = -\sqrt{x^2}\right)$$

$$= \lim_{x\to-\infty} \frac{\dfrac{-\sqrt{x^2-4}}{x^2}}{2}$$

$$= \lim_{x\to-\infty} \frac{-\sqrt{1-\dfrac{1}{x^2}}}{2}$$

$$= -\frac{\sqrt{1}}{2} = -\frac{1}{2}$$

4. From Chapter 6

$$y = \sqrt{x-1} = (x-1)^{\frac{1}{2}}; \ \frac{dy}{dx} = \frac{1}{2}(x-1)^{-\frac{1}{2}}$$

$$= \frac{1}{2(x-1)^{\frac{1}{2}}}$$

$$\frac{dy}{dx}\bigg|_{x=5} = \frac{1}{2(5-1)^{\frac{1}{2}}} = \frac{1}{2(4)^{\frac{1}{2}}} = \frac{1}{4}$$

At $x = 5$, $y = \sqrt{x-1} = \sqrt{5-1} = 2$; $(5, 2)$

Slope of normal line = negative reciprocal

of $\left(\dfrac{1}{4}\right) = -4$

Equation of normal line:

$$y - 2 = -4(x - 5) \Rightarrow y = -4(x - 5) + 2 \text{ or}$$

$$y = -4x + 22.$$

5. From Chapter 4

See Figure DS-1.

Based on the graph of f:

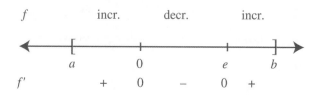

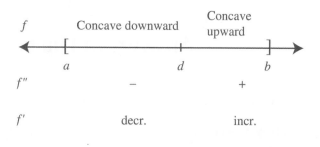

A possible graph of f'

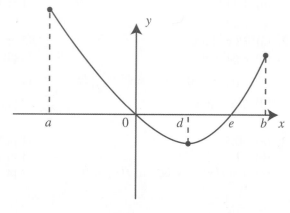

Figure DS-1

6. From Chapters 2 and 3

$$f(x) = |2xe^x| = \begin{cases} 2xe^x \text{ if } x \geq 0 \\ -2xe^x \text{ if } x < 0 \end{cases}$$

If $x \geq 0$, $f'(x) = 2e^x + e^x(2x) = 2e^x + 2xe^x$

$$\lim_{x \to 0^+} f'(x) = \lim_{x \to 0^+}(2e^x + 2xe^x) = 2e^0 + 0 = 2$$

7. From Chapter 7

$$\int \frac{1-x^2}{x^2}\,dx = \int \left(\frac{1}{x^2} - \frac{x^2}{x^2}\right)dx = \int \left(\frac{1}{x^2} - 1\right)dx$$

$$= \int (x^{-2} - 1)dx = \frac{x^{-1}}{-1} - x + c$$

$$= -\frac{1}{x} - x + c$$

! You can check the answer by differentiating your result.

8. From Chapter 8

$$\int_{-1}^{k}(2x-3)dx = x^2 - 3x\Big]_{-1}^{k}$$

$$= (k^2 - 3k) - ((-1)^2 - 3(-1))$$

$$= k^2 - 3k - (1+3)$$

$$= k^2 - 3k - 4$$

Set $k^2 - 3k - 4 = 6 \Rightarrow k^2 - 3k - 10 = 0$

$$\Rightarrow (k-5)(k+2) = 0 \Rightarrow k = 5 \text{ or } k = -2$$

You can check your answer by evaluating $\int_{-1}^{-2}(2x-3)$ and $\int_{-1}^{6}(2x-3)dx$

9. From Chapter 9

$$\text{Total distance} = \int_0^4 v(t) + \left|\int_4^5 v(t)dt\right|$$

$$= \frac{1}{2}(4)(20) + \left|\frac{1}{2}(2)(-10)\right|$$

$$= 40 + 10 = 50 \text{ feet}$$

10. From Chapter 8

$$h(x) = \int_{\pi/2}^{x} \sqrt{\sin t}\,dt \Rightarrow h'(x) = \sqrt{\sin x}$$

$$h'(\pi) = \sqrt{\sin \pi} = \sqrt{0} = 0$$

11. From Chapter 10

$$\text{Average value} = \frac{1}{\ln 2 - (-\ln 2)}\int_{-\ln 2}^{\ln 2} e^{-4x}\,dx$$

Let $u = -4x$; $du = -4dx$ or $\dfrac{-du}{4} = dx$

$$\int e^{-4x}\,dx = \int e^u\left(\frac{-du}{4}\right) = \frac{1}{4}e^u + c = \frac{-1}{4}e^{-4x} + c$$

$$\text{Average value} = \frac{1}{2\ln 2}\left[\frac{e^{-4x}}{-4}\right]_{-\ln x}^{\ln 2}$$

$$= \frac{1}{2\ln 2}\left[\left(\frac{e^{-4\ln 2}}{-4}\right) - \left(\frac{e^{-4(-\ln 2)}}{-4}\right)\right]$$

$$= \frac{1}{2\ln 2}\left[\frac{(e^{\ln 2})^{-4}}{-4} + \frac{(e^{\ln 2})^4}{4}\right]$$

$$= \frac{1}{2\ln 2}\left[\frac{2^{-4}}{-4} + \frac{2^4}{4}\right]$$

$$= \frac{1}{2\ln 2}\left(\frac{1}{-64} + 4\right)$$

$$= \frac{1}{2\ln 2}\left(\frac{255}{64}\right)$$

$$= \frac{255}{128\ln 2}$$

12. From Chapter 9

$$\int_{-1}^{5} f(x)dx = \int_{-1}^{1} f(x)dx + \int_{1}^{5}f(x)dx$$

$$= -\frac{1}{2}(2)(1) + \frac{1}{2}(2+4)(1)$$

$$= -1 + 3 = 2$$

13. From Chapter 3

$$y = (x+1)(x-3)^2;$$

$$\frac{dy}{dx} = (1)(x-3)^2 + 2(x-3)(x+1)$$

$$= (x-3)^2 + 2(x-3)(x+1)$$

$$\frac{dy}{dx}\Big|_{x=-1} = (-1-3)^2 + 2(-1-3)(-1+1)$$

$$= (-4)^2 + 0 = 16$$

14. From Chapter 2

$$h(x) = \begin{cases} \sqrt{x} & \text{if } x > 4 \\ x^2 - 12 & \text{if } x \le 4 \end{cases}$$

$$\lim_{x \to 4^+} h(x) = \lim_{x \to 4^+} \sqrt{x} = \sqrt{4} = 2$$

$$\lim_{x \to 4^-} h(x) = \lim_{x \to 4^-} (x^2 - 12) = (4^2 - 12) = 4$$

Since $\lim_{x \to 4^+} h(x) \ne \lim_{x \to 4^-} h(x)$, thus $\lim_{x \to 4} h(x)$

does not exist.

15. From Chapter 6

$$y = \cos(xy); \frac{dy}{dx} = [-\sin(xy)]\left(1y + x\frac{dy}{dx}\right)$$

$$\frac{dy}{dx} = -y\sin(xy) - x\sin(xy)\frac{dy}{dx}$$

$$\frac{dy}{dx} + x\sin(xy)\frac{dy}{dx} = -y\sin(xy)$$

$$\frac{dy}{dx}[1 + x\sin(xy)] = -y\sin(xy)$$

$$\frac{dy}{dx} = \frac{-y\sin(xy)}{1 + x\sin(xy)}$$

At $x = 0$, $y = \cos(xy) = \cos(0) = 1; (0, 1)$

$$\left.\frac{dy}{dx}\right|_{x=0, y=1} = \frac{-(1)\sin(0)}{1 + 0\sin(0)} = \frac{0}{1} = 0$$

Thus the slope of the tangent at $x = 0$ is 0.

16. From Chapter 8

Let $u = 3x; du = 3dx$ or $\frac{du}{3} = dx$

$$\int g(3x)dx = \int g(u)\frac{du}{3} = \frac{1}{3}\int g(u)du$$

$$= \frac{1}{3}f(u) + c = \frac{1}{3}f(3x) + c$$

$$\int_0^2 g(3x)dx = \frac{1}{3}[f(3x)]_0^2 = \frac{1}{3}f(6) - \frac{1}{3}f(0)$$

Thus, the correct choice is (A).

17. From Chapter 3

$$f'(x_1) = \lim_{\Delta x \to 0} \frac{f(x_1 + \Delta x) - f(x_1)}{\Delta x}$$

Thus $\lim_{\Delta x \to 0} \dfrac{\tan\left(\dfrac{\pi}{4} + \Delta x\right) - \tan\left(\dfrac{\pi}{4}\right)}{\Delta x}$

$$= \frac{d}{dx}(\tan x)_{x/4}$$

$$= \sec^2\left(\frac{\pi}{4}\right) = \left(\sqrt{2}\right)^2 = 2$$

18. From Chapter 4

  I. Since the graph of g is decreasing and then increasing, It is not monotonic.

  II. Since the graph of g is a smooth curve, g' is continuous,

  III. Since the graph of g is concave upward, $g'' > 0$.

Thus only statements II and III are true.

19. From Chapter 6

See Figure DS-2.

$$v(t) = t^2 - t$$

    Set $v(t) = 0 \Rightarrow t(t - 1) = 0 \Rightarrow$

    $t = 0$ or $t = 1$

$$a(t) = v'(t) = 2t - 1$$

    Set $a(t) = 0 \Rightarrow 2t - 1 = 0$ or $t = \dfrac{1}{2}$.

Since $v(t) < 0$ and $a(t) > 0$ on $\left(\dfrac{1}{2}, 1\right)$,

the speed of the particle is decreasing on

$\left(\dfrac{1}{2}, 1\right)$.

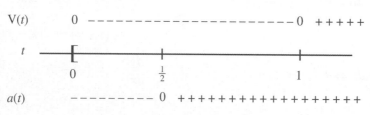

Figure DS-2

20. From Chapter 8

$$\int_\pi^x \sin(2t)dt = \left[\frac{-\cos(2t)}{2}\right]_\pi^x = \frac{-\cos(2x)}{2}$$

$$-\left(-\frac{\cos(2\pi)}{2}\right)$$

$$= -\frac{1}{2}\cos(2x) + \frac{1}{2}$$

21. From Chapter 1

See DS-3.

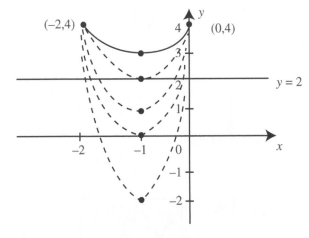

Figure DS-3

If $b = 2$, then $x = -1$ would be a solution for $f(x) = 2$.

If $b = 1$, 0 or -2, $f(x) = 2$ would have two solutions for $f(x) = 2$.

Thus, $b = 3$, choice (A).

22. From Chapter 9

To find points of intersection, set $y = x^2 - x = 0$
$\Rightarrow x(x - 1) = 0 \Rightarrow x = 0$ or $x = 1$. See Figure DS-4.

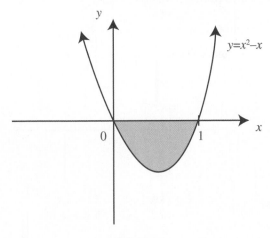

Figure DS-4

$$\text{Area} = \left|\int_0^1 (x^2 - x)dx\right| = \left|\frac{x^3}{3} - \frac{x^2}{2}\right]_0^1\right|$$

$$= \left|\left(\frac{1}{3} - \frac{1}{2}\right) - 0\right| = \left|-\frac{1}{6}\right|$$

$$= \frac{1}{6}$$

23. From Chapter 9

$\int_{-k}^k f(x)dx = 0 \Rightarrow f(x)$ is odd function,

i.e., $f(x) = -f(-x)$

Thus the graph in choice (D) is the only odd function.

24. From Chapter 7

Let $u = e^x + 1; du = e^x dx$

$$f(x) = \int \frac{e^x}{e^x + 1}dx = \int \frac{1}{u}du$$

$$= \ln|u| + c = \ln|e^x + 1| + c$$

$$f(0) = \ln|e^0 + 1| + c = \ln(2) + c \text{ and}$$

$$f(0) = \ln 2 \Rightarrow \ln(2) + c = \ln 2$$

$$\Rightarrow c = 0$$

Thus $f(x) = \ln(e^x + 1)$ and $f(\ln 2)$

$$= \ln(e^{\ln 2} + 1) = \ln(2 + 1) = \ln 3$$

25. From Chapter 10

$$\frac{dy}{dx} = 2\sin x \Rightarrow dy = 2\sin x dx$$

$$\int dy = \int 2\sin x dx \Rightarrow y = -2\cos x + c$$

$$\text{At } x = \pi, y = 2 \Rightarrow 2 = -2\cos \pi + c$$

$$\Rightarrow 2 = (-2)(-1) + c$$

$$\Rightarrow 2 = 2 + c \text{ or } c = 0.$$

Thus $y = -2\cos x$

26. From Chapter 5

Let z be the diagonal of a square.

$$\text{Area of a square } A = \frac{z^2}{2}$$

$$\frac{dA}{dt} = \frac{2z}{2}\frac{dz}{dt} = z\frac{dz}{dt}$$

Since $\frac{dA}{dt} = 4\frac{dz}{dt}; 4\frac{dz}{dt} = z\frac{dz}{dt} \Rightarrow z = 4$

Let s be a side of the square. Since the diagonal $z = 4$, $s^2 + s^2 = z^2$ or $2s^2 = 16$. Thus, $s^2 = 8$ or $s = 2 \times \sqrt{2}$.

27. From Chapter 4

The graph indicates that (1) $f(10) = 0$, (2) $f'(10) < 0$, since f is decreasing; and (3) $f''(10) > 0$, since f is concave upward.

Thus $f'(10) < f(10) < f''(10)$, choice (C).

28. From Chapter 8

I. $\int_a^c f(x)dx = \int_a^b f(x)dx + \int_b^c f(x)dx$

The statement is true, since the upper and lower limits of the integrals are in sequence, i.e., $a \to c = a \to b \to c$.

II. $\int_a^b f(x)dx = \int_a^c f(x)dx - \int_c^b f(x)dx$

$= \int_a^c f(x)dx + \int_b^c f(x)dx$

The statement is not always true.

III. $\int_b^c f(x)dx = \int_b^a f(x)dx - \int_c^a f(x)dx$

$= \int_b^a f(x)dx + \int_a^c f(x)dx$

The statement is true.

Thus only statements I and III are true.

Part B—Calculators are permitted.

76. From Chapter 9

$$\text{Area} = \int_1^k \sqrt{x}dx = \int_1^k x^{1/2}dx = \left[\frac{x^{3/2}}{3/2}\right]_1^k$$

$$= \left[\frac{2}{3}x^{3/2}\right]_1^k = \frac{2}{3}k^{3/2} - \frac{2}{3}(1)^{3/2}$$

$$= \frac{2}{3}k^{3/2} - \frac{2}{3} = \frac{2}{3}\left(k^{3/2} - 1\right)$$

Since $A = 8$, set $\frac{2}{3}\left(k^{3/2} - 1\right) = 8 \Rightarrow k^{3/2} - 1$

$= 12 \Rightarrow k^{3/2} = 13$ or $k = 13^{2/3}$

You can check your result by evaluating

$\int_1^{13^{2/3}} \sqrt{x}dx$ to obtain 8.

77. From Chapter 8

Since $g(x) = \int_{\pi/2}^x 2 \sin t \, dt$, then $g'(x) = 2 \sin x$

Set $g'(x) = 0 \Rightarrow 2 \sin x = 0 \Rightarrow x = \pi$, or 2π

$g''(x) = 2 \cos x$ and $g''(\pi) = 2 \cos \pi = -2$ and

$g''(2\pi) = 1$

Thus, g has a local minimum at $x = 2\pi$.

You can also approach the problem geometrically by looking at the area under the curve. See Figure DS-5.

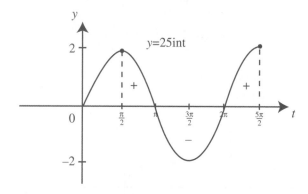

Figure DS-5

78. From Chapter 5

See Figure DS-6.

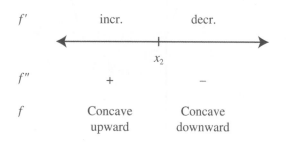

Figure DS-6

The graph of g indicates that a relative maximum occurs at $x = 2$, g is not differentiable at $x = 6$, since there is a *cusp* at $x = 6$ and g does not have a point of inflection at $x = -2$, since there is no tangent line at $x = -2$.

Thus, only statement I is true.

79. From Chapter 4

See Figure DS-7.

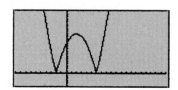

Figure DS-7

The graph of f is concave upward for $x < x_2$.

80. From Chapter 4

See Figure DS-8.

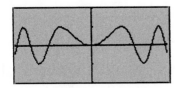

Figure DS-8

Enter $y_1 = \sin(x^2)$

Using the Inflection function of your calculator, you obtain four points of inflection on $[0, \pi]$. The points of inflection occur at $x = 0.81, 1.81, 2.52,$ and 3.07. Since $y_1 = \sin(x^2)$, is an even function, there is a total of eight points of inflection on $[-\pi, \pi]$. An alternate solution is to enter $y_2 = \dfrac{d^2}{dx^2}(y_1(x), x, 2)$. The graph of y_2 indicates that there are eight zeros on $[-\pi, \pi]$.

81. From Chapter 6

$$v(t) = \frac{t^3}{3} - 2t^2 + 5$$

$$a(t) = v'(t) = t^2 - 4t$$

See Figure DS-9.

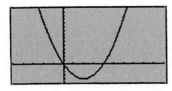

Figure DS-9

The graph indicates that the maximum acceleration occurs at the endpoint $t = 6$. $a(t) = t^2 - 4t$ and $a(6) = 6^2 - 4(6) = 12$

82. From Chapter 10

Amount of Water Leaked $= \displaystyle\int_0^5 10\ln(t + 1)dt$

Using your calculator, you obtain $10(6 \ln 6 - 5)$ which is approximately *57.506 gallons*.

83. From Chapter 6

$$y = x^3, x \geq 0; \frac{dy}{dx} = 3x^2$$

$$f'(x) = 12 \Rightarrow \frac{dy}{dx} = 3x^2 = 12 \Rightarrow x^2$$

$$= 4 \Rightarrow x = 2$$

Slope of normal = negative reciprocal of slope of tangent $= -\dfrac{1}{2}$

At $x = 2, y = x^3 = 2^3 = 8$; $(2, 8)$

Equation of normal line: $y - 8 = -\dfrac{1}{12}(x - 2)$

$$\Rightarrow y = -\frac{1}{12}(x - 2) + 8 \text{ or}$$

$$y = -\frac{1}{12}x + \frac{49}{6}.$$

84. From Chapter 4

Since $g(x) = \displaystyle\int_a^x f(t)dt, g'(x) = f(x)$.

See Figure DS-10.

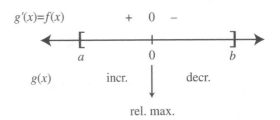

Figure DS-10

The only graph that satisfies the behavior of g is choice (A)

85. From Chapter 9

See Figure DS-11.

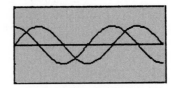

Figure DS-11

Using the Intersection function of the calculator, you obtain the intersection points at $x = 0.785398, 3.92699,$ and 7.06858.

$$\text{Area} = \int_{0.785398}^{3.92699} (\sin x - \cos x)dx$$

$$+ \int_{3.92699}^{7.06858} (\cos x - \sin x)dx$$

$$= 2.82843 + 2.82843 \approx 5.65685$$

You can also find the area by:

$$\text{Area} = \int_{.785398}^{7.06858} |\sin x - \cos x| dx \approx 5.65685$$

$$\approx 5.657.$$

86. From Chapter 10

$$\frac{dy}{dx} = ky \Rightarrow y = y_0 e^{kt}$$

Half-life $= 5730 \Rightarrow y = \frac{1}{2} y_0$ when $t = 5730$

Thus, $\frac{1}{2} y_0 = y_0 e^{k(5730)} \Rightarrow \frac{1}{2} = e^{5730k}$

$\ln\left(\frac{1}{2}\right) = \ln\left(e^{5730k}\right) \Rightarrow \ln\left(\frac{1}{2}\right) = 5730k$

$\ln 1 - \ln 2 = 5730k \Rightarrow -\ln 2 = 5730k$

$$k = \frac{-\ln 2}{5730}$$

87. From Chapter 6

$f\left(\frac{\pi}{2}\right) = 3 \Rightarrow \left(\frac{\pi}{2}, 3\right)$ is on the graph

$f'\left(\frac{\pi}{2}\right) = -1 \Rightarrow$ slope of the tangent at

$x = \frac{\pi}{2}$ is -1.

Equation of tangent line: $y - 3 = -1\left(x - \frac{\pi}{2}\right)$ or

$$y = -x + \frac{\pi}{2} + 3$$

Thus $f\left(\frac{\pi}{2} + \frac{\pi}{180}\right) \approx -\left(\frac{\pi}{2} + \frac{\pi}{180}\right) + \frac{\pi}{2} + 3$

$$\approx 3 - \frac{\pi}{180} \approx 2.98255 \approx 2.983$$

88. From Chapter 7

See Figure DS-12.

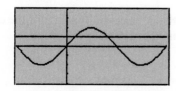

Figure DS-12

To find the points of intersection, set

$\sin 2x = \frac{1}{2} \Rightarrow 2x = \sin^{-1}\left(\frac{1}{2}\right)$

$\Rightarrow 2x = \frac{\pi}{6}$ or $2x = \frac{5\pi}{6} \Rightarrow x = \frac{\pi}{12}$ or $x = \frac{5\pi}{12}$

Volume of solid $= \pi\int_{\frac{\pi}{12}}^{\frac{5\pi}{12}} \left[\left(\sin 2x\right)^2 - \left(\frac{1}{2}\right)^2\right]dx$

Using your calculator, you obtain:

Volume of solid $\approx (0.478306)\pi \approx 1.50264$

$$\approx 1.503$$

89. From Chapter 4

See Figure DS-13.

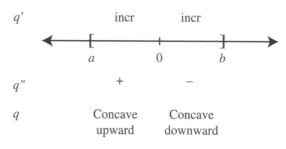

Figure DS-13

A change of concavity occurs at $x = 0$ for q. Thus, q has a point of inflection at $x = 0$. None of the other functions has a point of inflection.

90. From Chapter 6

$f(x) = \frac{\ln x}{x}; f'(x) = \frac{\left(\frac{1}{x}\right)(x) - (1)\ln x}{x^2}$

$= \frac{1}{x^2} - \frac{\ln x}{x^2}$

$y = -x^2; \frac{dy}{dx} = -2x$

Perpendicular tangents $\Rightarrow (f'(x))\left(\frac{dy}{dx}\right) = -1$

$\Rightarrow \left(\left(\frac{1}{x^2}\right) - \frac{\ln x}{x^2}\right)(-2x) = -1$

Using the Solve function on your calculator, you obtain $x \approx 1.37015 \approx 1.370$.

91. From Chapter 9

Length of a rectangle $= \frac{6 - 0}{3} = 2$

Midpoints are $x = 1, 3$ and 5 and $f(1) = 2$, $f(3) = 10$ and $f(5) = 26$

$$\int_0^6 f(x)dx \approx 2(2 + 10 + 26) \approx 2(38) = 76$$

92. From Chapter 10

    See Figure DS-14.

    To find points of intersection, set $x^2 = x + 2 \Rightarrow$
    $x^2 - x - 2 = 0 \Rightarrow x = 2$ or $x = -1$

    Area of cross section $= \left((x + 2) - x^2\right)^2$

    Volume of solid, $V = \int_{-1}^2 \left(x + 2 - x^2\right)^2 dx$

    Using your calculator, you obtain: $V = \dfrac{81}{10}$

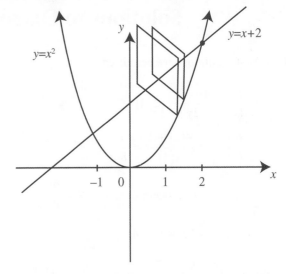

Figure DS-14

Solutions to Diagnostic Test—Section II

Part A—Calculators are permitted.

1. (a) $\dfrac{dy}{dx} = \dfrac{4x+1}{2y}; (2,4)$

$\left.\dfrac{dy}{dx}\right|_{(2,4)} = \dfrac{4(2)+1}{2(4)} = \dfrac{9}{8}$

Equation of tangent line: $y - 4 = \dfrac{9}{8}(x-2)$

or $y = \dfrac{9}{8}(x-2) + 4$

(b) $f(2.1) \approx \dfrac{9}{8}(2.1-2) + 4 \approx \dfrac{0.9}{8} + 4$

$\approx 4.1125 \approx 4.113$

(c) $2y\,dy = (4x+1)dx$

$\int 2y\,dy = \int (4x+1)dx$

$y^2 = 2x^2 + x + c; f(2) = 4$

$4^2 = 2(2)^2 + 2 + c \Rightarrow c = 6$

Thus $y^2 = 2x^2 + x + 6$ or $y = \pm\sqrt{2x^2 + x + 6}$

Since the point (2, 4) is on the graph of f,

$y = \sqrt{2x^2 + x + 6}$

(d) $y = \sqrt{2x^2 + x + 6}$

$f(2.1) = \sqrt{2(2.1)^2 + 2.1 + 6} = \sqrt{16.92}$

$\approx 4.11339 \approx 4.113$

2. (a) The amount of oil leaked out after 6 minutes

$= \int_0^6 10 \sin\left(\pi t/12\right)dt$

$= \left[\dfrac{-10\cos\left(\pi t/12\right)}{\pi/12}\right]_0^6$

$= \left[-\dfrac{120}{\pi}\cos\left(\pi t/12\right)\right]_0^6$

$= \dfrac{120}{\pi} \approx 38.1972$ gallons ≈ 38 gallons.

(b) Average amount of oil leaked out per minute from $t = 0$ to $t = 6$:

$= \dfrac{1}{6-0}\int_0^6 10 \sin\left(\pi t/12\right)dt = \dfrac{1}{6}\left(\dfrac{120}{\pi}\right)$

$= 6.3662 \approx 6$ gallons.

(c) The amount of oil in the drum at t

$f(t) = 100 - \int_0^{t_1} 10 \sin\left(\pi x/12\right)dx$

(d) Let a be the value of t:

$100 - \int_0^a 10 \sin\left(\pi t/12\right)dt = 40$

$100 - \left[\left(-\dfrac{120}{\pi}\right)\cos\left(\pi t/12\right)\right]_0^a = 40$

$100 - \left\{\left(-\dfrac{120}{\pi}\right)\cos\left(a\pi/12\right)\right.$

$\left. -\left[\left(-\dfrac{120}{\pi}\right)\cos(0)\right]\right\} = 40$

$100 + \left(\dfrac{120}{\pi}\right)\cos\left(a\pi/12\right) - \left(\dfrac{120}{\pi}\right) = 40$

$\left(\dfrac{120}{\pi}\right)\cos\left(a\pi/12\right) = \left(\dfrac{120}{\pi}\right) + 40 - 100$

$\cos\left(a\pi/12\right) = \left(\dfrac{120}{\pi} - 60\right)\left(\dfrac{\pi}{120}\right)$

$\cos\left(a\pi/12\right) = \dfrac{(-\pi+2)}{2} \approx -0.570796$

$a\pi/12 \approx \cos^{-1}(-0.570796) \approx 2.17827$

$a = (2.17827)\left(\dfrac{12}{\pi}\right) \approx 8.32038$

$a \approx 8$ minutes

3. (a) $f(x) = xe^{2x}$

$f'(x) = e^{2x} + x(e^{2x})(2) = e^{2x} + 2xe^{2x}$

$= e^{2x}(1 + 2x)$

Set $f'(x) = 0 \Rightarrow e^{2x}(1 + 2x) = 0$.

Since $e^{2x} > 0$, thus $1 + 2x = 0$ or $x = -0.5$

(b) $f'(x) = e^{2x} + 2xe^{2x}$

$f''(x) = (e^{2x})2 + 2e^{2x} + 2x(e^{2x})(2)$

$= 2e^{2x} + 2e^{2x} + 4xe^{2x} = 4e^{2x} + 4xe^{2x}$

$= 4e^{2x}(1 + x)$

Set $f''(x) = 0 \Rightarrow 4e^{2x}(1 + x) = 0$

Since $e^{2x} > 0$, thus $1 + x = 0$ or $x = -1$.

(c) $\lim\limits_{x\to\infty} xe^{2x} = \infty$, since xe^{2x} increases without bound as x approaches ∞.

$\lim\limits_{x\to-\infty} xe^{2x} = \lim\limits_{x\to-\infty} \dfrac{x}{e^{-2x}}$

as $x \to -\infty$, the numerator $\to -\infty$

as $x \to -\infty$, the denominator $e^{-2x} \to \infty$

However, the denominator increases at a much greater rate and thus $\lim\limits_{x \to -\infty} xe^{2x} = 0$.

(d) Since as $x \to \infty$, xe^{2x} increases without bound, f has no absolute maximum value. From part (a) $f(x)$ has one critical point at $x = -0.5$. Since $f'(x) = e^{2x}(1 + 2x)$, $f'(x) < 0$ for $x < -0.5$ and $f'(x) > 0$ for $x > -0.5$, thus f has a relative minimum at $x = -0.5$, and it is the absolute minimum because $x = -0.5$ is the only critical point on an open interval. The absolute

minimum value is $-0.5e^{2(-0.5)} = -\dfrac{1}{2e}$

(e) $f(x) = xe^{ax}, a > 0$

$f'(x) = e^{ax} + x(e^{ax})(a) = e^{ax} + axe^{ax}$

$= e^{ax}(1 + ax)$

Set $f'(x) = 0 \Rightarrow e^{ax}(1 + ax) = 0$ or $x = -\dfrac{1}{a}$. If

$x < -\dfrac{1}{a}, f'(x) < 0$ and if $x > -\dfrac{1}{a}, f'(x) > 0$.

Thus $x = -\dfrac{1}{a}$ is the only critical point, and

f has an absolute minimum at $x = -\dfrac{1}{a}$.

$f\left(-\dfrac{1}{a}\right) = \left(-\dfrac{1}{a}\right)e^{a\left(-\frac{1}{a}\right)} = -\dfrac{1}{a}e^{-1} = -\dfrac{1}{ae}$.

The absolute minimum value of f is $-\dfrac{1}{ae}$ for all $a > 0$.

Part B—No calculators

4. (a) See Figure DS-15.

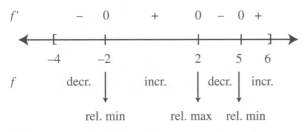

Figure DS-15

Since f increases on $(-2, 2)$ and decreases on $(2, 5)$, f has a relative maximum at $x = 2$

(b) Since f decreases on $(-4, -2)$ and increases on $(-2, 2)$, f has a relative minimum at $x = -2$. And f decreases on $(2, 5)$ and increases on $(5, 6)$, f has a relative minimum at $x = 5$.

(c) See Figure DS-16.

Since f' is increasing on the intervals $(-4, 0)$ and $(4, 6)$, $f'' > 0$ on $(-4, 0)$ and $(4, 6)$.

(d) A change of concavity occurs at $x = 0$ and at $x = 4$. (See Figure DS-16).

Thus f has a point of inflection at $x = 0$ and at $x = 4$.

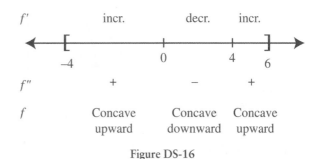

Figure DS-16

(e) See Figure DS-17.

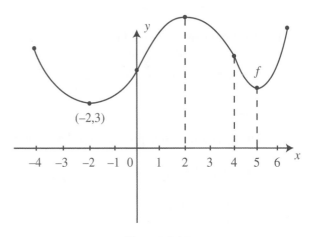

Figure DS-17

5. See Figure DS-18 on page 38.

(a) Area of $R = \displaystyle\int_0^2 x^3\,dx = \dfrac{x^4}{4}\bigg]_0^2 = \dfrac{2^4}{4} - 0 = 4$

(b) Volume of solid $= \pi\displaystyle\int_0^2 (x^3)^2\,dx = \pi\left[\dfrac{x^7}{7}\right]_0^2$

$= \dfrac{2^7(\pi)}{7} = \dfrac{128\pi}{7}$

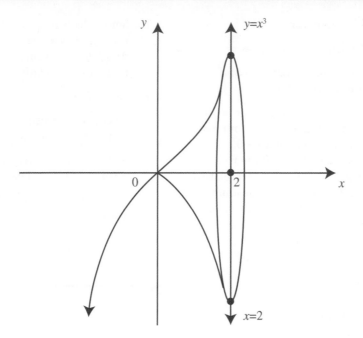

Figure DS-18

(c) $\pi \int_0^a (x^3)^2 \, dx = \frac{1}{2}\left(\frac{128\pi}{7}\right)$

$\pi\left[\dfrac{x^7}{7}\right]_0^a = \dfrac{64\pi}{7}\,;\; \dfrac{\pi a^7}{7} = \dfrac{64\pi}{7}\,;$

$a^7 = 64 = 2^6\,;\; a = 2^{6/7}$

(d) Area of cross section $= \left(x^3\right)^2 = x^6$

Volume of solid $= \displaystyle\int_0^2 x^6 \, dx = \left.\dfrac{x^7}{7}\right]_0^2 = \dfrac{128}{7}.$

6. (a) $x^2 y^2 = 4$

Differentiating using product and chain rules:

$2xy^2 + (x^2)\, 2y\, \dfrac{dy}{dx} = 0$

$2x^2 y\, \dfrac{dy}{dx} = -2xy^2$

$\dfrac{dy}{dx} = \dfrac{-2xy^2}{2x^2 y} = \dfrac{-y}{x}$

(b) $\left.\dfrac{dy}{dx}\right|_{(1,-2)} = \dfrac{-(-2)}{1} = 2$

Equation of tangent: $y - (-2) = 2(x - 1)$

$\Rightarrow y + 2 = 2x - 2$

or $y = 2x - 4.$

(c) Slope of normal $= \dfrac{-1}{\text{slope of tangent}} = \dfrac{-1}{2}$

Equation of normal: $y - (-2) = -\dfrac{1}{2}(x - 1)$

$\Rightarrow y + 2 = -\dfrac{1}{2}x + \dfrac{1}{2}$

or $y = -\dfrac{1}{2}x - \dfrac{3}{2}$

(d) $y = \dfrac{1}{2}x + 2$; $m = \dfrac{1}{2}$ and $\dfrac{dy}{dx} = \dfrac{-y}{x}$

Set $\dfrac{-y}{x} = \dfrac{1}{2} \Rightarrow -2y = x$

$x^2 y^2 = 4$; substitute $x = -2y$

$(-2y)^2 y^2 = 4$; $4y^2 \cdot y^2 = 4$;

$4y^4 = 4$; $y^4 = 1$

$y = \pm 1$

If $y = 1$, $x^2 y^2 = 4 \Rightarrow x^2(1)^2 = 4 \Rightarrow$

$x^2 = 4 \Rightarrow x = \pm 2$

If $y = -1$, $x^2 y^2 = 4 \Rightarrow x^2(-1)^2 = 4 \Rightarrow$

$x^2 = 4 \Rightarrow x = \pm 2$

Possible Points for P are: $(2, 1)$, $(2, -1)$, $(-2, 1)$, and $(-2, -1)$.

Since $\dfrac{dy}{dx} = \dfrac{-y}{x}$, the only points to which the

tangent line has a slope of $\dfrac{1}{2}$ are $(2, -1)$ and

$(-2, 1)$, since the x and y coordinates must have opposite signs.

SCORING AND INTERPRETATION

Scoring Sheet for Diagnostic Test

Section I—Part A

$$\underline{\hspace{6cm}} \times 1.2 \quad = \underline{\hspace{6cm}}$$

No. Correct $\qquad\qquad\qquad$ Subtotal A

$$\underline{\hspace{6cm}} \times (0.25) \times 1.2 = \underline{\hspace{6cm}}$$

No. Incorrect $\qquad\qquad\qquad$ Subtotal B

$$\text{Part A (Subtotal A} - \text{Subtotal B)} = \underline{\hspace{4cm}}$$

$\qquad\qquad\qquad\qquad\qquad\qquad\qquad\qquad\qquad$ Subtotal C

Section I—Part B

$$\underline{\hspace{6cm}} \times 1.2 \quad = \underline{\hspace{6cm}}$$

No. Correct $\qquad\qquad\qquad$ Subtotal D

$$\underline{\hspace{6cm}} \times (0.25) \times 1.2 = \underline{\hspace{6cm}}$$

No. Incorrect $\qquad\qquad\qquad$ Subtotal E

$$\text{Part B (Subtotal D} - \text{Subtotal E)} = \underline{\hspace{4cm}}$$

$\qquad\qquad\qquad\qquad\qquad\qquad\qquad\qquad\qquad$ Subtotal F

Section II—Part A (Each question is worth 9 points.)

$$\underline{\hspace{3cm}} + \underline{\hspace{3cm}} + \underline{\hspace{3cm}} = \underline{\hspace{4cm}}$$

Q#1 $\qquad\quad$ Q#2 $\qquad\quad$ Q#3 $\qquad\quad$ Subtotal G

Section II—Part B (Each question is worth 9 points.)

$$\underline{\hspace{3cm}} + \underline{\hspace{3cm}} + \underline{\hspace{3cm}} = \underline{\hspace{4cm}}$$

Q#1 $\qquad\quad$ Q#2 $\qquad\quad$ Q#3 $\qquad\quad$ Subtotal H

Total Raw Score (Subtotals C + F + G + H) = ☐

Approximate Conversion Scale:	
Total Raw Score	**Approximate AP Grade**
75–108	5
60–74	4
45–59	3
31–44	2
0–30	1

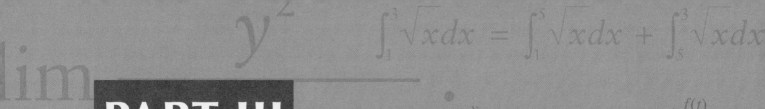

PART III

COMPREHENSIVE REVIEW

Chapter 1
Review of Pre-Calculus

1.1 LINES

Main Concepts: *Slope of a Line, Equations of a Line, Parallel and Perpendicular Lines*

Slope of a Line

Given two points A (x_1, y_1) and B (x_2, y_2), the *slope* of the line passing through the two given points is defined as

$$m = \frac{y_2 - y_1}{x_2 - x_1} \text{ where } (x_2 - x_1) \neq 0$$

Note that if $(x_2 - x_1) = 0$, then $x_2 = x_1$ which implies that points A and B are on a vertical line parallel to the y-axis and thus, the slope is *undefined*.

Example 1

Find the slope of the line passing through the points $(3, 2)$ and $(5, -4)$. Using the definition $m = \frac{y_2 - y_1}{x_2 - x_1}$, the slope of the line is $m = \frac{-4 - 2}{5 - 3} = \frac{-6}{2} = -3$.

Example 2

Find the slope of the line passing through the points $(-5, 3)$ and $(2, 3)$. The slope $m = \frac{3 - 3}{2 - (-5)} = \frac{0}{2 + 5} = \frac{0}{7} = 0$. This implies that the points $(-5, 3)$ and $(2, 3)$ are on a horizontal line parallel to the x-axis.

Example 3

Here is a summary of 4 different orientations of lines and their slopes:

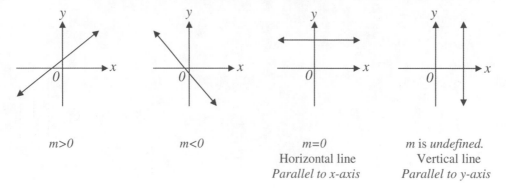

$m>0$ $m<0$ $m=0$
Horizontal line
Parallel to x-axis m is *undefined.*
Vertical line
Parallel to y-axis

Figure 1.1-1

Equations of Lines

$y = mx + b$	*Slope-intercept form* of a line where m is its slope and b is y-intercept.
$y - y_1 = m(x - x_1)$	*Point-slope form* of a line where m is the slope and (x_1, y_1) is a point on the line.
$Ax + By + C = 0$	*General form* of a line where A, B and C are constants and A and B are not *both* equal to 0.

Example 1

Write an equation of the line through the points $(-2, 1)$ and $(3, -9)$. The slope of line passing through $(-2, 1)$ and $(3, -9)$ is $m = \dfrac{-9 - 1}{3 - (-2)} = \dfrac{-10}{5} = -2$. Using the point-slope form and the point $(-2, 1)$,

$y - 1 = -2[x - (-2)]$
$y - 1 = -2(x + 2)$ or $y = -2x - 3$
An equation of the line is $y = -2x - 3$.

Example 2

An equation of a line l is $2x + 3y = 12$. Find the slope, the x-intercept and the y-intercept of line l.

Begin by expressing the equation $2x + 3y = 12$ in *slope-intercept form.*

$$2x + 3y = 12$$
$$3y = -2x + 12$$
$$y = \frac{-2}{3}x + 4$$

Therefore, m, the slope of line l, is $\dfrac{-2}{3}$ and b, the y-intercept, is 4. To find the x-intercept, set $y = 0$ in the original equation $2x + 3y = 12$. Thus, $2x + 0 = 12$ and $x = 6$. The x-intercept of line l is 6.

Example 3

Equations of *vertical* and *horizontal* lines involve only a single variable. Here are several examples:

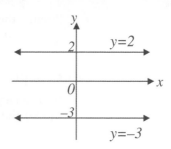

Figure 1.1-2

• Write clearly. If the reader (the person grading your test) can't read your handwriting, you're in trouble.

Parallel and Perpendicular Lines

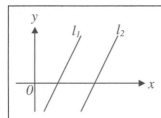

Figure 1.1-3

Given two non-vertical lines l_1 and l_2 with slopes m_1 and m_2 respectively.

Lines l_1 and l_2 are parallel if and only if $m_1 = m_2$.

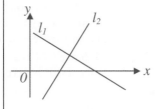

Figure 1.1-4

Lines l_1 and l_2 are perpendicular if and only if $m_1 m_2 = -1$.

Example 1

Write an equation of the line through the point $(-1, 3)$ and parallel to the line $3x - 2y = 6$.

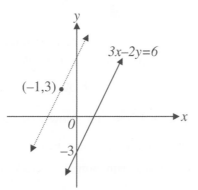

Figure 1.1-5

Begin by expressing $3x - 2y = 6$ in *slope-intercept form.*

$$3x - 2y = 6$$
$$-2y = -3x + 6$$
$$y = \frac{-3}{-2}x + \frac{6}{-2}$$
$$y = \frac{3}{2}x - 3$$

Therefore, the slope of the line $3x - 2y = 6$ is $m = \frac{3}{2}$ and the slope of the line parallel to the line $3x - 2y = 6$ is also $\frac{3}{2}$. Since the line parallel to $3x - 2y = 6$ passes through the point $(-1, 3)$, you can use the point-slope form and obtain the equation $y - 3 = \frac{3}{2}[x - (-1)]$ or $y - 3 = \frac{3}{2}(x + 1)$.

Example 2

Write an equation of the perpendicular bisector of the line segment joining the points $A(3, 0)$ and $B(-1, 4)$.

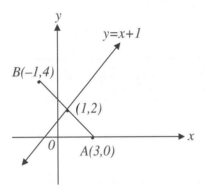

Figure 1.1-6

Begin by finding the midpoint of $\overline{AB}$.

Midpoint $= \left(\dfrac{3 + (-1)}{2}, \dfrac{0 + 4}{2}\right) = (1, 2)$. The

slope of $\overline{AB}$ is $m = \dfrac{4 - 0}{-1 - 3} = -1$. Therefore,

the perpendicular bisector of $\overline{AB}$ has a slope of 1. Since the perpendicular bisector of $\overline{AB}$ passes through the midpoint, you could use the *point-slope form* and obtain $y - 2 = 1(x - 1)$ or $y - 2 = x - 1$ or $y = x + 1$.

Example 3

Write an equation of the circle with center at $C(-2, 1)$ and tangent to the line l having the equation $x + y = 5$.

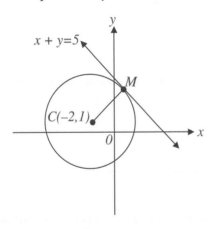

Figure 1.1-7

Let M be the point of tangency. Express the equation $x + y = 5$ in slope-intercept form and obtain $y = -x + 5$. Thus, the slope of line l is -1. Since $\overline{CM}$ is a radius drawn to the point of tangency, it is perpendicular to line l, and the slope of $\overline{CM}$ is 1. Using the point-slope formula, the equation of $\overline{CM}$ is $y - 1 = 1[x - (-2)]$ or $y = x + 3$. To find the coordinates of point M, solve the two equations $y = -x + 5$ and $y = x + 3$ simultaneously. Thus, $-x + 5 = x + 3$ which is equivalent to $2 = 2x$ or $x = 1$.

Substituting $x = 1$ into $y = x + 3$, you have $y = 4$. Therefore, the coordinates of M are $(1, 4)$. Since $\overline{CM}$ is the radius of the circle, you should find the length of $\overline{CM}$ by using the distance formula $d = \sqrt{(x_2 - x_1)^2 + (y_2 - y_1)^2}$.

Thus, $CM = \sqrt{[1 - (-2)]^2 + (4 - 1)^2} = \sqrt{18}$. Now that you know both the radius of the circle $\left(r = \sqrt{18}\right)$ and its center, $(-2, 1)$, use the formula $(x - h)^2 + (y - k)^2 = r^2$ to find an equation of the circle. Thus, an equation of the circle is $(x - (-2))^2 + (y - 1)^2 = 18$ or $(x + 2)^2 + (y - 1)^2 = 18$.

- Even functions are symmetrical with respect to the y-axis. That means you only need to do one side of the graph and then reflect it to get the other side.

1.2 ABSOLUTE VALUES AND INEQUALITIES

Main Concepts: *Absolute Values, Inequalities and The Real Number Line, Solving Absolute Value Inequalities, Solving Polynomial Inequalities, Solving Rational Inequalities*

Absolute Values

Let a and b be real numbers.

1. $|a| = \begin{cases} a, & \text{if } a \geq 0 \\ -a, & \text{if } a < 0 \end{cases}$

3. $|a - b| = |b - a|$

2. $|ab| = |a||b|$

4. $\sqrt{a^2} = |a| = \begin{cases} a, & \text{if } a \geq 0 \\ -a, & \text{if } a < 0 \end{cases}$

Example 1

Solve for x: $|3x - 12| = 18$.

    Depending on whether the value of $(3x - 12)$ is positive or negative, the equation $|3x - 12| = 18$ could be written as $3x - 12 = 18$ or $3x - 12 = -18$. Solving both equations, you have $x = 10$ or $x = -2$. (*Be sure to check both answers in the original equation.*) The solution set for x is $\{-2, 10\}$.

Example 2

Solve for x: $|2x - 12| = |4x + 24|$.

    The given equation implies that either $2x - 12 = 4x + 24$ or $2x - 12 = -(4x + 24)$. Solving both equations, you have $x = -18$ or $x = -2$. Checking $x = -18$ with the original equation: $|2(-18) - 12| = |4(-18) + 24|$ or $|-36 - 12| = |-72 + 24|$ or $|-48| = |-48|$. Checking $x = -2$ with the original equation, you have $|-16| = |16|$. Thus, the solution set for x is $\{-18, -2\}$.

Example 3

Solve for x: $|11 - 3x| = 1 - x$.

    Depending on the value of $(11 - 3x)$—whether it is greater than or less than 0—the given equation could be written as $11 - 3x = 1 - x$ or $11 - 3x = -(1 - x)$. Solving both equations, you have $x = 5$ and $x = 3$. Checking $x = 5$ with the original equation yields $|11 - 3(5)| = 1 - 5$ or $|-4| = -4$ which is *not* possible. Checking $x = 3$ with the original equation shows that $|11 - 3(3)| = 1 - 3$ or $|-2| = -2$ which is also *not* possible. Thus, the solution for x is the empty set $\{\ \}$. You could also solve the equation using a graphing calculator.

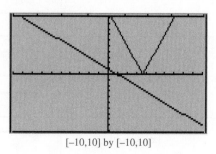

[-10,10] by [-10,10]

Figure 1.2-1

Enter $y1 = |11 - 3x|$ and $y2 = 1 - x$. The two graphs do not intersect, thus, no common solution.

Inequalities and the Real Number Line

Properties of Inequalities:

Let a, b, c, d, and k be real numbers:

1. If $a < b$ and $b < c$, then $a < c$.
   e.g., $-7 < 2$ and $2 < 5 \Rightarrow -7 < 5$

2. If $a < b$ and $c < d$, then $a + c < b + d$.
   e.g., $5 < 7$ and $3 < 6 \Rightarrow 5 + 3 < 7 + 6$

3. If $a < b$ and $k > 0$, then $ak < bk$.
   e.g., $3 < 5$ and $2 > 0 \Rightarrow 3(2) < 5(2)$

4. If $a < b$ and $k < 0$, then $ak > bk$.
   e.g., $3 < 5$ and $2 < 0 \Rightarrow 3(-2) > 5(-2)$

Example 1

Solve the inequality $6 - 2x \leq 18$ and sketch the solution on the real number line.

Solving the inequality $6 - 2x \leq 18$
$$-2x \leq 12$$
$$x \geq -6$$

Therefore, the solution set is the interval $[-6, \infty)$ or expressing the solution set in set notation: $\{x \mid x \geq -6\}$.

Example 2

Solve the double inequality $-15 \leq 3x + 6 < 9$ and sketch the solution on the real number line.

Solving the double inequality $-15 \leq 3x + 6 < 9$
$$-21 \leq 3x < 3$$
$$-7 \leq x < 1$$

Therefore, the solution set is the interval $[-7, 1)$ or expressing the solution in set notation: $\{x \mid -7 \leq x < 1\}$.

Example 3

Here is a summary of the different types of intervals on a number line:

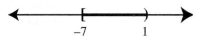

Interval Notation	Set Notation	Graph
$[a, b]$	$\{x \mid a \leq x \leq b\}$	
(a, b)	$\{x \mid a < x < b\}$	
$[a, b)$	$\{x \mid a \leq x < b\}$	
$(a, b]$	$\{x \mid a < x \leq b\}$	
$[a, \infty)$	$\{x \mid x \geq a\}$	
(a, ∞)	$\{x \mid x > a\}$	
$(-\infty, b]$	$\{x \mid x \leq b\}$	
$(-\infty, b)$	$\{x \mid x < b\}$	
$(-\infty, \infty)$	$\{x \mid x \text{ is a real number}\}$	

Solving Absolute Value Inequalities

Let a be a real number such that $a \geq 0$

$|x| \geq a \Leftrightarrow (x \geq a \text{ or } x \leq -a)$ and $|x| > a \Leftrightarrow (x > a \text{ or } x < a)$

$|x| \leq a \Leftrightarrow (-a \leq x \leq a)$ and $|x| < a \Leftrightarrow (-a < x < a)$

Example 1

Solve the inequality $|3x - 6| \leq 15$ and sketch the solution on the real number line. The given inequality is equivalent to

$$-15 \leq 3x - 6 \leq 15$$
$$-9 \leq 3x \leq 21$$
$$-3 \leq x \leq 7$$

Therefore, the solution set is the interval $[-3, 7]$ or written in set notation $\{x| -3 \leq x \leq 7\}$.

Example 2

Solve the inequality $|2x + 1| > 9$ and sketch the solution on the real number line. The inequality $|2x + 1| > 9$ implies that

$$2x + 1 > 9 \text{ or } 2x + 1 < -9$$

Solving the two inequalities on the above line, you have $x > 4$ or $x < -5$. Therefore, the solution set is the union of the two disjoint intervals $(4, \infty) \cup (-\infty, -5)$ or writing the solution in set notation: $\{x| (x > 4) \text{ or } (x < -5)\}$.

Example 3

Solve the inequality $|1 - 2x| \leq 7$ and sketch the solution on the real number line. The inequality $|1 - 2x| \leq 7$ implies that

$$-7 \leq 1 - 2x \leq 7$$
$$-8 \leq -2x \leq 6$$
$$4 \geq x \geq -3$$
$$-3 \leq x \leq 4$$

Therefore, the solution set is the interval $[-3, 4]$ or writing the solution in set notation: $\{x| -3 \leq x \leq 4\}$.

[-7.9, 7.9] by [-5, 10]

Figure 1.2-2

Note: You can solve an absolute value inequality by using a graphing calculator. For instance, in example 3, enter y1 = $|1 - 2x|$ and y2 = 7. The graphs intersect at $x = -3$ and 4, and y1 is below y2 on the interval $(-3, 4)$. Since the inequality is $\leq$, the solution set is $[-3, 4]$.

Solving Polynomial Inequalities

1. Write the given inequality in standard form with the polynomial on the left and zero on the right.
2. Factor the polynomial if possible.
3. Find all zeros of the polynomial.
4. Using the zeros on a number line, determine the test intervals.
5. Select an x-value from each interval and substitute it in the polynomial.
6. Check the *endpoints* of each interval with the inequality.
7. Write the solution to the inequality.

Example 1

Solve the inequality $x^2 - 3x \geq 4$.

Steps: 1. Write in standard form: $x^2 - 3x - 4 \geq 0$
2. Factor polynomial: $(x - 4)(x + 1)$
3. Find zeros: $(x - 4)(x + 1) = 0$ implies that $x = 4$ and $x = -1$

4. Determine intervals:
$(-\infty, -1)$ and $(-1, 4)$ and $(4, \infty)$

5. Select an x-value in each interval and evaluated polynomial at that value:

Selected Interval	Factor x-value	Factor $(x + 1)$	Polynomial $(x - 4)$	$(x - 4)(x + 1)$
$(-\infty, -1)$	-2	$-$	$-$	$+$
$(-1, 4)$	0	$+$	$-$	$-$
$(4, \infty)$	6	$+$	$+$	$+$

Therefore the intervals $(-\infty, -1)$ and $(4, \infty)$ make $(x - 4)(x + 1) > 0$.

6. Check end-points:
Since the inequality $x^2 - 3x - 4 \geq 0$ is greater than or equal to 0, both end-points $x = -1$ and $x = 4$ are included in the solution.
7. Write solution: The solution is $(-\infty, -1] \cup [4, \infty)$.

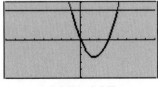

[-8,8] by [-5,5]

Figure 1.2-3

Note: The inequality $x^2 - 3x \geq 4$ could have been solved using a graphing calculator. Enter $y1 = x^2 - 3x$ and $y2 = 4$. The graph of y1 is above y2 on $(-\infty, -1)$ and $(4, \infty)$. Since the inequality is $\geq$, the solution set is $(-\infty, -1]$ or $[4, \infty)$.

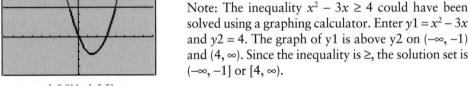

• Label everything in a diagram including axes, origin, function, lines, intercepts (if appropriate), intersection points, and special points.

Example 2

Solve the inequality $x^3 - 9x < 0$ using a graphing calculator.

Steps: 1. Enter $y = x^3 - 9x$ into your graphing calculator.
2. Find the zeros of y: $x = -3, 0$ and 3.
3. Determine the intervals on which $y < 0$: $(-\infty, -3)$ and $(0, 3)$.
4. Check if the end-points satisfy the inequality. Since the inequality is strictly less than 0, the end-points are not included in the solution.
5. Write the solution to the inequality. The solution is $(-\infty, -3)$ $\cup (0, 3)$.

[−10,10] by [−15,15]

Figure 1.2-4

Example 3

Solve the above inequality $x^3 - 9x < 0$ algebraically.

Steps: 1. Write in standard form: $x^3 - 9x < 0$ is already in standard form.
2. Factor polynomial: $x(x - 3)(x + 3)$
3. Find zeros: $x(x - 3)(x + 3) = 0$ implies that $x = 0$, $x = 3$ and $x = -3$.

4. Determine intervals:
$(-\infty, -3), (-3, 0), (0, 3)$ and $(3, \infty)$

5. Select an x-value and evaluate polynomial:

Interval	Selected x-value	Factor x	Factor $(x + 3)$	Factor $(x - 3)$	Polynomial $x(x - 3)(x + 3)$
$(-\infty, -3)$	−5	−	−	−	−
$(-3, 0)$	−1	−	+	−	+
$(0, 3)$	1	+	+	−	−
$(3, \infty)$	6	+	+	+	+

Therefore, the intervals $(-\infty, -3)$ and $(0, 3)$ make $x(x - 3)(x + 3) < 0$.

8. Check end-points:
Since the inequality $x^3 - 9x < 0$ is strictly less than 0, none of the endpoints $x = -3$, 0 and 3 are included in the solution.
9. Write the solution: The solution is $(-\infty, -3) \cup (0, 3)$.

Solving Rational Inequalities

1. Rewrite the given inequality so that all the terms are on the left and only zero is on the right.
2. Find the least common denominator and combine all the terms on the left into *a single fraction.*
3. Factor the numerator and the denominator if possible.
4. Find all x-values for which the numerator or the denominator is zero.
5. Put these x-values on a number line; determine the test intervals.
6. Select an x-value from each interval and substitute it in the fraction.
7. Check the *endpoints* of each interval with the inequality.
8. Write the solution to the inequality.

Example 1

Solve the inequality $\dfrac{2x-5}{x-3} \le 1$.

Steps: 1. Rewrite: $\dfrac{2x-5}{x-3} - 1 \le 0$

2. Combine: $\dfrac{2x-5-x+3}{x-3} \le 0 \Leftrightarrow \dfrac{x-2}{x-3} \le 0$

3. Set numerator and denominator equal to 0 and solve for x: $x = 2$ or 3.

4. Determine intervals:
$(-\infty, 2), (2, 3)$ and $(3, \infty)$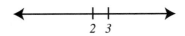

5. Select x-value and evaluate fraction:

Interval	Selected x-value	$(x-2)$	$(x-3)$	Fraction $\dfrac{x-2}{x-3}$
$(-\infty, 2)$	0	−	−	+
$(2, 3)$	2.5	+	−	−
$(3, \infty)$	6	+	+	+

Therefore, the interval $(2, 3)$ makes the fraction < 0.

6. Check endpoints:
At $x = 3$, the fraction is undefined. Thus the only endpoint is $x = 2$. Since the inequality is less than or equal to 0, $x = 2$ is included in the solution.

7. Write solution: The solution is the interval $[2, 3)$.

Example 2

Solve the inequality $\dfrac{2x-5}{x-3} \le 1$ using a graphing calculator.

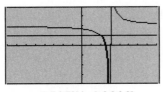

[−7.9,79] by [−3.8,3.8]

Figure 1.2-5

1. Enter $y1 = \dfrac{2x-5}{x-3}$ and $y2 = 1$.

2. Find the intersection points: $x = 2$. Note that at $x = 3$, $y1$ is undefined.)

3. Determine the intervals on which $y1$ is below $y2$: The interval is $(2, 3)$

4. Check if the endpoints satisfy the inequality. Since the inequality is less than or equal to 1, the endpoint at $x = 2$ is included in the solution.

5. Write the solution to the inequality. The solution is the interval $[2, 3)$.

Example 3

Solve the inequality $\dfrac{1}{x} \ge x$ using a graphing calculator.

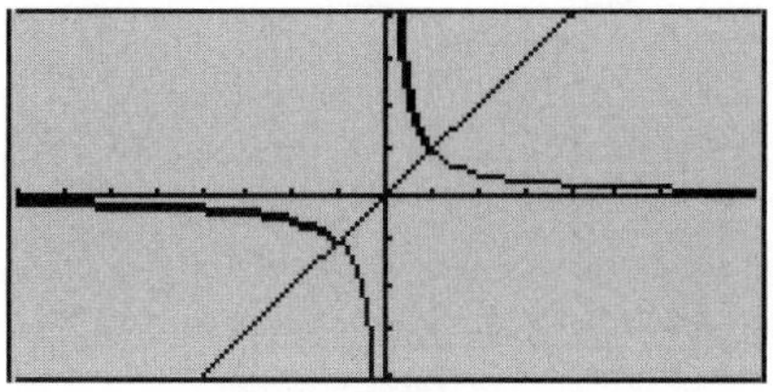

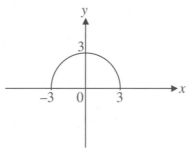

[-8,8] by [-4,4]

Figure 1.2-6

1. Enter $y1 = \dfrac{1}{x}$ and $y2 = x$.
2. Find the intersection points: at $x = -1$ and 1. Note that $x = 0$, y1 is undefined.)
3. Determine the intervals on which y1 $\geq$ y2. The interval are $(-\infty, -1)$ and $(0, 1)$.
4. Check if the end-points satisfy the inequality. Since the inequality is greater than or equal to x, the endpoints at $x = -1$ and 1 are included in the solution.
5. Write the solution to the inequality. The solution is the interval $(-\infty, -1] \cup (0, 1]$.

1.3 FUNCTIONS

Main Concepts: *Definition of a Function, Operations on Functions, Inverse Functions, Trigonometric and Inverse Trigonometric Functions, Exponential and Logarithmic Functions*

Definition of a Function

A function f is a set of ordered pairs (x, y) in which for every x coordinate there is *one and only one* corresponding y coordinate. We write $f(x) = y$.

The domain of f is the set of all possible values of x and the range of f is the set of all values of y.

Vertical Line Test

If all vertical lines pass through the graph of an equation in at most one point, then the equation is a function.

Example 1

Given $y = \sqrt{9 - x^2}$, where $\sqrt{}$ denotes the positive square root, sketch the graph of the equation, determine if the equation is a function and find the domain and range of the equation.

Figure 1.3-1

Since the graph of $y = \sqrt{9 - x^2}$ passes the vertical line test, the equation is a function. Let $y = f(x)$. The expression $\sqrt{9 - x^2}$ implies that $9 - x^2 \geq 0$. By inspection, note that $-3 \leq x \leq 3$. Thus the domain is $[-3, 3]$. Since $f(x)$ is defined for all values of $x \in [-3, 3]$ and $f(-3) = 0$ is the minimum value and $f(0) = 3$ is the maximum value, the range of $f(x)$ is $[0, 3]$.

Example 2

Given $f(x) = x^2 - 4x$, find $f(-3)$, $f(-x)$ and $\dfrac{f(x + h) - f(x)}{h}$.

$$f(-3) = (-3)^2 - 4(-3) = 9 + 12 = 21$$

$$f(-x) = (-x)^2 - 4(-x) = x^2 + 4x$$

$$\frac{f(x + h) - f(x)}{h} = \frac{(x + h)^2 - 4(x + h) - (x^2 - 4x)}{h}$$

$$= \frac{x^2 + 2hx + h^2 - 4x - 4h - x^2 + 4x}{h}$$

$$= \frac{2hx + h^2 - 4h}{h} = 2x + h - 4.$$

- Given the function $f(x) = \begin{cases} \dfrac{x^2 - 9}{x - 3} & \text{if } x \neq 3 \\ 0 & \text{if } x = 3 \end{cases}$, $f(x)$ is discontinuous at $x = 3$,

  but the $\lim\limits_{x \to 3} f(x) = 6$.

Operations on Functions

Let f and g be two given functions. Then for all x in the intersection of the domains of f and g, the *sum*, *difference*, *product*, and *quotient* of f and g are defined as:

$$(f + g)(x) = f(x) + g(x)$$

$$(f - g)(x) = f(x) - g(x)$$

$$(fg)(x) = f(x)g(x)$$

$$\left(\frac{f}{g}\right)(x) = \frac{f(x)}{g(x)}, \; g(x) \neq 0$$

The composition of f with g is:

$$(f \circ g)(x) = f[g(x)]$$

where the domain of $f \circ g$ is the set containing all x in the domain of g for which $g(x)$ is in the domain of f.

Example 1

Given $f(x) = x^2 - 4$ and $g(x) = x - 5$, find

(a) $(f \circ g)(-1)$ (b) $(g \circ f)(-1)$ (c) $(f + g)(-3)$ (d) $(f - g)(1)$

(e) $(fg)(2)$ (f) $\left(\dfrac{f}{g}\right)(0)$ (g) $\left(\dfrac{f}{g}\right)(5)$ (h) $\left(\dfrac{g}{f}\right)(4)$.

(a) $(f \circ g)(x) = f[g(x)] = f(x - 5) = (x - 5)^2 - 4 = x^2 - 10x + 21.$
     Thus $(f \circ g)(-1) = (-1)^2 - 10(-1) + 21 = 1 + 10 + 21 = 32.$

     Or $(f \circ g)(-1) = f[g(-1)] = f(-6) = 32$

(b) $(g \circ f)(x) = g[f(x)] = g(x^2 - 4) = (x^2 - 4) - 5 = x^2 - 9.$
     Thus $(g \circ f)(-1) = (-1)^2 - 9 = 1 - 9 = -8.$

(c) $(f + g)(x) = (x^2 - 4) + (x - 5) = x^2 + x - 9.$ Thus $(f + g)(-3) = -3.$

(d) $(f - g)(x = (x^2 - 4) - (x - 5) = x^2 - x + 1.$ Thus $(f - g)(1) = 1.$

(e) $(fg(x) = (x^2 - 4)(x - 5) = x^3 - 5x^2 - 4x + 20.$ Thus $(fg)(2) = 0.$

(f) $\left(\dfrac{f}{g}\right)(x) = \dfrac{x^2 - 4}{x - 5}$, $x \neq 5$. Thus $\left(\dfrac{f}{g}\right)(0) = \dfrac{4}{5}$.

(g) Since $g(5) = 0$, $x = 5$ is *not* in the domain of $\left(\dfrac{f}{g}\right)$, $\left(\dfrac{f}{g}\right)(5)$ is *undefined*.

(h) $\left(\dfrac{g}{f}\right)(x) = \dfrac{x - 5}{x^2 - 4}$, $x \neq 2$ or -2. Thus $\left(\dfrac{g}{f}\right)(4) = -\dfrac{1}{12}$.

Example 2

Given $h(x) = \sqrt{x}$ and $k(x) = \sqrt{9 - x^2}$:

   (a) find $\left(\dfrac{h}{k}\right)(x)$ and indicate its domain; and

   (b) find $\left(\dfrac{h}{k}\right)(x)$ and indicate its domain.

(a) $\left(\dfrac{h}{k}\right)(x) = \dfrac{\sqrt{x}}{\sqrt{9 - x^2}}$

   The domain of $h(x)$ is $[0, \infty)$ and the domain of $k(x)$ is $[-3, 3]$.

   The intersection of the two domains is $[0, 3]$. However, $k(3) = 0$.

   Therefore the domain of $\left(\dfrac{h}{k}\right)$ is $[0, 3)$.

   Note that $\dfrac{\sqrt{x}}{\sqrt{9 - x^2}}$ is not equivalent to $\sqrt{\dfrac{x}{9 - x^2}}$ outside of the domain $[0, 3)$.

(b) $\left(\dfrac{h}{k}\right)(x) = \dfrac{\sqrt{9 - x^2}}{\sqrt{x}}$

   The intersection of the two domains is $[0, 3]$. However, $h(0) = 0$.

   Therefore the domain of $\left(\dfrac{h}{k}\right)$ is $(0, 3]$.

Example 3

Given the graphs of functions $f(x)$ and $g(x)$:

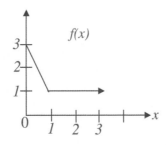

Figure 1.3-2

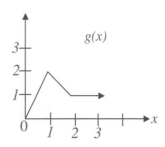

Figure 1.3-3

Find (a) $(f + g)(1)$ (b) $(fg)(0)$ (c) $\left(\dfrac{f}{g}\right)(0)$ (d) $f[g(3)]$

(a) $(f + g)(1) = f(1) + g(1) = 3$.   (b) $(fg)(0) = f(0)g(0) = 3(0) = 0$

(c) $\left(\dfrac{f}{g}\right)(0) = \dfrac{f(0)}{g(0)} = \dfrac{3}{0}$ *undefined.*

(d) $f[g(3)] = f(1) = 1.$

Inverse Functions

Given a function f, the inverse of f (if it exists) is a function g such that $f(g(x)) = x$ for every x in the domain of g and $g(f(x)) = x$ for every x in the domain of f. The function g is written as f^{-1}. Thus: $f[f^{-1}(x)] = x$ and $f^{-1}[f(x)] = x$.

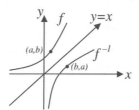

The graphs of f and f^{-1} are *reflections* of each other in the line $y = x$. The point (a, b) is on the graph of f if and only if the point (b, a) is on the graph of f^{-1}.

Figure 1.3-4

A function f is *one-to-one* if for any two points x_1 and x_2 in the domain such that $x_1 \neq x_2$, then $f(x_1) \neq f(x_2)$.

Equivalent Statements: Given a function f,
1. The function f has an inverse.
2. The function f is one-to-one.
3. Every horizontal line passes through the graph of f at most once.

Finding the inverse of a function f:
1. Check if f has an inverse, i.e., f is one-to-one or passes the horizontal line test.
2. Replace $f(x)$ by y.
3. Interchange the variables x and y.
4. Solve for y.
5. Replace y by $f^{-1}(x)$.
6. Indicate the domain of $f^{-1}(x)$ as the range of $f(x)$.
7. Verify $f^{-1}(x)$ by checking if $f[f^{-1}(x)] = f^{-1}[f(x)] = x$.

Example 1

Given the graph of $f(x)$, find (a) $f^{-1}(0)$, (b) $f^{-1}(1)$ and (c) $f^{-1}(3)$.

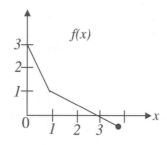

(a) By inspection, $f(3) = 0$. Thus, $f^{-1}(0) = 3$.
(b) Since $f(1) = 1$, $f^{-1}(1) = 1$.
(c) Since $f(0) = 3$, $f^{-1}(3) = 0$.

Figure 1.3-5

Example 2

Determine if the given function has an inverse:
(a) $f(x) = x^3 + x - 2$ (b) $f(x) = x^3 - 2x + 1$

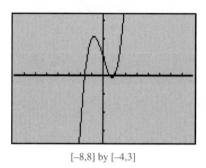

[−10,10] by [10,10]

Figure 1.3-6

(a) By inspection, the graph of $f(x) = x^3 + x - 2$ is strictly increasing which implies that $f(x)$ is one-to-one. (You could also use the horizontal line test.) Therefore, $f(x)$ has an inverse function.

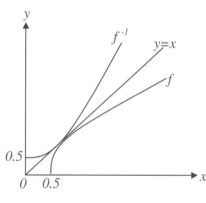

[−8,8] by [−4,3]

Figure 1.3-7

(b) By inspection, the graph of $f(x) = x^3 - 2x + 1$ fails the horizontal line test. Thus, $f(x)$ has no inverse function.

Example 3

Find the inverse function of $f(x) = \sqrt{2x - 1}$.

Figure 1.3-8

1. Since $f(x)$ a strictly increasing function, the inverse function exists.

2. Let $y = f(x)$. Thus, $y = \sqrt{2x - 1}$.

3. Interchange x and y. You have
$$x = \sqrt{2y - 1}.$$

4. Solve for y. Thus, $y = \dfrac{x^2 + 1}{2}$.

5. Replace y by $f^{-1}(x)$. You have
$$f^{-1}(x) = \frac{x^2 + 1}{2}.$$

6. Since the range of $f(x)$ is $[0, \infty)$, the domain of $f^{-1}(x)$ is $[0, \infty)$.

7. Verify $f^{-1}(x)$ by checking:

Since $x > 0$, $\sqrt{x^2} = x$. $f[f^{-1}(x)] = f\left(\dfrac{x^2 + 1}{2}\right) = \sqrt{2\left(\dfrac{x^2 + 1}{2}\right) - 1} = x$;

$f^{-1}[f(x)] = f^{-1}\left(\sqrt{2x - 1}\right) = \dfrac{\sqrt{2x - 1}^{\,2} + 1}{2} = x$

- Organize your solution so that the reader can follow your line of reasoning. Write all formulas used and indicate all major steps taken.

Trigonometric and Inverse Trigonometric Functions

$y = \sin x$

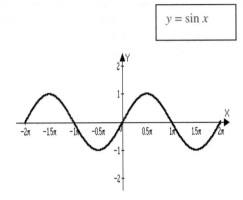

Domain: $\{-\infty < x < \infty\}$
Range: $\{-1 \le y \le 1\}$ Amplitude: 1
Frequency: 1   Period: 2π

Figure 1.3-9

$y = \sin^{-1} x$

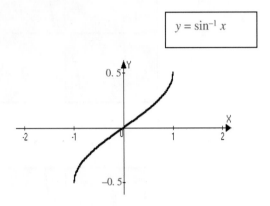

Domain: $\{-1 \le x \le 1\}$
Range: $\left\{-\pi/2 \le y \le \pi/2\right\}$

Figure 1.3-10

$y = \cos x$

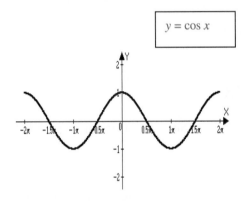

Domain: $\{-\infty < x < \infty\}$
Range: $\{-1 \le y \le 1\}$ Amplitude: 1
Frequency: 1   Period: 2π

Figure 1.3-11

$y = \cos^{-1} x$

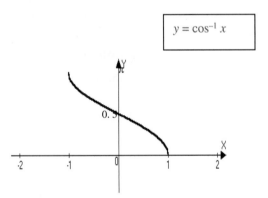

Domain: $\{-1 \le x \le 1\}$
Range: $\{0 \le y \le \pi\}$

Figure 1.3-12

$y = \tan x$

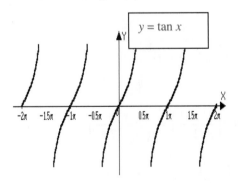

Domain: $\left\{\text{all } x \ne \pm\pi/2, \pm 3\pi/2, \dots\right\}$
Range: $\{-\infty < y < \infty\}$
Frequency: 1   Period: π

Figure 1.3-13

$y = \tan^{-1} x$

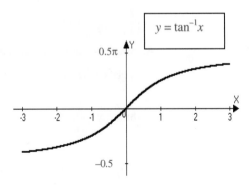

Domain: $\{-\infty < x < \infty\}$
Range: $\left\{-\pi/2 < y < \pi/2\right\}$

Figure 1.3-14

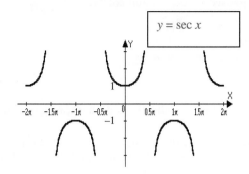

$y = \sec x$

Domain: $\{$ all $x \neq \pm \frac{\pi}{2}, \pm \frac{3\pi}{2}, \dots \}$

Range: $\{y \leq -1 \text{ and } y \geq 1\}$

Frequency: 1   Period: 2π

Figure 1.3-15

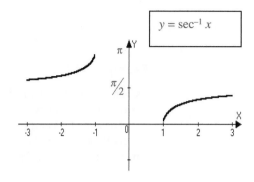

$y = \sec^{-1} x$

Domain: $\{x \leq -1 \text{ or } x \geq 1\}$

Range: $\{0 \leq y \leq \pi, y \neq \frac{\pi}{2} \}$

Figure 1.3-16

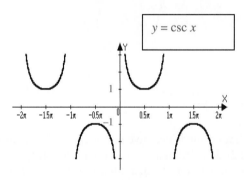

$y = \csc x$

Domain: $\{$ all $x \neq 0, \pm\pi, \pm 2\pi \}$

Range: $\{y \leq -1 \text{ and } y \geq 1\}$

Frequency: 1   Period: 2π

Figure 1.3-17

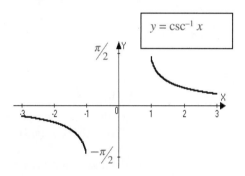

$y = \csc^{-1} x$

Domain: $\{x \leq -1 \text{ or } x \geq 1\}$

Range: $\left\{ -\frac{\pi}{2} \leq y \leq \frac{\pi}{2}, y \neq 0 \right\}$

Figure 1.3-18

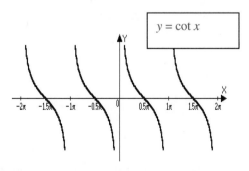

$y = \cot x$

Domain: $\{$ all $x \neq 0, \pm\pi, \pm 2\pi \}$

Range: $\{-\infty < y < \infty\}$

Frequency: 1 Period: π

Figure 1.3-19

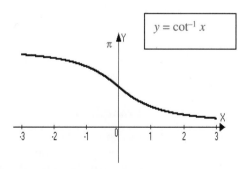

$y = \cot^{-1} x$

Domain: $\{-\infty < x < \infty\}$

Range: $\{0 < y < \pi\}$

Figure 1.3-20

Formulas for using a calculator to get $\sec^{-1}x$, $\csc^{-1}x$, and $\cot^{-1}x$:

$$\sec^{-1}x = \cos^{-1}(1/x)$$
$$\csc^{-1}x = \sin^{-1}(1/x)$$
$$\cot^{-1}x = \pi/2 - \tan^{-1}x$$

Example 1

Sketch the graph of the function $y = 3\sin 2x$. Indicate its domain, range, amplitude, period and frequency.

The domain is all real numbers. The range is $[-3, 3]$. The amplitude is 3, which is the coefficient of $\sin 2x$. The frequency is 2, the coefficient of x, and the period is $(2\pi) \div$ (the frequency), thus $(2\pi) \div 2 = \pi$. (See Figure 1.3-21.)

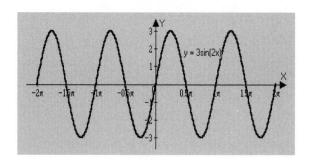

Figure 1.3-21

Example 2

Solve the equation $\cos x = -0.5$ if $0 \le x \le 2\pi$.

Note that $\cos(\pi/3) = 0.5$ and that cosine is negative in the 2nd and 3rd quadrants. Since $\cos x = -0.5$, x must be in the 2nd or 3rd quadrants with a reference angle of $\pi/3$. In the 2nd quadrant, $x = \pi - (\pi/3) = 2\pi/3$ and in the 3rd quadrant, $x = \pi + (\pi/3) = 4\pi/3$.

Thus $x = 2\pi/3$ or $4\pi/3$. (See Figure 1.3-22.)

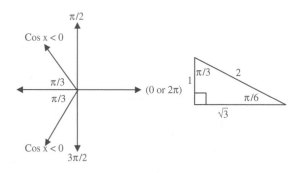

Figure 1.3-22

Example 3

Evaluate $\tan^{-1}(3)$.

Using your graphing calculator, enter $\tan^{-1}(3)$ and the result is 1.2490457724. Note that the range of $\tan^{-1}0\ x$ is $(-\pi/2, \pi/2)$ and $-\pi/2 \le 1.2490457724 \le \pi/2$. Thus $\tan^{-1}(3) \approx 1.2490457724$.

Example 4

Evaluate $\sin\left[\cos^{-1}\left(\dfrac{\sqrt{3}}{2}\right)\right]$.

Note that $\cos^{-1}\left(\dfrac{\sqrt{3}}{2}\right) = \pi/6$, and thus, $\sin(\pi/6) = 0.5$. Or you could use a calculator and enter $\sin\left[\cos^{-1}\left(\dfrac{\sqrt{3}}{2}\right)\right]$ and get 0.5.

Exponential and Logarithmic Functions

Exponential Function with base a: $f(x) = a^x$ where $a > 0$ and $a \neq 1$.
Domain: {all real numbers}. Range: $\{y \mid y > 0\}$. Y-intercept: (0, 1). Horizontal Asymptote: x-axis. Behavior: strictly increasing. (See Figure 1.3-23.)

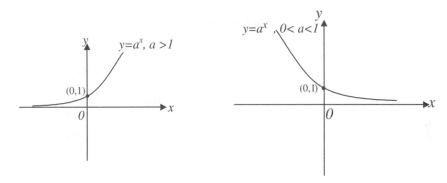

Figure 1.3-23

Properties of Exponents:
Given $a > 0$, $b > 0$ and x and y are real numbers, then

$$a^x \cdot a^y = a^{(x+y)}$$

$$a^x \div a^y = a^{(x-y)}$$

$$(a^x)^y = a^{xy}$$

$$(ab)^x = a^x \cdot b^x$$

$$\left(\frac{a}{b}\right)^x = \frac{a^x}{b^x}$$

Logarithmic Function with base a: $y = \log_a x$ if and only if $a^y = x$ where $x > 0$, $a > 0$ and $a \neq 1$. (See Figure 1.3-24.)

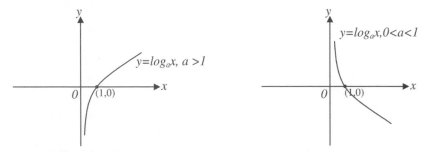

Figure 1.3-24

Domain: $\{x \mid x > 0\}$. Range: {all real numbers}. X-intercept: (1, 0). Vertical Asymptote: y-axis. Behavior: strictly increasing.

Note that $y = \log_a x$ and $y = a^x$ are inverse functions (i.e., $\log_a (a^x) = a^{(\log_a x)} = x$.) (See Figure 1.3-25.)

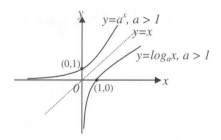

Figure 1.3-25

Properties of Logarithms:

Given x, y, and a are positive numbers with $a \neq 1$ and n is a real number, then

$$\log_a (xy) = \log_a x + \log_a y$$

$$\log_a \left(\frac{x}{y}\right) = \log_a x - \log_a y$$

$$\log_a x^n = n \log_a x$$

Note that $\log_a 1 = 0$, $\log_a a = 1$ and $\log_a a^x = x$.

The Natural Base e:

$$e \approx 2.71828182846 \ldots$$

The expression $\left(1 + \dfrac{1}{x}\right)^x$ approaches the number e as x gets larger and larger.

An equivalent expression is $(1 + h)^{1/h}$. The expression $(1 + h)^{1/h}$ also approaches e as h approaches 0.

Exponential Function with base e: $f(x) = e^x$
The Natural Logarithmic Function: $f(x) = \ln x = \log_e x$ where $x > 0$.
Note that $y = e^x$ and $y = \ln x$ are inverse functions: $(e^{\ln x} = \ln (e^x) = x)$
Also note that $e^0 = 1$, $\ln 1 = 0$, and $\ln e = 1$. (See Figure 1.3-26.)

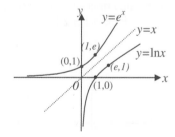

Figure 1.3-26

Properties of the Natural Logarithmic and Exponential Functions:

Given x and y are real numbers, then

$$e^x \cdot e^y = e^{(x+y)}$$

$$e^x \div e^y = e^{(x-y)}$$

$$(e^x)^y = e^{xy}$$

$$\ln (xy) = \ln x + \ln y$$

$$\ln \left(\frac{x}{y}\right) = \ln x - \ln y$$

$$\ln x^n = n \ln x$$

Change of Base Formula:

$$\log_a x = \frac{\ln x}{\ln a} \text{ where } a > 0 \text{ and } a \neq 1$$

Example 1

Sketch the graph of $f(x) = \ln (x - 2)$

Note that the domain of $f(x)$ is $\{x \,|\, x > 2\}$ and that $f(3) = \ln(1) = 0$ and thus, the x-intercept is 3. (See figure 1.3-27.)

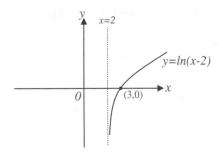

Figure 1.3-27

Example 2

Evaluate (a) $\log_2 8$, (b) $\log_5 \dfrac{1}{25}$, and (c) $\ln e^5$.

(a) Let $n = \log_2 8$ and thus, $2^n = 8 = 2^3$. Therefore $n = 3$.

(b) Let $n = \log_5 \dfrac{1}{25}$, and thus, $5^n = \dfrac{1}{25} = 5^{-2}$. Therefore, $n = -2$.

(c) You know that $y = e^x$ and $y = \ln x$ are inverse functions. Thus, $\ln e^5 = 5$.

Example 3

Express $\ln [x(2x + 5)^3]$ as the sum and multiple of logarithms.

$$\ln [x(2x + 5)^3] = \ln x + \ln (2x + 5)^3$$
$$= \ln x + 3 \ln (2x + 5)$$

Example 4

Solve $2e^{x+1} = 18$ to the nearest thousandth.

$$2e^{x+1} = 18$$
$$e^{x+1} = 9$$
$$\ln (e^{x+1}) = \ln 9$$
$$x + 1 = \ln 9$$
$$x = 1.197$$

Example 5

Solve $3 \ln 2x = 12$ to the nearest thousandth.

$$3 \ln 2x = 12$$
$$\ln 2x = 4$$
$$e^{\ln 2x} = e^4$$
$$2x = e^4$$
$$x = e^4/2 = 27.299$$

1.4 GRAPHS OF FUNCTIONS

Main Concepts: *Increasing and Decreasing Functions; Intercepts and Zeros; Odd and Even Functions; Shifting, Reflecting, and Stretching Functions*

Increasing and Decreasing Functions

Given a function f defined on an interval:

- f is increasing on an interval if $f(x_1) < f(x_2)$ whenever $x_1 < x_2$ for any x_1 and x_2 in the interval
- f is decreasing on an interval if $f(x_1) > f(x_2)$ whenever $x_1 < x_2$ for any x_1 and x_2 in the interval
- f is constant on an interval if $f(x_1) = f(x_2)$ for any x_1 and x_2 in the interval.

A function value $f(c)$ is called a relative minimum of f if there exists an interval (a,b) in the domain of f containing c such that $f(c) \leq f(x)$ for all $x \in (a,b)$.

A function value $f(c)$ is called a relative maximum of f if there exists an interval (a,b) in the domain of f containing c such that $f(c) \geq f(x)$ for all $x \in (a,b)$ (See Figure 1.4-1.)

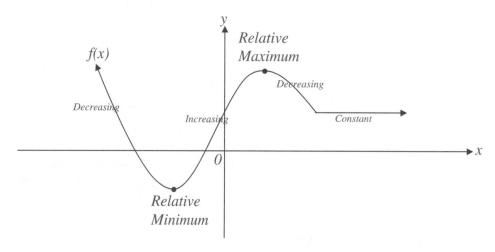

Figure 1.4-1

In the following examples, using your graphing calculator, determine the intervals over which the given function is increasing, decreasing or constant. Indicate any relative minimum and maximum values of the function.

Example 1: $f(x) = x^3 - 3x + 2$

The function $f(x) = x^3 - 3x + 2$ is increasing on $(-\infty, -1)$ and $(1, \infty)$, decreasing on $(-1, 1)$.

A relative minimum value of the function is 0 occurring at the point (1,0) and a relative maximum value is 4 located at the point (−1,4). (See Figure 1.4-2.)

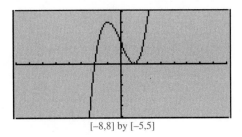

[−8,8] by [−5,5]

Figure 1.4-2

Example 2: $g(x) = (x − 1)^3$

Note that $g(x) = (x − 1)^3$ is increasing for the entire domain $(−\infty, \infty)$ and it has no relative minimum or relative maximum values. (See Figure 1.4-3.)

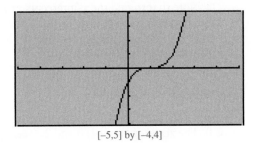

[−5,5] by [−4,4]

Figure 1.4-3

Example 3: $f(x) = \dfrac{x}{x − 2}$

The function f is decreasing on the intervals $(−\infty, 2)$ and $(2, \infty)$ and it has no relative minimum or relative maximum values. (See Figure 1.4-4.)

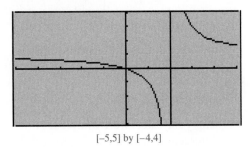

[−5,5] by [−4,4]

Figure 1.4-4

• The $\displaystyle\lim_{h\to 0} \frac{\sin(\pi + h) − \sin \pi}{h}$ is equivalent to $\dfrac{d}{dx} \sin x \big|_{x=\pi}$ which is $\cos \pi$ or $−1$.

Intercepts and Zeros

Given a function f, if $f(a) = 0$, then the point $(a, 0)$ is an x-intercept of the graph of the function, and the number a is called a zero of the function.

If $f(0) = b$, then b is the y-intercept of the graph of the function. (See Figure 1.4-5.)

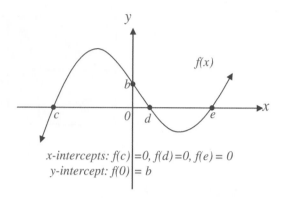

x-intercepts: $f(c) = 0$, $f(d) = 0$, $f(e) = 0$
y-intercept: $f(0) = b$

Figure 1.4-5

Note that to find the x-intercepts or zeros of a function, you should set $f(x) = 0$ and to find the y-intercept, let x be 0 (i.e., find $f(0)$.)

In the following examples, find the x-intercepts, y-intercept, and zeros of the given function if they exist.

Example 1: $f(x) = x^3 - 4x$

Using your graphing calculator, note that the x-intercepts are $-2, 0, 2$ and the y-intercept is 0. The zeros of f are $-2, 0$ and 2. (See Figure 1.4-6.)

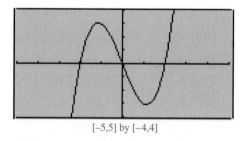

[−5,5] by [−4,4]

Figure 1.4-6

Example 2: $f(x) = x^2 - 2x + 4$

Using your calculator, you see that the y-intercept is $(0, 4)$ and the function f has no x-intercept or zeros. (See Figure 1.4-7.)

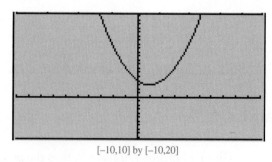

[−10,10] by [−10,20]

Figure 1.4-7

Odd and Even Functions

A function f is an even function if $f(-x) = f(x)$ for all x in the domain. The graph of an even function is symmetrical with respect to the y-axis. If a point (a,b) is on the graph, so is the point $(-a,b)$. If a function is a polynomial with only even powers, then it is an even function. (See Figure 1.4-8.)

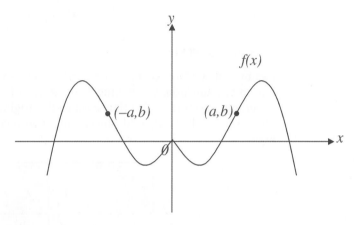

Figure 1.4-8

A function f is an odd function if $f(-x) = -f(x)$ for all x in the domain. The graph of an odd function is symmetrical with respect to the origin. If a point (a, b) is on the graph, so is the point $(-a, -b)$. If a function is a polynomial with only odd powers and a zero constant, then it is an odd function. (See Figure 1.4-9.)

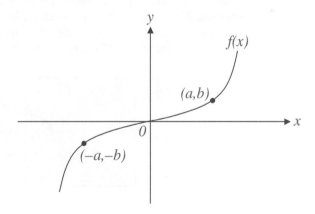

Figure 1.4-9

In the following example, determine if the given functions are even, odd or neither.

Example 1: $f(x) = x^4 - x^2$

Begin by examining $f(-x)$. Since $f(-x) = (-x)^4 - (-x)^2 = x^4 - x^2$, $f(-x) = f(x)$. Therefore, $f(x) = x^4 - x^2$ is an even function. Or using your graphic calculator, you see that the graph of $f(x)$ is symmetrical with respect to the y-axis. Thus, $f(x)$ is an even function. Or, since f has only even powers, it is an even function. (See Figure 1.4-10.)

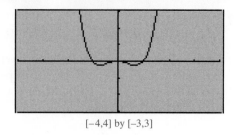

[−4,4] by [−3,3]

Figure 1.4-10

Example 2: $g(x) = x^3 + x$

Examine $g(-x)$. Note that $g(-x) = (-x)^3 + (-x) = -x^3 - x = -g(x)$. Therefore, $g(x) = x^3 + x$ is an odd function. Or looking at the graph of $g(x)$ in your calculator, you see that the graph is symmetrical with respect to the origin. Therefore, $g(x)$ is an odd function. Or, since $g(x)$ has only odd powers and a zero constant, it is an odd function. (See Figure 1.4-11.)

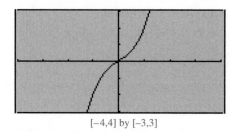

[−4,4] by [−3,3]

Figure 1.4-11

Example 3: $h(x) = x^3 + 1$

Examine $h(-x)$. Since $h(-x) = (-x)^3 + 1 = -x^3 + 1$, $h(-x) \neq h(x)$ which indicates that $h(x)$ is not even. Also, $-h(x) = -x^3 - 1$; therefore, $h(-x) \neq -h(x)$ which implies that $h(x)$ is not odd. Using your calculator, you notice that the graph of $h(x)$ is not symmetrical respect to the y-axis or the origin. Thus, $h(x)$ is neither even nor odd. (See Figure 1.4-12.)

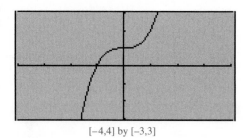

[−4,4] by [−3,3]

Figure 1.4-12

Shifting, Reflecting, and Stretching Graphs

Vertical and Horizontal Shifts

Given $y = f(x)$ and $a > 0$, the graph of

$y = f(x) + a$ is a vertical shift of the graph of $y = f(x)$ a units upward.

$y = f(x) - a$ is a vertical shift of the graph of $y = f(x)$ a units downward. (See Figure 1.4-13.)

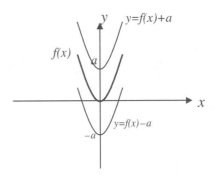

Figure 1.4-13

$y = f(x - a)$ is a horizontal shift of the graph of $y = f(x)$ a units to the right.

$y = f(x + a)$ is a horizontal shift of the graph of $y = f(x)$ a units to the left. (See Figure 1.4-14.)

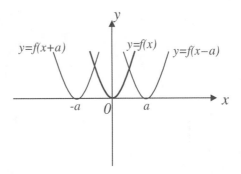

Figure 1.4-14

Reflections about the x-Axis, y-Axis, and the Origin

Given $y = f(x)$, then the graph of

$y = -f(x)$ is a reflection of the graph of $y = f(x)$ about the x-axis. (See Figure 1.4-15.)

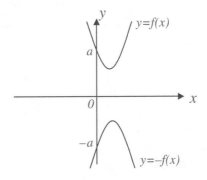

Figure 1.4-15

$y = f(-x)$ is a reflection of the graph of $y = f(x)$ about the y-axis. (See Figure 1.4-16.)

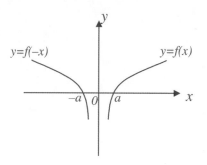

Figure 1.4-16

$y = -f(-x)$ is a reflection of the graph of $y = f(x)$ about the origin. (See Figure 1.4-17.)

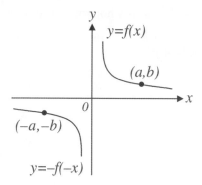

Figure 1.4-17

Stretching Graphs

Given $y = f(x)$, the graph of

$y = af(x)$ where $a > 1$ is a vertical stretch of the graph of $y = f(x)$, and

$y = af(x)$ where $0 < a < 1$ is a vertical shrink of the graph of $y = f(x)$. (See Figure 1.4-18.)

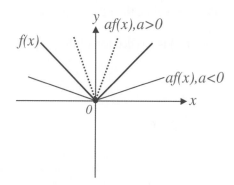

Figure 1.4-18

Example 1

Sketch the graphs of the given functions and verify your results with your graphing calculator: $f(x) = x^2$, $g(x) = 2x^2$ and $p(x) = (x - 3)^2 + 2$.

Note that $g(x)$ is a vertical stretch of $f(x)$ and that $p(x)$ is a horizontal shift of $f(x)$ 3 units to the right followed by a vertical shift of 2 units upward. (See Figure 1.4-19.)

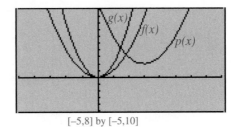

[−5,8] by [−5,10]

Figure 1.4-19

Example 2

Figure 1.4-20 contains the graphs of $f(x) = x^3$, $h(x)$, and $g(x)$. Find an equation for $h(x)$ and an equation for $g(x)$.

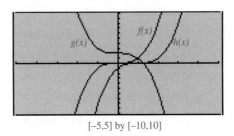

[−5,5] by [−10,10]

Figure 1.4-20

The graph of $h(x)$ is a horizontal shift of the graph of $f(x)$ one unit to the right. Therefore, $h(x) = (x - 1)^3$. The graph of $g(x)$ is a reflection of the graph of $f(x)$ about the x-axis followed by a vertical shift 2 units upward. Thus, $g(x) = -x^3 + 2$.

Example 3

Given $f(x)$ as shown in Figure 1.4-21, sketch the graph of $f(x - 2)$, $f(x) + 1$ and $2f(x)$.

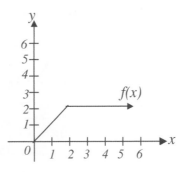

Figure 1.4-21

Note that (a) $f(x - 2)$ is a horizontal shift of $f(x)$ 2 units to the right, (b) $f(x) + 1$ is a vertical shift of $f(x)$ 1 unit upward, and (c) $2f(x)$ is a vertical stretch of $f(x)$ by a factor of 2. (See Figure 1.4-22.)

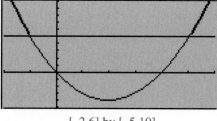

Figure 1.4-22

1.5 RAPID REVIEW

1. If line l is parallel to the line $y - 3x = 2$, find m_l.

   Answer: $m_l = 3$

2. If line l is perpendicular to the line $2y + x = 6$, find m_l.

   Answer: $m_l = 2$

3. If $x^2 + y = 9$, find the x-intercepts and y-intercepts.

   Answer: The x-intercepts are ± 3 (by setting $y = 0$) and the y-intercept is 9 (by setting $x = 0$).

4. Simplify (a) $\ln(e^{3x})$ and (b) $e^{\ln(2x)}$.

   Answer: Since $y = \ln x$ and $y = e^x$ are inverse functions, thus $\ln(e^{3x}) = 3x$ and $e^{\ln(2x)} = 2x$

5. Simplify $\ln\left(\dfrac{1}{x}\right)$.

   Answer: Since $\ln\left(\dfrac{a}{b}\right) = \ln(a) - \ln(b)$, thus $\ln\left(\dfrac{1}{x}\right) = \ln(1) - \ln x = -\ln x$.

6. Simplify $\ln(x^3)$.

   Answer: Since $\ln(a^b) = b \ln a$, thus $\ln(x^3) = 3 \ln x$.

7. Solve the inequality $x^2 - 4x > 5$, using your calculator.

   Answer: Let y1 $= x^2 - 4x$ and y2 $= 5$. Look at the graph and see where y1 is above y2. Solution is $\{x : x < -1 \text{ or } x > 5\}$. (See Figure 1.5-1.)

[-2,6] by [-5,10]

Figure 1.5-1

8. Evaluate $\sin\left(\dfrac{\pi}{6}\right)$, $\tan\left(\dfrac{\pi}{4}\right)$, and $\cos\left(\dfrac{\pi}{6}\right)$.

   Answer: $\sin\left(\dfrac{\pi}{6}\right) = \dfrac{1}{2}$, $\tan\left(\dfrac{\pi}{4}\right) = 1$, and $\cos\left(\dfrac{\pi}{6}\right) = \dfrac{\sqrt{3}}{2}$.

9. Find the domain of $f(x) = \dfrac{\sqrt{x^2 - 1}}{x - 2}$.

Answer: The domain of f is $\{x : |x| \geq 1 \text{ and } x \neq 2\}$.

10. Is the function $f(x) = x^4 - x^2$ even, odd, or neither?

Answer: $f(x)$ is an even function since the exponents of x are all even.

1.6 PRACTICE PROBLEMS

Part A—The use of a calculator is not allowed.

1. Write an equation of a line passing through the point $(-2, 5)$ and parallel to the line $3x - 4y + 12 = 0$.

2. The vertices of a triangle are $A(-2, 0)$, $B(0, 6)$ and $C(4, 0)$. Find an equation of a line containing the median from vertex A to $\overline{BC}$.

3. Write an equation of a circle whose center is at $(2, -3)$ and tangent to the line $y = -1$.

4. Solve for x: $|x - 2| = 2x + 5$

5. Solve the inequality $|6 - 3x| < 18$ and sketch the solution on the real number line.

6. Given $f(x) = x^2 + 3x$, find $\dfrac{f(x + h) - f(x)}{h}$ in simplest form.

7. Determine which of the following equations represent y as a function of x:
   (1) $xy = -8$ (2) $4x^2 + 9y^2 = 36$
   (3) $3x^2 - y = 1$ (4) $y^2 - x^2 = 4$.

8. If $f(x) = x^2$ and $g(x) = \sqrt{25 - x^2}$, find $(f \circ g)(x)$ and indicate its domain.

9. Given the graphs of f and g in Figures 1.6-1 and 1.6-2, evaluate:
   (1) $(f - g)(2)$ (2) $(f \circ g)(1)$ (3) $(g \circ f)(0)$

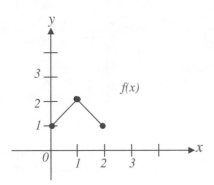

Figure 1.6-1

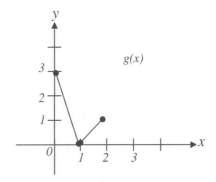

Figure 1.6-2

10. Find the inverse of the function $f(x) = x^3 + 1$.

11. Sketch the graph of the equation $y = 3 \cos (\frac{1}{2}) x$ in the interval $-2\pi \leq x \leq 2\pi$ and indicate the amplitude, frequency and period.

12. On the same set of axes, sketch the graphs of:
    (1) $y = \ln x$ (2) $y = \ln (-x)$ (3) $y = -\ln (x + 2)$

Part B—Calculators are permitted.

13. Solve the inequality $|2x + 4| \leq 10$.

14. Solve the inequality $x^3 - 2x > 1$.

15. Evaluate $\tan \left(\arccos \dfrac{\sqrt{2}}{2} \right)$.

16. Solve for x to the nearest thousandth: $e^{2x} - 6e^x + 5 = 0$.

17. Solve for x to the nearest thousandth: $3 \ln 2x - 3 = 12$.

18. Solve the inequality $\dfrac{2x - 1}{x + 1} \leq 1$.

19. Determine if the function $f(x) = -2x^4 + x^2 + 5$ is even, odd, or neither.

20. Given the function $f(x) = x^4 - 4x^3$, determine the intervals over which the function is increasing, decreasing, or constant. Find all zeros of $f(x)$ and indicate any relative minimum and maximum values of the function.

1.7 SOLUTIONS TO PRACTICE PROBLEMS

1. Rewrite the equation $3x - 4y + 12 = 0$ in $y = mx + b$ form: $y = \frac{3}{4}x + 3$. Thus, the slope of the line is $\frac{3}{4}$. Since line l is parallel to this line, the slope of line l must also be $\frac{3}{4}$. Line l also passes through the point $(-2, 5)$. Therefore, an equation of line l is $y - 5 = \frac{3}{4}(x + 2)$.

2. Let M be the midpoint of $\overline{BC}$. Using the midpoint formula, you will find the coordinates of M to be $(2, 3)$. The slope of median $\overline{AM}$ is $\frac{3}{4}$. Thus, an equation of $\overline{AM}$ is $y - 3 = \left(\frac{3}{4}\right)(x - 2)$.

3. Since the circle is tangent to the line $y = -1$, the radius of the circle is 2 units. Therefore, the equation of the circle is $(x - 2)^2 + (y + 3)^2 = 4$.

4. The two derived equations are $x - 2 = 2x + 5$ and $x - 2 = -2x - 5$. From $x - 2 = 2x + 5$, $x = -7$ and from $x - 2 = -2x - 5$, $x = -1$. However, substituting $x = -7$ into the original equation $|x - 2| = 2x + 5$ results in $9 = -9$ which is not possible. Thus the only solution is -1.

5. The inequality $|6 - 3x| < 18$ is equivalent to $-18 < 6 - 3x < 18$. Thus, $-24 < -3x < 12$. Dividing through by -3 and reversing the inequality sign, you have $8 > x > -4$ or $-4 < x < 8$.

6. Since $f(x + h) = (x + h)^2 + 3(x + h)$, the expression $\dfrac{f(x + h) - f(x)}{h}$ is equivalent to

$$\frac{\left[(x + h)^2 + 3(x + h)\right] - \left[x^2 + 3x\right]}{h}$$

$$= \frac{\left(x^2 + 2xh + h^2 + 3x + 3h\right) - x^2 - 3x}{h}$$

$$= \frac{2xh + h^2 + 3h}{h} = 2x + h + 3.$$

7. The graph of equation (2) $4x^2 + 9y^2 = 36$ is an ellipse and the graph of (4) $y^2 - x^2 = 4$ is a hyperbola intersecting the y-axis at two distinct points. Both of these graphs fail the vertical line test. Only the graphs of equations (1) $xy = -8$ (a parabola) and (3) $3x^2 - y = 1$ (a hyperbola in the 2nd and 4th quadrant) pass the vertical line test. Thus, only (1) $xy = -8$ and (3) $3x^2 - y = 1$ are functions.

8. The domain of $g(x)$ is $-5 \le x \le 5$, and the domain of $f(x)$ is the set of all real numbers. Therefore, the domain of $(f \circ g)(x) = \left(\sqrt{25 - x^2}\right)^2 = 25 - x^2$ is the interval $-5 \le x \le 5$.

9. From the graph, $(f - g)(2) = f(2) - g(2) = 1 - 1 = 0$, $(f \circ g)(1) = f[g(1)] = f(0) = 1$, and $(g \circ f)(0) = g[f(0)] = g(1) = 0$.

10. Let $y = f(x)$ and thus $y = x^3 + 1$. Switch x and y and obtain $x = y^3 + 1$. Solve for y and you will have $y = (x - 1)^{\frac{1}{3}}$. Thus $f^{-1}(x) = (x - 1)^{\frac{1}{3}}$.

11. The amplitude is 3, frequency is $\frac{1}{2}$, and period is 4π. (See Figure 1.7-1.)

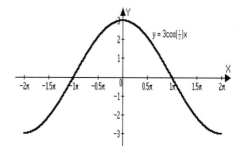

Figure 1.7-1

12. Note that (1) $y = \ln x$ is the graph of the natural logarithmic function. (2) $y = \ln(-x)$ is the reflection about the y-axis. (3) $y = -\ln(x + 2)$ is a horizontal shift 2 units to the left followed by a reflection about the x-axis. (See Figure 1.7-2.)

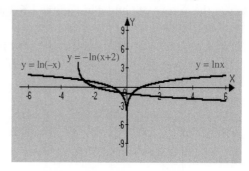

Figure 1.7-2

13. Enter into your calculator $y1 = |2x + 4|$ and $y2 = 10$. Locate the intersection points. They occur at

$x = -7$ and 3. Note that $y1$ is below $y2$ from $x = -7$ to 3. Since the inequality is less than or equal to, the solution is $-7 \leq x \leq 3$. (See Figure 1.7-3.)

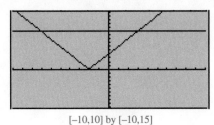

[−10,10] by [−10,15]

Figure 1.7-3

14. Enter into your calculator $y1 = x^3 - 2x$ and $y2 = 1$. Find the intersection points. The points are located at $x = -1, -0.618$ and 1.618. Since $y1$ is above $y2$ in the intervals $-1 < x < -0.618$ and $x > 1.618$ excluding the end points, the solution to the inequality are the intervals $-1 < x < -0.618$ and $x > 1.618$. (See Figure 1.7-4.)

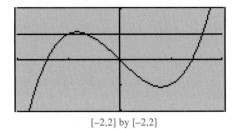

[−2,2] by [−2,2]

Figure 1.7-4

15. Enter $\tan\left(\arccos\dfrac{\sqrt{2}}{2}\right)$ into your calculator and obtain 1. (Note that $\arccos\dfrac{\sqrt{2}}{2} = \pi/4$ and $\tan(\pi/4) = 1$.)

16. Factor $e^{2x} - 6e^x + 5 = 0$ as $(e^x - 5)(e^x - 1) = 0$. Thus $(e^x - 5) = 0$ or $(e^x - 1) = 0$ resulting in $e^x = 5$ and $e^x = 1$. Taking the natural log of both sides yields $\ln(e^x) = \ln 5 \approx 1.609$ and $\ln(e^x) = \ln 1 = 0$. Therefore to the nearest thousandth, $x = 1.609$ or 0. [Note that $\ln(e^x) = x$.]

17. The equation $3 \ln 2x - 3 = 12$ is equivalent to $\ln 2x = 5$. Therefore, $e^{\ln 2x} = e^5$, $2x = e^5 \approx 148.413159$ and $x \approx 74.207$.

18. Enter $y1 = \dfrac{2x - 1}{x + 1}$ and $y2 = 1$ into your calculator. Note that $y1$ is below $y2 = 1$ on the interval

$(-1, 2)$. Since the inequality is $\leq$ which includes the end point at $x = 2$, the solution is $(-1, 2]$. (See Figure 1.7-5.)

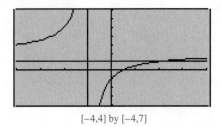

[−4,4] by [−4,7]

Figure 1.7-5

19. Examine $f(-x)$ and $f(-x) = -2(-x)^4 + (-x)^2 + 5 = -2x^4 + x^2 + 5 = f(x)$. Therefore, $f(x)$ is an even function. Note that the graph of $f(x)$ is symmetrical with respect to the y-axis; thus, $f(x)$ is an even function. (See Figure 1.7-6.)

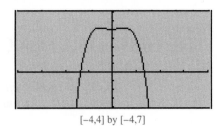

[−4,4] by [−4,7]

Figure 1.7-6

20. Enter $y1 = x^4 - 4x^3$ into your calculator and examine the graph. Note that the graph is decreasing on the interval $(-\infty, 3)$ and increasing on $(3, \infty)$. The function crosses the x-axis at 0 and 4. Thus, the zeros of the function are 0 and 4. There is one relative minimum point at $(3, -27)$. Thus, the relative minimum value for the function is -27. There is no relative maximum. (See Figure 1.7-7.)

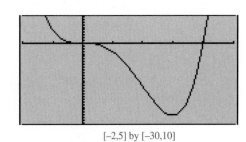

[−2,5] by [−30,10]

Figure 1.7-7

Chapter 2

Limits and Continuity

2.1   THE LIMIT OF A FUNCTION

Main Concepts: *Definition and Properties of Limits, Evaluating Limits, One-sided Limits, Squeeze Theorem*

Definition and Properties of Limits

Definition of Limit

Let f be a function defined on an open interval containing a, except possibly at a itself. Then $\lim\limits_{x \to a} f(x) = L$ (read as the limit of $f(x)$ as x approaches a is L) if for any $\varepsilon > 0$, there exists a $\delta > 0$ such that $|f(x) - L| < \varepsilon$ whenever $|x - a| < \delta$.

Properties of Limits

Given $\lim\limits_{x \to a} f(x) = L$ and $\lim\limits_{x \to a} g(x) = M$ and L, M, a, c and n are real numbers, then

1. $\lim\limits_{x \to a} c = c$

2. $\lim\limits_{x \to a} \left[cf(x) \right] = c \lim\limits_{x \to a} f(x) = cL$

3. $\lim\limits_{x \to a} \left[f(x) \pm g(x) \right] = \lim\limits_{x \to a} f(x) \pm \lim\limits_{x \to a} g(x) = L + M$

4. $\lim\limits_{x \to a} \left[f(x) \cdot g(x) \right] = \lim\limits_{x \to a} f(x) \cdot \lim\limits_{x \to a} g(x) = L \cdot M$

5. $\lim\limits_{x \to a} \dfrac{f(x)}{g(x)} = \dfrac{\lim\limits_{x \to a} f(x)}{\lim\limits_{x \to a} g(x)} = \dfrac{L}{M}, M \neq 0$

6. $\lim\limits_{x \to a} \left[f(x) \right]^n = \left(\lim\limits_{x \to a} f(x) \right)^n = L^n$

Evaluating Limits

If f is a continuous function on an open interval containing the number a, then $\lim_{x \to a} f(x) = f(a)$.

Common techniques in evaluating limits are:

1. substituting directly
2. factoring and simplifying
3. multiplying the numerator and denominator of a rational function by the conjugate of either the numerator or denominator
4. using a graph or a table of values of the given function.

Example 1

Find the limit: $\lim_{x \to 5} \sqrt{3x + 1}$

Substituting directly: $\lim_{x \to 5} \sqrt{3x + 1} = \sqrt{3(5) + 1} = 4$.

Example 2

Find the limit: $\lim_{x \to \pi} 3x \sin x$

Using the product rule, $\lim_{x \to \pi} 3x \sin x = \left(\lim_{x \to \pi} 3x\right)\left(\lim_{x \to \pi} \sin x\right) = (3\pi)(\sin \pi) = (3\pi)(0) = 0$.

Example 3

Find the limit: $\lim_{t \to 2} \dfrac{t^2 - 3t + 2}{t - 2}$

Factoring and simplifying: $\lim_{t \to 2} \dfrac{t^2 - 3t + 2}{t - 2} = \lim_{t \to 2} \dfrac{(t - 1)(t - 2)}{(t - 2)} = \lim_{t \to 2} (t - 1) = (2 - 1)$

$= 1$. (Note that had you substituted $t = 2$ directly in the original expression, you would have obtained a zero in both the numerator and denominator.)

Example 4

Find the limit: $\lim_{x \to b} \dfrac{x^5 - b^5}{x^{10} - b^{10}}$.

Factoring and simplifying: $\lim_{x \to b} \dfrac{x^5 - b^5}{x^{10} - b^{10}} = \lim_{x \to b} \dfrac{x^5 - b^5}{(x^5 - b^5)(x^5 + b^5)}$

$$= \lim_{x \to b} \dfrac{1}{x^5 + b^5} = \dfrac{1}{b^5 + b^5} = \dfrac{1}{2b^5}$$

Example 5

Find the limit: $\lim_{t \to 0} \dfrac{\sqrt{t + 2} - \sqrt{2}}{t}$

Multiplying both the numerator and the denominator by the conjugate of the numerator,

$\left(\sqrt{t + 2} + \sqrt{2}\right)$, yields $\lim_{t \to 0} \dfrac{\sqrt{t + 2} - \sqrt{2}}{t} \left(\dfrac{\sqrt{t + 2} + \sqrt{2}}{\sqrt{t + 2} + \sqrt{2}}\right) = \lim_{t \to 0} \dfrac{t + 2 - 2}{t\left(\sqrt{t + 2} + \sqrt{2}\right)}$

$$= \lim_{t \to 0} \dfrac{t}{t\left(\sqrt{t + 2} + \sqrt{2}\right)} = \lim_{t \to 0} \dfrac{1}{\left(\sqrt{t + 2} + \sqrt{2}\right)} = \dfrac{1}{\sqrt{0 + 2} + \sqrt{2}} = \dfrac{1}{2\sqrt{2}}$$

$= \dfrac{1}{2\sqrt{2}}\left(\dfrac{\sqrt{2}}{\sqrt{2}}\right) = \dfrac{\sqrt{2}}{4}$. (Note that substituting 0 directly into the original expression would have produced a 0 in both the numerator and denominator.)

Example 6

Find the limit: $\lim\limits_{x\to0}\dfrac{3\sin 2x}{2x}$

Enter $y1 = \dfrac{3\sin 2x}{2x}$ in the calculator. You see that the graph of $f(x)$ approaches 3 as x approaches 0. Thus, the $\lim\limits_{t\to0}\dfrac{3\sin 2x}{2x} = 3$. (Note that had you substituted $x=0$ directly in the original expression, you would have obtained a zero in both the numerator and denominator.) (See Figure 2.1-1.)

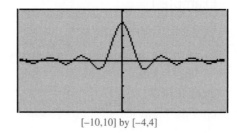

[−10,10] by [−4,4]

Figure 2.1-1

Example 7

Find the limit: $\lim\limits_{x\to3}\dfrac{1}{x-3}$

Enter $y1 = \dfrac{1}{x-3}$ into your calculator. You notice that as x approaching 3 from the right, the graph of $f(x)$ goes higher and higher, and that as x approaching 3 from the left, the graph of $f(x)$ goes lower and lower. Therefore, $\lim\limits_{x\to3}\dfrac{1}{x-3}$ is undefined. (See Figure 2.1-2.)

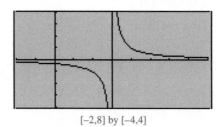

[−2,8] by [−4,4]

Figure 2.1-2

- Always indicate what the final answer is, e.g., "The maximum value of f is 5." Use complete sentences whenever possible.

One-Sided Limits

Let f be a function and a is a real number. Then the right-hand limit: $\lim\limits_{x\to a^+} f(x)$ represents the limit of f as x approaches a from the right, and left-hand limit: $\lim\limits_{x\to a^-} f(x)$ represents the limit of f as x approaches a from the left.

Existence of a Limit

Let f be a function and let a and L be real numbers. Then the two-sided limit $\lim\limits_{x \to a} f(x) = L$ if and only if the one-sided limits exist and $\lim\limits_{x \to a^+} f(x) = \lim\limits_{x \to a^-} f(x) = L$.

Example 1

Given $f(x) = \dfrac{x^2 - 2x - 3}{x - 3}$, find the limits (a) $\lim\limits_{x \to 3^+} f(x)$, (b) $\lim\limits_{x \to 3^-} f(x)$, and (c) $\lim\limits_{x \to 3} f(x)$.

Substituting $x = 3$ into $f(x)$ leads to a 0 in both the numerator and denominator. Factor $f(x)$ as $\dfrac{(x - 3)(x + 1)}{(x - 3)}$ which is equivalent to $(x + 1)$ where $x \neq 3$. Thus, (a) $\lim\limits_{x \to 3^+} f(x) = \lim\limits_{x \to 3^+} (x + 1) = 4$, (b) $\lim\limits_{x \to 3^-} f(x) = \lim\limits_{x \to 3^-} (x + 1) = 4$, and (c) since the one-sided limits exist and are equal, $\lim\limits_{x \to 3^+} f(x) = \lim\limits_{x \to 3^-} f(x) = 4$, therefore the two-sided limit $\lim\limits_{x \to 3} f(x)$ exists and $\lim\limits_{x \to 3} f(x) = 4$. (Note that $f(x)$ is undefined at $x = 3$, but the function gets arbitrarily close to 4 as x approaches 3. Therefore the limit exists. (See Figure 2.1-3.)

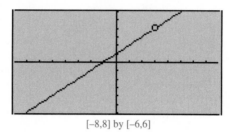

[–8,8] by [–6,6]

Figure 2.1-3

Example 2

Given $f(x)$ as illustrated in the accompanying diagram (Figure 2.1-4.) Find the limits (a) $\lim\limits_{x \to 0^+} f(x)$, (b) $\lim\limits_{x \to 0^-} f(x)$, and (c) $\lim\limits_{x \to 0} f(x)$.

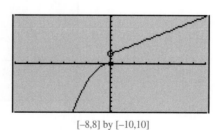

[–8,8] by [–10,10]

Figure 2.1-4

(a) As x approaches 0 from the left, $f(x)$ gets arbitrarily close to 0. Thus, $\lim\limits_{x \to 0^-} f(x) = 0$.

(b) As x approaches 0 from the right, $f(x)$ gets arbitrarily close to 2. Therefore, $\lim\limits_{x \to 0^+} f(x) = 2$. Note that $f(0) \neq 2$.

(c) Since $\lim\limits_{x \to 0^+} f(x) \neq \lim\limits_{x \to 0^-} f(x)$, $\lim\limits_{x \to 0} f(x)$ does not exist.

Example 3

Given the greatest integer function $f(x) = [x]$, Find the limits (a) $\lim\limits_{x \to 1^+} f(x)$, (b) $\lim\limits_{x \to 1^-} f(x)$, and (c) $\lim\limits_{x \to 1} f(x)$.

a. Enter $y1 = \text{int}(x)$ in your calculator. You see that as x approaches 1 from the right, the function stays at 1. Thus, $\lim\limits_{x \to 1^+} [x] = 1$. Note that $f(1)$ is also equal 1. (b) As x approaches 1 from the left, the function stays at 0. Therefore, $\lim\limits_{x \to 1^-} [x] = 0$. Notice that $\lim\limits_{x \to 1^-} [x] \neq f(1)$. (c) Since $\lim\limits_{x \to 1^-} [x] \neq \lim\limits_{x \to 1^+} [x]$, therefore, $\lim\limits_{x \to 1} [x]$ does not exist. (See Figure 2.1-5.)

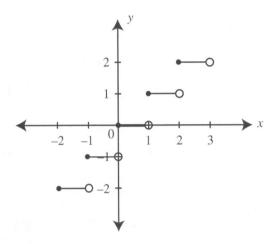

Figure 2.1-5

Example 4

Given $f(x) = \dfrac{|x|}{x}$, $x \neq 0$, find the limits (a) $\lim\limits_{x \to 0^+} f(x)$, (b) $\lim\limits_{x \to 0^-} f(x)$, and (c) $\lim\limits_{x \to 0} f(x)$.

(a) From inspecting the graph, $\lim\limits_{x \to 0^+} = \dfrac{|x|}{x} = 1$, (b) $\lim\limits_{x \to 0^-} = \dfrac{|x|}{x} = -1$, and (c) since $\lim\limits_{x \to 0^+} \dfrac{|x|}{x}$

$\neq \lim\limits_{x \to 0^-} \dfrac{|x|}{x}$, therefore, $\lim\limits_{x \to 0} = \dfrac{|x|}{x}$ does not exist. (See Figure 2.1-6.)

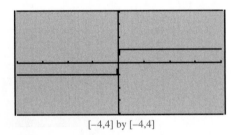

[−4,4] by [−4,4]

Figure 2.1-6

Example 5

If $f(x) = \begin{cases} e^{2x} & \text{for } -4 \leq x < 0 \\ xe^x & \text{for } 0 \leq x \leq 4 \end{cases}$, find $\lim\limits_{x \to 0} f(x)$.

$\lim\limits_{x \to 0^+} f(x) = \lim\limits_{x \to 0^+} xe^x = 0$ and $\lim\limits_{x \to 0^-} f(x) = \lim\limits_{x \to 0^-} e^{2x} = 1$.

Thus $\lim\limits_{x \to 0} f(x)$ does not exist.

• Remember $\ln(e) = 1$ and $e^{\ln 3} = 3$ since $y = \ln x$ and $y = e^x$ are inverse functions.

Squeeze Theorem

If f, g, and h are functions defined on some open interval containing a such that $g(x) \leq f(x) \leq h(x)$ for all x in the interval except possibly at a itself, and $\lim_{x \to a} g(x) = \lim_{x \to a} h(x) = L$, then $\lim_{x \to a} f(x) = L$.

Theorems on Limits

(1) $\lim_{x \to 0} \dfrac{\sin x}{x} = 1$ and (2) $\lim_{x \to 0} \dfrac{\cos x - 1}{x} = 0$

Example 1

Find the limit if it exists: $\lim_{x \to 0} \dfrac{\sin 3x}{x}$

Substituting 0 into the expression would lead to $\dfrac{0}{0}$. Rewrite $\dfrac{\sin 3x}{x}$ as $\dfrac{3}{3} \cdot \dfrac{\sin 3x}{x}$ and

thus, $\lim_{x \to 0} \dfrac{\sin 3x}{x} = \lim_{x \to 0} \dfrac{3 \sin 3x}{3x} = 3 \lim_{x \to 0} \dfrac{\sin 3x}{3x}$. As x approaches 0, so does $3x$. There-

fore, $3 \lim_{x \to 0} \dfrac{\sin 3x}{3x} = 3 \lim_{3x \to 0} \dfrac{\sin 3x}{3x} = 3(1) = 3$. (Note that $\lim_{3x \to 0} \dfrac{\sin 3x}{3x}$ is equivalent to

$\lim_{x \to 0} \dfrac{\sin x}{x}$ by replacing $3x$ by x.) Verify your result with a calculator. (See Figure 2.1-7.)

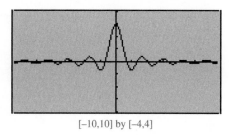

[−10,10] by [−4,4]

Figure 2.1-7

Example 2

Find the limit if it exists: $\lim_{h \to 0} \dfrac{\sin 3h}{\sin 2h}$.

Rewrite $\dfrac{\sin 3h}{\sin 2h}$ as $\dfrac{3\left(\dfrac{\sin 3h}{3h}\right)}{2\left(\dfrac{\sin 2h}{2h}\right)}$. As h approaches 0, so do $3h$ and $2h$. Therefore,

$\lim_{h \to 0} \dfrac{\sin 3h}{\sin 2h} = \dfrac{3 \lim_{3h \to 0} \dfrac{\sin 3h}{3h}}{2 \lim_{2h \to 0} \dfrac{\sin 2h}{2h}} = \dfrac{3(1)}{2(1)} = \dfrac{3}{2}$. (Note that substituting $h = 0$ into the original

expression would have produced $\dfrac{0}{0}$.) Verify your result with a calculator. (See Figure 2.1-8.)

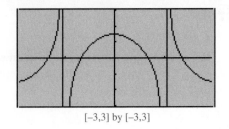

[−3,3] by [−3,3]

Figure 2.1-8

Example 3

Find the limit if it exists: $\lim\limits_{y\to 0} \dfrac{y^2}{1 - \cos y}$.

Substituting 0 in the expression would lead to $\dfrac{0}{0}$. Multiplying both the numerator and

denominator by the conjugate $(1 + \cos y)$ produces $\lim\limits_{y\to 0} \dfrac{y^2}{1 - \cos y} \cdot \dfrac{(1 + \cos y)}{(1 + \cos y)} =$

$\lim\limits_{y\to 0} \dfrac{y^2(1 + \cos y)}{1 - \cos^2 y} = \lim\limits_{y\to 0} \dfrac{y^2(1 + \cos y)}{\sin^2 y} = \lim\limits_{y\to 0} \dfrac{y^2}{\sin^2 y} \cdot \lim\limits_{y\to 0}(1 + \cos^2 y) =$

$\lim\limits_{y\to 0}\left(\dfrac{y}{\sin y}\right)^2 \cdot \lim\limits_{y\to 0}(1 + \cos^2 y) = \left(\lim\limits_{y\to 0} \dfrac{y}{\sin y}\right)^2 \cdot \lim\limits_{y\to 0}(1 + \cos^2 y) = (1)^2(1 + 1) = 2.$

(Note that $\lim\limits_{y\to 0} \dfrac{y}{\sin y} = \lim\limits_{y\to 0} \dfrac{1}{\dfrac{\sin y}{y}} = \dfrac{\lim\limits_{y\to 0}(1)}{\lim\limits_{y\to 0} \dfrac{\sin y}{y}} = \dfrac{1}{1} = 1.$) Verify your result with a

calculator. (See Figure 2.1-9.)

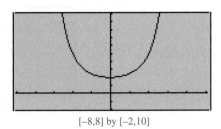

[−8,8] by [−2,10]

Figure 2.1-9

Example 4

Find the limit if it exists: $\lim\limits_{x\to 0} \dfrac{3x}{\cos x}$.

Using the quotient rule for limits, you have $\lim\limits_{x\to 0} \dfrac{3x}{\cos x} = \dfrac{\lim\limits_{x\to 0}(3x)}{\lim\limits_{x\to 0}(\cos x)} = \dfrac{0}{1} = 0.$ Verify

your result with a calculator. (See Figure 2.1-10.)

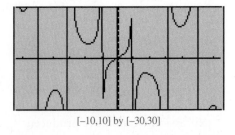

[−10,10] by [−30,30]

Figure 2.1-10

2.2 LIMITS INVOLVING INFINITIES

Main Concepts: *Infinite Limits (as* x → a*), Limits at Infinity (as* x → ∞*), Horizontal and Vertical Asymptotes*

Infinite Limits (as $x \to a$)

If f is a function defined at every number in some open interval containing a, except possibly at a itself, then

(1) $\lim\limits_{x \to a} f(x) = \infty$ means that $f(x)$ increases without bound as x approaches a,

(2) $\lim\limits_{x \to a} f(x) = -\infty$ means that $f(x)$ decreases without bound as x approaches a.

Limit Theorems

(1) If n is a positive integer, then

   (a) $\lim\limits_{x \to 0^+} \dfrac{1}{x^n} = \infty$

   (b) $\lim\limits_{x \to 0^-} \dfrac{1}{x^n} = \begin{cases} \infty & \text{if } n \text{ is even} \\ -\infty & \text{if } n \text{ is odd} \end{cases}$

(2) If the $\lim\limits_{x \to a} f(x) = c,\ c > 0$, and $\lim\limits_{x \to a} g(x) = 0$, then

$$\lim_{x \to a} \frac{f(x)}{g(x)} = \begin{cases} \infty & \text{if } g(x) \text{ approaches } 0 \text{ through positive values} \\ -\infty & \text{if } g(x) \text{ approaches } 0 \text{ through negative values} \end{cases}$$

(3) If the $\lim\limits_{x \to a} f(x) = c,\ c < 0$, and $\lim\limits_{x \to a} g(x) = 0$, then

$$\lim_{x \to a} \frac{f(x)}{g(x)} = \begin{cases} -\infty & \text{if } g(x) \text{ approaches } 0 \text{ through positive values} \\ \infty & \text{if } g(x) \text{ approaches } 0 \text{ through negative values} \end{cases}$$

(Note that limit theorems 2 and 3 hold true for $x \to a^+$ and $x \to a^-$.)

Example 1

Evaluate the limit: (a) $\lim\limits_{x \to 2^+} \dfrac{3x - 1}{x - 2}$ and (b) $\lim\limits_{x \to 2^-} \dfrac{3x - 1}{x - 2}$

The limit of the numerator is 5 and the limit of the denominator is 0 through positive values. Thus, $\lim\limits_{x \to 2^+} \dfrac{3x - 1}{x - 2} = \infty$. (b) The limit of the numerator is 5 and the limit of the denominator is 0 through negative values. Therefore, $\lim\limits_{x \to 2^-} \dfrac{3x - 1}{x - 2} = -\infty$. Verify your result with a calculator. (See Figure 2.2-1.)

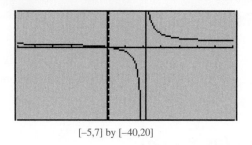

[−5,7] by [−40,20]

Figure 2.2-1

Example 2

Find: $\lim\limits_{x \to 3^-} \dfrac{x^2}{x^2 - 9}$

Factor the denominator obtaining $\lim\limits_{x \to 3^-} \dfrac{x^2}{x^2 - 9} = \lim\limits_{x \to 3^-} \dfrac{x^2}{(x - 3)(x + 3)}$. The limit of the numerator is 9 and the limit of the denominator is $(0)(6) = 0$ through negative values.

Therefore, $\lim\limits_{x \to 3^-} \dfrac{x^2}{x^2 - 9} = -\infty$. Verify your result with a calculator. (See Figure 2.2-2.)

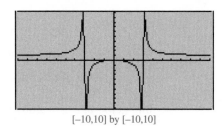

[−10,10] by [−10,10]

Figure 2.2-2

Example 3

Find: $\lim\limits_{x \to 5^-} \dfrac{\sqrt{25 - x^2}}{x - 5}$

Substituting 5 into the expression leads to $\frac{0}{0}$. Factor the numerator $\sqrt{25 - x^2}$ into $\sqrt{(5 - x)(5 + x)}$. As $x \to 5^-$, $(x - 5) < 0$. Rewrite $(x - 5)$ as $-(5 - x)$. As $x \to 5^-$, $(5 - x) > 0$ and thus, you may express $(5 - x)$ as $\sqrt{(5 - x)^2} = \sqrt{(5 - x)(5 - x)}$. Therefore, $(x - 5) = -(5 - x) = -\sqrt{(5 - x)(5 - x)}$. Substituting these equivalent expressions into

the original problem, you have $\lim\limits_{x \to 5^-} \dfrac{\sqrt{25 - x^2}}{x - 5} = \lim\limits_{x \to 5^-} \dfrac{\sqrt{(5 - x)(5 + x)}}{\sqrt{(5 - x)(5 - x)}}$

$= -\lim\limits_{x \to 5^-} \dfrac{\sqrt{(5 - x)(5 + x)}}{(5 - x)(5 - x)} = -\lim\limits_{x \to 5^-} \sqrt{\dfrac{(5 + x)}{(5 - x)}}$. The limit of the numerator is 10 and the

limit of the denominator is 0 through positive values. Thus, the $\lim\limits_{x \to 5^-} \dfrac{\sqrt{25 - x^2}}{x - 5} = -\infty$.

Example 4

Find: $\lim\limits_{x \to 2^-} \dfrac{[x] - x}{2 - x}$, where $[x]$ is the greatest integer value of x.

As $x \to 2^-$, $[x] = 1$. The limit of the numerator is $(1 - 2) = -1$. As $x \to 2^-$, $(2 - x) = 0$ through

positive values. Thus, $\lim\limits_{x \to 2^-} \dfrac{[x] - x}{2 - x} = -\infty$.

- Do easy questions first. The easy ones are worth the same number of points as the hard ones.

Limits at Infinity (as $x \to \pm\infty$)

If f is a function defined at every number in some interval (a, ∞), then $\lim\limits_{x \to \infty} f(x) = L$

means that L is the limit of $f(x)$ as x increases without bound.

If f is a function defined at every number is some interval $(-\infty, a)$, then $\lim\limits_{x \to -\infty} f(x) = L$

means that L is the limit of $f(x)$ as x decreases without bound.

Limit Theorem

If n is a positive integer, then

(a) $\lim\limits_{x \to \infty} \dfrac{1}{x^n} = 0$

(b) $\lim\limits_{x \to -\infty} \dfrac{1}{x^n} = 0$

Example 1

Evaluate the limit: $\lim\limits_{x \to \infty} \dfrac{6x - 13}{2x + 5}$

Divide every term in the numerator and denominator by the highest power of x, and in this case, it is x and obtain:

$$\lim_{x \to \infty} \frac{6x - 13}{2x + 5} = \lim_{x \to \infty} \frac{6 - \dfrac{13}{x}}{2 + \dfrac{5}{x}} = \frac{\lim\limits_{x \to \infty}(6) - \lim\limits_{x \to \infty}\dfrac{13}{x}}{\lim\limits_{x \to \infty}(2) + \lim\limits_{x \to \infty}\left(\dfrac{5}{x}\right)} = \frac{\lim\limits_{x \to \infty}(6) - 13\lim\limits_{x \to \infty}\left(\dfrac{1}{x}\right)}{\lim\limits_{x \to \infty}(2) + 5\lim\limits_{x \to \infty}\left(\dfrac{1}{x}\right)}$$

$$= \frac{6 - 13(0)}{2 + 5(0)} = 3.$$

Verify your result with a calculator. (See Figure 2.2-3.)

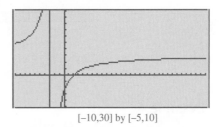

[−10,30] by [−5,10]

Figure 2.2-3

Example 2

Evaluate the limit: $\lim\limits_{x \to -\infty} \dfrac{3x - 10}{4x^3 + 5}$

Divide every term in the numerator and denominator by the highest power of x. In

this case, it is x^3. Thus, $\lim\limits_{x \to -\infty} \dfrac{3x - 10}{4x^3 + 5} = \lim\limits_{x \to -\infty} \dfrac{\dfrac{3}{x^2} - \dfrac{10}{x^3}}{4 + \dfrac{5}{x^3}} = \dfrac{0 - 0}{4 + 0} = 0$. Verify your result

with a calculator. (See Figure 2.2-4.)

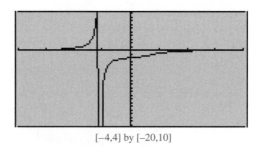

[−4,4] by [−20,10]

Figure 2.2-4

Example 3

Evaluate the limit: $\lim\limits_{x \to \infty} \dfrac{1 - x^2}{10x + 7}$

Divide every term in the numerator and denominator by the highest power of x. In this

case, it is x^2. Therefore, $\lim\limits_{x \to \infty} \dfrac{1 - x^2}{10x + 7} = \lim\limits_{x \to \infty} \dfrac{\dfrac{1}{x^2} - 1}{\dfrac{10}{x} + \dfrac{7}{x^2}} = \dfrac{\lim\limits_{x \to \infty}\left(\dfrac{1}{x^2}\right) - \lim\limits_{x \to \infty}(1)}{\lim\limits_{x \to \infty}\left(\dfrac{10}{x}\right) + \lim\limits_{x \to \infty}\left(\dfrac{7}{x^2}\right)}$. The limit

of the numerator is −1 and the limit of the denominator is 0. Thus, $\lim\limits_{x \to \infty} \dfrac{1 - x^2}{10x + 7} = -\infty$.

Verify your result with a calculator. (See Figure 2.2-5.)

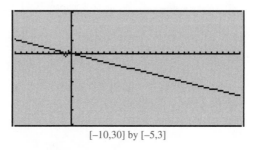

[−10,30] by [−5,3]

Figure 2.2-5

Example 4

Evaluate the limit: $\lim\limits_{x \to -\infty} \dfrac{2x + 1}{\sqrt{x^2 + 3}}$

As $x \to -\infty$, $x < 0$ and thus, $x = -\sqrt{x^2}$. Divide the numerator and denominator by x (not x^2 since the denominator has a square root.) Thus, you have $\lim\limits_{x \to -\infty} \dfrac{2x + 1}{\sqrt{x^2 + 3}}$

$= \lim\limits_{x \to -\infty} \dfrac{\dfrac{2x + 1}{x}}{\dfrac{\sqrt{x^2 + 3}}{x}}$. Replacing the x below $\sqrt{x^2 + 3}$ by $\left(-\sqrt{x^2}\right)$, you have $\lim\limits_{x \to -\infty} \dfrac{2x + 1}{\sqrt{x^2 + 3}}$

$= \lim\limits_{x \to -\infty} \dfrac{\dfrac{2x + 1}{x}}{\dfrac{\sqrt{x^2 + 3}}{-\sqrt{x^2}}} = \lim\limits_{x \to -\infty} \dfrac{2 + \dfrac{1}{x}}{-\sqrt{1 + \dfrac{3}{x^2}}} = \dfrac{\lim\limits_{x \to -\infty}(2) - \lim\limits_{x \to -\infty}\dfrac{1}{x}}{-\sqrt{\lim\limits_{x \to -\infty}(1) + \lim\limits_{x \to -\infty}\left(\dfrac{3}{x^2}\right)}} = \dfrac{2}{-1} = -2.$

Verify your result with a calculator. (See Figure 2.2-6.)

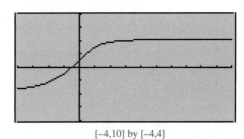

[-4,10] by [-4,4]

Figure 2.2-6

• Remember that $\ln\left(\dfrac{1}{x}\right) = \ln(1) - \ln x = -\ln x$ and $y = e^{-x} = \dfrac{1}{x^x}$.

Vertical and Horizontal Asymptotes

A line $y = b$ is called a horizontal asymptote for the graph of a function f if either $\lim\limits_{x \to \infty} f(x) = b$ or $\lim\limits_{x \to -\infty} f(x) = b$.

A line $x = a$ is called a vertical asymptote for the graph of a function f if either $\lim\limits_{x \to a^+} f(x) = +\infty$ or $\lim\limits_{x \to a^-} f(x) = +\infty$

Example 1

Find the horizontal and vertical asymptotes of the function $f(x) = \dfrac{3x + 5}{x - 2}$.

To find the horizontal asymptotes, examine the $\lim\limits_{x \to \infty} f(x)$ and the $\lim\limits_{x \to -\infty} f(x)$.

The $\lim\limits_{x \to \infty} f(x) = \lim\limits_{x \to \infty} \dfrac{3x + 5}{x - 2} = \lim\limits_{x \to \infty} \dfrac{3 + \dfrac{5}{x}}{1 - \dfrac{2}{x}} = \dfrac{3}{1} = 3$, and the $\lim_{x \to -\infty} f(x) = \lim_{x \to -\infty} \dfrac{3x + 5}{x - 2} = \lim_{x \to -\infty} \dfrac{3 + \dfrac{5}{x}}{1 - \dfrac{2}{x}} = \dfrac{3}{1} = 3.$

Thus, $y = 3$ is a horizontal asymptote.

To find the vertical asymptotes, look for x values such that the denominator $(x - 2)$ would be 0, in this case, $x = 2$. Then examine:

(a) $\lim_{x \to 2^+} f(x) = \lim_{x \to 2^+} \dfrac{3x + 5}{x - 2} = \dfrac{\lim_{x \to 2^+}(3x + 5)}{\lim_{x \to 2^+}(x - 2)}$, the limit of the numerator is 11 and the

limit of the denominator is 0 through positive values, and thus, $\lim_{x \to 2^+} \dfrac{3x + 5}{x - 2} = \infty.$

(b) $\lim_{x \to a^-} f(x) = \lim_{x \to 2^-} \dfrac{3x + 5}{x - 2} = \dfrac{\lim_{x \to 2^-}(3x + 5)}{\lim_{x \to 2^-}(x - 2)}$, the limit of the numerator is 11 and the

limit of the denominator is 0 through negative values, and thus, $\lim_{x \to 2^-} \dfrac{3x + 5}{x - 2} = -\infty.$

Therefore, $x = 2$ is a vertical asymptote.

Example 2

Using your calculator, find the horizontal and vertical asymptotes of the function

$f(x) = \dfrac{x}{x^2 - 4}.$

Enter $y1 = \dfrac{x}{x^2 - 4}$. The graphs shows that as $x \to \pm\infty$, the function approaches 0, thus

$\lim_{x \to \infty} f(x) = \lim_{x \to -\infty} f(x) = 0.$ Therefore, a horizontal asymptote is $y = 0$ (or the x-axis.)

For vertical asymptotes, you notice that $\lim_{x \to 2^+} f(x) = \infty$, $\lim_{x \to 2^-} f(x) = -\infty$, and $\lim_{x \to -2^+} f(x) = \infty$,

$\lim_{x \to -2^-} f(x) = -\infty.$ Thus, the vertical asymptotes are $x = -2$ and $x = 2$. (See Figure 2.2-7.)

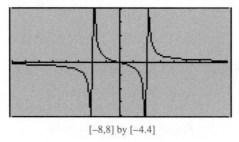

[−8,8] by [−4.4]

Figure 2.2-7

Example 3

Using your calculator, find the horizontal and vertical asymptotes of the function

$f(x) = \dfrac{x^3 + 5}{x}.$

Enter $y1 = \dfrac{x^3 + 5}{x}$. The graph of $f(x)$ shows that as x increases in the first quadrant, $f(x)$ goes higher and higher without bound. As x moves to the left in the 2nd quadrant, $f(x)$ again goes higher and higher without bound. Thus, you may conclude that $\lim_{x \to \infty} f(x) = \infty$ and $\lim_{x \to -\infty} f(x) = \infty$ and thus, $f(x)$ has no horizontal asymptote. For vertical asymptotes, you notice that $\lim\limits_{x \to 0^+} f(x) = \infty$, and $\lim\limits_{x \to 0^-} f(x) = -\infty$. Therefore, the line $x = 0$ (or the y-axis) is a vertical asymptote. (See Figure 2.2-8.)

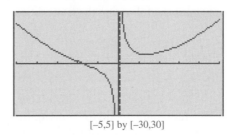

[–5,5] by [–30,30]

Figure 2.2-8

Relationship between the limits of rational functions as $x \to \infty$ and horizontal asymptotes:

Given $f(x) = \dfrac{p(x)}{q(x)}$, then

(1) if the degree of $p(x)$ is same as the degree of $q(x)$, then $\lim\limits_{x \to \infty} f(x) = \lim\limits_{x \to -\infty} f(x) = \dfrac{a}{b}$ where a is the coefficient of the highest power of x in $p(x)$ and b is the coefficient of the highest power of x in $q(x)$. The line $y = \dfrac{a}{b}$ is a horizontal asymptote. See example 1, above.

(2) if the degree of $p(x)$ is smaller than the degree of $q(x)$, then $\lim\limits_{x \to \infty} f(x) = \lim\limits_{x \to -\infty} f(x) = 0$. The line $y = 0$ (or x-axis) is a horizontal asymptote. See example 2, above.

(3) if the degree of $p(x)$ is greater than the degree of $q(x)$, then $\lim\limits_{x \to \infty} f(x) = \pm\infty$ and $\lim\limits_{x \to -\infty} f(x) = \pm\infty$. Thus, $f(x)$ has no horizontal asymptote. See example 3, above.

Example 4

Using your calculator, find the horizontal asymptotes of the function $f(x) = \dfrac{2 \sin x}{x}$.

Enter $y1 = \dfrac{2 \sin x}{x}$. The graph shows that $f(x)$ oscillates back and forth about the x-axis. As $x \to \pm\infty$, the graph of gets closer and closer to the x-axis which implies that $f(x)$ approaches 0. Thus, the line $y = 0$ (or the x-axis) is a horizontal asymptote. (See Figure 2.2-9.)

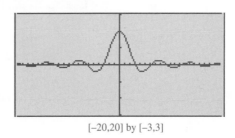

[–20,20] by [–3,3]

Figure 2.2-9

- When entering a rational function into a calculator, use parentheses for both the numerator and denominator, e.g., $(x–2) \div (x+3)$.

2.3 CONTINUITY OF A FUNCTION

Continuity of a Function at a Number: A function f is said to be continuous at a number a if the following three conditions are satisfied:

1. $f(a)$ exists
2. $\lim_{x \to a} f(x)$ exists
3. $\lim_{x \to a} f(x) = f(a)$

The function f is said to be discontinuous at a if one or more these three conditions are not satisfied and a is called the point of discontinuity.

Continuity of a Function over an Interval: A function is continuous over an interval if it is continuous at every point in the interval.

Theorems on Continuity

1. If the functions f and g are continuous at a, then the functions $f + g$, $f - g$, and f/g, $g(a) \neq 0$, are also continuous at a.
2. A polynomial function is continuous everywhere.
3. A rational function is continuous everywhere, except at points where the denominator is zero.
4. *Intermediate-Value Theorem:* If a function f is continuous on a closed interval $[a, b]$ and k is a number with $f(a) \leq k \leq f(b)$, then there exists a number c in $[a, b]$ such that $f(c) = k$.

Example 1

Find the points of discontinuity of the function $f(x) = \dfrac{x + 5}{x^2 - x - 2}$.

Since $f(x)$ is a rational function, it is continuous everywhere, except at points where the denominator is 0. Factor the denominator and set it equal to 0: $(x - 2)(x + 1) = 0$. Thus $x = 2$ or $x = -1$. The function $f(x)$ is undefined at $x = -1$ and at $x = 2$. Therefore, $f(x)$ is discontinuous at these points. Verify your result with a calculator. (See Figure 2.3-1.)

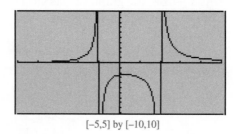

[–5,5] by [–10,10]

Figure 2.3-1

Example 2

Determine the intervals on which the given function is continuous:

$$f(x) = \begin{cases} \dfrac{x^2 + 3x - 10}{x - 2}, & x \neq 2 \\ 10, & x = 2 \end{cases}$$

Check the three conditions of continuity at $x = 2$:

Condition 1: $f(2) = 10$. Condition 2: $\lim\limits_{x \to 2} \dfrac{x^2 + 3x - 10}{x - 2} = \lim\limits_{x \to 2} \dfrac{(x + 5)(x - 2)}{x - 2}$
$= \lim\limits_{x \to 2}(x + 5) = 7$. Condition 3: $f(2) \neq \lim\limits_{x \to 2} f(x)$. Thus, $f(x)$ is discontinuous at $x = 2$. The function is continuous on $(-\infty, 2)$ and $(2, \infty)$. Verify your result with a calculator. (See Figure 2.3-2.)

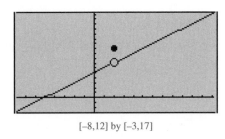

[–8,12] by [–3,17]

Figure 2.3-2

Remember that $\dfrac{d}{dx}\left(\dfrac{1}{x}\right) = -\dfrac{1}{x^2}$ and $\displaystyle\int \dfrac{1}{x}\, dx = \ln|x| + c$.

Example 3

For what value of k is the function $f(x) = \begin{cases} x^2 - 2x, & x \leq 6 \\ 2x + k, & x > 6 \end{cases}$ continuous at $x = 6$?

For $f(x)$ to be continuous at $x = 6$, it must satisfy the three conditions of continuity. Condition 1: $f(6) = 6^2 - 2(6) = 24$. Condition 2: $\lim\limits_{x \to 6^-}(x^2 - 2x) = 24$; thus $\lim\limits_{x \to 6^-}(2x + k)$ must also be 24 in order for the $\lim\limits_{x \to 6} f(x)$ to equal 24. Thus, $\lim\limits_{x \to 6^-}(2x + k) = 24$ which implies $2(6) + k = 24$ and $k = 12$. Therefore, if $k = 12$, condition (3) $f(6) = \lim\limits_{x \to 6} f(x)$ is also satisfied.

Example 4

Given $f(x)$ as shown in Figure 2.3-3, (a) find $f(3)$ and $\lim\limits_{x \to 3} f(x)$, and (b) determine if $f(x)$ is continuous at $x = 3$? Explain why.

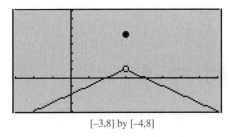

[–3,8] by [–4,8]

Figure 2.3-3

The graph of $f(x)$ shows that $f(3) = 5$ and the $\lim\limits_{x \to 3} f(x) = 1$. Since $f(3) \neq \lim\limits_{x \to 3} f(x)$, therefore $f(x)$ is discontinuous at $x = 3$.

Example 5

If $g(x) = x^2 - 2x - 15$, using the Intermediate Value Theorem show that $g(x)$ has a root in the interval $[1, 7]$.

Begin by finding $g(1)$ and $g(7)$, and $g(1) = -16$ and $g(7) = 20$. If $g(x)$ has a root, then $g(x)$ crosses the x-axis, i.e., $g(x) = 0$. Since $-16 \leq 0 \leq 20$, by the Intermediate Value Theorem, there exists at least one number c in $[1, 7]$ such that $g(c) = 0$. The number c is a root of $g(x)$.

Example 6

A function f is continuous on $[0, 5]$ and some of the values of f are shown below.

x	0	3	5
f	-4	b	-4

If $f(x) = -2$ has no solution on $[0, 5]$ then b could be

    (A) 3   (B) 1   (C) 0   (D) -2   (E) -5

If $b = -2$, then $x = 3$ would be a solution for $f(x) = -2$.
If $b = 0, 1$, or 3, $f(x) = -2$ would have two solutions for $f(x) = -2$.
Thus, $b = -5$, choice (E). (See Figure 2.3-4.)

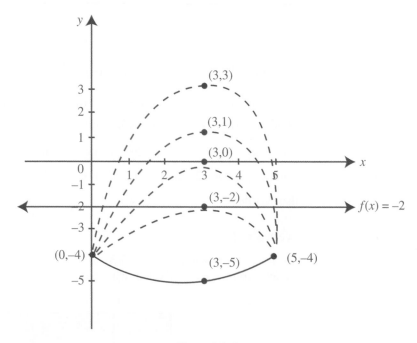

Figure 2.3-4

2.4   RAPID REVIEW

1. Find $f(2)$ and $\lim_{x \to 2} f(x)$ and determine if f is continuous at $x = 2$. (See Figure 2.4-1 on page 93.)

    Answer: $f(2) = 2$, $\lim_{x \to 2} f(x) = 4$, and f is discontinuous at $x = 2$.

2. Evaluate $\lim_{x \to a} \dfrac{x^2 - a^2}{x - a}$.

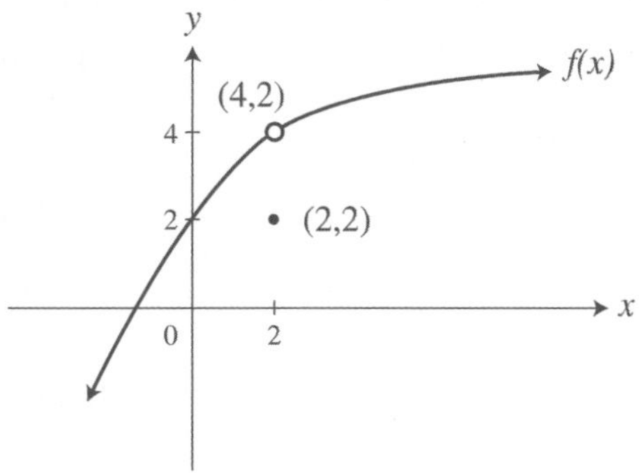

Figure 2.4-1

Answer: $\lim\limits_{x \to a} \dfrac{(x + a)(x - a)}{x - a} = 2a.$

3. Evaluate $\lim\limits_{x \to \infty} \dfrac{1 - 3x^2}{x^2 + 100x + 99}.$

Answer: The limit is −3, since the polynomials in the numerator and denominator have the same degree.

4. Determine if $f(x) = \begin{cases} x + 6 & \text{for } x < 3 \\ x^2 & \text{for } x \geq 3 \end{cases}$ is continuous at $x = 3$.

Answer: The function f is continuous, since $f(3) = 9$, $\lim\limits_{x \to 3^+} f(x) = \lim\limits_{x \to 3^-} f(x) = 9$ and $f(3) = \lim\limits_{x \to 3} f(x).$

5. If $f(x) = \begin{cases} e^x & \text{for } x \neq 0 \\ 5 & \text{for } x = 0 \end{cases}$, find $\lim\limits_{x \to 0} f(x).$

Answer: $\lim\limits_{x \to 0} f(x) = 1$, since $\lim\limits_{x \to 0^+} f(x) = \lim\limits_{x \to 0^-} f(x) = 1.$

6. Evaluate $\lim\limits_{x \to 0} \dfrac{\sin 6x}{\sin 2x}.$

Answer: The limit is $\dfrac{6}{2} = 3$, since $\lim\limits_{x \to 0} \dfrac{\sin x}{x} = 1.$

7. Evaluate $\lim\limits_{x \to 5^-} \dfrac{x^2}{x^2 - 25}.$

Answer: The limit is −∞, since $(x^2 - 25)$ approaches 0 through negative values.

8. Find the vertical and horizontal asymptotes of $f(x) = \dfrac{1}{x^2 - 25}.$

Answer: The vertical asymptotes are $x = \pm 5$, and the horizontal asymptote is $y = 0$, since $\lim\limits_{x \to \pm\infty} f(x) = 0.$

2.5 PRACTICE PROBLEMS

Part A—The use of a calculator is not allowed.

Find the limits of the following:

1. $\lim\limits_{x \to 0}(x - 5) \cos x$

2. If b ≠ 0, evaluate $\lim\limits_{x \to b} \dfrac{x^3 - b^3}{x^6 - b^6}$

3. $\lim\limits_{x \to 0} \dfrac{2 - \sqrt{4 - x}}{x}$

4. $\lim\limits_{x \to \infty} \dfrac{5 - 6x}{2x + 11}$

5. $\lim\limits_{x \to -\infty} \dfrac{x^2 + 2x - 3}{x^3 + 2x^2}$

6. $\lim\limits_{x \to \infty} \dfrac{3x^2}{5x + 8}$

7. $\lim\limits_{x \to -\infty} \dfrac{3x}{\sqrt{x^2 - 4}}$

8. If $f(x) = \begin{cases} e^x & \text{for } 0 \le x < 1 \\ x^2 e^x & \text{for } 1 \le x \le 5 \end{cases}$, find $\lim\limits_{x \to 1} f(x)$.

9. $\lim\limits_{x \to \infty} \dfrac{e^x}{1 - x^3}$

10. $\lim\limits_{x \to 0} \dfrac{\sin 3x}{\sin 4x}$

11. $\lim\limits_{t \to 3^+} \dfrac{\sqrt{t^2 - 9}}{t - 3}$

12. The graph of a function f is shown in Figure 2.5-1.

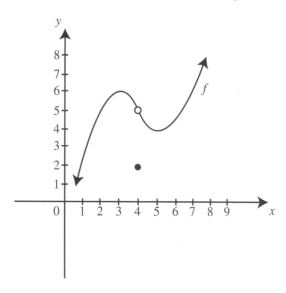

Figure 2.5-1

Which of the following statements is/are true?

I. $\lim\limits_{x \to 4^-} f(x) = 5$

II. $\lim\limits_{x \to 4} f(x) = 2$

III. $x = 4$ is not in the domain of f

Part B—Calculators are allowed.

13. Find the horizontal and vertical asymptotes of the graph of the function $f(x) = \dfrac{1}{x^2 + x - 2}$.

14. Find the limit: $\lim\limits_{x \to 5^+} \dfrac{5 + [x]}{5 - x}$ when $[x]$ is the greatest integer of x.

15. Find the points of discontinuity of the function
$$f(x) = \dfrac{x + 1}{x^2 + 4x - 12}.$$

16. For what value of k is the function
$$g(x) = \begin{cases} x^2 + 5, & x \le 3 \\ 2x - k, & x > 3 \end{cases} \text{ continuous at } x = 3?$$

17. Determine if $f(x) = \begin{cases} \dfrac{x^2 + 5 - x - 14}{x - 2}, & \text{if } x \ne 2 \\ 12, & \text{if } x = 2 \end{cases}$
is continuous at $x = 2$. Explain why or why not.

18. Given $f(x)$ as shown in Figure 2.5-2, find

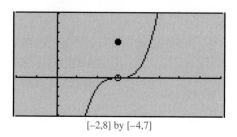

[−2,8] by [−4,7]

Figure 2.5-2

a) $f(3)$
b) $\lim\limits_{x \to 3^+} f(x)$
c) $\lim\limits_{x \to 3^-} f(x)$
d) $\lim\limits_{x \to 3} f(x)$
e) Is $f(x)$ continuous at $x = 3$? Explain why or why not.

19. A function f is continuous on $[-2,2]$ and some of the values of f are shown below:

x	−2	0	2
$f(x)$	3	b	4

If f has only one root, r, on the closed interval $[-2,2]$, and $r \ne 0$, then a possible value of b is

(A) −3   (B) −2   (C) −1   (D) 0   (E) 1

20. Evaluate $\lim\limits_{x \to 0} \dfrac{1 - \cos x}{\sin^2 x}$.

2.6 CUMULATIVE REVIEW PROBLEMS

21. Write an equation of the line passing through the point $(2, -4)$ and perpendicular to the line $3x - 2y = 6$.

22. The graph of a function f is shown in Figure 2.6-1. Which of the following statements is/are true?

   I. $\lim\limits_{x \to 4^-} f(x) = 3$.

   II. $x = 4$ is not in the domain of f.

   III. $\lim\limits_{x \to 4} f(x)$ does not exist.

23. Evaluate $\lim\limits_{x \to 0} \dfrac{|3x - 4|}{x - 2}$.

24. Find $\lim\limits_{x \to 0} \dfrac{\tan x}{x}$.

25. Find the horizontal and vertical asymptotes of $f(x)$

$$= \frac{x}{\sqrt{x^2 + 4}}.$$

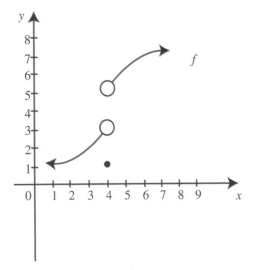

Figure 2.6-1

2.7 SOLUTIONS TO PRACTICE PROBLEMS

Part A—No calculators are permitted.

1. Using the product rule,

$$\lim_{x \to 0}(x - 5)(\cos x) = \left[\lim_{x \to 0}(x - 5)\right]\left[\lim_{x \to 0} \cos x\right]$$

$$= (0 - 5)(\cos 0) = (-5)(1) = -5.$$

(Note that $\cos 0 = 1$.)

2. Rewrite $\lim\limits_{x \to b} \dfrac{x^3 - b^3}{x^6 - b^6}$ as

$$\lim_{x \to b} \frac{x^3 - b^3}{(x^3 - b^3)(x^3 + b^3)} = \lim_{x \to b} \frac{1}{x^3 + b^3}.$$

Substitute $x = b$ and obtain $\dfrac{1}{b^3 + b^3} = \dfrac{1}{2b^3}$.

3. Substituting $x = 0$ into the expression $\dfrac{2 - \sqrt{4 - x}}{x}$

leads to $\dfrac{0}{0}$ which is an indeterminate form. Thus, multiply both the numerator and denominator by the conjugate $\left(2 + \sqrt{4 - x}\right)$ and obtain

$$\lim_{x \to 0} \frac{2 - \sqrt{4 - x}}{x} \left(\frac{2 + \sqrt{4 - x}}{2 + \sqrt{4 - x}}\right)$$

$$= \lim_{x \to 0} \frac{4 - (4 - x)}{x\left(2 + \sqrt{4 - x}\right)} = \lim_{x \to 0} \frac{x}{x\left(2 + \sqrt{4 - x}\right)}$$

$$= \lim_{x \to 0} \frac{1}{\left(2 + \sqrt{4 - x}\right)} = \frac{1}{\left(2 + \sqrt{4 - (0)}\right)} = \frac{1}{4}$$

4. Since the degree of the polynomial in the numerator is the same as the degree of the polynomial in the denominator,

$$\lim_{x \to \infty} \frac{5 - 6x}{2x + 11} = -\frac{6}{2} = -3.$$

5. Since the degree of the polynomial in the numerator is 2 and the degree of the polynomial in the denominator is 3,

$$\lim_{x \to \infty} \frac{x^2 + 2x - 3}{x^3 + 2x^2} = 0.$$

6. The degree of the monomial in the numerator is 2 and the degree of the binomial in the denominator is 1. Thus, $\lim\limits_{x \to \infty} \dfrac{3x^2}{5x + 8} = \infty$.

7. Divide every term in both the numerator and denominator by the highest power of x and in

this case, it is x. Thus, you have $\lim\limits_{x \to -\infty} \dfrac{\dfrac{3x}{x}}{\dfrac{\sqrt{x^2 - 4}}{x}}$.

As $x \to -\infty$, $x = -\sqrt{x^2}$. Since the denominator involves a radical, rewrite the expression as

$$\lim_{x \to -\infty} \frac{\dfrac{3x}{x}}{\dfrac{\sqrt{x^2 - 4}}{-\sqrt{x^2}}} = \lim_{x \to -\infty} \frac{3}{-\sqrt{1 - \dfrac{4}{x^2}}}$$

$$= \frac{3}{-\sqrt{1 - 0}} = -3$$

8. $\lim\limits_{x \to 1^+} f(x) = \lim\limits_{x \to 1^+}(x^2 e^x) = e$ and $\lim\limits_{x \to 1^-} f(x)$
$= \lim\limits_{x \to 1^-}(e^x) = e$. Thus $\lim\limits_{x \to 1} f(x) = e$.

9. $\lim\limits_{x \to \infty} e^x = \infty$ and $\lim\limits_{x \to \infty}(1 - x^3) = \infty$. However, as $x \to \infty$; the rate of increase of e^x is much greater than the rate of decrease of $(1 - x^3)$. Thus $\lim\limits_{x \to \infty} \dfrac{e^x}{1 - x^3} = -\infty$.

10. Divide both numerator and denominator by x and obtain $\lim\limits_{x \to 0} \dfrac{\dfrac{\sin 3x}{x}}{\dfrac{\sin 4x}{x}}$. Now rewrite the limit as

$$\lim_{x \to 0} \frac{3\dfrac{\sin 3x}{3x}}{4\dfrac{\sin 4x}{4x}} = \frac{3}{4}\lim_{x \to 0}\frac{\dfrac{\sin 3x}{3x}}{\dfrac{\sin 4x}{4x}}.$$ As x approaches

0, so do $3x$ and $4x$. Thus, you have

$$\frac{3}{4}\frac{\lim\limits_{3x \to 0}\dfrac{\sin 3x}{3x}}{\lim\limits_{4x \to 0}\dfrac{\sin 4x}{4x}} = \frac{3(1)}{4(1)} = \frac{3}{4}.$$

11. As $t \to 3^+$, $(t - 3) > 0$ and thus $(t - 3) = \sqrt{(t - 3)^2}$.

Rewrite the limit as $\lim\limits_{t \to 3^+} \dfrac{\sqrt{(t - 3)(t + 3)}}{\sqrt{(t - 3)^2}}$

$= \lim\limits_{t \to 3^+} \dfrac{\sqrt{(t + 3)}}{\sqrt{(t - 3)}}$. The limit of the numerator is

$\sqrt{6}$ and the denominator is approaching 0 through

positive values. Thus, $\lim\limits_{t \to 3^+} \dfrac{\sqrt{t^2 - 9}}{t - 3} = \infty$.

12. The graph of f indicates that:
I. $\lim\limits_{x \to 4^-} f(x) = 5$ is true.
II. $\lim\limits_{x \to 4} f(x) = 2$ is false. $\left(\text{The } \lim\limits_{x \to 4} f(x) = 5\right)$.
III. "$x = 4$ is not in the domain of f" is false since $f(4) = 2$.

Part B—Calculators are permitted.

13. Examining the graph in your calculator, you notice that the function approaches the x-axis as $x \to \infty$ or as $x \to -\infty$. Thus, the line $y = 0$ (the x-axis) is a horizontal asymptote. As x approaches 1 from either side, the function increases or decreases without bound. Similarly, as x approaches -2 from either side, the function increases or decreases without bound. Therefore, $x = 1$ and $x = -2$ are vertical asymptotes. (See Figure 2.7-1.)

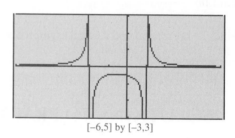

[−6,5] by [−3,3]

Figure 2.7-1

14. As $x \to 5^+$, the limit of the numerator $(5 + [5])$ is 10 and as $x \to 5^+$, the denominator approaches 0 through negative values. Thus, the $\lim\limits_{x \to 5^+} \dfrac{5 + [x]}{5 - x}$ $= -\infty$.

15. Since $f(x)$ is a rational function, it is continuous everywhere except at values where the denominator is 0. Factoring and setting the denominator equal to 0, you have $(x + 6)$ $(x - 2) = 0$. Thus, the points of discontinuity are at $x = -6$ and $x = 2$. Verify your result with a calculator. (See Figure 2.7-2.)

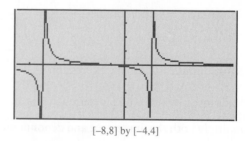

[−8,8] by [−4,4]

Figure 2.7-2

16. In order for $g(x)$ to be continuous at $x = 3$, it must satisfy the three conditions of continuity:

(1) $g(3) = 3^2 + 5 = 14$, (2) $\lim\limits_{x \to 3^+} (x^2 + 5) = 14$ and $\lim\limits_{x \to 3^-} (2x - k) = 6 - k$, and the two one-sided limits must be equal in order for $\lim\limits_{x \to 3} g(x)$ to exist. Therefore, $6 - k = 14$ and $k = -8$. Now, $g(3) = \lim\limits_{x \to 3} g(x)$ and condition 3 is satisfied.

17. Checking with the three conditions of continuity: Condition 1 $f(2) = 12$, condition 2

$$\lim_{x \to 2} \frac{x^2 + 5x - 14}{x - 2} = \lim_{x \to 2} \frac{(x + 7)(x - 2)}{x - 2} =$$

$\lim\limits_{x \to 2} (x + 7) = 9$, and condition 3 $f(2) \neq \lim\limits_{x \to 2} (x + 7)$. Therefore, $f(x)$ is discontinuous at $x = 2$.

18. The graph indicates that (a) $f(3) = 4$, (b) $\lim\limits_{x \to 3^+} f(x) = 0$, (c) $\lim\limits_{x \to 3^-} f(x) = 0$, (d) $\lim\limits_{x \to 3} f(x) = 0$, and (e) therefore, $f(x)$ is not continuous at $x = 3$ since $f(3) \neq \lim\limits_{x \to 3} f(x)$.

19. (See Figure 2.7-3.) If $b = 0$, then $r = 0$, but r cannot be 0. If $b = -3, -2,$ or -1 f would have more than one root. Thus $b = 1$. Choice (e).

20. Substituting $x = 0$ would lead to $\frac{0}{0}$. Substitute $(1 - \cos^2 x)$ in place of $\sin^2 x$ and obtain

$$\lim_{x \to 0} \frac{1 - \cos x}{\sin^2 x} = \lim_{x \to 0} \frac{1 - \cos x}{(1 - \cos^2 x)} =$$

$$\lim_{x \to 0} \frac{1 - \cos x}{(1 - \cos x)(1 + \cos x)} = \lim_{x \to 0} \frac{1}{(1 + \cos x)} =$$

$\dfrac{1}{1 + 1} = \dfrac{1}{2}$. Verify your result with a calculator. (See Figure 2.7-4.)

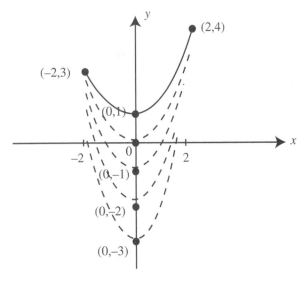

Figure 2.7-3

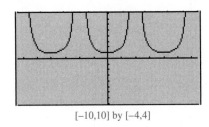

[-10,10] by [-4,4]

Figure 2.7-4

2.8 SOLUTIONS TO CUMULATIVE REVIEW PROBLEMS

21. Rewrite $3x - 2y = 6$ in $y = mx + b$ form which is $y = \dfrac{3}{2} x - 3$. The slope of this line whose equation is $y = \dfrac{3}{2} x - 3$ is $m = \dfrac{3}{2}$. Thus, the slope of a line perpendicular to this line is $m = -\dfrac{2}{3}$. Since the perpendicular line passes through the point $(2, -4)$, therefore, an equation of the perpendicular line is

$y - (-4) = -\dfrac{2}{3}(x - 2)$ which is equivalent to

$y + 4 = -\dfrac{2}{3}(x - 2)$

22. The graph indicates that $\lim\limits_{x \to 4^-} f(x) = 3$, $f(4) = 1$, and $\lim\limits_{x \to 4} f(x)$ does not exist. Therefore, only statement III is true.

23. Substituting $x = 0$ into $\dfrac{|3x - 4|}{x - 2}$, you obtain $\dfrac{4}{-2} = -2$.

24. Rewrite $\lim\limits_{x \to 0} \dfrac{\tan x}{x}$ as $\lim\limits_{x \to 0} \dfrac{\frac{\sin x}{\cos x}}{x}$ which is equivalent to $\lim\limits_{x \to 0} \dfrac{\sin x}{x \cos x}$ which is equal to

$$\lim_{x\to 0}\frac{\sin x}{x}\cdot\lim_{x\to 0}\frac{1}{\cos x}=(1)(1)=1.$$

25. To find horizontal asymptotes, examine the $\lim_{x\to\infty}f(x)$ and the $\lim_{x\to-\infty}f(x)$. The $\lim_{x\to\infty}f(x)$

$$=\lim_{x\to\infty}\frac{x}{\sqrt{x^2+4}}.$$ Dividing by the highest

power of x (and in this case, it's x), you obtain

$$\lim_{x\to\infty}\frac{\dfrac{x}{x}}{\dfrac{\sqrt{x^2+4}}{x}}.$$ As $x\to\infty$, $\sqrt{x^2}$ Thus, you have

$$\lim_{x\to\infty}\frac{\dfrac{x}{x}}{\dfrac{\sqrt{x^2+4}}{\sqrt{x^2}}}=\lim_{x\to\infty}\frac{1}{\sqrt{\dfrac{x^2+4}{x^2}}}$$

$$=\lim_{x\to\infty}\frac{1}{\sqrt{1+\dfrac{4}{x^2}}}=1.$$ Thus, the line $y=1$ is a

horizontal asymptote. The $\lim_{x\to-\infty}f(x)$

$$=\lim_{x\to-\infty}\frac{x}{\sqrt{x^2+4}}.$$ As $x\to-\infty$, $x=-\sqrt{x^2}$. Thus,

$$\lim_{x\to-\infty}\frac{x}{\sqrt{x^2+4}}=\lim_{x\to-\infty}\frac{\dfrac{x}{x}}{\dfrac{\sqrt{x^2+4}}{-\sqrt{x^2}}}$$

$$=\lim_{x\to-\infty}\frac{1}{-\sqrt{1+\dfrac{4}{x^2}}}=-1.$$ Therefore, the line

$y=-1$ is a horizontal asymptote. As for vertical asymptotes, $f(x)$ is continuous and defined for all real numbers. Thus, there is no vertical asymptote.

Chapter 3

Differentiation

3.1 DERIVATIVES OF ALGEBRAIC FUNCTIONS

Main Concepts: *Definition of the Derivative of a Function; Power Rule; The Sum, Difference, Product, and Quotient Rules; The Chain Rule*

Definition of the Derivative of a Function

The derivative of a function f, written as f', is defined as

$$f'(x) = \lim_{h \to 0} \frac{f(x+h) - f(x)}{h},$$

if this limit exists. (Note that $f'(x)$ is read as f prime of x.)

Other symbols of the derivative of a function are:

$$D_x f, \frac{d}{dx} f(x), \text{ and if } y = f(x), y', \frac{dy}{dx}, \text{ and } D_x y.$$

Let m_{tangent} be the slope of the tangent to a curve $y = f(x)$ at a point on the curve. Then

$$m_{\text{tangent}} = f'(x) = \lim_{h \to 0} \frac{f(x+h) - f(x)}{h}$$

$$m_{\text{tangent}} (\text{at } x = a) = f'(a) = \lim_{h \to 0} \frac{f(a+h) - f(a)}{h} \text{ or } \lim_{x \to a} \frac{f(x) - f(a)}{x - a}. \text{ (See Figure 3.1-1.)}$$

Given a function f, if $f'(x)$ exists at $x = a$, then the function f is said to be differentiable at $x = a$. If a function f is differentiable at $x = a$, then f is continuous at $x = a$. (Note that the converse of the statement is not necessarily true, i.e., if a function f is continuous at $x = a$, then f may or may not be differentiable at $x = a$.) Here are several examples of functions that are not differentiable at a given number $x = a$). (See Figures 3.1-2 to 3.1-5 on the next page.)

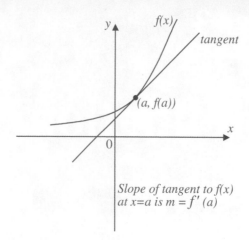

Slope of tangent to $f(x)$
at $x=a$ is $m = f'(a)$

Figure 3.1-1

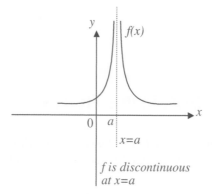

f is discontinuous
at $x=a$

Figure 3.1-2

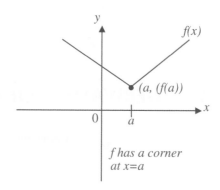

f has a corner
at $x=a$

Figure 3.1-3

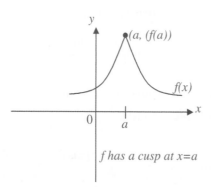

f has a cusp at $x=a$

Figure 3.1-4

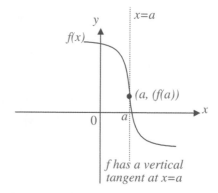

f has a vertical
tangent at $x=a$

Figure 3.1-5

Example 1

If $f(x) = x^2 - 2x - 3$, find (a) $f'(x)$ using the definition of derivative, (b) $f'(0)$, (c) $f'(1)$, and (d) $f'(3)$.

(a) Using the definition of derivative, $f'(x) = \lim\limits_{h \to 0} \dfrac{f(x + h) - f(x)}{h}$

$$= \lim_{h \to 0} \frac{[(x + h)^2 - 2(x + h) - 3] - [x^2 - 2x - 3]}{h}$$

$$= \lim_{h \to 0} \frac{[x^2 + 2xh + h^2 - 2x - 2h - 3] - [x^2 - 2x - 3]}{h} = \lim_{h \to 0} \frac{2xh + h^2 - 2h}{h}$$

$$= \lim_{h \to 0} \frac{h(2x + h - 2)}{h} = \lim_{h \to 0}(2x + h - 2) = 2x - 2.$$

(b) $f'(0) = 2(0) - 2 = -2$ (c) $f'(1) = 2(1) - 2 = 0$ and (d) $f'(3) = 2(3) - 2 = 4$.

Example 2

Evaluate $\lim_{h \to 0} \dfrac{\cos(\pi + h) - \cos(\pi)}{h}$

The expression $\lim_{h \to 0} \dfrac{\cos(\pi + h) - \cos(\pi)}{h}$ is equivalent to the derivative of the function $f(x) = \cos x$ at $x = \pi$, i.e., $f'(\pi)$. The derivative of $f(x) = \cos x$ at $x = \pi$ is equivalent to the slope of the tangent to curve of $\cos x$ at $x = \pi$. The tangent is parallel to the

x-axis. Thus, the slope is 0 or $\lim_{h \to 0} \dfrac{\cos(\pi + h) - \cos(\pi)}{h} = 0$.

Or, using an algebraic method, note that $\cos(a + b) = \cos(a)\cos(b) - \sin(a)\sin(b)$.

Then rewrite $\lim_{h \to 0} \dfrac{\cos(\pi + h) - \cos(\pi)}{h} = \lim_{h \to 0} \dfrac{\cos(\pi)\cos(h) - \sin(\pi)\sin(h) - \cos(\pi)}{h}$

$$= \lim_{h \to 0} \frac{-\cos(h) - (-1)}{h} = \lim_{h \to 0} \frac{-\cos(h) + 1}{h} = \lim_{h \to 0} \frac{-[\cos(h) - 1]}{h} = -\lim_{h \to 0} \frac{[\cos(h) - 1]}{h} = 0.$$

(See Figure 3.1-6.)

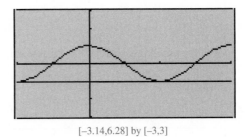

[−3.14,6.28] by [−3,3]

Figure 3.1-6

Example 3

If the function $f(x) = x^{2/3} + 1$, find all points where f is not differentiable.

The function $f(x)$ is continuous for all real numbers and the graph of $f(x)$ forms a "cusp" at the point $(0, 1)$. Thus, $f(x)$ is not differentiable at $x = 0$. See Figure 3.1-7.

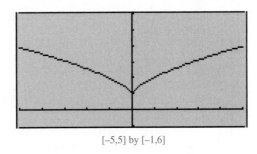

[−5,5] by [−1,6]

Figure 3.1-7

Example 4

Using a calculator, find the derivative of $f(x) = x^2 + 4x$ at $x = 3$.

There are several ways to find $f'(3)$, using a calculator. One way is to use the nDeriv function of the calculator. From the main (Home) screen, select F3-Calc and then select nDeriv. Enter nDeriv $(x^2 + 4x, x)|x = 3$. The result is 10.

> • Always write out all formulas in your solutions.

Power Rule

If $f(x) = c$ where c is a constant, then $f'(x) = 0$.
If $f(x) = x^n$ where n is a real number, then $f'(x) = nx^{n-1}$.
If $f(x) = cx^n$ where c is a constant and n is a real number, then $f'(x) = cnx^{n-1}$.

Summary of Derivatives of Algebraic Functions:

$$\frac{d}{dx}(c) = 0, \quad \frac{d}{dx}(x^n) = nx^{n-1}, \quad \text{and} \quad \frac{d}{dx}(c^n) = cnx^{n-1}$$

Example 1

If $f(x) = 2x^3$, find (a) $f'(x)$, (b) $f'(1)$ and (c) $f'(0)$
Note that (a) $f'(x) = 6x^2$, (b) $f'(1) = 6(1)^2 = 6$, and (c) $f'(0) = 0$.

Example 2

If $y = \dfrac{1}{x^2}$, find (a) $\dfrac{dy}{dx}$ and (b) $\left.\dfrac{dy}{dx}\right|_{x=0}$ $\left(\text{which represents } \dfrac{dy}{dx} \text{ at } x = 0.\right)$

Note that (a) $y = \dfrac{1}{x^2} = x^{-2}$ and thus, $\dfrac{dy}{dx} = -2x^{-3} = \dfrac{-2}{x^3}$ and (b) $\left.\dfrac{dy}{dx}\right|_{x=0}$ does not exist

because the expression $\dfrac{-2}{0}$ is undefined.

Example 3

Here are several examples of algebraic functions and their derivatives:

Function	Written in cx^n form	Derivative	Derivative with Positive Exponents
$3x$	$3x^1$	$3x^0 = 3$	3
$-5x^7$	$-5x^7$	$-35x^6$	$-35x^6$
$8\sqrt{x}$	$8x^{\frac{1}{2}}$	$4x^{-\frac{1}{2}}$	$\dfrac{4}{x^{\frac{1}{2}}}$ or $\dfrac{4}{\sqrt{x}}$
$\dfrac{1}{x^2}$	x^{-2}	$-2x^{-3}$	$\dfrac{-2}{x^3}$
$\dfrac{-2}{\sqrt{x}}$	$\dfrac{-2}{x^{\frac{1}{2}}} = -2x^{\frac{-1}{2}}$	$x^{\frac{-3}{2}}$	$\dfrac{1}{x^{\frac{3}{2}}}$ or $\dfrac{1}{\sqrt{x^3}}$
$-x^{\frac{1}{3}}$	$-x^{\frac{1}{3}}$	$-\dfrac{1}{3}x^{\frac{-2}{3}}$	$\dfrac{-1}{3x^{\frac{2}{3}}}$ or $\dfrac{-1}{3\sqrt[3]{x^2}}$

Example 4

Using a calculator, find $f'(x)$ and $f'(3)$ if $f(x) = \dfrac{1}{\sqrt{x}}$.

There are several ways of finding $f'(x)$ and $f'(9)$ using a calculator. One way to use the d(differentiate) function. Go to Home screen. Select F3-Calc and then select d(differentiate). Enter $d(1/\sqrt{(x)}, x)$. The result is $f'(x) = \dfrac{-1}{2x^{\frac{3}{2}}}$. To find $f'(3)$, enter

$d(1/\sqrt{(x)}, x)\big|x = 3$. The result is $f'(3) = -\dfrac{1}{54}$.

The Sum, Difference, Product, and Quotient Rules

If u and v are two differentiable functions, then

$$\frac{d}{dx}(u \pm v) = \frac{du}{dx} \pm \frac{dv}{dx} \qquad \text{Sum \& Difference Rules}$$

$$\frac{d}{dx}(uv) = v\frac{du}{dx} + u\frac{dv}{dx} \qquad \text{Product Rule}$$

$$\frac{d}{dx}\left(\frac{u}{v}\right) = \frac{v\dfrac{du}{dx} - u\dfrac{dv}{dx}}{v^2}, v\neq 0 \qquad \text{Quotient Rule}$$

Summary of Sum, Difference, Product and Quotient Rules:

$$\left(u \pm v\right)' = u' \pm v' \qquad \left(uv\right)' = u'v + v'u \qquad \& \qquad \left(\frac{u}{v}\right)' = \frac{u'v - v'u}{v^2}$$

Example 1

Find $f'(x)$ if $f(x) = x^3 - 10x + 5$.
Using the sum and difference rules, you can differentiate each term and obtain $f'(x) = 3x^2 - 10$. Or using your calculator, select the d(differentiate) function and enter $d(x^3 - 10x + 5, x)$ and obtain $3x^2 - 10$.

Example 2

If $y = (3x - 5)(x^4 + 8x - 1)$, find $\dfrac{dy}{dx}$.

Using the product rule $\dfrac{d}{dx}(uv) = v\dfrac{du}{dx} + u\dfrac{dv}{dx}$, let $u = (3x - 5)$ and $v = (x^4 + 8x - 1)$.

Then $\dfrac{dy}{dx} = (3)(x^4 + 8x - 1) + (4x^3 + 8)(3x - 5) = (3x^4 + 24x - 3) + (12x^4 - 20x^3 +$

$24x - 40) = 15x^4 - 20x^3 + 48x - 43$. Or you can use your calculator and enter $d((3x - 5)$ $(x^4 + 8x - 1), x)$ and obtain the same result.

Example 3

If $f(x) = \dfrac{2x - 1}{x + 5}$, find $f'(x)$.

Using the quotient rule $\left(\dfrac{u}{v}\right)' = \dfrac{u'v - v'u}{v^2}$, let $u = 2x - 1$ and $v = x + 5$. Then $f'(x) =$

$$\frac{(2)(x + 5) - (1)(2x - 1)}{(x + 5)^2} = \frac{2x + 10 - 2x + 1}{(x + 5)^2} = \frac{11}{(x + 5)^2}, x \neq -5.$$ Or you can use

your calculator and enter $d((2x - 1)/(x + 5), x)$ and obtain the same result.

Example 4

Using your calculator, find an equation of the tangent to the curve $f(x) = x^2 - 3x + 2$ at $x = 5$.

Find the slope of the tangent to the curve at $x = 5$ by entering $d(x^2 - 3x + 2, x)|x = 5$. The result is 7. Compute $f(5) = 12$. Thus, the point $(5,12)$ is on the curve of $f(x)$. An equation of the line whose slope $m = 7$ and passing through the point $(5,12)$ is $y - 12 = 7(x - 5)$.

- Remember that $\dfrac{d}{dx} \ln x = \dfrac{1}{x}$ and $\int \ln x \, dx = x \ln x - x + c$. The integral formula is not usually tested in the AB exam.

The Chain Rule

If $y = f(u)$ and $u = g(x)$ are differentiable functions of u and x respectively, then

$$\frac{d}{dx}[f(g(x))] = f'(g(x)) \cdot g'(x) \text{ or } \frac{dy}{dx} = \frac{dy}{du} \cdot \frac{du}{dx}$$

Example 1

If $y = (3x - 5)^{10}$, find $\dfrac{dy}{dx}$.

Using the chain rule, let $u = 3x - 5$ and thus, $y = u^{10}$. Then, $\dfrac{dy}{du} = 10u^9$ and $\dfrac{du}{dx} = 3$.

Since $\dfrac{dy}{dx} = \dfrac{dy}{du} \cdot \dfrac{du}{dx}$, $\dfrac{dy}{dx} = (10u^9)(3) = 10(3x - 5)^9(3) = 30(3x - 5)^9$. Or you can use

your calculator and enter $d((3x - 5)^{10}, x)$ and obtain the same result.

Example 2

If $f(x) = 5x\sqrt{25 - x^2}$, find $f'(x)$.

Rewrite $f(x) = 5x \sqrt{25 - x^2}$ as $f(x) = 5x(25 - x^2)^{\frac{1}{2}}$. Using the product rule,

$$f'(x) = (25 - x^2)^{\frac{1}{2}} \frac{d}{dx}(5x) + (5x)\frac{d}{dx}(25 - x^2)^{\frac{1}{2}} = 5(25 - x^2)^{\frac{1}{2}} + (5x)\frac{d}{dx}(25 - x^2)^{\frac{1}{2}}.$$

To find $\dfrac{d}{dx}(25 - x^2)^{\frac{1}{2}}$, use the chain rule and let $u = 25 - x^2$.

Thus, $\dfrac{d}{dx}(25 - x^2)^{\frac{1}{2}} = \dfrac{1}{2}(25 - x^2)^{-1/2}(-2x) = \dfrac{-x}{(25 - x^2)^{\frac{1}{2}}}.$ Substituting this quantity

back into $f'(x)$, you have

$$f'(x) = 5(25 - x^2)^{\frac{1}{2}} + (5x)\left(\frac{-x}{(25 - x^2)^{\frac{1}{2}}}\right) = \frac{5(25 - x^2) - 5x^2}{(25 - x^2)^{\frac{1}{2}}} = \frac{125 - 10x^2}{(25 - x^2)^{\frac{1}{2}}}.$$

Or you can use your calculator and enter $d\left(5x\sqrt{25-x^2}, x\right)$ and obtain the same result.

Example 3

If $y = \left(\dfrac{2x-1}{x^2}\right)^3$, find $\dfrac{dy}{dx}$.

Using the chain rule, let $u = \left(\dfrac{2x-1}{x^2}\right)$. Then $\dfrac{dy}{dx} = 3\left(\dfrac{2x-1}{x^2}\right)^2 \dfrac{d}{dx}\left(\dfrac{2x-1}{x^2}\right)$.

To find $\dfrac{d}{dx}\left(\dfrac{2x-1}{x^2}\right)$, use the quotient rule.

Thus, $\dfrac{d}{dx}\left(\dfrac{2x-1}{x^2}\right) = \dfrac{(2)(x^2)-(2x)(2x-1)}{(x^2)^2} = \dfrac{-2x^2+2x}{x^4}$. Substituting this quantity

back into $\dfrac{dy}{dx} = 3\left(\dfrac{2x-1}{x^2}\right)^2 \dfrac{d}{dx}\left(\dfrac{2x-1}{x^2}\right) = 3\left(\dfrac{2x-1}{x^2}\right)^2 \dfrac{-2x^2+2x}{x^4} = \dfrac{-6(x-1)(2x-1)^2}{x^7}$.

An alternate solution is to use the product rule and rewrite $y = \left(\dfrac{2x-1}{x^2}\right)^3$ as

$y = \dfrac{(2x-1)^3}{(x^2)^3} = \dfrac{(2x-1)^3}{x^6}$ and use the quotient rule. Another approach is to express

$y = (2x-1)^3(x^{-6})$ and use the product rule. Of course, you can always use your calculator if you are permitted to do so.

3.2 DERIVATIVES OF TRIGONOMETRIC, INVERSE TRIGONOMETRIC, EXPONENTIAL, AND LOGARITHMIC FUNCTIONS

Main Concepts: *Derivatives of Trigonometric Functions, Derivatives of Inverse Trigonometric Functions, Derivatives of Exponential and Logarithmic Functions*

Derivatives of Trigonometric Functions

Summary of Derivatives of Trigonometric Functions:

$$\dfrac{d}{dx}(\sin x) = \cos x \qquad\qquad \dfrac{d}{dx}(\cos x) = -\sin x$$

$$\dfrac{d}{dx}(\tan x) = \sec^2 x \qquad\qquad \dfrac{d}{dx}(\cot x) = -\csc^2 x$$

$$\dfrac{d}{dx}(\sec x) = \sec x \tan x \qquad\qquad \dfrac{d}{dx}(\csc x) = -\csc x \cot x.$$

Note that the derivatives of *cosine, cotangent,* and *cosecant* all have a negative sign.

Example 1

If $y = 6x^2 + 3\sec x$, find $\dfrac{dy}{dx}$.

$\dfrac{dy}{dx} = 12x + 3\sec x \tan x.$

Example 2

Find $f'(x)$ if $f(x) = \cot(4x - 6)$.

Using the chain rule, let $u = 4x - 6$. Then $f'(x) = [-\csc^2(4x - 6)][4] = -4\csc^2(4x - 6)$.

Or using your calculator, enter $d(1/\tan(4x - 6), x)$ and obtain $\dfrac{-4}{\sin^2(4x - 6)}$ which is an equivalent form.

Example 3

Find $f'(x)$ if $f(x) = 8\sin(x^2)$.

Using the chain rule, let $u = x^2$. Then $f'(x) = [8\cos(x^2)][2x] = 16x\cos(x^2)$.

Example 4

If $y = \sin x \cos(2x)$, find $\dfrac{dy}{dx}$.

Using the product rule, let $u = \sin x$ and $v = \cos(2x)$.

Then $\dfrac{dy}{dx} = \cos x \cos(2x) + [-\sin(2x)](2)(\sin x) = \cos x \cos(2x) - 2\sin x \sin(2x)$.

Example 5

If $y = \sin[\cos(2x)]$, find $\dfrac{dy}{dx}$.

Using the chain rule, let $u = \cos(2x)$. Then

$$\frac{dy}{dx} = \frac{dy}{du} \cdot \frac{du}{dx} = \cos[\cos(2x)] \frac{d}{dx}[\cos(2x)].$$

To evaluate $\dfrac{d}{dx}[\cos(2x)]$, use the chain rule again by making another u-substitution,

this time for $2x$. Thus, $\dfrac{d}{dx}[\cos(2x)] = [-\sin(2x)]2 = -2\sin(2x)$. Therefore,

$$\frac{dy}{dx} \cos[\cos(2x)](-2\sin(2x)) = -2\sin(2x)\cos[\cos(2x)].$$

Example 6

Find $f'(x)$ if $f(x) = 5x \csc x$.

Using the product rule, let $u = 5x$ and $v = \csc x$. Then
$f'(x) = 5\csc x + (-\csc x \cot x)(5x) = 5\csc x - 5x(\csc x)(\cot x)$.

Example 7

If $y = \sqrt{\sin x}$, find $\dfrac{dy}{dx}$.

Rewrite $y = \sqrt{\sin x}$ as $y = (\sin x)^{1/2}$. Using the chain rule, let $u = \sin x$. Thus,

$$\frac{dy}{dx} = \frac{1}{2}(\sin x)^{\frac{-1}{2}}(\cos x) = \frac{\cos x}{2(\sin x)^{\frac{1}{2}}} = \frac{\cos x}{2\sqrt{\sin x}}.$$

Example 8

If $y = \dfrac{\tan x}{1 + \tan x}$, find $\dfrac{dy}{dx}$.

Using the quotient rule, let $u = \tan x$ and $v = (1 + \tan x)$. Then,

$$\frac{dy}{dx} = \frac{(\sec^2 x)(1 + \tan x) - (\sec^2 x)(\tan x)}{(1 + \tan x)^2} = \frac{\sec^2 x + (\sec^2 x)(\tan x) - (\sec^2 x)(\tan x)}{(1 + \tan x)^2}$$

$$= \frac{\sec^2 x}{\left(1 + \tan x\right)^2}, \text{ which is equivalent to } \frac{\dfrac{1}{\left(\cos x\right)^2}}{\left(1 + \dfrac{\sin x}{\cos x}\right)^2}$$

$$= \frac{\dfrac{1}{\left(\cos x\right)^2}}{\left(\dfrac{\cos x + \sin x}{\cos x}\right)^2} = \frac{1}{\left(\cos x + \sin x\right)^2}.$$

Note: For all of the above exercises, you can find the derivatives by using a calculator provided that you are permitted to do so.

Derivatives of Inverse Trigonometric Functions

Summary of Derivatives of Inverse Trigonometric Functions:

Let *u* be a differentiable function of *x*, then

$$\frac{d}{dx}\sin^{-1} u = \frac{1}{\sqrt{1 - u^2}}\frac{du}{dx}, |u| < 1 \qquad \frac{d}{dx}\cos^{-1} u = \frac{-1}{\sqrt{1 - u^2}}\frac{du}{dx}, |u| < 1$$

$$\frac{d}{dx}\tan^{-1} u = \frac{1}{1 + u^2}\frac{du}{dx} \qquad \frac{d}{dx}\cot^{-1} u = \frac{-1}{1 + u^2}\frac{du}{dx}$$

$$\frac{d}{dx}\sec^{-1} u = \frac{1}{|u|\sqrt{u^2 - 1}}\frac{du}{dx}, |u| > 1 \qquad \frac{d}{dx}\csc^{-1} u = \frac{-1}{|u|\sqrt{u^2 - 1}}\frac{du}{dx}, |u| > 1.$$

Note that the derivatives of $\cos^{-1} x$, $\cot^{-1} x$ and $\csc^{-1} x$ all have a "−1" in their numerators.

Example 1
If $y = 5 \sin^{-1}(3x)$, find $\dfrac{dy}{dx}$.

Let $u = 3x$. Then $\dfrac{dy}{dx} = (5)\dfrac{1}{\sqrt{1 - (3x)^2}}\dfrac{du}{dx} = \dfrac{5}{\sqrt{1 - (3x)^2}}(3) = \dfrac{15}{\sqrt{1 - 9x^2}}.$

Or using a calculator, enter $d[5 \sin^{-1}(3x), x]$ and obtain the same result.

Example 2
Find $f'(x)$ if $f(x) = \tan^{-1}\sqrt{x}$.

Let $u = \sqrt{x}$. Then $f'(x) = \dfrac{1}{1 + (\sqrt{x})^2}\dfrac{du}{dx} = \dfrac{1}{1 + x}\left(\dfrac{1}{2}x^{\frac{-1}{2}}\right) = \dfrac{1}{1 + x}\left(\dfrac{1}{2\sqrt{x}}\right)$

$$= \dfrac{1}{2\sqrt{x}(1 + x)}.$$

Example 3
If $y = \sec^{-1}(3x^2)$, find $\dfrac{dy}{dx}$.

Let $u = 3x^2$. Then $\dfrac{dy}{dx} = \dfrac{1}{|3x^2|\sqrt{(3x^2)^2 - 1}}\dfrac{du}{dx} = \dfrac{1}{3x^2\sqrt{9x^2 - 1}}(6x) = \dfrac{2}{x\sqrt{9x^2 - 1}}.$

Example 4

If $y = \cos^{-1}\left(\dfrac{1}{x}\right)$, find $\dfrac{dy}{dx}$.

Let $u = \left(\dfrac{1}{x}\right)$. Then $\dfrac{dy}{dx} = \dfrac{-1}{\sqrt{1 - \left(\dfrac{1}{x}\right)^2}} \dfrac{du}{dx}$.

Rewrite $u = \left(\dfrac{1}{x}\right)$ as $u = x^{-1}$. Then $\dfrac{du}{dx} = -1x^{-2} = \dfrac{-1}{x^2}$.

Therefore, $\dfrac{dy}{dx} = \dfrac{-1}{\sqrt{1 - \left(\dfrac{1}{x}\right)^2}} \dfrac{du}{dx} = \dfrac{-1}{\sqrt{1 - \left(\dfrac{1}{x}\right)^2}} \dfrac{-1}{x^2} = \dfrac{1}{\sqrt{\dfrac{x^2-1}{x^2}}\left(x^2\right)} = \dfrac{1}{\dfrac{\sqrt{x^2-1}\left(x^2\right)}{|x|}}$

$= \dfrac{1}{|x|\sqrt{x^2-1}}$.

Note: For all of the above exercises, you can find the derivatives by using a calculator provided that you are permitted to do so.

Derivatives of Exponential and Logarithmic Functions

Summary of Derivatives of Exponential and Logarithmic Functions:

Let u be a differentiable function of x, then

$$\frac{d}{dx}\left(e^u\right) = e^u \frac{du}{dx} \qquad\qquad \frac{d}{dx}\left(a^u\right) = a^u \ln a \frac{du}{dx}, a > 0 \,\&\, a \neq 1$$

$$\frac{d}{dx}\left(\ln u\right) = \frac{1}{u}\frac{du}{dx}, u > 0 \qquad \frac{d}{dx}\left(\log_a u\right) = \frac{1}{u \ln a}\frac{du}{dx}, a > 0 \,\&\, a \neq 1.$$

For the following examples, find $\dfrac{dy}{dx}$ and verify your result with a calculator.

Example 1

$y = e^{3x} + 5xe^3 + e^3$

$\dfrac{dy}{dx} = \left(e^{3x}\right)(3) + 5e^3 + 0 = 3e^{3x} + 5e^3$ (Note that e^3 is a constant.)

Example 2

$y = xe^x - x^2 e^x$

Using the product rule for both terms, you have

$\dfrac{dy}{dx} = (1)e^x + \left(e^x\right)x - \left[(2x)e^x + \left(e^x\right)x^2\right] = e^x + xe^x - 2xe^x - x^2 e^x = e^x - xe^x - x^2 e^x$

$= -x^2 e^x - xe^x + e^x = e^x\left(-x^2 - x + 1\right).$

Example 3

$y = 3^{\sin x}$

Let $u = \sin x$. Then, $\dfrac{dy}{dx} = \left(3^{\sin x}\right)(\ln 3)\dfrac{du}{dx} = \left(3^{\sin x}\right)(\ln 3)\cos x = (\ln 3)\left(3^{\sin x}\right)\cos x.$

Example 4

$y = e^{(x^3)}$

Let $u = x^3$. Then, $\dfrac{dy}{dx} = \left[e^{(x^3)}\right]\dfrac{du}{dx} = \left[e^{(x^3)}\right]3x^2 = 3x^2\,e^{(x^3)}$.

Example 5

$y = (\ln x)^5$

Let $u = \ln x$. Then, $\dfrac{dy}{dx} = 5(\ln x)^4\,\dfrac{du}{dx} = 5(\ln x)^4\left(\dfrac{1}{x}\right) = \dfrac{5(\ln x)^4}{x}$.

Example 6

$y = \ln(x^2 + 2x - 3) + \ln 5$

Let $u = x^2 + 2x - 3$. Then, $\dfrac{dy}{dx} = \dfrac{1}{x^2 + 2x - 3}\,\dfrac{du}{dx} + 0 = \dfrac{1}{x^2 + 2x - 3}\,(2x + 2)$

$= \dfrac{2x + 2}{x^2 + 2x - 3}$.

(Note that $\ln 5$ is a constant. Thus the derivative of $\ln 5$ is 0.)

Example 7

$y = 2x\ln x + x$

Using the product rule for the first term,

you have $\dfrac{dy}{dx} = (2)\ln x + \left(\dfrac{1}{x}\right)(2x) + 1 = 2\ln x + 2 + 1 = 2\ln x + 3$.

Example 8

$y = \ln(\ln x)$

Let $u = \ln x$. Then, $\dfrac{dy}{dx} = \dfrac{1}{\ln x}\,\dfrac{du}{dx} = \dfrac{1}{\ln x}\left(\dfrac{1}{x}\right) = \dfrac{1}{x\ln x}$.

Example 9

$y = \log_5(2x + 1)$

Let $u = 2x + 1$. Then $\dfrac{dy}{dx} = \dfrac{1}{(2x + 1)\ln 5}\,\dfrac{du}{dx} = \dfrac{1}{(2x + 1)\ln 5}\cdot(2) = \dfrac{2}{(2x + 1)\ln 5}$.

Example 10

Write an equation of the line tangent to the curve of $y = e^x$ at $x = 1$.

The slope of the tangent to the curve $y = e^x$ at $x = 1$ is equivalent to the value of the derivative of $y = e^x$ evaluated at $x = 1$. Using your calculator, enter $d(e\char94(x), x)|x = 1$ and obtain e. Thus, $m = e$, the slope of the tangent to the curve at $x = 1$. At $x = 1$, $y = e^1 = e$, and thus the point on the curve is $(1, e)$. Therefore, the equation of the tangent is $y - e = e(x - 1)$ or $y = ex$. (See Figure 3.2-1.)

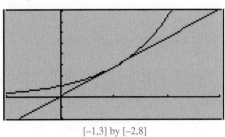

[-1,3] by [-2,8]

Figure 3.2-1

• Guess, if you can eliminate some of the choices in a multiple-choice question.

3.3 IMPLICIT DIFFERENTIATION

Procedure for Implicit Differentiation: Given an equation containing the variables x and y for which you cannot easily solve for y in terms of x, you can find $\dfrac{dy}{dx}$ by:

Steps: 1. Differentiate each term of the equation with respect to x.

2. Move all terms containing $\dfrac{dy}{dx}$ to the left side of the equation and all other terms to the right side.

3. Factor out $\dfrac{dy}{dx}$ on the left side of the equation.

4. Solve for $\dfrac{dy}{dx}$.

Example 1

Find $\dfrac{dy}{dx}$ if $y^2 - 7y + x^2 - 4x = 10$.

Step 1: Differentiate each term of the equation with respect to x. (Note y is treated as a function of x.) $2y\dfrac{dy}{dx} - 7\dfrac{dy}{dx} + 2x - 4 = 0$

Step 2: Move all terms containing $\dfrac{dy}{dx}$ to the left side of the equation and all other terms to the right: $2y\dfrac{dy}{dx} - 7\dfrac{dy}{dx} = -2x + 4$

Step 3: Factor out $\dfrac{dy}{dx}$: $\dfrac{dy}{dx}(2y - 7) = -2x + 4$

Step 4: Solve for $\dfrac{dy}{dx}$: $\dfrac{dy}{dx} = \dfrac{-2x + 4}{2y - 7}$

Example 2

Given $x^3 + y^3 = 6xy$, find $\dfrac{dy}{dx}$.

Step 1: Differentiate each term with respect to x: $3x^2 + 3y^2\dfrac{dy}{dx} = (6)y + \left(\dfrac{dy}{dx}\right)(6x)$

Step 2: Move all $\dfrac{dy}{dx}$ terms to the left side: $3y^2\dfrac{dy}{dx} - 6x\dfrac{dy}{dx} = 6y - 3x^2$

Step 3: Factor out $\dfrac{dy}{dx}$: $\dfrac{dy}{dx}(3y^2 - 6x) = 6y - 3x^2$

Step 4: Solve for $\dfrac{dy}{dx}$: $\dfrac{dy}{dx} = \dfrac{6y - 3x^2}{3y^2 - 6x} = \dfrac{2y - x^2}{y^2 - 2x}$

Example 3

Find $\dfrac{dy}{dx}$ if $(x + y)^2 - (x - y)^2 = x^5 + y^5$

Step 1: Differentiate each term with respect to x:

$$2(x + y)\left(1 + \frac{dy}{dx}\right) - 2(x - y)\left(1 - \frac{dy}{dx}\right) = 5x^4 + 5y^4\frac{dy}{dx}$$

Distributing $2(x + y)$ and $-2(x - y)$, you have

$$2(x + y) + 2(x + y)\frac{dy}{dx} - 2(x - y) + 2(x - y)\frac{dy}{dx} = 5x^4 + 5y^4\frac{dy}{dx}$$

Step 2: Move all $\dfrac{dy}{dx}$ terms to the left side:

$$2(x + y)\frac{dy}{dx} + 2(x - y)\frac{dy}{dx} - 5y^4\frac{dy}{dx} = 5x^4 - 2(x + y) + 2(x - y)$$

Step 3: Factor out $\dfrac{dy}{dx}$:

$$\frac{dy}{dx}\left[2(x + y) + 2(x - y) - 5y^4\right] = 5x^4 - 2x - 2y + 2x - 2y$$

$$\frac{dy}{dx}\left[2x + 2y + 2x - 2y - 5y^4\right] = 5x^4 - 4y$$

$$\frac{dy}{dx}\left[4x - 5y^4\right] = 5x^4 - 4y$$

Step 4: Solve for $\dfrac{dy}{dx}$: $\dfrac{dy}{dx} = \dfrac{5x^4 - 4y}{4x - 5y^4}$

Example 4

Write an equation of the tangent to the curve $x^2 + y^2 + 19 = 2x + 12y$ at $(4, 3)$

The slope of the tangent to the curve at $(4, 3)$ is equivalent to the derivative $\dfrac{dy}{dx}$ at $(4, 3)$.
Using implicit differentiation, you have

$$2x + 2y\frac{dy}{dx} = 2 + 12\frac{dy}{dx}$$

$$2y\frac{dy}{dx} - 12\frac{dy}{dx} = 2 - 2x$$

$$\frac{dy}{dx}(2y - 12) = 2 - 2x$$

$$\frac{dy}{dx} = \frac{2 - 2x}{2y - 12} = \frac{1 - x}{y - 6} \quad \text{and} \quad \left.\frac{dy}{dx}\right|_{(4,3)} = \frac{1 - 4}{3 - 6} = 1$$

Thus the equation of the tangent is $y - 3 = (1)(x - 4)$ or $y - 3 = x - 4$.

Example 5

Find $\dfrac{dy}{dx}$, if $\sin(x + y) = 2x$

$$\left[\cos(x + y)\left(1 + \frac{dy}{dx}\right)\right] = 2$$

$$1 + \frac{dy}{dx} = \frac{2}{\cos(x + y)}$$

$$\frac{dy}{dx} = \frac{2}{\cos(x + y)} - 1$$

3.4 APPROXIMATING A DERIVATIVE

Given a continuous and differentiable function, you can find the approximate value of a derivative at a given point numerically. Here are two examples.

Example 1

The graph of a function f on $[0, 5]$ is shown in Figure 3.4-1. Find the approximate value of $f'(3)$. (See Figure 3.4-1.)

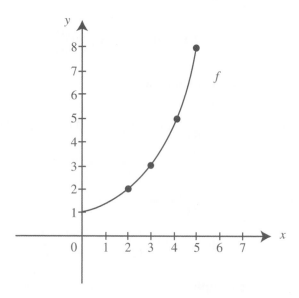

Figure 3.4-1

Since $f'(3)$ is equivalent to the slope of the tangent to $f(x)$ at $x = 3$, there are several ways you can find its approximate value.

Method 1: Using slope of the line segment joining the points at $x = 3$ and $x = 4$.

$$f(3) = 3 \text{ and } f(4) = 5$$

$$m = \frac{f(4) - f(3)}{4 - 3} = \frac{5 - 3}{4 - 3} = 2$$

Method 2: Using the slope of the line segment joining the points at $x = 2$ and $x = 3$.

$$f(2) = 2 \text{ and } f(3) = 3$$

$$m = \frac{f(2) - f(2)}{3 - 2} = \frac{3 - 2}{3 - 2} = 1$$

Method 3: Using the slope of the line segment joining the points at $x = 2$ and $x = 4$.

$$f(2) = 2 \text{ and } f(4) = 5$$

$$m = \frac{f(4) - f(2)}{4 - 2} = \frac{5 - 2}{4 - 2} = \frac{3}{2}$$

Note that $\frac{3}{2}$ is the average of the results from methods 1 and 2.

Thus $f'(3) \approx 1, 2$ or $\frac{3}{2}$ depending on which line segment you use.

Example 2

Let f be a continuous and differentiable function. Selected values of f are shown below. Find the approximate value of f' at $x = 1$.

x	-2	-1	0	1	2	3
f	1	0	1	1.59	2.08	2.52

You can use the difference quotient $\dfrac{f(a + h) - f(a)}{h}$ to approximate $f'(a)$.

$$\text{Let } h = 1; \quad f'(1) \approx \frac{f(2) - f(1)}{2 - 1} \approx \frac{2.08 - 1.59}{1} \approx 0.49$$

$$\text{Let } h = 2; \quad f'(1) \approx \frac{f(3) - f(1)}{3 - 1} \approx \frac{2.52 - 1.59}{2} \approx 0.465$$

Or, you can use the symmetric difference quotient $\dfrac{f(a + h) - f(a - h)}{2h}$ to approximate $f'(a)$.

$$\text{Let } h = 1; \quad f'(1) \approx \frac{f(2) - f(0)}{2 - 0} \approx \frac{2.08 - 1}{2} \approx 0.54$$

$$\text{Let } h = 2; \quad f'(1) \approx \frac{f(3) - f(-1)}{3 - (-1)} \approx \frac{2.52 - 0}{4} \approx 0.63$$

Thus, $f'(3) \approx 0.49, 0.465, 0.54$ or 0.63 depending on your method.

Note that f is decreasing on $(-2, -1)$ and increasing on $(-1, 3)$. Using the symmetric difference quotient with $h = 3$ would not be accurate. (See Figure 3.4-2.)

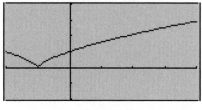

[–2,4] by [–2,4]

Figure 3.4-2

- Remember that the $\displaystyle\lim_{x \to 0} \frac{\sin 6x}{\sin 2x} = \frac{6}{2} = 3$ because the $\displaystyle\lim_{x \to 0} \frac{\sin x}{x} = 1$.

3.5 DERIVATIVES OF INVERSE FUNCTIONS

Let f be a one-to-one differentiable function with inverse function f^{-1}. If $f'(f^{-1}(a)) \neq 0$, then the inverse function f^{-1} is differentiable at a and

$$\left(f^{-1}\right)'(a) = \frac{1}{f'(f^{-1}(a))}. \quad \text{(See Figure 3.5-1.)}$$

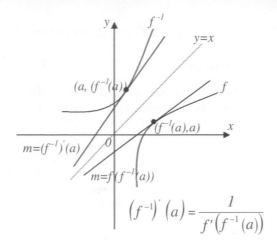

$$\left(f^{-1}\right)'(a) = \frac{1}{f'\left(f^{-1}(a)\right)}$$

Figure 3.5-1

If $y = f^{-1}(x)$ so that $x = f(y)$, then $\dfrac{dy}{dx} = \dfrac{1}{\dfrac{dx}{dy}}$ with $\dfrac{dx}{dy} \neq 0$.

Example 1

If $f(x) = x^3 + 2x - 10$, find $(f^{-1})'(x)$

Step 1: Check if $(f^{-1})'(x)$ exists. $f'(x) = 3x^2 + 2$ and $f'(x) > 0$ for all real values of x. Thus $f(x)$ is strictly increasing which implies that $f(x)$ is $1 - 1$. Therefore $(f^{-1})'(x)$ exists.

Step 2: Let $y = f(x)$ and thus $y = x^3 + 2x - 10$.

Step 3: Interchange x and y to obtain the inverse function $x = y^3 + 2y - 10$.

Step 4: Differentiate with respect to y: $\dfrac{dx}{dy} = 3y^2 + 2$

Step 5: Apply formula $\dfrac{dx}{dy} = \dfrac{1}{\dfrac{dx}{dy}}$.

$$\frac{dx}{dy} = \frac{1}{\dfrac{dx}{dy}} = \frac{1}{3y^2 + 2} . \text{ Thus, } \left(f^{-1}\right)'(x) = \frac{1}{3y^2 + 2}$$

Example 2

Example 1 could have been done by using implicit differentiation.

Step 1: Let $y = f'(x)$, and thus $y = x^3 + 2x - 10$.

Step 2: Interchange x and y to obtain the inverse function $x = y^3 + 2y - 10$.

Step 3: Differentiate each term implicitly with respect to x.

$$\frac{d}{dx}(x) = \frac{d}{dx}\left(y^3\right) + \frac{d}{dx}(2y) - \frac{d}{dx}(-10)$$

$$1 = 3y^2 \frac{dy}{dx} + 2\frac{dy}{dx} - 0$$

Step 4: Solve for $\dfrac{dy}{dx}$.

$$1 = \dfrac{dy}{dx}\left(3y^2 + 2\right)$$

$$\dfrac{dy}{dx} = \dfrac{1}{3y^2 + 2} . \text{ Thus } \left(f^{-1}\right)'(x) = \dfrac{1}{3y^2 + 2}$$

Example 3

If $f(x) = 2x^5 + x^3 + 1$, find (a) $f(1)$ and $f'(1)$ and (b) $(f^{-1})(4)$ and $(f^{-1})'(4)$.
Enter $y1 = 2x^5 + x^3 + 1$. Since $y1$ is strictly increasing, thus $f(x)$ has an inverse.

(a) $f(1) = 2(1)^5 + (1)^3 + 1 = 4$
$f'(x) = 10x^4 + 3x^2$
$f'(1) = 10(1)^4 + 3(1)^2 = 13$

(b) Since $f(1) = 4$ implies the point $(1,4)$ is on the curve $f(x) = 2x^5 + x^3 + 1$, therefore the point $(4,1)$ (which is the reflection of $(1,4)$ on $y = x$) is on the curve $(f^{-1})(x)$. Thus $(f^{-1})(4) = 1$

$$\left(f^{-1}\right)'(4) = \dfrac{1}{f'(1)} = \dfrac{1}{13}$$

Example 4

If $f(x) = 5x^3 - x + 8$, find $(f^{-1})'(8)$.
Enter $y1 = 5x^3 - x + 8$. Since $y1$ is strictly increasing near $x = 8$, $f(x)$ has an inverse near $x = 8$.
Note that $f(0) = 5(0)^3 - 0 + 8 = 8$ which implies the point $(0,8)$ is on the curve of $f(x)$.
Thus, the point $(8,0)$ is on the curve of $(f^{-1})(x)$.

$$f'(x) = 15x^2 - 1$$
$$f'(0) = -1$$

Therefore $\left(f^{-1}\right)'(8) = \dfrac{1}{f'(0)} = \dfrac{1}{-1} = -1.$

- Leave a multiple-choice question blank if you have no clue. You don't have to answer every question to get a 5 on the AP Calculus AB exam.

3.6   HIGHER ORDER DERIVATIVES

If the derivative f' of a function f is differentiable, then the derivative of f' is the second derivative of f represented by f'' (reads as f double prime). You can continue to differentiate f as long as there is differentiability.

Some of the Symbols of Higher Order Derivatives:

$$f'(x), f''(x), f'''(x), f^{(4)}(x)$$

$$\dfrac{dy}{dx}, \dfrac{d^2y}{dx^2}, \dfrac{d^3y}{dx^3}, \dfrac{d^4y}{dx^4}$$

$$y', y'', y''', y^{(4)}$$

$$D_x(y), D_x^2(y), D_x^3(y), D_x^4(y)$$

Note that $\dfrac{d^2y}{dx^2} = \dfrac{d}{dx}\left(\dfrac{dy}{dx}\right)$ or $\dfrac{dy'}{dx}$.

Example 1

If $y = 5x^3 + 7x - 10$, find the first four derivatives.

$$\frac{dy}{dx} = 15x^2 + 7; \ \frac{d^2y}{dx^2} = 30x; \ \frac{d^3y}{dx^3} = 30; \ \frac{d^4y}{dx^4} = 0$$

Example 2

If $f(x) = \sqrt{x}$, find $f''(4)$.

Rewrite: $f(x) = \sqrt{x} = x^{1/2}$ and differentiate: $f'(x) = \dfrac{1}{2}x^{-1/2}$

Differentiate again:

$$f''(x) = -\frac{1}{4}x^{-3/2} = \frac{-1}{4x^{3/2}} = \frac{-1}{4\sqrt{x^3}} \ \text{and} \ f''(4) = \frac{-1}{4\sqrt{4^3}} = -\frac{1}{32}$$

Example 3

If $y = x \cos x$, find y''.
Using the product rule, $y' = (1)(\cos x) + (x)(-\sin x) = \cos x - x\sin x$

$$y'' = -\sin x - [(1)(\sin x) + (x)(\cos x)] = -\sin x - \sin x - x\cos x$$

$$= -2\sin x - x\cos x$$

Or, you can use a calculator and enter $d(x*\cos x, x, 2)$ and obtain the same result.

3.7 RAPID REVIEW

1. If $y = e^{x^3}$, find $\dfrac{dy}{dx}$.

   Answer: Using the chain rule, $\dfrac{dy}{dx} = \left(e^{x^2}\right)(2x)$.

2. Evaluate $\lim\limits_{h \to 0} \dfrac{\cos\left(\dfrac{\pi}{6} + h\right) - \cos\left(\dfrac{\pi}{6}\right)}{h}$.

   Answer: The limit is equivalent to $\dfrac{d}{dx}\cos x\Big|_{x=\frac{\pi}{6}} = -\sin\left(\dfrac{\pi}{6}\right) = -\dfrac{1}{2}$.

3. Find $f'(x)$ if $f(x) = \ln(3x)$.

   Answer: $f'(x) = \dfrac{1}{3x}(3) = \dfrac{1}{x}$.

4. Find the approximate value of $f'(3)$. (See Figure 3.7-1.)

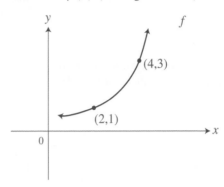

Figure 3.7-1

Answer: Using the slope of the line segment joining $(2,1)$ and

$(4,3)$, $f'(3) \approx \dfrac{3-1}{4-2} = 1$.

5. Find $\dfrac{dy}{dx}$ if $xy = 5x^2$.

Answer: Using implicit differentiation, $1y + x\dfrac{dy}{dx} = 10x$. Thus $\dfrac{dy}{dx} = \dfrac{10x - y}{x}$.

6. If $y = \dfrac{5}{x^2}$, find $\dfrac{d^2y}{dx^2}$.

Answer: Rewrite $y = 5x^{-2}$. Then

$\dfrac{dy}{dx} = -10x^{-3}$ and $\dfrac{d^2y}{dx^2} = 30x^{-4} = \dfrac{30}{x^4}$.

7. Using a calculator, write an equation of the line tangent to the graph $f(x) = -2x^4$ at the point where $f'(x) = -1$.

Answer: $f'(x) = -8x^3$. Using a calculator, enter Solve $(-8x\^3 = -1, x)$ and

obtain $x = \dfrac{1}{2} \Rightarrow f'\left(\dfrac{1}{2}\right) = -1$. Using your calculator $f\left(\dfrac{1}{2}\right) = -\dfrac{1}{8}$. Thus tangent

is $y + \dfrac{1}{8} = -1\left(x - \dfrac{1}{2}\right)$.

3.8 PRACTICE PROBLEMS

Part A—The use of a calculator is not allowed.

Find the derivative of each of the following functions.

1. $y = 6x^5 - x + 10$

2. $f(x) = \dfrac{1}{x} + \dfrac{1}{\sqrt[3]{x^2}}$

3. $y = \dfrac{5x^6 - 1}{x^2}$

4. $y = \dfrac{x^2}{5x^6 - 1}$

5. $f(x) = (3x - 2)^5 (x^2 - 1)$

6. $y = \sqrt{\dfrac{2x + 1}{2x - 1}}$

7. $y = 10 \cot(2x - 1)$

8. $y = 3x\sec(3x)$

9. $y = 10 \cos\lfloor \sin(x^2 - 4) \rfloor$

10. $y = 8 \cos^{-1}(2x)$

11. $y = 3e^5 + 4xe^x$

12. $y = \ln(x^2 + 3)$

Part B—Calculators are allowed.

13. Find $\dfrac{dy}{3x}$, if $x^2 + y^3 = 10 - 5xy$.

14. The graph of a function f on $[1, 5]$ is shown in Figure 3.8-1. Find the approximate value of $f'(4)$.

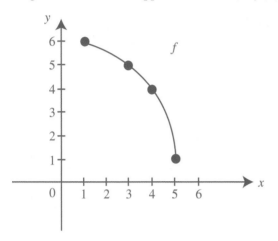

Figure 3.8-1

15. Let f be a continuous and differentiable function. Selected values of f are shown below. Find the approximate value of f' at $x = 2$.

x	–1	0	1	2	3
f	6	5	6	9	14

16. If $f(x) = x^5 + 3x - 8$, find $(f^{-1})'(-8)$.

17. Write an equation of the tangent to the curve $y = \ln x$ at $x = e$.

18. If $y = 2x\sin x$, find $\dfrac{d^2y}{dx^2}$ at $x = \dfrac{\pi}{2}$.

19. If the function $f(x) = (x - 1)^{2/3} + 2$, find all points where f is not differentiable.

20. Write an equation of the normal line to the curve $x \cos y = 1$ at $\left(2, \dfrac{\pi}{3}\right)$.

3.9 CUMULATIVE REVIEW PROBLEMS

("Calculator" indicates that calculators are permitted)

21. Find $\displaystyle\lim_{h\to 0} \dfrac{\sin\left(\dfrac{\pi}{2} + h\right) - \sin\left(\dfrac{\pi}{2}\right)}{h}$.

22. If $f(x) = \cos^2(\pi - x)$, find $f'(0)$.

23. Find $\displaystyle\lim_{x\to\infty} \dfrac{x - 25}{10 + x - 2x^2}$.

24. (Calculator) Let f be a continuous and differentiable function. Selected values of f are shown below. Find the approximate value of f' at $x = 1$.

x	0	1	2	3	4	5
f	3.9	4	4.8	6.5	8.9	11.8

25. (Calculator) If $f(x) = \begin{cases} \dfrac{x^2 - 9}{x - 3}, & x \neq 3, \\ 3, & x = 3 \end{cases}$ determine if $f(x)$ is continuous at $x = 3$.) Explain why or why not.

3.10 SOLUTIONS TO PRACTICE PROBLEMS

Part A—No calculators.

1. Applying the power rule, $\dfrac{dy}{dx} = 30x^4 - 1$.

2. Rewrite $f(x) = \dfrac{1}{x} + \dfrac{1}{\sqrt[3]{x^2}}$

   as $f(x) = x^{-1} + x^{-2/3}$.

Differentiate,

$$f'(x) = -x^{-2} - \dfrac{2}{3}x^{-5/3} = -\dfrac{1}{x^2} - \dfrac{2}{3\sqrt[3]{x^5}}$$

3. Rewrite

$$y = \dfrac{5x^6 - 1}{x^2} \text{ as } y = \dfrac{5x^6}{x^2} - \dfrac{1}{x^2} = 5x^4 - x^{-2}.$$

Differentiate,

$$\frac{dy}{dx} = 20x^3 - (-2)x^{-3} = 20x^3 + \frac{2}{x^3}.$$

An alternate method is to differentiate

$$y = \frac{5x^6 - 1}{x^2} \text{ directly, using the quotient rule.}$$

4. Applying the quotient rule,

$$\frac{dy}{dx} = \frac{(2x)(5x^6 - 1) - (30x^5)(x^2)}{(5x^6 - 1)^2}$$

$$= \frac{10x^7 - 2x - 30x^7}{(5x^6 - 1)^2}$$

$$= \frac{-20x^7 - 2x}{(5x^6 - 1)^2} = \frac{-2x(10x^6 + 1)}{(5x^6 - 1)^2}$$

5. Applying the product rule, $u = (3x - 2)^5$ and $v = (x^2 - 1)$ and then the chain rule,

$$f'(x) = [5(3x - 2)^4(3)][x^2 - 1] + [2x][(3x - 2)^5]$$

$$= 15(x^2 - 1)(3x - 2)^4 + 2x(3x - 2)^5$$

$$= (3x - 2)^4[15(x^2 - 1) + 2x(3x - 2)]$$

$$= (3x - 2)^4[15x^2 - 15 + 6x^2 - 4x]$$

$$= (3x - 2)^4(21x^2 - 4x - 15)$$

6. Rewrite $y = \sqrt{\dfrac{2x + 1}{2x - 1}}$ as $y = \left(\dfrac{2x + 1}{2x - 1}\right)^{\frac{1}{2}}$.

Applying first the chain rule and then the quotient rule,

$$\frac{dy}{dx} = \frac{1}{2}\left(\frac{2x + 1}{2x - 1}\right)^{-\frac{1}{2}}\left[\frac{(2)(2x - 1) - (2)(2x + 1)}{(2x - 1)^2}\right]$$

$$= \frac{1}{2}\frac{1}{\left(\dfrac{2x + 1}{2x - 1}\right)^{\frac{1}{2}}}\left[\frac{-4}{(2x - 1)^2}\right]$$

$$= \frac{1}{2}\frac{1}{\dfrac{(2x + 1)^{\frac{1}{2}}}{(2x - 1)^{\frac{1}{2}}}}\left[\frac{-4}{(2x - 1)^2}\right]$$

$$= \frac{-2}{(2x + 1)^{\frac{1}{2}}(2x - 1)^{\frac{3}{2}}}$$

Note: $\left(\dfrac{2x + 1}{2x - 1}\right)^{\frac{1}{2}} = \dfrac{(2x + 1)^{\frac{1}{2}}}{(2x - 1)^{\frac{1}{2}}}$,

if $\dfrac{2x + 1}{2x - 1} > 0$ which implies $x < -\dfrac{1}{2}$

or $x > \dfrac{1}{2}$.

An alternate method of solution is to write

$$y = \frac{\sqrt{2x + 1}}{2x - 1} \text{ and use the quotient rule.}$$

Another method is to write $y = (2x + 1)^{\frac{1}{2}}$

$(2x - 1)^{\frac{1}{2}}$ and use the product rule.

7. Let $u = 2x - 1$, $\dfrac{dy}{dx} = 10\left[- \csc^2(2x - 1)\right](2)$

$$= -20 \csc^2(2x - 1)$$

8. Using the product rule,

$$\frac{dy}{dx} = (3[\sec(3x)]) + [\sec(3x) \tan(3x)](3)[3x]$$

$$= 3 \sec(3x) + 9x \sec(3x) \tan(3x) = 3 \sec(3x)$$
$$[1 + 3x \tan(3x)]$$

9. Using the chain rule, let $u = \sin(x^2 - 4)$.

$$\frac{dy}{dx} = 10(- \sin[\sin(x^2 - 4)]) [\cos(x^2 - 4)] (2x)$$

$$= -20x \cos(x^2 - 4) \sin[\sin(x^2 - 4)]$$

10. Using the chain rule, let $u = 2x$.

$$\frac{dy}{dx} = 8\left(\frac{-1}{\sqrt{1 - (2x)^2}}\right)(2) = \frac{-16}{\sqrt{1 - 4x^2}}$$

11. Since $3e^5$ is a constant, thus its derivative is 0.

$$\frac{dy}{dx} = 0 + (4) (e^x) + (e^x) (4x)$$

$$= 4e^x + 4xe^x = 4e^x(1 + x)$$

12. Let $u = (x^2 + 3)$, $\dfrac{dy}{dx} = \left(\dfrac{1}{x^2 + 3}\right)(2x)$

$$= \frac{2x}{x^2 + 3}$$

Part B—Calculators are permitted.

13. Using implicit differentiation, differentiate each term with respect to x.

$$2x + 3y^2 \frac{dy}{dx} = 0 - \left[(5)(y) + \frac{dy}{dx}(5x) \right]$$

$$2x + 3y^2 \frac{dy}{dx} = -5y - 5x\frac{dy}{dx}$$

$$3y^2 \frac{dy}{dx} + 5x \frac{dy}{dx} = -5y - 2x$$

$$\frac{dy}{dx}(3y^2 + 5x) = -5y - 2x$$

$$\frac{dy}{dx} = \frac{-5y - 2x}{3y^2 + 5x} \text{ or } \frac{dy}{dx} = \frac{-(2x + 5y)}{5x + 3y^2}$$

14. Since $f'(4)$ is equivalent to the slope of the tangent to $f(x)$ at $x = 4$, there are several ways you can find its approximate value.

Method 1: Using the slope of the line segment joining the points at $x = 4$ and $x = 5$.

$f(5) = 1$ and $f(4) = 4$

$$m = \frac{f(5) - f(4)}{5 - 4} = \frac{1 - 4}{1} = -3$$

Method 2: Using the slope of the line segment joining the points at $x = 3$ and $x = 4$.

$f(3) = 5$ and $f(4) = 4$

$$m = \frac{f(4) - f(3)}{4 - 3} = \frac{4 - 5}{4 - 3} = -1$$

Method 3: Using the slope of the line segment joining the points at $x = 3$ and $x = 5$.

$f(3) = 5$ and $f(5) = 1$

$$m = \frac{f(5) - f(3)}{5 - 3} = \frac{1 - 5}{5 - 3} = -2$$

Note that -2 is the average of the results from methods 1 and 2. Thus $f'(4) \approx -3, -1$ or -2 depending on which line segment you use.

15. You can use the difference quotient

$$\frac{f(a + h) - f(a)}{h} \text{ to approximate } f'(a).$$

Let $h = 1$; $f'(2) \approx \frac{f(3) - f(2)}{3 - 2} \approx \frac{14 - 9}{3 - 2} \approx 5$

Or, you can use the symmetric difference quotient

$$\frac{f(a + h) - f(a - h)}{2h} \text{ to approximate } f'(a).$$

Let $h = 1$; $f'(2) \approx \frac{f(3) - f(1)}{2 - 0} \approx \frac{14 - 6}{2} \approx 4$

Thus, $f'(2) \approx 4$ or 5 depending on your method.

16. Enter $y1 = x^5 + 3x - 8$. The graph of $y1$ is strictly increasing. Thus $f(x)$ has an inverse. Note that $f(0) = -8$. Thus the point $(0, -8)$ is on the graph of $f(x)$ which implies that the point $(-8, 0)$ is on the graph of $f^{-1}(x)$.

$f'(x) = 5x^4 + 3$ and $f'(0) = 3$

Since $(f^{-1})'(-8) = \frac{1}{f'(0)}$, thus $(f^{-1})'(-8) = \frac{1}{3}$.

17. $\frac{dy}{dx} = \frac{1}{x}$ and $\left. \frac{dy}{dx} \right|_{x=e} = \frac{1}{e}$

Thus the slope of the tangent to $y = \ln x$ at

$x = e$ is $\frac{1}{e}$. At $x = e$, $y = \ln x = \ln e = 1$, which means the point $(e, 1)$ is on the curve of $y = \ln x$. Therefore, an equation of the tangent is

$y - 1 = \frac{1}{e}(x - e)$ or $y = \frac{x}{e}$. (See Figure 3.10-1.)

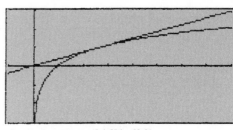

[-1,8] by [3,3]

Figure 3.10-1

18. $\frac{dy}{dx} = (2)(\sin x) + (\cos x)(2x) = 2\sin x + 2x\cos x$

$\dfrac{d^2y}{dx^2} = 2\cos x + [(2)(\cos x) + (-\sin x)(2x)]$

$\qquad = 2\cos x + 2\cos x - 2x\sin x$

$\qquad = 4\cos x - 2x\sin x$

$\dfrac{d^2y}{dx^2}\Big|_{x=\pi/2} = 4\cos\left(\dfrac{\pi}{2}\right) - 2\left(\dfrac{\pi}{2}\right)\left(\sin\left(\dfrac{\pi}{2}\right)\right)$

$\qquad = 0 - 2\left(\dfrac{\pi}{2}\right)(1) = -\pi$

Or, using a calculator, enter $d(2x - \sin(x), x, 2)$

$x = \dfrac{\pi}{2}$ and obtain $-\pi$.

19. Enter $y1 = (x - 1)^{2/3} + 2$ in your calculator. The graph of $y1$ forms a cusp at $x = 1$. Therefore, f is not differentiable at $x = 1$.

20. Differentiate with respect to x:

(1) $\cos y + \left[(-\sin y)\dfrac{dy}{dx}\right](x) = 0$

$\cos y - x\sin y\dfrac{dy}{dx} = 0$

$\dfrac{dy}{dx} = \dfrac{\cos y}{x\sin y}$

$\dfrac{dy}{dx}\Big|_{x=2, y=\pi/3} = \dfrac{\cos\left(\pi/3\right)}{(2)\sin\left(\pi/3\right)} = \dfrac{1/2}{2\left(\sqrt{3}/2\right)} = \dfrac{1}{2\sqrt{3}}$

Thus, the slope of the tangent to the curve at $\left(2, \pi/3\right)$ is $m = \dfrac{1}{2\sqrt{3}}$.

The slope of the normal line to the curve at $\left(2, \pi/3\right)$ is $m = -\dfrac{2\sqrt{3}}{1} = -2\sqrt{3}$.

Therefore an equation of the normal line is

$y - \pi/3 = -2\sqrt{3}(x - 2)$.

3.11 SOLUTIONS TO CUMULATIVE REVIEW PROBLEMS

21. The expression $\lim\limits_{h\to 0}\dfrac{\sin\left(\pi/2 + h\right) - \sin\left(\pi/2\right)}{h}$ is the derivative of $\sin x$ at $x = \pi/2$ which is the slope of the tangent to $\sin x$ at $x = \pi/2$. The tangent to $\sin x$ at $x = \pi/2$ is parallel to the x-axis.

Therefore the slope is 0, i.e.,

$\lim\limits_{h\to 0}\dfrac{\sin\left(\pi/2 + h\right) - \sin\left(\pi/2\right)}{h} = 0.$

An alternate method is to expand $\sin\left(\pi/2 + h\right)$ as $\sin\left(\pi/2\right)\cos h + \cos\left(\pi/2\right)\sin h.$

Thus, $\lim\limits_{h\to 0}\dfrac{\sin\left(\pi/2 + h\right) - \sin\left(\pi/2\right)}{h}$

$= \lim\limits_{h\to 0}\dfrac{\sin\left(\pi/2\right)\cos h + \cos\pi/2\sin h - \sin\left(\pi/2\right)}{h}$

$= \lim\limits_{h\to 0}\dfrac{\sin\left(\pi/2\right)[\cos h - 1] + \cos\pi/2\sin h}{h}$

$= \lim\limits_{h\to 0}\sin\left(\pi/2\right)\left(\dfrac{\cos h - 1}{h}\right) - \lim\limits_{h\to 0}\cos\left(\pi/2\right)\left(\dfrac{\sin h}{h}\right)$

$= \sin\left(\pi/2\right)\lim\limits_{h\to 0}\left(\dfrac{\cos h - 1}{h}\right) - \cos\left(\pi/2\right)\lim\limits_{h\to 0}\left(\dfrac{\sin h}{h}\right)$

$= \left[\sin\left(\pi/2\right)\right] 0 + \cos\left(\pi/2\right)(1) = \cos\left(\pi/2\right) = 0$

22. Using the chain rule, let $u = (\pi - x)$. Then, $f'(x) = 2\cos(\pi - x)[-\sin(\pi - x)](-1)$
$= 2\cos(\pi - x)\sin(\pi - x)$
$f'(0) = 2\cos\pi\sin\pi = 0.$

23. Since the degree of the polynomial in the denominator is greater than the degree of the polynomial in the numerator, the limit is 0.

24. You can use the difference quotient $\dfrac{f(a + h) - f(a)}{h}$ to approximate $f'(a)$.

Let $h = 1$; $f'(2) \approx \dfrac{f(3) - f(2)}{3 - 2}$

$\approx \dfrac{6.5 - 4.8}{1} \approx 1.7.$

Let $h = 2$; $f'(2) \approx \dfrac{f(4) - f(2)}{4 - 2}$

$\approx \dfrac{8.9 - 4.8}{2} \approx 2.05.$

Or, you can use the symmetric difference quotient $\dfrac{f(a + h) - f(a - h)}{2h}$ to approximate $f'(a)$.

Let $h = 1$; $f'(2) \approx \dfrac{f(3) - f(1)}{3 - 1}$

$\approx \dfrac{6.5 - 4}{2} \approx 1.25$

Let $h = 2$; $f'(2) \approx \dfrac{f(4) - f(0)}{4 - 0}$

$\approx \dfrac{8.9 - 3.9}{4} \approx 1.25$

Thus, $f'(2) \approx 1.7$, 2.05, or 1.25 depending on your method.

25. (See Figure 3.11-1.) Checking the three conditions of continuity:

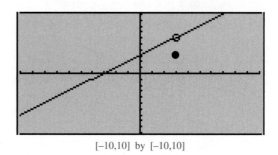

[−10,10] by [−10,10]

Figure 3.11-1

(1) $f(3) = 3$

(2) $\lim\limits_{x \to 3} \dfrac{x^2 - 9}{x - 3} = \lim\limits_{x \to 3}\left(\dfrac{(x + 3)(x - 3)}{(x - 3)} \right)$

$= \lim\limits_{x \to 3}(x + 3) = (3) + 3 = 6.$

(3) Since $f(3) \neq \lim\limits_{x \to 3} f(x)$, $f(x)$ is discontinous at $x = 3$.

Chapter 4

Graphs of Functions and Derivatives

4.1 ROLLE'S THEOREM, MEAN VALUE THEOREM, AND EXTREME VALUE THEOREM

Main Concepts: *Rolle's Theorem, Mean Value Theorem, Extreme Value Theorem*

> • Set your calculator to Radians and change it to Degrees if/when you need to. Don't forget to change it back to Radians after you're finished using it in Degrees.

Rolle's Theorem and Mean Value Theorem

Rolle's Theorem: If f is a function that satisfies the following three conditions:

1. f is continuous on a closed interval $[a, b]$
2. f is differentiable on the open interval (a, b)
3. $f(a) = f(b) = 0$

then there exists a number c in (a, b) such that $f'(c) = 0$. (See Figure 4.1-1.)

Note that if you change condition 3 from $f(a) = f(b) = 0$ to $f(a) = f(b)$, the conclusion of Rolle's Theorem is still valid.

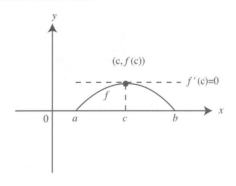

Figure 4.1-1

Mean Value Theorem: If f is a function that satisfies the following conditions:

1. f is continuous on a closed interval $[a, b]$
2. f is differentiable on the open interval (a, b)

then there exists a number c in (a, b) such that

$$f'(c) = \frac{f(b) - f(a)}{b - a}. \text{ (See Figure 4.1-2.)}$$

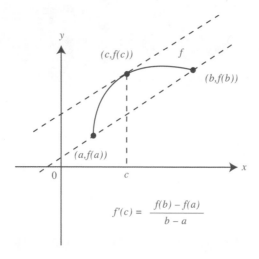

Figure 4.1-2

Example 1

If $f(x) = x^2 + 4x - 5$, show that the hypotheses of Rolle's Theorem are satisfied on the interval $[-4, 0]$ and find all values of c that satisfy the conclusion of the theorem. Check the three conditions in the hypothesis of Rolle's Theorem:

(1) $f(x) = x^2 + 4x - 5$ is continuous everywhere since it is polynomial.
(2) The derivative $f'(x) = 2x + 4$ is defined for all numbers and thus is differentiable on $(-4, 0)$.
(3) $f(0) = f(-4) = -5$. Therefore, there exists a c in $(-4, 0)$ such that $f'(c) = 0$. To find c, set $f'(x) = 0$. Thus $2x + 4 = 0 \Rightarrow x = -2$, i.e., $f'(-2) = 0$. (See Figure 4.1-3.)

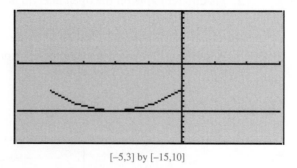

[−5,3] by [−15,10]

Figure 4.1-3

Example 2

Let $f(x) = \dfrac{x^3}{3} - \dfrac{x^2}{2} - 2x + 2$. Using Rolle's Theorem, show that there exists a number c in the domain of f such that $f'(c) = 0$. Find all values of c.

Note $f(x)$ is a polynomial and thus $f(x)$ is continuous and differentiable everywhere. Enter $y1 = \dfrac{x^3}{3} - \dfrac{x^2}{2} - 2x + 2$. The zero's of $y1$ are approximately -2.3, 0.9 and 2.9 i.e. $f(-2.3) = f(0.9) = f(2.9) = 0$. Therefore, there exists at least one c in the interval $(-2.3, 0.9)$ and at least one c in the interval $(0.9, 2.9)$ such that $f'(c) = 0$. Use d(differentiate) to find $f'(x)$: $f'(x) = x^2 - x - 2$. Set $f'(x) = 0 \Rightarrow x^2 - x - 2 = 0$ or $(x - 2)(x + 1) = 0$.

Thus $x = 2$ or $x = -1$, which implies $f'(2) = 0$ and $f'(-1) = 0$. Therefore the values of c are -1 and 2. (See Figure 4.1-4.)

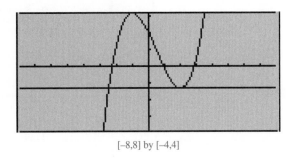

[−8,8] by [−4,4]

Figure 4.1-4

Example 3

The points $P(1, 1)$ and $Q(3, 27)$ are on the curve $f(x) = x^3$. Using the Mean Value Theorem, find c in the interval $(1, 3)$ such that $f'(c)$ is equal to the slope of the secant $\overline{PQ}$.

The slope of secant $\overline{PQ}$ is $m = \dfrac{27 - 1}{3 - 1} = 13$. Since $f(x)$ is defined for all real numbers, $f(x)$ is continuous on $[1, 3]$. Also $f'(x) = 3x^2$ is defined for all real numbers. Thus $f(x)$ is differentiable on $(1,3)$. Therefore, there exists a number c in $(1, 3)$ such that $f'(c) = 13$. Set $f'(c) = 13 \Rightarrow 3(c)^2 = 13$ or $c^2 = \dfrac{13}{3}$ $c = \pm\sqrt{\dfrac{13}{3}}$. Since only $\sqrt{\dfrac{13}{3}}$ is in the interval $(1, 3)$, thus $c = \sqrt{\dfrac{13}{3}}$. (See Figure 4.1-5.)

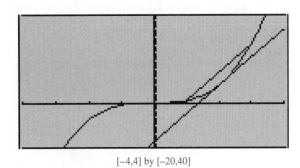

[−4,4] by [−20,40]

Figure 4.1-5

Example 4

Let f be the function $f(x) = (x - 1)^{\frac{2}{3}}$. Determine if the hypotheses of the Mean Value Theorem are satisfied on the interval $[0,2]$ and if so, find all values of c that satisfy the conclusion of the theorem.

Enter $y1 = (x - 1)^{\frac{2}{3}}$. The graph $y1$ shows that there is a cusp at $x = 1$. Thus, $f(x)$ is not differentiable on $(0, 2)$ which implies there may or may not exist a c in $(0,2)$ such that $f'(c) = \dfrac{f(2) - d(0)}{2 - 0}$. The derivative $f'(x) = \dfrac{2}{3}(x-1)^{-\frac{1}{3}}$ and $\dfrac{f(2) - f(0)}{2 - 0} =$

$\dfrac{1-1}{2} = 0$. Set $\dfrac{2}{3}(x-1)^{\frac{1}{3}} = 0 \Rightarrow x = 1$. Note f is not differentiable $(a+x=1)$. Therefore c does not exist. (See Figure 4.1-6.)

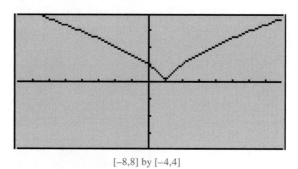

[−8,8] by [−4,4]

Figure 4.1-6

- The formula for finding the area of an equilateral triangle is $area = \dfrac{s^2\sqrt{3}}{4}$ where s is the length of a side. You might need this to find the volume of a solid whose cross sections are equilateral triangles.

Extreme Value Theorem

Extreme Value Theorem: If f is a continuous function on a closed interval $[a,b]$, then f has both a maximum and a minimum value on the interval.

Example 1

If $f(x) = x^3 + 3x^2 - 1$, find the maximum and minimum values of f on $[-2,2]$. Since $(f(x)$ is a polynomial, it is a continuous function everywhere. Enter $y1 = x^3 + 3x^2 - 1$. The graph of $y1$ indicates that f has a minimum of -1 at $x = 0$ and a maximum value of 19 at $x = 2$. (See Figure 4.1-7.)

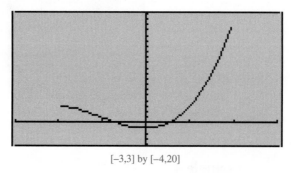

[−3,3] by [−4,20]

Figure 4.1-7

Example 2

If $f(x) = \dfrac{1}{x^2}$, find any maximum and minimum values of f on $[0,3]$. Since $f(x)$ is a rational function, it is continuous everywhere except at values where the denominator is 0.

In this case, at $x = 0$, $f(x)$ is undefined. Since $f(x)$ is not continuous on $[0,3]$, the Extrema Value Theorem may not be applicable. Enter $y1 = \dfrac{1}{x^2}$. The graph of $y1$ shows that as $x \to 0^+$, $f(x)$ increases without bound (i.e., $f(x)$ goes to infinity). Thus f has no maximum value. The minimum value occurs at the endpoint $x = 3$ and the minimum value is $\dfrac{1}{9}$. (See Figure 4.1-8.)

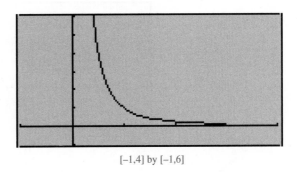

[−1,4] by [−1,6]

Figure 4.1-8

4.2 DETERMINING THE BEHAVIOR OF FUNCTIONS

Main Concepts: *Test for Increasing and Decreasing Functions, First Derivative Test and Second Derivative Test for Relative Extrema, Test for Concavity and Points of Inflection*

Test for Increasing and Decreasing Functions

Let f be a continuous function on the closed interval $[a,b]$ and differentiable on the open interval (a,b).

1. If $f'(x) > 0$ on (a, b), then f is increasing on $[a,b]$
2. If $f'(x) < 0$ on (a, b), then f is decreasing on $[a,b]$
3. If $f'(x) = 0$ on (a, b), then f is constant on $[a,b]$

Definition: Let f be a function defined at a number c. Then c is a critical number of f if either $f'(c) = 0$ or $f'(c)$ does not exist. (See Figure 4.2-1.)

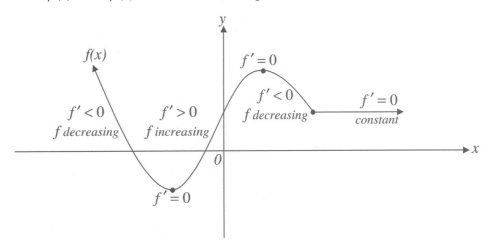

Figure 4.2-1

Example 1

Find the critical numbers of $f(x) = 4x^3 + 2x^2$.

To find the critical numbers of $f(x)$, you have to determine where $f'(x) = 0$ and where $f'(x)$ does not exist. Note $f'(x) = 12x^2 + 4x$, and $f'(x)$ is defined for all real numbers. Let $f'(x) = 0$ and thus $12x^2 + 4x = 0$ which implies $4x(3x + 1) = 0 \Rightarrow x = -1/3$ or $x = 0$. Therefore the critical numbers of f are 0 and $-1/3$. (See Figure 4.2-2.)

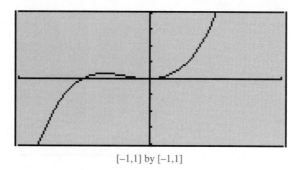

[−1,1] by [−1,1]

Figure 4.2-2

Example 2

Find the critical numbers of $f(x) = (x - 3)^{2/5}$.

$f'(x) = \dfrac{2}{5}(x - 3)^{-3/5} = \dfrac{2}{5(x - 3)^{3/5}}$. Note that $f'(x)$ is undefined at $x = 3$ and that $f'(x)$

$\neq 0$. Therefore, 3 is the only critical number of f. (See Figure 4.2-3.)

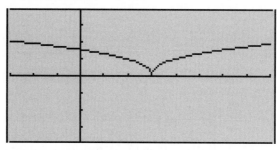

[−3,8] by [−4,4]

Figure 4.2-3

Example 3

The graph of f' on (1,6) is shown in Figure 4.2-4. Find the intervals on which f is increasing or decreasing.

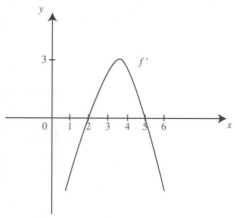

Figure 4.2-4

Solution: See Figure 4.2-5.

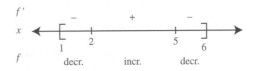

Figure 4.2-5

Thus, f is decreasing on [1,2] and [5,6] and increasing on [2,5].

Example 4

Find the open intervals on which $f(x) = (x^2 - 9)^{2/3}$ is increasing or decreasing.

Step 1: Find the critical numbers of f.

$$f'(x) = \frac{2}{3}(x^2 - 9)^{-1/3}(2x) = \frac{4x}{3(x^2 - 9)^{1/3}}$$

Set $f'(x) = 0 \Rightarrow 4x = 0$ or $x = 0$.
Since $f'(x)$ is a rational function, $f'(x)$ is undefined at values where the denominator is 0. Thus, set $x^2 - 9 = 0 \Rightarrow x = 3$ or $x = -3$. Therefore the critical numbers are $-3, 0,$ and 3.

Step 2: Determine intervals.

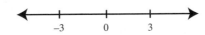

Intervals are $(-\infty, -3)$, $(-3, 0)$, $(0, 3)$ and $(3, -\infty)$.

Step 3: Set up a table.

Interval	$(-\infty, -3)$	$(-3, 0)$	$(0, 3)$	$(3, \infty)$
Test Point	−5	−1	1	5
$f'(x)$	−	+	−	+
$f(x)$	decr	incr	decr	incr

Step 4: Write a conclusion. Therefore $f(x)$ is increasing on [−3,0] and [3,∞) and decreasing on (−∞,−3] & [0,3]. (See Figure 4.2-6.)

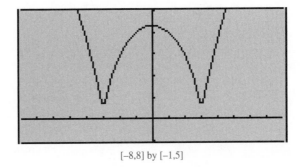

[−8,8] by [−1,5]

Figure 4.2-6

Example 5

The derivative of a function f is given as $f'(x) = \cos(x^2)$. Using a calculator, find the values of x on $\left[-\dfrac{\pi}{2}, \dfrac{\pi}{2}\right]$ such that f is increasing. (See Figure 4.2-7.)

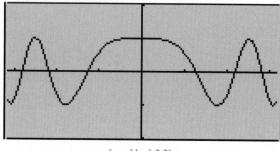

[-π,π] by [-2,2]

Figure 4.2-7

Using the zero function of the calculator, you obtain $x = 1.25331$ is a zero of f' on $\left[0, \dfrac{\pi}{2}\right]$. Since $f'(x) = \cos(x^2)$ is an even function, $x = -1.25331$ is also a zero on $\left[-\dfrac{\pi}{2}, 0\right]$. (See Figure 4.2-8.)

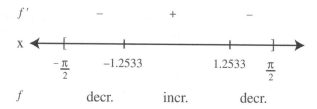

Figure 4.2-8

Thus f is increasing on $[-1.2533, 1.2533]$.

- Bubble in the right grid. You have to be careful in filling in the bubbles especially when you skip a question.

First Derivative Test and Second Derivative Test for Relative Extrema

First Derivative Test for Relative Extrema:

Let f be a continuous function and c be a critical number of f. (Figure 4.2-9.)

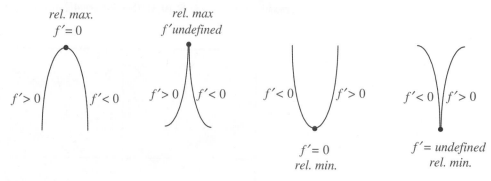

Figure 4.2-9

1. If $f'(x)$ changes from positive to negative at $x = c$ ($f' > 0$ for $x < c$ and $f' < 0$ for $x > c$), then f has a relative maximum at c.
2. If $f'(x)$ changes from negative to positive at $x = c$ ($f' < 0$ for $x < c$ and $f' > 0$ for $x > c$), then f has a relative minimum at c:

Second Derivative Test for Relative Extrema:

Let f be a continuous function at a number c.

1. If $f'(c) = 0$ and $f''(c) < 0$, then $f(c)$ is a relative minimum.
2. If $f'(c) = 0$ and $f''(c) > 0$, then $f(c)$ is a relative minimum.
3. If $f'(c) = 0$ and, $f''(c) = 0$, then the test is inconclusive. Use the first Derivative Test.

Example 1

See Figure 4.2-10. The graph of f', the derivative of a function f is shown in Figure 4.2-10. Find the relative extrema of f.

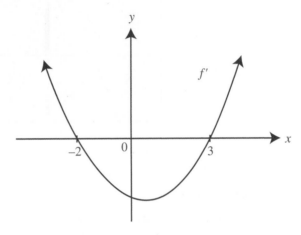

Figure 4.2-10

Solution: See Figure 4.2-11.

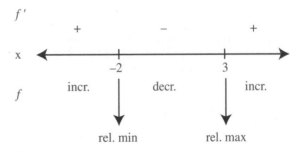

Figure 4.2-11

Thus f has a relative minimum at $x = -2$, and a relative maximum at $x = 3$.

Example 2

Find the relative extrema for the function $f(x) = \dfrac{x^3}{3} - x^2 - 3x$.

Step 1: Find $f'(x)$.

$$f'(x) = x^2 - 2x - 3$$

Step 2: Find all critical numbers of $f(x)$.
Note that $f'(x)$ is defined for all real numbers.
Set $f'(x) = 0$: $x^2 - 2x - 3 = 0 \Rightarrow (x - 3)(x + 1) = 0 \Rightarrow x = 3$ or $x = -1$.

Step 3: Find $f''(x)$: $f''(x) = 2x - 2$.

Step 4: Apply the Second Derivative Test.
$f''(3) = 2(3) - 2 = 4 \Rightarrow f(3)$ is a relative minimum.
$f''(-1) = 2(-1) - 2 = -4 \Rightarrow f(-1)$ is a relative maximum.
$f(3) = \dfrac{3^3}{3} - (3)^2 - 3(3) = -9$ and $f(-1) = \dfrac{5}{3}$.

Therefore, -9 is a relative minimum value of f and $\dfrac{5}{3}$ is a relative maximum value. (See Figure 4.2-12.)

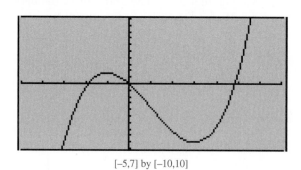

[−5,7] by [−10,10]

Figure 4.2-12

Example 3

Find the relative extrema for the function $f(x) = (x^2 - 1)^{2/3}$.
Using the First Derivative Test:

Step 1: Find $f'(x)$.
$$f'(x) = \frac{2}{3}(x^2 - 1)^{-1/3}(2x) = \frac{4x}{3(x^2 - 1)^{1/3}}.$$

Step 2: Find all critical numbers of f.
Set $f'(x) = 0$. Thus $4x = 0$ or $x = 0$.
Set $x^2 - 1 = 0$. Thus $f'(x)$ is undefined at $x = 1$ and $x = -1$. Therefore the critical numbers are $-1, 0, 1$.

Step 3: Determine intervals.

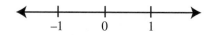

The intervals are $(-\infty, -1)$, $(-1, 0)$, $(0, 1)$, and $(1, \infty)$.

Step 4: Set up a table.

Interval	$(-\infty, -1)$	$x = -1$	$(-1, 0)$	$x = 0$	$(0, 1)$	$x = 1$	$(1, \infty)$
Test Point	−2		−1/2		1/2		2
$f'(x)$	−	undefined	+	0	−	undefined	+
$f(x)$	decr	rel min	incr	rel max	decr	rel min	incr

Step 5: Write a conclusion

Using the First Derivative Test, note that $f(x)$ has a relative maximum at $x = 0$ and relative minimum at $x = -1$ and $x = 1$.

Note that $f(-1) = 0$, $f(0) = 1$ and $f(1) = 0$. Therefore, 1 is a relative maximum value and 0 is a relative minimum value. (See Figure 4.2-13.)

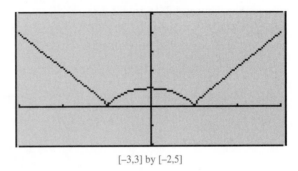

[-3,3] by [-2,5]

Figure 4.2-13

• Don't forget the constant, C, when you write the antiderivative after evaluating an indefinite integral, e.g., $\int \cos x\, dx = \sin x + C$.

Test for Concavity and Points of Inflection

Test for Concavity:

Let f be a differentiable function.

1. If $f'' > 0$ on an interval I, then f is concave upward on I.
2. If $f'' < 0$ on an interval I, then f is concave downward on I.

See Figures 4.2-14 and 4.2-15.

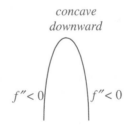

concave downward

$f'' < 0$ $f'' < 0$

Figure 4.2-14

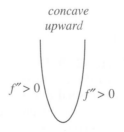

concave upward

$f'' > 0$ $f'' > 0$

Figure 4.2-15

A point P on a curve is a point of inflection if

1. the curve has a tangent line at P, and
2. the curve changes concavity at P (from concave upward to downward or from concave downward to upward).

See Figures 4.2-16 to 4.2-18.

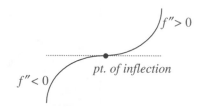

Figure 4.2-16

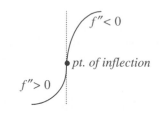

Figure 4.2-17

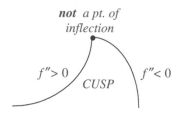

Figure 4.2-18

Note that if a point $(a, f(a))$ is a point of inflection, the $f''(c) = 0$ or $f''(c)$ does not exist. (The converse of the statement is not necessarily true.)

Note: There are some textbooks that define a point of inflection as a point where the concavity changes and do not require the existence of a tangent at the point of inflection. In that case, the point at the *cusp* in Figure 4.2-18 would be a point of inflection.

Example 1

See Figure 4.2-19. The graph of f', the derivative of a function f is shown in Figure 4.2-19 on page 135. Find the points of inflection of f and determine where the function f is concave upward and where it is concave downward on $[-3,5]$.

Solution: See Figure 4.2-20 on page 135.

Thus f is concave upward on $[-3,0)$ and $(3,5]$, and is concave downward on $(0,3)$.

There are two points of inflection: one at $x = 0$ and the other at $x = 3$.

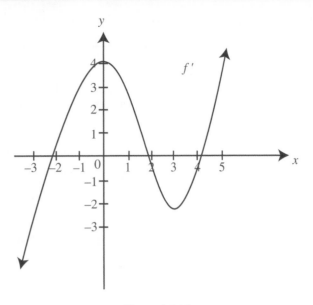

Figure 4.2-19

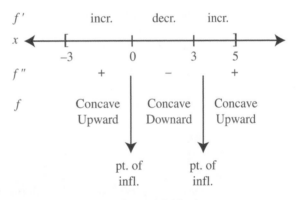

Figure 4.2-20

Example 2

Using a calculator, find the values of x at which the graph of $y = x^2 e^x$ changes concavity.

Enter $y_1 = x\char94 2 * e\char94 x$ and $y_2 = d(y_1(x), x, 2)$. The graph of y_2, the second derivative of y, is shown in Figure 4.2-21. Using the Zero function, you obtain $x = -3.41421$ and $x = -0.585786$. (See Figures 4.2-21 and 4.2-22.)

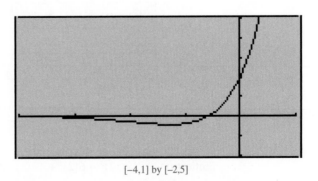

[−4,1] by [−2,5]

Figure 4.2-21

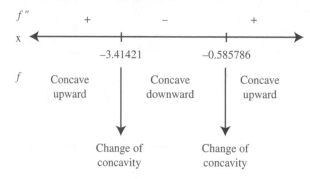

Figure 4.2-22

Thus, f changes concavity at $x = -341421$ and $x = -0.585786$.

Example 3

Find the points of inflection of $f(x) = x^3 - 6x^2 + 12x - 8$ and determine the intervals where the function f is concave upward and where it is concave downward.

Step 1: Find $f'(x)$ and $f''(x)$.

$$f'(x) = 3x^2 - 12x + 12$$
$$f''(x) = 6x - 12$$

Step 2: Set $f''(x) = 0$

$$6x - 12 = 0$$
$$x = 2$$

Note that $f''(x)$ is defined for all real numbers.

Step 3: Determine intervals.

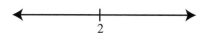

The intervals are $(-\infty, 2)$ and $(2, \infty)$.

Step 4: Set up a table.

Interval	$(-\infty, 2)$	$x = 2$	$(2, \infty)$
Test Point	0		5
$f''(x)$	−	0	+
$f(x)$	concave downward	point of inflection	concave upward

Since $f(x)$ has change of concavity at $x = 2$, the point $(2, f(2))$ is a point of inflection. $f(2) = (2)^3 - 6(2)^2 + 12(2) - 8 = 0$.

Step 5: Write a conclusion.
Thus $f(x)$ is concave downward on $(-\infty, 2)$, concave upward on $(2, \infty)$ and $f(x)$ has a point of inflection at $(2,0)$. (See Figure 4.2-23.)

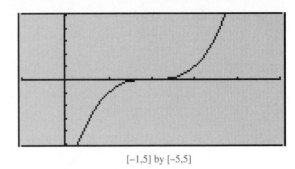

[−1,5] by [−5,5]

Figure 4.2-23

Example 4

Find the points of inflection of $f(x) = (x - 1)^{\frac{2}{3}}$ and determine the intervals where the function f is concave upward and where it is concave downward.

Step 1: Find $f'(x)$ and $f''(x)$.

$$f'(x) = \frac{2}{3}(x - 1)^{-\frac{1}{3}} = \frac{2}{3(x - 1)^{\frac{1}{3}}}$$

$$f''(x) = -\frac{2}{9}(x - 1)^{-\frac{1}{3}} = \frac{-2}{9(x - 1)^{\frac{4}{3}}}$$

Step 2: Find values of x where $f''(x) = 0$ or $f''(x)$ is undefined.
Note that $f''(x) \neq 0$ and that $f''(1)$ is undefined.

Step 3: Determine intervals.

1

The intervals are $(-\infty, 1)$, and $(1, \infty)$.

Step 4: Set up a table.

Interval	$(-\infty, 1)$	$x = 1$	$(1, \infty)$
Test Point	0		2
$f''(x)$	−	undefined	−
$f(x)$	concave downward	no change of inflection	concave downward

Note that $f(x)$ has no change of concavity at $x = 1$, f does not have a point of inflection.

Step 5: Write a conclusion.
Therefore $f(x)$ is concave downward on $(-\infty, \infty)$ and has no point of inflection. (See Figure 4.2-24.)

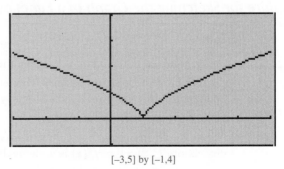

[−3,5] by [−1,4]

Figure 4.2-24

Example 5
The graph of *f* is shown in Figure 4.2-25 and *f* is twice differentiable, which of the following statements is true:

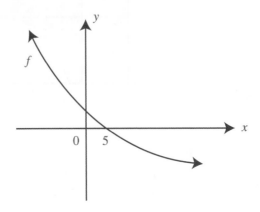

Figure 4.2-25

(A) $f(5) < f'(5) < f''(5)$

(B) $f''(5) < f'(5) < f(5)$

(C) $f'(5) < f(5) < f''(5)$

(D) $f'(5) < f''(5) < f(5)$

(E) $f''(5) < f(5) < f'(5)$

The graph indicates that (1) $f(5) = 0$, (2) $f'(5) < 0$, since *f* is decreasing; and (3) $f''(5) < 0$, since *f* is concave upward. Thus $f'(5) < f(5) < f''(5)$, choice (C).

> • Move on. Don't linger on a problem too long. You can earn many more points from other problems.

4.3   SKETCHING THE GRAPHS OF FUNCTIONS

Main Concepts: *Graphing without Calculators, Graphing with Calculators*

Graphing without Calculators

General Procedure for Sketching the Graph of a Function

Steps:

1. Determine the domain and if possible the range of the function $f(x)$.
2. Determine if the function has any symmetry i.e., if the function is even $(f(x) = f(-x))$; odd $(f(x) = -f(-x))$; or periodic $(f(x + p) = f(x))$
3. Find $f'(x)$ and $f''(x)$.
4. Find all critical numbers ($f'(x) = 0$ or $f'(x)$ is undefined) and possible points of inflection ($f''(x) = 0$ or $f''(x)$ is undefined).

5. Using the numbers in Step 4, determine the intervals on which to analyze $f(x)$.

6. Set up a table using the intervals, to
   (a) determine where $f(x)$ is increasing or decreasing.
   (b) find relative and absolute extrema.
   (c) find points of inflection.
   (d) determine the concavity of $f(x)$ on each interval.

7. Find any horizontal, vertical, or slant asymptotes.

8. If necessary, find the x-intercepts, the y-intercepts, and a few selected points.

9. Sketch the graph.

Example

Sketch the graph of $f(x) = \dfrac{x^2 - 4}{x^2 - 25}$.

Step 1: Domain: all real numbers $x \neq \pm 5$.

Step 2: Symmetry: $f(x)$ is an even function ($f(x) = f(-x)$); symmetrical with respect to y-axis.

Step 3: $f'(x) = \dfrac{(2x)(x^2 - 25) - (2x)(x^2 - 4)}{(x^2 - 25)^2} = \dfrac{-42x}{(x^2 - 25)^2}$

$f''(x) = \dfrac{-42(x^2 - 25)^2 - 2(x^2 - 25)(2x)(-42x)}{(x^2 - 25)^4} = \dfrac{42(3x^2 + 25)}{(x^2 - 25)^3}$

Step 4: Critical numbers:
$f'(x) = 0 \Rightarrow -42x = 0$ or $x = 0$
$f'(x)$ is undefined at $x = \pm 5$ which are not in the domain.

Possible points of inflection:
$f''(x) \neq 0$ and $f''(x)$ is undefined at $x = \pm 5$ which are not in the domain.

Step 5: Determine Intervals:

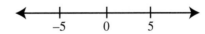

Intervals are $(-\infty, -5)$, $(-5, 0)$, $(0, 5)$ & $(5, \infty)$

Step 6: Set up a table:

Intervals	$(-\infty, -5)$	$x = -5$	$(-5, 0)$	$x = 0$	$(0, 5)$	$x = 5$	$(5, \infty)$
$f(x)$		undefined		4/25		undefined	
$f'(x)$	+	undefined	+	0	−	undefined	−
$f''(x)$	+	undefined	−	−	−	undefined	+
conclusion	incr concave upward		incr concave downward	rel max	decr concave downward		decr concave upward

Step 7: Vertical asymptote: $x = 5$ and $x = -5$
Horizontal asymptote: $y = 1$

Step 8: y-intercept: $\left(0, \dfrac{4}{25}\right)$

x-intercept: $(-2, 0)$ and $(2, 0)$

See Figure 4.3-1.

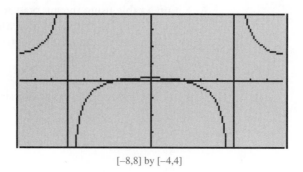

[−8,8] by [−4,4]

Figure 4.3-1

Graphing with Calculators

Example 1

Using a calculator, sketch the graph of $f(x) = -x^{5/3} + 3x^{2/3}$ indicating all relative extrema, points of inflection, horizontal and vertical asymptotes, intervals where $f(x)$ is increasing or decreasing, and intervals where $f(x)$ is concave upward or downward.

1. Domain: all real numbers; Range: all real numbers
2. No symmetry
3. Relative Minimum (0,0); Relative Maximum (1.2,2.03); Points of Inflection (−0.6,2.56)
4. No asymptote.
5. $f(x)$ is decreasing on $(-\infty,0]$, $[1.2,\infty)$; and increasing on $(0,1.2)$
6. Evaluating the $f''(x)$ on either side of the point of inflection (−0.6,2.56)

$$d\left(-x \wedge \left(\frac{5}{3}\right) + 3 * x \wedge \left(\frac{2}{3}\right), x, 2\right) \; x = -2 \rightarrow 0.19$$

$$d\left(-x \wedge \left(\frac{5}{3}\right) + 3 * x \wedge \left(\frac{2}{3}\right), x, 2\right) \; x = -1 \rightarrow -4.66$$

$\Rightarrow f(x)$ is concave upward on $(-\infty,-0.6)$ and concave downward on $(-0.6,\infty)$ (See Figure 4.3-2.)

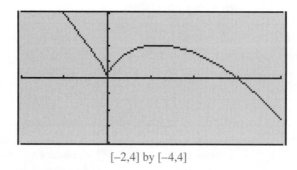

[−2,4] by [−4,4]

Figure 4.3-2

Example 2

Using a calculator, sketch the graph of $f(x) = e^{-x^2/2}$; indicating all relative minimum and maximum points; points of inflection, vertical and horizontal asymptotes, intervals on which $f(x)$ is increasing, decreasing, concave upward or concave downward.

1. Domain: all real numbers; Range $(0,1]$
2. Symmetry: $f(x)$ is an even function, and thus is symmetrical with respect to the y-axis.
3. Relative maximum: $(0,1)$
   No relative minimum
   Points of inflection: $(-1,0.6)$ and $(1,0.6)$
4. $y = 0$ is a horizontal asymptote; no vertical asymptote
5. $f(x)$ is increasing on $(-\infty,0]$ and decreasing on $[0,\infty)$
6. $f(x)$ is concave upward on $(-\infty,-1)$ and $(1,\infty)$; and concave downward on $(-1,1)$

See Figure 4.3-3.

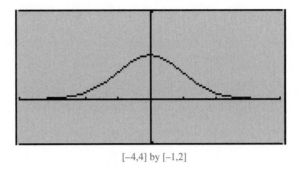

[−4,4] by [−1,2]

Figure 4.3-3

- When evaluating a definite integral, you don't have to write a constant C, e.g., $\int_1^3 2x\,dx = x^2\big|_1^3 = 8$. Notice, no C.

4.4   GRAPHS OF DERIVATIVES

The functions f, f', and f'' are interrelated, and so are their graphs. Therefore, you can usually infer from the graph of one of the three functions (f, f', or f'') and obtain information about the other two. Here are some examples.

Example 1

The graph of a function f is shown in Figure 4.4-1. Which of the following is true for f on (a,b)?

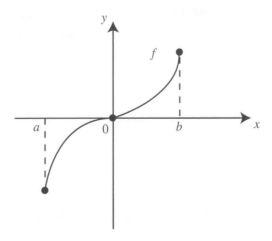

Figure 4.4-1

I. $f' \geq 0$ on (a,b)
II. $f'' > 0$ on (a,b)

Solution:

I. Since f is strictly increasing, $f' \geq 0$ on (a,b) is true.
II. The graph is concave downward on (a,0) and upward on (0,b). Thus $f'' > 0$ on (0,b) only. Therefore only statement I is true.

Example 2

Given the graph of f' in Figure 4.4-2, find where the function f (a) has its relative maximum(s) or relative minimums, (b) is increasing or decreasing, (c) has its point(s) of inflection, (d) is concave upward or downward, and (e) if $f(-2) = f(2) = 1$ and $f(0) = -3$, draw a sketch of f.

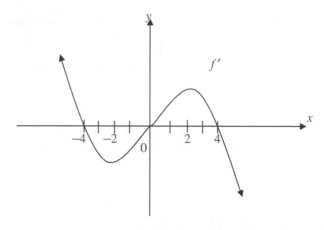

Figure 4.4-2

(a) Summarize the information of f' on a number line:

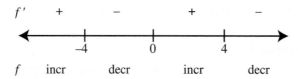

The function f has a relative maximum at $x = -4$ and at $x = 4$; and a relative minimum at $x = 0$.

(b) The function f is increasing on interval $(-\infty, -4]$ and $[0,4]$, and f is decreasing on $[-4,0]$ and $[4,\infty)$.

(c) Summarize the information of f' on a number line:

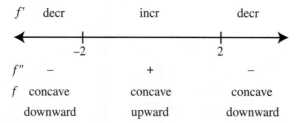

A change of concavity occurs at $x = -2$ and at $x = 2$ and f' exists at $x = -2$ and at $x = 2$, which implies that there is a tangent line to the graph of f at $x = -2$ and at $x = 2$. Therefore, f has a point of inflection at $x = -2$ and at $x = 2$.

(d) The graph of f is concave upward on the interval $(-2,2)$ and concave downward on $(-\infty,-2)$ and $(2,\infty)$.

(e) A sketch of the graph of f is shown in Figure 4.4-3.

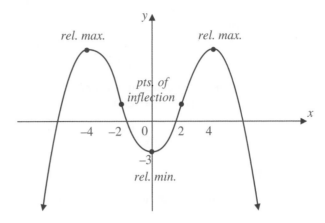

Figure 4.4-3

Example 3

Given the graph of f' in Figure 4.4-4, find where the function f (a) has a horizontal tangent, (b) has its relative extrema, (c) is increasing or decreasing, (d) has a point of inflection, and (e) is concave upward or downward.

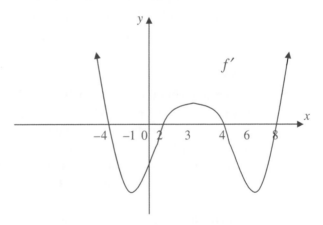

Figure 4.4-4

(a) $f'(x) = 0$ at $x = -4, 2, 4, 8$. Thus f has a horizontal tangent at these values.

(b) Summarize the information of f' on a number line:

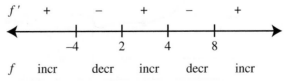

The first Derivative Test indicates that f has a relative maximum at $x = -4$ and 4; and f has a relative minimum at $x = 2$ and 8.

(c) The function f is increasing on $(-8,-4]$, $[2,4]$ and $[8,\infty)$ and is decreasing on $[-4,2]$ and $[4,8]$.

(d) Summarize the information of f' on a number line:

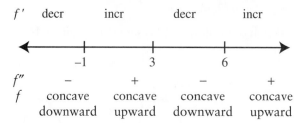

A change of concavity occurs at $x = -1$, 3, and 6. Since $f'(x)$ exists, f has a tangent at every point. Therefore, f has a point of inflection at $x = -1$, 3, and 6.

(e) The function f is concave upward on $(-1,3)$ and $(6,\infty)$ and concave downward on $(-\infty,-1)$ and $(3,6)$.

Example 4

A function f is continuous on the interval $[-4,3]$ with $f(-4) = 6$ and $f(3) = 2$ and the following properties:

Intervals	$(-4,-2)$	$x = -2$	$(-2,1)$	$x = 1$	$(1,3)$
f'	–	0	–	undefined	+
f''	+	0	–	undefined	–

(a) Find the intervals on which f is increasing or decreasing.
(b) Fund where f has its absolute extrema.
(c) Find where f has the points of inflection.
(d) Find the intervals on where f is concave upward or downward.
(e) Sketch a possible graph of f.

Solution:

(a) The graph of f is increasing on $[1,3]$ and decreasing on $[-4,-2]$ and $[-2,1]$.
(b) At $x = -4$, $f(x) = 6$. The function decreases until $x = 1$ and increases back to 2 at $x = 3$. Thus, f has its absolute maximum at $x = -4$ and its absolute minimum at $x = 1$.
(c) A change of concavity occurs at $x = -2$, and since $f'(-2) = 0$ which implies a tangent lines exists at $x = -2$, thus f has a point of infection at $x = -2$.
(d) The graph of f is concave upward on $(-4,-2)$ and concave downward on $(-2,1)$ and $(1,3)$.
(e) A possible sketch of f is shown in Figure 4.4-5.

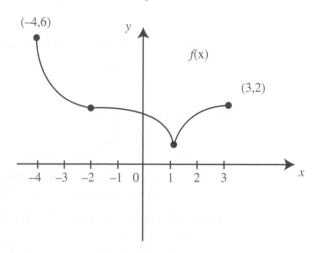

Figure 4.4-5

Example 5

If $f(x) = \left|\ln(x + 1)\right|$, find $\lim\limits_{x \to 0^-} f'(x)$. (See Figure 4.4-6.)

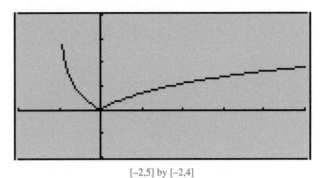

[–2,5] by [–2,4]

Figure 4.4-6

The domain of f is $(-1, \infty)$.

$f(0) = \left|\ln(0 + 1)\right| = \left|\ln(1)\right| = 0$

$$f(x) = \left|\ln(x + 1)\right| = \begin{cases} \ln(x + 1) & \text{if } x > 0 \\ -\ln(x + 1) & \text{if } x > 0 \end{cases}.$$

Thus, $f'(x) = \begin{cases} \dfrac{1}{x + 1} & \text{if } x > 0 \\ -\dfrac{1}{x + 1} & \text{if } x > 0 \end{cases}$

Therefore, $\lim\limits_{x \to 0^-} f'(x) = \lim\limits_{x \to 0^-}\left(-\dfrac{1}{x + 1}\right) = -1$.

4.5 RAPID REVIEW

1. If $f'(x) = x^2 - 4$, find the intervals where f is decreasing. (See Figure 4.5-1.)

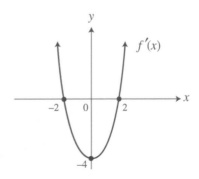

Figure 4.5-1

Answers: Since $f'(x) < 0$ if $-2 < x < 2$, f is decreasing on $(-2,2)$.

2. If $f''(x) = 2x - 6$ and f' is continuous, find the values of x where f has a point of inflection. (See Figure 4.5-2.)

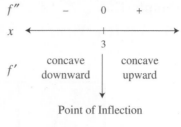

Figure 4.5-2

Answers: Thus f has a point of inflection at $x = 3$.

3. See Figure 4.5-3. Find the values of x where f has a change of concavity.

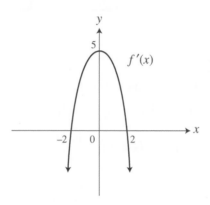

Figure 4.5-3

Answers: f has a change of concavity at $x = 0$. See Figure 4.5-4.

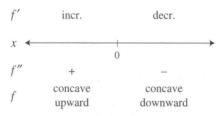

Figure 4.5-4

4. See Figure 4.5-5. Find the values of x where f has a relative minimum.

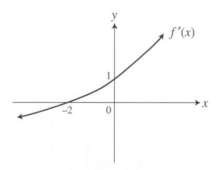

Figure 4.5-5

Answers: Thus, *f* has a relative minimum at $x = -2$. See Figure 4.5-6.

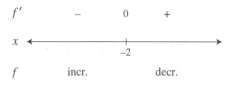

Figure 4.5-6

5. See Figure 4.5-7. Given *f* is twice differentiable, arrange $f(10)$, $f'(10)$, $f''(10)$ from smallest to largest.

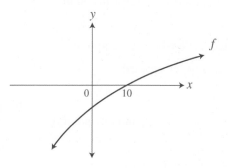

Figure 4.5-7

Answers: $f(10) = 0$, $f'(10) > 0$ since *f* is increasing and $f''(10) < 0$ since *f* is concave downward. Thus the order is $f''(10)$, $f(10)$, $f'(10)$.

6. See Figure 4.5-8. Find the values of *x* where f' is concave up.

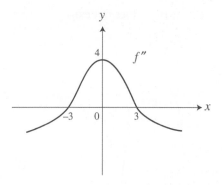

Figure 4.5-8

Answers: Thus, f' is concave upward on $(-\infty, 0)$. See Figure 4.5-9.

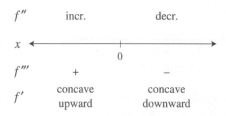

Figure 4.5-9

4.6 PRACTICE PROBLEMS

Part A—The use of a calculator is not allowed.

1. If $f(x) = x^3 - x^2 - 2x$, show that the hypotheses of Rolle's Theorem are satisfied on the interval $[-1,2]$ and find all values of c that satisfy the conclusion of the theorem.

2. Let $f(x) = e^x$. Show that the hypotheses of the Mean Value Theorem are satisfied on $[0, 1]$ and find all values of c that satisfy the conclusion of the theorem.

3. Determine the intervals in which the graph of $f(x) = \dfrac{x^2 + 9}{x^2 - 25}$ is concave upward or downward.

4. Given $f(x) = x + \sin x \ 0 \le x \le 2\pi$, find any points of inflection of f.

5. Show that the absolute minimum of $f(x) = \sqrt{25 - x^2}$ on $[-5,5]$ is 0 and the absolute maximum is 5.

6. Given the function f in Figure 4.6-1, identify the points where:

   (a) $f' < 0$ and $f'' > 0$,   (b) $f' < 0$ and $f'' < 0$,

   (c) $f' = 0$ (d) f'' does not exist.

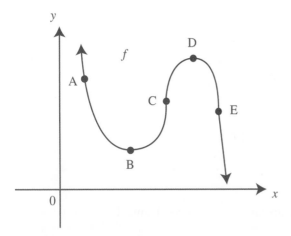

Figure 4.6-1

7. Given the graph of f'' in Figure 4.6-2, determine the values of x at which the function f has a point of inflection. (See Figure 4.6-2.)

8. If $f''(x) = x^2(x + 3)(x - 5)$, find the values of x at which the graph of f has a change of concavity.

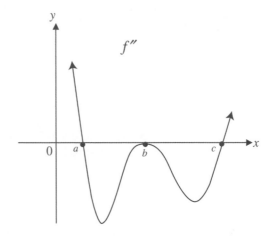

Figure 4.6-2

9. The graph of f' on $[-3,3]$ is shown in Figure 4.6-3.

   Find the values of x on $[-3,3]$ such that (a) f is increasing and (b) f is concave downward.

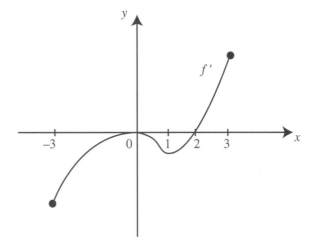

Figure 4.6-3

10. The graph of f is shown in Figure 4.6-4 on page 149 and f is twice differentiable. Which of the following has the largest value:

    (A) $f(-1)$

    (B) $f'(-1)$

    (C) $f''(-1)$

    (D) $f(-1)$ and $f'(-1)$

    (E) $f'(-1)$ and $f''(-1)$

    Sketch the graphs of the following functions indicating any relative and absolute extrema, points of inflection, intervals on which the function is increasing, decreasing, concave upward or concave downward.

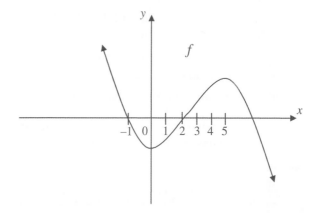

Figure 4.6-4

11. $f(x) = x^4 - x^2$

12. $f(x) = \dfrac{x + 4}{x - 4}$

Part B—Calculators are permitted.

13. Given the graph of f' in Figure 4.6-5, determine at which of the four values of x (x_1, x_2, x_3, x_4) does f have

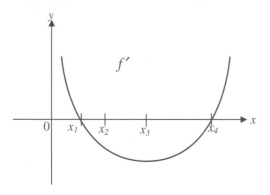

Figure 4.6-5

(a) the largest value,

(b) the smallest value,

(c) a point of inflection,

(d) and at which of the four values of x does f'' have the largest value.

14. Given the graph of f in Figure 4.6-6, determine at which values of x is

(a) $f'(x) = 0$

(b) $f''(x) = 0$

(c) f' a decreasing function.

Figure 4.6-6

15. A function f is continuous on the interval $[-2,5]$ with $f(-2) = 10$ and $f(5) = 6$ and the following properties:

Intervals	(−2,1)	x = 1	(1,3)	x = 3	(3,5)
f'	+	0	−	undefined	+
f''	−	0	−	undefined	+

(a) Find the intervals on which f is increasing or decreasing.

(b) Find where f has its absolute extrema.

(c) Find where f has points of inflection.

(d) Find the intervals where f is concave upward or downward.

(e) Sketch a possible graph of f.

16. Given the graph of f' in Figure 4.6-7, find where the function f (a) has its relative extrema (b) is increasing or decreasing (c) has its point(s) of inflection, (d) is concave upward or downward, and (e) if $f(0) = 1$ and $f(6) = 5$, draw a sketch of f.

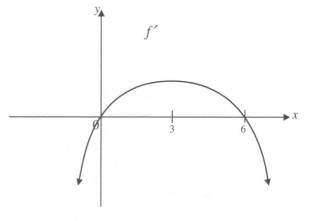

Figure 4.6-7

17. If $f(x) = |x^2 - 6x - 7|$, which of the following statements about f are true?

    I. f has a relative maximum at $x = 3$.

    II. f is differentiable at $x = 7$.

    III. f has a point of inflection at $x = -1$.

18. How many points of inflection does the graph of $y = \cos(x^2)$ have on the interval $[-\pi, \pi]$?

Sketch the graphs of the following functions indicating any relative extrema, points of inflection, asymptotes, and intervals where the function is increasing, decreasing, concave upward, or concave downward.

19. $f(x) = 3e^{-x^2/2}$

20. $f(x) = \cos x \sin^2 x \ [0, 2\pi]$

4.7 CUMULATIVE REVIEW PROBLEMS

"Calculator" indicates that calculators are permitted.

21. Find $\dfrac{dy}{dx}$ if $(x^2 + y^2)^2 = 10xy$

22. Evaluate $\displaystyle\lim_{x \to 0} \dfrac{\sqrt{x + 9} - 3}{x}$

23. Find $\dfrac{d^2y}{dx^2}$ if $y = \cos(2x) + 3x^2 - 1$

24. (Calculator) Determine the value of k such that the function

$$f(x) = \begin{cases} x^2 - 1, x \le 1 \\ 2x + k, x > 1 \end{cases} \text{ is continuous for all}$$

real numbers.

25. A function f is continuous on the interval $[-1, 4]$ with $f(-1) = 0$ and $f(4) = 2$ and the following properties:

Intervals	$(-1,0)$	$x = 0$	$(0,2)$	$x = 2$	$(2,4)$
f'	$+$	undefined	$+$	0	$-$
f''	$+$	undefined	$-$	0	$-$

(a) Find the intervals on which f is increasing or decreasing.

(b) Find where f has its absolute extrema.

(c) Find where f has points of inflection.

(d) Find where intervals on where f is concave upward or downward.

(e) Sketch a possible graph of f.

4.8 SOLUTIONS TO PRACTICE PROBLEMS

Part A—No calculators.

1. Condition 1: Since $f(x)$ is a polynomial, it is continuous on $[-1, 2]$.

   Condition 2: Also, $f(x)$ is differentiable on $[-1, 2]$ because $f'(x) = 3x^2 - 2x - 2$ is defined for all numbers in $[-1, 2]$.

   Condition 3: $f(-1) = f(2) = 0$. Thus $f(x)$ satisfies the hypotheses of Rolle's Theorem which means there exists a c in $[-1, 2]$ such that $f'(c) = 0$. Set $f'(x) = 3x^2 - 2x - 2 = 0$. Solve $3x^2 - 2x - 2 = 0$, using the quadratic formula and obtain

   $x = \dfrac{1 \pm \sqrt{7}}{3}$. Thus $x \approx 1.215$ or -0.549 and

   both values are in the interval $(-1, 2)$. Therefore

   $c = \dfrac{1 \pm \sqrt{7}}{3}$.

2. Condition 1: $f(x) = e^x$ is continuous on $[0, 1]$.

   Condition 2: $f(x)$ is differentiable on $[0, 1]$ since $f'(x) = e^x$ is defined for all numbers in $[0, 1]$. Thus, there exists a number c in $[0, 1]$ such

   that $f'(c) = \dfrac{e^1 - e^0}{1 - 0} = (e - 1)$. Set $f'(x) = e^x = (e - 1)$. Thus $e^x = (e - 1)$. Take $\ln$ of both sides. $\ln(e^x) = \ln(e - 1) \Rightarrow x = \ln(e - 1)$. Thus $x \approx 0.541$ which is in the $(0, 1)$. Therefore $c = \ln(e - 1)$.

3. $f(x) = \dfrac{x^2 + 9}{x^2 - 25}, f'(x)$

$= \dfrac{2x(x^2 - 25) - (2x)(x^2 + 9)}{(x^2 - 25)^2}$

$= \dfrac{-68x}{(x^2 - 25)^2}$ and

$f''(x) = \dfrac{-68(x^2 - 25)^2 - 2(x^2 - 25)(2x)(-68x)}{(x^2 - 25)^4}$

$= \dfrac{68(3x^2 + 25)}{(x^2 - 25)^3}$

Set $f'' > 0$. Since $(3x^2 + 25) > 0, \Rightarrow (x^2 - 25)^3 > 0$ $\Rightarrow x^2 - 25 > 0$, so $x < -5$ or $x > 5$. Thus $f(x)$ is concave upward on $(-\infty, -5)$ and $(5, \infty)$ and concave downward on $(-5, 5)$.

4. Step 1: $f(x) = x + \sin x, f'(x) = 1 + \cos x, f''(x) = -\sin x$.

   Step 2: Set $f''(x) = 0 \Rightarrow -\sin x = 0$ or $x = 0, \pi, 2\pi$

   Step 3: Check intervals.

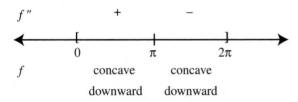

   Step 4: Check for tangent line:

   At $x = \pi, f'(x) = 1 + (-1) = 0 \Rightarrow$ there is a tangent line at $x = \pi$.

   Step 5: Thus (π, π) is a point of inflection.

5. Step 1: Rewrite $f(x)$ as $f(x) = (25 - x^2)^{1/2}$.

   Step 2: $f'(x) = \dfrac{1}{2}(25 - x^2)^{-1/2}(-2x)$

   $= \dfrac{-x}{(25 - x^2)^{1/2}}$

   Step 3: Find critical numbers. $f'(x) = 0$; at $x = 0$; and $f'(x)$ is undefined at $x = \pm 5$.

   Step 4:
   $$f''(x) = \dfrac{(-1)(25 - x^2)^{1/2} - \dfrac{1}{2}(25 - x^2)^{-1/2}(-2x)(-x)}{(25 - x^2)}$$

   $$= \dfrac{-1}{(25 - x)^{1/2}} - \dfrac{x^2}{(25 - x^2)^{3/2}}$$

$f'(0) = 0$ and $f''(0) = -\dfrac{1}{5}$ (and $f(0) = 5$) $\Rightarrow (0, 5)$ is a relative maximum. Since $f(5)$ and $f(-5)$ are both undefined, use the First Derivative Test. The domain of f is $[-5, 5]$.

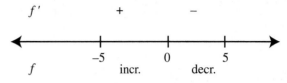

Since $x = -5$ and $x = 5$ are endpoints of $[-5, 5]$, and $f(-5) = f(5) = 0$, and there are no other relative minimum points, thus 0 is the absolute minimum value. Similarly, since there is only one relative maximum value and it is greater than $f(x)$ at the endpoints, the point $(0, 5)$ is the absolute maximum point and 5 is the absolute maximum value.

6. (a) Point A $f' < 0 \Rightarrow$ decreasing and $f'' > 0 \Rightarrow$ concave upward.

   (b) Point E $f' < 0 \Rightarrow$ decreasing and $f'' < 0 \Rightarrow$ concave downward.

   (c) Point B and D $f' = 0 \Rightarrow$ horizontal tangent.

   (d) Point C f'' does not exist $\Rightarrow$ vertical tangent.

7. A change in concavity $\Rightarrow$ a point of inflection. At $x = a$, there is a change of concavity; f'' goes from positive to negative $\Rightarrow$ concavity changes from upward to downward. At $x = c$, there is a change of concavity; f'' goes from negative to positive $\Rightarrow$ concavity changes from downward to upward. Therefore f has two points of inflection, one at $x = a$ and the other at $x = c$.

8. Set $f(x) = 0$. Thus $x^2(x + 3)(x - 5) = 0 \Rightarrow x = 0$, $x = -3$ or $x = 5$. (See Figure 4.8-1.)

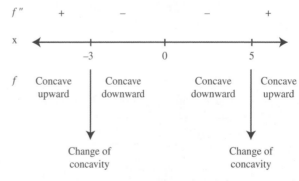

Figure 4.8-1

Thus f has a change of concavity at $x = -3$ and at $x = 5$.

9. See Figure 4.8-2.

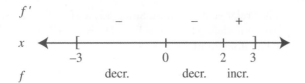

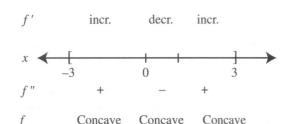

Figure 4.8-2

Thus f is increasing on [2,3] and concave downward on (0,1)

10. The correct answer is (A)

$f(-1) = 0$; $f'(-1) < 0$ since f is decreasing and $f''(-1) < 0$ since f is concave downward. Thus $f(-1)$ has the largest value.

11. Step 1: Domain: all real numbers.

Step 2: Symmetry: Even function $(f(x) = f(-x))$; symmetrical with respect to the y-axis.

Step 3: $f'(x) = 4x^3 - 2x$ and $f''(x) = 12x^2 - 2$.

Step 4: Critical numbers:

$f'(x)$ is defined for all real numbers. Set $f'(x) = 4x^3 - 2x = 0 \Rightarrow 2x(2x^2 - 1) = 0 \Rightarrow x = 0$ or $x = \pm\sqrt{1/2}$.

Possible points of inflection:

$f''(x)$ is defined for all real numbers. Set $f''(x) = 12x^2 - 2 = 0 \Rightarrow 2(6x^2 - 1) = 0 \Rightarrow x = \pm\sqrt{1/6}$.

Step 5: Determine intervals:

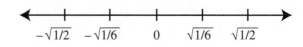

Intervals are: , $\left(-\infty,-\sqrt{1/2}\right)$, $\left(-\sqrt{1/2},-\sqrt{1/6}\right)$, $\left(-\sqrt{1/6},0\right)$, $\left(0,\sqrt{1/6}\right)$, $\left(\sqrt{1/6},\sqrt{1/2}\right)$, $\left(\sqrt{1/2},\infty\right)$.

Since $f'(x)$ is symmetrical with respect to the y-axis, you only need to examine half of the intervals.

Step 6: Set up a table (See Table 4.8-1.)

Step 7: Sketch the graph. (See Figure 4.8-3.)

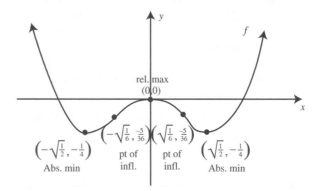

Figure 4.8-3

12. Step 1: Domain: all real numbers $x \neq 4$.

Step 2: Symmetry: none

Step 3: Find f' and f''.

$$f'(x) = \frac{(1)(x - 4) - (1)(x + 4)}{(x - 4)^2}$$

$$= \frac{-8}{(x - 4)^2}, f''(x) = \frac{16}{(x - 4)^3}$$

Step 4: Critical numbers:

$f'(x) \neq 0$ and $f'(x)$ is undefined at $x = 4$.

Table 4.8-1

Intervals	$x = 0$	$\left(0, \sqrt{1/6}\right)$	$x = \sqrt{1/6}$	$\left(\sqrt{1/6}, \sqrt{1/2}\right)$	$x = \sqrt{1/2}$	$\left(\sqrt{1/2}, \infty\right)$
$f(x)$	0		-5/36		-1/4	
$f'(x)$	0	-	-	-	0	+
$f''(x)$	-	-	0	+	+	+
conclusion	rel max	decr concave downward	decr pt. of inflection	decr concave upward	rel min	incr concave upward

The function has an absolute minimum value of (-1/4) and no absolute maximum value.

Step 5: Determine intervals.

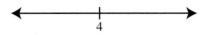

Intervals are $(-\infty, 4)$ and $(4, \infty)$.

Step 6: Set up table as below:

Interval	$(-\infty,4)$	$(4,\infty)$
f'	−	−
f''	−	+
conclusion	Decr Concave downward	Incr Concave upward

Step 7: Horizontal asymptote:

$$\lim_{x\to\pm\infty}\frac{x+4}{x-4} = 1;\text{ Thus, } y = 1 \text{ is a}$$

horizontal asymptote.

Vertical asymptote:

$$\lim_{x\to 4^+}\frac{x+4}{x-4} = \infty \text{ and } \lim_{x\to 4^-}\frac{x+4}{x-4} = -\infty;$$

Thus, $x = 4$ is a vertical asymptote.

Step 8: x-intercept: Set $f'(x) = 0 \Rightarrow x + 4 = 0$; $x = -4$

y-intercept: Set $x = 0 \Rightarrow f(x) = -1$.

Step 9: Sketch the graph. (See Figure 4.8-4.)

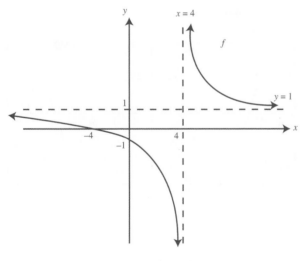

Figure 4.8-4

13. (a)

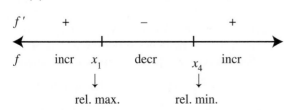

The function f has the largest value (of the four choices) at $x = x_1$.

(b) And f has the smallest value at $x = x_4$.

(c)

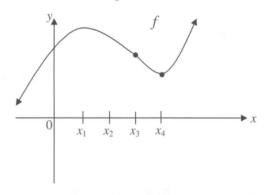

A change of concavity occurs at $x = x_3$, and $f'(x_3)$ exists which implies there is a tangent to f at $x = x_3$. Thus, at $x = x_3$, f has a point of inflection.

(d) The function f'' represents the slope of the tangent to f'. The graph indicates that the slope of the tangent to f' is the largest at $x = x_4$. (See Figure 4.8-5.)

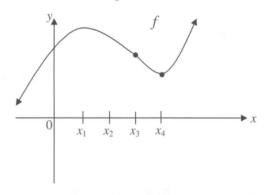

Figure 4.8-5

14. (a) Since $f'(x)$ represents the slope of the tangent, $f'(x) = 0$ at $x = 0$, and $x = 5$.

(b) At $x = 2$, f has a point of inflection which implies that if $f''(x)$ exists, $f''(x) = 0$. Since $f'(x)$ is differentiable for all numbers in the domain, $f''(x)$ exists, and $f''(x) = 0$ at $x = 2$.

(c) Since the function f is concave downwards on $(2,\infty)$, $f'' < 0$ on $(2,\infty)$ which implies f' is decreasing on $(2,\infty)$.

15. (a) The function f is increasing on the intervals $[-2,1]$ and $[3,5]$.

(b) The absolute maximum occurs at $x = 1$, since it is a relative maximum, $f(1) > f(-2)$ and $f(5) < f(-2)$. Similarly, the absolute minimum occurs at $x = 3$, since it is a relative minimum, and $f(3) < f(5) < f(-2)$.

(c) No point of inflection. (Note that at $x = 3$ f has a cusp.)

Note: Some textbooks define a point of inflection as a point where the concavity changes and do not require the existence of a tangent. In that case, at $x = 3$, f has a point of inflection.

(d) Concave upward on (3, 5) and concave downward on (−2, 3).

(e) A possible graph is shown in Figure 4.8-6.

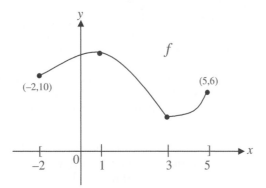

Figure 4.8-6

16. (a)

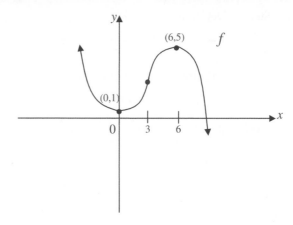

Figure 4.8-7

The function f has its relative minimum at $x = 0$ and its relative maximum at $x = 6$.

(b) The function f is increasing on [0,6] and decreasing on (−∞,0] and [6,∞).

(c)

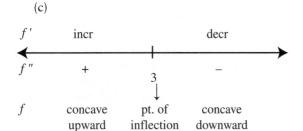

Since $f'(3)$ exists and a change of concavity occurs at $x = 3$, f has a point of inflection at $x = 3$.

(d) Concave upward on (−∞,3) and downward on (3,∞).

(e) Sketch a graph. (See Figure 4.8-7.)

17. See Figure 4.8-8.

The graph of f indicates that a relative maximum occurs at $x = 3$, f is not differentiable at $x = 7$, since there is a *cusp* at $x = 7$ and f does not have a point of inflection at $x = -1$, since there is no tangent line at $x = -1$. Thus, only statement I is true.

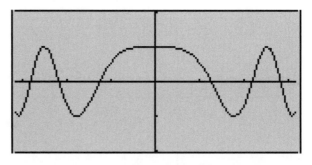

[−5,10] by [−5,20]

Figure 4.8-8

18. See Figure 4.8-9.

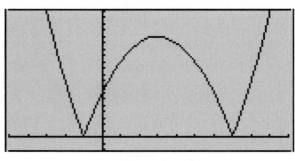

[−π,π] by [−2,2]

Figure 4.8-9

Enter $y_1 = \cos(x^2)$

Using the Inflection function of your calculator, you obtain three points of inflection on [0, π]. The points of inflection occur at $x = 1.35521$, 2.1945 and 2.81373. Since $y_1 = \cos(x^2)$, is an even function; there is a total of 6 points of inflection on [−π, π]. An alternate solution is to enter $y_2 = \dfrac{d^2}{dx^2}(y_1(x), x, 2)$. The graph of y_2 indicates that there are 6 zero's on [−π, π].

19. Enter $y_1 = 3 * e \wedge (-x \wedge 2/2)$. Note that the graph has a symmetry about the y-axis. Using the functions of the calculator, you will find:

(a) a relative maximum point at $(0,3)$, which is also the absolute maximum point;

(b) points of inflection at $(-1,1.819)$ and $(1,1.819)$;

(c) $y = 0$ (the x-axis) a horizontal asymptote;

(d) y_1 increasing on $(-\infty,0]$ and decreasing on $[0,\infty)$; and

(e) y_1 concave upward on $(-\infty,-1)$ and $(1,\infty)$ and concave downward on $(-1,1)$. (See Figure 4.8-10.)

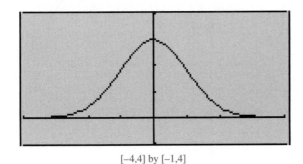

[−4,4] by [−1,4]

Figure 4.8-10

20. (See Figure 4.8-11.) Enter $y_1 = \cos(x) * (\sin(x))$ $\wedge 2$. A fundamental domain of y_1 is $[0,2\pi]$. Using the functions of the calculator, you will find:

(a) relative maximum points at $(0.955,0.385)$, $(\pi,0)$ and $(5.328,0.385)$ and relative minimum points at $(2.186,-0.385)$ and $(4.097,-0.385)$;

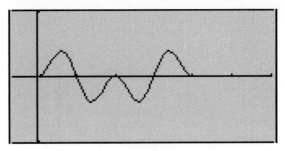

[−1,9.4] by [−1,1]

Figure 4.8-11

(b) points of inflection at $(0.491,0.196)$, $\left(\dfrac{\pi}{2},0\right)$, $(2.651,-0.196)$, $(3.632,-0.196)$, $\left(\dfrac{3\pi}{2},0\right)$ and $(5.792,0.196)$;

(c) no asymptote;

(d) function is increasing on intervals $(0,0.955)$, $(2.186,\pi)$ and $(4.097,5.328)$ and decreasing on intervals $(0.955,2.186)$, $(\pi,4.097)$ and $(5.328,2\pi)$;

(e) function is concave upwards on intervals $(0,0.491)$, $\left(\dfrac{\pi}{2},2.651\right)$, $\left(3.632,\dfrac{3\pi}{2}\right)$, and $(5.792, 2\pi)$ and concave downward on the intervals $\left(0.491,\dfrac{\pi}{2}\right)$, , $(2.651,3.632)$ and $\left(\dfrac{3\pi}{2},5.792\right)$.

4.9 SOLUTIONS TO CUMULATIVE REVIEW PROBLEMS

21. $(x^2 + y^2)^2 = 10xy$

$$2(x^2 + y^2)\left(2x + 2y\frac{dy}{dx}\right) = 10y + (10x)\frac{dy}{dx}$$

$$4x(x^2 + y^2) + 4y(x^2 + y^2)\frac{dy}{dx} = 10y + (10x)\frac{dy}{dx}$$

$$4y(x^2 + y^2)\frac{dy}{dx} - (10x)\frac{dy}{dx} = 10y - 4x(x^2 + y^2)$$

$$\frac{dy}{dx}\left(4y(x^2 + y^2) - 10x\right) = 10y - 4x(x^2 + y^2)$$

$$\frac{dy}{dx} = \frac{10y - 4x(x^2 + y^2)}{4y(x^2 + y^2) - 10x} = \frac{5y - 2x(x^2 + y^2)}{2y(x^2 + y^2) - 5x}$$

22. $\displaystyle\lim_{x \to 0}\frac{\sqrt{x + 9} - 3}{x} = \lim_{x \to 0}\frac{\left(\sqrt{x + 9} - 3\right)}{x} \cdot \frac{\left(\sqrt{x + 9} + 3\right)}{\left(\sqrt{x + 9} + 3\right)}$

$$= \lim_{x \to 0}\frac{(x + 9) - 9}{x\left(\sqrt{x + 9} + 3\right)}$$

$$= \lim_{x \to 0}\frac{x}{x\left(\sqrt{x + 9} + 3\right)}$$

$$= \lim_{x \to 0}\frac{1}{\sqrt{x + 9} + 3} = \frac{1}{\sqrt{0 + 9} + 3}$$

$$= \frac{1}{3 + 3} = \frac{1}{6}.$$

23. $y = \cos(2x) + 3x^2 - 1$

$\dfrac{dy}{dx} = \left[-\sin(2x)\right](2) + 6x = -2\sin(2x) + 6x$

$\dfrac{d^2y}{dx^2} = -2(\cos(2x))(2) + 6 = -4\cos(2x) + 6.$

24. (Calculator) The function f is continuous everywhere for all values of k except possibly at $x = 1$. Checking with the three conditions of continuity at $x = 1$:

(1) $f(1) = (1)^2 - 1 = 0$

(2) $\lim\limits_{x \to 1^+}(2x + k) = 2 + k$, $\lim\limits_{x \to 1^-}(x^2 - 1) = 0$;
thus $2 + k = 0 \Rightarrow k = -2$. Since
$\lim\limits_{x \to 1^+} f(x) = \lim\limits_{x \to 1^-} f(x) = 0$, therefore
$\lim\limits_{x \to 1} f(x) = 0.$

(3) $f(1) = \lim\limits_{x \to 1} f(x) = 0$. Thus, $k = -2$.

25. (a) Since $f' > 0$ on $(-1,0)$ and $(0,2)$, the function f is increasing on the intervals $[-1,0]$ and $[0,2]$. And $f' < 0$ on $(2,4)$, f is decreasing on $[2,4]$.

(b) The absolute maximum occurs at $x = 2$, since it is a relative maximum and it is the only relative extremum on $(-1,4)$. The absolute minimum occurs at $x = -1$, since

$f(-1) < f(4)$ and the function has no relative minimum on $[-1,4]$.

(c) A change of concavity occurs at $x = 0$. However, $f'(0)$ is undefined, which implies f may or may not have a tangent at $x = 0$. Thus f may or may not have a point of inflection at $x = 0$.

(d) Concave upward on $(-1,0)$ and concave downward on $(0,4)$.

(e) A possible graph is shown in Figure 4.9-1.

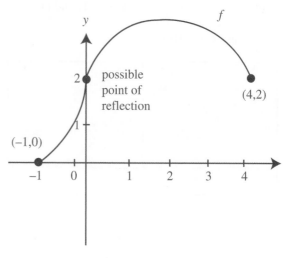

Figure 4.9-1

Chapter 5

Applications of Derivatives

5.1 RELATED RATE

Main Concepts: *General Procedure for Solving Related Rate Problems, Common Related Rate Problems, Inverted Cone (Water Tank) Problem, Shadow Problem, Angle of Elevation Problem*

General Procedure for Solving Related Rate Problems

1. Read the problem and if appropriate, draw a diagram.
2. Represent the given information and the unknowns by mathematical symbols.
3. Write an equation involving the rate of change to be determined. (If the equation contains more than one variable, it may be necessary to reduce the equation to one variable.)
4. Differentiate each term of the equation with respect to time.
5. Substitute all known values and known rates of change into the resulting equation.
6. Solve the resulting equation for the desired rate of change.
7. Write the answer and, if given, indicate the units of measure.

Common Related Rate Problems

Example 1

When area of a square is increasing twice as fast as its diagonals, what is the length of a side of the square?

Let z represent the diagonal of the square. The area of a square is $A = \dfrac{z^2}{2}$.

$$\frac{dA}{dt} = 2z\frac{dz}{dt}\left(\frac{1}{2}\right) = z\frac{dz}{dt}.$$

Since $\dfrac{dA}{dt} = 2\dfrac{dz}{dt}$, $2\dfrac{dz}{dt} = z\dfrac{dz}{dt} \Rightarrow z = 2$

Let s be a side of the square. Since the diagonal $z = 2$, then $s^2 + s^2 = z^2$

$$\Rightarrow 2s^2 = 4 \Rightarrow s^2 = 4 \Rightarrow s^2 = 2 \text{ or } s = \sqrt{2}.$$

Example 2

Find the surface area of a sphere at the instant when the rate of increase of the volume of the sphere is nine times the rate of increase of the radius.

Volume of a sphere: $V = \dfrac{4}{3} \pi r^3$; Surface area of a sphere: $S = 4\pi r^2$

$$V = \frac{4}{3} \pi r^3; \frac{dV}{dt} = 4r^2 \frac{dr}{dt}$$

Since $\dfrac{dV}{dt} = 9 \dfrac{dr}{dt}$, you have $9 \dfrac{dr}{dt} = 4\pi r^2 \dfrac{dr}{dt}$ or $9 = 4\pi r^2$.

Since $S = 4\pi r^2$, thus the surface area is $S = 9$ square units.

Note: At $9 = 4\pi r^2$, you could solve for r and obtain $r^2 = \dfrac{9}{4\pi}$ or $r = \dfrac{3}{2} \dfrac{1}{\sqrt{\pi}}$. You could

then substitute $r = \dfrac{3}{2} \dfrac{1}{\sqrt{\pi}}$ into the formula for surface area $s = 4\pi r^2$ and obtain 9. These

steps are of course correct but not necessary.

Example 3

The height of a right circular cone is always three times the radius. Find the volume of the cone at the instant when the rate of increase of the volume is twelve times the rate of increase of the radius.

Let r, h be the radius and height of the cone respectively.

Since $h = 3r$, the volume of the cone $V = \dfrac{1}{3} \pi r^2 h = \dfrac{1}{3} \pi r^2 (3r) = \pi r^3$.

$$V = \pi r^3; \frac{dV}{dt} = 3\pi r^2 \frac{dr}{dt}.$$

When $\dfrac{dV}{dt} = 12 \dfrac{dr}{dt}$, $12 \dfrac{dr}{dt} = 3\pi r^2 \dfrac{dr}{dt} \Rightarrow 4 = \pi r^2 \Rightarrow r = \dfrac{2}{\sqrt{\pi}}$.

Thus $V = \pi r^3 = \pi \left(\dfrac{2}{\sqrt{\pi}} \right)^3 = \pi \left(\dfrac{8}{\pi \sqrt{\pi}} \right) = \dfrac{8}{\sqrt{\pi}}$.

> • Go with your first instinct if you are unsure. Usually that's the correct one.

Inverted Cone (Water Tank) Problem

A water tank is in the shape of an inverted cone. The height of the cone is 10 meters and the diameter of the base is 8 meters as shown in Figure 5.1-1. Water is being pumped into the tank at the rate of 2 m³/min. How fast is the water level rising when the water is 5 meters deep? (See Figure 5.1-1 on page 159.)

Solution:

Step 1: Define the variables. Let V be the volume of water in the tank; h be the height of the water level at t minutes; r be the radius of surface of the water at t minutes; and t be the time in minutes.

Step 2: Given: $\dfrac{dV}{dt} = 2$ m³/min. Height = 10 m, diameter = 8 m

Find: $\dfrac{dh}{dt}$ at $h = 5$.

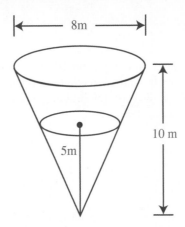

Figure 5.1-1

Step 3: Set up an equation $V = \dfrac{1}{3}\pi r^2 h$.

Using similar triangles, you have $\dfrac{4}{10} = \dfrac{r}{h} \Rightarrow 4h = 10r$; or $r = \dfrac{2h}{5}$. See Figure 5.1-2.

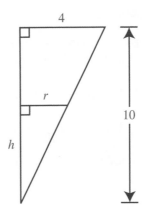

Figure 5.1-2

Thus, you can reduce the equation to one variable:

$$V = \frac{1}{3}\pi\left(\frac{2h}{5}\right)^2 h = \frac{4}{75}\pi h^3$$

Step 4: Differentiate both sides of the equation with respect to t.

$$\frac{dV}{dt} = \frac{4}{75}\pi(3)h^2\frac{dh}{dt} = \frac{4}{25}\pi h^2\frac{dh}{dt}$$

Step 5: Substituting known values.

$$2 = \frac{4}{25}\pi h^2\frac{dh}{dt}; \frac{dh}{dt} = \left(\frac{25}{2}\right)\frac{1}{\pi h^2}\ \text{m/min}$$

Evaluating $\dfrac{dh}{dt}$ at $h = 5$; $\left.\dfrac{dh}{dt}\right|_{h=5} = \left(\dfrac{25}{2}\right)\dfrac{1}{\pi(5)^2}\ \text{m/min}$

$$= \frac{1}{2\pi}\ \text{m/min}.$$

Step 6: Thus, the water level is rising at $\dfrac{1}{2\pi}$ m/min when the water is 5 m high.

Shadow Problem

A light on the ground 100 feet from a building is shining at a 6-foot tall man walking away from the streetlight and towards the building at the rate of 4 ft/sec. How fast is his shadow on the building growing shorter when he is 40 feet from the building? See Figure 5.1-3.

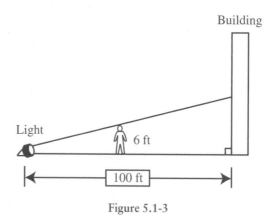

Figure 5.1-3

Solution:

Step 1: Let s be the height of the man's shadow; x be the distance between the man and the light; and t be the time in seconds.

Step 2: Given: $\dfrac{dx}{dt} = 4$ ft/sec; man is 6 ft tall; distance between light and building = 100 ft. Find $\dfrac{ds}{dt}$ at $x = 60$.

Step 3: See Figure 5.1-4. Write an equation using similar triangles, you have:

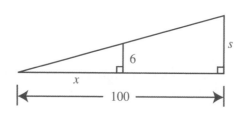

Figure 5.1-4

$$\frac{6}{s} = \frac{x}{100}; \quad s = \frac{600}{x} = 600x^{-1}$$

Step 4: Differentiate both sides of the equation with respect to t.

$$\frac{ds}{dt} = (-1)(600)x^{-2}\frac{dx}{dt} = \frac{-600}{x^2}\frac{dx}{dt} = \frac{-600}{x^2}(4) = \frac{-2400}{x^2} \text{ ft/sec}$$

Step 5: Evaluate $\dfrac{ds}{dt}$ at $x = 60$.

Note: when the man is 40 ft from the building, x (distance from the light) is 60 ft.

$$\left.\frac{ds}{dt}\right|_{x=60} = \frac{-2400}{(60)^2} \text{ ft/sec} = -\frac{2}{3} \text{ ft/sec}$$

Step 6: The height of the man's shadow on the building is changing at $-\frac{2}{3}$ ft/sec .

> • Indicate units of measure, e.g., the velocity is 5 m/sec *or* the volume is 25 in³.

Angle of Elevation Problem

A camera on the ground 200 meters away from a hot air balloon records the balloon rising into the sky at a constant rate of 10 m/sec. How fast is the camera's angle of elevation changing when the balloon is 150 m in the air? See Figure 5.1-5.

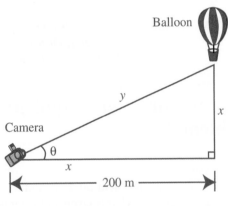

Figure 5.1-5

Step 1: Let x be the distance between the balloon and the ground; θ be the camera's angle of elevation; and t be the time in seconds.

Step 2: Given: $\frac{dx}{dt} = 10$ m/sec; distance between camera and the point on the ground where the balloon took off is 200 m, $\tan \theta = \frac{x}{200}$.

Step 3: Find $\frac{d\theta}{dt}$ at $x = 150$ m.

Step 4: Differentiate both sides with respect to t.

$$\sec^2 \theta \frac{d\theta}{dt} = \frac{1}{200} \frac{dx}{dt}; \frac{d\theta}{dt} = \frac{1}{200}\left(\frac{1}{\sec^2 \theta}\right)(10) = \frac{1}{20 \sec^2 \theta}$$

Step 5: $\sec \theta = \frac{y}{200}$ and at $x = 150$

Using the Pythagorean Theorem: $y^2 = x^2 + (200)^2$

$$y^2 = (150)^2 + (200)^2$$

$$y = \pm 250$$

Since $y > 0$, then $y = 250$. Thus, $\sec \theta = \frac{250}{200} = \frac{5}{4}$.

$$\text{Evaluating } \left.\frac{d\theta}{dt}\right|_{x=150} = \frac{1}{20\sec^2\theta} = \frac{1}{20\left(\dfrac{5}{4}\right)^2} \text{ radian/sec}$$

$$= \frac{1}{20\left(\dfrac{5}{4}\right)^2} = \frac{1}{20\left(\dfrac{25}{16}\right)} = \frac{1}{\dfrac{125}{4}} = \frac{4}{125} \text{ radian/sec}$$

$$\text{or } .032 \text{ radian/sec}$$

$$\approx 1.833 \text{ deg/sec}$$

Step 6: The camera's angle of elevation changes at approximately 1.833 deg/sec when the balloon is 150 m in the air.

5.2   APPLIED MAXIMUM AND MINIMUM PROBLEMS

Main Concepts: *General Procedure for Solving Applied Maximum and Minimum Problems, Distance Problem, Area and Volume Problems, Business Problems*

General Procedure for Solving Applied Maximum and Minimum Problems

Steps:
1. Read the problem carefully and if appropriate, draw a diagram.
2. Determine what is given and what is to be found and represent these quantities by mathematical symbols.
3. Write an equation that is a function of the variable representing the quantity to be maximized or minimized.
4. If the equation involves other variables, reduce the equation to a single variable that represents the quantity to be maximized or minimized.
5. Determine the appropriate interval for the equation (i.e., the appropriate domain for the function) based on the information given in the problem.
6. Differentiate to obtain the first derivative and to find critical numbers.
7. Apply the First Derivative Test or the Second Derivative Test by finding the second derivative.
8. Check the function values at the end points of the interval.
9. Write the answer(s) to the problem and, if given, indicate the units of measure.

Distance Problems

Find the shortest distance between the point $A\ (19, 0)$ and the parabola $y = x^2 - 2x + 1$.

Solution:

Step 1: Draw a diagram. See Figure 5.2-1.
Step 2: Let $P(x, y)$ be the point on the parabola and let Z represents the distance between points $P(x, y)$ and $A(19, 0)$.
Step 3: Using the distance formula,

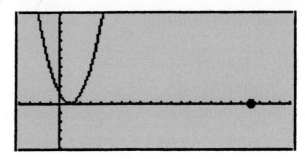

Figure 5.2-1

$$Z = \sqrt{(x-19)^2 + (y-0)^2} = \sqrt{(x-19)^2 + (x^2 - 2x + 1 - 0)^2}$$

$$= \sqrt{(x-19)^2 + \left((x-1)^2\right)^2} = \sqrt{(x-19)^2 + (x-1)^4}$$

(Special case: In distance problems, the distance and the square of the distance have the same maximum and minimum points). Thus, to simplify computations, let $L = Z^2 = (x-19)^2 + (x-1)^4$. The domain of L is $(-\infty, \infty)$.

Step 4: Differentiate $\dfrac{dL}{dx} = 2(x-19)(1) + 4(x-1)^3(1)$

$$= 2x - 38 + 4x^3 - 12x^2 + 12x - 4 = 4x^3 - 12x^2 + 14x - 42$$

$$= 2(2x^3 - 6x^2 + 7x - 21)$$

$\dfrac{dL}{dx}$ is defined for all real numbers.

Set $\dfrac{dL}{dx} = 0$; $2x^3 - 6x^2 + 7x - 21 = 0$. The factors of 21 are $\pm 1, \pm 3, \pm 7$ and ± 21.

Using Synthetic Division, $2x^3 - 6x^2 + 7x - 21 = (x-3)(2x^2 + 7) = 0 \Rightarrow x = 3$. Thus the only critical number is $x = 3$.
(Note: Step 4 could have been done using a graphing calculator.)

Step 5: Apply the First Derivative Test.

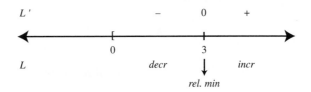

Step 6: Since $x = 3$ is the only relative minimum point in the interval, it is the absolute minimum.

Step 7: At $x = 3$, $Z = \sqrt{(3-19)^2 + (3^2 - 2(3) + 1)^2} = \sqrt{(-16)^2 + (4)^2}$

$$= \sqrt{272} = \sqrt{16}\sqrt{17} = 4\sqrt{17}. \text{ Thus, the shortest distance is } 4\sqrt{17}.$$

• Simplify numeric or algebraic expressions only if the question asks you to do so.

Area and Volume Problems

Example—Area Problem

The graph of $y = -\frac{1}{2}x + 2$ encloses a region with the x-axis and y-axis in the first quadrant. A rectangle in the enclosed region has a vertex at the origin and the opposite vertex on the graph of $y = -\frac{1}{2}x + 2$. Find the dimensions of the rectangle so that its area is a maximum.

Solution:

Step 1: Draw a diagram. (See Figure 5.2-2.)

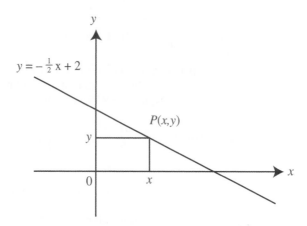

Figure 5.2-2

Step 2: Let $P(x, y)$ be the vertex of the rectangle on the graph of $y = -\frac{1}{2}x + 2$.

Step 3: Thus the area of the rectangle is:

$$A = xy \text{ or } A = x\left(-\frac{1}{2}x + 2\right) = -\frac{1}{2}x^2 + 2x$$

The domain of A is $[0,4]$.

Step 4: Differentiate.

$$\frac{dA}{dx} = -x + 2$$

Step 5: $\frac{dA}{dx}$ is defined for all real numbers.

Set $\frac{dA}{dx} = 0 \Rightarrow -x + 2 = 0; \ x = 2$

$A(x)$ has one critical number $x = 2$.

Step 6: Apply Second Derivative Test

$$\frac{d^2A}{dx^2} = -1 \Rightarrow A(x) \text{ has a relative maximum point at } x = 2; A(2) = 2.$$

Since $x = 2$ is the only relative maximum, it is the absolute maximum. (Note at the endpoints: $A(0) = 0$ & $A(4) = 0$)

Step 7: At $x = 2$, $y = -\frac{1}{2}(2) + 2 = 1$

Therefore the length of the rectangle is 2, and its width is 1.

Example—Volume Problem (with calculator)

If an open box is to be made using a square sheet of tin, 20 inches by 20 inches, by cutting a square from each corner and folding the sides up; find the length of a side of the square being cut so that the box will have a maximum volume.

Solution:

Step 1: Draw a diagram. (See Figure 5.2-3.)

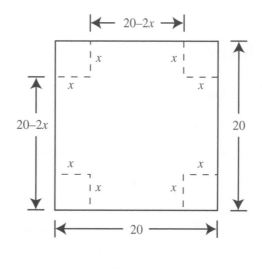

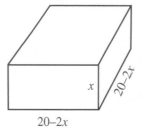

Figure 5.2-3

Step 2: Let x be the length of a side of the square to be cut from each corner.

Step 3: The volume of the box is $V = x(20 - 2x)(20 - 2x)$.

The domain of V is $[0, 10]$.

Step 4: Differentiate $V(x)$.

Entering $d(x * (20 - 2x) * (20 - 2x), x) = 4(x - 10)(3x - 10)$.

Step 5: $V'(x)$ is defined for all real numbers:

Set $V'(x) = 0$ by entering: solve $(4(x - 10)(3x - 10) = 0, x)$, and obtain $x = 10$ or $x = \dfrac{10}{3}$. The critical numbers of $V(x)$ are $x = 10$ and $x = \dfrac{10}{3}$. $V(10) = 0$ and $V\left(\dfrac{10}{3}\right) = 592.59$. Since $V(10) = 0$, you need to test only $x = \dfrac{10}{3}$.

Step 6: Using the Second Derivative Test, $d(x * (20 - 2x) * (20 - 2x), x, 2)|\, x = \dfrac{10}{3}$. and obtain -80. Thus, $V\left(\dfrac{10}{3}\right)$ is a relative maximum. And since it is the only relative maximum on the interval, it is the absolute maximum. (Note at the other endpoint $x = 0$, $V(0) = 0$).

Step 7: Therefore, the length of a side of the square to be cut is $x = \dfrac{10}{3}$.

> • The formula for the average value of a function f from $x = a$ to $x = b$ is
> $$\frac{1}{b-a}\int_a^b f(x)dx.$$

Business Problems

Summary of Formulas:

1. $P = R - C$: Profit = Revenue − Cost

2. $R = xp$: Revenue = (Units Sold)(Price Per Unit)

3. $\overline{C} = \dfrac{C}{x}$, Average Cost $= \dfrac{\text{Total Cost}}{\text{Units produced/Sold}}$

4. $\dfrac{dR}{dx}$ = Marginal Revenue ≈ Revenue from selling one more unit

5. $\dfrac{dP}{dx}$ = Marginal Profit ≈ Profit from selling one more unit

6. $\dfrac{dC}{dx}$ = Marginal Cost ≈ Cost of producing one more unit

Example 1

Given the cost function $C(x) = 100 + 8x + 0.1x^2$,
(a) find the marginal cost when $x = 50$; and (b) find the marginal profit at $x = 50$, if the price per unit is $20.

Solution:

(a) Marginal cost is $C'(x)$. Enter $d(100 + 8x + 0.1x^2, x)|x = 50$ and obtain $18.

(b) Marginal profit is $P'(x)$

$P = R - C$

$P = 20x - (100 + 8x + 0.1x^2)$. Enter $d(20x - (100 + 8x + 0.1x^2, x)|x = 50$ obtain 2.

> • Carry all decimal places and round only at the final answer. Round to 3 decimal places unless the question indicates otherwise.

Example 2

Given the cost function $C(x) = 500 + 3x + 0.01x^2$ and the demand function (the price function) $p(x) = 10$, find the number of units produced in order to have maximum profit.

Solution:

Step 1: Write an equation.

Profit = Revenue − Cost

$P = R - C$

Revenue = (Units Sold)(Price Per Unit)

$R = xp(x) = x(10) = 10x$

$P = 10x - (500 + 3x + 0.01x^2)$

Step 2: Differentiate.

Enter $d(10x - (500 + 3x + 0.01x^2, x)$ and obtain $7 - 0.02x$.

Step 3: Find critical numbers.

Set $7 - 0.02x = 0 \Rightarrow x = 350$.

Critical number is $x = 350$.

Step 4: Apply Second Derivative Test.

Enter $d(10x - (500 + 3x + 0.01x^2), x, 2)|x = 350$ and obtain -02.

Since $x = 350$ is the only relative maximum, it is the absolute maximum.

Step 5: Write a Solution

Thus, producing 350 units will lead to maximum profit.

5.3 RAPID REVIEW

1. Find the instantaneous rate of change at $x = 5$ of the function $f(x) = \sqrt{2x - 1}$.

Answer: $f(x) = \sqrt{2x - 1} = (2x - 1)^{\frac{1}{2}}$

$f(x) = \frac{1}{2}(2x - 1)^{\frac{1}{2}}(2) = (2x - 1)^{-\frac{1}{2}}$

$f'(5) = \frac{1}{3}$

2. If the diameter of a circle h is increasing at a constant rate of 0.1 cm/sec, find the rate of change of the area of the circle when the diameter is 4 cm.

Answer: $A = \pi r^2 = \left(\frac{h}{2}\right)^2 = \frac{1}{4}\pi h^2$

$\frac{dA}{dt} = \frac{1}{2}\pi h\frac{dh}{dt} = \frac{1}{2}\pi(4)(0.1) = 0.2\,\pi\,\text{cm}^2/\text{sec}$.

3. The radius of a sphere is increasing at a constant rate of 2 inches per minute. In terms of the surface area, what is the rate of change of the volume of the sphere?

Answer: $V = \frac{4}{3}\pi r^3; \frac{dr}{dt} = 4\pi r^2\frac{dr}{dt}$ since $S = \pi r^2, \frac{dV}{dt} = 2S$ in.^{3}/min.

4. Using your calculator, find the shortest distance between the point $(4, 0)$ and the line $y = x$. (See Figure 5.3-1.)

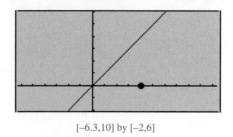

[−6.3,10] by [−2,6]

Figure 5.3-1

Answer:

$$S = \sqrt{(x-4)^2 + (y-0)^2} = \sqrt{(x-4)^2 + x^2}$$

Enter $y1 = ((x-4)\wedge 2 + x\wedge 2)\wedge(.5)$ and $y2 = d(y1(x), x)$

Use the Zero function for $y2$ and obtain $x = 2$. Use the Value function for $y1$ at $x = 2$ and obtain $y1 = 2.82843$. Thus the shortest distance is approximately 2.828.

5.4 PRACTICE PROBLEMS

Part A—The use of a calculator is not allowed.

1. A spherical balloon is being inflated. Find the volume of the balloon at the instant when the rate of increase of the surface area is eight times the rate of increase of the radius of the sphere.

2. A 13-foot ladder is leaning against a wall. If the top of the ladder is sliding down the wall at 2 ft/sec, how fast is the bottom of the ladder moving away from the wall, when the top of the ladder is 5 feet from the ground? (See Figure 5.4-1.)

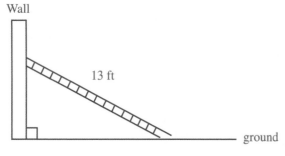

Figure 5.4-1

3. Air is being pumped into a spherical balloon at the rate of 100 cm³/sec. How fast is the diameter increasing when the radius is 5 cm?

4. A man 5 feet tall is walking away from a streetlight hung 20 feet from the ground at the rate of 6 ft/sec. Find how fast his shadow is lengthening.

5. A water tank in the shape of an inverted cone has an altitude of 18 feet and a base radius of 12 feet. If the tank is full and the water is drained at the rate of 4 ft³/min, how fast is the water level dropping when the water level is 6 feet high?

6. Two cars leave an intersection at the same time. The first car is going due east at the rate of 40 mph and the second is going due south at the rate of 30 mph. How fast is the distance between the two cars increasing when the first car is 120 miles from the intersection?

7. If the perimeter of an isosceles triangle is 18 cm, find the maximum area of the triangle.

8. Find a number in the interval (0,2) such that the sum of the number and its reciprocal is the absolute minimum.

9. An open box is to be made using a cardboard 8 cm by 15 cm by cutting a square from each corner and folding the sides up. Find the length of a side of the square being cut so that the box will have a maximum volume.

10. What is the shortest distance between the point $\left(2, -\dfrac{1}{2}\right)$ and the parabola $y = -x^2$?

11. If the cost function is $C(x) = 3x^2 + 5x + 12$, find the value of x such that the average cost is a minimum.

12. A man with 200 meters of fence plans to enclose a rectangular piece of land using a river on one side and a fence on the other three sides. Find the maximum area that the man can obtain.

Part B—Calculators are allowed.

13. A trough is 10 meters long and 4 meters wide. (See Figure 5.4-2.)

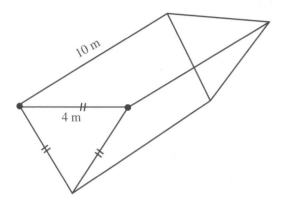

Figure 5.4-2

The two sides of the trough are equilateral triangles. Water is pumped into the trough at 1 m³/ min. How fast is the water level rising when the water is 2 meters high?

14. A rocket is sent vertically up in the air with the position function $s = 100t^2$ where s is measured in meters and t in seconds. A camera 3000 m away is recording the rocket. Find the rate of change of the angle of elevation of the camera 5 sec after the rocket went up.

15. A plane lifts off from a runway at an angle of 20°. If the speed of the plane is 300 mph, how fast is the plane gaining altitude?

16. Two water containers are being used. (See Figure 5.4-3.)

One container is in the form of an inverted right circular cone with a height of 10 feet and a radius at the base of 4 feet. The other container is a right circular cylinder with a radius of 6 feet and a height of 8 feet. If water is being drained from the conical container into the cylindrical container at the rate of 15 ft³/min, how fast is the water level falling in the conical tank when the water level in the conical tank is 5 feet high? How fast is the water level rising in the cylindrical container?

17. The wall of a building has a parallel fence that is 6 feet high and 8 feet from the wall. What is the length of the shortest ladder that passes over the fence and leans on the wall? (See Figure 5.4-4.)

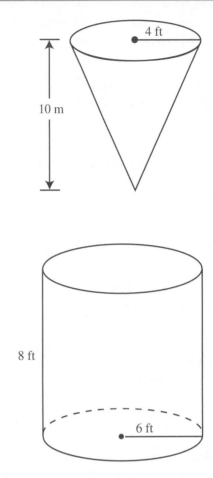

Figure 5.4-3

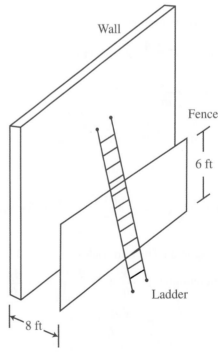

Figure 5.4-4

18. Given the cost function $C(x) = 2500 + 0.02x + 0.004x^2$, find the product level such that the average cost per unit is a minimum.

19. Find the maximum area of a rectangle inscribed in an ellipse whose equation is $4x^2 + 25y^2 = 100$.

20. A right triangle is in the first quadrant with a vertex at the origin and the other two vertices on the x- and y-axes. If the hypotenuse passes through the point $(0.5, 4)$, find the vertices of the triangle so that the length of the hypotenuse is the shortest.

5.5 CUMULATIVE REVIEW PROBLEMS

"Calculator" indicates that calculators are permitted.

21. If $y = \sin^2(\cos(6x - 1))$, find $\dfrac{dy}{dx}$.

22. Evaluate $\displaystyle\lim_{x \to \infty} \dfrac{100/x}{-4 + x + x^2}$.

23. The graph of f' is shown in Figure 5.5-1. Find where the function f: (a) has its relative extrema or absolute extrema; (b) is increasing or decreasing; (c) has its point(s) of inflection; (d) is concave upward or downward; and (e) if $f(3) = -2$, draw a possible sketch of f. (See Figure 5.5-1.)

24. (Calculator) At what values(s) of x does the tangent to the curve $x^2 + y^2 = 36$ have a slope of -1.

25. (Calculator) Find the shortest distance between the point $(1, 0)$ and the curve $y = x^3$.

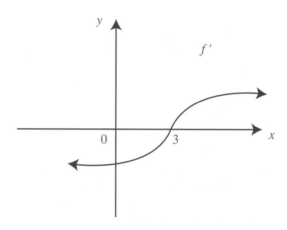

Figure 5.5-1

5.6 SOLUTIONS TO PRACTICE PROBLEMS

Part A—No calculators.

1. Volume: $V = \dfrac{4}{3}\pi r^3$; Surface Area: $S = 4\pi r^2$

$$\frac{dS}{dt} = 8\pi r \frac{dr}{dt}$$

Since $\dfrac{dS}{dt} = 8\dfrac{dr}{dt}, 8\dfrac{dr}{dt} = 8\pi r\dfrac{dr}{dt} \Rightarrow 8 = 8\pi r$

or $r = \dfrac{1}{\pi}$.

At $r = \dfrac{1}{\pi}, V = \dfrac{4}{3}\pi\left(\dfrac{1}{\pi}\right)^3 = \dfrac{4}{3\pi^2}$ cubic units.

2. Pythagorean Theorem yields $x^2 + y^2 = (13)^2$.

Differentiate: $2x\dfrac{dx}{dt} + 2y\dfrac{dy}{dt} = 0 \Rightarrow \dfrac{dy}{dt}$

$= \dfrac{-x}{y}\dfrac{dx}{dt}$.

At $x = 5$, $(5)^2 + y^2 = 13 \Rightarrow y = \pm 12$, since $y > 0$, $y = 12$.

Therefore, $\dfrac{dy}{dt} = -\dfrac{5}{12}(-2)$ ft/sec $= \dfrac{5}{6}$ ft/sec.

The ladder is moving away from the wall at $\dfrac{5}{6}$ ft/sec when the top of the ladder is 5 feet from the ground.

3. Volume of a sphere is $V = \dfrac{4}{3}\pi r^3$.

Differentiate: $\dfrac{dV}{dt} = \left(\dfrac{4}{3}\right)(3)\pi r^2\dfrac{dr}{dt} = 4\pi r^2\dfrac{dr}{dt}$.

Substitute: $100 = 4\pi(5)^2\dfrac{dr}{dt} \Rightarrow \dfrac{dr}{dt} = \dfrac{1}{\pi}$ cm/sec.

Let x be the diameter. Since $x = 2r$, $\dfrac{dx}{dt} = 2\dfrac{dr}{dt}$.

Thus $\dfrac{dx}{dt}\bigg|_{r=5} = 2\left(\dfrac{1}{\pi}\right)$ cm/sec $= \dfrac{2}{\pi}$ cm/sec. The diameter is increasing at $\dfrac{2}{\pi}$ cm/sec when the radius is 5 cm.

4. See Figure 5.6-1. Using similar triangles, with y the length of the shadow you have:

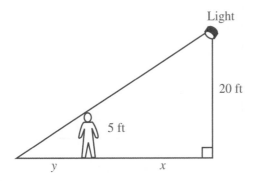

Figure 5.6-1

$$\frac{5}{20} = \frac{y}{y+x} \Rightarrow 20y = 5y + 5x \Rightarrow 15y$$
$$= 5x \text{ or } y = \frac{x}{3}.$$

Differentiate: $\dfrac{dy}{dt} = \dfrac{1}{3}\dfrac{dx}{dt} \Rightarrow \dfrac{dy}{dt} = \dfrac{1}{3}(6)$
$$= 2 \text{ ft/sec.}$$

5. See Figure 5.6-2. Volume of a cone $V = \dfrac{1}{3}\pi r^2 h$.

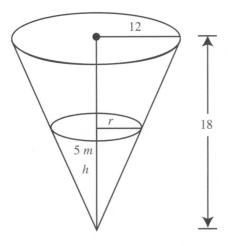

Figure 5.6-2

Using similar triangles, you have $\dfrac{12}{18} = \dfrac{r}{h} \Rightarrow 2h$

$= 3r$ or $r = \dfrac{2}{3}h$, thus reducing the equation to

$$V = \frac{1}{3}\pi\left(\frac{2}{3}h\right)^2(h) = \frac{4\pi}{27}h^3.$$

Differentiate: $\dfrac{dV}{dt} = \dfrac{4}{9}\pi h^2 \dfrac{dh}{dt}$. Substituting

known values: $-4 = \dfrac{4\pi}{9}(6)^2\dfrac{dh}{dt}$

$\Rightarrow -4 = 16\pi\dfrac{dh}{dt}$ or $\dfrac{dh}{dt} = -\dfrac{1}{4\pi}$ ft/min

The water level is dropping at $\dfrac{1}{4\pi}$ ft/min when $h = 6$ ft.

6. See Figure 5.6-3. Step 1. Using the Pythagorean Theorem, you have $x^2 + y^2 = z^2$. You also have $\dfrac{dx}{dt} = 40$ and $\dfrac{dy}{dt} = 30$.

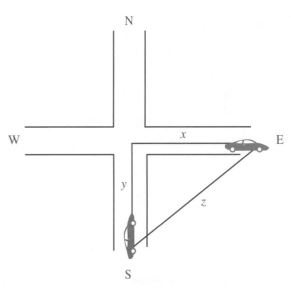

Figure 5.6-3

Step 2. Differentiate: $2x\dfrac{dx}{dt} + 2y\dfrac{dy}{dt} = 2z\dfrac{dz}{dt}$.
At $x = 120$, both cars have traveled 3 hours and thus, $y = 3(30) = 90$. By the Pythagorean Theorem, $(120)^2 + (90)^2 = z^2 \Rightarrow z = 150$.

Step 3. Substitute all known values into the equation:
$$2(120)(40) + 2(90)(30) = 2(150)\frac{dz}{dt}$$
Thus $\dfrac{dz}{dt} = 50$ mph.

Step 4. The distance between the two cars is increasing at 50 mph at $x = 120$.

7. See Figure 5.6-4. Step 1. Applying the Pythagorean Theorem, you have $x^2 = y^2 + (9-x)^2 \Rightarrow y^2 = x^2 - (9-x)^2 = x^2 - (81 - 18x + x^2) = 18x - 81 = 9(2x-9)$, or $y = \pm\sqrt{9(2x-9)} = \pm 3\sqrt{(2x-9)}$

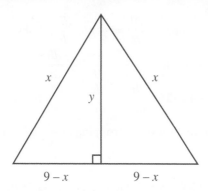

Figure 5.6-4

since $y > 0$, $y = 3\sqrt{(2x - 9)}$. The area of the

triangle $A = \dfrac{1}{2}\left(3\sqrt{2x - 9}\right)(18 - 2x) = \left(3\sqrt{2x - 9}\right)$

$(9 - x) = 3(2x - 9)^{\frac{1}{2}}(9 - x)$.

Step 2. $\dfrac{dA}{dx} = \dfrac{3}{2}(2x - 9)^{-\frac{1}{2}}(2)(9 - x)$

$\qquad + (-1)(3)(2x - 9)^{\frac{1}{2}}$

$\qquad = \dfrac{3(9 - x) - 3(2x - 9)}{\sqrt{2x - 9}}$

$\qquad = \dfrac{54 - 9x}{\sqrt{2x - 9}}$

Step 3. Set $\dfrac{dA}{dx} = 0 \Rightarrow 54 - 9x = 0$; $x = 6$

$\dfrac{dA}{dx}$ is undefined at $x = \dfrac{9}{2}$. The critical numbers are $\dfrac{9}{2}$, 6.

Step 4. First Derivative Test

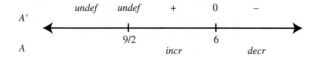

Thus at $x = 6$, the area A is a relative maximum.

$$A(6) = 3\sqrt{2(6) - 9}(9 - 6) = 9\sqrt{3}.$$

Step 5. Check endpoints. The domain of A is $\left[\dfrac{9}{2}, 9\right] A\left(\dfrac{9}{2}\right) = 0$; and $A(9) = 0$.

Therefore, the maximum area of an isosceles triangle with the perimeter of 18 cm is $9\sqrt{3}$ cm. (Note, at $x = 6$, the triangle is an equilateral triangle.)

8. See Figure 5.6-5. Step 1. Let x be the number and $\dfrac{1}{x}$ be its reciprocal.

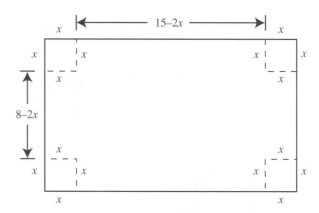

Figure 5.6-5

Step 2. $S = x + \dfrac{1}{x}$ with $0 < x < 1$.

Step 3. $\dfrac{ds}{dx} = 1 + (-1)x^{-2} = 1 - \dfrac{1}{x^2}$

Step 4. Set $\dfrac{ds}{dx} = 0$

$\qquad \Rightarrow 1 - \dfrac{1}{x^2} = 0$

$\qquad \Rightarrow x = \pm 1$, since the domain is $(0,2)$, thus $x = 1$.

$\qquad \dfrac{ds}{dx}$ is defined for all x in $(0,2)$.

$\qquad$ Critical number is $x = 1$.

Step 5. Second Derivative Test: $\dfrac{d^2s}{dx^2} = \dfrac{2}{x^3}$ and

$\qquad \left.\dfrac{d^2s}{dx^2}\right|_{x=1} = 2.$

Thus at $x = 1$, s is a relative minimum. Since it is the only relative extremum, thus, at $x = 1$, it is the absolute minimum.

9. Step 1. Volume $V = x(8 - 2x)(15 - 2x)$ with $0 \leq x \leq 4$.

Step 2. Differentiate: Rewrite as $V = 4x^3 - 46x^2 + 120x$

$\qquad \dfrac{dV}{dx} = 12x^2 - 92x + 120$

Step 3. Set $V = 0 \Rightarrow 12x^2 - 92x + 120 = 0$ $\Rightarrow 3x^2 - 23x + 30 = 0$. Using the quadratic formula, you have $x = 6$ or $x = \dfrac{5}{3}$. And $\dfrac{dV}{dx}$ is defined for all real numbers.

Step 4. Second Derivative Test.

$$\frac{d^2V}{dx^2} = 24x - 92; \left.\frac{d^2V}{dx^2}\right|_{x=6}$$

$$= 52 \text{ and } \left.\frac{d^2V}{dx^2}\right|_{x=\frac{5}{3}} = -52$$

Thus at $x = \frac{5}{3}$ is a relative maximum.

Step 5. Check endpoints.

At $x = 0$, $V = 0$ and at $x = 4$, $V = 0$.

Therefore, at $x = \frac{5}{3}$, V is the absolute maximum.

10. See Figure 5.6-6. Step 1. Distance Formula:

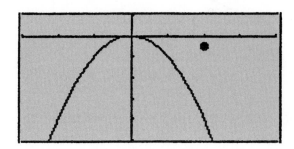

Figure 5.6-6

$$Z = \sqrt{(x - 2)^2 + \left(y - \left(-\frac{1}{2}\right)\right)^2}$$

$$= \sqrt{(x - 2)^2 + \left(-x^2 + \frac{1}{2}\right)^2}$$

$$= \sqrt{x^2 - 4x + 4 + x^4 - x^2 + \frac{1}{4}}$$

$$= \sqrt{x^4 - 4x + \frac{17}{4}}$$

Step 2. Let $S = Z^2$, since S and Z have the same maximums and minimums.

$$S = x^4 - 4x + \frac{17}{4}; \frac{dS}{dx} = 4x^3 - 4$$

Step 3. Set $\frac{dS}{dx} = 0$; $x = 1$ and $\frac{dS}{dx}$ is defined for all real numbers.

Step 4. Second Derivative Test: $\frac{d^2S}{dx^2} = 12x^2$

and $\left.\frac{d^2S}{dx^2}\right|_{x=1} = 12$. Thus at $x = 1$, Z is a

minimum and since it is the only relative extrema, it is the absolute minimum

Step 5. At $x = 1$, $Z = \sqrt{(1)^4 - 4(1) + \frac{17}{4}} = \sqrt{\frac{5}{4}}$.

Therefore, the shortest distance is $\sqrt{\frac{5}{4}}$.

11. Step 1. Average Cost $\overline{C} = \frac{C(x)}{x} = \frac{3x^2 + 5x + 12}{x}$

$$= 3x + 5 + \frac{12}{x}$$

Step 2. $\frac{d\overline{C}}{dx} = 3 - 12x^{-2} = 3 - \frac{12}{x^2}$

Step 3. Set $\frac{d\overline{C}}{dx} = 0 \Rightarrow 3 - \frac{12}{x^2} = 0 \Rightarrow 3 - \frac{12}{x^2}$

$\Rightarrow x \pm 2$. Since $x > 0$, $x = 2$ and $\overline{C}(2)$

$= 17$. $\frac{d\overline{C}}{dx}$ is undefined at $x = 0$ which is

not in the domain.

Step 4. Second Derivative Test:

$$\frac{d^2\overline{C}}{dx^2} = \frac{24}{x^3} \text{ and } \left.\frac{d^2\overline{C}}{dx^2}\right|_{x=2} = 3$$

Thus at $x = 2$, the average cost is a minimum

12. See Figure 5.6-7. Step 1. Area $A = x(200 - 2x) = 200x - 2x^2$ with $0 \le x \le 100$

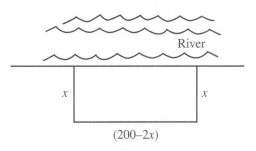

Figure 5.6-7

Step 2. $A'(x) = 200 - 4x$

Step 3. Set $A'(x) = 0 \Rightarrow 200 - 4x = 0$; $x = 50$

Step 4. Second Derivative Test

$A''(x) = -4$; Thus at $x = 50$, the area is a relative maximum.

$A(50) = 5000 \text{ m}^2$.

Step 5. Check endpoints

$A(0) = 0$ and $A(100) = 0$; Therefore at $x = 50$, the area is the absolute maximum and 5000 m^2 is the maximum area.

13. Step 1. Let h be the height of the trough and 4 be a side of one of the two equilateral triangles. Thus, in a 30–60 right triangle,

$h = 2\sqrt{3}$.

Step 2. Volume V = (area of the triangle) · 10

$$= \left[\frac{1}{2}(h)\left(\frac{2}{\sqrt{3}}h\right)\right]10 = \frac{10}{\sqrt{3}}h^2$$

Step 3. Differentiate with respect to t.

$$\frac{dV}{dt} = \left(\frac{10}{\sqrt{3}}\right)(2)h\frac{dh}{dt}$$

Step 4. Substitute known values

$$1 = \frac{20}{\sqrt{3}}(2)\frac{dh}{dt} ; \quad \frac{dh}{dt} = \frac{\sqrt{3}}{40} \text{ m/min}.$$

The water level is rising $\frac{\sqrt{3}}{40}$ m/min when the water level is 2 m high.

14. See Figure 5.6-8. Step 1. $\tan\theta = S/3000$

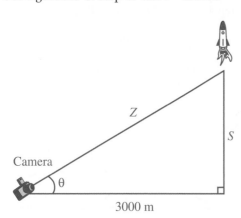

3000 m

Figure 5.6-8

Step 2. Differentiate with respect to t.

$$\sec^2\theta \frac{d\theta}{dt} = \frac{1}{3000}\frac{dS}{dt} ; \quad \frac{d\theta}{dt}$$

$$= \frac{1}{3000}\left(\frac{1}{\sec^2\theta}\right)\frac{dS}{dt}$$

$$= \frac{1}{3000}\left(\frac{1}{\sec^2\theta}\right)(200t)$$

Step 3. At $t = 5$; $S = 100(5)^2 = 2500$;

Thus $Z^2 = (3000)^2 + (2500)^2 = 15{,}250{,}000$. Therefore $Z = \pm500\sqrt{61}$, since $Z > 0$, $Z = 500\sqrt{61}$. Substitute known values into the question:

$$\frac{d\theta}{dt} = \frac{1}{3000}\left(\frac{1}{\frac{500\sqrt{61}}{3000}}\right)^2(1000),$$

since $\sec\theta = \frac{Z}{3000}$.

$$\frac{d\theta}{dt} = 0.197 \text{ radian/sec}$$

The angle of elevation is changing at 0.197 radian/sec, 5 seconds after lift off.

15. See Figure 5.6-9. $\sin 20° = \dfrac{h}{300t}$

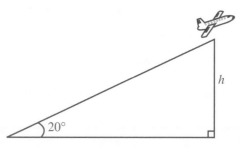

Figure 5.6-9

$$h = (\sin 20°)\,300t; \quad \frac{dh}{dt} = (\sin 20°)(300) \approx$$

102.61 mph. The plane is gaining altitude at 102.61 mph.

16. $V_{\text{come}} = \dfrac{1}{3}\pi r^2 h$

Similar triangles: $\dfrac{4}{10} = \dfrac{r}{h} \Rightarrow 5r = 2h$ or $r = \dfrac{2h}{5}$

$$V_{\text{come}} = \frac{1}{3}\pi\left(\frac{2h}{5}\right)^2 h = \frac{4\pi}{75}h^3; \frac{dV}{dt} = \frac{4\pi}{75}(3)h^2\frac{dh}{dt}.$$

Substitute known values: $-15 = \dfrac{4\pi}{25}(5)^2\dfrac{dh}{dt}$;

$$-15 = 4\pi\frac{dh}{dt}; \frac{dh}{dt} = \frac{-15}{4\pi} \approx -1.19 \text{ ft/min}$$

The water level in the cone is falling at

$\dfrac{-15}{4\pi}$ ft/min ≈ -1.19 ft/min when the water level

is 5 feet high.

$V_{\text{cyclinder}} = \pi R^2 H = \pi(6)2\,H = 36\,\pi H.$

$$\frac{dV}{dt} - 36\pi\frac{dH}{dt}; \frac{dH}{dt} = \frac{1}{36\pi}\frac{dV}{dt}; \frac{dH}{dt}$$

$$= \frac{1}{36\pi}(15) = \frac{5}{12\pi} \text{ ft/min}$$

≈ 0.1326 ft/min or 1.592 in./min

The water level in the cylinder is rising at

$\dfrac{5}{12\pi}$ ft/min ≈ 0.1326 ft/min.

17. Step 1. Let x be the distance of the foot of the ladder from the higher wall. Let y be the height of the point where the ladder touches the higher wall. The slope of the ladder is $m = \dfrac{y-6}{0-8}$ or

$$m = \dfrac{6-0}{8-x}.$$

Thus $\dfrac{y-6}{-8} = \dfrac{6}{8-x} \Rightarrow (y-6)(8-x) = -48$

$$\Rightarrow 8y - xy - 48 + 6x = -48 \Rightarrow y(8-x) = -6x$$

$$\Rightarrow y = \dfrac{-6x}{8-x}$$

Step 2. Pythagorean Theorem: $l^2 = x^2 + y^2 = x^2 + \left(\dfrac{-6x}{8-x}\right)^2$

Since $l > 0$, $l = \sqrt{x^2 + \left(\dfrac{-6x}{8-x}\right)^2}$, $x > 8$

Step 3. Enter $y_1 = \sqrt{\{x^\wedge 2 + [(-6*x)/(8-x)]^\wedge 2\}}$. The graph of y_1 is continuous on the interval $x > 8$. Use the minimum function of the calculator and obtain $x = 14.604$; $y = 17.42$. Thus the minimum value of l is 19.731 or the shortest ladder is approximately 19.731 feet.

18. Step 1. Average Cost $\overline{C} = \dfrac{C}{x}$; Thus $\overline{C}(x)$

$$= \dfrac{2500 + 0.02x + 0.004x^2}{x}$$

$$= \dfrac{2500}{x} + 0.02 + .004x$$

Step 2. Enter $y_1 = \dfrac{2500}{x} + .02 + .004*x$

Step 3. Use the Minimum function in the calculator and obtain $x = 790.6$.

Step 4. Verify the result with the First Derivative Test. Enter $y_2 = d(2500/x + .02 + 004x, x)$; Use the Zero function and obtain $x = 790.6$. Thus $\dfrac{d\overline{C}}{dx} = 0$; at $x = 790.6$. Apply the First Derivative Test:

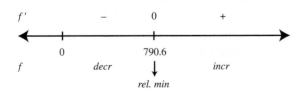

Thus the minimum average cost per unit occurs at $x = 790.6$ (The graph of the average cost function is shown in Figure 5.6-10.)

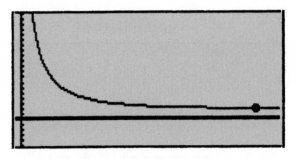

Figure 5.6-10

19. See Figure 5.6-11. Step 1. Area $A = (2x)(2y)$; $0 \le x \le 5$ and $0 \le y \le 2$.

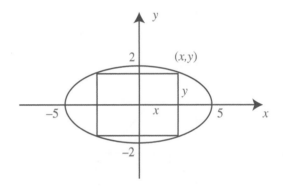

Figure 5.6-11

Step 2. $4x^2 + 25y^2 = 100$; $25y^2 = 100 - 4x^2$

$$y^2 = \dfrac{100 - 4x^2}{25} \Rightarrow y = \pm\sqrt{\dfrac{100 - 4x^2}{25}}$$

Since $y \ge 0$

$$y = \sqrt{\dfrac{100 - 4x^2}{25}} = \dfrac{\sqrt{100 - 4x^2}}{5}$$

Step 3. $A = (2x)\left(\dfrac{2}{5}\right)\left(\sqrt{100 - 4x^2}\right)$

$$= \dfrac{4x}{5}\sqrt{100 - 4x^2}$$

Step 4. Enter $y_1 = \dfrac{4x}{5}\sqrt{100 - 4x^2}$

Use the Maximum function and obtain $x = 3.536$ and $y_1 = 20$.

Step 5. Verify the result with the First Derivative Test.

Enter $y_2 = d\left(\dfrac{4x}{5}\sqrt{100 - 4x^2}, x\right)$. Use

Zero function and obtain $x = 3.536$.

Note that:

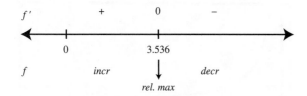

The function f has only one relative extrema. Thus it is the absolute extrema. Therefore, at $x = 3.536$, the area is 20 and the area is the absolute maxima.

20. See Figure 5.6-12. Step 1. Distance formula: $l^2 = x^2 + y^2$; $x > 0.5$ and $y > 4$

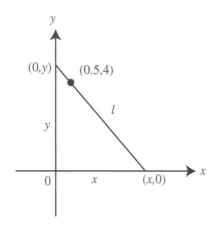

Figure 5.6-12

Step 2. The slope of the hypotenuse:

$$m = \dfrac{y - 4}{0 - 0.5} = \dfrac{-4}{x - 0.5}$$

$$\Rightarrow (y - 4)(x - 0.5) = 2$$

$\Rightarrow xy - 0.5y - 4x + 2$
$= 2;\ y(x - 0.5) = 4x$

$$y = \dfrac{4x}{x - 0.5}$$

Step 3. $l^2 = x^2 + \left(\dfrac{4x}{x - 0.5}\right)^2$;

$$l = \pm\sqrt{x^2 + \left(\dfrac{4x}{x - 0.5}\right)^2}$$

Since $l > 0$, $l = \sqrt{x^2 + \left(\dfrac{4x}{x - 0.5}\right)^2}$

Step 4. Enter $y_1 = \sqrt{x^2 + \left(\dfrac{4x}{x - 0.5}\right)^2}$ and use the minimum function of the calculator and obtain $x = 2.5$.

Step 5. Apply the First Derivative Test.

Enter $y_2 = d(y_1(x), x)$ and use the zero function and obtain $x = 2.5$.

Note that:

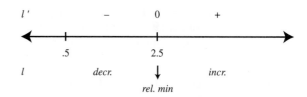

Since f has only one relative extremum, it is the absolute extremum.

Step 6. Thus at $x = 2.5$, the length of the hypotenuse is the shortest. At $x = 2.5$, $y = \dfrac{4(2.5)}{2.5 - 0.5} = 5$. The vertices of the triangle are $(0,0)$, $(2.5,0)$ and $(0,5)$.

5.7 SOLUTIONS TO CUMULATIVE REVIEW PROBLEMS

21. Rewrite: $y = \left[\sin(\cos(6x - 1))\right]^2$

Thus $\dfrac{dy}{dx} = 2\left[\sin(\cos(6x - 1))\right]\left[\cos(\cos(6x - 1))\right]$

$\left[-\sin(6x - 1)\right](6)$

$= -12\sin(6x - 1)\left[\sin(\cos(6x - 1))\right]$

$\left[\cos(\cos(6x - 1))\right]$

22. As $x \to \infty$, the numerator $\dfrac{100}{x}$ approaches 0 and the denominator increases without bound (i.e. ∞). Thus the $\lim\limits_{x\to\infty}\dfrac{100/x}{-4 + x + x^2} = 0$.

23. (a) Summarize the information of f' on a number line.

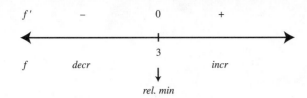

Since f has only one relative extremum, it is the absolute extremum. Thus at $x = 3$, it is an absolute minimum.

(b) The function f is decreasing as the interval $(-\infty, 3)$ and increasing on $(3, \infty)$.

(c)

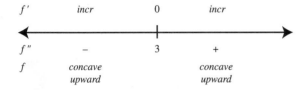

no change of concavity $\Rightarrow$ no point of inflection.

(d) The function f is concave upward for the entire domain $(-\infty, \infty)$.

(e) Possible sketch of graph for $f(x)$. See Figure 5.7-1.

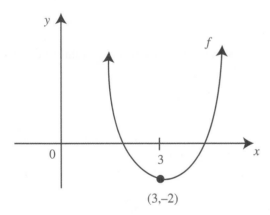

$(3, -2)$

Figure 5.7-1

24. (Calculator) See Figure 5.7-2.

Step 1. Differentiate: $2x + 2y \dfrac{dy}{dx} = 0 \Rightarrow \dfrac{dy}{dx}$

$$= -\frac{x}{y}$$

Step 2. Set $\dfrac{dy}{dx} = -1 \Rightarrow \dfrac{-x}{y} = -1 \Rightarrow y = x$

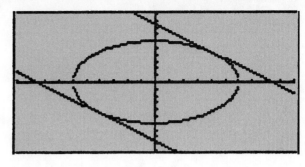

Figure 5.7-2

Step 3. Solve for y: $x^2 + y^2 = 36 \Rightarrow y^2 = 36 - x^2$;

$$y = \pm\sqrt{36 - x^2}$$

Step 4. Thus, $y = x \Rightarrow \pm\sqrt{36 - x^2} = x \Rightarrow 36 - x^2$

$$= x^2 \Rightarrow 36 = 2x^2 \text{ or } x = \pm 3\sqrt{2}$$

25. (Calculator) See Figure 5.7-3.

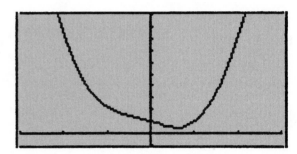

Figure 5.7-3

Step 1. Distance formula: $z = \sqrt{(x - 1)^2 + (x^3)^2}$

$$= \sqrt{(x - 1)^2 + x^6}$$

Step 2. Enter $y_1 = \sqrt{((x - 1) \wedge 2 + x \wedge 6)}$. Use the Minimum function of the calculator and obtain $x = .65052$ and $y_1 = .44488$. Verify the result with the First Derivative Test. Enter $y_2 = d(y_1(x), x)$ and use the Zero Function and obtain $x = .65052$.

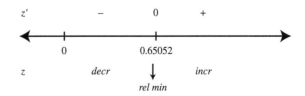

Thus the shortest distance is approximately 0.445.

Chapter 6

More Applications of Derivatives

6.1   TANGENT AND NORMAL LINES

Main Concepts: *Tangent Lines, Normal Lines*

Tangent Lines

If the function y is differentiable at $x = a$, then the slope of the tangent line to the graph of y at $x = a$ is given as $m_{(\text{tangent at } x=a)} = \dfrac{dy}{dx}\bigg|_{x=a}$.

Types of Tangent Lines:

Horizontal Tangents $\left(\dfrac{dy}{dx} = 0\right)$. (See Figure 6.1-1.)

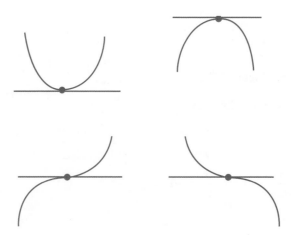

Figure 6.1-1

Vertical Tangents $\left(\dfrac{dy}{dx}\text{ does not exist but }\dfrac{dx}{dy} = 0\right)$. (See Figure 6.1-2.)

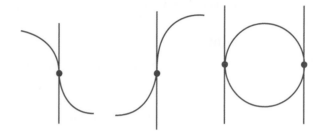

Figure 6.1-2

Parallel Tangents $\left(\left.\dfrac{dy}{dx}\right|_{x=a} = \left.\dfrac{dy}{dx}\right|_{x=c}\right)$. (See Figure 6.1-3.)

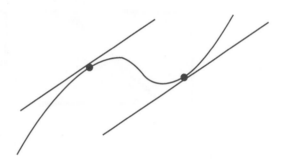

Figure 6.1-3

Example 1

Write an equation of the line tangent to the graph of $y = -3 \sin 2x$ at $x = \dfrac{\pi}{2}$. (See Figure 6.1-4.)

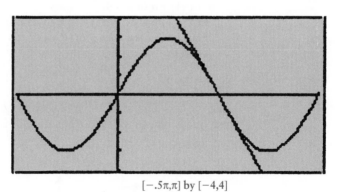

$[-.5\pi,\pi]$ by $[-4,4]$

Figure 6.1-4

$$y = -3 \sin 2x; \frac{dy}{dx} = -3[\cos(2x)]\,2 = -6 \cos(2x)$$

$$\text{slope of tangent}\left(\text{at } x = \frac{\pi}{2}\right): \left.\frac{dy}{dx}\right|_{x=\pi/2} = -6 \cos\left[2\left(\frac{\pi}{2}\right)\right] = -6 \cos \pi = 1.$$

$$\text{Point of tangency: At } x = \frac{\pi}{2}, y = -3 \sin(2x) = -3 \sin\left[2\left(\frac{\pi}{2}\right)\right] = -3 \sin(\pi) = 0.$$

Therefore $\left(\dfrac{\pi}{2}, 0\right)$ is the point of tangency.

Equation of Tangent: $y - 0 = 1\left(x - \dfrac{\pi}{2}\right)$ or $y = x - \dfrac{\pi}{2}$.

Example 2

If the line $y = 6x + a$ is tangent to the graph of $y = 2x^3$, find the value(s) of a.

Solution:

$$y = 2x^3; \frac{dy}{dx} = 6x^2. \text{ (See Figure 6.1-5.)}$$

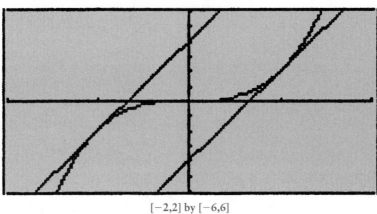

$[-2,2]$ by $[-6,6]$

Figure 6.1-5

The slope of the line $y = 6x + a$ is 6.

Since $y = 6x + a$ is tangent to the graph of $y = 2x^3$, thus $\dfrac{dy}{dx} = 6$ for some values of x.

Set $6x^2 = 6 \Rightarrow x^2 = 1$ or $x = \pm 1$.
At $x = -1$, $y = 2x^3 = 2(-1)^3 = -2$; $(-1,-2)$ is a tangent point. Thus, $y = 6x + a \Rightarrow -2 = 6(-1) + a$ or $a = 4$.
At $x = 1$, $y = 2x^3 = 2(1)^3 = 2$; $(1,2)$ is a tangent point.
Thus $y = 6x + a \Rightarrow 2 = 6(1) + a$ or $a = -4$.
Therefore, $a = \pm 4$.

Example 3

Find the coordinates of each point on the graph of $y^2 - x^2 - 6x + 7 = 0$ at which the tangent line is vertical. Write an equation of each vertical tangent. (See Figure 6.1-6.)

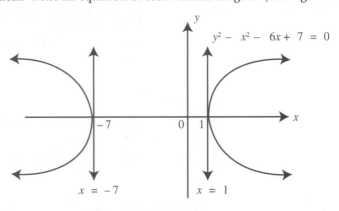

Figure 6.1-6

Step 1: Find $\dfrac{dy}{dx}$

$$y^2 - x^2 - 6x + 7 = 0$$

$$2y\frac{dy}{dx} - 2x - 6 = 0$$

$$\frac{dy}{dx} = \frac{2x + 6}{2y} = \frac{x + 3}{y}$$

Step 2: Find $\dfrac{dy}{dx}$

Vertical tangent $\Rightarrow \dfrac{dx}{dy} = 0$

$$\frac{dx}{dy} = \frac{1}{\dfrac{dy}{dx}} = \frac{1}{\dfrac{(x+3)}{y}} = \frac{y}{x+3}$$

Set $\dfrac{dx}{dy} = 0 \Rightarrow y = 0$.

Step 3: Find points of tangency.
At $y = 0$, $y^2 - x^2 - 6x + 7 = 0$ becomes $-x^2 - 6x + 7 = 0 \Rightarrow x^2 + 6x - 7 = 0$
$\Rightarrow (x + 7)(x - 1) = 0 \Rightarrow x = -7$ or $x = 1$.
Thus the points of tangency are $(-7, 0)$ and $(1, 0)$

Step 4: Write equation for vertical tangents:
$x = -7$ and $x = 1$.

Example 4

Find all points on the graph of $y = |xe^x|$ at which the graph has a horizontal tangent.

Step 1: Find $\dfrac{dy}{dx}$

$$y = |xe^x| = \begin{cases} xe^x & \text{if } x \geq 0 \\ -xe^x & \text{if } x < 0 \end{cases}$$

$$\frac{dy}{dx} = \begin{cases} e^x + xe^x & \text{if } x \geq 0 \\ -e^x + xe^x & \text{if } x < 0 \end{cases}$$

Step 2: Find the x-coordinate of points of tangency.

Horizontal Tangent $\Rightarrow \dfrac{dy}{dx} = 0$

If $x \geq 0$, set $e^x + xe^x = 0 \Rightarrow e^x(1 + x) = 0$
$\Rightarrow x = -1$ but $x \geq 0$, therefore, no solution.
If $x = 0$, set $-e^x - xe^x = 0 \Rightarrow -e^x(1 + x) = 0$
$\Rightarrow x = -1$.

Step 3: Find points of tangency.

At $x = -1$, $y = -xe^x = -(-1)e^1 = \dfrac{1}{e}$.

Thus at the point $\left(-1, \dfrac{1}{e}\right)$, the graph has a horizontal tangent.

(See Figure 6.1-7.)

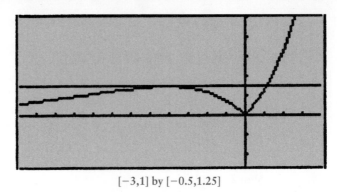

[−3,1] by [−0.5,1.25]

Figure 6.1-7

Example 5

Using your calculator, find the value(s) of x to the nearest hundredth at which the slope of the line tangent to the graph of $y = 2 \ln(x^2 + 3)$ is equal to $-\dfrac{1}{2}$. (See Figure 6.1-8 and 6.1-9.)

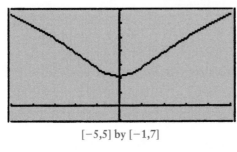

[−5,5] by [−1,7]

Figure 6.1-8

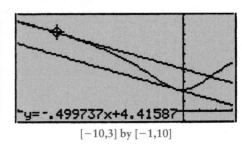

[−10,3] by [−1,10]

Figure 6.1-9

Step 1: Enter $y_1 = 2 * \ln(x\verb|^|2 + 3)$

Step 2: Enter $y_2 = d(y_1(x), x)$ and enter $y^3 = -\dfrac{1}{2}$

Step 3: Using the Intersection function of the calculator for y_2 and y_3, you obtain $x = -7.61$ or $x = -0.39$.

Example 6

Using your calculator, find the value(s) of x at which the graphs of $y = 2x^2$ and $y = e^x$ have parallel tangents.

Step 1: Find $\dfrac{dy}{dx}$ for both $y = 2x^2$ and $y = e^x$

$$y = 2x^2; \frac{dy}{dx} = 4x$$

$$y = e^x; \frac{dy}{dx} = e^x$$

Step 2: Find the *x-coordinate* of the points of tangency. Parallel tangents ⇒ slopes are equal.

Set $4x = e^x \Rightarrow 4x - e^x = 0$

Using the Solve function of the calculator, enter Solve $(4x - e^{\wedge}(x) = 0, x)$ and obtain $x = 2.15$ and $x = 0.36$.

- Watch out for different units of measure, e.g., the radius, r, is 2 feet, find $\dfrac{dr}{dt}$ in inches per second.

Normal Lines

The normal line to the graph of f at the point (x_1, y_1) is the line perpendicular to the tangent line at (x_1, y_1). (See Figure 6.1-10.)

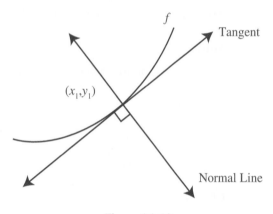

Figure 6.1-10

Note that the slope of the normal line and the slope of the tangent line at any point on the curve are negative reciprocals provided that both slopes exist.

$$(m_{\text{normal line}})(m_{\text{tangent line}}) = -1.$$

Special Cases: See Figure 6.1-11.

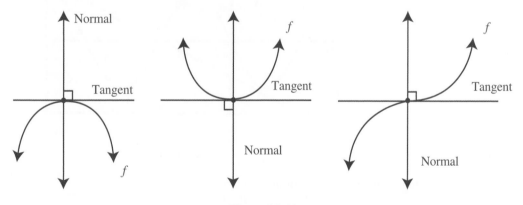

Figure 6.1-11

At these points, $m_{\text{tangent}} = 0$; but m_{normal} does not exist.
See Figure 6.1-12.

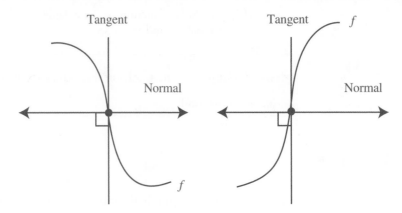

Figure 6.1-12

At these points, m_{tangent} does not exist; however $m_{\text{normal}} = 0$.

Example 1

Write an equation for each normal to the graph of $y = 2 \sin x$ for $0 \le x \le 2\pi$ that has a slope of $\dfrac{1}{2}$.

Step 1: Find m_{tangent}

$$y = 2 \sin x; \frac{dy}{dx} = 2 \cos x$$

Step 2: Find m_{normal}

$$m_{\text{normal}} = -\frac{1}{m_{\text{tangent}}} = -\frac{1}{2 \cos x}$$

Set $m_{\text{normal}} = \dfrac{1}{2} \Rightarrow -\dfrac{1}{2 \cos x} = \dfrac{1}{2} \Rightarrow \cos x = -1$

$\Rightarrow x = \cos^{-1}(-1)$ or $x = \pi$. (See Figure 6.1-13.)

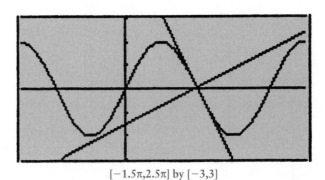

$[-1.5\pi, 2.5\pi]$ by $[-3,3]$

Figure 6.1-13

Step 3: Write equation of normal line.

At $x = \pi$, $y = 2 \sin x = 2(0) = 0$; $(\pi, 0)$

Since $m = \dfrac{1}{2}$, equation of normal is:

$$y - 0 = \frac{1}{2}(x - \pi) \text{ or } y = \frac{1}{2}x - \frac{\pi}{2}.$$

Example 2

Find the point on the graph of $y = \ln x$ such that the normal line at this point is parallel to the line $y = -ex - 1$.

Step 1: Find m_{tangent}

$$y = \ln x; \frac{dy}{dx} = \frac{1}{x}$$

Step 2: Find m_{normal}

$$m_{\text{normal}} = \frac{-1}{m_{\text{tangent}}} = \frac{-1}{1/x} = -x$$

slope of $y = -ex - 1$ is $-e$.
Since normal is parallel to the line $y = -ex - 1$, set $m_{\text{normal}} = -e$
$\Rightarrow -x = -e$ or $x = e$.

Step 3: Find point on graph. At $x = e$, $y = \ln x = \ln e = l$. Thus the point of the graph of $y = \ln x$ at which the normal is parallel to $y = -ex - 1$ is (e, 1). (See Figure 6.1-14.)

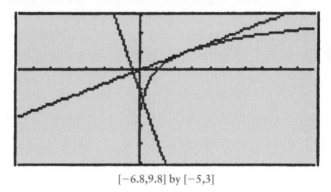

[−6.8,9.8] by [−5,3]

Figure 6.1-14

Example 3

Given the curve $y = \frac{1}{x}$: (a) write an equation of the normal to the curve $y = \frac{1}{x}$ at the point $\left(2, \frac{1}{2}\right)$ and (b) does this normal intersect the curve at any other point? If yes, find the point.

Step 1: Find m_{tangent}

$$y = \frac{1}{x}; \frac{dy}{dx} = (-1)(x^{-2}) = -\frac{1}{x^2}$$

Step 2: Find m_{normal}

$$m_{\text{normal}} = \frac{-1}{m_{\text{tangent}}} = \frac{-1}{-1/x^2} = x^2$$

At $\left(2, \frac{1}{2}\right)$, $m_{\text{normal}} = 2^2 = 4$.

Step 3: Write equation of normal

$$m_{\text{normal}} = 4; \left(2, \frac{1}{2}\right)$$

Equation of normal: $y - \frac{1}{2} = 4(x - 2)$, or $y = 4x - \frac{15}{2}$

Step 4: Find other points of intersection.

$$y = \frac{1}{x}; y = 4x - \frac{15}{2}$$

Using the Intersection function of your calculator, enter $y_1 = \frac{1}{x}$ and

$y_2 = 4x - \frac{15}{2}$ and obtain $x = -0.125$ and $y = -8$. Thus, the normal line intersect the graph of $y = \frac{1}{x}$ at the point $(-0.125, -8)$ as well.

> • Remember that $\int 1 dx = x + C$ and $\frac{d}{dx}(1) = 0$.

6.2 LINEAR APPROXIMATIONS

Main Concepts: *Tangent Line Approximation, Estimating the nth Root of a Number, Estimating the Value of a Trigonometric Function of an Angle*

Tangent Line Approximation

An equation of the tangent line to a curve at the point $(a, f(a))$ is:

$y = f(a) + f'(a)(x - a)$; providing that f is differentiable at a. See Figure 6.2-1.

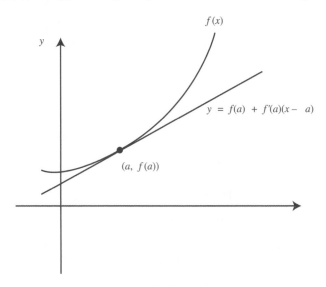

Figure 6.2-1

Tangent Line Approximation (or Linear Approximation):

Since the curve of $f(x)$ and the tangent line are close to each other for points near $x = a$, $f(x) \approx f(a) + f'(a)(x - a)$

Example 1

Write an equation of the tangent line to $f(x) = x^3$ at $(2,8)$. Use the tangent line to find the approximate values of $f(1.9)$ and $f(2.01)$.

Differentiate $f(x)$: $f'(x) = 3x^2$; $f'(2) = 3(2)^2 = 12$. Since f is differentiable at $x = 2$, thus an equation of the tangent at $x = 2$ is:

$$y = f(2) + f'(2)(x - 2)$$
$$y = (2)^3 + 12(x - 2) = 8 + 12x - 24 = 12x - 16$$
$$f(1.9) \approx 12(1.9) - 16 = 6.8$$
$$f(2.01) \approx 12(2.01) - 16 = 8.12. \text{ (See Figure 6.2-2.)}$$

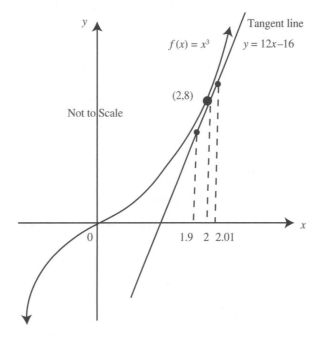

Figure 6.2-2

Example 2

If f is a differentiable function and $f(2) = 6$ and $f'(2) = -\dfrac{1}{2}$, find the approximation value of $f(2.1)$.

Using tangent line approximation, you have

(a) $f(2) = 6 \Rightarrow$ the point of tangency is $(2,6)$

(b) $f'(2) = -\dfrac{1}{2} \Rightarrow$ the slope of the tangent at $x = 2$ is $m = -\dfrac{1}{2}$.

(c) the equation of the tangent is $y - 6 = -\dfrac{1}{2}(x - 2)$ or $y = -\dfrac{1}{2}x + 7$

(d) thus $f(2.1) \approx -\dfrac{1}{2}(2.1) + 7 \approx 5.95$.

Example 3

The slope of a function at any point (x, y) is $-\dfrac{x + 1}{y}$. The point $(3,2)$ is on the graph of f. (a) Write an equation of the line tangent to the graph of f at $x = 1$. (b) Use the tangent line in part (a) to approximate $f(3.1)$.

(a) Let $y = f(x)$, then $\dfrac{dy}{dx} = -\dfrac{x + 1}{y}$

$$\left. \dfrac{dy}{dx} \right|_{x=3, y=2} = -\dfrac{3 + 1}{2} = -2.$$

Equation of tangent: $y - 2 = -2(x - 3)$ or $y = -2x + 8$

(b) $f(3.1) \approx -2(3.1) + 8 \approx 1.8$.

Estimating the *n*th Root of a Number

Another way of expressing the tangent line approximation is:

$f(a + \Delta x) \approx f(a) + f'(a)\Delta x$; where Δx is a relatively small value.

Example 1

Find the approximation value of $\sqrt{50}$ using linear approximation.

Using $f(a + \Delta x) \approx f(a) + f'(a)\Delta x$, let $f(x) = \sqrt{x}$; $a = 49$ and $\Delta x = 1$.

Thus $f(49 + 1) \approx f(49) + f'(49)(1) \approx \sqrt{49} + \frac{1}{2}(49)^{-\frac{1}{2}}(1) \approx 7 + \frac{1}{14} \approx 7.0714$.

Example 2

Find the approximate value of $\sqrt[3]{62}$ using linear approximation.

Let $f(x) = x^{\frac{1}{3}}$, $a = 64$, $\Delta x = -2$. Since $f'(x) = \frac{1}{3}x^{-\frac{2}{3}} = \frac{1}{3x^{\frac{2}{3}}}$ and

$f'(64) = \frac{1}{3(64)^{\frac{2}{3}}} = \frac{1}{48}$, you can use $f(a + \Delta x) \approx f(a) + f'(a)\Delta x$. Thus

$f(62) = f(64 - 2) \approx f(64) + f'(64)(-2) \approx 4 + \frac{1}{48}(-2) \approx 3.958$.

- Use calculus notations and not calculator syntax, e.g., write $\int x^2 dx$ and not $\int(x^\wedge 2, x)$.

Estimating the Value of a Trigonometric Function of an Angle

Example

Approximate the value of $\sin 31°$.

Note: You must express the angle measurement in radians before applying linear approximations. $30° = \frac{\pi}{6}$ radians and $1° = \frac{\pi}{180}$ radians.

Let $f(x) = \sin x$, $a = \frac{\pi}{6}$ and $\Delta x = \frac{\pi}{180}$.

Since $f'(x) = \cos x$ and $f'\left(\frac{\pi}{6}\right) = \cos\left(\frac{\pi}{6}\right) = \frac{\sqrt{3}}{2}$, you can use linear approximations:

$$f\left(\frac{\pi}{6} + \frac{\pi}{180}\right) \approx f\left(\frac{\pi}{6}\right) + f'\left(\frac{\pi}{6}\right)\left(\frac{\pi}{180}\right)$$

$$\approx \sin\frac{\pi}{6} + \left[\cos\left(\frac{\pi}{6}\right)\right]\left(\frac{\pi}{180}\right)$$

$$\approx \frac{1}{2} + \frac{\sqrt{3}}{2}\left(\frac{\pi}{180}\right) \approx 0.515.$$

6.3 MOTION ALONG A LINE

Main Concepts: *Instantaneous Velocity and Acceleration, Vertical Motion, Horizontal Motion*

Instantaneous Velocity and Acceleration

Position Function: $s(t)$

Instantaneous Velocity: $v(t) = s'(t) = \dfrac{ds}{dt}$

If particle is moving to the right →, then $v(t) > 0$.
If particle is moving to the left ←, then $v(t) < 0$.

Acceleration: $a(t) = v'(t) = \dfrac{dv}{dt}$ or $a(t) = s''(t) = \dfrac{d^2 s}{dt^2}$

Instantaneous speed: $|v(t)|$

Example 1

The position function of a particle moving on a straight line is $s(t) = 2t^3 - 10t^2 + 5$. Find (a) the position, (b) instantaneous velocity, (c) acceleration and (d) speed of the particle at $t = 1$.

Solution

    (a) $s(1) = 2(1)^3 - 10(1)^2 + 5 = -3$
    (b) $v(t) = s'(t) = 6t^2 - 20t$
        $v(1) = 6(1)^2 - 20(1) = -14$
    (c) $a(t) = v'(t) = 12t - 20$
        $a(1) = 12(1) - 20 = -8$
    (d) Speed $= |v(t)| = |v(1)| = 14$

Example 2

The velocity function of a moving particle is $v(t) = \dfrac{t^3}{3} - 4t^2 + 16t - 64$ for $0 \le t \le 7$.

What are the minimum and maximum acceleration of the particle on $0 \le t \le 7$?

$$v(t) = \frac{t^3}{3} - 4t^2 + 16t - 64$$

$$a(t) = v'(t) = t^2 - 8t + 16$$

See Figure 6.3-1. The graph of $a(t)$ indicates that:

    (1) The minimum acceleration occurs at $t = 4$ and $(a)(4) = 0$.
    (2) The maximum acceleration occurs at $t = 0$ and $a(0) = 16$.

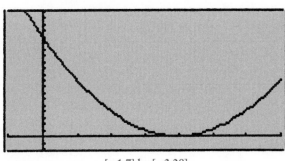

[−1,7] by [−2.20]

Figure 6.3-1

Example 3

The graph of the velocity function is shown in Figure 6.3-2.

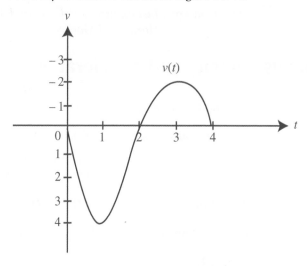

Figure 6.3-2

(a) when is the acceleration 0?
(b) when is the particle moving to the right?
(c) when is the speed the greatest?

Solution:

(a) $a(t) = v'(t)$ and $v'(t)$ is the slope of tangent to the graph of v.
    At $t = 1$ and $t = 3$, the slope of the tangent is 0.
(b) For $2 < t < 4$, $v(t) > 0$. Thus the particle is moving to the right during $2 < t < 4$.
(c) Speed $= |v(t)|$ at $t = 1$, $v(t) = -4$.
    Thus speed at $t = 1$ is $|-4| = 4$ which is the greatest speed for $0 \le t \le 4$.

> • Use only the four specified capabilities of your calculator to get your answer: plotting graph, finding zeros, calculating numerical derivatives, and evaluating definite integrals. All other built-in capabilities can only be used to *check* your solution.

Vertical Motion

Example

From a 400-foot tower, a bowling ball is dropped. The position function of the bowling ball $s(t) = -16t^2 + 400$, $t \ge 0$ is in seconds. Find:

(a) the instantaneous velocity of the ball at $t = 2$ sec
(b) the average velocity for the first 3 sec
(c) when the ball will hit the ground

Solution

(a) $v(t) = s'(t) = -32t$
    $v(2) = -32(2) = -64$ ft/sec

(b) Average velocity $= \dfrac{s(3) - s(0)}{3 - 0} = \dfrac{\left(-16(3)^2 + 400\right) - (0 + 400)}{3}$

    $= -48$ ft/sec

(c) When the ball hits the ground, $s(t) = 0$.
Thus set $s(t) = 0 \Rightarrow -16t^2 + 400 = 0$; $16t^2 = 400$; $t^2 = 25$; $t = \pm 5$
Since $t \geq 0$, $t = 5$. The ball hits the ground at $t = 5$ sec.

• Remember that the volume of a sphere is $v = \dfrac{4}{3}\pi r^3$ and the surface area is $s = 4\pi r^2$. Note that $v' = s$.

Horizontal Motion

Example

The position function of a particle moving on a straight line is $s(t) = t^3 - 6t^2 + 9t - 1$, $t \geq 0$. Describe the motion of the particle.

Step 1. Find $v(t)$ and $a(t)$. $v(t) = 3t^2 - 12t + 9$
$a(t) = 6t - 12$

Step 2. Set $v(t)$ and $a(t) = 0$.
Set $v(t) = 0 \Rightarrow 3t^2 - 12t + 9 = 0 \Rightarrow 3(t^2 - 4t + 3) = 0$
$\Rightarrow 3(t - 1)(t - 3) = 0$ or $t = 1$ or $t = 3$.
Set $a(t) = 0 \Rightarrow 6t - 12 = 0 \Rightarrow 6(t - 2) = 0$ or $t = 2$.

Step 3. Determine the directions of motion. See Figure 6.3-3.

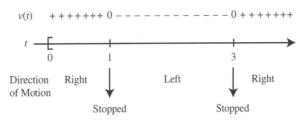

Figure 6.3-3

Step 4. Determine acceleration. See Figure 6.3-4.

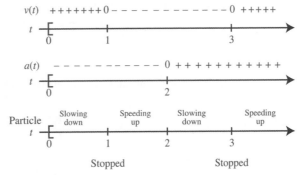

Figure 6.3-4

Step 5. Draw the motion of the particle. See Figure 6.3-5.
$s(0) = -1$, $s(1) = 3$, $s(2) = 1$ and $s(3) = -1$

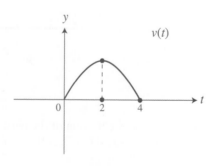

Figure 6.3-5

At $t = 0$, the particle is at -1 and moving to the right. It slows down and stops at $t = 1$ and at $t = 3$. It reverses direction (moving to the left) and speeds up until it reaches 1 at $t = 2$. It continues moving left but slows down and it stops at -1 at $t = 3$. Then it reverses direction (moving to the right) again and speeds up indefinitely. (Note: "Speeding up" is defined as when $|v(t)|$ increases and "slowing down" is defined as when $|v(t)|$ decreases.)

6.4 RAPID REVIEW

1. Write an equation of the normal line to the graph $y = e^x$ at $x = 0$.

   Answer: $\dfrac{dy}{dx}\Big|_{x=0}\ e^x = e^x\big|_{x=0} = e^0 = 1 \Rightarrow m_{normal} = -1$.

   At $x = 0$, $y = e^0 = 1 \Rightarrow$ you have the point $(0,1)$.
   Equation of normal $y - 1 = -1(x - 0)$ or $y = -x + 1$.

2. Using your calculator, find the values of x at which the functions $y = -x^2 + 3x$ and $y = \ln x$ have parallel tangents.

   Answer: $y = -x^2 + 3x \Rightarrow \dfrac{dy}{dx} = -2x + 3$

   $y = \ln x \Rightarrow \dfrac{dy}{dx} = \dfrac{1}{x}$

   Set $-2x + 3 = \dfrac{1}{x}$. Using the Solve function on your calculator, enter

   $\text{Solve}\left(-2x + 3 = \dfrac{1}{x}, x\right)$ and obtain $x = 1$ or $x = \dfrac{1}{2}$.

3. Find the linear approximation of $f(x) = x^3$ at $x = 1$ and use the equation to find $f(1.1)$.

   Answer: $f(1) = 1 \Rightarrow (1,1)$ is on the tangent line and $f'(x) = 3x^2 \Rightarrow f'(1) = 3$.
   $y - 1 = 3(x - 1)$ or $y = 3x - 2$
   $f(1.1) \approx 3(1.1) - 2 \approx 1.3$.

4. See Figure 6.4-1.
   (a) When is the acceleration zero? (b) is the particle moving to the right or left?

Figure 6.4-1

Answer: (a) $a(t) = v'(t)$ and $v'(t)$ is the slope of the tangent. Thus, $a(t) = 0$ at $t = 2$.
(b) Since $v(t) \geq 0$, the particle is moving to the right.

5. Find the maximum acceleration of the particle whose velocity function is $v(t) = t^2 + 3$ on the interval $0 \leq t \leq 4$.

Answer: $a(t) = v'(t) = 2(t)$ on the interval $0 \leq t \leq 4$, $a(t)$ has its maximum value at $t = 4$. Thus $a(t) = 8$. The maximum acceleration is 8.

6.5 PRACTICE PROBLEMS

Part A—The use of a calculator is not allowed.

1. Find the linear approximation of $f(x) = (1 + x)^{\frac{1}{4}}$ at $x = 0$ and use the equation to approximate $f(0.1)$.

2. Find the approximate value of $\sqrt[3]{28}$ using linear approximation.

3. Find the approximation value of $\cos 46°$ using linear approximation.

4. Find the point on the graph of $y = |x^3|$ such that the tangent at the point is parallel to the line $y - 12x = 3$.

5. Write an equation of the normal to the graph of $y = e^x$ at $x = \ln 2$.

6. If the line $y - 2x = b$ is tangent to the graph $y = -x^2 + 4$, find the value of b.

7. If the position function of a particle is $s(t) = \dfrac{t^3}{3} - 3t^2 + 4$, find the velocity and position of particle when its acceleration is 0.

8. The graph in Figure 6.5-1 represents the distance in feet covered by a moving particle in

t seconds. Draw a sketch of the corresponding velocity function.

9. The position function of a moving particle is shown in Figure 6.5-2. For which value(s) of t (t_1, t_2, t_3) is:

(a) the particle moving to the left?

(b) the acceleration negative?

(c) the particle moving to the right and slowing down?

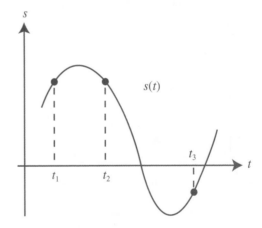

Figure 6.5-2

10. The velocity function of a particle is shown in Figure 6.5-3.

(a) when does the particle reverse direction?

(b) when is the acceleration 0?

(c) When is the speed the greatest?

11. A ball is dropped from the top of a 640-foot building. The position function of the ball is $s(t) = -16t^2 + 640$, where t is measured in seconds and $s(t)$ is in feet. Find:

(a) The position of the ball after 4 seconds.

(b) The instantaneous velocity of the ball at $t = 4$.

(c) The average velocity for the first 4 seconds.

(d) When the ball will hit the ground.

(e) The speed of the ball when it hits the ground.

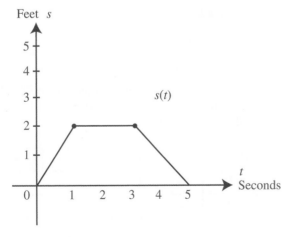

Figure 6.5-1

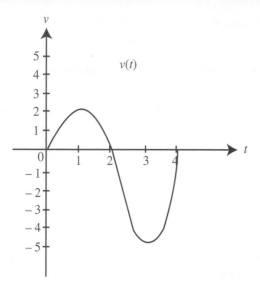

v(t)

Figure 6.5-3

12. The graph of the position function of a moving particle is shown. See Figure 6.5-4.

(a) What is the particle's position at $t = 5$?

(b) When is the particle moving to the left?

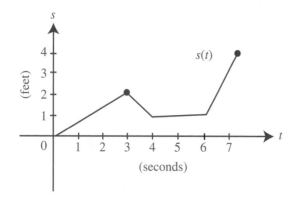

Figure 6.5-4

(c) When is the particle standing still?

(d) When does the particle have the greatest speed?

Part B—Calculators are permitted.

13. The position function of a particle moving on a line is $s(t) = t^3 - 3t^2 + 1$, $t \geq 0$ where t is measured in seconds and s in meters. Describe the motion of the particle.

14. Find the linear approximation of $f(x) = \sin x$ at $x = \pi$. Use the equation to find the approximate value of $f\left(\dfrac{181\pi}{180}\right)$.

15. Find the linear approximation of $f(x) = \ln(1 + x)$ at $x = 2$.

16. Find the coordinates of each point on the graph of $y^2 = 4 - 4x^2$ at which the tangent line is vertical. Write an equation of each vertical tangent.

17. Find the value(s) of x at which the graphs of $y = \ln x$ and $y = x^2 + 3$ have parallel tangents.

18. The position functions of two moving particles are $s_1(t) = \ln t$, and $s_2(t) = \sin t$, a and the domain of both functions is $1 \leq t \leq 8$. Find the values of t such that the velocities of the two particles are the same.

19. The position function of a moving particle on a line is $s(t) = \sin(t)$ for $0 \leq t \leq 2\pi$. Describe the motion of the particle.

20. A coin is dropped from the top of a tower and hits the ground 10.2 seconds later. The position function is given as $s(t) = -16t^2 + v_0 t + s_0$, where s is measured in feet, t in seconds and v_0 is the initial velocity and s_0 is the initial position. Find the approximate height of the building to the nearest foot.

 ## 6.6 CUMULATIVE REVIEW PROBLEMS

"Calculator" indicates that calculators are permitted.

21. Find $\dfrac{dy}{dx}$ if $y = x \sin^{-1}(2x)$.

22. Given $f(x) = x^3 - 3x^2 + 3x - 1$ and the point $(1,2)$ is on the graph of $f^{-1}(x)$. Find the slope of the tangent line to the graph of $f^{-1}(x)$ at $(1,2)$.

23. Evaluate $\displaystyle\lim_{x \to 100} \dfrac{x - 100}{\sqrt{x} - 10}$.

24. A function f is continuous on the interval $[-1,8]$ with $f(0) = 0$, $f(2) = 3$, and $f(8) = \frac{1}{2}$ and the following properties:

Intervals	(−1,2)	x = 2	(2,5)	x = 5	(5,8)
f′	+	0	−	−	−
f″	−	−	−	0	+

(a) Find the intervals on which f is increasing or decreasing.

(b) Find where f has its absolute extrema.

(c) Find where f has the points of inflection.

(d) Find the intervals on where f is concave upward or downward.

(e) Sketch a possible graph of f.

25. The graph of the velocity function of a moving particle for $0 \le t \le 8$ is shown in Figure 6.6-1. Using the graph:

    (a) estimate the acceleration when $v(t) = 3$ ft/sec.

    (b) the time when the acceleration is a minimum.

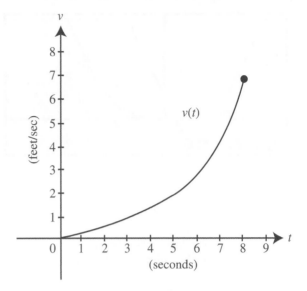

Figure 6.6-1

6.7 SOLUTIONS TO PRACTICE PROBLEMS

Part A—No calculators.

1. Equation of tangent line: $y = f(a) + f'(a)(x - a)$

$$f'(x) = \frac{1}{4}(1 + x)^{-3/4}(1) = \frac{1}{4}(1 + x)^{-3/4}$$

$$f'(0) = \frac{1}{4} \text{ and } f(0) = 1;$$

Thus, $y = 1 + \frac{1}{4}(x - 0) = 1 + \frac{1}{4}x$.

$$f(0.1) = 1 + \frac{1}{4}(0.1) = 1.025.$$

2. $f(a + \Delta x) \approx f(a) + f'(a)\Delta x$

Let $f(x) = \sqrt[3]{x}$ and $f(28) = f(27 + 1)$.

Then $f'(x) = \frac{1}{3}(x)^{-2/3}$

and $f'(27) = \frac{1}{27}$ and $f(27) = 3$.

$$f(27 + 1) \approx f(27) + f'(27)(1) \approx 3 +$$

$$\left(\frac{1}{27}\right)(1) \approx 3.\overline{037}.$$

3. $f(a + \Delta x) \approx f(a) + f'(a)\Delta x$. Convert to radians:

$$\frac{46}{180} = \frac{a}{\pi} \Rightarrow a = \frac{23\pi}{90} \text{ and } 1° = \frac{\pi}{180}; 45° = \frac{\pi}{4}.$$

Let $f(x) = \cos x$ and $f(45°) =$

$$f\left(\frac{\pi}{4}\right) = \cos\left(\frac{\pi}{4}\right) = \frac{\sqrt{2}}{2}$$

Then $f'(x) = -\sin x$ and $f'(45°) =$

$$f'\left(\frac{\pi}{4}\right) = -\frac{\sqrt{2}}{2}$$

$$f(46°) = f\left(\frac{23\pi}{90}\right) = f\left(\frac{\pi}{4} = \frac{\pi}{180}\right)$$

$$f\left(\frac{\pi}{4} + \frac{\pi}{180}\right) \approx f\left(\frac{\pi}{4}\right) + f'\left(\frac{\pi}{4}\right)\left(\frac{\pi}{180}\right) \approx$$

$$\frac{\sqrt{2}}{2} + \left(\frac{\sqrt{2}}{2}\right)\left(\frac{\pi}{180}\right) \approx \frac{\sqrt{2}}{2} - \frac{\pi\sqrt{2}}{360}$$

4. Step 1: Find m_{tangent}

$$y = |x^3| = \begin{cases} x^3 & \text{if } x \ge 0 \\ -x^3 & \text{if } x < 0 \end{cases}$$

$$\frac{dy}{dx} = \begin{cases} 3x^2 & \text{if } x > 0 \\ -3x^2 & \text{if } x < 0 \end{cases}$$

Step 2: Set $m_{\text{tangent}} = $ slope of line $y - 12x = 3$.
Since $y - 12x = 3 \Rightarrow y = 12x + 3$,
then $m = 12$.
Set $3x^2 = 12 \Rightarrow x \pm 2$ since $x \ge 0$, $x = 2$.
Set $-3x^2 = 12 \Rightarrow x^2 = -4$. Thus ϕ.

Step 3: Find the point on the curve.
(See Figure 6.7-1.)

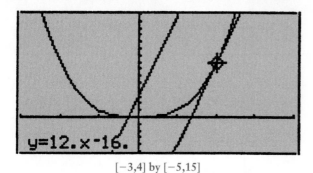

$y=12.x-16.$

[−3,4] by [−5,15]

Figure 6.7-1

At $x = 2$, $y = x^3 = 2^3 = 8$.
Thus the point is (2,8).

5. Step 1: Find m_{tangent}

$$y = e^x; \frac{dy}{dx} = e^x$$

$$\left.\frac{dy}{dx}\right|_{x=\ln 2} = e^{\ln 2} = 2$$

Step 2: Find m_{normal}

$$\text{At } x = \ln_2, m_{\text{normal}} = \frac{-1}{m_{\text{tangent}}} = -\frac{1}{2}$$

Step 3: Write equation of normal
At $x = \ln 2$, $y = e^x = e^{\ln 2} = 2$. Thus the point of tangency is (ln 2, 2).
The equation of normal:

$$y - 2 = -\frac{1}{2}(x - \ln 2) \text{ or}$$

$$y = -\frac{1}{2}(x - \ln 2) + 2.$$

6. Step 1: Find m_{tangent}

$$y = -x^2 + 4; \frac{dy}{dx} = -2x.$$

Step 2: Find the slope of line $y - 2x = b$
$y - 2x = b \Rightarrow y = 2x + b$ or $m = 2$.

Step 3: Find point of tangency. Set $m_{\text{tangent}} = $ slope of line $y - 2x = b - 2x = 2 \Rightarrow x = -1$.
At $x = -1$, $y = -x^2 + 4 = -(-1)^2 + 4 = 3$; (−1, 3).

Step 4: Find b.
Since the line $y - 2x = b$ passes through the point (−1, 3), thus $3 - 2(-1) = b$ or $b = 5$.

7. $v(t) = s'(t) = t^2 - 6t; a(t) = v'(t) = s''(t) = 2t - 6$
Set $a(t) = 0 \Rightarrow 2t - 6 = 0$ or $t = 3$.

$$v(3) = (3)^2 - 6(3) = -9; s(3) = \frac{(3)^3}{3} - 3(3)^2 + 4 = -14.$$

8. On the interval (0, 1), the slope of the line segment is 2. Thus the velocity $v(t) = 2$ ft/sec. On (1, 3), $v(t) = 0$ and on (3, 5), $v(t) = -1$. See Figure 6.7-2.

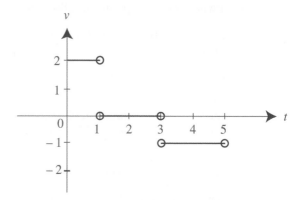

Figure 6.7-2

9. (a) At $t = t_2$, the slope of the tangent is negative. Thus, the particle is moving to the left.

 (b) At $t = t_1$, and at $t = t_2$, the curve is concave downward $\Rightarrow \frac{d^2 s}{dt^2} = $ acceleration is negative.

 (c) At $t = t_1$, the slope > 0 and thus the particle is moving to the right. The curve is concave downward $\Rightarrow$ the particle is slowing down.

10. (a) At $t = 2$, $v(t)$ changes from positive to negative, and thus the particle reverses its direction.

 (b) At $t = 1$, and at $t = 3$, the slope of the tangent to the curve is 0. Thus the acceleration is 0.

 (c) At $t = 3$, speed is equal to $|-5| = 5$ and 5 is the greatest speed.

11. (a) $s(4) = -16(4)^2 + 640 = 384$ ft

 (b) $v(t) = s'(t) = -32t$
 $v(4) = -32(4)$ ft/sec $= -128$ ft/sec

 (c) Average Velocity $= \dfrac{s(4) - s(0)}{4 - 0}$

 $= \dfrac{384 - 640}{4} = -64$ ft/sec

 (d) Set $s(t) = 0 \Rightarrow -16t^2 + 640 = 0 \Rightarrow 16t^2 = 640$
 or $t = \pm 2\sqrt{10}$.
 Since $t \geq 0$, $t = +2\sqrt{10}$ or $t \approx 6.32$ sec.

 (e) $\left|v(2\sqrt{10})\right| = \left|-32(2\sqrt{10})\right| = \left|-64\sqrt{10}\right|$ ft sec

 or ≈ 202.39 ft/sec

12. (a) At $t = 5$, $s(t) = 1$

(b) For $3 < t < 4$, $s(t)$ decreases. Thus, the particle moves to the left when $3 < t < 4$.

(c) When $4 < t < 6$, the particle stays at 1.

(d) When $6 < t < 7$, speed = 2 ft/sec, the greatest speed, which occurs where s has the greatest slope.

Part B—Calculators are permitted.

13. Step 1. $v(t) = 3t^2 - 6t$
    $a(t) = 6t - 6$

Step 2. Set $v(t) = 0 \Rightarrow 3t^2 - 6t = 0 \Rightarrow 3t(t - 2) = 0$,
    or $t = 0$ or $t = 2$
    Set $a(t) = 0 \Rightarrow 6t - 6 = 0$ or $t = 1$.

Step 3. Determine the directions of motion. See Figure 6.7-3.

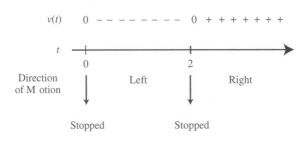

Figure 6.7-3

Step 4. Determine acceleration. See Figure 6.7-4.

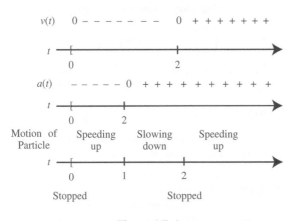

Figure 6.7-4

Step 5. Draw the motion of the particle. See Figure 6.7-5. $s(0) = 1$, $s(1) = -1$ and $s(2) = -3$.

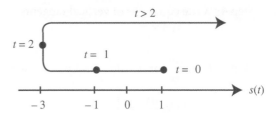

Figure 6.7-5

The particle is initially at 1 ($t = 0$). It moves to the left speeding up until $t = 1$, when it reaches -1. Then it continues moving to the left, but slowing down until $t = 2$ at -3. The particle reverses direction, moving to the right and speeding up indefinitely.

14. Linear approximation: $y = f(a) + f'(a)(x - a)$
    $a = \pi$
    $f(x) = \sin x$ and $f(\pi) = \sin \pi = 0$
    $f'(x) = \cos x$ and $f'(\pi) = \cos \pi = -1$.
    Thus $y = 0 + (-1)(x - \pi)$ or $y = -x + \pi$.

$f\left(\dfrac{181\pi}{180}\right)$ is approximately:

$$y = -\left(\dfrac{181\pi}{180}\right) + \pi = \dfrac{-\pi}{180} \text{ or } \approx -0.0175.$$

15. $y = f(a) + f'(a)(x - a)$
    $f(x) = \ln(1 + x)$ and $f(2) = \ln(1 + 2) = \ln 3$
    $f'(x) = \dfrac{1}{1 + x}$ and $f'(2) = \dfrac{1}{1 + 2} = \dfrac{1}{3}$.

    Thus $y = \ln 3 + \dfrac{1}{3}(x - 2)$.

16. Step 1: Find $\dfrac{dy}{dx}$.

$$y^2 = 4 - 4x^2$$

$$2y\dfrac{dy}{dx} = -8x \Rightarrow \dfrac{dy}{dx} = \dfrac{-4x}{y}$$

Step 2: Find $\dfrac{dx}{dy}$.

$$\dfrac{dx}{dy} = \dfrac{1}{dy/dx} = \dfrac{1}{-4x/y} = \dfrac{-y}{4x}$$

Set $\dfrac{dx}{dy} = 0 \Rightarrow \dfrac{-y}{4x} = 0$ or $y = 0$.

Step 3: Find points of tangency
    At $y = 0$, $y^2 = 4 - 4x^2$ becomes $0 = 4 - 4x^2$
    $\Rightarrow x = \pm 1$.
    Thus points of tangency are $(1, 0)$ and $(-1, 0)$

Step 4: Write equations of vertical tangents
$x = 1$ and $x = -1$.

17. Step 1: Find $\dfrac{dy}{dx}$ for $y = \ln x$ and $y = x^2 + 3$

$y = \ln x; \dfrac{dy}{dx} = \dfrac{1}{x}$

$y = x^2 + 3; \dfrac{dy}{dx} = 2x$

Step 2: Find the x-coordinate of point(s) of tangency.
Parallel tangents $\Rightarrow$ slopes are equal

Set Set $\dfrac{1}{x} = 2x$.

Using the Solve function of your calculator,

enter solve $\left(\dfrac{1}{x} = 2x, x \right)$ and obtain

$x = \dfrac{\sqrt{2}}{2}$ or $x = \dfrac{-\sqrt{2}}{2}$. Since for $y = \ln x$,

$x > 0$, thus $x = \dfrac{\sqrt{2}}{2}$.

18. $s_1(t) = \ln t$ and $s_1'(t) = \dfrac{1}{t}$; $1 \le t \le 8$

$s_2(t) = \sin(t)$ and $s_2'(t) = \cos(t)$; $1 \le t \le 8$

Enter $y_1 = \dfrac{1}{x}$ and $y_2 = \cos(x)$. Use the Intersection function of the calculator and obtain $t = 4.917$ and $t = 7.724$.

19. Step 1. $s(t) = \sin t$
$v(t) = \cos t$
$a(t) = -\sin t$

Step 2. Set $v(t) = 0 \Rightarrow \cos t = 0$; $t = \dfrac{\pi}{2}$ and $\dfrac{3\pi}{2}$.

Set $a(t) = 0 \Rightarrow -\sin t = 0$; $t = \pi$ and 2π.

Step 3. Determine the directions of motion. See Figure 6.7-6.

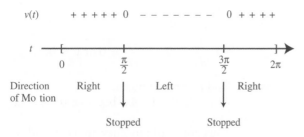

Figure 6.7-6

Step 4. Determine acceleration. See Figure 6.7-7.

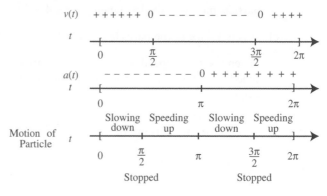

Figure 6.7-7

Step 5. Draw the motion of the particle. See Figure 6.7-8.

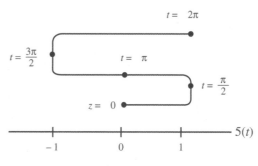

Figure 6.7-8

The particle is initially at 0, $s(0) = 0$. It moves to the right but slows down to a stop at 1 when

$t = \dfrac{\pi}{2}$, $s\left(\dfrac{\pi}{2}\right) = 1$. It then turns and moves to the

left speeding up until it reaches 0, when $t = \pi$, $s(\pi) = 0$ and continues to the left but slowing down

to a stop at -1 when $t = \dfrac{3\pi}{2}$, $s\dfrac{3\pi}{2} = -1$. It then

turns around again, moving to the right, speeding up to 1 when $t = 2\pi$, $s(2\pi) = 0$.

20. $s(t) = -16t^2 + v_0 t + s_0$.
$s_0 =$ height of building and $v_0 = 0$.
Thus $s(t) = -16t^2 + s_0$.
When the coin hits the ground, $s(t) = 0$, $t = 10.2$.
Thus, set $s(t) = 0 \Rightarrow -16t^2 + s_0 = 0 \Rightarrow -16(10.2)^2 + s_0 = 0$
$s_0 = 1664.64$ ft. The building is approximately 1665 ft tall.

6.8 SOLUTIONS TO CUMULATIVE REVIEW PROBLEMS

21. Using product rule, let $u = x$; $v = \sin^{-1}(2x)$.

$$\frac{dy}{dx} = (1)\sin^{-1}(2x) + \frac{1}{\sqrt{1-(2x)^2}}(2)(x)$$

$$= \sin^{-1}(2x) - \frac{2x}{\sqrt{1-4x^2}}$$

22. Let $y = f(x) \Rightarrow y = x^3 - 3x^2 + 3x - 1$.
To find $f^{-1}(x)$, switch x and y: $x = y^3 - 3y^2 + 3y - 1$

$$\frac{dx}{dy} = 3y^2 - 6y + 3;$$

$$\frac{dy}{dx} = \frac{1}{dx/dy} = \frac{1}{3y^2 - 6y + 3}$$

$$\left.\frac{dy}{dx}\right|_{y=2} = \frac{1}{3(2)^2 - 6(2) + 3} = \frac{1}{3}$$

23. Substituting $x = 0$ into the expression $\frac{x-100}{\sqrt{x}-10}$

would lead to $\frac{0}{0}$. Multiply both numerator and denominator by the conjugate of the denominator $\left(\sqrt{x}+10\right)$:

$$\lim_{x \to 100} \frac{(x-100)}{(\sqrt{x}-10)} \cdot \frac{(\sqrt{x}+10)}{(\sqrt{x}+10)} =$$

$$\lim_{x \to 100} \frac{(x-100)(\sqrt{x}+10)}{(x-100)}$$

$$\lim_{x \to 100}\left(\sqrt{x}+10\right) = 10 + 10 = 20.$$

An alternative solution is to factor the numerator:

$$\lim_{x \to 100} \frac{(\sqrt{x}-10)(\sqrt{x}+10)}{(\sqrt{x}-10)} = 20.$$

24. (a) $f' > 0$ on $(-1,2)$, f is increasing on $(-1,2)$
$f' < 0$ on $(2,8)$, f is decreasing on $(2,8)$

(b) At $x = 2$, $f' = 0$ and $f'' < 0$, thus at $x = 2$, f has a relative maximum. Since it is the only relative extremum on the interval, it is an absolute maximum. Since f is a continuous function on a closed interval and at its endpoints $f(-1) < 0$ and $f(8) = \frac{1}{2}$, thus f has an absolute minimum at $x = -1$.

(c) At $x = 5$, f has a change of concavity and f' exists at $x = 5$.

(d) $f'' < 0$ on $(-1,5)$, f is concave downward on $(-1,5)$.
$f'' > 0$ on $(5,8)$, f is concave upward on $(5,8)$.

(e) A possible graph of f is given in Figure 6.8-1.

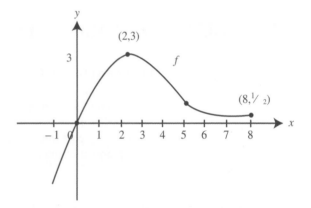

Figure 6.8-1

25. (a) $v(t) = 3$ ft/sec at $t = 6$. The tangent line to the graph of $v(t)$ at $t = 6$ has a slope of approximately $m = 1$. (The tangent passes through the points $(8,5)$ and $(5,0)$; thus $m = 1$). Therefore the acceleration is 1 ft/sec².

(b) The acceleration is a minimum at $t = 0$, since the slope of the tangent to the curve of $v(t)$ is the smallest at $t = 0$.

Chapter 7

Integration

7.1 EVALUATING BASIC INTEGRALS

Main Concepts: *Antiderivatives and Integration Formulas, Evaluating Integrals*

> • Answer all parts of a question from Section II even if you think your answer to an earlier part of the question might not be correct. Also, if you don't know the answer to part one of a question, and you need it to answer part two, just make it up and continue.

Antiderivatives and Integration Formulas

Definition: A function F is an antiderivative of another function f if $F'(x) = f(x)$ for all x in some open interval. Any two antiderivatives of f differ by an additive constant C. We denote the set of antiderivatives of f by $\int f(x)dx$, called the indefinite integral of f.

Integration Rules:

1. $\int f(x)dx = F(x) + C \Leftrightarrow F'(x) = f(x)$

2. $\int a f(x)\, dx = a\int f(x)\, dx$

3. $\int -f(x)\, dx = -\int f(x)\, dx$

4. $\int [f(x) \pm g(x)]\, dx = \int f(x)\, dx \pm \int g(x)dx$

Differentiation Formulas:

1. $\dfrac{d}{dx}(x) = 1$

2. $\dfrac{d}{dx}(ax) = a$

Integration Formulas:

1. $\int 1dx = x + c$

2. $\int a\, dx = ax + c$

Differentiation Formulas (cont.):

3. $\dfrac{d}{dx}\left(x^n\right) = nx^{n-1}$

4. $\dfrac{d}{dx}\left(\cos x\right) = -\sin x$

5. $\dfrac{d}{dx}\left(\sin x\right) = \cos x$

6. $\dfrac{d}{dx}\left(\tan x\right) = \sec^2 x$

7. $\dfrac{d}{dx}\left(\cot x\right) = -\csc^2 x$

8. $\dfrac{d}{dx}\left(\sec x\right) = \sec x \tan x$

9. $\dfrac{d}{dx}\left(\csc x\right) = -\csc x\left(\cot x\right)$

10. $\dfrac{d}{dx}\left(\ln x\right) = \dfrac{1}{x}$

11. $\dfrac{d}{dx}\left(e^x\right) = e^x$

12. $\dfrac{d}{dx}\left(a^x\right) = \left(\ln a\right)a^x$

13. $\dfrac{d}{dx}\left(\sin^{-1} x\right) = \dfrac{1}{\sqrt{1 - x^2}}$

14. $\dfrac{d}{dx}\left(\tan^{-1} x\right) = \dfrac{1}{1 + x^2}$

15. $\dfrac{d}{dx}\left(\sec^{-1} x\right) = \dfrac{1}{|x|\sqrt{x^2 - 1}}$

Integration Formulas (cont.):

3. $\displaystyle\int x^n dx = \dfrac{x^{n+1}}{n + 1} + c,\, n \neq -1$

4. $\displaystyle\int \sin x\, dx = -\cos x + c$

5. $\displaystyle\int \cos x\, dx = \sin x + c$

6. $\displaystyle\int \sec^2 x\, dx = \tan x + c$

7. $\displaystyle\int \csc^2 x\, dx = -\cot x + c$

8. $\displaystyle\int \sec x\left(\tan x\right)dx = \sec x + c$

9. $\displaystyle\int \csc x\left(\cot x\right)dx = -\csc x + c$

10. $\displaystyle\int \dfrac{1}{x}\, dx = \ln|x| + c$

11. $\displaystyle\int e^x dx = e^x + c$

12. $\displaystyle\int a^x dx = \dfrac{a^x}{\ln a} + c\quad a > 0, a \neq 1$

13. $\displaystyle\int \dfrac{1}{\sqrt{1 - x^2}}\, dx = \sin^{-1} x + c$

14. $\displaystyle\int \dfrac{1}{1 + x^2}\, dx = \tan^{-1} x + c$

15. $\displaystyle\int \dfrac{1}{|x|\sqrt{x^2 - 1}}\, dx = \sec^{-1} x + c$

More Integration Formulas:

16. $\displaystyle\int \tan x\, dx = \ln|\sec x| + c \text{ or } -\ln|\cos x| + c$

17. $\displaystyle\int \cot x\, dx = \ln|\sin x| + c \text{ or } -\ln|\csc x| + c$

18. $\displaystyle\int \sec x\, dx = \ln|\sec x + \tan x| + c$

19. $\displaystyle\int \csc x\, dx = \ln|\csc x - \cot x| + c$

20. $\displaystyle\int \ln x\, dx = x \ln|x| - x + c$

21. $\displaystyle\int \dfrac{1}{\sqrt{a^2 - x^2}}\, dx = \sin^{-1}\left(\dfrac{x}{a}\right) + c$

22. $\displaystyle\int \dfrac{1}{a^2 + x^2}\, dx = \dfrac{1}{a}\tan^{-1}\left(\dfrac{x}{a}\right) + c$

23. $\displaystyle\int \dfrac{1}{x\sqrt{x^2 + a^2}}\, dx = \dfrac{1}{a}\sec^{-1}\left|\dfrac{x}{a}\right| + c \text{ or } \dfrac{1}{a}\cos^{-1}\left|\dfrac{a}{x}\right| + c$

24. $\int \sin^2 x \, dx = \dfrac{x}{2} - \dfrac{\sin(2x)}{4} + c.$ Note: $\sin^2 x = \dfrac{1 - \cos 2x}{2}$

Note: After evaluating an integral, always check the result by taking the derivative of the answer (i.e., taking the derivative of the antiderivative).

- Remember that the volume of a right-circular cone is $v = \dfrac{1}{3}\pi r^2 h$ where r is the radius of the base and h is the height of the cone.

Evaluating Integrals

Integral	Rewrite	Antiderivative
$\int x^3 dx$		$\dfrac{x^4}{4} + c$
$\int dx$	$\int 1 dx$	$x + c$
$\int 5dx$		$5x + c$
$\int \sqrt{x} \, dx$	$\int x^{1/2} dx$	$\dfrac{x^{3/2}}{3/2} + c$ or $\dfrac{2x^{3/2}}{3} + c$
$\int x^{5/2} dx$		$\dfrac{x^{7/2}}{7/2} + c$ or $\dfrac{2x^{7/2}}{7} + c$
$\int \dfrac{1}{x^2} dx$	$\int x^{-2} dx$	$\dfrac{x^{-1}}{-1} + c$ or $\dfrac{-1}{x} + c$
$\int \dfrac{1}{\sqrt[3]{x^2}} dx$	$\int \dfrac{1}{x^{2/3}} dx = \int x^{-2/3} dx$	$\dfrac{x^{1/3}}{1/3} + c$ or $3\sqrt[3]{x} + c$
$\int \dfrac{x+1}{x} dx$	$\int \left(1 + \dfrac{1}{x}\right) dx$	$x + \ln|x| + c$
$\int x(x^5 + 1)dx$	$\int (x^6 + x)dx$	$\dfrac{x^7}{7} + \dfrac{x^2}{2} + c$

Example 1

Evaluate $\int (x^5 - 6x^2 + x - 1)dx$

Apply the formula $\int x^n dx = \dfrac{x^{n+1}}{n+1} + c,\ n \neq 1$.

$\int (x^5 - 6x^2 + x - 1)dx = \dfrac{x^6}{6} - 2x^3 + \dfrac{x^2}{2} - x + c$

Example 2

Evaluate $\int \left(\sqrt{x} + \dfrac{1}{x^3} \right) dx$

Rewrite $\int \left(\sqrt{x} + \dfrac{1}{x^3} \right) dx$ as $\int \left(x^{1/2} + x^{-3} \right) dx = \dfrac{x^{3/2}}{3/2} + \dfrac{x^{-2}}{-2} + c$

$$= \dfrac{2}{3} x^{3/2} - \dfrac{1}{2x^2} + c$$

Example 3

If $\dfrac{dy}{dx} = 3x^2 + 2$, and the point $(0,-1)$ lies on the graph of y, find y.

Since $\dfrac{dy}{dx} = 3x^2 + 2$, then y is an antiderivative of $\dfrac{dy}{dx}$. Thus

$y = \int (3x^2 + 2)dx = x^3 + 2x + c$. The point $(0,-1)$ is on the graph of y.

Thus $y = x^3 + 2x + c$ becomes $-1 = 0^3 + 2(0) + c$ or $c = -1$. Therefore, $y = x^3 + 2x - 1$.

Example 4

Evaluate $\int \left(1 - \dfrac{1}{\sqrt[3]{x^4}} \right) dx$

Rewrite as $\int \left(1 - \dfrac{1}{x^{4/3}} \right) dx = \int \left(1 - x^{-4/3} \right) dx$

$$= x - \dfrac{x^{-1/3}}{-1/3} + c = x + \dfrac{3}{\sqrt[3]{x}} + c$$

Example 5

Evaluate $\int \dfrac{3x^2 + x - 1}{x^2} dx$

Rewrite as $\int \left(3 + \dfrac{1}{x} - \dfrac{1}{x^2} \right) dx = \int \left(3 + \dfrac{1}{x} - x^{-2} \right) dx$

$$= 3x + \ln|x| - \dfrac{x^{-1}}{-1} + c = 3x + \ln|x| + \dfrac{1}{x} + c$$

Example 6

Evaluate $\int \sqrt{x}(x^2 - 3)dx$

Rewrite $\int x^{1/2}(x^2 - 3)dx = \int \left(x^{5/2} - 3x^{1/2}\right)dx$

$$= \frac{x^{7/2}}{7/2} - \frac{3x^{3/2}}{3/2} + c = \frac{2}{7}x^{7/2} - 2\sqrt{x^3} + c$$

Example 7

Evaluate $\int (x^3 - 4 \sin x)dx$

$\int (x^3 - 4 \sin x)dx = \dfrac{x^4}{4} + 4 \cos x + c$

Example 8

Evaluate $\int (4 \cos x - \cot x)dx$

$\int (4 \cos x - \cot x)dx = 4 \sin x - \ln|\sin x| + c$

Example 9

Evaluate $\int \dfrac{\sin x - 1}{\cos x}dx$

Rewrite $\int \left(\dfrac{\sin x}{\cos x} - \dfrac{1}{\cos x}\right)dx = \int (\tan x - \sec x)dx = \int \tan x\, dx - \int \sec x\, dx$

$$= \ln |\sec x| - \ln |\sec x + \tan x| + c = \ln \left|\frac{\sec x}{\sec x + \tan x}\right| + c$$

$$\text{or} -\ln |\sin x + 1| + c$$

Example 10

Evaluate $\int \dfrac{e^{2x}}{e^x}dx$

Rewrite the integral as $\int e^x dx = e^x + c$

Example 11

Evaluate $\int \dfrac{3}{1 + x^2}dx$

Rewrite as $3\int \dfrac{1}{1 + x^2}dx = 3 \tan^{-1} x + c$

Example 12

Evaluate $\int \dfrac{1}{\sqrt{9 - x^2}}dx$

Rewrite as $\int \dfrac{1}{\sqrt{3^2 - x^2}}dx = \sin^{-1}\left(\dfrac{x}{3}\right) + c$

Example 13

Evaluate $\int 7^x dx$

$\int 7^x dx = \dfrac{7^x}{\ln 7} + c$

!

Reminder: You can always check the result by taking the derivative of the answer.

7.2 INTEGRATION BY U-SUBSTITUTION

Main Concepts: *The U-Substitution Method, U-Substitution and Algebraic Functions, U-Substitution and Trigonometric Functions, U-Substitution and Inverse Trigonometric, U-Substitution and Logarithmic and Exponential Functions*

The U-Substitution Method

The Chain Rule for Differentiation:

$$\frac{d}{dx} F(g(x)) = f(g(x))g'(x) \text{ where } F' = f$$

The Integral of a Composite Function:

If $f(g(x))$ and f' are continuous and $F' = f$, then

$$\int f(g(x))g'(x)\,dx = F(g(x)) + c$$

Making a U-Substitution:

Let $u = g(x)$; then $du = g'(x)\,dx$

$$\int f(g(x))g'(x)\,dx = \int f(u)\,du = F(u) + c = F(g(x)) + c$$

Procedure for Making a U-Substitution:

Steps:
1. Given $f(g(x))$; Let $u = g(x)$
2. Differentiate: $du = g'(x)\,dx$
3. Rewrite the integral in terms of u.
4. Evaluate the integral.
5. Replace u by $g(x)$.
6. Check your result by taking the derivative of the answer.

U-Substitution and Algebraic Functions

Another Form of the Integral of a Composite Function:

If f is a differentiable function, then

$$\int (f(x))^n f'(x)\,dx = \frac{(f(x))^{n+1}}{n+1} + c, n \neq -1$$

Making a U-Substitution:

Let $u = f(x)$; then $du = f'(x)\,dx$.

$$\int (f(x))^n f'(x)\,dx = \int u^n\,du = \frac{u^{n+1}}{n+1} + c = \frac{(f(x))^{n+1}}{n+1} + c, n \neq -1$$

Example 1

Evaluate $\int x(x + 1)^{10}\,dx$

Step 1. Let $u = x + 1$; then $x = u - 1$

Step 2. Differentiate: $du = dx$

Step 3. Rewrite: $\int (u-1)u^{10}\, du = \int (u^{11} - u^{10})\, du$

Step 4. Integrate: $\dfrac{u^{12}}{12} - \dfrac{u^{11}}{11} + c$

Step 5. Replace u: $\dfrac{(x+1)^{12}}{12} - \dfrac{(x+1)^{11}}{11} + c$

Step 6. Differentiate and Check: $\dfrac{12(x+1)^{11}}{12} - \dfrac{11(x+1)^{10}}{11} = (x+1)^{11} - (x+1)^{10}$

$$= (x+1)^{10}(x+1-1) = (x+1)^{10}\,x \text{ or } x(x+1)^{10}$$

Example 2

Evaluate $\int x\sqrt{x-2}\, dx$

Step 1. Let $u = x - 2$; then $x = u + 2$

Step 2. Differentiate $du = dx$

Step 3. Rewrite: $\int (u+2)\sqrt{u}\, du = \int (u+2)u^{1/2}\, du = \int \left(u^{3/2} + 2u^{1/2}\right) du$

Step 4. Integrate: $\dfrac{u^{5/2}}{5/2} + \dfrac{2u^{3/2}}{3/2} + c$

Step 5. Replace: $\dfrac{2(x-2)^{5/2}}{5} + \dfrac{4(x-2)^{3/2}}{3} + c$

Step 6. Differentiate and Check: $\left(\dfrac{5}{2}\right)\dfrac{2(x-2)^{3/2}}{5} + \left(\dfrac{3}{2}\right)\dfrac{4(x-2)^{1/2}}{3}$

$$= (x-2)^{3/2} + 2(x-2)^{1/2}$$

$$= (x-2)^{1/2}[(x-2) + 2] = (x-2)^{1/2}\,x \text{ or } x\sqrt{x-2}$$

Example 3

Evaluate $\int (2x-5)^{2/3}\, dx$

Step 1. Let $u = 2x - 5$

Step 2. Differentiate: $du = 2dx \Rightarrow \dfrac{du}{2} = dx$

Step 3. Rewrite: $\int u^{2/3}\dfrac{du}{2} = \dfrac{1}{2}\int u^{2/3}\, du$

Step 4. Integrate: $\dfrac{1}{2}\left(\dfrac{u^{5/3}}{5/3}\right) + c = \dfrac{3u^{5/3}}{10} + c$

Step 5. Replace u: $\dfrac{3(2x-5)^{5/3}}{10} + c$

Step 6. Differentiate and Check: $\left(\dfrac{3}{10}\right)\left(\dfrac{5}{3}\right)(2x-5)^{2/3}(2) = (2x-5)^{2/3}$

Example 4

Evaluate $\int \dfrac{x^2}{\left(x^3 - 8\right)^5}\,dx$

Step 1. Let $u = x^3 - 8$

Step 2. Differentiate: $du = 3x^2dx \Rightarrow \dfrac{du}{3} = x^2dx$

Step 3. Rewrite: $\int \dfrac{1}{u^5}\dfrac{du}{3} = \dfrac{1}{3}\int \dfrac{1}{u^5}\,du = \dfrac{1}{3}\int u^{-5}\,du$

Step 4. Integrate: $\dfrac{1}{3}\left(\dfrac{u^{-4}}{-4}\right) + c$

Step 5. Replace u: $\dfrac{1}{-12}\left(x^3 - 8\right)^{-4} + c$ or $\dfrac{-1}{12\left(x^3 - 8\right)^4} + c$

Step 6. Differentiate and Check: $\left(-\dfrac{1}{12}\right)(-4)\left(x^3 - 8\right)^{-5}\left(3x^2\right) = \dfrac{x^2}{\left(x^3 - 8\right)^5}$

U-Substitution and Trigonometric Functions

Example 1

Evaluate $\int \sin 4x\ dx$

Step 1. Let $u = 4x$

Step 2. Differentiate: $du = 4dx$ or $\dfrac{du}{4} = dx$

Step 3. Rewrite: $\int \sin u\ \dfrac{du}{4} = \dfrac{1}{4}\int \sin u\ du$

Step 4. Integrate: $\dfrac{1}{4}\left(-\cos u\right) + c = -\dfrac{1}{4}\cos u + c$

Step 5. Replace u: $-\dfrac{1}{4}\cos\left(4x\right) + c$

Step 6. Differentiate and Check: $\left(-\dfrac{1}{4}\right)\left(-\sin 4x\right)\left(4\right) = \sin 4x$

Example 2

Evaluate $\int 3\left(\sec^2 x\right)\sqrt{\tan x}\ dx$

Step 1. Let $u = \tan x$

Step 2. Differentiate: $du = \sec^2 x\ dx$

Step 3. Rewrite: $3\int \left(\tan x\right)^{\frac{1}{2}}\sec^2 x\ dx = 3\int u^{\frac{1}{2}}du$

Step 4. Integrate $3\dfrac{u^{\frac{3}{2}}}{\frac{3}{2}} + c = 2u^{\frac{3}{2}} + c$

Step 5. Replace u: $2\left(\tan x\right)^{\frac{3}{2}} + c$ or $2\tan^{\frac{3}{2}} x + c$

Step 6. Differentiate and Check: $(2)\left(\dfrac{3}{2}\right)\left(\tan^{\frac{1}{2}} x\right)\left(\sec^2 x\right) = 3\left(\sec^2 x\right)\sqrt{\tan x}$

Example 3

Evaluate $\int 2x^2 \cos(x^3)\,dx$

Step 1. Let $u = x^3$

Step 2. Differentiate $du = 3x^2\,dx \Rightarrow \dfrac{du}{3} = x^2 dx$

Step 3. Rewrite: $2\int \left[\cos(x^3)\right]x^2 dx = 2\int \cos u\,\dfrac{du}{3} = \dfrac{2}{3}\int \cos u\,du$

Step 4. Integrate: $\dfrac{2}{3}\sin u + c$

Step 5. Replace u: $\dfrac{2}{3}\sin(x^3) + c$

Step 6. Differentiate & Check: $\dfrac{2}{3}\left[\cos(x^3)\right]3x^2 = 2x^2\cos(x^3)$

- Remember that the area of a semi-circle is $\dfrac{1}{2}\pi r^2$ Don't forget the $\dfrac{1}{2}$. If the cross sections of a solid are semi-circles, the integral for the volume of the solid will involve $\left(\dfrac{1}{2}\right)^2$ which is $\dfrac{1}{4}$.

U-Substitution and Inverse Trigonometric Functions

Example 1

Evaluate $\int \dfrac{dx}{\sqrt{9 - 4x^2}}$

Step 1. Let $u = 2x$

Step 2. Differentiate $du = 2x; \dfrac{du}{2} = dx$

Step 3. Rewrite: $\int \dfrac{1}{\sqrt{9 - u^2}}\,\dfrac{du}{2} = \dfrac{1}{2}\int \dfrac{du}{\sqrt{3^2 - u^2}}$

Step 4. Integrate: $\dfrac{1}{2}\sin^{-1}\left(\dfrac{u}{3}\right) + c$

Step 5. Replace u: $\dfrac{1}{2}\sin^{-1}\left(\dfrac{2x}{3}\right) + c$

Step 6. Differentiate and Check: $\dfrac{1}{2}\,\dfrac{1}{\sqrt{1 - (2x/3)^2}} \cdot \dfrac{2}{3} = \dfrac{1}{3}\,\dfrac{1}{\sqrt{1 - 4x^2/9}}$

$$= \dfrac{1}{\sqrt{9}}\,\dfrac{1}{\sqrt{1 - 4x^2/9}} = \dfrac{1}{\sqrt{9(1 - 4x^2/9)}} = \dfrac{1}{\sqrt{9 - 4x^2}}$$

Example 2

Evaluate $\int \dfrac{1}{x^2 + 2x + 5}\, dx$

Step 1. Rewrite: $\int \dfrac{1}{(x^2 + 2x + 1) + 4} = \int \dfrac{1}{(x + 1)^2 + 2^2}\, dx = \int \dfrac{1}{2^2 + (x + 1)^2}\, dx$

Let $u = x + 1$

Step 2. Differentiate: $du = dx$

Step 3. Rewrite: $\int \dfrac{1}{2^2 + u^2}\, du$

Step 4. Integrate: $\dfrac{1}{2} \tan^{-1}\left(\dfrac{u}{2}\right) + c$

Step 5. Replace u: $\dfrac{1}{2} \tan^{-1}\left(\dfrac{x + 1}{2}\right) + c$

Step 6. Differentiate and Check: $\left(\dfrac{1}{2}\right) \dfrac{1\left(\frac{1}{2}\right)}{1 + [(x + 1)/2]^2} = \left(\dfrac{1}{4}\right) \dfrac{1}{1 + (x + 1)^2/4}$

$\left(\dfrac{1}{4}\right) \dfrac{4}{4 + (x + 1)^2} = \dfrac{1}{x^2 + 2x + 5}$.

- If the problem gives you the diameter of a sphere is 6 and you are using formulas such as $v = \dfrac{4}{3}\pi r^3$ or $s = 4\pi r^2$, don't forget that $r = 3$.

U-Substitution and Logarithmic and Exponential Functions

Example 1

Evaluate $\int \dfrac{x^3}{x^4 - 1}\, dx$

Step 1. Let $u = x^4 - 1$

Step 2. Differentiate: $du = 4x^3 dx \Rightarrow \dfrac{du}{4} = x^3 dx$

Step 3. Rewrite: $\int \dfrac{1}{u} \dfrac{du}{4} = \dfrac{1}{4} \int \dfrac{1}{u}\, du$

Step 4. Integrate: $\dfrac{1}{4} \ln|u| + c$

Step 5. Replace u: $\dfrac{1}{4} \ln|x^4 - 1| + c$

Step 6. Differentiate & Check: $\left(\dfrac{1}{4}\right) \dfrac{1}{x^4 - 1} \left(4x^3\right) = \dfrac{x^3}{x^4 - 1}$.

Example 2

Evaluate $\int \dfrac{\sin x}{\cos x + 1}\, dx$

Step 1. Let $u = \cos x + 1$

Step 2. Differentiate: $du = -\sin x\, dx \Rightarrow -du = \sin x\, dx$

Step 3. Rewrite: $\int \dfrac{-du}{u} = -\int \dfrac{du}{u}$

Step 4. Integrate: $-\ln|u| + c$

Step 5. Replace u: $-\ln|\cos x + 1| + c$

Step 6. Differentiate and Check: $-\left(\dfrac{1}{\cos x + 1}\right)(-\sin x) = \dfrac{\sin x}{\cos x + 1}$.

Example 3

Evaluate $\int \dfrac{x^2 + 3}{x - 1}\, dx$

Step 1. Rewrite $\dfrac{x^2 + 3}{x - 1} = x + 1 + \dfrac{4}{x - 1}$; by dividing $(x^2 + 3)$ by $(x - 1)$.

$$\int \dfrac{x^2 + 3}{x - 1}\, dx = \int \left(x + 1 + \dfrac{4}{x - 1}\right) dx = \int (x + 1)\, dx + \int \dfrac{4}{x - 1}\, dx$$

$$= \dfrac{x^2}{2} + x + 4\int \dfrac{1}{x - 1}\, dx$$

Let $u = x - 1$.

Step 2. Differentiate: $du = dx$

Step 3. Rewrite: $4\int \dfrac{1}{u}\, du$

Step 4. Integrate: $4 \ln|u| + c$

Step 5. Replace u: $4 \ln|x - 1| + c$

$$\int \dfrac{x^2 + 3}{x - 1}\, dx = \dfrac{x^2}{2} + x + 4 \ln|x - 1| + c$$

Step 6. Differentiate and Check:

$$\dfrac{2x}{2} + 1 + 4\left(\dfrac{1}{x - 1}\right) + c = x + 1 + \dfrac{4}{x - 1} = \dfrac{x^2 + 3}{x - 1}.$$

Example 4

Evaluate $\int \dfrac{\ln x}{3x}\, dx$

Step 1. Let $u = \ln x$

Step 2. Differentiate: $du = \dfrac{1}{x}\, dx$

Step 3. Rewrite: $\dfrac{1}{3}\int u\, dx$

Step 4. Integrate $\left(\dfrac{1}{3}\right)\dfrac{u^2}{2} + c = \dfrac{1}{6}u^2 + c$

Step 5. Replace u: $\dfrac{1}{6}\left(\ln x\right)^2 + c$

Step 6. Differentiate and Check: $\dfrac{1}{6}(2)(\ln x)\left(\dfrac{1}{x}\right) = \dfrac{\ln x}{3x}$.

Example 5

Evaluate $\int e^{(2x-5)}dx$

Step 1. Let $u = 2x - 5$

Step 2. Differentiate: $du = 2dx \Rightarrow \dfrac{du}{2} = dx$

Step 3. Rewrite: $\int e^u\left(\dfrac{du}{2}\right) = \dfrac{1}{2}\int e^u du$

Step 4. Integrate: $\dfrac{1}{2}e^u + c$

Step 5. Replace u: $\dfrac{1}{2}e^{(2x-5)} + c$

Step 6. Differentiate and Check: $\dfrac{1}{2}e^{2x-5}(2) = e^{2x-5}$.

Example 6

Evaluate $\int \dfrac{e^x}{e^x + 1}\,dx$

Step 1. Let $u = e^x + 1$

Step 2. Differentiate: $du = e^x\,dx$

Step 3. Rewrite: $\int \dfrac{1}{u}\,du$

Step 4. Integrate: $\ln|u| + c$

Step 5. Replace u: $\ln|e^x + 1| + c$

Step 6. Differentiate and Check: $\dfrac{1}{e^x + 1} \cdot e^x = \dfrac{e^x}{e^x + 1}$.

Example 7

Evaluate $\int xe^{3x^2}dx$

Step 1. Let $u = 3x^2$

Step 2. Differentiate: $du = 6x\,dx \Rightarrow \dfrac{du}{6} = x\,dx$

Step 3. Rewrite: $\int e^u \dfrac{du}{6} = \dfrac{1}{6}\int e^u du$

Step 4. Integrate: $\dfrac{1}{6}e^u + c$

Step 5. Replace u: $\dfrac{1}{6}e^{3x^2} + c$

Step 6. Differentiate and Check: $\dfrac{1}{6}\left(e^{3x^2}\right)(6x) = xe^{3x^2}$.

Example 8

Evaluate $\int 5^{(2x)}\,dx$

Step 1. Let $u = 2x$

Step 2. Differentiate: $du = 2dx \Rightarrow \dfrac{du}{2} = dx$

Step 3. Rewrite: $\int 5^u\,\dfrac{du}{2} = \dfrac{1}{2}\int 5^u\,du$

Step 4. Integrate: $\dfrac{1}{2}\left(5^u\right)/\ln 5 + c = 5^u/2\ln 5 + c$

Step 5. Replace u: $\dfrac{5^{2x}}{2\ln 5} + c$

Step 6. Differentiate and Check: $\left(5^{2x}\right)(2)\ln 5/2\ln 5 = 5^{2x}$.

Example 9

Evaluate $\int x^3 5^{\left(x^4\right)}\,dx$

Step 1. Let $u = x^4$

Step 2. Differentiate: $du = 4x^3\,dx \Rightarrow \dfrac{du}{4} = x^3\,dx$

Step 3. Rewrite: $\int 5^u\,\dfrac{du}{4} = \dfrac{1}{4}\int 5^u\,du$

Step 4. Integrate: $\dfrac{1}{4}\left(5^u\right)/\ln 5 + c$

Step 5. Replace u: $\dfrac{5^{x^4}}{4\ln 5} + c$

Step 6. Differentiate and Check: $5^{\left(x^4\right)}\left(4x^3\right)\ln 5/4\ln 5 = x^3 5^{\left(x^4\right)}$.

Example 10

Evaluate $\int (\sin \pi x)e^{\cos \pi x}\,dx$

Step 1. Let $u = \cos \pi x$

Step 2. Differentiate: $du = -\pi \sin \pi x\,dx;\; -\dfrac{du}{\pi} = \sin \pi x\,dx$

Step 3. Rewrite: $\int e^u\left(\dfrac{-du}{\pi}\right) = -\dfrac{1}{\pi}\int e^u\,du$

Step 4. Integrate: $-\dfrac{1}{\pi}e^u + c$

Step 5. Replace u: $-\dfrac{1}{\pi} e^{\cos \pi x} + c$

Step 6. Differentiate and Check: $-\dfrac{1}{\pi} \left(e^{\cos \pi x} \right)\left(-\sin \pi x \right)\pi = \left(\sin \pi x \right)e^{\cos \pi x}$.

7.3   RAPID REVIEW

1. Evaluate $\displaystyle\int \dfrac{1}{x^2}\, dx$.

   Answer: Rewrite as $\displaystyle\int x^{-2}dx = \dfrac{x^{-1}}{-1} + c = -\dfrac{1}{x} + c$.

2. Evaluate $\displaystyle\int \dfrac{x^3 - 1}{x}\, dx$.

   Answer: Rewrite as $\displaystyle\int \left(x^2 - \dfrac{1}{x} \right)dx = \dfrac{x^3}{3} - \ln|x| + c$.

3. Evaluate $\displaystyle\int x\sqrt{x^2 - 1}\,dx$.

   Answer: Rewrite as $\displaystyle\int x\left(x^2 - 1 \right)^{\frac{1}{2}} dx$. Let $u = x^2 - 1$.

   Thus $\dfrac{du}{2} = x\,dx \Rightarrow \dfrac{1}{2}\displaystyle\int u^{\frac{1}{2}}\,du = \dfrac{1u^{\frac{3}{2}}}{2\,\frac{3}{2}} + c = \dfrac{1}{3}\left(x^2 - 1 \right)^{\frac{3}{2}} + c$.

4. Evaluate $\displaystyle\int \sin x\, dx$

   Answer: $-\cos x + c$.

5. Evaluate $\displaystyle\int \cos(2x)\,dx$

   Answer: Let $u = 2x$ and obtain $\dfrac{1}{2}\sin 2x + c$.

6. Evaluate $\displaystyle\int \dfrac{\ln x}{x}\, dx$

   Answer: Let $u = \ln x$; $du = \dfrac{1}{x}\, dx$ and obtain $\dfrac{\left(\ln x \right)^2}{2} + c$.

7. Evaluate $\displaystyle\int x e^{x^2}\, dx$

   Answer: Let $u = x^2$; $\dfrac{du}{2} = x\,dx$ and obtain $\dfrac{e^{x^2}}{2} + c$.

7.4   PRACTICE PROBLEMS

Evaluate the following integrals in problems 1 to 20. No calculators allowed. (However, you may use calculators to check your results.)

1. $\displaystyle\int \left(x^5 + 3x^2 - x + 1 \right)dx$

2. $\displaystyle\int \left(\sqrt{x} - \dfrac{1}{x^2} \right)dx$

3. $\displaystyle\int x^3\left(x^4 - 10 \right)^5 dx$

4. $\displaystyle\int x^3 \sqrt{x^2 + 1}\,dx$

5. $\int \dfrac{x^2 + 5}{\sqrt{x - 1}}\,dx$

6. $\int \tan\left(\dfrac{x}{2}\right) dx$

7. $\int x \csc^2(x^2)\,dx$

8. $\int \dfrac{\sin x}{\cos^3 x}\,dx$

9. $\int \dfrac{1}{x^2 + 2x + 10}\,dx$

10. $\int \dfrac{1}{x^2}\sec^2\left(\dfrac{1}{x}\right) dx$

11. $\int (e^{2x})(e^{4x})\,dx$

12. $\int \dfrac{1}{x \ln x}\,dx$

13. $\int \ln(e^{5x+1})\,dx$

14. $\int \dfrac{e^{4x} - 1}{e^x}\,dx$

15. $\int (9 - x^2)\sqrt{x}\,dx$

16. $\int \sqrt{x}\left(1 + x^{\frac{3}{2}}\right)^4 dx$

17. If $\dfrac{dy}{dx} = e^x + 2$ and the point $(0,6)$ is on the graph of y, find y.

18. $\int -3e^x \sin(e^x)\,dx$

19. $\int \dfrac{e^x - e^{-x}}{e^x + e^{-x}}\,dx$

20. If $f(x)$ is the antiderivative of $\dfrac{1}{x}$ and $f(1) = 5$, find $f(e)$.

7.5   CUMULATIVE REVIEW PROBLEMS

"Calculator" indicates that calculators are permitted.

21. The graph of the velocity function of a moving particle for $0 \le t \le 10$ is shown in Figure 7.5-1.

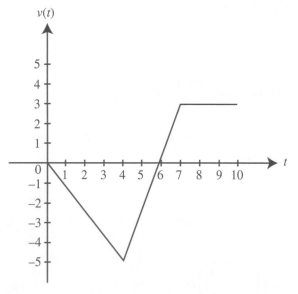

Figure 7.5-1

(a) At what value of t is the speed of the particle the greatest?

(b) At what time is the particle moving to the right?

22. Air is pumped into a spherical balloon, whose maximum radius is 10 meters. For what value of r is the rate of increase of the volume a hundred times that of the radius?

23. Evaluate $\int \dfrac{\ln^3(x)}{x}\,dx$

24. (Calculator) The function f is continuous and differentiable on the interval $[0,2]$ with $f''(x) > 0$ for all x in the interval $[0,2]$. Some of the points on the graph are shown below.

x	0	0.5	1	1.5	2
$f(x)$	1	1.25	2	3.25	5

Which of the following is the best approximation for $f'(1)$?

(a) $f'(1) < 2$

(b) $0.5 < f'(1) < 1$

(c) $1.5 < f'(1) < 2.5$

(d) $2.5 < f'(1) < 3.5$

(e) $f'(1) > 2$

25. The graph of the function f'' on the interval $[1,8]$ is shown in Figure 7.5-2. At what value(s) of t on the open interval $(1,8)$, if any, does the graph of the function f':

(a) have a point of inflection?

(b) have a relative maximum or minimum?

(c) concave upward?

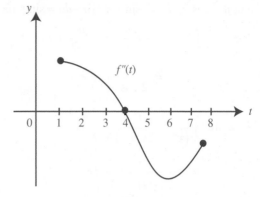

Figure 7.5-2

7.6 SOLUTIONS TO PRACTICE PROBLEMS

No calculators except for verifying your results.

1. $\dfrac{x^6}{6} + x^3 - \dfrac{x^2}{2} + x + c$

2. Rewrite:

$$\int \left(x^{1/2} - x^{-2}\right) dx = \dfrac{x^{3/2}}{3/2} - \dfrac{x^{-1}}{-1} + c = \dfrac{2x^{3/2}}{3} + \dfrac{1}{x} + c$$

3. Let $u = x^4 - 10 \; du = 4x^3 \, dx$ or $\dfrac{du}{4} = x^3 dx$.

   Rewrite: $\int u^5 \dfrac{du}{4} = \dfrac{1}{4}\int u^5 du = \left(\dfrac{1}{4}\right)\dfrac{u^6}{6} + c$

   $$= \dfrac{\left(x^4 - 10\right)^6}{24} + c$$

4. Let $u = x^2 + 1 \Rightarrow (u - 1) = x^2$ and

   $du = 2x \, dx$ or $\dfrac{du}{2} = x \, dx$

   Rewrite: $\int x^2 \sqrt{x^2 + 1}\,(x \, dx) = \int (u - 1)\sqrt{u}\,\dfrac{du}{2}$

   $$= \dfrac{1}{2}\int (u - 1)u^{1/2} du = \dfrac{1}{2}\int \left(u^{3/2} - u^{1/2}\right) du$$

   $$= \dfrac{1}{2}\left(\dfrac{u^{5/2}}{5/2} - \dfrac{u^{3/2}}{3/2}\right) + c = \dfrac{u^{5/2}}{5} - \dfrac{u^{3/2}}{3} + c$$

   $$= \dfrac{\left(x^2 + 1\right)^{5/2}}{5} - \dfrac{\left(x^2 + 1\right)^{3/2}}{3} + c$$

5. Let $u = x - 1; \; du = dx$ and $(u + 1) = x$

   Rewrite:

   $$\int \dfrac{(u + 1)^2 + 5}{\sqrt{u}}\,du = \int \dfrac{u^2 + 2u + 6}{u^{1/2}}\,du$$

   $$= \int \left(u^{3/2} + 2u^{1/2} + 6u^{-1/2}\right) du$$

   $$= \dfrac{u^{5/2}}{5/2} + \dfrac{2u^{3/2}}{3/2} + \dfrac{6u^{1/2}}{1/2} + c$$

   $$= \dfrac{2(x - 1)^{5/2}}{5} + \dfrac{4(x - 1)^{3/2}}{3}$$

   $$+ 12(x - 1)^{1/2} + c$$

6. Let $u = \dfrac{x}{2}; \; du = \dfrac{1}{2}dx$ or $2du = dx$

   Rewrite: $\int \tan u \,(2du) = 2\int \tan u \, du$

   $$= -2 \ln|\cos u| + c$$

   $$= -2 \ln\left|\cos \dfrac{x}{2}\right| + c$$

7. Let $u = x^2; \; du = 2x \, dx$ or $\dfrac{du}{2} = x \, dx$

   Rewrite: $\int \csc^2 u \,\dfrac{du}{2} = \dfrac{1}{2}\int \csc^2 u \, du$

   $$= -\dfrac{1}{2}\cot u + c$$

   $$= -\dfrac{1}{2}\cot\left(x^2\right) + c$$

8. Let $u = \cos x$; $du = -\sin x\, dx$ or $-du = \sin x\, dx$

Rewrite: $\int \dfrac{-du}{u^3} = -\int \dfrac{du}{u^3} = -\dfrac{u^{-2}}{-2} + c$

$$= \dfrac{1}{2\cos^2 x} + c$$

9. Rewrite $\int \dfrac{1}{(x^2 + 2x + 1) + 9}\, dx$

$$= \int \dfrac{1}{(x+1)^2 + 3^2}\, dx$$

Let $u = x + 1$; $du = dx$

Rewrite $\int \dfrac{1}{u^2 + 3^2}\, du = \dfrac{1}{3}\tan^{-1}\left(\dfrac{u}{3}\right) + c$

$$= \dfrac{1}{3}\tan^{-1}\left(\dfrac{x+1}{3}\right) + c$$

10. Let $u = \dfrac{1}{x}$; $du = \dfrac{-1}{x^2}\, dx$ or $-du = \dfrac{1}{x^2}\, dx$

Rewrite: $\int \sec^2 u(-du) = -\int \sec^2 u\, du$

$$= -\tan u + c$$

$$= -\tan\left(\dfrac{1}{x}\right) + c$$

11. Rewrite $\int e^{(2x+4x)}\, dx = \int e^{6x}\, dx$

Let $u = 6x$; $du = 6\, dx$ or $\dfrac{du}{6} = dx$

Rewrite $\int e^u\, \dfrac{du}{6} = \dfrac{1}{6}\int e^u\, du = \dfrac{1}{6}e^u + c$

$$= \dfrac{1}{6}e^{6x} + c$$

12. Let $u = \ln x$; $du = \dfrac{1}{x}\, dx$

Rewrite $\int \dfrac{1}{u}\, du = \ln|u| + c = \ln|\ln x| + c$

13. Since e^x and $\ln x$ are inverse functions:

$\int \ln\left(e^{5x+1}\right) dx = \int (5x + 1) dx = \dfrac{5x^2}{2} + x + c$

14. Rewrite $\int \left(\dfrac{e^{4x}}{e^2} - \dfrac{1}{e^x}\right) dx = \int (e^{3x} - e^{-x}) dx$

$$= \int e^{3x}\, dx - \int e^{-x}\, dx$$

Let $u = 3x$; $du = 3\, dx$;

$\int e^{3x}\, dx = \int e^u\left(\dfrac{du}{3}\right) = \dfrac{1}{3}e^u + c_1 = \dfrac{1}{3}e^{3x} + c$

Let $v = -x$; $dv = -dx$;

$\int e^{-x}\, dx = \int e^v(-dv) = -e^v + c_2 = -e^{-x} + c_2$

Thus $\int e^{3x}\, dx - \int e^{-x}\, dx = \dfrac{1}{3}e^{3x} + e^{-x} + c$

Note: c_1 and c_2 are arbitrary constants, and thus $c_1 + c_2 = c$.

15. Rewrite $\int (9 - x^2)x^{1/2}\, dx = \int \left(9x^{1/2} - x^{5/2}\right) dx$

$$= \dfrac{9x^{3/2}}{3/2} - \dfrac{x^{7/2}}{7/2} + c$$

$$= 6x^{3/2} - \dfrac{2x^{7/2}}{7} + c$$

16. Let $u = 1 + x^{3/2}$; $du = \dfrac{3}{2}x^{1/2}\, dx$ or

$$\dfrac{2}{3}\, du = x^{1/2}\, dx = \sqrt{x}\, dx$$

Rewrite: $\int u^4\left(\dfrac{2}{3}\, du\right) = \dfrac{2}{3}\int u^4\, du = \dfrac{2}{3}\left(\dfrac{u^5}{5}\right) + c$

$$= \dfrac{2\left(1 + x^{3/2}\right)^5}{15} + c$$

17. Since $\dfrac{dy}{dx} = e^x + 2$, then $y = \int (e^x + 2) dx$

$$= e^x + 2x + c.$$

The point $(0, 6)$ is on the graph of y. Thus, $6 = e^0 + 2(0) + c \Rightarrow 6 = 1 + c$ or $c = 5$. Therefore, $y = e^x + 2x + 5$.

18. Let $u = e^x$; $du = e^x\, dx$

Rewrite: $-3\int \sin(u) du = -3(-\cos u) + c$

$$= 3\cos(e^x) + c$$

19. Let $u = e^x + e^{-x}$; $du = (e^x - e^{-x})\, dx$

Rewrite: $\int \dfrac{1}{u}\, du = \ln|u| + c = \ln|e^x + e^{-x}| + c$

$$\text{or} = \ln\left|e^x + \dfrac{1}{e^x}\right| + c$$

$$= \ln\left|\dfrac{e^{2x} + 1}{e^x}\right| + c$$

$$= \ln|e^{2x} + 1| - \ln|e^x| + c$$

$$= \ln|e^{2x} + 1| - x + c$$

20. Since $f(x)$ is the antiderivative of $\dfrac{1}{x}$,

$$f(x) = \int \frac{1}{x}\,d = \ln|x| + c.$$

Given $f(1) = 5$; thus $\ln(1) + c = 5 \Rightarrow 0 + c = 5$ or $c = 5$.

Thus, $f(x) = \ln|x| + 5$ and $f(e) = \ln(e) + 5$ $= 1 + 5 = 6$.

7.7 SOLUTIONS TO CUMULATIVE REVIEW PROBLEMS

"Calculator" indicates that calculators are permitted.

21. (a) At $t = 4$, speed is 5 which is the greatest on $0 \le t \le 10$.

(b) The particle is moving to the right when $6 < t < 10$.

22. $V = \dfrac{4}{3}\pi r^3;\ \dfrac{dV}{dt} = \left(\dfrac{4}{3}\right)(3)\pi r^2 \dfrac{dr}{dt} = 4\pi r^2 \dfrac{dr}{dt}$

If $\dfrac{dV}{dt} = 100\,\dfrac{dr}{dt}$, then $100\,\dfrac{dr}{dt}$

$$= 4\pi r^2 \frac{dr}{dt} \Rightarrow 100 = 4\pi r^2$$

or $r = \pm\sqrt{\dfrac{25}{\pi}} = \pm\dfrac{5}{\sqrt{\pi}}$.

Since $r \ge 0$, $r = \dfrac{5}{\sqrt{\pi}}$ meters.

23. Let $u = \ln x;\ du = \dfrac{1}{x}\,dx$

Rewrite: $\displaystyle\int u^3\,du = \dfrac{u^4}{4} + c = \dfrac{(\ln x)^4}{4} + c$

$$= \frac{\ln^4(x)}{4} + c$$

24. Label given points as A, B, C, D and E.

Since $f''(x) > 0 \Rightarrow f$ is concave upward for all x in the interval $[0,2]$.

Thus $m_{\overline{BC}} < f'(1) < m_{\overline{CD}};\ m_{\overline{BC}} = 1.5$ and $m_{\overline{CD}} = 2.5$

Therefore $1.5 < f'(1) < 2.5$, choice (c). See Figure 7.7-1.

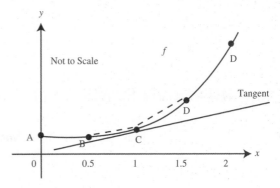

Figure 7.7-1

25. (a) f'' is decreasing on $[1,6] \Rightarrow f''' < 0 \Rightarrow f'$ is concave downward on $[1,6)$ and f'' is increasing on $(6,8] \Rightarrow f'''$ is concave upward on $(6,8]$.

Thus, at $x = 6$, f' has a change of concavity. Since f' exists at $x = 6$ (which implies there is a tangent to the curve of f' at $x = 6$), f' has a point of inflection at $x = 6$.

(b) $f'' > 0$ on $[1,4) \Rightarrow f'$ is increasing and $f'' < 0$ on $(4,8] \Rightarrow f'$ is decreasing. Thus at $x = 4$, f' has a relative maximum at $x = 4$. There is no relative minimum.

(c) f'' is increasing on $(6,8] \Rightarrow f''' > 0 \Rightarrow f'$ is concave upward on $(6,8]$.

Chapter 8

Definite Integrals

8.1 RIEMANN SUMS AND DEFINITE INTEGRALS

Main Concepts: *Sigma Notation, Definition of a Riemann Sum, Definition of a Definite Integral, and Properties of Definite Integrals*

Sigma Notation or Summation Notation

$$\sum_{i=1}^{n} a_1 + a_2 + a_3 + \ldots + a_n$$

where i is the index of summation, l is the lower limit and n is the upper limit of summation. (**Note:** The lower limit may be any non-negative integer $\leq n$.)

Examples

$$\sum_{i=5}^{7} i^2 = 5^2 + 6^2 + 7^2$$

$$\sum_{k=0}^{3} 2k = 2(0) + 2(1) + 2(2) + 2(3)$$

$$\sum_{i=-1}^{3} (2i + 1) = -1 + 1 + 3 + 5 + 7$$

$$\sum_{k=1}^{4} (-1)^{k}(k) = -1 + 2 - 3 + 4$$

Summation Formulas

If n is a positive integer, then:

1. $\displaystyle\sum_{i=1}^{n} a = an$

2. $\displaystyle\sum_{i=1}^{n} i = \frac{n(n + 1)}{2}$

3. $\displaystyle\sum_{i=1}^{n} i^2 = \frac{n(n + 1)(2n + 1)}{6}$

4. $\displaystyle\sum_{i=1}^{n} i^3 = \frac{n^2(n + 1)^2}{4}$

5. $\displaystyle\sum_{i=1}^{n} i^4 = \frac{n(n + 1)(6n^3 + 9n^2 + n - 1)}{30}$

Example

Evaluate $\displaystyle\sum_{i=1}^{n} \frac{i(i + 1)}{n}$

Rewrite $\displaystyle\sum_{i=1}^{n} \frac{i(i + 1)}{n}$ as $\dfrac{1}{n}\displaystyle\sum_{i=1}^{n}(i^2 + i) = \dfrac{1}{n}\left(\displaystyle\sum_{i=1}^{n} i^2 + \displaystyle\sum_{i=1}^{n} i\right)$

$$= \frac{1}{n}\left(\frac{n(n + 1)(2n + 1)}{6} + \frac{n(n + 1)}{2}\right)$$

$$= \frac{1}{n}\left[\frac{n(n + 1)(2n + 1) + 3n(n + 1)}{6}\right] = \frac{(n + 1)(2n + 1) + 3(n + 1)}{6}$$

$$= \frac{(n + 1)[(2n + 1) + 3]}{6} = \frac{(n + 1)(2n + 4)}{6}$$

$$= \frac{(n + 1)(n + 2)}{3}$$

(**Note:** This question has not appeared in an AP Calculus AB Exam in recent years).

- Remember in exponential growth/decay problems, the formulas are
$\dfrac{dy}{dx} = ky$ and $y = y_0 e^{kt}$.

Definition of a Riemann Sum

Let f be defined on $[a, b]$ and x_1's be points on $[a, b]$ such that $x_0 = a$, $x_n = b$ and $a < x_1 < x_2 < x_3 \ldots < x_{n-1} < b$. The points $a, x_1, x_2, x_3, \ldots x_{n+1}, b$ form a partition of f denoted as Δ on $[a, b]$. Let Δx_i be the length of the ith interval $[x_{i-1}, x_i]$ and c_i be any point in the ith interval. Then the Riemann sum of f for the partition is $\displaystyle\sum_{i=1}^{n} f(c_i)\Delta x_i$.

Example 1

Let f be a continuous function defined on $[0, 12]$ as shown below.

x	0	2	4	6	8	10	12
$f(x)$	3	7	19	39	67	103	147

Find the Riemann sum for $f(x)$ over $[0,12]$ with 3 subdivisions of equal length and the midpoints of the intervals c_i's.

Length of an interval $\Delta x_i = \dfrac{12 - 0}{3} = 4$. (See Figure 8.1-1.)

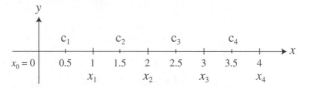

Figure 8.1-1

$$\text{Riemann sum} = \sum_{i=1}^{3} f(c_i)\Delta x_i = f(c_1)\Delta x_1 + f(c_2)\Delta x_2 + f(c_3)\Delta x_3$$

$$= 7(4) + 39(4) + 103(4) = 596$$

The Riemann sum is 596.

Example 2

Find the Riemann sum for $f(x) = x^3 + 1$ over the interval $[0,4]$ using 4 subdivisions of equal length and the midpoints of the intervals as c_i's. (See Figure 8.1-2.)

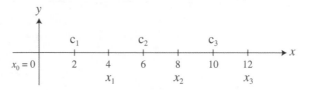

Figure 8.1-2

Length of an interval $\Delta x_i = \dfrac{b - a}{n} = \dfrac{4 - 0}{4} = 1; c_i = 0.5 + (i = 1) = i - 0.5$

$$\text{Riemann sum} = \sum_{i=1}^{4} f(c_i)\Delta x_i = \sum_{i=1}^{4}\left[(i - 0.5)^3 + 1\right]1 = \sum_{i=1}^{4}(i - 0.5)^3 + 1$$

Enter $\sum\left((i - 0.5)^3 + 1, i, 1, 4\right) = 66$.

The Riemann sum is 66.

Definition of a Definite Integral

Let f be defined on $[a, b]$ with the Riemann sum for f over $[a, b]$ written as $\sum_{i=1}^{n} f(c_i)\Delta x_i$.

If $\max \Delta x_i$ is the length of the largest subinterval in the partition and the $\displaystyle\lim_{\max \Delta x_i \to 0} \sum_{i=1}^{n} f(c_i)\Delta x_i$ exists, then the limit is denoted by:

$$\lim_{\max \Delta x_i \to 0} \sum_{i=1}^{n} f(c_i)\Delta x_i = \int_a^b f(x)dx$$

$\int_a^b f(x)dx$ is the definite integral of f from a to b.

Example 1

Using a midpoint Riemann sum with three subdivisions of equal length to find the approximate value of $\int_0^6 x^2 dx$.

$$\Delta x = \frac{6-0}{3} = 2, f(x) = x^2$$

midpoints are $x = 1$, 3 and 5.

$$\int_0^6 x^2 dx \approx f(1)\Delta x + f(3)\Delta x + f(5)\Delta x \approx 1(2) + 9(2) + 25(2)$$
$$\approx 70.$$

Example 2

Using the limit of the Riemann sum, find $\int_1^5 3x\,dx$.

Using n subintervals of equal lengths, the length of an interval

$$\Delta x_i = \frac{5-1}{n} = \frac{4}{n}; x_i = 1 + \left(\frac{4}{n}\right)i$$

$$\int_1^5 3x\,dx = \lim_{\max \Delta x_i \to 0} \sum_{i=1}^n f(c_i)\Delta x_i$$

Let $c_i = x_i$; $\max \Delta x_i \to 0 \Rightarrow n \to \infty$

$$\int_1^5 3x\,dx = \lim_{n\to\infty} \sum_{i=1}^n f\left(1 + \frac{4i}{n}\right)\left(\frac{4}{n}\right) = \lim_{n\to\infty} \sum_{i=1}^n 3\left(1 + \frac{4i}{n}\right)\left(\frac{4}{n}\right)$$

$$= \lim_{n\to\infty} \frac{12}{n}\sum_{i=1}^n \left(1 + \frac{4i}{n}\right) = \lim_{n\to\infty} \frac{12}{n}\left(n + \frac{4}{n}\left[n\left(\frac{n+1}{2}\right)\right]\right)$$

$$= \lim_{n\to\infty} \frac{12}{n}\left(n + 2(n+1)\right) = \lim_{n\to\infty} \frac{12}{n}(3n+2) = \lim_{n\to\infty}\left(36 + \frac{24}{n}\right) = 36$$

Thus $\int_1^5 3x\,dx = 36$.

(**Note:** This question has not appeared in an AP Calculus AB Exam in recent years.)

Properties of Definite Integrals

1. If f is defined on $[a, b]$, and the limit $\lim_{\max \Delta x_i \to 0} \sum_{i=1}^n f(x_i)\Delta x_i$ exists, then f is integrable on $[a, b]$.
2. If f is continuous on $[a, b]$, then f is integrable on $[a, b]$.

If $f(x)$, $g(x)$, $h(x)$ are integrable on $[a, b]$, then

3. $\int_a^a f(x)dx = 0$

4. $\int_a^b f(x)dx = -\int_b^a f(x)$

5. $\int_a^b cf(x)dx = c\int_a^b f(x)dx$ when c is a consonant.

6. $\int_a^b [f(x) \pm g(x)]dx = \int_a^b f(x)dx \pm \int_a^b g(x)dx$

7. $\int_a^b f(x)dx \geq 0$ provided $f(x) \geq 0$ on $[a, b]$

8. $\int_a^b f(x)dx \geq \int_a^b g(x)dx$ provided $f(x) \geq g(x)$ on $[a, b]$

9. $\left|\int_a^b f(x)dx\right| \leq \int_a^b |f(x)|dx$

10. $\int_a^b g(x)dx \le \int_a^b f(x)dx \le \int_a^b h(x)dx$; provided $g(x) \le f(x) \le h(x)$ on $[a, b]$

11. $m(b\text{-}a) \le \int_a^b f(x)dx \le M(b\text{-}a)$; provided $m \le f(x) \le M$ on $[a, b]$

12. $\int_a^c f(x)dx = \int_a^b f(x)dx + \int_b^c f(x)dx$; provided $f(x)$ is integrable on an interval containing a, b, c.

Examples

1. $\int_\pi^\pi \cos x\,dx = 0$

2. $\int_1^5 x^4 dx = -\int_5^1 x^4 dx$

3. $\int_{-2}^7 5x^2 dx = 5\int_{-2}^7 x^2 dx$

4. $\int_0^4 (x^3 - 2x + 1)dx = \int_0^4 x^3 dx - 2\int_0^4 x\,dx + \int_0^4 1\,dx$

5. $\int_1^5 \sqrt{x}\,dx = \int_1^3 \sqrt{x}\,dx + \int_3^5 \sqrt{x}\,dx$

note: Or $\int_1^3 \sqrt{x}\,dx = \int_1^5 \sqrt{x}\,dx + \int_5^3 \sqrt{x}\,dx$

$\int_a^c = \int_a^b + \int_b^c$ a, b, c do not have to be arranged from smallest to largest.

The remaining properties are best illustrated in terms of the area under the curve of the function as discussed in the next section.

> • Don't forget that $\int_0^{-3} f(x)dx = -\int_{-3}^0 f(x)dx$.

8.2 FUNDAMENTAL THEOREMS OF CALCULUS

Main Concepts: *The First Fundamental Theorem of Calculus, The Second Fundamental Theorem of Calculus*

First Fundamental Theorem of Calculus

If f is continuous on $[a, b]$ and F is an antiderivative of f on $[a, b]$, then

$$\int_a^b f(x)dx = F(b) - F(a).$$

Note $F(b) - F(a)$ is often denoted as $F(x)]_a^b$.

Example 1

Evaluate $\int_0^2 (4x^3 + x - 1)dx$

$$\int_0^2 (4x^3 + x - 1)dx = \frac{4x^4}{4} + \frac{x^2}{2} - x\Big]_0^2 = x^4 + \frac{x^2}{2} - x\Big]_0^2$$

$$= \left(2^4 + \frac{2^2}{2} - 2\right) - (0) = 16$$

Example 2

Evaluate $\int_{-\pi}^{\pi} \sin x \, dx$

$$\int_{-\pi}^{\pi} \sin x \, dx = -\cos x \Big]_{-\pi}^{\pi} = [-\cos \pi] - [-\cos(-\pi)]$$
$$= [-(-1)] - [-(-1)] = (1) - (1) = 0$$

Example 3

If $\int_{-2}^{k} (4x + 1) \, dx = 30, \, k > 0$, find k.

$$\int_{-2}^{k} (4x + 1) \, dx = 2x^2 + x \Big]_{-2}^{k} = (2k^2 + k) - \left(2(-2)^2 - 2\right)$$
$$= 2k^2 + k - 6$$

Set $2k^2 + k - 6 = 30 \Rightarrow 2k^2 + k - 36 = 0$

$$\Rightarrow (2k + 9)(k - 4) = 0 \text{ or } k = -\frac{9}{2} \text{ or } k = 4.$$

Since $k > 0, \, k = 4$.

Example 4

If $f'(x) = g(x)$ and g is a continuous function for all real values of x, express $\int_{2}^{5} g(3x) \, dx$ in terms of f.

Let $u = 3x; \, du = 3dx$ or $\dfrac{du}{3} = dx$

$$\int g(3x) \, dx = \int g(u) \frac{du}{3} = \frac{1}{3} \int g(u) \, du = \frac{1}{3} f(u) + c$$

$$= \frac{1}{3} f(3x) + c$$

$$\int_{2}^{5} g(3x) \, dx = \frac{1}{3} f(3x) \Big]_{2}^{5} = \frac{1}{3} f(3(5)) - \frac{1}{3} f(3(2))$$

$$= \frac{1}{3} f(15) - \frac{1}{3} f(6).$$

Example 5

Evaluate $\int_{0}^{4} \dfrac{1}{x - 1} \, dx$

Cannot evaluate using the First Fundamental Theorem of Calculus since $f(x) = \dfrac{1}{x - 1}$ is discontinuous at $x = 1$.

Example 6

Using a graphing calculator, evaluate $\int_{-2}^{2} \sqrt{4 - x^2} \, dx$.

Using a TI-89 graphing calculator, enter $\int \left(\sqrt{(4 - x\wedge2)}, x, -2, 2 \right)$ and obtain 2π.

Second Fundamental Theorem of Calculus

If f is continuous on $[a, b]$ and $F(x) = \int_a^x f(t)dt$, then $F'(x) = f(x)$ at every point x in $[a, b]$.

Example 1

Evaluate $\int_{\pi/4}^{x} \cos(2t)dt$

Let $u = 2t; du = 2dt$ or $\dfrac{du}{2} = dt$

$$\int \cos(2t)dt = \int \cos u \, \frac{du}{2} = \frac{1}{2}\int \cos u \, du$$

$$= \frac{1}{2}\sin u + c = \frac{1}{2}\sin(2t) + c$$

$$\int_{\pi/4}^{x} \cos(2t)dt = \frac{1}{2}\sin(2t)\Big]_{\pi/4}^{x}$$

$$= \frac{1}{2}\sin(2x) - \frac{1}{2}\sin\left(2\left(\frac{\pi}{4}\right)\right)$$

$$= \frac{1}{2}\sin(2x) - \frac{1}{2}\sin\left(\frac{\pi}{2}\right)$$

$$= \frac{1}{2}\sin(2x) - \frac{1}{2}$$

Example 2

If $h(x) = \int_3^x \sqrt{t + 1}\,dt$, find $h'(8)$.

$h'(x) = \sqrt{x + 1}; h'(8) = \sqrt{8 + 1} = 3.$

Example 3

Find $\dfrac{dy}{dx}$; if $y = \int_1^{2x} \dfrac{1}{t^3}dt$.

Let $u = 2x$; then $\dfrac{du}{dx} = 2$.

Rewrite: $y = \int_1^{u} \dfrac{1}{t^3}dt$

$$\frac{dy}{dx} = \frac{dy}{du} \cdot \frac{du}{dx} = \frac{1}{u^3} \cdot (2) = \frac{1}{(2x)^3} \cdot 2 = \frac{1}{4x^3}$$

Example 4

Find $\dfrac{dy}{dx}$; if $y = \int_{x^2}^{1} \sin t \, dt$.

Rewrite: $y = -\int_1^{x^2} \sin t \, dt$

Let $u = x^2$; then $\dfrac{du}{dx} = 2x$

Rewrite: $y = -\displaystyle\int_1^u \sin t\, dt$

$$\frac{dy}{dx} = \frac{dy}{du} \cdot \frac{du}{dx} = (-\sin u)2x = (-\sin x^2)2x = -2x\sin(x^2)$$

Example 5

Find $\dfrac{dy}{dx}$; if $y = \displaystyle\int_x^{x^2} \sqrt{e^t + 1}\, dt$.

$$y = \int_x^0 \sqrt{e^t + 1}\, dt + \int_0^{x^2} \sqrt{e^t + 1}\, dt \quad y = -\int_0^x \sqrt{e^t + 1}\, dt + \int_0^{x^2} \sqrt{e^t + 1}\, dt$$

$$= \int_0^{x^2} \sqrt{e^t + 1}\, dt - \int_0^x \sqrt{e^t + 1}\, dt$$

Since $y = \displaystyle\int_0^{x^2} \sqrt{e^t + 1}\, dt - \int_0^x \sqrt{e^t + 1}\, dt$

$$\frac{dy}{dx} = \left(\frac{d}{dx}\int_0^{x^2} \sqrt{e^t + 1}\, dt\right) - \left(\frac{d}{dx}\int_0^x \sqrt{e^t + 1}\, dt\right)$$

$$= \left(\sqrt{e^{x^2} + 1}\right)\frac{d}{dx}\left(x^2\right) - \left(\sqrt{e^x + 1}\right)$$

$$= 2x\sqrt{e^{x^2} + 1} - \sqrt{e^x + 1}$$

Example 6

$F(x) = \displaystyle\int_1^x (t^2 - 4)\, dt$, integrate to find $F(x)$ and then differentiate to find $F'(x)$.

$$F(x) = \frac{t^3}{3} - 4t\Big]_1^x = \left(\frac{x^3}{3} - 4x\right) - \left(\frac{1^3}{3} - 4(1)\right)$$

$$= \frac{x^3}{3} - 4x + \frac{11}{3}$$

$$F'(x) = 3\left(\frac{x^2}{3}\right) - 4 = x^2 - 4.$$

8.3 EVALUATING DEFINITE INTEGRALS

Main Concepts: *Definite Integrals Involving Algebraic Functions; Definite Integrals Involving Absolute Volume; Definite Integrals Involving Trigonometric, Logarithmic, and Exponential Functions; Definite Integrals Involving Odd and Even Functions*

- If the problem asks you to determine the concavity of f' (not f), you need to know if f'' is increasing or decreasing or if f''' is positive or negative.

Definite Integrals Involving Algebraic Functions

Example 1

Evaluate: $\int_1^4 \dfrac{x^3 - 8}{\sqrt{x}}\, dx$

Rewrite: $\int_1^4 \dfrac{x^3 - 8}{\sqrt{x}}\, dx = \int_1^4 \left(x^{5/2} - 8x^{-1/2}\right)dx$

$$= \dfrac{x^{7/2}}{7/2} - \dfrac{8x^{1/2}}{1/2}\Bigg]_1^4 = \dfrac{2x^{7/2}}{7} - 16x^{1/2}\Bigg]_1^4$$

$$= \left(\dfrac{2(4)^{7/2}}{7} - 16(4)^{1/2}\right) - \left(\dfrac{2(1)^{7/2}}{7} - 16(1)^{1/2}\right) = \dfrac{142}{7}$$

Verify your result with a calculator.

Example 2

Evaluate: $\int_0^2 x\left(x^2 - 1\right)^7 dx$

Begin by evaluating the indefinite integral $\int x\left(x^2 - 1\right)^7 dx$.

Let $u = x^2 - 1$; $du = 2x\,dx$ or $\dfrac{du}{2} = x\,dx$

Rewrite: $\int \dfrac{u^7 du}{2} = \dfrac{1}{2}\int u^7 du = \dfrac{1}{2}\left(\dfrac{u^8}{8}\right) + c = \dfrac{u^8}{16} + c$

$$= \dfrac{\left(x^2 - 1\right)^8}{16} + c$$

Thus the definite integral $\int_0^2 x\left(x^2 - 1\right)^7 dx = \dfrac{\left(x^2 - 1\right)^8}{16}\Bigg]_0^2$

$$= \dfrac{\left(2^2 - 1\right)^8}{16} - \dfrac{\left(0^2 - 1\right)^8}{16} = \dfrac{3^8}{16} - \dfrac{(-1)^8}{16} = \dfrac{3^8 - 1}{16} = 410$$

Verify your result with a calculator.

Example 3

Evaluate $\int_{-8}^{-1} \left(\sqrt[3]{y} + \dfrac{1}{\sqrt[3]{y}}\right)dy$

Rewrite: $\int_{-8}^{-1} \left(y^{1/3} + \dfrac{1}{y^{1/3}}\right)dy = \int_{-8}^{-1} \left(y^{1/3} + y^{-1/3}\right)dy$

$$= \dfrac{y^{4/3}}{4/3} + \dfrac{y^{2/3}}{2/3}\Bigg]_{-8}^{-1} = \dfrac{3y^{4/3}}{4} + \dfrac{3y^{2/3}}{2}\Bigg]_{-8}^{-1}$$

$$= \left(\dfrac{3(-1)^{4/3}}{4} + \dfrac{3(-1)^{2/3}}{2}\right) - \left(\dfrac{3(-8)^{4/3}}{4} + \dfrac{3(-8)^{2/3}}{2}\right)$$

$$= \left(\dfrac{3}{4} + \dfrac{3}{2}\right) - (12 + 6) = \dfrac{-63}{4}$$

Verify your result with a calculator.

Definite Integrals Involving Absolute Value

Example 1

Evaluate: $\int_1^4 |3x - 6| \, dx$

Set $3x - 6 = 0$; $x = 2$; Thus $|3x - 6| = \begin{cases} 3x - 6 & \text{if } x \geq 2 \\ -(3x - 6) & \text{if } x < 2 \end{cases}$

Rewrite Integral:

$$\int_1^4 |3x - 6| \, dx = \int_1^2 -(3x - 6) \, dx + \int_2^4 (3x - 6) \, dx$$

$$= \left[\frac{-3x^2}{2} + 6x \right]_1^2 + \left[\frac{3x^2}{2} - 6x \right]_2^4$$

$$= \left(\frac{-3(2)^2}{2} + 6(2) \right) - \left(\frac{-3(1)^2}{2} + 6(1) \right)$$

$$+ \left(\frac{3(4)^2}{2} - 6(4) \right) - \left(\frac{3(2)^2}{2} - 6(2) \right)$$

$$= (-6 + 12) - \left(-\frac{3}{2} + 6 \right) + (24 - 24) - (6 - 12)$$

$$= 6 - 4\frac{1}{2} + 0 + 6 = \frac{15}{2}$$

Verify your result with a calculator.

Example 2

Evaluate $\int_0^4 |x^2 - 4| \, dx$

Set $x^2 - 4 = 0$; $x = \pm 2$

Thus $|x^2 - 4| = \begin{cases} x^2 - 4 & \text{if } x \geq 2 \text{ or } x \leq -2 \\ -(x^2 - 4) & \text{if } -2 < x < 2 \end{cases}$

Thus $\int_0^4 |x^2 - 4| \, dx = \int_0^2 -(x^2 - 4) \, dx + \int_2^4 (x^2 - 4) \, dx$

$$= \left[\frac{-x^3}{3} + 4x \right]_0^2 + \left[\frac{x^3}{3} - 4x \right]_2^4$$

$$= \left(\frac{-2^3}{3} + 4(2) \right) - (0) + \left(\frac{4^3}{3} - 4(4) \right) - \left(\frac{2^3}{3} - 4(2) \right)$$

$$= \left(\frac{-8}{3} + 8 \right) + \left(\frac{64}{3} - 16 \right) - \left(\frac{8}{3} - 8 \right) = 16$$

Verify your result with a calculator.

Definite Integrals Involving Trigonometric, Logarithmic, and Exponential Functions

Example 1

Evaluate $\int_0^\pi (x + \sin x)\,dx$

Rewrite: $\int_0^\pi (x + \sin x)\,dx = \dfrac{x^2}{2} - \cos x \Big]_0^\pi = \left(\dfrac{\pi^2}{2} - \cos \pi\right) - (0 - \cos 0)$

$$= \dfrac{\pi^2}{2} + 1 + 1 = \dfrac{\pi^2}{2} + 2$$

Verify your result with a calculator.

Example 2

Evaluate $\int_{\pi/4}^{\pi/2} \csc^2(3t)\,dt$

Let $u = 3t$; $du = 3dt$ or $\dfrac{du}{3} = dt$

Rewrite the indefinite integral $= \int \csc^2 u \, \dfrac{du}{3} = -\dfrac{1}{3} \cot u + c$

$$= -\dfrac{1}{3} \cot(3t) + c$$

$$\int_{\pi/4}^{\pi/2} \csc^2(3t)\,dt = -\dfrac{1}{3} \cot(3t)\Big]_{\pi/4}^{\pi/2}$$

$$= -\dfrac{1}{3}\left[\cot\left(\dfrac{3\pi}{2}\right) - \cot\left(\dfrac{3\pi}{4}\right)\right]$$

$$= -\dfrac{1}{3}\left[0 - (-1)\right] = -\dfrac{1}{3}$$

Verify your result with a calculator.

Example 3

Evaluate: $\int_1^e \dfrac{\ln t}{t}\,dt$

Let $u = \ln t$, $du = \dfrac{1}{t}\,dt$

Rewrite: $\int \dfrac{\ln t}{t}\,dt = \int u\,du = \dfrac{u^2}{2} + c = \dfrac{(\ln t)^2}{2} + c$

$$\int_1^e \dfrac{\ln t}{t}\,dt = \dfrac{(\ln t)^2}{2}\Big]_1^e = \dfrac{(\ln e)^2}{2} - \dfrac{(\ln 1)^2}{2}$$

$$= \dfrac{1}{2} - 0 = \dfrac{1}{2}$$

Verify your result with a calculator.

Example 4

Evaluate: $\int_{-1}^2 xe^{(x^2+1)}\,dx$

Let $u = x^2 + 1$; $du = 2x\,dx$ or $\dfrac{du}{2} = x\,dx$

$$\int xe^{(x^2+1)}dx = \int e^u \frac{du}{2} = \frac{1}{2}e^u + c = \frac{1}{2}e^{(x^2+1)} + c$$

Rewrite: $\displaystyle\int_{-1}^{2} xe^{(x^2+1)}dx = \frac{1}{2}e^{(x^2+1)}\Bigg]_{-1}^{2} = \frac{1}{2}e^5 - \frac{1}{2}e^2$

$$= \frac{1}{2}e^2\left(e^3 - 1\right)$$

Verify your result with a calculator.

Definite Integrals Involving Odd and Even Functions

If f is an even function, that is, $f(-x) = f(x)$, and is continuous on $[-a, a]$, then

$$\int_{-a}^{a} f(x)dx = 2\int_{0}^{a} f(x)dx$$

If f is an odd function, that is, $F(x) = -f(-x)$, and is continuous on $[-a, a]$ then

$$\int_{-a}^{a} f(x)dx = 0$$

Example 1

Evaluate: $\displaystyle\int_{-\pi/2}^{\pi/2} \cos x\,dx$

Since $f(x) = \cos x$ is an even function,

$$\int_{-\pi/2}^{\pi/2} \cos x\,dx = 2\int_{0}^{\pi/2} \cos x\,dx = 2[\sin x]_{0}^{\pi/2} = 2\left[\sin\left(\frac{\pi}{2}\right) - \sin(0)\right]$$

$$= 2(1 - 0) = 2$$

Verify your result a calculator.

Example 2

Evaluate: $\displaystyle\int_{-3}^{3} \left(x^4 - x^2\right)dx$

Since $f(x) = x^4 - x^2$ is an even function, i.e., $f(-x) = f(x)$, thus

$$\int_{-3}^{3}\left(x^4 - x^2\right)dx = 2\int_{0}^{3}\left(x^4 - x^2\right)dx = 2\left[\frac{x^5}{5} - \frac{x^3}{3}\right]_{0}^{3}$$

$$= 2\left[\left(\frac{3^5}{5} - \frac{3^3}{3}\right) - 0\right] = \frac{396}{5}$$

Verify your result with a calculator.

Example 3

Evaluate: $\displaystyle\int_{-\pi}^{\pi} \sin x\,dx$

Since $f(x) = \sin x$ is an odd function, i.e., $f(-x) = -f(x)$, thus

$$\int_{-\pi}^{\pi} \sin x \, dx = 0$$

Verify your result algebraically.

$$\int_{-\pi}^{\pi} \sin x \, dx = -\cos x\Big]_{-\pi}^{\pi} = (-\cos \pi) - [-\cos(-\pi)]$$

$$= [-(-1)] - [-(-1)] = (1) - (1) = 0$$

You can also verify the result with a calculator.

Example 4

If $\int_{-k}^{k} f(x)dx = 2\int_{0}^{k} f(x)dx$ for all values of k, then which of the following could be the graph of f? See Figure 8.3-1.

(A)
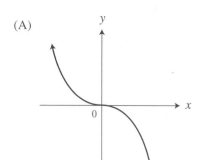

(B)
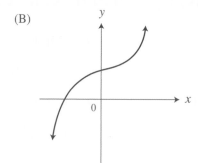

(C)
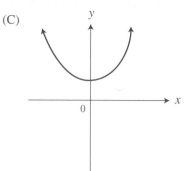

(D)
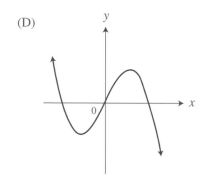

(E)
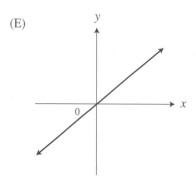

Figure 8.3-1

$$\int_{-k}^{k} f(x)dx = \int_{-k}^{0} f(x)dx + \int_{0}^{k} f(x)dx$$

Since $\int_{-k}^{k} f(x)dx = 2\int_{0}^{k} f(x)dx$, then $\int_{0}^{k} f(x)dx = \int_{-k}^{0} f(x)dx$

Thus f is an even function. Choice (c).

 ## 8.4 RAPID REVIEW

1. Evaluate $\int_{\pi/2}^{x} \cos t \, dt$.

   Answer: $\sin t\Big]_{x/2}^{x} = \sin x - \sin\left(\dfrac{\pi}{2}\right) = \sin x - 1.$

2. Evaluate $\int_0^1 \dfrac{1}{x+1}\,dx$

   Answer: $\ln(x+1)\big]_0^1 = \ln 2 - \ln 1 = \ln 2.$

3. If $G(x) = \int_0^x (2t+1)^{3/2}\,dt$, find $G'(4)$.

   Answer: $G'(x) = (2x+1)^{3/2}$ and $G'(4) = 9^{3/2} = 27.$

4. If $\int_1^k 2x\,dx = 8$, find k.

   Answer: $x^2\big]_1^k = 8 \Rightarrow k^2 - 1 = 8 \Rightarrow k = \pm 3.$

5. If $G(x)$ is a antiderivative of $(e^x + 1)$ and $G(0) = 0$, find $G(1)$.

   Answer: $G(x) = e^x + x + c$

   $G(0) = e^0 + 0 + c = 0 \Rightarrow c = -1.$

   $G(1) = e^1 + 1 - 1 = e.$

6. If $G'(x) = g(x)$, express $\int_0^2 g(4x)\,dx$ in terms of $G(x)$.

   Answer: Let $u = 4x;\ \dfrac{du}{4} = dx.$

   $\int g(u)\dfrac{du}{4} = \dfrac{1}{4}G(u).$ *Thus* $\int_0^2 (4x)dx = \dfrac{1}{4}G(4x)\Big]_0^2 = \dfrac{1}{4}\big[G(8) - G(0)\big].$

8.5   PRACTICE PROBLEMS

Part A—The use of a calculator is not allowed.

Evaluate the following definite integrals.

1. $\int_{-1}^0 (1 + x - x^3)\,dx$

2. $\int_6^{11} (x-2)^{1/2}\,dx$

3. $\int_1^3 \dfrac{t}{t+1}\,dt$

4. $\int_0^6 |x - 3|\,dx$

5. If $\int_0^k (6x - 1)\,dx = 4$, find k.

6. $\int_0^\pi \dfrac{\sin x}{\sqrt{1 + \cos x}}\,dx$

7. If $f'(x) = g(x)$ and g is a continuous function for all real values of x, express $\int_1^2 g(4x)$ in terms of f.

8. $\int_{\ln 2}^{\ln 3} 10e^x\,dx$

9. $\int_e^{e^2} \dfrac{1}{t+3}\,dt$

10. If $f(x) = \int_{-\pi/4}^x \tan^2(t)\,dt$, find $f'\left(\dfrac{\pi}{6}\right)$.

11. $\int_{-1}^1 4xe^{x^2}\,dx$

12. $\int_{-\pi}^\pi (\cos x - x^2)\,dx$

Part B—Calculators are permitted.

13. Find k if $\int_0^2 (x^3 + k)\,dx = 10$

14. Evaluate $\int_{-1.2}^{3.1} 2\theta \cos\theta\,d\theta$ to the nearest 100th.

15. If $y = \int_1^{x^3} \sqrt{t^2 + 1}\,dt$, find $\dfrac{dy}{dx}$.

16. Use a midpoint Riemann sum with four subdivisions of equal length to find the approximate value of $\int_0^8 (x^3 + 1)\,dx$.

17. Given $\int_{-2}^{2} g(x)dx = 8$ and $\int_{0}^{2} g(x)dx = 3$

 find (a) $\int_{-2}^{0} g(x)dx$

 (b) $\int_{2}^{-2} g(x)dx$

 (c) $\int_{0}^{-2} 5g(x)dx$

 (d) $\int_{-2}^{-2} 2g(x)dx$

18. Evaluate: $\int_{0}^{1/2} \dfrac{dx}{\sqrt{1 - x^2}}$

19. Find $\dfrac{dy}{dx}$ if $y = \int_{\cos x}^{\sin x} (2t + 1)dt$

20. Let f be a continuous function defined on $[0, 35]$ with selected values as shown below:

x	0	5	10	15	20	25	30
$f(x)$	1.4	2.6	3.4	4.1	4.7	5.2	5.7

 Use a midpoint Riemann sum with three subdivisions of equal length to find the approximate value of $\int_{0}^{30} f(x)dx$.

8.6   CUMULATIVE REVIEW PROBLEMS

21. Evaluate $\lim\limits_{x \to -\infty} \dfrac{\sqrt{x^2 - 4}}{3x - 9}$

22. Find $\dfrac{dy}{dx}$ at $x = 3$ if $y = \ln|x^2 - 4|$.

23. The graph of f', the derivative of f, $-6 \le x \le 8$ is shown in Figure 8.6-1.

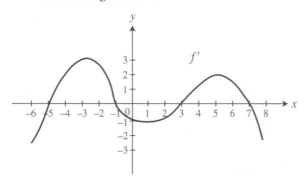

Figure 8.6-1

 (a) Find all values of x such that f attains a relative maximum or a relative minimum.

 (b) Find all values of x such that f is concave upward.

 (c) Find all values of x such that f has a change of concavity.

24. (Calculator) Given the equation $9x^2 + 4y^2 - 18x + 16y = 11$, find the points on the graph where the equation has a vertical or horizontal tangent.

25. (Calculator) Two corridors, one 6 *feet* wide and another 10 *feet* wide meet at a corner. See Figure 8.6-2. What is the maximum length of a pipe of negligible thickness that can be carried horizontally around the corner?

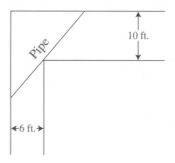

Figure 8.6-2

8.7   SOLUTIONS TO PRACTICE PROBLEMS

Part A—No calculators.

1. $\int_{-1}^{0} (1 + x - x^3)dx = x + \dfrac{x^2}{2} - \dfrac{x^4}{4} \Big]_{-1}^{0}$

 $= 0 - \left[(-1) + \dfrac{(-1)^2}{2} - \dfrac{(-1)^4}{4}\right]$

 $= \dfrac{3}{4}$

2. Let $u = x - 2$ $du = dx$

$$\int (x-2)^{\frac{1}{2}} dx = \int u^{\frac{1}{2}} du = \frac{2u^{\frac{3}{2}}}{3} + c$$

$$= \frac{2}{3}(x-2)^{\frac{3}{2}} + c$$

Thus $\int_6^{11} (x-2)^{\frac{1}{2}} dx = \frac{2}{3}(x-2)^{\frac{3}{2}}\Big]_6^{11}$

$$= \frac{2}{3}\left[(11-2)^{\frac{3}{2}} - (6-2)^{\frac{3}{2}}\right]$$

$$= \frac{2}{3}(27-8) = \frac{38}{3}$$

3. Let $u = t + 1$; $du = dt$ and $t = u - 1$.

Rewrite: $\int \frac{t}{t+1} dt = \int \frac{u-1}{u} du$

$$= \int \left(1 - \frac{1}{u}\right) du$$

$$= u - \ln|u| + c$$

$$= t + 1 - \ln|t + 1| + c$$

$\int_1^3 \frac{t}{t+1} dt = \left[t + 1 - \ln|t+1|\right]_1^3$

$$= \left[(3) + 1 - \ln|3+1|\right]$$

$$- \left((1) + 1 - \ln|1+1|\right)$$

$$= 4 - \ln 4 - 2 + \ln 2$$

$$= 2 - \ln 4 + \ln 2$$

$$= 2 - \ln(2)^2 + \ln 2$$

$$= 2 - 2\ln 2 + \ln 2$$

$$= 2 - \ln 2$$

4. Set $x - 3 = 0$; $x = 3$.

$$|x - 3| = \begin{cases} (x-3) \text{ if } x \geq 3 \\ -(x-3) \text{ if } x < 3 \end{cases}$$

$\int_0^6 |x-3| dx = \int_0^3 -(x-3) dx + \int_3^6 (x-3) dx$

$$= \left[\frac{-x^2}{2} + 3x\right]_0^3 + \left[\frac{x^2}{2} - 3x\right]_3^6$$

$$= \left(-\frac{(3)^2}{2} + 3(3)\right) - 0$$

$$+ \left(\frac{6^2}{2} - 3(6)\right) - \left(\frac{3^2}{2} - 3(3)\right)$$

$$= \frac{9}{2} + \frac{9}{2} = 9$$

5. $\int_0^k (6x-1) dx = 3x^2 - x\Big]_0^k = 3k^2 - k$

Set $3k^2 - k = 4 \Rightarrow 3k^2 - k - 4 = 0$

$$\Rightarrow (3k-4)(k+1) = 0$$

$$\Rightarrow k = \frac{4}{3} \text{ or } k = -1$$

Verify your results by evaluating

$\int_0^{\frac{4}{3}} (6x-1) dx$ and $\int_0^{-1} (6x-1) dx$.

6. Let $u = 1 + \cos x$; $du = -\sin x\, dx$ or $-du = \sin x\, dx$.

$$\int \frac{\sin x}{\sqrt{1 + \cos x}} dx = \int \frac{-1}{\sqrt{u}}(du) = -\int \frac{1}{u^{\frac{1}{2}}} du$$

$$= -\int u^{-\frac{1}{2}} du = -\frac{u^{\frac{1}{2}}}{\frac{1}{2}} + c$$

$$= -2u^{\frac{1}{2}} + c$$

$$= -2(1 + \cos x)^{\frac{1}{2}} + c$$

$\int_0^\pi \frac{\sin x}{\sqrt{1+\cos x}} dx = -2(1+\cos x)^{\frac{1}{2}}\Big]_0^\pi$

$$= -2\left[(1 + \cos \pi)^{\frac{1}{2}}\right.$$

$$\left. - (1 + \cos 0)^{\frac{1}{2}}\right]$$

$$= -2[0 - 2^{\frac{1}{2}}] = 2\sqrt{2}$$

7. Let $u = 4x$; $du = 4\, dx$ or $\frac{du}{4} = dx$

$$\int g(4x) dx = \int g(u) \frac{du}{4} = \frac{1}{4} \int g(u) du$$

$$= \frac{1}{4} f(u) + c$$

$$= \frac{1}{4} f(4x) + c$$

$\int_1^2 g(4x) dx = \frac{1}{4} f(4x)\Big]_1^2$

$$= \frac{1}{4} f(4(2)) - \frac{1}{4} f(4(1))$$

$$= \frac{1}{4} f(8) - \frac{1}{4} f(4).$$

8. $\int_{\ln 2}^{\ln 3} 10e^x dx = 10e^x\Big]_{\ln 2}^{\ln 3} = 10\left[(e^{\ln 3}) - (e^{\ln 2})\right]$

$$= 10(3 - 2) = 10.$$

9. Let $u = t + 3$; $du = dt$.

$$\int \frac{1}{t+3}\,dt = \int \frac{1}{u}\,du = \ln|u| + c = \ln|t+3| + c$$

$$\int_e^{e^2} \frac{1}{t+3}\,dt = \ln|t+3|\Big]_e^{e^2}$$

$$= \ln(e^2 + 3) - \ln(e + 3)$$

$$= \ln\left(\frac{e^2+3}{e+3}\right)$$

10. $f'(x) = \tan^2 x$; $f'\left(\dfrac{\pi}{6}\right) = \tan^2\left(\dfrac{\pi}{6}\right) = \left(\dfrac{1}{\sqrt{3}}\right)^2 = \dfrac{1}{3}$.

11. Let $u = x^2$; $du = 2x\,dx$ or $\dfrac{du}{2} = x\,dx$

$$\int 4xe^{x^2}\,dx = 4\int e^u\left(\frac{du}{2}\right)$$

$$= 2\int e^u\,du = 2e^u + c = 2e^{x^2} + c$$

$$\int_{-1}^1 4xe^{x^2}\,dx = 2e^{x^2}\Big]_{-1}^1$$

$$= 2\left[e^{(1)^2} - e^{(-1)^2}\right] = 2(e - e) = 0$$

Note that $f(x) = 4xe^{x^2}$ is an odd function. Thus $\int_{-a}^a f(x)\,dx = 0$.

12. $\displaystyle\int_{-\pi}^{\pi} \left(\cos x - x^2\right)dx = \sin x - \frac{x^3}{3}\Big]_{-\pi}^{\pi}$

$$= \left(\sin \pi - \frac{\pi^3}{3}\right)$$

$$- \left(\sin(-\pi) - \frac{(-\pi)^3}{3}\right)$$

$$= -\frac{\pi^3}{3} - \left(0 - \frac{-\pi^3}{3}\right)$$

$$= -\frac{2\pi^3}{3}$$

Note that $f(x) = \cos x - x^2$ is an even function. Thus you could have written

$$\int_{-\pi}^{\pi} \left(\cos x - x^2\right)dx = 2\int_0^{\pi}\left(\cos x - x^2\right)dx \quad\text{and}$$

obtain the same result.

Part B—Calculators are permitted.

13. $\displaystyle\int_0^2 (x^3 + k)dx = \frac{x^4}{4} + kx\Big]_0^2 = \left(\frac{2^4}{4} + k(2)\right) - 0$

$$= 4 + 2k$$

Set $4 + 2k = 10$ and thus $k = 3$.

14. Enter $\int(2x * \cos(x), x, -1.2, 3.1)$ and obtain $-4.70208 \approx -4.702$.

15. $\dfrac{d}{dx}\left(\displaystyle\int_1^{x^3} \sqrt{t^2 + 1}\, dt\right) = \sqrt{(x^3)^2 + 1}\,\dfrac{d}{dx}(x^3)$

$$= 3x^2\sqrt{x^6 + 1}.$$

16. $\Delta x = \dfrac{8 - 0}{4} = 2$ Midpoints are $x = 1, 3, 5$ and 7.

$$\int_0^{12} (x^3 + 1)dx \approx (1^3 + 1)(2) + (3^3 + 1)(2)$$

$$+ (5^3 + 1)(2) + (7^3 + 1)(2)$$

$$\approx (2)(2) + (28)(2) + (126)(1)$$

$$+ (344)(2) = 874$$

17. (a) $\displaystyle\int_{-2}^0 g(x)dx + \int_0^2 g(x)dx = \int_{-2}^2 g(x)dx$

$$\int_{-2}^0 g(x)dx + 3 = 8. \text{ Thus } \int_{-2}^0 g(x)dx = 5$$

(b) $\displaystyle\int_2^{-2} g(x)dx) = -\int_{-2}^2 g(x)dx = -8$

(c) $\displaystyle\int_0^{-2} 5g(x)dx = 5\int_0^{-2} g(x)dx$

$$= 5\left(-\int_{-2}^0 g(x)dx\right)$$

$$= 5(-5) = -25$$

(d) $\displaystyle\int_{-2}^2 2g(x)dx = 2\int_{-2}^2 g(x)dx = 2(8) = 16$

18. $\displaystyle\int_0^{\frac{1}{2}} \frac{dx}{\sqrt{1 - x^2}} = \sin^{-1}(x)\Big]_0^{\frac{1}{2}}$

$$= \sin^{-1}\left(\frac{1}{2}\right) - \sin^{-1}(0)$$

$$= \frac{\pi}{6} - 0 = \frac{\pi}{6}$$

19. $\displaystyle\int_{\cos x}^{\sin x} (2t + 1)dt = \int_0^{\sin x} (2t + 1)dt$

$$- \int_0^{\cos x} (2t + 1)dt$$

$$\frac{dy}{dx} = \frac{d}{dx}\left(\int_{\cos x}^{\sin x} (2t + 1)\right) = (2\sin x + 1)\frac{d}{dx}$$

$$\sin x - (2\cos x + 1)\frac{d}{dx}(\cos x)\bigg)$$

$$= (2\sin x + 1)\cos x$$

$$- (2\cos x + 1)(-\sin x)$$

$$= 2\sin x \cos x + \cos x + 2\sin x \cos x$$

$$+ \sin x = 4\sin x \cos x + \cos x + \sin x.$$

20. $\Delta x = \dfrac{30 - 0}{3} = 10$

Midpoints are $x = 5$, 15 and 25.

$\int_0^{30} f(x)dx \approx [f(5)]10 + [f(15)]10 + [f(25)]10$

$\approx (2.6)(10) + (4.1)(10) + (5.2)(10)$

$\approx 119.$

8.8 SOLUTIONS TO CUMULATIVE REVIEW PROBLEMS

21. As $x \to -\infty$, $x = -\sqrt{x^2}$

$\displaystyle\lim_{x \to -\infty} \frac{\sqrt{x^2 - 4}}{3x - 9} = \lim_{x \to -\infty} \frac{\sqrt{x^2 - 4}/-\sqrt{x^2}}{(3x - 9)/x}$

$= \displaystyle\lim_{x \to -\infty} \frac{-\sqrt{(x^2 - 4)/x^2}}{3 - (9/x)}$

$= \displaystyle\lim_{x \to -\infty} \frac{-\sqrt{1 - (4/x^2)}}{3 - 9/x}$

$= \dfrac{-\sqrt{1 - 0}}{3 - 0} = -\dfrac{1}{3}.$

22. $y = \ln|x^2 - 4|$, $\dfrac{dy}{dx} = \dfrac{1}{(x^2 - 4)}(2x)$

$\dfrac{dy}{dx}\bigg|_{x=3} = \dfrac{2(3)}{(3^2 - 4)} = \dfrac{6}{5}$

23. (a) See Figure 8.8-1.

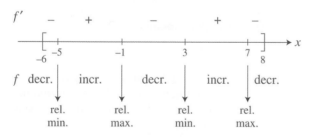

Figure 8.8-1

The function f has a relative minimum at $x = -5$ and $x = 3$, and f has a relative maximum at $x = -1$ and $x = 7$.

(b) See Figure 8.8-2.

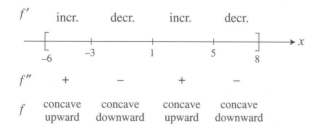

Figure 8.8-2

The function f is concave upward on intervals $(-6, -3)$ and $(1, 5)$.

(c) A change of concavity occurs at $x = -3$, $x = 1$ and $x = 5$.

24. (Calculator) Differentiate both sides of $9x^2 + 4y^2 - 18x + 16y = 11$.

$18x + 8y\dfrac{dy}{dx} - 18 + 16\dfrac{dy}{dx} = 0$

$8y\dfrac{dy}{dx} + 16\dfrac{dy}{dx} = -18x + 18$

$\dfrac{dy}{dx}(8y + 16) = -18x + 18$

$\dfrac{dy}{dx} = \dfrac{-18x + 18}{8y + 16}$

Horizontal tangent $\Rightarrow \dfrac{dy}{dx} = 0$

Set $\dfrac{dy}{dx} = 0 \Rightarrow -18x + 18 = 0$ or $x = 1$

At $x = 1$, $9 + 4y^2 - 18 + 16y = 11$

$4y^2 + 16y - 20 = 0$

Using a calculator, enter solve $(4y^2 + 16y - 20 = 0, y)$; obtaining $y = -5$ or $y = 1$.

Thus each of the points at $(1, 1)$ and $(1, -5)$ the graph has a horizontal tangent at each point.

Vertical tangent $\Rightarrow \dfrac{dy}{dx}$ is undefined.

Set $8y + 16 = 0 \Rightarrow y = -2$.

At $y = -2$, $9x^2 + 16 - 18x - 32 = 11$

$9x^2 - 18x - 27 = 0$

Enter solve $(9x^2 - 8x - 27 = 0, x)$ and obtain $x = 3$ or $x = -1$.

Thus at each of the points $(3, -2)$ and $(-1, -2)$, the graph has a vertical tangent. (See Figure 8.8-3.)

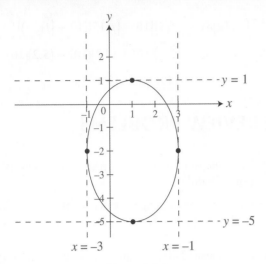

Figure 8.8-3

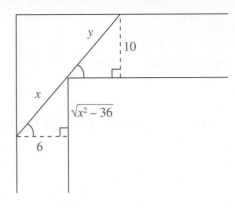

Figure 8.8-4

25. (Calculator)

Step 1. See Figure 8.8-4. Let $P = x + y$ where P is the length of the pipe and x and y are as shown. The minimum value of P is the maximum length of the pipe to be able to turn in the corner. By similar triangles, $\dfrac{y}{10} = \dfrac{x}{\sqrt{x^2 - 36}}$ and thus

$$y = \frac{10x}{\sqrt{x^2 - 36}}, x > 6$$

$$P = x + y = x + \frac{10x}{\sqrt{x^2 - 36}}$$

Step 2. Find the minimum value of P.

Enter $y_1 = x + 10 * x / \left(\sqrt{\ } \left(x^\wedge 2 - 36 \right) \right)$.

Use the Minimum function of the calculator and obtain the minimum point (9.306, 22.388).

Step 3. Verify with the First Derivative Test.

Enter $y_2 = (y_1(x), x)$ and observe. (See Figure 8.8-5.)

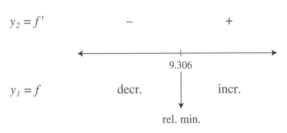

Figure 8.8-5

Step 4. Check endpoints.

The domain of x is $(6, \infty)$

Since at $x = 9.306$ is the only relative extremum, it is the absolute minimum. Thus the maximum length of the pipe is 22.388 feet.

Chapter 9

Areas and Volumes

9.1   THE FUNCTION $F(x) = \int_a^x f(t)dt$

The Second Fundamental Theorem of Calculus defines

$$F(x) = \int_a^x f(t)dt$$

and states that if f is continuous on $[a,b]$, then $F'(x) = f(x)$ for every point x in $[a,b]$.
If $f \geq 0$, then $F \geq 0$. $F(x)$ can be interpreted geometrically as the area under the curve of
f from $t = a$ to $t = x$. (See Figure 9.1-1.)

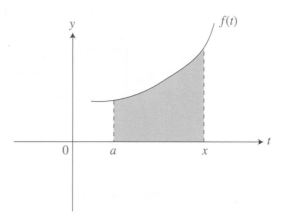

Figure 9.1-1

If $f < 0$, $F < 0$. $F(x)$ can be treated as the negative value of the area between the curve of
f and the *t-axis* from $t = a$ to $t = x$. (See Figure 9.1-2.)

Example 1
If $f(x) = \int_0^x 2 \cos t \ dt$ for $0 \leq x \leq \pi$, find the value(s) of x where f has a local minimum.

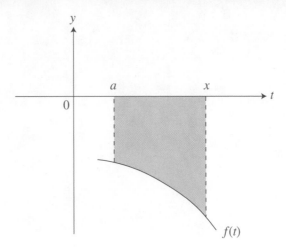

Figure 9.1-2

Method 1:

Since $f(x) = \int_0^x 2 \cos t\, dt$, $f'(x) = 2 \cos x$.

Set $f'(x) = 0$; $2 \cos x = 0$, $x = \dfrac{\pi}{2}$ or $\dfrac{3\pi}{2}$.

$f''(x) = -2 \sin x$ and $f''\left(\dfrac{\pi}{2}\right) = -2$ and $f''\left(\dfrac{3\pi}{2}\right) = 2$

Thus at $x = \dfrac{3\pi}{2}$, f has a local minimum.

Method 2:

You can solve this problem geometrically by using area. See Figure 9.1-3.

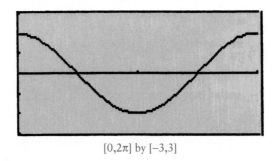

[0,2π] by [−3,3]

Figure 9.1-3

The area "under the curve" is above the t-axis on $\left[0, \dfrac{\pi}{2}\right]$ and below the x-axis on $\left[\dfrac{\pi}{2}, \dfrac{3\pi}{2}\right]$. Thus the local minimum occurs at $\dfrac{3\pi}{2}$.

Example 2

Let $p(x) = \int_0^x f(t)\, dt$ and the graph of f is shown in Figure 9.1-4.

(a) Evaluate: $p(0)$, $p(1)$, $p(4)$
(b) Evaluate: $p(5)$, $p(7)$, $p(8)$
(c) At what value of t does p have a maximum value?

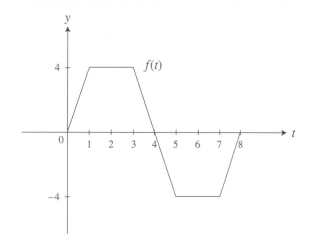

Figure 9.1-4

(d) On what interval(s) is p decreasing?

(e) Draw a sketch of the graph of p.

Solution:

(a) $p(0) = \int_0^0 f(t)\,dt = 0$

$p(1) = \int_0^1 f(t)\,dt = \dfrac{(1)(4)}{2} = 2$

$p(4) = \int_0^4 f(t)\,dt = \dfrac{1}{2}(2 + 4)(4) = 12$

(**Note:** $f(t)$ forms a trapezoid from $t = 0$ to $t = 4$.)

(b) $p(5) = \int_0^5 f(t)\,dt = \int_0^4 f(t)\,dt + \int_4^5 f(t)\,dt$

$= 12 - \dfrac{(1)(4)}{2} = 10$

$p(7) = \int_0^7 f(t)\,dt = \int_0^4 f(t)\,dt + \int_4^5 f(t)\,dt + \int_5^7 f(t)\,dt$

$= 12 - 2 - (2)(4) = 2$

$p(8) = \int_0^8 f(t)\,dt = \int_0^4 f(t)\,dt + \int_4^8 f(t)\,dt$

$= 12 - 12 = 0$

(c) Since $f \geq 0$ on the interval $[0,4]$, p attains a maximum at $t = 4$.

(d) Since $f(t)$ is below the *x-axis* from $t = 4$ to $t = 8$, if $x > 4$,

$\int_0^x f(t)\,dt = \int_0^4 f(t)\,dt + \int_4^x f(t)\,dt$ where $\int_4^x f(t)\,dt < 0$.

Thus p is decreasing on the interval $(4, 8)$.

(e) $p(x) = \int_0^x f(t)\,dt$. See Figure 9.1-5 for a sketch.

x	0	1	2	3	4	5	6	7	8
$p(x)$	0	2	6	10	12	10	6	2	0

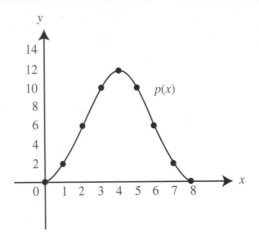

Figure 9.1-5

- Remember differentiability implies continuity, but the converse is not true, i.e., continuity does not implies differentiability, e.g., as in the case of a cusp or a corner.

Example 3

The position function of a moving particle on a coordinate axis is:

$$s = \int_0^t f(x)\,dx \text{ feet.}$$

The function f is a differentiable function and its graph is shown below in Figure 9.1-6.

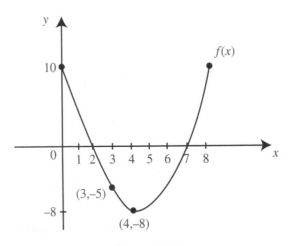

Figure 9.1-6

(a) What is the particle's velocity at $t = 4$?
(b) What is the particle position at $t = 3$?
(c) When is the acceleration zero?
(d) When is the particle moving to the right?
(e) At $t = 8$, is the particle on the right side or left side of the origin?

Solution:

(a) Since $s = \int_0^t f(x)\,dx$, then $v(t) = s'(t) = f(t)$

Thus $v(4) = -8\ ft$.

(b) $s(3) = \int_0^3 f(x)\,dx = \int_0^2 f(x)\,dx + \int_2^3 f(x)\,dx = \frac{1}{2}(10)(2) - \frac{1}{2}(1)(5) = \frac{15}{2}$

(c) $a(t) = v'(t)$. Since $v'(t) = f'(t)$, $v'(t) = 0$ at $t = 4$. Thus $a(4) = 0$.

(d) The particle is moving to the right when $v(t) > 0$. Thus the particle is moving to the right on intervals $(0, 2)$ and $(7, 8)$

(e) The area of f below the *x-axis* from $x = 2$ to $x = 7$ is larger then the area of f above the *x-axis* from $x = 0$ to $x = 2$ and $x = 7$ to $x = 8$. Thus $\int_0^8 f(x)\,dx < 0$ and the particle is on the left side of the origin.

• Don't forget that $(fg)' = f'g + g'f$ and *not* $f'g'$. However, $\lim(fg) = (\lim f)\,(\lim g)$

9.2 APPROXIMATING THE AREA UNDER A CURVE

Main Concepts: *Rectangular Approximations, Trapezoidal Approximations*

Rectangular Approximations

If $f \ge 0$, the area under the curve of f can be approximated using three common types of rectangles: left-endpoint rectangles, right-endpoint rectangles, or midpoint rectangles. (See Figure 9.2-1.)

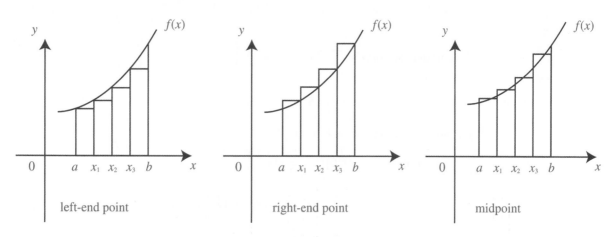

Figure 9.2-1

The area under the curve using n rectangles of equal length is approximately:

$$\sum_{i=1}^{n} \left(\text{area of rectangle}_i\right) = \begin{cases} \displaystyle\sum_{i=1}^{n} f(x_{i-1})\Delta x & \text{left-endpoint rectangles} \\[2ex] \displaystyle\sum_{i=1}^{n} f(x_i)\Delta x & \text{right-endpoint rectangles} \\[2ex] \displaystyle\sum_{i=1}^{n} f\left(\frac{x_i + x_{i-1}}{2}\right)\Delta x & \text{midpoint rectangles} \end{cases}$$

where $\Delta x = \dfrac{b - a}{n}$ and $a = x_0 < x_1 < x_2 < \ldots < x_n = b$

If f is increasing on $[a,b]$, then left-endpoint rectangles are inscribed rectangles and the right-endpoint rectangles are circumscribed rectangles. If f is decreasing on $[a,b]$, then left-endpoint rectangles are circumscribed rectangles and the right-endpoint rectangles are inscribed. Furthermore,

$$\sum_{i=1}^{n} \text{inscribed rectangle}_i \le \text{area under the curve} \le \sum_{i=1}^{n} \text{circumscribed rectangle}_i.$$

Example 1

Find the approximate area under the curve of $f(x) = x^2 + 1$ from $x = 0$ to $x = 2$. Using 4 left-endpoint rectangles of equal length. (See Figure 9.2-2.)

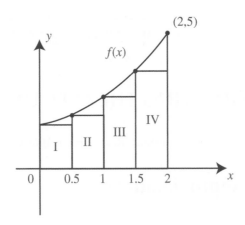

Figure 9.2-2

Let Δx_i be the length of ith rectangle. The length $\Delta x_i = \dfrac{2 - 0}{4} = \dfrac{1}{2}$; $x_{i-1} = \dfrac{1}{2}(i - 1)$

Area under the curve $\approx \displaystyle\sum_{i=1}^{4} f(x_{i-1})\Delta x_i = \sum_{i=1}^{4} \left(\left(\dfrac{1}{2}(i - 1)\right)^2 + 1\right)\left(\dfrac{1}{2}\right)$

Enter $\sum \left(\left(\left(.5(x - 1)\right)^2 + 1\right)* .5, x, 1, 4\right)$ and obtain 3.75.

Or, finding the area of each rectangle:

$$\text{Area of Rect}_\text{I} = \left(f(0)\right)\Delta x_1 = (1)\left(\dfrac{1}{2}\right) = \dfrac{1}{2}$$

$$\text{Area of Rect}_\text{II} = f(0.5)\Delta x_2 = \left((0.5)^2 + 1\right)\left(\dfrac{1}{2}\right) = 0.625$$

$$\text{Area of Rect}_\text{III} = f(1)\Delta x_3 = \left(1^2 + 1\right)\left(\dfrac{1}{2}\right) = 1$$

$$\text{Area of Rect}_\text{IV} = f(1.5)\Delta x_4 = \left(1.5^2 + 1\right)\left(\dfrac{1}{2}\right) = 1.625$$

Area of $(\text{Rect}_\text{I} + \text{Rect}_\text{II} + \text{Rect}_\text{III} + \text{Rect}_\text{IV}) = 3.75$
   Thus the approximate area under the curve of $f(x)$ is 3.75.

Example 2

Find the approximate area under the curve of $f(x) = \sqrt{x}$ from $x = 4$ to $x = 9$ using 5 right-endpoint rectangles. (See Figure 9.2-3.)

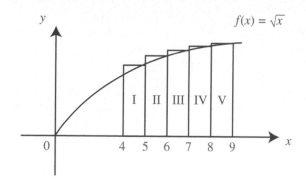

Figure 9.2-3

Let Δx_i be the length of ith rectangle. The length $\Delta x_i = \dfrac{9-4}{5} = 1$; $x_i = 4 + (1)i = 4 + i$

$$\text{Area of Rect}_{\text{I}} = f(x_1)\Delta x_1 = f(5)(1) = \sqrt{5}$$

$$\text{Area of Rect}_{\text{II}} = f(x_2)\Delta x_2 = f(6)(1) = \sqrt{6}$$

$$\text{Area of Rect}_{\text{III}} = f(x_3)\Delta x_3 = f(7)(1) = \sqrt{7}$$

$$\text{Area of Rect}_{\text{IV}} = f(x_4)\Delta x_4 = f(8)(1) = \sqrt{8}$$

$$\text{Area of Rect}_{\text{V}} = f(x_5)\Delta x_5 = f(9)(1) = \sqrt{9} = 3$$

$$\sum_{i=1}^{5}\left(\text{Area of Rect}_i\right) = \sqrt{5} + \sqrt{6} + \sqrt{7} + \sqrt{8} + 3 \approx 13.16$$

Or, using $\sum$ notation:

$$\sum_{i=1}^{5} f(x_i)\Delta x_i = \sum_{i=1}^{5} f(4 + i)(1) = \sum_{i=1}^{5} \sqrt{4 + 1}$$

Enter $\sum\left(\sqrt{(4 + x)}, x, 1, 5\right)$ and obtain 13.16

Thus the area under the curve is approximately 13.16.

Example 3

The function f is continuous on $[1,9]$ and $f > 0$. Selected values of f are given below:

x	1	2	3	4	5	6	7	8	9
$f(x)$	1	1.41	1.73	2	2.37	2.45	2.65	2.83	3

Using 4 midpoint rectangles, approximate the area under the curve of f for $x = 1$ to $x = 9$. (See Figure 9.2-4.)

Let Δx_i be the length of ith rectangle. The length $\Delta x_i = \dfrac{9 - 1}{4} = 2$.

$$\text{Area of Rect}_{\text{I}} = f(2)(2) = (1.41)2 = 2.82$$

$$\text{Area of Rect}_{\text{II}} = f(4)(2) = (2)2 = 4$$

$$\text{Area of Rect}_{\text{III}} = f(6)(2) = (2.45)2 = 4.90$$

$$\text{Area of Rect}_{\text{IV}} = f(8)(2) = (2.83)2 = 5.66$$

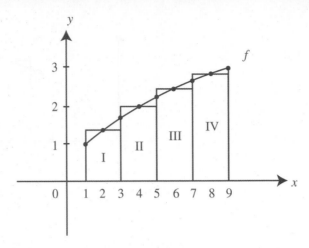

Figure 9.2-4

Area of $(\text{Rect}_{\text{I}} + \text{Rect}_{\text{II}} + \text{Rect}_{\text{III}} + \text{Rect}_{\text{IV}}) = 2.82 + 4 + 4.90 + 5.66 = 17.38$.
Thus the area under the curve is approximately 17.38.

Trapezoidal Approximations

Another method of approximating the area under a curve is to use trapezoids. See Figure 9.2-5.

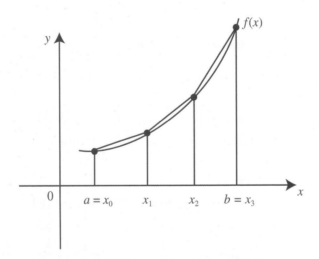

Figure 9.2-5

Formula for Trapezoidal Approximation:

If f is continuous, the area under the curve of f from $x = a$ to $x = b$ is:

$$\text{Area} \approx \frac{b-a}{2n}\left[f(x_0) + 2f(x_1) + 2f(x_2) \cdots + 2f(x_{n-1}) + f(x_n)\right]$$

Example 1

Find the approximate area under the curve of $f(x) = \cos\left(\dfrac{x}{2}\right)$ from $x = 0$ to $x = \pi$, using

4 trapezoids. (See Figure 9.2-6.)

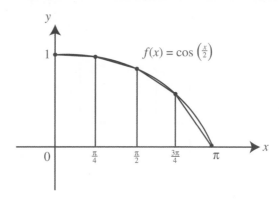

Figure 9.2-6

Since $n = 4$, $\Delta x = \dfrac{\pi - 0}{4} = \dfrac{\pi}{4}$

Area under the curve:

$$\approx \frac{\pi}{4} \cdot \frac{1}{2}\left[\cos(0) + 2\cos\left(\frac{\pi/4}{2}\right) + 2\cos\left(\frac{\pi/2}{2}\right) + 2\cos\left(\frac{3\pi/4}{2}\right) + \cos\left(\frac{\pi}{2}\right)\right]$$

$$\approx \frac{\pi}{8}\left[\cos(0) + 2\cos\left(\frac{\pi}{8}\right) + 2\cos\left(\frac{\pi}{4}\right) + 2\cos\left(\frac{3\pi}{8}\right) + \cos\left(\frac{\pi}{2}\right)\right]$$

$$\approx \frac{\pi}{8}\left[1 + 2(.9239) + 2\left(\frac{\sqrt{2}}{2}\right) + 2(.3827) + 0\right] \approx 1.9743$$

- When using a graphing calculator in solving a problem, you are required to write the setup that leads to the answer. For example, if you are finding the volume of a solid, you must write the definite integral and then use the calculator to compute the numerical value, e.g., Volume $= \pi\int_0^3 (5x)^2 dx = 225\pi$. Simply indicating the answer without writing the integral would only get you a point for the answer but not the credits for the work.

9.3 AREA AND DEFINITE INTEGRALS

Main Concepts: *Area under a Curve Area between Two Curves*

Area under a Curve

If $y = f(x)$ is continuous and non-negative on $[a,b]$, then the area under the curve of f from a to b is:

Area $= \int_a^b f(x)\,dx.$

If f is continuous and $f < 0$ on $[a,b]$, then the area under the curve from a to b is:

Area $= -\int_a^b f(x)\,dx.$ See Figure 9.3-1.

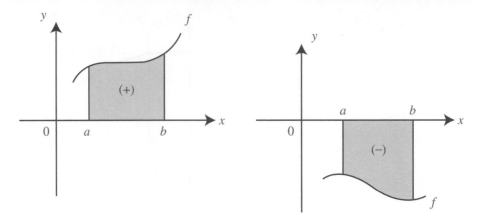

Figure 9.3-1

If $x = g(y)$ is continuous and non-negative on $[c, d]$, then the area under the curve of g from c to d is:

$$\text{Area} = \int_c^d g(y)\,dy. \text{ See Figure 9.3-2.}$$

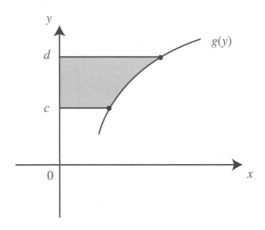

Figure 9.3-2

Example 1

Find the area under the curve of $f(x) = (x - 1)^3$ from $x = 0$ to $x = 2$.

Step 1. Sketch the graph of $f(x)$. See Figure 9.3-3.

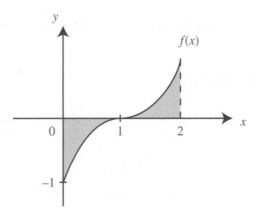

Figure 9.3-3

Step 2. Set up integrals:

$$\text{Area} = \left| \int_0^1 f(x)\,dx \right| + \int_1^2 f(x)\,dx.$$

Step 3. Evaluate integrals:

$$\left| \int_0^1 (x-1)^3\,dx \right| = \left| \frac{(x-1)^4}{4} \right]_0^1 \right| = \left| -\frac{1}{4} \right| = \frac{1}{4}$$

$$\int_1^2 (x-1)^3\,dx = \frac{(x-1)^4}{4} \right]_1^2 = \frac{1}{4}$$

Thus the total area is $\dfrac{1}{4} + \dfrac{1}{4} = \dfrac{1}{2}$.

Another solution is to find the area using a calculator.

Enter $\int \left(abs((x-1)^{\wedge}3), x, 0, 2 \right)$ and obtain $\dfrac{1}{2}$.

Example 2

Find the area of the region bounded by the graph of $f(x) = x^2 - 1$, the lines $x = -2$ and $x = 2$ and the x-axis.

Step 1. Sketch the graph of $f(x)$. See Figure 9.3-4.

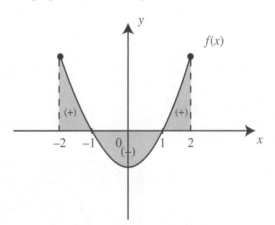

Figure 9.3-4

Step 2. Set up integrals.

$$\text{Area} = \int_{-2}^{-1} f(x)\,dx + \left| \int_{-1}^{1} f(x)\,dx \right| + \int_1^2 f(x)\,dx.$$

Step 3. Evaluate the integrals:

$$\int_{-2}^{-1} (x^2 - 1)\,dx = \frac{x^3}{3} - x \right]_{-2}^{-1} = \frac{2}{3} - \left(-\frac{2}{3} \right) = \frac{4}{3}$$

$$\left| \int_{-1}^{1} (x^2 - 1)\,dx \right| = \left| \frac{x^3}{3} - x \right]_{-1}^{1} \right| = \left| -\frac{2}{3} - \left(\frac{2}{3} \right) \right| = \left| -\frac{4}{3} \right| = \frac{4}{3}$$

$$\int_1^2 (x^2 - 1)\,dx = \frac{x^3}{3} - x \right]_1^2 = \frac{2}{3} - \left(-\frac{2}{3} \right) = \frac{4}{3}$$

Thus the total area = total area = $\dfrac{4}{3} + \dfrac{4}{3} + \dfrac{4}{3} = 4$.

Note: Since $f(x) = x^2 - 1$ is an even function, you can use the symmetry of the graph and set area $= 2\left(\left|\int_0^1 f(x)\,dx\right| + \int_1^2 f(x)\,dx\right)$.

An alternate solution is to find the area using a calculator.
    Enter $\int (abs(x\wedge 2 - 1), x, -2, 2)$ and obtain 4.

Example 3

Find the area of the region bounded by $x = y^2$, $y = -1$ and $y = 3$. See Figure 9.3-5.

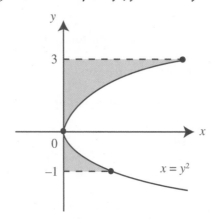

Figure 9.3-5

$$\text{Area} = \int_{-1}^{3} y^2\,dy = \left.\dfrac{y^3}{3}\right]_{-1}^{3} = \dfrac{3^3}{3} - \dfrac{(-1)^3}{3} = \dfrac{28}{3}.$$

Example 4

Using a calculator, find the area bounded by $f(x) = x^3 + x^2 - 6x$ and the *x-axis*. See Figure 9.3-6.

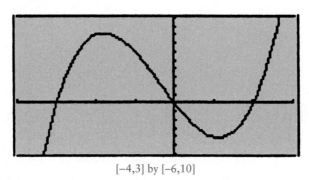

[−4,3] by [−6,10]

Figure 9.3-6

Step 1. Enter $y_1 = x\wedge 3 + x\wedge 2 - 6x$

Step 2. Enter $\int (abs(x\wedge 3 + x\wedge 2 - 6 * x), x, -3, 2)$ and obtain 21.083.

Example 5

The area under the curve $y = e^x$ from $x = 0$ to $x = k$ is 1. Find the value of k.

Area $= \int_0^k e^x\,dx = \left.e^x\right]_0^k - e^k - e^0 = e^k - 1 \Rightarrow e^k = 2$. Take ln of both sides:

$\ln(e^k) = \ln 2$; $k = \ln 2$.

Example 6

The region bounded by the *x-axis*, and the graph of $y = \sin x$ between $x = 0$ and $x = \pi$ is divided into 2 regions by the line $x = k$. The area of the region $0 \leq x \leq k$ is twice the area of the region $k \leq x \leq \pi$, find k. (See Figure 9.3-7.)

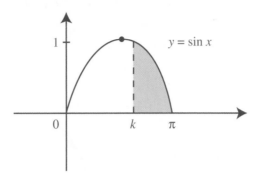

Figure 9.3-7

$$\int_0^k \sin x \, dx = 2\int_k^\pi \sin x \, dx$$

$$-\cos x\Big]_0^k = 2\big[-\cos x\big]_k^\pi$$

$$-\cos k - \big(-\cos(0)\big) = 2\big(-\cos \pi - \big(-\cos k\big)\big)$$

$$-\cos k + 1 = 2\big(1 + \cos k\big)$$

$$-\cos k + 1 = 2 + 2\cos k$$

$$-3\cos k = 1$$

$$\cos k = -\frac{1}{3}$$

$$k = \arccos\left(-\frac{1}{3}\right) = 1.91063.$$

Area between Two Curves

Area Bounded by Two Curves: See Figure 9.3-8.

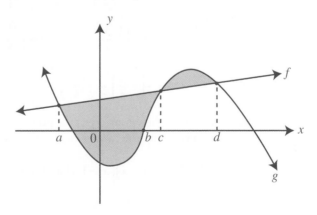

Figure 9.3-8

$$\text{Area} = \int_a^c \big[f(x) - g(x)\big]dx + \int_c^d \big[g(x) - f(x)\big]dx$$

Note: $\text{Area} = \int_a^d \big(\text{upper curve} - \text{lower curve}\big)dx$

Example 1

Find the area of the region bounded by the graphs of $f(x) = x^3$ and $g(x) = x$. (See Figure 9.3-9.)

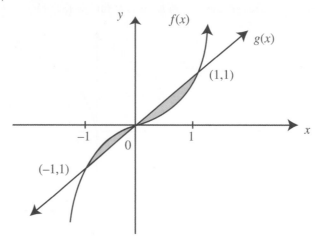

Figure 9.3-9

Step 1. Sketch the graphs of $f(x)$ and $g(x)$.

Step 2. Find the points of intersection.

Set $f(x) = g(x)$

$x^3 = x$

$x(x^2 - 1) = 0$

$x(x - 1)(x + 1) = 0$

$x = 0, 1, -1$

Step 3. Set up integrals.

$$\text{Area} = \int_{-1}^{0} (f(x) - g(x))dx + \int_{0}^{1} (g(x) - f(x))dx$$

$$= \int_{-1}^{0} (x^3 - x)dx + \int_{0}^{1} (x - x^3)dx$$

$$= \left[\frac{x^4}{4} - \frac{x^2}{2}\right]_{-1}^{0} + \left[\frac{x^2}{2} - \frac{x^4}{4}\right]_{0}^{1}$$

$$= 0 - \left(\frac{(-1)^4}{4} - \frac{(-1)^2}{2}\right) + \left(\frac{1^2}{2} - \frac{1^4}{4}\right) - 0$$

$$= -\left(-\frac{1}{4}\right) + \frac{1}{4} = \frac{1}{2}.$$

Note: You can use the symmetry of the graphs and let area $= 2\int_{0}^{1}(x - x^3)dx$. An alternate solution is to find the area using a calculator.

Enter $\int (abs(x \wedge 3 - x), x, -1, 1)$ and obtain $\frac{1}{2}$.

Example 2

Find the area of the region bounded by the curve $y = e^x$, the *y-axis* and the line $y = e^2$.

Step 1. Sketch a graph. See Figure 9.3-10.

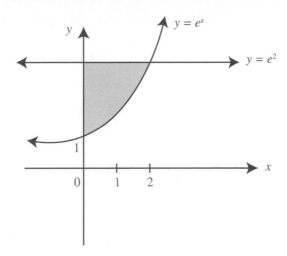

Figure 9.3-10

Step 2. Find the point of intersection. Set $e^2 = e^x \Rightarrow x = 2$.

Step 3. Set up an integral:

$$\text{Area} = \int_0^2 (e^2 - e^x)\,dx = (e^2)x - e^x \Big]_0^2$$

$$= (2e^2 - e^2) - (0 - e^0)$$

$$= e^2 + 1.$$

Or using a calculator, enter $\int ((e \wedge (2) - e \wedge (x)), x, 0, 2)$ and obtain $(e^2 + 1)$.

Example 3

Using a calculator, find the area of the region bounded by $y = \sin x$ and $y = \dfrac{x}{2}$ between $0 \le x \le \pi$.

Step 1. Sketch a graph. See Figure 9.3-11.

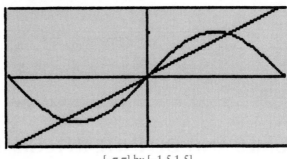

$[-\pi, \pi]$ by $[-1.5, 1.5]$

Figure 9.3-11

Step 2. Find the points of intersection.

Using the Intersection function of the calculator, the intersection points are $x = 0$ and $x = 1.89549$.

Step 3. Enter nInt($\sin(x) - .5x, x, 0, 1.89549$) and obtain $0.420798 \approx 0.421$.

(Note: You could also use the $\int$ function on your calculator and get the same result.)

Example 4

Find the area of the region bounded by the curve $xy = 1$ and the lines $y = -5$, $x = e$ and $x = e^3$.

Step 1. Sketch a graph. See Figure 9.3-12.

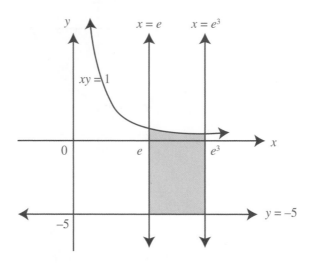

Figure 9.3-12

Step 2. Set up an integral:

$$\text{Area} = \int_{e}^{e^3} \left(\frac{1}{x} - (-5) \right) dx$$

Step 3. Evaluate the integral:

$$\text{Area} = \int_{e}^{e^3} \left(\frac{1}{x} - (-5) \right) dx = \int_{e}^{e^3} \left(\frac{1}{x} + 5 \right) dx$$

$$= \ln|x| + 5x \Big]_{e}^{e^3} = \left[\ln(e^3) + 5(e^3) \right] - \left[\ln(e) + 5(e) \right]$$

$$= 3 + 5e^3 - 1 - 5e = 2 - 5e + 5e^3.$$

• Remember: if $f' > 0$, then f is increasing and if $f'' > 0$, then the graph of f is concave upward.

9.4 VOLUMES AND DEFINITE INTEGRALS

Main Concepts: *Solids with Known Cross Sections, The Disc Method, The Washer Method*

Solids with Known Cross Sections

If $A(x)$ is the area of a cross section of a solid and $A(x)$ is continuous on $[a,b]$, then the volume of the solid from $x = a$ to $x = b$ is:

$$V = \int_{a}^{b} A(x)\, dx$$

See Figure 9.4-1.

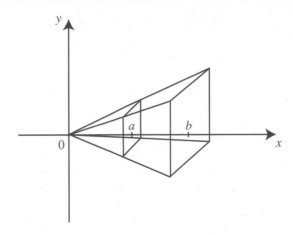

Figure 9.4-1

Note: A cross section of a solid is perpendicular to the height of the solid.

Example 1

The base of a solid is the region enclosed by the ellipse $\dfrac{x^2}{4} + \dfrac{y^2}{25} = 1$. The cross sections are perpendicular to the *x-axis* and are isosceles right triangles whose hypotenuse are on the ellipse. Find the volume of the solid. See Figure 9.4-2.

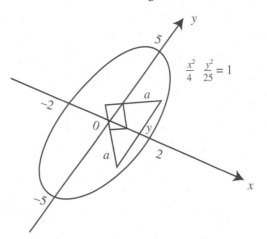

Figure 9.4-2

Step 1. Find the area of a cross section $A(x)$.

Pythagorean Theorem: $a^2 + a^2 = (2y)^2$
$$2a^2 = 4y^2$$
$$a = \sqrt{2}y,\ a > 0$$

$$A(x) = \frac{1}{2}a^2 = \frac{1}{2}\left(\sqrt{2}y\right)^2 = y^2$$

Since $\dfrac{x^2}{4} + \dfrac{y^2}{25} = 1$, $\dfrac{y^2}{25} = 1 - \dfrac{x^2}{4}$ or $y^2 = 25 - \dfrac{25x^2}{4}$

$$A(x) = 25 - \frac{25x^2}{4}$$

Step 2. Set up an integral.

$$V = \int_{-2}^{2}\left(25 - \frac{25x^2}{4}\right)dx$$

Step 3. Evaluate the integral.

$$V = \int_{-2}^{2}\left(25 - \frac{25x^2}{4}\right)dx = 25x - \frac{25}{12}x^3\Big]_{-2}^{2}$$

$$= \left(25(2) - \frac{25}{12}(2)^3\right) - \left(25(-2) - \frac{25}{12}(-2)^3\right)$$

$$= \frac{100}{3} - \left(-\frac{100}{3}\right) = \frac{200}{3}.$$

The volume of the solid is $\frac{200}{3}$.

Verify your result with a graphing calculator.

Example 2

Find the volume of a pyramid whose base is a square with a side of 6 *feet long*, and a height of 10 *feet*. See Figure 9.4-3.

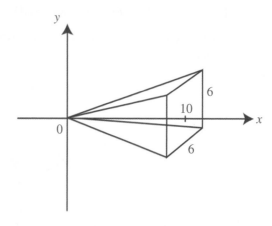

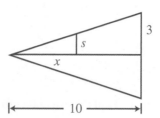

Figure 9.4-3

Step 1. Find the area of a cross section $A(x)$. Note each cross section is a square of side 2s.

Similar triangles: $\dfrac{x}{s} = \dfrac{10}{3} \Rightarrow s = \dfrac{3x}{10}$

$$A(x) = (2s)^2 = 4s^2 = 4\left(\frac{3x}{10}\right)^2 = \frac{9x^2}{25}$$

Step 2. Set up an integral.

$$V = \int_{0}^{10}\frac{9x^2}{25}\,dx$$

Step 3. Evaluate the integral.

$$V = \int_0^{10} \frac{9x^2}{25}\, dx = \frac{3x^3}{25}\Bigg]_0^{10} = \frac{3(10)^3}{25} - 0 = 120.$$

The volume of the pyramid is $120\ ft^3$.

Example 3

The base of a solid is the region enclosed by a triangle whose vertices are $(0,0)$, $(4,0)$ and $(0,2)$. The cross sections are semicircles perpendicular to the x-axis. Using a calculator, find the volume of the solid. (See Figure 9.4-4.)

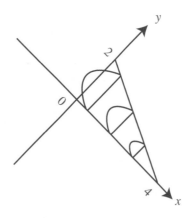

Figure 9.4-4

Step 1. Find the area of a cross section. Equation of the line passing through

$$(0,2) \text{ and } (4,0): y = mx + b; m = \frac{0-2}{4-0} = -\frac{1}{2}; b = 2$$

$$y = -\frac{1}{2}x + 2$$

$$\text{Area of semicircle} = \frac{1}{2}\pi r^2; \quad r = \frac{1}{2}y = \frac{1}{2}\left(-\frac{1}{2}x + 2\right) = -\frac{1}{4}x + 1$$

$$A(x) = \frac{1}{2}\pi\left(\frac{y}{2}\right)^2 = \frac{\pi}{2}\left(-\frac{1}{4}x + 1\right)^2.$$

Step 2. Set up an integral.

$$V = \int_0^4 A(x)\,dx = \int_0^4 \frac{\pi}{2}\left(-\frac{1}{4}x + 1\right)^2.$$

Step 3. Evaluate the integral.

Enter $\int\left(\left(\frac{\pi}{2}\right) * (-.25x + 1)^\wedge 2, x, 0, 4\right)$ and obtain 2.0944.

Thus the volume of the solid is 2.0944.

> • Remember: if $f' < 0$, then f is decreasing and if $f'' < 0$, then the graph of f is concave downward.

The Disc Method

The volume of a solid of revolution using discs:

Revolving about the *x-axis*:

$$V = \pi\int_a^b (f(x))^2\, dx, \quad f(x) = \text{radius}$$

Revolving about the *y-axis*:

$$V = \pi\int_c^d (g(y))^2\, dx, \quad g(y) = \text{radius}$$

See Figure 9.4-5.

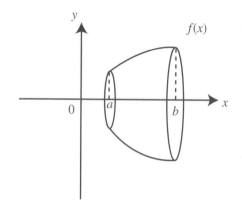

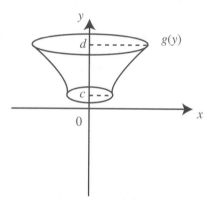

Figure 9.4-5

Revolving about a line *y = k:*

$$V = \pi\int_a^b (f(x) - k)^2\, dx, \quad \text{where } |f(x) - k| = \text{radius}$$

Revolving about the *a* line *x = h:*

$$V = \pi\int_c^d (g(y) - h)^2\, dy, \quad \text{where } |g(y) - h| = \text{radius}$$

See Figure 9.4-6 on page 257.

Example 1

Find the volume of the solid generated by revolving the region bounded by the graph of $f(x) = \sqrt{x - 1}$, the *x-axis* and the line $x = 5$ about the *x-axis*.

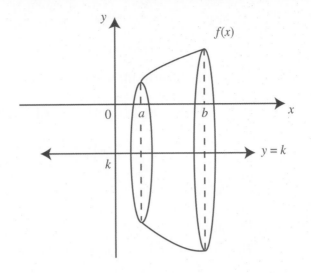

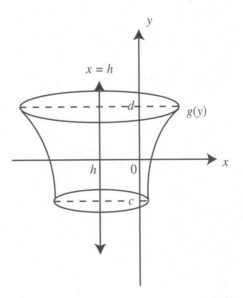

Figure 9.4-6

Step 1. Draw a sketch. See Figure 9.4-7.

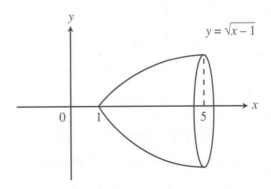

Figure 9.4-7

Step 2. Determine the radius of a disc from a cross section.

$$r = f(x) = \sqrt{x-1}$$

Step 3. Set up an integral.

$$V = \pi \int_1^5 (f(x))^2 \, dx = \pi \int_1^5 \left(\sqrt{x} - 1\right)^2 dx$$

Step 4. Evaluate the integral.

$$V = \pi \int_1^5 \left(\sqrt{x} - 1\right)^2 dx = \pi[(x - 1)]_1^5 = \pi\left[\frac{x^2}{2} - x\right]_1^5$$

$$= \pi\left(\left(\frac{5^2}{2} - 5\right) - \left(\frac{1^2}{2} - 1\right)\right) = 8\pi$$

Verify your result with a calculator.

Example 2

Find the volume of the solid generated by revolving the region bounded by the graph of $y = \sqrt{\cos x}$ where $0 \leq x \leq \frac{\pi}{2}$, and the x-axis about the x-axis.

Step 1. Draw a sketch. See Figure 9.4-8.

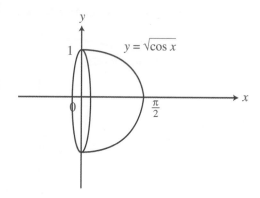

Figure 9.4-8

Step 2. Determine the radius from a cross section.

$$r = f(x) = \sqrt{\cos x}$$

Step 3. Set up an integral.

$$V = \pi \int_0^{\pi/2} \left(\sqrt{\cos x}\right)^2 dx = \pi \int_0^{\pi/2} \cos x \, dx.$$

Step 4. Evaluate the integral.

$$V = \pi \int_0^{\pi/2} \cos x \, dx = \pi[\sin x]_0^{\pi/2} = \pi\left(\sin\left(\frac{\pi}{2}\right) - \sin 0\right) = \pi.$$

Thus the volume of the solid is π.

Verify your result with a calculator.

Example 3

Find the volume of the solid generated by revolving the region bounded by the graph of $y = x^2$, the y-axis, and the line $y = 6$ about the y-axis.

Step 1. Draw a sketch. See Figure 9.4-9.

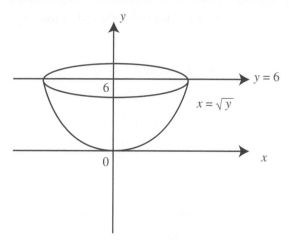

Figure 9.4-9

Step 2. Determine the radius from a cross section.

$$y = x^2 \Rightarrow x = \pm\sqrt{y}$$

$x = \sqrt{y}$ is the part of the curve involved in the region.

$$r = x = \sqrt{y}$$

Step 3. Set up an integral.

$$V = \pi\int_0^6 x^2 dy = \pi\int_0^6 \left(\sqrt{y}\right)^2 dy = \pi\int_0^6 y\, dy.$$

Step 4. Evaluate the integral.

$$V = \pi\int_0^6 y\, dy = \pi\left[\frac{y^2}{2}\right]_0^6 = 18\pi.$$

The volume of the solid is 18π.

Verify your result with a calculator.

Example 4

Using a calculator, find the volume of the solid generated by revolving the region bounded by the graph of $y = x^2 + 4$, the line $y = 8$ about the line $y = 8$.

Step 1. Draw a sketch. See Figure 9.4-10.

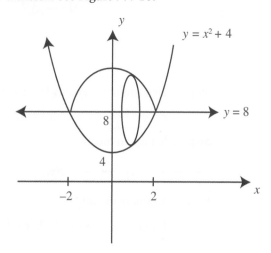

Figure 9.4-10

Step 2. Determine the radius from a cross section.

$$r = 8 - y = 8 - (x^2 + 4) = 4 - x^2$$

Step 3. Set up an integral.

To find the intersection points, set $8 = x^2 + 4 \Rightarrow x = \pm 2$.

$$V = \pi \int_{-2}^{2} \left(4 - x^2\right)^2 dx$$

Step 4. Evaluate the integral.

Enter $\int \left(\pi\left(4 - x\wedge 2\right)\wedge 2, x, -2, 2\right)$ and obtain $\dfrac{512}{15}\pi$.

Thus the volume of the solid is $\dfrac{512}{15}\pi$.

Verify your result with a calculator.

Example 5

Using a calculator, find the volume of the solid generated by revolving the region bounded by the graph of $y = e^x$, the y-axis, the lines $x = \ln 2$ and $y = -3$ about the line $y = -3$.

Step 1. Draw a sketch. See Figure 9.4-11.

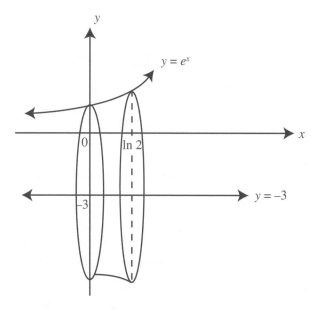

Figure 9.4-11

Step 2. Determine the radius from a cross section.

$$r = y - (-3) = y + 3 = e^x + 3.$$

Step 3. Set up an integral.

$$V = \pi \int_{0}^{\ln 2} \left(e^x + 3\right)^2 dx.$$

Step 4. Evaluate the integral.

Enter $\int \left(\pi\left(e\wedge(x) + 3\right)\wedge 2, x, 0 \ln(2)\right)$ and obtain $\pi\left(9 \ln 2 + \dfrac{15}{2}\right) \approx 13.7383\pi$

The volume of the solid is approximately 13.7383π.

• Remember: if f' is increasing, then $f'' > 0$ and the graph of f is concave upward.

The Washer Method

The volume of a solid (with a hole in the middle) generated by revolving a region bounded by 2 curves:

About the *x-axis*:

$$V = \pi \int_a^b \left[(f(x))^2 - (g(x))^2 \right] dx; \text{ where } f(x) = \text{outer radius \& } g(x) = \text{inner radius}$$

About the *y-axis*:

$$V = \pi \int_c^d \left[(p(y))^2 - (q(y))^2 \right] dy; \text{ where } p(y) = \text{outer radius \& } q(y) = \text{inner radius}$$

About a line *x = h*:

$$V = \pi \int_a^b \left[(R(x))^2 - (r(x))^2 \right] dx; \text{ where } R(x) = \text{outer radius \& } r(x) = \text{inner radius}$$

About a line *y = k*:

$$V = \pi \int_c^d \left[(R(y))^2 - (r(y))^2 \right] dy; \text{ where } R(y) = \text{outer radius \& } r(y) = \text{inner radius}$$

Example 1

Using the Washer Method, find the volume of the solid generated by revolving the region bounded by $y = x^3$ and $y = x$ in the first quadrant about the *x*-axis.

Step 1. Draw a sketch. See Figure 9.4-12.

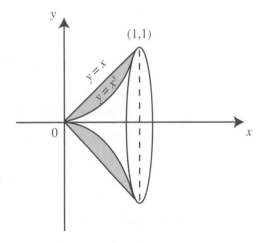

Figure 9.4-12

To find the points of intersection, set $x = x^3 \Rightarrow x^3 - x = 0$ or $x(x^2 - 1) = 0$ or $x = -1$, 0, 1. In the first quadrant $x = 0, 1$.

Step 2. Determine the outer and inner radii of a washer, whose outer radius = x; and inner radius = x^3.

Step 3. Set up an integral.

$$V = \int_0^1 \left[x^2 - \left(x^3 \right)^2 \right] dx$$

Step 4. Evaluate the integral.

$$V = \int_0^1 \left(x^2 - x^6 \right) dx = \pi \left[\frac{x^3}{3} - \frac{x^7}{7} \right]_0^1$$

$$= \pi \left(\frac{1}{3} - \frac{1}{7} \right) = \frac{4\pi}{21}$$

Verify your result with a calculator.

Example 2

Using the Washer Method and a calculator, find the volume of the solid generated by revolving the region in Example 1 about the line $y = 2$.

Step 1. Draw a sketch. See Figure 9.4-13.

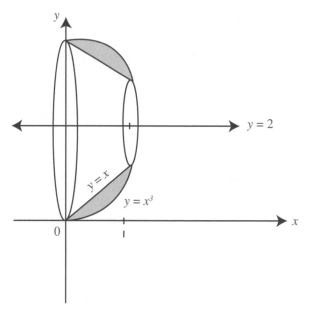

Figure 9.4-13

Step 2. Determine the outer & inner radii of a washer.

The outer radius = $(2 - x^3)$ and inner radius = $(2 - x)$.

Step 3. Set up an integral.

$$V = \pi \int_0^1 \left[\left(2 - x^3 \right)^2 - \left(2 - x^2 \right) \right] dx$$

Step 4. Evaluate the integral.

Enter $\int \left(\pi * \left(\left(2 - x \wedge 3 \right) \wedge 2 - \left(2 - x \right) \wedge 2 \right), x, 0, 1 \right)$ and obtain $\frac{17\pi}{21}$.

The volume of the solid is $\frac{17\pi}{21}$.

Example 3

Using the Washer Method and a calculator, find the volume of the solid generated by revolving the region bounded by $y = x^2$ and $x = y^2$ about the y-axis.

Step 1. Draw a sketch. See Figure 9.4-14.

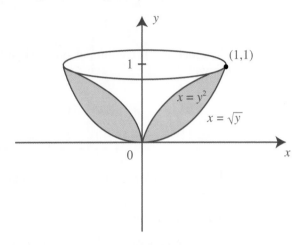

Figure 9.4-14

Intersection points: $y = x^2$; $x = y^2 \Rightarrow y = \pm\sqrt{x}$

Set $x^2 = \sqrt{x} \Rightarrow x^4 = x \Rightarrow x^4 - x = 0 \Rightarrow x(x^3 - 1) = 0 \Rightarrow x = 0$ or $x = 1$

$x = 0$, $y = 0$ $(0,0)$

$x = 1$, $y = 1$ $(1,1)$.

Step 2. Determine the outer and inner radii of a washer, whose outer radius: $x = \sqrt{y}$, and inner radius: $x = y^2$.

Step 3. Set up an integral.

$$V = \pi\int_0^1 \left(\left(\sqrt{y}\right)^2 - \left(y^2\right)^2 \right) dy$$

Step 4. Evaluate the integral

Enter $\int \pi * \left(\left(\sqrt{\ }(y)\right)^{\wedge}2 - (y^{\wedge}2)^{\wedge}2 \right), y, 0, 1)$ and obtain $\dfrac{3\pi}{10}$.

The volume of the solid is $\dfrac{3\pi}{10}$.

9.5 RAPID REVIEW

1. If $f(x) = \int_0^x g(t)\,dt$ and the graph of g is shown in Figure 9.5-1. Find $f(3)$.

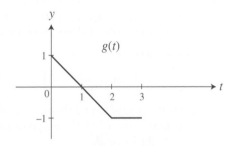

Figure 9.5-1

1110 • Comprehensive Review

Answer: $f(3) = \int_0^3 g(t)dt = \int_0^1 g(t)dt + \int_1^3 g(t)dt$

$= 0.5 - 1.5 = -0.5.$

2. The function f is continuous on $[1,5]$ and $f > 0$ and selected values of f are given below.

x	1	2	3	4	5
$f(x)$	2	4	6	8	10

Using 2 midpoint rectangles, approximate the area under the curve of f for $x = 1$ to $x = 5$.

Answer: Midpoints are $x = 2$ and $x = 4$ and the width of each rectangle $= \dfrac{5-1}{2} = 2.$

Area ≈ Area of Rect$_1$ + Area of Rect$_2$ ≈ $4(2) + 8(2)$ ≈ 24.

3. Set up an integral to find the area of the regions bounded by the graphs of $y = x^3$ and $y = x$. Do not evaluate the integral.

Answer: Graphs intersect at $x = -1$ and $x = 1$. See Figure 9.5-2.

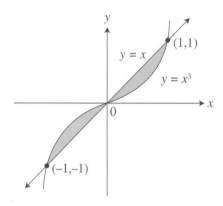

Figure 9.5-2

$$\text{Area} = \int_{-1}^0 \left(x^3 - x\right)dx + \int_0^1\left(x - x^3\right)dx$$

Or, using symmetry, Area $= 2\int_0^1\left(x - x^3\right)dx.$

4. The base of a solid is the region bounded by the lines $y = x$, $x = 1$, and the *x-axis*. The cross sections are squares perpendicular to the *x-axis*. Set up an integral to find the volume of the solid. Do not evaluate the integral.

Answer: Area of cross section $= x^2$

Volume of solid $= \int_0^1 x^2 dx.$

5. Set up an integral to find the volume of a solid generated by revolving about the *x-axis* the region bounded by the graph of $y = \sin x$, where $0 \le x \le \pi$ and the *x-axis*. Do not evaluate the integral.

Answer: Volume $= \pi\int_0^\pi \left(\sin x\right)^2 dx.$

6. The area under the curve of $y = \dfrac{1}{x}$ from $x = a$ to $x = 5$ is approximately 0.916 where $1 \le a < 5$. Using your calculator, find a.

$$\text{Answer: } \int_a^5 \dfrac{1}{x}\, dx = \ln x\Big]_a^5 = \ln 5 - \ln a = 0.916$$

$$\ln a = \ln 5 - 0.916 \approx .693$$

$$a \approx e^{0.693} \approx 2.$$

9.6   PRACTICE PROBLEMS

Part A—The use of a calculator is not allowed.

1. Let $F(x) = \int_0^x f(t)\,dt$ where the graph of f is given in Figure 9.6-1.

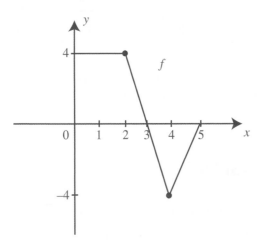

Figure 9.6-1

a. Evaluate $F(0)$, $F(3)$, and $F(5)$.
b. On what interval(s) is F decreasing?
c. At what value of t does F have a maximum value?
d. On what interval is F concave up?

2. Find the area of the region(s) enclosed by the curve $f(x) = x^3$, the x-axis, and the lines $x = -1$ and $x = 2$.

3. Find the area of the region(s) enclosed by the curve $y = |2x - 6|$, the x-axis, and the lines $x = 0$ and $x = 4$.

4. Find the approximate area under the curve $f(x) = \dfrac{1}{x}$ from $x = 1$ to $x = 5$, using four right-endpoint rectangles of equal lengths.

5. Find the approximate area under the curve $y = x^2 + 1$ from $x = 0$ to $x = 3$, using the Trapezoidal Rule with $n = 3$.

6. Find the area of the region bounded by the graphs $y = \sqrt{x}$, $y = -x$ and $x = 4$.

7. Find the area of the region bounded by the curves $x = y^2$ and $x = 4$.

8. Find the area of the region bounded by the graphs of all four equations:
$$f(x) = \sin\left(\dfrac{x}{2}\right); \ x\text{-axis; and the lines, } x = \dfrac{\pi}{2}$$
and $x = \pi$.

9. Find the volume of the solid obtained by revolving about the x-axis, the region bounded by the graph of $y = x^2 + 4$, the x-axis, the y-axis, and the line $x = 3$.

10. The area under the curve $y = \dfrac{1}{x}$ from $x = 1$ to $x = k$ is 1. Find the value of k.

11. Find the volume of the solid obtained by revolving about the y-axis the region bounded by $x = y^2 + 1$, $x = 0$, $y = -1$ and $y = 1$.

12. Let R be the region enclosed by the graph $y = 3x$, the x-axis and the line $x = 4$. The line $x = a$ divides region R into two regions such that when the regions are revolved about the x-axis, the resulting solids have equal volume. Find a.

Part B—Calculators are allowed.

13. Find the volume of the solid obtained by revolving about the x-axis the region bounded by the graphs of $f(x) = x^3$ and $g(x) = x^2$.

14. The base of a solid is a region bounded by the circle $x^2 + y^2 = 4$. The cross of the solid sections are perpendicular to the x-axis and are equilateral triangles. Find the volume of the solid.

15. Find the volume of the solid obtained by revolving about the y-axis, the region bounded by the curves $x = y^2$ and $y = x - 2$.

For Problems 16 thru 19, find the volume of the solid obtained by revolving the region as described below. See Figure 9.6-2.

16. R_1 about the x-axis.

17. R_2 about the y-axis.

18. R_1 about the line $\overleftrightarrow{BC}$.

19. R_2 about the line $\overleftrightarrow{AB}$.

20. The function $f(x)$ is continuous on $[0, 12]$ and the selected values of $f(x)$ are shown below.

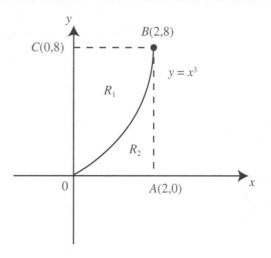

Figure 9.6-2

x	0	2	4	6	8	10	12
$f(x)$	1	2.24	3	3.61	4.12	4.58	5

Find the approximate area under the curve of f from 0 to 12 using three midpoint rectangles.

9.7 CUMULATIVE REVIEW PROBLEMS

"Calculator" indicates that calculators are permitted.

21. If $\int_{-a}^{a} e^{x^2}\, dx = k$, find $\int_{0}^{a} e^{x^2}\, dx$ in terms of k.

22. A man wishes to pull a log over a 9 foot high garden wall as shown. See Figure 9.7-1.

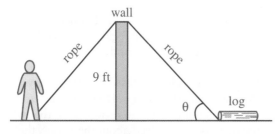

Figure 9.7-1

He is pulling at a rate of 2 ft/sec. At that rate is the angle between the rope and the ground changing when there are 15 feet of rope between the top of the wall and the log?

23. (Calculator) Find a point on the parabola $y = \dfrac{1}{2}x^2$ that is closest to the point $(4, 1)$.

24. The velocity function of a particle moving along the x-axis is $v(t) = t\cos(t^2 + 1)$ for $t \geq 0$.

   (a) If at $t = 0$, the particle is at the origin, find the position of the particle at $t = 2$.

   (b) Is the particle moving to the right or left at $t = 2$?

   (c) Find the acceleration of the particle at $t = 2$ and determine if the velocity of the particle is increasing or decreasing. Explain why.

25. (Calculator) Given $f(x) = xe^x$ and $g(x) = \cos x$, find:

   (a) the area of the region in the first quadrant bounded by the graphs $f(x)$, $g(x)$, and $x = 0$.

   (b) The volume obtained by revolving the region in part (a) about the x-axis.

9.8 SOLUTIONS TO PRACTICE PROBLEMS

Part A—No calculators.

1. (a) $F(0) = \int_0^0 f(t)\,dt = 0.$

   $F(3) = \int_0^3 f(t)\,dt = \dfrac{1}{2}(3+2)(4) = 10.$

   $F(5) = \int_0^5 f(t)\,dt = \int_0^3 f(t)\,dt + \int_3^5 f(t)\,dt$

   $\qquad = 10 + (-4) = 6.$

   (b) Since $\int_3^b f(t)\,dt \le 0$, F is decreasing on the interval $(3,5]$.

   (c) At $t = 3$, F has a maximum value.

   (d) $F'(x) = f(x)$, $F'(x)$ is increasing on $(4,5)$ which implies $F \le (x) > 0$. Thus F is concave upwards on $(4,5)$.

2. See Figure 9.8-1.

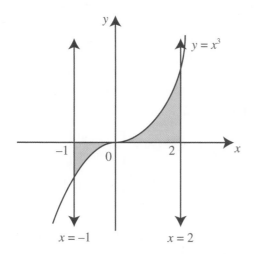

Figure 9.8-1

$A = \left|\int_{-1}^0 x^3\,dx\right| + \int_0^2 x^3\,dx$

$\quad = \left|\dfrac{x^4}{4}\right]_{-1}^0\right| + \left[\dfrac{x^4}{4}\right]_0^2 = \left|0 - \dfrac{(-1)^4}{4}\right| + \left(\dfrac{2^4}{4} - 0\right)$

$\quad = \dfrac{1}{4} + 4 = \dfrac{17}{4}$

3. See Figure 9.8-2.

   Set $2x - 6 = 0$; $x = 3$ and

   $f(x) = \begin{cases} 2x - 6 & \text{if } x \ge 3 \\ -(2x - 6) & \text{if } x < 3 \end{cases}$

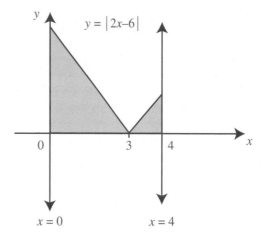

Figure 9.8-2

$A = \int_0^3 -(2x - 6)\,dx + \int_3^4 (2x - 6)\,dx$

$\quad = \left[-x^2 + 6x\right]_0^3 + \left[x^2 - 6x\right]_3^4 = \left[-(3)^2 + 6(3)\right]$

$\qquad - 0 + \left[4^2 - 6(4)\right] - \left[3^2 - 6(3)\right]$

$\quad = 9 + 1 = 10.$

4. See Figure 9.8-3.

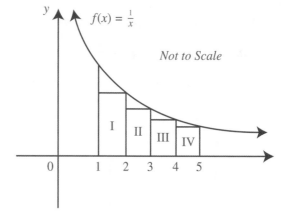

Figure 9.8-3

Length of $\Delta x_t = \dfrac{5 - 1}{4} = 1$

Area of $\text{Rect}_{\text{I}} = f(2)\Delta x_1 = \dfrac{1}{2}(1) = \dfrac{1}{2}$

Area of $\text{Rect}_{\text{II}} = f(3)\Delta x_2 = \dfrac{1}{3}(1) = \dfrac{1}{3}$

Area of $\text{Rect}_{\text{III}} = f(4)\Delta x_3 = \dfrac{1}{4}(1) = \dfrac{1}{4}$

Area of Rect$_{IV}$ = $f(5)\Delta x_4 = \dfrac{1}{5}(1) = \dfrac{1}{5}$

Total Area = $\dfrac{1}{2} + \dfrac{1}{3} + \dfrac{1}{4} + \dfrac{1}{5} = \dfrac{77}{60}$.

5. See Figure 9.8-4.

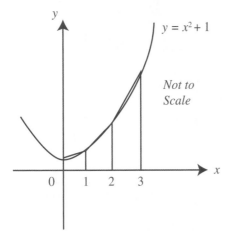

$y = x^2 + 1$

Not to Scale

Figure 9.8-4

Trapezoid Rule = $\dfrac{b-a}{2n}(f(a) + 2f(x_1)$
$+ 2f(x_2) + f(b))$

$A = \dfrac{3-0}{2(3)}(f(0) + 2f(1) + 2f(2) + f(3))$

$= \dfrac{1}{2}(1 + 4 + 10 + 10) = \dfrac{25}{2}$.

6. See Figure 9.8-5.

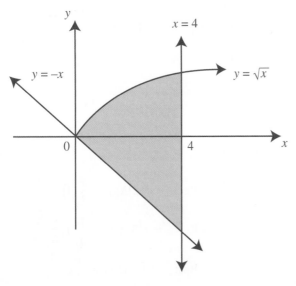

$x = 4$

$y = -x$

$y = \sqrt{x}$

Figure 9.8-5

$A = \int_0^4 \left(\sqrt{x} - (-x)\right) dx = \int_0^4 \left(x^{\frac{1}{2}} + x\right) dx$

$= \left[\dfrac{2x^{\frac{3}{2}}}{3} + \dfrac{x^2}{2}\right]_0^4 = \left(\dfrac{2(4)^{\frac{3}{2}}}{3} + \dfrac{4^2}{2}\right) - 0$

$= \dfrac{16}{3} + 8 = \dfrac{40}{3}$

7. See Figure 9.8-6.

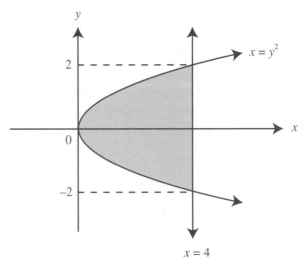

$x = y^2$

$x = 4$

Figure 9.8-6

Intersection points: $4 = y^2 \Rightarrow y = \pm 2$

$A = \int_{-2}^2 (4 - y^2)dy = \left[4y - \dfrac{y^3}{3}\right]_{-2}^2$

$= \left(4(2) - \dfrac{2^3}{3}\right) - \left(4(-2) - \dfrac{(-2)^3}{3}\right)$

$= \left(8 - \dfrac{8}{3}\right) - \left(-8 + \dfrac{8}{3}\right)$

$= \dfrac{16}{3} + \dfrac{16}{3} = \dfrac{32}{3}$

You can use the symmetry of the region and obtain the area = $2\int_{-2}^2 (4 - y^2)dy$. An alternative method is to find the area by setting up an integral with respect to the *x-axis* and expressing $x = y^2$ as $y = \sqrt{x}$ and $y = -\sqrt{x}$.

8. See Figure 9.8-7.

$A = \int_{\pi/2}^{\pi} \sin\left(\dfrac{x}{2}\right) dx$

Let $u = \dfrac{x}{2}$ and $du = \dfrac{dx}{2}$ or $2\,du = dx$

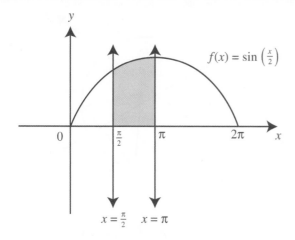

Figure 9.8-7

$$\int \sin\left(\frac{x}{2}\right)dx = \int \sin u(2du) = 2\int \sin u \, du$$

$$= -2\cos u + c = -2\cos\left(\frac{x}{2}\right) + c$$

$$A = \int_{\pi/2}^{\pi} \sin\left(\frac{x}{2}\right)dx = -2\cos\left(\frac{x}{2}\right)\Bigg]_{\pi/2}^{\pi}$$

$$= -2\left[\cos\left(\frac{\pi}{2}\right) - \cos\left(\frac{\pi/2}{2}\right)\right]$$

$$= -2\left(\cos\left(\frac{\pi}{2}\right) - \cos\left(\frac{\pi}{4}\right)\right)$$

$$= -2\left(0 - \frac{\sqrt{2}}{2}\right) = \sqrt{2}$$

9. See Figure 9.8-8.

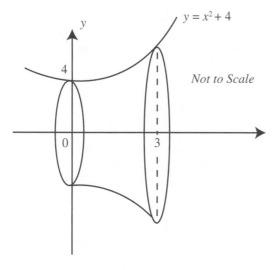

Figure 9.8-8

Disc Method:

$$V = \pi\int_0^3 (x^2 + 4)^2\,dx = \pi\int_0^3 (x^4 + 8x^2 + 16)\,dx$$

$$= \pi\left[\frac{x^5}{5} + \frac{8x^3}{3} + 16x\right]_0^3$$

$$= \pi\left[\frac{3^5}{5} + \frac{8(3)^3}{3} + 16(3)\right] - 0 = \frac{843}{5}\,\pi.$$

10. Area $= \int_1^k \frac{1}{x}\,dx = \ln x\Big]_1^k = \ln k - \ln 1 = \ln k$

Set $\ln k = 1$. Thus $e^{\ln k} = e^1$ or $k = e$.

11. See Figure 9.8-9.

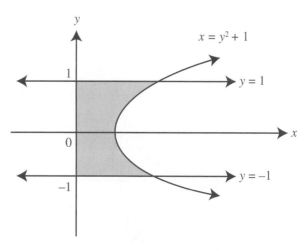

Figure 9.8-9

Disc Method:

$$V = \pi\int_{-1}^1 (y^2 + 1)^2\,dy = \pi\int_{-1}^1 (y^4 + 2y^2 + 1)\,dy$$

$$= \pi\left[\frac{y^5}{5} + \frac{2y^3}{3} + y\right]_{-1}^1$$

$$= \pi\left[\left(\frac{1^5}{5} + \frac{2(1)^3}{3} + 1\right)\right.$$

$$\left. - \left(\frac{(-1)^5}{5} + \frac{2(-1)^3}{3} + (-1)\right)\right]$$

$$= \pi\left(\frac{28}{15} + \frac{28}{15}\right) = \frac{56\pi}{15}.$$

Note: You can use the symmetry of the region and find the volume by

$$2\pi\int_0^1 (y^2 + 1)^2\,dy.$$

12. Volume of solid by revolving R:

$$V_R = \int_0^4 \pi(3x)^2\,dx = \pi\int_0^4 9x^2\,dx = \pi\left[3x^3\right]_0^4$$

$$= 192\pi.$$

Set $\int_0^a \pi(3x)^2\,dx = \dfrac{192\pi}{2}$

$$\Rightarrow 3a^3\pi = 96\pi$$

$$a^3 = 32$$

$$a = (32)^{1/3} = 2(2)^{2/3}.$$

You can verify your result by evaluating $\int_0^{2(2)^{2/3}} \pi(3x)^2\,dx$. The result is 96π.

Part B—Calculators are permitted.

13. See Figure 9.8-10.

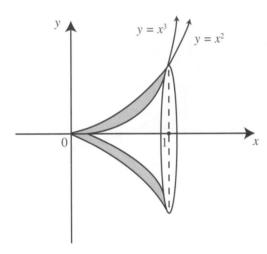

Figure 9.8-10

Step 1. Washer Method

Points of intersection: Set $x^3 = x^2 \Rightarrow x^3 - x^2 = 0 \Rightarrow x^2(x-1) = 0$ or $x = 0$ or $x = 1$. Outer radius $= x^2$; Inner radius $= x^3$.

Step 2. $V = \pi\int_0^1\left(\left(x^2\right)^2 - \left(x^3\right)^2\right)dx$

$$= \pi\int_0^1\left(x^4 - x^6\right)dx$$

Step 3. Enter $\int\left(\pi(x^4 - x^6), x, 0, 1\right)$ and obtain $\dfrac{2\pi}{35}$.

14. See Figure 9.8-11.

Step 1. $x^2 + y^2 = 4 \Rightarrow y^2 = 4 - x2 \Rightarrow$
$y = \pm\sqrt{4 - x^2}$

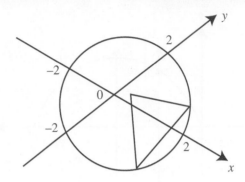

Figure 9.8-11

Let $s = $ a side of an equilateral triangle

$$s = 2\sqrt{4 - x^2}.$$

Step 2. Area of a cross section:

$$A(x) = \frac{s^2\sqrt{3}}{4} = \frac{\left(2\sqrt{4 - x^2}\right)^2\sqrt{3}}{4}.$$

Step 3. $V = \int_{-2}^2\left(2\sqrt{4 - x^2}\right)^2\dfrac{\sqrt{3}}{4}\,dx$

$$= \int_{-2}^2 \sqrt{3}(4 - x^2)\,dx$$

Step 4. Enter $\int\left(\sqrt{}(3) * (4 - x\wedge 2), x, -2, 2\right)$

and obtain $\dfrac{32\sqrt{3}}{3}$.

15. See Figure 9.8-12.

Step 1. Washer Method

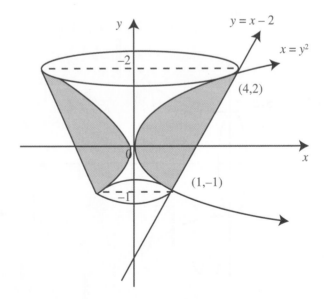

Figure 9.8-12

Points of Intersection: $y = x - 2 \Rightarrow$
$x = y + 2$

Set $y^2 = y + 2 \Rightarrow y^2 - y - 2 = 0 \Rightarrow (y - 2)$
$(y + 1) = 0$ or $y = -1$ or $y = 2$.

Outer radius = $y + 2$ and inner
radius = y^2.

Step 2. $V = \pi \int_{-1}^{2} \left((y + 2)^2 - (y^2)^2 \right) dy$.

Step 3. Enter $\pi \int \left((y + 2) \wedge 2 - y \wedge 4, y, -1, 2 \right)$

and obtain $\dfrac{72}{5} \pi$.

16. See Figure 9.8-13.

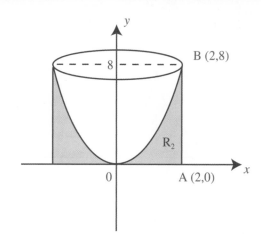

Figure 9.8-14

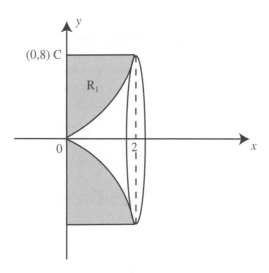

Figure 9.8-13

Step 1. Washer Method

$y = 8$, $y = x^3$

Outer radius = 8; Inner radius = x^3

$V = \pi \int_{0}^{2} \left(8^2 - (x^3)^2 \right) dx$

Step 2. Enter $\int \pi (8 \wedge 2 - x \wedge 6, x, 0, 2)$

and obtain $\dfrac{768\pi}{7}$.

17. See Figure 9.8-14.

Using the Washer Method:

Outer radius: $x = 2$ and Inner radius: $x = y^{1/3}$

$V = \pi \int_{0}^{8} \left(2^2 - \left(y^{1/3} \right)^2 \right) dy$

Using your calculator, you obtain $V = \dfrac{64\pi}{5}$.

18. See Figure 9.8-15.

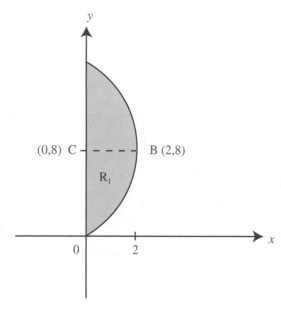

Figure 9.8-15

Step 1. Disc Method:

Radius $= \left(8 - x^3 \right)$

$V = \pi \int_{0}^{2} \left(8 - x^3 \right)^2 dx$

Step 2. Enter $\int \left(\pi * \left(8 - x \wedge 3 \right) \wedge 2, x, 0, 2 \right)$

and obtain $\dfrac{576\pi}{7}$.

19. See Figure 9.8-16.

Using the Disc Method:

Radius $= 2 - x = \left(2 - y^{1/3} \right)$

$V = \pi \int_{0}^{8} \left(2 - y^{1/3} \right)^2 dy$

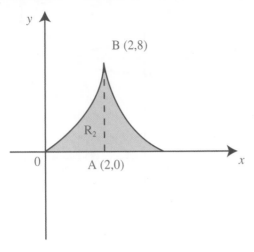

Figure 9.8-16

Using your calculator, you obtain $V = \dfrac{16\pi}{5}$.

20. Area $\approx \displaystyle\sum_{i=1}^{3} f(x_i)\Delta x_i$

x_i = midpoint of the ith interval.

Length of $\Delta x_i = \dfrac{12-0}{3} = 4$

Area of Rect$_I = f(2)\Delta x_1 = (2.24)(4) = 8.96$

Area of Rect$_{II} = f(6)\Delta x_2 = (3.16)(4) = 14.44$

Area of Rect$_{III} = f(10)\Delta x_3 = (4.58)(4) = 18.32$

Total Area $= 8.96 + 14.44 + 18.32 = 41.72$

The area under the curve is approximately 41.72.

9.9 SOLUTIONS TO CUMULATIVE REVIEW PROBLEMS

21. (See Figure 9.9-1.) $\displaystyle\int_{-a}^{a} e^{x^2}\,dx = \int_{-a}^{0} e^{x^2}\,dx + \int_{0}^{a} e^{x^2}\,dx$

Since e^{x^2} is an even function, thus

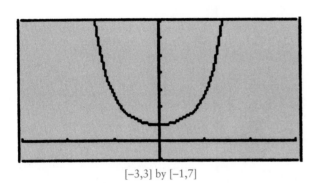

[−3,3] by [−1,7]

Figure 9.9-1

$\displaystyle\int_{-a}^{0} e^{x^2}\,dx = \int_{0}^{a} e^{x^2}\,dx.$

$k = 2\displaystyle\int_{0}^{a} e^{x^2}\,dx$ and $\displaystyle\int_{0}^{a} e^{x^2}\,dx = \dfrac{k}{2}.$

22. See Figure 9.9-2.

$\sin\theta = \dfrac{9}{x}$

Differentiate both sides:

$\cos\theta\,\dfrac{d\theta}{dt} = (9)(-x^{-2})\dfrac{dx}{dt}$

when $x = 15$, $9^2 + y^2 = 15^2 \Rightarrow y = 12$

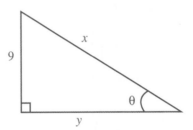

Figure 9.9-2

Thus $\cos\theta = \dfrac{12}{15} = \dfrac{4}{5};\quad \dfrac{dx}{dt} = -2$ ft/sec.

$\dfrac{4}{5}\dfrac{d\theta}{dt} = 9\left(-\dfrac{1}{15^2}\right)(-2)$

$= \dfrac{d\theta}{dt} = \dfrac{18}{15^2}\dfrac{5}{4} = \dfrac{1}{10}$ radian/sec.

23. See Figure 9.9-3.

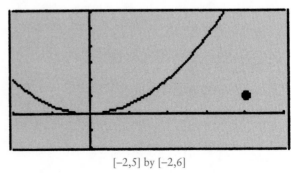

[−2,5] by [−2,6]

Figure 9.9-3

Step 1. Distance Formula

$$L = \sqrt{(x-4)^2 + (y-1)^2}$$

$$= \sqrt{(x-4)^2 + \left(\frac{x^2}{2} - 1\right)^2}$$

where the domain of x is all real numbers.

Step 2. Enter $y_1 = \sqrt{((x-4)^2 + (.5x^2 - 1)^2)}$

Enter $y_2 = d(y_1(x), x)$

Step 3. Use the Zero Function and obtain $x = 2$ for y_2.

Step 4. Use the First Derivative Test. (See Figures 9.9-4 and 9.9-5.)

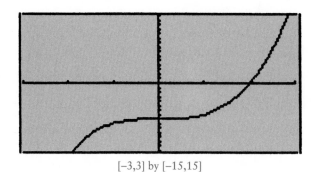

[−3,3] by [−15,15]

Figure 9.9-4

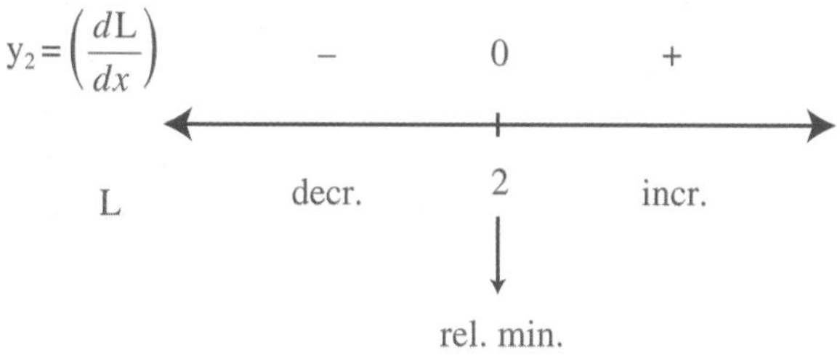

$y_2 = \left(\dfrac{dL}{dx}\right)$

— 0 +

L   decr.   2   incr.

rel. min.

Figure 9.9-5

At $x = 2$, L has a relative mimimum.

Since at $x = 2$, L has the only relative extremum, it is an absolute minimum.

Step 5. At $x = 2$, $y = \dfrac{1}{2}(x^2) = \dfrac{1}{2}(2^2) = 2$

Thus the point on $y = \dfrac{1}{2}(x^2)$ closest to the point $(4,1)$ is the point $(2,2)$.

24. (a) $s(0) = 0$ and

$$s(t) = \int v(t)\,dt = \int t\cos(t^2 + 1)\,dt.$$

Enter $\int (x * \cos(x \wedge 2 + 1), x)$

and obtain $\dfrac{\sin(x^2 + 1)}{2}$.

Thus $s(t) = \dfrac{\sin(t^2 + 1)}{2} + c.$

Since $s(0) = 0 \Rightarrow \dfrac{\sin(0^2 + 1)}{2} + c = 0$

$\Rightarrow \dfrac{.841471}{2} + c = 0$

$\Rightarrow c = -0.420735 \approx -0.421$

$s(t) = \dfrac{\sin(t^2 + 1)}{2} - 0.420735$

$s(2) = \dfrac{\sin(2^2 + 1)}{2} - 0.420735$

$= -0.900197 \approx -0.900$

(b) $v(2) = 2\cos(2^2 + 1) = 2\cos(5) = 0.567324$

Since $v(2) > 0$, the particle is moving to the right at $t = 2$.

(c) $a(t) = v'(t)$

Enter $d(x * \cos(x \wedge 2 + 1), x)|x = 2$ and obtain 7.95506.

Thus, the velocity of the particle is increasing at $t = 2$, since $a(2) > 0$.

25. See Figure 9.9-6.

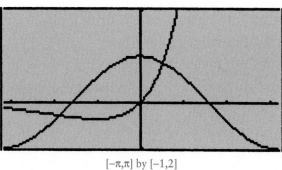

[−π,π] by [−1,2]

Figure 9.9-6

(a) Point of Intersection: Use the Intersection Function of the calculation and obtain $(0.517757, 0.868931)$

$$\text{Area} = \int_0^{0.51775} \left(\cos x - xe^x \right) dx$$

Enter $\int \left(\cos(x) - x * e \wedge (x), x, 0, .51775 \right)$ and obtain $.304261$.

The area of the region is approximately 0.304.

(b) Step 1. Washer Method:

Outer radius $= \cos x$ and Inner radius $= x\,e^x$

$$V = \pi \int_0^{0.51775} \left[\left(\cos x \right)^2 - \left(xe^x \right)^2 \right] dx$$

Step 2. Enter $\int \left(\pi \left((\cos(x) \wedge 2) - (x * e \wedge (x)) \wedge 2 \right), x, 0.51775 \right)$ and obtain 1.16678.

The volume of the solid is approximately 1.167.

Chapter 10

More Applications of Definite Integrals

10.1 AVERAGE VALUE OF A FUNCTION

Main Concepts: *Mean Value Theorem for Integrals, Average Value of a Function on* [a,b]

Mean Value Theorem for Integrals

Mean Value Theorem for Integrals:

If f is continuous on $[a,b]$, then there exists a number c in $[a,b]$ such that $\int_a^b f(x)\,dx = f(c)(b-a)$. See Figure 10.1-1.

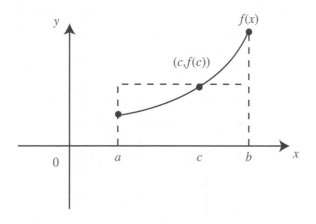

Figure 10.1-1

Example 1

Given $f(x) = \sqrt{x-1}$, verify the hypotheses of the Mean Value Theorem for Integrals for f on $[1, 10]$ and find the value of c as indicated in the theorem.

The function f is continuous for $x \geq 1$, thus:

$$\int_1^{10} \sqrt{x-1}\,dx = f(c)(10-1)$$

$$\frac{2(x-1)^{\frac{3}{2}}}{3}\Bigg]_1^{10} = 9f(c)$$

$$\frac{2}{3}\left[(10-1)^{\frac{3}{2}} - 0\right] = 9f(c)$$

$$18 = 9f(c);\ 2 = f(c);\ 2 = \sqrt{c-1};\ 4 = c-1$$

$$5 = c$$

Example 2

Given $f(x) = x^2$, verify the hypotheses of the Mean Value Theorem for Integrals for f on $[0, 6]$ and find the value of c as indicated in the theorem.

Since f is a polynomial, it is continuous everywhere, thus:

$$\int_0^6 x^2\,dx = f(c)(6-0)$$

$$\frac{x^3}{3}\Bigg]_0^6 = f(c)6$$

$$72 = 6f(c);\ 12 = f(c);\ 12 = c^2$$

$$c = \pm\sqrt{12} = \pm 2\sqrt{3}\left(\pm 2\sqrt{3} \approx \pm 3.4641\right)$$

Since only $2\sqrt{3}$ is in the interval $[0, 6]$, $c = 2\sqrt{3}$.

- Remember: if f' is decreasing, then $f'' < 0$ and the graph of f is concave downward.

Average Value of a Function on $[a,b]$

Average Value of a Function on an Interval:

If f is a continuous function on $[a,b]$, then the Average Value of f on $[a,b]$

$$= \frac{1}{b-a}\int_a^b f(x)\,dx.$$

Example 1

Find the average value of $y = \sin x$ between $x = 0$ to $x = \pi$.

$$\text{Average value} = \frac{1}{\pi - 0}\int_0^\pi \sin x\,dx$$

$$= \frac{1}{\pi}\left[-\cos x\right]_0^\pi = \frac{1}{\pi}\left[-\cos \pi - (-\cos(0))\right]$$

$$= \frac{1}{\pi}\left[1 + 1\right] = \frac{2}{\pi}.$$

Example 2

The graph of a function f is shown in Figure 10.1-2. Find the average value of f on [0,4].

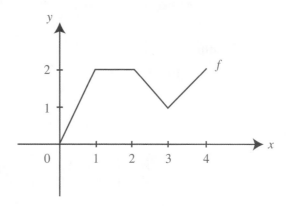

Figure 10.1-2

$$\text{Average value} = \frac{1}{4-0}\int_0^4 f(x)\,dx$$

$$= \frac{1}{4}\left(1+2+\frac{3}{2}+\frac{3}{2}\right) = \frac{3}{2}.$$

Example 3

The velocity of a particle moving on a line is $v(t) = 3t^2 - 18t + 24$. Find the average velocity from $t = 1$ to $t = 3$.

$$\text{Average velocity} = \frac{1}{3-1}\int_1^3 \left(3t^2 - 18t + 24\right)dt$$

$$= \frac{1}{2}\left[t^3 - 9t^2 + 24t\right]_1^3$$

$$= \frac{1}{2}\left[\left(3^3 - 9(3^2) + 24(3)\right) - \left(1^3 - 9(1^2) + 24(1)\right)\right]$$

$$= \frac{1}{2}(18 - 16) = \frac{1}{2}(2) = 1.$$

Note: The average velocity for $t = 1$ to $t = 3$ is $\dfrac{s(3) - s(1)}{2}$, which is equivalent to the computation above.

10.2   DISTANCE TRAVELED PROBLEMS

Summary of Formulas:

Position Function: $s(t);\ s(t) = \int v(t)\,dt$

Velocity: $v(t) = \dfrac{ds}{dt};\ v(t) = \int a(t)\,dt$

Acceleration: $a(t) = \dfrac{dv}{dt}$

Speed: $\left|v(t)\right|$

Displacement from t_1 to $t_2 = \int_{t_1}^{t_2} v(t)\,dt = s(t_2) - s(t_1)$

Total Distance Traveled from t_1 to $t_2 = \int_{t_1}^{t_2} |v(t)|\,dt$

Example 1

See Figure 10.2-1.

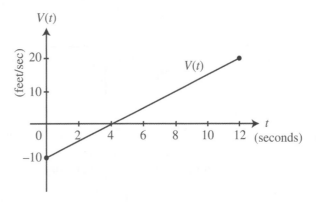

Figure 10.2-1

The graph of the velocity function of a moving particle is shown in Figure 10.2-1. What is the total distance traveled by the particle during $0 \le t \le 12$?

$$\text{Total Distance Traveled} = \left| \int_0^4 v(t)\,dt \right| + \int_4^{12} v(t)\,dt$$

$$= \frac{1}{2}(4)(10) + \frac{1}{2}(8)(20) = 20 + 80 = 100 \; feet.$$

Example 2

The velocity function of a moving particle on a coordinate line is $v(t) = t^2 + 3t - 10$ for $0 \le t \le 6$. Find (a) the displacement by the particle during $0 \le t \le 6$, and (b) the total distance traveled during $0 \le t \le 6$.

(a) $\text{Displacement} = \int_{t_1}^{t_2} v(t)\,dt$

$$= \int_0^6 (t^2 + 3t - 10)\,dt = \frac{t^3}{3} + \frac{3t^2}{2} - 10t \Big]_0^6$$

$$= 66.$$

(b) $\text{Total Distance Traveled} = \int_{t_1}^{t_2} |v(t)|\,dt$

$$= \int_0^6 |t^2 + 3t - 10|\,dt$$

Let $t^2 + 3t - 10 = 0 \Rightarrow (t + 5)(t - 2) = 0 \Rightarrow t = -5$ or $t = 2$

$$|t^2 + 3t - 10| = \begin{cases} -(t^2 + 3t - 10) & \text{if } 0 \le t \le 2 \\ t^2 + 3t - 10 & \text{if } t > 2 \end{cases}$$

$$\int_0^6 |t^2 + 3t - 10| \, dt = \int_0^2 -(t^2 + 3t - 10) \, dt + \int_2^6 (t^2 + 3t - 10) \, dt$$

$$= \left[\frac{-t^3}{3} - \frac{3t^2}{2} + 10t \right]_0^2 + \left[\frac{t^3}{3} + \frac{3t^2}{2} - 10t \right]_2^6$$

$$= \frac{34}{3} + \frac{232}{3} = \frac{266}{3} \approx 88.667$$

The total distance traveled by the particle is $\dfrac{266}{3}$ or approximately 88.667.

Example 3

The velocity function of a moving particle on a coordinate line is $v(t) = t^3 - 6t^2 + 11t - 6$. Using a calculator, find (a) the displacement by the particle during $1 \le t \le 4$, and (b) the total distance traveled by the particle during $1 \le t \le 4$.

(a) Displacement $= \displaystyle\int_{t_1}^{t_2} v(t) \, dt$

$$= \int_1^4 (t^3 - 6t^2 + 11t - 6) \, dt$$

Enter $\displaystyle\int (x\wedge 3 - 6x\wedge 2 + 11x - 6, x, 1, 4)$ and obtain $\dfrac{9}{4}$.

(b) Total Distance Traveled $= \displaystyle\int_{t_1}^{t_2} |v(t)| \, dt$.

Enter $y_1 = x \wedge 3 - 6x \wedge 2 + 11x - 6$ and use the Zero Function to obtain x-intercepts at $x = 1, 2, 3$.

$$|v(t)| = \begin{cases} v(t) & \text{if } 1 \le t \le 2 \text{ and } 3 \le t \le 4 \\ -v(t) & \text{if } 2 < t < 3 \end{cases}$$

Total Distance Traveled $= \displaystyle\int_1^2 v(t) \, dt + \int_2^3 -v(t) \, dt + \int_3^4 v(t) \, dt$.

Enter $\displaystyle\int (y_1(x), x, 1, 2)$ and obtain $\dfrac{1}{4}$.

Enter $\displaystyle\int (-y_1(x), x, 2, 3)$ and obtain $\dfrac{1}{4}$.

Enter $\displaystyle\int (y_1(x), x, 3, 4)$ and obtain $\dfrac{9}{4}$.

Thus, total distance traveled is $\left(\dfrac{1}{4} + \dfrac{1}{4} + \dfrac{9}{4} \right) = \dfrac{11}{4}$.

Example 4

If the acceleration function of a moving particle on a coordinate line is $a(t) = -4$ and $v_0 = 12$ for $0 \le t \le 8$. Find the total distance traveled by the particle during $0 \le t \le 8$.

$$a(t) = -4$$

$$v(t) = \int a(t) \, dt = \int -4 \, dt = -4t + c$$

Since $v_0 = 12 \Rightarrow -4(0) + c = 12$ or $c = 12$

Thus $v(t) = -4t + 12$

$$\text{Total Distance Traveled} = \int_0^8 |-4t + 12|\, dt$$

Let $-4t + 12 = 0 \Rightarrow t = 3$.

$$|-4t + 12| = \begin{cases} -4t + 12 & \text{if } 0 \le t \le 3 \\ -(-4t + 12) & \text{if } t > 3 \end{cases}$$

$$\int_0^8 |-4t + 12|\, dt = \int_0^3 (-4t + 12)\, dt + \int_3^8 -(-4t + 12)\, dt$$

$$= \left[-12t^2 + 12t\right]_0^3 + \left[2t^2 - 12t\right]_3^8$$

$$= 18 + 50 = 68$$

Total distance traveled by the particle is 68.

Example 5

The velocity function of a moving particle on a coordinate line is $v(t) = 3\cos(2t)$ for $0 \le t \le 2\pi$. Using a calculator.

    (a) Determine when the particle is moving to the right.

    (b) Determine when the particle stops.

    (c) The total distance traveled by the particle during $0 \le t \le 2\pi$.

Solution:

    (a) The particle is moving to the right when $v(t) > 0$.

Enter $y_1 = 3\cos(2x)$. Obtain $y_1 = 0$ when $t = \dfrac{\pi}{4}, \dfrac{3\pi}{4}, \dfrac{5\pi}{4}$ and $\dfrac{7\pi}{4}$.

The particle is moving to the right when:

$$0 < t < \frac{\pi}{4}, \quad \frac{3\pi}{4} < t < \frac{5\pi}{4}, \quad \frac{7\pi}{4} < t < 2\pi.$$

    (b) The particle stops when $v(t) = 0$.

Thus the particle stops at $t = \dfrac{\pi}{4}, \dfrac{3\pi}{4}, \dfrac{5\pi}{4}$ and $\dfrac{7\pi}{4}$.

    (c) Total distance traveled $= \displaystyle\int_0^{2\pi} |3\cos(2t)|\, dt$

Enter $\int (abs(3\cos(2x)), x, 0, 2\pi)$ and obtain 12.

The total distance traveled by the particle is 12.

10.3   DEFINITE INTEGRAL AS ACCUMULATED CHANGE

Main Concepts: *Business Problems, Temperature Problems, Leakage Problems, Growth Problems*

Business Problems

$$P(x) = R(x) - C(x) \qquad \text{Profit} = \text{Revenue} - \text{Cost}$$

$$R(x) = px \qquad\qquad\quad \text{Revenue} = (\text{price})(\text{items sold})$$

$$P'(x) \qquad \text{Marginal Profit}$$
$$R'(x) \qquad \text{Marginal Revenue}$$
$$C'(x) \qquad \text{Marginal Cost}$$

$P'(x)$, $R'(x)$, and $C'(x)$ are the instantaneous rates of change of profit, revenue and cost respectively.

Example 1

The marginal profit of manufacturing and selling a certain drug is $P'(x) = 100 - 0.005x$. How much profit should the company expect if it sells 10,000 units of this drug?

$$P(t) = \int_0^t P'(x)\,dx$$

$$= \int_0^{10,000} (100 - 0.005x)\,dx$$

$$= 100x - \frac{0.005x^2}{2}\Big]_0^{10,000}$$

$$= \left(100(10,000) - \frac{0.005}{2}(10,000)^2\right)$$

$$= 750,000.$$

> • If $f''(a) = 0$, f may or may not have a point of inflection at $x = a$, e.g., as in the function $f(x) = x^4$, $f''(0) = 0$, *but* at $x = 0$, f has an absolute minimum.

Example 2

If the marginal cost of producing x units of a commodity is $C'(x) = 5 + 0.4x$.

Find (a) the marginal cost when $x = 50$.

(b) the cost of producing the first 100 units.

Solution:

(a) marginal cost at $x = 50$:
$$C'(50) = 5 + 0.4(50) = 5 + 20 = 25.$$

(b) cost of producing 100 units:

$$C(t) = \int_0^t C'(x)\,dx$$

$$= \int_0^{100} (5 + 0.4x)\,dx$$

$$= 5x - 0.2x^2\Big]_0^{100}$$

$$= \left(5(100) + 0.2(100)^2\right) - 0 = 2500.$$

Temperature Problems

Example

On a certain day, the changes in the temperature in a greenhouse beginning at 12 noon are represented by $f(t) = \sin\left(\frac{t}{2}\right)$ degree Fahrenheit, where t is the number of hours elapsed after 12 noon. If at 12 noon, the temperature is 95°F, find the temperature in the greenhouse at 5 p.m.

Let $F(t)$ represent the temperature of the greenhouse.

$$F(0) = 95°F$$

$$F(t) = 95 + \int_0^t f(x)\,dx$$

$$F(5) = 95 + \int_0^5 \sin\left(\frac{x}{2}\right)dx$$

$$= 95 + \left[-2\cos\left(\frac{x}{2}\right)\right]_0^5 = 95 + \left[-2\cos\left(\frac{5}{2}\right) - (-2\cos(0))\right]$$

$$= 95 + 3.602 = 98.602$$

The temperature in the greenhouse at 5 p.m. is 98.602°F.

Leakage Problems

Example

Water is leaking from a faucet at the rate of $l(t) = 10e^{-0.5t}$ *gallons/per hour*, where t is measured in *hours*. How many gallons of water will have leaked from the faucet after a 24 *hour* period?

Let $L(x)$ represent the number of gallons that have leaked after x *hours*.

$$L(x) = \int_0^x l(t)\,dt = \int_0^2 10e^{-0.5t}dt.$$

Using your calculator, enter $\int \left(10e \wedge (-0.5x), x, 0, 24\right)$ and obtain 19.9999. Thus, the number of gallons of water that have leaked after x hours is approximately 20 gallons.

• You are permitted to use the following 4 built-in capabilities of your calculator to obtain an answer: plotting the graph of a function, finding the zeros of a function, finding the numerical derivative of a function, and evaluating a definite integral. All other capabilities of your calculator can only be used to *check* your answer. For example, you may *not* use the built-in Inflection function of your calculator to find points of inflection. You must use calculus using derivatives and showing change of concavity.

Growth Problems

Example

In a farm, the animal population is increasing at a rate which can be approximately represented by $g(t) = 20 + 50\ln(2 + t)$, where t is measured in years. How much will the animal population increase to the nearest tens between the 3rd and 5th year?

Let $G(x)$ be the increase in animal population after x years.

$$G(x) = \int_0^x g(t)\,dt$$

Thus, the population increase between the 3rd and 5th years

$$= G(5) - G(3)$$

$$= \int_0^5 \left(20 + 50 \ln(2 + t)\, dt - \int_0^3 \left(20 + 50 \ln(2 + t)\, dt\right)\right)$$

$$= \int_3^5 \left[20 + 50 \ln(2 + t)\right] dt$$

Enter $\int (20 + 50 \ln(2 + x), x, 3, 5)$ and obtain 218.709.

Thus the animal population will increase by approximately 220 between the 3rd and 5th years.

10.4 DIFFERENTIAL EQUATIONS

Main Concepts: *Exponential Growth/Decay Problems, Separable Differential Equations*

Exponential Growth/Decay Problems

1. If $\dfrac{dy}{dt} = ky$, then the rate of change of y is proportional to y.

2. If y is a differentiable function of t with $y > 0$ and $\dfrac{dy}{dt} = ky$, then $y(t) = y_0 e^{kt}$; where

    y_0 is the initial value of y and k is constant. If $k > 0$, then k is a growth constant and if $k < 0$, then k is the decay constant.

Example 1—Population Growth

If the amount of bacteria in a culture at any time increases at a rate proportional to the amount of bacteria present and there are 500 bacteria after one day and 800 bacteria after the third day:

(a) approximately how many bacteria are there initially, and

(b) approximately how many bacteria are there after 4 days?

Solution:

(a) Since the rate of increase is proportional to the amount of bacteria present,

Then:

$\dfrac{dy}{dt} = ky$ where y is the amount of bacteria at any time

Therefore this is an exponential growth/decay model: $y(t) = y_0 e^{kt}$

Step 1. $y(1) = 500$ and $y(3) = 800$

$500 = y_0 e^{1k}$ and $800 = y_0 e^{3k}$

Step 2. $500 = y_0 e^{k} \Rightarrow y_0 = \dfrac{500}{e^k} = 500\, e^{-k}$

Substitute $y_0 = 500e^{-k}$ into $800 = y_0 e^{3k}$

$$800 = (500)(e^{-k})(e^{3k})$$

$$800 = 500e^{2k} \Rightarrow \frac{8}{5} = e^{2k}.$$

Take the ln of both sides:

$$\ln\left(\frac{8}{5}\right) = \ln\left(e^{2k}\right)$$

$$\ln\left(\frac{8}{5}\right) = 2k$$

$$k = \frac{1}{2}\ln\left(\frac{8}{5}\right) = \ln\sqrt{\frac{8}{5}}$$

Step 3. Substitute $k = \frac{1}{2}\ln\left(\frac{8}{5}\right)$ into one of the equations

$$500 = y_0 e^k$$

$$500 = y_0 e^{\ln\left(\sqrt{\frac{8}{5}}\right)}$$

$$500 = y_0\left(\sqrt{\frac{8}{5}}\right)$$

$$y_0 = \frac{500}{\sqrt{\frac{8}{5}}} = 125\sqrt{10} \approx 395.285;$$

Thus, there are 395 bacteria present initially.

(b) $y_0 = 125\sqrt{10}$, $k = \ln\sqrt{\frac{8}{5}}$

$$y(t) = y_0 e^{kt}$$

$$y(t) = \left(125\sqrt{10}\right)e^{\left(\ln\sqrt{\frac{8}{5}}\right)t} = \left(125\sqrt{10}\right)\left(\frac{8}{5}\right)^{1/2}$$

$$y(4) = \left(125\sqrt{10}\right)\left(\frac{8}{5}\right)^{4/2} = \left(125\sqrt{10}\right)\left(\frac{8}{5}\right)^2 \approx 1011.93$$

Thus there are approximately 1011 bacteria present after 4 days.

• Get a good night sleep the night before. Have a light breakfast before the exam.

Example 2—Radioactive Decay

Carbon-14 has a half-life of 5750 years. If initially there are 60 grams of carbon-14, how many grams are left after 3000 years?

Step 1. $y(t) = y_0 e^{kt} = 60e^{kt}$

Since half-life is 5750 years, $30 = 60\,e^k(5750) \Rightarrow \frac{1}{2} = e^{5750k}$

$$\ln\left(\frac{1}{2}\right) = \ln\left(e^{5750k}\right)$$

$$-\ln 2 = 5750k$$

$$\frac{-\ln 2}{5750} = k$$

Step 2. $y(t) = y_0 e^{kt}$

$$y(t) = 60e^{\left[\frac{-\ln 2}{5750}\right]t}$$

$$y(3000) = 60e^{\left[\frac{-\ln 2}{5750}\right](3000)}$$

$$y(3000) \approx 41.7919$$

Thus, there will be approximately 41.792 grams of carbon-14 after 3000 years.

Separable Differential Equations

General Procedure:

1. Separate the variables: $g(y)\, dy = f(x)\, dx$
2. Integrate both sides: $\int g(y)\, dy = \int f(x)\, dx$
3. Solve for y to get a general solution.
4. Substitute given conditions to get a particular solution.
5. Verify your result by differentiating.

Example 1

Given $\dfrac{dy}{dx} = 4x^3 y^2$ and $y(1) = -\dfrac{1}{2}$, solve the differential equation.

Step 1. Separate the variables: $\dfrac{1}{y^2}\, dy = 4x^3 dx$

Step 2. Integrate both sides: $\int \dfrac{1}{y^2}\, dy = \int 4x^3 dx;\ -\dfrac{1}{y} = x^4 + c$

Step 3. General solution: $y = \dfrac{-1}{x^4 + c}$

Step 4. Particular solution: $-\dfrac{1}{2} = \dfrac{-1}{1 + c} \Rightarrow c = 1;\ y = \dfrac{-1}{x^4 + 1}$

Step 5. Verify result by differentiating

$$y = \frac{-1}{x^4 + 1} = (-1)(x^4 + 1)^{-1}$$

$$\frac{dy}{dx} = (-1)(-1)(x^4 + 1)^{-2}(4x^3) = \frac{4x^3}{(x^4 + 1)^2}$$

Note: $y = \dfrac{-1}{x^4 + 1}$ implies $y^2 = \dfrac{1}{(x^4 + 1)^2}$

Thus $\dfrac{dy}{dx} = \dfrac{4x^3}{(x^4 + 1)^2} = 4x^3 y^2$.

Example 2

Find a solution of the differentiation equation $\dfrac{dy}{dx} = x \sin(x^2); \; y(0) = -1$.

Step 1. Separate variables: $dy = x \sin(x^2)\, dx$

Step 2. Integrate both sides: $\displaystyle\int dy = \int x \sin(x^2)\, dx; \; \int dy = y$

Let $u = x^2; \; du = 2x\, dx$ or $\dfrac{du}{2} = x\, dx$

$$\int x \sin(x^2)\, dx = \int \sin u \left(\frac{du}{2}\right) = \frac{1}{2}\int \sin u\, du = -\frac{1}{2}\cos u + c$$

$$= -\frac{1}{2}\cos(x^2) + c$$

Thus: $y = -\dfrac{1}{2}\cos(x^2) + c$.

Step 3. Substitute given condition:

$$y(0) = -1; \; -1 = -\frac{1}{2}\cos(0) + c; \; -1 = \frac{-1}{2} + c; \; -\frac{1}{2} = c$$

Thus, $y = -\dfrac{1}{2}\cos(x^2) - \dfrac{1}{2}$.

Step 4. Verify result by differentiating:

$$\frac{dy}{dx} = \frac{1}{2}\left[\sin(x^2)\right](2x) = x \sin(x^2).$$

Example 3

If $\dfrac{d^2y}{dx^2} = 2x + 1$ and at $x = 0$, $y' = -1$ and $y = 3$, find a solution of the differential equation.

Step 1. Rewrite: $\dfrac{d^2y}{dx^2}$ as $\dfrac{dy'}{dx}$; $\dfrac{dy'}{dx} = 2x + 1$.

Step 2. Separate variables: $dy' = (2x + 1)\, dx$.

Step 3. Integrate both sides: $\displaystyle\int dy' = \int (2x + 1)\, dx; \; y' = x^2 + x + c_1$.

Step 4. Substitute given condition: At $x = 0$, $y' = -1$; $-1 = 0 + 0 + c_1 \Rightarrow c_1 = -1$.

Thus $y' = x^2 + x - 1$.

Step 5. Rewrite: $y' = \dfrac{dy}{dx}$; $\dfrac{dy}{dx} = x^2 + x - 1$.

Step 6. Separate variables: $dy = (x^2 + x - 1)\, dx$.

Step 7. Integrate both sides: $\displaystyle\int dy = \int (x^2 + x - 1)\, dx$

$$y = \frac{x^3}{3} + \frac{x^2}{2} - x + c_2.$$

Step 8. Substitute given condition: At $x = 0$, $y = 3$; $3 = 0 + 0 - 0 + c_2 \Rightarrow c_2 = 3$

Therefore $y = \dfrac{x^3}{3} + \dfrac{x^2}{2} - x + 3$.

Step 9. Verify result by differentiating: $y = \dfrac{x^3}{3} + \dfrac{x^2}{2} - x + 3$

$$\frac{dy}{dx} = x^2 + x - 1; \ \frac{d^2y}{dx^2} = 2x + 1.$$

Example 4

Find the general solution of the differential equation $\dfrac{dy}{dx} = \dfrac{2xy}{x^2 + 1}$.

Step 1. Separate variables:

$$\frac{dy}{y} = \frac{2x}{x^2 + 1}\,dx.$$

Step 2. Integrate both sides: $\displaystyle\int \frac{dy}{y} = \int \frac{2x}{x^2 + 1}\,dx$ (let $u = x^2 + 1$; $du = 2x\,dx$)

$$\ln|y| = \ln(x^2 + 1) + c_1$$

Step 3. General Solution: solve for y

$$e^{\ln|y|} = e^{\ln(x^2+1)+c_1}$$

$$|y| = e^{\ln(x^2+1)} \cdot e^{c_1}; \ |y| = e^{c_1}(x^2 + 1)$$

$$y = \pm e^{c_1}(x^2 + 1)$$

The general solution is $y = c(x^2 + 1)$.

Step 4. Verify result by differentiating:

$$y = c(x^2 + 1)$$

$$\frac{dy}{dx} = 2cx = 2x\frac{c(x^2 + 1)}{(x^2 + 1)} = \frac{2xy}{x^2 + 1}.$$

Example 5

Write an equation for the curve that passes through the point $(3, 4)$ and has a slope at any point (x, y) as $\dfrac{dy}{dx} = \dfrac{x^2 + 1}{2y}$.

Step 1. Separate variables: $2y\,dy = (x^2 = 1)\,dx$.

Step 2. Integrate both sides: $\displaystyle\int 2y\,dy = \int (x^2 + 1)\,dx$; $y^2 = \dfrac{x^3}{3} + x + c$.

Step 3. Substitute given condition: $4^2 = \dfrac{3^3}{3} + 3 + c \Rightarrow c = 4$

Thus $y^2 = \dfrac{x^3}{3} + x + 4$.

Step 4. Verify the result by differentiating: $2y\dfrac{dy}{dx} = x^2 + 1$

$$\frac{dy}{dx} = \frac{x^2 + 1}{2y}.$$

10.5   RAPID REVIEW

1. Find the average value of $y = \sin x$ on $[0, \pi]$.

   Answer: Average value $= \dfrac{1}{\pi - 0}\displaystyle\int_0^\pi \sin x\, dx$

   $$= \frac{1}{\pi}\left[-\cos x\right]_0^\pi = \frac{2}{\pi}$$

2. Find the total distance traveled by a particle during $0 \le t \le 3$ whose velocity function is shown in Figure 10.5-1.

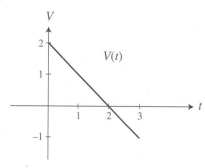

Figure 10.5-1

   Answer: The Total Distance Traveled $= \displaystyle\int_0^2 v(t)\,dt + \left|\int_2^3 v(t)\,dt\right|$

   $$= 2 + 0.5 = 2.5$$

3. Oil is leaking from a tank at the rate of $f(t) = 5e^{-0.1t}$ gallons/hour, where t is measured in hours. Write an integral to find the total number of gallons of oil that will have leaked from the tank after 10 hours. Do not evaluate the integral.

   Answer: Total number of gallons leaked $= \displaystyle\int_0^{10} 5e^{-0.1t}\,dt$

4. How much money should Mary invest at 7.5% interest a year compounded continuously, so that Mary will have \$100,000 after 20 *years*.

   Answer: $y(t) = y_0 e^{kt}$, $k = 0.075$ and $t = 20$. $y(20) = 100{,}000 = y_0 e^{(0.075)(20)}$. Thus you obtain $y_0 \approx 22313$, using a calculator.

5. Given $\dfrac{dy}{dx} = \dfrac{x}{y}$ and $y(1) = 0$, solve the differential equation.

   Answer: $y\,dy = x\,dx \Rightarrow \displaystyle\int y\,dy \Rightarrow \dfrac{y^2}{2} = \dfrac{x^2}{2} + c \Rightarrow 0 = \dfrac{1}{2} + c \Rightarrow c = -\dfrac{1}{2}$.

   Thus $\dfrac{y^2}{2} = \dfrac{x^2}{2} - \dfrac{1}{2}$ or $y^2 = x^2 - 1$.

10.6   PRACTICE PROBLEMS

Part A—The use of a calculator is not allowed.

1. Find the value of c as stated in the Mean Value Theorem for Integrals for $f(x) = x^3$ on $[2,4]$.

2. The graph of f is shown in Figure 10.6-1. Find the average value of f on $[0,8]$.

3. The position function of a particle moving on a coordinate line is given as $s(t) = t^2 - 6t - 7$, $0 \le t$

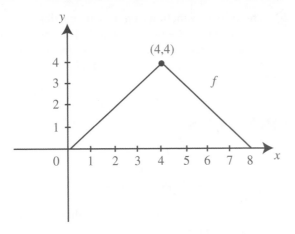

Figure 10.6-1

≤ 10. Find the displacement and total distance traveled by the particle from $1 \le t \le 4$.

4. The velocity function of a moving particle on a coordinate line is $v(t) = 2t + 1$ for $0 \le t \le 8$. At $t = 1$, its position is -4. Find the position of the particle at $t = 5$.

5. The rate of depreciation for a new piece of equipment at a factory is given as $p(t) = 50t - 600$ for $0 \le t \le 10$, where t is measured in years. Find the total loss of value of the equipment over the first 5 years.

6. The acceleration of a moving particle on a coordinate line is $a(t) = -2$ for $0 \le t \le 4$, and the initial velocity $v_0 = 10$. Find the total distance traveled by the particle during $0 \le t \le 4$.

7. The graph of the velocity function of a moving particle is shown in Figure 10.6-2. What is the total distance traveled by the particle during $0 \le t \le 12$?

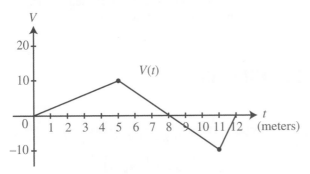

Figure 10.6-2

8. If oil is leaking from a tanker at the rate of $f(t) = 10e^{0.2t}\ dt$ gallons per hour where t is measured in hours, how many gallons of oil will have leaked from the tanker after the first 3 hours?

9. The change of temperature in a cup of coffee measured in degrees Fahrenheit in a certain room is represented by the function
$$f(t) = -\cos\left(\frac{t}{4}\right) \text{ for } 0 \le t \le 5, \text{ where } t \text{ is}$$
measured in minutes. If the temperature of the coffee is initially 92°F, find its temperature after the first 5 minutes.

10. If the *half-life* of a radioactive element is 4500 years, and initially there are 100 grams of this element, approximately how many grams are left after 5000 years?

11. Find a solution of the differential equation:
$$\frac{dy}{dx} = x\cos(x^2); \ y(0) = \pi$$

12. If $\dfrac{d^2 y}{dx^2} = x - 5$ and at $x = 0$, $y' = -2$ and $y = 1$, find a solution of the differential equation.

Part B—Calculators are permitted.

13. Find the average value of $y = \tan x$ from
$$x = \frac{\pi}{4} \text{ to } x = \frac{\pi}{3}.$$

14. The acceleration function of a moving particle on a straight line is given by $a(t) = 3e^{2t}$, t is measured in seconds, and the initial velocity is $\dfrac{1}{2}$. Find the displacement and total distance traveled by the particle in the first 3 seconds.

15. The sales of an item in a company follows an exponential growth/decay model, where t is measured in months. If the sales drop from 5000 units in the first months to 4000 units in the third month, how many units should the company expect to sell during the seventh month?

16. Find an equation of the curve that has a slope for $\dfrac{2y}{x + 1}$ at the point (x, y) and passes through the point $(0,4)$.

17. The population in a city is approximately 750,000 in 1980, and growing at a rate of 3% per year. If the population growth follows an exponential growth model, find the city's population in the year 2002.

18. Find a solution of the differential equation $4e^y = y' - 3xe^y$ and $y(0) = 0$.

19. How much money should a person invest at 6.25% interest compounded continuously so that the person will have $50,000 after 10 years?

20. The velocity function of a moving particle is given as $v(t) = 2 - 6e^{-t}$, $t \geq 0$ and t is measured in seconds. Find the total distance traveled by the particle during the first 10 seconds.

10.7 CUMULATIVE REVIEW PROBLEMS

("Calculator" indicates that calculators are permitted)

21. If $3e^y = x^2y$, find $\dfrac{dy}{dx}$.

22. Evaluate $\displaystyle\int_0^1 \dfrac{x^2}{x^3 + 1}\, dx$.

23. The graph of a continuous function f which consists of three line segments on $[-2, 4]$ is shown in Figure 10.7-1. If $F(x) = \displaystyle\int_{-2}^x f(t)\, dt$ for $-2 \leq x \leq 4$,

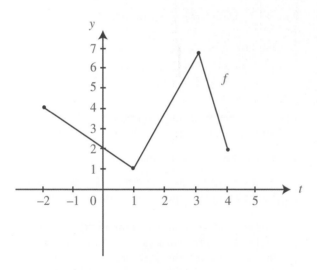

Figure 10.7-1

(a) find $F(-2)$ and $F(0)$.

(b) find $F'(0)$ and $F'(2)$.

(c) find the value of x such that F has a maximum on $[-2,4]$.

(d) on which interval is the graph of F concave upward.

24. (Calculator) The slope of a function $y = f(x)$ at any point (x, y) is $\dfrac{y}{2x + 1}$ and $f(0) = 2$.

(a) Write an equation of the line tangent to the graph of f at $x = 0$.

(b) Use the tangent in part (a) to find the approximate value of $f(0.1)$.

(c) Find a solution $y = f(x)$ for the differential equation.

(d) Use the result in part (c), find $f(0.1)$.

25. (Calculator) Let R be the region in the first quadrant bounded by $f(x) = e^x - 1$ and $g(x) = 3 \sin x$.

(a) Find the area of region R.

(b) Find the volume of the solid obtained by revolving R about the x-axis.

(c) Find the volume of the solid having R as its base and its cross sections are semicircles perpendicular to the x-axis.

10.8 SOLUTIONS TO PRACTICE PROBLEMS

Part A—No calculators.

1. $\displaystyle\int_2^4 x^3\, dx = f(c)(4 - 2)$

$\displaystyle\int_2^4 x^3\, dx = \dfrac{x^4}{4}\Big]_2^4 = \left(\dfrac{4^2}{4}\right) - \left(\dfrac{2^4}{4}\right) = 60$

$2f(c) = 60 \Rightarrow f(c) = 30$

$c^3 = 30 \Rightarrow c = (30)^{1/3}$.

2. Average Value $= \dfrac{1}{8 - 0}\displaystyle\int_0^8 f(x)\, dx$

$= \dfrac{1}{8}\left(\dfrac{1}{2}(8)(4)\right) = 2.$

3. Displacement $= s(4) - s(1) = -15 - (-12) = -3.$

Distance Traveled $= \displaystyle\int_1^4 |v(t)|\, dt$

$v(t) = s'(t) = 2t - 6$

Set $2t - 6 = 0 \Rightarrow t = 3$

$$|2t - 6| = \begin{cases} -(2t - 6) & \text{if } 0 \le t < 3 \\ 2t - 6 & \text{if } 3 \le t \le 10 \end{cases}$$

$$\int_1^4 |v(t)| \, dt = \int_1^3 -(2t - 6) \, dt + \int_3^4 (2t - 6) \, dt$$

$$= \left[-t^2 + 6t \right]_1^3 + \left[t^2 - 6t \right]_3^4$$

$$= 4 + 1 = 5.$$

4. Position Function $s(t) = \int v(t) \, dt$

$$= \int (2t + 1) \, dt$$

$$= t^2 + t + c$$

$$s(1) = -4 \Rightarrow (1)^2 + 1 + c$$

$$= -4 \text{ or } c = -6$$

$$s(t) = t^2 + t - 6.$$

$$s(5) = 5^2 + 5 - 6 = 24.$$

5. Total Loss $= \int_0^5 p(t) \, dt = \int_0^5 (50t - 600) \, dt$

$$= 25t^2 - 600t \Big]_0^5 = 2375.$$

6. $v(t) = \int a(t) \, dt = \int -2 \, dt = -2t + c$

$$v_0 = 10 \Rightarrow -2(0) + c = 10 \text{ or } c = 10$$

$$v(t) = -2t + 10.$$

Distance Traveled $= \int_0^4 |v(t)| \, dt.$

Set $v(t) = 0 \Rightarrow -2t + 10 = 0$ or $t = 5.$

$|-2t + 10| = -2t + 10$ if $0 \le t < 5$

$$\int_0^4 |v(t)| \, dt = \int_0^4 (-2t + 10) \, dt$$

$$= -t^2 + 10t \Big]_0^4 = 24.$$

7. Total Distance Traveled

$$= \int_0^8 v(t) \, dt + \left| \int_8^{12} v(t) \right|$$

$$= \frac{1}{2} (8)(10) + \frac{1}{2} (4)(10)$$

$$= 60 \text{ meters.}$$

8. Total Leakage $= \int_0^3 10 e^{0.2t} \, dt = 50 e^{0.2t} \Big]_0^3$

$$= 91.1059 - 50$$

$$= 41.1059 \approx 41 \text{ gallons}$$

9. Total change in temperature

$$= \int_0^5 -\cos\left(\frac{t}{4}\right) dt$$

$$= -4 \sin\left(\frac{t}{4}\right) \Big]_0^5$$

$$= -3.79594 - 0$$

$$= -3.79594°\text{F}.$$

Thus the temperature of coffee after 5 minutes is $(92 - 3.79594) \approx 88.204°\text{F}$

10. $y(t) = y_0 e^{kt}$

Half-life $= 4500$ years $\Rightarrow \dfrac{1}{2} = e^{4500k}$

Take ln of both sides:

$$\ln\left(\frac{1}{2}\right) = \ln e^{4500k} \Rightarrow$$

$$-\ln 2 = 4500k \text{ or}$$

$$k = \frac{-\ln 2}{4500}$$

$$y(t) = 100 \, e^{\left(\frac{-\ln 2}{4500}\right)(5000)} = 25\left(2^{\frac{8}{9}}\right) \approx 46.29.$$

There are approximately 46.29 grams left.

11. Step 1. Separate variables: $dy = x \cos(x^2) \, dx$

Step 2. Integrate both sides: $\int dy = \int x \cos(x^2) \, dx.$

$$\int dy = y$$

$$\int x \cos(x^2) \, dx = \text{Let } u = x^2;$$

$$du = 2x \, dx, \frac{du}{2} = x \, dx$$

$$\int x \cos(x^2) \, dx = \int \cos u \, \frac{du}{2}$$

$$= \frac{\sin u}{2} + c = \frac{\sin(x^2)}{2} + c.$$

Thus $y = \dfrac{\sin(x^2)}{2} + c$

Step 3. Substitute given values.

$$y(0) = \frac{\sin(0)}{2} + c = \pi \Rightarrow c = \pi$$

$$y = \frac{\sin(x^2)}{2} + \pi.$$

Step 4. Verify result by differentiating

$$\frac{dy}{dx} = \frac{\cos(x^2)(2x)}{2} = x \cos(x^2).$$

12. Step 1. Rewrite $\dfrac{d^2y}{dx^2}$ as $\dfrac{dy'}{dx}$

$$\frac{dy'}{dx} = x - 5$$

Step 2. Separate variables: $dy' = (x - 5)\,dx$

Step 3. Integrate both sides: $\int dy' = \int(x - 5)\,dx$

$$y' = \frac{x^2}{2} - 5x + c_1$$

Step 4. Substitute given values:

At $x = 0$, $y' = \dfrac{0}{2} - 5(0)$

$$+ c_1 = -2 \Rightarrow c_1 = -2$$

$$y' = \frac{x^2}{2} - 5x - 2$$

Step 5. Rewrite: $y' = \dfrac{dy}{dx}$; $\dfrac{dy}{dx} = \dfrac{x^2}{2} - 5x - 2$.

Step 6. Separate variables:

$$dy = \left(\frac{x^2}{2} - 5x - 2\right)dx.$$

Step 7. Integrate both sides:

$$\int dy = \int\left(\frac{x^2}{2} - 5x - 2\right)dx$$

$$y = \frac{x^3}{6} - \frac{5x^2}{2} - 2x + c_2.$$

Step 8. Substitute given values:

At $x = 0$, $y = 0 - 0 - 0 + c_2 = 1 \Rightarrow c_2 = 1$

$$y = \frac{x^3}{6} - \frac{5x^2}{2} - 2x + 1.$$

Step 9. Verify result by differentiating

$$\frac{dy}{dx} = \frac{x^2}{2} - 5x - 2$$

$$\frac{d^2y}{dx^2} = x - 5.$$

Part B—Calculators are permitted.

13. Average Value $= \dfrac{1}{\frac{\pi}{3} - \frac{\pi}{4}}\displaystyle\int_{\pi/4}^{\pi/3} \tan x\,dx$

Enter $= \left(\dfrac{1}{\frac{\pi}{3} - \frac{\pi}{4}}\right)\displaystyle\int\left(\tan x, x\,\frac{\pi}{4},\frac{\pi}{3}\right)$

and obtain $\dfrac{6\ln(2)}{\pi} \approx 1.32381$.

14. $v(t) = \displaystyle\int a(t)\,dt$

$$= \int 3e^{2t} = \frac{3}{2} e^{2t} + c$$

$$v(0) = \frac{3}{2} e^0 + c = \frac{1}{2}$$

$$\Rightarrow \frac{3}{2} + c = \frac{1}{2} \text{ or } c = -1$$

$$v(t) = \frac{3}{2} e^{2t} - 1$$

Displacement $= \displaystyle\int_0^3\left(\frac{3}{2} e^{2t} - 1\right)dt$

Enter $\displaystyle\int\left(\frac{3}{2} * e^\wedge(2x) - 1, x, 0, 3\right)$

and obtain 298.822.

Distance Traveled $= \displaystyle\int_0^3 |v(t)|\,dt$

Since $\dfrac{3}{2} e^{2t} - 1 > 0$ for $t \geq 0$,

$$\int_0^3 |v(t)|\,dt = \int_0^3\left(\frac{3}{2} e^{2t} - 1\right)dt = 298.822.$$

15. Step 1. $y(t) = y_0 e^{kt}$

$y(1) = 5000 \Rightarrow 5000 = y_0 e^k \Rightarrow y_0$
$= 5000e^{-k}$

$y(3) = 4000 \Rightarrow 4000 = y_0 e^{3k}$

Substituting $y_0 = 5000e^{-k}$, 4000
$= (5000e^{-k})e^{3k}$

$4000 = 5000e^{2k}$

$$\frac{4}{5} = e^{2k}$$

$$\ln\left(\frac{4}{5}\right) = \ln(e^{2k}) = 2k$$

$$k = \frac{1}{2} \ln\left(\frac{4}{5}\right) \approx -0.111572.$$

Step 2. $5000 = y_0 e^{-0.111572}$

$y_0 = (5000)e^{0.111572} \approx 5590.17$

$y(t) = (5590.17)e^{-0.111572t}$

Step 3. $y(7) = (5590.17)e^{-0.111572(7)} \approx 2560$

Thus sales for the 7th month are approximately 2560 units.

16. Step 1. Separate variables:

$$\frac{dy}{dx} = \frac{2y}{x+1}$$

$$\frac{dy}{2y} = \frac{dx}{x+1}$$

Step 2. Integrate both sides:

$$\int \frac{dy}{2y} = \int \frac{dx}{x+1}$$

$$\frac{1}{2}\ln|y| = \ln|x+1| + c.$$

Step 3. Substitute given value (0,4):

$$\frac{1}{2}\ln(4) = \ln(1) + c$$

$$\ln 2 = c$$

$$\frac{1}{2}\ln|y| - \ln|x+1| = \ln 2$$

$$\ln\left|\frac{y^{1/2}}{x+1}\right| = \ln 2$$

$$e^{\ln\left|\frac{y^{1/2}}{x+1}\right|} = e^{\ln 2}$$

$$\frac{y^{1/2}}{x+1} = 2$$

$$y^{1/2} = 2(x+1)$$

$$y = (2)^2(x+1)^2$$

$$y = 4(x+1)^2.$$

Step 4. Verify result by differentiating:

$$\frac{dy}{dx} = 4(2)(x+1) = 8(x+1)$$

Compare with $\dfrac{dy}{dx} = \dfrac{2y}{x+1}$

$$= \frac{2\left(4(x+1)^2\right)}{(x+1)}$$

$$= 8(x+1).$$

17. $y(t) = y_0 e^{kt}$

$y_0 = 750,000$

$y(22) = (750,000)e^{(0.03)(22)}$

$$\approx \begin{cases} 1.45109E6 \approx 1,451,090 \text{ using an TI-89} \\ 1,451,094 \text{ using an TI-85.} \end{cases}$$

18. Step 1. Separate variables:

$$4e^y = \frac{dy}{dx} - 3xe^y$$

$$4e^y + 3xe^y = \frac{dy}{dx}$$

$$e^y(4+3x) = \frac{dy}{dx}$$

$$(4+3x)\,dx = \frac{dy}{e^y} = e^{-y}dy$$

Step 2. Integrate both sides:

$$\int (4+3x)\,dx = \int e^{-y}dy$$

$$4x + \frac{3x^2}{2} = -e^{-y} + c$$

switch sides: $e^{-y} = -\dfrac{3x^2}{2} - 4x + c$

Step 3. Substitute given value: $y(0)=0 \Rightarrow e^0 = 0$
$-0 + c \Rightarrow c = 1$

Step 4. Take ln of both sides:

$$e^{-y} = -\frac{3x^2}{2} - 4x + 1$$

$$\ln(e^{-y}) = \ln\left(-\frac{3x^2}{2} - 4x + 1\right)$$

$$y = -\ln\left(1 - 4x - \frac{3x^2}{2}\right).$$

Step 5. Verify result by differentiating:
Enter $d(-\ln(1 - 4x - 3(x^2)/2), x)$ and
obtain $\dfrac{-2(3x+4)}{3x^2 + 8x - 2}$,
Which is equivalent to $e^y(4+3x)$.

19. $y(t) = y_0 e^{kt}$

$k = 0.0625$, $y(10) = 50,000$

$50,000 = y_0 e^{10(0.0625)}$

$$y_0 = \frac{50,000}{e^{0.625}} \approx \begin{cases} \$26763.1 \text{ using an TI-89} \\ \$26763.071426 \approx \$26763.07 \\ \quad \text{using an TI-85.} \end{cases}$$

20. Set $v(t) = 2 - 6e^{-t} = 0$. Using the Zero Function on your calculator, compute $t = 1.09861$.

Distance Traveled $= \int_0^x |v(t)|\,dt = 10$

$$|2 - 6e^{-t}| = \begin{cases} -(2 - 6e^{-t}) \text{ if } 0 \le t < 1.09861 \\ 2 - 6e^{-t} \text{ if } t \ge 1.09861 \end{cases}$$

$$\int_0^{10} |2 - 6e^{-t}| \, dt = \int_0^{1.09861} -(2 - 6e^{-t}) \, dt$$

$$+ \int_{1.09861}^{10} (2 - 6e^{-t}) \, dt$$

$$= 1.80278 + 15.803$$

Alternatively, use the nInt Function on the calculator.

Enter nInt($abs(2 - 6e^{\wedge}(-x))$, x, 0, 10) and obtain the same result.

10.9 SOLUTIONS TO CUMULATIVE REVIEW PROBLEMS

21. $3e^y = x^2 y$

$$3e^y \frac{dy}{dx} = 2xy + \frac{dy}{dx}(x^2)$$

$$3e^y \frac{dy}{dx} - \frac{dy}{dx} x^2 = 2xy$$

$$\frac{dy}{dx}(3e^y - x^2) = 2xy$$

$$\frac{dy}{dx} = \frac{2xy}{3e^y - x^2}$$

22. Let $u = x^3 + 1$; $du = 3x^2 \, dx$ or $\dfrac{du}{3} = x^2 dx$

$$\int \frac{x^2}{x^3 + 1} \, dx = \int \frac{1}{u} \frac{du}{3} = \frac{1}{3} \ln|u|$$

$$+ c = \frac{1}{3} \ln|x^3 + 1| + c$$

$$\int_0^1 \frac{x^2}{x^3 + 1} \, dx = \frac{1}{3} \ln|x^3 + 1| \Big|_0^1$$

$$= \frac{1}{3} (\ln 2 - \ln 1) = \frac{\ln 2}{3}.$$

23. (a) $F(-2) = \int_{-2}^{-2} f(t) \, dt = 0$

$$F(0) = \int_{-2}^0 f(t) \, dt = \frac{1}{2}(4 + 2)2 = 6$$

(b) $F'(x) = f(x)$; $F'(0) = 2$ and $F'(2) = 4$

(c) Since $f > 0$ on $[-2,4]$, F has a maximum value at $x = 4$.

(d) The function f is increasing on $(1,3)$ which implies that $f' > 0$ on $(1,3)$.

Thus, F is concave upward on $(1,3)$. (Note: f' is equivalent to the 2nd derivative of F.)

24. (a) $\dfrac{dy}{dx} = \dfrac{y}{2x + 1}$; $f(0) = 2$

$$\frac{dy}{dx}\Big|_{x=0} = \frac{2}{2(0) + 1} = 2 \Rightarrow m = 2 \text{ at } x = 0$$

$y - y_1 = m(x - x_1)$

$y - 2 = 2(x - 0) \Rightarrow y = 2x + 2$

The equation of the tangent to f at $x = 0$ is $y = 2x + 2$.

(b) $f(0.1) = 2(0.1) + 2 = 2.2$

(c) Solve the differential equation: $\dfrac{dy}{dx} = \dfrac{y}{2x + 1}$

Step 1. Separate variables

$$\frac{dy}{y} = \frac{dx}{2x + 1}$$

Step 2. Integrate both sides

$$\int \frac{dy}{y} = \int \frac{dx}{2x + 1}$$

$$\ln|y| = \frac{1}{2} \ln|2x + 1| + c$$

Step 3. Substitute given values $(0,2)$

$$\ln 2 = \frac{1}{2} \ln 1 + c \Rightarrow c = \ln 2$$

$$\ln|y| = \frac{1}{2}|2x + 1| + \ln 2$$

$$\ln|y| - \frac{1}{2}|2x + 1| = \ln 2$$

$$\ln \left| \frac{y}{(2x + 1)^{1/2}} \right| = \ln 2$$

$$e^{\ln \left| \frac{y}{(2x+1)^{1/2}} \right|} = e^{\ln 2}$$

$$\frac{y}{(2x + 1)^{1/2}} = 2$$

$$y = 2(2x + 1)^{1/2}.$$

Step 4. Verify result by differentiating

$$y = 2(2x + 1)^{1/2}$$

$$\frac{dy}{dx} = 2\left(\frac{1}{2}\right)(2x+1)^{-\frac{1}{2}}(2)$$

$$= \frac{2}{\sqrt{2x+1}} \cdot$$

Compare this with:

$$\frac{dy}{dx} = \frac{y}{2x+1} = \frac{2(2x+1)^{\frac{1}{2}}}{2x+1}$$

$$= \frac{2}{\sqrt{2x+1}} \cdot$$

Thus the function is $y = f(x) = 2(2x+1)^{\frac{1}{2}}$.

(d) $f(x) = 2(2x+1)^{\frac{1}{2}}$

$$f(0.1) = 2(2(0.1)+1)^{\frac{1}{2}} = 2(1.2)^{\frac{1}{2}} \approx 2.19089$$

25. See Figure 10.9-1.

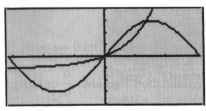

[−π,π] by [−4,4]

Figure 10.9-1

(a) Intersection points: Using the Intersection Function on the calculator, you have $x = 0$ and $x = 1.37131$.

$$\text{Area of } R = \int_0^{1.37131} \left[3\sin x - (e^x - 1)\right] dx$$

Enter $\int(3\sin(x)) - (e\wedge(x) - 1), x, 0,$ 1.37131) and obtain 0.836303.

The area of region R is approximately 0.836.

(b) Using the Washer Method, volume of

$$R = \pi \int_0^{1.37131} \left[(3\sin x)^2 - (e^x - 1)^2\right] dx$$

Enter $\pi \int ((3\sin(x))\wedge 2 - (e\wedge(x) - 1)\wedge 2, x, 0,$ 1.37131) and obtain 2.54273π or 7.98824.

The volume of region R is 7.988.

(c) Volume of Solid $= \pi \int_0^{1.37131}$ (Area of Cross Section) dx

$$\text{Area of Cross Section} = \frac{1}{2}\pi r^2$$

$$= \frac{1}{2}\pi \left(\frac{1}{2}(3\sin x - (e^x - 1))\right)^2$$

Enter $\left(\frac{\pi}{2}\right)\frac{1}{4} * \int ((3\sin(x)) - (e\wedge(x) - 1))\wedge 2,$

$x, 0, 1.37131)$ and obtain 0.077184π or 0.24248.

The volume of the solid is approximately 0.077184π or 0.242.

PART IV

APPENDIXES

Appendix I

Formulas and Theorems

1. Quadratic Formula:

$$ax^2 + b + c = 0 \ (a \neq 0)$$

$$x = \frac{-b \pm \sqrt{b^2 - 4ac}}{2a}$$

2. Distance Formula:

$$d = \sqrt{(x_2 - x_1)^2 + (y_2 - y_1)^2}$$

3. Equation of a Circle:

$x^2 + y^2 = r^2$ center at $(0,0)$ and radius $= r$

4. Equation of an Ellipse:

$$\frac{x^2}{a^2} + \frac{y^2}{b^2} = 1 \text{ center at } (0,0)$$

$$\frac{(x - h)^2}{a^2} + \frac{(y - k)^2}{b^2} = 1 \text{ center at } (h, k)$$

5. Area and Volume Formulas:

Figure	Area Formula
Trapezoid	$\frac{1}{2}$ [base$_1$ + base$_2$] (height)
Parallelogram	(base)(height)
Equilateral Triangle	$\frac{s^2\sqrt{3}}{4}$
Circle	πr^2 (circumference $= 2\pi r$)

Solid	Volume	Surface Area
Sphere	$\frac{4}{3}\pi r^3$	$4\pi r^2$
Right Circular Cylinder	$\pi r^2 h$	$2\pi rh$
Right Circular Cone	$\frac{1}{3}\pi r^2 h$	Lateral S.A.: $\pi r\sqrt{r^2 + h^2}$ Total S.A.: $\pi r^2 + \pi r\sqrt{r^2 + h^2}$

6. Special Angles:

Angle Function	0°	$\frac{\pi}{6}$ 30°	$\frac{\pi}{4}$ 45°	$\frac{\pi}{3}$ 60°	$\frac{\pi}{2}$ 90°	π 180°	$\frac{3\pi}{2}$ 270°	2π 360°
Sin	0	$\frac{1}{2}$	$\frac{\sqrt{2}}{2}$	$\frac{\sqrt{3}}{2}$	1	0	−1	0
Cos	1	$\frac{\sqrt{3}}{2}$	$\frac{\sqrt{2}}{2}$	$\frac{1}{2}$	0	−1	0	1
Tan	0	$\frac{\sqrt{3}}{3}$	1	$\sqrt{3}$	Undefined	0	Undefined	0

7. Double Angles:

- $\sin 2\theta = 2\sin\theta \cos\theta$
- $\cos 2\theta = \cos^2 \theta - \sin^2 \theta$ or
  $1 - 2\sin^2 \theta$ or $2\cos^2 \theta - 1$
- $\cos^2 \theta = \dfrac{1 + \cos 2\theta}{2}$
- $\sin^2 \theta = \dfrac{1 - \cos 2\theta}{2}$

8. Pythagorean Identities:

- $\sin^2 \theta + \cos^2 \theta = 1$
- $1 + \tan^2 \theta = \sec^2 \theta$
- $1 + \cot^2 \theta = \csc^2 \theta$

9. Limits:

$$\lim_{x \to \infty} \frac{1}{x} = 0 \qquad \lim_{x \to 0} \frac{\cos x - 1}{x} = 0$$

$$\lim_{x \to 0} \frac{\sin x}{x} = 1 \qquad \lim_{x \to \infty} \left(1 + \frac{1}{h}\right)^h = e$$

$$\lim_{h \to 0} \frac{e^h - 1}{h} = 1 \qquad \lim_{x \to 0} (1 + x)^{\frac{1}{x}} = e$$

10. Rules of Differentiation:

a. Definition of the Derivative of a Function:

$$f'(x) = \lim_{h \to 0} \frac{f'(x + h) - f(x)}{h}$$

b. Power Rule: $\dfrac{d}{dx}(x^n) = nx^{n-1}$

c. Sum & Difference Rules:

$$\frac{d}{dx}(u \pm v) = \frac{du}{dx} \pm \frac{du}{dx}$$

d. Product Rule:

$$\frac{d}{dx}(uv) = v\frac{du}{dx} + u\frac{dv}{dx}$$

e. Quotient Rule:

$$\frac{d}{dx}\left(\frac{u}{v}\right) = \frac{v\dfrac{du}{dx} - u\dfrac{dv}{dx}}{v^2}, v \neq 0$$

Summary of Sum, Difference, Product and Quotient Rules:

$$(u \pm v)' = u' \pm v' \qquad (uv)' = u'v + v'u$$

$$\left(\frac{u}{v}\right)' = \frac{u'v - v'u}{v^2}$$

f. Chain Rule:

$$\frac{d}{dx}[f(g(x))] = f'(g(x)) \cdot g'(x)$$

$$\text{or } \frac{dy}{dx} = \frac{dy}{du} \cdot \frac{du}{dx}$$

11. Inverse Function and Derivatives:

$$(f^{-1})'(x) = \frac{1}{f'(f^{-1}(x))} \text{ or } \frac{dy}{dx} = \frac{1}{dx/dy}$$

12. Differentiation and Integration Formulas:

Integration Rules

a. $\int f(x)dx = F(x) + C \Leftrightarrow F'(x) = f(x)$

b. $\int af(x)dx = a\int f(x)dx$

c. $\int -f(x)dx = -\int f(x)dx$

d. $\int [f(x) \pm g(x)]dx = \int f(x)dx \pm \int g(x)dx$

Differentiation Formulas:

a. $\dfrac{d}{dx}(x) = 1$

b. $\dfrac{d}{dx}(ax) = a$

c. $\dfrac{d}{dx}(x^n) = nx^{n-1}$

d. $\dfrac{d}{dx}(\cos x) = -\sin x$

e. $\dfrac{d}{dx}(\sin x) = \cos x$

f. $\dfrac{d}{dx}(\tan x) = \sec^2 x$

g. $\dfrac{d}{dx}(\cot x) = -\csc^2 x$

h. $\dfrac{d}{dx}(\sec x) = \sec x \tan x$

i. $\dfrac{d}{dx}(\csc x) = -\csc x(\cot x)$

j. $\dfrac{d}{dx}(\ln x) = \dfrac{1}{x}$

k. $\dfrac{d}{dx}(e^x) = e^x$

l. $\dfrac{d}{dx}(a^x) = (\ln a)a^x$

m. $\dfrac{d}{dx}(\sin^{-1} x) = \dfrac{1}{\sqrt{1 - x^2}}$

n. $\dfrac{d}{dx}(\tan^{-1} x) = \dfrac{1}{1 + x^2}$

o. $\dfrac{d}{dx}(\sec^{-1} x) = \dfrac{1}{|x|\sqrt{x^2 - 1}}$

Integration Formulas:

a. $\int 1\,dx = x + c$

b. $\int a\,dx = ax + c$

c. $\int x^n\,dx = \dfrac{x^{n+1}}{n + 1} + c, n \neq -1$

d. $\int \sin x\,dx = -\cos x + c$

e. $\int \cos x\,dx = \sin x + c$

f. $\int \sec^2 x\,dx = \tan x + c$

g. $\int \csc^2 x\,dx = -\cot x + c$

h. $\int \sec x(\tan x)\,dx = \sec x + c$

i. $\int \csc x(\cot x)\,dx = -\csc x + c$

j. $\int \dfrac{1}{x}\,dx = \ln|x| + c$

k. $\int e^x\,dx = e^x + c$

l. $\int a^x\,dx = \dfrac{a^x}{\ln a} + c \quad a > 0, a \neq 1$

m. $\int \dfrac{1}{\sqrt{1 - x^2}}\,dx = \sin^{-1} x + c$

n. $\int \dfrac{1}{1 + x^2}\,dx = \tan^{-1} x + c$

o. $\int \dfrac{1}{|x|\sqrt{x^2 - 1}}\,dx = \sec^{-1} x + c$

More Integration Formulas:

a. $\int \tan x\,dx = \ln|\sec x| + c \text{ or } -\ln|\cos x| + c$

b. $\int \cot x\,dx = \ln|\sin x| + c \text{ or } -\ln|\csc x| + c$

c. $\int \sec x\,dx = \ln|\sec x + \tan x| + c$

d. $\int \csc x\,dx = \ln|\csc x - \cot x| + c$

e. $\int \ln x\,dx = x \ln|x| - x + c$

f. $\int \dfrac{1}{\sqrt{a^2 - x^2}}\,dx = \sin^{-1}\left(\dfrac{x}{a}\right) + c$

g. $\int \dfrac{1}{a^2 + x^2}\,dx = \dfrac{1}{a}\tan^{-1}\left(\dfrac{x}{a}\right) + c$

h. $\int \dfrac{1}{x\sqrt{x^2 - a^2}}\,dx = \dfrac{1}{a}\sec^{-1}\left|\dfrac{x}{a}\right| + c \text{ or}$

$\dfrac{1}{a}\cos^{-1}\left|\dfrac{a}{x}\right| + c$

i. $\int \sin^2 x\,dx = \dfrac{x}{2} - \dfrac{\sin(2x)}{4} + c.$

Note: $\sin^2 x = \dfrac{1 - \cos 2x}{2}$

Note: After evaluating an integral, always check the result by taking the derivative of the answer (i.e., taking the derivative of the antiderivative).

13. The Fundamental Theorems of Calculus

$$\int_a^b f(x)dx = F(b) - F(a), \text{ where } F'(x) = f(x).$$

If $F(x) = \int_a^x f(t)dt$, then $F'(x) = f(x)$.

14. Trapezoidal Approximation:

$$\int_a^b f(x)dx \approx \frac{b-a}{2n}\left[\begin{array}{l} f(x_0) + 2f(x_1) + 2f(x_2)\ldots \\ + 2f(x_{n-1}) + f(x_n) \end{array}\right]$$

15. Average Value of a Function:

$$f(c) = \frac{1}{b-a}\int_a^b f(x)dx$$

16. Mean Value Theorem:

$$f'(c) = \frac{f(b) - f(a)}{b-a} \text{ For some } c \text{ in (a,b)}$$

17. Mean Value Theorem for Integrals:

$$\int_a^b f(x)dx = f(c)(b-a) \text{ For some } c \text{ in (a,b)}$$

18. Area Bounded by 2 Curves:

$$\text{Area} = \int_{x_1}^{x_2}(f(x) - g(x))dx, \text{ where } f(x) \geq g(x)$$

19. Volume of a Solid with Known Cross Section:

$$V = \int_a^b A(x)dx, \text{ where } A(x) \text{ is the cross section.}$$

20. Disc Method:

$$V = \pi\int_a^b (f(x))^2 dx, \text{ where } f(x) = \text{radius}$$

21. Washer Method:

$$V = \pi\int_a^b\left((f(x))^2 - (g(x))^2\right)dx$$

where $f(x)$ = outer radius and $g(x)$ = inner radius

22. Distance Traveled Formulas:

- Position Function: $s(t)$; $s(t) = \int v(t)dt$

- Velocity: $v(t) = \dfrac{ds}{dt}$; $v(t) = \int a(t)dt$

- Acceleration: $a(t) = a(t$

- Speed: $|v(t)|$

- Displacement from t_1 to $t_2 = \int_{t_1}^{t_2} v(t)dt$

$$= s(t_2) - s(t_1)$$

- Total Distance Traveled from t_1 to

$$t_2 = \int_{t_1}^{t_2} |v(t)|dt$$

23. Business Formulas:

$P(x) = R(x) - C(x)$	Profit = Revenue − Cost
$R(x) = px$	Revenue = (price) (items sold)
$P'(x)$	Marginal Profit
$R'(x)$	Marginal Revenue
$C'(x)$	Marginal Cost

$P'(x)$, $R'(x)$, $C'(x)$ are the instantaneous rates of change of profit, revenue and cost respectively.

24. Exponential Growth/Decay Formulas:

$$\frac{dy}{dt} = ky, y > 0 \text{ and } y(t) = y_0 e^{kt}$$

Appendix II

Special Topic: Slope Fields

Slope field is a relatively new topic in AP Calculus. It has been part of the AP Calculus BC curriculum for the past several years. It will be introduced in the AP Calculus AB curriculum beginning with the academic year 2003–2004.*

A *slope field* (or a *direction field*) for a first-order differential equation is a graphic representation of the slopes of a family of curves. It consists of a set of short line segments drawn on a pair of axes. These line segments are the tangents to a family of solution curves for the differential equation at various points. The tangents show the direction in which the solution curves will follow. Slope fields are useful in sketching solution curves without having to solve a differential equation algebraically.

Example 1

If $\dfrac{dy}{dx} = 0.5x$, draw a slope field for the given differential equation.

Solution:

Step 1: Set up a table of values for $\dfrac{dy}{dx}$ for selected values of x.

x	-4	-3	-2	-1	0	1	2	3	4
$\dfrac{dy}{dx}$	-2	-1.5	-1	-0.5	0	0.5	1	1.5	2

Note that since $\dfrac{dy}{dx} = 0.5x$, the numerical value of $\dfrac{dy}{dx}$ is independent of the value of y. For example, at the points $(1,-1)$, $(1,0)$, $(1,1)$, $(1,2)$, $(1,3)$ and at all the points whose x-coordinates are 1, the numerical value of $\dfrac{dy}{dx}$ is 0.5 regardless of their y-coordinates. Similarly, for all the points whose x-coordinates are 2 (e.g., $(2,-1)$, $(2,0)$, $(2,3)$, etc.),

---

*This topic will not appear on the AP Calculus AB Exam until, at the earliest, May 2004.

$\dfrac{dy}{dx} = 1$. Also, remember that $\dfrac{dy}{dx}$ represents the slopes of the tangent lines to the curve at various points. You are now ready to draw these tangents.

Step 2: Draw short line segments with the given slopes at the various points. The slope field for the differential equation $\dfrac{dy}{dx} = 0.5x$ is shown in Figure A-1.

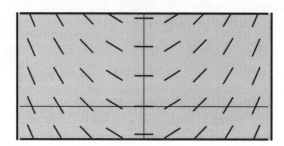

Figure A-1

Example 2

Figure A-2 shows a slope field for one of the differential equations given below. Identify the equation.

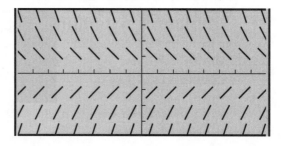

Figure A-2

(a) $\dfrac{dy}{dx} = 2x$ (b) $\dfrac{dy}{dx} = -2x$ (c) $\dfrac{dy}{dx} = y$

(d) $\dfrac{dy}{dx} = -y$ (e) $\dfrac{dy}{dx} = x + y$

Solution:

If you look across horizontally at any row of tangents, you'll notice that the tangents have the same slope. (Points on the same row have the same y-coordinate but different x-coordinates.) Therefore, the numerical value of $\dfrac{dy}{dx}$ (which represents the slope of the tangent) depends solely on the y-coordinate of a point and it is independent of the x-coordinate. Thus only choice (c) and choice (d) satisfy this condition. Also notice that the tangents have a negative slope when $y > 0$ and have a positive slope when $y < 0$.

Therefore, the correct choice is (c) $\dfrac{dy}{dx} = -y$.

Example 3

A slope field for a differential equation is shown in Figure A-3.

Draw a possible graph for the particular solution $y = f(x)$ to the differential equation function, if (a) the initial condition is $f(0) = -2$ and (b) the initial condition is $f(0) = 0$.

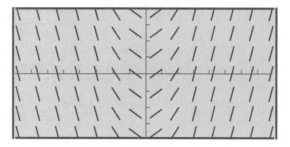

Figure A-3

Solution:

Begin by locating the point $(0, -2)$ as given in the initial condition. Follow the flow of the field and sketch the graph of the function. Repeat the same procedure with the point $(0, 0)$. See the curves as shown in Figure A-4.

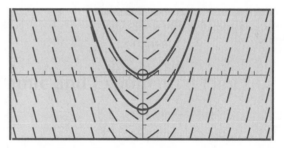

Figure A-4

Example 4

Given the differential equation $\dfrac{dy}{dx} = -xy$.

(a) draw a slope field for the differential equation at the 15 points indicated on the provided set of axes in Figure A-5.

(b) sketch a possible graph for the particular solution $y = f(x)$ to the differential equation with the initial condition $f(0) = 3$

(c) find, algebraically, the particular solution $y = f(x)$ to the differential equation with the initial condition $f(0) = 3$.

Solution:

(a) Set up a table of values for $\dfrac{dy}{dx}$ at the 15 given points.

	x = -2	x = -1	x = 0	x = 1	x = 2
y = 1	2	1	0	-1	-2
y = 2	4	2	0	-2	-4
y = 3	6	3	0	-3	-6

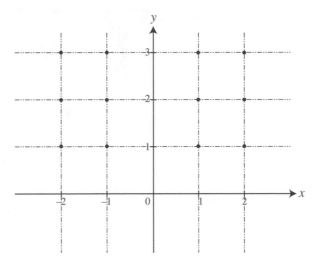

Figure A-5

Then sketch the tangents at the various points as shown in Figure A-6.

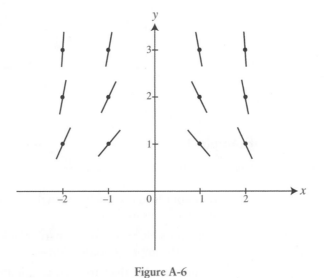

Figure A-6

(b) Locate the point (0,3) as indicated in the initial condition. Follow the flow of the field and sketch the curve as shown in Figure A-7.

(c) Step 1: Rewrite $\dfrac{dy}{dx} = -xy$ as $\dfrac{dy}{y} = -x\ dx$.

Step 2: Integrate both sides $\displaystyle\int \dfrac{dy}{y} = \int -x\,dx$ and obtain $\ln|y| = -\dfrac{x^2}{2} + c$.

Step 3: Apply the exponential function to both sides and obtain $e^{\ln|y|} = e^{\frac{x^2}{2}+c}$

Step 4: Simplify the equation and get $y = \left(e^{\frac{x^2}{2}}\right)\!\left(e^c\right) = \dfrac{e^c}{e^{\frac{x^2}{2}}}$.

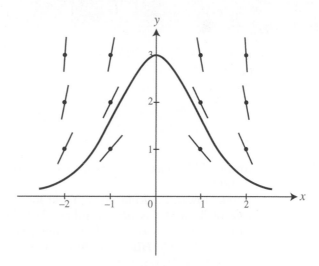

Figure A-7

Let $k = e^c$ and you have $y = \dfrac{k}{e^{\frac{x^2}{2}}}$.

Step 5: Substitute initial condition $(0, 3)$ and obtain $k = 3$. Thus you have $y = \dfrac{3}{e^{\frac{x^2}{2}}}$.

Appendix III

Bibliography

Advanced Placement Program Course Description. New York: The College Board, 2000.

Anton, Howard. *Calculus*. New York: John Wiley & Sons, 1984.

Apostol, Tom M. *Calculus*. Waltham, MA: Blaisdell Publishing Company, 1967.

Berlinski, David. *A Tour of the Calculus*. New York: Pantheon Books, 1995.

Boyer, Carl B. *The History of the Calculus and Its Conceptual Development*. New York: Dover, 1959.

Finney, R., Demana, F. D., Waits, B. K., Kennedy, D. *Calculus Graphical, Numerical, Algebraic*. New York: Scott Foresman Addison Wesley, 1999.

Kennedy, Dan. *Teacher's Guide–AP Calculus*. New York: The College Board, 1997.

Larson, R. E., Hostetler, R. P., Edwards, B. H. *Calculus*. New York: Houghton Mifflin Company, 1998.

Leithold, Louis. *The Calculus with Analytic Geometry*. New York: Harper & Row, 1976.

Sawyer, W.W. *What Is Calculus About?* Washington, DC: Mathematical Association of America, 1961.

Spivak, Michael. *Calculus*. New York: W. A. Benjamin, Inc., 1967.

Stewart, James. *Calculus*. New York: Brooks/Cole Publishing Company, 1995.

Appendix IV

Websites

www.collegeboard.org/ap/calculus

http://www.maa.org/features/mathed_disc.html

http://www.askdrmath.com/

http://www.askdrmath.com/calculus/calculus.html

http://www.askdrmath.com/library/topics/svcalc/

http://www-history.mcs.st-and.ac.uk/history/HistTopics/The_rise_of_calculus.html

http://mathforum.com/epigone/ap-calc/

http://www.sparknotes.com/math/calcab/.dir/

"In a hole in the ground there lived a hobbit."

"I am an invisible man."

"Many years later, as he faced the firing squad, Colonel Aureliano Buendía was to remember that distant afternoon when his father took him to discover ice."

5 Steps to a 5

Writing the AP English Essay

We called him Old Yeller.

"I have been afraid of putting air in a tire ever since I saw a tractor tire blow up and throw Newt Hardbines's father over the top of the Standard Oil sign."

"It was the best of times, it was the worst of times...."

st night I dreamt I went Manderly again."

"All this happened, more or less."

Call me Ishmael.

Preface

5 Steps to a 5, Writing the AP English Essay: A Personal Trainer for the AP English Student is meant to be a supplement to both the AP English Language and Composition and the AP English Literature and Composition courses. There is no way to take the place of the instruction, interaction, feedback, and growth that takes place in the English classroom. What we hope to accomplish in this text is similar to what a personal trainer can do in the gym: provide those eager and willing to learn with information and activities designed to increase writing endurance and to enhance, fine tune, and shape the writing muscles being used in the AP English classroom.

Although specifically designed for the AP English student, the concepts, strategies, techniques, and skills examined in this book can easily be applied to college-level writing assignments across the curriculum.

Acknowledgments

Our love and appreciation to Leah and Allan for their constant support and encouragement. Our very special thanks to the many English instructors and English students who were so gracious and cooperative in granting us access to their expertise and their writing. We particularly would like to acknowledge the following educators: Diane Antonucci, Joyce Bisso, Mrs. Curran, Sandi Forsythe, Scott Honig, Barbara Inners, Mike Kramer, Margaret Rice, Joan Rosenberg, Ed Schmieder, Joanne Seale, Conni Shelnut, Doris Valliante, Rosemary Varade, Karl Zemer, and Pat Zippel.

The following students were willing to be risk-takers in allowing their writings to be incorporated into the pages of this book. They, and all of our students, are the primary reason why all of us do the work we do.

Matthew Bergman
Kate Boicourt
Jaime Burke
Alyssa Dunn
Jessica Fisher
Allison Ivans
Adam Katz
Karin Katz
Adam Kaufman
Josh Kazdin
Brian Kelly
Michael Kleinman
Daniel Lange
Tamara Lee
Michelle Rinke
Sally Robley

Dana Schenendorf
Carly Seidman
Jamelle Sing
Matthew Singer
Lenny Slutsky
Limor Spector
Alex Stein
Matthew Stoff
Lindsey Thalheim
Michael Tolkin
Danielle Tumminio
Deborah Wassel
Diana Watral
Amanda Weingarten
Zachary Zwillinger

PART I

INTRODUCTION TO THE TRAINING PROGRAM

Chapter 1

Get with the Program

"The task of a writer consists in being able to make something out of an idea."
—Thomas Mann

MEET YOUR TRAINERS

Welcome to our writing training program. Obviously, if you've decided to purchase and read this book, you already have an interest in writing. Good for you. Now, take a moment to clarify for yourself why you feel the need for training. (Check those that apply.) Perhaps:

____ You want to do well in your AP English class.
____ You freeze when writing timed essays.
____ You have trouble finding the right things to say.
____ You don't like to write exam essays.
____ You can't finish an exam essay on time.
____ You frequently have writer's block.

You might also have chosen this text because you're interested in or unsure about one or more of the following aspects of the writing process. (Check those that apply.)

____ pointers
____ planning
____ models
____ exercises
____ standards
____ evaluation

We're betting that you checked off more than one of these items. With this in mind, we're going to help you address each of these areas of concern about writing. Think of us as your AP Writing personal trainers. You have the ability, and you certainly have the desire and will. Together, we will develop and strengthen those writing muscles you need to compose effective AP English essays.

It is important to understand that the purpose of this training is to help you to develop as an AP writer throughout the year, NOT just for performance on a single exam at the end of the term. But, obviously, if you train with a specific goal in mind, your performance on the exam should be enhanced.

Having said that, there are probably many questions that you would like to ask about AP English essays. Here are a few that students have asked over the years.

QUESTIONS ABOUT THE AP ENGLISH ESSAY

What's the Difference Between the "Average High School English Essay" and One Termed an "Advanced Placement English Essay?"

You can begin to answer this question yourself just by deciding which of the following is an average high school essay and which is an AP English essay.

A

Verbal prowess has certainly played a great role in history. An individual's language is instrumental in the formation of his personal identity just as the language of a given culture plays a large part in the formation of its communal identity. Language can be a key to success in both personal and public causes. Back in the early 1800's, a young black slave, Phyllis Wheatley, set herself apart through poetry and led her readers to a fuller awareness of the plight of slaves in the United States. In the later 1800's, a very eloquent ex-slave, Frederick Douglass spoke on behalf of his race, expertly manipulating his words into an extremely effective weapon. Douglass' mastery of language earned him great respect, an invitation to the White House and the ear of the American public. In the mid-1900's, people like Martin Luther King, Jr. and Malcolm X continued Douglass' legacy through their own communication and speaking skills. These public figures and artists illustrate that those who can speak and write well readily earn people's respect, thus developing their own individuality and ability to fight for the success of their cause.

B

I have a very good friend who speaks really well. He is an example of how speaking correctly can lead to bigger and better things. He was always using words such as "like," "you know," "ain't." We all use these words when we talk to each other, but our teachers always telling us that adults in the business world don't like us to use slang like this. So, when my friend set up an appointment to interview for a summer job, we all told him not to use these words. He shrugged it off and didn't listen to us, and he didn't get the job. The second job he went to interview for was different. He didn't use those words, and he got the job. This goes to show that language can be the key to success.

So, which one did you pick as the AP English paragraph? We were fairly certain that you'd choose **A**. Now, here is the difficult part. <u>Why</u> did you pick it as the AP sample? Quickly list three reasons.

1. _____

2. _____

3. _____

Do your reasons include any of the following?

____ clear thesis
____ diction (word choice)
____ sentence variety
____ examples and details

_____ organization
_____ syntax (sentence structure)
_____ topic adherence
_____ vocabulary

You may not have used our exact words, but you probably did identify a couple of these points. Good, you DO know what an upper-level essay is. Now our job, <u>and yours</u>, is to provide opportunities for you to practice and develop the knowledge, skills, and techniques that will allow you to write a variety of successful AP English essays consistently.

What Does AP Have to Say About What an AP English Essay Actually Is?

<u>The College Board directly states that one of the goals of an AP English course is to have students become "practiced, logical, and honest writers."</u> In other words, the AP English student is expected to read, think, plan, write, and revise so that the ideas presented are clear, appropriate, and effective for the chosen purpose and audience.

In general, an AP English essay will demonstrate the writer's ability to do the following:

1. Think through an idea.
2. Plan the presentation of his or her own claim (thesis, assertion, main point).
3. Draft a text that is logically organized to effectively support the writer's idea(s) and purpose.

The AP English student <u>must</u> be able to write a well-developed, timed essay, which is most often a critical analysis, argument, or exposition in response to a specific prompt. Those who create AP English courses and exams also expect the student writer to use the elements of syntax, diction, and rhetoric appropriate to the writer's purpose and audience.

Specifically, the student who elects to take the AP English Language or Literature exam in May will be required to do the following:

ENGLISH LANGUAGE	ENGLISH LITERATURE
Part I	
1 hour multiple choice	1 hour multiple choice
Part II	
One essay that analyzes the structure of a prose piece	One essay based on given prose passage(s)

One essay that analyzes the effect of a prose piece

One argumentative essay based on a given text

One essay based on given poetry selection(s)

One essay applied to a chosen full-length work (prose or drama)

What's the Difference Between the AP English Language and the AP English Literature Essays?

Basically, the AP English Language course concentrates on reading prose from various time periods, written to achieve many different purposes. The emphasis is on writing expository, analytical, and argumentative essays.

In general, Language essays are based on nonfiction works. You may be asked to do any of the following:

- Identify the author's purpose.
- Identify the audience.
- Identify and analyze the rhetorical strategies and/or language resources used by the author to achieve his or her purpose.

AND/OR

- Defend, refute, or qualify the author's position on a given subject.

In contrast, AP Literature students read a wide range of literary works of differing genres, and the assigned essays require the writer to focus on a given piece of literature, be it prose, poetry, or drama. The emphasis is on writing analytical, expository, and argumentative essays based on the literature.

Most often, literature essays are based on prose and poetry, although selections from drama may be included. For each, you may be asked to do any of the following.

- Analyze the techniques the author uses to produce a particular effect, reveal a character, develop a concept, etc. in the work.
- Compare and contrast two pieces of literature.

AND/OR

- Compose an essay based on a given topic that must be supported with specific references to a full-length literary work of your choice.

As we progress through this text, we look carefully at the various essay formats and requirements of each course.

What Are the Expectations of the AP English Essay?

> Before addressing this question, it is important to define two terms used throughout this book. The first is PROMPT. A prompt is the professional word that indicates the "question" on which your instructor or exam creator requires you to base an assigned essay. It is your essay assignment. The second is RUBRIC. A rubric is the professional word for a set of rating standards employed by the reader(s) of a given essay.

In Chapter 5 we work with the process of reading and working the essay prompts. Right now, let's take a close look at rubrics used for evaluating an AP English essay. For both Language and Literature the <u>high</u> rated essays are assigned either a 9 or an 8. The <u>middle</u> range essays receive anywhere from 7 to 5. (There are rare instances when a 7 could be said to be in the high range.) Those essays rated 4 to 1 are considered <u>low</u> range.

It is important to note that AP English essays on the AP exam are rated with numbers ranging from 9 to 1 for each of the exam's three essays. The AP English essays are also characterized as high, middle, and low range. With a specific formula, these scores are combined with the multiple choice score, and converted into an overall rating of the complete exam that ranges from 5 to 1.

A generic set of AP Language rubrics would look like this:

A <u>9</u> essay has all the qualities of an 8 essay, and the <u>writing style</u> is especially <u>impressive</u>, as is the analysis of the specifics related to the prompt and the text.

An <u>8</u> will <u>effectively</u> and <u>cohesively</u> address the prompt. It will analyze and/or argue the elements called for in the question. And, it will do so using appropriate evidence from the given text. The essay will also show the writer's <u>ability to control language well</u>.

A <u>7</u> essay has all the properties of a 6, only with a <u>more complete</u>, well-developed analysis/argument or a more mature writing style.

A **6** essay <u>adequately</u> addresses the prompt. The analysis and/or argument is on target and makes use of appropriate specifics from the text. However, these elements are less fully developed than scores in the 7, 8, 9 range. The writer's ideas are expressed with clarity, but the writing may have a few errors in syntax and/or diction.

A **5** essay demonstrates that the writer <u>understands the prompt</u>. The analysis/argument is generally understandable but is limited or uneven. The writer's ideas are expressed clearly with a few errors in syntax or diction.

A **4** essay is <u>an inadequate response</u> to the prompt. The writer's analysis/argument of the text indicates a misunderstanding, an oversimplification, or a misrepresentation of the given passage. The writer may use evidence that is inappropriate or insufficient to support the analysis/argument.

A **3** essay is a lower 4 because it is <u>even less effective</u> in addressing the prompt. It is also less mature in its syntax and organization.

A **2** essay indicates <u>little success in speaking to the prompt</u>. The writer may misread the question, only summarize the passage, fail to develop the required analysis/argument, or simply ignore the prompt and write about another topic. The writing may also lack organization and control of language and syntax. (***Note:*** **No matter how good the summary, it will never rate more than a 2.**)

A **1** essay is a lower 2 because it is even <u>more simplistic, disorganized,</u> and <u>lacking in control of language</u>.

Although similar, there are specific differences between the Literature and Language rubrics. Here is a generic set of rubrics for an AP English Literature essay.

A **9** essay has all the qualities of an 8 essay, and the writing style is <u>especially impressive</u>, as is the <u>relationship between the text and the subtext</u> and the <u>inclusion of supporting detail</u>.

An **8** essay will <u>effectively and cohesively</u> address the prompt. It will refer to the appropriate text and provide specific and relevant references from the text to illustrate and support the writer's thesis as related to the prompt. The essay will indicate the writer's ability to perceive the relationship between text and subtext in a clear and mature writing style.

A **7** essay has all the properties of a 6, only with <u>more well-developed</u> analysis/discussion related to the prompt or a more mature writing style.

A <u>6</u> essay <u>adequately</u> addresses the prompt. The analysis/discussion is on target and makes use of appropriate references from the chosen literary work to support the thesis. However, these elements are less fully developed than scores in the 7, 8, or 9 range. The writer's ideas are expressed with clarity, but the writing may have a few errors in syntax and/or diction.

A <u>5</u> essay demonstrates that the writer <u>understands the prompt's requirements</u>. The analysis/discussion of the text and how it relates to the prompt is generally understandable, but it is limited or uneven. The writer's ideas are expressed clearly with a few errors in syntax and/or diction.

A <u>4</u> essay is <u>an inadequate response</u> to the prompt. The writer's analysis/discussion of the text and how it relates to the prompt indicates a misunderstanding, an oversimplification, or a misrepresentation of the chosen literary work. The writer may use evidence that is inappropriate or insufficient to support his or her thesis.

A <u>3</u> essay is a lower 4 because it is <u>even less effective</u> in addressing the text and how it relates to the prompt. It is also less mature in its syntax and organization.

A <u>2</u> essay indicates <u>little success in speaking to the prompt</u>. The writer may misread the question, choose an unacceptable literary work, only summarize the selection, fail to develop the required analysis, or simply ignore the prompt and write about another topic altogether. (*Note:* **No matter how good the summary may be, it will NEVER rate more than a 2.**)

A <u>1</u> essay is a lower 2 because it is even <u>more simplistic, disorganized, off topic, and lacking in control of language</u>.

Although each essay is rated on a scale of 9 to 1, your final AP English exam score is going to be a 5, 4, 3, 2, or a 1. If you'd like to transpose these numbers into letter grades, you could use the following as a guide.

ESSAYS	**EXAM**
9 = A+ / A	5 = A
8 = A / A−	4 = B
7 = B+ / B	3 = C
6 = B− / C+	2 = D
5 = C / C+	1 = F
4 = C−	
3 = D+	
2 = D	
1 = F	

So, if you receive a 7 on an AP English essay, you can think of it in terms of receiving a letter grade of B+ or an A–.

Is It Difficult to Write an Effective AP English Essay?

When we watch an athlete jumping hurdles, skiing down a precipitous slope, winning at Wimbledon, hitting a home run, or completing the marathon, we often say, "Wow, that sure looks easy." When we go to an art gallery and see a photograph by Ansel Adams or Annie Leibowitz or a painting by Pablo Picasso, we often hear people say, "I can do this. There's nothing to it."

However, doing something well is not always easy.

What is done well "appears" smooth and effortless. However, the observer is unaware of the hours, days, months, and sometimes years of practice, rehearsal, editing, and "tweaking" that go into the event or presentation.

The same is true of writing. Your favorite novelists, journalists, poets, playwrights, song writers, screenwriters, and essayists work their way through a process of observing, thinking, planning, prewriting, writing, and revision. Once their final draft is presented, you read it as a smooth, seamless piece of work. Try not to think of writing in terms of difficulty. Think of it as an ongoing process that becomes clearer and smoother with practice. Easy!

How Is This Book Going to Work?

Just as the title says—this book will be your personal training manual for writing the AP English essay. Because we're going to be your personal AP writing trainers, we will ask you to do the first thing any good trainer would do. We're going to ask you to assess your needs. First, why are you here? What do you hope to gain from spending time and effort working your way through this text? (These goals may be related to those items you checked off at the beginning of this chapter.)

My primary goals are:

_____

_____

_____

_____

Make certain your goals are reasonable and realistic. For example, having a primary goal of winning the Nobel Prize in Literature during your year as an AP English student is not realistic—a terrific dream, but not a reasonable goal for this year.

The next step is to create a profile of you as a writer. To do this, you need to answer the following questions.

MY PERSONAL WRITING PROFILE

	Yes	No
I enjoy writing.	____	____
I find writing assignments intimidating.	____	____
I become nervous when I have to write a timed essay.	____	____
I have problems figuring out how to begin my essays.	____	____
I have difficulty organizing my ideas clearly.	____	____
I always revise my essays before handing in the final draft when possible.	____	____
I usually run out of time when writing a timed essay.	____	____
I have problems finding appropriate evidence in the given texts to support my thesis.	____	____
I often wander off the topic.	____	____
I often don't know when to stop writing.	____	____
I don't like to revise my writing.	____	____
I do my best writing under pressure.	____	____
I have taken other AP courses.	____	____
I have problems writing for specific purposes (i.e. exposition, analysis, argument)	____	____
AP English exam essay prompts scare me.	____	____
For my nontimed class essays, I always have one of my peers read my essay before I hand it in.	____	____

When I write an essay that allows for planning and revision, I usually receive a ____ high, ____ middle, or ____ low grade.

When I write a timed essay under controlled conditions, I usually receive a ____ high, ____ middle, or ____ low grade.

What frustrates me most about writing in general is _____

_____

_____

What frustrates me most about timed writing is _____

_____

_____

I do my best writing when _____

_____

_____

Take a few moments to consider your responses. If you answered these questions honestly, you have created a fairly accurate profile of yourself as a writer. Are you satisfied with your writing portrait? If you are, you don't need us—give this book to a friend! If you're not (to be honest, almost no one ever is), commit yourself to a training program—and invite a friend to work out with you.

ABOUT THE BASIC TRAINING PROGRAM

THE BASIC TRAINING PROGRAM

If you are planning to use this text to its fullest, you need to look at it as a "basic training program" to develop your AP English writing potential.

You need to:

- **Make a commitment.**
- **Remember that patience is a <u>must</u>.**
- **Assess your writing strengths and weaknesses.**
- **Remember that AP English writing fitness enables you to**
  - **Write up to your potential**
  - **Write routine course assignments with understanding and effectiveness**
  - **Write under pressure**
  - **Understand unexpected and unfamiliar writing situations**
  - **Endure and withstand writing stress**
  - **Progress toward your goal of becoming a successful AP English student**

- **Know the basics**
  - ○ **Modes of discourse**
  - ○ **Rhetorical strategies and techniques**
- **Establish a writing "exercise" program and routine**
  - ○ **Read and work different types of AP English prompts**
  - ○ **Plan and prewrite**
  - ○ **Write the introduction**
  - ○ **Write the body of the essay**
  - ○ **Write the conclusion**
- **Evaluate progress and make adjustments**
  - ○ **Practice writing sample AP English exam essays**

Acting as your personal writing trainers, we have created a program to help you reach those goals you listed at the start of this section. **Remember, this book does <u>not</u> replace your AP English instructor, and it does <u>not</u> replace the work you must consistently and responsibly study and complete in your own AP English class.**

We highly recommend that you work your way through the entire book. However, be aware that this training program is designed to "pump up" all AP English students. Therefore, it will be up to you to make the important decisions about which chapters and sections of chapters to complete and how much time you will devote to any given chapter, section or activity.

Throughout this text you will find a few icons that indicate special notes and suggestions for you to consider.

This icon indicates special notes or comments that can be of help in strengthening your writing skills.

This icon indicates a particular writing activity that will introduce or strengthen a specific skill or writing technique.

This icon introduces general warm-up and work-out exercises within each chapter.

Important terms are printed in **bold,** as are important definitions, which are also highlighted for you. We indicate the location specific practice exercises in two ways: 1) The beginning of each new exercise is <u>underlined</u>; and 2) the different parts of the exercise are bulleted (•) for you to easily recognize them.

Reaching higher levels of achievement demands training, practice, and commitment. You've already taken the first step in your training to be an accomplished AP English essay writer. **Now, let's get to work.**

PART II

KNOW THE BASICS

WRITING AEROBICS

Chapter 2

The First Set of Basic Exercises for Your Writing Routine

The Four Modes of Discourse

*"Find a subject you care about and which you in your
heart feel others should care about."*
—Kurt Vonnegut, Jr.

THE BASICS

As your writing trainers, we recommend that you begin with the basics. In any physical training program, if your personal trainer told you to do five sets of *crunches,* and you didn't have the foggiest idea what a *crunch* was, you would certainly ask, "What are you talking about?" Your trainer would not only explain what it is, but he or she would also demonstrate this exercise for you to practice. Then, you'd give it a try. Slowly at first, doing only a very few. Once comfortable, you would move on to the next step. This process also holds true with our writing training program.

The first set of basics is for you to become familiar with the **four modes of discourse.** Think of these activities as "breathing exercises" for AP English writers. Don't let the professional language throw you. **Remember that a mode refers to a method or form used, and discourse is the technical term for conversation. Therefore, a mode of discourse is simply a method a writer uses to have a conversation with a particular reader/audience.**

You are already acquainted with the four modes of discourse. They are:

- **Exposition**—writing that explains or informs
- **Narration**—writing that tells a story

- **Description**—writing that appeals to the five senses
- **Argument/persuasion**—writing that presents a position in hopes that the reader will accept an assertion

So, there you have it, the four modes of discourse: exposition, narration, description, and argument.

As a warm-up exercise, let's look at four sentences that revolve around the same event. We're betting you can easily identify the mode of discourse of each statement.

Warm-up 1

_____**1.** Last night I took the train into the city with a couple of old friends to see Herman Overact as the lead in *The Crucible* at the Humongous Theater, and we had a terrific time.

_____**2.** Herman Overact's performance in Arthur Miller's *The Crucible* is an acting event not to be missed.

_____**3.** Herman Overact is playing the lead role in Arthur Miller's *The Crucible* at the Humongous Theater for the next 6 weeks.

_____**4.** Last evening, the sold-out audience buzzed with excitement as it stared wide-eyed at the stage in rapt anticipation of the appearance of Herman Overact in Miller's *The Crucible*.

That was easy enough, wasn't it? But, wait a second. Let's take a closer look at these rather simple sentences. Didn't each of them contain information, and didn't each assume that the reader would accept what was stated? Yes, to both questions. If that's the case, how can you correctly identify each of the sentences as being a specific mode of discourse?

Be aware that most writing experts agree that **a writer rarely uses only a single mode of discourse.** However, even though more than one mode may be employed, there is a **dominant mode** that fits the author's specific purpose. **The key word here is PURPOSE—why the author composed each of these sentences.** With this in mind, take another look at these four sentences. The primary purpose is what determines the primary mode of discourse. (Want to check your answers? 1. narration; 2. argument; 3. exposition; 4. description.)

Now, using this basic information, complete the following set: identify the dominant mode of discourse of each of the following excerpts. Read each carefully, keeping in mind that every author writes with a purpose. Whether you're dealing with an entire book or with a single sentence, **once you determine what the author's purpose is in a given context, you know what the dominant mode of discourse is.** Remember to ask yourself: What is the author's purpose?

Warm-up 2

_____Gertrude Stein liked to say that America entered the twentieth century ahead of the rest of the world. In 1933, in *The Autobiography of Alice B. Toklas,* she put it more strongly—that America actually created the new century.
—R. W. B. Lewis, "Writers at the Century's Turn,"
appearing in *The Writing Life*

R. W. B. Lewis tells his reader about the thoughts of Gertrude Stein. Therefore, the dominant mode of discourse is **exposition** (although you might like to argue about what Ms. Stein had to say about America).

* * * *

_____My other hangout, strategically located near the front door, was under the porch, behind the blue hydrangeas. I could see the postman's hairy legs and black socks, the skirts of my mother's bridge friends, and sometimes hear bits of forbidden conversation. . . .
—Frances Mayes, *Bella Tuscany*

In this short excerpt, Ms. Mayes attempts to have her readers sense her immediate surroundings and begin to feel her life as a child. This is an example of **description.**

* * * *

_____. . . we should not be surprised to find that [certain contemporary historians] have overlooked a tremendous contribution in the distant past that was both Celtic and Catholic, a contribution without which European civilization would have been impossible.
—Thomas Cahill, *How the Irish Saved Civilization*

Here Thomas Cahill presents a very **arguable** assertion. You can be sure that there are people who will want to agree, disagree, or qualify his thesis.

* * * *

_____I, myself, was having a terrible time reading the paper, so yesterday morning, I went to Birmingham to get my eyes checked, and lo and behold, I had on Wilbur's glasses and he had on mine. We are getting different colored ones next time.

—Fanny Flagg, *Fried Green Tomatoes at the Whistle Stop Cafe*

Fanny Flagg relates a brief <u>episode that has a beginning, a middle, and an end</u>. Although quite short; that's **narration.**

* * * *

_____So why do I write, torturing myself to put it down? Because in spite of myself I've learned some things. Without the possibility of action, all knowledge comes to one labeled "file and forget," and I can neither file nor forget.

—Ralph Ellison, *Invisible Man*

Writing in the first person, Mr. Ellison is telling his reader about <u>why he has to write</u>. Although this excerpt appears in a full-length narrative, the dominant purpose of this selection is **exposition.**

* * * *

- <u>As your next warm-up exercise</u>, identify the mode of discourse of each of the following.

Warm-up 3

_____The cold air stung us and we played till our bodies glowed. Our shouts echoed in the silent street.

—James Joyce, "Araby"

* * * *

_____A buoy is nothing but a board four or five feet long, with one end turned up; it is a reversed school-house bench, with one of the supports left and the other removed.

—Mark Twain, *Life on the Mississippi*

* * * *

_____It is rather for us to be here dedicated to the great task remaining before us—that from these honored dead we take increased devotion to that cause for which they gave the last full measure of devotion—that we here highly resolve that these dead shall not have died in vain—that this nation, under God, shall have a new birth of freedom—and that government of the people, by the people, for the people, shall not perish from the earth.

—Abraham Lincoln, "Address at the Dedication of Gettysburg Cemetery as a War Memorial"

* * * *

_____The journey took about a week each way, and each day had my parents both in its grip. Riding behind my father I could see that the road had him by the shoulders, by the hair under his driving cap. It took my mother to make him stop. I inherited this nervous energy in the way I can't stop writing on a story.

—Eudora Welty, *One Writer's Beginnings*

* * * *

_____The law can only do so much in removing the burden of living vigilantly and responsibly, for our own sake and for our children's. So click off the Internet and go for a brisk walk. You look as though you could use some exercise.

—George F. Will, "Sex, Fat and Responsibility," *Newsweek*, July 7, 1997

* * * *

_____Beside us, on an overstuffed chair, absolutely motionless, was a platinum-blond woman in her forties, wearing a black silk dress and a strand of pearls. Her long legs were crossed; she supported her head on her fist.

—Annie Dillard, *Teaching a Stone to Talk*

* * * *

_____So I was a lucky child too. I played with a set of paper dolls called "The Family of Dolls," four in number, who came with the factory-assigned names of Dad, Mom, Sis, and Junior. . . . Now I've replaced the dolls with a life.

—Barbara Kingsolver, "Stone Soup," *High Tide in Tucson*

_____I learned this, at least, by my experiment; that if one advances confidently in the direction of his dreams, and endeavors to live the life which he has imagined, he will meet with a success unexpected in common hours.

—Henry David Thoreau, *Walden*

_____Antigua used to have a splendid library, but in The Earthquake (everyone talks about it that way—The Earthquake; we Antiguans, for I am one, have a great sense of things, and the more meaningful the thing, the more meaningless we make it) the library building was damaged.

—Jamaica Kincaid, *A Small Place*

_____Partially covering his shaggy blond hair was one of those blue baseball caps with gold braid on the bill and a sailfish patch sewn onto the peak. Covering his eyes and part of his face was a pair of those stupid-looking '50s-style wrap-around sunglasses.

—Cherokee Paul McDonald, "A View from the Bridge,"
Sunshine Magazine

(You can find the answers on page 1383.)

You should give yourself time to practice this recognition skill as you read your academic assignments, as you peruse periodicals, and as you read for pure enjoyment. Stop every so often to ask yourself what the author's purpose is for the entire selection or for a specific portion of it. Then categorize it as exposition, narration, description, or argument. Why not invite a group of your peers to practice with you? As with any skill, the more you practice, the easier it becomes.

* * * *

If you can recognize the modes of discourse, you should be able to identify them in your own writing. Because we're only doing basic exercises at this point, <u>try your hand at composing a set of sentences</u>, each of which revolves around the same subject but with a different purpose.

Warm-up 4: Follow Our Lead

For example: <u>Subject: my love of shoes</u>

Exposition: I own several pairs of Kangaroo sneakers. They take up most of the shoe space in my closet. But, I can never have enough of them.

Narration: Yesterday, I saw an ad in the newspaper for a 60 percent sale on Kangaroo sneakers at the Bullseye department store. I can't resist either Kangaroo sneakers or a bargain, so I called two of my friends, and off we went. You would not believe the fun we had. Crowds, choices, credit cards, and lunch. My closet has never been so colorfully stuffed.

Description: My closet is boxed in by shoes. Shoes lined up on the top shelf, shoes straddling a rack on the floor, and shoes nestling in hanging pockets on the door. I like to think of it as my Kangaroo cage.

Argument: I've owned many different brands of sneakers, but none is as comfortable, colorful, long-wearing, and reasonably priced as Kangaroos. No other sneaker even comes close.

- <u>Now, it's your turn.</u>

write-a-mins

My subject is _____

Exposition: _____

_____

_____

_____

_____

Narration: _____

_____

_____

_____

_____

Description: _____

_____

_____

_____

_____

Argument: _____

_____

_____

_____

_____

If you have any doubt, or if you would like to check your "take" on your samples with the ideas of others, why not invite your peer group to complete this exercise and cross check and discuss them with each other? If you would like to post these samples, you can go to our Website <www.clearestideas.com> and log them on for comments and identification from other students across the nation.

Chapter 3

"Stretching" and "Aerobic" Exercises for Your Writing Routine

Rhetorical Strategies

"Why do writers write? Because it isn't there."
—Thomas Berger

The second section of this book is like the stretching and aerobic exercises you do before you get down to the nitty-gritty fitness routine of building strength and flexibility and sculpting your muscles. So far you've been introduced to the first set of writing exercises in our training program: recognizing the four modes of discourse and writing examples of these (exposition, narration, description, and argument). Now, it's time to become familiar with the next set of writing aerobics.

RHETORICAL STRATEGIES

This second set of exercises will develop and strengthen your knowledge of rhetorical strategies.

 **Keep in mind that your familiarity with the professional terminology used in the course will contribute to your strength and flexibility when analyzing texts and writing about them.**

The first term you must become comfortable with is **rhetorical strategy.** Simply, rhetoric is the method a writer or speaker uses to communicate ideas to an audience. And, you know what a strategy is; it's a plan or a course of action taken to reach a goal. Therefore, **a rhetorical**

strategy is the specific approach or approaches a writer employs to achieve an intended purpose. Before going any further, it's important to understand what **purpose** is. Purpose is the reason why you or any other person chooses to communicate with an audience—the goal, the intended effect. The basic purposes are:

- **To inform**
- **To entertain**
- **To question**
- **To argue**
- **To elicit an emotional response**

It doesn't matter whether it's Shakespeare, Strindberg, Steinbeck, or Sally Student, every author has a desire to explain, narrate, describe, or argue a specific topic. HOW the writer accomplishes this is called a rhetorical strategy. Rhetorical strategies include:

- **Cause/effect**
- **Classification/division**
- **Contrast/comparison**
- **Definition**
- **Description**
- **Exemplification**
- **Narration**
- **Process/analysis**

It doesn't matter how long or short the piece of writing is, an author will use one or more of these strategies to develop an overall purpose. One of the writer's first considerations MUST be the audience. For example, if a mathematician wanted to explain a mathematical principle to a general audience, the speaker or writer might contrast and compare several familiar objects or phenomena and narrate a personal story to illustrate the principle. However, if addressing a mathematics symposium, the speaker might choose to use process and analysis. It's all a matter of choice and knowing who the audience is.

In this chapter we work with the personal essay form and prewriting activities using the rhetorical strategies in writing personal essays. If you can perform these exercises well, you can duplicate the process in formal, academic essays. AND, you will be more easily able to handle essay assignments that ask you to analyze a given text.

EXEMPLIFICATION

The most frequently used rhetorical strategy is exemplification/example. Whatever the subject, course, level of sophistication, or audience, examples are of utmost importance. The fundamental ways a writer can illustrate, support, and clarify ideas include referring to a:

- **sample**
- **detail**
- **person**
- **typical event**

Here are two very brief excerpts from longer works that illustrate the use of examples.

Even very inconsistent discipline may fit a child to live in an inconsistent world. A Balinese mother would play on her child's fright by shouting warnings against nonexistent dangers: "Look out! Fire! . . . Snake! . . . Tiger!" The Balinese system required people to avoid strange places without inquiring why.

—Margaret Mead, *A Way of Seeing*

The subject of this piece is obviously discipline, and Ms. Mead uses the example of a Balinese mother to illustrate how Balinese children are trained to avoid danger.

The new bread-and-circuses approach to mall building was ventured in 1985 by the four Ghermezian brothers . . . builders of Canada's $750 million West Edmonton Mall, which included a water slide, an artificial lake, a miniature-golf course, a hockey rink, and forty-seven rides in an amusement park known as Fantasyland.

—David Guterson, "Enclosed. Encyclopedic. Endured. The Mall of America," *Harper's Magazine*

Mr. Guterson's subject is a particular type of mall—the "bread and circus mall." He chooses to exemplify what this type of mall is with the West Edmonton Mall.

* * * *

Our first exercise is a practice in recognizing the use of examples when you see it. It's easy AND quick. For our purposes, here, we are only going to concentrate on an excerpt. Just take your favorite magazine or newspaper and read what you ordinarily read in this periodical, and choose ONE of the articles to work with.

Warm-up 1

- The subject of the article is _____.
- The purpose of the article is _____.
- The audience for this article is _____.
- I've chosen to work with paragraph_____, and this paragraph uses (#) _____ examples.

Repeat this exercise with other readings until you feel familiar and comfortable with the task of recognizing examples when you see them. Also, be aware of the use of examples in your classroom texts. Remember that checking with a peer can be helpful to both of you.

This next exercise will work with your ability and flexibility to choose a subject and appropriate examples to illustrate it. Keep in mind that the only way a writer can honestly work with an idea is to choose something that is personally familiar or important. For example, suppose a writer chose the subject "my personal writing idiosyncrasies," with the purpose of illustrating these quirks to a general audience. What could be some examples of personal idiosyncrasies? How about biting nails, playing with hair, tapping a pen, scratching the head, crossing and uncrossing legs, saying "okay" at the ends of sentences, brushing back hair, humming while writing, doodling using only circles . . . You get the idea.

Okay, it's time for you to cite your examples.

Warm-up 2

- My subject is _____.
- My purpose is _____

_____.

- My audience is _____.

- Possible examples of the subject are _____

_____

_____

_____

Easy, right? The next step is to choose which of the examples would best illustrate and support the subject and purpose.

> At this time, we would like to introduce you to *OUR WRITER* who will be authoring the writing samples we use throughout Chapters 3 and 4. He will be following the text and will complete the exercises just as you will. You will be able to read his responses and our comments on his writing.

So, our writer decides to use <u>tapping a pen</u>, <u>brushing back hair</u>, <u>humming while writing</u>, and <u>doodling using only circles</u>.

You already have your subject, purpose, audience, and possible examples in mind; now you need to choose which of these examples will BEST serve your subject/purpose. Most college level or AP essays are about 500 to 800 words long. You can't cover everything in an essay of this length. So, you have to choose to work with a limited number of examples. Remember, our writer chose four. Go back to your list of possibles. Given the limits of this personal essay, which examples would you choose that would BEST support and illustrate your subject and purpose?

- _____

- _____

- _____

- _____

Good, you've chosen your examples. Now, you need to make some decisions about organization.

<u>This is your next exercise</u>. How will you present your examples to your audience? You can choose from among the following organizational patterns:

✓ spatial (where it fits within a physical area)
✓ chronological (time sequence, from first to last)
✓ most important to least important
✓ the one I want to emphasize first

✓ least important to most important
✓ the one I want to emphasize last

Because our writer's purpose is to show the reader the quirky movements he goes through during the process of beginning to write, the choice is chronological order: brushing back hair, tapping the pen, doodling using circles, and finally humming while writing. <u>Now, it's your turn.</u>

Warm-up 3

- I'm going to use the following organizational

  pattern: _____

- In the order they will be used, my examples are:

_____

_____

_____

You're beginning to work up some writing steam now. Stay with it. Having chosen the organizational pattern and the examples that fit it, the writer is ready to construct the thesis statement. Let's review. We've decided on a subject, purpose, audience, appropriate examples, and their organization. How does the writer let the reader know all of this in a single sentence? **The writer creates a thesis statement or assertion.**

Not wishing to give away all of the examples at once, our writer composes the following thesis statement: *Before actually putting pen to paper, I perform a peculiar prewriting ritual*. This sentence does its job. We know the subject—quirky prewriting activity. We are aware of the purpose—illustrate the ritual. We don't know the specific examples that the writer will develop, but we <u>are</u> expecting some, and we are expecting these examples to be in chronological order because of the use of the word *Before*.

Following this demonstration, you should be able to construct a thesis statement that lets your chosen audience know the subject, sense the purpose, and recognize the organization of your examples.

- Here's my thesis: _____

_____

_____

_____

_____

Checklist

Does this statement clearly indicate the

subject/topic?____yes ____no

Does this statement give the reader a clear idea of the purpose?

____yes ____no

Does this statement indicate the actual examples that will be developed?

____yes ____no

Does this statement hint at the examples that will be used?

____yes ____no

Does this statement give the reader an idea of the organization?

____yes ____no

With the answers to each of these questions in mind, you may want to revise your thesis statement.

- Here is my revised thesis: _____

_____

_____

_____

_____.

If you were to read the complete essay based on our writer's thesis, you would be asking yourself how well the writer performs each of the above exercises, and you would also need to ask yourself the following:

- Do the examples adequately support the thesis?
- Are the examples representative of indicated categories?
- Are the examples relevant to the purpose?

It doesn't matter for which class or for which topic, if the requirement is to use examples to develop a subject, you can use these exercises in developing your presentation. If you can easily perform these exercises for brief texts, you can easily perform them for longer texts.

CONTRAST/COMPARISON

Another rhetorical strategy available to you is **contrast/comparison (c/c)**. Next to exemplification, contrast/comparison is the most widely used method of development for essays in the academic world. As an AP English student, you're already very familiar with comparison and contrast. **Contrast is interested in the differences, and comparison is interested in the similarities. It's rather important to know that the term *comparison* is often used alone when referring to BOTH types of analysis.** (Yes, it is also analysis because you are taking something apart.) Here are three brief excerpts that illustrate contrast/comparison.

> If there ever were two cultures in which differences of the [uses of space] are marked, it is in the educated (public school) English and the middle-class Americans. One of the basic reasons for this wide disparity is that in the United States, we use space as a way of classifying people and activities; whereas, in England, it is the social system that determines who you are.
>
> —Edward T. Hall, *The Hidden Dimension*

Mr. Hall's subject is the use of space, and, in this instance, he chooses to **contrast** different strata of English and American culture.

* * * *

> Different as [Grant and Lee] were—in background, in personality, in underlying aspiration—these two great soldiers had much in common. Under everything else, they were marvelous fighters. Furthermore, their fighting qualities were really very much alike.
>
> —Bruce Catton, "Grant and Lee: A Study in Contrasts,"
> *The American Story*

The subject for Mr. Catton is Grant and Lee. In this excerpt, he concentrates on the **similarities** between the two fighters.

* * * *

> Young men, in the conduct and manage of actions, embrace more than they can hold; stir more than they can quiet; fly to the end, without consideration of the means and degrees; pursue some few examples which they have chanced upon absurdity; care not to innovate, which draws unknown inconveniences; use extreme remedies at first; and, that which doubleth all errors, will not acknowledge or retract them; like an unready horse that will neither stop nor turn. Men of age object too much, consult too long, adventure too little, repent too soon, and seldom drive business home to the full period, but content themselves with a mediocrity of success.
>
> —Francis Bacon, "Of Youth and Age"

The subject of Bacon's presentation is most probably youth and age, and in this excerpt the basis of **comparison** is the actions of young and older men with regard to success in business.

* * * *

Our first contrast/comparison (c/c) exercise will involve your recognizing contrast/comparison when you see it. As with examples, this activity is quick and easy. Again, using your favorite periodical or newspaper, locate an article that seems to use c/c. Choose an excerpt from this article to work with.

Warm-up 4

- The subject of the article is _____.
- The basis for comparison is _____.
- The purpose of the article is _____.
- The audience for this article is _____.
- I've chosen to work with paragraph _____.
- There are (#) _____ items being _____ compared _____ contrasted _____ compared & contrasted.
- These items are _____.

Repeat this exercise with other readings until you feel familiar and comfortable with the task of recognizing contrast/comparison when you see it.

A clear comparison depends not only on choosing two things that can be compared, and being aware of your purpose and audience, but also on a balanced organization. There are THREE primary ways to organize a c/c presentation: subject-by-subject, point-by-point, and the combination approach.

The subject-by-subject pattern presents the details about the first item and then the details about the second. For example, our writer wants to compare two film directors. The areas to consider might include subject matter, cinematography, handling of actors, or handling of script. The subject-by-subject method presents all of the points about the first director and then all of the points about the second. An example might look like this:

I. First Director
    A. Subject matter   C. Handling of actors
    B. Cinematography   D. Handling of scripts

II. Second Director
A. Subject matter
B. Cinematography
C. Handling of actors
D. Handling of scripts

On the other hand, organizing the presentation point-by-point, the writer discusses one point at a time, going back and forth between the two. The outline might look like the following example.

I. Subject Matter
A. First director
B. Second director
II. Cinematography
A. First director
B. Second director

III. Handling of Actors
A. First Director
B. Second director
IV. Handling of Scripts
A. First director
B. Second director

In longer texts, a writer may choose to employ a combination of these two approaches. But, it is rare to see this method of presentation in shorter pieces of writing.

NO MATTER WHICH ORGANIZATIONAL PATTERN YOU CHOOSE, MAKE CERTAIN THAT YOU FOLLOW IT THROUGHOUT YOUR ESSAY.

This exercise will further develop your ability and flexibility to choose a subject for comparison, the areas to be compared and the organization of the presentation. Remember to choose a subject that is familiar to you and of interest. You've seen what our writer has done; now it's your turn to practice this exercise.

Warm-up 5

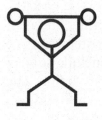

- I would like to compare _____ to _____.

- My purpose is to _____.

- My audience is _____.

- The basis for comparison is _____.

- The points I could include are _____

  _____

  _____

  _____

Before planning the organization, make certain to choose points that are relevant to both items being compared. Circle those points that you have decided BEST suit your subject, basis for comparison, and purpose.

- I have decided to use the_____subject-by-subject_____point-by-point approach.
- Below is a brief outline.

_____

_____

_____

_____

_____

_____

ULTA-MINDS

Don't work in a vacuum. Share your ideas with one or more of your AP classmates. Share them with your AP instructor. The more input you can gather the better. The more practice you can fit in the better.

Our writer chooses to employ the subject-by-subject method, and the resulting thesis statement is: *Sam Peckinpah and Ingmar Bergman are two film directors with completely different styles.* This thesis is on target. We know the subject—Sam Peckinpah and Ingmar Bergman. We know the basis for comparison—styles of directing. We are aware of the purpose—to compare the two directors. We don't know the specific organizational pattern at this time, but we could conclude that it will be subject-by-subject based on the way the sentence is worded.

Using this sample as a starting point, you should be able to construct a thesis statement that will let your reader know the subject, basis for comparison and the general purpose.

- Here is my thesis: _____

_____

_____

_____

_____.

Checklist

Does this thesis clearly indicate the subject

for comparison? ____yes ____no

Does this statement indicate the basis for comparison?

____yes ____no

Does the statement give a general idea as to purpose?

____yes ____no

Does the statement give a hint of the organization?

____yes ____no

With the answers to each of these questions in mind, you may wish to revise your thesis.

• I've decided to revise my original thesis. Here is the revision:

_____

_____

_____

_____

_____.

If you were to read the complete c/c essay based on our writer's thesis, you would be asking yourself how well the writer performs each of the above exercises, and you would also need to ask yourself the following.

• Are the points for each subject developed adequately?
• Are the points relevant to the purpose and thesis?
• Is each of the body paragraphs balanced, using the pattern established in the first body paragraph?

* * * *

Here's an exercise that may even prove to be helpful as you make decisions about which colleges you want to attend.

1. List those qualities you think are important in a college or university.
2. List the colleges that interest you.
3. Set up an organizational outline or chart just as you did in the last exercise.

You could choose to set up your comparison using college-by-college or quality-by-quality. Not only will you get further practice with the basics of contrast/comparison, but you will also be performing needed investigations to make an informed decision about your choice of a college or university.

CAUSE AND EFFECT

You know about cause and effect. If you exercise your body every day, you will grow stronger and more flexible. If you perform the writing exercise diligently, your writing will become more clear, more mature, and more confident. **That's cause and effect (c/e). As a result of *A*, *B* occurs.** This linkage of events occurs along a timeline. Whether you're trying to figure out why your car is guzzling gas, the causes of road rage, the result of using hair spray as an insect repellent, or the influence of one novelist on another, you are involved with cause and effect.

Below are a few brief excerpts that make use of cause and effect. When considering causes, keep in the following in mind. There are

- primary causes
- contributing causes
- immediate causes
- remote causes.

For example, if someone were to ask you why you're applying to college, you could respond in any number of ways:

✓ My parents are forcing me to apply. (immediate)
✓ My grandmother went to college. (remote)
✓ I want to have a successful career in ichthyology. (primary)
✓ I like the sound of "college graduate." (contributing)

The same situation holds true for effects or consequences of actions. There are primary and secondary effects as well as immediate and remote.

✓ My parents will be happy. (immediate)
✓ My kids will go to college. (remote)
✓ I will be the head of a new Marine World. (primary)
✓ People will respect me. (contributing)

Below are three brief excerpts which make use of cause and effect.

Some of this shift away from words—toward images—can be attributed to our ever-growing multilingual population. But for many people,

reading is passé or impractical or, like, so totally unnecessary in this day and age.

—Linton Weeks, "The No-Book Report: Skim It and Weep," *The Washington Post*, May 14, 2001

The subject of this passage is reading, and Mr. Weeks is interested in at least two reasons why the population is reading less.

* * * *

Actually, no one can understand the action of Mrs. Parks unless he realizes that eventually the cup of endurance runs over, and the human personality cries out, "I can take it no longer." Mrs. Park's refusal to move back was her intrepid affirmation that she had had enough.

—Martin Luther King, Jr., *Stride Toward Freedom*

Martin Luther King, Jr.'s subject here is Mrs. Parks and the reasons she refused to move to the back of the bus. While we are not told in this selection the immediate cause of her refusal, we are certainly hearing Reverend King's belief as to the primary cause.

* * * *

In Ireland, as food historian Reay Tannahill describes it, 'the potato famine meant more than food scarcity.' It meant no seed potatoes from which to grow next year's crop. It meant that the pig or cow which would normally have been sold to pay the rent had to be slaughtered, because there was nothing to fatten it on.

—Mary Talbot, "The Potato: How It Shaped the World," *Newsweek*, October 12, 1991

In these sentences, Ms. Talbot's subject is the Irish potato famine and, not only its primary result, but also its secondary effects.

* * * *

As we have been doing, <u>this exercise will build your strength in recognizing the use of cause and effect when you see it</u>. Take the periodical you read most often and find an ad that really captures your attention and probably makes use of cause and effect. (Just a hint—almost every ad in existence uses c/e.)

Warm-up 6

• The subject of the ad is _____.

• The purpose of the ad is _____.

- The audience for this ad is _____.

- The ad is more interested in _____ cause(s) _____ effects(s)

- From what I can deduce, the cause(s) in this ad is/are _____

  _____

  _____

  (Place a *P* above a primary cause, a *C* above contributing causes, *I* for immediate, and *R* for remote.)

- The ad indicates the following effect(s): _____

  _____

  _____

  (Place a *P* above a primary effect, an *S* for secondary, an *I* for immediate, and an *R* for remote.)

We recommend that you also do this exercise using your own textbooks, especially in the sciences and history. You'll find that they are chock full of examples of cause and effect. This should provide you with myriad possibilities to practice, practice, practice, both alone and with your peers.

Okay, so you can easily recognize cause and effect when you see it. But, can you, as a writer, choose a subject and determine how you are going to examine cause and effect in relation to it? Well, work through this next exercise, and you'll no doubt find it easier to do this choosing and deciding.

For example, our writer has chosen a subject—vegetarianism—and has decided to inform the reader about the effects that becoming a vegetarian has had on his life. Given this subject, purpose, and audience, the best course of action would be to emphasize EFFECT. The question remains whether to choose one effect or several. To start the process, our writer lists all those effects which immediately come to mind: old friends and family think I'm weird; I become very good friends with my neighborhood greengrocer; I feel better; I have less guilt about food; I save money; I sleep better; I no longer fear being a vegetarian; I make new friends; I lose weight; I create my own vegetarian website; I add new shelves of vegetarian cookbooks to my library; my refrigerator looks like a large green salad. . . . Need we go on?

Knowing that a decision has to be made, our writer spends some time thinking about the list of consequences. "Do I want to concentrate only on the primary effect? Do I want to develop the primary, plus the secondary? Or, do I want to consider the immediate effect and forget about the remote ones?" The choice is made! Our writer will concentrate on just one effect—the response of his friends and family. This will entail both immediate as well as remote consequences. And, our writer is aware not to settle for one cause or effect when there could be more

Now you try it. We'll give you the subject this time. Your subject is **the popularity of a TV show, movie, rock star, book. (Choose one.)**

Warm-up 7

- My specific subject is _____.
- My audience is _____.
- My purpose is _____.
- I'm going to **emphasize** _____ cause, _____ effect, _____ causes, _____ effects.
- I believe I'll use one or more of the following in relation to what I decided to emphasize:

____ primary cause	____ primary effect
____ contributing cause(s)	____ secondary effect(s)
____ immediate cause	____ immediate effect
____ remote cause(s)	____ remote effect(s)

Don't write that thesis statement just yet. You still need to make some decisions about your organization. Do you want to present your ideas in chronological order, from most to least important, or vice versa? Our writer has decided to use chronological order. What arrangement will you use to organize your ideas?

____ chronological ____ most to least important

____ least to most important

It's now time to write that thesis statement. Our writer thinks, doodles for a while, scribbles a bit, writes a first draft, thinks, and finally writes the following revised thesis: *My family and friends no longer see me as the potential Himalayan hermit they first imagined when they became aware that I had become a vegetarian.* Notice the indicators of chronology: *no longer, first imagine, when.* Notice also that this sentence gives the reader fair warning that what follows is going to center on the effect on family and friends.

Okay. You have all of the needed information about your own subject in front of you. Your job is to compose your own thesis statement for a cause and effect presentation.

Warm-up 8

- My initial thesis is _____
  _____
  _____
  _____
  _____.

Checklist

Does this thesis statement clearly indicate the
   subject? ____yes ____no

Does this statement make it clear to the reader that this is a cause and
   effect presentation? ____yes ____no

Does the give the reader a general idea as to purpose? ____yes ____no

Does the statement give the reader an idea as to what the emphasis
   will be? ____yes ____no

Does the statement give an indication what the organization will be?
   ____yes ____no

   With these answers in hand, you may want to revise your original
thesis statement.

- Here's my revised thesis: _____
  _____
  _____
  _____
  _____.

   If you were to read a complete cause and effect essay based on our
writer's thesis, as in any analysis of a text, you would ask yourself how
and how well the author performs the tasks you have been practicing.
You would also need to ask yourself the following.

- Have the causes and effects been clearly connected to the subject?
- Given the subject and purpose, are there any obvious or needed causes
  or effects that are missing?
- Is the organization appropriate for the subject and purpose?

CLASSIFICATION AND DIVISION

Classification and division are true work horses of rhetorical strategies. You can find yourself using classification and division for almost any purpose and for almost any subject. **Basically, classification is the process of grouping items together that share important characteristics. Classification goes from specific to general, from small groups or examples to larger, more general categories. Division goes from the whole (general) to the parts (specific categories, groups, examples).** It may be easier to visualize the difference between the two if we take a look at a football team. If I wanted to discuss the <u>TYPES</u> of football teams, I would be dealing with <u>classification</u>. However, if I wanted to examine the <u>ORGANIZATION</u> of a football team or who is on the team, I would be using <u>division</u>.

Here are two brief excerpts that use classification and/or division.

Aaron takes me only to art films. That's what I call them, anyway: strange movies with vague poetic images I don't always understand, long dreamy movies about a distant Technicolor past, even longer black-and-white movies about the general meaninglessness of life. . . . Pete takes me only to movies that he thinks have redeeming social value.
—Susan Allen Toth, "Cinematypes," *Harper's Magazine,* 1980

Here is a rather interesting passage. Although the subject of the entire essay might very well be this writer's two friends and informing the reader how she relates to each, this particular section is about the types of movies the two friends like: art movies and movies with "redeeming social value." And, even though most instructors will advise you to choose a classification principle that has more than two categories associated with it, in this instance, Ms. Toth is referring to only two. Each of these will probably have subclasses.

* * * *

I spend a great deal of my time thinking about the power of language— the way it can evoke emotion, a visual image, a complex idea, or a simple truth. Language is the tool of my trade. And I use them all—all the Englishes I grew up with.
—Amy Tan, "Mother Tongue," *Threepenny Review,* 1990

It's quite obvious from this very short bit of text that Ms Tan's subject is language, her purpose to inform, and her classification is going to revolve around several types of English.

* * * *

Now, you try it. Following our routine, the first classification exercise will provide you with practice recognizing classification when you see it. Take a close look at your history and science textbooks. We guarantee that you will find examples of classification in these books. Because you're using a textbook, the purpose is obviously to inform a student audience.

Warm-up 9

- I chose to look in the following textbook: _____.

- I located one, and its subject is _____.

- The basis for the classification (classification principle) is _____ _____ .

- There are _____ groups within this classification principle.

Don't stop with just one sample; try many, and get your AP classmates to do some with you. They're easy to find and will give you and your peers valuable practice.

Not only do you need to be aware of the above guidelines, but you must also be certain that your groupings are:

✓ Uniform—This is the principle on which the groups are created. It's the umbrella under which all of your categories fit.
✓ Consistent—All the categories truly fit into the principle you've created.
✓ Exclusive—No category overlaps another.
✓ Complete—All of the examples you're including in your presentation are grouped into the appropriate category based on your purpose

As an example, suppose our writer decides to compose a humorous essay that classifies certain types of dogs.

✓ The basis for the classification will be how dogs view themselves in relation to their owners.
✓ The categories will be: 1) those who see themselves as king or queen; 2) those who see their owners as king or queen; and 3) those who see themselves as court jester.
✓ We may have a problem with number 3. Is it possible that 3 overlaps with 2? Yes. Our writer realizes that a court jester is under the control of the king or queen. So, it will be a subclass of 2.

Try this easy one yourself. Consider your friends as the subject for a classification essay.

Warm-up 10

- My subject is <u>my friends</u>.
- My purpose is _____.
- My audience is _____.
- My classification principle is _____
  _____.
- My categories are: _____
  _____.

Checklist

I've checked to see that all the categories fit
   into my principle of classification.

_____yes _____no

I've made certain no category overlaps with any other. _____yes _____no

The next step in prewriting the classification essay is to consider the organization and the details. Think about how to present the material. Based on purpose and audience, decide among chronological, logical (how the groups relate to each other and to the classification principle), least to most important or vice versa. That done, choose which details will BEST support the thesis and purpose.

With this information in mind, our writer chooses the logical approach for organizing his material and decides that the details will all revolve around relationships—dog to owner and owner to dog. Our writer creates this thesis statement: ***Anyone who has ever owned or been owned by a dog is familiar with the two basic categories of man's best friend: dogs who believe they are king and dogs who believe their owners are king.*** The juxtaposition of dog, ownership, and king places the subject and principle of classification into a humorous vein for a general audience. Rightfully, the reader will be expecting the writer to provide subgroups and appropriate examples within each subgroup.

<u>You're next</u>. Go back to your prewriting notes above. Consider that information, plus the need to <u>decide on an organizational pattern and appropriate details</u>.

Warm-up 11

- I've decided to use the following as my organizational pattern _____ chronological ___ logical
  ___ least to most important

- I chose this organizational pattern because _____

  _____ .

- Some of the appropriate subgroups I should include are:

  _____

  _____

  _____

- This is the first draft of my thesis statement: _____

  _____

  _____

  _____

  _____

Carefully read your thesis and ask yourself if the purpose is clear, if the subject and principle of classification is given, as well as an indication of the organization and possible subgroups. Once you've done this, ask yourself whether or not the first draft of your thesis statement needs to be revised. If it does, rewrite below.

- This is my revised thesis: _____

  _____

  _____

  _____

  _____ .

PROCESS

If you were to take a careful look at the work you've just done in the last section of this chapter, you could not help but notice that we provide you with instructions about HOW to do the prewriting work for the classification/division essay. This is a demonstration of a process that just happens to be the next rhetorical strategy we will develop. **Process analysis is the method of describing how to perform a task or explaining how something works by breaking it down into the chronologically ordered steps that lead to the goal.** We use this strategy quite often, from telling someone how to set the VCR, to cookbook instructions on baking a cake; from telling your friend how to get a particular teacher to allow him to hand in a paper late, to explaining to your parents why you did not do well on a math exam. You might have noticed that there may be **two types of process analysis,** and you would be right. Each serves a specific purpose.

✓ Process analysis that is **directive** provides step-by-step instructions.
✓ Process analysis that is **informative** explains how something works or is done.

Take a look at the following excerpts that use process analysis.

> If you don't know where to begin [the letter], start with the present moment: I'm sitting at the kitchen table on a rainy Saturday morning. Everyone is gone and the house is quiet. Let your simple description of the present moment lead to something else, let the letter drift gently along.
>
> —Garrison Keillor, *We Are Still Married*

Mr. Keillor's subject is how to write a letter. From this brief excerpt, it seems the process analysis will be **directive** because the author is beginning to give the chronologically ordered steps for writing a letter.

* * * *

> In personal situations, complaints may come the way of vague statements. . . . While there may be more serious relationship issues at hand, there is a specific way to help the situation. What you want to do is to have him get as specific as possible about what is bothering him.
>
> —David Lieberman, *Get Anyone to Do Anything: Never Feel Powerless Again–With Psychological Secrets to Control and Influence Every Situation*

Even the title of this author's book gives a clear indication that we are dealing with process. Notice that the writer uses the phrase *there is a specific way*. This is a clue that this part of the text is using a **directive** process analysis. And, from other wording in this selection, informative analysis is also possible.

* * * *

It's time for you to try recognizing process analysis. As we've said before, you can find examples of this strategy almost anywhere. Why not use your textbooks, especially in such "lab courses" as biology, chemistry, or physics. That's easy pickin's. For more sophisticated practice, try locating examples in the magazines and periodicals you read. For every example you can pinpoint, determine the following:

Warm-up 12

- The text I found this example of process analysis in is _____ _____.
- The subject is _____.
- The audience is _____.
- The purpose is (What is the reader supposed to do with this information?): _____.
- The process analysis is primarily_____directive _____informative.

Our now famous writer is in a sarcastic mood and has decided to write a process essay about drivers' tests. Because this will be for a general audience, and because the writer wants to be a bit humorous, the specific subject will be how NOT to pass a driver's test. Going for humor, our author will use a directive approach.

You're up! Think about important events in your life: holidays, birthdays, other celebrations. What processes are involved? Think about activities in your life, those you like and those you dislike: dining with your parents' friends, meeting with your date's parents, dealing with an angry teacher, enjoying a baseball game, eating pizza, and so on.

Warm-up 13

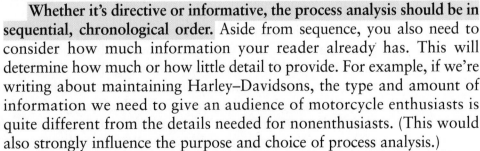

- My subject is _____.
- My audience is _____.
- My purpose is _____.
- My approach will be_____directive_____informative.

Whether it's directive or informative, the process analysis should be in sequential, chronological order. Aside from sequence, you also need to consider how much information your reader already has. This will determine how much or how little detail to provide. For example, if we're writing about maintaining Harley–Davidsons, the type and amount of information we need to give an audience of motorcycle enthusiasts is quite different from the details needed for nonenthusiasts. (This would also strongly influence the purpose and choice of process analysis.)

Our writer knows that his audience is one that has experience as drivers; therefore, they have a good idea what a driver's test is like. He decides to use the following steps in sequence.

1. Be on time.
2. Be familiar with your test car.
3. Greet your inspector.
4. Listen to the instructor at all times.
5. Keep your eyes on the road.
6. Keep your hands on the wheel.
7. Precisely follow the inspector's instructions.
8. Say a prayer of thanks when you finish.

Step right up! You know your subject, audience, and purpose. Now, consider how much your readers already know about your subject. This should give you an idea about the type of information and how much added detail you must provide.

Warm-up 14

- The steps in the order I would like to use them are:

1. _____

2. _____

3. _____

4. _____

5. _____

6. _____

7. _____

8. _____

You don't have to use all eight steps; in fact, you might very well use fewer or even more. This is all dependent on your purpose, audience, and length of presentation.

Once this is completed, it's time to write the thesis statement for the process analysis. Our writer has thought about all of the prewriting activities so far and has written the following thesis: ***Having been through the trials, tribulations, and pitfalls of this American rite of passage, I believe I'm wise enough to advise prospective highway jockeys how NOT to pass their driver's test.*** Drivers' tests, a humorous purpose, a general audience, and a directive process analysis are all indicated in this sentence.

You can do this. Using the information from the prewriting you've already developed, try your hand at composing the thesis statement for your process analysis essay.

Warm-up 15

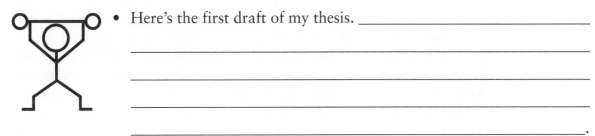

- Here's the first draft of my thesis. _____

_____

_____

_____

_____.

Checklist

As you have done with the previous strategies, carefully reread your thesis and complete each of the following:

My subject is clearly indicated.____yes____no

It's easy to see what my purpose is.____yes____no

It is obvious that the process analysis will be directive or informative.

____yes____no

This thesis statement gives the reader a clear idea that what follows

will be a process analysis essay.____yes____no

Once you've answered these brief questions, you can easily see whether or not your first draft needs revision.

- Here's the second draft of my thesis statement. _____

_____

_____

_____

_____.

Remember to practice often and with your classmates. Feedback from others taking the AP English course can be of great help in honing your skills.

DEFINITION

Now that you are up to speed with the all of the rhetorical strategies we've had you working with, you're ready to refine your skills with the strategy of definition. **Basically, a definition is the meaning of a word.** However, you know and we know that it's not this simple. For example, we've all been in situations where we've said to someone, "I don't know what you mean." And, we all know that the person who defines the word for us can choose to be **denotative/objective, acting like a dictionary, or connotative/subjective, giving you her personal meaning and relationship with the word.** So, if I asked you what the word *educated* means, you could provide a definition as if you were *Webster's Dictionary* (denotative/objective), or you could define it the way you personally see and relate to it (connotative/subjective).

Here are two excerpts by writers who are making use of definition.

> Being a hippie is not about putting a flower in your hair and dancing around in your bare feet. Being a hippie means approaching life's obstacles in a way that promotes freedom, peace, love, and respect for our earth and all of mankind.
>
> —Katherine Marie DiFillippo, "Love or Haight,"
> *Making Sense, A New Rhetorical Reader*

Based on these two sentences, it is obvious that Ms DiFillippo's subject is the definition of the word *hippie*. It is also quite clear that she is developing a **connotative/subjective** definition of the term.

* * * *

> . . . in a very real sense, crime is a legal concept: what makes some conduct criminal, and other conduct not, is the fact that some, but not others, are "against the law"
> Crimes, then, are forbidden acts. But they are forbidden in a special way.
>
> —Lawrence M. Friedman,
> *Crime and Punishment in American History*

This excerpt from Mr. Friedman's book clearly indicates the subject to be the meaning of the concept *crime*. At this point, it seems that the definition is **denotative/objective**.

* * * *

If you take a close look at textbooks, you will find many, many examples of definition. However, the real challenge is finding examples of definition used in TV commercials and in the ads in the regular reading you do in magazines and periodicals.

VITA-MINDS

Here's a good idea. Collect examples of the various rhetorical strategies that you locate in your own reading. Identify each and underline key words or phrases that support your identification. You could also do this with ads you find in magazines. Place all of these excerpts in an envelope that you tape inside the back cover of this book. It will prove to be a marvelous review tool for you.

The objective and subjective distinctions aren't the only things you need to be aware of when dealing with definition. You must consider the following.

✓ Purpose (Do you want to inform or to argue a point?)
✓ Audience (What do your readers know about this subject?)
✓ Tone (Do you want to be serious, humorous, or a combination of the two?)
✓ Developing the definition (Have you used one or more of the following?)

- Examples
- Description
- Comparisons
- Negative comparisons
- Classification or division
- Cause and effect
- Narration
- Historical background

Let's assume that you have made all of the necessary decisions reviewed above. Where do you go from here? The first thing you must do is to construct a brief definition that states the word or concept, the class or group to which it belongs, and how it is different from all others in that category.

WORD/CONCEPT	+	CLASS	+	DIFFERENTIATION
For example: SUV	+	is a car	+	that serves as a combination family car, pick-up truck, and sports vehicle.

Therefore, the definition is: *An SUV is a car that serves as a combination family car, pick-up truck, and sports vehicle.*

Our well-practiced writer has decided to define the term *bugdust*. Term = bugdust, class = expletive, differentiation = original, personally invented so that the user can avoid using unacceptable four-letter words in tense situations. Our writer has also chosen a subjective, humorous approach to inform a general audience, and will use examples, cause and effect, and historical background to develop the definition.

<u>Step up to the plate</u>. Now, you choose a subject. How about choosing a word that has special meaning only to you, or to you and your family or friends? How about a current slang word?

Warm-up 16

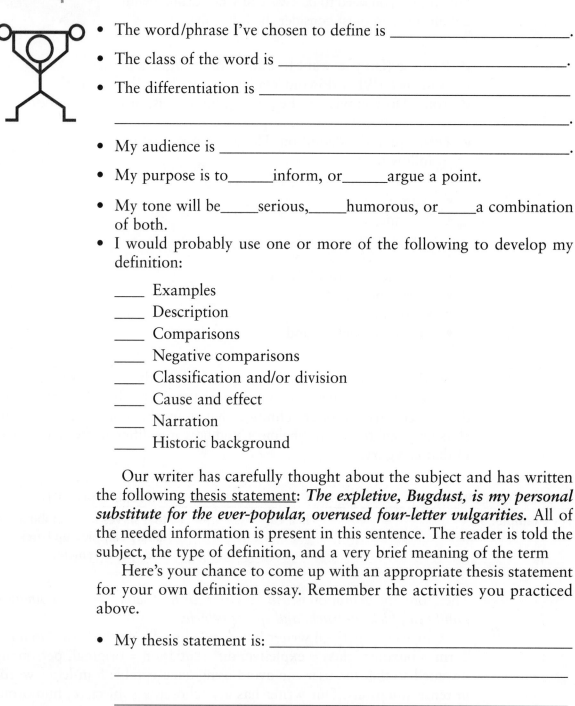

- The word/phrase I've chosen to define is _____.

- The class of the word is _____.

- The differentiation is _____

  _____.

- My audience is _____.

- My purpose is to_____inform, or_____argue a point.

- My tone will be_____serious,_____humorous, or_____a combination of both.

- I would probably use one or more of the following to develop my definition:

  ____ Examples
  ____ Description
  ____ Comparisons
  ____ Negative comparisons
  ____ Classification and/or division
  ____ Cause and effect
  ____ Narration
  ____ Historic background

Our writer has carefully thought about the subject and has written the following <u>thesis statement</u>: ***The expletive, Bugdust, is my personal substitute for the ever-popular, overused four-letter vulgarities.*** All of the needed information is present in this sentence. The reader is told the subject, the type of definition, and a very brief meaning of the term

Here's your chance to come up with an appropriate thesis statement for your own definition essay. Remember the activities you practiced above.

- My thesis statement is: _____

  _____

  _____

  _____.

Checklist

Have you made it clear to your reader what the parameters are for your term?____yes ____no

Is it also clear that your presentation will be objective or subjective? ____yes ____no

If you've answered "no" to either of these questions, you will need to revise.

• My revised thesis is: _____

_____

_____

_____

_____.

DESCRIPTION

We've saved two of the most creative rhetorical strategies until now so that you would have a great many skills to pull from your writing routine. The first of these is **description. A writer uses description to recreate a person, place, thing, or idea in ways that appeal to the senses.** We use description everyday in many ways, from readings in textbooks to telling a friend over the phone about a new jacket, from telling the insurance company about the damages to a car, to recreating a feeling of happiness.

The description can be either informative or impressionistic/ evocative.

• An informative description is the one that is factual, practical, and to the point. (The house is a two-story, white colonial with a black roof, black shutters on the windows, and a red front door.)
• The impressionistic/evocative description appeals to the reader's senses, intellect and emotions. (The wind moaned as if the night were in pain.)

Carefully read the following excerpts that make use of description.

> I can call back the solemn twilight and mystery of the deep woods, the earthy smells, the faint odors of the wild flowers, the sheen of the rain-washed foliage, the rattling clatter of drops when the wind shook the trees, the far-off hammering of woodpeckers and the muffled drumming of wood pheasants in the remoteness of the forest, the snapshot glimpses of disturbed wild creatures scurrying through the grass—I can

call back the prairie, and its loneliness and peace, and a vast hawk hanging motionless in the sky, with its wings spread wide and the blue of the vault showing through the fringe of their end feathers. I can see the woods in their autumn dress, the oaks purple, the hickories washed with gold, the maples and the sumachs luminous with crimson fires, and I can hear the rustle made by the fallen leaves as we plowed through them. I can see the blue clusters of wild grapes hanging among the foliage of the saplings, and I remember the taste of them and the smell. I know how the wild blackberries looked, and how they tasted, and . . . the pawpaws, the hazelnuts, and the persimmons; and I can feel the thumping rain upon my head, of hickory nuts and walnuts when we were out in the frosty days . . .

—Mark Twain, *Autobiography*

From the very first line, the reader is taken into the "deep woods" of Mark Twain's memory. The author vividly recreates this woodland scene by means of **impressionistic/evocative** description such as "snapshot glimpses of disturbed wild creatures," "solemn twilight," "sumachs luminous with crimson fires."

* * * *

And this is how I see the East. I have seen its secret places and have looked into its very soul; but now I see it always from a small boat, a high outline of mountains, blue and afar in the morning; like faint mist at noon; a jagged wall of purple at sunset. I have the feel of the oar in my hand, the vision of the scorching blue sea in my eyes. And I see a bay, a wide bay, smooth as glass and polished like ice, shimmering in the dark. A red light burns far off upon the gloom of the land, and the night is soft and warm. We drag at the oars with aching arms, and suddenly a puff of wind, a puff faint and tepid and laden with strange odors of blossoms, of aromatic wood, comes out of the still night—the first sigh of the East on my face. That I can never forget. It was impalpable and enslaving, like a charm, like a whispered promise of mysterious delight.

—Joseph Conrad, "The East"

Joseph Conrad is also recreating a locale from his memory. This scene is of his recollections of the "East." Notice phrases like "impalpable and enslaving, like a charm," "jagged wall of purple sunset." These are just two examples of the **impressionistic/evocative** description used throughout this excerpt.

* * * *

Both of these authors illustrate what a vivid description can be. Not only have they chosen their subjects with care, but they have also completed several other important steps in composing a successful description. First, it is obvious that they chose a <u>dominant impression</u> they want their readers to feel. For Twain, it is a connection to nature, and for Conrad, it is a sense of strangeness and mystery. Second, they each carefully chose their organizational pattern. This pattern can be any of the following.

✓ Chronological (time sequence)
✓ Spatial (positions from a particular point of view)
✓ Most noticeable feature (details in relation to this feature)
✓ Importance (details used to reinforce the most important feature)
   Both Twain and Conrad use a spatial organization.

To give yourself practice recognizing these different types of description, the dominant impression, and the methods an author can employ to create a description, try a few of the following:

- Find an interesting photograph in a magazine or newspaper.
   Determine the subject and ask yourself:
   ○ What is the dominant impression?
   ○ Do you think the photographer intended to be factual or evocative?
   ○ Is the photograph emphasizing sequence, location, a very noticeable feature, an important feature?
   ○ You can also do this with your own photographs. Search your albums and photograph collections. We're certain you'll find many from which to choose.
- As you're reading your favorite periodical, notice description. Choose a specific excerpt and ask the same questions as above: subject, dominant impression, type, organization. You can also do this with the books you're reading outside of class or for class assignments.

As for writing a description, suppose our writer chooses to describe a traffic jam on the way to entering a tunnel. The writer makes the following decisions:

✓ The audience will be a general one.
✓ The purpose will be to evoke the feeling of being caught in the jam.
   Therefore, impressionistic description is in order.
✓ The organizational pattern will be spatial.
✓ The dominant impression will be anger and frustration.

<u>Take your position.</u> <u>Choose a person, place, thing, idea to describe.</u> Make the types of choices our writer did above. Perhaps you'd like to describe your room, a favorite place, riding your favorite amusement

park ride, winning a game, meeting your date for the first time, your favorite car, a frustrating experience, or so on.

Warm-up 17

- My subject is _____.

- I will create a description that is _____ informative _____ evocative.

- The dominant impression will be _____.

- My organization pattern will be ____ chronological ____ spatial ____ most noticeable feature ____ most important feature.

Once these choices are made, you need to consider the language you will need to create the description. If you wanted to write an informative description of a house, you would use <u>objective and denotative language</u>—in other words, language that keeps the writer's personal feelings, and so forth, out of the situation. Just the cold, hard facts are given, as in scientific journals, hard news articles, and accident reports. On the other hand, if you wanted to interject your personal attitudes, and so forth into a depiction of a house, you would choose primarily subjective and connotative language. A 1955 Chevy convertible can be a vintage, prized possession, or it can be an old, scrappy jalopy. **Choices depend on purpose and audience.**

Although a description can make use of both objective and subjective language, if an author employs subjective language, this can include <u>figurative language</u>, such as

✓ Direct comparison (metaphor)
✓ Indirect comparison (simile)
✓ Concrete words
✓ Imagery
✓ Onomatopoeia

Our writer is "champing at the bit" to create his description of the traffic jam leading into a tunnel. Because the preliminary choices have all been made, all he needs to do is to compose the thesis statement. *Here I am caught for the umpteenth time in the never-ending traffic jam that leads to the Lincoln Tunnel. I usually tap my fingers on the steering wheel, listen to the radio, and kind of space out. However, this time I feel like a piece of meat slowly being forced through a grinder to form a sausage.* Okay. This is one unhappy, frustrated, and hopeless commuter. It is quite obvious from the predominantly subjective, connotative, and figurative language that this is an impressionistic description organized in a spatial pattern.

Practice time! Using your own prewriting information, compose the first draft of your thesis statement for your descriptive essay.

Warm-up 18

- My thesis is _____
  _____
  _____
  _____
  _____ .

Checklist

Carefully reread your thesis statement and answer the following questions:

- My subject is clearly indicated. ____yes ____no
- It is clear that my description will be predominantly ____ informative, ____ impressionistic.
- My reader gets a clear indication of the dominant impression I'm going to work toward. ____yes ____no
- I've also indicated to my reader that the description will be predominantly ____ objective, ____ subjective.
- I've given my reader an indication what my organizational pattern will be. ____yes ____no

If you've answered "no" to any of these questions, you need to revise your thesis.

- Here is my revised thesis statement: _____
  _____
  _____
  _____
  _____ .

NARRATION

Our next-to-last rhetorical strategy is **narration.** Everyone loves a story and loves to be told stories. It's in our genes. It's one of those things that makes us human. And, it is one of those writing strategies that can really make an assertion "come alive." **In narration, a writer tells or retells a sequence of events within a particular time frame for a specific purpose.** You know the routine. A story needs a beginning, a middle, and an end. As a rhetorical strategy, a narrative can be of any length, from an simple anecdote to the complete presentation.

No matter what the purpose, time frame, or sequence, a narration needs a <u>point of view</u>. The choices include:

- First person (I, we, us),
- Stream-of-consciousness, an off-shoot of first person, allows the reader to enter the mind of the narrator and be privy to the working of his mind.
- Third person (he, she, they, them).
  ○ with third person objective, the narrator acts as a reporter;
  ○ with third person omniscient, the narrator knows all.

Can you identify the characteristics of narration we've just mentioned in each of the excerpts below?

> One day General Littlefield picked our company out of the whole regiment and tried to get it mixed up by putting it through one movement after another as fast as we could execute them: squads right, squads left . . . etc. In about three minutes one hundred and nine men were marching in one direction and I was marching away from them at a right angle of forty degrees, all alone. "Company, halt!" shouted General Littlefield. "That man is the only man who has it right!" I was made a corporal for my achievement.
> —James Thurber, "University Days,"
> *My Life and Hard Times*

In this first person anecdote, Mr. Thurber relates a personal tale that has a beginning, a middle, and an end.

* * * *

> My guardian angel was a light sleeper. He saved me from speeding cars, playground fights, and mercury splashing on my face. That was in fifth grade when we stole balls of mercury from the science teacher to shine coins and belt buckles. Finished, we closed one eye and flung the mercury at each other and giggled all the way to lunch.
> —Gary Soto, "The Guardian Angel," *A Summer Life*

Mr. Soto uses first person to narrate this brief episode that is obviously part of a much longer work. Even in its brevity, the story has a beginning, a middle, and an ending.

* * * *

Writing a narrative demands its own special prewriting routines. Before composing a narrative, you need to decide on each of the following:

- The point to be made (commonly termed the *theme*)
- The point of view
- The temporal basis for the story (setting)
  - the time
  - the place, the major sequence of events (plot)
- The major sequence of events
- The characters/people in the story
- The primary tension of the story (conflict)
- The major details necessary for the story

In James Thurber's first person anecdote, a boot camp event is used to illustrate the old adage: the best laid plans often go awry. The time is the recent past, the setting a military encampment, and the sequence of events is quite clear. The tension centers on whether or not the general will succeed in confusing the company of men to whom he has given a series of marching directions. Although brief, details of the types of orders given, the number of men, dialog, and the indication of time all contribute to the liveliness and believability of the story.

Mr. Soto tells his brief, first person episode to illustrate the childhood obliviousness of danger and repercussions of danger. The time is the recent past, the setting an elementary school science room, and the sequence of events is logical and clear. The tension centers around the fifth grade narrator and his friends playing with the dangerous metal—mercury. Soto's details in this very short tale contribute to the sense of place and childhood abandon.

You are not going to write a complete narrative in this activity, but you will do some of the prewriting necessary to compose it successfully. Our writer has chosen to illustrate a combination of the two points made by Mr. Thurber and Mr. Soto. The best laid plans of a child unaware of consequences can go awry quite quickly.

To illustrate this point to a general audience, our writer uses the first person point of view to relate a story about his taking his father's car without permission and without a driver's license.

The time is the recent past, and the place is an urban neighborhood. The major sequence of events is as follows.

1. Parents take car to church
2. Narrator walks to church and takes car
3. Narrator plans to return car to same spot before the end of the service
4. Narrator picks up friends
5. Car runs out of gas
6. Motorist offers to help but only to take narrator back to the church to meet parents

We could go on, but you get the idea. The characters are obviously going to be the narrator, his parents, his friends, and the motorist, and, oh yes, the police and the pastor. The primary tension is going to revolve around getting the car back before the narrator's parents leave the church after the service.

Get ready, get set. Go! This is now your practice time. You are going to do the prewriting for your own narrative. If you can't immediately think of a point you'd like to make or a story you'd like to tell, how about an incident that you've either been a part of or witnessed that could be used to illustrate an aspect of being a student, a younger or older sibling, the oldest or youngest child, the only child, parental mishaps, getting even, the joy of winning, brotherhood, friendship, and so forth.

Warm-up 19

- The point I want to make is _____
  _____
  _____.

- To illustrate this point, I will tell a story that focuses on _____
  _____
  _____.

- I will tell this story using the following point of view: ____1st person ____3rd person objective, ____3rd person omniscient, ____ stream of consciousness

- The major sequence of events: _____
  _____
  _____

- The temporal basis of my story will consist of

    A. The time: _____

    B. The place: _____

- The characters/people in my narrative will be _____

    _____

    _____.

- The primary tension will revolve around _____

    _____

    _____.

Once this information is in place, you can begin to think about the opening that will contain your thesis. Our writer has written the following, which contains the thesis. *I was tremendously angry that Mom and Dad would decide to ruin MY secret plans to accommodate their own needs. I would NOT be denied. Therefore, I schemed, without parental permission and without a driver's license.*
<u>Pick up your pen, or put your fingers on the keyboard.</u> What will you write to introduce your thesis?

- Here's my thesis and the surrounding sentences that will get my narrative up and running. _____

    _____

    _____

    _____

    _____

    _____

    _____

    _____

    _____.

Checklist

Do your thesis and surrounding sentences

- introduce your audience to the focus of the story?___yes ____no

- give a hint as to the point of the story? ____yes ____no
- make it clear what the point of view is? ____yes ____no
- introduce the setting? ____yes ____no
- introduce the major character(s)? ____yes ____no
- give an indication of the tension in the story? ____yes ____no

If you answered "no" to any of these questions, you need to revise.

- Here's my revised thesis and the surrounding sentences.

_____

_____

_____

_____

_____

_____

_____

_____.

ARGUMENT

The last rhetorical strategy we will work with is **argument. In a very real sense, ALL writing is argument because all writers attempt to have their readers believe and accept the point being made by their presentations.** We argue with ourselves and the world around us countless times each day as we make our ways in life. There are those who draw a fine line between argument and persuasion; wherein, <u>argument employs logical reasoning</u> to get the audience to accept the assertion, and <u>persuasion uses a combination of logic and emotion.</u> **For our purposes here, we use the term *argument* to cover both argument and persuasion.**

You would construct an argument if you wanted: 1) to express you own assertion; 2) to qualify or oppose another's point of view; or 3) to convince an audience to alter its own stand on an issue. Below are three brief excerpts from longer pieces. Can you identify into which of these three categories each of these selections belongs?

> **In sum, intercollegiate athletics has come to have too pronounced an effect on colleges and universities—and on society—to be treated with benign neglect.**
>
> —James J. Shulman and William G. Bowen,
> *The Game of Life: College Sports and Educational Values*

Shulman and Bowen are expressing their own opinion about the effect of intercollegiate sports on higher education and society.

* * * *

> But if we cannot ourselves hold to the principle that the right to express views must be defended even when the views offend listeners, including ACLU members, we can hardly call on governments to follow that principle.
>
> —Abba P. Lerner, ACLU's Grievous Mistake,"
> *The New York Times*, 1978

Based on this sentence, we can conclude that Mr. Lerner is qualifying an already existing position of others.

* * * *

> Institutions stop teaching and set aside entire weeks for [comprehensive final] tests. Some even give students extra days without classes before exam week to prepare. Legends of all-nighters . . . abound. Clearly, many alumni have fond memories of these academic hell weeks—of having survived and proved themselves. Yet maybe this great tradition is dysfunctional.
>
> —Karl L. Schilling and Karen Maitland Schilling,
> "Final Exams Discourage True Learning,"
> *Chronicle of Higher Education*, February 2, 1994

In this example, Mr. and Mrs. Schilling are making known to their audience their personal opinion about days being set aside for final exam prep on college campuses.

* * * *

Recognition time! You should allow yourself some practice time recognizing arguments when you see them—their subjects, points of view and purpose.

1. The easiest thing is to go to your school newspaper and read the editorial page and the letters to the editor. This, alone, will provide more than enough practice material.
2. Want still more? Do the same thing with your local newspaper.
3. During election season, why not take a look at the TV ads of politicians running for office. This is a truly fertile field to harvest.

Once you know your subject, your purpose, and the type of audience you'll be writing for, you can continue with the prewriting routine by deciding on what type of argument you'll construct. Are you going to base it on your own reputation and experience? Will you construct your argument based on logic or reason? Or, do you want to appeal to the emotions of your audience?

Our writer is interested in the "winner takes all" versus the "proportional" forms of representation in government assemblies and parliaments. Based on his own experience, observation, and research, our writer has quite strong feelings about the value, honesty, and viability of proportional representation. He would very much like to defend his own assertion about the two different forms. He is not an expert in either field but has done some in-depth reading and has watched a number of Public Broadcasting specials on the topic. Because of this, he decides against using an argument that is based on his own experience and reputation in this area. Therefore, he must choose between the other two types. Because his audience is a general one and one with myriad opinions and backgrounds, our writer believes an appeal to logic and reason will provide his best argument.

<u>Feel the ideas kick into gear. It's time for you to take a stand.</u> Choose a subject or issue about which you have a strong opinion.

Warm-up 20

- An issue/subject I have a strong opinion about is _____

  _____

  _____.

- The purpose of my argument will be to_____express and

  defend my own assertion_____qualify or oppose another's

  point of view_____convince my audience to change its mind

  or behavior.

- My audience is _____.

- I will base my argument on____personal reputation and experience,

  ____logic and reason, or____emotions of the audience.

That done, the next steps include making a quick list of the following:

1. The reasons why you hold your strong opinion
2. Who would agree with you
3. Who would disagree with you
4. Reasons why they would disagree with you

A most important step involves your taking a careful look at these lists and determining whether you will use the inductive or the deductive approach to the organization of your argument.

> To review quickly, **inductive reasoning** (specific to general) **draws conclusions or generalizations based on specific examples/events that are truly representative of the general area being examined. Deductive reasoning** (general to specific) **is developed by presenting specific examples that are drawn from the generalization about the subject.**

Our writer has made his list and has chosen to use the deductive approach to organizing his argument. His generalization is that the proportional form of representation is more democratic than the "winner takes all" form. His list of reasons why he holds this opinion, those who agree with him, and those who disagree with him will all provide the possible specifics to support his assertion.

<u>What's your decision?</u> Think about your subject, and complete the following:

Warm-up 21

- Three major reasons why I have hold this opinion are:

    1. _____

    2. _____

    3. _____

- I think the following would agree with me: _____

    _____

    _____

- These people or groups would agree with me because _____

    _____

    _____.

- I believe the following would disagree with me: _____

_____

_____

- These people or groups would disagree with me because _____

_____

_____.

- I have decided to use the____deductive approach____inductive approach.

This preliminary information will provide you with enough material to both compose your thesis statement and write your outline and first draft. For our purposes, we will only write the thesis. Our writer's thesis statement is: *Polls indicate that most Americans believe that when a politician wins an election, the true voice of the people will be represented in the government. However, true representation of the people's voices lies in proportional representation.* This is certainly not an emotional statement of our writer's assertion, but it does indicate his strong position regarding representation in government. It also makes it clear that he knows there is a large number of people who would oppose him. Given the generalization made, the reader can expect a **deductive** argument.

Take a deep breath; consider your preliminary information; compose! That's your task at this time. Just as our writer did, you need to think and to write the first draft of your thesis statement.

Warm-up 22

- Here is my thesis statement: _____

_____

_____

_____

_____

_____

Checklist

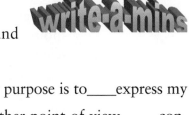

- My thesis clearly presents the subject and my position.____yes____no

- My thesis gives a clear indication that my purpose is to____express my own opinion,____qualify or oppose another point of view, ____convince my audience to change its mind or behavior.

- My thesis indicates that I will base my argument on____my own reputation and experience,____logic and reason,____emotions of my reader.

- I indicate to my reader that my argument will be____inductive, ____deductive.

    If you've answered "no" to any of these questions, you need to revise. Rethink and rewrite.

- Here is my revised thesis: _____

_____

_____

_____

_____

    Although you are not going to write a complete argumentative essay at this time, it is very important to review an absolute requirement for a valid argument. **If you want your audience to accept your opinion, you must make certain to avoid logical fallacies.** These errors in reasoning can easily lead your audience to suspect both your assertion and your support for it. Some of the most common logical fallacies are the following.

- <u>Non sequitur argument</u>: This Latin phrase means "does not follow." This is the argument that has a conclusion that does not follow from the premise. (Example: Bob drives a Mercedes convertible. He must have a great deal of money and live in a mansion.)
- <u>Begging the question</u>: Here is a mistake in which the writer assumes in his assertion/premise/thesis something that really needs to be proved. (Example: All good citizens know the Constitution's Bill of Rights. Therefore, a test on the Bill of Rights should be given to all those registering to vote.)

- <u>Circular reasoning</u>: This mistake in logic restates the premise rather than giving a reason for holding that premise. (Example: Science should be required of all students because all students need to know science.)

- <u>Strawman argument</u>: Here is a technique we've all seen and heard used by politicians seeking election. The speaker/writer attributes false or exaggerated characteristics or behaviors to the opponent and attacks him on those falsehoods or exaggerations. (Example: You say you are for allowing only people over twenty-one to vote. I'll never understand why mean, simple-minded activists like you are willing to deny democratic freedoms to millions of citizens.)

- <u>Ad hominem argument</u>: This literally means to "argue against the man." This technique attacks the person rather than dealing with the issue under discussion. (Example: We all know that Romulus was forced to leave college. How can we trust his company with our investments.)

- <u>Hasty generalization</u>: A person who makes a hasty generalization draws a conclusion about an entire group based on evidence which is too scant or insufficient. (Example: The well-known computer expert found a virus in his own PC. All computers must be contaminated with this virus.)

- <u>Overgeneralization</u>: This is what we call stereotyping in most cases. Here, the writer/speaker draws a conclusion about a large number of people, ideas, things, etc. based on very limited evidence. (Example: All members of the Wooden Peg Club are not to be trusted.) Words such as *all, never, always, every,* are usually indicative of overgeneralization. It's best to use and to look for qualifiers (*some, seem, appear, often, perhaps, frequently,* etc.), which indicate that the writer has an awareness of the complexities of the topic or group under discussion.

- <u>Post hoc argument</u>: This fallacy cites an unrelated event that occurred earlier as the cause of a current situation. (Example: I had an argument with my best friend the night before my driver's test; therefore, I blame her for my failure.)

- <u>Either/or argument</u>: With this fallacy, the writer asserts that there are only two possibilities, when, in reality, there are more. (Example: Tomorrow is my chemistry final; therefore, I must study all night, or I will fail the course.)

Hundreds of books contain instructions on how to construct an argument, and your own AP English instructor will undoubtedly spend some time going over argument and having you write and analyze many samples. But, before leaving this rhetorical strategy, we would recommend that when writing, revising, and analyzing an argument, you check to see if the following are part of the presentation:

A General Checklist for Argumentative Essays

_____ 1. A clearly developed thesis is evident.

_____ 2. Facts are distinguished from opinions.

_____ 3. Opinions are supported and qualified.

_____ 4. The speaker develops a logical argument and avoids fallacies in reasoning.

_____ 5. Support for facts is tested, reliable, and authoritative.

_____ 6. The speaker does not confuse appeals to logic and emotion.

_____ 7. Opposing views are represented in a fair and undistorted way.

_____ 8. The argument reflects a sense of audience.

_____ 9. The argument reflects an identifiable voice and point of view.

_____ 10. The piece reflects the image of a speaker with identifiable qualities (honesty, sincerity, authority, intelligence, etc.).

A TOTAL WORKOUT

If you want to turn the individual warm-up exercises suggested in this chapter into a full out workout, try this: Choose an artifact—something made by humans—and explore it using each of the rhetorical strategies we've just reviewed. With this artifact as your subject, write a series of thesis statements that make assertions about the item, one for each of these strategies.

This is a drawing of the artifact:

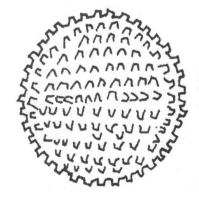

Diameter = 1⅝"
Weight = 3 oz.

Color = dark green
Material = hard rubber

Here are the sample statements using the various rhetorical strategies.

Cause/effect: When I squeeze this little green, rubber ball, my hands tingle.

Classification: This is a green, hard rubber sphere which is used for hand exercise and rehabilitation.

Contrast/comparison: This green rubber ball is smaller than an orange but larger than a golf ball.

Exemplification: This ball was given to me by my personal trainer to strengthen my tennis grip.

Definition: The hand massager is a hard rubber ball with small rubber extensions around the entire sphere used to strengthen hand muscles.

Narration: One day my personal trainer Percival presented me with this perfectly precious green rubber ball.

Process: To get maximum benefit from the hand massager, grip it firmly in the palm of the hand and squeeze and release in four sets of fifty.

Description: The hand massager is like a round, hard, flattened pinecone.

Argument: Everyone should own and use the hand massager.

In this chapter, we have concentrated your efforts on a review of the rhetorical strategies and the skills connected to prewriting and constructing the thesis statement for a personal essay. We are certain that you will be able to apply these skills to the more complex task of composing a complete personal essay. And, if you can utilize these strategies in a personal essay, you can recognize and analyze them in the writings of others.

it was the best of times, we called
it was the worst of times...."
call me ishmael.

Chapter 4

"Stretching" and "Aerobic" Exercises for Your Writing Routine

Rhetorical Devices, Techniques, and Writing Style

*"One of the most difficult things is the first paragraph. . . .
Once I get it, the rest just comes out very easily."*
—Gabriel García Márquez

This next set of writing warm-up exercises will have you reviewing and working with rhetorical devices and techniques and, then, writing style. In the previous chapter, you flexed those muscles that recognize and develop material according to a specific rhetorical pattern or strategy. If a rhetorical strategy is the carefully developed plan for achieving a specific writing purpose, then rhetorical devices are the tools and mechanisms the writer employs to produce that plan, and the rhetorical technique is the manner in which the author uses these tools or devices.

As an example, let's examine a simple task: draw a square. The equipment includes a straight edge, a pencil, and a piece of paper. In writing parlance, to "draw a square" would be the writing purpose, deciding whether to draw it free hand, to use a template, or to trace it would be the rhetorical strategies, and the listed equipment would be the rhetorical devices. These are the tools that enable you to develop that strategy. How the person positions the paper, holds the straight edge and places it on the paper, how the person holds the pen and draws the line would ALL be referred to as rhetorical techniques (in some cases, this is termed *style*).

RHETORICAL DEVICES

Let's begin with rhetorical devices, those writing tools and mechanisms that an author uses to develop a specific strategy. Because this section of the book is concerned with stretching and flexing exercises, we will not be examining all of the possible rhetorical devices. (You may be interested in knowing that there are over 60 of them.) We will have you working out with the most often used and analyzed of the rhetorical devices in an AP, freshman college level English course, whether in composition or in literature.

Here is the list of the most used and referred to rhetorical devices and figures of speech that you will be working with during your warm-up activities.

Alliteration	Hyperbole	Parallelism
Allusion	Metaphor	Personification
Analogy	Metonymy/Synecdoche	Rhetorical Question
Antithesis	Onomatopoeia	Simile
Apostrophe	Oxymoron	Understatement/Litotes
Epithet		

Circle those terms that you know; those you currently can both recognize and use in your own writing. These are the devices you will most probably skip over or just briefly review. For the rest, carefully work your way through each set of exercises. In mostly alphabetical order, we provide a definition, an example, and practice for each of the terms. At the end of this section, there is a self-test that will allow you to evaluate your working knowledge of these particular rhetorical devices.

* * * *

ALLITERATION is the repetition of the initial consonant sounds in a group of words. For example, Tommy towed the tiny truck to the town dump. Repeating the "t" sound is an obvious use of alliteration. Now, you try one by filling in the missing letter in the following sentence. The _____ ong, _____ ow _____ incoln _____ urched ahead after the _____ ight turned green. Easy, right? The initial consonant sound being repeated is _____ ?

Warm-up 1

- <u>How about trying an original one on your own?</u>

  _____

  _____.

  The initial consonant used in this sentence is

  _____.

- Here's an example of alliteration I found in my reading: _____

_____

The initial consonant used in this example is ____.

* * * *

ALLUSION is an indirect reference to another idea, person, place, event, artwork, etc. to enhance the meaning of the work in which it appears. Allusions can be mythological, biblical, historical, literary, political, or contemporary. The writer assumes that the audience or a specific part of the audience will have knowledge of the item to which he or she refers. For example, if a writer were to refer to his or her subject in these terms: "The killer wore the mark of Cain as he stalked his brother," it is assumed that the reader would be assuming his readers are familiar with the biblical story of Cain and Abel. As you read your favorite periodicals or as you read your class assignments, be aware of allusions and jot down a few as practice and review.

Warm-up 2

- <u>Here's an example of an allusion that I found in my own reading.</u>
  This is the statement that contains the allusion:

  _____

  _____.

  I found this in _____.

  The allusion is to _____.

- Here is an original allusion I created: _____

  _____

  _____

  The allusion is to _____.

* * * *

ANALOGY is comparison between two different items that an author may use to describe, define, explain, etc. by indicating their similarities. Here's an example from Gary Soto's *A Summer Life*. "The asphalt softened, the lawns grew spidery brown, and the dogs crept like shadows." Did you recognize the two analogies? The appearance of the lawns is compared to spiders, and the way dogs walk is compared to shadows.

Can you spot the analogy in the following selection from Norman Mailer's *The Armies of the Night?* ". . . even the pale institutional green paint of the walls would be the same. Perhaps even the prison would not be so dissimilar." Here, _____ is being compared to _____. (If you saw that the walls or the room were being compared to a prison you're right on track.)

<u>You're on your own</u>. Take those periodicals you read regularly; take your class assignments; we're certain you will be able to locate many, many examples of analogy—some using "like" and "as"; others not.

Warm-up 3

- An example of an analogy I found was in _____
_____.

The statement reads "_____

_____

_____

_____."

In this example, _____ is

compared to _____.

- Here is an example I created: _____

_____

_____.

In this example, _____ is

compared to _____.

* * * *

ANTITHESIS is just that—two opposing ideas presented in a parallel manner. For example, we've all used the expression, *Sometimes I love . . . , and sometimes I hate. . . .* Notice the parallel structure of the opposing ideas. There is probably no better example of this device than the opening of Charles Dickens' *A Tale of Two Cities.*

It was the best of times, it was the worst of times, it was the age of wisdom, it was the age of foolishness, it was the epoch of belief, it was the epoch of incredulity, it was the season of Light, it was the season of Darkness . . .

The strength of the parallelism lies with its grammatical structure, "It was the . . . ," where each opposing side is structured with the same pattern.

Can you recognize the antithesis in this statement from Alexander Pope?

To err is human, to forgive, divine.

The parallel structure is created with _____.
(If you recognized the use of infinitives, you've got the idea.)

Give it a try. This may not be the easiest rhetorical device to find on a casual basis, but keep your eyes open and your mind alert. You may find examples in speeches that you are reading in your history class, essays in your English class, or ads in your favorite periodicals. They're out there.

Warm-up 4

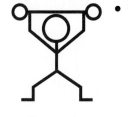

- Eureka! I found an example of antithesis. I located it in _____

_____.

The statement is "_____

_____

_____

_____."

The two opposites are _____ and _____.

The parallel structure is created by _____.

- Here's my own antithesis: _____

_____

_____.

The two opposites are _____ and _____.

The parallel structure is created by _____.

* * * *

APOSTROPHE is a device or figure of speech that is most frequently found in poetry. When a writer employs apostrophe, he or she speaks directly to an abstract person, idea, or ideal. It is used to exhibit strong emotions. Here is an example from Yeats:

Be with me Beauty, for the fire is dying.

Can you recognize the direct address to "Beauty" and the strong emotional content of the line? This is apostrophe.

Can you pick out the apostrophe in the following from Shakespeare?

Blow, winds, and crack your cheeks.

Simple enough, isn't it? Here the Bard is directly speaking to the "winds" in an imperative appeal.

Try your hand at recognizing apostrophe.

Warm-up 5

- First, can you spot this figure of speech in the following lines from a Sir Philip Sidney sonnet?

    With how sad steps, O Moon, thou climb'st the skies!
    How silently, and with how wan a face!

    The apostrophe is centered on _____.

    The emotion is quite evident with the use of the _____.
    (Good for you if you recognized the moon as the apostrophe and the exclamation point as the indicator of emotion.)

- Second, can you find an example of apostrophe in your literature text?

    I found an example in _____ by _____.

    The line(s) reads "_____

    _____

    _____."

    The apostrophe centers on _____.

    The emotional aspect is indicated by _____.

* * * *

An EPITHET is an adjective or adjective phrase that an author uses to describe the perceived nature of a noun by accentuating one of its dominant characteristics, whether real or metaphorical. Ancient Greece used epithets to characterize their gods and goddesses. For example, in *The Iliad* you can find among the many examples "grey-eyed Athena," "The wide-ruling King warned the priest . . ." Sports figures often acquire epithets, such as "Wilt the Stilt" Chamberlain, "Broadway" Joe Namath, "Mean" Joe Greene, and "Air" Jordan.

Unfortunately, today, epithets are too often used as a weapon for verbal abuse. These abusive phrases can be obscene, sexist, racist, prejudicial, jingoistic, or discriminatory. In this context, Robert Ingersoll said, ". . . epithets are the arguments of malice." When dealing with epithets be aware of their connotative implications.

Can you pick out the epithet in this sentence? *The dark woman smiled at her dark-eyed lover.* (If you recognized that "dark-eyed lover" was an epithet, you've got the idea.)

<u>Step up to the plate</u>. Go to the sports section of your newspaper or a sports magazine and see if you can spot examples of epithets.

Warm-up 6

- I located an example of an epithet in _____.
  Here's the complete statement that contains the epithet.

  "_____

  _____."

  The subject of this epithet is _____.

  The actual epithet is _____.

  This example treats its subject in a ____ positive ____ negative manner.

* * * *

So, you've tuned to the TV broadcast of your favorite football team's Sunday afternoon game. The commentators are excited to tell the audience what a <u>great</u> game it's going to be, with the two <u>unbeatable</u> quarterbacks of these two <u>super</u> teams battling it out on their way to winning the <u>greatest</u> of sports trophies, the <u>immortal</u> coach Lombardi trophy. Zap! You've just been the victim of hyperbole. **You know HYPERBOLE. This** is exaggeration or overstatement to emphasize a point or to achieve a specific effect that can be serious, humorous, sarcastic, or even ironic. The writer needs to be aware of the dangers of overuse, and the reader should be aware that the hyperbolic word or phrase should not be taken literally.

In another example, Robert Burns emphasizes the depth of his love when he says it will last "until all the seas run dry." (That's a lot of loving and a long, long time.) Hyperbole is a mainstay of advertising: the paper towel that is as strong as iron; the kitchen knife that can slice through a silver dollar; the auto sale of a lifetime. We're certain that you can also find hyperbole in song lyrics, ads, and ordinary conversations.

Become an hyperbole detective. Read, look, and listen carefully. We know you are going to discover many examples, one of which you will note below.

Warm-up 7

- I found this example of hyperbole in/when _____

_____ .

Here's the actual hyperbole: _____

_____

_____ .

The hyperbole is emphasizing _____ .

I think the intended effect is ____ serious, ____ humorous,

____ sarcastic, ____ ironic.

- Here's one I created: _____

_____

_____ .

The hyperbole is emphasizing _____ .

I want the intended effect to be ____ serious, ____ humorous,

____ sarcastic, ____ ironic.

* * * *

The other side of hyperbole is UNDERSTATEMENT. When a writer wishes to minimize the obvious importance or seriousness of someone or something, he uses understatement, assuming that the audience knows the subject's significance. As with hyperbole, the intended effect of understatement can be serious, humorous, sarcastic, or ironic. In many cases, it indicates politeness, humility, or tact. To hear a firefighter describe the rescue of a family from its fiery home as "*just doing my job*" is an example of understatement. Here, the firefighter is being humble about his bravery, and the effect on the audience is ironic.

Be careful. There is a danger that the use or overuse of understatement can be taken as flippant, when that is not the intended effect. If a weather reporter were to comment on a dangerous hurricane as a "little rain shower," she or he might be seen as sarcastic and insensitive.

In presenting an argument, especially to a hostile audience, understatement may prove useful in getting your opinion heard. When writing a letter to the editor opposing the building of a theater next to a school, it may be best to refer to your opponents, not as "hedonistic heathens," but rather as "theater lovers."

One of the most famous examples of understatement is Marc Antony's many references to Brutus and the other conspirators in Shakespeare's *Julius Caesar* as ". . . all honorable men."

Take a stand. You will be able to find examples of understatement in your favorite periodicals and in song lyrics. List one example below.

Warm-up 8

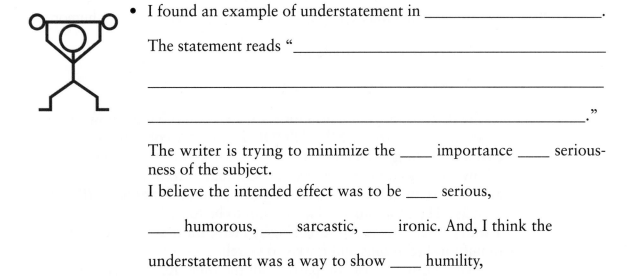

- I found an example of understatement in _____.

  The statement reads "_____

  _____

  _____."

  The writer is trying to minimize the ____ importance ____ seriousness of the subject.

  I believe the intended effect was to be ____ serious,

  ____ humorous, ____ sarcastic, ____ ironic. And, I think the

  understatement was a way to show ____ humility,

  ____ politeness, ____ tact, ____ none of these.

* * * *

A special type of understatement is LITOTES. Used for emphasis or affirmation, litotes asserts a point by denying the opposite. For example, *Tornadoes are not unheard of in Nebraska during the summer.* Compare this with *Tornadoes occur frequently in Nebraska during the summer.* (In the first, "<u>not</u> unheard of" is a denial of the opposite of "frequently," which is used in the second sentence.) Litotes can have the same intended effect as any understatement. As another example, compare these two sentences: 1) Our family did not fail to have its usual tension-filled vacation; 2) Our family had a tension-filled vacation. (The first sentence seems more modest in its intent and more sarcastic than the second.)

Can you spot the litotes in the following statement? *Eating that pint of chocolate chip cookie dough ice cream certainly didn't do my diet any good.* (The dieter is affirming the opposite of doing good.)

<u>Now is the time not to give up.</u> (An example of litotes, by the way.) As you read materials for your classes, try your hand at locating an example of litotes.

Warm-up 9

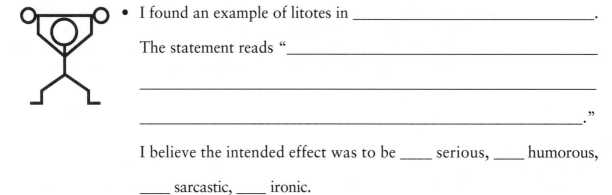

- I found an example of litotes in _____.

The statement reads "_____

_____

_____."

I believe the intended effect was to be ____ serious, ____ humorous,

____ sarcastic, ____ ironic.

* * * *

By this time in your educational career, you probably know this next definition by heart. **A METAPHOR is a direct comparison between two unlike things,** such as "Thine eyes are stars of morning." (Longfellow) In this comparison, *eyes* are compared to morning stars. And, **a SIMILE is an indirect comparison of two unlike things using *like* or *as,*** such as "The short story is like a room to be furnished; the novel is like a warehouse." (Isaac Bashevis Singer) Here, short stories are compared to unfurnished rooms and novels to warehouses.

We do this type of comparison all the time. Remember our examination of **analogy.** If you're watching a film in a cold movie theater, you could use a metaphor and say, "This place is a freezer." Or, you could use a simile and say, "This place is like a freezer."

Whether used in poetry or prose, both metaphors and similes engage the imagination of the reader and can make the strange or abstract familiar and concrete. However, it's wise to remember that a little goes a long way—all things in moderation. Also, be wary of:

1. mixed metaphors/similes, comparisons that do not fit together (I'm such a poor cook that I feel like a bull in a china shop.);
2. inappropriate metaphors/similes, comparisons that bring up unwanted associations (The popularity of our rock band is spreading like cancer.); and clichés, comparisons that have been overused (That outfit is as old as the hills.).

Remember, a successful writer will always choose material and devices with the purpose and audience in mind.

<u>Now it's time to put on your thinking caps</u>. (Metaphor, if you please.) This should be an easy set of exercises for you. You're going to find examples of metaphors and similes in three different places: in your literature book's poetry section, in your favorite periodical's main article, and in an ad.

Warm-up 10

- I found a ____ metaphor, ____ simile in the

  poem "_____" by

  _____.

  The metaphor/simile is "_____."

  _____ is being compared to _____.

- I found a ____ metaphor, ____ simile in an article titled

  "_____" that appeared in the _____

  issue of _____ magazine.

  The metaphor/simile is "_____."

  _____ is compared to _____.

- I found a ____ metaphor, ____ simile in an ad for

  _____ that appeared in the _____

  issue of _____ magazine.

The metaphor/simile is "_____."

_____ is compared to _____.

* * * *

Metonymy is another widely used figure of speech. Here is a familiar example. *Today, the White House issued a statement congratulating Congress on its passage of the new energy bill.* You know and we know that the White House did NOT speak, but rather a spokesperson representing the President of the United States. In this case, our close association of the presidency with the White House allows this statement to make sense to us. **METONYMY, therefore, is a metaphor in which the actual subject is represented by an item with which it is closely associated.** Can you identify the metonymic word/phrase in this old adage? *The pen is mightier than the sword.* (If you identified *pen* for words/writing and *sword* for violence/war, you understand what metonymy is.)

SYNECDOCHE is a metaphor that uses a part to represent the whole. Here's a familiar example, *I just got a new set of wheels.* Here the new car is represented by a part of the vehicle, its wheels. Carefully read this example by Joseph Conrad, "Jump, boys, and bear a hand!" It's obvious to the reader that Conrad uses "hand" as a synecdoche to have the speaker exhort his crew to get busy and use their hands and skills to achieve a goal. Can you identify the synecdoche in this phrase: "many moons ago . . ."? (Sure, you recognize that *moons* is being used to represent the passage of months, the cycle of the moon being a part of the monthly passage of time.)

It's important to note that in current literary circles, metonymy is also employed to refer to synecdoche.

<u>Take your mark.</u> Find examples of metonymy and synecdoche in your current class readings and periodicals. By the way, advertising loves these two devices. Pen two samples below. (Metonymy, here.)

Warm-up 11

• I found an example of metonymy in _____.

Here's the actual statement. "_____

_____

_____."

The author uses _____ to

represent _____.

- I also found an example of synecdoche in _____.

  Here's the actual statement. "_____

  _____

  _____."

  The author uses _____ to

  represent _____.

* * * *

Beep. Beep. Pow. Zap. Swoosh. We've all seen, read, and heard these words in cartoons, in fiction, in poetry, and on the radio. These are very simple examples of a figure of speech termed **onomatopoeia**. Don't let the word frighten you off. **ONOMATOPOEIA is simply the word imitating the sound that is being made.** Here are some further examples: *buzz, sizzle, lisp, murmur, hiss, roar, splat.* Look carefully at *I quickly swallowed my coffee.* Now, compare it with *I gulped my coffee.* Can you feel the difference between the two? The second sentence uses <u>onomatopoeia</u> to bring you into the scene to actually hear the sound of the speaker drinking and being rushed.

<u>Don't sigh</u>. (Onomatopoeia, here.) Now, it's your turn. Turn to your literature texts and your favorite periodicals to find examples of onomatopoeia. Advertising also makes great use of this figure of speech.

Warm-up 12

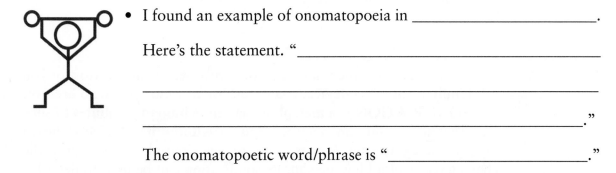

- I found an example of onomatopoeia in _____.

  Here's the statement. "_____

  _____

  _____."

  The onomatopoetic word/phrase is "_____."

  It is being used to imitate the sound of _____.

* * * *

Oxymoron is another figure of speech borrowed from the Greek. An **OXYMORON is a paradoxical image created by using two contradictory terms together, such as *bittersweet, jumbo shrimp, pretty ugly.*** A writer employs an oxymoron for one or more of the following reasons:

- to produce an effect,
- to indicate the complexity of the subject,
- to emphasis a subject's attributes,
- to be humorous.

Jonathan Swift uses an oxymoron when he states, "I do make humbly bold to present them with a short account . . ." (To be humble and bold at the same time is oxymoronic.) As always, the writer must be aware of his or her purpose and audience and use this device in moderation.

Recognition time. Using your textbooks for English, social studies, and science, look for examples of oxymoron as you read. You will also find them in political speeches, comedy routines, advertising, and song lyrics.

Warm-up 13

- Hooray! I located one in _____.

Here's the statement that contains the oxymoron. "_____

_____

_____."

The oxymoron is "_____"

I believe that the author's intended purpose is ____ to indicate the complexity of the subject ____, to emphasize a subject's attributes, ____ to be humorous (ironic, sarcastic, cynical, witty).

* * * *

Personification is the final figure of speech we examine. Most of you are familiar with this device. However, for those of you who are not, **PERSONIFICATION is a metaphor that gives human attributes to subjects that are nonhuman, abstract, and/or without life.** We've all heard or used the expression, *love is blind.* In this example, love is given the characteristics of a blind person. Personification can be used to describe, explain, define, argue, or narrate. It can also help clarify abstract ideas.

Can you spot the personification in this example from Shakespeare's *Romeo and Juliet*? "Arise fair sun, and kill the envious moon/Who is already sick and pale with grief . . ." (There are two examples in these two lines. *Sun* is compared to a hunter/killer, while the *moon* is compared to an envious person who is sickly and grieving.) As you can readily see, the use of personification here allows the reader to use his or her imagination much more than with straight reporting.

Warm-up 14

<u>Give your literary muscles a stretch</u>. (Personification, right?)

- Using only the ads in your favorite periodicals, locate examples of personification. Record one of them below.

I found an example of personification in an ad for _____.

The actual line reads "_____."

In this example _____ is

compared to a _____.

My example doesn't have an actual line, but the ad implies that a

_____ is compared to _____.

- Using your literary texts or editorials in your newspaper, locate examples of personification. Record one of them below.

I found an example of personification in _____.

The actual line reads "_____."

In this example _____ is

compared to a _____.

* * * *

Parallelism is a rhetorical device used to emphasize a set or series of ideas or images. **In PARALLEL STRUCTURE, the writer employs grammatically similar constructions to create a sense of balance that allows the audience to compare and contrast the parallel subjects.** These constructions can be words, phrases, clauses, sentences, paragraphs, and whole sections of a longer work. If you go back to our entry for *antithesis*, you will find an excellent of example of parallelism in the excerpt from Dickens' *A Tale of Two Cities*. "It was the best of times . . ." The wide range of antithetical ideas are juxtaposed using parallel structure. The repetition of "It was the" balances all of these opposing thoughts.

In Martin Luther King, Jr.'s "I Have a Dream" speech that he delivered in front of the Lincoln Memorial in 1963, the reader can see the parallelism the audience heard that day. Each major paragraph begins with "I have a dream that . . ." This parallel structure united and emphasized the equal importance of his main points and helped develop his purpose of exhorting the hundreds of thousands in attendance at this civil rights rally.

Can you identify the parallelism in this statement by Aristotle?

For the end of a theoretical science is truth, but the end of a practical science is performance.

(Right. . . . *the end of a* _____ *is* _____ repeats in both halves of the sentence to emphasize the equal importance of the subjects while remaining different.)

To read, to locate, to record, that is your assignment. (Parallelism using an infinitive, correct?) Okay, grab your textbooks and your periodicals. As you read, keep your eyes open for examples of parallelism. Speeches and writing that tries to exhort an audience are good sources.

Warm-up 15

Record one of your finds below.

• I located an example of parallelism in _____.

This is the statement that contains parallelism. "_____

_____

_____."

The parallel structure is based on the following construction:

_____.

* * * *

The **rhetorical question** is the final rhetorical device on our stretching and flexing exercise list. **If you pose a question to an audience and do not expect an answer or do not intend to provide one, you have constructed a RHETORICAL QUESTION.** This device provides a mechanism for the author to get his audience to think about a situation. For example, Ernest Dowson asks, "Where are they now, the days of wine and roses?" One of the more famous rhetorical questions in the world of advertising is "Got milk?" The National Dairy Farmers of America do not expect us to answer that question directly, but they do hope the advertising campaign will encourage the public to both think about milk and buy it.

Can you recognize both the rhetorical question asked by Marcus Aurelius and its purpose? "For if we lose the ability to perceive our faults, what is the good of living on?"

- Do you understand that Aurelius does not intend to either receive a response or to give one to the question?
- Is it clear to you that the author wants to exhort his audience to really think about their faults?"

(If you answered yes to both questions, you have a working knowledge of rhetorical questions.)

You don't want to give up now do you? (That's a rhetorical question alright.) Be aware of the device of rhetorical questions when you read your texts. Often, the writers of textbooks will ask a rhetorical question before beginning a new subject or section. Advertisers frequently turn to the rhetorical question to push their products. Watch for them. Record one of your finds below.

Warm-up 16

- I located a rhetorical question in _____.

  Here's the actual question. "_____

  _____

  _____."

  The subject of the question is _____.

  The author most probably wants the reader to think about _____

  _____.

Parenthesis is our final term (and, we bet you thought **rhetorical question** was) in this section. This sentence, by the way, contains an example of parenthesis. Take a closer look. **PARENTHESIS is a construction (word, phrase, another sentence) that is placed as an unexpected aside in the middle of the rest of the sentence.** For example: *If you pick up the kids at 5:00 (by the way, you're a dear for doing this) we can all meet for dinner at the Clubhouse Restaurant.*

Parenthesis can be set off in two ways:

- By parenthesis ( ) *The reporter assumed that what the eye-witness said was either true or (at least) closer to the truth than the tale of the accused.*
- By dashes—This tends to be a bit more forceful than parenthesis.
  The members of the symphonic chorus all said how great—Ouch, how I hate that word!—the European tour was and how much they learned form their experience.

For more examples of the dash, consider the excerpt at the end of this chapter.

A writer who decides to employ parenthesis needs to be aware that this intrusion into the middle of the sentence can be a little startling because it is introduced suddenly and is not actually part of the syntax of the rest of the sentence. Parenthesis, with its unexpected "dropping in of the writer," provides the reader with a kind of immediacy and spontaneity. It's almost as if the writer and the reader were involved in a private conversation. The parenthesis can also provide a specific context precisely when it is needed rather than wait for the following sentence or two. For example: *His guitar (he always thought of it as his right arm) was missing again.*

It's now time for you to practice (Oh, no, not again!) recognizing and constructing examples of parenthesis.

Warm-up 17

- Here's an example of parenthesis that I found: _____

_____

_____

_____.

I located this example in _____.

This example makes use of _____, and the result is to

_____ be more conversational _____ provide added information in the immediate context.

- Here is my own example of parenthesis: _____

_____

_____

_____.

This example makes use of _____, and the result is to

_____ be more conversational _____ provide added information in the immediate context.

SELF-TEST

Carefully read each of the following statements and identify the rhetorical device/figure of speech contained in each. Some may contain more than one device. You may choose from among these terms:

Alliteration	Hyperbole	Parenthesis
Allusion	Metaphor	Personification
Analogy	Metonymy/Synecdoche	Rhetorical question
Antithesis	Onomatopoeia	Simile
Apostrophe	Oxymoron	Understatement/Litotes
Epithet	Parallelism	

_____ 1. The village went to sleep, window by window. (Edmund Gilligan)

_____ 2. You are as cold and pitiless as your own marble. (Nathaniel Hawthorne)

_____ 3. But if possibility of evil be to exclude good, no good ever can be done. (Samuel Johnson)

_____ 4. Frankly, my dear, I don't feel like dining out.

_____ 5. The true nature of man, his true good, true virtue, and true religion are things which cannot be known separately. (Blaise Pascal)

_____ 6. Clang battleaxe, and crash brand! Let the King reign. (Alfred, Lord Tennyson)

_____ 7. His first irresistible notion was that the whole China Sea had climbed on the bridge. (Joseph Conrad)

_____ 8. Roll on, thou dark blue ocean, roll. (George Gordon, Lord Byron)

_____ 9. He employs over one hundred hands on his ranch in Wyoming.

_____ 10. Over the cobbles he clatters and clangs in the dark inn-yard. (Alfred Noyes)

_____ 11. And called for flesh and wine to feed his spears. (Alfred, Lord Tennyson)

_____ 12. Who among you would choose not to attend the rally?

_____ 13. The winner of the Indie 500 told reporters that the win was not his but the result of teamwork.

_____ 14. Sat gray-haired Saturn, quiet as a stone. (John Keats)

_____ 15. The setting sun—red tail-light of the departing day. (Richard Kinney)

_____ 16. The furrow followed free. (Samuel Taylor Coleridge)

_____ 17. Look, he's winding up the watch of his wit; / By and by it will strike. (Shakespeare)

_____ 18. There are millions of people waiting to get through the door.

_____ 19. Ask not what your country can do for you; ask what you can do for your country. (John F. Kennedy)

_____ 20. [to Hero,] Thou pure impiety and impious purity . . . (Shakespeare)

(You will find the answers to this self-test on pages 1383–1384.)

RHETORICAL TECHNIQUES

Now that you've flexed your rhetorical device muscles, you need to move on to the next part of your training routine—**rhetorical techniques. RHETORICAL TECHNIQUES are HOW you use these tools, when, where, how often.** It all has to do with choice—choices the writer makes when presenting a particular subject to a specific audience for a specific purpose. These choices revolve around the following:

✓ diction   ✓ tone and attitude
✓ syntax   ✓ point of view
    ✓ organization

Diction

Let's begin this set of exercises with **diction. You may know DICTION as** *word choice.* **It's the conscious decision the author makes when choosing vocabulary to create an intended effect.** There is almost an infinite number of ways to describe diction. Some of the most often used terms are *formal, informal, poetic, heightened* (used for special ceremonies and events), *pretentious, slang, colloquial, ordinary, simple, complex,* etc. A perceptive writer is always aware of the audience, purpose, AND is sensitive to the connotation and denotation of word choice. It makes a difference.

For example, let's suppose you are writing some e-mails or instant messages to several people, including your grandmother, about your birthday celebration.

- How would you describe this event in an instant message to a friend who lives two states away from you?
- How would you describe it in an e-mail to your closest friend from camp?
- And, how would you describe the day's party to your grandmother?

We're betting that your word choice and selection of detail would be quite different in each scenario. Now, you have the idea. It's using the right word in the right place.

Let's look at a situation together. You wake up in the morning with a toothache. You call your dentist and say, "My tooth aches." What kind of pain are you experiencing? Is it sharp, piercing, throbbing, grinding, stabbing, shooting, gnawing, burning, excruciating, agonizing, tortuous, racking, unbearable? Each one of these words has its own denotation and connotation. Do you want to indicate to the dentist that you need immediate relief, even before seeing him or her? Do you want the dentist to see you right away? Is it an emergency? Can it wait? Are you afraid? What is it you want to convey about this toothache? MAKE A CHOICE. Because this toothache is <u>unbearable</u>, you want relief even before you see the dentist. And, because it is <u>excruciating, stabbing</u> pain, you need to see the dentist <u>ASAP, if not sooner</u>. If you look at the underlined words, it becomes clear that the choices made are indicative of a cry for immediate help. **This is diction.**

As another example, look at the following statements about fog.

1. *Fog forms in the same way as clouds. In fact, fog is a cloud that is on the ground, or with its bottom very near the ground.*
2. *Mists of fog rolled in waves through the tunnels of streets girded with a chain of street lamps.*
3. *The fog comes in on little cat feet.*

- Which one of these statements is atmospheric and almost gloomy?

  _____

- Which one is not threatening, but rather soft and appealing?

  _____

- Which one is matter-of-fact, straight to the point, simple?

  _____

The first statement is straightforward, using ordinary language and is from an encyclopedia entry provided by *USA Today*.com. The second compares fog to surf and includes images of chains and girding. It is not matter-of-fact, but vivid and edgy. This is from a short story by Isaac Babel titled "Guy de Maupassant." And, the third statement has fog portrayed as a small, gentle cat. This is a line from Carl Sandberg's poem "Fog." Each one of these examples, all with fog as the subject, has a definite effect and purpose. And, that effect is created, and its purpose is developed via diction.

Carefully read each of the following passages.

The skeletal passage:

> There was a very loud rap song coming from another car. It was so loud the driver could hear every beat and syllable even with his windows rolled up. The lyrics this so-called artist sang were off-color to say the least.

The fleshed-out passage:

> A rap song was pounding out of the Camaro with such astounding volume, Roger Too White could hear every single vulgar intonation of it even with the Lexus's windows rolled up. *How'm I spose a love her . . .* —sang or chanted, or recited, or whatever you were supposed to call it, the guttural voice of a rap artist named Doctor Rammer Doc Doc, if it wasn't utterly ridiculous to call him an artist. (*A Man in Full,* Tom Wolff)

• <u>Let's consider the diction in the two versions.</u>

Is the subject the same? _____ yes _____ no

Is the sequencing the same? _____

Is the effect the same? _____

(The answer to the first question is yes. For the second question, the answer is for the most part, yes. In answer to the third, definitely not. The effect of the first is one of basic disapproval. The effect of the second is blunt, forceful, and prosecutorial. In the first, there is little specificity and few words to indicate disapproval and how strong it is. However, the second passage has specifics regarding makes of cars, names of characters, and sample of lyrics. Words and phrases, such as "astounding volume," "vulgar intonation," "guttural voice," and "utterly ridiculous" all contribute to the overall effect of searing disapproval. This is the result of diction.)

* * * *

Syntax

Syntax and **diction** are usually considered together, so we'll continue that tradition. **Basically, SYNTAX is the grammatical structure of sentences.** We do not mean the strict grammatical construction that you learned in the lower grades. We mean the carefully chosen sentence structure and variety a writer uses to develop the subject, purpose, and/or effect. For example, "I read that article last night," and "That article I read last night" use exactly the same words and are equally valid sentences, but the structure and the effect of each is different. This is syntax. To discuss syntax, you should have a working knowledge of each of the terms in the following list of basics.

✓ phrases (*at the same time*)
✓ main clauses (*Horatio watches the "Today" show.*)
✓ subordinate clauses (*before Horatio goes to work*)
✓ declarative sentence (*Horatio watches.*)
✓ imperative sentence (*Horatio must watch.*)
✓ exclamatory sentence (*Horatio really watches!*)
✓ interrogative sentence (*Does Horatio watch the "Today" show?*)
✓ simple sentence (*Horatio watches the "Today" show.*)
✓ compound sentence (*Horatio watches the "Today" show, and he eats his breakfast at the same time.*)
✓ complex sentence (*As Horatio eats his breakfast, he watches the "Today" show.*)
✓ compound–complex sentence (*Before he goes to work, Horatio eats his breakfast, and he watches the "Today" show at the same time.*)
✓ loose sentence (*Horatio watches the "Today" show, and he eats his breakfast at the same time.*)
✓ periodic sentence (*Before going to work and while eating his breakfast, Horatio watches the "Today" show.*)
✓ inverted sentence (*The "Today" show Horatio does watch.*)
✓ paragraphing
✓ punctuation and spelling

If you are not comfortable with any of these items, we suggest, as always, you consult with your English instructor. You may also want to consult the handbook section of an English composition book, Strunk and White's *The Elements of Style,* or one of the websites we list at the end of this book.

<u>Wrap your know-how around this exercise</u>. See if you can combine the following short, simple sentences into an example of the specified sentence type.

Warm-up 18

- *The pilot flew the plane. The plane landed smoothly. The plane landed at O'Hare Airport. The passengers were quite happy. The passengers had been on a long trip. The plane landed safely.*

Combine these brief sentences to create the following:

Compound sentence: _____

_____

_____ .

Complex sentence: _____

_____

_____ .

Compound–complex sentence: _____

_____

_____ .

Periodic sentence: _____

_____

_____ .

(If you would like to check your sentences with the ones we constructed, you can check them out on page 1384.)

The words an author chooses and how those words are arranged and organized creates the intended meaning and effect. Syntactical patterns heighten the literary experience because they help lead the reader to "get" the emotional and intellectual connotations of the actual text. When presenting ideas to an audience, the writer should consider what will best create the desired meaning and effect. The noted short story writer Isaac Babel said, "No iron spike can pierce a human heart as icily as a period in the right place."

✓ Do you want to sound like a poet? Try unusual or inverted word order. Imitating Robert Frost, a writer could state, "Whose books these belong to I think I know." This is more unusual than the ordinary "I believe I know who owns these books."

✓ Sentence length can also add to the effect. For example, notice the different "feel" you get from the same information presented using two different sentence length patterns.

1. "I drive. I have a driving problem. The problem is speed. This problem leads to something. It leads to getting tickets. These tickets could lead to suspension of my driver's license. I must slow down. I must control my need to speed."

2. "I have this need to speed that has led to two speeding tickets over the past year. If I don't slow down, I'm going to end up having my driver's license suspended."

✓ The use of punctuation within sentences is another contributing factor in the development of meaning and effect.

✓ Interruptions inside sentences can have a direct effect on the meaning. (parentheticals, direct address, apostrophes, exclamations, quotations, etc.)

✓ Parallel structure can help create balance and emphasis.

✓ A shift in word order can indicate that an important idea is being presented.

Take a deep breath and practice recognizing diction and syntax and their effects. Carefully read the following passage from Washington Irving's *Rip Van Winkle* and answer the questions that follow.

Warm-up 19

In a long ramble of the kind on a fine autumnal day, Rip had unconsciously scrambled to one of the highest parts of the Kaatskill Mountains. He was after his favorite sport squirrel shooting, and the still solitudes had echoed and re-echoed with the reports of his gun. Panting and fatigued, he threw himself, late in the afternoon, on a green knoll, covered with mountain herbage, that crowded the brow of a precipice. From an opening between the trees, he could overlook all the lower country for many a mile of rich woodland. He saw at a distance the lordly Hudson, far, far below him, moving on its silent but majestic course, with the reflection of a purple cloud, or the sail of a lagging bark, here and there sleeping on its glassy bosom, and at last losing itself in the blue highlands.

- This passage contains _____ sentences.

  Sentences _____ and _____ begin with prepositional phrases.

  Sentence _____ begins with a participial phrase.

  Sentences _____ and _____ begin with the subject.

The two compound sentences are _____ and _____.

Sentences _____ and _____ are simple.

The only complex sentence is _____.

There are _____ loose sentences and _____ periodic sentences.

Based on this information, I can describe these sentences as ____ all similar, ____ varied.

- This main subject of this passage is _____.

    Its purpose is to ____ inform, ____ amuse, ____ describe, ____ argue.

    The sentences in the passage ____ do, ____ do not contain many descriptive phrases set off by commas.

    The two items given the most coverage in this excerpt are

    _____ and _____.

- An example of personification can be found in sentence _____.

- The diction can be described as: (Check all that apply.)
    ____ slang   ____ poetic   ____ ironic
    ____ ordinary   ____ complex   ____ witty
    ____ graceful   ____ simple   ____ economical
    ____ artful   ____ torrid   ____ conversational

- Based on all of the above information, I can conclude that the overall effect of this passage is
    ____ wicked   ____ wise   ____ refreshing
    ____ gritty   ____ clever   ____ spicy
    ____ lyrical   ____ austere   ____ haunting
    ____ forceful   ____ indifference

(You can find the answers to these questions on page 1384.)

* * * *

Tone and attitude are the combination of diction, syntax, and rhetorical devices combined to create the specific written work. **If you want to discuss an author's perception about a subject and its presentation to an audience, you are involved with TONE and ATTITUDE.** The concept here may best be understood by thinking of "tone of voice." Consider how many different meanings the word "yes" can have simply by changing your voice or combining it with body language. A writer doesn't have this available; therefore, he or she must use words and structure to do the same thing.

Generally speaking, most writing programs divide tone into three categories:

- **Informal tone** is used in everyday writing and speaking and in informal writing. It includes:
    slang
    colloquialisms
    regional expressions
        (Example: We were really ticked off when we missed the train to the city.)

- **Semi-formal tone** is the what students use in assigned essays for their classes. This includes:
    standard vocabulary
    conventional sentence structure
    few or no contractions
        (Example: We were quite annoyed when we missed the train to the city.)

- **Very formal tone** is what you would find in a professional, scholarly journal or a paper presented at an academic conference. In this situation, you might find:
    polysyllabic words
    professional jargon
    complex syntax that you would not use in ordinary conversations or informal writing
        (Example: Unable to catch the commuter train into the city because of a series of miscalculations, we found ourselves in a state of annoyance.)

An author's attitude also includes his or her relationship to his audience as well as to his or her subject. When discussing a writer's attitude toward the reader, consider if he is:

✓ Talking down to the audience as an advisor
✓ Talking down to the audience as a satirist
✓ Talking to the audience as an equal
✓ Talking up to the audience as a subordinate or supplicant.

Tone and attitude can be described in myriad ways. Some of the more frequent descriptors are:

bitter	objective	idyllic
sardonic	naïve	compassionate

sarcastic	joyous	reverent
ironic	whimsical	lugubrious
mocking	wistful	elegiac
scornful	nostalgic	gothic
satiric	humorous	macabre
indifferent	astonished	reflective
scathing	pedantic	maudlin
confidential	didactic	sentimental
factual	inspiring	patriotic
informal	remorseful	admiring
facetious	disdainful	detached
critical	laudatory	angry
resigned	mystified	sad

It important to note that a combination of two of these describers is sometimes used, such as "That editorial was critical and didactic."

- <u>Create your own review</u>. Carefully read this fictitious movie review and answer the questions that follow.

Warm-up 20

Little Miss Muffet is a perfunctory sci-fi thriller boasting one or two harrowing and confusing plot turns. Ms Muffet is toyed with, not acted, by Sandi Curls, who is often a jump ahead of her nemesis—though not always of the audience. The problem with <u>Muffet</u> is that it's heavy on plot and lurid teasers but light on character development. <u>Miss Muffet</u> frightens away any and all interested spiders.

The tone of this review is basically ____informal, ____semiformal, ____formal.

Using the list of describers, I would use the following word(s) to characterize the tone of the review: _____.

These are the words/phrases that help develop this tone. _____

_____

_____

(If you are interested in our answers, you can find them on page 1385.)

To really flex and strength your tone and attitude muscles, you can apply the activity above to real review of movies, TV shows, theater, recordings, art work, books, technology, etc. Use your highlighter or pen to underline those words/phrases that create the tone and attitude you perceive. You might want to keep a collection of favorites for review purposes or to share with your classmates. It's good practice.

Another flexing activity you can try is to take a very simple sentence, such as "The car came down the street" and create several different kinds of tone by changing the verb and adding different describers (adjectives, adverbs, metaphors, similes).

* * * *

ORGANIZATION

How do you organize your clothes closet? It might be even closer to the truth if we asked, "Do you organize your closet?" In any event, would the organization—or lack of it—tell us something about you? We're betting it would. Likewise, how you organize your English notebook can tell a perceptive observer a good deal about your study habits, interests in the field of English, and your willingness to complete assignments.

So, too, with writing. **The way an author presents ideas to an audience is termed ORGANIZATION.** Having practiced with the different rhetorical strategies, you should be familiar with the following organizational patterns that are most often used:

✓ chronological   ✓ contrast/comparison   ✓ specific to general
✓ cause/effect   ✓ least to most important   ✓ most important to least
✓ spatial   ✓ general to specific   ✓ flashback/fast forward

It should be added that readers respond to organizational patterns. They become aware of the way an author perceives the subject and the world around that subject, and, because of this, the purpose, effect and tone of the piece are further developed.

POINT OF VIEW

Point of view is a companion technique to organization. You have all had experience identifying it in literary works. **POINT OF VIEW is the method the writer uses to narrate the story.** They are:

✓ *First person:* The narrator is the main character of the tale.
   (I played tennis.)
✓ *Third person objective:* The narrator is an uninvolved reporter.
   (She played tennis.)

✓ *Third person omniscient:* The narrator is an all-knowing onlooker who tells the reader what the character is thinking, gives background information, and provides material unknown to the characters. (She played tennis unaware that a scout from her first-choice college was in the stands.)

✓ *Stream-of-consciousness:* The reader is placed inside the mind of the character and is privy to all his random or spontaneous thoughts. (Virginia Woolf's *To the Lighthouse*)

✓ *Interior monologue:* A type of stream-of-consciousness, it lets the reader in on a character's on-going thoughts, perception, commentary about a particular subject. (i.e., Hamlet's soliloquy: "To be or not to be . . .")

* * * *

When you talk about a writer's choices and the pattern of these choices you are in the world of literary style.

STYLE

"It's not my style." "Have you seen the style section of the newspaper?" "She dresses with such style." "What style house is that?" "I love standup comedy, but I don't really like the slap-stick style of comedy." Sound familiar? We use or hear or see the word *style* almost everyday. But, if you were to ask someone to define style, chances are that person would have a difficult time putting it into words. So, we'll do it for you. **STYLE is the unique way an author consistently presents ideas. An author's choice of diction, syntax, imagery, rhetorical devices, structure, and content all contribute to a particular style.** It's an author's writing pattern, if you will. Writing style can vary from author to author, subject to subject, period to period, and even among the same author's different works.

If you were given an empty room and asked to make it your own, what would you do with it? What would you use the room for? What color would you paint the walls? What would be your major piece of furniture? What would be your other pieces of furniture and accessories? How would you light the room? What would you put on the walls and the windows?

You get the idea. Once the room is finished to your specifications, it is yours; it is your style. Thinking about and discussing writing style is very similar to the above process. Any writer comes to the blank page with an idea and purpose in mind. **The writer's style is the result of all the decisions made about HOW to present <u>that</u> idea to achieve <u>that</u> purpose.**

This is true whether you are examining your own writing style or that of a professional writer. Before going any further, here is a list of those items that literary analysts consider when looking at style:

- ✓ subject matter
- ✓ purpose
- ✓ organization
- ✓ point of view
- ✓ diction

- ✓ syntax
- ✓ rhetorical devices and figures of speech
- ✓ attitude
- ✓ tone

You're already familiar with the flexing and stretching exercises for these items. So, as this part of the chapter progresses, you will be examining and practicing how to use them when discussing writing style.

Your first style exercise may be difficult, but don't refuse to do it. This exercise is about YOUR writing style. If you come across a term that you are unfamiliar or uncomfortable with, check the index of this book or the handbook section of your writing textbook, or ask your AP English instructor. One of these sources is bound to clear things up for you.

Warm-up 21

- Take one of your essays from your portfolio and complete the following inventory.

My subject is _____.

I use the following mode of discourse: _____.

The primary rhetorical strategy I use to develop my subject is

_____.

My purpose is _____.

My audience is _____.

The essay has _____ paragraphs.

Total number of sentences = _____	Sentences beginning with I/SHE/HE/IT = _____
Simple sentences = _____	Sentences beginning with A or THE = _____
Compound sentences = _____	Sentences beginning with a subordinate clause = _____
Complex sentences = _____	Sentences beginning with a participial phrase = _____

Compound–complex sentences = _____   Sentences beginning with a gerund = _____

Sentences beginning with an infinitive phrase = _____

I use a lot of:

simple, monosyllabic words. _____ yes _____ no

complicated, polysyllabic words. _____ yes _____ no

jargon and/or clichés. _____ yes _____ no

passive voice. _____ yes _____ no

My essay contains the following rhetorical devices: (Check the devices you find times the number of times you use that device in this essay. For example: x analogy × 3)

_____ parallelism × _____   _____ hyperbole × _____

_____ rhetorical question   _____ understatement

× _____   × _____

_____ analogy × _____   _____ antithesis × _____

The essay also has the following figures of speech: (identify, plus times used; for example: x simile × 7)

_____ alliteration × _____   _____ allusion × _____

_____ apostrophe × _____   _____ metonymy × _____

_____ epithet × _____   _____ metaphor × _____

_____ onomatopoeia × _____   _____ oxymoron × _____

_____ personification × _____   _____ simile × _____

I've read over my complete essay, and I like the following sentence(s) the most. _____

_____

_____

_____

_____

Now, here is a difficult question. Why do you like this sentence? Be honest. No one will see this if you don't want them to. _____

_____

_____

If you had to describe or categorize your own writing, what would you choose from the list below? (Circle all that apply.)

formal	informal	simple	reader-friendly	earnest
simple	complicated	austere	authentic	dreary
effective	interesting	fluent	focused	talky
artful	eloquent	wise	substantive	self-indulgent
distinctive	memorable	strong	revealing	melodramatic
blunt	haunting	compelling	enlightening	elitist
economical	elegant	balanced	thorough	affected
edgy	fresh	bold	contrived	opinionated
dramatic	imaginative	surprising	hyperbolic	abrasive
striking	impassioned	forceful	overdone	flippant
honest	insightful	gutsy	forced	idiosyncratic
dense	gritty	ironic	obvious	insubstantial
paradoxical	funny	witty	formulaic	underdone
amusing	entertaining	delightful	unconvincing	forgettable
offbeat	endearing	refreshing	gimmicky	lackluster
outrageous	spicy	subtle	ordinary	anemic
graceful	serious	provocative	trite	narrow
urbane	thoughtful	sarcastic	lurid	pedestrian
profound	intimate	ironic	shallow	labored
sensuous	lush	dreamy	sophomoric	awkward
lyrical	rhapsodic	sympathetic	simplistic	hackneyed
rambling	repetitive	sentimental	maudlin	purple
corny	abstract	cerebral	pedantic	stiff
preachy	lofty	bookish	wordy	grandiose
pompous	pretentious	tiresome	grim	nasty
pejorative	morbid	moralizing	uneven	predictable
down-to-earth			thought-provoking	

Quite a list isn't it? Actually, this is only about one-third of the descriptors we've seen used to discuss literary style. Don't panic. We are not going to have you working out with each of these terms. However, this list is a handy one to have when you begin to think and talk about your writing style or that of another.

To return to your writing style. If you completed the above activities, you have a pretty good idea about how you write in ONE, SPECIFIC instance. If you continue to employ these same tactics in most of your other writing, you could say you have a definite style.

You would use this same process if you wanted to examine the writing style of a particular writer. For example, many English instructors, literary critics and general readers characterize the writing of Ernest Hemingway as having:

✓ simple grammar
✓ realistic dialog
✓ accessible diction
✓ austere word choice
✓ blunt descriptions
✓ short, declarative sentences

As another example, when describing the writing style of Isaac Babel, one writer described Babel's style as exhibiting:

✓ economy of words
✓ construction of images from unusual pairings
✓ juxtaposing disparate items.

This writer sees Babel's style as tightly tied to the mood of the narrator, his sense of selfhood, his family, the history of his people, and the political situation in which he finds himself. Finally, Isaac Babel's style is characterized as "lush without being over the top." With practice, you, too, should be able to examine a writer's work and to describe and characterize the literary style.

TOTAL WORKOUT

No pain, no gain. Here's the final exercise for this chapter.

• Carefully read the passage below and answer the questions that follow. Take a deep breath . . .

True!—nervous—very, very dreadfully nervous I had been and am; but why will you say that I am mad? The disease had sharpened my senses—not destroyed—not dulled them. Above all was the sense of hearing acute. I heard all things in the heaven and in the earth. I heard many things in hell. How, then, am I mad? Hearken! And observe how healthily—how calmly I can tell you the whole story.

It is impossible to say how first the idea entered my brain; but once conceived, it haunted me day and night. Object there was none. Passion there was none. I loved the old man. He had never wronged me. He had never given me insult. For his gold I had no desire. I think it was his eye! Yes, it was this! He had the eye of a vulture—a pale blue eye, with a film over it. Whenever it fell upon me, my blood ran cold; and so by degrees—very gradually—I made up my mind to take the life of the old man, and thus rid myself of the eye forever. Now, this is the point. You fancy me mad. Madmen know nothing.

But you should have seen how wisely I proceeded—with what caution—with what foresight—with what dissimulation I went to work! And every night, about midnight, I turned the latch of his door and opened it—oh so gently! And then, when I had made an opening sufficient for my head, I put in a dark lantern, all closed, closed, that no light shone out, and then I thrust in my head. Oh, you would have laughed to see how cunningly I thrust it in! I moved slowly—very, very slowly, so that I might not disturb the old man's sleep. It took me an hour to place my whole head within the opening so far that I could see him as he lay upon his bed. Ha! Would a madman have been so wise as this? And then, when my head was well in the room, I undid the lantern cautiously—oh, so cautiously—cautiously (for the hinges creaked)—I undid it just so much that a single thin ray fell upon the vulture eye. And this I did for seven long nights—every night just at midnight—but I found the eye always closed; and so it was impossible to do the work; for it was not the old man who vexed me, but his Evil Eye. And every morning, when the day broke, I went boldly into the chamber, and spoke courageously to him, calling him by name in a hearty tone, and inquiring how he has passed the night. So you see he would have been a very profound old man, indeed, to suspect that every night, just at twelve, I looked in upon him while he slept.

1. The subject of this passage is _____.

2. The purpose of this passage is to ____ inform, ____ describe, ____ entertain, ____ argue.

3. The passage is told from which point of view? ____ 1st, ____ 3rd objective, ____ 3rd omniscient, ____ stream-of-consciousness, ____ interior monolog

4. Which two punctuation marks, not used often by most writers, does this author use quite frequently? _____ and _____. (Note: There are three uses for dashes: 1) indicating sudden change; 2) making parenthetical or explanatory material stand out; and 3) summarizing preceding material.)

5. The author uses the dash to _____

_____.

6. An exclamation point is used to indicate sudden or strong emotions. The author of this excerpt employs the exclamation point to indicate

   _____ sudden, _____ strong emotions.

7. With your answer to question 6 in mind, why can the use of the exclamation point after "—oh so gently" be termed ironic? _____

   _____

8. In the phrase "—oh, so cautiously—cautiously (for the hinges creaked)," why would the author use the actual ( ) rather than more dashes? _____

   _____

9. To which two senses does this passage focus its attention? _____

   and _____

10. Check the rhetorical devices found in this excerpt.
    _____ alliteration   _____ allusion   _____ apostrophe
    _____ analogy   _____ antithesis   _____ litotes
    _____ metaphor   _____ metonymy   _____ onomatopoeia
    _____ oxymoron   _____ parallelism   _____ personification
    _____ rhetorical question   _____ simile

11. Does this passage use punctuation that contributes to the development of the meaning and effect? _____ yes _____ no

12. Does the passage use interrupters that contribute to the development of the meaning and effect? _____ yes _____ no

13. The sentences in this excerpt are _____ all similar _____ varied.

14. The passage _____ does _____ does not contain many descriptive phrases.

15. Which words does the author repeat frequently in this passage?

    _____

16. The diction can be described as (check those that apply)

    ____ economical   ____ ordinary   ____ ironic

    ____ simple   ____ complex   ____ witty

    ____ conversational

17. Based on all of the above information, I can conclude that the overall effect of this passage is (check those that apply)

    ____ chilling   ____ indifferent   ____ lyrical

    ____ suspenseful   ____ torrid   ____ austere

18. Based on my close reading of this passage, I can describe the author's style as (check those that apply):

    ____ anemic   ____ abstract   ____ simple

    ____ hyperbolic   ____ ordinary   ____ flippant

    ____ frivolous   ____ dramatic   ____ spare

    ____ sensuous   ____ compelling   ____ complex

(You can find the answers to these questions on page 1385.)

Your warm-up exercises are now completed. You have reviewed and practiced with the basics of **modes of discourse** in Chapter 2, **rhetorical strategies** in Chapter 3, and **rhetorical devices and techniques,** and the elements of **literary style** in this chapter. You are now ready to step up to a full-fledged writing routine. It is important to keep in mind that you can always return to these warm-up activities and flex those writing muscles that can become stiff and flabby if not used regularly.

YOUR RHETORICAL KEYSTONE

MODES OF DISCOURSE

(method a writer uses to have a conversation with a particular reader/audience)

Exposition   Narration   Description   Argument

RHETORICAL STRATEGIES

(plan for achieving a specific writing purpose)

Example   Cause/effect   Contrast/comparison   Division/classification
Process   Description   Narration   Argument   Definition

RHETORICAL DEVICES

(tools and mechanisms the writer employs to develop the strategy)

The most used and referred to rhetorical devices and figures
of speech include:

Alliteration	Hyperbole	Parallelism
Allusion	Metaphor	Personification
Analogy	Metonymy/synecdoche	Rhetorical question
Antithesis	Onomatopoeia	Simile
Apostrophe	Oxymoron	Understatement/litotes
Epithet		

RHETORICAL TECHNIQUES

(choices and HOW the author uses rhetorical devices)

These choices revolve around the following:

Diction	Syntax
Tone/attitude	Organization

Point of view

WRITING EXERCISE PROGRAM AND ROUTINE

Chapter 5

Reading and Working Different Types of AP English Prompts

"Do not open the mouth until the brain is in gear."
(A.A.)

The same also could be said for those preparing to write an AP English essay. **Do not write your AP English essay until your brain is in gear.** Getting your brain in gear starts with deconstructing the prompt.

Continuing with our personal training metaphor, if you have a personal physical trainer, he or she has carefully prepared a specific routine that tells you what to do when you go to the gym for your workout. It clearly states the exercise, the number of repetitions, and the number of sets. To ignore these instructions is to place your physical well-being in jeopardy. The same principle holds true for addressing the AP English essay prompt. It doesn't matter if it's a prompt for a Literature essay or for a Language essay; each assumes that you will read both the prompt and the given text carefully. **The expectation is that you will recognize and pay attention to key terms. Not only are you to recognize these important words, but you are also to have a working familiarity with them. These are the keys to your planning and writing your AP English essay.**

KEY WORDS AND PHRASES

If you are like most of our students, your first question will probably be, "Okay, but just what are these key words or phrases?" **The "key words and phrases" are all related to the two general purposes emphasized by both AP English courses: analysis and argumentation, and they are examined in Chapters 2, 3, and 4 of this book.** If you have skipped any of these sections, you should go back and make certain you are familiar with the material covered in each of these three chapters. For a really quick review, go to the chart at the end of Chapter 4.

Throughout this chapter, and the ones to follow in this section of the book, we not only give you formats, ideas, activities, and thought-provoking questions to consider, but we also model the process for you with actual student samples and commentary on them.

WHAT CONSTITUTES AN AP ENGLISH PROMPT OR QUESTION?

Remember, a prompt is just that, a suggestion, or hint, or timely instruction as to what is expected of you as a writer in a specific circumstance. As we have said before, the two major writing tasks that AP English courses are preparing for are: 1) analysis of text; and 2) argumentation. Therefore, AP English essay prompts are aimed at developing and evaluating your skills in writing the essay of analysis or a clearly presented and supported argument.

Generally, you could say that the AP English prompt is made up of THREE parts:

SUBJECT + VERB + OBJECT. Sound familiar? You're right; it looks like the basic components of a sentence. And, if you keep this idea in mind, you'll not easily forget to look for each of these three parts when you begin to deconstruct any given prompt.

- **The SUBJECT refers to the given text on which both the prompt and your essay are based.** For example:
    - _____ Read the following passage from . . .
    - _____ In her book, the author makes the following observation about . . .
    - _____ In the following passage, the speaker discusses . . .
    - _____ Read the following poem . . .
    - _____ Read the following short story . . .
    - _____ Writers often highlight . . .
    - _____ The author wrote . . .

- **The VERB specifically tells you what to do with the given text.** For example:
    - _____ Analyze the rhetorical techniques or strategies . . .
    - _____ Defend, challenge, or qualify the writer's ideas . . .
    - _____ Analyze how the poet uses imagery . . .
    - _____ Analyze how the author uses literary techniques or devices . . .

____ Choose a literary work and show how . . .

____ Discuss the poem's controlling metaphor . . .

____ Explain how . . .

____ Other verbs that could be used include: compare, contrast, evaluate, explain, justify, relate, describe, identify and discuss, identify and explain.

- **The OBJECT is the GOAL. It makes it clear what the overall purpose of your essay is to be.** For example:

    ____ . . . Two conflicts within one character illuminating the meaning

    ____ . . . Reveals the speaker's response to . . .

    ____ . . . Author's rhetorical purpose in the passage as a whole . . .

    ____ . . . Author's exploration of . . .

    ____ . . . Expression of the attitude of the speaker . . .

    ____ . . . Revelation of character . . .

    ____ . . . Retelling of an experience . . .

A fourth component of an AP prompt that MUST be considered is the recognition of KEY WORDS and PHRASES. These are clues that let you know what the creator of the prompt is looking for in the organization and structure of your presentation. For example:

- Consider such <u>stylistic devices</u> as: diction, imagery, syntax, pacing, structure, tone and selection of detail.
- Using your own knowledge and experiences or readings . . .
- Choose a <u>suitable</u> literary work . . .
- Choose a work of literary <u>merit</u> . . .
- Consider <u>formal elements</u> such as structure, syntax, diction and imagery . . .
- Consider <u>literary elements</u> such as point of view, selection of detail, figurative language . . .
- Consider such <u>poetic elements</u> as imagery, metaphor, rhythm, form and rhyme . . .

A fifth and final component that many prompts contain is the <u>inclusion of incidental data</u>. These are remarks that are made about the given text that can often prove to be quite helpful in both your understanding and analysis of the text. Pay attention to such information as titles, author's name, date of publication, the genre of the text, and any other background that the test maker provides. If the information is given to you, it must be important in your consideration of the text and the preparation of your essay.

NOTE: When a prompt reads "such as," you can choose from among the ideas presented, or you can choose to develop your own ideas, strategies and devices. But, be aware that you MUST adhere to the requirements dictated by the prompt. If it asks for more than one item, you cannot develop only one. No matter how well you develop this one idea, it will fall short of the basic requirements of the prompt.

Once you know what is expected, you will be able to

- Read in a more directed manner;
- Be sensitive to those details that will apply;
- Write an essay that adheres to the given topic.

Ready. Set. It's Time to Strengthen Your "Deconstructing Muscles."

The following are two AP English prompts from past exams. Using your "prompt deconstructing" knowledge, carefully read and notate each prompt and answer the questions that follow.

A. In the following passage from a letter to her daughter, Lady Wortley Montague (1689–1762) discusses the education of her daughter. Read the passage carefully. Then write an essay in which you analyze how Lady Montague uses rhetorical strategies and stylistic devices to convey her views about the role of knowledge played in the lives of women of her time. (AP Language, 1996)

1. Highlight the subject of the prompt.
2. Underline the key verb(s) of the prompt.
3. Bracket the object/goal of the prompt.

4. The topic of the letter is _____.

5. The letter is one that is written from a _____ to her _____.

6. The historical context is the _____15th–16th, _____16th–17th, _____17th–18th centuries.

7. Will the time period play a necessary role in how the writer addresses the text? _____ yes _____ no

8. Can the writer choose to address ONLY rhetorical strategies? _____ yes _____ no

9. Can the writer choose to compose an essay about his/her views concerning knowledge and education? _____ yes _____ no

<u>Check your responses with ours.</u> The subject of the prompt is clearly Lady Montague's letter to her daughter, and the key verb is ANALYZE. The object/goal of this analysis is the use of rhetorical strategies and stylistic devices. The topic of the letter written from a mother to her daughter is the education of young women. The historical context of the 17th and 18th centuries would have no real bearing on how the writer addresses the analysis of the text. The prompt makes it clear that the writer must address BOTH rhetorical strategies and stylistic devices. Because this is an essay of analysis, the writer DOES NOT discuss his or her personal views about knowledge and education.

B. **Carefully read the following passage from George Eliot's novel *Middlemarch* (1871). Then write an essay in which you characterize the narrator's attitude toward Dorothea Brooke and analyze the literary techniques used to convey the attitude. Support your analysis with specific references to the passage. (AP Literature, 1998)**

1. Highlight the **subject** of the prompt.
2. Underline the **key verb(s)** of the prompt.
3. Bracket the **object/goal** of the prompt.

4. For this prompt, is it important to pay close attention to the time period of novel's setting? _____ yes _____ no

5. Is the writer expected to address all of the possible literary techniques in this passage? _____ yes _____ no

6. Based on the demands of the prompt, can the essay be an abstract discussion? _____ yes _____ no

7. Based on the demands of the prompt, can the writer discuss his or her own attitude toward Dorothea? _____ yes _____ no

<u>Compare your responses with ours.</u> The subject of this prompt is George Eliot's novel *Middlemarch*, and the key verbs are CHARAC-TERIZE and ANALYZE. The narrator's attitude toward Dorothea Brooke and the literary techniques used to convey the attitude are the two objects/ goals of the key verbs. Even though the date of the novel is provided, it is not important to the type of analysis demanded by the prompt. If the test makers wanted the writer to address all of the possible literary techniques used in the passage, they would have specified ALL. Based on a careful reading and deconstruction of the prompt, the writer should be able to clearly see that an abstract discussion will NOT meet the basic requirements, and neither will a discussion of the writer's personal attitude toward Dorothea.

You Should Now Feel Prompted to Give Your "Prompt Deconstructing Muscles" a Workout.

Carefully read and notate each of the following prompts and answer the questions which follow.

A. **The following passage is in the introduction to Martin Luther King, Jr.'s** *Why We Can't Wait,* **a book that describes the social conditions and the attitudes of many Black Americans in the 1960s. After reading the passage carefully, write an essay that describes the rhetorical purpose of the passage and analyzes its stylistic, narrative, and persuasive devices. (AP Language, 1989)**

1. Highlight the **subject** of the prompt.
2. Underline the **key verb(s)** of the prompt.
3. Bracket the **object/goal** of the prompt.

4. The historical context is _____.

5. The writer needs to recognize the author's _____.

6. The two key verbs in this prompt are _____ and _____.

7. The three devices that must be addressed are _____, _____, and _____.

8. Does the prompt allow the writer to choose from among these three devices? ____ yes ____ no

B. **Read the following two poems carefully, noting that the second includes an allusion to the first. Then write a well-organized essay in** which you discuss their similarities and differences. In your essay, be sure to consider both theme and style. (AP Literature, 1988)

1. Highlight the **subject** of the prompt.
2. Underline the **key verb(s)** of the prompt.
3. Bracket the **object/goal** of the prompt.
4. The primary strategy demanded for your essay is ____ cause/ effect, ____ argument, ____ contrast/comparison, ____ description, ____ narration.
5. The major clue given to the writer in this prompt is that poem #2 contains an _____ to poem #1.
6. Can the writer choose to write about only theme or only style? ____ yes ____ no

(You can find the answers to these questions on pages 1385–1386.)

Introducing an Added Set to Your Training Routine

As we progress through Part II of the book, we address two specific essay prompts, one for Language and one for Literature. For each, we deconstruct the prompt, notate the text, plan the essay, and write each section of the presentation. In many situations, we will be using actual student-written material.

> Let us introduce you to our two sample prompts.

ENGLISH LANGUAGE AND COMPOSITION

In "A Presidential Candidate," Mark Twain makes his own "modest proposal." Carefully read the text and identify the author's purpose. Then write a well-organized essay in which you analyze Twain's use of rhetorical devices and strategies to achieve his purpose and create humor. You may wish to consider such items as diction, selection of detail, irony, and tone.

Here's What a Deconstruction of This Prompt Would Look Like.

English Language and Composition

In "A Presidential Candidate," Mark Twain makes his own "modest proposal." Carefully read the text and identify the author's purpose. Then write a well-organized essay in which you analyze Twain's [use of rhetorical devices and strategies to achieve his purpose and create humor.] You may wish to consider such items as diction, selection of detail, irony, and tone.

1. The subject is Mark Twain's "A Presidential Candidate."
2. The key verbs are identify, analyze.
3. The object/goal is the purpose and humor and how it is achieved and created.
4. As I read the text, I will pay close attention to diction, selection of detail, irony, and tone, although I could have chosen others.

ENGLISH LITERATURE AND COMPOSITION

In "Dover Beach," Matthew Arnold presents an argument for fidelity and love. In a well-developed essay, discuss the techniques Arnold employs to develop his persuasive poem. Refer to such tools of the poet's craft as diction, organization, meter, poetic devices, and imagery.

Here's What a Deconstruction of This Prompt Would Look Like.

English Literature and Composition

In "Dover Beach," Matthew Arnold presents an argument for fidelity and love. In a well-developed essay discuss the [techniques Arnold employs to develop his persuasive poem.] Refer to such tools of the poet's craft as diction, organization, meter, poetic devices, and imagery.

1. The subject of this prompt is Matthew Arnold's "Dover Beach."
2. The key verb is discuss.
3. The object/goal is the development of the argument.
4. As I read the poem, I want to pay close attention to poetic form, imagery, figurative language, and rhetorical strategies, or others.

After the careful reading and deconstruction of the prompt, the writer is now ready to move on to the prewriting and planning of the essay.

It was the best of times,
it was the worst of times....
ast night I dreamt I went
to Man
"All this happened,

Chapter 6

Prewriting and Planning

"A good essay is like a sharpened pencil. It has a point."
(A.A.)

You can sharpen that pencil using a mechanical or electrical sharpener or just a plain, old penknife. (By the way, the word *penknife* got its name from the small knife that was used to sharpen the ends of quills that would be used as pens.)

Just as a sharpened point of a pencil will produce a fine, clear line, your sharpened writing skills will allow you to present your ideas in a clear and compelling AP English essay. This chapter will provide you with information and practice exercises that will both develop and strengthen your prewriting and planning skills. As your writing trainers, we lead you through the actual process of reading, notating, and organizing your thoughts and materials for an AP English essay.

PREWRITING

Prewriting is the process that generates the raw material on which you will base your essay. It can be a messy piece of business, but this messiness can lead to a well-developed and appealingly designed presentation. From your many years of experience as an English student, you are probably familiar with the prewriting process. This includes:

- Highlighting ✓   See sample prompts.
- Underlining ✓   See sample prompts.
- Bracketing [✓]   See sample prompts.
- Determining the   Given in the prompt. See sample
  subject 🗐   prompts.
- Deciding on   Determined by the prompt.
  a strategy 🗐   See sample prompts.

- Writing margin notes

  Jot down questions, responses, identifications, etc. in the margins. See sample texts.

- Concept mapping

  and }

  Concept wheels

  Group related ideas, examples, points, etc. around a major point. Use circles, squares and lines to connect specifics to the topic or major point. See sample texts.

- Charting

  List ideas, examples, etc. under major headings. See sample texts.

- Questioning

  Identify who, what, when, where, why, and how. This technique works quite well for informative and explanatory essays.

- Free writing

  For a set period of time (such as 5–10 minutes), jot down anything about your subject that comes to mind. The important thing is not to stop for the entire time period. This is a good mind-juggling technique for those essay assignments that do not involve timed writing. It's not particularly useful for an essay exam situation.

- Brainstorming

  This is a good group pre-writing activity in which the people in the group try to come up with as many possible words or phrases or ideas that can be associated with a given subject. It is not really practical for a timed essay. (Yes, you can brainstorm by yourself.)

NOTATING THE TEXT

After deconstructing the prompt, the next step is to notate the text, using any of the above techniques that are appropriate and comfortable for you. The notating process demands your active involvement with the text. You need to:

1. Quickly read to get the gist of the text.

Completing items 2 through 5 should not take any longer than 2–3 minutes.

2. Take a moment to clarify your take on the text (your response to subject, tone, style, etc.).
3. Check the title, etc. for any useable peripheral information.
4. Jot down any general thoughts and observations in the top margin area.
5. Go back to the prompt and choose those elements with which you are comfortable and that seem appropriate for the required task.
6. Then, go back to the text for a truly close second reading.

Carefully completing item 7 will point you in the direction of the development of your essay.

7. Notate those elements, details, examples, etc. that illustrate the devices, techniques, and ideas on which you've chosen to focus.

With the notated text in front of you, planning the organization of your essay will prove to be a quick and easy task as you complete items 8 through 10.

8. Categorize your notes. This simply means deciding which information you will link to each of the major elements that you're developing.
9. Develop the sequence in which you will present each element or major point.
10. Decide on which examples, details, etc. you will use to develop each element or major idea and in what order you will place specifics.
11. Last, decide on which rhetorical strategy will be your controlling organizational pattern.

After all of these preliminary steps have been completed, the writer should find it fairly easy to construct a clear and workable <u>thesis statement</u>.

With the pre-writing and basic planning completed, you've

- decided what you are going to write about;
- thought about the elements of the prompt you will deal with;
- thought about the purpose of the essay;
- made a decision about the tone you will take.

You're now in a position to construct a thesis statement that makes the reader aware of the writer's assertion and purpose. In other words, the thesis statement will clearly indicate the subject and controlling idea of the essay. It should also give the reader some idea as to the pattern of development (rhetorical strategy) and the direction the essay will take in relation to the subject and controlling idea. Here are a few examples of good thesis statements created by AP English students:

- Goodwin and Dickens create two images of the famous London fog [subject] that are at radically opposite ends of the "fog spectrum." [controlling idea]
- In Alice Walker's novel *The Color Purple,* the heroine, Celie, [subject] grows and develops tremendously as an individual as she undergoes major spiritual and psychological transformations. [controlling idea]
- Attempting to convince the white man to deal fairly with Native Americans, [subject] Chief Seattle appeals to the pride and reason of Governor Isaac I. Stevens in a speech that reminds the Governor that, though weak, Native Americans are not powerless. [controlling idea]

Here's a Self-Control Exercise for Your Own Thesis Statements.

write-a-mins

1. Locate at least three of your own AP English essays and write down the thesis statement for each.

A. _____

_____

_____

B. _____

_____

_____

C. _____

_____

_____

2. Underline the subject of each thesis statement.

3. Bracket the controlling idea of each thesis statement.

4. Is the subject clear in each statement? ____ yes ____ no

5. Is the controlling idea clear in each statement? ____ yes ____ no

6. If you answered *no* to either number 4 or 5, or both, you need to revise. Don't neglect this or pooh-pooh it. Revision practice can only help your thesis writing skills improve.

OUR TWO SAMPLE TEXTS

Read and think with us as we work our way through this sample text. Pay attention to the notes in the margins and the words, phrases and sentences in the text that are bracketed. After notating the text, we manipulate these notes into statements about the text, and based on these notes and statements, we write the thesis statement.

Language Sample

A Presidential Candidate
by Mark Twain

as it appeared in *The New York Evening Post* (June 9, 1879)

I have pretty much made up my mind to run for President. What the country wants is a candidate who cannot be injured by investigation of his past history, so that the enemies of the party will be unable to rake up anything against him that nobody ever heard of before. If you know the worst about a candidate, to begin with, every attempt to spring things on him will be checkmated. Now I am going to enter the field with an open record. I am going to own up in advance to all the wickedness I have done, and if any Congressional committee is disposed to prowl around my biography in the hope of discovering any dark and deadly deed that I have secreted, why—let it prowl.

In the first place, I admit that I treed a rheumatic grandfather of mine in the winter of 1850. He was old and inexpert in climbing trees, but with the heartless brutality that is characteristic of me I ran him out of the front door in his nightshirt at the point of a shotgun, and caused him to bowl up a maple tree, where he remained all night, while I emptied shot into his legs. I did this because he snored. I will do it again if I ever have another grandfather. I am as inhuman now as I was in 1850. I candidly acknowledge that I ran away at the battle of Gettysburg. My friends have tried to smooth over this fact by asserting that I did so for the purpose of imitating Washington, who went into the woods at Valley Forge for the purpose of saying his prayers. It was a miserable subterfuge. I struck out in a straight line for the Tropic of Cancer because I was scared. I wanted my country saved, but I preferred to have somebody else save it. I entertain that preference yet. If the bubble reputation can be obtained only at the cannon's mouth, I am willing to go there for it, provided the cannon is empty. If it is loaded my immortal and inflexible purpose is to get over the fence and go home. My invariable practice in war has been to bring out of every fight two-thirds more men than when I went in. This seems to me to be Napoleonic in its grandeur.

My financial views are of the most decided character, but they are not likely, perhaps, to increase my popularity with the advocates of inflation. I do not insist upon the special supremacy of rag money or hard money. The great fundamental principle of my life is to take any kind I can get.

The rumor that I buried a dead aunt under my grapevine was correct. The vine needed fertilizing, my aunt had to be buried, and I dedicated her to this high purpose. Does that unfit me for the Presidency? The Constitution of our country does not say so. No other citizen was ever considered unworthy of this office because he enriched his grapevines with his dead relatives. Why should I be selected as the first victim of an absurd prejudice?

I admit also that I am not a friend of the poor man. I regard the poor man, in his present condition, as so much wasted raw material. Cut up and properly canned, he might be made useful to fatten the natives of the cannibal islands and to improve our export trade with that region. I shall recommend legislation upon the subject in my first message. My campaign cry will be: "Desiccate the poor workingman; stuff him into sausages."

These are about the worst parts of my record. On them I come before the country. If my country don't want me, I will go back again. But I recommend myself as a safe man—a man who starts from the basis of total depravity and proposes to be fiendish to the last.

Here Is What a Deconstruction of This Text Would Look Like.

A Presidential Candidate
by Mark Twain

as it appeared in *The New York Evening Post* (June 9, 1879)

parody

regional   I have <u>pretty much made up my mind</u> to run for President. What the [non-humorous] country wants is a candidate who cannot be injured by investigation of [honest] his past history, so that the enemies of the party will be unable to rake up anything against him that nobody ever heard of before. If you know the worst about a candidate, to begin with, every attempt to spring things

will tell on him will be checkmated. Now I am going to enter the field with an

his sins   open record. I am going to own up in advance to all the wickedness I have done, and if any Congressional committee is disposed to <u>prowl</u> [regional] <u>around</u> my biography in the hope of discovering any dark and deadly deed that I have secreted, why—let it prowl. [regional]

experiences	In the first place, I admit that I treed a rheumatic grandfather of mine in the winter of 1850. He was old and inexpert in climbing trees, but
1	with the heartless brutality that is characteristic of me I ran him out of
exaggerates	the front door in his nightshirt at the point of a shotgun, and caused him
improbable	to bowl up a maple tree, where he remained all night, while I emptied

family tale

In the first place, I admit that I treed a rheumatic grandfather of mine in the winter of 1850. He was old and inexpert in climbing trees, but with the heartless brutality that is characteristic of me I ran him out of the front door in his nightshirt at the point of a shotgun, and caused him to bowl up a maple tree, where he remained all night, while I emptied shot into his legs. I did this because he snored. I will do it again if I ever have another grandfather. I am as inhuman now as I was in 1850. I candidly acknowledge that I ran away at the battle of Gettysburg. My friends have tried to smooth over this fact by asserting that I did so for the purpose of imitating Washington, who went into the woods at Valley Forge for the purpose of saying his prayers. It was a miserable subterfuge. I struck out in a straight line for the Tropic of Cancer because I was scared. I wanted my country saved, but I preferred to have somebody else save it. I entertain that preference yet. If the bubble reputation can be obtained only at the cannon's mouth, I am willing to go there for it, provided the cannon is empty. If it is loaded my immortal and inflexible purpose is to get over the fence and go home. My invariable practice in war has been to bring out of every fight two-thirds more men than when I went in. This seems to me to be Napoleonic in its grandeur.

My financial views are of the most decided character, but they are not likely, perhaps, to increase my popularity with the advocates of inflation. I do not insist upon the special supremacy of rag money or hard money. The great fundamental principle of my life is to take any kind I can get.

The rumor that I buried a dead aunt under my grapevine was correct. The vine needed fertilizing, my aunt had to be buried, and I dedicated her to this high purpose. Does that unfit me for the Presidency? The Constitution of our country does not say so. No other citizen was ever considered unworthy of this office because he enriched his grapevines with his dead relatives. Why should I be selected as the first victim of an absurd prejudice?

Margin annotations:

experiences
1 exaggerates improbable
2
historical references
war tale
war experience
exaggeration and irony
exaggeration
economic view
2nd family tale
irony and sarcasm
rhetorical questions
opinion

family tale
opinion

opinion

re: the

common man

opposite

views

I admit also that I am not a friend of the poor man. I regard the poor man, in his present condition, as so much wasted raw material. Cut up and properly canned, he might be made useful to fatten the natives of the cannibal islands and to improve our export trade with that region. I shall recommend legislation upon the subject in my first message. My campaign cry will be: "Desiccate the poor workingman; stuff him into sausages."

allusion to "A Modest Proposal"

informal

These are about the worst parts of my record. On them I come before the country. If my country don't want me, I will go back again. But I recommend myself as a safe man—a man who starts from the basis of total depravity and proposes to be fiendish to the last.

total opposite of how politicians end their speeches

Using the notes, the writer can easily complete each of the following planning points.

1. The purpose of "A Presidential Candidate" is to parody campaign speeches.
2. The tone/attitude of the selection is sarcastic, ironic, humorous.
3. The rhetorical devices used to develop the purpose and attitude include:

Device	Location
1. exaggeration	1. ¶2-grandfather, ¶4-aunt, ¶5-the poor
2. irony	2. ¶2-war exp., ¶3-finance, ¶4-burial
3. choice of details	3. (see irony) ¶2-Washington ¶4-Constitution, ¶5-allusion
4. informal diction	4. ¶1-"pretty much own up . . ." ¶1-"prowl around," ¶2-"bowl up," ¶6-". . . don't want me"
5. rhetorical questions	5. ¶2 (2 examples)

3. "A Presidential Candidate" resembles a typical speech made by a political candidate today in several ways: 1) references to personal and moral standing; 2) family background; 3) position on the economy; 4) position on the common man; and 5) war experiences and patriotism.

4. "A Presidential Candidate" does NOT resemble a typical speech made by a political candidate today in several ways. First, rather than emphasizing the "good," he's done, Twain focuses on the "wrongs" he's committed. Second, he takes the absurdly opposite positions on the usual political issues. Third, rather than lofty language, his diction is informal and folksy.

Using the above information, the writer is in a position to write a clear **thesis statement**.

> In "A Presidential Candidate," Mark Twain makes his own "modest proposal" [**subject**] with a parody of the typical political campaign speech. [**controlling idea**]

Literature Sample

As we did with the previous sample, read and think with us as we work our way through this sample poem. Pay attention to the notes in the margins and the words, phrases and lines that are bracketed. After notating the text, we manipulate these notes into statements about the poem, and based on these notes and statements, we write the thesis statement.

Dover Beach by Matthew Arnold (1867)

The sea is calm tonight,
The tide is full, the moon lies fair
Upon the straits; on the French coast the light
Gleams and is gone; the cliffs of England stand,
Glimmering and vast, out in the tranquil bay.   5
Come to the window, sweet is the night air!
Only, from the long line of spray
Where the sea meets the moon-blanched land,
Listen! you hear the grating roar
Of pebbles which the waves draw back, and fling,   10
At their return, up the high strand,
Begin, and cease, and then again begin,
With tremulous cadence slow, and bring
The eternal note of sadness in.

Sophocles long ago   15
Heard it on the Aegean, and it brought
Into his mind the turbid ebb and flow
Of human misery; we
Find also in the sound a thought,
Hearing it by this distant northern sea.

The Sea of Faith   *20*
Was once, too, at the full, and round earth's shore
Lay like the folds of a bright girdle furled.
But now I only hear
Its melancholy, long, withdrawing roar,
Retreating, to the breath   *25*
Of the night wind, down the vast edges drear
And naked shingles of the world.

Ah, love, let us be true
To one another! for the world, which seems
To lie before us like a land of dreams,   *30*
So various, so beautiful, so new,
Hath really neither joy, nor love, nor light,
Nor certitude, nor peace, nor help for pain;
And we are here as on a darkling plain
Swept with confused alarms of struggle and flight,   *35*
Where ignorant armies clash by night.

Here Is What a Deconstruction of This Poem Would Look Like.

Dover Beach by Matthew Arnold (1867)

Positive		Positive
= calm/full/tranquil	The sea is calm to-night,	night = moon/fair/light/
	The tide is full, the moon lies fair	gleams/glimmering
	Upon the straits; on the French coast the light	
	Gleams and is gone; the cliffs of England stand,	
	Glimmering and vast, out in the tranquil bay. *5*	
Look!---	Come to the window, sweet is the night air!	sweet-night
senses	Only, from the long line of spray	
	Where the sea meets the moon-blanched land,	contrast—sea & land
Listen!---	Listen! you hear the grating roar	onomatopoeia
	Of pebbles which the waves draw back, and fling, *10*	
	At their return, up the high strand,	
	Begin, and cease, and then again begin,	caesuras & enjambment
Meter is slow	With tremulous cadence slow, and bring	for contrast
	The eternal note of sadness in.	go/stop/go pattern
why?---	Sophocles long ago *15*	
	Heard it on the Aegean, and it brought--------------- allusion	

Into his mind the turbid ebb and flow   contrast

what sadness? Of human misery; we

Find also in the sound a thought,

Hearing it by this distant northern sea.   20

Negative   The Sea of Faith   --metaphor? religion?   Negative

Sea = turbid/distant/   Was once, too, at the full, and round earth's shore   night = drear/naked

misery/north   Lay like the folds of a bright girdle furled.

But now I only hear

Its melancholy, long, withdrawing roar,   assonance-sound/slow   25

Retreating, to the breath

Of the night wind, down the vast edges drear

And naked shingles* of the world.

Ah, love, let us be true ------------------------------------ ** theme—his plea**

To one another! for the world, which seems   not real—dreams   30

To lie before us like a land of dreams,

So various, so beautiful, so new,

Hath really neither joy, nor love, nor light,   repetition and contrast

Nor certitude, nor peace, nor help for pain;   positive to negative

Simile in last 3 lines And we are here as on a darkling plain   35

Swept with confused alarms of struggle and flight,

Where ignorant armies clash by night.   contrast—sea to land
                                                      starts and ends with
                                                      night/no light

                                                      *shingles = beaches

Using the notes written in the margins of the poem, the writer easily
constructs the following mapping/chart.

CONTRASTS

	Sea	/	Land	(Diction and Imagery)
stanza 1	calm		confused	
	light		darkling	*stanza 4*
	tranquil		struggle & clash	

stanza 2 { Sophocles/Aegean long ago / Lovers / Northern sea now

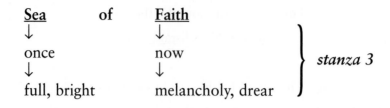

Sea   of   Faith
↓   ↓
once   now   } *stanza 3*
↓   ↓
full, bright   melancholy, drear

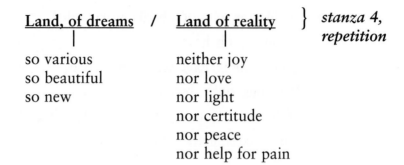

<u>Land, of dreams</u>   /   <u>Land of reality</u>   } *stanza 4,*
        | | *repetition*
so various   neither joy
so beautiful   nor love
so new   nor light
                         nor certitude
                         nor peace
                         nor help for pain

DEVICES / TECHNIQUES

Caesura—lines 9–12—all of stanzas 1 and 4
    Begin/cease/begin (contrast)
    go/stop/go = the waves
Enjambment—lines 15–20—longer cadence = thoughts
Metaphor—lines 20–27—Sea of Faith = disillusionment
Simile—lines 29–36—like a land of dreams + as on a darkling plain
    (contrast)

THEMES

Life is a battle.
Life is ebb and flow.   ------}   Only love is
Life is universal.   constantly in contrast
                                     to war/misery/darkness

OBSERVATIONS

Moves from positive to negative
Moves from specific to universal to specific
Moves from light to dark
Moves from look to listen
ebb & flow of sea = ebb/flow of their love

climax = lines 27–28: his appeal that love is the only contrast to
    misery and pain.
    love and loving are the only certainties in life.

Using the above information, the writer is in a position to write a clear **thesis statement.**

Matthew Arnold's poem "Dover Beach" is a study in contrasts **[subject]** developed to convince his beloved of the value of love and loyalty. **[controlling idea]**

A Note About Note-Taking Styles

You have no doubt noticed that the notation, prewriting, and planning styles of the two samples above are quite different. (At least, we hope you've noticed.) This was done purposely to illustrate the very important point that **there is no single, correct way to read, notate, prewrite, and plan any essay.** The important factor here is that you do the close reading, etc. and that you do it using strategies and techniques that are comfortable for you. As the old Nike ad said, "Just do it!"

With the prewriting and planning completed, you're ready to write your essay.

Chapter 7

Introducing the Essay

"Composing is not a linear process, though what it creates has linear form."
—*Anne Berthoff,* The Making of Meaning

Composing has its peaks and valleys, ups and downs, circuitous and bumpy highways and byways, and getting from point A to point Z can be like walking or driving backward. However, the important thing is to arrive at your destination with both you and your reader safely intact.

One of the important steps to help smooth out the literary ride is to create a clear, informative, and interesting opening paragraph. By now, you have had experiences with many English instructors who have correctly told you that an introduction has a specific job to do. And, by now, you must feel that you're fairly expert at constructing these opening salvos for your essays.

However, humor your trainers, and take a few moments to review what you've been taught in the past. Specifically the introductory paragraph or opening should indicate:

- **What is to follow;**
- **The topic you will address;**
- **Your position on the subject;**
- **Why the reader should be at all interested in the subject;**
- **Why your reader should pay any attention to your take on this subject.**

In other words, you, the writer, have to make your intentions clear, grab your reader's interest and imply the significance of your subject. You've also practiced many times over the "formula" for the construction of the opening paragraph. An introductory paragraph must

contain an introduction to the subject plus any needed background information, such as dates, statistics, scenario, etc. plus an indication of the organizational pattern of the essay plus a thesis statement.

Okay. So, supposedly, you know what your writing job is and how it should be accomplished. If that is true, why bother strengthening your skills for writing the introduction? Why? Because you're maturing as a writer, and you want to be treated and taken seriously as an adult writer with something interesting to say about important topics. There's more to the writing life than three-word sentences and five-sentence paragraphs. There's a whole world of adventurous openings just waiting for you to write them and curious readers whose interests can be piqued.

You're also familiar with the old cliché "You can't judge a book by its cover." But, let's be honest here. No matter how hard we may try not to, we DO draw immediate conclusions about people, events, presentations, etc. based on the initial impression or impact on us. And, when it comes to writing, a reader is quick to throw down or ignore a text that does not capture his or her attention within the first few lines. Therefore, YOU, THE WRITER, have to grab the attention of your intended reader in that introductory paragraph or section.

We say introductory paragraph or section because the length of your introduction depends on the length of the entire text. A short essay needs one opening paragraph, perhaps two at times. However, a longer work, such as a research paper, demands several paragraphs, and a book may require an entire chapter or two. No matter the text and the length of the introduction, it is important to ease your reader into the subject. Get them comfortable in the passenger seat and strap them in for the ride.

There are several techniques for introducing the subject of your essay. These include:

- **Analogy** _____ Present a comparison between your subject and something with which your reader is most probably familiar.

- **Anecdote** _____ Choose a brief incident that relates to your subject and tells the story.

- **Dialog** _____ Include a brief piece of conversation that is related to your subject and that will lead to your assertion.

- **Explicit and direct statement of the assertion** _____ Go right to the subject and assertion of your essay and state it clearly. This type of opening is especially useful for those writing assignments that are reports, essays in science or history, or for essay assignments that present difficulties to both your and your reader.

- **Interesting fact or detail** _____ Choose an interesting historical reference, a statistic, or a specific detail and indicate how it is related to your subject.

- **Question** _____ Ask a broad question and indicate how it could be related to your subject/ assertion. The question can be a regular question for which you will provide an answer, or it could be rhetorical.

- **Quotation** _____ Find a quotation that is related to your subject and indicate how it is related to your thesis. Quotations can come from within the text being discussed or from another source.

- **Startling remark** _____ This should be a real attention grabber. However, make certain that it is actually related to your subject and your assertion about it.

> **Remember that no matter which opening gambit you choose to employ, that introduction should be one that is <u>specifically tuned</u> to your subject, assertion, purpose, and audience.**

THE PROFESSIONALS DO IT

Let's take a close look at a series of introductions written by professionals. Writers of fiction and nonfiction frequently use the same techniques to involve their readers. Just as we often jump to conclusions about individuals or situations based on first impressions, so, too, do readers often jump to conclusions about continuing to read a work. It is imperative for an author to capture and coerce his or her reader to be actively involved from the beginning. Take a look at these examples, both fiction and nonfiction, and concentrate on the writer's craft as you read.

J. D. Salinger from *The Catcher in the Rye*

If you really want to hear about it, the first thing you'll probably want to know is where I was born, and what my lousy childhood was like, and how my parents were occupied and all before they had me, and all that David Copperfield kind of crap, but I don't feel like going into it, if you really want to know the truth.

Comments: (question)

This first person opening draws the reader into the passage by posing an implied question on the part of the reader—if you really want to hear about it—and then by answering it—I don't feel like going into it—thereby raising the reader's curiosity. Stylistically, the speaker mixes literary allusion and colloquialisms, indicating a complex character. The concept of truth hints at the thematic elements of the novel.

Mark Twain from *The Adventures of Huckleberry Finn*

You don't know about me, without you have read a book by the name of "The Adventures of Tom Sawyer," but that ain't no matter. That book was made by Mr. Mark Twain, and he told the truth, mainly. There was things which he stretched, but mainly he told the truth. That is nothing. I never seen anybody but lied, one time or another, without it was Aunt Polly, or the widow, or maybe Mary. Aunt Polly, Tom's Aunt Polly she is—and Mary, and the Widow Douglas, is all told about in that book—which is mostly a true book; with some stretchers, as I said before.

Comments: (dialog)

Here is one of the most famous openings in all of American literature. Twain's first person narrative is made immediately compelling as Huck introduces himself to the reader. The reference to *The Adventures of Tom Sawyer* and to Twain, himself; the informality and regional English; plus Huck's obvious desire to tell his story, all provide a sense of time and place and draw the audience into the story.

Rita Mae Brown from *Rita Will: Memoir of a Literary Rabble-Rouser*

My mother was mucking stalls at Hanover Shoe Farm outside of Hanover, Pennsylvania, within a shout of the Mason–Dixon line, when her water broke. Had the hospital not been nearby, I would have been born in a manger. Perhaps I came into the world knowing Jesus had already done that, and since he suffered for all of us I saw no reason to be redundant.

Comments: (anecdote)

Ms. Brown's first person anecdote introduces herself to the reader as a straight-talking, ironic and humorous individual. It also lets the reader know that this is going to be a type of memoir.

F. Scott Fitzgerald from *The Great Gatsby*

In my younger and more vulnerable years my father gave me some advice that I've been turning over in my mind ever since.

"Whenever you feel like criticizing any one," he told me, "just remember that all the people in this world haven't had the advantages that you've had."

He didn't say any more, but we've always been unusually communicative in a reserved way, and I understood that he meant a great deal more than that. In consequence, I'm inclined to reserve all judgments, a habit that has opened up many curious natures to me and also made me the victim of not a few veteran bores.

Comments: (quotation and anecdote)

This opening employs a quotation and an anecdote to introduce the themes of the novel and the narrator. The reader infers that judgment, consequences, communication, vulnerability and victimization will all be important in this work.

Jane Austen from *Pride and Prejudice*

It is a truth universally acknowledged, that a single man in possession of a good fortune must be in want of a wife. However little known the feelings or views of such a man may be on his first entering a neighborhood, this truth is so well fixed in the minds of the surrounding families, that he is considered as the rightful property of someone or other of their daughters.

Comments: (explicit statement)

The opening sentence is also the assertion upon which the novel is developed. There is no doubt in the reader's mind about the subject matter or focus of the novel. The pleasant surprise is the understated humor in the first paragraph which alludes to a witty and wry tone toward the subject.

Thomas Jefferson from *The Declaration of Independence*

When in the course of human events, it becomes necessary for one people to dissolve the political bands which have connected them with another, and to assume among the powers of the earth, the separate and equal station to which the Laws of Nature and of Nature's God entitle them, a decent respect to the opinions of mankind requires that they should declare the causes which impel them to the separation.

Comments: (direct plus explicit)

In his opening, Jefferson is forceful and direct. Without hyperbolic language, or interesting tales and references, he makes it clear to the world the exact purpose and assertion of his declaration.

Richard Wright from *Native Son*

Brrrrrrrriiiiiiiiiiiiiiiinnng!
An alarm clock clanged in the dark and silent room. A bed spring creaked.
A woman's voice sang out impatiently: "Bigger, shut that thing off!"

Comments: (dialog)

This tidbit of dialog, as emphatic as the alarm clock itself, emphasizes the demands made on the main character who has yet to be met. The brevity of the introduction and the simplicity of syntax and diction establish the elemental quality of the work.

Albert Camus from *The Stranger*

Mother died today. Or, maybe, yesterday; I can't be sure. The telegram from the Home says: YOUR MOTHER PASSED AWAY. FUNERAL TOMORROW. DEEP SYMPATHY. Which leaves the matter doubtful; it could have been yesterday.

Comments: (startling remark)

Certainly this novel opens with a startling observation. Perhaps it is the objectivity of the speaker that is so shocking and compelling that we must read on. On another level, the opening is analogous to the entire existential movement: death, uncertainty, isolation, the inadequacy of communication and the absurdity of time and life, are the basis tenets of the philosophy Camus will explore in the novel.

Calvin Trillin from "Comforting Thoughts" in *Enough's Enough (And Other Rules of Life)*

First I read a study in Meriden, Connecticut, which indicated that talking to yourself is a perfectly legitimate way of getting comfort during a difficult time. Then I saw an item about research at Yale demonstrating that stress seems to be reduced in some people by exposing them to aromas of certain desserts. Then I started talking to myself about desserts with aromas I find soothing. Then I felt a lot better. Isn't science grand?

Comments: (interesting facts plus rhetorical question)

Mr. Trillin's citing of the two research studies and his use of the rhetorical question to end the opening paragraph easily and humorously indicate the subject, the assertion and the tone the essay will take.

Louisa May Alcott from *Little Women*

"Christmas won't be Christmas without any presents," grumbled Jo, lying on the rug.

"It's so dreadful to be poor!" sighed Meg, looking down at her old dress.

"I don't think it's fair for some girls to have plenty of pretty things and other girls nothing at all," added little Amy, with an injured sniff.

"We've got father and mother and each other," said Beth contentedly, from her corner.

Comments: (dialog)

Totally dependent on dialog, this opening introduces four diverse characters with incredible economy. Each personality is defined, the conflicts are enumerated, the ideal is presented, and the reader is given the opportunity to identify with the speaker of his choice.

David Sedaris's Opening of "Diary of a Smoker" in *Barrel Fever*

I rode my bike to the boat pond in Central Park, where I bought myself a cup of coffee and sat down on a bench to read. I lit a cigarette and was enjoying myself when the woman seated twelve feet away, on the other side of the bench, began waving her hands before her face. I thought she was fighting off a bee.

She fussed at the air and called out, "Excuse me, do you mind if we make this a no-smoking bench?"

Comments: (dialog plus anecdote)

David Sedaris uses this first person anecdote that includes dialog to introduce the reader to both his subject and his assertion. It is obvious to any reader that Mr. Sedaris is not at all happy with those who would impose their no-smoking mania on others.

Camille Paglia from "Rock as Art" in *Sex, Art and American Culture*

> Rock is eating its young. Rock musicians are America's most wasted natural resource.

Comments: (analogy plus startling statement)

Containing two startling analogies, this quite brief pair of sentences is the opening salvo to an essay in which Ms. Paglia will obviously be arguing in favor of the importance of "rock."

OUR SAMPLE WRITERS

As a first example, the writer for our Mark Twain prompt has written the following three opening paragraphs.

A

Honesty and *politics*. For the cynic in each of us, these are two mutually exclusive terms. Each time we hear a politician say, "I want to be perfectly clear," we know to take what is said with a grain of salt. Mark Twain plays with our political cynicism in "A Presidential Candidate," an essay that parodies the stereotypical campaign speech.

B

We've all heard the following before, haven't we? "Trust me. I only want to be your public servant. I will always work for the common good of all." It's so familiar and so shallow that the political cynic in each of us responds, "<u>Sure</u> we should. <u>Sure</u> he does. <u>Sure</u> he will." Aware of this cynicism, Mark Twain plays with our political suspicions in "A Presidential Candidate," a parody of the typical campaign speech.

C

Barely 51 percent of those eligible to vote did so in the last presidential election. Do you wonder why? Perhaps it's the result of voters distrusting politicians. Mark Twain plays with this cynicism of the electorate in "A Presidential Candidate," an essay that parodies the stereotypical political campaign speech.

Comments

Opening **A** uses a brief quotation to introduce the context of the essay; whereas, opening **B** employs a rhetorical question and two bits of dialog to grab the reader's attention and to indicate the subject. Last, opening **C** presents an interesting, if not startling, statistic and a rhetorical question to engage and lead the reader to the assertion. After thoughtfully considering each of these introductions and the purpose of the essay, our writer has chosen to use opening **B.** This is a choice that could certainly be changed in a writing situation that allows for revision. However, in a timed essay exam, opening **B** would be our first AND final choice because it lends itself most directly to both the assertion and the tone the writer wishes to take.

For our <u>second example</u>, the writer for the "Dover Beach" prompt has composed the following three opening paragraphs.

A

"Ah, love, let us be true to one another!" says Matthew Arnold. What a line! One can almost hear him asking his beloved what her sign is. And yet, this impassioned and shameless plea for requited love works, and it works because of the diction, poetic devices, and imagery Arnold presents in "Dover Beach." The poor girl doesn't have a chance.

B

From "calm to clash, from light to darkling, from sea to land," Matthew Arnold's poem "Dover Beach" is a study in contrast. This contrast is necessary to convince his love to be true, and it is developed throughout the poem by an increasingly negative progression of examples. This organizational pattern is enhanced by the form and structure of the lines. Arnold also appeals to the senses to bring his love to see the urgency of his desire and passion. The metaphors and allusions all reiterate his position, that love and lovemaking are the only things of certainty in an ignorant and hostile world.

C

It seems there is nothing new under the sun after all. Whenever young men are endangered by war, they are driven to counter the threat of death with the experience of life. In *A Streetcar Named Desire*, Blanche DuBois says "the opposite of death is desire" and this seems especially appropriate to remember when reading Matthew Arnold's poem, "Dover Beach." Through poetic devices, symbols, and repetition, the poet argues for love and fidelity.

Comments

All three opening paragraphs include author, title, and genre. Each addresses the major points of the prompt and indicates the writer's understanding of task and text. Opening **A** refers to a quotation from the poem to help establish the voice of the writer. The tone of the essay is clear and engaging. Opening **B** immediately makes reference to the entire poem with specific details and delineates the direction the essay will take. It is clear and academic and indicates a level of confidence on the part of the writer. Opening **C** links one literary work with another and incorporates an outside quotation to illustrate an analogous insight about the poem.

In a timed situation, the writer would be most comfortable developing example **B** because it already has established the format of the essay. Sequence and progression help to control literary analysis and keep the writer on track. Example **A** might be more fun to write, but it could be difficult to maintain tone, and the desire to be clever could get in the way of the task. Likewise, opening **C** could prove limiting because of its focus on the last stanza as the controlling idea. Each of these openings would be suitable for an untimed essay, but for this, opening **B** is the choice.

STUDENT SAMPLES

Professional writers make their living doing this kind of stuff, but what about the ordinary student who is stuck writing an essay in answer to a specific assignment or prompt? To find out, read the following student samples.

Student A

The culmination of moral reconciliation and spiritual awakening is most evident at the end of Toni Morrison's Song of Solomon. *This gradual enlightenment, rather than a sudden epiphany, is portrayed through Milkman, the heroic character of the novel.*

Comments

This brief, but on-target, introduction indicates a student writer who is in control of his or her subject. Not only does the writer state the subject and purpose of the essay, but he or she also employs mature diction and presents insights using phrases such as *moral reconciliation and spiritual awakening,* and *rather than a sudden epiphany* to point out an inherent contrast.

Student B

In her op-ed piece, "Pretty Poison," Maureen Dowd examines and modifies Anna Quindlen's earlier insight into the categorized life span of a woman, that is, "pre-Babe, Babe, and post-Babe." Reflecting on the new "Botox-injection craze," Dowd facetiously updates Quindlen's classifications to, "pre-Babe, Babe, Botox-Babe, and Cher." Ms. Dowd employs a variety of rhetorical devices to expose the absurdity of the female ideal of presenting herself as a younger, more attractive woman than she believes she is.

Comments

This introduction clearly presents both the subject and purpose together with the writer's definite attitude toward Ms. Dowd's and Ms. Quindlen's topics that this student refers to with quotations from the op-ed column. Using words such as *craze, facetiously,* and *absurdity,* the reader also becomes aware of an upcoming "prickly" analysis of the columnist's presentation.

Student C

The reader of Norman Mailer's passage walks away with great empathy for Benny "Kid" Paret and a better understanding of what it was like in that arena the night of his massacre. Mailer's diction, syntax, and use of specific animal imagery recreates this event with a dichotomous tone and a sense of the bestiality of the "sweet science."

Comments

Here is a student who has a definite point of view and is not afraid to make that point of view known to the reader who is brought immediately into the essay. The writer's tone is obvious from the very beginning with the use of words such as *massacre,* and *bestiality,* and, the thesis incorporates the prompt without a bland restatement of its purpose and object.

Student D

In sixth grade, when most boys fantasize about becoming famous baseball players, I dreamed, among other things, about being a contestant on <u>Jeopardy</u>. Athletics interested me, but I suspected that fame and fortune would be more assured if I pursued the game show route. Now, six years later, I was actually auditioning for <u>Teen Jeopardy</u>. At last, I would have the opportunity to mentally spar with the other contestants and relate my own droll anecdote to Alex Trebek. Dreams can come true.

Comments

This is an intriguing opening to a personal essay. The student's use of anecdote immediately sets the informal and personal tone of the essay as it piques the reader's curiosity. Will the writer's dream come true? What happened on *Teen Jeopardy*?

TOTAL WORKOUT

Enough of just looking at others. It's time to stretch and maximize your own opening skills.

Go to your writing folder or portfolio and choose THREE opening paragraphs.

- Either rewrite or copy and paste each of the openings on a separate sheet of paper and answer the following questions:

  1. The subject of the essay is _____.

  2. My purpose is _____.

  3. My audience is _____.

  4. My assertion is _____.

  5. I used the following opening technique(s) in my opening _____.

  6. I believe the opening is good just the way it is. ____ yes ____ no

7. If you answered *no* to question 6, what technique do you think would be a better choice?

_____.

- Choose ONE of the introductions and complete the following:

1. Using three different techniques, rewrite the opening THREE different ways below.

Technique _____ Rewrite: _____

_____

_____

_____

_____

_____

_____

Technique _____ Rewrite: _____

_____

_____

_____

_____

_____

_____

Technique _____ Rewrite: _____

_____

_____

_____

_____

_____

_____

2. Which technique do you think works best? _____

3. Why do you believe this method is best? _____

4. Ask one of your peers to read each opening and see whether or not he or she agrees with your choice.

5. Do you think revising your introduction would make your essay

   even better? ____ yes ____ no. Why?_____

_____

Can you feel the burn? Well, before you cool down, here's another item to consider when deciding on your opening. If you are given a writing assignment that involves several classes and several steps, from planning to first draft to peer review to revision, you can take a great deal of time to consider and reconsider your introduction. This is the time to experiment and to be creative. However, in a timed situation, you will have to think quickly and decisively. The more practice you allow yourself in the untimed essays, the better you will be in the stressful and demanding timed writing environments.

Note: **You can read the complete essays by our two sample writers on pages 1335–1337 in Chapter 9.**

Chapter 8

Writing the Body of the Essay and the Supporting Syntax

"What is written without effort is read without pleasure."
—*Samuel Johnson*

Yes! We are going to acknowledge that you have been putting in a great deal of effort so far. But, the operative phrase here is "so far." You've only just begun. With the close reading, prewriting, planning, and introduction completed, you're set to write the body of your essay.

Don't doubt yourself. You ARE ready to write the body of your essay. You know your audience, your purpose, your assertion, and your rhetorical strategy. You know the major points that support your assertion, you know the sequence of your specific examples that illustrate each of your major points, and you've engaged your reader. Now what?

Here's what—decide on your organizing principle. That's the basic pattern that you'll use to develop your presentation. You're already familiar with these patterns; you've been using them for years. You just need to put them in specific context. **Each rhetorical strategy lends itself to a specific organizational structure.** These are:

- <u>Chronological order</u> deals with items in the time order in which they occur. The two strategies that use this pattern are <u>narration</u> and <u>process</u>.
- <u>Spatial order</u> details items as they appear in a particular environment: from right to left, top to bottom, front to back, etc. This pattern is most often used in <u>description</u>.
- <u>Subject by subject</u> discusses each subject in a separate paragraph or section.
  <u>Point by point</u> examines each point in a separate paragraph or section. These patterns are used with <u>contrast/comparison</u>.
- <u>Categorizing</u> is the process of placing items in groups and examining each one of the categories and the items in it. Obviously, the rhetorical strategy that demands this pattern is <u>classification</u>.

- A single cause leading to a single effect or multiple effects
  Multiple causes leading to a single effect or multiple effects
  A single effect and the single or multiple cause(s)
  Multiple effects and the single or multiple cause(s)
  These patterns are best used for the cause/effect strategy
- Most important to least important or vise versa can be used in to organize almost any of the rhetorical strategies, especially analysis, explanation and cause/effect.
- Deduction is a pattern that works from the general (thesis) to specific/supporting details, while induction works from the specific examples/details to the general (thesis). Argumentation is the strategy that most often consciously employs these two patterns.

Note: The organizational pattern is usually given to the writer in the very wording of the timed AP English essay prompt. However, when you are given a writing assignment that does not call for a specific type of organizational pattern, you will have to decide on the best one, based on your thinking, prewriting and planning.

Remember that each major point must play an important part in developing and supporting your assertion. In most instances, you discuss, analyze each major point, and support or illustrate it with specific examples, statistics, details, textual references, etc. For each point:

- Introduce it.
- Describe it.
- Discuss how it is connected to the assertion/claim/thesis.

You always want to be aware of your thesis, your purpose, and your audience. Each paragraph in the body of your essay has to move your reader closer and closer to your goal, your final destination (your assertion), and you've got to do this making certain to show the interconnectedness among each of your major points with what we call "connective tissue," and what others term transitional elements.

OUR BODY SAMPLES

Language

"A Presidential Candidate"

Informal diction contributes to the overall humor of this parody. Most of us expect a modicum of seriousness and dignity from our political candidates. And, we expect this to be evident in their speeches and writing. To the contrary, Twain uses "folksy" and regional words and phrases throughout the essay. In paragraph one, avoiding lofty language, the author writes "pretty much made up my mind" to tell his audience that he has made a decision, and he invites Congressional scrutiny with "let it prowl." Paragraph two has Twain's grandfather "bowling up" a tree when he is chased from his house by the narrator. Using his own method to appeal to the common man, the candidate says, "If my country don't want me . . ."

Exaggeration also plays a major role in the creation of this humorous take-off on campaign speeches. The anecdote about the author and his grandfather is in every way over the top. Treeing and shooting his grandfather with buckshot is both ludicrous and highly improbable. The absurdity continues in paragraph four with the tale of his burying his dead aunt "under my grapevine." In paragraph five, Twain takes a wide and caustic swing at political candidates who promise to stand up for the common man. He says, ". . . I regard the poor man, in his present condition, as so much wasted raw material." The author's outrageous suggestion to kill and cannibalize "the poor workingman . . ." and ". . . stuff him into sausages," would have made Jonathan Swift very proud.

Almost all of Twain's selection of details contributes to the irony of this piece. We expect heroic details of the candidate's war experiences, but this candidate describes and admits his cowardice in the face of battle, even while making a tongue-in-cheek reference to Washington. Instead of claiming to be a financial virgin as most candidates do, Twain readily characterizes himself as money hungry and willing to get it any way he can. Adding to the irony that is the basis for the announcement, Twain makes references to the U.S. Constitution and asks rhetorical questions about both his fitness for the presidency and his being a "victim of absurd prejudices."

Analysis of the Body of the Essay

topic sentence   <u>Informal diction contributes to the overall</u> | humor | of | this parody. | Most   transition

of us expect a modicum of seriousness and dignity from our political candidates. And, we expect this to be evident in their speeches and writing. To the contrary, Twain uses "folksy" and regional words and phrases throughout the essay. In paragraph one, avoiding lofty language,

ex. 1   the author writes "pretty much made up my mind" to tell his audience

ex. 2   that he has made a decision, and he invites Congressional scrutiny with

ex. 3   "let it prowl." Paragraph two has Twain's grandfather "bowling up" a tree when he is chased from his house by the narrator. And, in his final paragraph, the author uses his own method to appeal to the common man

ex. 4   when says, "If my country don't want me . . ."

topic sentence   Exaggeration also plays a major role in the creation of this humorous take-off on campaign speeches. The anecdote about the author and

ex. 1   his grandfather is in everyway over-the-top. Treeing and shooting his grandfather with buckshot is both ludicrous and highly improbable.

ex. 2   The absurdity continues in paragraph four with the tale of his burying his dead aunt "under my grapevine." In paragraph five, Twain takes a wide and caustic swing at political candidates who promise to stand up

ex. 3   for the common man. He says, ". . . I regard the poor man, in his pres-

ex. 4   ent condition, as so much wasted raw material." The author's outrageous suggestion to kill and cannibalize "the poor workingman . . ."

good allusion   and ". . . stuff him into sausages," would have made **Jonathan Swift very proud.**

topic sentence   Almost all of Twain's selection of details contributes to the irony of this piece. [We expect heroic tales of the candidate's war experiences, but this candidate describes and admits his cowardice in the face of

ex. 1 & 2   battle, even while making a tongue-in-cheek reference to Washington. Instead of claiming to be a financial virgin, as most candidates do, Twain

ex. 3   readily characterizes himself as money hungry and willing to get it any way he can.] Adding to the irony that is the basis for the announcement,

ex. 4   Twain makes references to the U.S. Constitution and asks rhetorical questions about both his fitness for the presidency and his being a "vic-

ex. 5 & 6   tim of absurd prejudices."

Comments

Because this is an AP English prompt that demands a specific type of response, the body paragraphs almost organize themselves. Pay close attention to the topic sentences, each of which markedly refer the reader to the thesis of the essay. Notice that each of the major points is developed using specific references to the text. For example, the first body paragraph contains four examples of informal diction, each of which is connected to the idea of humor and parody. The second body paragraph discusses the exaggeration Twain employs with three specific references to the text. The last major point concerns irony, and the writer examines this device by citing six textual references.

It is important to note that the textual references are NOT merely listed. They are incorporated into the framework of the paragraph, via both citations and comments, to support and illustrate each topic sentence (underlined). As an example, look carefully at the second and third sentences of paragraph three (bracketed). Including the reader in the comments, the writer vests the audience in the subject and tone of "A Presidential Candidate" and in the AP English essay, itself.

Last, the continuity is maintained throughout with clear transitions and echo words—what we term connecting tissue (blocked). Repeating key words *humor* and *parody* ties the first body paragraph to the opening paragraph. *Also* and *this,* together with the phrase *humorous take-off,* refer to the previous paragraphs and are, therefore, the key transitions in the second paragraph. Connecting the third paragraph to the prompt and the other preceding paragraphs are the transitional words *Twain's* and *this piece.* Rather than repeating Mark Twain over and over, the writer uses echo words, such as *author, narrator, this candidate.* And, Twain's essay is referred to as *announcement, remarks, absurdity, caustic swing, parody, take-off.*

Literature

"Dover Beach"

Drawing his images from nature, Arnold creates a romantic scene that will later be contrasted in the final stanza. As he implores his love to look from the window at the world beneath them, the poet introduces the sea and the land, and the diction positions them as the dominant contradictory symbols of the poem. Although it is night, "moon, fair, light, gleams, and glimmering" all illuminate the "calm, full, and tranquil bay." And yet, in his description of the "sweet night," Arnold includes the word, "only" to imply something other than the idyllic vision. This change in mood is meant to make his beloved uneasy, so she will be receptive to him later when he proposes an antidote to the ensuing negative examples.

To further his position, Arnold juxtaposes the sea and the "moon-blanched land," light and dark, and seeing and hearing. Now he orders his love to "Listen!" as well as look. This imperative is also for the reader, and we can hear, through onomatopoeia, the "grating roar" of the pebbles breaking the quiet tone. The following lines, 10–14, depend on sound devices and punctuation to develop contrast. A succession of caesuras breaks the iambic meter and makes the speaker and reader start and stop and start again, much like the rhythm of the waves themselves which "begin, and cease, and then again, begin." Perhaps, Arnold is using this pattern as a parallel to the lovers' relationship. It, too, may have its high and low tides.

Allusions to Sophocles and the Aegean allow Arnold to move from the immediate and specific images of the first stanza to a more general argument. Like the eternal sea, human misery is a common experience, and this example from the past will make his argument for loyalty and love more poignant and universal. His diction now is negative; the sea is "turbid, distant and northern." It is possible his love has also been remote and cold. Again, one can infer that the "ebb and flow" may refer to inconstancies the lovers have endured.

The third stanza introduces a more abstract metaphor, linking religion and nature. This "Sea of Faith" reveals the speaker's loss of belief and his disillusionment. With this negative example, Arnold contrasts the once "bright girdle furled with full faith" and the now "melancholy, drear, and naked" beaches swept by the "breath of night wind." This analogy seems developed to elicit both empathy and response on the part of his beloved. He has lost everything—God and Nature, but she can be his salvation because, by implication, he still believes in her. She will be his faith, his light, his constant sea.

As the poem reaches its climax, the speaker again moves from the general to the specific. He returns to the present and implores his beloved to accept his fervent plea: "Ah, love, let us be true to one another!" Arnold emphasizes this assertion by contrasting it with the concluding lines of the poem. Only this line is a simple direct imperative. The rest of the stanza is a complex set of similes that reiterate the major points of the speaker's argument.

In the first stanza, the couple was literally on the land, but, now, the world is "like a land of dreams." Repetition reinforces what the dream may be: "so various, so beautiful, so new." Immediately, this line is contrasted with a negative series focusing not on the dream, but on the reality: "neither joy, nor love, nor light, nor certitude, nor peace, nor help for pain." The final simile, "as on a darkling plain, where ignorant armies clash by night," is a direct contrast to the first stanza's softly lit sea, solitude, and serenity. Arnold puts the final touch on his argument by implying that they, the lovers who are true, therefore, must be everything positive and enlightened because they are in sharp contrast to the images and techniques presented throughout the poem.

Analysis of the Body of the Essay

topic sentence — Drawing his images from nature, Arnold creates a romantic scene that will be contrasted in the final stanza. As he implores his love to look from the window at the world beneath them, the poet introduces the sea and the land, and the diction positions them as the dominant contradictory symbols of the poem. Although it is night, "moon, fair, light, gleams, and glimmering" all illuminate the "calm, full, and tranquil

reference — bay." And yet, in his description of the "sweet night," Arnold includes

reference — the word, "only" to imply something other than the idyllic vision. This

reference — change in mood is meant to make his beloved uneasy, so she will be receptive to him later when he proposes an antidote to the ensuing neg-

connection to thesis — ative examples.

To further his position, Arnold juxtaposes the sea and the "moon-blanched land", light and dark, and seeing and hearing. Now he orders his love to "Listen!" as well as look. This imperative is also for the

ref. — reader, and we can hear, through onomatopoeia, the "grating roar" of the pebbles breaking the quiet tone. The following lines, 10–14, depend on sound devices and punctuation to develop contrast. A succession of

reference — caesuras breaks the iambic meter and makes the speaker/reader start

example — and stop and start again, much like the rhythm of the waves themselves

example — which "begin, and cease, and then again, begin." Perhaps, Arnold is using this pattern as a parallel to the lovers' relationship. It, too, may have its high and low tides.

topic — Allusions to Sophocles and the Aegean allow Arnold to move from

sentence — the immediate and specific images of the first stanza to a more general

universal — argument. Like the eternal sea, human misery is a common experience, and this example from the past will make his argument for loyalty and

idea love more poignant and universal. His <u>diction</u> now is negative; the sea

reference is "turbid, distant and northern." It is possible his love has also been remote and cold. Again, one can infer that the "ebb and flow" may refer

connection to thesis to inconstancies the lovers have endured.

ts   <u>The third stanza introduces a</u> more abstract metaphor, <u>linking reli-</u>

interp. <u>gion and nature.</u> This "Sea of Faith" reveals the speaker's loss of belief and his disillusionment. With this negative example, Arnold <u>contrasts</u>

reference the once "bright girdle furled with full faith" and the now "melancholy,

reference drear, and naked" beaches swept by the "breath of night wind." This <u>analogy</u> seems developed to elicit both empathy and response on the part of his beloved. He has lost everything—God and Nature, but she can be his salvation because, by implication, he still believes in her. She

interpretation will be his faith, his light, his constant sea.

ts   As the poem <u>reaches its climax, the speaker again moves from the gen-</u> <u>eral to the specific.</u> He returns to the present and implores his beloved to

ref. accept his fervent plea: "Ah, love, let us be true to one another!" Arnold emphasizes this assertion by <u>contrasting</u> it with the concluding lines of the poem. Only this line is a simple direct imperative. The rest of the stanza is a complex set of similes which reiterate the major points of the speak-er's argument.

    In the first stanza, the couple was literally on the land, but, now, the

ex. world is "like a land of dreams." <u>Repetition</u> reinforces what the dream may be: "so various, so beautiful, so new." Immediately, this line is <u>con-</u> <u>trasted</u> with a negative series focusing not on the dream, but on the real-

ex. ity: "neither joy, nor love, nor light, nor certitude, nor peace, nor help

ex. for pain." The final <u>simile</u>, "as on a darkling plain, where ignorant armies clash by night," is a direct <u>contrast</u> to the first stanza's softly lit sea, solitude, and serenity. <u>Arnold puts the</u> final touch <u>on his argument</u> <u>by implying that they, the lovers who are true, therefore, must be every-</u>

topic <u>thing positive and enlightened because they are in</u> sharp opposition <u>to</u>

sentence <u>the images and techniques presented throughout the poem.</u>

Comments

Obviously the writer of this essay has a clear understanding of the prompt and the poem. The paper is well focused, strongly based on the text, and clearly expressed. Specific references are appropriate and smoothly integrated into the essay. Topic adherence is reinforced throughout by echo words and connective tissue.

The essay's thesis, that the poem is developed by contrast to persuade the lover to her partner's viewpoint, is reiterated in each paragraph. The words, *contrast, contradictory,* and *opposition* are used to maintain this thread. Similarly, *argument, persuade, convince, point of view, position,* and *assertion* all focus the paper on its topic: the poem as an argument for reciprocal love. The illustrations of diction, meter, organization, metaphor, and similes relate the meaning of the poem and the essay directly to the prompt.

References to *now* and *then, again, first* and *last stanza, beginning, climax* and *concludes* serve as transitions to link and move the sections of the essay.

The level and thoroughness of analysis is the strength of the essay. The writer moves beyond the average paper by drawing a parallel between the movement of the lines and meter and the movement of the waves. This technical information is then carried over to the interpretive level with the insight that the ebb and flow of the sea might refer to the pattern of the relationship. The understanding and explanation of the use of contrast as a persuasive tool is also an upper level concept. The writer understands Arnold's real motivation for the poem and is aware of the emotional manipulation occurring. Including inferences shows the readers of the essay the depth of the writer's interpretive skills. The vocabulary, such as *juxtapose, idyllic, romantic, onomatopoeia, implication,* is used appropriately and also raises the level of the essay. Likewise, the sentence variety enhances the readability level.

The essay itself follows the pattern of the poem, and this approach maintains clarity. In addition, it opens and closes with direct references to the text that serve to unify the paper. The presentation is on task and accessible, reflecting good planning and prewriting efforts.

STUDENT SAMPLES

The transitions are bracketed for you.

Student A

["The Passionate Shepherd to His Love"] is very idyllic, flowery even. Marlowe uses words like "pleasures," "melodious," and "pretty lambs," for their connotative enhancements to the romantic tone of the poem. The line "And a thousand fragrant posies" is particularly powerful with its over-the-top image of a sea of flowers: "fragrant" with its hint of elegance, beauty, and grace, and "posies" reinforcing that image of soft, delicate, and perhaps gently swaying fields in which to frolic. The complete poetic mosaic, thus, creates a field of brightest colors, with the scent of sweet perfume and lazy bees droning overhead in this most romantic of rainbow paradises.

The second poem is the cynical twin of the first. Here, all the high-minded and romantic ideals are dashed into the "rocks grow[n] cold." Line by line, stanza by stanza, Sir Walter Raleigh's "The Nymph's Reply to the Shepherd" opposes the romantic attitude of the passionate shepherd of the first poem. The reply is: no, poor shepherd, you are a dreamer. "Cold," "gall," "fade," and "wither" are all chillingly clipped answers to the shepherd's lovesick plea. He would wither away, longing for the immortal nymph. Here, the poet presents a realistic (if somewhat pessimistic) viewpoint on life and love. The shepherd and the nymph become a metaphor for life and how nothing lasts forever; thus, everything is in vain.

This negative metaphor is developed by Raleigh's use of non-flowery, realistic diction. For example, "Soon break, soon wither, soon forgotten" is a far cry from the "posies" and fair lined slippers" of the first poem. The nymph's reply is cold and harsh with heart-breaking negative connotations for the shepherd and others who read the poem. Romanticism is challenged, calling to light the follies of the optimistic and pining fantasies of Christopher Marlowe's poem.

Comments

This successful contrast/comparison essay presents a thorough and well-organized series of points. They are substantiated by text and insightful interpretation. This student writer:

- demonstrates a thorough understanding of the prompt and its demands;
- clearly illustrates the differing attitudes towards life presented in the two poems;
- effectively develops comparison and contrast points;
- makes appropriate and meaningful references to the texts to support the analysis;
- uses inferences to draw conclusions about the underlying meaning of the poems;
- demonstrates strong topic adherence;
- employs a mature writing style.

Student B

From the very beginning, the specific tone of praise and empathy are established. The author's choice of words praises Paret and looks at him and at his fighting style with a sense of awe. Descriptive phrases, such as, "that he had an unusual ability to take a punch;" or that "he took three punches to the head in order to give back two." begin to lead an already shocked reader toward the inevitable ending. When Mailer uses the words "bouncing," "headache," and "bad maulings," an image of an animal springing from a fight pop into mind. However, this animal doesn't know when to give up, that is why he doesn't lose a fight; he just receives bad punches or beatings. Because of details and diction like these, the reader knows this man Benny Paret was special and would not give up, no matter what.

As one begins to read the second paragraph, the tone changes slightly. Paret is still proud; however, his showmanship is faltering. This, in turn, leads to his demise which is unlike any other. Much like his entire boxing career, Paret's death was brutal, but respectable. The first seven sentences in the second paragraph set the reader up for the climax. They detail the Kid's "first sign of weakness," and "inspired particular shame," allowing the reader to see that, as the Mailer states, "Paret began to wilt." For the first time the crowd sees him as human, a man, a man about to take the last beating of his life.

When the writer begins to narrate the actual mauling, or should I say killing, he goes into gory animalistic detail, comparing Paret to a "huge boxed rat" and Griffith to a "cat ready to rip the life out . . ." Right away, the reader begins to imagine this poor fighter trapped in the corner and this ogre beating away at him. Later on, Griffith's punches are compared to a "piston rod which has broken through the crankcase;" and to "a baseball bat demolishing a pumpkin," the pumpkin being Paret's head. All of a sudden, the reader not only visualizes this murder but hears the sounds that go with it, the sound of "goosh" or "whoosh," two sounds that aren't very pleasant when talking about a human being's head. Describing the force needed to pull Griffith away, Mailer talks about his uncontrollable power, much like a rabid animal in real life, one with no feelings, just waiting to win. Griffith is portrayed as a man with no remorse.

The last paragraph really hits home, making the reader say, "Wow" or "Oh, my G-d." The idea of Paret dying on his feet, and the impact left on the crowd is almost overpowering. When Mailer chooses the word "hover" a certain heavy feeling just kind of hangs with the reader. The Kid's death is slow and admirable. The metaphor "sank slowly" like a "large ship which turns . . ." gives a feeling of respect, the kind we give to great ships that sink at sea. In the last sentence, "the sound of Griffith's . . . chopping into a wet log," brutally drives home and reminds the reader of the relentless beating Paret sustained before he died.

Comments

The body of this student essay indicates a writer who understood both Mailer's text and how to analyze the rhetorical strategies used by the author. This sample is a good model of an essay that smoothly integrates details and specific references into both the sentence and the paragraph.

Paragraph 1 points out Mailer's use of descriptive words and phrases, cites specific examples, AND comments about the purpose and effect of these citations. Paragraph 2 provides an example of another form of citation. Here the writer refers to WHERE in the text the reference occurs. Note also how smoothly the details are integrated into the sentences. In paragraph 3, specific references are linked to the student writer's main points, and he correctly makes use of the ellipsis. The final body paragraph also uses the ellipsis correctly and well when the writer pulls out just the phrases of a metaphor he needs to make a point. And, don't forget to take note of the sequential transitional phrases we've blocked for you.

Take a Deep Breath. It's Time for Your Body-Building Routine

Go to your current writing portfolio or folder and choose one of your essays to examine closely.

1. The title of the essay is _____.

2. The subject of the essay is _____

   _____.

3. The purpose is _____.

4. The audience is _____.

5. My thesis statement is located in paragraph _____. It is

   _____

   _____

   _____

6. I have _____ major points in this essay. They are:

   _____   _____

   _____   _____

_____   _____

_____   _____

7. I've used the following organization method(s) to develop my points. (Check all that apply)

____ Chronological order
____ Spatial order
____ Subject by subject
____ Point by point examines
____ Categorizing
____ A single cause leading to a single effect or multiple effects
____ Multiple causes leading to a single effect or multiple effects
____ A single effect and the single or multiple cause(s)
____ Multiple effects and the single or multiple cause(s)
____ Most important to least important or vise versa
____ Deduction
____ Induction

8. My essay has _____ paragraphs.

9. The transitional elements in each of my paragraphs are:

¶ 2 _____

¶ 3 _____

¶ 4 _____

¶ 6 _____

¶ 7 _____

¶ 8 _____

¶ 9 _____

¶ 10 _____

10. Each of my paragraphs has a topic sentence. ____ yes ____ no

11. Each of my body paragraphs has specific examples, references, etc. to support both my thesis and the topic sentence. ____ yes ____ no

12. I've made certain to avoid just listing examples, references, etc.

_____ yes _____ no

13. I've connected each of my examples, or references, or points to the subject of my essay. _____ yes _____ no

14. If I had the opportunity to rewrite any of the body paragraphs of this essay, I would choose to rewrite paragraph _____ because _____.

15. Here's my revision: _____

_____

_____

_____

_____

_____

_____

_____

_____

_____

_____

_____

> *Note:* We strongly urge you to work through this and other writing and revising activities with members of your English class or members of your peer reading group. Having other readers provide you with feedback and vice versa is vital for strengthening your writing skills.

SUPPORTING SYNTAX

Remember that part of your responsibility as a writer is clarity, whether you're composing the opening of your essay, the body, or its conclusion. As writing trainers, we can tell you that there are particular syntax problems that you should be aware of and that you should try to avoid if you want to insure this clarity. Consider the following:

1. Incorporating Quotations and References from the Text into a Sentence

There are several techniques that allow you to place a specific textual reference in the sentence.

- The reference to the speaker or writer or character; for example, *According to Mark Twain . . .*
- Citing the location of the reference; for example, lines 3–5 of paragraph 2 pose a rhetorical question.
- Placing the reference inside the sentence to illustrate a point; for example, *Dickens' diction such as "somber," "wasted," and "suffocating" establishes the motif of illness and death.*
- A general reference; for example, *In the first part of the poem . . .*
- Beginning a sentence with a quotation; for example, *"But why you ask me, should this tale be told/to men grown old, or who are growing old?"* signals a transition in the poem.
- Splitting references; for example, *"An insurmountable precipice"* faces Hester in her quest for equality, and mustering courage, she is able to *"start back from a deep chasm."*
- AVOID THE LAUNDRY LIST. For example, There is frequent use of assonance in the poem, such as *"woe," "bemoan," "Lone," and "o'er."* (This list is NOT linked to any meaning or point being made.) The solution: With such words as *"woe," "bemoan," "lone,"* and *"o'er,"* the poet's assonance approximates the sounds of someone lamenting.

We recommend that you use a combination of the above techniques in any given essay. We also want to stress the importance of making certain that you link any and all of your references to a specific point you are making.

2. Using Transitions

Why worry about transitions? Simple. They constitute the primary connective tissue within the body of your essay. Transitions will

- connect the various parts of the essay to both your thesis and to the preceding paragraph;
- enable you to move from one thought to another without confusing your reader;
- set up a sequence, if needed;
- indicate cause and effect; and
- delineate the areas of contrast and comparison.

Below Is a Brief Listing of Frequently Used Transitional Words and Phrases

- Most often used and most "natural" transitions in sentences or brief sequences of sentences: *and, but, or, nor, for, yet*
- Some other commonly used transitions between paragraphs or sections of longer works:

    _____ (numerical) *first, second, third, primarily*, etc.
    _____ (sequential) *then, finally, next*
    _____ (additional) *furthermore, moreover, again, also, similarly*
    _____ (illustrative) *for example, for instance, to illustrate*
    _____ (contrast, comparison, alternative) *on the other hand, nevertheless, conversely, instead, however, still*
    _____ (cause and effect) *therefore, consequently, as a result, accordingly*
    _____ (affirmation) *of course, obviously, indeed*

3. Active and Passive Voice

You've probably heard this more often than you can remember—"Avoid the passive voice." And, most of the time, you've ignored this piece of advice or used the passive voice without realizing it. Well, we're asking you NOT to ignore it and NOT to use if at all possible. Nothing can add a deadening quality to your writing more than passive voice.

We know; we know; you want to sound as "intelligent" as you possibly can, and using long, involved sentences with multisyllabic words that only a thesaurus could love is the way to do it. WRONG! Knowing your material and presenting it clearly is your best bet.

Just What Is ACTIVE and PASSIVE VOICE?

To answer this question, look at the following sentences:

The car was driven by Paul.

1. What is the subject? _____

2. What is the verb tense? _____

3. Is the verb simple or compound? _____

4. What is the prepositional phrase? _____

5. How many words are in the sentence? _____

Paul drove the car.

1. What is the subject? _____

2. What is the verb tense? _____

3. Is the verb simple or compound? _____

4. Is there a prepositional phrase? _____

5. How many words are in the sentence? _____

Which of the two sentences has the subject of the sentence doing the

action? _____

Which one has the subject being acted upon? _____

When the writing lets the reader know that the subject is <u>doing the acting</u>, you have ACTIVE VOICE. When the subject is acted upon or is the goal of the action, and, therefore, NOT responsible, you have PASSIVE VOICE.

With this in mind, identify which of the two sentences above is active and which one is passive. Without a doubt, we know you chose the <u>second as active</u> and the <u>first as passive</u>.

Here's another example:

The new free trade agreement was signed last night.

Who signed the treaty? Whom do we blame if the agreement falters? We don't know, do we? Passive voice avoids responsibility. It is a primary tool of those who wish to obfuscate or those who lack confidence and decisiveness.

Why not give the true picture and write:

Last night, the President of the United States and the President of Mexico signed a new free trade agreement.

4. More "Avoiders"

There are two AP English "idiosyncrasies" we would like to see every student avoid.

1. Avoid this type of phrase: *Poe uses diction . . .*

   A writer doesn't <u>use</u> diction. His or her word choice is <u>categorized</u> as diction. Therefore, the proper phrasing would be: *Poe's diction . . .*

2. Avoid the judgmental qualifiers; for example, *Wordsworth's <u>masterful</u> use of the English language. . . ; The <u>magnificent</u> argument . . .*

   Masterful and *magnificent* are qualifiers. You may be at a later date, but at this point in your academic career, you are NOT in a position to make this type of judgment. They are just empty fillers and do nothing to enhance your essay.

   The solution: *Wordsworth's use of language . . .*
   This argument . . .

Chapter 9

Writing the Conclusion of the Essay and Revising

"Writing is easy. All you have to do is sit down in front of the computer and open a vein."
—Red Smith

"Leave 'em wantin' more." That's a piece of advice most performers are given early in their career. We'd like to give you a similar, yet somewhat different, piece of advice. "Leave 'em feelin' satisfied." You've made an assertion and provided support for that assertion in the body of your essay. And, you want the reader to leave your presentation understanding your point of view and accepting your evidence in support of it. You also want your reader to sense a kind of closure and not feel as if left swinging in the breeze. The obvious way to provide this sense of security and closure is to compose an appropriate conclusion.

The old, tried-and-true conclusion is the all too familiar one. It usually begins with "In summary," or "In conclusion," or "Finally" followed by a review of the thesis and major points made in the presentation. Although this might be useful in an extended and complex essay, it is not needed, nor is it recommended, for a 500–1000-word presentation in a response to a college-level writing prompt, whether timed or untimed.

With that in mind, you no doubt are asking yourself, "Okay, if not a summary, what should I write?" You could try one of the following:

- Link your conclusion to something you said in the introduction.
- Link your idea to a more universal point.
- Relate a personal experience or idea to your thesis.
- Link your thesis to the world of your reader.
- Challenge your reader.
- End with a rhetorical question or imperative statement.
- Use an anecdote to reinforce a major point in your essay.
- End with an important line from the original text.

Your conclusion should leave the reader with a sense of you as a person with a voice and a valid, interesting point of view. This is your last chance to make an impression. Don't lose the opportunity. Consider the following samples from students' essays.

OUR SAMPLE CONCLUSIONS

Language

"A Presidential Candidate"

Throughout "A Presidential Candidate," Mark Twain focuses on his negative qualities rather than on the good, which is the usual MO for a political candidate. He enumerates absurdly opposite positions to the usual campaign promises. I only wish every candidate for political office could read this parody. As a matter of fact, I think I will e-mail this to all my representatives who hold national, state, and local offices. Thanks, Mr. Twain.

Comments

This conclusion links the final remarks to the more universal point of current politicians needing to reconsider their own approaches to addressing the electorate. The conclusion ends with a personal challenge that the writer makes to himself.

Sample Conclusion from the "Dover Beach" Prompt

"Ah, love, let us be true," pleads the speaker and we can imagine the lovers, just the two of them, together, in the present, against the dark past and unknown future.

Comments

Highlighting the most important line of the poem, this conclusion succinctly summarizes the essential contrasts presented in the introduction to the essay.

STUDENT SAMPLES

Student A

Throughout history, the rich and famous have enjoyed privileges that the common man hasn't been allowed. Many current headline stories reveal the depth to which money and fame can infect the justice system. Meanwhile, those clothed in "rags" continue to get shafted by a system that they do not influence nor control.

Comments

This conclusion aggressively finalizes the writer's position. With no re-hashing of the prompt and no repetition of the thesis, this student leaves his reader with an implied challenge–do you dare to agree or disagree with me?

Student B

In any case, that's what it comes down to. The Calvinists believed that wealth was a sign from God that a man had been pre-selected to reside in heaven. So, our wealthy folks are really heaven-sent. Perfect angels don't need laws anyway, right?

Comments

Using a sarcastic rhetorical question to end this essay is a thought-provoking way for this student writer to make his or her own voice and point of view heard loudly and clearly.

Okay, You've Completed Your Warmup Conclusion Activities. It's Now Time for the Real Workout

You're going to be examining the <u>same three essays</u> you've been working with in Chapters 7 and 8 to complete this exercise set.

1. For each of the conclusions cite the transitional element that connects the ending to the body of the essay.

   Essay #1: _____

   Essay #2: _____

   Essay #3: _____

2. What technique(s) did you use to create each of your conclusions?

Essay	*Technique*
1 _____ 2 _____ 3 _____	Link your conclusion to something you said in the introduction.
1 _____ 2 _____ 3 _____	Link your idea to a more universal point.
1 _____ 2 _____ 3 _____	Relate a personal experience or idea to your thesis.
1 _____ 2 _____ 3 _____	Link your thesis to the world of your reader.
1 _____ 2 _____ 3 _____	Challenge your reader.
1 _____ 2 _____ 3 _____	End with a rhetorical question or imperative statement.
1 _____ 2 _____ 3 _____	Use an anecdote to reinforce a major point in your essay.
1 _____ 2 _____ 3 _____	Use a quotation from the original text.

3. Have you avoided "In summary," "In conclusion," etc. in each of your conclusions?

   1 ____ yes ____ no; 2 ____ yes ____ no;

   3 ____ yes ____ no

4. Select one of your three conclusions and rewrite it using TWO different techniques.

5. I chose the conclusion to essay _____ 1 _____ 2 _____ 3.

6. For the conclusion to essay _____ I've decided to use the following techniques:

   Technique 1: _____

   Technique 2: _____

7. On a separate sheet of paper rewrite the conclusion using the two different techniques.

8. Of the three different conclusions, including my original, to essay _____, the one I like best is _____ the original _____ the conclusion using technique 1 _____ the conclusion using technique 2.

9. I think my choice is the best conclusion because _____ _____ _____.

REVISION

The process you just completed is a type of revision. But, this is just one of many ways to go about reworking your essay. To give you an idea of some of these methods, we'd like to examine the real work of revision. To examine the real work of revision (and, as some would say, the real work of writing), we are going to provide you with several different methods that you could employ to revise your essays.

1. Here Is a Very Simple Method

This is a quick overview that you can do alone or with a peer reader. You should consider and take notes, where and when necessary, as you consider each of the following.

RECONSIDER YOUR OPENING PARAGRAPH.

1. Is there a clear thesis statement?
2. Does it somehow grab the interest of your reader?
3. In what tense are you going to present your ideas?

ORGANIZATION

1. What is the purpose of your essay?
2. What rhetorical strategies, techniques and devices do you use to achieve this purpose?
3. Is your essay presented as FORMAL or INFORMAL?
4. Are there transitional words/phrases connecting the body paragraphs to each other?
5. Do you have an ending that naturally evolves from your essay?

SYNTAX

1. Are all verbs in the same tense? Is there a reason for any verb to be a different tense?
2. Do all words/phrases adhere to the essay being formal or informal?
3. Does EACH pronoun have a CLEAR ANTECEDENT?
4. Is there a clear reason for every COMMA used in the essay?
5. Examine the beginning of each sentence. Is there an overuse of a type of opening? If there is, work on changing some to achieve variety.
6. Do you have a variety of sentence types? Simple? Compound? Complex? Compound–complex?

2. Here's a More Involved and Involving Revision Method That Can Provide Valuable Feedback.

1. What is the subject of your essay?
2. What do you hope your reader will come away with after having read your essay?
3. With the answers to the above questions in mind, what is the thesis statement? Quote it exactly.
4. How have you ordered the development of the support for your claim? Is it in chronological order, spatial, least important to most important, etc.? List the major points in your essay in the order that each appears.
5. Does each of your paragraphs, other than the first, have a transitional word or phrase?

List them:

PARAGRAPH #   TRANSITION WORD/PHRASE

2

3

4

5

6

7

8

9

10

6. Take a really close look at your introductory paragraph(s). Is it made very clear to your reader what the subject of this essay is? Does it contain the thesis/claim? Does the last sentence of the introduction lead easily to the next section of your essay?

7. Take a close look at your conclusion. Does it bring closure to your essay in such a way that your reader should feel he or she knows your point of view, attitude, and why he or she should care about it?

8. Let's call this next part of the revising process **COAP**ing.

   CUT: bracket all the best or most workable sentences and CUT OUT everything else.

   ORDER: put these pieces in the best order, decide what your main point is; put in transitions.

   ADD: do any additional writing that is needed.

   POLISH: make the sentences smooth and readable.

   • Cut unnecessary words and phrases
   • Clarify anything that isn't clear.
   • Combine any sentences that lend themselves to combining, for greater flow and variety.
   • Correct typos, spelling, punctuation, and grammar.

9. And last, but most important, **READ YOUR ESSAY OUT LOUD TO SOMEONE, AND SOMEONE MUST READ IT OUT LOUD TO YOU.** (Do this for your first draft and all other drafts.)

10. As a result of this reading aloud, have you located any major errors that need to be revised? If so, list them.

3. For a Writing Assignment Specifically Related to Literary Texts, the Following Method Might Be Useful.

1. The text(s) I am working with is/are _____.

2. My essay is ____ formal ____ informal.

3. The thesis/claim of my essay is _____.

4. I have made certain to include the title(s) and author(s) of my texts.

   They are _____.

5. The main rhetorical strategy I use to develop my essay is
   ____ contrast/comparison, ____ exposition,
   ____ definition, ____ cause/effect, ____ process,
   ____ classification, ____ analysis, ____ description.

7. I have also made use of the following:
   ____ contrast/comparison, ____ examples,
   ____ definition, ____ cause/effect, ____ process,
   ____ classification, ____ analysis, ____ description.

8. I organize my essay around _____ character relationships,
   _____ conflicts, _____ significance of setting, _____
   the writer's use of symbols, _____ the writer's manipulation of
   his/her point of view, _____ the development of imagery.

9. I have made _____ specific references to my first text, _____
   _____ and _____ specific references to my second
   text, _____.

10. When referring to printed text, each one of my references cites the
    appropriate LINE, PARAGRAPH, STANZA, or PAGE, depending
    on whether it is prose or poetry. Here are my references:

Reference #	Page #	Paragraph #	Line #	Stanza #
_____	_____	_____	_____	_____
_____	_____	_____	_____	_____
_____	_____	_____	_____	_____

11. Below are the transition words/phrases I use between paragraphs.

PARAGRAPH #	TRANSITION WORD/PHRASE
2	
3	
4	
5	
6	
7	
8	
9	
10	

12. My ending makes a final statement rather than summarizing what
    I've already said. ____ YES   ____ NO

OUR WRITERS' SAMPLE ESSAYS

Essay in Response to the Prompt for Mark Twain's "A Presidential Candidate"

We've all heard the following before, haven't we? "Trust me. I only want to be your public servant. I will always work for the common good of all." It's so familiar and so shallow that the political cynic in each of us responds, "<u>Sure</u> we should. <u>Sure</u> he does. <u>Sure</u> he will." Aware of this cynicism, Mark Twain plays with our political suspicions in "A Presidential Candidate," a parody of the typical campaign speech.

Informal diction contributes to the overall humor of this parody. Most of us expect a modicum of seriousness and dignity from our political candidates. And, we expect this to be evident in their speeches and writing. To the contrary, Twain uses "folksy" and regional words and phrases throughout the essay. In paragraph one, avoiding lofty language, the author writes "pretty much made up my mind" to tell his audience that he has made a decision, and he invites Congressional scrutiny with "let it prowl." Paragraph two has Twain's grandfather "bowling up" a tree when he is chased from his house by the narrator. And, in his final paragraph, the author uses his own method to appeal to the common man when says, "If my country don't want me . . ."

Exaggeration also plays a major role in the creation of this humorous take-off on campaign speeches. The anecdote about the author and his grandfather is in every way over the top. Treeing and shooting his grandfather with buckshot is both ludicrous and highly improbable. The absurdity continues in paragraph four with the tale of his burying his dead aunt "under my grapevine." In paragraph five, Twain takes a wide and caustic swing at political candidates who promise to stand up for the common man. He says, ". . . I regard the poor man, in his present condition, as so much wasted raw material." The author's outrageous suggestion to kill and cannibalize "the poor workingman . . ." and ". . . stuff him into sausages," would have made Jonathan Swift very proud.

Almost all of Twain's selection of details contributes to the irony of this piece. We expect heroic tales of the candidate's war experiences, but this candidate describes and admits his cowardice in the face of battle, even while making a tongue-in-cheek reference to Washington. Instead of claiming to be a financial virgin, as most candidates do, Twain readily characterizes himself as money hungry and willing to get it any way he can. Adding to the irony that is the basis for the announcement, Twain makes references to the U.S. Constitution and asks rhetorical questions about both his fitness for the presidency and his being a "victim of absurd prejudices."

Throughout "A Presidential Candidate," Mark Twain focuses on his negative qualities rather than on the positive which is the usual MO for a political candidate. He enumerates absurdly opposite positions to the usual campaign promises. I only wish every candidate for political office could read this parody. As a matter of fact, I think I will e-mail this to all my representatives who hold national, state, and local offices. Thanks, Mr. Twain.

Essay in Response to the Prompt for "Dover Beach"

From "calm to clash, from light to darkling, from sea to land," Matthew Arnold's poem, "Dover Beach" is a study in contrast. This contrast, developed throughout the poem by a progression of increasingly negative examples, is necessary to convince his love to be true. In addition, poetic devices and techniques enable Arnold to encourage his love to see the urgency of his desire and passion. Metaphors, allusions, organization, and appeals to the senses reinforce his argument, that love and love-making are the only things of certainty in an ignorant and hostile world.

This contrast is a subtle way to persuade his love to his point of view. By gradually leading her to realize that life is, and always has been, filled with "misery and uncertainty," he establishes his argument that only their commitment to one another can counteract the inevitable struggle and disillusionment of life.

Drawing his images from nature, Arnold creates a romantic scene that will later be contrasted in the final stanza. As he implores his love to look from the window at the world beneath them, the poet introduces the sea and the land, and the diction positions them as the dominant contradictory symbols of the poem. Although it is night, "moon, fair, light, gleams, and glimmering" all illuminate the "calm, full, and tranquil bay." And yet, in his description of the " sweet night," Arnold includes the word, "only" to imply something other than the idyllic vision. This change in mood is meant to make his beloved uneasy, so she will be receptive to him later when he proposes an antidote to the ensuing negative examples.

To further his position, Arnold juxtaposes the sea and the "moon-blanched land," light and dark, and seeing and hearing. Now he orders his love to "Listen!" as well as look. This imperative is also for the reader, and we can hear, through onomatopoeia, the "grating roar" of the pebbles breaking the quiet tone. The following lines, 10–14, depend on sound devices and punctuation to develop contrast. A succession of caesuras breaks the iambic meter and makes the speaker and reader start and stop and start again, much like the rhythm of the waves themselves, which "begin, and cease, and then again, begin." Perhaps, Arnold is using this pattern as a parallel to the lovers' relationship. It, too, may have its high and low tides.

Allusions to Sophocles and the Aegean allow Arnold to move from the immediate and specific images of the first stanza to a more general argument. Like the eternal sea, human misery is a common experience, and this example from the past will make his argument for loyalty and love more poignant and universal. His diction now is negative; the sea is "turbid, distant and northern." It is possible his love has also been remote and cold. Again, one can infer that the "ebb and flow" may refer to inconstancies the lovers have endured.

The third stanza introduces a more abstract metaphor, linking religion and nature. This "Sea of Faith" reveals the speaker's loss of belief and his disillusionment. With this negative example, Arnold contrasts the once "bright girdle furled with full faith" and the now "melancholy, drear, and naked" beaches swept by the "breath of night wind." This analogy seems developed to elicit both empathy and response on the part of his beloved. He has lost everything—God and Nature, but she can be his salvation because, by implication, he still believes in her. She will be his faith, his light, his constant sea.

As the poem reaches its climax, the speaker again moves from the general to the specific. He returns to the present and implores his beloved to accept his fervent plea: "Ah, love, let us be true to one another!" Arnold emphasizes this assertion by contrasting it with the concluding lines of the poem. Only this line is a simple direct imperative. The rest of the stanza is a complex set of similes that reiterate the major points of the speaker's argument.

In the first stanza, the couple was literally on the land, but, now, the world is "like a land of dreams." Repetition reinforces what the dream may be: "so various, so beautiful, so new." Immediately, this line is contrasted with a negative series focusing not on the dream, but on the reality: "neither joy, nor love, nor light, nor certitude, nor peace, nor help for pain." The final simile, "as on a darkling plain, where ignorant armies clash by night," is a direct contrast to the first stanza's softly lit sea, solitude, and serenity. Arnold puts the final touch on his argument by implying that they, the lovers who are true, therefore, must be everything positive and enlightened because they are in sharp contrast to the negative images and techniques presented throughout the poem.

"Ah, love, let us be true," pleads the speaker, and we can imagine the lovers, just the two of them, together, in the present, against the dark past and unknown future.

PART IV

TRAINING SUPPLEMENTS

Chapter 10

The College Application Essay

> *"Blot out, correct, insert, refine,*
> *Enlarge, diminish, interline;*
> *Be mindful, when intervention fails,*
> *To scratch your head, and bite your nails."*
> —Jonathan Swift

Finally, the moment of truth is at hand. You've been exercising your mental muscles, and it's time to put yourself to the test by writing your college application essay. If you're like most students, applying to the college of your choice is a little like trying out for the Olympics—many are called, but few are chosen. But, remember that your trainers are here with you, and you're going to be just fine. If you apply those writing skills that you have been developing and strengthening throughout this book, you should come through these Olympian trials with ease. Let's begin your college application routine by answering a few basic questions that most students have about this process.

Why Do Colleges Want an Essay? Isn't It Just More Work for Them?

Actually, admissions people tell us they look forward to this part of the application requirements. After all, this is the time that they finally have a chance to hear your voice. And, this is the time that you have to make certain that this voice of yours is heard clearly and emphatically. The college essay is the part of the application that you can control and use to your advantage.

What Do Colleges Look for in the Application Essay?

There are many things that an essay reveals to the reader. First and foremost, of course, it conveys the level of your writing ability. Colleges want students who are articulate, conscientious, and creative. The level of your essay is an indicator of your academic strengths.

In addition, the essay reveals particular aspects of your personality. As you know from the other sections of this book, choice is a critical aspect of the writing process. How you choose to approach the essay, what you choose to write about, and the style you choose to employ all indicate who you are.

How Much Does the Essay Count in the Admissions Process?

Trust us, it counts. Although there is no single mathematical formula for weighting the essay, it is certainly a major determining factor in the acceptance process. If you are applying to a highly competitive school, it is safe to assume that the other applicants are just as proficient and well-rounded as you. (One of our students, a valedictorian accepted at an Ivy League school, was amazed to discover that nearly every classmate in his English class had been valedictorian in his or her high school.) **Because grades, scores, and activities are fairly objective information, it falls to the essay to separate one bright student from another.**

If you are a strong student who writes an exceptional paper, you have absolutely increased your chances of acceptance. If, on the other hand, you are a strong student who writes a weak paper, you are likely to be dropped a notch in the admissions process.

How Do I Get Started Writing the Application Essay?

There are two basic approaches you can take. The <u>first</u> is the: I've got a burning passion, funniest ever, scariest, life-altering perfect story to tell, I've always known I was going to write about it, and this is my chance, don't stop me now–approach.

To which we reply: Good. You're halfway there. Keep an open mind and we'll try to work that one of a kind story into a solid college essay.

The <u>second</u> approach is probably more common. Help, I don't know what to write about. I'll never be able to do this. Where do I start. Would you write it for me–approach.

To which we reply: Good. That's what your trainers are going to help you overcome.

Let's get started. Set aside some time, make yourself comfortable and face your future. First, gather the applications from the colleges of your choice and analyze the tasks they expect you to fulfill.

A SAMPLING OF SOME TYPICAL COLLEGE ESSAY QUESTIONS

This section introduces you to the most common questions you will encounter. It also deconstructs the question and provides suggestions for approaching the task. We have indicated the specific college requir-

ing the questions, but, obviously, we could not list questions for all the schools you may be considering. Be aware that many, many, schools use the same questions or variations on the topics we examine. In fact, many schools use the Common Application form, and we cover these questions in this chapter. Even if you are not planning to apply to one of the schools we refer to, it is very important to read all the questions.

Sometimes reading a prompt in a different format will trigger a response in you and start you on the path to delineating your essay for the college of your choice. There's an added bonus: thinking about each of these topics will prepare those of you who choose to go on a personal interview. These ideas are representative of what you may be asked, and, how terrific, you'll have all the right answers because you've been exercising your minds throughout the application process.

Question

Choose and discuss a quotation or personal motto that reflects your values and beliefs and tells us something about the kind of person you are.

—Cornell University

The choice of quotation can determine the tone and style of your essay. If you already have a personal favorite, go for it. If not, here are some tips:

- Pick up a copy of *Bartlett's Familiar Quotations* and randomly skim through it.
- Go online to various quotation sites and plug in topics of interest to you.
- Reflect on your favorite songs and extract lines as possibilities.
- Review the novels, plays, and poems you have studied for great lines or mottos.
- Think of family sayings and their implications.

Remember, the idea is not only about choosing a quotation with potential, but it is also about what that quotation reveals about your values and you as a person. Always give credit to the source of your choice.

No pain, but real gain. It's time to stretch *your own* quotable memory.

FAVORITE	WHAT IT REVEALS ABOUT ME
Quotations	
Lyrics	
Mottos and Aphorisms	

Question

> *You have just completed your 300-page autobiography. Please submit page 217.*
>
> **—University of Pennsylvania**

This question allows you to reveal your future plans and aspirations. You must realize that the page number implies that you have lived a good portion of your life already. The voice you choose should reflect a level of maturity and reflection. You can utilize any or all of the rhetorical strategies and literary techniques to create your scenario and persona. Be creative. Use such techniques as dialogue, symbol, epiphany, mood, and tone to develop your essay. Remember, it must reveal you and your values.

Practice This Set with Your Imagination in High Gear

My age when I'm writing this autobiography is _____

My age on page 217 will be _____.

Because page 300 is the end of the book, my circumstances at that time

will be (be specific) _____

_____

_____

My personal circumstances on page 217 will be (be specific) _____

_____

_____

What this page (217) will reveal about me. _____

_____

_____

Question

Indicate a person who has had a significant influence on you, and explain that influence.

—Harvard University

Generally speaking, this question refers to real people with whom you have interacted. The pitfall of this question is that many students choose family members, which is perfectly fine, but it is often difficult to separate personal emotion from the point of the essay. By all means, choose honestly, but remember that the admissions committee will be reading many, many, inspirational testaments to relatives. **Avoid being sentimental, and focus on the influence and its power in your life.**

Question

Describe a character in fiction, an historical figure, or a creative work (as in art, music, science, etc.) that has had an influence on you and explain that influence.

—Harvard University

This related question is easier for some students because it may not be as emotionally linked as the previous choice. Be honest. Do not choose a character that you think will impress the reader. Choose one that you truly respond to (remember how passionate Holden Caulfield was when he said he wanted to meet Eustacia Vye? He really let us in on his most private longings and values.)

Once again, **it is not just the character or work that you must address, but also the nature of the influence and its effect on you.**

Be Honest When You Do This Next Exercise

<u>MY MOST INFLUENTIAL PERSON</u>
<u>(or character, or work of art, etc.)</u>

Who: _____

Why: _____

Influence: _____

_____

Circumstance or episode I recall that illustrates this influence:

_____

_____

_____

_____

Its effect on me:

_____

_____

Question

Recall an occasion when you took a risk that you now know was the right thing to do.

—University of Pennsylvania

This question requires that you reflect on the risk and explore the long term effects of your decision. To construct a complete response, you must explain the nature of the risk, the reasons you took it, and how, with the benefit of time, you now know that you made the right decision. **It is always a plus if you can relate that decision to your current personality and explain how it will benefit you in your college experience.**

Lower Your Application Essay Risk by Completing the Following Chart

THE RISK   WHY TAKEN   SPECIFICS   RIGHT OR NOT

Question

What is your favorite word and why?
— University of Virginia

A very challenging and creative question that is deceptive in its simplicity. Your choice will reveal your understanding of nuance and tone. It's a great question to have fun with—but don't jump to easy and trite responses. Think and explore the possibilities of language . . . and of course, be yourself.

Sure, You Have a Word for It. Here's Another Memory-Stretching Exercise

WORD   DEFINITION(S)   WHY IT'S A FAVORITE

Question

Have you witnessed a person who is close to you doing something you considered seriously wrong? Describe the circumstances, your thoughts, and how you chose to respond. If you discussed it with a person, was his/her justification valid? In retrospect, what, if anything, would you have done differently and why?

— Duke University

Not for the faint-hearted, this question is very personal and you need to consider all the requirements carefully. You must isolate a moral problem, share an intimate relationship, analyze your situation and response. You may reveal more than you realize. Pay careful attention to your tone—avoid pomposity and preaching. If applicable, remember to address the other person's rationale and its validity. And then, you must include how time has or has not altered your view of the episode. An essay this complex is a rich opportunity if you are comfortable with it. If not, avoid it completely.

Here's Your Chance to Play Judge and Jury

The Offense: Your Circumstances:

Who: Your thoughts:

What: Your response:

Where   Your reflections over time

Why:

* * * *

The following questions are for **you** to examine and think about. Follow the form of the previous examples. These should give you a clear idea of the scope and variety of writing opportunities available to you. Really flex your muscles—write the answers in note form or talk them out with yourself or a good listener. This is your strength training, and it will pay off. The more familiar you are with the process, the less nervous you will be, and the more confident a writer you'll become.

Amherst College Question

Please respond to one of the following quotations. We are eager to know more about you as a person. We hope to find out who you are, how you think, what you think about, and how you choose to express yourself.

1. *"We seek [community] more often than we find it; we find it in odd and surprising ways; it is real but is also fragile, uncertain, and sometimes ambiguous."* Amherst College President Tom Gerety, Commencement Address 1994.

2. *"There is no use in trying," said Alice; "one can't believe impossible things." "I dare say you haven't much practice," said the Queen. "When I was your age, I always did it for half an hour a day. Why, sometimes I believed six impossible things before breakfast."* Lewis Carroll, <u>Alice's Adventures in Wonderland</u>.

University of Virginia Questions

Look out any window in your home. What would you change and why?

What form of discrimination most concerns you?

Technophobe or technophile?

Massachusetts Institute of Technology Questions

Life brings many disappointments as well as satisfactions. Could you tell us about a time in your life when you experienced disappointment, or faced difficult or trying circumstances?

Make up a question that is personally relevant to you, state it clearly, and answer it. Feel free to use your imagination, recognizing that those who read it will not mind being entertained.

Duke University Question

What has been your most profound or surprising intellectual experience?

Emory University Question

Of the activities in which you have been involved, which has meant the most to you, and why?

The Johns Hopkins University Question

Please respond to the following, using whatever space and medium you like. If you had only 10 dollars or the equivalent in another currency, to plan a day's adventure, where would you go, what would you do, and who would you take with you?

Princeton University Questions

If you were given one year to spend in service on behalf of others, what would you choose to do, and why?

What is the most difficult decision you've had to make? How did you go about making it?

What idea, invention, discovery, or creation do you think has had the biggest impact on your life so far?

What is the most difficult decision you've had to make? How did you go about making it?

What particular accomplishment up to this point in your life has given you the greatest satisfaction? Briefly explain.

Columbia University Question

Write an essay that conveys to the reader a sense of who you are. Possible topics include, but are not limited to, experiences that have shaped your life, the circumstances of your upbringing, your most meaningful intellectual achievement, the way you see the world—the people in it, events great and small, everyday life—or any personal theme that appeals to your imagination. Please remember that we are concerned not only with the substance of your prose but with your writing style as well.

Yale University Question

We ask you to write a personal essay that will help us to know you better. In the past, candidates have written about their families, intellectual and extracurricular interests, ethnicity or culture, school and community events to which they have had strong reactions, people who have influ-

enced them, significant experiences, personal aspirations, or topics that spring entirely from their imaginations. You should feel confident that in writing about what matters to you, you are bound to convey a strong sense of who you are.

YOUR OWN PERSONAL INTERVIEW

Take a break. You deserve one after all these warmups. While you're cooling down, consider that by now you should be very comfortable with the various types of questions you may encounter. Now it's time to personalize your workout. For this training, we're going to put you through a personal interview—with <u>yourself</u>!

What follows is a fairly random list of categories that we want you to fill in with specifics. We've mixed the list up so that you can think in clusters, intuitive reactions, or spontaneous responses. Feel free to add to the list or to modify it to suit your needs. Come back to the list—let it marinate in your brain. This is the fun part. Be loose—pull out all the stops—brag—exaggerate—be witty, serious, clever, academic—let your mind free-associate as you brainstorm. Don't just give one word answers—search for the potential in your answers. We guarantee that by the time you've worked your way through the interview, you will have many, many, ideas for your college essays. (Of course, your responses are just a springboard to more fully developed explanations.)

The list is to combat writer's block and make you aware of how interesting and unique you really are.

Begin Here . . .

My favorite movie(s) are: (why?)
I wish I knew . . . (person or character)
I wish I knew . . . (ideas)
My goals are:
I can't live without:
The greatest thrill for me would be:
The song that moves me most is: (why?)
My dream job would be:
A pet story or memory:
A unique talent I have:
Something I'm ashamed of is:
Best friends or old friends or lost friends or new friends:
Colors in my life:

The greatest gadget:
A secret desire I have is:
The most moving thing I have ever read or heard or seen is:
If I could change one thing:
The best of times:
The worst of times:
Rituals:
The things or people that make me laugh:
A practical joke:
A disaster, (comic or real or imagined):
Driving:
Temptation—(avoided or given in to):
The things or people that make me cry:
Things that fill me with wonder:
What a character!
My unsung hero:
I'm so frustrated by:
The best thing I ever learned:
First loves:
I'm outraged by:
I have to change:
My favorite paintings or artists are:
My secret haunt:
A time period I wish I had lived in and why:
The best book I've read this year is: (why)
I'm proudest of:
I'd like to meet:
An ethical dilemma I faced:
An injustice:
I did it!
There will never be another . . .
I'm a survivor:
The joys of nature:
A challenge I met:
Something I hated . . . until:
My favorite place on earth:
My creed or I believe:
I won't part with:
Just once I'd like to:
I soar when . . .
An opinion I changed and why:
Sports and me—what a team:
I love . . .

Words I love:
Words I hate:
The greatest gift:
An emotional tug of war:
The weakest link:
Stick with me kid, I'm going places:
Most people don't know this, but I'm . . .
Food, glorious food:
But you can't choose your family . . . or can you?
My road not taken:
The sweetest sounds I ever heard:
Time is on my side because:
Not all lessons are in class:
I took a chance:
I get a kick out of:
I need . . .

Well, student, do you know thyself? We bet you know more about yourself than you realized. And of course this is an exercise you can do anywhere, anytime, with multiple repetitions and an entirely different set of answers. Up the ante—play with the list in a humorous vein. Then change and provide serious answers for the queries. Change again and try to fill it out for someone else. **The goal here is to have you work the material to suit the question.**

WORKING THE MATERIAL

This is the skill we want you to develop and refine.

After you have spent serious time with the questions and informal time with the personal interview, it's time to pre-write your essay. Now you have to choose an episode or belief or activity that is critical to who you are. For example, let's assume that dance is your passion. Using <u>dance</u> as your frame of reference, and with a few specific questions in mind, **work the material:**

1. First, list several broad contexts to consider, such as: a challenge, a triumph, a fear, a hope.
2. Next, decide on your topic, or passion, or episode. (We've chosen dance.) Prepare yourself thoroughly with all aspects of your choice: your actions, reactions, sights, people, sounds, places emotions, etc.
3. Now, mold the information to fit the question. For example, using DANCE as your topic,

- An *academic lesson* might evolve from a choreographer's direction.
- You might discuss a *social challenge* in terms of an audition.
- Your most *treasured recreational moments* might be when you are moving to the music.
- Your *ethical goal* might be to bring dance to underprivileged children.
- A *personal or spiritual triumph* might be a difficult sequence you've mastered.
- An injury might force you to examine your *occupational goals.*

We're sure you get the idea. You take the basic area you're going to write about and tweak and modify it until it suits your purposes. (Make certain you adapt your essay to the specific needs of each of the college to which you are applying.) In other words, we've looked at the big picture, and now you are going to focus the scene into a tight shot that will be intense, alive, and unique to you. And, when you do this, the admissions readers will truly hear **your voice.**

A FEW NOTES ABOUT WRITING THE COLLEGE APPLICATION ESSAY

It's time to get to the nitty-gritty of writing the essay. Just as repetition strengthens your writing muscles, it also makes your form smoother and more graceful. Spend a few minutes reviewing the following points with us.

First and foremost, BE YOURSELF! The college admissions officers want to get to know a real person, someone they would like to meet and talk with. It is this genuine character who has to catch their attention. If you are whimsical, be playful; if you are academic, be scholarly; if you are forthright, be direct. There is no single approach to success.

Remember that first impressions do count. Make the opening of your essay reach out and grab the reader. After all, your paper has to be heard above all the others yet to be read.

Carefully read and deconstruct the question being asked of you. The personal essay is usually one that is centered on a character-building event or experience. The questions could be related to such ideas as:

- An important person
- A character in a novel
- A decisive moment

Some applications will allow for a creative project, or ask you to explore a personal issue, or explore a passion of yours. If you feel comfortable with your creative side, you could write a:

- Poem
- Song lyric
- Dramatic scene
- Parody

Once you have your question, consider the following when thinking about and planning your essay:

- How does the episode/event/idea you choose connect in some way to what you're going to do in this college?
- Be positive NOT negative. Of course, you can be critical of an issue, but be careful. Often your subtext and diction reveal more about you than you may realize. Avoid whining, blaming, and ranting. For example, don't write about how your math teacher hated you and that's why your grades were low, but you showed him and got a tutor and passed to spite him.
- Be careful with emotional topics. It is easy to be maudlin or overly sentimental. Try not to write about divorce, family deaths, personal losses or defeats. This is not to trivialize these life-altering occurrences, but to make you aware that it is very difficult to relate a personal emotion of this nature to a universal understanding for the reader.
- Don't be cutesy; it can backfire on you. There's a fine line between cutesy and clever. If in doubt, leave it out. For example, avoid writing a "recipe" for a successful college student—1 cup of hard work, 2 tablespoons extracurricular activities, a dash of spunk, etc. This may have been fresh once, but it is trite and ineffectual now.
- Stay away from straight autobiographical chronologies. BORING!
- Write something you're comfortable with. You will know it so well that the examples and details will ring true and flow easily.
- Try for something a little obscure, a small turning point that made a big difference. The uniqueness will be charming.
- Write a tight, polished gem of an essay instead of a sweeping global paper that will be vague and general. You don't have to include everything you know.

When you finally have a chance or you have the idea fixed in your head, write the first draft. Remember to:

- Write with focus and a clear voice;
- Pay attention to clarity of thought, organization, and syntax;

- Engage the reader;
- Elucidate, illuminate your idea with details, examples, anecdotes;
- Try to keep it in present tense if at all possible;
- Use the active voice;
- Keep it short;
- Do not sound like a thesaurus. Nothing is more awkward or makes the readers laugh as much as the misuse of pompous and inappropriate words. Be natural in your writing. Imagine you are having a conversation with the reader.

The well-worn advice of your many English instructors works very well here. Try to begin your essay with one of these:

- A real quotation you like;
- A piece of dialog;
- A rhetorical question;
- A startling statement;
- An engaging anecdote;
- A challenge.

And last, once you've written the first draft:

- **LET SOMEONE ELSE READ IT BACK TO YOU OUT LOUD.** (We can't stress this strongly enough.)
- Ask for comments and suggestions from your instructor(s) and those whom you consider can offer good advice and from those who really know you. (Take advice, but don't let them change your style or voice. They had their chance; this is your essay.)
- **REVISE.**
- Let someone else read the revision back to you **out loud.**
- If needed, revise and revise again.
- **PROOFREAD!**

Quite a workout! By now you should feel the burn, and begin to see the results of your hard work. Take a break and read some successful college essays written by your peers.

SAMPLE STUDENT ESSAYS

Although there are as many different personal essays as there are writers, a quality paper conveys confidence, clarity, control, and creativity. The following papers exhibit AP-level strengths and are typical of strong and successful essays. Each student was accepted to his or her college of choice.

We've reprinted the essays as written and have added commentary to illustrate the strengths of the essays.

Sample Essay A: Self-generated Topic

Bulldogs have it easy. They're long since retired from the first bull baiting contests, which started in England in 1200, and they don't do much anymore. One of these continually relaxing animals lives in my home. My family and I affectionately call her Daffodil. She resides in our linen closet, atop a mass of unused comforters, pillows, and sheets, and, on average, sleeps twenty-two hours each day. In some of my more slothful moments, I have pondered what a bargain it would be to trade all earthly pleasures for the constant idleness and lack of responsibility that my dog enjoys, though I always find my present state to be superior.

During the rare occasions when Daffodil is awake, she sits upright in a regal posture, her massive head positioned between her bow legs for maximum Feng-Shui effect. Gazing off at apostrophic ideals, she resembles a philosopher. When consulted for advice, she sits and ponders with a stare that Oppenheimer might have given when ruminating over sub-atomic theory. Aside from her role as family philosopher, she also serves as a social worker and teacher. She listens to all problems, no matter how trivial, and teaches the art of reticence and patience. There is something to be said for her wisdom in these matters.

Out in the real world, Daffodil would hardly be successful. Sometimes she is antisocial, and as I have already pointed out, she is lazy. But from her, I have derived some important life lessons. Her stoic nature and calm acceptance of her surroundings are excellent examples of her teachings, which I employ in my life. When helping friends, I bear the same ponderous look and offer my taciturn, minimalist wisdom only after hearing the whole story. (From speaking to Daffodil, I know that simply talking about problems is often a better remedy than any advice.) She has set an existentialist example for me: very often she seeks and finds a beam of sunlight that passes through the smallest break in the window shades. Watching her bask serenely in this tiny square of warmth demonstrates the proper way to seek out the best of the present, and to savor it completely. She can often be seen enjoying every morsel of food she encounters, devouring not only what is in her bowl, but licking the bowl itself and the floor until she is satisfied that she has extracted every bit of pleasure from that very moment in her existence.

Partly as a result from all this eating in her spare time, Daffodil is Buddha-like in appearance. But she is no false idol, only a friend and a teacher. In the end, her greatest lesson to me has been one that I stumbled on myself. I looked to Daffodil amusingly for advice, but her gift to me has been the confidence that I should look for inspiration in the strangest of places, even in the upstairs linen closet.

Commentary

This is an excellent essay for the following reasons.

<u>Paragraph 1</u>: The opening is unique and intriguing. We want to read more. The tone—light, informative, and slightly tongue-in-cheek, is established early and indicates the warm and open personality of the writer.

<u>Paragraph 2</u>: Original details and images, such as the first sentence, enliven the description of Daffodil in a vivid and unusual manner. These images also reveal the breadth of the writer. Humor and allusions, the juxtaposing of Oppenheimer and Feng Shui, and the use of Daffodil as a foil for the candidate, provide the reader with a sense of the bright, observant, and charmingly quirky writer. The final sentence about wisdom provides the transition to the third paragraph's topic.

<u>Paragraph 3</u>: The vocabulary is mature and appropriately used. Syntactical constructions are varied and natural. Every detail and image

rings true. The reader is carried by the genuine nature of the essay. This is a writer who probably has pondered philosophy and the meaning of life. And he has the wisdom and maturity to see in it through a unique lens. He understands the gifts he has received: the simple and the true, the friend and the teacher, and the known and the now.

Paragraph 4: The unity and structure of the essay is well planned—alternating Daffodil and the writer and returning to the opening of the essay with a twist of insight as conclusion. The essay is a delight! The readers want to know this candidate who shows such insight, self-awareness, and whimsy.

Sample Essay B

I consider myself a connoisseur of paper. I've grown sensitive to its feel, its color, its holistic perfection in blocks and pads, its singular simplicity in sheets. There is an unmistakable potential in a new notebook, freshly cut, tightly bound, ready for the world outside the factory. And now I sit, writing upon that same threshold, writing the concluding remarks to my own manufacture, writing as I have throughout. I've always had an intimate awareness of paper. As a baby I fell asleep each night grasping not a doll but a tissue. It was, however, only until I had learned how to write that my true love affair began. Paired with a pen and a pad, I brazenly trumpeted out into the bungalow colonies and retirement communities of my childhood in search of contents for my "important papers," as I called them. Unlike other great epic journeymen, I didn't strive for just one end. I marched through Elysian Fields and Aeolian winds for a purpose far broader than, say, a home and a wife in Ithaca or a golden fleece. In my tiny hand there was a world of uncertainty, and I committed myself to fill that void. Inspiration breathed through many lungs: news of eye surgeries and cocktail parties, visiting relatives and trips to the supermarket. To me, any news was fit to print, and I was fit to print it all.

This brand of literary liberty, in which I had so freely indulged, had left me with an intrinsic and indomitable desire to write and to write and to write. It was also this intellectual attribute that hastened a great change in third grade. Having finished the first long term report of my school career, in my mind a truly stunning intellectual work about penguins, I handed the rough draft to my mother to check for minor problems.

"Wait. I don't know what you're talking about. You have to make it clearer," she said.

And, so we embarked upon the great revision of my penguin report, a watershed in my literary "career." So grand was the impact of this lesson in clarity and communication that it still plagues me today, even as I write this essay, the final work of my childhood. Through alternating episodes of anger and tears, my mother and I slowly rewrote the entire paper, sentence by excruciating sentence. This personal reformation would culminate with a very short poem written in reaction to the flamboyant graffiti of New York's SOHO district. In small gray print on rolled computer paper, its coherence stood in drastic contrast to the sprawling run-on sentences of years preceding. High school has left me an amalgamation of these ways. As such, I find a wide open future ahead—as a journalist or a linguist, a presidential speechwriter or international lawyer, a writer of any sort. Whatever I become, whenever I become it, I will find my peace among books and reams and sheets of paper.

Commentary

This is a top-notch essay for the following reasons:

Paragraph 1: The opening statement, almost poetic in its rhythm and imagery, prepares the reader for an unusual and interesting paper. There is a subtle comparison between the unprinted paper and its potential and the applicant and his potential. Writing in a mock heroic style, the applicant reveals his control of humor, allusion, metaphor, and diction. There is a very fine mix of scholarship and gentle self-mockery.

Paragraph 2: The first person narrative moves freely and light-heartedly. The incorporation of dialog adds to the understanding of our writer and his future epiphany. The self-deprecating tone adds to the humor and keeps the paper modest and light. The maturity of the sentence structure and vocabulary is a nice foil to the third grade penguin paper.

Paragraph 3: Connecting the point of the essay and the subject of the essay, this paragraph brings the reader from the young journeyman to the present writer. The essay is intelligent and thoughtful.

Paragraph 4: The conclusion masterfully unites the goals, personality, and original thesis of the essay. Well done!

Sample Essay C: A Personal Challenge

It was a warm summer afternoon in August, and from what I remember, the atmosphere of the small place we were in was definitely not a comfortable one. The air was thick and moist, the sun was hot and potent. Here in this room were five individuals awaiting a challenge. And I, Lindsay, the only female, was one of them.

After eight long years of preparation, I stood on that hard wooden floor facing the judges who were about to decide my fate. I thought to myself, "Am I ready? Am I good enough? Am I going to pass?" Trying to conceal the glut of emotions running through my fear-filled body, I quickly forced myself to smile; however, my anxiety was completely revealed by the apprehensive expression plastered across my face.

At that brief but significant moment, my name was finally called. "Lindsay," a judge said. "You're up." So with my stomach churning and legs trembling, I quickly hurried to the black X in the center of the room, turned around and faced the mirrored wall behind me. I could see the reflection of my Sensei in the glass, and as my eyes met his, I realized how important this day was. "If I could only show them what I'm capable of," I thought to myself, "then maybe, just maybe, I would finally become a Black Belt."

While standing with the other students before the judges and my teacher, I reviewed the entire test in my mind. Each student completed five dance-like self-defense moves, otherwise known as Katas. When it was my turn to start with the fifth Kata, the very last Kata, my mind suddenly went blank. However, what I didn't realize was that, because I had practiced these sequences so many times, the movements had actually become part of me. As soon as my teacher shouted, "Yoi!" (a command to assume the starting position), the Kata came back to me naturally. Although I was able to finish, I wasn't sure if every aspect of the test I had just completed was absolutely perfect. But even still, I was sure that I had tried my best, giving the judges my utmost attention and showing them, with great spirit, what I was capable of accomplishing.

Suddenly, I was brought back to reality when my Sensei reentered the room. He came in carrying four black belts. That meant one of us had not passed. After we stood facing each other in silence for what seemed like an eternity, he summoned one of the judges to join us. It was then that I saw it. It was then that I knew I had passed. As the judge approached me, he carried a black belt. The happiness I felt at that moment was ineffable. I was so proud of myself. Although I had so many other responsibilities in my life, I had still persevered in order to make my dream of becoming a Black Belt a reality.

Upon tying the black belt around my waist, I realized the significance of what I had just accomplished. Suddenly, I was instilled with feelings of pride, self-confidence, and the personal fulfillment of achieving a life-long goal. And, then it hit me. At that instant, I began to comprehend the genuine spiritual aspects of karate. Through the years, my teacher had always guided me by saying, "Seek perfection of character. Be faithful in all your endeavors. Respect others. And refrain from violent behavior." I heard these words every time I met with him, and, although the actual words had been branded into my mind, until that afternoon, I had very little conception of their meaning. Until this point, my main mental objective was to memorize these phrases; my physical one, to master the corporal aspects of karate. But now that I had passed the test, I knew that all was going to change. The second that judge handed over my belt, not only did I begin to understand the "true" meaning of karate, but I began to feel it as well.

Now that I am a Black Belt, I have begun to teach other children, hoping to instill in them the same qualities that my teacher had instilled in me. Being on the "opposite side of the fence" has done more than just show me that I can teach. It has really shown me that I have so much more to learn. Oscar Wilde once said, "The true Black Belt is the white belt of a beginner, stained by the dried blood and sweat of the owner." And for me, becoming a Black Belt is more than just the means to an end. Only now am I truly beginning.

Commentary

Paragraph 1: The essay immediately introduces the candidate and draws the reader into the challenge. The topic of the essay is delineated and the difficulty of the situation foreshadowed by the writers diction: not comfortable, thick and moist, hot and potent.

Paragraph 2: The writer controls the emotion of this section by maintaining strong topic adherence. The personal questions involve the reader, who subconsciously looks forward to or supplies the unspoken answers.

Paragraph 3: Details and strong images "show" rather than "tell" the experience. Now that the stage is set, the writer establishes the thematic statement of the essay—"If I could now only show them what I'm really capable of." Obviously, the essay is also intended to show what she is capable of.

Paragraph 4: Informative and detailed, this body paragraph reveals the character of the writer, persistent, qualified, self-effacing, spirited.

Paragraph 5: The speaker's passion for her subject, her emotions and responses are vividly expressed through her choice of topic.

Paragraph 6: This lifts the essay into the higher range. Here, the speaker clarifies her values and is honestly reflective of own progress and maturity. She moves from the physical to the mental and spiritual planes and indicates to the reader that a sensitive, thoughtful, and committed student has written the essay. The ability to make the abstract concrete is the writer's strength.

Paragraph 7: The final statement synthesizes the concepts of the piece and the personality of the writer. Scholarship, insight, and the ability to apply a specific experience as a metaphor for a personal philosophy, all indicate a fine candidate. As she concludes strongly, "Only now am I truly beginning." We can feel confident that this effort will help open the door to the college of her choice.

A Final Thought: This essay's strength is its controlled development. We move logically through the experience to its conclusion. Along the way we follow the emotional and cognitive development of the writer. Focused and deliberate, ending with a highly affirmative statement, the essay builds nicely and indicates a clarity of thought. The vocabulary and syntax are appropriate and effective for their purpose.

Sample Essay D: Personal Memoir

Ms. Skipper was a whale of a woman. She was enormous, walking sideways to get through the classroom door. She wore the typical fat lady's dress, blue with hundreds of little red flowers. She was possibly the scariest woman you ever saw. Her chin folded into her neck, which disappeared where her broad shoulders met the rest of her oversized body. None of that ever mattered. Ms. Skipper was Queen of her castle, and boy, did she love her fourth grade subjects. There was never a moment when she didn't have time to cheer us on or make us laugh. Despite her intimidating appearance, my fourth grade teacher was the funniest and sweetest woman I have ever met. That's the reason I remember the mistake I made that early morning eight years ago.

The class was studying electricity. It was a unit I had been looking forward to all year. Sure the Native Americans and long division were interesting subjects, but this, this was special. I still remember the excitement I felt every morning as I walked into class. There wasn't a fourth grader in the school who knew circuits better than I did. Whether it was particle flow, negative charge, or interface transit molecule acceleration, I was an electrical master equaling the great Mr. Thomas Edison.

For those few weeks there was only one thing I loved more than electricity. Her name was Roxanne. She got my heart racing faster than a game of schoolyard dodge ball. And so it came to the final exam of our unit. We would be working with actual electrical equipment; wires, batteries, and light bulbs. We would also be working in groups.

For me that meant just one thing, maybe, just maybe, if I were lucky, I would be paired with Roxanne. She was a goddess with beautiful green eyes, long curly locks of brown hair, and a smile bigger than an ocean. My heart skipped a beat every time I heard her name. I remember thinking; "I wouldn't even know what to say to her."

"Brian and Stacey, Peter and Kim, David and Justin." As each group was called out I knew my chances were increasing. "Marisa and Nicole, Daniel and Tom," and then . . . "Alex and Roxy," as Ms. Skipper called her!

I almost fell out of my chair. My excitement climbed to dangerous levels, until I realized something terrifying. I actually had to talk to Roxanne. A bead of sweat lined my upper lip. I painfully cracked all ten of my knuckles. God, I was nervous.

We started our work, building circuits and making connections. Light bulbs illuminated the room. Roxanne and I were getting along great. I was a genuine

Casanova. Then I made the terrible mistake that still haunts me to this day. We had just finished building a circuit composed of a light bulb and two unprotected wires. Trying to impress Roxanne, I arched my hairless chest and declared, "I wonder what would happen if I stuck these in the electrical outlet."

Roxanne gave me a look, flashed a smile, and said, "I don't know, but I dare you to find out."

I knew it was a bad idea. I was a prisoner of my own desires. With just the slightest of youthful hesitation, I murmured "What could possibly happen?" and plugged the wires in.

Crack! Fizzle! BAMB!

The bulb exploded with whirls of acrid smoke as red-tinged sparks sputtered over the rows of desks. The entire class gasped in unison as they turned and stared. Worst of all, Ms. Skipper was furious. She charged across the room (imagine that) and pulled me away yelling as only she could. Worst of all, she said the three words that no student ever wants to hear, "Stay after class." For the rest of the day I sat hunched over my desk, nervously awaiting my fate.

It seemed like an eternity until the bell, but finally it rang. All the students cheerfully packed up their belongings and left, all of them, except me. Ms. Skipper sat at her desk. I sat at mine. The room was eerily quiet, even the birds had stopped singing. The tension was killing me. I had to do something. I slowly got up from my chair and walked over to Ms. Skipper's desk. I began to cry. I'm not sure how another teacher would have handled the situation but Ms. Skipper opened her arms and brought me into her enormous body.

She didn't tell me I was a bad kid, or that I was a troublemaker. There would be no phone call home. Ms. Skipper told me I was lucky to be alive. The electric shock could have sent me flying across the room. She told me how frightened I had made her and how disappointed she was with my behavior. If you thought I was crying before she spoke, you should have seen me after. I apologized. Ms. Skipper forgave me and reminded me that everyone makes mistakes. I was dismissed but still the crying continued.

I collected my things and I left the room bleary-eyed. All I could think about was getting home. I just wanted the day to end. I had made a fool of myself in front of Roxanne. I was sure she would never talk to me again. Nothing could have made the day worse. I was wrong. As I left the room, I heard laughing. Roxanne and her friends had come back for a forgotten coat. They had been standing just outside the room. There I was, tears running down my face and the love of my life was staring me straight in the eye. Roxanne looked at me for a moment and then darted through the door.

To this day I swear she was laughing as I ran down the hall. I didn't speak to Roxanne for the rest of the year but if you love a happy ending, she was my date for the fifth grade dance.

The lessons I learned that day remain with me even now. Taking risks is an important part of life, even when the outcomes may blow up in your face. I feel challenged when faced with uncertainty. My interests may have changed from electricity to history and politics but I still get that thrill from learning. My youthful curiosity hasn't died but rather matured through high school.

What I took with me from, not just that day, but the whole year, is what Ms. Skipper taught us about being comfortable with who we are, that appearances are irrelevant. I made the mistake of sacrificing my own values in the face of beauty. I don't think Ms. Skipper would hold me accountable for the mistakes by a schoolboy romantic, but I do believe there is something to learn from every experience. Ask me today whom I have fonder memories of and the answer can be given without hesitation. It's the lady in the big flowered dress, who bestowed perfect papers with red lipstick kisses. Roxanne and Ms. Skipper were diametrical opposites; one a physical beauty, and the other a beautiful spirit. I can now see the beauty in all our imperfections.

Commentary

This is a strong essay for the following reasons:

Paragraph 1: The opening clearly establishes the topic and tone of the essay, as well as the writing skills of the applicant. The memoir is so smooth and real, that the reader quickly identifies with the writer. The descriptions and observations are lively and concrete. The unabashed affection for his teacher is an endearing quality of the essay.

Paragraphs 2–11: The body of the narrative rapidly develops—the plot is universal and specific at the same time. The diction, dialog, and events prove the wisdom of writing about what is true and real to you. His details, cracking his knuckles, puffing out his hairless chest, bring the essay to life. We laugh and ache for the writer. We care about him and can't wait to see what happens next. The essay also demonstrates how a small and seemingly insignificant event can be developed into a very unique and effective piece of writing.

Paragraphs 12–17: Concluding his memoir, the writer reintroduces the subject of his essay, Mrs. Skipper. The episode, which stood on its own charm, now serves to illustrate an important lesson and turning point. Sweetly poignant and adolescently humorous, the essay is a wonderful vehicle for the writer's voice. And, the admissions committee listened and accepted him.

Sample Essay E: A Specific Page from Your Autobiography (p. 217)

... keep myself from crying. All my life, I have gone by instinct, by my raw emotions. Textbooks do not contain a chapter on how to keep your hands from shaking while giving an injection. No amount of reading can make it easier to look into their eyes, as you know for certain that there's nothing more you can do.

After sixteen years, it was still just as difficult as the first time I had done it. I lifted his tiny, lifeless body off the table. As always, I was instantly brought back to the age of fifteen, the first time I'd ever had to hold an animal that was no longer living. I expected his body to be stiff and cold. But his body was still warm, his fur just as soft. As I lifted him into my arms, his head drooped over to one side and his flaccidity was the only true sign that he was dead. Even as I held him, I still envisioned him breathing, and as I held my old stethoscope to his chest, I heard phantom heartbeats that I knew couldn't possibly be there. How could my mind still be playing tricks on me after so many years?

It's hard to tell what's real and what's not anymore. If after ten years of practicing medicine I still couldn't tell for sure whether an animal was dead or not, how could I be sure that anything was really the way I saw it?

I washed my hands, threw off my scrubs, and dashed to my car. A storm was approaching, and I wanted to be home. When I pulled into the garage, I didn't even notice I had left the door open. I simply ran inside and before my husband even realized who was charging at him, I wrapped my arms around him and smiled, thankful that I could be there with him. He simply smiled back, and without any words, he understood that I'd had a hard day at work. He walked me to the den where our three-year-old terror was sleeping like an angel on the couch. I sat down beside him, stroking his back and before I knew it, my husband was walking back into the den carrying a tray holding two cups of cocoa and a plate of marshmallows. He built a fire, settled himself onto the couch, and I nestled beside him.

Before we were married, the most exciting moments of my life were when I graduated from veterinary school, and any time I saw an animal I treated walk out of the hospital perfectly healed. Now, I reveled in moments like these. The quiet warmth radiating throughout our house, the gentle breathing of my baby lying beneath my old baby blanket, the familiar smell of my husband's sweater, and the silence of snowflakes outside as each one waltzed its way to the ground. I was in bliss until I heard the buzzing of my pager on the countertop in the cold kitchen upstairs. My eyelids sank, and I drew in a deep breath as my husband clutched my hand. I stood up and looked at him, and again with no words, he let go his tight grasp and stared into the glowing fire as I plodded my way up the stairs.

The storm made it almost impossible to see, but then, covered in a thick layer of ice and snow, I saw the old familiar sign of the animal hospital and I smiled. As much as I wanted to be home, I had an impulse to run into the hospital and save the day. A dog that had been hit by a car that skidded over a patch of black ice was brought in to the hospital. I put on a pair of scrubs and prepped myself for surgery. Standing over the dog for three hours, I did all I possibly could to save him. At 12:32 A.M. I pronounced him dead. I took off my surgical mask and stared at him as the technicians disconnected him from the machines. His paws still had snow stuck to them. I picked some off, and as it melted in my hand, I glanced over at the line of cages along the wall. The little dog I had treated earlier was sitting up, staring at me. I laughed at his overgrown ears and walked over to his cage. His tail wagged so wildly that it was hitting the walls of the cage, making a thunderous noise against the steel. I lifted him up and cradled him in my arms. He fell asleep and at that moment, I felt it had all been worth it. The long *hours, the studying, the fights about when I would go back to work—it was all worth it because now that one of my patients felt comfortable enough to fall asleep my arms, I could go home and tell my husband that I had a good day.*

Commentary

This is an powerful essay for the following reasons:

Paragraph 1: The writer cleverly includes words ostensibly left over from the previous page, to add to the verisimilitude of the essay. The actual entry reads beautifully—setting, plot, conflict, characterization, and theme are foreshadowed. The topic is painful, yet holds us.

Paragraph 2: The development of the storyline reveals the intelligence and sensitivity of the subject. Every word is carefully chosen—obviously the applicant is a gifted creative writer who consciously develops her themes and images.

Paragraph 3: Posing the questions of life and death, reality and delusion, this brief entry is crucial to the character.

Paragraphs 4 and 5: The writer shows her skills and command of imagery and symbol. She develops the scene, with its literal and figurative storm, and contrasts its coldness and death, with the warmth of life, love, and home. The maturity of the piece, which could have deteriorated into bathos, is her strength. Her use of a retrospective voice helps to create this distance and addresses the flashback aspect of the essay prompt.

Paragraph 6: Once again, the diction and use of detail, such as the snow melting on the paw, raise this essay from the pitfall of cliché and attest to the compassion and sensitivity of the writer. Who wouldn't want to have this writer as a member of their academic community?

A Few Final Illustrations

The following bits and pieces from myriad college essays illustrate the limitless venues for you to explore. They also should re-emphasize the variety of writing styles encountered by the admissions people.

❖ *In my opinion, my entire being—my soul, my inner essence, my thoughts, my actions, my mannerisms, my heart—can all be interpreted through my hands. Take a look at my hands on any given day, and you are bound to learn at least one thing about me. They are* my tools, strong, small, and precise. Often, they are stained with acrylic paint, or chalk, or a leaky pen. Nourished by cool, wet clay and the smell of turpentine, my fingers pinch the forearm of the sculpture as it narrows down to the wrist. I extend forward the figure's long arms by using my palms to press the shoulders inward. I use the pads of my fingers to transform conspicuous lines into dimpled flesh. My long nail scrapes out a collarbone and a dramatically arched spine. My fingers draw soft rolls on the sculpture's body to create skin as soft as velvet drapery and masses as voluminous as water. Hours later, I find pieces of hardened clay hiding underneath my nails.

❖ The summer of my junior year I was both anxious and eager. It would be the first I did not spend with my close-knit group of summer girlfriends. When we literally made the decision to go our separate ways, I was frightened. I suddenly became unsure of my social skills and worried that it would be difficult to make new friends. The choice to separate was a risk that I now know was the most important risk I have taken to this point in my life. It opened my eyes to a world of prejudices that I had been sheltered from my entire life.

❖ I decided to celebrate my birthday in the same hall that I made to reference to in earlier chapters. It is the hall that lies deep within my mind; a hall that I can visit in search of inspiration and assurance. In this "Hall of Heroes" stand those whose lives I seek to emulate. Strolling down the hall and gazing at the great men and women who stand before me, I cannot help but feel like a lesser man in orbit among giants.

❖ The travel website, expedia.com advertises low cost vacations to exotic resorts in Tahiti this year. A much more adventuresome holiday awaits me, however, and it's right in my living room. To me, playing the piano is as exciting, fresh, and relaxing as a fancy vacation because unlike a packaged getaway, it can be custom tailored to my mood or desire.

❖ I have finally discovered it. It is everything they said it would be. It is an element more valuable than platinum, more malleable than gold, and more brilliant than all the diamonds in the limitless heavens. I have finally discovered it: metaphoric "Jello," my passion for learning. The connection between Jello and learning embodies the belief that there is always room to broaden one's horizon through exploration. Jello comes in a spectrum of diverse flavors: orange, raspberry, grape, lemon and lime. The opportunities in school also come in many flavors: math, history, art, science and language. There's always room for learning.

❖ When I finally decided to take AP Bio, it really was one of the best decisions of my high school career . . . The work was difficult, and I worked harder than I have ever worked in my life to keep my grades up. I studied and I went to extra help—two experiences which were fairly new to me. After I got the hang of it, it became a puzzle to me; an exciting enigma that was both challenging and enjoyable. I learned more about the world around me than I had ever thought possible. I found myself answering rhetorical questions uttered over the lunch table like, "Where do hiccups come from?" and "Why can't I make up missed sleep on the weekends?" Eventually my friends learned to keep their biology-related questions to themselves, for fear of my actually knowing the answer.

I became a Bio Nerd. I saw ADP on a license plate and thought adenosine diphosphate; the obvious answer to "Which kind of worm would you rather be?" was clearly "annelids!" I enjoyed every minute of it.

❖ I listen. The music begins. The notes and melodies ring in my ears. I am dancing—dancing as free as an autumn leaf blowing in the wind. I am so involved in the music that nothing else around me matters. I am untouchable. When I stretch my arm, the energy spills out the tips of my fingers. From my pointed toes to the expression on my face, my whole body is in tune with the rhythm of the music. I am no longer a person. I am movement and energy and life.

❖ The wind whooshed through the trees behind me, rushing up the waves into parachutes ready to envelop little children playing inside. I ran to the water and dove in. Of those who live near the water, some love it and some hate it. Me? I hated it.

❖ A wrong turn on the N-12 traveling to the Sabi Sabi Desert in the East Rand led us through the most desolate part of South Africa. The people stared at our car passing down the sandy path that served as a road, with their faces shiny and dark under the hot African sun. They were alone with nothing, absolutely nothing in the middle of a vast expanse of land. This was the face of poverty, and the only thing separating me from them was the pane of glass out of which I stared, observed, and remained silent.

❖ "cause I'm the naked cowboy, coming to a town near you," he sang, as I filmed him for a documentary I was creating for the William H. Cosby Future Filmmakers Workshop at NYU. The "naked cowboy," singing in Times Square in New York City on a cold winter day, has no fear. He has confidence and self-respect. How else would he be able to stand outside, nearly nude, serenading strangers?

Well, do you want to read more? We did, and so did the admissions committees. Each snippet was part of a successful essay. Your break is over; time for you to go for the burn. Set those applications on fire and do yourself proud. **You're ready!**

Appendix

- ## Bibliography of Recommended Authors and Texts
- ## Answers to Questions on Practice Activities
- ## Glossary of Terms
- ## Websites of Interest to the AP English Student

Writers don't choose their craft; they need to write in order to face the world.
—*Alice Hoffman*

BIBLIOGRAPHY OF RECOMMENDED AUTHORS AND TEXTS

The following is a very selected listing of authors, both past and present. Each of these writers presents ideas in original, thought-provoking, and enlightening ways. Our recommendation is that you read as many and as much of them as you can. The more you read and examine these writers and their works, the better prepared you will be for informed thinking, discussing, and writing the AP English essay. And, there is another mind-expanding benefit. You will become much more aware of the challenging and compelling world of ideas that surrounds you. We invite you to accept our invitation to this complex universe.

Suggested Classical Works and Authors

Homer	*The Iliad, The Odyssey*
The Bible	"Genesis," "Exodus," "Matthew"
Sophocles	*Antigone, Oedipus Rex*
Euripides	*Medea*
Aristotle	"On the Nature of Tragedy"
Plato	"The Apology," "The Allegory of the Cave"
Swift	*Gulliver's Travels*
Voltaire	*Candide*
Molière	*Tartuffe, The Misanthrope*
Racine	*Phaedra*
Milton	"L'Allegro," "Il Penseroso," "On His Blindness," *Paradise Lost*
Pope	"An Essay on Man," "An Essay on Criticism," "The Rape of the Lock"

Suggested Realistic Works and Authors

Chaucer	*The Canterbury Tales*
Fyodor Dostoevsky	*Crime and Punishment*
Leo Tolstoy	*Anna Karenina*
Anton Chekhov	*The Cherry Orchard*
Ernest Hemingway	*The Sun Also Rises*
Henrik Ibsen	*Hedda Gabler, A Doll's House*

Suggested Romantic Works and Authors

Anonymous	*Beowulf*
Boccaccio	*The Decameron*
Cervantes	*Don Quixote*
Shakespeare	*Hamlet, King Lear, Twelfth Night*
Goethe	*Faust*
Hawthorne	*The Scarlet Letter*
Brontë	*Jane Eyre*
Hugo	*Les Miserables*

Suggested Romantic Poets

Anonymous	The Ballads—Scottish and British
Shakespeare	The Sonnets
Robert Burns	"To a Mouse," "John Anderson," "My Jo," "A Red, Red, Rose"
William Blake	"A Poison Tree," "The Sick Rose," "London," "The Chimney Sweep"

William Wordsworth	"Tintern Abbey," "My Heart Leaps Up," "London, 1802," "The World Is Too Much With Us," "I Wondered Lonely As a Cloud," "Ode on Intimations of Immortality," "Preface to the Lyrical Ballads"
Samuel Taylor Coleridge	"Kubla Khan," "The Frost at Midnight," "The Rime of the Ancient Mariner"
George Gordon, Lord Byron	"Sonnet on Chillon," "When We Two Parted," "Maid of Athens," "The Isles of Greece," "She Walks in Beauty"
Percy Bysshe Shelley	"Ode to the West Wind," "To a Skylark," "Ozymandias"
John Keats	"On First Looking Into Chapman's Homer," "Ode to a Nightingale," "Ode on a Grecian Urn," "When I Have Fears That I May Cease to Be"
Alfred, Lord Tennyson	"Ulysses"
Robert Browning	"My Last Duchess," "Pippa's Song," "Soliloquy of the Spanish Cloister"

Suggested Impressionistic Works and Authors

Henry James	*The American, Washington Square*
Joseph Conrad	*Heart of Darkness, The Secret Sharer,* "The Lagoon"
Katherine Mansfield	"Bliss"
Kate Chopin	"Story of an Hour" *The Awakening*

Suggested Naturalistic Works and Authors

James Joyce	*Dubliners*
Eugene O'Neill	*Desire Under the Elms, The Hairy Ape, The Iceman Cometh*
T. S. Eliot	"The Hollow Men," "The Love Song of J. Alfred Prufrock"
Franz Kafka	*Metamorphosis, The Trial*
Tennessee Williams	*A Streetcar Named Desire, Cat on a Hot Tin Roof*
Frank Norris	*The Octopus*
Stephen Crane	*Maggie, A Girl of the Streets*
Upton Sinclair	*The Jungle*

Recommended Poets

Matthew Arnold	Seamus Haeney
W. H. Auden	Galway Kinnell

Elizabeth Bishop

Gwendolyn Brooks

e e cummings

T. S. Eliot

Lawrence Ferlinghetti

Robert Francis

Robert Graves

Donald Hall

Maxine Kumin

Pablo Neruda

Sharon Olds

Wilfred Owen

Linda Pastan

May Swenson

Edna St. Vincent Millay

Dylan Thomas

Recommended Authors

Chinua Achebe	*Things Fall Apart*
Aeschylus	*Orestia*
Margaret Atwood	*The Handmaid's Tale*
Jane Austin	*Pride and Prejudice, Sense and Sensibility*
James Baldwin	*Go Tell It on the Mountain*
Charlotte Brontë	*Jane Eyre*
Emily Brontë	*Wuthering Heights*
Albert Camus	*The Stranger*
Willa Cather	*My Antonia, One of Ours, Death Comes to the Archbishop*
Anton Chekhov	*The Cherry Orchard*
Kate Chopin	*The Awakening*
Sandra Cisneros	*The House on Mango Street*
Joseph Conrad	*Heart of Darkness, Lord Jim, The Secret Sharer*
Stephen Crane	*The Red Badge of Courage*
Don Delillo	*White Noise*
Charles Dickens	*Great Expectations, A Tale of Two Cities*
Fyodor Dostoevski	*Crime and Punishment*
Theodore Dreiser	*An American Tragedy, Sister Carrie*
George Eliot	*Silas Marner, Middlemarch*
Ralph Ellison	*Invisible Man*
Euripides	*Medea*
William Faulkner	*As I Lay Dying, The Sound and the Fury*
Henry Fielding	*Tom Jones*
F. Scott Fitzgerald	*The Great Gatsby*
Gustave Flaubert	*Madame Bovary*
E. M. Forster	*A Passage to India*
Thomas Hardy	*Jude the Obscure, Tess of the D'Ubervilles*
Nathaniel Hawthorne	*The Scarlet Letter*
Joseph Heller	*Catch-22*
Ernest Hemingway	*The Sun Also Rises*
Homer	*The Iliad, The Odyssey*

Zora Neale Hurston	*Their Eyes Were Watching God*
Aldous Huxley	*Brave New World*
Henrik Ibsen	*A Doll's House, Ghosts, Hedda Gabler*
Kazuo Ishiguro	*The Remains of the Day*
Henry James	*The Turn of the Screw, The American*
James Joyce	*A Portrait of the Artist as a Young Man*
Franz Kafka	*Metamorphosis, The Trial*
Ken Kesey	*One Flew Over the Cuckoo's Nest*
Maxine Hong Kingston	*The Woman Warrior*
D. H. Lawrence	*Sons and Lovers*
Gabriel Garcia Márquez	*One Hundred Years of Solitude*
Herman Melville	*Moby Dick, Billy Budd*
Arthur Miller	*Death of a Salesman, The Crucible*
Toni Morrison	*Beloved, Song of Solomon*
V. S. Naipul	*A Bend in the River*
Eugene O'Neill	*Desire Under the Elms, Long Day's Journey into Night*
George Orwell	*1984*
Tim O'Brien	*The Things They Carried*
Alan Paton	*Cry, the Beloved Country*
Jean Rhys	*Wide Sargasso Sea*
Jean-Paul Sartre	*No Exit, Nausea*
William Shakespeare	*Hamlet, King Lear, Macbeth, Othello, Twelfth Night*
George Bernard Shaw	*Major Barbara, Man and Superman, Pygmalion*
Mary Shelley	*Frankenstein*
Sophocles	*Antigone, Oedipus Rex*
John Steinbeck	*The Grapes of Wrath, Of Mice and Men, Cannery Row*
Tom Stoppard	*Rosencrantz and Guildenstern Are Dead*
Jonathan Swift	*Gulliver's Travels*
Amy Tan	*The Kitchen God's Wife*
Lee Tolstoy	*Anna Karenina*
Mark Twain	*The Adventures of Huckleberry Finn*
Voltaire	*Candide*
Kurt Vonnegut	*Slaughterhouse Five*
Alice Walker	*The Color Purple*
Edith Wharton	*Ethan Frome, The House of Mirth*
Oscar Wilde	*The Importance of Being Earnest*
Thornton Wilder	*Our Town*
Tennessee Williams	*A Streetcar Named Desire, The Glass Menagerie*
Virginia Woolf	*To the Lighthouse, A Room of One's Own*
Richard Wright	*Native Son*

Personal Writing: Journals, Autobiographies, Diaries

Maya Angelou	Mary McCarthy
Annie Dillard	Samuel Pepys
Frederick Douglas	Richard Rodriguez
Lillian Hellman	May Sarton
Helen Keller	Richard Wright
Martin Luther King, Jr.	Malcolm X
Maxine Hong Kingston	

Biographies and Histories

Walter Jackson Bate	Winston Churchill
James Boswell	Shelby Foote
Thomas Carlyle	George Trevelyan
Bruce Catton	Barbara Tuchman

Journalists and Essayists

Joseph Addison	Ellen Goodman
Michael Arlen	Pauline Kael
Matthew Arnold	Garrison Keillor
Francis Bacon	John McPhee
Russell Baker	N. Scott Momaday
Harold Bloom	Anna Quindlen
G. K. Chesterton	John Ruskin
Kenneth Clark	Marjorie Sandor
Joan Didion	Susan Sontag
Maureen Dowd	Richard Steele
Nora Ephron	Henry David Thoreau
Ann Fadiman	Calvin Trillin
Paul Russell	Eudora Welty
William Hazlett	E. B. White
John Holt	Paul Zimmer

Political Writing and Satire

Hannah Arendt	John Stuart Mill
Simone de Beauvoir	Sir Thomas More
W. E. B. DuBois	Lincoln Steffens
William F. Buckley	Jonathan Swift
Thomas Hobbes	Alexis de Tocqueville
Thomas Jefferson	Tom Wolfe

John Locke   T. H. White
Machiavelli

Naturalists, Scientists, Adventurers

Edward Abbey   Verlyn Klinkenborf
Rachel Carson   Barry Lopez
Charles Darwin   Peter Matthiessen
Loren Eisley   Margaret Mead
Stephen Jay Gould   Carl Sagan
William Least Heat-Moon

Writers Known for Their Fiction and Nonfiction

Zora Neale Hurston   George Orwell
Charlotte Perkins Gilman   Virginia Woolf
Norman Mailer

ANSWERS TO QUESTIONS ON PRACTICE ACTIVITIES

Chapter 2

Examples of Modes of Discourse in Warm-Up 3 on Pages 1182–1184

Description, exposition/description, argument, narration, argument, description, narration, argument, exposition, description

Chapter 4

The Rhetorical Devices/Figures of Speech Used in the Self-Test on Pages 1251–1252

1. metonymy, metaphor, personification
2. simile
3. parallelism
4. allusion (the film, *Gone with the Wind*)
5. parallelism, antithesis
6. onomatopoeia, apostrophe
7. metaphor, personification, hyperbole
8. onomatopoeia, apostrophe, metaphor, personification
9. metonymy
10. onomatopoeia, alliteration

11. metaphor, personification, synecdoche
12. rhetorical question, litotes
13. understatement
14. epithet, simile
15. metaphor, epithet
16. alliteration
17. metaphor, alliteration
18. hyperbole
19. parallelism
20. oxymoron

Answers to Sentence Combination Activity in Warm-up 18 on Page 1256

Compound sentence: After a long flight, the pilot landed the plane at O'Hare airport, and the passengers were quite happy for the safe and smooth landing.

Complex sentence: After a long trip, the passengers were quite happy that the pilot landed the plane safely and smoothly at O'Hare Airport.

Compound–complex sentence: The pilot landed the plane at O'Hare airport, and after a long trip, the passengers were quite happy that the landing was a safe and smooth one.

Periodic sentence: After a long trip, and after a safe and smooth landing by the pilot at O'Hare Airport, the passengers were quite happy.

Practice Activity re: Rip Van Winkle Excerpt in Warm-up 19 on Pages 1257–1258

There are five sentences.
Sentences 1 and 4 begin with prepositional phrases.
Sentence 3 begins with a participial phrase.
Sentences 2 and 5 being with the subject.
The two compound sentences are 2 and 5.
Sentences 1 and 4 are simple.
Sentence 3 is the only complex sentence.
The excerpt's subject is the Kaatskill Mountains.
The purpose is to describe.
The sentences do contain many descriptive phrases set off by commas.
The mountains and the Hudson River are the two items given the most coverage.
Personification is found in sentence 5.
The diction can be described as poetic, complex, graceful, and artful.
The overall effect of the passage is lyrical.

Practice Activity re: Tone in Warm-up 20 on Page 1260

Tone is informal.

Words that characterize the tone of the review: critical and sarcastic.

Words/phrases that help develop the tone: *perfunctory, harrowing and confusing, toyed with, not acted, problem, lurid teasers, light on character development, frightens away.*

Answers to Style Questions in Total Workout on Pages 1266–1269, Which Is an Excerpt from Edgar Allen Poe's "The Tell-Tale Heart"

1. A man tells the reader his plans for killing an old man.
2. To entertain
3. 1st
4. Dash and exclamation point
5. Make parentheticals stand out and for explanatory information
6. Strong emotions
7. "Gentle" and followed by an indication of strong or sudden emotion do not go together; they in opposition
8. To go from cautiously moving to a hearing situation is unexpected and not grammatically connected to the rest of the sentence.
9. Sight and sound
10. Metaphor, rhetorical question, analogy, parallelism, onomatopoeia, litote, personification
11. Yes
12. Yes
13. Varied
14. Does not
15. *Mad, you, madman, cautiously, very, eye, old man*
16. Ironic, complex, conversational
17. Chilling, suspenseful
18. Hyperbolic, dramatic, compelling, complex

Chapter 5

Prompt A on Page 1278

1. A passage from the introduction to Martin Luther King's *Why We Can't Wait.*
2. Describes, analyzes
3. Rhetorical purpose of the passage, the stylistic, narrative, and persuasive devices

4. Social conditions and attitudes of Black Americans in the 1960s
5. Rhetorical purpose
6. Describes and analyzes
7. Stylistic, narrative and persuasive devices
8. No

Prompt B on Page 1279

1. Two poems
2. Discuss
3. Similarities, differences
4. Contrast/comparison
5. Allusion
6. No

GLOSSARY OF TERMS

Allegory   A work that functions on a symbolic level.

Alliteration   The repetition of initial consonant sounds, such as "Peter Piper picked a peck of pickled peppers."

Allusion   A reference contained in a work.

Assertion   Your thesis, the point you wish to make in your essay.

Cacophony   Harsh and discordant sounds in a line or passage in a literary work.

Character   Those who carry out the action of the plot in literature. Major, minor, static, and dynamic are types of characters.

Comic relief   The inclusion of a humorous character or scene to contrast with the tragic elements of a work, thereby intensifying the next tragic event.

Conflict   A clash between opposing forces in a literary work, such as man versus man; man versus nature; man versus god; man versus self.

Connotation   The interpretive level of a word based on its associated images rather than its literal meaning.

Deconstruct   To break something into its parts, to identify the components of a text and to decipher each of their meanings within a given context.

Denotation   The literal or dictionary meaning of a word.

Diction   The author's choice of words.

Euphony   The pleasant, mellifluous presentation of sounds in a literary work.

Exposition   Background information presented in a literary work.

Figurative language   That body of devices that enables the writer to operate on levels other than the literal one. It includes metaphor, simile, symbol, motif, hyperbole, and others.

Flashback   A device that enables a writer to refer to past thoughts, events, and episodes.

Form   The shape or structure of a literary work.

Hyperbole   Extreme exaggeration. In "My Love is Like a Red, Red Rose," Burns speaks of loving "until all the seas run dry."

Image   A verbal approximation of a sensory impression, concept or emotion.

Imagery   The total effect of related sensory images in a work of literature.

Irony   An unexpected twist or contrast between what happens and what was intended or expected to happen. It involves dialog and situation, and can be intentional or unplanned. Dramatic irony centers around the ignorance of those involved while the audience is aware of the circumstance.

Metaphor   A direct comparison between dissimilar things. "Your eyes are stars" is an example.

Metonymy   A figure of speech in which a representative term is used for a larger idea (The pen is mightier than the sword.)

Monologue   A speech given by one character (Hamlet's "To be or not to be . . .").

Motif   The repetition or variations of an image or idea in a work that is used to develop theme or characters.

Narrator   The speaker of a literary work.

Onomatopoeia   Words that sound like the sound they represent (hiss, gurgle, bang).

Oxymoron   An image of contradictory term (bittersweet, pretty ugly, giant economy size).

Parable   A story that operates on more than one level and usually teaches a moral lesson. (*The Pearl* by John Steinbeck is a fine example. See Allegory.)

Parody   A comic imitation of a work that ridicules the original.

Pathos   The aspects of a literary work that elicit pity from the audience.

Personification   The assigning of human qualities to inanimate objects or concepts (Wordsworth personifies "the sea that bares her bosom to the moon" in the poem "London 1802.")

Plot   A sequence of events in a literary work.

Point of view   The method of narration in a work.

Rhetorical question   One that does not expect an explicit answer. It is used to pose an idea to be considered by the speaker or audience. (Ernest Dowson asks, "Where are they now the days of wine and roses?")

Satire   A mode of writing based on ridicule, which criticizes the foibles and follies of society without necessarily offering a solution (Jonathan Swift's *Gulliver's Travels* is a great satire, which exposes mankind's condition.)

Setting   The time and place of a literary work.

Simile   An indirect comparison that uses the words *like* or *as* to link the differing items in the comparison. ("Your eyes are like stars.")

Stage directions   The specific instructions a playwright includes concerning sets, characterization, delivery, etc. (See *Hedda Gabler* by Ibsen.)

Stanza   A unit of a poem, similar in rhyme, meter, and length to other units in the poem.

Structure   The organization and form of a work.

Style   The unique way an author presents his ideas. Diction, syntax, imagery, structure, and content all contribute to a particular style.

Symbol   Something in a literary work that stands for something else. (Plato has the light of the sun symbolize truth in "The Allegory of the Cave.")

Synecdoche   A figure of speech that utilizes a part as representative of the whole. ("All hands on deck" is an example.)

Syntax   The grammatical structure of prose and poetry.

Theme   The underlying ideas the author illustrates through characterization, motifs, language, plot, etc.

Tone   The author's attitude toward his or her subject.

Understatement   The opposite of exaggeration. It is a technique for developing irony and/or humor where one writes or says less than intended.

Voice   The author's distinct, unique, recognizable style. Voice can also refer to *active* or *passive* when referring to whether the subject of the sentence is doing the acting or is being acted upon.

WEBSITES OF INTEREST TO THE AP ENGLISH STUDENT

Please note that these Websites are up and running as of the date of publication of this book. We can only hope that they are still operational when you go to use them. If they are not, please contact your authors. If you find any truly wonderful Websites that you think should be added to our listing, please contact us. Your feedback is always welcome. We can be found at our Website: <www.clearestideas.com>

Comnet: <http://webster.comnet.edu/grammar> an all-purpose grammar site

Arts and Letters Daily: <www.aldaily.com> a daily newsletter about arts and letters with links to many related sites

Google: <www.google.com> one of the best, if not the best, free
search engines that finds topics according to the most hits; indexes
the largest number of Web pages

Northern Light Search: <www.nlsearch.com> searches both full-text
articles + huge number of Web pages; can sort results into folders
according to your category, source, etc.

WebCrawler: <http://webcrawler.com> operates by searching the Web
to construct index for later use or by surfing in real time

Alta Vista: <www.altavista.com> claims to be able to index and search
over 21 million Web pages and Usenet news groups very quickly

HotBot: <www.hotbot.com> Ranked #1 of all search engines in
number of sites in its index

AP Central: <www.Apcentral.collegeboard.com> Advanced
Placement's home Website

Garble: <www.garbl.home.attbi.com/writing/process.htm> annotated
directory of websites that can help you during the writing process

Dogpile: <www.dogpile.com> a terrific search engine that finds topics
via categories and other search engines

Bowling Green University Writer's Lab:
<www.bgsu.edu/offices/acen/writerslab> super site

Purdue On-Line Writing Lab (OWL): <http://owl.english.purdue.edu>
an incredibly helpful on-line writing center with a huge set of links

University of Missouri's Online Writery:
<http://www.missouri.edu/~writery> very user friendly with terrific
graphics

Marist College Academic Learning Center User-friendly Instructional
Network (ALCUIN): <http://academic.marist.edu/alcuin/main.html>
a terrific instructional resource

Rensselear Polytechnic Writing Center: <http://www.rpi.edu/web/
writingcenter> good for advice on mechanics and style

Syracuse University Writing Center: <http://wrt.syr.edu/
thewritingcenter.html> good for writing skills across the curriculum

A+ Research and Writing: <http://ipl.si.umich.edu/div/teen/aplus>
comprehensive guide to writing research papers

University of Michigan's Sweetland Writing Center:
<www.lsa.umich.edu/swc/help/help.html> user friendly and quite
comprehensive

Writing @ Colorado State University:
<http://writing.colostate.edu/resources> links to other Internet-based
resources provides access to a wide range of resources for writers,
many annotated cites

Index

A

abolitionists 153, 160
abolition movement 349
absolute value (math) 893–895
active/passive voice (Eng.) 1324–1326
Addison, Joseph 1382
Aeschylus 1380
affirmative action 566
agenda-setting 566
Age of Enlightenment 355
Alien and Sedition Acts 138, 141, 349
allegory 1386
alliteration 1234
allusion 1235
amendment(s) 566
American
Colonization Society 349
Expeditionary Forces (AEF) 349
Federation of Labor (AFL) 349
Indian Movement (AIM) 79, 349
Revolution 113–118, 122–129
amicus curiae brief 566
analogy 1235, 1236
Angelou, Maya 1382
animal(s)
learning and behavior 774–778, 811
Anti-Federalists 566
antithesis 1236–1237
apostrophe (poetic device) 1238
appellate jurisdiction 566
apportionment 566
appropriations 566
area
and volume 1083–1109
Aristotle 1378
Arnold, Matthew 1379, 1382
Articles of Confederation 127–128, 132, 566
assertion 1386
at-large 566
Auden, W. H. (Wystan Hugh) 1379

B

Bacon, Francis 1382
Baldwin, James 1380
Bataan Death March 350
Battle(s)
of Bull Run 352
of Fredericksburg 357
of Gettysburg 357
of Guadalcanal 359
Bay of Pigs 350
Bear Flag Revolt 350
Beauvoir, Simone de 1382
Berlin Wall 351
bicameral legislatures 351, 566
bill(s) 566
of attainder 566
Bill of Rights 77, 134–135, 351, 566
BIOLOGY 595–840
black(s)
civil rights (nationalism) 351
Blake, William 1378
blanket primary 566
"Bleeding Kansas" 351

block grant 566
Boccaccio, Giovanni 1378
Bonus Army 351
Boston
Massacre 351
Tea Party 79, 351
Boswell, James 1382
brief 566
orders 566
Brontë, Charlotte 1378
Browning, Robert 1379
Brown v. Board of Education of Topeka 78, 305, 566
Bryan, William Jennings 211
Buchanan, James 166
Bull Moose Party 351–352
Bull Run, Battles of 352
bureaucracy 522–524, 566
bureaucratic theory 566
Burns, Robert 1378
Burr, Aaron 144
Bush, George H. 339–341
Bush, George W. 344
Byron, George Gordon 1379

C

Cabinet Departments 566
cacophony 1386
CALCULUS 889–1153
Calhoun, John C. 163–164
Camp David Accords 352
Camus, Albert 1380
carpetbaggers 352
Carson, Rachel 1383
Carter, Jimmy 331–333
categorical grant 566
Cather, Willa 1380
Catton, Bruce 1382
caucus 566
cell 621–625
division 653–661, 801–802
Central Powers 352
Cervantes, Miguel de 1378
character (comp.) 1386
Chaucer, Geoffrey 1378
Chavez, Cesar 79
checks and balances 566
Chekhov, Anton 1378, 1380
CHEMISTRY 609–617, 800
Cherokee (Indians) 352
Chesterton, G. K. 1382
Churchill, Winston 1382
civil
Civil Rights Act of 1866 352
Civil Rights Act of 1964 (employment) 352
Civil Service Reform Act of 1883 352
liberties 537–543, 566
rights 305–306, 314–316, 543–545, 566
service 210
Civil War (U.S.) 79, 171–178
Clark, Kenneth 1382
Clay, Henry 164
Clayton Antitrust Act 352
Cleveland, Grover 79, 197, 211, 217
Clinton, William Jefferson (Bill) 78, 341–344

closed primary 566
cloture rule 567
Cold War 290–298, 317–318, 352–353
Coleridge, Samuel Taylor 1379
college
application essay 1341–1375
colonies, English 99–102, 107–110, 113–118
colonies, French 98–99
colonies, Spanish 98–99
comic relief 1386
Committees of Correspondence 353
Common Sense 353
comparable worth 567
Compromise of 1850 353
concluding the essay 1327–1337
concurrent
jurisdiction 567
powers 567
Confederate States of America 353
Confederation, Articles of 127–128, 132, 566
conference committee 567
conflict 1386
Congress of Industrial Organizations (CIO) 353
congressional districting 567
Connecticut Compromise 567
connotation 1386
Conrad, Joseph 1380
conservative 567
constituent 567
Constitution (U.S.) 132–134, 452–457, 567
constitutional
courts 567
law 567
Continental Army 353
continuity (math)
of a function 936–938
Coolidge, Calvin 251–252
cooperative federalism 567
Copperheads 353
courts of appeal 567
Coxey, General Jacob S.
Coxey's Army 354
Crane, Stephen 1379, 1380
Crusades 97
Cuban missile crisis 354
cummings, e e 1380

D

dark horse (candidate) 354
Darwin, Charles 1383
Dawes Act 354
Declaration of Independence (U.S.) 123–124, 567
deconstruction 1280
deficit 567
definite integrals 1064–1076, 1121–1133
delegated powers 567
democracy 567
Democrat(s)
Democratic Party 354
Democratic-Republicans 354
democratic government theories 446–447
denotation 1386

derivative(s)
applications 1003–1013, 1024–1038
détente 354
devolution 567
Dickens, Charles 1380
diction 1252–1254
differentiation (math) 945–962
direct primary 567
disc method 1102–1106
discretionary spending 567
dissenting opinion 567
district courts 567
Dostoevski (Dostoevsky), Feodor (Fyodor) 1378
double jeopardy 567
Douglas, Stephen A. 165–167
Dred Scott v. Sandford 166, 355
Dreiser, Theodore 1380
dual federalism 567
Dutch 99

E

ecology 782–792, 811–812
Eisenhower, Dwight David 77, 78, 296–298, 304–306, 317
Eisenhower Doctrine 355
Eisley, Loren 1383
elastic clause 567
elections 485–492
Electoral College 355, 567
Eliot, George 1380
Eliot, T. S. (Thomas Stearns) 1379
elitist theory 567
Emancipation Proclamation 355
Emergency Quota Act of 1921 355
eminent domain 568
England
English colonies 99–102, 107–110, 113–118
entitlement program 568
environmental impact statement 568
epithet 1239
equal protection clause 568
"Era of Good Feelings" 355
essay(s)
body and syntax 1308–1309
expectations 1168–1170
"prompts" 1274–1279
euphony 1386
Euripides 1378
evolution 701–712, 808–809
executive
branch 516–524
order 568
privilege 568
exposition 1386
ex post facto law 568
extradition 568

F

Faulkner, William 1380
federal agencies
Federal Reserve System 356
Federal Trade Commission (FTC) 79

federalism 461–466
Federalists 79, 134, 135, 144, 356, 568
federal system (gov.) 568
Fielding, Henry 1380
Fifteenth Amendment 356
figurative language 1387
filibuster 568
Fillmore, Millard 166
fireside chats 356
fiscal policy 568
Fitzgerald, F. Scott 1380
flashback 1387
Flaubert, Gustave 1380
Food and Drug Act 356
Foote, Shelby 1382
Ford, Gerald R. 330–331
foreign policy 556–558
form (Eng.) 1387
forms of government 446
Forster, E. M. 1380
Fort Sumter (South Carolina) 356
Fourteen Points 356–357
Fourteenth Amendment 357
Fredericksburg, Virginia (Battle of) 357
freedmen 357
freedom ride(r)s 357
free trade 135
French
and Indian War(s) 113, 357
colonies 98–99
Revolution 136
FTC (Federal Trade Commission) 79
Fugitive Slave Act 76, 357
full faith and credit clause 568
function(s) (math) 899–938
graphs 910–918, 969–991
limits 922–935
fundamental theorem(s) of calculus 1068–1071

G

Gadsden Purchase 357
general election(s) 568
gerrymandering 568
Gettysburg, Pennsylvania (Battle of) 357
Gilded Age 359
Goethe, Johann Wolfgang von 1378
gold standard 358
Gould, Stephen Jay 1383
Government, United States 405–571
Grange (movement) 358
Grant, Ulysses S. (Simpson) 177, 185
graphs and graphing (math)
calculators 986–987
without calculators 984–986
grassroots 568
Graves, Robert 1380
Great
Awakening 110, 152, 358
Compromise 358
Depression 262–274
Migration
African-Americans
North 358
Society 314, 358

H

Harding, Warren G. (Gamaliel) 78, 250–251
Hardy, Thomas 1380
Harlem Renaissance 257, 359
Hatch Act 568
Hawthorne, Nathaniel 1378
Hayes, Rutherford B. (Birchard) 186
Haymarket (Square) Riot 359
Head Start 359
Hemingway, Ernest 1378
heredity 665–676, 807–808
Hessian mercenaries 359
Hobbes, Thomas 1382
Holocaust 359
Homer 1378
Homestead Act 359
Hoover, Herbert 258, 262, 266–267
House of Representatives
House Un-American Activities Committee 359–360
Hugo, Victor 1378
Huguenots 360
Hull House 360
human
physiology 741–757, 810–811
reproduction 762–770
Huxley, Aldous 1381
hyperbole 1387
hyperpluralism 568

I

Ibsen, Henrik 1378
image 1387
imagery (lit.) 1387
immigration 207–208, 254
impeachment 568
imperialism 216–223
implied powers 568
incumbent 569
indentured servants 100, 360
industrial development (U.S.) 150–151, 201–208
Industrial Workers of the World (IWW) 360
inequalities (math) 894–899
integration (math) 1046–1059
interest group(s) 496–498
internment camps 360
Interstate Commerce Act 360
Intolerable (Coercive) Acts 360–361
introductory paragraph 1294–1307
Iran
hostage crisis 361
Iran-Contra affair 361
Iron Curtain 361
irony 1387
isolationism 361

Guadalcanal (Battle of) 359
Guadaloupe-Hidalgo, Treaty of 359

J

Jackson, Andrew 154–156
Jacksonian Era 153–156
James, Henry 1379, 1381
Jay Treaty 361
Jazz Age 256–257, 361
Jefferson, Thomas 79, 124
Johnson, Andrew 178, 182, 184–185
Johnson, Lyndon B. (Baines) 79,
    313–314, 318–319
Joyce, James 1379, 1381
judicial branch 528–534
judicial review 569

K

Kafka, Franz 1379
Kansas-Nebraska Act of 1854 362
Keats, John 1379
Kennedy, John F. (Fitzgerald) 77, 78,
    312–313, 315, 317–318
Kennedy, Robert 315
Knights of Labor 362
Know-Nothing Party 362
Korean War 362
Ku Klux Klan 362

L

labor unions 205–206, 362
laboratory experiments (biol.)
    798–812
law making process 510–511
Lawrence, David Herbert 1381
League of Nations 362–363
legislative branch 505–512
Lend-Lease Act 363
Lewis and Clark Expedition 363
liberal 569
Lincoln, Abraham 166–167, 176–178,
    181
line item veto 569
litotes 1242
lobby 569
Locke, John 1383
Louisiana Purchase 143
Lusitania 363–364

M

MacArthur, Douglas 243
Machiavelli, Niccoló 1383
Mailer, Norman 1383
mandates 569
Manhattan Project 364
manifest destiny 159–168, 190–198,
    217, 364
Marbury v. Madison 142, 364, 456–457,
    569
March on Washington 364

Marshall Plan 292, 364
mass media 499–502
McCarran-Walter Act 364
McCarthy, Joseph 295–296
McCarthyism 296, 364
McCulloch v. Madison 569
McKinley, William 219–222
Mead, Margaret 1383
Medicare (Act) 364
Melville, Herman 1381
mercantilism 105–106, 135, 364
metaphor 1242–1244
metonymy 1244–1245
Mexican War 160–163
Middle East
    and U.S. affairs 331–332, 335,
        340–341
Middle Passage 364
Mill, John Stuart 1382
Millay, Edna St. Vincent 1380
Miller, Arthur 1381
Miranda v. Arizona 569
Missouri Compromise 76, 147,
    163, 365
Model T 365
moderate (pol. sci.) 569
Molasses Act 365
molecular genetics 683–695
Molière 1378
monologue 1387
Monroe, James
    Monroe Doctrine 151, 365
More, Sir Thomas 1382
Morrill (Land Grant) Act 365
Morrison, Toni 1381
motif 1387
muckrakers 365

N

NAACP (National Association for the
    Advancement of Colored People)
    365
NAFTA (North American Free Trade
    Agreement) 365, 569
narrator 1387
National
    Association for the Advancement of
        Colored People (NAACP) 365
    Labor Relations Board (NLRB) 366
    Organization for Women (NOW)
        367
national debt 569
Native Americans 97–99, 151–152,
    194–195
NATO (North Atlantic Treaty
    Organization) 366
Navigation Acts 366
necessary and proper clause 569
New
    Deal 77, 262–274, 366
    Frontier 312–313, 367
Nixon, Richard Milhous
    77, 78, 312, 320, 325–330
NLRB (National Labor Relations Board)
    366
North
    American Free Trade Agreement
        (NAFTA) 365, 569

Atlantic Treaty Organization (NATO)
    366
Northwest Ordinances 367
NOW (National Organization for
    Women) 367

O

O'Neill, Eugene 1379
onomatopoeia 1245
OPEC (Organization of Petroleum
    Exporting Countries) 368
open
    -door policy 368
    primary 570
Oregon Treaty 368
organization 1261, 1308–1309
Organization of
    Petroleum Exporting Countries
        (OPEC) 368
Orwell, George 1381, 1383
oxymoron 1246

P

PAC (political action committee) 570
Paine, Thomas 123
Panama Canal 222, 368
Panic of 1837 368
parable 1387
parallelism (Eng.) 1247–1248
pardon 570
parenthesis (comp.) 1250
parody 1387
pathos 1387
Paton, Alan 1381
Pentagon Papers 79, 368
Pepys, Samuel 1382
personification 1246
photosynthesis 641–649, 802–804
physiology, human 741–757, 810–811
Pierce, Franklin 164–165
plant systems 731–737,
    809–810
plot 1387
point of view 1261–1262
policy making 552–558
political
    action committee(s) (PAC) 570
    development 469–471
    party, parties 474–480, 570
    spectrum 472
Polk, James Knox 161–162
populism 195–198
pork barrel legislation 570
Potsdam Conference 369
pre-calculus 889–921
president, presidency (U.S.
    powers 519–521
president pro tempore 570
prewriting 1281–1293
procedural due process 570
progressivism 227–234, 369
proportional representation 369
public policy 570
Puritans 78, 369

Index

R

Racine, Jean 1378
radical (math) 570
reactionary 570
Reagan, Ronald 333–335
reapportionment 570
recall 370, 570
Reconstruction 181–186, 370
Red Scare 370
referendum 570
representative democracy 570
reproduction 762–770
    human 762–770
Republican Party 371
reserved powers 570
respiration 630–637, 804–805
revenue sharing 570
rhetorical
    question 1249
    writing strategies 1187–1232,
        1308–1309
rider 570
Roe v. Wade 317, 371
Roosevelt Corollary 371
Roosevelt, Franklin Delano (FDR)
    76–77, 267–272, 279–280,
    282–283, 290
Roosevelt, Theodore 79, 220, 222–223,
    231–234
Rough Riders 371

S

Sagan, Carl 1383
Sartre, Jean-Paul 1381
satire (lit.) 1388
Scopes trial 372
secession 372
Second Bank of the United States
    (Second National Bank) 372
separation of powers 571
setting (lit.) 1388
Shakespeare, William 1378
Shaw, George Bernard 1381
Shays, Daniel
    Shays's Rebellion 129
Shelley, Mary Godwin 1381
Shelley, Percy Bysshe 1379
Sherman Antitrust Act 373
simile 1242–1244
Sinclair, Upton 78, 1379
Sioux (Indians) 373
sit-ins 373
slave(s), slavery 77–78, 106–107, 133,
    147, 153, 160, 162–168
slope (math) 889–892
Social Darwinism 373
Social Security
    Act 373
Sons of Liberty 373
Sophocles 1378
Spanish
    -American War 218–222, 374
    colonies 98–99
spoils system 209–212, 374
Sputnik 374

stage directions 1388
Stamp Act 374
stanza 1388
Steele, Richard 1382
Steffens, Lincoln 1382
Steinbeck, John 1381
Stoppard, Tom 1381
strict constructionist 571
structure 1388
style (comp.) 1262–1266
Sumpter, Fort 356
supremacy clause 571
Supreme Court 529–534
Swift, Jonathan 1378
symbol(s)
    literature 1388
synecdoche 1244–1245
syntax 1255–1258

T

Taft-Hartley Act 375
Taft, William Howard 232–233, 249
Tammany Hall 375
Tariff of 1816 375
taxonomy
    and classification 717–727
Taylor, Zachary 162–163
Teapot Dome scandal 78, 375
Tennessee Valley Authority (TVA)
    376
Tennyson, Alfred 1379
Tet offensive 376
theme 1388
Thirteenth Amendment 376
Thomas, Dylan 1380
Thoreau, Henry David 1382
time line
    U.S. history 103, 119–120, 130, 139,
        148, 157, 168–169, 179, 187, 199,
        213–214, 224, 235, 236, 245–246,
        259, 275–276, 287–288, 300, 309,
        322–323, 336–337, 346
Tocqueville, Alexis de 1382
Tolstoy, Leo 1378
tone (lit.) 1258–1261
Townshend Acts 79, 376
Trail of Tears 376
Treaty of Guadalupe Hidalgo
    359
triangular trade system 377
Truman, Harry S. 76, 284, 291, 304
    Truman Doctrine 377
Tuchman, Barbara 1382
TVA (Tennessee Valley Authority) 376
Twain, Mark 1381
Tweed, William Marcy
    "Boss" 211–212

U

understatement 1241
unicameral (one-house) legislature
    377
U.S. GOVERNMENT 405–571
U.S. HISTORY 122–380

V

vertical integration 378
Vietnam War 77, 318–321
voice 1324–1326
Voltaire 1378
volume (math)
    washer method 1107–1109

W

Walker, Alice 1381
War of 1812 144–147
washer method 1107–1109
Washington, George 123, 126
Watergate affair 327–330, 379
Webster, Daniel
    Webster-Hayne debate 379
Welty, Eudora 1382
Whig Party 156, 379
Whiskey Rebellion 379
White, E. B. 1382
Wilder, Thornton 1381
Williams, Tennessee 1381
Wilmot Proviso 378
Wilson, Woodrow 79, 234, 239–240,
    243–244
Wolfe, Tom 1382
women's suffrage 230–231
Woolf, Virginia 1381, 1383
Wordsworth, William 1379
World War I 238–244
World War II 278–286
Wright, Richard 1381
writ of habeas corpus 571
WRITING (Eng.) 1161–1389
    basics 1179–1186

Y

Yalta Conference 380
yellow journalism 380
Yorktown, Virginia (Battle of) 380

Z

Zenger, Peter 77
Zimmermann note (telegram) 380